Masterplots

Fourth Edition

Masterplots

Fourth Edition

Volume 10
The Savage Mind—That Was Then, This Is Now

Editor
Laurence W. Mazzeno
Alvernia College

SALEM PRESS
Pasadena, California   Hackensack, New Jersey

Editor in Chief: Dawn P. Dawson

Editorial Director: Christina J. Moose   *Editorial Assistant:* Brett S. Weisberg
Development Editor: Tracy Irons-Georges   *Research Supervisor:* Jeffry Jensen
Project Editor: Desiree Dreeuws   *Research Assistant:* Keli Trousdale
Manuscript Editors: Constance Pollock,   *Production Editor:* Joyce I. Buchea
Judy Selhorst, Andy Perry   *Design and Graphics:* James Hutson
Acquisitions Editor: Mark Rehn   *Layout:* William Zimmerman

Cover photo: Marco Polo (The Granger Collection, New York)

Library of Congress Cataloging-in-Publication Data

Masterplots / editor, Laurence W. Mazzeno. — 4th ed.
     v.   cm.
    Includes bibliographical references and indexes.
    ISBN 978-1-58765-568-5 (set : alk. paper) — ISBN 978-1-58765-578-4 (v. 10 : alk. paper)
  1. Literature—Stories, plots, etc.   2. Literature—History and criticism.   I. Mazzeno, Laurence W.
   PN44.M33 2010
   809—dc22

                       2010033931

Fourth Edition
First Printing

Contents

Complete List of Titles ccclxv

The Savage Mind—*Claude Lévi-Strauss* 5127
Scaramouche—*Rafael Sabatini* 5129
The Scarlet Letter—*Nathaniel Hawthorne* 5132
Schindler's List—*Thomas Keneally*. 5136
The Scholar-Gipsy—*Matthew Arnold* 5138
The School for Husbands—*Molière* 5140
The School for Scandal—*Richard Brinsley
    Sheridan* 5143
The School for Wives—*Molière* 5147
The Screwtape Letters—*C. S. Lewis* 5150
Sea Garden—*H. D.* 5153
The Sea of Grass—*Conrad Richter* 5156
The Sea-Wolf—*Jack London* 5159
The Seagull—*Anton Chekhov* 5162
A Season in Hell—*Arthur Rimbaud* 5166
A Season in Rihata—*Maryse Condé* 5168
The Seasons—*James Thomson* 5171
Seatonian Poems *and* A Song to David—
    Christopher Smart 5174
The Second Mrs. Tanqueray—*Arthur Wing
    Pinero* 5176
The Second Sex—*Simone de Beauvoir* 5179
The Second Shepherds' Play—*Wakefield Master*. . . 5182
The Secret Agent—*Joseph Conrad* 5185
Seeing Things—*Seamus Heaney* 5188
Seize the Day—*Saul Bellow* 5191
Sejanus His Fall—*Ben Jonson* 5194
Self-Portrait in a Convex Mirror—*John Ashbery*. . . 5197
The Self-Tormentor—*Terence*. 5199
El Señor Presidente—*Miguel Ángel Asturias* 5202
Sense and Sensibility—*Jane Austen* 5205
A Sentimental Education—*Gustave Flaubert* 5208
A Sentimental Journey—*Laurence Sterne* 5212
A Separate Peace—*John Knowles* 5215
Set This House on Fire—*William Styron* 5218
Seven Against Thebes—*Aeschylus* 5221
Seven Pillars of Wisdom—*T. E. Lawrence* 5224
The Seven Who Were Hanged—
    Leonid Andreyev 5226
Seventeen—*Booth Tarkington*. 5229
Sexual Politics—*Kate Millett* 5232
Shadows on the Rock—*Willa Cather* 5234

The Shawl—*Cynthia Ozick* 5237
She—*H. Rider Haggard*. 5239
She Stoops to Conquer—*Oliver Goldsmith*. 5242
The Sheep Well—*Lope de Vega Carpio* 5245
The Sheltered Life—*Ellen Glasgow* 5248
The Sheltering Sky—*Paul Bowles* 5251
The Shepheardes Calender—*Edmund Spenser* . . . 5254
The Shining—*Stephen King*. 5257
Ship of Fools—*Katherine Anne Porter* 5260
The Shipping News—*E. Annie Proulx* 5263
Shirley—*Charlotte Brontë* 5266
Shoeless Joe—*W. P. Kinsella* 5268
The Shoemaker's Holiday—*Thomas Dekker* 5271
The Shoes of the Fisherman—*Morris West* 5274
Shōgun—*James Clavell*. 5277
Show Boat—*Edna Ferber* 5280
A Shropshire Lad—*A. E. Housman*. 5283
Shroud for a Nightingale—*P. D. James*. 5285
The Sickness unto Death—*Søren Kierkegaard* . . . 5287
Siddhartha—*Hermann Hesse* 5290
The Siege of Rhodes—*Sir William Davenant* 5293
The Sign in Sidney Brustein's Window—
    Lorraine Hansberry 5295
The Sign of Four—*Sir Arthur Conan Doyle* 5298
The Significance of the Frontier in American
    History—*Frederick Jackson Turner* 5302
Silas Marner—*George Eliot*. 5304
Silence—*Shūsaku Endō* 5307
Sinners in the Hands of an Angry God—
    Jonathan Edwards 5310
Sir Charles Grandison—*Samuel Richardson* 5312
Sir Gawain and the Green Knight—*Pearl-Poet*. . . 5316
The Sirens of Titan—*Kurt Vonnegut* 5319
Sister Carrie—*Theodore Dreiser* 5321
Sister Philomène—*Edmond de Goncourt* and
    Jules de Goncourt 5325
Six Characters in Search of an Author—
    Luigi Pirandello 5328
Six Degrees of Separation—*John Guare* 5332
The Skin of Our Teeth—*Thornton Wilder* 5334
Slaughterhouse-Five—*Kurt Vonnegut*. 5338
The Sleepwalkers—*Hermann Broch* 5340
Slouching Towards Bethlehem—*Joan Didion* 5344
Slow Homecoming—*Peter Handke*. 5346

The Small House at Allington—
  Anthony Trollope 5349
Smoke—Ivan Turgenev 5353
The Snake Pit—Sigrid Undset 5356
Snow Country—Yasunari Kawabata 5359
Snow Falling on Cedars—David Guterson 5362
Snow White—Donald Barthelme 5364
Snow-Bound—John Greenleaf Whittier 5367
The Snows of Kilimanjaro, and Other Stories—
  Ernest Hemingway 5369
So Big—Edna Ferber 5371
The Social Contract—Jean-Jacques Rousseau 5374
Society and Solitude—Ralph Waldo Emerson 5377
Sohrab and Rustum—Matthew Arnold 5380
Solaris—Stanisław Lem 5382
The Solitudes—Luis de Góngora y Argote 5385
A Son of the Middle Border—Hamlin Garland . . . 5388
The Song of Hiawatha—Henry Wadsworth
  Longfellow 5391
The Song of Roland—Unknown 5394
Song of Solomon—Toni Morrison 5398
The Song of the Lark—Willa Cather 5401
The Song of the World—Jean Giono 5404
Songs of Innocence and of Experience—
  William Blake 5407
Sonnets for Helen—Pierre de Ronsard 5410
Sonnets from the Portuguese—Elizabeth Barrett
  Browning 5412
Sonnets of Michelangelo—Michelangelo 5415
Sonnets of Shakespeare—William Shakespeare . . . 5418
Sonnets to Orpheus—Rainer Maria Rilke 5421
Sons and Lovers—D. H. Lawrence 5424
Sophie's Choice—William Styron 5427
The Sorrows of Young Werther—Johann
  Wolfgang von Goethe 5430
The Sot-Weed Factor—John Barth 5433
Soul Mountain—Gao Xingjian 5436
The Souls of Black Folk—W. E. B. Du Bois 5439
The Sound and the Fury—William Faulkner 5441
The Sound of Waves—Yukio Mishima 5444
South Wind—Norman Douglas 5447
Spain, Take This Cup from Me—César Vallejo . . . 5450
The Spanish Friar—John Dryden 5452
The Spanish Tragedy—Thomas Kyd 5455
The Spectator—Joseph Addison and Sir Richard
  Steele 5458
Speculations About Jakob—Uwe Johnson 5461
The Spirit of the Laws—Montesquieu 5464
The Spoils of Poynton—Henry James 5466

Spoon River Anthology—Edgar Lee Masters 5470
The Sport of the Gods—Paul Laurence Dunbar . . . 5472
The Sportswriter—Richard Ford 5475
Spring Awakening—Frank Wedekind 5477
The Spy—James Fenimore Cooper 5481
The Spy Who Came in from the Cold—
  John le Carré 5485
The Stand—Stephen King 5488
The Star of Seville—Unknown 5491
Steppenwolf—Hermann Hesse 5494
Steps—Jerzy Kosinski 5498
Steps to the Temple—Richard Crashaw 5500
The Stone Angel—Margaret Laurence 5503
The Stone Diaries—Carol Shields 5506
The Stones of Venice—John Ruskin 5508
The Story of an African Farm—Olive Schreiner . . . 5511
The Story of Burnt Njal—Unknown 5514
The Story of Gösta Berling—Selma Lagerlöf 5518
Storyteller—Leslie Marmon Silko 5521
The Strange Case of Dr. Jekyll and Mr. Hyde—
  Robert Louis Stevenson 5523
Strange Interlude—Eugene O'Neill 5526
Strange Stories from a Chinese Studio—
  Pu Songling 5529
The Stranger—Albert Camus 5531
Stranger in a Strange Land—Robert A. Heinlein . . . 5534
Strangers and Brothers series—C. P. Snow 5537
Strangers on a Train—Patricia Highsmith 5540
The Street—Ann Lane Petry 5543
Street Scene—Elmer Rice 5546
A Streetcar Named Desire—Tennessee Williams . . . 5549
Studs Lonigan—James T. Farrell 5552
A Study in Scarlet—Sir Arthur Conan Doyle 5556
A Study of History—Arnold Toynbee 5559
The Subjection of Women—John Stuart Mill 5561
Suddenly Last Summer—Tennessee Williams 5564
Sula—Toni Morrison 5567
Summa Theologica—Thomas Aquinas 5570
The Sun Also Rises—Ernest Hemingway 5572
The Sunken Bell—Gerhart Hauptmann 5576
The Sunlight Dialogues—John Gardner 5579
The Suppliants—Aeschylus 5582
The Suppliants—Euripides 5585
Surfacing—Margaret Atwood 5588
The Surrounded—D'Arcy McNickle 5591
Swallow Barn—John Pendleton Kennedy 5593
The Swiss Family Robinson—Johann David Wyss
  and Johann Rudolf Wyss 5596
Sybil—Benjamin Disraeli 5599

Contents

Tala—*Gabriela Mistral* 5603

A Tale of a Tub—*Jonathan Swift* 5605

The Tale of Genji—*Murasaki Shikibu* 5608

A Tale of Two Cities—*Charles Dickens* 5611

The Talented Mr. Ripley—*Patricia Highsmith* 5615

Tales of Ise—*Unknown* 5617

Tales of Odessa—*Isaac Babel* 5620

Tales of Soldiers and Civilians—
    Ambrose Bierce 5622

Tales of the South Pacific—*James A. Michener* . . . 5624

The Talisman—*Sir Walter Scott* 5627

Talley Family Saga—*Lanford Wilson* 5631

Tamar—*Robinson Jeffers* 5634

Tamburlaine the Great—*Christopher Marlowe* 5637

The Taming of the Shrew—*William
    Shakespeare* 5640

Tarr—*Wyndham Lewis* 5643

Tartuffe—*Molière* 5647

The Task—*William Cowper* 5649

A Taste of Honey—*Shelagh Delaney* 5652

Tell Me a Riddle—*Tillie Olsen* 5655

The Tell-Tale Heart—*Edgar Allan Poe* 5657

The Tempest—*William Shakespeare* 5660

The Temple—*George Herbert* 5663

The Temple of the Golden Pavilion—
    Yukio Mishima 5666

The Temptation of Saint Anthony—
    Gustave Flaubert 5668

The Tenant of Wildfell Hall—*Anne Brontë* 5672

Tender Is the Night—*F. Scott Fitzgerald* 5675

Tess of the D'Urbervilles—*Thomas Hardy* 5678

Tevye the Dairyman—*Sholom Aleichem* 5682

Tex—*S. E. Hinton* 5684

Thanatopsis—*William Cullen Bryant* 5687

That Evening Sun—*William Faulkner* 5689

That Was Then, This Is Now—*S. E. Hinton* 5692

Complete List of Titles

Volume 1

Publisher's Note v
List of Contributors vii
Contents xix
Complete List of Titles. xxiii

About a Boy—*Nick Hornby*. 1
Abraham and Isaac—*Unknown* 4
Abraham Lincoln—*Carl Sandburg* 6
Absalom, Absalom!—*William Faulkner* 9
Absalom and Achitophel—*John Dryden* 12
The Absentee—*Maria Edgeworth*. 15
The Accidental Tourist—*Anne Tyler*. 19
The Acharnians—*Aristophanes* 22
Ada or Ardor—*Vladimir Nabokov*. 25
Adam Bede—*George Eliot* 28
The Admirable Crichton—*Sir James Barrie* 31
Adolphe—*Benjamin Constant* 34
Adonais—*Percy Bysshe Shelley* 38
The Adventures of Augie March—*Saul Bellow* 40
Adventures of Huckleberry Finn—*Mark Twain* 43
The Adventures of Peregrine Pickle—
   Tobias Smollett 47
The Adventures of Roderick Random—
   Tobias Smollett 51
The Adventures of Tom Sawyer—*Mark Twain* . . 54
The Adventurous Simplicissimus—*Hans Jakob*
   Christoffel von Grimmelshausen 58
Aeneid—*Vergil*. 60
Aesop's Fables—*Aesop* 64
The Affected Young Ladies—*Molière*. 66
The Afternoon of a Faun—*Stéphane Mallarmé* 69
Against the Grain—*Joris-Karl Huysmans*. . . . 72
The Age of Anxiety—*W. H. Auden* 75
The Age of Innocence—*Edith Wharton* 78
The Age of Reason—*Thomas Paine* 81
Agnes Grey—*Anne Brontë*. 84
Ajax—*Sophocles*. 87
The Albany Cycle—*William Kennedy*. 91
Alcestis—*Euripides* 94
The Alchemist—*Paulo Coelho* 97
The Alchemist—*Ben Jonson* 100
Alcools—*Guillaume Apollinaire* 103

Aleck Maury, Sportsman—*Caroline Gordon* 105
The Alexandria Quartet—*Lawrence Durrell* 109
Alias Grace—*Margaret Atwood* 112
Alice's Adventures in Wonderland—
   Lewis Carroll 114
All Fall Down—*James Leo Herlihy* 118
All Fools—*George Chapman*. 120
All for Love—*John Dryden* 123
All Hallows' Eve—*Charles Williams* 126
All Men Are Brothers—*Shi Naian* 129
All My Sons—*Arthur Miller* 132
All Quiet on the Western Front—
   Erich Maria Remarque 135
All That Fall—*Samuel Beckett* 138
All the King's Men—*Robert Penn Warren*. 141
All's Well That Ends Well—
   William Shakespeare 144
Almanac of the Dead—*Leslie Marmon Silko* 148
Almayer's Folly—*Joseph Conrad* 151
Alton Locke—*Charles Kingsley* 154
Always Coming Home—*Ursula K. Le Guin*. . . . 157
Amadeus—*Peter Shaffer* 160
Amadís of Gaul—*Vasco de Lobeira* 162
The Amazing Adventures of Kavalier and Clay—
   Michael Chabon. 165
The Ambassadors—*Henry James* 168
Amelia—*Henry Fielding* 171
The American—*Henry James* 175
American Buffalo—*David Mamet* 178
The American Commonwealth—*James Bryce*. . . . 181
The American Notebooks—
   Nathaniel Hawthorne 183
American Pastoral—*Philip Roth* 185
The American Scholar—*Ralph Waldo Emerson* 188
An American Tragedy—*Theodore Dreiser*. 190
Amores—*Ovid* 193
Amoretti—*Edmund Spenser* 196
Amphitryon—*Plautus* 199
Amphitryon 38—*Jean Giraudoux* 202
Amsterdam—*Ian McEwan* 204
Anabasis—*Saint-John Perse* 207
Anabasis—*Xenophon* 209

Anatomy of Criticism—*Northrop Frye.* 212
The Anatomy of Melancholy—*Robert Burton.* 215
And Quiet Flows the Don—*Mikhail Sholokhov* 217
And Then There Were None—*Agatha Christie* 219
Andersen's Fairy Tales—*Hans Christian
    Andersen.* 222
Andersonville—*MacKinlay Kantor* 227
Andria—*Terence* 230
Andromache—*Euripides* 233
Andromache—*Jean Racine.* 235
Angela's Ashes—*Frank McCourt* 239
Angels and Insects—*A. S. Byatt* 241
Angels in America—*Tony Kushner.* 244
Angle of Repose—*Wallace Stegner* 248
Animal Dreams—*Barbara Kingsolver.* 251
Animal Farm—*George Orwell.* 253
Anna Christie—*Eugene O'Neill* 256
Anna Karenina—*Leo Tolstoy.* 259
Anna of the Five Towns—*Arnold Bennett* 262
Annals—*Tacitus* 266
Annie Allen—*Gwendolyn Brooks* 269
Annie John—*Jamaica Kincaid.* 272
Another Country—*James Baldwin.* 274
Antigone—*Jean Anouilh* 277
Antigone—*Sophocles.* 280
The Antiquary—*Sir Walter Scott.* 282
Antony and Cleopatra—*William Shakespeare* 284
Apologia pro Vita Sua—*John Henry Newman.* 288
The Apostle—*Sholem Asch.* 290
Appointment in Samarra—*John O'Hara.* 293
The Apprenticeship of Duddy Kravitz—
    Mordecai Richler 296
The Arabian Nights' Entertainments—*Unknown* . . . 299
The Arbitration—*Menander* 304
Arcadia—*Sir Philip Sidney.* 307
Areopagitica—*John Milton.* 311
Ariel—*Sylvia Plath.* 313
Der arme Heinrich—*Hartmann von Aue* 315
The Armies of the Night—*Norman Mailer* 318
Arms and the Man—*George Bernard Shaw* 321
Arrowsmith—*Sinclair Lewis* 324
The Art of Fiction—*Henry James* 327
Art of Love—*Ovid* 329
The Art of Poetry—*Horace.* 332
The Artamonov Business—*Maxim Gorky* 334
As I Lay Dying—*William Faulkner* 337
As You Like It—*William Shakespeare* 340
Ash Wednesday—*T. S. Eliot* 343
Ashes—*Stefan Żeromski* 345

The Aspern Papers—*Henry James* 348
The Assistant—*Bernard Malamud* 350
L'Assommoir—*Émile Zola.* 353
Astrophel and Stella—*Sir Philip Sidney* 356
Atala—*François-René de Chateaubriand* 359
Atalanta in Calydon—*Algernon Charles
    Swinburne* 361
Atlas Shrugged—*Ayn Rand.* 364
Atonement—*Ian McEwan* 368
Aucassin and Nicolette—*Unknown* 371
August 1914—*Aleksandr Solzhenitsyn.* 373
Aurora Leigh—*Elizabeth Barrett Browning* 376
The Autobiography of Alice B. Toklas—
    Gertrude Stein. 379
The Autobiography of an Ex-Coloured Man—
    James Weldon Johnson 382
Autobiography of Benjamin Franklin—
    Benjamin Franklin. 385
Autobiography of Benvenuto Cellini—
    Benvenuto Cellini 388
Autobiography of John Stuart Mill—
    John Stuart Mill 391
The Autobiography of Malcolm X—*Malcolm X.* . . . 394
The Autobiography of Miss Jane Pittman—
    Ernest J. Gaines. 397
The Autobiography of W. E. B. Du Bois—
    W. E. B. Du Bois. 400
The Autocrat of the Breakfast-Table—
    Oliver Wendell Holmes 403
The Awakening—*Kate Chopin.* 406
The Awkward Age—*Henry James* 409

Baal—*Bertolt Brecht* 413
Babbitt—*Sinclair Lewis* 416
The Bacchae—*Euripides* 419
The Bachelors—*Muriel Spark* 422
Back to Methuselah—*George Bernard Shaw* 426
Badenheim 1939—*Aharon Appelfeld* 429
The Bald Soprano—*Eugène Ionesco* 432
Bambi—*Felix Salten* 435
Barabbas—*Pär Lagerkvist* 437
The Barber of Seville—*Pierre-Augustin Caron de
    Beaumarchais* 440
Barchester Towers—*Anthony Trollope.* 443
Barnaby Rudge—*Charles Dickens.* 446
Baron Münchausen's Narrative of His Marvellous
    Travels and Campaigns in Russia—*Rudolf Erich
    Raspe* 450
Barren Ground—*Ellen Glasgow* 453

Barrio Boy—*Ernesto Galarza* 456
Barry Lyndon—*William Makepeace Thackeray* 459
Bartholomew Fair—*Ben Jonson* 462
Batouala—*René Maran* 466
The Bay of Silence—*Eduardo Mallea* 469
The Bean Trees—*Barbara Kingsolver* 472
The Beaux' Stratagem—*George Farquhar* 474
The Beaver Coat—*Gerhart Hauptmann* 477
Bech—*John Updike* 480
Becket—*Jean Anouilh* 483
The Bedbug—*Vladimir Mayakovsky* 486
The Beet Queen—*Louise Erdrich* 489
The Beggar Maid—*Alice Munro* 492
The Beggar's Opera—*John Gay* 494
Being and Nothingness—*Jean-Paul Sartre* 497
Being and Time—*Martin Heidegger* 500
Being There—*Jerzy Kosinski* 503
Bel-Ami—*Guy de Maupassant* 506
Belinda—*Maria Edgeworth* 509
A Bell for Adano—*John Hersey* 512

The Bell Jar—*Sylvia Plath* 514
La Belle Dame sans Merci—*John Keats* 517
Bellefleur—*Joyce Carol Oates* 519
Bells in Winter—*Czesław Miłosz* 521
Beloved—*Toni Morrison* 524
Ben-Hur—*Lew Wallace* 527
A Bend in the River—*V. S. Naipaul* 530
Benito Cereno—*Herman Melville* 533
Beowulf—*Unknown* 537
Bérénice—*Jean Racine* 540
Berlin Alexanderplatz—*Alfred Döblin* 542
The Berlin Stories—*Christopher Isherwood* 545
The Betrothed—*Alessandro Manzoni* 548
Betsey Brown—*Ntozake Shange* 551
Between the Acts—*Virginia Woolf* 554
Bevis of Hampton—*Unknown* 557
Beyond Freedom and Dignity—*B. F. Skinner* 561
Beyond Good and Evil—*Friedrich Nietzsche* 563
The Big Rock Candy Mountain—
   Wallace Stegner 566

Volume 2

Contents lvii
Complete List of Titles lxi

The Big Sky—*A. B. Guthrie, Jr.* 569
The Big Sleep—*Raymond Chandler* 572
The Biglow Papers—*James Russell Lowell* 575
Billy Bathgate—*E. L. Doctorow* 577
Billy Budd, Foretopman—*Herman Melville* 580
Biographia Literaria—*Samuel Taylor Coleridge* . . 584
The Birds—*Aristophanes* 587
The Birth of Tragedy out of the Spirit of Music—
   Friedrich Nietzsche 590
The Birthday Party—*Harold Pinter* 592
The Black Arrow—*Robert Louis Stevenson* 595
Black Boy—*Richard Wright* 598
Black Elk Speaks—*Black Elk* and
   John G. Neihardt 601
Black Lamb and Grey Falcon—*Rebecca West* 604
Black Narcissus—*Rumer Godden* 606
The Black Swan—*Thomas Mann* 609
Black Thunder—*Arna Bontemps* 611
Bleak House—*Charles Dickens* 614
Bless Me, Ultima—*Rudolfo Anaya* 617
The Blind Assassin—*Margaret Atwood* 620

Blindness—*José Saramago* 622
Blindness and Insight—*Paul de Man* 625
Blithe Spirit—*Noël Coward* 627
The Blithedale Romance—*Nathaniel Hawthorne* . . . 630
Blonde—*Joyce Carol Oates* 633
Blood Wedding—*Federico García Lorca* 636
The Bluest Eye—*Toni Morrison* 639
The Bohemians of the Latin Quarter—
   Henri Murger 642
Bonjour Tristesse—*Françoise Sagan* 645
The Book of Evidence—*John Banville* 648
The Book of Illusions—*Paul Auster* 650
The Book of Laughter and Forgetting—
   Milan Kundera 653
The Book of Songs—*Confucius* 656
Book of Songs—*Heinrich Heine* 658
The Book of the City of Ladies—
   Christine de Pizan 661
The Book of the Courtier—
   Baldassare Castiglione 664
The Book of the Dead—*Unknown* 668
Book of the Duchess—*Geoffrey Chaucer* 670
The Book of Theseus—*Giovanni Boccaccio* 673
The Border Trilogy—*Cormac McCarthy* 677

Boris Godunov—*Alexander Pushkin*. 681

The Borough—*George Crabbe*. 684

The Bostonians—*Henry James*. 686

Boswell's London Journal, 1762-1763—
    James Boswell. 690

The Braggart Soldier—*Plautus*. 692

Brand—*Henrik Ibsen*. 695

Brave New World—*Aldous Huxley*. 697

Bread and Wine—*Ignazio Silone*. 701

Break of Noon—*Paul Claudel*. 704

Breakfast at Tiffany's—*Truman Capote* 707

Breakfast of Champions—*Kurt Vonnegut* 710

Breathing Lessons—*Anne Tyler* 713

The Bride of Lammermoor—*Sir Walter Scott* 716

The Bride Price—*Buchi Emecheta*. 719

The Bride's Tragedy *and* Death's Jest-Book—
    Thomas Lovell Beddoes 722

Brideshead Revisited—*Evelyn Waugh* 725

The Bridge—*Hart Crane* 728

The Bridge of San Luis Rey—*Thornton Wilder* . . . 731

The Bridge on the Drina—*Ivo Andrić* 734

A Brief History of Time—*Stephen Hawking*. 736

Brighton Rock—*Graham Greene* 739

Britannicus—*Jean Racine* 742

Broad and Alien Is the World—*Ciro Alegría* 745

The Broken Jug—*Heinrich von Kleist* 748

The Bronze Horseman—*Alexander Pushkin*. 751

Brother Ass—*Eduardo Barrios*. 754

The Brothers—*Terence* 756

The Brothers Ashkenazi—*Israel Joshua Singer* . . . 759

The Brothers Karamazov—*Fyodor Dostoevski* 762

Brown Girl, Brownstones—*Paule Marshall* 766

The Browning Version—*Terence Rattigan*. 769

Brut—*Layamon*. 771

Buddenbrooks—*Thomas Mann* 774

Bullet Park—*John Cheever*. 777

The Bulwark—*Theodore Dreiser*. 780

A Burnt-Out Case—*Graham Greene*. 783

Bury My Heart at Wounded Knee—*Dee Brown* . . . 786

Bus Stop—*William Inge* 789

The Business of Fancydancing—*Sherman Alexie* . . . 792

Bussy d'Ambois—*George Chapman*. 794

Cadastre—*Aimé Césaire* 798

Cadmus—*Unknown*. 800

Caesar and Cleopatra—*George Bernard Shaw*. . . . 803

Cain—*Lord Byron* 806

The Caine Mutiny—*Herman Wouk*. 809

Cakes and Ale—*W. Somerset Maugham* 812

Caleb Williams—*William Godwin* 815

Call It Sleep—*Henry Roth* 818

The Call of the Wild—*Jack London* 821

Camel Xiangzi—*Lao She*. 824

Camille—*Alexandre Dumas*, fils 827

Cancer Ward—*Aleksandr Solzhenitsyn*. 829

Candida—*George Bernard Shaw*. 832

Candide—*Voltaire* 835

Cane—*Jean Toomer* 838

Cannery Row—*John Steinbeck*. 841

The Cannibal—*John Hawkes*. 844

The Canterbury Tales—*Geoffrey Chaucer* 847

Canto general—*Pablo Neruda* 850

Cantos—*Ezra Pound* 853

Captain Blood—*Rafael Sabatini* 856

Captain Horatio Hornblower—*C. S. Forester* 858

Captains Courageous—*Rudyard Kipling*. 861

The Captain's Daughter—*Alexander Pushkin* 864

The Captives—*Plautus* 868

The Caretaker—*Harold Pinter* 870

Carmen—*Prosper Mérimée* 873

Carmina—*Catullus* 875

Carrie—*Stephen King*. 877

Cass Timberlane—*Sinclair Lewis* 880

The Castle—*Franz Kafka*. 883

The Castle of Otranto—*Horace Walpole* 886

Castle Rackrent—*Maria Edgeworth* 889

Cat and Mouse—*Günter Grass*. 892

Cat on a Hot Tin Roof—*Tennessee Williams*. 895

Catch-22—*Joseph Heller* 898

The Catcher in the Rye—*J. D. Salinger* 901

Catiline—*Ben Jonson*. 904

Cat's Cradle—*Kurt Vonnegut*. 907

Cawdor—*Robinson Jeffers* 910

Cecilia—*Fanny Burney*. 913

Celestina—*Fernando de Rojas* 917

The Cenci—*Percy Bysshe Shelley* 920

Ceremony—*Leslie Marmon Silko* 923

Ceremony in Lone Tree—*Wright Morris* 926

The Chairs—*Eugène Ionesco*. 928

Chaka—*Thomas Mofolo* 931

The Changeling—*Thomas Middleton* and
    William Rowley 933

The Changing Light at Sandover—*James Merrill* . . . 937

Charles Demailly—*Edmond de Goncourt* and
    Jules de Goncourt 940

Charms—*Paul Valéry*. 943

The Charterhouse of Parma—*Stendhal*. 946

Chéri—*Colette* 949

The Cherokee Night—*Lynn Riggs* 952
The Cherry Orchard—*Anton Chekhov* 955
The Chevalier de Maison-Rouge—*Alexandre
    Dumas, père,* and *Auguste Maquet* 958
Chicago Poems—*Carl Sandburg* 962
The Chickencoop Chinaman—*Frank Chin.* 964
Child of God—*Cormac McCarthy* 967
Childe Harold's Pilgrimage—*Lord Byron* 969
Children of a Lesser God—*Mark Medoff* 973
The Children of Herakles—*Euripides* 975
Children of the Game—*Jean Cocteau* 978
The Children's Hour—*Lillian Hellman* 981
The Chimeras—*Gérard de Nerval* 984
Chita—*Lafcadio Hearn.* 987
The Chocolate War—*Robert Cormier* 990
The Chosen—*Chaim Potok.* 992
Christabel—*Samuel Taylor Coleridge* 996
A Christmas Carol—*Charles Dickens* 999
Chronicles—*Jean Froissart* 1002
The Chronicles of Narnia—*C. S. Lewis.* 1005
The Chrysanthemums—*John Steinbeck* 1011
The Cid—*Pierre Corneille* 1013
The Cider House Rules—*John Irving.* 1016
Cinna—*Pierre Corneille* 1020
Cinq-Mars—*Alfred de Vigny* 1023
The City of God—*Saint Augustine* 1026
The City of the Sun—*Tommaso Campanella* 1028
Civil Disobedience—*Henry David Thoreau* 1031
Civilization and Its Discontents—
    Sigmund Freud. 1033
Clarissa—*Samuel Richardson.* 1036
The Clayhanger Trilogy—*Arnold Bennett* 1039
Clear Light of Day—*Anita Desai* 1042
Cligès—*Chrétien de Troyes* 1045
A Clockwork Orange—*Anthony Burgess* 1049

Close Range—*Annie Proulx* 1051
The Closed Garden—*Julien Green* 1053
The Clouds—*Aristophanes* 1057
Cloudsplitter—*Russell Banks* 1059
The Clown—*Heinrich Böll* 1062
The Cocktail Party—*T. S. Eliot* 1064
Cold Comfort Farm—*Stella Gibbons* 1068
Cold Mountain—*Charles Frazier.* 1071
Collected Poems—*Marianne Moore* 1073
The Collector—*John Fowles* 1076
Color of Darkness—*James Purdy.* 1079
The Color Purple—*Alice Walker* 1081
The Colossus, and Other Poems—*Sylvia Plath.* . . . 1084
The Comedy of Errors—*William Shakespeare* 1086
Commentaries—*Julius Caesar* 1089
Common Sense—*Thomas Paine* 1091
The Communist Manifesto—*Karl Marx* and
    Friedrich Engels 1094
The Company of Women—*Mary Gordon* 1096
The Compleat Angler—*Izaak Walton.* 1099
The Complete Poems of Emily Dickinson—
    Emily Dickinson 1101
The Complete Tales of Uncle Remus—
    Joel Chandler Harris. 1107
Comus—*John Milton* 1110
The Concubine—*Elechi Amadi* 1113
Confessions—*Saint Augustine* 1116
Confessions—*Jean-Jacques Rousseau* 1119
Confessions of an English Opium Eater—
    Thomas De Quincey 1121
Confessions of Felix Krull, Confidence Man—
    Thomas Mann 1125
The Confessions of Nat Turner—*William Styron* . . . 1128
The Confidence Man—*Herman Melville* 1132
The Confidential Clerk—*T. S. Eliot* 1136

Volume 3

Contents xcv
Complete List of Titles xcix

Coningsby—*Benjamin Disraeli.* 1139
The Conjure Woman—*Charles Waddell
    Chesnutt* 1142
A Connecticut Yankee in King Arthur's Court—
    Mark Twain. 1145
The Conscience of the Rich—*C. P. Snow.* 1149

The Conscious Lovers—*Sir Richard Steele.* 1151
The Conservationist—*Nadine Gordimer* 1155
The Consolation of Philosophy—*Boethius* 1157
Consuelo—*George Sand* 1160
Continental Drift—*Russell Banks.* 1163
Conversation in the Cathedral—
    Mario Vargas Llosa 1166
Coplas on the Death of His Father—
    Jorge Manrique 1168

Coriolanus—*William Shakespeare* 1171

The Cornerstone—*Zoé Oldenbourg*. 1174

The Corsican Brothers—*Alexandre Dumas*, père. . . 1177

The Cossacks—*Leo Tolstoy* 1180

Cotton Comes to Harlem—*Chester Himes* 1183

The Count of Monte-Cristo—*Alexandre
   Dumas, père* 1186

The Counterfeiters—*André Gide* 1190

The Countess Cathleen—*William Butler Yeats* 1194

A Country Doctor—*Sarah Orne Jewett*. 1197

The Country Girls Trilogy and Epilogue—
   Edna O'Brien 1200

The Country of the Pointed Firs—
   Sarah Orne Jewett 1204

The Country Wife—*William Wycherley*. 1207

Couples—*John Updike* 1211

The Courtesan—*Pietro Aretino* 1214

The Courtship of Miles Standish—*Henry
   Wadsworth Longfellow*. 1217

Cousin Bette—*Honoré de Balzac*. 1220

Cousin Pons—*Honoré de Balzac* 1223

Crabwalk—*Günter Grass* 1227

Cranford—*Elizabeth Gaskell* 1229

The Cream of the Jest—*James Branch Cabell* 1232

Crime and Punishment—*Fyodor Dostoevski* 1235

Crimes of the Heart—*Beth Henley* 1239

The Crisis—*Winston Churchill* 1241

The Critic—*Richard Brinsley Sheridan*. 1244

The Critique of Judgment—*Immanuel Kant* . . . 1247

Critique of Practical Reason—*Immanuel Kant*. . . 1250

Critique of Pure Reason—*Immanuel Kant* 1252

The Crock of Gold—*James Stephens* 1255

Crome Yellow—*Aldous Huxley*. 1258

Crotchet Castle—*Thomas Love Peacock* 1260

Crow—*Ted Hughes* 1263

The Crucible—*Arthur Miller* 1266

Cry, the Beloved Country—*Alan Paton*. 1269

The Crying of Lot 49—*Thomas Pynchon*. 1272

Culture and Anarchy—*Matthew Arnold* 1274

Cupid and Psyche—*Unknown*. 1277

Custer Died for Your Sins—*Vine Deloria, Jr.*. . . . 1280

The Custom of the Country—*Edith Wharton*. 1283

Cuttlefish Bones—*Eugenio Montale* 1286

Cyclops—*Euripides*. 1288

Cymbeline—*William Shakespeare* 1291

The Cypresses Believe in God—*José María
   Gironella* 1294

Cyrano de Bergerac—*Edmond Rostand* 1296

Cyropaedia—*Xenophon* 1299

Daisy Miller—*Henry James*. 1302

Dame Care—*Hermann Sudermann* 1305

The Damnation of Theron Ware—
   Harold Frederic 1307

The Dance of Death—*August Strindberg* 1311

A Dance to the Music of Time—*Anthony Powell*. . . 1314

Dancing at Lughnasa—*Brian Friel* 1322

Dangerous Acquaintances—*Pierre Choderlos de
   Laclos* 1324

Daniel Deronda—*George Eliot* 1328

Danton's Death—*Georg Büchner* 1331

Daphnis and Chloë—*Longus* 1334

The Dark Journey—*Julien Green* 1337

Dark Laughter—*Sherwood Anderson*. 1339

Darkness at Noon—*Arthur Koestler* 1342

Das Kapital—*Karl Marx* 1345

Daughter of Fortune—*Isabel Allende*. 1347

David Copperfield—*Charles Dickens*. 1350

The Day of the Locust—*Nathanael West* 1354

De Profundis—*Oscar Wilde*. 1357

Dead Souls—*Nikolai Gogol*. 1359

Death and the King's Horseman—
   Wole Soyinka 1362

Death Comes for the Archbishop—
   Willa Cather 1365

Death in the Afternoon—*Ernest Hemingway*. . . . 1368

A Death in the Family—*James Agee* 1371

Death in Venice—*Thomas Mann* 1373

Death of a Hero—*Richard Aldington* 1377

Death of a Salesman—*Arthur Miller* 1380

The Death of Artemio Cruz—*Carlos Fuentes* 1383

The Death of Empedocles—*Friedrich Hölderlin*. . . 1386

The Death of Ivan Ilyich—*Leo Tolstoy* 1390

The Death of the Heart—*Elizabeth Bowen* 1393

The Death of Virgil—*Hermann Broch* 1396

The Death Ship—*B. Traven*. 1399

The Decameron—*Giovanni Boccaccio* 1403

Decline and Fall—*Evelyn Waugh* 1408

The Decline of the West—*Oswald Spengler* 1412

The Deerslayer—*James Fenimore Cooper* 1414

The Defence of Guenevere, and Other Poems—
   William Morris 1417

Defence of Poesie—*Sir Philip Sidney*. 1420

A Defence of Poetry—*Percy Bysshe Shelley* 1423

Defender of the Faith—*Philip Roth*. 1425

Deirdre—*James Stephens* 1428

Deirdre—*William Butler Yeats* 1431

Deirdre of the Sorrows—*John Millington
   Synge* 1434

Dejection—*Samuel Taylor Coleridge* 1436

Delia—*Samuel Daniel*. 1438

A Delicate Balance—*Edward Albee* 1441

Deliverance—*James Dickey*. 1444

Delphine—*Madame de Staël* 1446

Delta Wedding—*Eudora Welty* 1450

Demian—*Hermann Hesse*. 1452

Democracy—*Henry Adams* 1455

Democracy—*Joan Didion*. 1458

Democracy in America—*Alexis de Tocqueville* . . . 1460

Democratic Vistas—*Walt Whitman* 1463

The Demon—*Mikhail Lermontov*. 1466

The Deptford Trilogy—*Robertson Davies* 1469

Descent into Hell—*Charles Williams*. 1473

The Descent of Man—*Charles Darwin*. 1476

Desert—*J. M. G. Le Clézio* 1479

Desire in Language—*Julia Kristeva* 1481

Desire Under the Elms—*Eugene O'Neill*. 1484

The Devil upon Two Sticks—*Alain-René
    Lesage* 1487

The Devil's Elixirs—*E. T. A. Hoffmann*. 1490

The Devotion of the Cross—*Pedro Calderón
    de la Barca* 1493

Dhalgren—*Samuel R. Delany*. 1496

The Dialogic Imagination—*Mikhail Bakhtin* 1499

The Dialogues of Plato—*Plato* 1501

Diana of the Crossways—*George Meredith* 1504

Diary—*Samuel Pepys* 1508

The Diary of a Country Priest—*Georges
    Bernanos* 1510

The Diary of a Young Girl—*Anne Frank* 1512

The Diary of Anaïs Nin—*Anaïs Nin* 1514

The Dining Room—*A. R. Gurney, Jr.* 1517

Dinner at Antoine's—*Frances Parkinson Keyes* . . . 1520

Dinner at the Homesick Restaurant—
    Anne Tyler 1522

The Dinner Party—*Claude Mauriac* 1525

The Disciple—*Paul Bourget* 1527

Discipline and Punish—*Michel Foucault* 1531

Discourse on Method—*René Descartes* 1533

Disgrace—*J. M. Coetzee* 1536

The Dispossessed—*Ursula K. Le Guin* 1539

District and Circle—*Seamus Heaney* 1542

The Divan—*Hafiz* 1544

The Divine Comedy—*Dante* 1546

The Divine Fire—*May Sinclair* 1551

Divine Love and Wisdom—*Emanuel
    Swedenborg* 1554

Diving into the Wreck—*Adrienne Rich*. 1556

Do Androids Dream of Electric Sheep?—
    Philip K. Dick 1558

Doctor Faustus—*Thomas Mann* 1561

Doctor Faustus—*Christopher Marlowe*. 1564

Doctor Pascal—*Émile Zola* 1568

Doctor Thorne—*Anthony Trollope* 1572

Doctor Zhivago—*Boris Pasternak* 1575

Dodsworth—*Sinclair Lewis*. 1579

Dog Soldiers—*Robert Stone* 1583

Dog Years—*Günter Grass* 1585

A Doll's House—*Henrik Ibsen* 1588

Dom Casmurro—*Joaquim Maria Machado
    de Assis* 1591

Dombey and Son—*Charles Dickens* 1594

Dominique—*Eugène Fromentin* 1597

Don Carlos, Infante of Spain—
    Friedrich Schiller 1600

The Don Flows Home to the Sea—
    Mikhail Sholokhov 1603

Don Juan—*Lord Byron* 1606

Don Juan Tenorio—*José Zorrilla y Moral* 1610

Don Quixote de la Mancha—*Miguel de
    Cervantes*. 1613

Don Segundo Sombra—*Ricardo Güiraldes*. 1618

Doña Bárbara—*Rómulo Gallegos*. 1621

Dona Flor and Her Two Husbands—
    Jorge Amado 1623

Doña Perfecta—*Benito Pérez Galdós*. 1626

Donald Duk—*Frank Chin*. 1628

The Double-Dealer—*William Congreve* 1631

Dover Beach—*Matthew Arnold*. 1633

Down There—*Joris-Karl Huysmans* 1635

Dracula—*Bram Stoker* 1638

Dragon Seed—*Pearl S. Buck* 1641

Dramatis Personae—*Robert Browning* 1644

Dream of the Red Chamber—*Cao Xueqin* 1647

The Dream Songs—*John Berryman* 1651

Drums Along the Mohawk—*Walter D.
    Edmonds* 1653

Dubliners—*James Joyce* 1656

The Duchess of Malfi—*John Webster* 1659

Duino Elegies—*Rainer Maria Rilke* 1662

Dulce et Decorum Est—*Wilfred Owen* 1665

The Dumb Waiter—*Harold Pinter* 1668

The Dunciad—*Alexander Pope* 1670

Dune series—*Frank Herbert* 1673

Dust Tracks on a Road—*Zora Neale Hurston* . . . 1677

Dutchman—*Amiri Baraka* 1679

The Dynasts—*Thomas Hardy*. 1682

Earth—*Émile Zola*. 1686

The Earthly Paradise—*William Morris* 1689

Earthsea Trilogy—*Ursula K. Le Guin* 1692

East of Eden—*John Steinbeck* 1695

Eastward Ho!—*George Chapman, Ben Jonson,*
  and John Marston 1699

Eat a Bowl of Tea—*Louis H. Chu*. 1702

Volume 4

Contents cxxxiii

Complete List of Titles cxxxvii

Eclogues—*Vergil* 1705

The Edge of the Storm—*Agustín Yáñez* 1708

The Edible Woman—*Margaret Atwood* 1712

The Education of Henry Adams—*Henry Adams* . . 1714

Edward II—*Christopher Marlowe* 1717

The Effect of Gamma Rays on Man-in-the-Moon
  Marigolds—*Paul Zindel* 1720

Effi Briest—*Theodor Fontane*. 1723

Egmont—*Johann Wolfgang von Goethe* 1726

The Egoist—*George Meredith* 1729

El Zarco, the Bandit—*Ignacio Manuel
  Altamirano* 1732

The Elder Statesman—*T. S. Eliot* 1736

Elective Affinities—*Johann Wolfgang
  von Goethe* 1738

Electra—*Euripides* 1742

Electra—*Hugo von Hofmannsthal* 1744

Electra—*Sophocles* 1747

The Elegy of Lady Fiammetta—
  Giovanni Boccaccio 1750

Elegy Written in a Country Churchyard—
  Thomas Gray. 1753

Ellen Foster—*Kaye Gibbons* 1756

Elmer Gantry—*Sinclair Lewis* 1759

Éloges, and Other Poems—*Saint-John Perse* . . . 1762

The Emigrants—*W. G. Sebald* 1764

The Emigrants of Ahadarra—*William Carleton* . . 1766

Émile—*Jean-Jacques Rousseau* 1769

Emilia Galotti—*Gotthold Ephraim Lessing* . . . 1772

Eminent Victorians—*Lytton Strachey*. 1774

Emma—*Jane Austen* 1777

The Emperor Jones—*Eugene O'Neill*. 1782

Empire Falls—*Richard Russo*. 1785

Empire of the Sun—*J. G. Ballard*. 1788

Enamels and Cameos—*Théophile Gautier* 1790

Encheiridion—*Epictetus* 1793

The End of the Road—*John Barth* 1796

Endgame—*Samuel Beckett* 1799

Endymion—*John Keats*. 1801

Endymion, the Man in the Moon—*John Lyly*. . . . 1804

Enemies—*Isaac Bashevis Singer* 1806

An Enemy of the People—*Henrik Ibsen* 1809

The English Patient—*Michael Ondaatje* 1813

The Enneads—*Plotinus* 1815

The Enormous Room—*E. E. Cummings* 1817

An Enquiry Concerning Human Understanding—
  David Hume 1820

An Enquiry Concerning Political Justice—
  William Godwin 1823

Epicœne—*Ben Jonson* 1825

Epigrams—*Martial* 1829

Epigrams—*Meleager* 1831

Epistles—*Horace* 1833

Epitaph of a Small Winner—*Joaquim Maria
  Machado de Assis* 1836

Epithalamion—*Edmund Spenser* 1839

Equus—*Peter Shaffer* 1841

Erec and Enide—*Chrétien de Troyes* 1844

Erewhon—*Samuel Butler* 1848

An Essay Concerning Human Understanding—
  John Locke 1850

An Essay on Criticism—*Alexander Pope* 1853

An Essay on Man—*Alexander Pope* 1856

Essays—*Francis Bacon*. 1858

The Essays—*Michel Eyquem de Montaigne* 1860

Essays of Elia *and* Last Essays of Elia—
  Charles Lamb 1863

Esther Waters—*George Moore* 1866

Ethan Frome—*Edith Wharton* 1869

Ethics—*Baruch Spinoza* 1872

Eugene Onegin—*Alexander Pushkin* 1875

Eugénie Grandet—*Honoré de Balzac*. 1878

The Eunuch—*Terence* 1882

Euphues, the Anatomy of Wit—*John Lyly* 1885

The Eustace Diamonds—*Anthony Trollope*. . . . 1888

Evangeline—*Henry Wadsworth Longfellow* 1891

The Eve of St. Agnes—*John Keats* 1894

Evelina—*Fanny Burney* 1896

Every Man in His Humour—*Ben Jonson* 1900

Every Man out of His Humour—*Ben Jonson* 1903
Everyman—*Unknown* 1907
Everything Is Illuminated—*Jonathan Safran
    Foer.* 1910
The Executioner's Song—*Norman Mailer* 1912
Exiles—*James Joyce* 1915
Exodus—*Leon Uris* 1918
The Expedition of Humphry Clinker—*Tobias
    Smollett.* 1920
Explosion in a Cathedral—*Alejo Carpentier* 1924

A Fable—*William Faulkner* 1927
A Fable for Critics—*James Russell Lowell* 1930
The Fables—*Jean de La Fontaine.* 1933
The Faerie Queene—*Edmund Spenser* 1936
Fahrenheit 451—*Ray Bradbury.* 1939
Fail-Safe—*Eugene Burdick* and *Harvey Wheeler.* . . 1942
The Fair Maid of Perth—*Sir Walter Scott.* 1945
The Faithful Shepherdess—*John Fletcher* 1949
The Fake Astrologer—*Pedro Calderón de
    la Barca* 1951
Falconer—*John Cheever* 1954
The Fall—*Albert Camus* 1956
The Fall of the House of Usher—
    Edgar Allan Poe 1959
The Family at Gilje—*Jonas Lie.* 1963
The Family of Pascual Duarte—
    Camilo José Cela. 1966
The Family Reunion—*T. S. Eliot* 1968
The Far Field—*Theodore Roethke* 1971
Far from the Madding Crowd—*Thomas Hardy.* . . . 1974
Far Tortuga—*Peter Matthiessen* 1977
A Farewell to Arms—*Ernest Hemingway* 1980
Farewell to Manzanar—*Jeanne Wakatsuki
    Houston* and *James D. Houston* 1983
The Farming of Bones—*Edwidge Danticat.* 1985
Fateless—*Imre Kertész* 1988
The Father—*August Strindberg* 1991
Father and Son—*Edmund Gosse* 1995
The Fathers—*Allen Tate.* 1998
Fathers and Sons—*Ivan Turgenev.* 2001
Faultline—*Sheila Ortiz Taylor* 2005
Faust—*Johann Wolfgang von Goethe.* 2007
Fear and Loathing in Las Vegas—*Hunter S.
    Thompson* 2010
Fear and Trembling—*Søren Kierkegaard.* 2012
Fear of Flying—*Erica Jong.* 2014
The Federalist—*Alexander Hamilton,
    James Madison,* and *John Jay* 2016

Felix Holt, the Radical—*George Eliot* 2019
The Fellowship of the Ring—*J. R. R. Tolkien* . . . 2022
The Female Quixote—*Charlotte Lennox* 2026
The Feminine Mystique—*Betty Friedan* 2029
Fences—*August Wilson* 2031
Ferdydurke—*Witold Gombrowicz.* 2034
Ficciones, 1935-1944—*Jorge Luis Borges* 2037
The Field of Vision—*Wright Morris* 2040
Fiesta in November—*Eduardo Mallea* 2042
The Fifth Child—*Doris Lessing.* 2045
The Fifth Horseman—*José Antonio Villarreal* . . . 2048
The Filostrato—*Giovanni Boccaccio* 2051
Final Payments—*Mary Gordon.* 2054
The Financier—*Theodore Dreiser* 2057
Finn Cycle—*Unknown* 2059
Finnegans Wake—*James Joyce* 2063
The Fire Next Time—*James Baldwin.* 2066
The Firebugs—*Max Frisch* 2069
The First Circle—*Aleksandr Solzhenitsyn* 2071
First Poetic Works *and* New Poetic Works—
    Alfred de Musset 2074
The Fisher Maiden—*Bjørnstjerne Bjørnson* 2077
Five Women Who Loved Love—*Ihara Saikaku* . . . 2079
The Fixer—*Bernard Malamud* 2081
A Flag for Sunrise—*Robert Stone* 2084
Flaubert's Parrot—*Julian Barnes* 2087
The Flies—*Mariano Azuela.* 2089
The Flies—*Jean-Paul Sartre* 2092
The Floating Opera—*John Barth* 2095
The Floating World—*Cynthia Kadohata* 2098
Flowers for Algernon—*Daniel Keyes.* 2101
Flowers of Evil—*Charles Baudelaire.* 2104
F.O.B.—*David Henry Hwang.* 2107
The Folks—*Ruth Suckow* 2110
Foma Gordeyev—*Maxim Gorky* 2112
Fontamara—*Ignazio Silone* 2115
Fool for Love—*Sam Shepard* 2118
The Fool of Quality—*Henry Brooke* 2120
Fools Crow—*James Welch* 2123
for colored girls who have considered suicide/
    when the rainbow is enuf—*Ntozake Shange.* . . 2126
For the Union Dead—*Robert Lowell* 2129
For Whom the Bell Tolls—*Ernest Hemingway.* . . . 2132
Foreign Affairs—*Alison Lurie* 2135
The Foreign Girl—*Florencio Sánchez* 2137
The Forsyte Saga—*John Galsworthy.* 2140
Fortunata and Jacinta—*Benito Pérez Galdós* . . . 2143
The Fortunes of Nigel—*Sir Walter Scott* 2147
The Forty Days of Musa Dagh—*Franz Werfel* . . . 2150

Foucault's Pendulum—*Umberto Eco* 2154

The Foundation Trilogy—*Isaac Asimov* 2157

The Fountainhead—*Ayn Rand* 2161

The Four Horsemen of the Apocalypse—
Vicente Blasco Ibáñez 2164

Four Quartets—*T. S. Eliot* 2166

Frankenstein—*Mary Wollstonecraft Shelley* 2169

Franny and Zooey—*J. D. Salinger* 2172

Free Fall—*William Golding* 2174

Freedom or Death—*Nikos Kazantzakis* 2177

The French Lieutenant's Woman—*John Fowles* . . . 2180

The French Revolution—*Thomas Carlyle* 2183

Friar Bacon and Friar Bungay—*Robert Greene* . . . 2185

Frithiof's Saga—*Esaias Tegnér* 2188

The Frogs—*Aristophanes* 2190

From Here to Eternity—*James Jones* 2193

The Fruit of the Tree—*Edith Wharton* 2196

Gabriela, Clove and Cinnamon—*Jorge Amado* . . . 2199

Galileo—*Bertolt Brecht* 2202

The Gambler—*Fyodor Dostoevski* 2206

The Garden Party—*Katherine Mansfield* 2209

The Gardener's Dog—*Lope de Vega Carpio* 2212

Gargantua and Pantagruel—*François Rabelais* 2215

The Gates of Ivory—*Margaret Drabble* 2219

The Gaucho Martín Fierro—*José Hernández* 2221

A General Introduction to Psychoanalysis—
Sigmund Freud 2224

The "Genius"—*Theodore Dreiser* 2227

Georgics—*Vergil* 2230

Germinal—*Émile Zola* 2233

Germinie Lacerteux—*Edmond de Goncourt* and
Jules de Goncourt 2236

The Ghost Sonata—*August Strindberg* 2239

Ghosts—*Henrik Ibsen* 2242

Giant—*Edna Ferber* 2245

Giants in the Earth—*O. E. Rölvaag* 2248

The Gift of the Magi—*O. Henry* 2251

Gil Blas—*Alain-René Lesage* 2253

The Gilded Age—*Mark Twain* and *Charles
Dudley Warner* 2256

Gilead—*Marilynne Robinson* 2260

Giles Goat-Boy—*John Barth* 2262

The Gilgamesh Epic—*Unknown* 2265

Girl with a Pearl Earring—*Tracy Chevalier* 2268

Volume 5

Contents clxxi

Complete List of Titles clxxv

The Glass Bead Game—*Hermann Hesse* 2271

The Glass Key—*Dashiell Hammett* 2274

The Glass Menagerie—*Tennessee Williams* 2277

Glengarry Glen Ross—*David Mamet* 2279

Go Down, Moses—*William Faulkner* 2282

Go Tell It on the Mountain—*James Baldwin* 2285

Goblin Market—*Christina Rossetti* 2289

The God of Small Things—*Arundhati Roy* 2292

God's Little Acre—*Erskine Caldwell* 2295

The Gold-Bug—*Edgar Allan Poe* 2297

The Gold Bug Variations—*Richard Powers* 2299

The Golden Apples—*Eudora Welty* 2302

The Golden Ass—*Lucius Apuleius* 2304

The Golden Bough—*Sir James George Frazer* 2307

The Golden Bowl—*Henry James* 2310

Golden Boy—*Clifford Odets* 2313

The Golden Fruits—*Nathalie Sarraute* 2315

The Golden Notebook—*Doris Lessing* 2317

Gone with the Wind—*Margaret Mitchell* 2320

The Good Companions—*J. B. Priestley* 2324

The Good Earth—*Pearl S. Buck* 2327

A Good Man Is Hard to Find, and Other Stories—
Flannery O'Connor 2330

The Good Soldier—*Ford Madox Ford* 2332

The Good Soldier Švejk—*Jaroslav Hašek* 2335

Good-bye, Mr. Chips—*James Hilton* 2338

Gorboduc—*Thomas Norton* and
Thomas Sackville 2340

Grace Abounding to the Chief of Sinners—
John Bunyan 2343

A Grain of Wheat—*Ngugi wa Thiong'o* 2346

Grand Hotel—*Vicki Baum* 2349

The Grandissimes—*George Washington Cable* . . . 2352

The Grandmothers—*Glenway Wescott* 2355

The Grapes of Wrath—*John Steinbeck* 2358

The Gravedigger's Daughter—*Joyce Carol
Oates* 2361

Gravity's Rainbow—*Thomas Pynchon* 2364

Great Expectations—*Charles Dickens* 2367

The Great Galeoto—*José Echegaray y
Eizaguirre* 2370

The Great Gatsby—*F. Scott Fitzgerald* 2373
The Great Santini—*Pat Conroy* 2376
The Great Testament—*François Villon* 2379
The Greek Passion—*Nikos Kazantzakis* 2382
Green Grow the Lilacs—*Lynn Riggs* 2385
Green Henry—*Gottfried Keller* 2388
Green Hills of Africa—*Ernest Hemingway* 2391
The Green House—*Mario Vargas Llosa* 2393
Green Mansions—*W. H. Hudson* 2396
Greene's Groatsworth of Wit Bought with a
    Million of Repentance—*Robert Greene* 2399
Grendel—*John Gardner* 2401
Grimm's Fairy Tales—*Jacob Grimm* and
    Wilhelm Grimm 2404
Group Portrait with Lady—*Heinrich Böll* 2406
Growth of the Soil—*Knut Hamsun* 2409
Guard of Honor—*James Gould Cozzens* 2412
Guest the One-Eyed—*Gunnar Gunnarsson* 2415
The Guide—*R. K. Narayan* 2417
The Gulag Archipelago, 1918-1956—*Aleksandr
    Solzhenitsyn* 2420
Gulliver's Travels—*Jonathan Swift* 2423
Guy Mannering—*Sir Walter Scott* 2427
Guy of Warwick—*Unknown* 2430

The Hairy Ape—*Eugene O'Neill* 2434
Hakluyt's Voyages—*Richard Hakluyt* 2436
The Hamlet—*William Faulkner* 2439
Hamlet, Prince of Denmark—*William
    Shakespeare* 2443
A Handful of Dust—*Evelyn Waugh* 2446
The Handmaid's Tale—*Margaret Atwood* 2449
Hard Times—*Charles Dickens* 2452
Harmonium—*Wallace Stevens* 2455
The Harp-Weaver, and Other Poems—*Edna
    St. Vincent Millay* 2458
Harry Potter novels—*J. K. Rowling* 2461
The Haunting of Hill House—*Shirley Jackson* 2466
Havelok the Dane—*Unknown* 2469
A Hazard of New Fortunes—*William Dean
    Howells* 2472
Headlong Hall—*Thomas Love Peacock* 2475
The Heart Is a Lonely Hunter—*Carson
    McCullers* 2478
Heart of Aztlán—*Rudolfo Anaya* 2482
Heart of Darkness—*Joseph Conrad* 2485
The Heart of Midlothian—*Sir Walter Scott* 2488
The Heart of the Matter—*Graham Greene* 2492
Heartbreak House—*George Bernard Shaw* 2495

Heat and Dust—*Ruth Prawer Jhabvala* 2499
The Heat of the Day—*Elizabeth Bowen* 2502
Hedda Gabler—*Henrik Ibsen* 2505
The Heidi Chronicles—*Wendy Wasserstein* 2508
The Heights of Macchu Picchu—
    Pablo Neruda 2512
Heimskringla—*Snorri Sturluson* 2514
The Heirs of Columbus—*Gerald Vizenor* 2516
Helen—*Euripides* 2520
Henderson the Rain King—*Saul Bellow* 2523
Henry IV—*Luigi Pirandello* 2526
Henry IV, Part I—*William Shakespeare* 2528
Henry IV, Part II—*William Shakespeare* 2531
Henry V—*William Shakespeare* 2534
Henry VI, Part I—*William Shakespeare* 2538
Henry VI, Part II—*William Shakespeare* 2541
Henry VI, Part III—*William Shakespeare* 2545
Henry VIII—*William Shakespeare* and
    John Fletcher 2548
The Heptameron—*Marguerite de Navarre* 2551
Hercules and His Twelve Labors—*Unknown* 2554
Hereward the Wake—*Charles Kingsley* 2557
Herland—*Charlotte Perkins Gilman* 2560
A Hero of Our Time—*Mikhail Lermontov* 2563
The Hero with a Thousand Faces—
    Joseph Campbell 2567
The Heroes of Romances—*Nicolas Boileau-
    Despréaux* 2569
Heroides—*Ovid* 2572
Herzog—*Saul Bellow* 2573
Hesperides—*Robert Herrick* 2576
High Fidelity—*Nick Hornby* 2579
A High Wind in Jamaica—*Richard Hughes* 2582
Hippolytus—*Euripides* 2585
Hiroshima—*John Hersey* 2587
The History of England—*Thomas Babington
    Macaulay* 2591
The History of Henry Esmond, Esquire, a
    Colonel in the Service of Her Majesty
    Q. Anne—*William Makepeace Thackeray* 2594
The History of Herodotus—*Herodotus* 2597
A History of New York—*Washington Irving* 2600
The History of Pendennis—*William Makepeace
    Thackeray* 2602
History of Plymouth Plantation—
    William Bradford 2606
The History of Rome—*Livy* 2608
The History of the Decline and Fall of the
    Roman Empire—*Edward Gibbon* 2610

A History of the English-Speaking Peoples—
Winston Churchill 2612
History of the Kings of Britain—*Geoffrey of
Monmouth* 2615
History of the Peloponnesian War—*Thucydides* . . . 2618
The Hive—*Camilo José Cela* 2620
Hizakurige—*Jippensha Ikku* 2623
H.M.S. Pinafore—*W. S. Gilbert* 2625
The Hobbit—*J. R. R. Tolkien* 2627
Holy Sonnets—*John Donne* 2630
Homage to Mistress Bradstreet—*John
Berryman* 2632
Homebody/Kabul—*Tony Kushner* 2634
Homeward—*Æ* 2637
The Homewood Trilogy—*John Edgar Wideman* . . . 2640
Homo Faber—*Max Frisch* 2643
The Honorary Consul—*Graham Greene* 2645
Hopscotch—*Julio Cortázar* 2647
Horace—*Pierre Corneille* 2650
The Horse's Mouth—*Joyce Cary* 2653
Hotel du Lac—*Anita Brookner* 2656
The Hotel New Hampshire—*John Irving* 2659
The Hound of the Baskervilles—*Sir Arthur
Conan Doyle* 2661
The Hours—*Michael Cunningham* 2664
The House by the Churchyard—*Joseph Sheridan
Le Fanu* 2666
The House by the Medlar Tree—
Giovanni Verga 2669
A House for Mr. Biswas—*V. S. Naipaul* 2673
The House in Paris—*Elizabeth Bowen* 2676
House Made of Dawn—*N. Scott Momaday* 2679
The House of Blue Leaves—*John Guare* 2682
A House of Gentlefolk—*Ivan Turgenev* 2685
The House of Life—*Dante Gabriel Rossetti* 2688
The House of Mirth—*Edith Wharton* 2691
The House of the Seven Gables—*Nathaniel
Hawthorne* 2694
The House of the Spirits—*Isabel Allende* 2697
The House on Mango Street—*Sandra Cisneros* . . . 2700
The House on the Hill—*Cesare Pavese* 2703
Housekeeping—*Marilynne Robinson* 2705
How Green Was My Valley—*Richard Llewellyn* . . . 2708
How Stella Got Her Groove Back—
Terry McMillan 2711
How the García Girls Lost Their Accents—
Julia Alvarez 2714
Howards End—*E. M. Forster* 2716

Howl—*Allen Ginsberg* 2719
Hudibras—*Samuel Butler* 2722
Hugh Selwyn Mauberley—*Ezra Pound* 2725
The Human Beast—*Émile Zola* 2728
The Human Comedy—*William Saroyan* 2731
The Human Condition—*Hannah Arendt* 2734
The Human Factor—*Graham Greene* 2736
The Human Stain—*Philip Roth* 2739
Humboldt's Gift—*Saul Bellow* 2742
The Hunchback of Notre Dame—*Victor Hugo* 2745
Hunger—*Knut Hamsun* 2749
Hunger of Memory—*Richard Rodriguez* 2751
Huon of Bordeaux—*Unknown* 2753
Hyde Park—*James Shirley* 2756
Hydriotaphia, Urn-Burial—*Sir Thomas
Browne* 2759
Hymn to Intellectual Beauty—*Percy Bysshe
Shelley* 2761
Hymns—*Callimachus* 2764
Hypatia—*Charles Kingsley* 2766

I Am the Cheese—*Robert Cormier* 2771
I and Thou—*Martin Buber* 2774
I, Claudius—*Robert Graves* 2776
I Know Why the Caged Bird Sings—
Maya Angelou 2779
The Iceman Cometh—*Eugene O'Neill* 2782
The Idea of Order at Key West—
Wallace Stevens 2785
The Idiot—*Fyodor Dostoevski* 2787
Idylls—*Theocritus* 2790
Idylls of the King—*Alfred, Lord Tennyson* 2793
If He Hollers Let Him Go—*Chester Himes* 2797
If Not Now, When?—*Primo Levi* 2800
If on a Winter's Night a Traveler—*Italo Calvino* . . . 2803
Ignez de Castro—*António Ferreira* 2805
Iliad—*Homer* 2808
Illness as Metaphor—*Susan Sontag* 2812
Imaginary Conversations of Literary Men and
Statesmen—*Walter Savage Landor* 2814
The Imaginary Invalid—*Molière* 2817
The Imitation of Christ—*Thomas à Kempis* 2820
Immensee—*Theodor Storm* 2822
The Immoralist—*André Gide* 2825
The Importance of Being Earnest—*Oscar Wilde* . . . 2828
In a Free State—*V. S. Naipaul* 2831
In Cold Blood—*Truman Capote* 2833
In Country—*Bobbie Ann Mason* 2836

Volume 6

Contents ccix
Complete List of Titles ccxiii

In Dubious Battle—*John Steinbeck* 2839
In Memoriam—*Alfred, Lord Tennyson* 2841
In the Heart of the Seas—*Shmuel Yosef Agnon* . . . 2844
In the Time of the Butterflies—*Julia Alvarez* 2847
In the Wilderness—*Sigrid Undset* 2850
Incidents in the Life of a Slave Girl—
    Harriet Jacobs 2853
Independence Day—*Richard Ford* 2855
Independent People—*Halldór Laxness* 2857
Indian Summer—*William Dean Howells* 2861
Indiana—*George Sand* 2864
The Informer—*Liam O'Flaherty* 2867
The Inheritors—*William Golding* 2870
The Inspector General—*Nikolai Gogol* 2873
The Interpretation of Dreams—*Sigmund Freud* . . . 2876
The Interrogation—*J. M. G. Le Clézio* 2879
The Intruder—*Maurice Maeterlinck* 2881
Intruder in the Dust—*William Faulkner* 2885
Inundación castálida—*Sor Juana Inés de
    la Cruz* 2887
Invisible Man—*Ralph Ellison* 2890
The Invisible Man—*H. G. Wells* 2893
Iolanthe—*W. S. Gilbert* 2896
Ion—*Euripides* 2899
Iphigenia in Aulis—*Euripides* 2902
Iphigenia in Tauris—*Euripides* 2904
Irish Melodies—*Thomas Moore* 2907
Islands in the Stream—*Ernest Hemingway* 2910
Israel Potter—*Herman Melville* 2913
The Italian—*Ann Radcliffe* 2916
The Itching Parrot—*José Joaquín Fernández
    de Lizardi* 2921
Ivanhoe—*Sir Walter Scott* 2924

J. B.—*Archibald MacLeish* 2928
Jack of Newbery—*Thomas Deloney* 2931
Jack Sheppard—*William Harrison Ainsworth* 2934
Jacques the Fatalist and His Master—
    Denis Diderot 2937
Jane Eyre—*Charlotte Brontë* 2940
Jasmine—*Bharati Mukherjee* 2944
Jason and the Golden Fleece—*Unknown* 2947
Jazz—*Toni Morrison* 2950
Jealousy—*Alain Robbe-Grillet* 2953

Jennie Gerhardt—*Theodore Dreiser* 2955
Jerusalem Delivered—*Torquato Tasso* 2959
The Jew of Malta—*Christopher Marlowe* 2962
Joe Turner's Come and Gone—*August
    Wilson* 2965
John Brown's Body—*Stephen Vincent Benét* 2968
John Halifax, Gentleman—*Dinah Maria
    Mulock* 2971
Jonathan Wild—*Henry Fielding* 2974
Jorrocks' Jaunts and Jollities—*Robert Smith
    Surtees* 2977
Joseph Andrews—*Henry Fielding* 2980
The Journal of a Tour to the Hebrides with
    Samuel Johnson, LL.D.—*James Boswell* 2983
A Journal of the Plague Year—*Daniel Defoe* 2986
Journal to Eliza—*Laurence Sterne* 2988
A Journey to the Centre of the Earth—
    Jules Verne 2990
Journey to the End of the Night—*Louis-
    Ferdinand Céline* 2993
The Journey to the West—*Wu Chengen* 2996
The Joy Luck Club—*Amy Tan* 2999
Jubilee—*Margaret Walker* 3002
Jude the Obscure—*Thomas Hardy* 3005
Julius Caesar—*William Shakespeare* 3008
July's People—*Nadine Gordimer* 3012
Juneteenth—*Ralph Ellison* 3014
The Jungle—*Upton Sinclair* 3017
The Jungle Books—*Rudyard Kipling* 3020
Juno and the Paycock—*Sean O'Casey* 3024
Jurgen—*James Branch Cabell* 3027

Kaddish for a Child Not Born—*Imre Kertész* 3031
Kalevala—*Elias Lönnrot* 3033
Kamouraska—*Anne Hébert* 3037
Kenilworth—*Sir Walter Scott* 3040
Kidnapped—*Robert Louis Stevenson* 3042
Kim—*Rudyard Kipling* 3045
Kindred—*Octavia E. Butler* 3048
Kinflicks—*Lisa Alther* 3051
A King and No King—*Francis Beaumont* and
    John Fletcher 3053
King Horn—*Unknown* 3056
King Johan—*John Bale* 3059
King John—*William Shakespeare* 3062
King Lear—*William Shakespeare* 3065
King Solomon's Mines—*H. Rider Haggard* 3069

The King, the Greatest Alcalde—*Lope de Vega Carpio* 3072
Kiss of the Spider Woman—*Manuel Puig* 3076
The Kitchen God's Wife—*Amy Tan* 3079
The Kite Runner—*Khaled Hosseini* 3081
The Knight of the Burning Pestle—*Francis Beaumont* 3084
The Knights—*Aristophanes* 3087
The Known World—*Edward P. Jones* 3090
Krapp's Last Tape—*Samuel Beckett* 3093
The Kreutzer Sonata—*Leo Tolstoy* 3095
Kristin Lavransdatter—*Sigrid Undset* 3099

The Labyrinth of Solitude—*Octavio Paz* 3103
Lady Chatterley's Lover—*D. H. Lawrence* 3105
The Lady from the Sea—*Henrik Ibsen* 3108
The Lady of the Lake—*Sir Walter Scott* 3111
Lady Windermere's Fan—*Oscar Wilde* 3114
The Lady's Not for Burning—*Christopher Fry* . . . 3117
The Lais of Marie de France—*Marie de France* . . 3120
Lalla Rookh—*Thomas Moore* 3125
Lancelot—*Chrétien de Troyes* 3128
Language, Truth, and Logic—*A. J. Ayer* 3131
Largo Desolato—*Václav Havel* 3134
The Last Chronicle of Barset—*Anthony Trollope* 3137
The Last Days of Pompeii—*Edward Bulwer-Lytton* 3140
The Last of the Mohicans—*James Fenimore Cooper* 3143
The Last of the Wine—*Mary Renault* 3146
The Last Picture Show—*Larry McMurtry* 3149
The Last Puritan—*George Santayana* 3152
The Last Temptation of Christ—*Nikos Kazantzakis* 3155
The Last Tycoon—*F. Scott Fitzgerald* 3157
The Late George Apley—*John P. Marquand* 3160
The Laugh of the Medusa—*Hélène Cixous* 3163
Laughter—*Henri Bergson* 3165
Lavengro—*George Henry Borrow* 3167
The Lay of Igor's Campaign—*Unknown* 3171
The Lay of the Last Minstrel—*Sir Walter Scott* . . . 3173
Lazarillo de Tormes—*Unknown* 3176
Leaves of Grass—*Walt Whitman* 3179
The Left Hand of Darkness—*Ursula K. Le Guin* . . . 3182
The Legend of Good Women—*Geoffrey Chaucer* 3185
The Legend of Sleepy Hollow—*Washington Irving* 3188

The Leopard—*Giuseppe Tomasi di Lampedusa* . . . 3191
Les Misérables—*Victor Hugo* 3194
Let Us Now Praise Famous Men—*James Agee* 3198
Letter from Birmingham City Jail—*Martin Luther King, Jr.* 3200
Letters from an American Farmer—*Michel-Guillaume Jean de Crèvecœur* 3202
Letters to His Son—*Lord Chesterfield* 3205
Leviathan—*Thomas Hobbes* 3207
The Liar—*Pierre Corneille* 3210
Liber Amoris—*William Hazlitt* 3213
Lie Down in Darkness—*William Styron* 3215
The Life and Extraordinary Adventures of Private Ivan Chonkin—*Vladimir Voinovich* 3217
Life and Times of Michael K—*J. M. Coetzee* 3219
Life Is a Dream—*Pedro Calderón de la Barca* 3222
The Life of Marianne—*Marivaux* 3225
Life of Pi—*Yann Martel* 3229
The Life of Samuel Johnson, LL.D.—*James Boswell* 3232
Life on the Mississippi—*Mark Twain* 3234
Ligeia—*Edgar Allan Poe* 3237
Light in August—*William Faulkner* 3240
Lightning—*Santō Kyōden* 3244
Like Water for Chocolate—*Laura Esquivel* 3247
Liliom—*Ferenc Molnár* 3249
Little Big Man—*Thomas Berger* 3252
The Little Clay Cart—*Sudraka* 3255
Little Dorrit—*Charles Dickens* 3257
The Little Foxes—*Lillian Hellman* 3260
The Little Prince—*Antoine de Saint-Exupéry* 3262
Little Women—*Louisa May Alcott* 3265
The Lives of the Poets—*Samuel Johnson* 3268
Locksley Hall—*Alfred, Lord Tennyson* 3271
Lolita—*Vladimir Nabokov* 3273
The Lone Ranger and Tonto Fistfight in Heaven—*Sherman Alexie* 3276
The Lonely Passion of Judith Hearne—*Brian Moore* 3278
Lonesome Dove—*Larry McMurtry* 3281
A Long and Happy Life—*Reynolds Price* 3284
Long Day's Journey into Night—*Eugene O'Neill* 3288
The Long Goodbye—*Raymond Chandler* 3291
The Long Journey—*Johannes V. Jensen* 3293
The Longest Journey—*E. M. Forster* 3297
A Longing for the Light—*Vicente Aleixandre* 3300
Look Back in Anger—*John Osborne* 3303
Look Homeward, Angel—*Thomas Wolfe* 3306

Looking Backward—*Edward Bellamy* 3309
Lord Jim—*Joseph Conrad* 3313
Lord of the Flies—*William Golding* 3316
Lorna Doone—*R. D. Blackmore* 3319
Loss and Gain—*John Henry Newman* 3322
Lost Horizon—*James Hilton* 3325
Lost Illusions—*Honoré de Balzac* 3328
A Lost Lady—*Willa Cather* 3332
The Lost Weekend—*Charles Jackson* 3334
The Lost World—*Randall Jarrell* 3337
The Lottery—*Shirley Jackson* 3340
Love for Love—*William Congreve* 3342
Love in a Wood—*William Wycherley* 3346
Love in the Time of Cholera—*Gabriel
    García Márquez* 3349
Love Medicine—*Louise Erdrich* 3351
The Love Song of J. Alfred Prufrock—
    T. S. Eliot 3354
The Love Suicides at Sonezaki—*Chikamatsu
    Monzaemon* 3356
The Lover—*Marguerite Duras* 3358

Love's Labour's Lost—*William Shakespeare* 3361
Loving—*Henry Green* 3364
The Lower Depths—*Maxim Gorky* 3367
Lucasta Poems—*Richard Lovelace* 3369
The Luck of Roaring Camp, and Other
    Sketches—*Bret Harte* 3372
Lucky Jim—*Kingsley Amis* 3374
The Lusiads—*Luis de Camões* 3377
The Lute—*Gao Ming* 3379
Lycidas—*John Milton* 3382
Lyrical Ballads—*William Wordsworth* and
    Samuel Taylor Coleridge 3384
Lysistrata—*Aristophanes* 3386

M. Butterfly—*David Henry Hwang* 3389
Ma Rainey's Black Bottom—*August Wilson* 3392
The Mabinogion—*Unknown* 3395
Mac Flecknoe—*John Dryden* 3399
Macbeth—*William Shakespeare* 3402
McTeague—*Frank Norris* 3405

Volume 7

Contents ccxlvii
Complete List of Titles ccli

Madame Bovary—*Gustave Flaubert* 3409
Mademoiselle de Maupin—*Théophile Gautier* 3413
The Madwoman of Chaillot—*Jean Giraudoux* 3416
Maggie—*Stephen Crane* 3418
The Magic Mountain—*Thomas Mann* 3421
The Magician of Lublin—*Isaac Bashevis Singer* . . . 3424
Magnalia Christi Americana—*Cotton Mather* 3427
The Magnificent Ambersons—*Booth Tarkington* . . . 3429
Magnificent Obsession—*Lloyd C. Douglas* 3432
The Magus—*John Fowles* 3435
The Mahabharata—*Unknown* 3437
The Maid of Honour—*Philip Massinger* 3441
The Maids—*Jean Genet* 3444
The Maid's Tragedy—*Francis Beaumont* and
    John Fletcher 3447
Main Currents in American Thought—*Vernon
    Louis Parrington* 3450
Main Street—*Sinclair Lewis* 3452
Main-Travelled Roads—*Hamlin Garland* 3455
Major Barbara—*George Bernard Shaw* 3457
The Making of Americans—*Gertrude Stein* 3460

The Malcontent—*John Marston* 3463
Malone Dies—*Samuel Beckett* 3466
The Maltese Falcon—*Dashiell Hammett* 3469
The Mambo Kings Play Songs of Love—
    Oscar Hijuelos 3472
Man and Superman—*George Bernard Shaw* 3475
A Man for All Seasons—*Robert Bolt* 3478
The Man of Feeling—*Henry Mackenzie* 3480
The Man of Mode—*Sir George Etherege* 3484
The Man Who Came to Dinner—*George S.
    Kaufman* and *Moss Hart* 3487
The Man Who Loved Children—
    Christina Stead 3490
The Man Who Was Thursday—
    G. K. Chesterton 3492
The Man with the Golden Arm—*Nelson Algren* . . . 3495
The Man Without a Country—*Edward Everett
    Hale* 3498
The Man Without Qualities—*Robert Musil* 3500
Manette Salomon—*Edmond de Goncourt* and
    Jules de Goncourt 3503
Manfred—*Lord Byron* 3507
Manhattan Transfer—*John Dos Passos* 3510
Manifesto of Surrealism—*André Breton* 3513

Manon Lescaut—*Abbé Prévost* 3516
Man's Fate—*André Malraux* 3519
Mansfield Park—*Jane Austen* 3522
The Mansion—*William Faulkner* 3525
Marat/Sade—*Peter Weiss* 3528
The Marble Faun—*Nathaniel Hawthorne* 3531
March—*Geraldine Brooks* 3534
Mardi, and a Voyage Thither—*Herman Melville* . . . 3536
Maria Magdalena—*Friedrich Hebbel* 3539
Marius the Epicurean—*Walter Pater* 3542
Marmion—*Sir Walter Scott* 3545
The Marquise of O——*Heinrich von Kleist* 3548
Marriage à la Mode—*John Dryden* 3550
The Marriage of Figaro—*Pierre-Augustin Caron
    de Beaumarchais* 3553
The Martian Chronicles—*Ray Bradbury* 3556
Martin Chuzzlewit—*Charles Dickens* 3558
Mary Barton—*Elizabeth Gaskell* 3562
The Masque of the Red Death—
    Edgar Allan Poe 3565
The Master and Margarita—*Mikhail Bulgakov* . . . 3568
The Master Builder—*Henrik Ibsen* 3571
"MASTER HAROLD" . . . and the Boys—
    Athol Fugard 3574
The Masters—*C. P. Snow* 3577
Maud—*Alfred, Lord Tennyson* 3580
Maud Martha—*Gwendolyn Brooks* 3583
Maurice—*E. M. Forster* 3586
Max Havelaar—*Multatuli* 3588
The Maxims—*François de La Rochefoucauld* 3592
The Maximus Poems—*Charles Olson* 3594
The Mayor of Casterbridge—*Thomas Hardy* 3596
The Mayor of Zalamea—*Pedro Calderón
    de la Barca* 3600
Measure for Measure—*William Shakespeare* 3603
Medea—*Euripides* 3607
Meditations—*Marcus Aurelius* 3609
Meditations on First Philosophy—
    René Descartes 3612
Mein Kampf—*Adolf Hitler* 3614
Melmoth the Wanderer—*Charles Robert
    Maturin* 3617
The Member of the Wedding—*Carson
    McCullers* 3621
Memed, My Hawk—*Yashar Kemal* 3624
Memento Mori—*Muriel Spark* 3627
Memoirs of a Physician—*Alexandre Dumas*, père
    and *Auguste Maquet* 3630
Memoirs of Hadrian—*Marguerite Yourcenar* 3634

Men and Women—*Robert Browning* 3637
The Menaechmi—*Plautus* 3640
The Merchant of Venice—*William
    Shakespeare* 3643
Meridian—*Alice Walker* 3646
The Merry Wives of Windsor—*William
    Shakespeare* 3649
Metamorphoses—*Ovid* 3651
The Metamorphosis—*Franz Kafka* 3653
Metamorphosis—*Edith Sitwell* 3656
Metaphysics—*Aristotle* 3659
Michael Kohlhaas—*Heinrich von Kleist* 3661
Midaq Alley—*Naguib Mahfouz* 3664
Mid-Channel—*Arthur Wing Pinero* 3667
Middle Passage—*Charles Johnson* 3669
Middlemarch—*George Eliot* 3672
Midnight's Children—*Salman Rushdie* 3676
A Midsummer Night's Dream—*William
    Shakespeare* 3679
The Mighty and Their Fall—*Ivy Compton-
    Burnett* 3682
The Mikado—*W. S. Gilbert* 3684
The Mill on the Floss—*George Eliot* 3687
The Mill on the Po—*Riccardo Bacchelli* 3691
Milton—*William Blake* 3693
The Minister's Black Veil—
    Nathaniel Hawthorne 3696
The Ministry of Fear—*Graham Greene* 3699
The Miracle Worker—*William Gibson* 3702
The Misanthrope—*Molière* 3704
Miscellanies—*Abraham Cowley* 3707
The Miser—*Molière* 3709
Miss Julie—*August Strindberg* 3712
Miss Lonelyhearts—*Nathanael West* 3715
Mister Roberts—*Thomas Heggen* 3718
Mistero Buffo—*Dario Fo* 3721
The Mistress of the Inn—*Carlo Goldoni* 3724
Mithridates—*Jean Racine* 3727
Moby Dick—*Herman Melville* 3730
A Modern Instance—*William Dean Howells* 3734
Modern Love—*George Meredith* 3737
A Modest Proposal—*Jonathan Swift* 3740
Moll Flanders—*Daniel Defoe* 3743
Molloy—*Samuel Beckett* 3746
A Mölna Elegy—*Gunnar Ekelöf* 3749
Money—*Martin Amis* 3751
The Monk—*Matthew Gregory Lewis* 3754
Monsieur Lecoq—*Émile Gaboriau* 3757
Mont-Oriol—*Guy de Maupassant* 3760

Mont-Saint-Michel and Chartres—
  Henry Adams 3764
A Month in the Country—Ivan Turgenev 3766
The Moon and Sixpence—W. Somerset
  Maugham. 3769
The Moon Is Down—John Steinbeck 3772
The Moonstone—Wilkie Collins 3775
Le Morte d'Arthur—Sir Thomas Malory 3779
Morte d'Urban—J. F. Powers 3782
The Mosquito Coast—Paul Theroux 3784
The Mother—Grazia Deledda 3787
Mother—Maxim Gorky 3790
Mother and Son—Ivy Compton-Burnett 3793
Mother Courage and Her Children—
  Bertolt Brecht 3796
Mother Hubberds Tale—Edmund Spenser 3799
The Moths, and Other Stories—Helena María
  Viramontes 3802
Mourning Becomes Electra—Eugene O'Neill . . . 3804
The Mousetrap—Agatha Christie. 3807
A Moveable Feast—Ernest Hemingway 3811
The Moviegoer—Walker Percy 3813
Mr. Cogito—Zbigniew Herbert 3816
Mr. Sammler's Planet—Saul Bellow 3819
Mrs. Dalloway—Virginia Woolf. 3821
Mrs. Dane's Defence—Henry Arthur Jones 3825
Mrs. Ted Bliss—Stanley Elkin 3828
Much Ado About Nothing—William
  Shakespeare 3831
Mumbo Jumbo—Ishmael Reed 3834
Murder in the Cathedral—T. S. Eliot 3837
Murder on the Orient Express—Agatha Christie . . . 3840
The Murder Room—P. D. James 3843
Mutiny on the Bounty—Charles Nordhoff and
  James Norman Hall 3846
My Ántonia—Willa Cather 3849
My Brilliant Career—Miles Franklin 3852
My Kinsman, Major Molineux—Nathaniel
  Hawthorne 3855
My Life and Hard Times—James Thurber 3858
My Name Is Asher Lev—Chaim Potok 3860
My Name Is Red—Orhan Pamuk 3863
Myra Breckinridge—Gore Vidal 3865
The Mysteries of Paris—Eugène Sue 3868
The Mysteries of Pittsburgh—Michael Chabon . . . 3871

The Mysteries of Udolpho—Ann Radcliffe 3874
The Mysterious Island—Jules Verne 3878
The Mystery of Edwin Drood—
  Charles Dickens 3881
The Myth of Sisyphus—Albert Camus 3884

The Naked and the Dead—Norman Mailer. . . . 3887
Naked Lunch—William S. Burroughs. 3890
The Naked Year—Boris Pilnyak 3893
The Name of the Rose—Umberto Eco 3895
Nana—Émile Zola. 3899
The Napoleon of Notting Hill—
  G. K. Chesterton 3902
The Narrative of Arthur Gordon Pym—
  Edgar Allan Poe 3905
Narrative of the Life of Frederick Douglass—
  Frederick Douglass 3908
The Narrow Road to the Deep North—
  Matsuo Bashō 3911
Nathan the Wise—Gotthold Ephraim Lessing . . . 3913
Native Son—Richard Wright 3916
The Natural—Bernard Malamud 3919
Nausea—Jean-Paul Sartre 3922
The Necklace—Guy de Maupassant 3925
A Nest of Simple Folk—Seán O'Faoláin. 3928
The Neuromancer Trilogy—William Gibson . . . 3931
Never Cry Wolf—Farley Mowat 3936
New Atlantis—Francis Bacon 3937
New Grub Street—George Gissing 3940
The New Héloïse—Jean-Jacques Rousseau . . . 3943
The New Life—Dante. 3946
A New Way to Pay Old Debts—
  Philip Massinger. 3949
The New York Trilogy—Paul Auster 3952
The Newcomes—William Makepeace
  Thackeray 3956
News from Nowhere—William Morris 3960
The Nibelungenlied—Unknown. 3962
Nicholas Nickleby—Charles Dickens 3966
Nick of the Woods—Robert Montgomery Bird. . . 3969
Nicomachean Ethics—Aristotle. 3974
The Nigger of the Narcissus—Joseph Conrad . . . 3976
Night—Elie Wiesel 3979
Night Flight—Antoine de Saint-Exupéry 3981

Volume 8

Contents cclxxxv
Complete List of Titles cclxxxix

'night, Mother—*Marsha Norman* 3985
The Night of the Iguana—*Tennessee Williams* 3987
Night Rider—*Robert Penn Warren* 3990
Nightmare Abbey—*Thomas Love Peacock* 3992
Nightwood—*Djuna Barnes* 3995
Nineteen Eighty-Four—*George Orwell* 3998
Ninety-two in the Shade—*Thomas McGuane* 4001
No Exit—*Jean-Paul Sartre* 4004
No-No Boy—*John Okada* 4006
No Trifling with Love—*Alfred de Musset* 4009
The Normal Heart—*Larry Kramer* 4012
North and South—*Elizabeth Bishop* 4014
North and South—*Elizabeth Gaskell* 4017
North of Boston—*Robert Frost* 4020
Northanger Abbey—*Jane Austen* 4023
Nostromo—*Joseph Conrad* 4026
Notes from the Underground—*Fyodor
    Dostoevski* 4030
Notes of a Native Son—*James Baldwin* 4033
The Novice—*Mikhail Lermontov* 4037
The Nun—*Denis Diderot* 4040
Nuns and Soldiers—*Iris Murdoch* 4042

O Pioneers!—*Willa Cather* 4046
Obasan—*Joy Kogawa* 4049
Oblomov—*Ivan Goncharov* 4051
The Obscene Bird of Night—*José Donoso* 4055
The Octopus—*Frank Norris* 4058
The Odd Couple—*Neil Simon* 4062
Ode—*William Wordsworth* 4064
Ode on a Grecian Urn—*John Keats* 4067
Ode to a Nightingale—*John Keats* 4069
Ode to Aphrodite—*Sappho* 4070
Ode to the West Wind—*Percy Bysshe Shelley* . . . 4073
Odes—*Pindar* 4075
Odyssey—*Homer* 4077
The Odyssey—*Nikos Kazantzakis* 4081
Oedipus at Colonus—*Sophocles* 4083
Oedipus Tyrannus—*Sophocles* 4086
Of Dramatic Poesie—*John Dryden* 4089
Of Grammatology—*Jacques Derrida* 4092
Of Human Bondage—*W. Somerset Maugham* 4094
Of Mice and Men—*John Steinbeck* 4098
Of Time and the River—*Thomas Wolfe* 4101

The Old Bachelor—*William Congreve* 4104
The Old Curiosity Shop—*Charles Dickens* 4107
Old Fortunatus—*Thomas Dekker* 4110
The Old Gringo—*Carlos Fuentes* 4113
The Old Maid—*Edith Wharton* 4115
The Old Man and the Sea—*Ernest Hemingway* . . . 4118
Old Mortality—*Sir Walter Scott* 4121
The Old Wives' Tale—*Arnold Bennett* 4125
The Old Wives' Tale—*George Peele* 4128
Oldtown Folks—*Harriet Beecher Stowe* 4131
Oliver Twist—*Charles Dickens* 4135
Omensetter's Luck—*William H. Gass* 4139
Omeros—*Derek Walcott* 4142
Omoo—*Herman Melville* 4144
On Heroes, Hero-Worship, and the Heroic in
    History—*Thomas Carlyle* 4147
On Liberty—*John Stuart Mill* 4150
On Sepulchres—*Ugo Foscolo* 4152
On the Genealogy of Morals—*Friedrich
    Nietzsche* 4154
On the Nature of Things—*Lucretius* 4156
On the Origin of Species by Means of Natural
    Selection—*Charles Darwin* 4159
On the Road—*Jack Kerouac* 4161
On the Soul—*Aristotle* 4164
On the Sublime—*Longinus* 4166
The Once and Future King—*T. H. White* 4168
One Day in the Life of Ivan Denisovich—
    Aleksandr Solzhenitsyn 4171
One Flew over the Cuckoo's Nest—*Ken Kesey* . . . 4175
One Hundred Years of Solitude—*Gabriel
    García Márquez* 4177
One of Ours—*Willa Cather* 4180
The Open Boat—*Stephen Crane* 4183
The Optimist's Daughter—*Eudora Welty* 4185
Oration on the Dignity of Man—*Giovanni Pico
    della Mirandola* 4188
The Orations—*Cicero* 4190
The Ordeal of Richard Feverel—
    George Meredith 4192
The Order of Things—*Michel Foucault* 4196
Ordinary People—*Judith Guest* 4198
Oresteia—*Aeschylus* 4201
Orfeo—*Poliziano* 4205
Orlando—*Virginia Woolf* 4207
Orlando Furioso—*Ludovico Ariosto* 4211
Orlando Innamorato—*Matteo Maria Boiardo* . . . 4214

Orley Farm—*Anthony Trollope* 4218

Oroonoko—*Aphra Behn*. 4222

Orpheus—*Jean Cocteau*. 4226

Orpheus and Eurydice—*Unknown* 4229

Oscar and Lucinda—*Peter Carey* 4231

Othello—*William Shakespeare* 4234

The Other One—*Colette* 4237

Other Voices, Other Rooms—*Truman Capote* 4240

Other Women—*Lisa Alther* 4243

Our Ancestors—*Italo Calvino* 4246

Our House in the Last World—*Oscar Hijuelos*. . . 4249

Our Mutual Friend—*Charles Dickens* 4252

Our Town—*Thornton Wilder* 4255

Out of Africa—*Isak Dinesen* 4258

Out of the Silent Planet—*C. S. Lewis* 4261

The Outsiders—*S. E. Hinton* 4264

The Overcoat—*Nikolai Gogol* 4266

The Ox-Bow Incident—*Walter Van Tilburg
    Clark* 4270

The Painted Bird—*Jerzy Kosinski*. 4273

Palace Walk—*Naguib Mahfouz* 4275

Pale Fire—*Vladimir Nabokov* 4278

Pale Horse, Pale Rider—*Katherine Anne
    Porter*. 4281

The Palm-Wine Drinkard—*Amos Tutuola* 4285

Pamela—*Samuel Richardson* 4288

Parable of the Sower *and* Parable of the
    Talents—*Octavia E. Butler* 4292

Parade's End—*Ford Madox Ford* 4295

Paradise—*Toni Morrison* 4298

Paradise Lost—*John Milton*. 4301

Paradise Regained—*John Milton* 4304

Paradox, King—*Pío Baroja* 4307

Parallel Lives—*Plutarch* 4310

Parlement of Foules—*Geoffrey Chaucer* 4313

Parzival—*Wolfram von Eschenbach* 4315

A Passage to India—*E. M. Forster* 4319

Passing—*Nella Larsen* 4322

The Passion According to G. H.—
    Clarice Lispector. 4325

The Passion Flower—*Jacinto Benavente y
    Martínez* 4328

Passions and Ancient Days—*Constantine P.
    Cavafy* 4330

Past and Present—*Thomas Carlyle* 4333

Paterson—*William Carlos Williams*. 4336

The Pathfinder—*James Fenimore Cooper* 4338

Patience—*W. S. Gilbert* 4342

Patience and Sarah—*Isabel Miller* 4345

Peace—*Aristophanes* 4348

The Peasants—*Władysław Reymont* 4350

Peder Victorious—*O. E. Rölvaag* 4353

Pedro Páramo—*Juan Rulfo* 4357

Pedro Sánchez—*José María de Pereda* 4360

Peer Gynt—*Henrik Ibsen* 4362

Pelle the Conqueror—*Martin Andersen Nexø* 4364

Pelléas and Mélisande—*Maurice Maeterlinck* 4367

Penguin Island—*Anatole France* 4370

Penrod—*Booth Tarkington* 4373

Pensées—*Blaise Pascal* 4375

The People, Yes—*Carl Sandburg*. 4378

Pepita Jiménez—*Juan Valera* 4380

Père Goriot—*Honoré de Balzac* 4383

Pericles, Prince of Tyre—*William Shakespeare*. . . 4386

The Persians—*Aeschylus* 4389

Personae—*Ezra Pound* 4392

Persuasion—*Jane Austen* 4395

Peter Ibbetson—*George du Maurier* 4398

Peter Pan—*Sir James Barrie* 4401

Peyton Place—*Grace Metalious* 4404

Phaedra—*Jean Racine* 4406

Pharsalia—*Lucan* 4409

The Phenomenology of Spirit—*Georg Wilhelm
    Friedrich Hegel*. 4412

The Phenomenon of Man—*Pierre Teilhard de
    Chardin*. 4415

Philaster—*Francis Beaumont* and
    John Fletcher 4418

The Philippics—*Demosthenes* 4421

Philoctetes—*Sophocles* 4423

Philosopher or Dog?—*Joaquim Maria
    Machado de Assis* 4426

Philosophical Investigations—*Ludwig
    Wittgenstein* 4429

Philosophy of Art—*Hippolyte Taine* 4432

Phineas Finn, the Irish Member—
    Anthony Trollope. 4434

Phineas Redux—*Anthony Trollope* 4438

The Phoenician Women—*Euripides* 4441

Phormio—*Terence*. 4444

The Piano Lesson—*August Wilson* 4447

The Piano Teacher—*Elfriede Jelinek* 4450

Pickwick Papers—*Charles Dickens*. 4453

Picture Bride—*Cathy Song* 4457

The Picture of Dorian Gray—*Oscar Wilde* 4459

Pierre—*Herman Melville* 4462

Piers Plowman—*William Langland*. 4466

Pilgrim at Tinker Creek—*Annie Dillard* 4469
The Pilgrim Hawk—*Glenway Wescott* 4471
Pilgrimage—*Dorothy Richardson*. 4474
The Pilgrimage of Charlemagne—*Unknown* 4476
The Pilgrim's Progress—*John Bunyan* 4479
The Pillars of Society—*Henrik Ibsen*. 4483
The Pilot—*James Fenimore Cooper* 4486
Pincher Martin—*William Golding* 4489
The Pioneers—*James Fenimore Cooper* 4492
The Pirates of Penzance—*W. S. Gilbert*. 4496
The Pit—*Frank Norris* 4499
The Plague—*Albert Camus*. 4502
The Plain-Dealer—*William Wycherley* 4506
Planet of the Apes—*Pierre Boulle* 4509
Plantation Boy—*José Lins do Rego*. 4512
Platero and I—*Juan Ramón Jiménez* 4515

The Playboy of the Western World—*John
    Millington Synge* 4518
The Plough and the Stars—*Sean O'Casey* 4520
The Plumed Serpent—*D. H. Lawrence* 4523
Plutus—*Aristophanes* 4526
Pnin—*Vladimir Nabokov* 4529
Poem of the Cid—*Unknown* 4532
Poems—*Sidney Lanier* 4535
Poems—*Sir Walter Ralegh* 4538
Poems and Ballads—*Algernon Charles
    Swinburne* 4540
Poems, Chiefly in the Scottish Dialect—
    Robert Burns 4543
Poetic Edda—*Unknown* 4545
Poetical Meditations—*Alphonse de Lamartine* . . . 4547
Poetics—*Aristotle* 4550

Volume 9

Contents cccxxiii
Complete List of Titles cccxxvii

Poetry of Campion—*Thomas Campion*. 4553
Poetry of Carducci—*Giosuè Carducci* 4555
Poetry of Carew—*Thomas Carew* 4557
Poetry of Clare—*John Clare* 4560
Poetry of du Bellay—*Joachim du Bellay* 4563
Poetry of George—*Stefan George* 4565
Poetry of Laforgue—*Jules Laforgue* 4568
Poetry of Machado—*Antonio Machado* 4570
Poetry of Mörike—*Eduard Mörike* 4572
Poetry of Skelton—*John Skelton* 4575
Poetry of Traherne—*Thomas Traherne* 4579
Poetry of Vaughan—*Henry Vaughan* 4582
Poetry of Verlaine—*Paul Verlaine* 4585
Point Counter Point—*Aldous Huxley* 4588
The Poisonwood Bible—*Barbara Kingsolver* 4591
Pollyanna—*Eleanor H. Porter* 4595
Polyeucte—*Pierre Corneille* 4597
Poly-Olbion—*Michael Drayton*. 4600
The Ponder Heart—*Eudora Welty*. 4603
Poor Folk—*Fyodor Dostoevski* 4605
Poor Richard's Almanack—*Benjamin Franklin* . . . 4608
Poor White—*Sherwood Anderson* 4610
The Poorhouse Fair—*John Updike* 4613
Porgy—*DuBose Heyward*. 4615
Portnoy's Complaint—*Philip Roth* 4618
Il porto sepolto—*Giuseppe Ungaretti* 4621

The Portrait of a Lady—*Henry James* 4623
Portrait of the Artist as a Young Dog—
    Dylan Thomas 4627
A Portrait of the Artist as a Young Man—
    James Joyce 4630
The Possessed—*Fyodor Dostoevski* 4633
Possession—*A. S. Byatt* 4637
The Postman Always Rings Twice—
    James M. Cain 4640
The Pot of Gold—*Plautus*. 4643
Power—*Lion Feuchtwanger*. 4645
The Power and the Glory—*Graham Greene* 4648
The Power of Darkness—*Leo Tolstoy*. 4651
Pragmatism—*William James* 4653
The Prairie—*James Fenimore Cooper* 4656
The Praise of Folly—*Desiderius Erasmus* 4660
Praisesong for the Widow—*Paule Marshall* 4662
A Prayer for Owen Meany—*John Irving* 4665
Preface to Shakespeare—*Samuel Johnson* 4668
Prejudices—*H. L. Mencken* 4670
The Prelude—*William Wordsworth* 4672
Preludes for Memnon—*Conrad Aiken* 4675
The Pretenders—*Ludovico Ariosto* 4677
Pride and Prejudice—*Jane Austen* 4680
The Prime of Miss Jean Brodie—
    Muriel Spark 4685
The Prince—*Niccolò Machiavelli*. 4688
The Prince and the Pauper—*Mark Twain*. 4690
The Prince of Homburg—*Heinrich von Kleist* 4694

The Princess—*Alfred, Lord Tennyson* 4697
The Princess Casamassima—*Henry James* 4700
The Princess of Clèves—*Madame de La Fayette* . . . 4703
Principia—*Sir Isaac Newton* 4707
Principia Ethica—*G. E. Moore* 4709
Principia Mathematica—*Bertrand Russell* and
   Alfred North Whitehead 4713
Principles of Political Economy—*John Stuart*
   Mill 4715
The Prisoner of Zenda—*Anthony Hope* 4717
The Private Life of the Master Race—
   Bertolt Brecht 4720
Private Lives—*Noël Coward* 4723
The Problems of Philosophy—*Bertrand*
   Russell 4725
The Professor's House—*Willa Cather* 4728
Prometheus Bound—*Aeschylus* 4731
Prometheus Unbound—*Percy Bysshe Shelley* . . . 4733
The Promised Land—*Henrik Pontoppidan* 4736
The Prophet—*Kahlil Gibran* 4739
Prosas Profanas, and Other Poems—
   Rubén Darío 4741
Proserpine and Ceres—*Unknown* 4743
Pseudolus—*Plautus* 4746
Purgatory—*William Butler Yeats* 4749
Purple Dust—*Sean O'Casey* 4752
Pygmalion—*George Bernard Shaw* 4754

Quartet in Autumn—*Barbara Pym* 4758
Queen Mab—*Percy Bysshe Shelley* 4761
Quentin Durward—*Sir Walter Scott* 4763
The Quest for Certainty—*John Dewey* 4767
The Quest for Christa T.—*Christa Wolf* 4770
The Quest of the Holy Grail—*Unknown* 4772
Quicksand—*Nella Larsen* 4775
The Quiet American—*Graham Greene* 4778
Quo Vadis—*Henryk Sienkiewicz* 4781

The Rabbit Angstrom novels—*John Updike* 4784
Rabbit Boss—*Thomas Sanchez* 4787
The Rainbow—*D. H. Lawrence* 4789
Raintree County—*Ross Lockridge, Jr.* 4792
A Raisin in the Sun—*Lorraine Hansberry* 4795
Ralph Roister Doister—*Nicholas Udall* 4798
Ramayana—*Vālmīki* 4801
Rameau's Nephew—*Denis Diderot* 4804
The Rape of Lucrece—*William Shakespeare* 4807
The Rape of the Lock—*Alexander Pope* 4810
Rappaccini's Daughter—*Nathaniel Hawthorne* . . . 4813

Rasselas—*Samuel Johnson* 4816
The Razor's Edge—*W. Somerset Maugham* 4819
The Real Life of Sebastian Knight—*Vladimir*
   Nabokov 4822
The Real Thing—*Tom Stoppard* 4825
Rebecca—*Daphne du Maurier* 4827
The Recruiting Officer—*George Farquhar* 4830
The Rector of Justin—*Louis Auchincloss* 4833
The Red and the Black—*Stendhal* 4836
The Red Badge of Courage—*Stephen Crane* 4839
Redburn—*Herman Melville* 4842
Reflections in a Golden Eye—*Carson*
   McCullers 4845
Reflections on the Revolution in France—
   Edmund Burke 4848
The Reivers—*William Faulkner* 4851
Relativity—*Albert Einstein* 4854
The Remains of the Day—*Kazuo Ishiguro* 4856
Remembrance of Things Past—*Marcel Proust* . . . 4859
The Renaissance—*Walter Pater* 4863
Renée Mauperin—*Edmond de Goncourt* and
   Jules de Goncourt 4866
Representative Men—*Ralph Waldo Emerson* 4868
Republic—*Plato* 4872
Requiem—*Anna Akhmatova* 4875
Requiem for a Nun—*William Faulkner* 4877
Resurrection—*Leo Tolstoy* 4880
The Return—*Walter de la Mare* 4884
The Return of the King—*J. R. R. Tolkien* 4887
The Return of the Native—*Thomas Hardy* 4890
The Revenge of Bussy d'Ambois—
   George Chapman 4894
The Revenger's Tragedy—*Thomas Middleton* . . . 4897
The Revolt of the Masses—*José Ortega y*
   Gasset 4900
Reynard the Fox—*Unknown* 4902
Rhadamistus and Zenobia—*Prosper Jolyot de*
   Crébillon 4905
Rhinoceros—*Eugène Ionesco* 4908
The Rhymes—*Gustavo Adolfo Bécquer* 4910
Rhymes—*Petrarch* 4913
Riceyman Steps—*Arnold Bennett* 4915
Richard II—*William Shakespeare* 4918
Richard III—*William Shakespeare* 4922
Riders in the Chariot—*Patrick White* 4925
Riders to the Sea—*John Millington Synge* 4929
The Right Stuff—*Tom Wolfe* 4931
Right You Are (If You Think So)—
   Luigi Pirandello 4934

Rights of Man—*Thomas Paine* 4936

The Rime of the Ancient Mariner—*Samuel Taylor Coleridge* 4938

The Ring and the Book—*Robert Browning* 4941

Rip Van Winkle—*Washington Irving* 4945

The Rise of Silas Lapham—*William Dean Howells* 4948

The Rising of the Moon—*Lady Augusta Gregory* 4952

Rites of Passage—*William Golding* 4955

The Rivals—*Richard Brinsley Sheridan* 4958

The Road—*Cormac McCarthy* 4961

Roan Stallion—*Robinson Jeffers* 4963

Rob Roy—*Sir Walter Scott* 4966

The Robe—*Lloyd C. Douglas* 4969

Robert Elsmere—*Mary Augusta Ward* 4972

Robin Hood's Adventures—*Unknown* 4975

Robinson Crusoe—*Daniel Defoe* 4978

The Rocking-Horse Winner—*D. H. Lawrence* . . . 4982

Roderick Hudson—*Henry James* 4984

The Romance of Leonardo da Vinci—*Dmitry Merezhkovsky* 4988

The Romance of the Forest—*Ann Radcliffe* 4991

Romance of the Three Kingdoms— *Luo Guanzhong* 4996

The Romantic Comedians—*Ellen Glasgow* 4998

Romeo and Juliet—*William Shakespeare* 5001

Romola—*George Eliot* 5005

Room at the Top—*John Braine* 5009

A Room of One's Own—*Virginia Woolf* 5011

A Room with a View—*E. M. Forster* 5014

Roots—*Alex Haley* 5017

The Rope—*Plautus* 5020

A Rose for Emily—*William Faulkner* 5023

Rosencrantz and Guildenstern Are Dead— *Tom Stoppard* 5025

Rosmersholm—*Henrik Ibsen* 5028

Roughing It—*Mark Twain* 5031

Rouse Up O Young Men of the New Age!— *Kenzaburō Ōe* 5033

Roxana—*Daniel Defoe* 5036

Rubáiyát of Omar Khayyám—*Edward FitzGerald* 5039

Rubyfruit Jungle—*Rita Mae Brown* 5042

Rumble Fish—*S. E. Hinton* 5045

R.U.R.—*Karel Čapek* 5047

Ruslan and Lyudmila—*Alexander Pushkin* 5050

The Sacred Fount—*Henry James* 5054

The Sacred Hoop—*Paula Gunn Allen* 5057

The Saga of Grettir the Strong—*Unknown* 5059

The Sailor Who Fell from Grace with the Sea— *Yukio Mishima* 5063

Saint Joan—*George Bernard Shaw* 5066

St. Peter's Umbrella—*Kálmán Mikszáth* 5069

Śakuntalā—*Kālidāsa* 5071

Salammbô—*Gustave Flaubert* 5074

'Salem's Lot—*Stephen King* 5077

The Salt Eaters—*Toni Cade Bambara* 5080

Samson Agonistes—*John Milton* 5083

Sanctuary—*William Faulkner* 5085

Sanine—*Mikhail Artsybashev* 5089

Sappho—*Alphonse Daudet* 5092

Sappho—*Franz Grillparzer* 5095

Sartor Resartus—*Thomas Carlyle* 5098

Sartoris—*William Faulkner* 5101

The Satanic Verses—*Salman Rushdie* 5103

Satires—*Nicolas Boileau-Despréaux* 5106

Satires—*Juvenal* 5109

Satires—*Lucian* 5112

Satires—*Persius* 5115

Satiromastix—*Thomas Dekker* 5118

The Satyricon—*Petronius* 5120

Saul—*Vittorio Alfieri* 5124

Volume 10

Contents
Complete List of Titles

Contents ccclxi

Complete List of Titles ccclxv

The Savage Mind—*Claude Lévi-Strauss* 5127

Scaramouche—*Rafael Sabatini* 5129

The Scarlet Letter—*Nathaniel Hawthorne* 5132

Schindler's List—*Thomas Keneally* 5136

The Scholar-Gipsy—*Matthew Arnold* 5138

The School for Husbands—*Molière* 5140

The School for Scandal—*Richard Brinsley Sheridan* 5143

The School for Wives—*Molière* 5147

The Screwtape Letters—*C. S. Lewis* 5150

Sea Garden—*H. D.* 5153

The Sea of Grass—*Conrad Richter* 5156

The Sea-Wolf—*Jack London* 5159

The Seagull—*Anton Chekhov* 5162

A Season in Hell—*Arthur Rimbaud* 5166

A Season in Rihata—*Maryse Condé* 5168

The Seasons—*James Thomson* 5171

Seatonian Poems *and A Song to David*—
    Christopher Smart 5174

The Second Mrs. Tanqueray—*Arthur Wing*
    Pinero 5176

The Second Sex—*Simone de Beauvoir* 5179

The Second Shepherds' Play—*Wakefield Master* . . 5182

The Secret Agent—*Joseph Conrad* 5185

Seeing Things—*Seamus Heaney* 5188

Seize the Day—*Saul Bellow* 5191

Sejanus His Fall—*Ben Jonson* 5194

Self-Portrait in a Convex Mirror—*John Ashbery* . . 5197

The Self-Tormentor—*Terence*. 5199

El Señor Presidente—*Miguel Ángel Asturias* 5202

Sense and Sensibility—*Jane Austen* 5205

A Sentimental Education—*Gustave Flaubert* 5208

A Sentimental Journey—*Laurence Sterne* 5212

A Separate Peace—*John Knowles* 5215

Set This House on Fire—*William Styron* 5218

Seven Against Thebes—*Aeschylus* 5221

Seven Pillars of Wisdom—*T. E. Lawrence* 5224

The Seven Who Were Hanged—
    Leonid Andreyev 5226

Seventeen—*Booth Tarkington*. 5229

Sexual Politics—*Kate Millett* 5232

Shadows on the Rock—*Willa Cather* 5234

The Shawl—*Cynthia Ozick* 5237

She—*H. Rider Haggard*. 5239

She Stoops to Conquer—*Oliver Goldsmith* 5242

The Sheep Well—*Lope de Vega Carpio* 5245

The Sheltered Life—*Ellen Glasgow* 5248

The Sheltering Sky—*Paul Bowles* 5251

The Shepheardes Calender—*Edmund Spenser* . . . 5254

The Shining—*Stephen King*. 5257

Ship of Fools—*Katherine Anne Porter* 5260

The Shipping News—*E. Annie Proulx* 5263

Shirley—*Charlotte Brontë* 5266

Shoeless Joe—*W. P. Kinsella* 5268

The Shoemaker's Holiday—*Thomas Dekker* 5271

The Shoes of the Fisherman—*Morris West* 5274

Shōgun—*James Clavell*. 5277

Show Boat—*Edna Ferber*. 5280

A Shropshire Lad—*A. E. Housman*. 5283

Shroud for a Nightingale—*P. D. James*. 5285

The Sickness unto Death—*Søren Kierkegaard* . . . 5287

Siddhartha—*Hermann Hesse* 5290

The Siege of Rhodes—*Sir William Davenant* 5293

The Sign in Sidney Brustein's Window—
    Lorraine Hansberry 5295

The Sign of Four—*Sir Arthur Conan Doyle* 5298

The Significance of the Frontier in American
    History—*Frederick Jackson Turner* 5302

Silas Marner—*George Eliot*. 5304

Silence—*Shūsaku Endō*. 5307

Sinners in the Hands of an Angry God—
    Jonathan Edwards 5310

Sir Charles Grandison—*Samuel Richardson* 5312

Sir Gawain and the Green Knight—*Pearl-Poet*. . . 5316

The Sirens of Titan—*Kurt Vonnegut* 5319

Sister Carrie—*Theodore Dreiser* 5321

Sister Philomène—*Edmond de Goncourt* and
    Jules de Goncourt 5325

Six Characters in Search of an Author—
    Luigi Pirandello 5328

Six Degrees of Separation—*John Guare* 5332

The Skin of Our Teeth—*Thornton Wilder* 5334

Slaughterhouse-Five—*Kurt Vonnegut*. 5338

The Sleepwalkers—*Hermann Broch* 5340

Slouching Towards Bethlehem—*Joan Didion* 5344

Slow Homecoming—*Peter Handke*. 5346

The Small House at Allington—
    Anthony Trollope 5349

Smoke—*Ivan Turgenev* 5353

The Snake Pit—*Sigrid Undset* 5356

Snow Country—*Yasunari Kawabata* 5359

Snow Falling on Cedars—*David Guterson* 5362

Snow White—*Donald Barthelme*. 5364

Snow-Bound—*John Greenleaf Whittier* 5367

The Snows of Kilimanjaro, and Other Stories—
    Ernest Hemingway. 5369

So Big—*Edna Ferber*. 5371

The Social Contract—*Jean-Jacques Rousseau* 5374

Society and Solitude—*Ralph Waldo Emerson* 5377

Sohrab and Rustum—*Matthew Arnold* 5380

Solaris—*Stanisław Lem*. 5382

The Solitudes—*Luis de Góngora y Argote* 5385

A Son of the Middle Border—*Hamlin Garland* . . . 5388

The Song of Hiawatha—*Henry Wadsworth*
    Longfellow 5391

The Song of Roland—*Unknown* 5394

Song of Solomon—*Toni Morrison* 5398

The Song of the Lark—*Willa Cather* 5401

The Song of the World—*Jean Giono* 5404

Songs of Innocence and of Experience—
    William Blake 5407

Sonnets for Helen—*Pierre de Ronsard* 5410
Sonnets from the Portuguese—*Elizabeth Barrett*
    Browning 5412
Sonnets of Michelangelo—*Michelangelo*. 5415
Sonnets of Shakespeare—*William Shakespeare* . . . 5418
Sonnets to Orpheus—*Rainer Maria Rilke* 5421
Sons and Lovers—*D. H. Lawrence* 5424
Sophie's Choice—*William Styron*. 5427
The Sorrows of Young Werther—*Johann*
    Wolfgang von Goethe 5430
The Sot-Weed Factor—*John Barth* 5433
Soul Mountain—*Gao Xingjian* 5436
The Souls of Black Folk—*W. E. B. Du Bois* 5439
The Sound and the Fury—*William Faulkner* 5441
The Sound of Waves—*Yukio Mishima* 5444
South Wind—*Norman Douglas*. 5447
Spain, Take This Cup from Me—*César Vallejo* . . 5450
The Spanish Friar—*John Dryden* 5452
The Spanish Tragedy—*Thomas Kyd* 5455
The Spectator—*Joseph Addison* and *Sir Richard*
    Steele. 5458
Speculations About Jakob—*Uwe Johnson* 5461
The Spirit of the Laws—*Montesquieu* 5464
The Spoils of Poynton—*Henry James* 5466
Spoon River Anthology—*Edgar Lee Masters* 5470
The Sport of the Gods—*Paul Laurence Dunbar* . . . 5472
The Sportswriter—*Richard Ford* 5475
Spring Awakening—*Frank Wedekind*. 5477
The Spy—*James Fenimore Cooper* 5481
The Spy Who Came in from the Cold—
    John le Carré. 5485
The Stand—*Stephen King*. 5488
The Star of Seville—*Unknown* 5491
Steppenwolf—*Hermann Hesse* 5494
Steps—*Jerzy Kosinski*. 5498
Steps to the Temple—*Richard Crashaw* 5500
The Stone Angel—*Margaret Laurence* 5503
The Stone Diaries—*Carol Shields* 5506
The Stones of Venice—*John Ruskin* 5508
The Story of an African Farm—*Olive Schreiner* . . . 5511
The Story of Burnt Njal—*Unknown* 5514
The Story of Gösta Berling—*Selma Lagerlöf* 5518
Storyteller—*Leslie Marmon Silko*. 5521
The Strange Case of Dr. Jekyll and Mr. Hyde—
    Robert Louis Stevenson 5523
Strange Interlude—*Eugene O'Neill*. 5526
Strange Stories from a Chinese Studio—
    Pu Songling 5529
The Stranger—*Albert Camus* 5531

Stranger in a Strange Land—*Robert A. Heinlein* . . . 5534
Strangers and Brothers series—*C. P. Snow* 5537
Strangers on a Train—*Patricia Highsmith* 5540
The Street—*Ann Lane Petry* 5543
Street Scene—*Elmer Rice*. 5546
A Streetcar Named Desire—*Tennessee Williams* . . . 5549
Studs Lonigan—*James T. Farrell* 5552
A Study in Scarlet—*Sir Arthur Conan Doyle*. 5556
A Study of History—*Arnold Toynbee* 5559
The Subjection of Women—*John Stuart Mill* 5561
Suddenly Last Summer—*Tennessee Williams* 5564
Sula—*Toni Morrison* 5567
Summa Theologica—*Thomas Aquinas* 5570
The Sun Also Rises—*Ernest Hemingway* 5572
The Sunken Bell—*Gerhart Hauptmann* 5576
The Sunlight Dialogues—*John Gardner* 5579
The Suppliants—*Aeschylus* 5582
The Suppliants—*Euripides* 5585
Surfacing—*Margaret Atwood*. 5588
The Surrounded—*D'Arcy McNickle* 5591
Swallow Barn—*John Pendleton Kennedy*. 5593
The Swiss Family Robinson—*Johann David Wyss*
    and *Johann Rudolf Wyss* 5596
Sybil—*Benjamin Disraeli* 5599

Tala—*Gabriela Mistral* 5603
A Tale of a Tub—*Jonathan Swift* 5605
The Tale of Genji—*Murasaki Shikibu* 5608
A Tale of Two Cities—*Charles Dickens* 5611
The Talented Mr. Ripley—*Patricia Highsmith* 5615
Tales of Ise—*Unknown* 5617
Tales of Odessa—*Isaac Babel*. 5620
Tales of Soldiers and Civilians—
    Ambrose Bierce. 5622
Tales of the South Pacific—*James A. Michener* . . . 5624
The Talisman—*Sir Walter Scott*. 5627
Talley Family Saga—*Lanford Wilson* 5631
Tamar—*Robinson Jeffers* 5634
Tamburlaine the Great—*Christopher Marlowe*. . . . 5637
The Taming of the Shrew—*William*
    Shakespeare 5640
Tarr—*Wyndham Lewis* 5643
Tartuffe—*Molière* 5647
The Task—*William Cowper*. 5649
A Taste of Honey—*Shelagh Delaney* 5652
Tell Me a Riddle—*Tillie Olsen* 5655
The Tell-Tale Heart—*Edgar Allan Poe* 5657
The Tempest—*William Shakespeare* 5660
The Temple—*George Herbert* 5663

The Temple of the Golden Pavilion—
   Yukio Mishima 5666
The Temptation of Saint Anthony—
   Gustave Flaubert 5668
The Tenant of Wildfell Hall—*Anne Brontë* 5672
Tender Is the Night—*F. Scott Fitzgerald* 5675

Tess of the D'Urbervilles—*Thomas Hardy* 5678
Tevye the Dairyman—*Sholom Aleichem* 5682
Tex—*S. E. Hinton* 5684
Thanatopsis—*William Cullen Bryant* 5687
That Evening Sun—*William Faulkner* 5689
That Was Then, This Is Now—*S. E. Hinton* 5692

Volume 11

Contents. cccxcix
Complete List of Titles. . . . . cdiii

Thebaid—*Statius* 5695
Their Eyes Were Watching God—*Zora Neale
   Hurston*. 5697
them—*Joyce Carol Oates* 5700
Thesmophoriazusae—*Aristophanes*. 5703
A Theory of Justice—*John Rawls*. 5706
The Theory of the Leisure Class—
   Thorstein Veblen 5708
Thérèse—*François Mauriac* 5710
Thérèse Raquin—*Émile Zola* 5714
These Jaundiced Loves—*Tristan Corbière* 5717
The Thin Man—*Dashiell Hammett* 5719
Things Fall Apart—*Chinua Achebe*. 5722
The Thirty-nine Steps—*John Buchan*. 5725
This Side of Paradise—*F. Scott Fitzgerald* 5728
This Sporting Life—*David Storey* 5730
Thomas and Beulah—*Rita Dove* 5733
A Thousand Acres—*Jane Smiley* 5735
Thousand Cranes—*Yasunari Kawabata* 5737
A Thousand Splendid Suns—*Khaled Hosseini* 5740
Three Lives—*Gertrude Stein* 5743
The Three Musketeers—*Alexandre Dumas, père* . . . 5746
The Three Sisters—*Anton Chekhov*. 5750
Three Soldiers—*John Dos Passos* 5753
Three Tall Women—*Edward Albee* 5756
The Threepenny Opera—*Bertolt Brecht* 5759
Through the Looking-Glass and What Alice
   Found There—*Lewis Carroll* 5762
Thus Spake Zarathustra—*Friedrich Nietzsche* 5766
Thyestes—*Seneca the Younger* 5768
Thyrsis—*Matthew Arnold*. 5771
Tiger at the Gates—*Jean Giraudoux* 5773
The Time Machine—*H. G. Wells* 5776
The Time of Your Life—*William Saroyan* 5780
The Time Quartet—*Madeleine L'Engle* 5782

Timon of Athens—*William Shakespeare* 5786
The Tin Drum—*Günter Grass* 5789
The Tin Flute—*Gabrielle Roy* 5792
Tinker, Tailor, Soldier, Spy—*John le Carré* 5795
'Tis Pity She's a Whore—*John Ford* 5798
The Titan—*Theodore Dreiser*. 5801
Titus Andronicus—*William Shakespeare* 5804
To a Skylark—*Percy Bysshe Shelley* 5808
To Autumn—*John Keats* 5811
To His Coy Mistress—*Andrew Marvell*. 5813
To Kill a Mockingbird—*Harper Lee* 5815
To the Lighthouse—*Virginia Woolf*. 5818
To Urania—*Joseph Brodsky*. 5822
Tobacco Road—*Erskine Caldwell* 5825
The Toilers of the Sea—*Victor Hugo* 5827
Tom Brown's School Days—*Thomas Hughes* 5830
Tom Jones—*Henry Fielding* 5833
Tono-Bungay—*H. G. Wells* 5837
Top Girls—*Caryl Churchill* 5840
Topdog/Underdog—*Suzan-Lori Parks* 5843
Torch Song Trilogy—*Harvey Fierstein* 5845
Tortilla Flat—*John Steinbeck* 5848
The Tower—*William Butler Yeats*. 5851
The Tower of London—*William Harrison
   Ainsworth*. 5853
The Town—*William Faulkner*. 5857
The Tragedy of King Christophe—*Aimé Césaire*. . . 5860
The Tragedy of Tragedies—*Henry Fielding* 5863
The Tragic Muse—*Henry James* 5866
The Tragic Sense of Life in Men and in
   Peoples—*Miguel de Unamuno y Jugo* 5869
Trainspotting—*Irvine Welsh* 5872
The Travels of Lao Ts'an—*Liu E* 5875
The Travels of Marco Polo—*Marco Polo* 5877
Travesties—*Tom Stoppard* 5881
Treasure Island—*Robert Louis Stevenson* 5884
A Tree Grows in Brooklyn—*Betty Smith* 5888
The Tree of Man—*Patrick White* 5891

The Tree of the Folkungs—*Verner von Heidenstam* 5894

The Trial—*Franz Kafka* 5897

The Trickster of Seville—*Tirso de Molina* 5902

Tristan and Isolde—*Gottfried von Strassburg* 5904

Tristia—*Osip Mandelstam* 5907

Tristram—*Edwin Arlington Robinson* 5910

Tristram Shandy—*Laurence Sterne* 5913

The Triumph of Death—*Gabriele D'Annunzio* 5917

Troilus and Cressida—*William Shakespeare* 5920

Troilus and Criseyde—*Geoffrey Chaucer* 5924

The Trojan Women—*Euripides* 5927

Tropic of Cancer—*Henry Miller* 5929

Tropic of Capricorn—*Henry Miller* 5932

Trout Fishing in America—*Richard Brautigan* 5935

A True History—*Lucian* 5938

The Truth Suspected—*Juan Ruiz de Alarcón* 5940

The Turn of the Screw—*Henry James* 5943

Twelfth Night—*William Shakespeare* 5946

The Twelve—*Aleksandr Blok* 5949

Twenty Thousand Leagues Under the Sea— *Jules Verne* 5952

Two Essays on Analytical Psychology— *Carl Jung* 5955

The Two Gentlemen of Verona— *William Shakespeare* 5957

The Two Noble Kinsmen—*William Shakespeare* and *John Fletcher* 5960

2001—*Arthur C. Clarke* 5962

The Two Towers—*J. R. R. Tolkien* 5965

Two Trains Running—*August Wilson* 5969

Two Treatises of Government—*John Locke* 5971

Two Women—*Alberto Moravia* 5974

Two Years Before the Mast—*Richard Henry Dana, Jr.* 5977

Typee—*Herman Melville* 5980

Typical American—*Gish Jen* 5983

The Ugly American—*William J. Lederer* and *Eugene Burdick* 5986

Ulysses—*James Joyce* 5989

Ulysses—*Alfred, Lord Tennyson* 5993

The Unbearable Bassington—*Saki* 5995

The Unbearable Lightness of Being—*Milan Kundera* 5997

Uncle Silas—*Joseph Sheridan Le Fanu* 6000

Uncle Tom's Cabin—*Harriet Beecher Stowe* 6004

Uncle Vanya—*Anton Chekhov* 6008

Under Fire—*Henri Barbusse* 6011

Under Milk Wood—*Dylan Thomas* 6014

Under the Greenwood Tree—*Thomas Hardy* 6017

Under the Net—*Iris Murdoch* 6020

Under the Volcano—*Malcolm Lowry* 6023

Under the Yoke—*Ivan Vazov* 6027

Under Two Flags—*Ouida* 6029

Under Western Eyes—*Joseph Conrad* 6033

The Underdogs—*Mariano Azuela* 6036

Understanding Media—*Marshall McLuhan* 6039

Undine—*Friedrich de la Motte-Fouqué* 6041

The Unfortunate Traveller—*Thomas Nashe* 6044

The Unnamable—*Samuel Beckett* 6047

An Unsuitable Job for a Woman—*P. D. James* 6050

The Unvanquished—*William Faulkner* 6053

Up from Slavery—*Booker T. Washington* 6056

U.S.A.—*John Dos Passos* 6059

The Use of Force—*William Carlos Williams* 6063

Utilitarianism—*John Stuart Mill* 6065

Utopia—*Thomas More* 6068

V.—*Thomas Pynchon* 6071

The Vagabond—*Colette* 6074

Vanity Fair—*William Makepeace Thackeray* 6076

The Varieties of Religious Experience— *William James* 6080

Vathek—*William Beckford* 6083

Venice Preserved—*Thomas Otway* 6086

Venus and Adonis—*William Shakespeare* 6089

The Vicar of Wakefield—*Oliver Goldsmith* 6091

Victory—*Joseph Conrad* 6094

A View from the Bridge—*Arthur Miller* 6097

View with a Grain of Sand—*Wisława Szymborska* 6100

Vile Bodies—*Evelyn Waugh* 6102

The Village—*Ivan Bunin* 6105

The Villagers—*Jorge Icaza* 6108

Villette—*Charlotte Brontë* 6111

A Vindication of the Rights of Woman, with Strictures on Political and Moral Subjects— *Mary Wollstonecraft* 6115

The Violent Bear It Away—*Flannery O'Connor* . . . 6118

The Violent Land—*Jorge Amado* 6121

The Virginian—*Owen Wister* 6124

The Virginians—*William Makepeace Thackeray* . . . 6127

The Visit—*Friedrich Dürrenmatt* 6130

Volpone—*Ben Jonson* 6132

Volupté—*Charles-Augustin Sainte-Beuve* 6136

The Voyage of the Beagle—*Charles Darwin* 6139

The Voyage Out—*Virginia Woolf* 6142

Waiting—*Ha Jin*. 6145
Waiting for Godot—*Samuel Beckett* 6148
Waiting for Lefty—*Clifford Odets* 6152
Waiting for the Barbarians—*J. M. Coetzee* 6154
Waiting to Exhale—*Terry McMillan* 6157
Walden—*Henry David Thoreau* 6159
Walden Two—*B. F. Skinner*. 6163
A Walk on the Wild Side—*Nelson Algren* 6165
Wallenstein—*Friedrich Schiller*. 6168
The Wanderer—*Alain-Fournier*. 6171
The Wandering Jew—*Eugène Sue* 6174
The Wandering Scholar from Paradise—
  Hans Sachs. 6176
The Wapshot Chronicle—*John Cheever* 6179
The Wapshot Scandal—*John Cheever* 6182
War and Peace—*Leo Tolstoy* 6186
The War of the Mice and the Crabs—*Giacomo
  Leopardi* 6191
The War of the Worlds—*H. G. Wells* 6193
War Trash—*Ha Jin* 6196
The Warden—*Anthony Trollope* 6199

Washington Square—*Henry James* 6202
The Wasps—*Aristophanes* 6205
The Waste Land—*T. S. Eliot* 6208
Watch on the Rhine—*Lillian Hellman* 6211
Water Music—*T. Coraghessan Boyle*. 6214
Waverley—*Sir Walter Scott*. 6217
The Waves—*Virginia Woolf*. 6220
The Way of All Flesh—*Samuel Butler* 6224
The Way of the World—*William Congreve*. . . . 6227
The Way We Live Now—*Anthony Trollope* 6230
The Wealth of Nations—*Adam Smith*. 6233
The Weary Blues—*Langston Hughes*. 6236
The Web and the Rock—*Thomas Wolfe* 6239
A Week on the Concord and Merrimack
  Rivers—*Henry David Thoreau* 6241
The Well—*Elizabeth Jolley*. 6243
The Well of Loneliness—*Radclyffe Hall* 6246
Westward Ho!—*Charles Kingsley* 6249
What Maisie Knew—*Henry James* 6253
What the Butler Saw—*Joe Orton*. 6256
When Rain Clouds Gather—*Bessie Head* 6258

Volume 12

Contents . . . . cdxxxvii
Complete List of Titles. . . . . cdxxxix

When We Dead Awaken—*Henrik Ibsen* 6261
Where Angels Fear to Tread—*E. M. Forster* 6263
Where I'm Calling From—*Raymond Carver*. . . . 6266
Where the Air Is Clear—*Carlos Fuentes* 6269
The White Album—*Joan Didion* 6271
The White Devil—*John Webster* 6273
The White Goddess—*Robert Graves* 6277
White-Jacket—*Herman Melville* 6279
White Teeth—*Zadie Smith* 6282
The Whitsun Weddings—*Philip Larkin* 6285
Who's Afraid of Virginia Woolf?—
  Edward Albee 6288
Wide Sargasso Sea—*Jean Rhys* 6291
Wieland—*Charles Brockden Brown* 6294
The Wild Ass's Skin—*Honoré de Balzac*. 6297
The Wild Duck—*Henrik Ibsen* 6301
The Wild Geese—*Mori Ōgai* 6304
The Wild Palms—*William Faulkner* 6306
Wilhelm Meister's Apprenticeship—*Johann
  Wolfgang von Goethe* 6310

Wilhelm Meister's Travels—*Johann Wolfgang
  von Goethe* 6313
The Will to Believe, and Other Essays in Popular
  Philosophy—*William James* 6316
William Tell—*Friedrich Schiller* 6318
The Wind in the Willows—*Kenneth Grahame* 6321
Wind, Sand, and Stars—*Antoine de
  Saint-Exupéry* 6324
The Wind-up Bird Chronicle—
  Haruki Murakami 6326
The Winds of War *and* War and Remembrance—
  Herman Wouk 6329
Winesburg, Ohio—*Sherwood Anderson* 6332
The Wings of the Dove—*Henry James* 6335
The Winter of Our Discontent—*John Steinbeck* . . . 6338
The Winter's Tale—*William Shakespeare* 6341
Winterset—*Maxwell Anderson* 6345
Wise Blood—*Flannery O'Connor* 6348
The Witches of Eastwick—*John Updike* 6350
Wives and Daughters—*Elizabeth Gaskell* 6354
Wizard of the Crow—*Ngugi wa Thiong'o* 6356
The Woman in the Dunes—*Kōbō Abe* 6358
The Woman in White—*Wilkie Collins* 6361

A Woman Killed with Kindness—
   Thomas Heywood 6365
The Woman of Rome—*Alberto Moravia* 6368
The Woman Warrior—*Maxine Hong Kingston* 6371
A Woman's Life—*Guy de Maupassant* 6374
Women Beware Women—*Thomas Middleton* 6377
Women in Love—*D. H. Lawrence* 6380
The Women of Brewster Place—*Gloria Naylor* . . . 6383
The Women of Trachis—*Sophocles*. 6386
Wonderland—*Joyce Carol Oates* 6389
Woodcutters—*Thomas Bernhard* 6392
The Woodlanders—*Thomas Hardy* 6395
Works and Days—*Hesiod*. 6398
The World According to Garp—*John Irving* 6400
The World as Will and Idea—
   Arthur Schopenhauer 6403
World Enough and Time—*Robert Penn Warren* . . . 6406
The World of the Thibaults—*Roger Martin
   du Gard*. 6409
The Would-Be Gentleman—*Molière* 6412
Woyzeck—*Georg Büchner* 6415
The Wreck of the Deutschland—*Gerard Manley
   Hopkins*. 6418
The Wretched of the Earth—*Frantz Fanon* 6420
Writing and Difference—*Jacques Derrida* 6423
Wuthering Heights—*Emily Brontë* 6426

Xala—*Ousmane Sembène* 6430

Year of Wonders—*Geraldine Brooks* 6433
The Yearling—*Marjorie Kinnan Rawlings* 6436
The Years—*Virginia Woolf* 6439
Yellow Back Radio Broke-Down—
   Ishmael Reed. 6443
The Yemassee—*William Gilmore Simms* 6445
Yonnondio—*Tillie Olsen* 6448
You Can't Go Home Again—*Thomas Wolfe* 6451
You Know Me Al—*Ring Lardner*. 6454
Youma—*Lafcadio Hearn* 6457
Young Goodman Brown—*Nathaniel Hawthorne*. . 6460
Yvain—*Chrétien de Troyes* 6462

Zadig—*Voltaire* 6467
Zaïre—*Voltaire* 6470
The Zoo Story—*Edward Albee* 6474
Zoot Suit—*Luis Miguel Valdez* 6476
Zorba the Greek—*Nikos Kazantzakis* 6479
Zuckerman Bound—*Philip Roth* 6482
Zuleika Dobson—*Max Beerbohm* 6485

Indexes
Author Index. 6491
Title Index 6519
Geographical Index 6551
Chronological List of Titles 6565
Genre Index 6595
Themes and Issues Index 6621

Masterplots

Fourth Edition

The Savage Mind

Author: Claude Lévi-Strauss (1908-2009)
First published: La Pensée sauvage, 1962 (English
   translation, 1966)
Type of work: Anthropology

Claude Lévi-Strauss, arguably the most prestigious cultural anthropologist of the second half of the twentieth century, continues to attract a large readership in both Europe and the United States. His prolific writings assert bold hypotheses and provocative explanations for the diverse ways in which human societies adapt to chaotic and challenging environments. In the tradition of Jean-Jacques Rousseau, whom he called our master and our brother, he typically praises premodern ways of life and denounces Western civilization as oppressive and destructive.

Influenced by Ferdinand de Saussure's structural linguistics, Lévi-Strauss considers every human culture as a structured universe composed of rules and logical organization, often operating at an unconscious level. Frequently he has been classified as belonging to the contemporary school of French structuralism, although he denies that he has much in common with most of the other writers and thinkers classified as structuralists.

The Savage Mind is often considered Lévi-Strauss's most influential and difficult work. The French title, *La Pensée sauvage*, is a pun not translatable in English. The word *pensée* can mean either "thought," "thinking," or the "pansy flower," whereas the word *sauvage* means either "savage," "primitive," or "wild." Thus, the French title could refer to the "wild pansy flower." In choosing the adjective *sauvage*, Lévi-Strauss was not denoting people with a special propensity for violence; his intention was to refer to the so-called primitive or savage societies, those societies that later anthropologists prefer to characterize in nonpejorative terms such as "premodern," "preliterate," or "precivilization." Rather than *The Savage Mind*, a more descriptive English title would have been "The Ways of Thinking of Premodern Peoples."

The major thesis of *The Savage Mind* is that no fundamental differences exist in the ways that modern humans and "primitive" peoples think and perceive reality, and that all mature humans with normally functioning brains are capable of complex thought, including critical analysis and inference about cause-and-effect relationships. Lévi-Strauss declares, therefore, that it is fallacious to assume a "dichotomy between logical and prelogical mentality," and that the "the savage mind is logical in the same sense and the same fashion as

ours" (of "nonprimitive" peoples). All cultures, moreover, contain common components, including myths and systems of classification, and the differences in the content of myths and classifications are primarily a result of variations in knowledge and technology.

In chapter 1, "The Science of the Concrete," Lévi-Strauss argues that primitive peoples utilize intellectual methods that are similar to those of modern peoples, including scientists. "This thirst for objective knowledge," he argues, "is one of the most neglected aspects of the thought of people we call primitive." Even Neolithic societies (which had invented agriculture) already had been heirs to a "long scientific tradition." More controversial is Lévi-Strauss's assertion that both modern science and tribal magic "require the same sort of mental operations," and that the only difference between the modern and the tribal operations of the mind are the kinds of problems each addresses. Rather than contrasting magic and science, therefore, he writes that it is better to "compare" the two as "parallel modes of acquiring knowledge." While conceding that modern science is more effective in producing knowledge that can be systematically assessed by empirical and quantitative methods, he insists that magic sometimes brings about good results.

Furthermore, in contrast to many anthropologists, Lévi-Strauss does not recognize a clear distinction between magic and religion. He describes religion as the "anthropomorphism of nature," or the idea that nature is in part controlled by a consciousness that resembles human consciousness, whereas magic is usually based on the assumption that humans can exercise some control over nature by means of rituals or physical objects. Viewing the two concepts as overlapping, Lévi-Strauss writes that there can be "no religion without magic any more" than there can be "magic without a trace of religion." The very notion of supernatural power, moreover, "exists only for a humanity which attributes supernatural powers to itself and in return ascribes the powers of its super-humanity to nature."

Lévi-Strauss emphasizes the importance of mythology within premodern cultures, and he also argues that myths reflect unconscious structures of the human mind. Rather than being fantasies or prelogical forms of thought, myths encompass "the totality of phenomena" and explain symbolically how things have become the way they are. Surprisingly, he avoids discussions of myths about gods and spirit beings, preferring instead to focus on those that deal with nature and wild animals. He points to, for example, Native American myths describing a distant time when humans and animals had become estranged from one another. He writes that these stories are "profound" because they account for one of the "tragic" conditions of the human condition: the inability to communicate with other species living on the same planet.

In chapter 4, "Totem and Myth," Lévi-Strauss presents a secular interpretation of totemism, which is the practice of kinship groups identifying with particular animals or other objects of nature. Rather than describing totemism as an early form of religion, as Émile Durkheim had, Lévi-Strauss conceptualizes totemism as essentially a system of classification by which preliterate peoples organize their relationships to the natural environment. He asserts that theorists such as Durkheim and Sir James George Frazer arbitrarily combined several "heterogeneous beliefs and customs" under the headings of totemism, then incorrectly interpreted these beliefs and customs through the lens of Judeo-Christian religions. He further argues that the castes of aristocratic societies, which are based on myths of a common ancestry, are equivalent to the myths of kinship clans in egalitarian tribal societies.

Lévi-Strauss recognizes that knowledge found in premodern societies is of a different order than that found in modern industrial societies. He writes that the latter utilize an engineering approach, thereby constructing knowledge that is specialized, empirical, and measurable. In contrast, premoderns used relatively simple tools and limited specialization of labor. Their approach was a form of bricolage, that is, putting things together using whatever comes to hand. Characterizing premodern societies as "cold," he observes that they have had almost no discernable experience with historical change, and because of this, they generally interpreted the universe from the timeless categories within nature. Unlike persons living in "hot" industrial societies, premoderns tended to have little interest in cultural changes, except perhaps in the area of practical technology. Lévi-Strauss insists that these cold cultures, rather than being only childlike stages of historical development, had endured for centuries as intelligent entities adapting to the environment.

It has often been observed by scholars that the social theories that focus on structure, by their nature, tend to describe human cultures as static, thereby downplaying historical change. Lévi-Strauss's focus on "prehistoric" societies further exacerbates this tendency. His structural approach is based on the premise that humans in all societies make sense of the universe by formulating structures of classifications that are based on dominant images observed within their experiences. He further argues that the human mind naturally classifies reality according to binary opposites, such as friend-enemy, edible-poisonous, goodness-evil, and strength-weakness. Once such dichotomies have been established, societies are then able to formulate more nuanced gradations, although binary opposites continue to provide the fundamental structures of human thought.

The final chapter of *The Savage Mind*, "History and Dialectic," is primarily an attack on Jean-Paul Sartre's difficult book *Critique de la raison dialectique, I: Théorie des ensembles pratiques* (1960; *Critique of Dialectical Reason, I: Theory of Practical Ensembles*, 1976), in which Sartre attempts to reconcile his earlier existentialism with a quasi-Marxist perspective of historical evolution. Lévi-Strauss is particularly critical of Sartre's downplaying of analytical reason in favor of dialectical reason, the conviction by Sartre that human societies progress dialectically (that is, through opposing forces) toward a communist utopia, just as Karl Marx had predicted. Lévi-Strauss accuses Sartre of building a "mystical conception" of history, and he argues that there exists only one valid kind of reason, the kind that is logical and rational.

In attacking Sartre's theories of history, Lévi-Strauss is actually expressing his disagreements with Marx as well as other Western thinkers who have conceptualized the past as a series of progressive stages from primitive cultures to modernity. Despite his commitment to Marx's vision of socialism, Lévi-Strauss accepts little of the Marxist paradigm of historical development, particularly the notion of a linear pattern toward an inevitable goal. Lévi-Strauss, moreover, writes that it is impossible to write a "total" history of humanity. Rather, historians and anthropologists can deal only with partial and incomplete aspects of the past; they are "doomed" to concentrate on singular and unique places, periods, events, or cultures. Disagreeing with theorists who have attempted to discover a common pattern for the evolution of all societies, Lévi-Strauss celebrates the diversity of historical experiences with a special fondness for the so-called primitive societies that have not pursued the path toward modernization.

Thomas Tandy Lewis

Further Reading

Barnard, Alan. *History and Theory in Anthropology.* New York: Cambridge University Press, 2000. A balanced survey of anthropological theories in their historical contexts that includes a helpful introduction to Lévi-Strauss's structuralism and to *The Savage Mind*.

Deliège, Robert. *Lévi-Strauss Today: An Introduction to Structural Anthropology*. New York: Berg, 2004. A useful overview of Lévi-Strauss's theories that emphasizes his influence on contemporary anthropology and other fields of study.

Hénaff, Marcel. *Claude Lévi-Strauss and the Making of Structural Anthropology*. Minneapolis: University of Minnesota Press, 1998. A scholarly analysis by a writer who shares Lévi-Strauss's appreciation for "primitive" societies. For advanced readers.

Lévi-Strauss, Claude, and Didier Eribon. *Conversations with Claude Lévi-Strauss*. Translated by Paul Wissing. Chicago: University of Chicago Press, 1991. Presents interesting questions and answers about Lévi-Strauss's life and ideas. Clearly and succinctly expresses the anthropologist's ideas.

Pace, David. *Claude Lévi-Strauss: The Bearer of Ashes*. Boston: Routledge & Kegan Paul, 1983. Presents concise and clear summaries of Lévi-Strauss's works. Chapters 6 and 7 are devoted primarily to *The Savage Mind*. Highly recommended.

Rothstein, Edward. "Claude Lévi-Strauss, 100, Dies: Altered Western Views of the 'Primitive.'" *The New York Times*, November 4, 2009. This obituary of Lévi-Strauss details his life and his influential career. A good article for students new to his work and for general readers.

Tremlett, Paul-François. *Lévi-Strauss on Religion: The Structuring Mind*. Oakville, Conn.: Equinox, 2008. A sympathetic critique of Lévi-Strauss's views on religious beliefs and practices and on the topics of spiritual beings, myths, magic, shamanism, and totemism.

Wiseman, Boris. *The Cambridge Companion to Lévi-Strauss*. New York: Cambridge University Press, 2009. A collection of fifteen commissioned articles by recognized scholars about various aspects of Lévi-Strauss's work and influence.

Scaramouche
A Romance of the French Revolution

Author: Rafael Sabatini (1875-1950)
First published: 1921
Type of work: Novel
Type of plot: Historical
Time of plot: 1789-1792
Locale: France

Principal characters:
ANDRE-LOUIS MOREAU, a young lawyer
QUINTIN DE KERCADIOU, Moreau's godfather
ALINE DE KERCADIOU, Quintin's niece
MADAME DE PLOUGASTEL, Quintin's cousin and Moreau's mother
PHILIPPE DE VILMORIN, Moreau's best friend, a seminary student
MARQUIS DE LA TOUR D'AZYR, a brigadier in Louis XVI's armies
M. BINET, head of a theatrical troupe
CLIMENE BINET, his daughter, an actress, and Moreau's fiancé
BERTRAND DES AMIS, a fencing academy owner

The Story:

Andre-Louis Moreau, a recent law school graduate, returns to the home of his godfather, Quintin de Kercadiou, in the small country village of Gavrillac. Moreau's parentage is unknown, but it is widely believed that Moreau is the illegitimate son of Kercadiou, who has also been raising his own niece Aline. Ambitious to join Versailles high society, Aline is being courted by the powerful and much older Marquis de La Tour d'Azur, considered one of the best swordsmen in France.

Moreau and the Kercadious are visited by a young priest, Philippe de Vilmorin, a devoted friend of Moreau. An idealist afire with the revolutionary spirit starting to sweep France,

Vilmorin hopes to persuade La Tour to provide reparations for the family of a peasant killed on the marquis's property. La Tour, however, tricks Vilmorin into a duel. The priest has no sword-fighting experience, and La Tour kills him.

Distraught and angry, Moreau vows to avenge Vilmorin's murder and take up his fight for freedom. Hoping to obtain justice for his friend, Moreau travels to the Palais de Justice in the city of Rennes, where his pleading falls on deaf ears. Moreau takes advantage of political gatherings and uses Vilmorin's arguments to incite the crowds in Rennes and nearby Nantes to take up the revolutionary cause. Moreau is charged with sedition and forced to flee for his life.

Moreau joins the Binet Troupe, an amateurish theatrical company that plays throughout the French countryside. Moreau starts as a stagehand but gradually begins to write new scenarios for the actors and takes on the acting role of Scaramouche, an impudent, sly comedic character. The troupe's fortunes begin to turn, and the company moves from makeshift outdoor theaters to real theaters to the Théâtre Feydau in Nantes, a provincial Comedie-Francaise, where it receives an enthusiastic reception.

M. Binet, the troupe's head, resents Moreau's growing influence and becomes further incensed at the engagement of Moreau to his daughter Climene. While initially infatuated with Moreau, Climene, with the support of her father, instigates an affair with La Tour, hoping the marquis will open doors for her in the great theaters of Paris. Aline, hearing of the affair, breaks off all contact with La Tour.

Nantes is alive with revolutionary fervor, and Moreau (as Scaramouche) starts inserting prorepublican lines into his nightly performances, further enraging Binet. Disgusted with Binet's political timidity and with Climene's sordid affair with his sworn enemy, Moreau concocts a scheme to avenge himself against La Tour. Knowing La Tour will be in the audience one night, Moreau creates a new scenario that denounces the marquis as a coward and calls upon the audience to fight for French freedom. A riot breaks out in the theater. Moreau shoots and wounds Binet, and he is forced to flee again.

Moreau escapes to Paris, where he is employed by fencing master Bertrand des Amis as an assistant. By reading fencing treatises and practicing at night, Moreau develops new techniques and ultimately surpasses Amis as a swordsman. When Amis is killed by German troops hired by King Louis XVI, Moreau takes over the academy. Meanwhile, Aline has moved to Paris to stay with Madame de Plougastel, Quintin's cousin.

Political unrest is sweeping Paris, and the National Assembly—composed of the nobility, the clergy, and the Third Estate (the common people and the bourgeoisie)—has been formed to draft a constitution. Members of the Third Estate, however, are being murdered by La Tour, who has been systematically provoking duels with them. Two members of the National Assembly—President Le Chapelier and Georges Danton—ask Moreau to join the assembly, not only for his political views but also for his excellent swordsmanship.

Moreau joins the assembly, and within a week he has either killed or wounded five aristocratic members. A few days later, he provokes a duel with La Tour. Aline, believing that La Tour is the superior swordsman, asks him not to duel with Moreau, but the marquis refuses, ending any hope he has of gaining her love. On the day of the duel, Moreau prevails, severely wounding the marquis in the arm. With his pride wounded, La Tour retires from the National Assembly and joins the royalist secret service.

In August, 1792, a mob storms the Tuileries palace, where King Louis XVI and Marie Antoinette are residing, ending the monarchy in France. Fearing for their safety, Aline and Madame de Plougastel try to flee Paris for Gavrillac, but they are turned back by guards. Kercadiou appeals to Moreau, who has continued to work for the National Assembly, to save the two women. When Moreau balks at saving Madame de Plougastel, the wife of a counterrevolutionary, Kercadiou confesses to Moreau that Madame de Plougastel is his mother.

With safe conduct passes in hand for the two women, Moreau returns to Paris to rescue them, only to find La Tour hiding from the mob in their home. Moreau refuses to save La Tour until Madame de Plougastel reveals to Moreau that La Tour is his father. The confession stuns both men, but Moreau hands a pass to La Tour, who escapes for Austria. Moreau then escorts both women from Paris. In the final chapter, Moreau, Aline, and Madame de Plougastel make plans to emigrate from France. Aline and Moreau finally confess their love for one another.

Critical Evaluation:

Although Rafael Sabatini had been steadily publishing novels, short stories, and biographies for twenty years, it was the publication of *Scaramouche* in 1921 that finally brought him literary fame. The novel, which had been rejected by seven publishers, became an instant international bestseller, prompting his American publisher, Houghton Mifflin, to reissue Sabatini's earlier works. To capitalize on *Scaramouche*'s sudden popularity, Sabatini quickly adapted the novel for the theater, and the first stage production opened in New York in 1922. A prolific writer, Sabatini continued to publish historical romances, including the very popular *Captain Blood* (1922) and its sequels, and throughout the 1920's and 1930's his fiction was consistently at the top of the best-seller lists.

Sabatini's stories of romantic adventures, gallant heroes, and spirited heroines provided escape from the ravages of World War I. In 1931, Sabatini published a sequel, *Scaramouche: The Kingmaker*, which was poorly received by critics and the public. *Scaramouche* and other major works by Sabatini have been periodically reissued, including new editions with scholarly introductions published by Norton in 2002.

Sabatini's historical romances, with their high adventure, ingenious plot twists, surprise endings, and melodrama, made them ideal for motion picture adaptations. The success of his novels on the screen increased Sabatini's popularity with the public. In 1923, Metro Pictures released a silent-film adaptation of *Scaramouche* starring Ramon Novarro, and in 1952 Metro-Goldwyn-Mayer (MGM) issued a lushly colored remake featuring Stewart Granger. The MGM version only loosely followed the plot of the novel, but it is considered one of the finest fencing pictures ever made. The film contains seven duels and the longest uncut sword fight (six and one-half minutes) in cinematic history.

Although Sabatini has fallen out of critical favor and little is now written about him, especially in the academic world, his best fiction—*Scaramouche, Captain Blood,* and *The Sea-Hawk* (1915)—rivals the historical fiction of Alexander Dumas, Rudyard Kipling, and Robert Louis Stevenson. His historical novels were influential during his lifetime, and Sabatini has continued to influence contemporary writers of historical fiction, most notably George MacDonald Fraser, author of the Flashman series. Many of Sabatini's plot devices (such as the wronged hero, piracy on the high seas, and court intrigue) are still used in historical fiction.

Fluent in six languages, Sabatini extensively researched historical characters and time periods before starting a new work, often relying on primary resources to do so. He preferred to write about historical eras of great social, economic, and political turmoil because they provided a dramatic backdrop to his stories. In *Scaramouche*, the upheaval of the French Revolution is finely detailed, and the carefully recounted events of the plot mirror what was happening in the revolution's early years. The narrative moves easily between lower-, middle-, and upper-class society in France from 1789 to 1792. Small details of eighteenth century life—the period's clothing, hairstyles, theatrical costumes, dueling etiquette, and so forth—are meticulously described. The novel's protagonist, Andre-Louis Moreau, encounters both

fictional characters and historical figures such as Maximilien Robespierre, Georges Danton, and King Louis XVI. To make the novel seem even more realistic, the narrator quotes from Moreau's letters and *Confessions* and refers to old newspapers and playbills on file in the Carnavet Museum.

Scaramouche's famous opening line, "He was born with a gift of laughter and a sense that the world was mad," sets the tone for this thrilling, swashbuckling romance. Divided into three sections, the novel traces the various careers of Moreau as a lawyer, comedic actor, fencing master, and politician. Impressively crafted, *Scaramouche* avoids the usual pitfalls of historical romances (formulaic plots, cardboard characters, and stilted dialogue) and instead presents an inventive, surprise-filled plot, fully developed characters, and witty and clever dialogue. Both the hero and the villain move beyond one-dimensional, stock characters. Moreau develops from a cynically disinterested law student into a revolutionary who embraces the French Revolution's ideals of liberty, equality, and fraternity. La Tour, while supporting the views of his class, is also a man of courage and honor. Although Aline is idealized, she too has a distinct, spirited personality and motives of her own.

The book's themes and characterization follow a pattern that Sabatini developed and used repeatedly in his better romantic historical novels. Like the protagonists Peter Blood (*Captain Blood*) and Sir Olivier Tressilian (*The Sea-Hawk*), Moreau is a good, intelligent, and innocent man who is accused of a crime he did not commit and branded an outlaw and fugitive. After acts of self-sacrifice and a series of daring adventures, he is able to reclaim his good name and place in society. The hero is also reunited at the end with the woman he loves. The overall theme of *Scaramouche* is justice, not only for Moreau and his murdered friend Vilmorin but also for all French people.

Debora J. Richey and Mona Y. Kratzert

Further Reading

Knight, Jesse F. "Rafael Sabatini: The Swashbuckler as Serious Artist." *Romanticist* 9/10 (1985/1986): 1-22. A lengthy discussion of the life and literary career of Sabatini. Provides a list of all his works, including his uncollected short stories and film adaptations of his novels.

McAlpin, Edwin A. "Sin and Its Consequences." In *Old and New Books as Life Teachers*. Garden City, N.Y.: Doubleday Doran, 1928. Summarizes the plot of *Scaramouche* and analyzes the novel's characters and themes.

Orel, Harold. *The Historical Novel from Scott to Sabatini: Changing Attitudes Toward a Literary Genre, 1814-1920.*

New York: St. Martin's Press, 1995. A collection of essays that traces the rise and fall in popularity of the historical novel from Sir Walter Scott to Sabatini.

Overton, Grant. "Salute to Sabatini." *Bookman* 60, no. 6 (February, 1925): 728-735. Written at the height of Sabatini's popularity, this tribute discusses the author's works, praising him as one of the few writers of historical fiction then remaining.

Pilkington, Ace G. "Reviving Sabatini." *Journal of the Utah Academy of Sciences, Arts, and Letters* 76 (1999): 245-257. Examines the characters and major themes of Sabatini's significant works while asserting that he is a greater writer than his critics generally claim.

Voorhees, Richard J. "The Return of Sabatini." *South Atlantic Quarterly* 78, no. 2 (Spring, 1979): 195-204. This respected scholar asserts that Sabatini's fiction is superior to the usual historic fiction of his time and deserves to be read again.

The Scarlet Letter

Author: Nathaniel Hawthorne (1804-1864)
First published: 1850
Type of work: Novel
Type of plot: Psychological realism
Time of plot: Early days of the Massachusetts Colony
Locale: Boston

Principal characters:
HESTER PRYNNE, a woman convicted of adultery
ARTHUR DIMMESDALE, a minister of the community
ROGER CHILLINGWORTH, a physician and Hester's husband
PEARL, Hester's daughter

The Story:

On a summer morning in Boston, in the early days of the Massachusetts Colony, a throng of curious people gather outside the jail in Prison Lane. They are there looking for Hester Prynne, who was found guilty of adultery by a court of stern Puritan judges. Condemned to wear on the breast of her gown the scarlet letter *A*, which stands for adulterer, she is to stand on the stocks before the meetinghouse for three hours so that her shame might be a warning and a reproach to all who see her. The crowd waits to see her ascend the scaffold with her child—the proof of the adultery, Hester's husband being absent—in her arms.

At last, escorted by the town beadle, the woman appears. She moves serenely to the steps of the scaffold and stands quietly under the staring eyes that watch her public disgrace. It is whispered in the gathering that she is spared the penalty of death or of branding only through the intercession of the Reverend Arthur Dimmesdale, into whose church she brought her scandalous sin.

While Hester stands on the scaffold, an elderly, almost deformed man appears out of the forest. When her agitation makes it plain that she recognizes him, he puts his finger to his lips as a sign of silence.

Hester's story is well known in the community. She is the daughter of an old family of decayed fortune; when she was young, her family married her to a husband who had great repute as a scholar. For some years, they lived in Antwerp. Two years later, the husband sent his wife alone across the ocean to the Massachusetts Colony, intending to follow her as soon as he could put his affairs in order. News came of his departure, but his ship was never heard of again. The young, attractive widow lived quietly in Boston until the time of her disgrace.

The scaffold of the pillory on which Hester stands is situated next to the balcony of the church where all the dignitaries of the colony sit to watch her humiliation. The ministers of the town call on her to name the man who is equally guilty; the most eloquent of those who exhorts her is Dimmesdale, her pastor. Hester refuses to name the father of her child, and she is led back to the prison after her period of public shame ends.

On her return to prison, Hester is found to be in a state of great nervous excitement. When at last medical aid is called, a man is found who professes knowledge of medicine. His name is Roger Chillingworth, he tells the jailer, and he recently arrived in town after a year of residence among the Indians. He is the stranger who appeared so suddenly from the forest that afternoon while Hester stood on the scaffold, and Hester recognized him immediately as her husband, the scholar Prynne. His ship was wrecked on the coast, and he was a captive among the Indians for many months. When he comes to Hester, he, too, asks her to name the father of her child. When she refuses, he tells her he will remain in Boston to practice medicine and that he will devote the rest of his life to discovering the identity of the man who dishonored him. He commands Hester not to betray the relationship between them.

When Hester's term of imprisonment is over, she finds a small house on the outskirts of town, far removed from other habitation. There, with her child, whom she names Pearl, she settles down to earn a living from needlework, an outcast from society. She still wears the scarlet emblem on the breast of her sober gowns, but she dresses her child in bright, highly ornamented costumes. As she grows up, Pearl proves to be a capricious, wayward child, hard to discipline. One day, Hester calls on Governor Bellingham to deliver a pair of embroidered gloves. She also wants to see him about the custody of Pearl, for there is a movement afoot among the strict church members to take the child away from her. In the garden of the governor's mansion, Hester finds the governor, Dimmesdale, and old Chillingworth. When the perverse child refuses to repeat the catechism, the governor thinks it necessary that she be reared apart from her mother. Dimmesdale argues persuasively, however, and in the end Hester is allowed to keep Pearl, who seems to be strangely attracted to the minister.

Chillingworth became intimately acquainted with Dimmesdale as both his parishioner and his doctor, for the minister has been in ill health ever since the physician came to town. The two men lodge in the same house, and the physician comes to know Dimmesdale's inmost thoughts and feelings. The minister is much plagued by his conscience and his feelings of guilt, but when he incorporates these ideas in generalities into his sermons, his congregation only thinks more highly of him. Slowly the conviction grows in Chillingworth that Dimmesdale is Pearl's father, and he conjures up for the sick man visions of agony, terror, and remorse.

One night, unable to sleep, Dimmesdale walks to the pillory where Hester stood in ignominy. He goes up the steps and stands for a long time in the same place. A little later Hester, who was watching at a deathbed, comes by with little Pearl. The minister calls them over, saying when they were there before he lacked the courage to stand beside them. As the three stand together, with Dimmesdale acknowledging himself as Pearl's father and Hester's partner in sin, Chillingworth watches them from the shadows.

Hester is so shocked by Dimmesdale's feeble and unhealthy condition that she determines to see her former husband and plead with him to free the sick minister from his evil influence.

One day, she meets the old physician gathering herbs in the forest and begs him to be merciful to his victim. Chillingworth, however, is inexorable; he will not forgo his revenge on the man who wronged him. Hester thereupon says that she will tell Dimmesdale their secret and warn him against his physician. A short time later, Hester and Pearl intercept Dimmesdale in the forest as he is returning from a missionary journey to the Indians. Hester confesses her true relationship with Chillingworth and warns the minister against the physician's evil influence. She and the clergyman decide to leave the colony together in secret, take passage on a ship then in the harbor, and return to the Old World. They plan to leave four days later, after Dimmesdale preaches the sermon on Election Day, when the new governor is to be installed.

Election Day is a holiday in Boston, and the port is lively with the unaccustomed presence of sailors from the ship in the harbor. In the crowd is the captain of the vessel, with whom Hester made arrangements for her own and Dimmesdale's passage. That morning, the captain informs Hester that Chillingworth also arranged for passage on the ship. Filled with despair, Hester turns away and goes with Pearl to listen to Dimmesdale's sermon.

Unable to find room within the church, she stands at the foot of the scaffold where at least she can hear the sound of his voice. As the procession leaves the church, everyone has words only of praise for the minister's inspired address. Dimmesdale walks like a man in a dream, and once he totters and almost falls. When he sees Hester and Pearl at the foot of the scaffold, he steps out of the procession and calls them to him. Then, taking them by the hand, he again climbs the steps of the pillory. Almost fainting, but with a voice terrible and majestic, the minister admits his guilt to the watching people. With a sudden motion, he tears the ministerial band from across his breast and sinks, dying, to the platform. When he thus exposes his breast, witnesses say that the stigma of the scarlet letter *A* was seen imprinted on the flesh above his heart.

Chillingworth, no longer able to wreak his vengeance on Dimmesdale, dies within the year, bequeathing his considerable property to Pearl. For a time, Hester disappears from the colony, but she returns alone years later to live in her humble thatched cottage and to wear as before the scarlet emblem on her breast. The scarlet letter, once her badge of shame, becomes an emblem of her tenderness and mercy—an object of veneration and reverence to those whose sorrows she alleviates by her deeds of kindness. At her death, she directs that the only inscription on her tombstone should be the letter *A*.

Critical Evaluation:

Since its publication in 1850, *The Scarlet Letter* has never been out of print, nor indeed out of favor with literary critics. It is inevitably included in listings of the five or ten greatest American novels, and it is considered the best of Nathaniel Hawthorne's writings. It may also be the most typical of his work, the strongest statement of his recurrent themes, and an excellent example of his craftsmanship.

The main theme in *The Scarlet Letter*, as in most of Hawthorne's work, is that of sin and its effects both on the individual and on society. It is frequently noted that Hawthorne's preoccupation with sin springs from the Puritan-rooted culture in which he lived and from his knowledge of two of his own ancestors who presided over bloody persecutions during the Salem witchcraft trials. It is difficult for readers from later times to comprehend the grave importance that seventeenth century New Englanders placed on transgression of the moral code. As Yvor Winters has pointed out, the Puritans, believing in predestination, viewed the commission of any sin as evidence of the sinner's corruption and preordained damnation. The harsh determinism and moralism of those early years softened somewhat by Hawthorne's day, and during the twelve years he spent in contemplation and semi-isolation, he worked out his own notions about human will and human nature. In *The Scarlet Letter*, Hawthorne proves to be closer to Paul Tillich than to Cotton Mather or Jonathan Edwards. Like Tillich, Hawthorne saw sin not as an act but as a state—what existentialists refer to as alienation and what Tillich describes as a threefold separation from God, other humans, and self. Such alienation needs no fire and brimstone as consequence; it is in itself a hell.

There is a certain irony in the way in which this concept is worked out in *The Scarlet Letter*. Hester Prynne's pregnancy forces her sin into public view, and she is compelled to wear the scarlet *A* as a symbol of her adultery. Yet, although she is apparently isolated from normal association with "decent" folk, Hester, having come to terms with her sin, is inwardly reconciled to God and self; she ministers to the needy among her townspeople, reconciling herself with others until some observe that her *A* now stands for "Able." Arthur Dimmesdale, her secret lover, and Roger Chillingworth, her secret husband, move much more freely in society than she can and even enjoy prestige: Dimmesdale as a beloved pastor, Chillingworth as a respected physician. However, Dimmesdale's secret guilt gnaws so deeply inside him that he is unable to make his peace with God or to feel at ease with his fellow citizens. For his part, Chillingworth permits vengeance to permeate his spirit so much that his alienation is absolute; he refers to himself as a "fiend," unable to impart forgiveness or to

change his profoundly evil path. His is the unpardonable sin—unpardonable not because God will not pardon, but because his own nature has become so depraved that he cannot repent or accept forgiveness.

Hawthorne clearly distinguishes between sins of passion and those of principle. Even Dimmesdale, traditional Puritan though he is, finally becomes aware of the difference.

We are not, Hester, the worst sinners in the world. There is one worse than even the polluted priest! That old man's revenge has been blacker than my sin. He has violated, in cold blood, the sanctity of a human heart. Thou and I, Hester, never did so.

Always more concerned with the consequences than with the cause of sin, Hawthorne to a remarkable extent anticipated Sigmund Freud's theories of the effects of guilt. Hester, whose guilt is openly known, grows through her suffering into an extraordinarily compassionate and understanding woman, a complete person who is able to come to terms with all of life, including sin. Dimmesdale, who yearns for the relief of confession but hides his guilt to safeguard his role as pastor, is devoured internally. Again like Freud, Hawthorne recognized that spiritual turmoil may produce physical distress. Dimmesdale's health fails and eventually he dies from no apparent cause other than guilt.

The characters in *The Scarlet Letter* are reminiscent of a number of Hawthorne's shorter works. Dimmesdale bears similarities to Young Goodman Brown who, having once glimpsed the darker nature of humankind, must forevermore view humanity as corrupt and hypocritical. There are also resemblances between Dimmesdale and Parson Hooper in "The Minister's Black Veil," who continues to perform the duties of his calling with eloquence and compassion but is permanently separated from the company of men by the veil that he wears as a symbol of secret sin. Chillingworth shows resemblances to Ethan Brand, the limeburner who finds the unpardonable sin in his own heart: "The sin of an intellect that triumphed over the sense of brotherhood with man and reverence for God, and sacrificed everything to its mighty claims!"

Hawthorne's craftsmanship is splendidly demonstrated in *The Scarlet Letter*. The structure is carefully unified, with three crucial scenes—at the beginning, the middle, and the end of the action—taking place on the scaffold. The scarlet *A* itself is repeatedly entwined into the narrative as a symbol of sin and shame, as a reminder of Hester's ability with the needle and her capability with people, and in Dimmesdale's case, as evidence of the searing effects of secret guilt. Hawthorne often anticipates later developments with hints or forewarnings: There is, for example, the suggestion that Pearl lacks complete humanity, perhaps because she has never known great sorrow, but at the end of the story when Dimmesdale dies, Hawthorne writes, "as [Pearl's] tears fell upon her father's cheek, they were the pledge that she would grow up amid human joy and sorrow, nor forever do battle with the world, but be a woman in it."

Hawthorne's skill as a symbolist is fully in evidence. As one critic has noted, there is hardly a concrete object in the book that does not do double duty as a symbol, among them the scarlet letter, the sunlight that eludes Hester, the scaffold of public notice, the armor in which Hester's shame and Pearl's selfishness are distorted and magnified. The four main characters themselves serve as central symbols in this, the greatest allegory of a master allegorist.

"Critical Evaluation" by Sally Buckner

Further Reading

Baym, Nina. *"The Scarlet Letter": A Reading.* Boston: Twayne, 1986. Full-length critical introduction that examines the setting, characters, and themes. One fascinating chapter treats the scarlet *A* as a character. Includes a chronology and extended bibliography.

Bloom, Harold, ed. *Hester Prynne.* Philadelphia: Chelsea House, 2004. Collection of essays focusing on the novel's protagonist.

_____. *Nathaniel Hawthorne's "The Scarlet Letter."* Updated ed. New York: Bloom's Literary Criticism, 2007. A compilation of essays examining the novel from various perspectives, including discussions of nature as a narrator, Hawthorne and the making of the middle class, and how the novel instituted the American romance tradition.

Colacurcio, Michael J. *New Essays on "The Scarlet Letter."* New York: Cambridge University Press, 1985. Offers a brief review of the different critical approaches brought to the novel from the time of its publication to the 1980's.

Gerber, John C., ed. *Twentieth-Century Interpretations of "The Scarlet Letter": A Collection of Critical Essays.* Englewood Cliffs, N.J.: Prentice-Hall, 1968. Twenty essays that explore background, form, techniques, and interpretations. Includes a useful chronology that pairs dates in Hawthorne's life with historical events.

Hawthorne, Nathaniel. *The Scarlet Letter: Complete, Authoritative Text with Biographical, Historical, and Cultural Contexts, Critical History, and Essays from Contemporary Critical Perspectives.* Edited by Ross C. Murfin. 2d ed. Boston: Bedford/St. Martin's, 2006. In addition to the text of the novel, this edition contains seven critical essays analyzing the book from psychoanalytic, feminist, and new historicist perspectives.

Millington, Richard H. *The Cambridge Companion to Nathaniel Hawthorne.* New York: Cambridge University Press, 2004. Collection of essays analyzing various aspects of Hawthorne's work, including discussions of Hawthorne and American masculinity, Hawthorne and the question of women, and "Love, Politics, Sympathy, and Justice in *The Scarlet Letter*" by Brook Thomas.

Pennell, Melissa McFarland. *Student Companion to Nathaniel Hawthorne.* Westport, Conn.: Greenwood Press, 1999. An introductory overview of Hawthorne's life and work designed for students and general readers. Includes a discussion of Hawthorne's contribution to American literature, analyses of his four major novels, a bibliography, and an index.

Person, Leland S. *The Cambridge Introduction to Nathaniel Hawthorne.* New York: Cambridge University Press, 2007. An accessible introduction to the author's life and works designed for students and general readers. It includes analysis of Hawthorne's fiction, with a separate chapter on *The Scarlet Letter.*

Turner, Arlin. *The Merrill Studies in "The Scarlet Letter."* Columbus, Ohio: Charles E. Merrill, 1970. Essays for the general reader, including pieces on Hawthorne's process of composition, reviews of the novel dating back to its publication in 1850, nineteenth century commentary, and a sampling of twentieth century critical approaches.

Weldon, Roberta. *Hawthorne, Gender, and Death: Christianity and its Discontents.* New York: Palgrave Macmillan, 2008. Weldon analyzes how Hawthorne depicts dying and his characters' reactions to death in *The Scarlet Letter* and in other fictional works.

Wineapple, Brenda. *Hawthorne: A Life.* New York: Knopf, 2003. A meticulously researched, evenhanded analysis of Hawthorne's often contradictory life that proposes that much of Hawthorne's fiction was autobiographical. Includes more than one hundred pages of notes, bibliography, and index.

Schindler's List

Author: Thomas Keneally (1935-   )
First published: 1982, as *Schindler's Ark*
Type of work: Novel
Type of plot: Historical realism
Time of plot: 1930's-1940's
Locale: Kracków, Poland; Brünnlitz, Czechoslovakia

Principal characters:
OSKAR SCHINDLER, a Czech manufacturer
ITZHAK STERN, his accountant
AMON GOETH, Nazi commandant of the Płaszów labor camp
HELEN HIRSCH, his maid

The Story:

Oskar Schindler, a Czech manufacturer and factory owner, is on his way to dine with Amon Goeth, Nazi commandant of the Płaszów labor camp outside Kracków, Poland, in 1943. Schindler's car travels on the broken Jewish gravestones that pave the road to Goeth's villa. Inside the villa, as Jewish musicians play unobtrusively, Goeth is surrounded by local police and prostitutes. Schindler encounters Goeth's maid, Helen Hirsch, who has been severely beaten by Goeth; terrified, she confides to Schindler about Goeth's frequent brutality and begs Schindler to find and save her younger sister.

It is now 1908, and Schindler is born in Zwittau, Austria (later part of Czechoslovakia), a small industrial town where people speak German. Schindler, whose favorite hobby is motorcycles, studies engineering and expects to take over his father's farm-machinery company. Soon, he marries Emilie, a farmer's daughter, but he is never faithful to her.

In the fall of 1939, Schindler moves to Kracków and meets Itzhak Stern, a Jewish accountant who has many valuable business insights and contacts. In November, Jews are required to register with the Nazis, and the restrictions and brutality against Jews begin. With Stern's advice, Schindler purchases an enamelware and cookware company called Deutsche Emailwaren Fabrik (Emalia) and initially employs 150 Jewish slave laborers. By the end of 1939, Schindler is often seen socializing with high-ranking Nazi officers and administrators, many of whom he bribes with rare black-market items to purchase their influence, protection, and support.

In early 1940, Kracków's Jews are forced into an overcrowded ghetto, while their Christian neighbors harass and spit at them. Despite vicious slogans and posters promising violent punishment for those who help Jews, Schindler assures his workers that they are safe with him.

Shortly thereafter, Schindler is arrested by the Nazis on a trumped up charge of some irregularity in his bookkeeping, but because of the intervention of bribed Nazi officials, Schindler is released. Later, however, when his workers

throw him a birthday party, Schindler is denounced for kissing a young female Jewish worker. He is rearrested but soon released because of intervention from ranking Nazi officials.

Schindler's office manager, Abraham Bankier, is missing, so Schindler uses bluster and bravado to retrieve him from the cattle cars departing for the death camps; while on horseback overlooking the grisly scene, he sees the brutal liquidation of the Kracków ghetto. His terrified eyes focus on one young girl in a scarlet coat, in front of whom the Nazis are shooting and bludgeoning people to death. After witnessing the cattle cars and the death of seven thousand people, Schindler fully realizes the Nazi's plan to exterminate all Jews.

Plunder, too, runs rampant in Poland, as Jewish jewelers are forced to appraise gold left behind in suitcases by fellow Jews on their way to death. So hard is it even for Jews to believe their imminent fate, that Schindler travels to Hungary to warn Jewish leaders there about the horrific reality of the camps.

Nazi commandant Goeth takes control of the Płaszów labor camp. His first act is to nonchalantly order the murder of a Jewish architect who had informed him that the Płaszów buildings are unstable. Goeth rules with an iron fist, and more than four thousand Jews who try to hide from incarceration in Płaszów are publically murdered in one night.

Schindler contracts with Goeth to take about eleven hundred of the Płaszów Jews and employ them as slave laborers at his factory. Schindler feeds and treats them far better than the remaining Jews are treated at Płaszów. As Płaszów's population reaches thirty thousand, others are able to join the relatively safe haven at Emalia. Goeth tortures and executes many of the remaining Jews, those who could not reach the safe haven of laborers now known as the Schindler Jews.

In 1944, when the Germans start losing the war, all of the murdered Jews at Płaszów are exhumed and cremated; flames, stench, and ash are everywhere. Of the 150,000 who came through Płaszów and its subsidiary camps, some eighty thousand died there. As more Jews arrive, the unhealthy ones are murdered. Fearing for their own safety, the Schindler Jews, aware of the liquidation, nervously continue to work at Emalia.

On a scalding summer day, Schindler demonstrates his humanity by insisting that cattle cars holding two thousand Jews en route to a death camp be hosed down with water to cool off the people jammed inside. As the Russians approach, Schindler decides to move his factory workers to a safer site in Brünnlitz, Czechoslovakia, where they will manufacture military shell-casings. Schindler convinces Goeth to "sell" him his Emalia workers, thus creating what is soon known as Schindler's list and ultimately saving the lives of about eight hundred men and three hundred women.

The Schindler men are successfully transported to Brünnlitz; the women (including Goeth's former maid, Helen Hirsch, and her sister) are mistakenly routed to Auschwitz. Weeks later, Schindler pays officials to release the women to his charge, marking the only time that a train with living passengers leaves a death camp during the Holocaust.

During the remaining months of the war, Schindler bribes and manipulates officials so that the Jews in his charge can survive; his factory produces no useable shells. At war's end, he exhorts his factory's German guards to return to their families peacefully and gives the remaining food and supplies to his Jewish workers.

After the war, Schindler is unsuccessful in business and is often bankrupt, but he is well cared for by his former employees. Honored as "Righteous Among the Nations" by Yad Vashem, the Israeli Holocaust Museum, Schindler spends his remaining years traveling between Germany and Israel. He dies in 1974 at the age of sixty-six and is buried in Jerusalem.

Critical Evaluation:

Winner of the prestigious Booker Prize for fiction in 1982, Thomas Keneally's novel *Schindler's List* is one of the most important literary works on the Holocaust. Ironically, the main controversy about the novel is whether it is really a novel at all. Keneally has stated that all people and events in the book are real and true ("I have attempted . . . to avoid all fiction"), although specific dialogue sometimes consists of "reasonable constructs" of "detailed recollections" of those present at the time; in other words, conversations in the novel have been filled in or shaped for clarity's sake, while remaining truthful to the memory of those present.

Keneally uses a literary technique called faction, that is, it is mostly fact with a small amount of fiction. *Schindler's List* is historically factual, yet as in any work of historical fiction, especially about such a mammoth event as the Holocaust, it requires some literary license with minor details. Keneally

uses no literary license, however, in his stark portrayal of the savage ways in which the perversion of even innocent language contributed to public Jew-hating during the Holocaust. For example, Keneally uses in the novel words such as "Aktions" (violent roundups of Jews into ghettos or death camps), "Selection" (at a moment's notice, Jews in death camps were sent either to the gas chamber or to filthy barracks), and both "Relocation" and "Special Treatment" (Jews were crammed into cattle cars en route to the death camps). All of this horror was intended to make the world *Judenrein*, or "Jew free."

Similarly, Keneally documents the posters plastered on the walls of the city, Kraców: "Jews—Lice—Typhus," "Whoever Helps a Jew, Helps Satan," and "Entrance Forbidden to Jews and Dogs." A falsely benign sign over the gas-chamber doors announces "Baths and Inhalation Rooms." Language reaches a hideous low point when hundreds of Płaszów children are marched off to the death trains, while their parents' hysterical screams are drowned out by loudspeakers that blare a popular song with the lyrics "Mummy, buy me a pony."

Originally published in England as *Schindler's Ark*, this title has the additional resonance of the Old Testament narrative of Noah who, under God's orders, built a huge boat to save the good of the world from the imminent, all-destroying Flood. However, just as there is no language powerful enough to encapsulate the great evil of the Nazis, particularly of tyrants like Amon Goeth, so there are no words to describe the profound altruism of those, like Schindler, who protected Jews during the war. This unlikely hero was a Nazi Party member, a rabid hedonist, and a womanizer, yet he built two arks of a sort, one in Kraców and one in Brünnlitz, to save some eleven hundred Jews.

Using tremendous restraint, Keneally wisely chooses not to guess at the alchemy of life experiences and personal psychology that motivated and shaped Schindler's—or Goeth's—choices and actions. Instead, he hints at the incremental realizations that seem to lead Schindler to his destiny.

After seeing firsthand the Kraców ghetto's liquidation, Schindler proclaims, "I was now resolved to do everything in my power to defeat the system." He follows through on this oath when soothing his workers at Brünnlitz, "You have nothing more to worry about. You're with me now," and announces that his best birthday present is the knowledge that the armaments his factory produced had failed all quality-control tests and, therefore, could neither maim nor kill anyone. Keneally does not try to solve the ageless mystery of the genesis of good and evil, but rather, he lets the question continue to intrigue humanity.

Had Keneally not wandered into a Beverly Hills luggage shop in 1980 and met Leopold "Poldek" Pfefferberg, a Schindler Jew eager to tell his story, the world might never have learned about Schindler's goodness. The 1993 film *Schindler's List*, directed by Steven Spielberg and winner of seven Academy Awards, brought Keneally's brilliant book, and the complex and heroic figure of Schindler, to stunning life for the world to admire.

Schindler's List is terrifying in its portrayal of the chilling inhumanity of humanity, but it also is inspiring because it demonstrates, through Schindler's altruism, that humans can do great things for each other. The grotesque early image of Jewish jewelers forced by the Nazis to weigh and grade a suitcase full of still-bloody gold teeth yanked from death-camp corpses later morphs into an altruistic image: One of the Schindler Jews has his gold dental work removed so that the gold can be melted down and shaped into a ring for Schindler. Inscribed on the ring is an extremely powerful verse from the Talmud: "He who saves a single life saves the world entire."

Howard A. Kerner

Further Reading

Brecher, Elinor J. *Schindler's Legacy: True Stories of the List Survivors*. New York: Penguin Books, 1994. An inspiring tribute to the Schindler Jews, thirty in particular, and the extraordinary accomplishments in their lives since being rescued by Oskar Schindler.

Crowe, David. *Oskar Schindler: The Untold Story of His Life, Wartime Activities, and the True Story Behind the List*. New York: Basic Books, 2004. This extremely thorough biography of Oskar Schindler, almost twice the length of *Schindler's List*, fills in many details about Schindler's early life, the war years, and his life after the war.

Keneally, Thomas. *Searching for Schindler*. New York: Doubleday, 2007. In this invaluable adjunct to his novel, Keneally describes the extraordinary process of interviewing at least fifty Schindler Jews from around the world and discusses his novel's adaptation into one of the most lauded films of all times.

Pemper, Mietek. *The Road to Rescue: The Untold Story of Schindler's List*. New York: Other Press, 2005. Serving as Amon Goeth's personal secretary and as a friend to Oskar Schindler during and after the war, Pemper is best qualified to offer a fascinating first-person account of the inner workings of the Nazi leadership and the creation of the life-giving Schindler's list.

Sauerberg, Lars Ole. "Fact-Flirting Fiction: Historiographical Potential or Involuntary Parody?" *European Journal of English Studies* 3, no. 2 (August, 1999): 190-205. This journal article examines the intersection of historical fiction, fiction, and history as it manifests in the novels, including *Schindler's List*, of writers such as Keneally.

Schindler, Emilie. *Where Light and Shadow Meet: A Memoir*. New York: W. W. Norton, 1996. A useful first-person account, by Schindler's wife, of day-to-day life with her husband, focusing on his great deeds but also on her own assistance in helping the Jews at Brünnlitz.

The Scholar-Gipsy

Author: Matthew Arnold (1822-1888)
First published: 1853
Type of work: Poetry

Matthew Arnold's "The Scholar-Gipsy," the major British Victorian poet's central poem, anticipates the crisis of the modernist period. The poem is testament to Arnold's preoccupation as a poet and a cultural critic: "this strange disease of modern life." Arnold returns to this theme throughout his work, including in his poetic masterpieces *Thyrsis* (1866) and "Dover Beach" (1867) and in his major work of prose criticism, *Culture and Anarchy* (1869). "The Scholar-Gipsy" serves as a template for Arnold's poetic and intellectual ca-

reer and epitomizes his paradoxical combination of Victorian vigor and social progressivism with a protomodernist sense of dissociation arising from religious doubt, social fragmentation, and ennui.

Written in a ten-line stanzaic pattern for a total of 250 lines, the poem is a major English pastoral elegy in the tradition of John Milton's "Lycidas" (1637) and Thomas Gray's "Elegy Written in a Country Churchyard" (1751). It bears the imprint of Arnold's classicism, with allusions to Vergil's

Aeneid (c. 29-19 B.C.E.; English translation, 1553) and its masterful conclusion in the form of an epic simile. At the same time, however, Arnold seems to undermine the sense of tradition, poetic or cultural, that he is seeking to maintain. The traditional pastoral elegy seeks to reaffirm a continuity between past and present and between the person who has died and the still-existing values that he or she had embodied.

The subject of Arnold's elegy is a legendary, poor Oxford University student of the seventeenth century who has abandoned his studies to learn the occult ways of the nomadic Roma, or gypsy, people. The Scholar-Gipsy is portrayed not as dead but as existing in an immortal twilight of the Romantic imagination. Moreover, rather than reinforce a sense of cultural continuity, Arnold is at pains to warn his elegiac "subject" away from deadening contact with the modern world, which is portrayed as radically alien in form and values from those he inhabits.

Arnold's unusual pastoral elegy begins well within the expectations of the genre. The poem's speaker addresses an unnamed shepherd and describes the timeless pastoral duties involved in the care and feeding of his flock. However, even the first stanza suggests something is amiss, as the speaker pictures the sheep at night on a "moon-blanched green" and then urges the symbolic shepherd to "again begin the quest." The moon becomes a symbol for the power of the imagination, and "quest" seems like a strong word for a simple shepherd's job of rounding up sheep. The speaker interjects himself into the poem in the second stanza, portraying himself seated in a field high in the Cumnor Hills overlooking his alma mater, Oxford University. The speaker becomes both participant and observer of the setting: He catalogs the flowers in the field but also mentions a decidedly unnatural object that he has brought with him: Joseph Glanvill's *The Vanity of Dogmatizing* (1661), which contains the original account of the Scholar-Gipsy.

In the subsequent four stanzas the natural world and pastoral convention disappear, as the speaker recounts the legend of the Scholar-Gipsy. Unsuccessful in knocking at "Preferment's door," the Scholar-Gipsy abandons Oxford University on a seeming whim "to learn the Gipsy lore." Though the Scholar-Gipsy is a product of the seventeenth century, his quest for a natural philosophy or mystic connection with the spirit manifest in nature seems more in accordance with the British Romantic movement of the late eighteenth and early nineteenth centuries. The Scholar-Gipsy seeks a power of imagination capable of creating and not simply reflecting reality. Like the prophet-wizard at the conclusion of Samuel Taylor Coleridge's poem "Kubla Khan" (1816), the Scholar-Gipsy wants to learn the gypsy "arts to

rule as they desired/ The Workings of men's brains" and, moreover, "the secret of their art,/ When fully learn'd, . . . to the world impart." The Scholar-Gipsy is a Romantic revolutionary who seeks to improve the world not through the industrial innovations of Victorian materialism but through a spiritual purification and reunification of humans with the universal spirit within nature.

The next seven stanzas continue the narrative of the Scholar-Gipsy's quest for a divine knowledge that could reconcile human and divine, matter and spirit. However, the Scholar-Gipsy is both present and absent in the passage. The poem recalls various sightings of its subject from the time he left Oxford to the poem's present. He appears on the banks of "the stripling Thames [River] at Bablock-hithe," with peasant children at play among the Cumnor Hills, amid the gypsy camps of Bagley Wood, and finally upon a "causeway chill" in the dead of winter. The Scholar-Gipsy—both a seemingly real person and figure of myth—appears and disappears in all seasons. Significantly, neither Arnold nor his speaker seem capable of imagining the Scholar-Gipsy's quest "for the spark from heaven to fall" from the Scholar-Gipsy's interior point of view. The subject of the poem remains oddly absent.

The poem's major break comes with the line "But what— I dream!" His imaginative reverie broken, the speaker at first acknowledges in accordance with nineteenth century realism that the Scholar-Gipsy must be long since dead and, in an allusion to Thomas Gray, "in some quiet churchyard laid." However, like Romantic poet John Keats, who endows a common bird with the immortality of the imagination in "Ode to a Nightingale" (1819), Arnold's speaker suddenly declares that the Scholar-Gipsy, too, lives on and has achieved his quest for immortality because he has remained untainted by contact with ennui and the spiritual desolation of the modern world: "O Life unlike to ours?/ Who fluctuate idly without term or scope." Arnold's speaker can imagine the possibility of imaginative transcendence and the validity of waiting for the "spark from Heaven"; however, he resolutely denies the possibility for his contemporaries, "Vague half-believers of our casual creeds," including even "our wisest," limited to mere lamentation for "the dying spark of hope."

The final five stanzas complete the break with the pastoral elegy and almost subvert literary tradition itself. In self-disgust, Arnold's speaker urges the Scholar-Gipsy to maintain his immortal spirit of transcendent imagination, which can only be accomplished by fleeing contact with the modern world, which is "feverish" and infected with "mental strife." The final two stanzas provide an epic simile for a modern world no longer capable of epic thought or in tune with the wisdom of classical tradition. The passage compares the modern audience in the antique garb of a "Tyrian trader," who has mastered the waves and commerce of material goods. However, the Scholar-Gipsy must maintain his distance to avoid the infection of modern life—like Iberian "[s]hy traffickers" of antiquity who traded with a more technologically advanced Tyrian culture but shunned actual contact with it to maintain their unity of culture—leaving their goods on the shore for Tyrian traders to pick up and leave their own trade-goods in return.

Luke Powers

Further Reading

Farell, John Philip. "'The Scholar-Gipsy' and the Continuous Life of Victorian Poetry." *Victorian Poetry* 43, no. 3 (Fall, 2005): 277-296. Argues that "The Scholar-Gipsy" is not a sign of Arnold's despair over the continuation of the English poetic tradition but an ultimately positive link in its "continuous" history.

Grob, Alan. *A Longing Like Despair: Arnold's Poetry of Pessimism*. Dover: University of Delaware Press, 2002. Grob finds the influence of German philosopher Arthur Schopenhauer on Arnold. Arnold's poetry, such as "The Scholar-Gipsy," illustrates Schopenhauer's dichotomy of the artist engaged in the paradoxical activity of trying to escape the experience of suffering while creating art about it.

Hamilton, Ian. *A Gift Imprisoned: The Poetic Life of Matthew Arnold*. New York: Basic Books, 1999. Hamilton, a poet and author of a definitive biography of poet Robert Lowell, examines Arnold's life as a deliberate renunciation of his poetic gift to focus on broad social causes. "The Scholar-Gipsy" epitomizes the tragic division in Arnold's life between timeless poet and prosaic man of his time.

Machann, Clinton. *Matthew Arnold: A Literary Life*. New York: St. Martin's Press, 1998. A succinct and well-articulated exposition of Arnold's intellectual and literary concerns, spanning his career in chronological chapters.

Mazzeno, Laurence W. *Matthew Arnold: The Critical Legacy*. Rochester, N.Y.: Camden House, 1999. Mazzeno surveys the critical response to Arnold. Resembles an annotated bibliography in that it treats its material item by item. A good resource for students new to Arnold and his work.

Moldstad, David. "The Imagination in *The Vanity of Dogmatizing* and 'The Scholar-Gipsy': Arnold's Reversal of Glanvill." *Victorian Poetry* 25, no. 2 (Summer, 1987): 159-172. Moldstad argues that Arnold did not merely use Joseph Glanvill's legend of the scholar-gypsy as a starting point for his own poem. Rather, Arnold reverses Glanvill's seventeenth century distrust of the imagination to a positive identification with the creative faculty capable of transcending the limitations of rationality.

Trotter, David. "Hidden Ground Within: Matthew Arnold's Lyric and Elegiac Poetry." *English Literary History* 44, no. 3 (Autumn, 1977): 526-553. Examines Arnold's development of the Romantic conceit of the gypsy (Roma) as social outsider. Trotter argues that "The Scholar-Gipsy," and Arnold's other early poetry, acts as a "hidden ground" or a personal zone exempt from Victorian materialism and positivism.

The School for Husbands

Author: Molière (1622-1673)
First produced: L'École des maris, 1661; first published, 1661 (English translation, 1732)
Type of work: Drama
Type of plot: Comedy of manners
Time of plot: 1660's
Locale: Paris

Principal characters:
SGANARELLE, a gentleman of means
ARISTE, his brother
ISABELLE, Sganarelle's ward
LÉONOR, her sister and Ariste's ward
VALÈRE, Isabelle's lover

The Story:

Léonor and Isabelle, orphaned on the death of their father, are committed by his deathbed wish to the guardianship of his friends Sganarelle and Ariste, with the additional charge that if Sganarelle and Ariste do not marry the young women, then the guardians are to provide suitable husbands for their wards. The two brothers have different ideas about the upbringing of the orphans. The elder, Ariste, chooses to conform to the fashions of the day but without going to extremes. He gives his ward, Léonor, the opportunity to attend balls and dances and meet the gallants of the city. Although he himself wishes to marry her, he loves Léonor sufficiently to leave the choice to her.

Sganarelle, in contrast, thinks that all this is foolish. Where Ariste hopes to govern only by affection, Sganarelle believes in the effectiveness of severity. He confines Isabelle strictly to her quarters and to household duties, thus keeping her from meeting any eligible young men. Determined to marry her himself, he hopes to discipline her to that end. When Sganarelle scoffs at his brother's leniency and predicts that he will in the end be tricked by so young a wife, Léonor declares that if she marries her guardian she will be faithful to him, but if she were to be Sganarelle's wife she would not be answerable for any of her actions.

Meanwhile, Valère, Sganarelle's new neighbor, has fallen in love with Isabelle, whom he has seen at a distance, and Isabelle reciprocates his love; however, with no means of communication neither knows the true feelings of the other. Isabelle finally works out a plan to test Valère. She tells Sganarelle about Valère's attentions and, knowing her guardian will then angrily accost Valère, declares that they are distasteful to her. Sganarelle asks Valère to cease molesting his ward and tells him that, even though Isabelle knows of Valère's hopes, his is an unrequited passion—her only wish is to find happiness in marrying her guardian. Valère senses in this message something more that Isabelle hopes to convey to him.

Sganarelle tells Isabelle that Valère has been crushed by her harsh message. Isabelle, under the pretense of returning a letter that, according to her story, an accomplice of Valère's had thrown into her chamber, persuades her guardian to deliver the note. Actually, it is a love letter that she has written to Valère. Sganarelle, taking her request as a touching example of model womanly behavior, delivers the letter, which tells of Isabelle's resolve to break free of her prison at any cost during the six days remaining before her enforced marriage to her guardian. Valère, making use of Sganarelle to take back to Isabelle words showing the sincerity of his attachment, declares that his only hope had been to make her his wife and that, although he now realizes the hopelessness of his suit, he will always love her. First he flatters Sganarelle as an opponent no one could possibly displace, and then he shows himself so completely crestfallen and hopeless in surrendering all thought of winning his fair prize that Sganarelle even comes to feel a little sorry for his rival.

Isabelle, trying to trick her guardian into appearing despi-

cable in the eyes of her lover, pretends to fear an attempt by Valère to force her from her chamber and carry her off before her marriage to Sganarelle. Bursting with pride at what he considers the womanly discretion of his ward, discretion obviously reflecting his own wisdom in her upbringing, Sganarelle offers to return to Valère and berate him for his bold and mischievous scheme. All turns out as Isabelle has hoped. In reply, Valère declares that if what Sganarelle reports is possibly true, then his passion is indeed hopeless. Sganarelle, to make matters perfectly clear, takes Valère directly to Isabelle to hear the cruel decision from her own lips. Using words that could be understood two ways, Isabelle and Valère declare their love for each other under the nose of their dupe. Then on Isabelle's order Valère departs, promising that in three days he will find a way to free her from her jailer. Sganarelle, however, cannot wait three days. Overjoyed at the exhibition of what he takes to be his ward's fond regard for him, he is eager to consummate the marriage. He tells Isabelle that the ceremony will be performed the next day.

Isabelle realizes that her last recourse is to commit herself unreservedly to her lover at once, but as she prepares for flight Sganarelle sees her and informs her that all preparations have been made for their union. Isabelle trumps up a story that she is about to leave the house to spend the night with a worthy friend, Lucrece, because Léonor, in desperation, has asked for the use of Isabelle's room that night. Against her better judgment, she declares, she has consented and has just locked her sister in. Isabelle pretends that Valère has really been Léonor's lover for more than a year but has abandoned her because he has become infatuated with Isabelle. She says that Léonor, hoping to win back Valère's love, plans to meet him in the lane near the house. Sganarelle, declaring this plan immodest, wants to drive Léonor out of the house at once. Isabelle restrains him, however, and persuades him to let her take the message to Léonor, after insisting that Sganarelle must hide himself and promise to let her sister leave without his speaking to her. Sganarelle agrees, secretly pleased at the thought of his brother's discomfiture over the wanton doings of his ward.

Isabelle, pretending to be Léonor, leaves the house. Curious, Sganarelle follows. He sees Valère and Isabelle meet and, after declaring their love, enter Valère's house. Thinking that Léonor is with Valère, and wishing to keep scandal from touching Isabelle through her sister, he hurriedly calls a magistrate and urges him to marry the pair. The magistrate is to wait, however, until Sganarelle can return with the bride's guardian to witness the ceremony.

Ariste cannot believe his ears when Sganarelle gloatingly insists that Léonor is with Valère, but he is induced nevertheless to accompany his brother. Valère, who has hidden Isabelle in a separate room, has the magistrate prepare a formal contract, to be signed by all parties present, indicating their consent to the marriage. Still under the delusion that the bride-to-be is his brother's ward, Léonor, Sganarelle agrees to the wedding; Ariste, placing the desires of his supposed ward above his own dreams, assents also.

Meanwhile, Léonor returns early from the ball she has attended. Ariste gently chides her for not confiding in him her love for Valère, but Léonor, amazed, protests that she loves only Ariste, her beloved guardian, whom she is ready to marry immediately. Angered, Sganarelle realizes too late the trick that Isabelle has played on him. All women, he declares, are to be disbelieved and shunned. In the schooling of husbands it is he and not his brother who has failed.

Critical Evaluation:

When Molière's theatrical troupe first performed his three-act comedy *The School for Husbands* in 1661, the author himself played the role of Sganarelle. At first glance, it may seem odd that Molière chose to play the role of an unsympathetic and egomaniacal character, but Sganarelle is a wonderful comic role. In all except one scene in this verse comedy Sganarelle dominates the stage, although his ability to dominate other characters proves to be illusory. Sganarelle is such a thoroughly unpleasant person that the audience wants to see him fail.

From the very beginning of this comedy, Molière contrasts Sganarelle's irrational attempts to limit Isabelle's actions with the more enlightened and tolerant attitude of his older brother, Ariste, toward his fiancé, Léonor. *The School for Husbands* begins with a dialogue between Sganarelle and Ariste. Sganarelle affirms that he has no interest in learning what others may think of his strange and inflexible behavior, but he grants to himself the right to criticize others. This hypocrisy immediately creates an unfavorable opinion of Sganarelle in the minds of Molière's viewers.

The play also features a marvelously ironic use of role reversal between these two brothers. Although Ariste is twenty years older than his brother, it is he and not Sganarelle who wears fashionable clothing and appreciates modern attitudes toward tolerance. Ariste does not object that Léonor spends money buying clothing for herself because this brings her pleasure, and Ariste is so well-to-do that he need not worry about such expenditures. He has no desire to "tyrannize" Léonor, and he is mature enough to realize that it would be better for him if she were to marry someone else rather than marry Ariste against her will. Ariste has no desire to be miserable in his marriage. Unless Léonor freely agrees to marry

him, Ariste prefers to remain a bachelor. Ariste's ideas on marriage are eminently sensible; he realizes that a marriage that is not based on equality and respect is doomed to unhappiness. Sganarelle, however, mocks Ariste's belief that a husband will be loved by his wife only if he respects her freedom and dignity. This comedy illustrates Ariste's wisdom and Sganarelle's folly.

Fate and a woman soon bring about Sganarelle's defeat. A very reasonable man named Valère loves Isabelle, but he does not realize that Sganarelle also hopes to marry her. As a result of his innocence and trust in the basic goodness of others, Valère speaks to Sganarelle of his passion for Isabelle. Valère correctly assumes that Isabelle has no desire to marry such a repulsive and insensitive man as Sganarelle. With supreme overconfidence, Sganarelle repeatedly makes the same mistake without realizing how his actions and comments will be interpreted or used by other characters. In the second act, he tells Valère that Isabelle wants nothing to do with him, but Valère correctly interprets this remark as a confirmation of her love for him. Sganarelle, being so sure that he cannot be fooled, is fooled. Sganarelle, who considers himself to be clever, falls for a trap prepared by Isabelle. She speaks of her anger (feigned) that Valère has thrown through her bedroom window a rock to which a love letter had been attached. She asks Sganarelle to return this letter unopened to Valère, and Sganarelle willingly does so, unwittingly delivering to Valère a love letter from Isabelle. Sganarelle's inflexibility and delusionary perception of reality lead to his unintentionally serving as the intermediary who helps to convince Valère of Isabelle's love for him. By an ironic twist of fate, the thoroughly unpleasant Sganarelle brings about the happy ending.

The third act of *The School for Husbands* contains many different levels of irony. As a result of his extreme vanity, Sganarelle does not realize that it is in his own self-interest to be flexible. He ensures his own failure, and the happiness of the two sympathetic couples, when he arranges for a notary to come to his house in order to prepare a marriage contract. The notary is delighted to have this new business, and he does not care who marries whom as long as he is paid. Molière's spectators realize that Sganarelle's perverse plan cannot succeed. Readers and theatergoers alike are amused in the third act when the self-righteous and ridiculous Sganarelle again criticizes Ariste for his complete faith in his fiancé, Léonor. Like Valère and Isabelle, Ariste also refuses to believe Sganarelle's preposterous claims. Ariste is trusting enough of the love that he and Léonor feel for each other that he dismisses Sganarelle's absurd charge that Léonor wishes to marry Valère.

While Sganarelle is busy berating his brother, Valère marries Isabelle, and it is clear to the audience that Ariste and Léonor will soon get married. Once the cooperative notary has finished composing the marriage contract for Valère and Isabelle, he can render the same professional service for Ariste and Léonor.

Léonor's servant Lisette speaks the last words in this comedy. After having listened to Sganarelle's irrational criticism of women, Lisette expresses the hope that men can profit from the moral lessons taught in the play. Men who respect women's freedom will attain happiness and true joy, whereas fanatics such as Sganarelle will never find pleasure in marriage.

"Critical Evaluation" by Edmund J. Campion

Further Reading

Ciccone, Anthony A. *The Comedy of Language: Four Farces by Molière*. Potomac, Md.: J. Porrua Turanzas, 1980. Discusses comic uses of language and the levels of irony in *The School for Husbands*. Examines the contrasts between the behavior of Ariste and that of Sganarelle.

Gaines, James F. *Social Structures in Molière's Theater*. Columbus: Ohio State University Press, 1984. Explores the differences between noble and middle-class values in Molière's comedies. Contrasts Sganarelle's obsessive desire to dominate his fiancé with the more enlightened views of his brother, Ariste.

Hawcroft, Michael. *Molière: Reasoning with Fools*. New York: Oxford University Press, 2007. Examines the characters in Molière's plays whom Hawcroft calls *raisonneurs*—the thoughtful, witty, and resourceful friends of the foolish protagonists. Analyzes the *raisonneur*'s role as brother and "sparring partner" in *The School for Husbands*.

Howarth, W. D. *Molière: A Playwright and His Audience*. New York: Cambridge University Press, 1982. Discusses performances by Molière's troupe and the critical reception of his comedies by Parisian theatergoers of his era. Explores the creative ways in which Molière employed theatrical conventions to create witty farces and comedies.

McCarthy, Gerry. *The Theatres of Molière*. New York: Routledge, 2002. Places Molière's life and work within the context of the French theater of his time. Discusses the productions of some of his plays, including the actors, scenery, and costumes.

Polsky, Zachary. *The Comic Machine, the Narrative Machine, and the Political Machine in the Works of Molière*. Lewiston, N.Y.: Edwin Mellen Press, 2003. Examines the nature of seventeenth century French comedy by analyzing the works of Molière. Discusses the moralism and political context of Molière's plays and describes the use of speech, voice, and body in their performance.

Scott, Virginia. *Molière: A Theatrical Life*. New York: Cambridge University Press, 2000. Chronicles Molière's life and provides an overview of his plays, placing them within the context of seventeenth century French theater.

Wadsworth, Philip A. *Molière and the Italian Theatrical Tradition*. York, S.C.: French Literature Publications, 1977. Discusses Molière's creative imitation of Italian theatrical tradition in his early farces. Contrasts Sganarelle's inflexibility with the more reasonable behavior of Ariste.

The School for Scandal

Author: Richard Brinsley Sheridan (1751-1816)
First produced: 1777; first published, 1780
Type of work: Drama
Type of plot: Comedy of manners
Time of plot: Eighteenth century
Locale: London

Principal characters:
SIR PETER TEAZLE, an elderly nobleman
LADY TEAZLE, his young wife
MARIA, Sir Peter's ward
SIR OLIVER SURFACE, Sir Peter's friend
JOSEPH SURFACE and CHARLES SURFACE, Sir Oliver's nephews
LADY SNEERWELL, Lady Teazle's friend
ROWLEY, Sir Peter's servant

The Story:

Lady Sneerwell, who in her youth was the target of slander, has set her life upon a course to reduce the reputations of other women to the level of her own. Aided by her intimate, Snake, she intrigues to involve the Teazles in scandal, to bring Joseph Surface's true character to light, to wreck the love between Charles and Maria, and to gain Charles for herself along with Sir Oliver's fortune. To her the world consists of nothing but scandal and scandalous intrigues, and she does her best to make her vision a reality. She is not successful, however, when she abuses Charles Surface to Sir Peter Teazle's ward Maria, who refuses to listen to her. Instead, Maria trustingly confides in Lady Candour, whose defense of a reputation ensures its complete annihilation.

Sometimes Sir Peter Teazle ponders the wisdom of his marriage to Lady Teazle, doubting the judgment of an old bachelor in marrying a young wife. Lady Teazle is a country-bred girl who is enjoying London life extravagantly and to the full. Sir Oliver Surface is concerned about his two nephews, his problem being the disposal of his great fortune. Sir Oliver has been abroad for the past fifteen years and feels that he does not know his nephews' real natures; he hopes by some stratagem to catch them unawares and thus be able to test their characters.

One day, Sir Peter and Lady Teazle quarrel because Sir Peter violently objects to her attendance at the home of Lady Sneerwell. Lady Teazle accuses Sir Peter of wishing to deprive her of all freedom and reminds him that he has promised to go to Lady Sneerwell's with her. He retorts that he will do so for only one reason, to look after his own character. When they arrive, Lady Sneerwell's rooms are full of people uttering libelous remarks about their enemies and saying even worse things about their friends. Sir Peter escapes as soon as possible.

When the rest of Lady Sneerwell's guests retire to the card room, leaving Maria and Joseph alone, Joseph once more presses his suit. He insinuates that Maria is in love with Charles and is thus running counter to Sir Peter's wishes. Lady Teazle walks in just as Joseph is on his knees avowing his honest love. Surprised, Lady Teazle tells Maria that she is wanted in the next room. After Maria leaves, Lady Teazle asks Joseph for an explanation of what she has seen, and he tells her that he was pleading with Maria not to tell Sir Peter of his tender concern for Lady Teazle.

Sir Oliver consults Rowley, Sir Peter's shrewd and observing servant, in an attempt to learn more about his nephews' characters. Rowley himself believes that Joseph does not have as good a character as his reputation seems to indicate and that Charles has a better one. Sir Oliver also consults Sir Peter, who declares that he is ready to stake his life on Joseph's honor. He is much put out, therefore, when Maria once more refuses to marry Joseph.

Sir Peter, Sir Oliver, and Rowley plan to test the worthiness of the nephews. Charles is, as usual, in dire need of money, and Sir Oliver arranges to accompany a moneylender who is going to see Charles; Sir Oliver will claim to be Mr. Premium, a man who can supply the money that Charles needs. When they arrive at Charles's lodging, a drinking party is in progress, and some of the guests are playing games of dice. Sir Oliver is not at all impressed with Trip, Charles's footman, who gives himself the airs of a fashionable man-about-town.

Upon investigating, Sir Oliver discovers that Charles has, with the exception only of the portraits of his ancestors, turned all of his inherited possessions into cash. Convinced that Charles is a scamp, Sir Oliver, still calling himself Premium, agrees to buy the paintings, and he purchases each picture as presented except his own portrait, which Charles will not sell for any amount of money. Sir Oliver is pleased by this fact and on that ground discounts Charles's reputation for extravagance. Charles receives a draft for eight hundred pounds for the portraits and immediately sends one hundred pounds to Mr. Stanley, a poor relation whose financial circumstances are even worse than his own.

During an assignation between Joseph Surface and Lady Teazle in Joseph's library, Joseph advises her to give her husband grounds for jealousy rather than to suffer his jealousy without cause. He argues that to save her reputation she must ruin it and that he is the man best able to help her. Lady Teazle considers such a doctrine very odd.

While they are talking, Sir Peter arrives unexpectedly, and Lady Teazle hides behind the screen that Joseph orders placed against the window. Joseph then pretends to be reading when Sir Peter walks in. Sir Peter has called to inform Joseph of his suspicions that Lady Teazle is having an affair with Charles; Sir Peter also shows Joseph two deeds he has brought with him, one settling eight hundred pounds a year on Lady Teazle for her independent use, the other giving her the bulk of his fortune at his death. Joseph's dissimulation before Sir Peter and Sir Peter's generosity to her are not lost on Lady Teazle. When Sir Peter begins to discuss Joseph's desire to wed Maria, Lady Teazle realizes that Joseph has been deceiving her.

Below stairs, Charles inopportunely demands entrance to the house to see his brother. Not wishing to see Charles, Sir Peter asks Joseph where he can hide. Sir Peter catches a glimpse of a petticoat behind the screen, but Joseph assures him that the woman behind the screen is only a French milliner who plagues him. Sir Peter hides in a closet, and Lady Teazle remains in her hiding place behind the screen.

When Charles comes in, he and Joseph discuss Lady Teazle and Sir Peter's suspicion that Charles is her lover. Charles mentions that he believes Joseph to be her favorite and recounts all the little incidents that lead him to think so. Embarrassed by this turn in the conversation, Joseph interrupts to say that Sir Peter is within hearing. Placed in a difficult position, Charles explains to Sir Peter that he has merely been playing a joke on Joseph. Sir Peter knows a good joke on Joseph, too, he says: Joseph is having an affair with a milliner. Charles decides that he wants to have a look at the milliner and pulls down the screen, revealing Lady Teazle. Joseph is undone because Lady Teazle refuses to agree with any of the excuses he makes. She angrily informs her husband of the whole nature of Joseph's intentions and departs. Sir Peter follows her, leaving Joseph to his own conscience.

Sir Oliver, masquerading as Mr. Stanley and badly in need of assistance, gains admittance to Joseph's apartment. Joseph refuses to help Mr. Stanley, saying that he receives very little money from Sir Oliver and claiming that he has advanced all his funds to Charles. After Sir Oliver leaves, Rowley, who is a party to the whole scheme, comes to tell Joseph that Sir Oliver has arrived in town.

Sir Oliver goes again to see Joseph. Still believing that his uncle is Mr. Stanley, Joseph is showing him out just as Charles enters. Charles, surprised to see the man he knows as Mr. Premium in his brother's apartment, also insists that he leave, but at that moment Sir Peter Teazle arrives and addresses Sir Oliver by his right name. Both Sir Oliver and Sir Peter are now aware of Joseph's real character. Charles, promising to try to reform, gets Maria and his uncle's inheritance as well. Lady Sneerwell is exposed by Snake, who is paid double to speak the truth, and Lady Teazle returns her diploma to the School for Scandal, of which Lady Sneerwell is president. Everyone is happy except Lady Sneerwell and Joseph Surface.

Critical Evaluation:

First performed at London's famous Drury Lane theater in 1777, *The School for Scandal* was staged a total of 261 times before the end of the eighteenth century and has been revived hundreds of times since, making it one of the most enduringly popular comedies in the English language. Accounting for the play's popularity is not difficult: Richard Brinsley Sheridan, who had succeeded the great David Garrick as manager of the Drury Lane theater in 1776, was

blessed with a keenly theatrical imagination and an instinctive sense of how best to please an audience. These talents are nowhere more evident than in *The School for Scandal*, which is, above all else, first-rate theater—a play graced by sparkling dialogue, a cast of memorable characters, and a complex plot that combines elements of high comedy, intrigue, and genuine feeling.

The ingredients that guarantee success on the stage, however, do not always guarantee critical esteem. Although critics have over the years had a great deal to say about William Shakespeare's *Twelfth Night: Or, What You Will* (pr. c. 1600-1602, pb. 1623) and Ben Jonson's *Volpone* (pr. 1605), they have had relatively little to say about *The School for Scandal*. Most discussions of the play, in fact, have focused less on literary analysis than on the question of Sheridan's success in rebelling against the sentimental comedies of his day and in recovering the spirit of such earlier Restoration comedies as William Congreve's *The Way of the World* (pr., pb. 1700). Unfortunately, when measured against these earlier plays, *The School for Scandal* has usually been found inferior—a comedy, as one critic trenchantly put it, in which the Restoration is unrestored.

It might be best to begin study of the play with the general disclaimer that *The School for Scandal* is not simply a Restoration comedy, it is another kind of comedy altogether—moral rather than satiric, basically humane and optimistic rather than hard edged and cynical. It is a comedy written for an audience whose basic assumptions about art, theater, and human nature made it radically different from the audience of Congreve's day.

The School for Scandal has been called a middle-class morality play, and in a sense that description is accurate. At play's end, good characters are rewarded and bad characters ("evil" is really too strong a word) are routed, thus providing the audience with two useful object lessons: Honesty and benevolence will, in the end, win out over duplicity and selfishness, and, as the surname of the brothers Charles and Joseph suggests, surface appearances are not always trustworthy indicators of inner character. It would be wrong, however, to assume that Sheridan was a moralist using comedy merely to sugarcoat his message. His primary goal in *The School for Scandal* was, without doubt, comic delight rather than moral instruction.

Although Sheridan's dialogue in *The School for Scandal* has often been celebrated, language in the play is less important as a source of its comedy than are plot and character. Creating interesting characters and placing them in situations that compel them to respond in particularly telling ways allows Sheridan to examine what writers of social comedy from Aristophanes to Woody Allen have never tired of examining: the abiding, perhaps even necessary, inconsistency in human society between surface and substance, appearance and reality, truth and fiction.

Lady Sneerwell and the members of her scandalous school are masters of social illusion. As a former victim of scandal herself, Lady Sneerwell understands only too well how fragile a thing reputation is. More to the point, perhaps, she has achieved an even more profound intuition: She has come to understand how all reputation—good or bad—is, from a purely social (rather than moral) perspective, a fiction, a contrivance of opinion. This understanding enables her to fashion the scheming hypocrite Joseph Surface into an admired man of sentiment and his good-hearted, although slightly profligate, brother Charles into a notorious libertine. That Joseph is by nature selfish and mercenary and Charles humane and generous is largely irrelevant within the sophisticated world of London high society, where surface is all that matters.

If *The School for Scandal* were another kind of comedy, Lady Sneerwell and her scandalmongering friends Mrs. Candour, Crabtree, and Sir Benjamin Backbite might be allowed to hold the stage. Their antics, as amply demonstrated in act 2, scene 1, amount to little more than niggling gossip. The Widow Ochre may use too much makeup and Miss Sallow may try "to pass for a girl at six-and-thirty," but these are relatively minor instances of affectation, and the point remains amusement rather than pain. Even the somewhat more serious matter of Lady Teazle's corruption by the school is played largely for laughs, and the prevailing tone throughout these scenes is one of childish naughtiness rather than true wickedness. A more concrete check on the goings-on is provided by the presence of Sir Peter and his young ward, Maria, both of whom display comically exasperated (but morally legitimate) dismay at the behavior of the scandalous characters.

Sheridan knew his audience, and he understood that moral comedy can flirt with sin but must never embrace it. Thus when the various schemes of Lady Sneerwell and Joseph proceed beyond the realm of detached amusement and begin to threaten the happiness of morally superior characters, the plot quickens toward resolution. This resolution comes about through the introduction of an outsider, Sir Oliver Surface, whose ability to penetrate social facades enables him to function as a kind of moral catalyst, and through two expertly crafted scenes in the fourth act. In the auction scene, Charles is shown to be a kind and generous man whose worst fault seems to be a fondness for cards and good company; in the famous screen scene that follows, Joseph is fully revealed as a smooth-tongued hypocrite. When the screen, that conventional yet effective stage device that both symbolizes and comments on the discrepancy between social fiction and moral truth, comes tumbling down, revealing a thoroughly abashed Lady Teazle, the audience can only respond with applause. Lady Teazle will soon resign her place in Lady Sneerwell's school, and Sir Peter will soon accept Charles as a proper husband for Maria, leaving Lady Sneerwell and Joseph with only each other—which seems perfectly appropriate punishment for them both.

"Critical Evaluation" by Michael Stuprich

Further Reading

Auburn, Mark. *Sheridan's Comedies: Their Contexts and Achievements*. Lincoln: University of Nebraska Press, 1977. Excellent study of Sheridan and his work provides a first-rate discussion of *The School for Scandal*.

Browne, Kevin Thomas. *Richard Brinsley Sheridan and Britain's School for Scandal: Interpreting His Theater Through Its Eighteenth-Century Social Context*. Lewiston, N.Y.: Edwin Mellen Press, 2006. Refutes criticism that Sheridan's plays are all style and no substance, arguing that the works depict how people from different social classes negotiate issues of British identity, such as money, gender, class, morality, and language. Chapter 4 is devoted to *The School for Scandal*.

Danziger, Marlies K. *Oliver Goldsmith and Richard Brinsley Sheridan*. New York: Frederick Unger, 1978. A good place to begin study of Sheridan and his work. Contains an excellent discussion of *The School for Scandal* and a useful bibliography.

Loftis, John. *Sheridan and the Drama of Georgian England*. Oxford, England: Basil Blackwell, 1976. Carefully researched and rewarding study by a leading scholar in the field places Sheridan's work firmly in the context of late eighteenth century theater and dispels many of the myths surrounding *The School for Scandal*. Highly recommended.

Morwood, James, and David Crane, eds. *Sheridan Studies*. New York: Cambridge University Press, 1995. Collection of essays examines Sheridan's theatrical and political careers. Topics addressed include theater in the age of Garrick and Sheridan, Sheridan's use of language, and the challenges of producing his plays. Two essays discuss *The School for Scandal*: "Sheridan, Congreve, and *The School for Scandal*," by Eric Rump, and "Sheridan, Molière, and the Idea of the School in *The School for Scandal*," by James Morwood.

O'Toole, Fintan. *A Traitor's Kiss: The Life of Richard Brinsley Sheridan*. London: Granta, 1997. Biography focuses on Sheridan's relationship to his native Ireland. Draws connections between Sheridan's life and his plays and provides a detailed examination of his political career.

Worth, Katharine. *Sheridan and Goldsmith*. New York: St. Martin's Press, 1992. Discusses the plays of Sheridan and Oliver Goldsmith in the context of eighteenth century theatrical traditions and practices. Includes a very good chapter on *The School for Scandal*.

The School for Wives

Author: Molière (1622-1673)
First produced: L'École des femmes, 1662; first published, 1663 (English translation, 1732)
Type of work: Drama
Type of plot: Comedy of manners
Time of plot: Seventeenth century
Locale: France

Principal characters:
ARNOLPHE (M. DE LA SOUCHE), a wealthy man
AGNÈS, his ward
HORACE, Agnès's lover
CHRYSALDE, Arnolphe's friend
ENRIQUE, Chrysalde's brother-in-law
ORONTE, Horace's father

The Story:

As Arnolphe tells his friend Chrysalde, if a man is not to be made to look like a fool by his wife, he must choose a wife who is ignorant of the ways of the world and in no danger of being admired by other men. Arnolphe, famous for his bitter ridicule of other men who are put to shame by the unfaithfulness of their wives, is determined that he will not find himself in a like position. For that reason, he proposes to marry Agnès, his young ward, whom he has protected from society. He thinks her such an ignorant girl and such a fool that she will make a perfect wife.

Agnès was placed in Arnolphe's care by her widowed foster mother. The girl had her early training in a convent to which Arnolphe sent her, and since then she has lived in a small cottage on his estate. Her life has been secluded in order that she might be kept safe from learning and from outside influences until she has reached an age for marriage. On a whim, Arnolphe has changed his name to Monsieur de la Souche, but Agnès is not aware of this fact, nor is she aware of Arnolphe's plan to marry her.

Before Arnolphe can inform Agnès of his wishes, Horace, the son of Arnolphe's friend Oronte, tells Arnolphe that he is in love with Agnès. Horace, knowing only that Agnès is the ward of one de la Souche, does not realize that Arnolphe and de la Souche are the same man. Horace asks Arnolphe not to tell anyone of the love affair because it must be kept a secret from both de la Souche and Horace's father. Arnolphe can only smother his rage in silence as he listens to the tale of Agnès's duplicity. Even though she is not aware that

Arnolphe plans to make her his wife, he already feels that she has been faithless to him and has shamed him. He decides that he must accuse her of sinning against him and must also tell her his plans immediately.

Agnès does not react to Arnolphe's accusations as he had anticipated. In her innocence, she tells him of the pleasure she finds in Horace's company. Arnolphe is relieved to learn that she has given her lover only kisses, for she is so innocent that she once asked if babies come from the ear. He orders her not to see Horace again, even telling her to slam the door in his face or throw stones at him if he attempts to see her. In addition, he lectures her on the role of women, wives in particular, and gives her a book of maxims to study so that she might be better prepared for marriage. The maxims express exactly Arnolphe's view of wives as the complete possessions of their husbands. Arnolphe tells Agnès that he intends to marry her, but she misunderstands and thinks that he means to give her in marriage. She is happy because she thinks she will be married to Horace.

Arnolphe learns from Horace that Agnès has obeyed orders and thrown a stone at him, but he learns also that the stone had a letter attached, a letter in which she professed her love for Horace. The young man is delighted. Still not knowing that his supposed friend is in reality Agnès's guardian, Horace asks Arnolphe for help in rescuing her from de la Souche.

Arnolphe decides to marry Agnès at once and sends for the notary. He is doubly miserable, because he feels betrayed and because he really loves the young woman. He becomes enraged when he learns of Horace's plan to gain admittance to Agnès's room, and he orders his servants to set upon Horace with clubs as he tries to climb to Agnès's window. He is horrified, however, when the servants return and tell him that they have beaten Horace too hard and have killed him.

Even though he hates the young man, Arnolphe is soon relieved to see Horace alive and not seriously injured. Horace tells Arnolphe that he pretended to be dead so that his attackers would leave him. Agnès, swearing that she is never going back to her prison cottage, has slipped out during the uproar. Horace, with no place to take her, asks Arnolphe to help him by hiding Agnès until they can be married. Arnolphe hides his face as he meets Agnès, and it is not until after Horace has gone that she recognizes Arnolphe as de la Souche. Still, her innocence makes her unafraid, and she tells Arnolphe that Horace is more to her liking for a husband than is Arnolphe. Swearing that she will have no one but Horace, she refuses to consider marrying Arnolphe in spite of his alternate threats and promises. At last Arnolphe declares angrily that he will send her to a convent, and he has his servants lock her up until a carriage can be secured.

Horace, ignorant of these developments, goes again to his friend Arnolphe, this time in great agitation. His father, Oronte, has arrived for a visit with his friend Enrique, the brother-in-law of Chrysalde. It is Oronte's purpose to marry Horace to Enrique's daughter, and Horace asks Arnolphe to persuade Oronte not to force the marriage. Although he promises to help Horace, Arnolphe does exactly the opposite. He tells Oronte that a father should never give in to a son, that a son should be made to bow to a parent's wishes. He insists that Horace and Enrique's daughter be married at once. Horace then learns that Arnolphe is in reality de la Souche and realizes that he has been betrayed.

Arnolphe has Agnès brought before the gathering because he wants to witness her grief and Horace's as they are separated forever. He is disappointed, however; to his astonishment, he learns that Agnès is Enrique's daughter. Enrique, years before, had secretly married the sister of Chrysalde. After her death, Enrique, forced to flee the country, had left his small daughter with a country woman. Too poor to provide for the child, the woman had in turn given Agnès to Arnolphe. Enrique had only recently learned of her whereabouts. As soon as he learned that she was with Arnolphe, he had arranged her betrothal to the son of his friend Oronte. Thus the lovers are united with the blessing of everyone but Arnolphe, who can only sputter and wring his hands. He has truly been betrayed.

Critical Evaluation:

The School for Wives was probably the most popular success of Molière's controversial career. When the play was first produced, Molière himself played Arnolphe, the middle-aged theorist of marriage, and Armande, his bride of less than a year, portrayed the ingenue, Agnès. Although the motif of the play is an old one and appears in Italian and Spanish tales, it is a fact that the problem of the ardent middle-aged lover and the bride half his age whom he has trained from girlhood was Molière's own. Perhaps this is why, in the last act, when Arnolphe pleads with the girl for her love, the comedy seems to drop away, exposing an agonized and aging man speaking desperate and moving words. The play is very funny, but it rings with truth and psychological realism beneath the humor and absurdity.

The School for Wives was Molière's first five-act comedy in verse, and generally its tone is realistic; the farcical action is confined, for the most part, to the servants. Although influenced by the traditional French farce and the Italian commedia dell'arte, the play is essentially a comedy of character, with an overlay of the comedy of manners. The theme is the old one that love conquers all and that the heart will always understand its own desires and will recognize the heart and soul destined to be joined with it. In an age of arranged marriages and subsequent philandering, Molière's conviction that marriage should be based on love would have been radical if it had not been integrated into the absurdities of the comedy.

The subsidiary themes of the play are that a young woman has a right to decent education commensurate with her intelligence and curiosity and that any attempt to keep her ignorant is in contempt of her privileges as a human being. At the beginning of the play, Arnolphe sympathetically presents his position: He is so exasperated by feminine coquetry that he feels the only safety is in marrying a fool. His greatest mistake is in carrying his attitude to ridiculous and wrongheaded extremes. With the single-mindedness of a pedant, he constructs a complete scheme for rearing the girl in a convent from the age of four so that she will be entirely untrained in the ways of the world. His pride in his scheme warns the audience of his eventual and inevitable downfall.

The play is witty and amusing, but it contains a surprisingly small amount of action. Mostly, it consists of speeches, many of them long and drawn out, the audience hearing about the action more than witnessing it. To Molière's contemporaries, however, such a comedy was subject to certain rules of decorum; all violent action was banned from the stage, and the audience's imagination filled in what was necessary. Although the play is often static, it is never dull; *The*

School for Wives is one of Molière's most delightful comedies.

Agnès is one of the most fascinating characters in any Molière comedy; if she sins, it is through lamblike ignorance and innocence, and her gradual awakening is a marvel of character portrayal. The revelation of her slowly developing temperament, all the stronger for its innocence and naïveté, is as touching as it is charming. At the same time, the pedant's personality undergoes a transformation, for he discovers, in spite of himself, the true nature of love. He, who has dismissed love and all of the accompanying nonsense as beneath him, finds that he is hopelessly in love with the young woman he has created. He has no choice but to eat his words and to suffer the consequences of his stupidity and blindness. His awkward gropings toward the manners and words of love become both his own punishment and the delight of the audience.

The moral point of the play rests in the fact that Arnolphe has deliberately sought to confine a human being, to limit her development unnaturally. Under the pretense of keeping her "simple," he has made her into a charming freak. The struggle is between the spontaneous and the rigid, a struggle that lends itself perfectly to comedy. The more Arnolphe treats life mechanically, the more his efforts backfire, for life reacts spontaneously to make the outcome of his elaborate schemes the opposite of his intentions. In Molière's plays, nature is always held up as a better guide than authority; human nature and human emotions must be allowed to take their own course. It is always the extreme position that causes unhappiness and eventual disaster. If human beings would avoid absurd obsessions, life would be smoother and more joyous for everybody concerned. Of course, it would also be duller, and it is this all-too-human tendency of people to embrace extreme points of view and absurd attitudes that provides Molière with his most brilliant comic creations.

Molière uses several clever devices to enliven his essentially simple plot. One is the fact that Arnolphe has taken the name of de la Souche. This allows Horace to make him the confidant of successive attempts to get Agnès out of old de la Souche's clutches. The complications of this misunderstanding are both absurd and hilarious. Another delightful and clever contrivance is the grotesque scurry of the denouement. The final scene of act 5 is filled with rapid-fire patter in which Chrysalde and Oronte, Horace's father, newly arrived on the scene with a person called Enrique, who has spent the last fourteen years in America, explain to all concerned that the rustic Agnès is actually Chrysalde's niece and the daughter of this Enrique. Enrique is a perfect and totally implausible deus ex machina, standing by, dumb as a fish, until just before the curtain falls to remark in three lines that he has no doubts about the identity of his daughter and consents to her marrying Horace. It is a daring and absurd conclusion to the play, but it provides the necessary happy ending for the young lovers and leaves Arnolphe sadder but wiser.

There is much excellent comedy in *The School for Wives*: the frenzy of Arnolphe, the leg pulling by Chrysalde, an absurd notary babbling in legal jargon, a saucy maid named Georgette, and the irony of the old man trying to win the love of a young woman he has tried to lock away from all eyes but his own. Chrysalde, in particular, is a satirist with a sense of humor, trying with a long merry tirade to laugh Arnolphe out of his obsession. The contrasts and contradictions of human behavior provide the basic, and often subtle, humor of the play, but Molière is never above farce, as in the opening scene when Alain and Georgette first refuse to let their master through the gate and then quarrel about which of them is to do it. As is often the case in Molière's comedies, much as in real life, the characters assume different guises, adopting different faces as they need them, then removing their masks and inventing new ones. The cloak of politeness falls, and the chaos beneath is hilariously revealed.

"Critical Evaluation" by Bruce D. Reeves

Further Reading

Calder, Andrew. *Molière: The Theory and Practice of Comedy.* London: Athlone Press, 1993. Examines connections between dramatic theory and theatrical performances of Molière's comedies. Discusses conflicts between ridiculous and sympathetic characters and the role of moral judgment in *The School for Wives*.

Guicharnaud, Jacques, ed. *Molière: A Collection of Critical Essays.* Englewood Cliffs, N.J.: Prentice-Hall, 1964. Contains numerous essays originally written by major critics in English or translated from French into English for this volume. Explores satire, parody, comedy of manners, and wit in Molière's comedies.

Hall, H. Gaston. *Comedy in Context: Essays on Molière.* Jackson: University Press of Mississippi, 1984. In twelve essays, an eminent Molière specialist examines such topics as comic images, social satire, and parody in *The School for Wives*.

Hawcroft, Michael. *Molière: Reasoning with Fools.* New York: Oxford University Press, 2007. Examines the characters in Molière's plays whom Hawcroft calls *raisonneurs*—the thoughtful, witty, and resourceful friends of the foolish protagonists. Analyzes the *raisonneur*'s role as friend and counselor in *The School for Wives*.

Koppisch, Michael S. *Rivalry and the Disruption of Order in Molière's Theater*. Madison, N.J.: Fairleigh Dickinson University Press, 2004. Argues that many of the characters in Molière's plays desperately want something they cannot have. Discusses Amolphe's desire to avoid cuckoldry in this light.

McCarthy, Gerry. *The Theatres of Molière*. New York: Routledge, 2002. Places Molière's life and work within the context of the French theater of his time. Discusses the productions of some of his plays, including their actors, scenery, and costumes.

Polsky, Zachary. *The Comic Machine, the Narrative Machine, and the Political Machine in the Works of Molière*. Lewiston, N.Y.: E. Mellen Press, 2003. Examines the nature of seventeenth century French comedy by analyzing the works of Molière. Discusses the moralism and political context of Molière's plays and describes the use of speech, voice, and body in their performance. Includes a detailed analysis of *The School for Wives*.

Scott, Virginia. *Molière: A Theatrical Life*. New York: Cambridge University Press, 2000. Chronicles Molière's life and provides an overview of his plays, placing them within the context of seventeenth century French theater.

Walker, Hallam. *Molière*. Updated ed. Boston: Twayne, 1990. Contains an excellent general introduction to Molière's comedies and an annotated bibliography of important critical studies on Molière. Examines images of marriage and the exploitation of women in *The School for Wives*.

The Screwtape Letters

Author: C. S. Lewis (1898-1963)
First published: 1941, serial; 1942, book
Type of work: Novel
Type of plot: Satire
Time of plot: Before and during World War II
Locale: England

Principal characters:
SCREWTAPE, a former tempter promoted to undersecretary in Hell's civil service
WORMWOOD, Screwtape's nephew, a tempter in training
THE PATIENT, the young Englishman to whom Wormwood is assigned
THE ENEMY, Hell's name for God
GLUBOSE, the devil assigned to the patient's mother
SLUMTRIMPET, the devil assigned to the patient's fiancé
TOADPIPE, secretary to Screwtape

The Story:

Screwtape, a senior devil in Hell's hierarchy, writes letters to his nephew Wormwood, who is attempting to corrupt his first mortal soul. The soul is that of a young Englishman whom the devils refer to as the "patient." Wormwood experiences a setback very early in his assignment, when the patient becomes a Christian. Undaunted, Screwtape advises several strategies to block the patient's movement forward. If the young man cannot be kept from going to church, he writes, Wormwood should lead him to regard other church members with disdain because of their various shortcomings. If he cannot be kept from praying, Wormwood should have him focus on himself and his feelings during prayer rather than on the "Enemy Above" (God).

Wormwood expresses joy at the outbreak of World War II, but Screwtape quickly corrects that attitude. Despite the wonderful suffering war can bring, he explains, war can also be quite dangerous since it leads people to reflect seriously on life and to prepare for death. Wormwood should keep the patient away from normal pleasures since they often lead back to the Enemy who invented them; pleasures are only allowed when they are distorted or taken in ways, times, or degrees that are forbidden by the Enemy. As the patient is slowly led away from the path of virtue, Screwtape warns Wormwood not to tempt him to any spectacular wickedness because sins that seem insignificant ensure a safer gradual path to eternal separation from the Enemy, whereas larger sins are likely to inspire repentance.

Unfortunately for Wormwood, when the patient is out for a solitary walk one day, he is surrounded by the presence of the Enemy (which Wormwood experiences as an asphyxiating cloud into which he cannot see) and is reconverted. Screwtape, ever adaptive to changing circumstances, advises that since the patient is now firmly resolved to live as a Christian, Wormwood should try to corrupt any of his developing virtues. The patient has now become humble, so Wormwood should corrupt his humility by making him proud of his humility or by making him dishonestly minimize the value of his gifts and talents. Since the patient is committed to attending church, he should be led to a church that waters down biblical teaching and encourages a lack of faith. Wormwood should also keep the patient's inclinations for doing good and his desire to grow in virtue firmly fixed in the realm of his imagination because these attitudes are quite harmless if they never reach his will and are never concretely put into action. Wormwood should also direct the patient's goodwill toward an abstract concept of humanity in general but direct the patient's lack of charity to his mother and the specific people he actually encounters in his life.

Things begin to seem worse for Wormwood because the patient falls in love with a young Christian woman. Screwtape encourages his nephew by reminding him that falling in love, like war and every other human event, is merely raw material that can be used by either side. Because the patient is now in the perilous company of mature Christians, Wormwood must lead him to be proud that he is part of such a fine group of spiritual people. He should also muddle the patient about the distinction between romantic love (which does not last) and fidelity and charity (which do last) in order to lay an unrealistic foundation for the patient's upcoming marriage and guarantee future marital problems.

While working as an air-raid warden, the patient is killed during a bombing attack; despite Screwtape and Wormwood's best efforts, he is now eternally beyond their grasp. At his death, his spiritual eyes are opened, and both he and Wormwood are able to see the angels who have assisted him throughout his life, as well as "Him" (Christ). Screwtape, furious with his nephew's defeat, expresses some pleasure at the thought that he may now devour Wormwood as punishment for his failure.

Critical Evaluation:

Written from a senior devil's point of view, *The Screwtape Letters* consists of thirty-one letters that focus on different issues in the art of temptation. The letters, which were first published serially in a weekly magazine in 1941, are linked by the ongoing narrative of the young man's ups and downs during his spiritual journey. In 1961, a new chapter to the book, "Screwtape Proposes a Toast," was appended. In it, Screwtape addresses a graduating class at the Tempters' Training College. Screwtape expresses delight in the increase of tyrannical regimes and the suppression of free peoples as a major way of destroying human beings' dignity and individuality. He also expounds on the distortions of the concept of equality in modern democracy: The idea that people should all be the same, without distinctive differences, has led to a wonderfully destructive mediocrity that penalizes excellence, especially in the area of education.

C. S. Lewis, a literature professor at Oxford and Cambridge, was a prolific writer whose various works fall into quite different categories, including literary criticism, philosophy, essays, poetry, theology, letters, and various genres of the novel. *The Screwtape Letters*, the third of his fourteen novels, established Lewis's reputation on both sides of the Atlantic and was soon considered a classic. The novel's popularity led to Lewis's appearance on the cover of *Time* on September 8, 1947, with the grinning figure of a devil (with horns and a pitchfork) depicted behind Lewis's left shoulder. The inscription on *Time*'s cover read, "Oxford's C. S. Lewis, His Heresy: Christianity."

A professed atheist for almost twenty years, Lewis converted to belief in God in 1929 and gradually came to accept all the traditional doctrines of Christian faith, including the existence of heaven, hell, angels, devils, and sin. He believed devils were supernatural beings, former angels who became enemies of God and therefore enemies of human beings and of all of God's creation. In this novel, however, Lewis's focus is not on a theological presentation of hell and devils but on the psychology of human beings and their moral choices.

With Screwtape as the first-person narrator, this epistolary novel derives much of its irony and satire from the inversion of traditionally accepted values. Evil becomes good and good becomes evil. The development of virtues is considered fatal, while the development of vices and sinful habits is highly desirable; love is despicable, and hate is heart-warming. The reversal occurs not just on the moral level but on the linguistic level as well. The spiritual "Enemy" or "Oppressor" is no longer the devil but God. Satan is called "Our Father Below," and the spiritual reward in this "Lowerarchy" is not the "Beatific Vision" but the "Miserific Vision."

Lewis does not offer a description of the geography of his fictional realm or of the devils who inhabit it but attempts instead to satirize Hell's spiritual atmosphere. He depicts it as a massive bureaucracy that includes an Intelligence Department for research, a Tempters' Training College, and a House of Correction for Incompetent Tempters. Similar to a totalitarian state, Hell has a bureaucratic headquarters that keeps dossiers on human beings and has its own Infernal Police to monitor the speech and activities of devils as they engage in their various tasks. This bureaucracy is characterized by envy, competition, resentment, ambition, self-glorification, and self-advancement. Although the devils are united in their quest to capture human souls, there are no friendships and thus no real unity among them. Lewis's petty, back-stabbing Hell is based on a choice of self over others—which is the basis of some moral choices people make—so his Hell sheds light primarily on the human condition.

Although Lewis's Hell is presented as a bureaucracy, it is also a place of punishment in which sinners undergo the same fate regardless of their sin: consumption by devils. This spiritual cannibalism graphically demonstrates Lewis's concept of the effect of sin. In yielding to temptation and sin, people yield their wills to the will of Hell, and, in yielding their wills, they yield their freedom. Lewis's symbolic rendering of the absorption of a weaker self by a stronger self is meant to reflect the loss of individuality and identity that occurs through wrong moral choices.

Another source of satiric humor is Lewis's penetrating critique of human pettiness and selfishness. The temptations advocated by Screwtape at times are linked to the traditional categories of the seven capital sins (pride, anger, envy, avarice, sloth, gluttony, and lust), but they also run the gamut of daily, trivial ways that people focus on themselves or elevate themselves to the detriment of others. At times, Lewis offers humorous but familiar instances of selfishness, such as the example of the woman who inconveniences her hostess by declining a prepared meal and asking instead to have only tea and toast, with very exact specifications about their preparation.

In addition to human foibles, Lewis also critiques social and cultural trends that detrimentally influence people's moral choices. A tendency to dismiss the past as full of ignorance means that the wisdom of the ancients is lost. Disdain for objectivity and Reason (almost always capitalized by Lewis) means that human beings, when faced with a new proposition or idea, tend to ask if it is progressive or old-fashioned, rather than asking if it is true or false. Lewis also cautions in several places against a glib acceptance of language used by politicians and media because often their goal is not to inform the public but to shape public opinion and perception.

Lewis is well known for clearly and simply explaining orthodox Christian doctrine, but in his fiction he does so in ways that are fresh and creative, as he translates traditional theological language into vernacular language. In *The Screwtape Letters*, his presentation of Christian morality and theology is lively and amusing, partly because of his unique, unorthodox narrative point of view but also because he understands the human condition so well. One does not need to accept Lewis's theological premises in order to appreciate his analysis of human behavior and cultural issues because his examples of self-centeredness and uncritical thinking are accessible to many readers.

Marsha Daigle-Williamson

Further Reading

Baggett, David, et al., eds. *C. S. Lewis as Philosopher.* Downer's Grove, Ill.: InterVarsity, 2008. Fifteen essays by philosophy professors on a variety of issues in Lewis's writings, with three on Hell and evil.

Christopher, Joe R. *C. S. Lewis.* New York: Twayne, 1987. Good introductory overview of Lewis as critic, philosopher, apologist, essayist, and novelist; discussion of each novel with reference to Lewis's affinity with other major authors, such as Dante and Edmund Spenser.

Clark, David. *C. S. Lewis: A Guide to His Theology.* Malden, Mass.: Blackwell, 2007. Succinct, clear description of Lewis's philosophical and religious thought in his fiction and nonfiction; discusses angels and devils in chapter 4. Good index, but very inadequate bibliography.

Green, Roger Lancelyn, and Walter Hooper. *C. S. Lewis: A Biography.* New York: Harcourt Brace Jovanovich, 1974. Excellent general introduction to Lewis's life and major works; discusses *The Screwtape Letters* in chapter 8.

Hooper, Walter. *C. S. Lewis: A Companion and Guide.* New York: HarperCollins, 1996. Indispensable book by Lewis's personal secretary that catalogs the background and provides a detailed summary for each work of fiction and nonfiction. Five helpful, comprehensive indexes at the end list Lewis's key ideas, people in the author's life, places of significance to him, and his publications, as well as providing a very detailed subject index.

Lindskoog, Kathryn. *C. S. Lewis: Mere Christian.* Rev. 4th ed. Chicago: Cornerstone, 1997. Emphasizes Christian themes in Lewis's fiction. Chapter 2 includes a section on Hell. Brief appendixes with time lines or the author's life and publications; good index.

Mills, David, ed. *The Pilgrim's Guide.* Grand Rapids, Mich.: Eerdmans, 1998. Seventeen essays by leading Lewis scholars on a variety of topics. A detailed time line that includes other authors and world events. Excellent annotated bibliography by Diana Pavlac Glyer.

Sea Garden

Author: H. D. (1886-1961)
First published: 1916
Type of work: Poetry

The poet Hilda Doolittle, born into a Moravian family in Bethlehem, Pennsylvania, was living in England when her first book, *Sea Garden*, was published. Restless by nature, she had left Bryn Mawr College after one year as a student and proceeded to educate herself in classical literature. Her former fiancé, the poet Ezra Pound, had helped initiate her attraction to the Greeks, and she soon followed him to London, where he was making a name for himself in bohemian and literary circles. It was Pound who, reading Doolittle's first poems in a London café, signed them at the bottom, "H. D. Imagiste," thus founding the Imagist movement in poetry and launching his friend's career under the more aurally pleasing pseudonym of her initials.

The principles of Imagism, as set forth by Pound, emphasize great concentration of language and subject matter. Like a Japanese haiku, the Imagist poem eschews verbiage and gives the reader a concrete and discrete image—or series of images—on which to focus. H. D.'s particular brand of Imagism blends her fascination with the world of classical antiquity and mythology with a drive toward both passion and austerity. The speaker is always a presence in her poems, and the speaker's relationship to the thing described is what the poem primarily conveys.

Sea Garden collects H. D.'s early Imagist poems. A slim volume, it is highly cohesive in its theme—enough so as to be an Imagist long poem. The predominant motif is the meeting and mating of contrary elements on an unearthly middle ground "where sea-grass tangles with/ shore-grass" ("Hermes of the Ways"). The emblems of this encounter are the flowers whose names and descriptions fill the book: "Sea Rose" (the first poem), "Sea Lily," "Sea Poppies," "Sea Violet," and "Sea Iris." Along with the flowers are invocations to mostly unnamed gods, goddesses, and godlike mortals, and poems describing the destructive and regenerative powers that natural forces (wind and water, primarily) have over natural objects such as trees, cliffs, and especially flowers.

The two powers, destructive and regenerative, are synonymous in H. D.'s philosophy and throughout *Sea Garden*. An example of the book's pairing of these two opposite ends of one thing is in a poem near the center of the volume, "Sheltered Garden." In this poem, the speaker "gasp[s] for breath," trapped in a mazelike garden of "scented pinks" that she likens to "pears wadded in cloth" or "melons smothered in straw." "It is better to taste of frost," she continues,

> the exquisite frost—
> than of wadding and dead grass.
> For this beauty,
> beauty without strength,
> chokes out life.

"O to blot out this garden," the poem ends, "to forget, to find a new beauty/ in some terrible/ wind-tortured place."

Critics and biographers of H. D. have focused extensively on her bisexuality and on the powerful influence of Sigmund Freud, a patriarch of psychoanalysis, who treated her in 1933 and again, briefly, in 1934. *Sea Garden* predates her analysis, and the reader can find in these poems the intense quest for an authoritative voice and the effort to recover the fragments of a more unified self that would bring H. D. to Freud nearly two decades later. As did Freud, H. D. had archaeological interests. Much of her poetic career was occupied with the attempt to invoke and inhabit the lost voices of an ancient past. Freud theorized that a matriarchal civilization once existed, predating the patriarchal world of history. The traces of this matriarchal world are all but lost. H. D. gestures toward such a civilization in poems such as "The Shrine," addressed to an unnamed, neglected goddess, a goddess of the sea whom "landsmen" call "useless" and blame for shipwrecks. "The Shrine," whose narrator could be female or male, reads at points like a protest against men's denigration and trivialization of female strength.

The motif of resuscitation informs virtually all the poems, which repeatedly address themselves to some neglected, nearly extinct iconic figure. The first such figure is the sea rose, "marred and with stint of petals," but far more "precious" than the ordinary garden rose or spice rose. "Can the spice-rose," asks the ending, "drip such acrid fragrance/ hardened in a leaf?" Questions like these hint that the speaker—and, by extension, the writer—is a revolutionary, a woman who rejects traditional roles, refusing to write "pretty" verses. The speaker will prefer, even revere, the bitter and attenuated over the lush and sweet and the blasted cliff over the fragrant forest. If she must be "wind-tortured" in the process of choosing such a preference, she will welcome that torment. In the end, the beaten thing (such as the goddess of "The Shrine") triumphs: "Yet though the whole wind/ slash at your bark,/ you are lifted up" ("Sea Lily").

The sea garden is a mythological realm, beyond this world yet filled with this world's passions. It is like the realm of the Greek gods. Its inhabitants are often androgynous or of undesignated gender. In one of the late poems, "Prisoner," one prisoner addresses another with whom he or she has fallen in love. Both seem to be prisoners of war. In the world of the sea garden, a world of water rather than land, radical combinations are possible, and the bounds of gender itself are in question. In an early poem, "The Contest," the speaker addresses a warrior or wrestler with a "male torso" in the first two sections. In part 3, the wrestler seems to answer back, describing the speaker's posture and "slight breast." Neither speaker is named, and gender remains uncertain despite the not entirely conclusive markers. The poem is on a high level of abstraction; the contest, apparently between two people, reads as a counterpoint of images.

It is such a purification, a stripping away, toward which these poems constantly strive. The sea flowers themselves, subjected to the battering of the waves, barely survive. What remains of them is curiously splendid. Austerity, in H. D.'s Imagism, often shades into luxuriance. Many of these spare poems are thick with flower names, descriptions of jewels, and descriptions of the face and body of the beloved. H. D. uses a lush and often esoteric vocabulary reminiscent of such late-nineteenth century aesthetes as Walter Pater and Oscar Wilde. She also shares their love of things Hellenic, their aura of sexuality, and their fascination with religious arcana. Her Poundian influence and her own literary inclination, however, always lead her back to simplicity, to the thing itself. The figure of the erotic martyr, which appears in H. D.'s poems and in the work of many authors of the late nineteenth century, represents the desire for purification, divestment, or stripping away rather than histrionic display.

"Spare us from loveliness," the speaker keeps crying in the poem "Orchard." Ambivalence about beauty drives the early work of H. D. to a continual refinement of imagery. That refinement is represented by nature at its barest, and the action of the wind on land. In a poem such as "The Cliff-Temple," the action of the wind is like the action of the poet on her own language, continually breaking things down, working to reveal essences. High places and unattainable gods are contrasted with forest underbrush and fallen fruit as the poet reminds herself to flee from luxury toward the difficult. The higher she climbs, the more removed is her goal. "O poplar," she cries in "Mid-day," an early poem,

> you are great
> among the hill-stones,
> while I perish on the path
> among the crevices of the rocks.

This despairing ending is revised in later poems. "The Cliff-Temple" ends with the speaker's almost matter-of-fact recognition that the journey will never end, nor the object be attained:

> Over me the wind swirls.
> I have stood on your portal
> and I know—
> you are further than this,
> still further on another cliff.

In *Sea Garden*, H. D. seems to be writing about her own career; the poems are all, in one way or another, about their own composing. Any extraneous matter has been eliminated, and even those poems that, according to biographer-critics, arose from the events of H. D.'s life seem to bear no relationship to anything in the external world. Her experience has been impersonalized, made into metaphors of poetic inspiration and poetic quest.

In the final poem of the volume, "Cities," the poet broadens her scope. The book's messianism, which is, in all but this poem, purely individual—the dream of a muse who comes to stay—culminates in the vision of a New Jerusalem for an entire community. An unnamed "we" (the reader presumes a society of artists) conspire to eradicate banality and resurrect the beauty of a forgotten era. The poem describes an ugly urban maze erected by the "maker of cities" above the old, gorgeous city of "arch upon perfect arch,/ of pillars and corridors that led out/ to strange court-yards and porches." The speaker wonders about the maker's motives, concluding that both he and the old city's inhabitants were put off by its splendor:

> For alas,
> he had crowded the city so full
> that men could not grasp beauty,
> beauty was over them,
> through them, about them,
> no crevice unpacked with the honey.

The new city, posits the speaker, was intended to foster human striving after beauty by removing it from reach but keeping it in sight. This same intention informs many of the poems in the volume. The poet repeatedly seeks to escape beauty and strive for the transcendent. In the context of "Cities," however, the idea has elitist and misanthropic implications: The speaker describes the new inhabitants as larvae, "disfigured, defaced," sleeping in their cells, crawling out "to attack our frail strength." "We," on the other hand, the few remaining former citizens, are bees who still hoard traces of honey, whose task it is to "recall the old splendour,/ await the new beauty of cities." Twice the speaker addresses the ugly new citizens with the very phrase the "landsmen" used against the goddess in "The Shrine": "You are useless."

Although a feminist interpretation is possible (the old city, with its feminine architectural shapes, is a matriarchal civilization, while the new one is a repressive patriarchal one), the inhabitants of the two cities are distinguished not by gender but by beauty and its appreciation. "We protect our strong race," says the speaker. The reader, who may detect in the poem the same elitist nostalgia that often informs the work of other famous modern poets such as T. S. Eliot and W. B. Yeats, may interpret the poem in terms of elitism rather than feminism. A certain tone running through the volume, one of self-dramatization and self-aggrandizement, culminates in this vision of a heavenly home for lovers of beauty.

The exacting reader may find the sea garden an airless and insular place, but there is no question of the beauty of these poems' highly concentrated imagery, of their rhythms and assonances, of their short, incantatory lines, or of H. D.'s singular achievement in defining the poetic movement known as Imagism. *Sea Garden* is a strong first volume by a poet who would move on to greater accomplishments; the work defines at the outset a career that would be marked by restlessness and a perpetual, mystical questing.

Natania Rosenfeld

Further Reading

Camboni, Marina, ed. *H. D.'s Poetry: "The Meanings That Words Hide"—Essays.* Brooklyn, N.Y.: AMS Press, 2003. Collection of essays covers topics such as figures of identity in H. D.'s early poetry, sapphic fragments in her work, and her poetic legacy.

Connor, Rachel. *H. D. and the Image.* New York: Manchester University Press, 2004. Examines how H. D.'s work was influenced by her experiences as a film editor, her writing about the cinema, and her appearances in avant-garde films.

DuPlessis, Rachel Blau. *H. D.: The Career of That Struggle.* Bloomington: Indiana University Press, 1986. Provides a succinct summary of H. D.'s life and work from a feminist viewpoint.

Friedman, Susan Stanford. *Psyche Reborn: The Emergence of H. D.* Bloomington: Indiana University Press, 1981. Extensive study examines H. D.'s development and influences, with an emphasis on feminist and psychoanalytic approaches.

Friedman, Susan Stanford, and Rachel Blau DuPlessis, eds. *Signets: Reading H. D.* Madison: University of Wisconsin Press, 1990. Collection gathers reminiscences of H. D., tributes to her work, and essays on her poetry by friends of H. D., scholars, and poets.

Guest, Barbara. *Herself Defined: The Poet H. D. and Her World.* New York: Quill, 1984. Eminently readable, fascinating biography—with fictional embellishments—is the work of an avant-garde poet who has read and researched H. D. with care and understanding.

H. D. *Collected Poems, 1912-1944.* Edited by Louis L. Martz. New York: New Directions, 1983. Vital for the serious reader of H. D., this book begins with all of *Sea Garden.* Includes an informative introduction that provides a good overview of the poet's work.

Hickman, Miranda B. *The Geometry of Modernism: The Vorticist Idiom in Lewis, Pound, H. D., and Yeats.* Austin: University of Texas Press, 2005. Examines the geometric imagery and ideas of vorticism, an early movement within the larger world of modernism whose chief proponent was British writer Wyndham Lewis. Discusses how the movement's ideas are reflected in the work of Lewis and his successors, including H. D.

Laity, Cassandra. "H. D.'s Early Decadent Masks and Images: *HER*; *Sea Garden.*" In *H. D. and the Victorian Fin de Siècle: Gender, Modernism, Decadence.* New York: Cambridge University Press, 1996. Examines how H. D. was influenced by decadent Romantic writers, such as Oscar Wilde and Algernon Charles Swinburne, whom other modernist writers deplored.

Taylor, Georgina. *H. D. and the Public Sphere of Modernist Women Writers, 1913-1946: Talking Women.* New York: Oxford University Press, 2001. Chronicles the activities of a small group of women writers, including H. D., who sought to defy social and literary convention, producing increasingly experimental work.

The Sea of Grass

Author: Conrad Richter (1890-1968)
First published: 1936
Type of work: Novel
Type of plot: Regional
Time of plot: 1885-1910
Locale: Southwestern United States

Principal characters:
COLONEL JIM BREWTON, a pioneer rancher
LUTIE, his wife
HAL, his nephew
BRICE CHAMBERLAIN, a lawyer
BROCK, Lutie's son by Brice Chamberlain

The Story:

Hal Brewton never forgets the day he stood on the railroad platform at Salt Fork, where he waited to meet Lutie Cameron, who was arriving from St. Louis to marry his uncle, Colonel Jim Brewton, the owner of the vast Cross B Ranch. Colonel Brewton is involved in a range war with nesters coming to rip the sod from the grazing lands in order to raise wheat.

On the day of Lutie's arrival, two of the colonel's cowhands are being tried for shooting at a homesteader on the Brewton range. Although the colonel's lawyer, Henry McCurtin, wins the case, the opposition lawyer, young Brice Chamberlain, protests indignantly that the victory will not be permanent. Colonel Brewton is contemptuous of the lawyer's warnings.

Lutie is a lovely woman, too lovely for that still-wild territory. When men see her, she wins them completely. Only Hal refuses to be moved by her charm. All that winter in an academy at Lexington, Missouri, he thinks of her as part of the destruction coming from the East to destroy the sea of grass he loves.

The following summer, he returns to a changed ranch house. Lutie filled it with furniture and flowers and planted a row of cottonwoods and tamarisks about it. Guests from the whole territory come and go. Officers from the Army posts, officials of the railroad companies, and neighboring ranchmen all find ample welcome at the home of Colonel and Mrs. Brewton.

The old-timers who knew the colonel before he married Lutie hope that she will settle down after having children. The babies are born, two boys and a girl; however, Lutie does not become any calmer. The third baby is scarcely in its cradle before she is dancing with Chamberlain as her favored partner. Colonel Brewton ignores the gossip that is whispered about Lutie.

Local politics concerning homesteading rights shift with the administration in Washington, D.C., for the territory depends upon appointments to its judicial staffs. For a while, Chamberlain has influential support from the government. Then, during another administration, the forces that back

Colonel Brewton are in power, and the incoming tide of settlers seems to be checked. Hal reads of the change with great pleasure, but when he returns to Salt Fork, he discovers that Chamberlain is still in his law office on the Salt Fork plaza. He learns that hundreds of settlers are waiting nearby for a change in government that will permit them to stake claims upon the miles of land held by men such as Colonel Brewton.

Lutie then calmly announces that she is leaving her husband and children. She explains that she has had enough of the flat grass country and the fighting between ranchers and homesteaders. She claims she will be able to get possession of her three children—Jimmy, Brock, and Sarah Beth—later, by court action.

The town is informed that Mrs. Brewton is leaving for a visit in St. Louis. Most of the people know better. Their feelings are confirmed when they see Chamberlain with a bag packed, ready to head East on the same train; but the colonel paces the station platform, a gun belt buckled under his broadcloth coat. Chamberlain does not board the train.

A few days later, the colonel sends Hal to Denver, to give Lutie a thousand dollars—he knows that his wife's cowardly lover has no intention of following her—but Hal can find no trace of Lutie in Denver. At the same time, a new administration appoints Chamberlain a judge of the district court. Back in Salt Fork, Hal sees the white-covered wagons of the emigrant trains moving westward into the range country. When Colonel Brewton plans to run the homesteaders off his land, a troop of cavalry from Fort Ewing is sent to guard him until all chances of his stopping the land grabbers are gone.

Studying for his medical degree, Hal spends three more years away from Salt Fork. When he returns, he discovers that his sea of grass is hopelessly despoiled. His uncle seems much older. The Brewton children are growing up wild, for their mother never sends for them.

One day, Hal sees Jimmy and Brock fighting in the dusty Salt Fork street. Then a nester among the onlookers calls out that he is betting on the Chamberlain brat. Hal hears for the first time the rumor that Brock is not his uncle's son. Hal fires at the nester but misses. When Colonel Brewton appears, the crowd, even the jeering nesters, grows quiet.

As young Brock grows older, he becomes the image of Chamberlain. It is obvious that he realizes the truth and resents it. He takes to gambling, drinking, and barroom brawling. At last, he is caught cheating in a card game. For that disgrace Colonel Brewton cannot forgive him, but he continues to indulge the boy and pay his debts. By that time, Hal is practicing medicine in Salt Fork. He is glad when Sarah Beth, who was away at school, returns and begins to look after her father.

One day, Brock shoots and kills Dutch Charley, who accused Brock of using a woman to help him cheat at cards. Brock is locked up, but Chamberlain soon gets him out of jail. When Brock returns home, he defies Colonel Brewton and says he is leaving the Brewton ranch to go to work for Chamberlain's interests. This last blow to the colonel's pride permanently wrecks his health.

Brock now takes the name of Chamberlain, an act that cuts the old colonel still more. Brock begins to ride wild, shooting up towns and staging reckless holdups. He becomes the talk of the Southwest for his daring lawlessness. At last, he is trapped by a posse of homesteaders and held at bay in a cabin by twenty or thirty vigilantes.

That same day, Lutie unexpectedly returns. She is fifteen years older, but she still carries herself with quiet self-possession. Lutie immediately assumes her place in her household as though she had been away for fifteen days, not for fifteen years.

Meanwhile, the colonel rides out to the cabin where Brock is holding off the sheriff and the armed and angry nesters. With Hal, who was summoned to attend a wounded deputy, he breaks through to Brock, who lies dying from a bullet wound in his lung. They bring his body back across desolate country scorching in raw sunlight, with nesters' families huddled about sagging shacks and plows rusting in fields where wheat will not grow in hot, rainless summers. Sand is beginning to drift among dugouts and rotting fence posts.

Brock is buried on the Brewton ranch. The stone inscribed with the name Brock Brewton is the old colonel's challenge to all gossip and speculation around Salt Fork. He and Lutie take up their life where she broke it off years previously, and no one ever dares ask either the colonel or his wife where she was. It seems to Hal that the colonel finds peace at last.

Critical Evaluation:

The use of Hal Brewton as the narrator in *The Sea of Grass* is extremely clever. He reminisces from the vantage point of being Salt Fork's physician. He sees many changes in the nearly fifty years he lives there. He is the nephew of Colonel Jim Brewton, whose stoicism he admires, and hence he is sympathetic both to him and more gradually to Lutie, whose beauty captivates him. He is Brock's cousin—nominally, at least—and therefore he narrates events in that conflicted youth's short life with muted emotion. Best of all, since Conrad Richter chose to present a quarter century's salient events in the lives of his triangle of central characters—Lutie, Brewton, and Brock—it is useful to have Hal periodically leave Salt Fork for schooling in the more settled East, so that, upon each return, he can observe dramatic changes and record them more emphatically. His objectivity, however, is tinged with melancholy; therefore his prose has lyric overtones, and his narration is often a kind of elegy. At the end of chapter 14, Hal imagines that Lutie is recalling Brock in her mind's eye as a yellow-haired baby again, "in the candlelight of a world that had vanished like last year's snow." Richter, who was a well-read author, assuredly wants his readers to hear echoes in these lines of the fifteenth century French poet François Villon's most famous line: "Mais où sont les neiges d'antan?" (But where are the snows of yesteryear?). Several critics have noted that Richter may also have been inspired to employ the kind of narrator he did by reading Willa Cather's novel *A Lost Lady* (1923), the narrator and heroine of which are very much like those in *The Sea of Grass*.

This short novel is compactly structured, with three numbered parts of almost exactly equal lengths. Each part, however, has a different number of chapters, perhaps to indicate the fact that separate dramatic segments presented in them carry different weights of import. Part 1, "Lutie," has five chapters; part 2, "The Colonel," seven chapters; and part 3, "Brock," three. Chapter 6, the shortest in the book, is also the most static. In it, Lutie leaves the town by train, and everyone else, including her husband, waits to see whether Brice Chamberlain will board it with her. However, nothing happens. The bleat of lambs in the shipping pen, though, reminds Hal of Lutie's three abandoned children. Chapter 15, the last, is also the longest. It skillfully ties up every plot strand in paragraph after paragraph, often out of chronological order for heightened effect. This chapter presents a memorable contrast between the Old West and the new: Lutie rather frenetically insists that Hal escort her to mass before asking him for details about Brock, who earlier derisively noted that the only thing not riddled with bullets from the posse's guns in his wretched hideout is a portrait of Christ.

Each of the three parts dramatizes a different kind of failure. Lutie, in part 1, fails her husband, for whatever reasons, and leaves him for her paramour, although she fails to find happiness with this man or even to set up a brief residence with him. The colonel, in part 2, prepares his loyal ranch hands to fight the "army" of nesters but fails to do so. Brock, in part 3, pursues a life with drinkers, town women, gamblers, and gunslingers, all of whom fail him, and he ends up being killed. The only other significantly active character, Chamberlain, relates to Lutie, the colonel, and Brock, but remains busy only in the shadows. He succeeds materially and professionally by failing Lutie, by legalizing the cause of the ruinously encroaching nesters, and by failing his son Brock. This novel, however, is less about failure than it is about Colonel Brewton's achieving tragically heroic stature through steady and responsible action. When Lutie leaves him, he tries to send her money for at least temporary help, and at the end he quietly welcomes her back into his life. (What marital success they may achieve is left to the reader to decide.) When the president sends the army to guard the nesters' encampment, Brewton, a former soldier, puts loyalty to the expanding nation foremost. When Brock is dying, Brewton races straight to him, offers what comfort he can, and buries him—on his land and as his son. Richter presents Brewton's reverence for the land sympathetically, but he shows it to be impractical in the face of inexorable Western settlement. Hence, there are two morals: One is romantic; the other is realistic. The romantic moral is that population explosions hurt nature. The realistic moral is that old ways must yield to the new.

Richter augments the unity of *The Sea of Grass* by repeating key words in describing characters, setting, and action. Lutie is lithe, slender, sparkling, with her head erect, and redolent of violet perfume. Almost monotonously, she is called gay—before that word lost its nonsexual meaning. Brewton is massive, dark, arrogant, implacable. His ropy, wine-dark hand and neck veins expand when he is outraged. Feisty Brock has feather blond hair and quick hands, whether he is playing the piano, dealing cards, or shooting. Richter stresses Chamberlain's blue eyes, blond hair, long legs, and brown-checked Eastern suit.

Musical motifs of imagery also ripple through the text. Most of the numerous similes and metaphors appropriately derive from natural elements. Thus, Brewton is likened to a stallion, a steer, granite; his eyes are fiery, stormy. The nesters, who are regularly demeaned by being depicted in dirty clothes, resemble a plague almost biblical in its advance and devastation. The most frequently repeated metaphor is naturally the one comparing the almost limitless prairie to a rippling sea, a sea of grass. Ultimately, this proves to be a sad metaphor, because in time the grass—which Brewton and

Hal love but which Lutie hates and hides from—will be, unlike the sea, gone.

"Critical Evaluation" by Robert L. Gale

Further Reading

Barnes, Robert J. *Conrad Richter*. Austin, Tex.: Steck-Vaughn, 1968. Considers Richter's fiction that has the Southwest as a setting. Especially valuable for its discussion of Richter's style and his use of deliberately repeated details in *The Sea of Grass*.

Estleman, Loren D. *The Wister Trace: Classic Novels of the American Frontier*. Ottawa, Ill.: Jameson Books, 1987. Analyzes *The Sea of Grass* as a prose poem about change and loss.

Gaston, Edwin W., Jr. *Conrad Richter*. Updated ed. Boston: Twayne, 1989. One of the best and most extensive treatments of Richter's plain life and creative versatility. The section on *The Sea of Grass* concerns its origins, plot, point of view, contrasting characters, themes of parenting and alienation, historical change, and unity of people and nature, and its relation to other fiction by Richter.

Johnson, David R. *Conrad Richter: A Writer's Life*. University Park: Pennsylvania State University Press, 2001. Johnson, aided by access to Richter's private papers, describes Richter's creative process; he places Richter's work within the context of America's "golden age" of mass-market magazine and novel publishing from the 1920's to the 1960's. Includes illustrations, bibliography, and index.

LaHood, Marvin J. *Conrad Richter's America*. The Hague, the Netherlands: Mouton, 1975. Highly academic treatise. Section on *The Sea of Grass* emphasizes the central characters and their different reactions to the land.

Pilkington, William T. "Conrad Richter." In *Fifty Western Writers: A Bio-Bibliographical Sourcebook*, edited by Fred Erisman and Richard W. Etulain. Westport, Conn.: Greenwood Press, 1982. Presents a brief biography of Richter, discusses his major themes, and surveys the extensive criticism of his work. Analyzes *The Sea of Grass* as a historical and a mythical drama of old and new ways, with Lutie as a reconciling influence.

Richter, Harvena. *Writing to Survive: The Private Notebooks of Conrad Richter*. Albuquerque: University of New Mexico Press, 1988. A fascinating interweaving of passages from Richter's many notebooks and his devoted daughter's intelligent commentary on these passages. Includes a complete bibliography of Richter's novels, short stories, short-story collections, nonfictional works, articles, and book reviews.

The Sea-Wolf

Author: Jack London (1876-1916)
First published: 1904
Type of work: Novel
Type of plot: Adventure
Time of plot: 1904
Locale: Pacific Ocean and the Bering Sea

Principal characters:
HUMPHREY "HUMP" VAN WEYDEN, an unwilling sailor aboard the *Ghost*
WOLF LARSEN, the captain of the *Ghost*
MUGRIDGE, the ship's cook
MAUD BREWSTER, a survivor picked up at sea

The Story:

When the ship in which he is a passenger sinks in a collision off the coast of California, Humphrey Van Weyden is picked up by the crew of Wolf Larsen's ship, the *Ghost*, a sailing vessel headed for seal hunting ranges in the Bering Sea. Larsen is a brute. Van Weyden witnesses the inhuman treatment of a sick mate, who dies shortly afterward. He sees a cabin boy badly beaten. In his own interview with the captain, he fares little better. Instead of promising to help him return to San Francisco, Wolf demands that Van Weyden sign as cabin boy and stay with his ship.

The crew sets to work taking in the topsails and jibs. From that moment Hump, as the crew called Van Weyden, learns things the hard way. He has to get his sea legs, and he has to learn the stoic indifference to pain and suffering that the sailors have mastered already. As cabin boy, he peels potatoes and washes greasy pots and pans. Mugridge, the cook, abuses him and robs him of his money. Only one man, Louis, seems to share Hump's feelings about the captain and his ship. Louis predicts that many deaths will result from the voyage. He said that Wolf is a violent, dangerous man and that the crew and seal hunters are vicious outcasts. Wolf does seem mad. He varies from moods of wild exultation to spells of extreme depression. In his cabin are classic books of literature, and when he speaks, he uses either excellent English or the lingo of the sailors. Sometimes he amuses himself by arguing with Hump. He claims that life is without meaning.

During a southeaster, Hump badly dislocates his knee, and Wolf unexpectedly allows Hump to rest for three days while he talks to him about philosophy and literature. When Hump returns to the galley, the cook is whetting his knife. Hump obtains a knife and begins whetting it also. Hump's actions so frighten the cowardly cook that Hump is no longer the victim of the cook's abuse.

Louis talks of the coming season with the seals. Moreover, he hints that trouble will come if the *Macedonia*, a sealing steamer, comes near. Captained by Death Larsen, the brother and enemy of Wolf, the *Macedonia* is a certain menace. As a prelude to things to come, an outbreak of fury takes place aboard the *Ghost*. First, Wolf and the mate beat a seaman named Johnson to a pulp because he complains of ill treatment; then Leach, the former cabin boy, beats the cook. Later, two hunters exchange shots, severely wounding each other, and Wolf beats them because they crippled themselves before the hunting season begins. Afterward, Wolf suffers from one of his periodic headaches. To Hump, life on shipboard is a tremendous experience in human cruelty and viciousness.

A few days later, the men try to mutiny. In the row that follows, Johansen, the mate, drowns, and Wolf is nearly killed. While Hump dresses Wolf's wounds, Wolf promotes him to mate in Johansen's place. Leach and Johnson would kill Wolf in a second, but he remains too wary for them. At the seal hunting grounds, a terrific storm costs them the lives of four men. The ship itself is beaten, its sails torn to shreds and portions of the deck swept into the sea.

When Leach and Johnson desert in a small skiff, Wolf starts out in pursuit. On the morning of the third day, an open boat is sighted. The boat contains a young woman and four men, survivors from a sinking steamer. Wolf takes them aboard, planning to make sailors of the men as he did of Hump. Shortly afterward, the *Ghost* overtakes Johnson and Leach. Refusing to pick them up, Wolf lets them struggle to get aboard until their small craft capsizes. He watches them drown without comment and then orders the ship's course set for a return to the seal hunting grounds.

The woman survivor is Maud Brewster, a rich woman and a poet. She is weak physically, as Hump was. Wolf resents the intimacy that springs up at once between Maud and Hump. He takes out his resentment by deciding to give the cook the first bath the cook has ever taken. At Wolf's orders, Mugridge is thrown into the water with a tow rope slung about his middle. At first, the cook flees madly about the ship, causing one man to break a leg and another to be injured in a fall. Then Mugridge is thrown into the sea. Before Wolf is ready to bring Mugridge back aboard ship, a shark bites off the cook's right foot at the ankle. Dragged aboard, Mugridge in his fury tries to bite Wolf's leg, and Wolf almost strangles him. Then Hump bandages the wounded man's leg. Maud looks on and nearly faints.

The *Macedonia* appears one day and robs Wolf's hunters of their day's catch of seals by cutting off the line of approach to the *Ghost*. In revenge, Wolf sets his men to work capturing hunters from the *Macedonia*. When the *Macedonia* gives chase, Wolf sails his ship into a fog bank. That night, Wolf tries to seize Maud, but Hump, awakening, runs his knife into Wolf's shoulder. At the same time, Wolf is overcome by one of his headaches, this seizure accompanied by blindness. Hump helps the captain to his bunk, and under the cover of darkness, he and Maud make their escape in an open boat. After days of tossing about on the open sea, they come to a small island. Using supplies they took from the *Ghost*, they set about making themselves houses and gathering food for the coming winter. One morning, Hump sees the wreck of the *Ghost* lying offshore. Going aboard, he discovers Wolf alone, his crew having deserted him to go aboard Death Larsen's ship. Wolf seems nearly insane and has only a desire to sleep. Hump steals some pistols and food, which he takes to the island. Hump, planning to repair the masts of the *Ghost*, begins work on the crippled ship. That night, Wolf undoes all Hump's work and casts the masts off the vessel.

Hump and Maud begin anew to refit the ship. One day, Wolf attempts to murder Hump, but during the struggle, he has a spasm and faints. While he is still unconscious, they handcuff him and shut him in the hold.

Then they move aboard the *Ghost*, and the work of refitting the vessel goes forward. Wolf has a stroke that paralyzes the right side of his body. Hump continues to repair the vessel. At last, it is able to sail. Wolf next loses the use of his muscles and lies in a coma. When he dies, Hump and Maud bury him at sea. By that time they are deeply in love. When a United States revenue cutter discovers them one day, they feel that their dangerous odyssey is at an end. They are, however, about to begin another journey together.

Critical Evaluation:

Jack London's talent for creating adventure stories made him one of the most popular writers of his time. His familiarity with adventure came from his own experience. He began making his own living at the age of fourteen. By the time he was able to live as a writer (with the publication of his collection of stories, *The Son of the Wolf*, 1900), London had worked a variety of menial jobs. He had been a seaman, a waterfront fighter, a coal shoveler, an oyster pirate, a wage slave in a laundry, and a gold prospector in the Klondike, to name a few. He also spent thirty days in prison for vagrancy. London

lived the seafaring life, and *The Sea-Wolf* portrays a vivid picture of the life on a sealing ship—from the technical details of steering a vessel in a blinding storm to violent encounters between seamen.

The Sea-Wolf is more than a simple adventure tale. It reflects philosophical ideas prevalent in London's time. In order to educate himself and improve his prospects, London read voraciously in all subjects. From Charles Darwin's *On the Origin of Species by Means of Natural Selection* (1859), London learned that in nature, living is a constant struggle, and organisms that have the ability to adapt to their environment survive. The works of nineteenth century philosopher Herbert Spencer taught him that human life is a matter of the survival of the fittest. The individual most likely to survive and dominate others would be much like the "superman," the man of superior intellectual and physical abilities who follows an amoral code as described by nineteenth century German philosopher Friedrich Nietzsche, another favorite of London. *The Sea-Wolf* portrays a struggle between civilization and raw nature. In the untamed, natural arena of the sea these two competing philosophies, embodied in Humphrey Van Weydon and Wolf Larsen, come into conflict.

The violently competitive environment on the *Ghost*, in which men struggle to establish their place in a pecking order based on physical strength, intimidation, courage, and aggression, seems to validate the worldview described by Spencer and Nietzsche. Larsen is close to the Nietzschean superman. Larsen is extraordinarily strong, with a body that strikes Humphrey with awe: "God made you well," he tells Larsen. Larsen may not be as learned as the formally educated Humphrey, but he impresses Humphrey by his breadth of knowledge, his thirst for reading in all subjects, and his keen understanding of human nature. He is an ardent individualist who follows the amoral code that suits him and the life he has led. To him human life has no individual value; for every one who dies many more are born. It is the nature of life to replenish itself. It is also the nature of life to kill so it can survive, to subdue the weak so it can remain strong. Larsen's uncompromisingly naturalistic code is realized in his cruel treatment of his men—dragging Mugridge the cook overboard, brutally beating two seal hunters, and allowing Johnson and Leach to drown.

London, however, cannot adhere completely to the philosophy of might makes right. In his wolf stories (*The Call of the Wild*, 1903, and *White Fang*, 1906), the law of nature, of survival of the fittest, dominates. In the social world in which humans interact, however, London was convinced that brutality could not be the only norm. During his time on the

Ghost, Humphrey fights to live by his civilized moral beliefs—the dignity of the individual, the need for compassion, and the value of human life. In frequent philosophical arguments with Larsen, Humphrey attempts to defend this moral code against Larsen's naturalistic beliefs. The brutal environment of the *Ghost* wears him down almost to the point of rejecting his moral code. Humphrey's love for Maud Brewster, however, encourages him to continue his moral struggle.

With Maud's appearance it seems that London sought to pander to the contemporary taste for sentimentalism, injecting feminine romance into his masculine adventure tale. Maud is a conventional female literary figure. Physically weak but morally courageous, she represents the humanistic values of a more civilized world. Under Maud's domestic influence, Humphrey's commitment to live morally is renewed. Humphrey becomes Maud's protector. They flee the *Ghost*, braving the open sea, in order to save Maud from Larsen's physical advances.

Although Humphrey is triumphant in the end, *The Sea-Wolf* does not completely reject Larsen's code. Larsen is London's most intriguing character, appealing and repugnant. He is an interesting combination of physical and mental power. His presence causes the book's most exciting dramatic scenes. Just as Larsen predicted, Humphrey's tenure on the *Ghost* makes him a better man. He becomes morally, mentally, and physically stronger, learning to be courageous and ingenuous in his effort to stay alive. At first sheltered and weakened by his upper-class privilege, Humphrey's nature is toughened through contact with Larsen's potent individualism.

Humphrey's humanism, however, has no influence on Larsen's brutal naturalistic philosophy. The once physically powerful man is made blind, deaf, and dumb by a brain tumor. His muscles slowly degenerate, leaving him paralyzed. In life he intentionally cut himself off from humanity through his excessive individualism and lack of compassion. Fittingly, he spends his last few hours in complete isolation, unable to see, hear, speak, or move.

The Sea-Wolf seems to demonstrate Darwinian principles. The balance that Humphrey strikes between body and spirit and between rugged individualism and humanistic compassion allows him to adapt to his changing environment more successfully than Larsen. The fittest survives.

"Critical Evaluation" by Heidi Kelchner

Further Reading

Auerbach, Jonathan. *Male Call: Becoming Jack London.* Durham, N.C.: Duke University Press, 1996. Auerbach reverses the trend of earlier London studies, emphasizing how London used his writing to reinvent himself. Above all, Auerbach argues, London wanted to become a successful author, and in that respect he shaped his life to suit his art. Chapter 6 focuses on *The Sea-Wolf.*

Cassuto, Leonard, and Jeanne Campbell Reesman, eds. *Rereading Jack London.* Stanford, Calif.: Stanford University Press, 1996. Essays on London as "representative man," his commitment to authorship, his portrayal of American imperialism, his handling of power, gender, and ideological discourse, his relationship to social Darwinism, and his status as writer/hero.

Doctorow, E. L. *Jack London, Hemingway, and the Constitution: Selected Essays.* New York: Random House, 1993. Doctorow, a major American novelist, provides a long and thoughtful reflection on London's politics and fiction; Doctorow is sympathetic but also critical of London's example.

Labor, Earle. *Jack London.* Boston: Twayne, 1974. Praises London's convincing portrayal of Wolf Larsen and of Humphrey's transformation from a weak, rich socialite to a dynamic he-man.

London, Jack. *Novels and Stories.* Notes and chronology by Donald Pizer. New York: Literary Classics of the United States, 1982. Uses text from the first editions. Includes notes on the texts, historical and geographical notes, maps, and notes on the stories.

Lundquist, James. *Jack London: Adventures, Ideas, and Fiction.* New York: Frederick Ungar, 1987. Suggests that the quality of London's stories arises from the risks he took and from his colorful personal experience. Traces London's intellectual leanings.

Sinclair, Andrew. *Jack: A Biography of Jack London.* New York: Harper & Row, 1977. Discusses the biographical detail in *The Sea-Wolf.* Describes London's marriages and affairs.

Stefoff, Rebecca. *Jack London: An American Original.* New York: Oxford University Press, 2002. Well-researched biography in which Stefoff describes London's life, beliefs, adventures, and writings, placing them within the social context of his times. Includes illustrations, bibliography, and index.

The Seagull

Author: Anton Chekhov (1860-1904)
First produced: Chayka, 1896; first published, 1904 (English translation, 1909)
Type of work: Drama
Type of plot: Impressionistic realism
Time of plot: Nineteenth century
Locale: Russia

Principal characters:
IRINA ARKADINA, an actor
KONSTANTIN TREPLEV, her son
PYOTR SORIN, her brother
ILYA SHAMRAEV, manager of his estate
POLINA, his wife
MASHA, their daughter
NINA ZARETCHYN, a young actor
BORIS TRIGORIN, an author
YEVGENY DORN, a doctor
SEMYON MEDVEDENKO, a schoolmaster

The Story:

One day Konstantin Treplev kills a seagull and places it at the feet of Nina, the beautiful young actor with whom he is hopelessly in love. He tells her that unless she can love him, he, too, will be lying dead at her feet. Nina, however, is not in love with Konstantin; she is infatuated with Trigorin, the famous novelist, who in turn is in love with Irina Arkadina, an actor and Konstantin's mother.

Konstantin hates Trigorin, looking upon him as a purveyor of empty phrases, a writer entirely different from what he himself hopes to become. Konstantin's ambition is to create new and more expressive literary forms, and he wrote a play in which Nina consents to appear. The performance, staged in the open air on the estate of Pyotr Sorin, Konstantin's uncle, is not exactly a success, although it possesses unquestioned literary merit. Madame Arkadina and Trigorin, who are present, refuse to take the production seriously. Trigorin is most impressed by the performance of nineteen-year-old Nina in the principal role.

Madame Arkadina's behavior at her son's play is typical of her attitude toward Konstantin in every aspect of their relationship. As a famous actor, whose popularity depends upon her keeping her youth and her good looks, she naturally is not overjoyed at the constant reminder that she is the mother of a twenty-five-year-old son. Consequently, she keeps Konstantin in the country, where he will not be seen and thus be associated with her in the public mind. Moreover, she gives him little or no money to spend, so that he is forced to wear the same suit for years until it is threadbare. Her brother, Pyotr Sorin, takes his sister to task on several occasions for her stinginess, but she pleads poverty, meaning, of course, that she prefers to spend her money on herself.

In spite of the way she treats him, Konstantin is greatly attached to his mother, so much so that he develops a morbid, unhealthy attitude toward his work and life in general. Occasionally he will lose his temper and quarrel violently with his mother. When he does so, she bursts into tears, and Konstantin is overcome promptly by feelings of remorse.

Konstantin is not the only unbalanced individual on the Sorin estate. Another is Masha, the daughter of Pyotr Sorin's manager, who is as hopelessly in love with Konstantin as he is with Nina. Although she is only a young girl, she dresses habitually in black—in mourning, she says, for her chronic unhappiness. Semyon Medvedenko, the schoolmaster, is in love with her, but he has only twenty-three rubles a month on which to support his mother, two sisters, and a brother. After two years, giving up all hope that Konstantin will ever notice her, Masha decides to marry Semyon. She has a child, but she is so indifferent to it that the schoolmaster takes care of the baby in addition to his other responsibilities.

Konstantin, like most young writers, knows many people who are willing to offer him advice on how he should write and what he should write about. Among these advisers is Yevgeny Dorn, the local doctor, who never wrote a line in his life, but who has theories about how it should be done. His idea is that Konstantin spends entirely too much time worrying about literary form, whereas literature is not a matter of form, good or bad, but of spontaneous ideas. Another dispenser of advice is the old man, Pyotr Sorin. He suggests that his nephew write a story called *The Man Who Wished*, based on Sorin's own life. He maintains that when he was young he wished to become an author but failed. Then he wanted to become an orator, but he spoke abominably. Finally he wanted to marry, but he never did. When Sorin is reminded that he also wished to become State Councilor and succeeded, he roars with laughter, claiming that he achieved the post with no effort of his own. The most complete analysis of the writer's art is made by the novelist, Trigorin. One day, while he is taking notes on the personal habits of the neurotic Masha, he is interrupted by Nina, who expresses the view that a writer's life must be a very fascinating one. He tells her that writing is merely a violent obsession that lays hold of a man and places him on a treadmill from which there is no escape. Against his will, almost, the writer of fiction is compelled to utilize everything in his experience for his next story. Even the seemingly trivial incident of the seagull that Konstantin shot, Trigorin views as material for a story. He begins to see Nina herself as the seagull and himself as the hunter. He realizes that Madame Arkadina will be furiously jealous of his interest in the younger woman. Fate plays into his hands when Nina promises to run away from home and join him in Moscow.

For nearly a year Nina is Trigorin's mistress in Moscow. After she has a child, who soon dies, Trigorin deserts her. Even her acting career is unsuccessful, consisting largely of a tour of country towns. All that time Konstantin follows Nina about, but the only encouragement he gets is an occasional letter that shows Nina's spirit near the breaking point.

At last, worn out and hungry, she comes to the Sorin estate, which awakens in her memories of her happy girlhood. Konstantin urges her to stay with him or to allow him to go away with her, but she refuses. She accepts an engagement for the winter with a second-rate repertory company at Eltz, and there she intends to go as the next step in her career as an actor. Out of her suffering she realizes that in any art it is not the honor and glory that matters—it is perseverance. Konstantin does not have that kind of strength, and when Nina, the seagull, flies out of his life forever, he locks himself in his room and puts a bullet through his head.

Critical Evaluation:

The Seagull was based on an event in Anton Chekhov's life. One afternoon, while he was taking a walk with his friend, Ilya Levitan, the landscape painter, he saw Levitan shoot a seagull that was flying over the river. Later, the moody painter, feeling scorned by the woman he loved, threw the dead seagull at her feet and threatened to kill himself. The play Chekhov made from this incident is perhaps the most elaborate and realistic analysis of the life of the artist ever presented in dramatic form; but all that almost any other dramatist would have selected as the material for his play takes place in Moscow between the third and fourth acts. What the audience sees is the effect of what took place, and in this lies the essence of what Chekhov has contributed to the art of the theater.

The first production of *The Seagull* on October 17, 1896, was a total disaster. The critics dismissed it as inept and even

absurd, and Chekhov, who fled the theater before the final curtain, accepted their verdict. One audience member, critic-playwright Vladimir Nemirovich-Danchenko, did not agree and determined to mount a second production of the play. Danchenko, at that time organizing the Moscow Art Theatre with Constantine Stanislavski, convinced his partner that the new Chekhov play had great potential and then he talked the playwright into allowing *The Seagull* a second chance. Their production of the play in 1898 was an enormous artistic, critical, and commercial success and led to that collaboration of playwright and theater that established the Moscow Art Theatre as one of the world's greatest, and stimulated the writing of Chekhov's last three dramatic masterpieces, *Dyadya Vanya* (1897; *Uncle Vanya*, 1914), *Tri sestry* (1901; *The Three Sisters*, 1920), and *Vishnyovy sad* (1904; *The Cherry Orchard*, 1908).

For all of the controversy provoked by the play, it is the most conventional of Chekhov's major plays. *The Seagull* is structured around romantic triangles (Arkadina-Trigorin-Nina, Konstantin-Nina-Trigorin, and, to a lesser extent, Masha-Konstantin-Medvedenko), activated by spite and jealousy, composed of incidents characteristic of popular melodrama (a failed suicide, a seduction and abandonment, a dead child, a successful suicide), and climaxed by an "obligatory scene" in which the main characters meet and resolve their conflicts in a face-to-face confrontation.

Chekhov's handling of this orthodox plot, however, is revolutionary and previews the formula he perfected in his last three masterworks. Konstantin's two suicide attempts and the melodramatic consequences of Nina's affair with Trigorin happen offstage. Chekhov deformalizes the play by undercutting the most intense moments with trivial details and apparently arbitrary bits of stage business—small talk, irrelevant comments and interjections, unexpected comical gestures, characters standing with their backs to the audience, and a game of "Lotto" while Konstantin prepares his suicide.

These deviations from traditional techniques are not merely novel stage gimmicks, however, but reflect Chekhov's basic dramatic and thematic purposes. He was not interested in theatrical action or excitement as such, but in the effects such incidents have on his people. Reality, he felt, does not consist of a series of dramatic climaxes but is, rather, a mundane process of day-to-day living in which the crucial events happen unobtrusively in the background. The important thing, therefore, is to explore and dramatize their continuing effects on the characters. Thus, even in the last plays, Chekhov does not abandon conventional dramatic structure but mutes it in order to concentrate on what he believed to be more important: real people living real lives.

The Seagull does, however, differ thematically from his later plays; it is the work in which Chekhov makes his definitive statement about the nature of creativity and the role of the artist in society. As both a practicing physician and a creative artist, Chekhov experienced great difficulty in reconciling the objective, practical world of medicine with the subjective, aesthetic environment of literature and theater. He already had analyzed the problem extensively in his fiction—notably in "A Boring Story" (1889), "The Grasshopper" (1892), and "The House with an Attic" (1896)—but *The Seagull* was his final, comprehensive exploration of the subject. Thus, it has a thematic clarity and rhetorical directness that differentiates it from its successors.

This is not to say that *The Seagull* is more simple or more obvious than the other works. The four major characters are exceedingly complicated; their relations to one another are subtle, ambiguous, and contradictory, and, although they are given ample opportunity to dramatize these complexities, it is for the audience to attempt the synthesis. Moreover, as completely individualized as the characters are, they embody basic attitudes toward life and art that are crucial to a final understanding and appreciation of the play.

Konstantin Treplev has three roles that he cannot reconcile—son, lover, and creative artist. His feelings about his mother are deep and ambivalent. He passionately craves her affection, yet he finds himself in an unequal competition with her; he desperately wants her to approve his creative efforts, yet he consciously advocates artistic notions that are antithetical to hers; he is fully aware of her egotism, pettiness, selfishness, and cruelty, yet he clings to a vision of her as a tender, considerate young mother.

Konstantin's relationship to Nina is equally unrealistic. At best theirs is an adolescent boy-girl flirtation; there is no indication that she was ever serious about him. In the early scenes of the play, as Konstantin tries to court her, she puts him off. Konstantin cannot see this; he insists on projecting his romantic fancies onto her and feels betrayed when she fails to respond. His sentimental longing for her is not unlike Masha's crush on him, and he has no more chance with Nina than Masha has with him.

As an artist Konstantin has two functions in the play: He is both a creative writer striving to find his own personal voice and a representative of the Symbolist movement. Thus, Chekhov can use him to comment on literary fashion while also developing his unique story. Although Arkadina speaks as much out of vindictiveness as conviction, her comments about Konstantin's play—"decadent raving," "pretensions to new forms"—echo opinions Chekhov expressed in his own correspondence. However, Konstantin is completely sincere in his advocacy of the new forms and thus represents a perennial artistic type, one who seeks to revolutionize the arts by finding new forms, not realizing, as Konstantin finally does, that form without content is pointless.

One of the many ironies in the play is the fact that the rival writers, Konstantin and Boris Trigorin, have the same problem: They have no real direction and nothing to say. If Konstantin is the abstract writer who, in an effort to capture essences in his writing, loses all humanity, Trigorin is the slick writer whose vision cannot go beyond the everyday lives of his trivial characters. He is in a permanent rut, and he knows it. Commercial success and the adulation of Arkadina and Nina are meaningless to him because he is honest enough to know that his work is frivolous when compared to that of truly serious writers.

Writing has, for Trigorin, almost become an unsatisfying but necessary compulsion. He carries his notebook with him and is constantly jotting notes until the audience gets the feeling that he only observes and never lives. When the dead seagull is presented to him, he makes notes for a story. Trigorin then acts out his story with Nina; life copies art and both are bereft of real intensity. Perhaps his affair with Nina is not merely a casual seduction but a vain attempt at direct experience. Trigorin would be a villain were he not so weak; he arouses contempt and pity, not anger. Like Konstantin, he needs others to support his deflated ego, but, unlike his rival, he lacks the strength even to kill himself.

Arkadina is a more complex figure than she seems at first glance. She, too, is an artist, but, as a performer, she has no interest in the opinion of posterity, nor, for that matter, does she have much interest in any aspect of the future. She sees herself as a beautiful young actor and clings tenaciously to that image in the face of reality. Her casual dismissal of time reveals an obsession with it. Arkadina is deeply insecure and very much afraid of age, sickness, poverty, and death. This fear shows in her suppression of all references to such things: her hostility toward her sick older brother, Sorin; her jealousy and fear of the truly young, especially Nina; her apparent flightiness; her domineering treatment of all underlings, including Trigorin; her stinginess; and, most of all, her attitude toward Konstantin. He is right in his belief that the major reason for her hostility toward him is that he reminds her that she is a middle-aged woman.

It is, however, through Nina, the seagull of Trigorin's unwritten short story, that Chekhov makes his definitive statement about creativity, and it is in her climactic interview with Konstantin that the major issues of the play are resolved. Although their external situations differ, they have both reached the crucial points in their artistic careers: They know what they can and must do if they are to realize their potentials.

Even though some of his stories have been published, Konstantin receives neither the critical acclaim nor the personal satisfaction he desires, and he understands why: His search for new forms led him into an artistic cul-de-sac. "Good literature," he muses, "is not a question of forms new or old, but of ideas that must pour freely from the author's heart." Konstantin's basic problem is that he has nothing to say "from the heart," and he knows it.

Konstantin is not stimulated by success, and Nina is hurt, but not defeated, by failure. She is almost ready to realize herself, but one final obstacle remains: She must get rid of her obsessive identification with the seagull of Trigorin's story. Therefore, Nina returns to Sorin's estate not to see Konstantin, as he desperately hopes, but to complete the purgation of this obsession by returning to its place of origin. To remain identified with the dead bird is to accept defeat; to free herself from it is to free herself from Trigorin's personal influence and his destructive attitudes. As she talks to Konstantin, she visibly shakes off the last vestiges of these pernicious influences. She goes from the stagestruck girl of the first act, who views acting as a way to "fame, resounding fame," to the mature woman who understands that the essential thing is the creative act itself: "One must know how to bear one's cross, and one must have faith," she proclaims: "When I think of my calling I do not fear life."

Konstantin has no such calling, and he is plunged into the final despair by her visit. Frustrated by his attempts to reach his mother, convinced that he will never write anything of value, all hopes for his relationship with Nina dashed, Konstantin kills himself. Nina, on the other hand, begins her life as a complete woman and a committed actor—to become, perhaps, a great one.

"Critical Evaluation" by Keith Neilson

Further Reading

Bristow, Eugene K., ed. *Anton Chekhov's Plays.* New York: W. W. Norton, 1977. An anthology of Chekhov's major plays, accompanied by thirteen critical articles. Of special interest is Thomas G. Winner's "Chekhov's *Sea Gull* and Shakespeare's *Hamlet:* A Study of a Dramatic Device."

Bunin, Ivan. *About Chekhov: The Unfinished Symphony.* Edited and translated by Thomas Gaiton Marullo. Evanston, Ill.: Northwestern University Press, 2007. Bunin, a writer and Nobel laureate, began a biography of Chekhov but did not complete it before he died in 1953. Although incomplete, the book provides intimate details of Chekhov at work, in love, and in relationships with other Russian writers.

Chekhov, Anton. *The Seagull.* Translated by Michael Frayn, with commentary and notes by Nick Worrall. London: Methuen, 2002. In addition to the text of the play, this edition offers a plot summary, commentary, critical perspective, and discussions of the play in its context, the seagull and the enchanted lake, the play-within-the-play, and other elements of the work.

Gottlieb, Vera, and Paul Allain, eds. *The Cambridge Companion to Chekhov.* New York: Cambridge University Press, 2000. Collection of essays about Chekhov, including a biography, an essay placing his life and work within the context of Russia, and a discussion of the playwright at the Moscow Art Theater. Also includes an essay on *The Seagull* by Thomas Kilroy.

Hingley, Ronald. *Chekhov: A Biographical and Critical Study.* New York: Barnes & Noble, 1950. A thoughtful study of all aspects of Chekhov's art, emphasizing his life. Chapters on Chekhov's connections with the Moscow Art Theater and his approach to drama are of special significance for understanding of *The Seagull.*

Jackson, Robert Louis, ed. *Chekhov: A Collection of Critical Essays.* Englewood Cliffs, N.J.: Prentice-Hall, 1967. Of the sixteen essays, nine are devoted to the theater of Chekhov, including the editor's "*The Seagull*: The Empty Well, the Dry Lake, and the Cold Cave."

Kataev, Vladimir. *If Only We Could Know: An Interpretation of Chekhov.* Edited and translated by Harvey Pitcher. Chicago: Ivan R. Dee, 2002. Kataev, a Russian scholar, offers interpretations of Chekhov's works, emphasizing the uniqueness and specificity of each incident and character. Includes the essay "Right in One's Own Way: *The Seagull.*"

Magarshak, David. *Chekhov the Dramatist.* New York: Hill & Wang, 1960. A thorough discussion of all of Chekhov's plays on such topics as direct action, transition, and indirect action. References to *The Seagull* place the play in a proper perspective within the playwright's general dramatic output.

Rayfield, Donald. *Anton Chekhov: A Life.* New York: Henry Holt, 1998. Comprehensive biography, offering a wealth of detail about Chekhov's life and work.

Valency, Maurice. *The Breaking String: The Plays of Anton Chekhov.* London: Oxford University Press, 1966. One of the best treatments of Chekhov's plays. Analyzes the general aspects of Chekhov's approach to theater and provides detailed discussion of all plays, including *The Seagull.*

A Season in Hell

Author: Arthur Rimbaud (1854-1891)
First published: Une Saison en enfer, 1873 (English
    translation, 1932)
Type of work: Poetry
Type of plot: Allegory

In the spring of 1873, Arthur Rimbaud wrote to a friend that he was preparing a "pagan book" with "half a dozen horror stories." He called the stories "stupid and innocent," but he added that his fate depended on them. A few months later, he took the finished manuscript to a printer in Brussels, who was to publish the work at the expense of Rimbaud's family. Rimbaud was not yet nineteen years old.

Rimbaud gave advance copies of *A Season in Hell* to his former mentor and lover, Paul Verlaine, and to a few other friends. Snubbed socially and artistically following a scandal that landed Verlaine in prison, Rimbaud burned the remaining copies of the book in a fireplace at his mother's house. He also burned a sheaf of his unpublished poems. He said he no longer thought about poetry. The boy who had been the talk of Paris at the age of sixteen—"an infant Shakespeare" in the words of novelist Victor Hugo—gave up poetry for a life of wandering and, eventually, running guns to rebel tribes in Africa.

Not until 1901, a full decade after Rimbaud's death, were the unsold copies of *A Season in Hell* discovered in a Brussels warehouse and sold to an admiring public. The apparently autobiographical nature of his "horror stories," which are really prose poems, only added to their appeal. His was the ultimate voice of tragic youth, of a poet risking all to attain the sublime vision that older poets only talked about.

In the opening paragraphs of the work, the speaker refers to the happier times of his childhood, to his first encounters with beauty and inspiration, and to the unspecified disaster that gave rise to his "book of the damned." (This speaker is a poet but not necessarily Rimbaud.) The first section, "Bad Blood," goes back to his peasant stock and his French heritage. It also refers to conflicts and retributions that evoke the Paris Commune of 1871 and the revolutionary spirit lingering when Rimbaud first arrived in the city later that year. Then comes the speaker's "Night in Hell," after he has died of world weariness. Following are two dreams, or "Deleria," in which the speaker reveals the secrets of his poetry.

The speaker returns to ordinary reality in the second half of the poem. In "The Impossible," he recognizes that others consider his dreams impossible. In "Lighting," he acknowl-edges that although he has lost all hope of entering a poetic heaven, he can begin to glimpse the light of everyday life. In "Morning," he listens to the music made by nations and rivers as they move onward. Finally, in "Farewell," the speaker sees the coming of autumn and, with the death of the year, the death of his youthful identity. He buries his imagination. He laughs off his past, as he thinks women laugh off unhappy loves. He prepares for a new relationship with reality when he will confront truth itself, body and soul.

The two episodes of delirium—in the word's etymological sense of deviation or deranging—come at the center of the poem and help to identify the speaker's deepest hopes and fears. The first episode is a dialogue between a Foolish Virgin and a Hellish Husband. In some sense they are no doubt Verlaine and Rimbaud, respectively, but they are allegorical figures as well. Jesus told the parable of the wise and foolish virgins, the women who were or were not prepared for the bridegroom who came in the night. In the biblical story, from Matthew, the bridegroom is the messiah, but in Rimbaud's version he is a parody savior. The section's original title, "False Conversion," already suggests the religious dimension of the story, as do earlier references to Jesus and Satan in the section describing the speaker's arrival in Hell.

The second delirium, "Alchemy of the Word," presents the speaker's dream of what poetry could be. He has made experiments with sounds, very much as an alchemist might experiment with elements. He has assigned a color to each vowel in an effort to create a whole new language for poetry. Now he dreams of a shape for each consonant and offers carefully crafted verses about a new age and a new relation between nature and humans. At the center is a new Tower of Babel and the song of a new age sung from its heights. The verses here are pure lyric, not the alexandrines of "The Drunken Boat" and many of Rimbaud's other major poems. However, all this is folly, he says, like the vanity of Ecclesiastes in the Hebrew Scriptures.

Assured that he has attained the glory of true song, if only for a moment, the speaker recognizes that the dream is done. He has greeted beauty where he found it and is ready to move on, back to the world of everyday life.

The completed poem, displaying the attractive notion of a despairing teenager tossing off brilliant experiments in the heat of passion, shows the marks of careful editing, making the work more unified and objective. Three fragments of Rimbaud's manuscript revisions were discovered in the twentieth century. As collected and translated by Wyatt Mason in the Modern Library edition (2002) of Rimbaud's poetry, they show that the author removed personal references to his sojourn in London with Verlaine and to the hallucinations he experienced there while smoking opium. He replaced them with the more general language of Heaven and Hell and allusions to such biblical figures as the Foolish Virgin and the melancholy preacher of Ecclesiastes. Denunciations of poets, both in specific and in general, are left out.

Most scholars now assume that Rimbaud had a mass of writing on hand when he conceived his pagan book and that he salted *A Season in Hell* with phrases composed during his days with Verlaine. Contemporaries remember having seen two lyrics included in the "Alchemy" section, and Rimbaud actually had written a sonnet, "Vowels." It began "Black A, White E, Red I, Green U, Blue O: vowels./ Someday I'll explain your burgeoning births."

Critics disagree about the overall unity and merit of *A Season in Hell*. However, almost all consider it a single poem and not a group of fragments. Critical opinion has long been divided. Those who read it as an allegory of Rimbaud's life—as does, for example, novelist Henry Miller in *The Time of the Assassins*—have found it the most compelling of his poems. Those who prefer the poet's more restrained experiments regard it as juvenile or self-indulgent. Paul Valèry, arguably the last of the French Symbolist poets with whom Rimbaud is most often grouped, complained that it offers nothing but exclamations and intensity. Most criticism has steered a middle course. The trend is to treat *A Season in Hell* as a commentary on the writing of poetry, indeed on the very possibility of writing poetry, and not just on one poet's personal life.

Critics tend to praise Rimbaud's virtuosity as he tries different verse forms and moves on to prose poems, continually seeking a closer match of form and content. Some find that he is deliberately uncouth when he wants to shock middle-class readers—*épater le bourgeoisie* in the French phrase. They suggest that the apparent unevenness of his poetry is there for a reason, that it shows the necessary indeterminacy of all human communications as well as the painful failures one person experienced in both life and art. Especially in France, some regard Rimbaud's verbal alchemy as an attempt to extend art into esoteric realms, but it seems more likely to have been made as a parody of the esoteric language that was fashionable at the time.

Rimbaud did not suddenly abandon verse for poetry in prose. On his first trip to Paris, he had discovered the "little poems in prose" of Charles Baudelaire, which had been posthumously published in 1869. Rimbaud's own experiments in the genre include "Deserts of Love" (1871). Forty of his later prose pieces, *Illuminations* (1880, 1886), had been collected after Rimbaud left Europe. Highly experimental, some are closer to the parables of novelists Franz Kafka and Jorge Luis Borges than to anything previously written.

For all its apparent spontaneity and unevenness, *A Season in Hell* remains an outstanding example of Symbolist poetry. More than half of the "celebrated citations" quoted in a recent French edition of Rimbaud's poetry are taken from this remarkable work of an eighteen-year-old genius.

Thomas Willard

Further Reading

Bloom, Harold, ed. *Arthur Rimbaud*. New York: Chelsea House, 1988. An extended selection of Rimbaud criticism that considers his work from his early free verse poems to *A Season in Hell*. Includes many slants on the possible meanings, aesthetics, poetics, and interpretations of Rimbaud's work.

Mason, Wyatt, ed. and trans. *Rimbaud Complete*. New York: Modern Library, 2002. A bilingual edition, separating prose from poetry and placing *A Season in Hell* in a series of increasingly ambitious experiments with prose poetry. Includes prefatory comments on Rimbaud's poetic project and the transformative role of *A Season in Hell*.

Nichol, Charles. *Somebody Else: Arthur Rimbaud in Africa*. London: Jonathan Cape, 1997. Though focusing on the last decade of the poet's life, this work includes a section on his early years and his efforts in prose poetry. A personal note at the end discusses Rimbaud's influence on Bob Dylan and others of the author's generation.

Oxenhandler, Neil. *Rimbaud: The Cost of Genius*. Columbus: Ohio State University Press, 2009. A comprehensive study of Rimbaud's poetry. Using psychoanalytic theory, suggests that *A Season in Hell* has an overall form reflecting the psychological processes that gave rise to it.

Perloff, Marjorie. *The Poetics of Indeterminacy: Rimbaud to Cage*. Evanston, Ill.: Northwestern University Press, 2000. This work contains only one chapter on Rimbaud but is highly useful in placing him within his historical context. Discusses his influence on modernist poets such as Gertrude Stein, Ezra Pound, and William Carlos Williams, and as a transitional force between Symbolism and modernism.

Robb, Graham. *Rimbaud: A Biography*. New York: Norton, 2000. Presents a "reconstruction of Rimbaud's life"; discusses the revolutionary impact his poetry has had on later writers and artists. Examines the influence of Rimbaud's early family life, in particular his relationship with his mother, and presents his checkered career after his abandonment of poetry at the age of twenty-one.

Steinmetz, Jean-Luc. *Arthur Rimbaud: Presence of an Enigma*. Translated by Jon Graham. New York: Welcome-

Rain, 2001. A comprehensive biography that focuses on Rimbaud's numerous self-contradictions and extremes of behavior, particularly in his stormy relationship with the older poet Paul Verlaine. The author analyzes Rimbaud's poetry primarily in its relation to the poet's life.

White, Edmund. *Rimbaud: The Double Life of a Rebel*. New York: Atlas, 2008. A concise, objective, and critical biography by a prominent literary critic. Includes White's own translations of the poems that he analyzes.

A Season in Rihata

Author: Maryse Condé (1937-   )
First published: Une Saison à Rihata, 1981 (English translation, 1988)
Type of work: Novel
Type of plot: Psychological realism
Time of plot: Late twentieth century
Locale: Rihata and Farokodoba, Africa

Principal characters:
ZEK, a forty-three-year-old manager of a bank agency
MARIE-HÉLÈNE, his wife
MADOU, Zek's younger half brother and minister for rural development
VICTOR, a man who kills Madou
MUTI, Victor's aunt
PRESIDENT TOUMANY, a dictator
SORY, a singer
DAWAD, the regional secretary
CHRISTOPHE, Zek and Marie-Hélène's nephew
SIA, Zek and Marie-Hélène's oldest daughter

The Story:

For two days, the residents of Rihata await the arrival of Madou. When he arrives in Rihata to commemorate the anniversary of President Toumany's overthrow of the previous government, Zek and several local officials greet him at the airport and take him to a reception in his honor. Afterward, Madou goes to Zek's home and tells Zek's wife, Marie-Hélène, that he plans to leave Rihata for the village of Farokodoba soon to meet with officials from a neighboring country as a representative of President Toumany.

Madou and Inawale, his chauffeur, arrive in Farokodoba. While Madou negotiates with the men representing Lopez de Arias, the leader of the neighboring country, Inawale wanders around the village, followed by a man named Victor. Victor convinces Inawale to go to a bar with him and puts a drug in Inawale's drink. Victor steals Inawale's money and gun, after trying to find out from him why Madou is in the village. Victor and two of his friends who were at the bar go to see Muti, Victor's aunt, and tell her what Victor did to Inawale. Muti is angry because she suspects that the police

will soon be looking for them. Her concerns prove to be justified. She is arrested after a Toumany supporter tells Madou of Muti's relationship with the individual who drugged and robbed Inawale. When Victor finds out that Muti was arrested and taken to Rihata, he goes there to assist her.

Upon arriving in Rihata, Victor goes to a bar. By coincidence, Zek enters the same bar. When Victor discovers his relationship to Madou, he follows Zek out of the bar. Victor tells Zek that he is heading to N'Daru, the capital, to see his brother, but that he needs a place to stay overnight. Zek allows him to stay in his garage. The following morning, Victor learns from Christophe, Zek's nephew, the location of Madou's residence. After leaving Zek's home, Victor heads to another bar. A procession of vehicles passes by the bar, and Victor finds out that people involved in the assault against Inawale are being taken to N'Daru in the procession. Victor heads back to Zek's house and sees Madou and Marie-Hélène talking with each other. Victor decides to kill Madou in retribution for Muti's arrest.

On Saturday, the market day, Zek, Christophe, and several public officials attend the name-giving ceremony for Sory's newborn son. Sory also invites Victor because it is customary to invite strangers to such events. Sory sings a song about greedy government officials, which offends Dawad, the regional secretary. Angry over Sory's song, Dawad has Sory arrested several days later. Madou attends a play supporting President Toumany that is put on by the ruling party's youth. During the performance, the lights go out and tracts criticizing President Toumany are placed on chairs. When the lights are turned back on and Madou sees a tract on his seat, he tears it up and leaves while the police search for the culprits.

The next day, the police bring three men who allegedly are responsible for the tracts to the police station. That day, Madou goes to Zek's home to see Marie-Hélène but finds out from her daughter Sia that Marie-Hélène is at the hospital giving birth. When Madou goes back to his villa, Victor is waiting for him with a gun. During the confrontation between Madou and Victor, Marie-Hélène's son is born; Zek names him Elikia, which means hope in his native language. When he goes home from the hospital, Zek learns from his neighbor that Madou was shot.

Victor is arrested immediately after shooting Madou. Marie-Hélène is discharged from the hospital, and Zek arrives to pick her up. When she and Zek go home, she begins to think about what happened to Madou. She wants him to live because of their past romantic relationship and his promise to assist Zek in obtaining a position as an embassy attaché.

Victor, Sory, and other individuals accused of antigovernment activities are transported to the police station in N'Daru to await trial. Marie-Hélène visits Madou in the hospital and tells him she has a son. He feels a sadness, for the happiest periods of his life were with her. Later, she returns to the hospital with Sia. Madou feels that Sia loves him and understands the relationship he had with her mother. When Madou's wife enters later that day, he convinces himself before he dies that he was a good husband for providing her with food, shelter, money, and clothes.

When Zek hears on the radio of his brother's death, he has mixed feelings. Zek decides he can forgive and forget about his brother's affair with his wife now that he is dead, yet he also laments that he might never obtain a position as an embassy attaché. Zek goes to his wife's bedroom and tells her the news about Madou. President Toumany decrees a national mourning period and orders the execution of all those involved with Madou's death. He believes that he can use Madou's death to his advantage to destroy enemies of the government and bring forth allies. Ironically, the president decides to appoint Madou as prime minister of the country, although he is dead.

Critical Evaluation:

A native of Guadeloupe who also lived in Africa, Maryse Condé received a doctorate in comparative literature from the Sorbonne in France. Her later novels include *Hérémakhonon* (1976; English translation, 1982), *Ségou: Les Murailles de terre* (1984; *Segu*, 1987), *Ségou II: La Terre en miettes* (1985; *The Children of Segu*, 1989), *Moi, Tituba, sorcière noire de Salem* (1985; *I, Tituba, Black Witch of Salem*, 1992), *La Vie scélérate* (1987; *Tree of Life*, 1992), and *Traversée de la mangrove* (1989; *Crossing the Mangrove*, 1995). Because of her exploration of race and experimentations in narrative technique, she has been compared to the Caribbean writer Aimé Césaire as well as to William Faulkner. Noting the influence of Faulkner and Césaire on her work, she points out in an interview,

> As far as *Crossing the Mangrove* is concerned, I had in mind and in fact on my desk was Faulkner's *As I Lay Dying* [1930]. It is strange that when I think of intertextuality, I have in mind two American writers [William Faulkner and Philip Roth]. I don't have any French writers in my mind. I don't have any Latin American writers in mind either. And I don't have any West Indian writers except Césaire, who is in everybody's mind.

The major theme of *A Season in Rihata* is the power of the past to influence and affect the lives of individuals in the present. Marie-Hélène seeks to resolve her guilt over the affair with Madou and a romantic relationship she had with Olnel, a Haitian man with whom her sister Delphine fell in love while they were students in France. Delphine, Christophe's mother, commits suicide when she realizes that Olnel, the father of her child, will never marry her. Christophe seeks to order his present world by finding out information regarding his biological mother and father so that he can have a sense of self and identity. Zek, too, is haunted by the past, feeling as if some failure within himself led to his wife's affair with his half brother. Madou tries to come to terms with his past and his guilt over the affair with Zek's wife and over the fact that several of her children may be his.

Another central theme is the search for fulfillment, expressed through the metaphor of motherhood. Throughout *A Season in Rihata*, characters seek out a mother figure to provide comfort and nurturing. Christophe is constantly searching for information about Delphine, but no one wants to provide him with it because the past is too painful. Marie-Hélène seeks a mother figure in the form of the African continent. She initially desires to leave her native Guadeloupe; she regards it as a "sterile womb" after her sister's death and, as a consequence, "Africa, Mother Africa, had appealed to her imagination and raised her expectations." Madou also seeks a mother figure. When he has been shot and is lying in the hospital, he regresses to an earlier womblike state: "He was lying in his mother's womb, far from the sound and the fury that the assassination attempt had triggered. He had returned to a time before childhood, before the creation of the world, before desire and sin. It was Eden." In this novel, the quest for the mother is symbolic of the desire for peace, security, love, and innocence, but often that quest is unfulfilled.

A third significant theme is political corruption in the emerging postcolonial world. Condé presents the ironic predicament in which the residents of Rihata find themselves: The black Africans who run the country are just as corrupt as the white Europeans who once ruled them, if not more so. Marie-Hélène expresses this sentiment in recounting her time in Rihata: "To think that twenty years earlier they had set the world to rights, talked about happiness for man and liberation for women. Now [she and Olnel] were both in countries largely destroyed by dictators, and they were compromising. Yes, compromising! What had gone wrong? What part of them had died with their youth?" She, Zek, and Madou all recognize the personal and political corruption that mars the dream of a truly free and independent African state.

Condé successfully treats a number of compelling issues in this novel. She examines both the public and the private lives of individuals living in a period of turmoil and change. Her success in dealing with such sensitive issues can be attributed to her narrative technique, for she tells the story from the viewpoints of the primary characters, enabling the reader to comprehend the complex nature of human desire, motivation, emotion, and thought. Exploring the reactions to postcolonial Africa from the perspectives of characters of different genders, educational backgrounds, and political views, Condé presents a moving, realistic, and unforgettable portrayal of life. Her work spans the past and the present, the Caribbean, Africa, and Europe, and the personal and the public realms of life in a well-crafted and thoroughly believable study of the human condition.

Sharon Lynette Jones

Further Reading

Alexander, Simone A. James. *Mother Imagery in the Novels of Afro-Caribbean Women*. Columbia: University of Missouri Press, 2001. Examines the complex images of motherhood in the work of Condé, Paule Marshall, and Jamaica Kincaid. Alexander maintains that these writers depict an "intricate trichotomous relationship" among the biological or surrogate mother, the mother lands of Africa and the Caribbean, and the mother countries of England, France, and/or North America that reflects their experiences with colonialism or colonial intervention.

Barbour, Sarah, and Gerise Herndon, eds. *Emerging Perspectives on Maryse Condé: A Writer of Her Own*. Trenton, N.J.: Africa World Press, 2006. Collection of essays interpreting Condé's novels. The editors' introduction places Condé's work within the context of political and theoretical discussions about women's writing, writing from the African diaspora, and global literature.

Broichhagen, Vera, Kathryn Lachman, and Nicole Simek, eds. *Feasting on Words: Maryse Condé, Cannibalism, and the Caribbean Text*. Princeton, N.J.: Latin American Studies, Princeton University, 2006. Includes an extended interview with Condé and ten critical essays by participants in a conference held at Princeton University in 2004. Some of the essays focus on her novel *Histoire de la femme cannibale* (2003; *The Story of the Cannibal Woman*, 2007), but others provide more general interpretations of her fiction.

Fulton, Dawn. *Signs of Dissent: Maryse Condé and Postcolonial Criticism*. Charlottesville: University of Virginia Press, 2008. Fulton interprets Condé's work from the perspective of postcolonial theory.

Hewitt, Leah D. "Inventing Antillean Narrative: Maryse Condé and Literary Tradition." *Studies in Twentieth Century Literature* 17, no. 1 (Winter, 1993): 79-96. A thoughtful analysis of the themes in Condé's works, including *A Season in Rihata*. Also examines Condé's narrative technique, pointing out the similarities between William Faulkner's *The Sound and the Fury* (1929) and Condé's *Crossing the Mangrove*.

Suk, Jeannie. *Postcolonial Paradoxes in French Caribbean Writing: Césaire, Glissant, Condé*. New York: Oxford University Press, 2001. A postcolonial analysis of works by French Caribbean writers. *A Season in Rihata* is discussed in chapter 4, "Archetypal Returns: *Heremakhonon* and *Une Saison a Rihata*."

The Seasons

Author: James Thomson (1700-1748)
First published: 1730; revised, 1744, 1746
Type of work: Poetry

A cycle of four long poems in blank verse with a brief concluding hymn, *The Seasons* celebrates the magnificence and harmony of nature as a manifestation of the Supreme Being. It embodies literary, philosophical, and theological ideas characteristic of the eighteenth century, yet it also prefigures the Romantic movement of the nineteenth century, particularly in its depictions of storms and wilderness. It enjoyed extraordinary popularity and influence in both centuries, and its impressive, picturesque landscapes made it a favorite text for illustration.

The poem evolved gradually, beginning with a short piece called "Winter," published in 1726. As he expanded and revised the work, James Thomson adopted the *Georgics* (c. 37-29 B.C.E.; English translation, 1589) of the ancient Roman poet Vergil as his literary model, finding there a precedent for his subject matter (nature), his four-part structure, and his elevated style. Standing in the middle ground between the pastoral and the epic, "georgic" verse was expected to use lofty diction in celebrating the earth's bounty. Whereas pastoral poetry uses nature artificially as stage scenery for the philosophizing of urbane shepherds, georgic poetry draws inspiration from the noble labors of the farmer. Thomson by no means restricts himself to the farm, however; he seeks in untamed nature a special quality that fascinated his age: the "sublime," the paradoxically uplifting experience of awe and even of terror.

Each of the four poems opens with conventional elements: an invocation to the poet's muse and an elegant address to his patron. Thereafter, each loosely adheres to a different structural principle. The first poem, "Spring," celebrates the influence of the season over the whole Chain of Being, starting with the lowest, inanimate matter, and ending with the highest of beings on earth, "Man." Thomson prefers not to depict nature for its own sake but to do so for what it teaches, and many of its glories become occasions for edifying digressions. After describing the breezes warming the soil, the poet argues for the dignity of his theme, for agriculture crowns the British Empire as it once crowned the Roman Empire. Describing a rainbow after a spring shower, he contrasts the scientific theory of Sir Isaac Newton with the dumb amazement of the ignorant swain. The thought of the virtues in herbs provokes a long discussion of humanity's lost innocence. In days of old, reason governed passion and even the lion was gentle, but, since the Flood, afflictions have beset humanity. Yet, humankind still neglects the "wholesome Herb" and consumes the flesh of harmless animals. Some readers have criticized the looseness that results from this circuitous method, and no doubt the long, cumulative process of composition worked against the development of a rigid structure, but this lack of architecture reflects Thomson's sense of nature, for the poem possesses an underlying coherence that may be discerned only intermittently beneath the wonderful variety of the surface.

Birds follow vegetation; the poem relates how, infused with love from the "Source of Beings," they mate and build nests, brood over their eggs, and at last teach their offspring the art of flight. This springtime diffusion of amorous passions dominates the rest of the poem, but it refuses to conduct—out of respect for female readers, says the poet—a detailed discussion of animals and gives rise instead to a lecture on the torments that befall youthful lovers and the happiness of those who join in marriage and bring forth a delightful "human blossom." Moralizing or "didactic" verse of this kind (besides being sanctioned by Thomson's literary model) was considered to be an integral part of the "topographical" poem, in which an impressive landscape becomes the occasion for profound and edifying meditation. Indeed, *The Seasons* inseparably intertwines description and didacticism, arguing throughout that our experience of nature inspires feeling, feeling inspires thought, and thought inspires praise of God.

"Summer," the longest of the four poems, traces a single day from morning to night, but it also uses the eye of imagination to describe the harsh climate of the tropics. The sun rules majestically over the summer day. All beings are its courtiers; his reign extends even to shining metals and gems that lie within the earth; ponds and oceans glitter with the sun's reflected light, yet nothing equals it. Having stirred the reader's wonder at the power of the sun, Thomson uses it for his devotional purpose: How, then, should he sing of God, its source? Yet, if men were silent, all creation would praise him. The theology of *The Seasons* has been a topic of controversy: Some interpret its God as deist, a Supreme Being who has revealed himself only in his creation. Here, however—

and at the end of "Summer"—Thomson insists that the human mind cannot fathom the deity, and his poem echoes passages from scripture that imply a traditional Christian position, despite the absence of references to Jesus Christ. His concern with the limitations of the human perspective reemerges in a subsequent passage when he emphasizes that, although science reveals that nature seethes with innumerable microscopic life-forms, as these lives are to us, so are human beings to the vast plan that comprehends all things.

The centerpiece of this poem is a reverie at noontime, when the poet retires in fancy to a grove and enjoys an idyllic landscape with a waterfall. The view is clearly idealized. Composed and almost framed, such landscapes show the influence of Renaissance artists such as Nicolas Poussin, Claude Lorrain, and Salvator Rosa. From within this dream setting, the imagination travels yet further to the jungles, groves, and savannahs of tropical lands. From a mountaintop in Africa, the poet watches a prodigious storm gather and break, washing over the continent and replenishing its rivers, and then recites the horrible fates that befall the people of the "torrid zone," impressing the reader with the awesome and sublime power of nature. Returning to England, another storm occasions two narrative episodes about lovers. The first issues a warning: Though innocent Celadon fears nothing, lightning slays his beloved Amelia. After the storm subsides, the poet recalls Damon, who cannot resist watching his beloved Musidora as she bathes, but at last flees, leaving her a pledge of his honor, which she finds and welcomes.

Patriotic sentiment represents another major theme in *The Seasons* that has a precedent in Vergil's *Georgics*. The earth's bounty testifies not only to the goodness of the Creator but also to the glory of the state and the empire. The afternoon portion of "Summer" is spent walking in the valley of the Thames, where the countryside's prosperity inspires the poet to enumerate its great kings, adventurers, soldiers, statesmen, philosophers, poets, and, finally, its beautiful women.

"Autumn" opens with an extended passage in praise of "industry," or labor. The sun's entry into Virgo and Libra (the scales) brings cloudy skies and ripe crops, and the keynote of this poem is harmony, not only nature's harmony within itself but also the human obligation to balance enjoyment of the earth's riches with self-discipline and virtue. Industry lifted humanity out of primitive barbarism and produced civilization; with civilization comes justice, the polity, and commerce. Thomson, however, only touches upon modern luxuries before turning the reader's attention to the tale of a poor and virtuous gleaner, an adaptation of the biblical book of Ruth. One day, when the maid Lavinia is gleaning the fields

of Palemon, a young nobleman notices her and falls in love. Amazed by her likeness to his old patron Acasto, he learns that she is in fact Acasto's daughter, and he makes her his wife.

Thomson then returns to a subject raised earlier in "Spring," namely, the morality of hunting. The peaceful muse spurns the hunter's triumph over the helpless hare or stag. Thomson is lenient, however; in "Spring," he concedes that skillful fishing is humane, and here he consents to hunting the "robber fox." After describing a vineyard and the various tasks involved in wine-making, the poet discusses precipitation and the origin of lakes and rivers. The 1730 version of the poem endorses the old, erroneous "percolation" theory, which states that sand and gravel draw the ocean's saltwater up to mountain springs, removing salt in the process. Later, Thomson inserted lines setting forth the condensation theory of astronomer Edmond Halley and shows the entire system of precipitation and drainage working harmoniously, demonstrating that science sustains rather than opposes faith in Providence. Nevertheless, scientific "Reason" needs to be informed by "Imagination," and later in the poem, in a sequence reminiscent of John Milton's *Il Penseroso* (1645), a fit of "philosophic melancholy" descends upon the poet. Let others pursue a life of activity; the poet's supreme pleasure is a simple rural retreat, where he can study nature and be caught up in philosophic rapture.

As in "Summer," the emphasis in "Winter" is on the season's extremes, and Thomson exploits the possibilities for sublime effects. This poem also, however, exalts the indoor pleasures of study and the contemplation of history, proceeding toward the final moral: When winter seems to have ruined everything and only human virtue survives the universal wreckage, spring returns and life awakens again, renewing hope.

Winter approaches with fierce storms of winds, hail, and blinding snow; an unfortunate swain loses his way and perishes while his family waits at home. This introduces a passage reflecting on the many miseries of human life, but the universal theme soon becomes the occasion to comment on a contemporary political problem. In 1729, a parliamentary committee was appointed to investigate allegations of torture in English jails. Thomson's plea on behalf of the abused prisoners is personal; nine members of the committee, whose unspoken purpose was to score points against the Whig government of Sir Robert Walpole, were subscribers to *The Seasons*.

"Winter" draws the reader into scenes of the utmost desolation: Wolves descend from the mountains, hunting down horses and bulls and even snatching infants out of their mother's arms. These horrors, however, enhance the appeal of the contemplative life that dominates the center of the poem. Although Thomson praises the simple virtue of the Swiss peasants known as Grisons, he would himself retire to more sophisticated and urbane pastimes, meditating on the heroes of ancient Greece and Rome. Their "ancient shades" parade before his eyes, and after them march the great English poets, with Thomson's revered contemporary Alexander Pope in the rear. The last portion of the poem returns to desolation, a shipwreck in the Northwest Passage and the Siberian wasteland, to prepare for the final note of life's resurrection. Frost, though seemingly ruinous, actually renovates the earth, and winter gestates the new life of spring.

The short, exuberant finale, "A Hymn on the Seasons," echoes Psalm 148 in its praise of God for revealing himself in his creation, though Thomson emphasizes each season as a distinct manifestation of God. The hymn functions as a synopsis of the devotional theme of the whole poem. In the end, however, when human words and voices fail, only "expressive Silence" remains.

Matthew Parfitt

Further Reading

Campbell, Hilbert H. *James Thomson*. Boston: Twayne, 1979. A convenient introduction to Thomson's life and works, with extensive commentary on *The Seasons*. Includes an annotated bibliography.

Cohen, Ralph. *The Unfolding of "The Seasons."* Baltimore: Johns Hopkins University Press, 1970. An exhaustive full-length study of the poem, arguing that the poem's literary merits and historical significance have been underestimated.

Goodman, Kevis. "The Microscopic Eye and the Noise of History in Thomson's *The Seasons*." In *Georgic Modernity and British Romanticism: Poetry and the Mediation of History*. New York: Cambridge University Press, 2004. Uses Thomson's reference to the "microscopic eye" in *The Seasons* to analyze the poem. Traces how the phrase, which originated in the natural science of the seventeenth century, was transformed in the eighteenth century to refer to a professional observer of public institutions and society.

Irlam, Shaun. "Vatic Tremors: Unworlding and Otherworldliness in James Thomson's *The Seasons*." In *Elations: The Poetics of Enthusiasm in Eighteenth-Century Britain*. Stanford, Calif.: Stanford University Press, 1999. Argues that the concept of enthusiasm was central to the aesthetics of early eighteenth century British literature. Traces the development of this concept and how it was reflected in Thomson's sentimental portrayal of the landscape in *The Seasons*.

Lethbridge, Stefanie. *James Thomson's Defence of Poetry: Intertextual Allusion in "The Seasons."* Tübingen, Germany: Niemeyer, 2003. Examines the allusions to Ovid, Vergil, John Milton, and other writers in the poem as well as its use of the genre conventions of pastoral poetry, romance literature, and sermons. Argues that Thomson intends *The Seasons* to defend poetry as a culturally relevant pursuit.

Sambrook, James, ed. Introduction to *James Thomson, "The Seasons."* New York: Oxford University Press, 1981. This authoritative critical edition of *The Seasons* offers a clear presentation of the complicated series of revisions that produced the final work. The introduction surveys the poem's principal subjects and the history of its composition and publication.

Spacks, Patricia Meyer. *The Varied God: A Critical Study of Thomson's "The Seasons."* Berkeley: University of California Press, 1959. A readable study of the significance of Thomson's revisions, showing how the moral and devotional purposes emerged.

Terry, Richard, ed. *James Thomson: Essays for the Tercentenary*. Liverpool, England: Liverpool University Press, 2000. The essays analyze the politics and aesthetics of Thomson's major poems, discuss the critical reception of his work after his death, and assess his influence on later writers. "*The Seasons* and the Politics of Opposition" by Glynis Ridley analyzes this poem, while another essay by W. B. Hutchings examines Thomson's landscape poetry.

Seatonian Poems *and* A Song to David

Author: Christopher Smart (1722-1771)
First published: 1750-1763; includes *On the Eternity of the Supreme Being*, 1750; *On the Immensity of the Supreme Being*, 1751; *On the Omniscience of the Supreme Being*, 1752; *On the Power of the Supreme Being*, 1754; *On the Goodness of the Supreme Being*, 1755; *Hymn to the Supreme Being, on Recovery from a Dangerous Fit of Illness*, 1756; *A Song to David*, 1763
Type of work: Poetry

Christopher Smart's Seatonian poems are those of his poems that won the Seatonian Prize at Cambridge University from 1750 to 1756. These poems cover the attributes of the "Supreme Being" to whom they are addressed—his Eternity, Immensity, Omniscience, Power, and Goodness. The poems are Miltonic not only in the structure of the verse but also in the largeness of vision they conjure up. The second of these in particular, *On the Immensity of the Supreme Being*, is a landmark of Miltonic adaptation. It begins with an avowal that God is best praised by poetry that, like nature itself, acknowledges "the grand thanksgiving" of creation. Its prevailing tone is humility; the center of the poem is God and not human beings. It is, in fact, a poem about human imperfection opposed to the plenitude of the created universe, and in this respect it is quite unlike the mainstream of eighteenth century poetry.

The beauty of the earth is praised for the evidence it gives of the nature of the deity. "Astonish'd into silence," the poet reflects on the variety, beauty, and multiplicity of creation, finding even in the bottom of the sea the evidence of a divine intention in "th' unplanted garden round/ Of vegetable coral, sea-flow'rs gay,/ And shrubs of amber from the pearl-pav'd bottom." Like the other Seatonian poems, this suggests that the works of civilization are far inferior to those of nature.

Smart's *Hymn to the Supreme Being* was written, as he said, to express his thanks for recovering from a dangerous illness. He begins by relating the sickness of David, a figure ever present in his mind. For Smart, David stands not only for the figure of the psalmist but also for the man who is both "the sovereign of myself and servant of the Lord." When he compares the sickness of David with his own illness, he sees that he has very little to recommend him to the special care of heaven. In going over his life he addresses himself constantly to the great themes of waste and sorrow. He finds that he has no special title to mercy, much less to divine notice, but it is

his discovery of this fact that both casts him down and lifts him up. His penitence and his union with a world of sinners, which he sums up as the "contrite heart," are the whole of the defense he offers of his past life. The poem is both a thanksgiving for and a praise of charity; it makes clear that the beneficiary is such only by the grace of heaven.

The figure of David is preeminent in Smart's *A Song to David*, a poem that is both a biography and a spiritual celebration of its subject. Smart begins by pointing out the excellence of David's character, which won for him material rewards. He outlines the courage and intelligence of his hero "arm'd in gallant faith." Yet above all other issues, and infinitely more meaningful than David's success as a warrior and a politician, is David's piety. It is his consecration to his religion that Smart particularly admires, and the poem is in substance in praise of this. The goodness of David he explains by reference to those occasions when the king showed mercy to his enemies: "To pity, to forgive, to save." Beyond this, according to the poet, is the perpetual prayer of David, the purity of his devotion, his fasting and fear of the Lord. Whether in warfare or in the employments of peace he is the paradigm of the virtuous man and the consecrated leader.

Like Milton, Smart appreciates in David another quality, that of poetic creativity. David as king elicits Smart's praises. David as the man of "perpetual prayer" draws his admiration, but David as the figure of the artist is perhaps even more central to the poet's vision. Smart writes of the "invention" of David, his capacity to make the form and the language of the Psalms convey the richness of his responses. He praises, too, the "conception" of the poet-king, his powers of imagination. His emotional quality is mentioned last, the "exaltations" that the poet, above all other men, manages to achieve and to express. David is in fact the model of the poet: He begins in contemplation and ends in creation. In this he repeats, indeed acts out, the first process of all, the creation of the world itself.

Thereafter Smart returns to the character of David, which he compiles from the stories of his reign as well as from the Psalms themselves. It is both the character of a man that is described and that of a symbol. The first of the allegorical qualities of soul that Smart attributes to David is serenity; it intimates the wish of the king for peace in his kingdom and on earth. The next of these is strength, to persist against the great odds of a divided people and hostile external forces. Smart then writes about the constancy, joy, and wisdom of his hero in terms that may be taken to reveal Smart's consciousness of his own tragic lack of these qualities. Writing shortly after a prolonged attack of insanity, in despair over his private and artistic life, Smart put into this poem a deep sense of the need for these qualities in life as in art.

One of the great themes of Smart's work as a whole is the appreciation of created things. This theme is explicitly connected to the idea of God as he is revealed by the things he has made. *A Song to David* leaves its first subject, the king himself, and turns to a lengthy consideration of this favorite and recurring theme. Smart himself can best convey the depth of his feelings for the plenitude of the created world:

> Trees, plants, and flow'rs—of virtuous root;
> Gem yielding blossom, yielding fruit,
> Choice gums and precious balm;
> Bless ye the nosegay in the vale,
> And with the sweetness of the gale
> Enrich the thankful psalm.

The "thankful psalm" is a good description of the essential character of Smart's work as a whole. He continually seizes upon the variety, beauty, and intelligibility of creation, and, as critics have pointed out, he does not spend as much poetic energy in contemplating his own condition as he does praising what he perceives by his senses. Smart praises the world of water and that of land, that of sky, and that of earth. He uses the ancient conception of the chain of being to give form to the feelings he tries to convey: From the world of shells and fishes to that of higher life he gives an outline of the harmonic order of the universe. Very little escapes this great catalog, even those inanimate things at the base of the pyramid of Being. After this interlude of praise, Smart returns to his ostensible subject, the Hebrew poet and king.

The height of David's achievement is summarized in Smart's concept of Adoration, the act of submitting the mortal to the immortal. This concluding section of the poem is a vital link connecting two subjects: the Hebraic tradition and the Christian. In a long and orchestral ending, Smart relates the qualities of David to those of Christ, and here the figure of the warrior and poet emerges as the forerunner of an even greater figure.

This outline would seem to indicate that Smart was almost totally involved in matters of religion, that his own religious mania succeeded, in spite of himself, in coloring all of his writing. The fact is that Smart found time to translate Horace and to provide a translation of the Roman poet of such high quality as to ensure its continuing use. Translation was a great eighteenth century craft, if not indeed an art, and Smart shows the same familiarity with the classical spirit as that shown by Alexander Pope and other masters of paraphrase. The *Odes of Horace* are simply and cleanly translated. Perhaps their most significant contribution is the expression of classical thought in Enlightenment language.

In addition to his religious poetry and his translation, Smart was able to work in minor veins of poetry. His poem "Of Jeoffrey, His Cat" is certainly slight, but it is strong evidence of Smart's ability to observe and to deduce: The cat is shown not with the automatic stare of the everyday but, as Smart sees it, "wreathing his body seven times round with elegant quickness." In many other minor poems Smart concentrates on his appreciation of the qualities of the senses. He writes about music in "On Gratitude" and celebrates the "Voice and Lyre" just as, in the religious poems, he celebrates all those things that bring beauty to life. In "An Epistle to John Sherratt, Esq." Smart writes that of all the offerings of which he can conceive, none so delights the mind as "gratitude expres'd in song." This thankfulness for the rewards of the senses is a constant theme in his work, and he relates it with equal constancy to the intention of God in creating a world full of aesthetic and moral delight.

In another poem he writes that "the sweets of Evening charm the mind." This is quite un-Miltonic in language and tone but very much related to Milton's consciousness of the nature and meaning of all things experienced by the mind. "Every thing that grows," Smart writes in this poem, is a reminder of "superior natures" and the highest sphere of imagination. In his work, whether it is about figures from history or the experiences of everyday life, he reiterates the constant theme of thankfulness for the variety and beauty of life. He reiterates, too, something substantially Miltonic: the conviction that all this beauty means something and that it is a key to an understanding of the nature of life itself.

Further Reading

Ainsworth, Edward G., and Charles E. Noyes. *Christopher Smart: A Biographical and Critical Study.* Columbia: University of Missouri Press, 1943. Scholarly study of Smart's life offers critical analyses of his major works, including illuminating commentary on the Seatonian poems and *A Song to David*. Especially informative regarding the reaction to Smart's work by his contemporaries.

Anderson, Frances. *Christopher Smart*. New York: Twayne, 1974. Provides an introductory overview, sketching Smart's life and giving some historical background to illuminate his accomplishments. Contains a brief discussion of the Seatonian poems and a chapter on *A Song to David*, stressing Smart's conscious imitation of the biblical psalmists in both.

Curry, Neil. *Christopher Smart*. Horndon, England: Northcote House/British Council, 2005. Presents a reappraisal of Smart's life and work, arguing that he is the most important English religious poet in the years between the works of George Herbert and Gerard Manley Hopkins. Maintains that Smart is a pivotal figure in eighteenth century English verse, asserting that his early work echoes that of John Milton while his later work anticipates the poetry of William Blake.

Dearnley, Moira. *The Poetry of Christopher Smart*. New York: Barnes & Noble, 1969. Includes lengthy chapters on the Seatonian poems and *A Song to David*. Stresses Smart's intense religious feelings, which inspired all his writings. Provides commentary on the structure of *A Song to David*.

Hawes, Clement, ed. *Christopher Smart and the Enlightenment*. New York: St. Martin's Press, 1999. Collection of essays reexamines Smart's legacy and his impact on twentieth century poetry. Includes a discussion of Smart's poetics, an examination of the treatment of confession in works by Smart and Jean-Jacques Rousseau, and analyses of some of Smart's poems.

Mounsey, Chris. *Christopher Smart: Clown of God*. Lewisburg, Pa.: Bucknell University Press, 2001. Biography offers new interpretations of Smart's life and work. Discusses the social, political, historical, and religious significance of his writings.

Smart, Christopher. *A Song to David*. Edited by J. B. Broadbent. Cambridge, England: Rampant Lions Press, 1960. Critical edition of the poem provides extensive commentary on its structure and analysis of Smart's technical skill and thematic aims.

The Second Mrs. Tanqueray

Author: Arthur Wing Pinero (1855-1934)
First produced: 1893; first published, 1895
Type of work: Drama
Type of plot: Social realism
Time of plot: 1890's
Locale: London and Surrey, England

Principal characters:
AUBREY TANQUERAY, a London socialite
CAYLEY DRUMMLE, his friend
PAULA, Aubrey's second wife
ELLEAN, Aubrey's daughter by a former marriage
CAPTAIN HUGH ARDALE, Ellean's suitor
MRS. ALICE CORTELYON, the Tanquerays' neighbor in Surrey

The Story:

Aubrey Tanqueray, a wealthy widower, is to be married to Paula Ray, a woman younger than he and of questionable character. Aubrey's first wife did not contribute a great deal to his happiness. A daughter, Ellean, was born to the Tanquerays shortly before the first Mrs. Tanqueray died of a fever, the only warmth, in the opinion of one of Aubrey's friends, ever to have come to the woman's body. Ellean has spent most of her life in a convent and is planning to take final vows.

Cayley Drummle, a friend of Aubrey, discusses with him the inadvisability of marriage between members of different social classes, but Aubrey, intent on having warmth and companionship in his home life, is resolute in his determination to marry Paula. Aubrey has momentary misgivings, however, when Paula appears late at night at his apartment. Such conduct does not become a lady, Aubrey charges; it will cause talk among the servants. Paula's opinion, indicative of her treatment of domestics, is that servants are merely machines to do chores and to appear for testimony in the divorce courts. Despite her glib pretenses, Paula, too, feels somewhat unsure about the social abyss that she and Aubrey are attempting to bridge. While she goes to put on her cloak,

Aubrey, reminded by his servant that he has not opened the day's mail, reads a letter from Ellean in which she tells him that she has communed with the spirit of her mother, who has admonished her to return to Aubrey in his loneliness. Perplexed, he is unable to foresee happiness between his daughter and his wife-to-be.

Two months after their marriage, the unhappiness of the Tanquerays in their domestic life is apparent to all their friends. Paula is bored with the inactivity of country life at Aubrey's house in Surrey, and Aubrey is apprehensive about Ellean and Paula's incompatibility. Both women wonder why their neighbors do not call on them.

Since her arrival, Ellean has become a barrier between her father and stepmother because of her life in the convent. Although Aubrey tries to throw the two women together, they soon show that they have nothing in common. When Cayley Drummle, who is staying at an adjoining estate, calls on the Tanquerays, he becomes the confidant of both Paula, who expresses her wishes for the life she knew before her marriage, and Aubrey, who expresses keen disappointment regarding Ellean's lack of interest in meeting eligible young men. Benevolent Drummle encourages Mrs. Cortelyon, his host at the neighboring estate and Aubrey's longtime friend, to call on Paula. Although Aubrey sees through Drummle's efforts, he appreciates Mrs. Cortelyon's visit and her invitation to have Ellean as her guest in Paris during the Easter holiday.

Paula resents Mrs. Cortelyon's attentions to Ellean, who makes no attempt to conceal her preference for a member of her father's social set. Mrs. Cortelyon makes the situation more awkward when she courteously and straightforwardly tells Paula that her memories of Aubrey's first wife can never be erased by the presence of another woman in the Tanqueray house.

Feeling excluded from her husband's life, Paula spitefully sends a letter to Sir George and Lady Orreyed, the latter a friend of Paula in her former way of life. Aubrey had earlier forbidden Paula to send an invitation to the Orreyeds because he does not wish to have Ellean associating with such boisterous and unconventional people.

Ellean goes to Paris with Mrs. Cortelyon, and the Orreyeds come to visit the Tanquerays. During their visit they insult their hosts because of the limited supply of liquor in the house, break furniture in the heat of a marital squabble, and loll about in unbecoming positions. Their crudeness is offensive to Paula, but having invited them she cannot, under the circumstances, ask them to leave; she can only hate them.

Although Aubrey's purpose in marrying Paula had been partly to show her kindness, he has been unable to do so because Paula, always on the defensive, will not accept his attentions. Drummle, having known Paula in her former situation, is seemingly capable of mellowing her. It is he who, on learning that Paula has intercepted letters from Mrs. Cortelyon and Ellean to Aubrey, convinces her that such conduct is only breeding much of the unhappiness that she is enduring. Paula gives the letters to Aubrey, who forgives her maliciousness in keeping the correspondence from him.

After Aubrey tells her of his disappointment and the frequent embarrassment he feels because of her common jokes and paltry cynicism, Paula admits that she has not been fair to him and Ellean, and she asks for another chance to prove herself when Ellean returns from Paris and London. Mrs. Cortelyon and Ellean return soon afterward, the older woman anxious because she has not heard from Aubrey regarding his reaction to Ellean's romance with Captain Hugh Ardale. The courtship has been the subject of the letters Paula was intercepting.

Deeply in love with Ardale, a British soldier stationed in India, Ellean approaches Paula to share the story of her good fortune. Paula rebuffs Ellean at first, saying that the girl is being kind only because she is soon to be married. Then, after confessing her bitter jealousy, Paula reconciles with Ellean and expresses her joy for Ellean in her newfound happiness.

Ardale, who has accompanied Ellean and Mrs. Cortelyon home from Paris, arrives at the Tanqueray house from a nearby hotel. Paula, after telling Ellean that she and Ardale have met before, says that she wants to talk with him about Ellean. Alone, Paula and Ardale recall the time when she had been his mistress. When Paula tells him that Aubrey must be informed of Ardale's past, Ardale threatens suicide if Paula interferes to prevent his marriage to Ellean.

Told of Paula and Ardale's past relationship, Aubrey refuses to allow Ellean to see Ardale again. Shocked by her father's attitude, Ellean guesses that Paula has influenced Aubrey against Ardale. When Ellean presses Paula for an explanation, Paula cannot bring herself to divulge her past life to her stepdaughter. Ellean then tells Paula that she can surmise what Paula has told Aubrey and that she has known from their first meeting that Paula is not a good woman.

Ardale sends a note to Paula, telling her that he is going back to Paris to await any word that she or Aubrey may want him to have and asking that they explain the situation to Ellean. After Aubrey has read the note, at Paula's request, they discuss philosophically what the future might hold for them together. Paula says that the only great distances in the world are those that people carry within themselves, the distances that separate husbands and wives, and she predicts that Aubrey will tire of her in the future.

Drummle returns to discuss with Aubrey the affair of Ellean and Ardale. As the men talk, Ellean appears and asks her father to go quickly to Paula. After he leaves, the young woman tells Drummle that when she went to Paula's room to apologize for her unkind remarks, she heard a body falling. Entering the room, she found Paula dying. Ellean says that she, in her unkindness, has helped to kill Paula.

Critical Evaluation:

Many scholars consider *The Second Mrs. Tanqueray* to be the first truly modern English play. Presenting a genuine social problem, this drama pictures people as they are in terms of their social prejudices and the difficulties arising from those biases. Other contributions that this play made to realistic English drama are the dramatist's use of the names of actual places in London and Surrey, the story's logically motivated action, and the exactness of the stage directions and descriptions of sets.

The Second Mrs. Tanqueray is one of the best examples in theatrical history of a play whose production was timely. Had it been written a few years earlier, it is doubtful that it would have gained a production or, if it had, that it would have met with anything but hostility and commercial failure. Presented even a few years later, after the early works of George Bernard Shaw and his realistic contemporaries, it is unlikely that its iconoclasm would have set it apart or that it would have enjoyed the instant masterpiece status accorded it by many of the best critics. In 1893, some of the Victorian moral rigidity began to give way to the more casual Edwardian lifestyle, and the influence of the new Continental theater was first being felt. The moment was ripe for a play that challenged Victorian social and moral postures but did not, finally, repudiate those attitudes and values.

Critics who have written about the play at some remove from the propitious time of its arrival, however, have been harsher in their appraisals. The most serious shortcoming of the play is that, seen from a modern perspective, it is too serious for a conventional well-made play but still lacks true depth because Pinero fails to pursue the moral and psychological implications of the characters and situations to their logical conclusions. In other words, Pinero has the material for a potentially important serious play, but, for reasons of personal taste or commercial wariness, he backs off and imposes a contrived but socially conventional conclusion on the work. To be specific, is the suicide of the heroine, Paula Tanqueray, the inevitable result of her character and circumstances, or is it simply a means by which Pinero sentimentally extricates himself from a situation too morally ambiguous for Victorian audiences to accept?

If the suicide can be justified, it must be seen as the result of an accumulation of factors: Paula's disillusionment with Aubrey and the realization that, although he loves her, he neither respects her nor considers her morally fit to associate with his daughter; her boredom with rural life and recognition of the fact that she will never be accepted by Aubrey's friends; her discovery that she has outgrown her old world but has no new one to enter; her lingering pain over her earlier breakup with Hugh Ardale, which is renewed by his return; her loss of Ellean's potential love; and, finally, her own feeling that she is getting old and will soon have nothing left. Aubrey vows they will make another "fresh start," but Paula knows better.

One can explain the motivation behind Paula's actions, but her behavior is not always dramatically convincing. For a woman of the world, she is too naïve and eager in her dealings with Ellean, her haughty and self-defeating handling of Mrs. Cortelyon seems artificial, her treatment of Aubrey frequently seems arbitrary and unnatural, and her moralistic decision to confess her previous affair with Ardale to her husband cannot be justified. The suicide is thus not the only problem in the play. In spite of some powerful and probing characterization, Paula exhibits behavior that too often seems to be necessitated by the shape of the plot rather than by the nature of the character.

Other characters also suggest complexities greater than those usually encountered in well-made plays. How much of Aubrey's love for Paula is genuine emotion and how much of it is rooted in an idealistic, moralistic desire to save and uplift a lost soul? How much influence does Aubrey's deceased first wife have on the Tanqueray household and especially on Ellean? And what about the relationship between Aubrey and his daughter? Is it completely within the normal father-daughter pattern? None of these provocative suggestions, however, is followed through. All remain tantalizing hints on the edge of the action, clues to character depths and complexities that are never explored.

Thus, however good *The Second Mrs. Tanqueray* may be, the reader constantly feels that it could have been much better. It is probably too much to expect Pinero to be an English Henrik Ibsen. Perhaps it is sufficient to say that, along with Henry Arthur Jones, Pinero brought a new seriousness to the British theater and that he helped to usher a new period of intense creativity onto the English stage.

Further Reading

Dawick, John. *Pinero: A Theatrical Life*. Niwot: University Press of Colorado, 1993. Comprehensive account of Pinero's personal and professional life is based in part on the writer's correspondence and unpublished materials from his literary estate. Discusses Pinero's plays and other writings within their theatrical and social contexts, including the Victorian concern about respectability. One chapter is devoted to a discussion of the production, presentation, and reception of *The Second Mrs. Tanqueray*.

Downer, Alan S. *The British Drama: A Handbook and Brief Chronicle*. New York: Appleton-Century-Crofts, 1950. Includes an examination of Pinero's life and works that focuses on him as a Victorian playwright with notable and innovative ideas.

Knight, G. Wilson. *The Golden Labyrinth: A Study of British Drama*. New York: W. W. Norton, 1962. Places Pinero's work in the context of the work of other playwrights of his time. Argues that Pinero addresses the sexual irregularities of both men and women with honesty in *The Second Mrs. Tanqueray* and discusses Pinero's handling of the technicalities of staging a play.

Powell, Kerry, ed. *The Cambridge Companion to Victorian*

and Edwardian Theatre. New York: Cambridge University Press, 2004. Collection of essays provides informative background on the theatrical context in which Pinero wrote.

Salerno, Henry F. Introduction to *The Second Mrs. Tanqueray*. In *English Drama in Transition: 1880-1920*. New York: Pegasus, 1968. Offers a well-written critical analysis of the play that includes information on Pinero's interests when he wrote it.

Wellwarth, George E. *The Maypole in the Strand: Sir Arthur Wing Pinero and Henry Arthur Jones, a Study*. New York: Vantage Press, 2001. Charts the careers of playwrights Pinero and Jones, provides commentaries on the plots of their plays, and offers contemporary criticism of their work, much of which was negative. Wellwarth is equally unimpressed, describing both men as prisoners of their times and middle-class backgrounds, traditionalists and sentimentalists who created a handful of insignificant farces.

The Second Sex

Author: Simone de Beauvoir (1908-1986)
First published: *Le Deuxième Sexe*, 1949 (English translation, 1953)
Type of work: Social criticism

The Second Sex is considered a pioneering treatment on the subject of women's personal and social freedom. Simone de Beauvoir, who was a prolific writer, was most famous for *The Second Sex* because of its profound impact upon the feminist movement. Though some feminists have concerns with the study, most continue to recognize it as a significant, perhaps even definitive, tract in the history of the modern women's movement. The essays also have been criticized by nonfeminists, with some justification. At times the work suffers from imprecise data and oversimplified generalizations. Generally, though, the work is considered one of substance, and later editions include corrected statistics.

The text, drawing upon a voluminous number of studies to explain the past and present condition of women in society, is not merely a biological and historical treatment. It is also an argument against the received views on the nature of women and an appeal for change. The work has two main ideas: First, borrowed directly from Jean-Paul Sartre, is the

famous notion of the other, a phenomenon acknowledging that woman sees herself only in relationship to man, while man does not recognize woman as an entity separate from himself. The second major idea is that woman is conditioned from birth to perform the role of a woman: thus, what is perceived as feminine nature is not innate but an artificial invention.

The book is divided into two parts: Book 1 treats "Facts and Myths," and book 2 examines "Woman's Life Today." In the first book, physical and historical facts that have contributed to the domination of women are cited in an attempt to show how these facts are related to myths about the nature of woman. The myths are a product of male domination, although women traditionally have accepted and then internalized the myths. Beauvoir's social, biological, and cultural survey begins by tracing the development of women throughout history. She argues that behaviors were inculcated into codes or mythologies as a result of woman's physical disadvantage in the division of labor, superstitions surrounding woman's bodily functions, and woman's functions involving reproduction and child care. Beauvoir also draws examples from literature, archetypes, and conventions in art to identify the way man has sought to define the concept of femininity through the ages and to thus perpetuate false beliefs about woman.

Beauvoir also points out that an existential viewpoint allows an understanding of how biology, economics, and popular wisdom have enabled male domination to flourish. In existential philosophy, man discovers himself by identifying with something else, and thus he transcends alienation. Woman experiences alienation far less affirmatively because she is prevented from discovering her autonomous, creative self by man, who regards her as his property. Specifically, man's role as warrior allows him to claim supremacy. Later cultural myths, especially the paradox of man's declaring respect for woman while declaring her inferiority, enables patriarchy—the rule of the father—to continue. Judaism's misogyny, firmly inculcated into Christian ideology, also contributes significantly to female oppression. This misogyny, reinforced by the Catholic Church fathers, lasted until the Renaissance, a time of slight advancement for woman with the advent of humanism.

In history, contradictions in woman's image abound. For example, there exists the idea that woman can be both perfect and evil, an idol and a servant, the source of truth and the source of untruth. Examples of such contradictions are comprehensive. Specifically, Beauvoir thoroughly covers the phenomenon of woman as myth in the work of five authors: Henri de Montherlant, D. H. Lawrence, Paul Claudel, André Breton, and Stendhal. From her examples, the ideal woman as protagonist incorporates perfectly the myths of the other. In daily life, societies and individuals define myths according to their needs and, Beauvoir reiterates, myths, based upon the point of view of men, are reinforced with woman's acquiescence.

The contradictions found in the image of woman are admirably exposed, and ample illustrations support the concept that woman is doomed by the culture's embracing of the idea of the incarnation of man's wishes and desires. This phenomenon keeps woman in a state of perpetual passivity. Usually, her situation disallows her the avenue of transcending her fate, but an awareness of the facts should aid in understanding the problem, thus avoiding perpetuation. Unfortunately, as is pointed out, exposition of the problem alone does not provide a solution.

The second part of *The Second Sex*, focusing on feminine experience and behavior predominately in twentieth century France, first traces the development of the female through life stages. Again, the antideterministic postulate from the first section, that woman is made, not born, is reemphasized. The idea of how woman's lack of choice forces her into social roles and psychological complexes created by history and myth is further expounded. First, the author, in admirably succinct statements, describes the adolescent response in both males and females to sexual drive. As far as sexual initiation, feminine sexuality is far more complicated than male sexuality. The girl both fears and desires male attention. Her experiences involve not only the erotic drive but also factors resulting from her situation.

As an adult, woman may adopt an image from the various roles man has foisted upon her, such as wife, mother, or prostitute. In the married state (the most accepted role), despite the appearance of equality in the institution of marriage, an inequality prevails, and the inequality has its roots in the husband's role as productive worker and the wife's role as mother. As long as the man holds the economic responsibility, the union is a farce. Beauvoir here shows her dedication to objectivity most profoundly. She characterizes woman in marriage as far less than blameless. The concept of marriage as the only avenue for woman has been so thoroughly internalized that women accept it without question as the only means open for them. The effect is that women eschew freedom, the fundamental right of human beings. The end result is marital unhappiness and sometimes adultery. Adultery is a pastime that helps society cope, but adultery does not solve society's problems.

To reshape their destiny, women will have to pursue endeavors other than escapist ones. Their salvation depends, the author rather ironically contends, upon a male liberator. The rather glum depiction of married life, although insightful at times, is supported mostly by evidence from literature, including letters and diaries, which are subjective. Those women who avoid marriage and become prostitutes are even more unhappy than their married sisters, because prostitution also is enslavement. Economically, marriage and prostitution are similar. The greatest difference between the two oppressed states is that the married woman is respected while the prostitute is reviled. The author uses the word *hetaera* to designate all women, married and unmarried, who use their bodies as capital. In the *hetaira* (a prostitute of the upper classes in ancient Greece), the concept of woman as myth is complete.

Married or unmarried love both give rise to various mental aberrations. Romantic love is always disappointing, and when love is not attained at all, woman may turn to adore divinity. The love of the divine has the same effect upon woman as romantic love and can only end in failure. Narcissism is the result of frustration and aggression. Possessiveness and jealousy are other painful effects.

The book also argues that disappointment in the sexual experience with men, and the sheer difficulties in obtaining men, affection, and protection, may create a situation for the development of lesbian tendencies. No clear boundaries exist, despite mythology to the contrary, between lesbians and women who are not lesbian, and the sexual behavior itself in not an aberration. To be free, woman must give up the idea of traditional love, and must cease to be a parasite. True love should allow for limitations. It should eschew worship, and essentially, become an interrelation, with both woman and man embracing their true selves. It is only with gainful employment that woman can find herself. Effort is the behavior most needed by women to assure their independence, and women may face myriad problems as a result, such as being torn between their profession and their sexual life.

As far as the formative years in childhood, the author first points out the disparity in the treatment of sons and daughters. The basic argument is that while a mother's influence on a son may be negative and ambiguous, the important quality is that no distinction is made for the son between his existence as a human being and as a human being who works. "Humanity is male," the author asserts. For the girl, a huge gap exists between her existence as a human being and her existence as a human being whose vocation is being female. To survive in the role of such artificiality, the girl must relinquish her childhood image of autonomy and accept the role of submission. In a society in which the community assumes much of the responsibility for raising the child, contradictory phenomena such as the role imposed on girls would dissolve in the face of examples of women who have escaped the role of submission. Girls would see women with careers. Thus, the traditional family perpetuates inequality.

Aging receives careful thought. First, aging means different things to men and women. Women, depending upon their self-image for identity, suffer substantially since erotic attractiveness is what provides them their life's opportunities. At some point during maturity, some women go through a stage in which they attempt to grasp a last opportunity by joining sects, clubs, charities, having another child, or obtaining a lover. During old age, the wisdom of a woman may be bitter or amused, but it will always be negative.

The condition of woman has remained much the same throughout history, and this condition is what is known as the "character" of woman. Woman's character is not determined by hormones nor a predetermination in the brain but rather is shaped by her social and cultural situations. Like other oppressed people, such as slaves, women are considered childish, devious, and emotional. Women may rise above their situations by way of collective effort.

In conclusion, Beauvoir calls upon both men and women to recognize each other as peers. Throughout the study, she demonstrates that if man has enjoyed superiority to woman, it is not solely because of his greater physical strength and his freedom from the duties of rearing offspring. It is also a result of his involvement in gainful employment, the constructing and revising of the world itself. When woman realizes that the world is not solely the domain of the male, then she is truly capable of being free, and will be able to engage in work, thus losing her passivity and all the characteristics that follow from the artificial feminine role. *The Second Sex* is an important social analysis that still commands respect as a cogent, insightful treatment of many of the major problems in gender history.

Dorie LaRue

Further Reading

Appignanesi, Lisa. *Simone de Beauvoir*. New York: Penguin Books, 1988. A significant appraisal of Beauvoir's concept of the independent woman. Appignanesi aptly explicates Beauvoir's existentialist ethics and her suppositions of woman's subjectivity.

Bair, Deirdre. *Simone de Beauvoir: A Biography*. New York: Summit Books, 1990. Reliable biography covering the philosophical life of Beauvoir as Beauvoir's inquiry into the nature of woman. Chapter 28 is an entertaining and edifying précis of *The Second Sex*.

Bieber, Konrad. *Simone de Beauvoir*. Boston: Twayne, 1979. A comprehensive, factual, and general presentation of Beauvoir's life and works, including a lucid overview of *The Second Sex*. Includes a good general bibliography.

Brosman, Catharine Savage. *Simone de Beauvoir Revisited*. Boston: Twayne, 1991. Introduces readers to the vocabulary and the existential concepts of Beauvoir's philosophy. Contains an important, succinct explication of *The Second Sex*.

Card, Claudia, ed. *The Cambridge Companion to Simone de Beauvoir*. New York: Cambridge University Press, 2003. Collection of essays focusing on Beauvior's philosophy, with references to *The Second Sex* throughout the book. Two essays devote particular attention to *The Second Sex*: "Complicity and Slavery in *The Second Sex*" by Susan James and "Simone de Beauvoir: (Re)counting the Sexual Difference" by Debra B. Bergoffen.

Crosland, Margaret. *Simone de Beauvoir: The Woman and Her Work*. London: Heinemann, 1992. A searching retrospective of Beauvoir's life and career. Crosland shows how Beauvoir's commitment to feminism in the late 1960's and early 1970's had developed in coincidence with feminism catching up to *The Second Sex*.

Hatcher, Donald L. *Understanding "The Second Sex."* New York: Peter Lang, 1984. Primarily a summary with comments on the essays. Excellent for those with no background in existential philosophy.

Moi, Toril. *Feminist Theory and Simone de Beauvoir*. Cambridge, Mass.: Blackwell, 1990. A concise investigation into the critical reception and critical implications of Beauvoir's work. Part of the Bucknell Lectures in Literary Theory series.

_____. *Simone de Beauvoir: The Making of an Intellectual Woman*. 2d. ed. New York: Oxford University Press, 2008. Chapter 3 recounts the hostile reception of Beauvoir's work by those in France and elsewhere who did not accord Beauvoir, as a woman, the intellectual strength and integrity of male philosophers. Chapter 6 juxtaposes Beauvoir's ethics of ambiguity and "alienation and the body" in *The Second Sex*.

Scarth, Fredrika. "*The Second Sex*: Ambiguity and the Body." In *The Other Within: Ethics, Politics, and the Body in Simone de Beauvoir*. Lanham, Md.: Rowman & Littlefield, 2004. Scarth's discussion of *The Second Sex* is part of her larger examination of Beauvoir's writings on the female body and on maternity.

Schwarzer, Alice. *After "The Second Sex": Conversations with Simone de Beauvoir*. Translated by Marianne Howarth. New York: Pantheon Books, 1984. Interviews with Beauvoir and Jean-Paul Sartre. Lively insights into *The Second Sex* and Beauvoir's relationship with Sartre.

Simons, Margaret A. *Beauvoir and "The Second Sex": Feminism, Race, and the Origins of Existentialism*. Lanham, Md.: Rowman & Littlefield, 1999. Simons searches for the origins of Beauvoir's existential philosophy, and in the process uncovers information about how African American author Richard Wright was Beauvoir's model of oppression and how *The Second Sex* influenced the philosophy of Jean-Paul Sartre.

The Second Shepherds' Play

Author: Wakefield Master (c. 1420-c. 1450)
First transcribed: Secunda Pastorum, fifteenth century
Type of work: Drama
Type of plot: Mystery and miracle play
Time of plot: The Nativity
Locale: Bethlehem and surrounding country

Principal characters:
FIRST SHEPHERD
SECOND SHEPHERD
THIRD SHEPHERD
MAK, a rascal
GILL, Mak's wife
AN ANGEL
MARY

The Story:

On the night of Christ's birth, a cold and lonely shepherd stands in the countryside near Bethlehem watching his flocks and bemoaning his lot in life. He is joined by another shepherd, who adds his lamentations to those of the first and points out that his lot is worse because he is married. The second shepherd complains that his wife, a fat, shrewish person, was once a sweet and charming girl, but that marriage changed her.

While they grumble, a third shepherd joins them. His chief complaint is the weather, for he thinks that never, since Noah's flood, was the season so bad. To ease their unhappy lot, the three begin to sing a song. After they sing, Mak comes into the field to join them. Mak is not very welcome, for he has a reputation as a thief, and the shepherds are somewhat fearful that he will steal something from them. Mak begs them to let him stay and tells a sad story of being hungry and unwelcome at home, even though he works hard to give his wife what she wants. The three shepherds give in and bid him lie down and spend the night with them.

After the three shepherds fall asleep, Mak arises and prepares to steal a sheep, first casting a spell over the shepherds to keep them from awakening. He goes to the fold, selects a fat ewe, and makes off with it to his house. Not daring to kill the sheep, lest the noise make the theft known, Mak and his wife Gill decide to hide the sheep in the cradle if anyone comes. In the meantime, Mak goes back to finish out his night's sleep with the shepherds and cover up his crime.

The next morning, Mak awakens with the shepherds, makes them note that he is taking nothing with him, and starts off toward his home. Not long after he reaches home, the shepherds, who missed their ewe, go to Mak's house to see if he or his wife stole the animal. According to plan, Mak and Gill hide the sheep in the cradle, and Gill pretends to have given birth to a son the night before. Although the accusers hunt all over the house, they find no sign of the sheep, not even a morsel of meat. After asking Mak's pardon and bidding good health to the new child in the cradle, the shepherds leave. Scarcely are they gone, when they remember they left no gifts for the baby. Returning to the house with a little gift, they look in the cradle and discover their stolen sheep. Mak and Gill try to explain that an evil spirit took their child and replaced it with the ewe. The shepherds are not taken in by the story, toss Mak in a sheet for punishment, and then depart with their sheep.

When the shepherds return to the fields, an angel appears to them and tells them of the birth of the Savior, who will overthrow the devil and restore the glory that was lost to man through Adam's fall. The shepherds, following the commands of the angel, make ready to visit the Christ child as it lay in a manger in Bethlehem, only a short distance away. They consider themselves lucky to have an opportunity to see the Messiah, who was prophesied in ages past.

Upon their arrival in Bethlehem, where they were led by the star, the three shepherds go to the stable where Mary and the Child are housed. The first shepherd, after greeting both the mother and the child, offers his gift of a bob of cherries. The second shepherd, not to be outdone as a giver of gifts, makes a little speech filled with respect and gives the child a bird to play with. The third shepherd also makes a short speech of reverence and then gives his gift, a ball. He urges the child to grow up and play at tennis.

After the shepherds give their gifts, Mary thanks them for the presents and the reverence. She also bids them to spread the news of Christ when they leave. The three shepherds depart to sing the good tidings to the world.

Critical Evaluation:

The Second Shepherds' Play is one of the best of the medieval mystery plays. Unlike the medieval morality play, which was allegorical in method and restricted to a few topics concerning salvation, the mystery play had much greater range in subject matter and characterization. Although originally limited to the dramatization of biblical events, mystery plays increasingly treated stories from Scripture and Church history with a good deal of latitude. The primary aim of this form of drama was the elucidation of biblical and traditional wisdom for the laity, but from the mystery play emerged the elements of Renaissance drama. In this evolutionary process, a group of plays called the Towneley cycle was very important and, of the Towneley plays, the most influential was *The Second Shepherds' Play.*

The mystery play had its origin in an antiphonal part of the mass for Easter called the *Quem quaeritis* (Whom do you seek?), which was the forerunner of liturgical innovations that used dialogue, adapted from Scripture, to enliven the worship. As the dialogues expanded, they were moved out of the mass proper, where they were becoming a distraction, to other services such as matins. When the practice was extended to Christmas and other feasts, the range of subjects and the scope of dialogues were correspondingly amplified.

Eventually, the dialogues began to incorporate materials that were irrelevant, sometimes even inappropriate, to the liturgy. These rudimentary plays were removed from the church to the courtyard and finally to the marketplace, where they slipped out of clerical control. Responsibility for the productions was assumed by the civil authorities and delegated to appropriate guilds; the Noah plays, for example, were assigned to shipbuilders. There followed a slow process of secularization, although biblical themes survived into the sixteenth century.

Early in the fourteenth century, it became customary to perform the plays on the feast of Corpus Christi. Many towns, especially in the north of England, developed cycles of plays covering the whole range of biblical history. The largest extant group is the York cycle, but there were impressive collections at Norwich, Coventry, Newcastle, Chester, and elsewhere.

The Wakefield cycle was the most impressive, partly because of the enormously talented contributions of a gifted playwright known only as the Wakefield Master. Known also as the Towneley cycle, because the manuscript was long at Towneley Hall in Lancashire, this group of plays developed in three parts. The first part is a series of rather simple plays, some of which seem to have been borrowed from the York cycle. The second part is a group of plays that were incorporated into the cycle in the early fifteenth century. The third part, added before the mid-fifteenth century, was the work of the Wakefield Master, who contributed several plays in a characteristic nine-line stanza and revised several others.

The Second Shepherds' Play is the most distinctive of the master's additions.

The historical importance of the work is in its departure from the devotional thrust of the mystery play. It is true that the mystery play long accommodated extraneous secular material as it developed into a more elaborate dramatic structure. It is even true that the humor, in the situation and in language, frequently became coarse. What is striking about *The Second Shepherds' Play* is basically a matter of proportion and individual talent. In this play, the secular component completely overwhelms the biblical. Although the focus of the play is on the Nativity and it concludes with a devout pageant, the intrigues among the shepherds, which dominate most of the play, are only tangentially related to the Nativity and are hugely entertaining in their own right.

In many mystery plays, the action moves quickly and easily between devotion and vulgar farce. *The Second Shepherds' Play* is more neatly divided and better controlled. The first part of the drama deals with the experiences of the shepherds, particularly with the conniving of Mak and his wife Gill. The dialogue of the three shepherds, as they complain of their lot, is full of cynical, comical reflections on their human situation. The plot of this section is simply the duping and their discovery of it. The tone is lighthearted, no great harm is done, and all is an excuse for good-humored repartee. The stanza of nine lines of different lengths accommodates short set speeches as well as rapid, witty interchanges.

The second part of the play, by way of contrast, involves the shepherds in gift-giving in the Christmas tableau. Ostensibly it is connected to the first part only by the presence of the same shepherds. Nevertheless, there are some surprising continuities. Despite the seriousness of the event, the poet maintains the same light touch and sensitivity to the mundane concerns of humankind. The tone, however, does not interfere with the solemnity of the scriptural occasion and with the appropriate decorum. Rather, the pageant gains a vitality all too often lacking in religious representations.

There is yet another connection between the two plots insofar as the story of Mak is a sort of secular parody of the Nativity. In the farcical plot, the shepherds do not give their gifts willingly but are conned out of them. When they finally approach the cradle, it is surrounded by the duplicitous Mak and Gill rather than Joseph and Mary, and the cradle contains not the Lamb of God but a real sheep. The main events of the play are a playful, but ultimately not blasphemous, secularization of the Christmas story. The Wakefield Master infused the Nativity into a pedestrian comedy and then transferred the joyous vitality of the farce to its solemn conclusion, thus stretching the mold of the mystery play in an unprecedented manner. As a result, *The Second Shepherds' Play* shares more with the kind of comedy that was to follow in the Renaissance than it does with its contemporaneous liturgical antecedents and neighbors.

"Critical Evaluation" by Edward E. Foster

Further Reading

Carpenter, Nan Cooke. "Music in the *Secunda Pastorum*." In *Medieval English Drama: Essays Critical and Contextual*, edited by Jerome Taylor and Alan H. Nelson. Chicago: University of Chicago Press, 1972. Asserts that music is an important element in the play's structure and a means of underscoring thematic statements.

Edminster, Warren. *The Preaching Fox: Festive Subversion in the Plays of the Wakefield Master*. New York: Routledge, 2005. Focuses on the festive elements in the plays, arguing that beneath their biblical surface these dramas make subversive comments about religion and politics. Maintains that the shepherds' complaints in *The Second Shepherds' Play* reflect the oppression of the peasantry by landlords and clergy.

Happé, Peter. *The Towneley Cycle: Unity and Diversity*. Cardiff: University of Wales Press, 2007. Detailed examination of the Towneley cycle, which includes *The Second Shepherds' Play*. Raises questions of authorship and the role of the Wakefield Master in the cycle's creation; provides a performance history; analyzes the cycle's language, style, and structure; and places the cycle in its historical and religious context.

Kinghorn, A. M. *Mediaeval Drama*. London: Evans Brothers, 1968. Devotes several pages to an analysis of the play, noting its humor, freshness, and realism.

Nelson, Alan H. "Some Configurations of Staging in Medieval English Drama." In *Medieval English Drama: Essays Critical and Contextual*, edited by Jerome Taylor and Alan H. Nelson. Chicago: University of Chicago Press, 1972. Examines scholarly understanding of the use of pageant wagons for the staging of mystery plays and discusses the unlikelihood of the plays' being staged in processions. Includes early illustrations.

Purdon, Liam O. *The Wakefield Master's Dramatic Art: A Drama of Spiritual Understanding*. Gainesville: University Press of Florida, 2003. Examines the Wakefield Master's contribution to the Towneley cycle by offering a detailed interpretation of the six plays and two revisions attributed to him. Focuses on the plays' treatment of the relationship between cooperatively serving God and serving self; maintains that cooperation is defined as either the proper use or the abuse of nature. Chapter 4 is devoted to a discussion of *The Second Shepherds' Play.*

Robinson, J. W. *Studies in Fifteenth-Century Stagecraft.* Kalamazoo: Medieval Institute Publications, Western Michigan University, 1991. One chapter contrasts the work of the Wakefield Master with that of the York realist. Examines *The Second Shepherds' Play* in detail, looking at structure, characterization, humor, and number imagery, among other topics.

Ross, Lawrence J. "Symbol and Structure in the *Secunda Pastorum.*" In *Medieval English Drama: Essays Critical and Contextual,* edited by Jerome Taylor and Alan H. Nelson. Chicago: University of Chicago Press, 1972. Argues for a unity that goes beyond the structural parallels of the two shepherds' plays to examine similarities in their language and the symbolic implications of the shepherds' gifts.

The Secret Agent
A Simple Tale

Author: Joseph Conrad (1857-1924)
First published: 1907
Type of work: Novel
Type of plot: Psychological realism
Time of plot: 1880's
Locale: London

Principal characters:
MR. VERLOC, a foreign secret agent
WINNIE, his English wife
STEVIE, her weak-minded brother
THE ASSISTANT COMMISSIONER, a London police official
CHIEF INSPECTOR HEAT
MR. VLADIMIR, First Secretary of an unnamed embassy
MICHAELIS and OSSIPON, anarchists

The Story:

Mr. Verloc is on his way to a certain foreign embassy, summoned there, to his astonishment and unease, at the unseemly hour of eleven in the morning. Ambling down the street, bulky and stolid, Mr. Verloc does not look very much like the agent provocateur that he is supposed to be. He keeps an obscure and ill-patronized little shop, behind which are quarters for his family. There he often entertains a group of London anarchists from whom he carefully keeps the secret that he is an embassy agent. He grumbles inwardly as he approaches the embassy, thinking how awkward it will be if any of his anarchist friends are to detect him in the act of entering such a place.

His appointment with Mr. Vladimir does nothing to improve his mood. In fact, his discontent deepens almost to a state of terror by the time of his departure. Mr. Verloc allowed himself to get comfortable, if not lazy, in the years since he settled in England as the agent of a foreign power; he never contemplated the possibility that he might lose his job. Now he finds himself being roundly abused and insulted for what First Secretary Vladimir is pleased to call his fatness, his slothfulness, and his general inefficiency. He is even

threatened with dismissal if he does not promptly promote some incident to upset English complacency. In short, Mr. Vladimir demands a dynamite outrage within a month and further specifies that it must be directed against some monument of learning and science—preferably the Greenwich Observatory.

Badly shaken, Mr. Verloc makes his way back to his shop in Soho. Rejoining his household in the room behind it, he manages to resume his usual demeanor of stolid reserve. When, soon after, his anarchist friends pay one of their calls, he betrays nothing to them of the frustration and fear that lurks behind his impassivity. He is not so successful with his wife. She is able to keep her own counsel, but she misses very little of what goes on about her.

Younger than her husband, Winnie Verloc married him for security rather than for love. It is not even her own security that she is concerned about but that of her unfortunate brother, whose passionate protector she is, ever since the days of their childhood. Now physically mature, Stevie remains childlike in other ways; he is easily excited and inarticulate, although generally softhearted and trusting. One of the people he trusts most is Mr. Verloc. His sister does a great deal to bring about this state of affairs; his mother, who is also being supported by Mr. Verloc, assists Winnie in impressing upon Stevie the idea that Mr. Verloc is good, that his wishes must be instantly carried out, and that he must be spared the slightest annoyance. Meanwhile, Mr. Verloc serenely goes his own way; insensitive to this anxious maneuvering to keep Stevie in his good graces, he largely ignores his brother-in-law even while tolerating his presence in the Verloc household.

To consolidate her son's position still further, the mother of Stevie and Winnie decides that before Mr. Verloc can tire of supporting both of his wife's relatives, she will move to an almshouse. Stevie misses her and begins moping. Seeking a remedy for her brother's moodiness, Winnie seizes upon what seems to her a happy expedient. The long walks of her husband, mysterious of purpose and destination, give Winnie an idea. Finding the right moment to make her request, she persuades her husband to take Stevie with him. To Winnie's gratification, this experiment soon becomes an established practice. With things apparently going so well, she sees no reason to object when Mr. Verloc makes a rather unexpected proposal regarding Stevie. Since Stevie is fond of Michaelis, an elderly anarchist who frequently visits the house, why not let the brother spend a few days with Michaelis at his retreat in the country?

Apparently pleased with this development, Stevie leaves to visit Michaelis, and the next few days pass without incident in the Verloc household. Late one afternoon, however, Mr. Verloc comes home from one of his walks more upset than Winnie ever saw him. He withdrew all of their money from the bank, and he mumbles vaguely about the necessity of leaving the country. Winnie tosses her head at this—he will go without her, she declares tartly. Mr. Verloc morosely ignores her wifely urgings that he eat his supper and change his slippers. He does not ignore, however, a distinguished-looking stranger who turns up presently and takes Mr. Verloc away. Winnie fails to recognize this caller as the Assistant Commissioner of London Police.

During their absence, a second stranger arrives. Winnie becomes more and more apprehensive upon learning that he is Chief Inspector Heat. When Heat learns that he was forestalled by his superior, he shows Winnie a cloth label bearing Stevie's name and address. Recognizing it as an identification tag placed in her brother's coat, she asks wildly where Heat found it. The return of Mr. Verloc, alone, interrupts their conversation. After Heat takes Mr. Verloc into another room, Winnie tries to overhear what they are saying. Almost mad with grief, she hears her husband tell how he trained Stevie to take part in a bombing attempt upon the Greenwich Observatory. Stevie, however, stumbled in the fog, exploding the bomb prematurely and blowing himself to bits.

After Heat leaves, Winnie faces her husband. White-faced and rigid, she hardly listens to his faltering explanation or his plan to turn state's evidence on the promise of a lighter penalty. When, exhausted, he finally drops on the couch, she seizes the carving knife and stabs him in the heart. Winnie runs aimlessly out into the dark and stumbles upon Comrade Ossipon, one of her husband's anarchist associates who has eyed her from time to time with admiration. After promising to help her, he discovers, with consternation, what occurred and that he might be implicated in the affair. Coaxing her onto a boat train, Ossipon waits until it starts to move; then he leaps off. With him, he takes the money that Winnie entrusted to his care.

A week passes. Ossipon does not enjoy his possession of Winnie's money; he feels heavily burdened by gloom and guilt. The feeling deepens as he reads a newspaper report of the suicide of a female passenger from a cross-channel boat. He is convinced that the last words of the dispatch will always haunt him since he alone knows the truth about Winnie's death, a deed that the newspaper calls a mystery of madness or of despair.

Critical Evaluation:

Although Joseph Conrad's literary reputation has been built largely on his nautical tales, such as *Lord Jim* (1990) and *Heart of Darkness* (1899), *The Secret Agent* marks a new creative direction for Conrad. It is a rather straightforward, realistic novel set in the heart of London, a city characterized by its filth, immorality, and despair. The novel has been identified as the prototypical serious spy novel. In the "Author's Note" written in 1920, thirteen years after the novel's original publication, Conrad acknowledges that he had been criticized "on the ground of sordid surroundings and the moral squalor of the tale." Populated by wretched political figures who believe in nothing but the absolute destruction of all principles and institutions, the world of the novel focuses upon the anarchical political plots disturbing 1880's England. The human condition, however, is of greater concern to Conrad.

A failed bombing of the Greenwich Observatory in 1894 served as the author's inspiration for the plot. Conrad recounts that he and fellow writer Ford Madox Ford recalled that one of the revolutionaries was "blown to bits for nothing even most remotely resembling an idea, anarchistic or other." Ford's casual observation, "Oh, that fellow was half an idiot. His sister committed suicide afterward," prompted Conrad's creation of Winnie Verloc and her half-witted brother, Stevie. Conrad admits that Mrs. Verloc is the imaginative center of his story. She and the city of London provide him with the appropriate forum for the discussion of lives of "utter desolation, madness and despair."

A mark of Conrad's fiction is his use of a controlling symbol that unifies the work. A symbolic scene also often functions as an expression of Conrad's themes. As the author pondered how he might bring together his ideas regarding politics, modern life, and the individuals caught up in it all, Conrad reports, "the vision of an enormous town presented itself, of a monstrous town . . . a cruel devourer of the world's light." London embodied for him the fragmentation, the isolation, the loneliness, and the inhumanity of contemporary society. The cab ride through the city as Winnie and Stevie accompany their mother to the almshouse is the scene that manifests all those qualities. The cabman's cruelty to his half-starved horse, Stevie's inappropriate outrage, and the indifference with which Winnie allows her mother to enter a life of loneliness and poverty point to Conrad's principal ideas. Other repeated symbols figure in the novel: the grotesque obesity of the main characters as a marker of immorality (only the Assistant Commissioner and Stevie—men somehow unaffected by the city's corrupting influences—are described as thin); the reference to human beings as body parts; Stevie's dismemberment; Stevie's endlessly drawing concentric circles, ironically the symbol of perfection.

Conrad's use of irony is another striking element in the novel. In many of his previous works, Conrad created a narrator—often similar to the *Heart of Darkness*'s Marlow figure—through whom he could speak. This narrator is merely a detached observer of the events he describes, uninvolved and distant from the people and the events of the story, enabling him to judge them. In *The Secret Agent*, the narrator's ironic tone allows him that distance. In the "Author's Note," Conrad observes that the "ironic treatment alone would enable me to say all I felt I would have to say in scorn as well as in pity." In mock-heroic language, he portrays the absurdity of the anarchists as they hold their regularly scheduled meetings in the security of Verloc's rather respectable and bourgeois household, accept their financial dependence upon generous aristocratic gentlewomen, and remain unaware of their absolute ignorance of the world they are supposedly out to save. This ironic scorn is not as appropriate in dealing with Winnie. In her case, Conrad uses distance and detachment, which prohibit the narrator from slipping into Dickensian sentimentality as she sacrifices her only love and hope for happiness—ironically with a young butcher, a foreshadowing of the role Winnie plays at the end of the novel—in ex-

change for her mother's and her brother's security. Even in Winnie's despair after murdering her husband, irony controls emotions. Comrade Ossipon, finally realizing that Winnie killed Verloc and that Verloc is not blown up as Ossipon thought, remarks how much she resembles her brother, whom he regards as degenerate. The idiot boy and his mad sister do not find a savior. Disgusted and fearful, Ossipon jumps from the moving train carrying Winnie to the Paris ferry, consigning her in her despair and utter loneliness to suicide. This story is told with a scrupulousness that appeals to judgment, not sentiment.

Conrad's greatest achievement in *The Secret Agent* is his vision of the human condition. His nineteenth century London teems with life and activity but is absolutely devoid of meaning and community. The Verlocs live in a tiny triangular island in a deserted Soho street cut off from the surrounding neighborhood. Although married for seven years, Winnie has never inquired into her husband's comings and goings, his friends, or his activities. She deems that life does not warrant too much looking into. Husband and wife hardly speak. Keeping Stevie quiet and occupied are of major concern to her. Winnie's mother wishes most to keep out of the way of Mr. Verloc, even to the point of consigning herself to the almshouse. There is no sense of social interaction, of communication, or of community. When in desperation Winnie seeks someone who might aid her escape from the gallows after she kills her husband, Winnie realizes her absolute aloneness in the world. She has no one to whom she can turn. Only coincidentally does she encounter Ossipon, who is on his way to visit the woman he thinks is recently widowed by the unfortunate accident in Greenwich Park. Ostensibly, he seeks to console, in truth he is looking for someone to support him. The one person Winnie thinks will help her only exploits her. Conrad's point in presenting this vision of modern life as fragmented and isolated is not to confirm it as the only possibility. Instead, he wishes to assert, through negative example, the ideal of a unified community.

"Critical Evaluation" by Laura Weiss Zlogar

Further Reading

Fleishman, Avrom. *Conrad's Politics: Community and Anarchy in the Fiction of Joseph Conrad*. Baltimore: Johns Hopkins University Press, 1967. The chapter on *The Secret Agent* discusses Conrad's portrayal of the modern world in fragmentation and his advocacy of social order and human community.

Hay, Eloise Knapp. *The Political Novels of Joseph Conrad: A Study*. Chicago: University of Chicago Press, 1963. Discusses how Conrad caricatures the aristocracy and mocks revolutionaries. Points out that Winnie Verloc suffers and faces despair alone, her condition made worse by anarchists.

Jordan, Elaine, ed. *Joseph Conrad*. New York: St. Martin's Press, 1996. An excellent introductory study of Conrad designed for students. The essays focus on three novels, *Heart of Darkness*, *Nostromo*, and *The Secret Agent*, analyzing these works from postcolonial feminist, Marxist, and other perspectives.

Kaplan, Carola M., Peter Mallios, and Andrea White, eds. *Conrad in the Twenty-First Century: Contemporary Approaches and Perspectives*. New York: Routledge, 2005. Collection of essays that analyze Conrad's depiction of postcolonialism, empire, imperialism, and modernism. "Reading *The Secret Agent* Now: The Press, the Police, and Premonition of Simulation" by Peter Lancelot Mallios focuses on this novel.

Karl, Frederick R. *A Reader's Guide to Joseph Conrad*. New York: Farrar, Straus & Giroux, 1969. Examines the novel's moral purpose, its characters, and its style. Argues that the book's concern is the moral corruption of all people.

Peters, John G. *The Cambridge Introduction to Joseph Conrad*. New York: Cambridge University Press, 2006. An introductory overview of Conrad, with information on his life, all of his works, and his critical reception.

Robert, Andrew Michael. *Conrad and Masculinity*. New York: St. Martin's Press, 2000. Uses modern theories about masculinity to analyze Conrad's work and explore the relationship of masculinity to imperialism and modernity. *The Secret Agent* is discussed in the chapter entitled "Masculinity, 'Woman' and Truth: *The Secret Agent*, *Under Western Eyes*, *Chance*."

Simmons, Allan H., and J. H. Stape, eds. *The Secret Agent: Centennial Essays*. New York: Rodopi, 2007. The thirteen essays offer various interpretations of *The Secret Agent*, including analyses of the representation of politics, death, London, Jews, degenerates, and opera in the novel.

Stape, J. H., ed. *The Cambridge Companion to Joseph Conrad*. New York: Cambridge University Press, 1996. Collection of essays discussing Conrad's life and analyzing his work, including discussions of Conradian narrative and his literary influences, and Conrad and the topics of imperialism and modernism. Jacques Berthoud's essay focuses on *The Secret Agent*.

Tillyard, E. M. W. "*The Secret Agent* Reconsidered." In *Conrad: A Collection of Critical Essays*, edited by Marvin Mudrick. Englewood Cliffs, N.J.: Prentice-Hall, 1966. Discusses Conrad's use of irony to create a necessary distance between the reader and the horrible lives of the characters.

Seeing Things

Author: Seamus Heaney (1939-   )
First published: 1991
Type of work: Poetry

Seeing Things, Seamus Heaney's tenth book of poems, is a collection united by the theme of movement between two worlds. The first and last poems in the book are translations; the opening poem is a translation of the "Golden Bough" passage from book 6 of the *Aeneid* (30-19 B.C.E.) that deals with obtaining the fruit on that bough to gain entrance to the underworld. The ending poem is a translation of a section in canto 3 of Dante's *Inferno* (c. 1320). It deals with crossing over to the underworld on Charon's boat. Thus the two translations that frame the book deal with access to the wonders and knowledge to be gained in another world. The poems in the book are clearly related to this introduction and conclu-

sion. They speak of ordinary things rendered in illuminating detail, which can lead to moments of transcendence or a crossing between two different worlds.

Seeing Things is divided into two distinct sections. In part 1, the lyrics are connected to the translations that deal with the entrance into another world; this is especially so in the first poem, "The Journey Back." The one who has returned from the other world is not an epic hero like Aeneas or Odysseus but a modern poet—Philip Larkin—who celebrated the ordinary world. Upon his return, he finds that "not a thing had changed." The dreary world of the street remains unaltered. He is also "Still my old self. Ready to knock one back." He may remain ordinary, "a-nine-to-five man," but he had "seen poetry." He had dwelt for a while in a world that is ruled by the imagination rather than the nine-to-five world. So there is some traffic between two very different worlds. It is a perfect introductory poem to the sequence.

"Markings" is a series of short poems on marking off things or defining them. For example, the first section speaks about the soccer field marked off by "four jackets," and the description is of an everyday event. It acquires a dream state as "Some limit had been passed," and the participants enter a world in which time is "extra, unforeseen and free." The terms come directly from the world of soccer, but they convey the sense of a magical moment beyond the confines of the ordinary world.

"Three Drawings" deals with common activities such as soccer and fishing; however, in stanzas 4 and 5 of "The Point," the ordinary game is, once more, transformed as the speaker asks the question "Was it you/ or the ball that kept going/ beyond you, amazingly/ higher and higher/ and ruefully free?" The freedom echoes "Markings," but now it is impossible to separate the boy and the ball; they have become one. It is a rueful freedom that evades capture and goes beyond the control of the boy or anyone else.

"Man and Boy" crisscrosses the worlds of father and son in its second section. A mower tells a boy to inform his father about his completed work on mowing the meadow. The boy becomes the poet's father who runs "at eye-level with weeds and stooks" to experience his father's death. The poet speaks of connecting with the "heat" and "quick legs" of that boy. The boy of the poem becomes the father carrying the boy who is now the poet. The generations are encapsulated in the crossing roles. The poet is the adult sympathizing with his then younger father. He is then turned into a child who is now described as "a witless elder escaped from the fire." The events that are described are commonplace, but the continual shifting of roles, a motion from one world to another, haunts human experience and is filled with wonder.

The title poem of the collection is divided into three parts. The second section, perhaps the most interesting, begins with a Joycean word, "Claritas." Joyce uses it in *A Portrait of the Artist as a Young Man* (1916) as one of the elements necessary for beauty; it is a "radiance," a revelation of the thing itself. Heaney then describes a scene of Jesus being baptized represented in a stone facade of the cathedral: "lines hard and thin and sinuous represent/ The flowing river." The scene is directly portrayed in its "utter visibility." However, the stone is "alive with what's invisible." Heaney then evokes an imaginative world of "stirred sand-grains" and "unshadowed stream"; the scene is created by the imagination rather than

by what is observed. The ending of the poem evokes another magical world beyond the facade on the cathedral but related to it. The heat is alive as it "wavered on the steps," and the "air we stood up to our eyes in wavered/ Like the zigzag hieroglyph for life itself." The most ordinary thing in this world—air—suddenly becomes alive and capable of symbolizing "life itself." It is a stunning poem and a perfect example of the method of the book as a whole.

"Pitchfork" is a detailed description of an ordinary farm tool; however, it reveals a world beyond it as well. The speaker of the poem asks an imagined observer to "see the shaft of a pitchfork sailing past/ Evenly, imperturbably through space." It is being controlled and aimed by the worker. That movement into space reveals a place where "perfection" can be imagined "Not in the aiming but the opening hand." The completion of this simple act leads to images of generosity and a "perfection" that can only be achieved by no longer trying to reach it or aim at it. This state clearly suggests the Zen achievement of mastery by not desiring.

"The Skylight" is another poem that plays with opposing perspectives. The woman in the poem desires "skylights" to open the roof and her world while the male speaker likes it "low and closed." He gives in and, when the slates are removed, "Sky entered and held surprise wide open." The speaker is not disgruntled by this change but transformed. He describes his new condition as a sick man who "Was lowered through the roof, had his sins forgiven,/ Was healed, took up his bed and walked away." The poem is humorous in tone, and while the speaker is renewed, he no longer is in possession of his snug room, as he is displaced after the transformation.

"Fosterling" is the last poem in the first part of the book. The speaker describes his affection for a picture of windmills with "heavy greenness" and filled with "in-placeness." The image of "heaviness" is transferred in the second stanza to the poet's own "heaviness of being." Poetry is now not "the music of what happens," as Heaney called it earlier, but "the doldrums of what happens." He speaks of having waited fifty years to "credit marvels," but with this faith all is transformed. The images are now of brightness and lightness; it is a time to be "dazzled." Faith in a world and experience beyond the ordinary transforms his perspective and opens a new world to him.

Part 2 is called "Squarings." The second poem in the "Lightenings" section is a definition of "lightenings." The speaker poses a few obvious definitions, such as "illumination," and then moves to a higher one. It is "A phenomenal instant when the spirit flares/ With pure exhilaration before death." This is immediately exemplified with the story of the good thief next to Christ on the cross. He is to be transported into a new world by the command of Jesus; however, he is still "untranslatable," since he remains "body racked." He aches for the transformation and has "nail craters" on his brain rather than his hands. The desired transformation is achieved by language, by the italicized words of Christ: "This Day thou shalt be with Me in Paradise." These words concentrate on the translation from one state to another by the means of language, the material of the poetic imagination.

Poem 18 plays with two types of life: bondage and freedom. A rope-man appears to a group of farmers with his wares to sell. He lives a life free of obligations and confinement. As a result, his life on the road "menaced them with freedoms/ They were going to turn their backs on." When the circle formed by the seller and the buyers breaks up, the farmers see the rope-man's "powerlessness" along with his supposed freedom. He breaks the magic circle that had been established and starts "loading." His freedom is only an illusion; his only power comes from his brief connection with those who have rejected freedom for a settled domestic life.

The second section of "lightenings" deals with an important element in Heaney's poetry. It describes a "reroofing" in elaborate detail. The verbs dominate: "roof it," "relocate the bedrock," "sink every impulse." There is an important turn in the last stanza. The poet-speaker demands that his place and art "Secure/ The bastion of sensation." It must deal with images, not ideas. So the last commands are "Do not waver/ Into language. Do not waver in it." The differences between the two are worth noting. To waver "into" language is to move away from things. To waver "in it" is to wallow in words and not what they are emblem of; it is to create an art that has no essential connection to the world.

Poem 8 is one of the best examples of the movement between two worlds. It describes an event recorded in the "annals" when a magical ship appeared to the monks of Clonmacnoise. The anchor of the ship "hooked itself on the altar rails." A crewman tries to release the anchor but fails to do so. The abbot then asks the monks to help because "This man can't bear our life here and will drown." The monks manage to free the ship "and the man climbed back/ Out of the marvellous as he had known it." An ordinary world is, to this mysterious traveler, "marvellous." What creates this sense of wonder is a change in perspective from one world to another. The poem is, perhaps, the most direct example of a movement between two worlds, a theme that dominates the book as a whole.

Poem 48 is the last in the sequence, and it unites many of the diverse worlds explored in the earlier poems. The poem plays with time and human knowledge of it. For example, what one anticipates in the future soon becomes the past, and one can only understand the present by the past. There is, apparently, a continual movement between states of time. After this definition, the poem shifts to images of a time "when light breaks over me" as it did on one occasion in the past. When that moment of illumination returns, "I'll be in step with what escaped me." The future is now united with present and past in a moment of true understanding and an obliteration of the earlier separateness. The book continually plays with different worlds that remain separate and distinct, and it is no accident that the last poem shows them coming together.

Seeing Things has an important place in Heaney's work as a whole. He began by writing poems about his rural background, then explored the political divisions that exist in Northern Ireland in his middle period, and in this work returns to a world of things. If those "things" are truly seen, they will be found to suggest other worlds and experiences related to but beyond them. It is his most rooted and his most transcendent book, but it also shows Heaney's refusal to be tied to one style or subject; he is continually renewing his style and his art.

James Sullivan

Further Reading

Bayley, John. "Seeing Things." Review of *Seeing Things*, by Seamus Heaney. *The New York Review of Books* 39 (June 25, 1992). An overview of the collection and its context within Heaney's oeuvre.

Bloom, Harold, ed. *Seamus Heaney*. Philadelphia: Chelsea House, 2002. An introductory analysis containing a biography, extracts from critical essays, thematic and structural analyses of Heaney's work, and an index of themes and ideas.

Garratt, Robert, ed. *Critical Essays on Seamus Heaney*. New York: G. K. Hall, 1995. Collection of essays, including analyses of Heaney's poetry, the feminine principle in his work, and comparisons of his poetry to that of Dante, William Butler Yeats, William Wordsworth, and James Joyce.

Heaney, Seamus. *Stepping Stones: Interviews with Seamus Heaney*. Edited by Dennis O'Driscoll. New York: Farrar, Straus and Giroux, 2008. In interviews conducted by O'Driscoll, Heaney reminisces about his life and discusses his poetry. Chapter 11 focuses on *Seeing Things*. Includes illustrations.

Jones, Chris. "Old English Escape Routes: Seamus Heaney, the Caedmon of the North." In *Strange Likeness: The Use of Old English in Twentieth Century Poetry.* New York: Oxford University Press, 2006. Examines how and why Heaney uses Old English language in his poetry.

Malloy, Catharine. "Seamus Heaney's *Seeing Things*: 'Retracing the Path Back.'" In *Seamus Heaney: The Shaping Spirit*, edited by Catharine Malloy and Phyllis Carey. Newark: University of Delaware Press, 1996. This analysis of *Seeing Things* focuses on Heaney's "artistic shaping," or how he refashions mythology, images, the influence of Dante and James Joyce, and other elements to create his unique poetry.

Nordin, Irene Gilsenan. *Crediting Marvels in Seamus Heaney's "Seeing Things."* Uppsala, Sweden: Uppsala University Press, 1999. Describes how, in *Seeing Things*, Heaney moves away from his earlier poetry, with its emphasis on the outer physicality of things, toward a concern with mental landscapes and the "thingness" of things. Recommended for advanced students of literature or philosophy.

Tobin, Daniel. *Passage to the Center: Imagination and the Sacred in the Poetry of Seamus Heaney.* Lexington: University Press of Kentucky, 1999. An examination of Heaney's poetry from the perspective of religion. Chapter 9 focuses on *Seeing Things*.

Seize the Day

Author: Saul Bellow (1915-2005)
First published: 1956
Type of work: Novel
Type of plot: Domestic realism
Time of plot: 1950's
Locale: New York City

Principal characters:
TOMMY WILHELM, the desperate protagonist
DR. ADLER, Tommy's father
DR. TAMKIN, Tommy's "mentor"

The Story:

Tommy Wilhelm descends from the twenty-third floor of the Gloriana Hotel and enters the lobby in search of his father. At the reception desk he collects the mail, buys a newspaper, and is told that his father, Dr. Adler, is already in the dining room having breakfast. Tommy braces himself to meet his father; a host of recollections bursting upon him. He is painfully aware of his father's contempt for him. The old man—now in his seventies—considers Tommy a failure.

In his middle forties, his marriage on the rocks, Tommy does not consider himself a failure, although his personal life is in shambles. Besides walking out on his wife, he lost his job at Rojax, is running into debt, and is learning about alimony payments. Tommy understands, vaguely, that part of his problem is that he is a dreamer, a man who trusts too many people and who has too little common sense.

He remembers his first failure, that of trying to be an actor in Hollywood. He trusted a so-called talent scout named Maurice Valence. He dropped out of college and went off to California on Valence's prompting. Tommy should have known that Valence was too anxious to assert his legitimacy,

and that, far from having a connection with the film business, he was just a fast-talking con artist who organized a ring of call girls. This first failure—one of many Tommy is to endure over the years—was the beginning of his father's low opinion of him.

His father, Dr. Adler, is having breakfast with a man named Perls, and Tommy suspects that the old man is trying to avoid him or to avoid being alone with him. Adler introduces Tommy to Perls and the conversation eventually centers on Tommy. His father is bragging about Tommy being an important man at Rojax, and Tommy suddenly realizes that his father is trying to promote himself as a father rather than praise Tommy as a son. Tommy is aggrieved as he hears himself reviewing his life story to this stranger. He is especially sensitive to Perls's and Adler's suspicions about Tommy's association with Dr. Tamkin. Tamkin, they declare, is either crazy or a crook, and Tommy is foolish for even talking to him, much less trusting the fellow. Tommy defends Tamkin, but in his heart he fears he has blundered in giving Tamkin power of attorney over his funds.

Laughing over Tamkin's schemes, Perls leaves the dining room. Alone with his father, Tommy speaks of his personal suffering—his marital problems and his impending financial ruin. By all this his father is unmoved, impatient with this apparent show of weakness and failure in his son. Adler rebukes Tommy, blaming him for his problems and advising him to develop a better sense of self-discipline.

Finally, when Tommy asks for some money, even in the form of a loan, Adler refuses, insisting that he does not want to get involved with Tommy's problems: He simply wants to be left alone.

On the way out Tommy meets Tamkin. Like Valence, Tamkin is a fast-talking con artist, but, unlike Valence, Tamkin raises the con to a transcendent level. His palaver is incessant, a convincing mixture of psychological insight and crass trickery. He convinced Tommy to invest his last seven hundred dollars in the commodities market and to make Tamkin the custodian of the funds. The chief commodity, lard, is now falling, and Tommy is sickened at the thought that he will soon be bankrupt. Meanwhile Tamkin comforts, cajoles, and wheedles. He lectures Tommy on the evils of money and of the pursuit of money, which is a form of aggression. Tamkin patronizes Tommy, telling him that neither Tamkin nor Tommy needs the money, that it is all a game. Tamkin seems to offer Tommy sympathy and understanding. Tommy's head distrusts Tamkin and his wiles, but Tommy's heart accepts the possibility of Tamkin's being honest.

Tommy and Tamkin are soon sitting in the commodities office, watching the numbers flash on the board. All the while, Tamkin is talking and talking. Despite all of his lies, falsehoods, and chicanery, Tamkin hits upon a truth. Seeing Tommy's agony of spirit, Tamkin advises him not to "marry suffering," to cease blaming himself and complaining of his wife's emasculating influence, and to try to be happy. Tommy needs to live for the here and now, to "live for today."

By the afternoon, lard falls and Tommy, staring at the commodities board in the brokerage office, sees himself wiped out. He looks for Tamkin, searching him out even in the bathroom, but the old charlatan is gone, disappeared, and Tommy finds himself alone, holding back tears.

In the final section, Tommy makes a desperate appeal to his father for help. He finds the old man in a steam room, enjoying the pleasures of a rubdown. Trying to keep his self-respect, Tommy pleads for help, not just for money this time, but for a kind word, a sense of understanding, comfort. None of these is his father able to give. In fact, Adler becomes irate. Furious, he calls Tommy a slob and tells him to get out of his life. Angry and hurt, Tommy goes out and receives his final rebuff from his former wife, Margaret. On the phone

she scolds him for sending his child-support check late and adds further abuse to his father's caustic rejection. Overwhelmed, Tommy wanders at last into a funeral chapel. There, unknown to the mourners, he weeps aloud for the dead, weeping for himself and for the death of love and human sympathy.

Critical Evaluation:

Seize the Day presents a character who is caught up in the impersonal American quest for money and success, yet who cannot ignore his own need for personal respect and compassion. A middle-aged Tommy Wilhelm is faced with the need to make money and to avoid looking like a failure, yet he longs for the solace of his father's approval. Tommy wants to listen to his heart, to trust even when that trust is foolish, as in his relationship with Dr. Tamkin. Tommy is an example of the long-suffering sensitive victim who, despite life's hardships, remains basically noble in a fragmented world. Tommy's plight is darkly comic—the poor soul who succumbs to the wiles of the fast-talking con artist and who is ultimately bereft of everything.

Tommy is a representative example of Saul Bellow's typical hero, a man trapped in the contradiction between desire and limitation, aspiration and ability. Such a hero experiences a conflict between head and heart. He is unable to reconcile the disparity between knowing and feeling. Tommy knows, for example, that Tamkin is not to be trusted, but he wants in his heart to trust him. Tommy sees his father's mean-spiritedness and contempt, but he wants his father's sympathy nevertheless.

Characteristically, Bellow depicts this contradiction not in naturalistic terms, as in the works of many of his contemporaries, but from a distinctly comic point of view. In this connection it is interesting to note that Bellow himself translated from the Yiddish the famous short story by Isaac Bashevis Singer, "Gimpel the Fool" (1953), a work spiritually akin to Bellow's point of view. Gimpel is the schlemiel, the loser with a soul, whose place in heaven is assured by his genuine humility, his acceptance of the essential holiness of life. Bellow's typical hero is, like Tommy, an intellectual schlemiel, aggrieved by the madness of contemporary life but unable to submit to it with the serenity of Gimpel. Tommy suffers, like Gimpel, not only because the world is pitiless and mad but also because he refuses to accept its madness, striving, instead, for some humanistic ideal. He wants sympathy; he demands it as a human being. He is thwarted by his father's heartlessness and by Tamkin's deceit.

Seize the Day is rich in character portrayals. Tamkin is a mix of the comic and the villainous. He cheats Tommy not only out of his money but also out of his beliefs in the possibility of honesty. Dr. Adler, whose name in German means "eagle," is a kind of predator, preying on his son's weakness as a way of nourishing his own self-image. Lofty, aristocratic, fiercely aloof, Adler divorces himself from human feelings.

In its concision, its taut depiction of character and event, and in its total immersion in its New York locale, *Seize the Day* is one of Bellow's outstanding novels. It serves as a good introduction to his work, containing the essential theme of the hero in moral conflict with the values of his society and told in a prose that combines erudition with slang, the analytically precise with the casually colloquial.

Edward Fiorelli

Further Reading

Atlas, James. *Bellow: A Biography*. New York: Random House, 2000. Atlas spent ten years working on this book, which some critics consider the definitive biography of Bellow. Atlas is particularly good at finding parallels between the tone of Bellow's novels and his mood at the time he wrote them.

Bach, Gerhard, ed. *The Critical Response to Saul Bellow*. Westport, Conn.: Greenwood Press, 1995. Collection of reviews and essays about Bellow's work that were published from the 1940's through the 1990's, including pieces by Delmar Schwartz, Robert Penn Warren, Alfred Kazin, and Granville Hicks. Contains articles about all of the major novels.

Braham, Jeanne. *A Sort of Columbus*. Athens: University of Georgia Press, 1984. Examines Bellow's novels as centering on the theme of discovery and how his heroes pursue a personal vision tempered by, yet transcending, the American experience.

Clayton, John. *Saul Bellow: In Defense of Man*. 2d ed. Bloomington: Indiana University Press, 1979. Discusses Bellow's characters as alienated and paranoid, yet acting in such a way as to affirm the brotherhood of man.

Codde, Philippe. *The Jewish American Novel*. West Lafayette, Ind.: Purdue University Press, 2007. Codde explains the reasons for the unprecedented success of novels written by Bellow and other Jewish American authors after World War II.

Eichelberger, Julia. "Renouncing the World's Business in *Seize the Day*." In *Prophets of Recognition: Ideology and the Individual in Novels by Ralph Ellison, Toni Morrison, Saul Bellow, and Eudora Welty*. Baton Rouge: Louisiana State University Press, 1999. Eichelberger finds similarities in *Seize the Day* and post-World War II American novels by Ellison, Morrison, and Welty. She maintains that in each novel "individuals seek a place within a public world" and demonstrate "suspicious humanism," or the ability to resist "dehumanizing cultural beliefs" and recognize each person's "own innate human value."

Kramer, Michael P., ed. *New Essays on "Seize the Day."* New York: Cambridge University Press, 1998. Contains six essays analyzing *Seize the Day*, including discussions about teaching the novel as a work of ethnic fiction, the cultural contexts of the novel, and "Death and the Post-Modern Hero/Schlemiel."

Newman, Judie. *Saul Bellow and History*. New York: St. Martin's Press, 1984. Provides a summary of critical opinions of Bellow's religious and psychological views of life. Newman sees Bellow as a novelist concerned with the effect of history on his protagonists.

Pifer, Ellen. *Saul Bellow Against the Grain*. Philadelphia: University of Pennsylvania Press, 1990. Argues that each of Bellow's heroes is in conflict with himself. The conflict between reason and religion ends with the hero's affirmation of a metaphysical or intuitive truth.

Sejanus His Fall

Author: Ben Jonson (1573-1637)
First produced: 1603; first published, 1605
Type of work: Drama
Type of plot: Tragedy
Time of plot: First century C.E.
Locale: Rome

Principal characters:
EMPEROR TIBERIUS
SEJANUS, his corrupt favorite
EUDEMUS, a physician and beautician
LIVIA, Tiberius's daughter-in-law
ARRUNTIUS, a righteous and indignant Roman citizen
SILIUS,
SABINUS,
CORDUS, and
LEPIDUS, noble Romans hostile to Tiberius's corrupt
  government
MACRO, a fiendish tool of the emperor

The Story:

Silius and Sabinus, respectable Roman citizens of the old stamp, meet and discuss the corruption of Tiberius's court. Both admire Agrippina, the widow of Germanicus. Although conscious of the prevalence of spies controlled by the emperor's loathsome favorite Sejanus, they show no personal fear. Arruntius and the historian Cordus, men of their kind, join them. Two of Sejanus's spies watch and plan to entrap these men devoted to freedom. Sejanus enters with a group of hangers-on and suitors. Arruntius and his friends observe the favorite with scorn. One of Sejanus's followers presents a suit from Eudemus, the physician of Livia, wife of the emperor's son Drusus. Sejanus sends for Eudemus privately and lays plans with him for the seduction of Livia.

When Tiberius, followed by Drusus, makes a public appearance, Sejanus bathes him in fulsome flattery, to the disgust of Arruntius and his friends. The emperor answers with a devious, hypocritical speech. After his departure, Drusus and Sejanus clash, and Drusus strikes him. Sejanus remains alone, promising himself to add revenge to his ambitious motives for the destruction of Drusus. Having found Livia a willing victim of corruption, Sejanus plots with her and Eudemus to poison Drusus. Sejanus works on the fears of Tiberius to persuade him to destroy Agrippina and the sons of Germanicus, who after Drusus are heirs to the empire; he also warns the emperor of the danger of Silius, Sabinus, and others. Tiberius consents to call the senate and to allow Sejanus to handle the destruction of Silius, his wife Sosia, and Cordus, leaving Sabinus and Arruntius for the future.

Arruntius and his friends, hearing that Drusus is dying, recalls the public blow given to Sejanus. Later, the senate convenes, with Drusus's death on all lips. Tiberius enters, to the amazement of the senators, who assumed grief would keep him from a political function. Tiberius delivers one of his hypocritical orations, punctuated by low-voiced comments from the undeceived Arruntius and his friends. Suddenly, without preliminary warning, Sejanus's puppets accuse Silius of treason. Recognizing the tyrant's trap and his own hopeless situation, Silius recalls his important services to Rome in peace and in war, formally accuses Tiberius of fraudulent conduct, and, mocking the tyrant's power, stabs himself. Tiberius hypocritically expresses regret that he is thus deprived of an opportunity to show mercy to an erring subject. Cordus is next accused and sentenced to prison. His books, histories of the Roman Republic, are sentenced to be burned. Arruntius growls at the senate's "brainless diligence" in attempting to destroy truth by book-burning.

At the conclusion of the senate meeting, Tiberius and Sejanus plan future moves to strengthen their hands; flushed with power and triumph, however, Sejanus makes a major mistake by asking to be allowed to marry Livia. Startled into suspicion, the emperor grunts ominously, then launches into a devious speech pointing out the dangers of such a match. Sejanus hastily withdraws his request but, still blinded by overconfidence, he urges Tiberius's retirement to Capri. Alone, he gloats over past successes and looks toward future triumphs, including the overthrow of the emperor himself. Tiberius, thoroughly suspicious, begins to work with a new tool, the villainous Macro, to undermine Sejanus. While the emperor retires to Capri, Macro begins his work by advising Caligula, one of the sons of Germanicus, to surrender himself to Tiberius, saying that he fears the plots of the powerful Sejanus.

The next victim of Sejanus is Sabinus. Arruntius is moved to wonder why Jove did not strike down the impious and ruthless favorite. Sejanus, having reached a dangerous state of intoxication with his own greatness, thinks himself superior not only to men but also to gods. Ominous events occur, but Sejanus scorns superstition and remains confident of success in his march to absolute power. Macro, with authority from Tiberius, causes the senate to convene again, apparently to confer new honors on Sejanus. Macro himself remains in the background but assumes control of the guards. As the senators gather for the session, Arruntius and Lepidus, a good old Roman unspotted by corruption, stand aside to observe the flatterers eager to get close enough to Sejanus to give his ears confidential whispers. Great rivalry follows to see who can sit close to him during the proceedings. When the senators are seated, a letter from the emperor is read aloud to them. Bit by bit this masterpiece of political deviousness shifts the majority of the hearers from fulsome support of Sejanus to suspicion, fear, and hostility. Flatterers who clamor to get near the favorite hastily shift their seats, all but a gouty one who struggles in vain to rise, much to the delight of Arruntius at seeing gout keep the flatterer "miserably constant." Macro enters, supported by the guards, and drags Sejanus from his seat, heaping violent personal indignities on him. Sejanus is hurried away to execution. Later reports tell of his body's being torn to pieces by the mob. Most horrible of all, the children of Sejanus are torn from his divorced wife, Apicata, and are killed. In agony and fury, Apicata accuses Livia and Eudemus of poisoning Drusus. Their death sentences are foretold.

Arruntius and Lepidus know that Rome exchanges one instrument of evil for another, as Macro is no improvement on Sejanus, and the venomous, reptilian emperor remains untouched. Arruntius, however, delivers a valedictory prophecy to all tyrants and, using the fall of Sejanus as an example, warns of the inevitability and terror of their destruction.

Critical Evaluation:

Ben Jonson, the author of *Sejanus His Fall*, was perhaps the foremost comic dramatist of the Elizabethan and Jacobean periods after William Shakespeare. Jonson was the primary purveyor of the "comedy of humours," in which a character possessed with a mania or obsessive trait drives the social order into comic disorder. Later in his career, Jonson wrote dark, moral comedies tinged with irony. *Volpone: Or, The Fox* (1605) and *The Alchemist* (1610) are two of Jonson's comic masterpieces.

Although Jonson is known primarily for his comedies, he ventured into tragedy. In his theory of tragedy, Jonson was a classicist. Classical tragedy focuses on the unities of time, place, and action. The classical tragedy should take place in a one-day period, be located in one place, and follow a few characters through a singular plot line. Classical tragedies have a chorus or group of characters who comment on the action, and they refrain from violent action onstage. Also, the classical hero is a noble person who falls after an error in judgment or as a result of some character flaw.

Sejanus His Fall was Jonson's first attempt at tragedy. It was performed in 1603 by the King's Men at the Globe Theatre. According to some sources, Shakespeare may have played the part of Tiberius. *Sejanus His Fall*, however, is far from a classical tragedy. In his preface to the play Jonson apologizes for not upholding the unity of time, but Jonson does more than break with this one unity. Instead of focusing on one day, the action in *Sejanus His Fall* spreads over several months. The locales change frequently. The cast is an assortment of characters caught in multiple sequences. The play lacks a chorus, and violent actions are graphically depicted on stage. Jonson could not hold to classical principles, and entertain Elizabethans, in writing his tragedy. Ironically, the play was not well received and was misunderstood by its contemporary audience. Today, it is seldom revived.

Nevertheless, *Sejanus His Fall* is worthy of critical acclaim. It is modern in its investigations of the machination of power, and it is deeply rooted in the primitive traditions of tragedy, which focus on the ritualistic dismemberment of a scapegoat figure. The greatness of the play does not lie in character portrayal, for Tiberius is the only character with complexity. Sejanus has no richness to his personality; he is not an interesting villain. The good characters, such as Lepidus and Arruntius, function primarily as choral commentators, comparing the past with the present; they are either ineffectual or impotent. Rather, our interest is drawn to the contest between two supreme Machiavellians, Tiberius and Sejanus, and to Jonson's suggestion that a corrupt and decadent society will inevitably produce a Tiberius and a Sejanus.

Jonson's drama brings the history of the Roman Empire into a thoroughly modern framework. His story is of a totalitarian machine ruled by a treacherous bureaucracy that is based on fear, betrayal, and deception. His characters lack psychological depth because they have no sense of self. They are victims of a historical process in which the machinery of the state turns the people against themselves. The times are out of joint, and there are no heroes or antiheroes to set them right. No grand avenger who upholds a sense of personal honor ever arises to redress the wrongs of Tiberius. Germanicus is mourned, but none of his kin has the will or the drive to seek retribution. Agrippina is so crushed that she can only tell her sons to suffer nobly. Even a hesitant avenger would be welcome in the cold world of spies. The state apparatus controls the populace thoroughly by means of fear of reprisal and the expediency of self-interest. There is not even a strong villain, for example a Richard III, to gloat.

Rome is ruled by Sejanus, a petty politician who lives in a world where evil is reduced to the trivial. Living in a world of soulless men who are forever seeking to follow the political tide, Sejanus uses uncertainty to control his followers. His supporters are honored one day and murdered the next. His network of spies makes the populace afraid. The emperor, the legitimate authority, hides behind his henchman, Sejanus. The honorable soldier, Silius, who fought for emperor and country, is discarded. Senators are fearful and silent. The good citizen, Lepidus, ignores the terror in order to save his own life. Even the gods are silent. Jonson vividly depicts the totalitarian state.

In this society even ostensibly free men are bought and sold. Sejanus puts political policy above blood ties. Macro sells out his own family. Honor, glory, family, kinship, loyalty, public responsibility—nothing has any meaning in the world of the treacherous bureaucracy. Power is centralized in a figurehead who passes out favors liberally and destroys his enemies. He, too, is a part of the system and just as replaceable as those he eliminates.

This usurpation of the body politic leads to the destruction of individuality. The individual becomes a subject of the power structure. In the play's imagery, the loss of the sense of self is seen in the fragmentation of the body. Faces are depicted as shifting; tongues are described as cleft; people's lips are divided from their hearts. The body of the individual and of the body politic suffers a condition in which body parts are out of control. The body also becomes a saleable commodity in a prostituted world order of deceptive transactions. Sejanus, once a male prostitute, figuratively prostitutes the whole body politic. In the end, the body imagery in the play is pronounced in the dismemberment of Sejanus, as the mob tears him to pieces in the reenactment of the ancient ritual of the expulsion of a scapegoat. In Jonson's bleak tragedy, however, expelling the source of evil is not enough. The whole system of the state is caught in a mechanism of repetition, evoking the traditional motif of the wheel of fortune. One devious bureaucrat replaces another.

Two traditional conventions inform the play: In addition to the motif of the revolving wheel of fortune is the classical idea of *hubris*. Together they cause Sejanus's fall. He falls when he is at the summit of success; his decline begins in act 3 when he suggests to Tiberius the marriage to Livia. These two somewhat contradictory ideas are suggested within the play: that Sejanus's fall is fated because everyone will eventually fall; and that Sejanus's pride, in his desire to become a god, caused his fall.

The great pessimism of *Sejanus His Fall* lies in the knowledge that Sejanus's downfall will lead to neither a personal renewal nor a cleansing of the state. Rome without Sejanus will be no less corrupt than Rome with him. Jonson creates in this play a nightmare world in which the body politic is in pieces and the state mechanism of treachery leads to a vicious circle of violence and suppression. Considered a minor and obscure work of Jonson, *Sejanus His Fall* remains powerful drama, rooted in ancient ritual and contemporary in its view of repressive totalitarian states.

"Critical Evaluation" by Paul Rosefeldt

Further Reading

Barrish, Jonas A. Introduction to *Sejanus*, by Ben Jonson. New Haven, Conn.: Yale University Press, 1965. Argues that Jonson moves between closet drama and popular theater but shows a departure from other contemporary playwrights by remaining faithful to his sources. Demonstrates how Jonson coats his history in a morality play format and reduces his characters to moral types.

Donaldson, Ian. *Jonson's Magic Houses: Essays in Interpretation.* New York: Oxford University Press, 1997. Donaldson, a Jonson scholar, provides new interpretations of Jonson's personality, work, and literary legacy.

Engel, Wilson F. "The Iron World of *Sejanus*." *Renaissance Drama* 11 (1980): 95-114. Shows how Jonson used a diverse collection of classical sources but wove them into a dynamic and coherent plot, producing a drama that vividly depicts the viciousness of a political age.

Harp, Richard, and Stanley Stewart, eds. *The Cambridge Companion to Ben Jonson.* New York: Cambridge University Press, 2000. Collection of essays about Jonson's life and career, including analyses of his comedies and late plays, a description of London and its theaters during Jonson's lifetime, and an evaluation of his critical heritage.

Lever, J. W. *The Tragedy of State.* New York: Methuen, 1971. Devotes a chapter to Roman tragedy, covering Jonson's *Sejanus His Fall.* Jonson is seen as different from other playwrights of his time in his concern for political instead of heroic personalities.

Loxley, James. *A Sourcebook.* New York: Routledge, 2002. An introductory overview of Jonson's life and work, particularly useful for students. Part 1 provides biographical information and places Jonson's life and work within the context of his times; part 2 discusses several works, including *Sejanus His Fall*; part 3 offers critical analysis of the themes in his plays, the style of his writing, and a comparison of his work to that of William Shakespeare.

McEvoy, Sean. *Ben Jonson, Renaissance Dramatist*. Edinburgh: Edinburgh University Press, 2008. McEvoy analyzes all of Jonson's plays, attributing their greatness to the playwright's commitment to the ideals of humanism during a time of authoritarianism and rampant capitalism in England. Chapter 3 focuses on his Roman tragedies, *Sejanus* and *Catiline*.

Sweeney, John G., III. "*Sejanus* and the People's Beastly Rage." *English Literary History* 48 (1981): 61-82. Shows how Jonson wrote a play that distances itself from the audience and does not give the viewers any characters with whom they may identify.

Self-Portrait in a Convex Mirror

Author: John Ashbery (1927-   )
First published: 1975
Type of work: Poetry

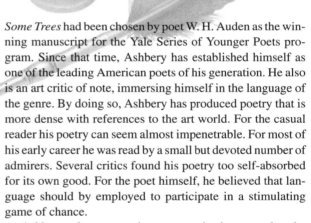

For John Ashbery, there is no memory or experience that can be taken at face value. There always exists more than meets the proverbial eye. The title poem of the collection *Self-Portrait in a Convex Mirror* is considered one of the most remarkable long contemporary poems written in the latter half of the twentieth century. It is an extraordinary autobiographical construction, though not traditional autobiography. Ashbery has no intention of revealing salacious details of his personal life. He is more concerned with revealing what cannot be truly revealed.

The title of Ashbery's collection, and the poem of the same name, is named for a Renaissance painting by Italian artist Parmigianino, whose *Self-Portrait in a Convex Mirror* (1524) has been recognized as a brilliant work of art. Ashbery was inspired by this painting after seeing it in person for the first time in 1959. In this collection, Ashbery ponders the nature of self-portraits and what they expose about the subject. He understands that distortion is inevitable, especially for a portrait that is revealed through a convex mirror. He takes aim at what may merely be an illusion, a beautiful illusion, yet not the truth that poets are supposedly in need of discovering. Ashbery concludes that words may not be able to fully describe what the poet senses about the nature of a painting, or about the nature of him- or herself. In a larger sense, then, Ashbery is contemplating how art itself is to be perceived.

In 1976, Ashbery was awarded a Pulitzer Prize, a National Book Award, and a National Book Critics Circle Award for his *Self-Portrait in a Convex Mirror*. Ashbery first burst onto the poetry scene in the 1950's. His 1956 collection

Some Trees had been chosen by poet W. H. Auden as the winning manuscript for the Yale Series of Younger Poets program. Since that time, Ashbery has established himself as one of the leading American poets of his generation. He also is an art critic of note, immersing himself in the language of the genre. By doing so, Ashbery has produced poetry that is more dense with references to the art world. For the casual reader his poetry can seem almost impenetrable. For most of his early career he was read by a small but devoted number of admirers. Several critics found his poetry too self-absorbed for its own good. For the poet himself, he believed that language should by employed to participate in a stimulating game of chance.

Ashbery, whose poetry is a maze, an intricate puzzle to be solved, has taken pride in his creative unpredictability and his unorthodox approach to poetry. By the early 1970's, he had published several provocative volumes, including *The Tennis Court Oath* (1962), *Rivers and Mountains* (1966), and *Three Poems* (1972). From the mid-1950's to the mid-1960's, he lived in Paris. During his Paris years, Ashbery absorbed everything French, including the language, the culture, the art, and the poetry. His poetry was dramatically altered by his years abroad. He was influenced by everything around him, including both "high" and "low" culture. Because of the breadth of his knowledge and the playfulness of his poetic approach, the poems incorporate a vast array of subjects. Because he is not tied to any one style, Ashbery demands much from himself and his readership. Taking inspiration from the poetry of the French Symbolists and the Surrealists and from the art of the French Impressionists and the American abstract expressionists, Ashbery built a poetic form that is both bold and, to a certain degree, reckless.

At first glance it seems that Ashbery throws together images with total abandon. It can be argued that chance and randomness play a major part in his poetic philosophy. For many critics and readers, Ashbery had been sabotaging American poetry, corrupting the nobility of what poetry can do. With *Self-Portrait in a Convex Mirror*, he forcefully and strategically presents a major collection that is chance personified. For many readers, poems are supposed to have resolutions. For much of the twentieth century, however, artists and writers found the idea of resolution to be a false god, a false hope. Turmoil was the order of the day, and art forms came to reflect the chaos that seemed to pervade life in the twentieth century. Ashbery felt compelled to jettison conventional poetry. The burning desire to take a subject and shape it into a presentable whole was not going to be his way of being a poet. For him, there really was no need to pursue, or to be the hunter as poet. Whatever entered his senses, his mind, and his life became the materials for his poems.

For this unique approach, Ashbery was considered a traitor to the genre. He became the outcast, the bad boy, the poet who deserted the people. While this trend in American poetry already had begun through such adventurous writers as Gertrude Stein, T. S. Eliot, and Wallace Stevens, Ashbery seemed to be taking poetry beyond the pale. While Stein is famous for her line "a rose is a rose is a rose," it could be said that Ashbery would change it to "a riddle is a riddle is a riddle." For his poetry, he incorporates the colloquial and weaves it together with impenetrable metaphysical phrasings. Whatever he has come across is likely to find its way into his verse.

Self-Portrait in a Convex Mirror includes thirty-five provocative and puzzling poems. He opens the collection with "As One Put Drunk into the Packet-Boat." In the second stanza the reader gets a glimpse into the idea of watching, of being receptive:

> New sentences were starting up. But the summer
> Was well along, not yet past the mid-point
> But full and dark with the promise of that fullness,
> That time when one can no longer wander away
> And even the least attentive fall silent
> To watch the thing that is prepared to happen.

There is reward in waiting, in standing pat. The reader who fights against Ashbery receives no reward at all. The poems are appropriate for those who open their minds to the possibility of a fresh course.

"Forties Flick" shows Ashbery's love for the cinema. He appreciates that artificiality can stand in for reality. He is intrigued by images in the dark.

> They had gone away into the plot of the story,
> The "art" part—knowing what important details
>   to leave out
> And the way character is developed. Things too real
> To be of much concern, hence artificial, yet now all
>   over the page,
> The indoors with the outside becoming part of you
> As you find you had never left off laughing at death,
> The background, dark vine at the edge of the porch.

In the poem "Mixed Feelings," Ashbery introduces the "pleasant smell of frying sausages" and instantly reflects on a photograph of girls who seem to be "lounging around/ An old fighter bomber, circa 1942 vintage." He puts himself in their lives and wonders what it would be like to meet them, but he is not "going to/ Waste any more time thinking about them." He is going to forget about them

> Until some day in the not too distant future
> When we meet possibly in the lounge of
>   a modern airport,
> They looking astonishingly young and fresh
>   as when this picture was made
> But full of contradictory ideas, stupid ones
>   as well as
> Worthwhile ones, but all flooding the surface
>   of our minds
> As we babble about the sky and the weather and
>   the forests of change.

The collection's title poem demands that the reader not look for easy explanations. The poet does not provide a comprehensible whole, and his work is more of an extended jumble in a hall of mirrors. A poem is never less than striking, yet it never provides an image one can trust. As Ashbery writes,

> Each person
> Has one big theory to explain the universe
> But it doesn't tell the whole story
> And in the end it is what is outside him
> That matters, to him and especially to us
> Who have been given no help whatever
> In decoding our own man-size quotient and must rely
> On second-hand knowledge.

Even though *Self-Portrait in a Convex Mirror* is Ashbery at his most accessible, he remains a poet who believes that creating a poem is far more important than the concrete conclusions that might be discerned by close readings.

Jeffry Jensen

Further Reading

Bloom, Harold, ed. *John Ashbery*. 1985. Reprint. Broomall, Pa.: Chelsea House, 2005. A solid collection of essays that delves into the way Ashbery makes poetry. Part of the Bloom's Major Poets series.

Herd, David. *John Ashbery and American Poetry*. New York: Palgrave, 2000. In addition to a balanced overview of the poet's career, Herd includes a striking discussion of the poem "Self-Portrait in a Convex Mirror."

Lehman, David, ed. *Beyond Amazement: New Essays on John Ashbery*. 1980. Reprint. Ithaca, New York: Cornell University Press, 2002. Several essays in this edited collection on Ashbery examine, among other topics, his approach to writing poetry, his metaphysical subjects, and his poetic "painting." Also includes an introduction to his poetry.

Shapiro, David. *John Ashbery: An Introduction to the Poetry*. New York: Columbia University Press, 1979. A thorough introduction to the poet that includes a detailed analysis of the title poem. Somewhat dated, but still useful.

Stamelman, Richard. "Poetry and Art Criticism in Ashbery's 'Self-Portrait in a Convex Mirror.'" *New Literary History* 15 (Spring, 1984): 607-630. An invigorating discussion of Ashbery's poem as it relates to the merging of poetry and art criticism.

The Self-Tormentor

Author: Terence (c. 190-159 B.C.E.)
First produced: Heautontimorumenos, 163 B.C.E. (English translation, 1598)
Type of work: Drama
Type of plot: Comedy
Time of plot: Fourteenth century B.C.E.
Locale: Countryside near Athens

Principal characters:
CHREMES, an old man
SOSTRATA, his wife
ANTIPHILA, his daughter
CLITIPHO, his son
CLINIA, a youth
MENEDEMUS, his father
SYRUS, Clitipho's servant
BACCHIS, a courtesan, Clitipho's mistress

The Story:

While Chremes's wife Sostrata is pregnant, Chremes tells her that if the child should be a girl she is to destroy it. Sostrata agrees, but when the baby turns out to be a daughter the poor woman does not have the heart to carry out her husband's command by herself. Instead, she gives the child to a poor Corinthian woman then living in Athens, who is to leave the child outside to die. Out of superstition, she also gives the woman a ring for her finger to accompany the child when it is left exposed.

The old Corinthian woman fails to carry out her instructions. Naming the child Antiphila, she rears the girl as her own. Antiphila grows up, well mannered and comely, and she is believed by everyone to be the old woman's own daughter.

Clinia, the son of Menedemus, sees Antiphila and falls desperately in love with her. Fearing the disapproval of his strict father, Clinia begins living with her in secret as though she is his wife. Menedemus at last discovers the affair, and by constantly chiding his son and accusing him of unmanly indolence, he finally causes the young man to go to the East and serve in the wars under the Persian king.

Shortly after Clinia leaves Athens, Menedemus comes to realize that he was unjust and cruel in his severity. To punish himself he sells all his possessions in Athens, purchases a farm in the country, and begins working both himself and his servants almost beyond endurance. Three months after his departure, Clinia returns, no longer able to tolerate his separation from Antiphila. Unaware of his father's change of heart, he keeps his return secret from Menedemus and is entertained by Clitipho, a boyhood friend and the son of Chremes. As soon as Clinia arrives, Clitipho sends his two slaves, Dromo and Syrus, into Athens to bring Antiphila to her lover. On the same day Chremes learns from Menedemus how much he wants his son to return and how generous he is determined to be to the young man when the opportunity does finally present itself. In fear of making Clinia audacious in his demands on Menedemus, however, Chremes refrains from telling the young man about his father's change of feeling.

That evening Syrus returns, bringing both Antiphila and a high-priced courtesan, Bacchis. Clitipho, unknown to his father, previously was deeply infatuated with Bacchis, and the cunning and bold Syrus decides that the youth's desire to see his mistress can be satisfied if Bacchis is introduced to Chremes as Clinia's mistress and Antiphila is to pretend to be a member of the courtesan's retinue.

Early the next day, Chremes goes to Menedemus and tells him of Clinia's arrival. The old man, overjoyed at the news, wants immediately to give his son full control over all his possessions. Chremes, however, counsels against such a move on the same grounds that he refrained from telling Clinia of his father's change of heart. Moreover, Chremes believes Bacchis to be Clinia's mistress, and he knows that her extravagant mode of living will quickly drain any admirer of all his possessions. The festivities of the night before alone cost Chremes dearly. What he does advise is that Menedemus should receive Clinia warmly, pretend to be ignorant of his affair with Bacchis, and allow himself to be tricked out of relatively small sums from time to time. This procedure, Chremes thinks, will keep Clinia at home and forestall the ruin of Menedemus.

Meanwhile, Syrus is hatching a plot to trick Chremes out of the ten minae that Bacchis demands as the price of her sojourn with Clitipho. The servant is gratified and amused when Chremes gives him apparent sanction for his deception by asking Syrus to contrive a way to deceive Menedemus into believing that Bacchis is not Clinia's mistress. Syrus, agreeing, cunningly proceeds with his own plot by telling Chremes that Antiphila's mother borrowed ten minae from Bacchis, leaving Antiphila as a pledge for the money. The old woman presumably dies, and Antiphila needs the money to purchase her freedom.

At that moment, however, Sostrata, Chremes' wife, discovers by means of the ring that Antiphila is her abandoned daughter. When this fact is revealed to Chremes, his first reaction is to chide his wife; but he is really pleased to recover his daughter now that his condition is improved financially.

At last Syrus hits upon a plan for deceiving both fathers by telling them the truth. He proposes that Bacchis and her retinue move to Menedemus's house on the pretext that she is Clitipho's mistress and that her affair with Clitipho must be concealed from Chremes. In addition, Antiphila is to be passed off as Clinia's mistress, and Clinia is to ask his father for ten minae to provide for the wedding. Chremes refuses to allow another to ransom his daughter for him, however, and gives Clitipho the ten minae. The rest of the plot proves acceptable as well, and Bacchis and her servants are moved to Menedemus's house.

Menedemus assumes that what he is told regarding Bacchis and Clitipho is designed to deceive him, but when he sees the two entering a bedchamber together without a word of protest from the observing Clinia, he grows troubled and tells Chremes what he saw. He also points out that Clinia made no effort to get money out of his father and seemed highly pleased when Menedemus agreed to his marriage with Antiphila. Thus, the whole truth comes out. Chremes, infuriated at first, threatens to settle the whole of his property on Antiphila. The sudden prospect of being left penniless leads Clitipho to reflect seriously on his mode of life, and he promises to abandon all courtesans and marry a virtuous woman. Under the gentle persuasion of Menedemus and Sostrata, Chremes finally agrees to let Antiphila marry Clinia, and in the end he promises to forgive even Syrus.

Critical Evaluation:

Although *The Self-Tormentor*, based on an earlier play by Menander, takes its primary force from its intricate plot, it is, like several of Terence's comedies, in some sense a problem play. The problem is whether undeviating strictness or affectionate tolerance is the best mode of rearing children. Menedemus begins by finding the apparent excesses of his son intolerable. Since his uncompromising reaction results in the loss of his son, his is clearly not the way Terence would recommend. Neither, however, is the old man's swing to the opposite extreme after his son leaves home. The implicit moral is that a flexible moderation between strictness and tolerance is best in rearing a son.

In the prologue to *The Self-Tormentor*, Terence explains that he turned the single plot of his source, a play by the Greek dramatist Menander, into a double one. *The Self-Tormentor* is certainly complicated. Admittedly, the comic effect depends on confusing the audience almost as much as the characters, but there should be an underlying sense that the playwright remains in control. This may not be the case with *The Self-Tormentor*, which is difficult to follow.

The play also has structural weaknesses. For example, in

most Roman comedies, the plans formulated by the clever slave dominate the action, but here, Syrus's schemes are not really productive. Terence seems to shift direction in the last part of the play, when he depends upon Sostrata, not Syrus, to bring about a restoration of order. If, as seems clear, the play was popular with Roman audiences, the reason must be its interesting characters, recognizable conflicts, and universal themes.

Terence's double plot operates through the skillful pairing of characters. There are two fathers, Menedemus, the title character, who believes that he has failed as a parent, and Chremes, who has complete faith in his own wisdom. Chremes must, in the tradition of comedy, be brought to self-knowledge, and Menedemus, who already recognizes his error, must be reunited with his son.

The two pairs of lovers are also contrasted. Clinia and Antiphila are both virtuous, idealistic, and capable of devotion. Only in birth and wealth are they unequal. That problem, in a comedy, is easily solved. Using a stock plot device, Terence arranges to have the young woman of good character but inferior station be recognized as the child of respectable parents. The only difference here is that this conventional recognition occurs in the middle of the action rather than at the end.

Unlike Clinia and Antiphila, Clitipho and Bacchis have no intention of marrying each other. As Bacchis admits to Antiphila, she is essentially a businesswoman, who uses her beauty and her charm in order to attain financial security. Clitipho will remain her lover only as long as he can pay. Besotted as he is, Clitipho understands the temporary nature of their relationship. At the end of the play, he does not object to being married off to an appropriate woman, as long as she is someone he likes.

Although each father quarrels with his son, it is ironic how much the sons resemble their fathers. Menedemus and Clinia are both men of principle. Clinia leaves home because he will not abandon the woman he loves, and Menedemus punishes himself because he knows that he violated his own standards of right and wrong. Similarly, Clitipho and Chremes are both less than honest. Clitipho deceives his father, and Chremes misleads his friend and neighbor. Both father and son are also impressed with their own cleverness. Neither of them realizes that one who is willing to lie to others may himself be deceived. Neither Chremes nor Clitipho is an evil person. Throughout the play, Chremes believes that he is acting in the best interests of Menedemus, and though he is anxious to keep his mistress nearby, Clitipho is also motivated by his desire to help his friend Clinia.

Though the young men are very different in some ways, they are alike in one important quality. Both of them love their fathers and will do almost anything to heal a breach with them. One reason for Clinia's return is surely his desire to make up matters with his father. As for Clitipho, when he is disinherited, he may regret being deprived of money and property, but he is devastated by the horrible suspicion that if Chremes could so easily reject him, it may be that he is not his father. The pain of losing a mistress is nothing, he realizes, when compared to the anguish he would suffer if he loses Chremes as a father.

Most analyses of *The Self-Tormentor* emphasize the theme of father-son relationships. However, unlike most other Roman comedies, this play has a strong but not shrewish female character, whose relationships with her husband and her offspring are of crucial importance. While she remains offstage during the first half of *The Self-Tormentor*, undoubtedly quite busy entertaining the three guests who are foisted upon her, when Sostrata finally enters, she takes charge of the play. She knows how to manipulate Chremes. First, with abject apologies, she admits her disobedience. When her girl child was born, she says, she failed to kill her, as Chremes ordered, and now their daughter reappears in the person of Antiphila. Then Sostrata stands submissive while Chremes first scolds her, then excuses her, since as a woman she cannot help being ignorant and excessively emotional. Then, as Sostrata expects, Chremes changes his mind. It would be nice, he thinks, to have a daughter. Sostrata gets her way. Sostrata is again a pivotal figure in the final scene of the play, first pleading with Chremes to take back their son, then speaking for Clitipho, who seems to have some foolish notion of arguing with his father. On her son's behalf, Sostrata agrees to a marriage; on her husband's behalf, she approves of the woman he likes.

In other ways, then, *The Self-Tormentor* more than makes up for its flaws. Within the context of the always difficult father-son relationships, Terence finds a way to warn against pride and hardheadedness, rashness and debauchery. His audiences may even have left the theater with some increased respect for matrons such as Sostrata.

"Critical Evaluation" by Rosemary M. Canfield Reisman

Further Reading

Brothers, A. J. "The Construction of Terence's *Heauton-timorumenos*." *Classical Quarterly* 30, no. 1 (1980): 94-119. Proposes a solution to a major critical problem by looking at the functions of Bacchis and Antiphila in the plot. A well-reasoned essay.

Duckworth, George E., ed. *The Complete Roman Drama.*

2 vols. New York: Random House, 1942. A classic edition. Duckworth's general introduction remains one of the best overviews of Roman drama. The introduction to *The Self-Tormentor* incorporates explanations of character motivation into a detailed plot summary.

Dutsch, Dorota M. *Feminine Discourse in Roman Comedy: On Echoes and Voices.* New York: Oxford University Press, 2008. Analyzes the dialogue of female characters in Terence's plays, noting its use of endearments, softness of speech, and emphasis on small problems. Questions whether Roman women actually spoke in such ways.

Forehand, Walter E. *Terence.* Boston: Twayne, 1985. One of the most readable studies of the playwright, with a systematic examination of each of his plays. Particular attention is given to the complicated plot of *The Self-Tormentor* and to the effective pairing of the characters. Includes an annotated bibliography of secondary sources.

Goldberg, Sander M. *Understanding Terence.* Princeton, N.J.: Princeton University Press, 1986. In the chapter "The *duplex comoedia*," *The Self-Tormentor* is carefully analyzed. Concludes that despite its convolutions, this play is essentially simple, designed for one purpose: that of "unmasking Chremes' hypocrisy." Includes bibliography.

Leigh, Matthew. *Comedy and the Rise of Rome.* New York: Oxford University Press, 2004. Analyzes the comedies of Plautus and Terence, placing them within the context of political and economic conditions in Rome during the third and second centuries B.C.E. Discusses how audiences of that time responded to these comedies.

Segal, Erich, ed. *Oxford Readings in Menander, Plautus, and Terence.* New York: Oxford University Press, 2001. Includes essays on the originality of Terence and his Greek models and on the intrigue of *The Self-Tormentor.*

El Señor Presidente

Author: Miguel Ángel Asturias (1899-1974)
First published: 1946 (English translation, 1963)
Type of work: Novel
Type of plot: Historical realism
Time of plot: Early twentieth century
Locale: Guatemala

Principal characters:
THE PRESIDENT, a cruel dictator
THE ZANY, a mentally disabled beggar
COLONEL JOSÉ SONRIENTE, killed by the Zany
GENERAL EUSEBIO CANALES, falsely implicated in the death of Colonel Sonriente
CAMILA, General Canales's daughter
MIGUEL ÁNGEL FACE, the president's confidential adviser
FEDINA DE RODAS, a young mother

The Story:

The Zany and his fellow homeless beggars lie sleeping in the shadow of the cathedral as night falls. Too poor to pay fines, they are generally undisturbed by the police, but Colonel Sonriente decides to amuse himself by tormenting the Zany, whose one comfort in his miserable life is memories of his mother. When the colonel awakens him by shouting, "Mother!" in his ear, the Zany jumps up and beats the colonel to death.

The beggars are rounded up by the police and tortured to reveal the identity of the murderer. Strangely enough, the correct answer, the Zany, does not seem to satisfy the police. Clearly, the authorities want to blame the crime on someone else.

Meanwhile, the Zany flees through the streets of the city until he falls and breaks his leg. He is attacked by a buzzard and would have died if not for the intervention of a mysterious, strikingly handsome man named Miguel Ángel Face.

Ángel Face is an unofficial adviser to the president, a ruthless tyrant. The president informs Ángel Face that he has a job for him, but a rather tricky one. A political enemy of the president, General Canales, is to be implicated in the murder of Colonel Sonriente, but it does not suit the president's purposes to have him arrested. Rather, Ángel Face is to force the general to become a fugitive by telling one of his servants that the police are on their way to arrest him.

After the general duly flees, Ángel Face, aided by the thugs Vasquez and Rodas, raids the general's house and kidnaps his daughter, Camila. The smooth-talking Ángel Face assures Camila that he helped the general escape out of the goodness of his heart and that he hides her away in a neighborhood inn to protect her from her father's enemies. Whatever his original intentions, this "line" soon comes close to being the truth, for Ángel Face finds himself facing a totally new emotion and motivation: love.

Rather than abusing Camila, Ángel Face becomes worried about her welfare. He tries to find a place for her to stay, starting with her uncle, Don Juan Canales. Here, however, Ángel Face begins to learn the consequences of living in a nation ruled by a tyrant, a tyrant for whom Ángel Face himself works. Camila's uncle refuses to help his niece for fear of being added to the president's list of enemies. Ángel Face is left with a defenseless, innocent girl for whom his affections and concern are growing by the hour.

In the meantime, the police make their official raid on General Canales's house. Finding no one there, they declare the general to be a fugitive fleeing the consequences of his crime and also begin to arrest persons suspected of helping him to escape (even though the plot to allow him to escape was the president's).

One of those arrested is Fedina de Rodas, wife of one of Ángel Face's henchmen. Fedina is thrown in prison along with her baby. Worse than her brutal torture is the suffering of her baby, who starves to death in her arms. Fedina is finally released from prison and forced to earn her living in a house of prostitution. All this befalls Fedina despite the fact that she knows nothing of the general's escape or of his whereabouts.

At that moment, in fact, the general is far from the city, hiding in a deserted hut in the countryside. Eventually he begins to meet some of the peasants living nearby, almost all of whom suffered greatly at the hands of the wealthy and powerful. Hearing their tales of exploitation, the general gradually realizes what a corrupt political system he has spent his life serving. Eventually the general escapes into the marshland, vowing to return and to fight for the people.

Back in the city, Ángel Face feels himself falling more and more in love with Camila. After nursing her through a near-fatal illness, he marries her and they set up house in the city. However, their happiness is marred by two factors. Camila's father, General Canales, dies (probably poisoned) on the eve of leading a band of rebels against the president, and Ángel Face falls into disfavor with the president because of his marriage to the daughter of the president's old enemy.

Indeed, the president takes his inevitable revenge. He first orders Ángel Face to go to Washington, D.C., on government business but has him arrested on the way. Camila never sees her husband again. At the end, Ángel Face languishes in prison, tortured by false rumors that his wife is the president's mistress.

Critical Evaluation:

Miguel Ángel Asturias is a leading figure in the phenomenon that has come to be known as the "Boom," the relatively sudden emergence of a large number of immensely talented fiction writers from Latin America. Scholars disagree about who started the Boom and who is its most important figure, but the fact that Asturias published his most famous novel, *El Señor Presidente*, in 1946, before many of his Latin American colleagues had even begun to write, and the fact that he won the Nobel Prize in Literature in 1967, indicates that he should be thought of as one of the earliest and one of the best Boom writers.

Although the Boom was not a school of writers with a set of goals in common, at least two major tendencies appear in much of their fiction. For one, Boom writers are among the most innovative of the twentieth century, blazing technical and stylistic trails. The way they write often seems as important to them and as interesting to the reader as that about which they write. However, they also take their subjects very seriously. The subject they address more than any other is politics, especially the relationship between the government and the governed. On both of these counts, Asturias shows himself to be a central figure in the Boom, and no better example than *El Señor Presidente* exists in his writing.

Asturias's theme is the most common one in Latin American political fiction: the relationship between the powerful and the powerless, victimizer and victim. In every case, Asturias's, and hence the readers', sympathies lie with the poor, weak victims of a political structure that rewards greed and cruelty and leaves everything else a waste.

At the top of the political-military power structure of Guatemala (never named in the novel) is the president (based on Manuel Estrada Cabrera), who rules by terror and by coercion. He perceives anyone with strength, talent, and the potential to be popular with the citizenry as an enemy and ruthlessly destroys him. Often this destruction, as in Ángel Face's case, takes some time in coming, and, before it arrives, the victim may believe himself to be favored by the president. To rise in the ranks, however—even by being especially loyal and useful to the president—is to acquire power. Those who live by power fear nothing so much as others with power. Thus, even the president's closest advisers and supporters are threats to his power and are always, ultimately, in danger of his wrath.

Fear pervades the tyrannical power structure of Guatemala, therefore, and its irrational nature is seen in the fact that not one of those arrested, brutalized, and often killed by the authorities poses a real threat to the president or, indeed, has done anything that could be interpreted as treasonous or even unpatriotic. This is true of Ángel Face, who rises to a position of power because of his loyalty to the president, of Camila, and of Fedina, whom the authorities know is innocent even before she is thrown in prison and tortured, and even of General Canales, for whose supposed treachery the president offers not a shred of evidence.

A few gleams of thematic light do penetrate this dark world of fear and oppression. Mothers still love their children. Persons of honor are still willing to die for the truth (as "Mosquito" does early in the novel when he refuses wrongly to implicate the general in Colonel Sonriente's death). Compassion and mercy still exist, although these are more frequently found among the poor and the powerless than among those who take their lessons from the president and make their way by force and intimidation.

The character who offers the most hope is Ángel Face. He rises to a position of great power and importance, and he has the intelligence and the talent to rise higher. Instead, knowing the dangers he faces, he chooses love and compassion.

Rather than moving the novel in an optimistic direction, though, Ángel Face's experience underscores the hopelessness of the situation. Clearly, the president wins out over everyone. Asturias holds out no promise for a better tomorrow. By the end of the novel, Guatemala is shown to be a society with two classes. In one class is the president, wielding all the power; in the other is everyone else.

Asturias began writing *El Señor Presidente* in the 1930's, in the middle of what has come to be called the age of modernism. Modernist novelists characteristically use much ambiguity, subtlety, and psychological penetration, qualities almost totally absent from Asturias's novel. Indeed, his themes are obvious, and even his major characters tend to be one-dimensional. Rather than being faults, however, these are deliberate technical strategies.

Asturias lives in the dark world that he writes about, and his desire to announce the horror of that world is too great to allow for such technical niceties as ambiguity. Evil is clearly evil in Asturias's novel and good clearly good, and the characters align themselves under one or the other heading. Even those characters who change over the course of time (especially Ángel Face and General Canales, who come to realize and react against the horrors of the government they serve) do so in easily perceived ways and stages. Even the passages in which realism seems to give way to the fantastic (the one in which the streets "chase" the Zany, for instance, and the one in which the chaotic deliriums of characters under torture are

described), Asturias is trying to convey plainly the evils of tyranny. This often imparts the feeling of a parable to this otherwise grimly realistic novel.

El Señor Presidente is not always a pleasant reading experience, but no reader can confuse Asturias's message: Power wielded by a single individual corrupts and destroys.

Dennis Vannatta

Further Reading

Barrueto, Jorge J. "A Latin American Indian Re-reads the Canon." *Hispanic Review* 72, no. 3 (Summer, 2004): 339-356. Barrueto critiques the novel from a postcolonial perspective, focusing on the significance of mimicry in Latin American literature, the concepts of surrealism and the otherness of non-Europeans in Asturias's work, and Asturias's ideas about Guatemalan politics.

Calan, Richard. *Miguel Ángel Asturias*. New York: Twayne, 1970. Calan devotes two lengthy chapters to *El Señor Presidente*, providing an overview of the major themes and technical strategies in the novel. In "Babylonian Mythology in *El Señor Presidente*," Calan argues that Asturias relies on themes and imagery derived not just from Mayan mythology, as scholars have long noted, but also from Babylonian mythology.

Campion, Daniel. "Eye of Glass, Eye of Truth: Surrealism in *El Señor Presidente*." *Hispanic Journal* 3 (Fall, 1981): 123-135. Campion analyzes Asturias's style of writing in the novel.

Martin, Gerald. "Miguel Ángel Asturias: *El Señor Presidente*." In *Landmarks of Modern Latin American Fiction*, edited by Philip Swanson. New York: Routledge, 1990. Provides a useful overview of the central issues in the novel.

Prieto, René. *Miguel Ángel Asturias' Archaeology of Return*. New York: Cambridge University Press, 1993. Prieto discusses the novel in the broader context of Asturias's life and work, specifically addressing surrealism, sexuality, and Dionysian elements in the novel.

Zimmerman, Marc. *Literature and Resistance in Guatemala: Textual Modes and Cultural Politics from "El Señor Presidente" to Rigoberta Menchú*. 2 vols. Athens: Ohio University Center for International Studies, 1995. Zimmerman examines the relationship among Guatemalan literature, politics, violence, and state repression during the last fifty years of the twentieth century, demonstrating how *El Señor Presidente* and other works of literature have influenced the nation's revolutionary political movements.

Sense and Sensibility

Author: Jane Austen (1775-1817)
First published: 1811
Type of work: Novel
Type of plot: Domestic realism
Time of plot: Early nineteenth century
Locale: England

Principal characters:
ELINOR DASHWOOD, a young woman of sense
MARIANNE DASHWOOD, her sister
JOHN DASHWOOD, her brother
FANNY DASHWOOD, his wife
EDWARD FERRARS, Fanny's brother
SIR JOHN MIDDLETON, a Dashwood relation
COLONEL BRANDON, Sir John's friend
JOHN WILLOUGHBY, a young man with whom Marianne
 falls in love
LUCY STEELE, a young woman who attracts Edward for a
 time
ROBERT FERRARS, Edward's brother

The Story:

When Mr. John Dashwood inherits his father's estate, it is his intention to provide comfortably for his stepmother and his half sisters. His wife, Fanny, has other ideas, however, and although she is independently wealthy, she cleverly prevents her husband from helping his relatives. When Fanny's brother, Edward Ferrars, begins to show an interest in Elinor, John's half sister, Fanny is determined to prevent any alliance between them. She makes life so uncomfortable for the older Mrs. Dashwood and her daughters that the ladies accept the offer of their relative, Sir John Middleton, to occupy a cottage on his estate.

Mrs. Dashwood, Elinor, and Marianne are happy in the cottage at Barton Park. There they meet Colonel Brandon, Sir John's thirty-five-year-old friend, who is immediately attracted to Marianne. She considers him too old and rejects his suit. Instead, she falls in love with John Willoughby, a young man visiting wealthy relatives on a neighboring estate.

Once, while the young people are preparing for an outing, Colonel Brandon is called away in a mysterious fashion. Elinor and Marianne are surprised later to hear that he has a daughter; at least that is the rumor they hear. Willoughby seems determined to give Marianne a bad impression of Colonel Brandon, which displeases Elinor. Shortly after the colonel's sudden departure, Willoughby himself leaves very suddenly and without explanation. Elinor cannot help being concerned about the manner of his departure, particularly since he did not make a definite engagement with Marianne.

A week later, Edward Ferrars appeared at the cottage for a visit. Elinor is strongly attracted to him, but Edward seems no more than mildly interested in her. After a short stay, he leaves the cottage without saying anything to give Elinor

hope. Meanwhile, Sir John invites to his home Miss Lucy Steele and her sister, two young ladies whom Elinor thinks vulgar and ignorant. She is therefore stunned when Lucy tells her that she is secretly engaged to Edward, whom she met while he was a pupil of Lucy's uncle. According to Lucy's story, they were engaged for four years, but Edward's mother would not permit him to marry. Since Edward has no money of his own and no occupation, they are forced to wait for Mrs. Ferrars's consent before they can announce their engagement. Concealing her unhappiness at this news, Elinor tells Lucy that she will help in any way she can.

A short time later, Elinor and Marianne are invited to London to visit friends. Marianne immediately writes to Willoughby to inform him that she is near. Although she writes two or three times, she gets no reply. One day, she meets him at a social event. He is with another young lady and treats Marianne courteously but coolly. The next morning, Marianne receives a letter from him telling her that he is sorry if she misunderstood his intentions and that he has long been engaged to someone else. All of her friends and relatives are furious with Willoughby. Although she is heartbroken, Marianne continues to defend him and to believe that he is blameless. She is comforted by Colonel Brandon, who is also in London.

The colonel privately tells Elinor Willoughby's story. The colonel had a ward, a young girl some believed to be his daughter, who is in reality the daughter of his brother's divorced wife. The colonel had to leave Barton Park so suddenly because he learned that his ward was seduced and then abandoned by Willoughby. When Elinor tells Marianne the news, her sister receives it with such sorrow that Elinor fears for her health. Colonel Brandon continues to be kind to Marianne, and it is obvious to everyone that he loves her deeply.

The young women stay on in London. A little later, their brother John and his wife take a house there. When the Misses Steele also arrive in town for a visit, Edward's mother learns at last that he and Lucy are engaged. Angrily, she settles what would have been Edward's inheritance on her other son, Robert, leaving Edward and Lucy with no means of support. Edward plans to study for the ministry, and Elinor arranges with Colonel Brandon that he become a curate on his estate so as to enable Edward and Lucy to be married.

Before Elinor and Marianne return home, they visit Cleveland, an estate between London and Barton Park. There Marianne becomes ill with a severe cold. Because she is anxious to see her mother, Colonel Brandon goes to fetch Mrs. Dashwood. Before they return, Willoughby, hearing of Marianne's illness, calls at the house. He admits to Elinor that he treated Marianne so shamefully because he has no money of his own and because his wealthy relative learned of the affair with Colonel Brandon's ward; as a result, his relative cut off his allowance, and he renounced Marianne to marry a wealthy young woman. He declares that he still loves Marianne and wishes her to know his story so that she will not think too harshly of him.

Marianne recovers from her illness and returns home with her mother and Elinor. After Elinor tells her Willoughby's story, Marianne continues to be sorrowful for him, but she no longer loves him.

After their return, Elinor learns from a servant that Mr. Ferrars and Lucy are married. She assumes that Edward married Lucy. Soon Edward appears at the cottage and tells the Dashwoods that the unscrupulous Lucy married his brother instead of him, since their mother disinherited Edward in favor of Robert. Edward comes to ask Elinor to marry him, and he has no trouble in gaining her consent as well as that of her mother. It remains only for him to secure a living. He goes to London to seek his mother's forgiveness. Because Mrs. Ferrars repudiated her son Robert after his marriage to Lucy, she feels a need for affection from one of her children. After much weeping and pleading, which fails to move Edward in his determination to marry Elinor, Mrs. Ferrars gives her consent to the wedding. After their marriage, they move into the parsonage that Colonel Brandon promised Edward some months before.

The colonel continues his quiet and gentle courtship of Marianne. At last, she recognizes his true worth, and they are married. When they move to his estate, the two sisters are near each other once more. Fanny and John are so pleased to be related to the colonel that Fanny even forgives Edward for marrying Elinor. Mrs. Dashwood is delighted at the good fortune of her children, and the families live in peace and contentment.

Critical Evaluation:

Jane Austen wrote this novel during an important transition in English cultural history when the sensible eighteenth century enlightenment ideas were giving way to the more sensitive romantic ideas of the nineteenth century. In *Sense and Sensibility*, she creates the two Dashwood sisters, Elinor and Marianne, to embody the extremes of relational and romantic personality. The story may sometimes seem to fit a predictable formula, in which common sense is pitted against emotional sensitivity, but Austen also makes keen observations about the way to go about attaining happiness.

The cool, rational elder sister, Elinor, falls deeply in love with her sister-in-law's brother, quiet, reserved Edward Ferrars. Elinor's sister-in-law Fanny regards Elinor as too poor for her wealthy brother, but he scorns his family's expectation that he marry a rich heir. Edward loves Elinor and he avoids her only because he secretly and foolishly engaged himself to Lucy Steele. This longtime clandestine engagement pains him when he realizes that he never loved Lucy. His gentleman's code of conduct, however, does not allow him to break his engagement, so he expects to have to marry Lucy even after he falls in love with Elinor. Elinor for her part is resigned to the prospect of often meeting Edward and Lucy as a married couple.

Lucy is a brilliantly portrayed character: a charming, intelligent, but completely heartless young woman who uses Edward to secure a position in upper-class society. As soon as Edward is disinherited by his angry mother and his brother Robert has better financial prospects, she shifts her affections and hopes to Robert.

Only because Lucy abandons honorable Edward does he become free to propose to Elinor. These lovers, who were guided by prudence and respect for social conventions, are finally united and win the happiness they desire because they honored the sensible values of society.

Meanwhile, the passionate, sensitive Marianne plunges into love with handsome, charming John Willoughby after he gallantly rescues her when she falls down a steep hill. He seems to be the perfect romantic hero. Everyone who sees them together agrees they seem perfectly matched in taste, values, and temperament. The two ignore rules of social conduct by spending many hours together and disregarding others. Marianne visits his home without a chaperone, and their ardent behavior misleads others into believing they are engaged even when they are not. After Marianne is abandoned by her seemingly ideal lover, it is long before she can accept what Willoughby did. Her first response is to become depressed and dangerously ill, and only slowly does she regain her health and will to live.

Courtship is the theme of all Austen's novels, but in *Sense and Sensibility*, the young ladies and gentlemen in love face dangerous challenges. Both Elinor's and Marianne's love affairs are threatened by mercenary forces intent on destroying their prospects of marriage. The obstacles to a marriage between reserved, sensible Elinor and Edward are his family's greed and pride as well as his earlier indiscretion in engaging himself. Passionate, romantic Marianne and Willoughby, after an intense attraction that causes them to ignore the barriers between them, suffer and end up bitterly regretting their behavior. Willoughby regrets having abandoned Marianne, "his secret standard of perfection in women," while she regrets having indulged her impulsive, irrational feelings for him.

Certainly, Austen is commenting on the relative value of sense and sensibility in the face of crisis, and clearly she prefers sense. The story vindicates sensible Elinor as a thoughtful, considerate person who, even while suffering from her own disappointed love, nurses and consoles her sister. Even while suffering, she can have the satisfaction of acting correctly, whereas Marianne is forced to condemn herself harshly for her past thoughtless self-absorption, her rudeness to others, her neglect of the rules of good conduct, and her self-destructiveness. Only after coming to this realization can Marianne find happiness with sensible Colonel Brandon, a steady, rational, kind older man.

In this novel, Austen critically examines the changing social values of England in the early nineteenth century. As Great Britain's colonial empire and Industrial Revolution created greater wealth and power in the early nineteenth century, traditional country values gradually gave way to newer, more cosmopolitan values. In the novel, plain-speaking, old-fashioned characters such as Sir John Middleton and his mother-in-law, Mrs. Jennings, seem at first rather vulgar and naïvely cheerful in their teasing about romance and enthusiasm for dinners and dances. In crisis situations, however, they prove to be good friends who care for the feelings of others and offer valued help to those in need. Mrs. Jennings's true affection for Elinor and Marianne becomes clear when she nurses Marianne through her serious illness.

In contrast to these simple, countrified types, Edward's mother, the elegant, sophisticated, and wealthy Mrs. Ferrars, and her daughter, Mrs. Fanny Dashwood, seem coldly calculating and cruel in their relations with others. They break promises and cast off needy relatives. Those aspiring to the wealth and sophistication of the Ferrars, such as Lucy Steele and Lady Middleton, also act in needlessly cruel and thoughtless ways. By contrasting old-fashioned manners with newer ones, Austen suggests that traditional ways are more trustworthy in times of need. She herself preferred life in a small country village and detested living in the elegant resort town of Bath, where sophisticated, leisured people gathered.

Austen's style adds a dramatically ironic dimension to the novel. Key characters reveal themselves in crisp, natural dialogue, at the same time showing readers that they do not completely understand themselves and their own values. Early in the story, Marianne declares to Elinor, "I have not known [Willoughby] long, indeed; but I am much better acquainted with him than I am with any other creature in the world, except yourself and mamma." Austen observes, "Marianne Dashwood was born to an extraordinary fate. She was born to discover the falsehood of her own opinions, and to counteract, by her conduct, her most favourite maxims."

"Critical Evaluation" by Patricia H. Fulbright

Further Reading

Austen, Jane. *Sense and Sensibility: Complete Text with Introduction, Historical Contexts, Critical Essays*. Edited by Beth Lau. Boston: Houghton Mifflin, 2002. In addition to the text, this volume contains background materials that place the novel within its social and historical context and four critical essays analyzing the work. It also features a twenty-two-page introduction by Lau, in which she explains why *Sense and Sensibility* is considered one of Austen's least successful novels.

Butler, Marilyn. *Jane Austen and the War of Ideas*. New York: Oxford University Press, 1987. Argues that this "unremittingly didactic" novel intends to oppose Marianne's idealistic values with the decisive correctness of Elinor's cautious civility. Asserts that Austen complicates this effort, however, by making Marianne too sympathetic.

Fergus, Jan. *Jane Austen and the Didactic Novel: "Northanger Abbey," "Sense and Sensibility," and "Pride and Prejudice."* Totowa, N.J.: Barnes & Noble, 1983. Very good in describing Austen's style and in situating her early novels in the tradition of eighteenth and early nineteenth century English fiction.

Honan, Park. *Jane Austen: Her Life*. London: Weidenfeld & Nicholson, 1987. Considered the standard biography, Honan's work carefully explains the context of Austen's novels, including a detailed discussion of the development of *Sense and Sensibility* through several drafts.

Lambdin, Laura Cooner, and Robert Thomas Lambdin, eds. *A Companion to Jane Austen Studies*. New York: Greenwood Press, 2000. A collection of twenty-two essays interpreting Austen's works. Includes two essays by Rebecca Stephens Duncan about *Sense and Sensibility*: "*Sense and Sensibility*: A Convergence of Readers/Viewers/Browsers" and "A Critical History of *Sense and Sensibility*."

Lauber, John. *Jane Austen*. New York: Twayne, 1993. A good basic discussion of the novel that uses the terms "sense" and "sensibility" to interpret and evaluate the characters' positive and negative qualities. Describes the novel as Austen's most passionate and darkly satirical. Contains a useful chronology and a short annotated bibliography.

Moler, Kenneth. *Jane Austen's Art of Allusion*. Lincoln: University of Nebraska Press, 1968. Considers the novel in relation to its literary antecedents, finding that Austen takes the conventional contrast of sense and sensibility and reworks it to show that both sides of the dichotomy have limitations. Asserts that the "sensible" Elinor is as much in need of self-knowledge as Marianne.

Mudrick, Marvin. *Jane Austen: Irony as Defense and Discovery*. Princeton, N.J.: Princeton University Press, 1952. Important early study of Austen's style and tone. Finds in *Sense and Sensibility* a youthful parody of romance dissolving uncomfortably into a mature, serious consideration of personal morality. Argues that Marianne is sacrificed to the restrictions of social propriety.

Perkins, Moreland. *Reshaping the Sexes in "Sense and Sensibility."* Charlottesville: University Press of Virginia, 1998. An analysis of the novel, focusing on its male and female characters. Perkins maintains that Elinor Dashwood is Austen's most intellectual and most "gender-dissonant" heroine.

Ruoff, Gene W. *Jane Austen's Sense and Sensibility*. New York: St. Martin's Press, 1992. Contains chapters on the historical and cultural context, critical reception of the text, theoretical perspectives, and a detailed interpretation of the novel, including a section on "women's lives and men's stories." A selected bibliography and index make this an especially useful study.

Todd, Janet M. *The Cambridge Introduction to Jane Austen*. New York: Cambridge University Press, 2006. Todd, an Austen scholar and editor of the author's work, provides an overview of Austen's life, novels, context, and reception. Includes a detailed discussion about each novel and provides a good starting point for the study of her major works.

Wiltshire, John. *Jane Austen and the Body*. New York: Cambridge University Press, 1992. Wiltshire argues that the "bodily condition" of Austen's heroines is as meaningful as their words and manners. Contrasts Marianne's "expressive" body (her exuberant health, dramatic illness, and quiet recovery) with Elinor's "nearly silent" body. Includes a useful bibliography.

A Sentimental Education

Author: Gustave Flaubert (1821-1880)
First published: L'Éducation sentimentale, 1869 (English translation, 1898)
Type of work: Novel
Type of plot: Naturalism
Time of plot: Nineteenth century
Locale: France

Principal characters:
FREDERIC MOREAU, a young student
MONSIEUR ARNOUX, a businessman
MADAME ARNOUX, his wife
MONSIEUR DAMBREUSE, a banker
MADAME DAMBREUSE, his wife
ROSANETTE, a mistress of many
DESLAURIERS, Frederic's friend
LOUISE ROQUE, Frederic's neighbor

The Story:

In 1840, the boat down the Seine to Nogent has among its passengers Frederic Moreau, who is returning home after finishing his course at the Collège de Sens and who has the prospect of a long vacation before beginning his law studies in Paris. Seeing on the boat an older man whose conversation is eagerly followed by a group of admirers, Frederic draws closer to hear what is being said. In a most worldly fashion, Monsieur Arnoux is holding forth on the subject of women.

He notices Frederic in the circle, and after he finishes speaking, he introduces himself to the young man and the two promenade for some time on deck. Arnoux invites Frederic to call on him when he arrives in Paris.

Frederic then goes up to the first-class deck to sit and reflect on his homecoming. There he sees an attractive woman knitting; Frederic thinks she is the most beautiful woman he has ever seen. She is a little older than he and has a demure manner; she never once looks directly at him, though they are alone on the deck. Frederic moves several times to see her from different angles. Finally she drops her ball of yarn, and Frederic retrieves it; her murmur of thanks is pleasant to hear. A few minutes later, a little girl approaches, and he knows the child is the woman's daughter. Then Arnoux appears on deck and Frederic learns that the woman is his wife. When the boat docks, he watches them drive away.

Madame Moreau, a widow, is glad to see her son; she has placed all her hopes in his future career in diplomacy. As soon as he decently can leave his mother, Frederic goes out to meet his friend Deslauriers, a young man who is also planning a legal career. The two friends discuss at great length their plans for their life in Paris in the fall.

When the time comes for Frederic to leave for Paris, a neighbor of the Moreaus, Monsieur Roque, gives him a letter for Monsieur Dambreuse, a rich Paris banker. Madame Moreau advises her son to call on Dambreuse as soon as he can, for the banker will be able to be of great help to a young lawyer. Bidding good-bye to his relatives and to his neighbor Louise Roque, a girl who has become his special friend during the summer, Frederic leaves for Paris and his studies at the university.

Deslauriers and Frederic take an apartment together and begin to attend lectures in law. Frederic finds it very difficult to keep his mind on his studies, however, for he thinks most of the time of Madame Arnoux. He finally receives an invitation to the Arnoux store, a large establishment dealing in paintings and other works of art. He is patient enough to establish an intimate relationship with Arnoux, hoping that eventually he will meet Arnoux's wife.

One night, Arnoux invites Frederic to a masquerade ball, and there Arnoux introduces him to Rosanette, an attractive woman whom her friends call la Maréchale. Frederic is sure that Rosanette is Arnoux's mistress. He is glad to learn about the liaison, thinking that it improves his chances of becoming friendly with Madame Arnoux.

When Frederic is finally invited to dine at the Arnoux home, he is happy to learn that Madame Arnoux remembers him perfectly. She is a friendly woman, but as time goes on Frederic sees little chance of his ever becoming more intimate with her. Even when he is regularly included in gatherings at the Arnoux country house, he makes no progress. He finally has to conclude that his friends are right: Madame Arnoux is a good woman.

So great is his preoccupation with the pursuit of Madame Arnoux that Frederic fails his examinations in the spring. Before he leaves for home he calls at the Dambreuse home, where he is well received. He vows to study hard, to forget about Madame Arnoux, and to try his luck in public life under the sponsorship of Monsieur Dambreuse. For a time, Frederic studies diligently and cultivates the Dambreuse family; he goes only occasionally to see Madame Arnoux. Eventually he passes his examinations, and he is admitted to the bar.

Before leaving Paris, he is included in a picnic held in honor of Madame Arnoux's birthday. During the party she seems put out with her husband, but Arnoux shrugs off his wife's pique and sends her back to the city with Frederic. As they leave, Arnoux gives his wife a bouquet, which she surreptitiously throws away. Thinking she has dropped it, Frederic picks it up and gives it to her in the carriage. As soon as they start off on their trip, she begs him to throw the flowers out the window. Never before has Frederic felt so close to her.

At Nogent, Frederic receives bad news: His mother's income has dwindled considerably because of the troubled politics of monarchical France, and she has been forced to sell some of her lands. Henceforth she will have only enough to live frugally. A worse blow falls when Frederic's rich uncle in Le Havre announces that he will not leave his wealth to Frederic. Feeling that he is ruined, with no income and no expectations, Frederic resigns himself to a dull life in Nogent and spends three years in almost complete idleness. His only friend is Louise Roque, who has grown into an attractive woman.

At last a telegram arrives to announce that the uncle in Le Havre has died without making a will and that Frederic is his only heir. Despite his mother's remonstrances, Frederic hastily prepares to return to Paris. He declares his love for Louise before he leaves, but all the while he is thinking of Madame Arnoux.

In Paris, Frederic takes a fashionable apartment and settles down to a life of ease. He again becomes an intimate of the Arnoux household and renews his friendship with Deslauriers. He agrees to furnish the money to found a journal of political opinion, his intention being to give employment to Deslauriers and at the same time to control a publication that will support his own future career in politics. When he learns that Arnoux is pressed financially, he lends money to him on the strength of Arnoux's promise to repay the debt in a few days. Arnoux never repays the money, however, and out of disappointment Deslauriers breaks off their friendship. Frederic consoles himself with his increasing intimacy with Madame Arnoux.

Little by little, Arnoux loses most of his money, and an oil company he founded goes bankrupt. He begins to spend less time at home and more with various mistresses. His wife becomes aware of his many affairs and turns to Frederic for sympathy. At last she agrees to meet him and spend an afternoon in his company.

With high hopes, Frederic rents a room for their rendezvous and fills it with expensive trinkets. He is to meet Madame Arnoux between 2:00 and 4:00, and on the appointed day he goes to the meeting place at 1:30. He waits until 6:30, but she does not appear. In despair he goes to see Rosanette, for to him it seems a just retaliation to make Arnoux's mistress his own. Unknown to Frederic, Madame Arnoux has not kept the appointment because her son is ill. Taking his illness as a sign from heaven, she is ashamed of her interest in Frederic.

During the riots that attend the overthrow of the French monarchy and the establishment of the republic, Frederic spends the time agreeably enough in the country with Rosanette. He returns to Paris only after he receives word that one of his friends has been wounded. Louise Roque arrives in Paris with her father; she has traveled there chiefly to find out what has happened to Frederic. When she finally sees Frederic, she understands that he is no longer interested in her.

While continuing his affair with Rosanette, Frederic takes another mistress, Madame Dambreuse. When the banker dies, Frederic decides to marry his widow, but the canny Dambreuse has left his money to his niece. Frederic thereupon gives up all thought of marrying the widow.

Frederic has many loves, but none is permanent. When he is nearly fifty years old, Madame Arnoux comes to see him. They agree that they had been right not to love carnally. Deslauriers, who has been a lawyer for twenty-five years in Nogent, comes to visit Frederic, and they talk over the past. Deslauriers had married Louise Roque, but she ran away with a singer. The old friends conclude that love is fickle, selfish, unhappy—like life itself.

Critical Evaluation:

A Sentimental Education, considered by some critics to be Gustave Flaubert's masterpiece, was without question one of the most influential French novels of the nineteenth century. The novel, for which Flaubert drew largely on autobiographical material, is the author's rewrite of a draft by the same title that he had written two decades earlier. The work represents his effort to produce a moral history of the men of his generation.

Flaubert's concern is with the organic growth of a personality and with the unfolding and discovery of the self. Education has, for Flaubert, the almost existential meaning of becoming through action. At the beginning of the book, the protagonist, Frederic Moreau, is little more than a potentiality, an empty page on which experience has yet to leave its mark. It is only as Frederic confronts the world and is forced to make choices and to react among other people that he develops into a complicated and tormented human being. The conflict is always between the man who was and the man who is about to be. To reflect this, the time sequence in the novel is poised between past and future, between the raw youth and the man of experience who is sadder and wiser but not necessarily better.

The question facing Frederic, particularly after he has moved to Paris, is whether he should become a man of the world, successful in love and business, and a man of action who is conventional in his behavior and opinions, or whether he should become a spectator of life, an outsider who remains aloof from the vanity of action and struggles to translate his ideal vision into artistic form. It is the same question that Flaubert himself faced: to be a man of the world, with all of his superficiality and convention, or a man of art, no longer of the real world. At the beginning, by necessity, Frederic stands on the sidelines, watching. He has not been able to enter society, knows few people, and has little money; so he watches the activities of others. This passive quality is emphasized by the repetition of verbs such as "he watched," "he contemplated," "he admired," and "he dreamed." Frederic seems to be a wallflower at a great and glorious ball. Then two events thrust him into the stream of action: love and the inheritance of a fortune from his uncle. With these, his real education begins.

Love is almost a pattern for all the lessons of life, according to the point of view expressed in this novel, and education, in the sense of "education for living," is synonymous with "sentimental education." The romantic or sentimental education of the hero thus assumes symbolic proportions. It is love through its many aspects, both sacred and profane, that opens up the world for Frederic Moreau. At first, his vision of love is ideal and pure, but as it becomes more earthbound and physical, he loses both his innocence and his idealism.

"I know nothing more noble," Flaubert once wrote, "than the contemplation of the world," and this novel provides such an opportunity for the reader. *A Sentimental Education* views the world in all of its sordid, beautiful, painful, and pleasurable complexity, and with consummate skill Flaubert presents his vision of the human condition. It is a view that many of his contemporaries considered shocking and disgusting but from which subsequent generations of readers have derived ironic, profound pleasure.

The heart of the novel is the love affair between Frederic and Madame Arnoux, a fictionalized version of the relationship between the young Flaubert and Elisa Schlesinger, the wife of a well-known music publisher, who is the prototype for the art dealer Monsieur Arnoux. The real-life relationship continued, off and on, for many years and was one of the central influences in the author's life. There is no doubt that the scene of Frederic's reunion with the white-haired Madame Arnoux had its counterpart in real life.

Just as Madame Arnoux is a portrait of Madame Schlesinger, so Frederic is a self-portrait of the author. The principal difference is that Flaubert acted on his dreams and learned to discipline himself in order to realize his ambitions. While Frederic is the ancestor of all the antiheroes of modern literature, Flaubert transcended the parts of himself that he gave to his hero and found in his literary vocation the strength that Frederic is never able to discover in himself.

It has been claimed that all the characters in the novel— from Frederic's friends to the many minor characters who fill out the spectacular picture of Parisian society—are based on real individuals whom Flaubert knew. Certainly Flaubert based the background events on history, and he did extensive research, particularly on the subject of the 1848 revolution, to ensure historical accuracy. He devoted as much care to describing an operation or a factory, however, as he did to writing about historical events. Where a lesser novelist might have let the tumultuous events of his background overpower the human story of his protagonists, Flaubert carefully kept a balance between the different parts of the novel; thus the historical events provide a counterpoint highlighting the personal adventures of his hero.

To later readers, perhaps the most fascinating aspect of *A Sentimental Education* is its detailed portrait of French society at the time that led to the coup d'état of 1851. The endless evenings of petty conversation in restaurants and fashionable salons, the bickering and plotting over finances, the quarreling over politics, the scheming of writers and artists to achieve notoriety and attention in periodicals—all are vividly drawn. Frederic wanders among the rich and well known as well as among the student class and the less rich, absorbing the lessons that the world around him has to offer. Flaubert's meticulous, graceful style renders the scenes sharply, even when his protagonist is suffering most acutely. The novel

gives the illusion of shapelessness, but it is actually carefully constructed. It is both a view of a society in the throes of change and a portrait of a human being discovering his own potential.

"Critical Evaluation" by Bruce D. Reeves

Further Reading

Brombert, Victor. *"L' Éducation sentimentale*: Profanation and the Permanence of Dreams." In *Critical Essays on Gustave Flaubert*, edited by Laurence M. Porter. Boston: G. K. Hall, 1986. Focuses on the theme of prostitution in the novel.

Cortland, Peter. *Sentiment in Flaubert's "Education sentimentale."* Muncie, Ind.: Ball State University Press, 1966. Focuses on analysis of the central character and includes an excellent discussion of the novel's opening scene. English translations and the original French are provided for quotations cited from the text.

Culler, Jonathan. *Flaubert: The Uses of Uncertainty.* Rev. ed. Ithaca, N.Y.: Cornell University Press, 1985. Classic, still highly relevant work examines Flaubert's narrative technique and use of irony. Provides both the original French and English translations for quotations from Flaubert's works.

Curry, Corrada Biazzo. *Description and Meaning in Three Novels by Gustave Flaubert.* New York: Peter Lang, 1997. Focuses on Flaubert's use of imagery in *Madame Bovary* (1857; English translation, 1886), *Salammbô* (1862; English translation, 1886), and *A Sentimental Education*. Demonstrates how his descriptive passages are subject to various possibilities of meaning and non-meaning.

Knight, Diana. *Flaubert's Characters: The Language of Illusion.* 1985. Reprint. New York: Cambridge University Press, 2009. Comparative study of Flaubert's fictional characters includes a valuable summary of earlier criticism. Chapter 5 offers a provocative interpretation of Frederic Moreau as an artist creating his life. Quotations from the novels appear in the original French.

Paulson, William. *"Sentimental Education": The Complexity of Disenchantment.* New York: Twayne, 1992. Comprehensive study of the novel presents concise background information on its literary and historical context as well as a clear discussion of Flaubert's narrative technique. Includes an excellent annotated bibliography.

Porter, Laurence M., ed. *A Gustave Flaubert Encyclopedia.* Westport, Conn.: Greenwood Press, 2001. Alphabetically arranged collection of articles focuses on Flaubert's literary works and their sources. Provides information about the places and characters in his fiction, nineteenth century history, and the writers who influenced and were influenced by Flaubert.

Troyat, Henri. *Flaubert*. Translated by Joan Pinkham. New York: Viking Press, 1992. Thorough, engrossing biography reconstructs Flaubert's life based on the novelist's prodigious correspondence with his family and friends.

Unwin, Timothy, ed. *The Cambridge Companion to Flaubert*. New York: Cambridge University Press, 2004. Collection of essays offers analyses of all of Flaubert's works as well as discussions of his life, his place in literary history, his writing process, and other aspects of his fiction. In the final essay, "Flaubert, Our Contemporary," noted novelist Mario Vargas Llosa assesses Flaubert's continued relevance.

Wall, Geoffrey. *Flaubert: A Life*. New York: Farrar, Straus, and Giroux, 2002. Critically acclaimed, highly readable narrative biography offers many previously unpublished details about Flaubert's life and works.

A Sentimental Journey

Author: Laurence Sterne (1713-1768)
First published: 1768, as *A Sentimental Journey Through France and Italy*
Type of work: Novel
Type of plot: Sentimental
Time of plot: 1760's
Locale: France

Principal characters:
MR. YORICK, a sentimental traveler
MADAME DE L——, a fellow traveler
MADAME DE R——, Madame de L——'s friend
COUNT DE B——, an admirer of Englishmen
LA FLEUR, a servant
MARIA, a country girl

The Story:

Mr. Yorick feels no kinship with all the different kinds of travelers—the Idle Travelers, the Inquisitive Travelers, the Travelers of Necessity, the Simple Travelers, and the rest. He is a Sentimental Traveler. As such, he collects sentimental adventures as other tourists collect postcards of the points of interest they visit. Mr. Yorick had started his journey because a man had asked him, with a sneer, if he had ever been in France. Yorick had just made some statement on the French and did not like being answered so tartly merely because he did not have firsthand experience. That same evening, he packed some clothes and left by boat for Calais.

While Yorick is having supper at an inn in Calais, a poor monk approaches him and begs alms for his monastery. Yorick rebuffs him with caustic and witty remarks. Later, Yorick sees the monk talking with an attractive woman who is also staying at the inn. Afraid the monk might tell her how rudely he has behaved, Yorick approaches the couple, apologizes to the monk, and offers his shell snuffbox to him as a peace offering. Now that Yorick has made friends with the monk and the lady, he plans to ask the lady to travel with him to Paris. He learns that her name is Madame de L——.

Proposing to make the trip to Paris in a private carriage, Yorick invites the lady to go with him to look over some of the vehicles for sale in a nearby courtyard. Their admiration of each other grows with unusual rapidity. Before Yorick has a chance to ask her to travel with him, however, she is called away by a message that her brother, Count de L——, has arrived. He has come to take her back to Belgium with him. Yorick is brokenhearted. In parting, Madame de L—— asks Yorick to visit her in Belgium if he passes through that country. She also gives him a letter of introduction to a good friend in Paris, Madame de R——.

The next day, Yorick sets off in a small carriage for Paris. His baggage falls out of the chaise several times, and he has an uncomfortable trip to Montriul. There, an innkeeper suggests he needs a servant, and Yorick sees that the man is quite right. He hires a young boy named La Fleur, whose greatest accomplishments are playing the flute and making love to the girls. La Fleur is delighted at the prospect of traveling around Europe with a generous and unpredictable English milord; he is only sad to have to say goodbye to all of his village sweethearts. Yorick is pleased with the lad's quickness and wit, and he is sure that the young Frenchman will be able to deal with any emergency arising along the way.

The first problem the travelers meet on their journey is a dead ass lying in the middle of the road. The horses refuse to pass the carcass, and La Fleur's horse throws him and runs away. Proceeding to the next town, they meet and talk with the owner of the poor dead animal. The owner had taken the ass with him from Germany to Italy and is very unhappy at its death, not so much because it had been a help to him but because he felt sure that the ass had loved him dearly and had been a good friend to him for many years.

In Paris, Yorick goes to the opera. A quotation from William Shakespeare pops into his mind, and he suddenly decides to go and buy the works of that writer. He enters a bookstore and finds a set on the counter. The books, however, are not for sale, having been sent to be re-bound for Count de B——, a great lover of English authors and Englishmen. In the shop, Yorick sees an attractive young girl who, he decides, must be a chambermaid. When she leaves the shop, he follows her and begins a conversation about the book she has bought. Yorick is surprised and pleased to discover that the young girl belongs to the household of Madame de R——. He tells her to inform her mistress that he will call the next day.

On returning to his rooms, Yorick learns from La Fleur that the police want to see him. In his rush out of England, he had forgotten to get a passport, and he had overlooked completely the fact that England and France were at war. He decides that he will have to get a passport, but he does not know how these matters are arranged in France. Madame de R—— is the only person in Paris to whom he carries a letter of introduction, and he does not want to bother the lady about the matter. The only other chance of help is from Count de B——, who, as he knows, likes Englishmen.

It takes Yorick some time to arrange to see the count; when he does, however, the count is most polite. As an amusing way to introduce himself, Yorick opens one of the volumes of Shakespeare, which had just been sent from the bookseller's. Turning to *Hamlet* and pointing to the passage about the jester Yorick, he says that is his name. The count is overcome with pleasure at meeting so famous a person, and nothing Yorick can say changes the count's mind. The count leaves the room and does not return for a long while. When he does, he presents Mr. Yorick with a passport that calls him the King's Jester. Realizing that he cannot correct the mistake without losing his passport, Yorick thanks the count and returns to his room.

The next day, Madame de R——'s chambermaid calls to see why Mr. Yorick has not visited her mistress as he had promised. Yorick explains about the passport and asks her to present his apology. Some hours later, after the girl has gone, the manager of the hotel comes in and objects to Yorick's having young ladies in his room. To keep from being evicted from the hotel, Yorick has to buy some lace from a young woman. He suspects that the manager pockets most of the profits from such sales.

On Sunday, La Fleur appears in a fine suit of clothes that he had bought secondhand. He asks if he might be allowed to have the day off, as he has made friends with a young woman he would like to see again that day. Yorick asks him to bring some food before he leaves for the day. Wrapped about the butter, which La Fleur brings with Yorick's dinner, is a piece of paper bearing some old printing. Yorick becomes interested in the story it tells and spends the whole day translating the faded characters to read the story of a luckless notary. Nevertheless, he is never to know the ending of the tale, for La Fleur had used the rest of the paper to wrap up a bouquet for his new friend.

Yorick has a fine time at parties to which he is invited by Count de B—— and the count's friends. Because he agrees with everyone to whom he talks and makes no remarks of his own, he is thought the finest wit in Paris. After several minor sentimental adventures, Yorick and La Fleur set out to travel through southern France. At Moulines, Yorick stops to see Maria, a poor unhappy girl who wanders about the country grieving for her dead father. He had heard of the girl from his old friend, Mr. Toby Shandy, who had met her several years before. Yorick sits down on a rock with Maria. Moved by her purity and sadness, he sheds a few tears with her.

Before ascending Mount Taurira, Yorick stops and has dinner with a pleasant peasant family. That night, he is forced to stay in a roadside inn. There is only one room in the inn, and Yorick has to share it with a French lady and her maid. In the room there are two large beds beside each other and, in a closet connected to the room, a cot. After much deliberation, the lady and Yorick take the big beds and send the maid into the closet. Yorick has to promise to stay in his bed and to keep silent all night. Unable to sleep, both Yorick and the lady begin talking. Afraid that something untoward might occur, the maid comes out of the closet and, unseen, stands between the two beds. Yorick stretches out his hand. With this sentimental gesture, Sterne ends abruptly the story of his sentimental journey.

Critical Evaluation:

The full title Lawrence Sterne gave his unconventional mixture of autobiography, travel impressions, and fiction—*A Sentimental Journey Through France and Italy*—is misleading. Sterne told of his travels through France, but he died of tuberculosis before writing the Italian section of his narrative. Sentimental, outrageous, and eccentric in its humorous effects, the novel is replete with delightful accounts and observations of whatever came into the author's mind. Like *The Life and Opinions of Tristram Shandy, Gent.* (1759-1767), the book broadened the scope of prose fiction for later writers by demonstrating that form and unified plot are not necessary for a successful novel.

In form and apparent subject, *A Sentimental Journey* follows in the tradition of the grand-tour novel. The depictions of scenes and persons, of escapades on the road, of the cultural adjustments required of an Englishman abroad, and of the things to be learned and the places to be visited were common, enjoyable reading matter for an eighteenth century audience. Sterne's grand tour, however, sports a delightful touch of irreverence. Its hero, Yorick, is not a typical young gentleman matriculating into a peripatetic finishing school but a low-key picaro buffeted by impulse and whimsy. Therefore, his "traveling" seems random. Unplanned, untimed, it accords perfectly with his sole principle, which, it seems, is to have no principle whatever except obedience to natural affections, to his growing sensibility, and his often unseemly passion. He prefers *filles de chambre* to cathedrals and a pretty face to a gallery portrait. Given his free-flowing nature, he does not seek to improve himself in accordance with a travel plan; he prefers to stumble over it in following his heart. The point Sterne makes is that a benevolent nature can be trusted not to err in promoting human goodness.

"Sentiment" and a host of such attendant words as "good nature," "sensibility," and "affections" were all terms with particular significance in Sterne's day. The doctrine of sensibility, popularized by the late seventeenth century Latitudinarian divines, urged an inherent goodness in human beings, a "sense" of moral absolutes that expresses itself in acts of charity and social benevolence. Championed philosophically by the third earl of Shaftesbury (in his *Characteristics of Men, Manners, Opinions, and Times*, 1711) and in fiction by Henry Fielding, this emphasis on good nature ran counter to the often equally influential tradition expounded by Thomas Hobbes in *Leviathan* (1651) and by Bernard de Mandeville in *The Fable of the Bees: Or, Private Vices, Public Benefits* (1714), a tradition that urged self-interest as the basis of all human action. These two forces collide in *A Sentimental Journey* as Sterne explores what it means to be a good person.

Sterne gave a sidelong glance at Hobbes in several of his characters: the huge oaf who deliberately blocks the view of a dwarf, the postilion who thrashes his horses, and even Yorick himself at the start of the novel when he refuses charity to a monk. Yet this "natural" cruelty—as Hobbes would have defined it—is contrasted with the virtues of a larger number of characters: the old French officer who assists the dwarf, the mourner who laments his dead animal, and the enlightened Yorick who guides the unfortunate Maria. Sterne recognizes only too well human beings' divided nature, in which good and evil are deeply intertwined, yet he wants to insist that the "deeper affections," the "eternal fountain of our feelings," as Yorick says, are also a primary impulse of inordinate strength.

Beneath the surface, *A Sentimental Journey* is something of an allegory, a type of metaphorical journey in which Yorick, and hence also the reader, discovers the primacy of human feeling. It is a travel not just through space and time but into sensibility itself, the common bond of all humanity. Yet on one level, the book is an outrageous comedy, and it is wise not to forget this. The famous ending ("When I stretched out my hand, I caught hold of the *fille de chambre's*—") and the mixed motives of its characters are reminders that Sterne wrote for delight as much as for instruction. The comedy, however, ought not to obscure a more serious intent in the book.

Sterne argues that there is a delicate line separating love from lust, if only because the "web of kindness" has "threads of love and desire . . . entangled with the piece." Too often, the temptation is to rend the whole web (as Yorick says) by drawing out the threads of love and desire, which results merely in people becoming heartless and cold. Instead, they ought to excuse occasional moral lapses in the interest of fostering greater love, for it is love alone that characterizes human beings in their best moments. This is the main point of Sterne's delightful Aristophanic fragment on the town of Abdera: There literature succeeds in making the most profligate town become devoted to Cupid. It is equally the point of Yorick's amorousness and of his belief that, once rekindled at Love's flame, he is all generosity and goodwill again. It underlies his celebration of freedom, La Fleur's Casanovan conquests, the Count de B——'s encomium on the fair sex, and, unforgettably, the French officer's noble lesson that mutual toleration teaches mutual love.

It could also be said that this message underlies Sterne's prose style inasmuch as readers, like Yorick, are sentimental travelers. The associative drift of the narrative precludes expectation; it demands instead that readers allow themselves to be taken wherever their sensibility chooses to take them. The novel demands to be read less with the head than with the heart. Many of the scenes, for example, play unabashedly on the emotions, just as Sterne plays on the readers' elementary sense of justice and distinction between what is right and wrong to score his points. In an intriguing way, therefore, *A Sentimental Journey* is not merely about a grand tour but is itself a grand tour. It is an education in the consistency of human nature, not its diversity. It is, like Euripides before Abdera, Sterne before the world.

"Critical Evaluation" by David B. Carroll

Further Reading

Bowden, Martha F. *Yorick's Congregation: The Church of England in the Time of Laurence Sterne*. Newark: University of Delaware Press, 2007. Examines the religious environment in which Sterne wrote his novels and sermons, explicating passages from his work to demonstrate how his experience of life in rural parishes informs his novels.

Brissenden, R. F. "The Sentimental Comedy: *A Sentimental Journey*." In *Virtue in Distress*. London: Macmillan, 1974. Argues that the primary purpose of *A Sentimental Journey* is to show the inextricable if ironic link between human beings' capacity for the social virtues of compassion and sympathy and their capacity for sexual responsiveness.

Gerard, W. B. *Laurence Sterne and the Visual Imagination*. Burlington, Vt.: Ashgate, 2006. A study of the illustrations by William Hogarth and other artists that complement Sterne's work. Examines the pictorial quality of Sterne's writing, describing how it inspires the visual imagination. Analyzes some of the illustrations for *A Sentimental Journey* and *Tristram Shandy*.

Howes, Alan B., ed. *Sterne: The Critical Heritage*. London: Routledge & Kegan Paul, 1974. A thorough and well-organized compilation of criticism, acclaim, and even accusations of plagiarism by Sterne's contemporaries in response to the publication of *A Sentimental Journey*. Discusses other works by Sterne.

Keymer, Thomas, ed. *The Cambridge Companion to Laurence Sterne*. New York: Cambridge University Press, 2009. Collection of specially commissioned essays analyzing Sterne's works and their key issues of sentimentalism, national identity, and gender. Some of the essays consider Sterne's life, milieu, literary career, and his subsequent influence on modernism. "*A Sentimental Journey* and the Failure of Feeling" by Keymer analyzes this novel.

Kraft, Elizabeth. *Laurence Sterne Revisited*. New York: Twayne, 1996. Provides a short biography and then devotes individual chapters to specific works, including *A Sentimental Journey*. The final chapter assesses Sterne's changing critical reputation.

Loveridge, Mark. *Laurence Sterne and the Argument About Design*. New York: Macmillan, 1982. Explores Sterne's use of pattern, design, and form, and places these concepts within the general cultural and literary context of his day. Chapter 7 deals exclusively with *A Sentimental Journey*.

Moglen, Helene. *The Philosophical Irony of Laurence Sterne*. Gainesville: University Press of Florida, 1975. Systematically discusses Sterne's use of stylistic and thematic irony in relation to character, theme development, and thematic unity. Explores the relevance of his novel to contemporary times.

New, Melvyn, ed. *Critical Essays on Laurence Sterne*. New York: G. K. Hall, 1998. Some of the essays focus on *A Sentimental Journey* and on sentimentality in Sterne's fiction.

Ross, Ian Campbell. *Laurence Sterne: A Life*. New York: Oxford University Press, 2001. This thorough and well-researched biography concentrates on the events of Sterne's life rather than on an analysis of his literary works. Includes a bibliography and an index.

A Separate Peace

Author: John Knowles (1926-2001)
First published: 1959
Type of work: Novel
Type of plot: Bildungsroman
Time of plot: 1942-1943 and 1958
Locale: New Hampshire

Principal characters:
GENE FORRESTER, a man reflecting on his experience in preparatory school
PHINEAS (FINNY), Gene's best friend
ELWIN "LEPER" LEPELLIER and BRINKER HADLEY, their classmates

The Story:

In 1958, Gene Forrester returns to his preparatory school, the Devon School, and reflects on the events that occurred there fifteen years prior. His memories start with the summer session of 1942 and end after a tragic event during the 1943 school year. Central to Gene's reflections is his relationship with his roommate and best friend Phineas, who most people affectionately call "Finny."

As a student, Gene is a far more dedicated and successful

than Finny, but he feels threatened by Finny's athleticism. Gene also envies his friend for several reasons, including his honesty and his ability to get away with almost anything: School administrators rarely punish Finny since they are quelled by his sincere charm. Gene also proves subject to Finny's charisma. The two often flout rules together, and in one instance they bike to the ocean. While there, Finny tells Gene that he considers Gene his best friend; Gene says nothing in return.

The summer of 1942 appears peaceful, and the students seem somehow apart from the rest of the world, which is plagued by the effects of World War II. On Finny's initiative, some students form the Super Suicide Society of the Summer Session. The society's members engage in daring actions, such as jumping from an enormous tree into the river below. Gene and Finny jump together, and Finny considers this jump symbolic of the solidarity of their friendship. Meanwhile, Gene's feelings of jealousy toward Finny grow; Gene feels irritated by Finny dragging him to Suicide Society meetings every night, especially when Gene wants to spend the evenings studying. Gene suspects that Finny, who is already more athletically gifted than he is, wants to sabotage Gene's academic studies so Gene will no longer best Finny in any way.

One night, Gene tells Finny he does not want to attend the society's meeting and expects a poor reaction from Finny. Instead, Finny simply tells Gene not to come along; he assumes Gene's scholastic abilities are natural and apologizes for preventing him from studying. Confident that Finny's intentions are pure, Gene decides to attend the meeting after all. At the meeting, Gene and Finny again climb the tree and prepare to jump. Gene's knees bend, the limb they are standing on trembles, and Finny plummets to the ground. The impact completely shatters the star athlete's leg.

Finny returns to his hometown, and Gene visits him there. He tells Finny that he shook the tree limb purposefully, but Finny refuses to believe him. Now in their final year, the students feel the pressure of the war. One day after Gene and Brinker Hadley (an influential classmate) shovel out some train tracks buried in snow, they watch recruits pass by and are inspired by the young men, who are not much older than themselves. During their return trip to Devon, they run into Elwin "Leper" Lepellier, a shy boy with a love for nature and skiing. Leper has spent the day skiing; this disgusts Brinker, who feels his fellow students are not sufficiently concerned about the war. Brinker suddenly decides to enlist, and Gene decides to do the same. Gene changes his mind, however, when he notices that Finny has returned, confined to crutches.

Brinker also does not enlist but instead resigns from most of his extracurricular activities since, in the light of the war, they seem frivolous. Finny encourages Gene to improve his physical abilities, and Gene does, viewing the commitment as an obligation to Finny because he destroyed Finny's physical prowess, even if unintentionally. The two roommates refuse to let Finny's accident and whatever caused it affect their friendship.

After watching a film showing troops on skis, Leper enlists. His shocked classmates imagine shy Leper committing amazing feats for the allies. Instead, Leper begins hallucinating and sees human limbs in arbitrary places. He deserts the Army before he can be discharged and sneaks back to Devon.

Brinker tries to convince Gene that, for Finny's own good, people must stop pitying him and make him confront the reality that he is crippled. Gene dislikes this suggestion. That evening, some of Brinker's friends force Finny and Gene into a building where students dressed in robes begin questioning Finny and Gene. They stage a trial to divine how Finny fell from the tree. The two friends clearly do not want to discuss the matter, but the other students press them. They even call Leper as a witness. Finny yells suddenly that he does not care about the outcome of the trial and hobbles off on his crutches. A loud crash follows. Finny has fallen down a large staircase, breaking his leg for a second time.

Staff members take Finny to the infirmary, and Gene follows. Once Finny is alone, Gene attempts to talk to him. Outraged, Finny asks Gene what else of his Gene plans to break. Gene returns the next day, and Finny apologizes for the way he treated Gene, explaining that the catalyst for his anger was his rejection from all military branches. Finny has spent the last few months trying to enlist, but, because of his leg, no organization will allow him entrance. Crying, Finny asks Gene if it was just an impulse to shake the tree branch, and Gene says it was an accident. Finny believes him.

After class, Gene returns to the infirmary. The doctor informs him that while he was setting the broken bone some marrow made its way into Finny's heart. As a result, Finny died. Gene does not cry for his friend. Instead, he reflects on how people and countries create their own enemies, as Gene once did with Finny. Gene remembers Finny for his sincerity and realizes the only enemy Gene had at school was himself.

Critical Evaluation:

John Knowles wrote in various prose forms, including the novel and short story, but *A Separate Peace* was his most celebrated work. Knowles based the novel on his experiences at his own preparatory school, Phillips Exeter Academy, a place Knowles loved for its natural beauty and atmosphere.

Rich in detail, the book presents readers with many complex themes, including individuality, denial, memory, and youth.

Knowles's work stresses the concept of individuality and, inherently, resisting conformity. Finny epitomizes individuality; his confidence and his choices often cause discomfort in others. Finny wears a pink shirt to dinner, uses the school tie as a belt, and shares his feelings openly about emotional subjects such as his friendship with Gene. These actions place him apart from his classmates, who wear their uniforms properly and do not reveal their vulnerabilities. Finny's sincerity also emphasizes his individuality: While most of his classmates act and speak as expected—properly and with regard to the addressed person's class and station—Finny speaks simply and honestly. He speaks freely even to members of the school's administration. While these adults seem taken aback, they never rebuke Finny for his behavior since his comments are sincere, confident, and always well intended.

Another topic central to *A Separate Peace* is denial. Finny's claim that there is no war functions as the most obvious example of denial in the novel. Since he cannot play an active role in the war because of his injury, he flatly and fervently argues the war is nothing more than a ploy concocted by fat, old, wealthy men. Knowles also poignantly explores the nuances of denial in the characters of Gene and Finny after the latter's fall from the tree. Gene is afraid to confront himself about why the limb shook, and Finny refuses to believe Gene's revelation that he jounced the limb on purpose. The two stay friends as long as the issue remains overlooked.

Gene and Finny's denial over the accident leads to significant pain, and the nature of Gene's actions must eventually be confronted. After Finny's leg breaks for the second time, he and Gene face reality together. Finny's resolve finally fades, and he confronts Gene, unleashing all the worries and concerns that have plagued him since his accident. Relieved that Finny acknowledges what Gene has always felt (that he shook the limb on purpose), the young men finally come to peace with themselves and one another. Because denial has been replaced by acknowledgment of the truth, Gene feels peace even after losing his best friend.

Since the novel is framed as a flashback to years past, another theme central to the novel is remembrance. The adult Gene seems unafraid of reliving the past in his memory since the truth of what transpired was uncovered years ago. Readers may doubt the objectivity of Gene's memories since he plays a central role in the story he narrates. By encapsulating the novel in memory, Knowles forces readers to question whether events transpired as Gene describes. Gene's sense of peace at the close of the book, coupled with his critical and reflective exploration of his younger self, tends to indicate that Gene's rendering of events is accurate. As a novel that encourages readers to value honesty and reality, several of the work's central themes would be discredited if Gene's version of events were unfaithful.

Knowles suggests that one's setting has incredible power to evoke memories. The novel opens with Gene describing, in detail, Devon's grounds. Including such details helps contextualize the story for readers, and Knowles expertly provides graphic descriptions of both natural objects (such as trees and rivers) and artificial structures (such as buildings on the Devon campus). These elements function as a framework for Gene to remember and, in many respects, relive the past.

The subject of youth is also fundamental to the novel. The story focuses on a group of young men who at first, in their junior year, seem protected from the war. Gene recalls that even some of the school staff made special allowances for the young men. During the summer of 1942, Gene and his friends came to represent pure freedom. They were carefree, and the older men (all too knowledgeable about the straining effects of war) admired these students' situation: Gene, Finny, Brinker, and the others were all young men on the brink of going off to war but still inhabited a pocket of time in which they could live joyfully. Gene and his friends were bursting with potential, the potential to live gloriously or to die sorrowfully. Some would live sadly, like Leper, whose mind broke under the pressure of war; some would die tragically, like Finny, without even setting foot on a battlefield. *A Separate Peace* reminds readers that, even though one matures, youth is still accessible through memory. Likewise, revisiting one's youth may create a sense of peace, a peace that is possible only with reflection.

Karley K. Adney

Further Reading

Bloom, Harold, ed. *John Knowles' "A Separate Peace."* Philadelphia: Chelsea House, 2000. This collection of scholarly essays explores the novel's themes, issues of perspective, the novel's structure, the influence of the novel, and its place in Knowles's body of work.

Bryant, Hallman Bell. *"A Separate Peace": The War Within.* Boston: Twayne, 1990. Places *A Separate Peace* in perspective for readers by studying life during World War II; builds a framework of understanding by incorporating Knowles's personal reflections on the novel.

_____, ed. *Understanding "A Separate Peace": A Student Casebook to Issues, Sources, and Historical Documents.*

Westport, Conn.: Greenwood Press, 2002. Collection of primary and secondary documents that contextualize Knowles's novel for readers. Includes some reflective pieces by Knowles, a section devoted to American preparatory schools, documents capturing life in the Army, and a section exploring concerns in Knowles's novel that remain contemporary, including the relationship between athletics and education, single-sex education, hazing, and even post-traumatic stress disorder.

Karson, Jill, ed. *Readings on "A Separate Peace."* San Diego, Calif.: Greenhaven Press, 1999. This collection provides a detailed analysis of symbolism in the novel. Contributors also explore the theme of freedom, the func-

tion of fear, and the novel's narrative structure, among other topics.

Sova, Dawn B. *Literature Suppressed on Social Grounds*. New York: Facts On File, 2006. Part of a series on book banning and censorship. Knowles's novel receives attention for the frequency with which it has been banned and challenged.

Whissen, Thomas R. *Classic Cult Fiction: A Companion to Popular Cult Literature*. New York: Greenwood Press, 1992. Whissen examines fifty novels that have received "cult classic" status and the reasons that each particular work—including Knowles's *A Separate Peace*—has inspired such passionate reader devotion.

Set This House on Fire

Author: William Styron (1925-2006)
First published: 1960
Type of work: Novel
Type of plot: Psychological realism
Time of plot: Mid-twentieth century
Locale: Sambuco, Italy

Principal characters:
CASS KINSOLVING, an expatriate alcoholic painter from the southern United States
PETER LEVERETT, an expatriate American lawyer and friend of Cass
MASON FLAGG, an American millionaire and friend of Cass and Peter
LUIGI MIGLIORE, an Italian police officer and Fascist humanist philosopher
FRANCESCA RICCI, an Italian peasant girl, loved by Cass but raped by Mason Flagg

The Story:

Peter Leverett, the first-person narrator of *Set This House on Fire*, is a lawyer in New York plagued by disturbing memories of and questions about events in Sambuco, Italy, several years earlier, which he partially observed and which culminated in the rape and murder of a young, beautiful Italian, Francesca Ricci, and in the death of Mason Flagg. Mason, a millionaire American temporarily in Sambuco, is found at the base of a cliff a few hours after the brutal attack on Francesca, and the Italian police decided an enraged, lustful Mason attacked Francesca and then killed himself in remorse. Having known Mason since their high school days some ten years earlier and believing him to be sexually obsessed but not a murderer, Peter has difficulty accepting the official explanation. After seeing a *New York Times* political cartoon drawn by Cass Kinsolving, another American who was in Sambuco when Mason and Francesca died, Peter

decides to contact Cass and get his version of what happened, particularly since Cass seems somehow to be involved.

Peter leaves New York for Virginia, where he grew up and where his parents still live, on his way to visit Cass in Charleston, South Carolina. In Virginia, Peter finds his hometown drastically changed and virtually unrecognizable, modernized and urbanized, and street names changed, such as "Bankhead Magruder Avenue" becoming "Buena Vista Terrace," prompting Peter's father to comment that "it's the California influence . . . it's going to get us all in the end."

In Charleston, Peter narrates, via personal flashback and quotation from Cass's comments and notebook, their experiences and observations prior to and after their arrival in Sambuco which, in totality, reconstruct the earlier reality and generate the truth about Francesca's rape and murder and Mason's death. First, Peter relates his school-based knowledge of Mason, a Northerner transplanted to Virginia because his unaffectionate movie-mogul father bought a plantation there, a place of entertainment for his movie-star friends. Peter also explains Mason's unusually close attachment to his alcoholic, virtually deserted mother and relates Mason's dismissal from school after his drunken seduction of a thirteen-year-old, imbecilic girl.

Peter then tells of his arrival in Sambuco on the afternoon before the murder, interrupting filming of a movie scene; a movie company was in Sambuco partially because of a tie to Mason. Next, Peter describes the movie crowd's raucous party and the mysterious scratches around Mason's face. He also observed Mason pursue and threaten to kill a young Italian girl who, with her dress torn, ran from his residence. Later, Peter observed Cass kiss this same girl (Francesca) and observed Mason receive a note that said, "You're in deep trouble. . . . I'm going to turn you into bait for buzzards. C." Peter then watched Mason humiliate a drunken Cass by coercing him to perform a "trained seal" act for the movie crowd (recite bawdy limericks, pantomime the behavior of a French whore, and sing "Old Black Joe," and do the "rebel yell," among other activities). Rescuing Cass from this humiliation, Peter went with him to deliver medicine (stolen from Mason) to Francesca's dying father. Peter then slept, awakening to the news of Francesca's rape and murder, and Mason's death.

Peter next presents Cass's account of his life prior to coming to Sambuco—his lower-class southern childhood, his determination to become a successful artist, his horrifying World War II experiences, and his subsequent mental problems, including an inability to successfully paint but desperate need to do so and an inability to avoid the alcohol consumption that seemed to dull the pain of his artistic failure but that actually only increased it. A successful painter in Charleston, Cass described himself as guilt-ridden and doubt-filled in Sambuco, haunted by dreams of his prior abuse of an African American family and unable to believe in any divine purpose for or control over the universe. Cass then explained that his love for Francesca and his desire to help her impoverished, dying father became his last means of escape from his depression and addiction. Cass said that Mason's rape of Francesca and his belief that Mason brutally attacked her a second time, killing her, led him to kill Mason, subsequently throwing his body over the cliff. Cass then learned that the second, more brutal attack on Francesca was by Saverio, the idiot of Sambuco, and that Luigi Migliore, Cass's Italian police officer-philosopher friend, concealed the evidence of Cass's attack and attributed Mason's death to suicide, because Luigi was convinced that "there had been in Sambuco

this day entirely too much suffering." Luigi believed that obtaining Cass's freedom would keep him "from the luxury of any more guilt" and force him to face his failings, conquer them, and salvage at least the remainder of his troubled life.

Cass related that he protested violently but eventually acquiesced, returning to the American South and gradually overcoming, at least somewhat, his artistic block, alcohol addiction, and depression. His talk with Peter thus leads him to understand the sexual obsessiveness that caused Mason to rape Francesca and helps him to understand the events in Sambuco that ended in Mason's death. Peter then returns to New York, reconciled to Mason's innocence of at least murder and to the tragically confused and violent inevitability of the events in Sambuco.

Critical Evaluation:

Set This House on Fire is William Styron's second novel, published nine years after *Lie Down in Darkness* (1951), the latter generating for Styron his reputation in the 1950's as America's most promising young novelist. Perhaps partly because of that reputation, *Set This House on Fire* represents Styron's desire to create an ambitious novel—lengthy, complex, graphically emotional, and often profound. However, since Styron's second novel is deceptively different from his first—in length, in location, and in extent of psychological portraiture—many critics found it disappointing, labeling it melodramatic, pretentious, vague, and unconvincing. These criticisms are undeserved, reflecting a failure to comprehend Styron's essential thematic concern and his fundamental technique.

Thematically, *Set This House on Fire* is completely a southern novel, but it is often unappreciated as such, given its symbolist (even allegorical) technique. This technique accounts for the Italian setting, Sambuco being a place of antiquity where characters are not constrained from confronting their primeval emotional and philosophical longings. Sambuco represents uncluttered human reality, unlike the modernized and urbanized hometown that Peter Leverett can no longer truly recognize or understand. In Sambuco, though, Peter can realize his true relationship to Mason Flagg (mutual dislike), and Cass Kinsolving can confront his guilt-ridden past and overcome it by purgative actions (serving as Mason's "slave" entertainer; helping the peasant father of Francesca, whom he associates with African Americans he abused in previous years; and murdering Mason).

The killing of Mason has been particularly misunderstood: Many critics fail to go beyond the symbolism of Mason's last name (Flagg, as in American flag, a symbol of America). Mason can also be understood in the context of the

Mason-Dixon line, specifically the northern side of that line, the Yankee side. His northern wealth, his northern upbringing, and his abrupt transplantation to Virginia via his father's carpetbaggerlike assumption of ownership of a Virginia plantation all connote Mason as a symbol of northern American commercial and industrial power, wealth, and corruption. In contrast, Cass Kinsolving is the "Dixon" part of the Mason-Dixon division. The name Kinsolving symbolizes the solving of problems created by his kinfolks, his southern ancestors. Born in North Carolina and most comfortable in Charleston, a center of Old South culture, Cass represents the South's strengths and weaknesses. He is heavily burdened by guilt over his treatment of African Americans, but he is violently opposed to the cultural superficiality, materialism, and sexual callousness of Mason. Like many southerners, Cass idolizes women, and his spiritual agonizing and artistic uncertainty are representative of southern intellectual and cultural nihilism as a result of the Civil War (symbolized by World War II in the novel). Thus, when Cass becomes Mason's "trained seal," he is doing penance for his symbolic enslavement of African Americans, and in helping Francesca's peasant father and killing Mason he is exacting revenge for the Civil War and northern material and sexual excesses. Thus, Cass regains his self-respect by his retribution against the North's oppression of the South as represented, in his mind, by Mason. He can then return to Charleston emotionally cleansed and able to productively paint and to continue his criticism of northern America via cartoons in *The New York Times*.

The novel's techniques often reflect the influence of other authors, such as Nathaniel Hawthorne and William Faulkner. Cass's constant psychological self-examination is clearly reminiscent of Robin Molineux in "My Kinsman, Major Molineux" (1832), for example, and the frequent use of flashbacks similarly echoes Hawthorne's obsessive self-examination techniques. Also, Styron repeatedly presents Cass's reveries in a state midway between sleeping and waking, in which he may be dreaming or daydreaming, with his repressed feelings of guilt exhibiting themselves in grotesquely altered forms. Styron presents Cass (and implicitly the South) as haunted by its treatment of African Americans. Peter's father touches on this while looking out at the ocean off Virginia's shore.

> That's where they came in, in the year 1619. Right out there. It was one of the saddest days in the history of man, I mean black *or* white. We're still paying for that day, and we'll be paying for it from right here on out. And there'll be blood shed, and tears.

Although skillfully disguised, symbolized, and put at a distance in Sambuco, the problem of America is the focal point of Styron's *Set This House on Fire*. Analogous to Hawthorne's dramatization of the effects of the excesses of American Puritanism, Styron dramatizes the continuing implications of America's racial history, acted out in profound psychological and physical microcosm in the conflict between Mason and Cass. *Set This House on Fire* is a profoundly Southern novel.

John L. Grigsby

Further Reading

Cologne-Brookes, Gavin. *The Novels of William Styron: From Harmony to History*. Baton Rouge: Louisiana State University Press, 1995. Examines the influence of the modernist movement on Styron's novels, exploring his psychological themes and analyzing his shifting patterns of discourse. Chapter 3 focuses on *Set This House on Fire*.

Fossum, Robert H. *William Styron*. Grand Rapids, Mich.: Eerdmans, 1968. Includes a thorough and perceptive chapter on *Set This House on Fire*. Notes the novel's existential bent and implications of purgatorial suffering.

Friedman, Melvin J. *William Styron*. Bowling Green, Ohio: Bowling Green State University Popular Press, 1974. Argues that the novel is a caricature of traditional detective fiction. Notes the importance of setting but incompletely explains the symbolism.

Hadaller, David. *Gynicide: Women in the Novels of William Styron*. Madison, N.J.: Fairleigh Dickinson University Press, 1996. Explores the treatment of women in Styron's fiction, with special emphasis on his handling of women's deaths and the meaning of these deaths. Argues that Styron's depictions force readers to question a society that victimizes women. Chapter 3 focuses on *Set This House on Fire*.

Pearce, Richard. *William Styron*. Minneapolis: University of Minnesota Press, 1971. Focuses on the class conflict implications in Styron's depiction of economic disparities and the violence underlying the superficial sophistication of American culture.

Ross, Daniel W., ed. *The Critical Response to William Styron*. Westport, Conn.: Greenwood Press, 1995. A collection of previously printed reviews and articles, as well as original essays, that chronologically trace the critical reception of Styron's novels.

Rubin, Louis D. *The Faraway Country: Writers of the Modern South*. Seattle: University of Washington Press, 1963.

One of the best analyses of the novel, depicting some of the southern themes implicit in it and sensitively analyzing the psychological portrait of Cass Kinsolving.

Ruderman, Judith. *William Styron.* New York: Ungar, 1987. A thorough study of the novel that utilizes prior criticism in effectively interpreting some of Styron's symbols. Astutely analyzes Mason Flagg's sexual obsessiveness.

West, James L. W., III, ed. *William Styron: A Life.* New York: Random House, 1998. A comprehensive biography that lucidly and cogently connects events in Styron's life to his fiction. An essential work for anyone who wishes to understand Styron and his writing.

Zetterberg Pettersson, Eva. *The Old World Journey: National Identity in Four American Novels from 1960 to 1973.* Uppsala, Sweden: Uppsala University Press, 2005. An analysis of *Set This House on Fire* and other novels about Americans traveling to Europe that were published in the 1960's and early 1970's. Demonstrates how the European journey is a means of raising questions about American identity.

Seven Against Thebes

Author: Aeschylus (525/524-456/455 B.C.E.)
First produced: Hepta epi Thēbas, 467 B.C.E. (English translation, 1777)
Type of work: Drama
Type of plot: Tragedy
Time of plot: Antiquity
Locale: Thebes

Principal characters:
ETEOCLES, the king of Thebes
POLYNICES, his brother
ANTIGONE and ISMENE, their sisters
A SPY
THEBAN WOMEN, the chorus

The Story:

After the ruin and exile of Oedipus, the king of Thebes, his sons, Eteocles and Polynices, fall into dispute, each brother claiming supreme authority in the city. The quarrel leads to a bloody civil war in which Eteocles is victorious. Banished from Thebes, Polynices goes to Argos. There he musters an army, led by six famous Argive heroes, for the purpose of returning and recapturing the city, which is restless under his brother's rule.

Thebes is besieged by the Argive warriors camped about its walls. Eteocles, consulting a seer, learns that his brother's army is planning to make a surprise night attack and, under cover of darkness, to scale the walls and overwhelm the defenders. Eteocles exhorts all Theban men, young and old, to stand bravely at their posts and to repel the attackers.

While he speaks, a spy reports to Eteocles that Polynices and his Argives have sworn to raze the city, their vows made with clasps of hands stained by blood dripping from the head of an ox sacrificed in solemn ritual. The spy also brings word that Polynices and the six Argive heroes drew lots to determine the city gates against which each of the seven would lead his band of attackers.

Upon hearing the spy's report, the Theban women call upon the gods and goddesses to protect Cadmus's sacred city from the onslaught of the besiegers. Eteocles rebukes the frightened women and declares that they are wasting their time with appeals to the gods at a time of imminent peril. He asserts that the Thebans must depend on their own courage and strength, not upon the unpredictable gods. Angrily he dismisses the women to attend to their children and weaving; they are to leave all other matters to their husbands and fathers.

Eteocles then chooses the six outstanding warriors of Thebes who will, with himself, defend the seven gates of the city against the seven Achaean warriors who swear each to take a gate of the city by storm. The king chooses the defending heroes carefully. Theban Melanippus will oppose Argive Tydeus; Polyphontes, Capaneus; Megareus, Eteocles of Argos; Hyperbius, Hippomedon; Actor, Parthenopaeus; and Lasthenes, Amphiaraus. Polynices is to be the seventh hero leading the attack against the seventh gate, so Eteocles announces that he will stand as his brother's opponent. Their combat, prince against prince, brother against brother, will determine the destiny of their ill-fated house.

Hearing his words, the Theban women again begin their wailing lament and warn him against the sin of fratricide. Eteocles, well aware of the blood bath that his family already suffered because of the curse of Pelops on Laius, his grandfather, ignores the city matrons. Defying the fickle gods, he declares that he is determined to remain the king of Thebes, even if his brother's death must be the price of his crown.

At Eteocles' mention of the curse upon his house, the Theban women deplore the sad story of Laius. Already cursed by Pelops, whose hospitality he desecrated, Laius was warned by Apollo that he would prosper only if he sired no child. In spite of the warning, however, he fathered a son, Oedipus. Later the child was abandoned in the wilderness, where he was saved from death by the intervention of an old household servant and reared to manhood by a good shepherd. Oedipus, in turn, defied prophecies of disaster and doom when he, unaware of his true identity, murdered Laius, his father, and subsequently married Jocasta, his mother. Two of the children of their ill-starred union were Eteocles and Polynices, whose rivalry caused untold suffering in Thebes. The women weep when they recall the years of strife and trouble brought upon their city by the doomed line of Cadmus.

Meanwhile the brazen clamor of arms and the shouts of men sound in the distance; the attack begins. While the women wait to learn the outcome of the assault, a messenger brings word that the defenders beat back the Argive warriors at six of the seven gates. The city is saved, he announces, but in the fighting at the seventh gate Eteocles and Polynices are both slain.

At the height of the attack, when the battle was fiercest, the brothers killed each other, thus fulfilling the prophecy of Oedipus that his sons would share glory by iron, that is to say, by the sword, not by gold. The only land over which they will rule will be the grave, and the soil that called them masters is now red with their blood.

The bodies of Eteocles and Polynices are carried into the city in preparation for their burial. Antigone and Ismene, sisters of the dead princes, mourn their violent deaths, while the Theban women sing a mournful dirge for the tragic ending of a great family, cursed by the gods but defiant of the doom forecast years before and then unhappily fulfilled.

In the middle of their laments, a herald appears to announce the decision of the Theban senate. Eteocles, the city fathers decree, was his country's friend; as such, his body is to receive final burial rites and to be interred within the royal tomb. Men will remember him as his city's champion and savior. Polynices, on the other hand, sowed dissension and civil strife. Demanding fit punishment for his crimes against the state, the senate proclaimed that his body should be thrown outside the city gates, where dogs and ravens can feast upon his flesh.

Antigone imperiously defies the city fathers. If no one else will give her brother a burial befitting his rank, she declares, she herself will bury him. It is her opinion, since he is the older son and therefore rightful heir to the throne, that he was no more right and no more wrong than Eteocles was in his beliefs and deeds.

Her brave defiance brings many sympathizing citizens to her side. Some declare that laws often change and what is one day right is often wrong tomorrow. The others, surrounding the corpse of Eteocles, maintain that they will obey the decree of the senate. In that division of public opinion more troubles are forecast for the unhappy city.

Critical Evaluation:

In this severely simple drama, in which all the action is described by messengers, Aeschylus presents the third and closing episode in the tragic legend of the royal house of Thebes. The plays dealing with the fate of Laius and of his son Oedipus unfortunately did not survive, but in the extant drama the deaths of Eteocles and his brother Polynices, sons of Oedipus and grandsons of Laius, are the culmination of three generations of violence, bloodshed, and agony that arose from Laius's ingratitude to Pelops. The delineation of the character of Eteocles in this play marks in Greek tragedy a new departure which was to be perfected by Sophocles and Euripides.

Seven Against Thebes was first produced as part of a Theban trilogy in 467 B.C.E., with which Aeschylus won first place in the Athenian drama competition. By then he had been writing tragedies for more than thirty years. Almost single-handedly he had fashioned an important art form out of the drama with his technical improvements and his gift for stirring dramatic poetry. Aeschylus was a very prominent playwright at that time, and younger men, such as Sophocles, were building on his achievements. Although *Seven Against Thebes* is a mature work, Aeschylus's finest triumphs were still to come.

The two other plays in this Theban series have not survived. Apparently they dealt with the legends of Laius and of Oedipus, the grandfather and the father of Eteocles and Polynices. *Seven Against Thebes* shows Aeschylus grappling with the theme of the blood curse. Laius was cursed because of his gross ingratitude to Pelops. Oedipus was cursed because he slew his father Laius and married his mother Jocasta; and he in turn cursed his sons Polynices and Eteocles for begrudging him food. This is the background for the fratricidal strife between the two, and for Eteocles' headstrong desire to fight his brother.

With Aeschylus a family curse is something almost palpable, a presence that hovers over a clan and works its doom. Each member of the family has free will, but that will is part of a whole that heads passionately for disaster. The audience sees this in Eteocles, a forerunner of the tragic hero; in Polynices; and in Antigone as she resolutely defies the edict of the Theban council by marching off to bury Polynices. Their fates are chosen, willed by themselves in full knowledge of the consequences, and yet they fit a broad pattern of calamity in the Theban Dynasty.

Seven Against Thebes falls into three sections, which diminish progressively in length. The first part handles Eteocles' preparations for battle, the second tells of the war's end and shows the mourning for the sons of Oedipus, while the third deals with Antigone's rebellion against the edict.

In the first section, the audience watches Eteocles in action as an effective leader in defending Thebes. His military address to the troops, his means of getting information about the enemy plans from seer and spy, the way he quells the panicky prayers of the Theban matrons, the type of men he chooses to defend the city gates, and his own willingness to fight, all point to an excellent general. If his right to rule Thebes is questionable, there is no doubt about the quality of his leadership in defending Thebes.

He is manly and disdainful of women who endanger the city through fright and weakness. Eteocles is not impious, for he sees the value of masculine piety in war, but he feels that men should rely chiefly on their own strength. There is, however, a barrier between him and heaven—the curse his father laid on him. He knows that he is doomed, but he takes every precaution to save Thebes. The patriotism of Aeschylus shines through the character of Eteocles. If it were not for his willful sin of fratricide, Eteocles might be an authentic tragic hero.

The second section underscores the idea of the blood curse, announces the Theban victory, and shows the mourning for Eteocles and Polynices. In the final section, with Antigone's defiance of the city elders, the audience realizes that the family curse does not end. Antigone is making a new crisis in burying her outcast brother. There is an echo of the brothers' feud in the way she leaves with Polynices' body while Ismene, following the edict, exits with the corpse of Eteocles.

It is significant that the audience sees the conflict between the brothers from the Theban point of view—from inside the city. The attackers are depicted as evildoers, as boastful, impious adventurers largely, each intent on sacking and burning the city and carrying off the women as slaves. The audience can understand the panic of the Theban chorus. Aeschylus knew from his experience in the Greek and Persian wars how

it felt to be assaulted by foreign troops who want to enslave one's homeland. He lived in a heroic era, and his dramas convey the grandeur of Periclean Athens.

Among other things, *Seven Against Thebes* is a rousing martial poem with a wide variety of poetic and rhetorical techniques. There is the military pep talk, the dithyrambic invocation of the gods, invective, choral odes, antithesis in choosing defenders, the dirge, stichomythia in the mourning of Antigone and Ismene, and debate between Antigone and the herald. From a poetic point of view the play is a tour de force.

This drama is usually seen as a prelude to *Oresteia* (458 B.C.E.; English translation, 1777), Aeschylus's greatest dramas, in which he again takes up the theme of the blood curse. *Seven Against Thebes* is a great work, and if it is not considered of the highest quality, the reason is that readers have the later plays of Aeschylus and the finest plays of Sophocles and Euripides for comparison.

"Critical Evaluation" by James Weigel, Jr.

Further Reading

Cameron, H. D. *Studies on the "Seven Against Thebes" of Aeschylus*. The Hague, the Netherlands: Mouton, 1971. One of the few books to concentrate specifically on this early and often slighted work of Aeschylus. Presumes some prior knowledge of the subject.

Conacher, D. J. *Aeschylus: The Earlier Plays and Related Studies*. Toronto, Ont.: University of Toronto Press, 1996. Devotes a chapter to an analysis of the play and its trilogy and includes three appendixes: "The Timing of Eteocles' Assignments at the Seven Gates," "'Eteocles' Fateful Decision': Various Views," and "Some Problems Concerning the End of *The Septem*."

Fritz, Kurt von. "The Character of Eteocles in Aeschylus's *Seven Against Thebes*." In *Aeschylus*, edited by Michael Lloyd. New York: Oxford University Press, 2007. An examination of Eteocles, whom Fritz describes as the "most strongly individualized of all Aeschylus's characters."

Herington, John. *Aeschylus*. New Haven, Conn.: Yale University Press, 1986. An excellent starting point. Stresses how the play depicts the conflict of two active principles by means of the struggle between Eteocles and Polynices. Notes that the play helped establish tragedy as a form.

Podlecki, Anthony J. *The Political Background of Aeschylean Tragedy*. Ann Arbor: University of Michigan Press, 1966. Relates the action of the play, which concerns conflicts between two would-be leaders of a Greek city-state, to the political disputes occurring in the Athens of Aeschylus's own time. Occasionally dated, crude analysis, but offers insights not readily available in other sources.

Rosenmeyer, Thomas. *The Art of Aeschylus*. Berkeley: University of California Press, 1982. Examines the play from a linguistic, stylistic, and aesthetic standpoint. Does not require any knowledge of ancient Greek to profit from its insight.

Winnington-Ingram, R. P. *Studies in Aeschylus*. New York: Cambridge University Press, 1983. Contains a compelling description of Eteocles as the "first man" of the European stage. Sheds light on Aeschylus's transmutation of his mythological sources and examines the conflict between the playwright's temperamental conservatism and the theme of conflict in the play. Occasionally abstruse and specialized.

Seven Pillars of Wisdom
A Triumph

Author: T. E. Lawrence (1888-1935)
First published: 1922
Type of work: History
Locale: Middle East

Principal personages:
T. E. LAWRENCE, the author
SHERIF FEISAL IBN HUSSEIN
FIELD MARSHAL EDMUND H. H. ALLENBY
SIR HENRY MCMAHON, high commissioner in Egypt
JEMAL PASHA, of Syria
SHERIF HUSSEIN, emir of Mecca

Unless the forces and countercurrents of world history change abruptly or virtually reverse themselves, it is unlikely that an Englishman will ever again have the opportunity to approximate the exploits and terrors, the sense of achievement and frustration, that T. E. Lawrence experienced and described in his *Seven Pillars of Wisdom*. This work is autobiographical history, lived by a most extraordinary and strangely gifted man.

The unusual qualities manifest in the author of *Seven Pillars of Wisdom* developed early. Lawrence's lifelong interest in archaeology and his field of special study at Oxford brought about his travels as a professional archaeologist in exploratory rambles through Syria, Egypt, and Northern Mesopotamia. When war broke out in 1914, Lawrence, who spoke perfect Arabic and who knew the region, served in British Intelligence in Egypt. In 1916, Captain Lawrence sought leave from these duties to try to bring about unity among the Arab chieftains in order to counteract the military and political activities of Turkey. *Seven Pillars of Wisdom* is concerned with these extraordinary years.

Following World War I, Lawrence's life fell into unusual patterns. Granted many military distinctions and special recognition for his achievements during the war years, he refused nearly every honor. For a time, he served as Arab consultant at peace conferences and as a political adviser to the colonial office of his government. By 1921, however, his secretive nature had asserted itself. He enlisted as an aircraftman under the name of Ross; he saw duty as Private T. E. Shaw in the tank corps; and he enlisted again as T. E. Shaw in the air force. Upon completion of this last tour of duty, he returned to England, only to lose his life in a motorcycle crash. His strange and unusual life was filled with adventure, heroic achievement, planned self-effacement, and an accidental conclusion.

Just as extraordinary were the events culminating in the final publication of *Seven Pillars of Wisdom*. Working from his own detailed notes, which he destroyed as he completed each major section of the book, Lawrence lost almost the entire first draft. Again he set about his task, this time writing from memory alone. Some of the work appeared as early as 1922 and in a limited edition in 1926. In the following year he issued an abridgement, *Revolt in the Desert*, for the general public. Following his death in 1935, the full text of *Seven Pillars of Wisdom* was released. Comparison of the complete work with *Revolt in the Desert* affords no good explanation for the author's insistence upon the delay in releasing the full text.

Strange, even quixotic, as some of the incidents of Lawrence's life and the fortunes of his principal publication may seem, the book itself is far more extraordinary and revealing: a detailed and absorbing recital of two years of striving, of attack and maneuver, of persuasion and rebuff, of privation and intense strain, which culminated in a large measure of success with partial victory of Arab forces over the common enemy, Turkey.

The title of this account is to some extent indicative of the complex mind of the author. Some years before, he selected the phrase from the first verse of the ninth chapter of the book of Proverbs: "Wisdom hath builded a house: she hath hewn out her seven pillars." At the time, he planned to use the title for a projected book about seven cities; later he transferred the title to the present work "as a memento" of his early literary enterprise; finally he added the subtitle, *Seven Pillars of Wisdom: A Triumph.* In essence, the full title suggests the transition from Lawrence the youthful archaeologist to Lawrence the expert in Arab affairs and in military plans and strategy.

This record of a two-year campaign is compact and explicit, although set down from memory. It consists of 122 closely written chapters—with an introduction, ten books, and an epilogue—totaling more than six hundred pages.

In the first seven chapters, Lawrence sketched what he termed the Foundations of Revolt. He described the Arab lands and their troubled peoples, the animosity between Turks and the other loosely knit groups, the lack of trust among various Arab clans, and the absence of fundamental understanding of all of these conflicting circumstances on the part of the British Foreign Office and key military leaders. Lawrence was convinced that the Arab revolt could succeed if the Arab leaders were properly advised.

After securing detachment from his foreign office assignment, he took off to interview Arab chieftains and leaders. He traveled far, on camelback and in Arab dress, to confer with Sherif Feisal Ibn Hussein and other prominent Arab chiefs in an effort to gather firsthand impressions of physical conditions, supplies, and military strength. With this information, Lawrence returned to his superior officers and reported that a tribal war would be feasible if it were adequately supplied logistically. His estimate of the situation was accepted, somewhat surprisingly, and preparations began for an attack on the Turks. A frontal assault soon proved foolhardy, however, because of the preponderant forces of the enemy. Thereafter, the Arabs under Feisal served often as an integral part of the British force and were successful in taking Medina, Akaba; in harassing the enemy by cutting railway communications; and in aiding in the capture of Damascus. By this time, the Turkish armies were scattered and the Eastern war drew to its end. Lawrence's efforts were expended. He departed as soon as possible, in order not to become involved in the stalemate of establishing authority.

As an account by one intimately acquainted with a successful military endeavor of great significance, *Seven Pillars of Wisdom* merits recognition and thorough study, for it is an excellent treatise of war conducted under extremely difficult conditions. Lawrence's book offers much more than mere history, however; the military story is little more than the framework upon which the author built a deeply absorbing analysis of this part of the Arab world, its people, its leaders, its weaknesses, and its hopes for the future. As a professional student of the past history of those areas, Lawrence chose to live among the people, to learn their ways, and to share their hardships. With this profoundly sympathetic background, Lawrence was singularly equipped to understand, to reconcile Arab psychology with Allied purposes, and to gain the confidence of justifiably suspicious Arab leaders. In the course of his account, Lawrence constantly describes, explains, and interprets. His style, although at times archaic or difficult, enables him to picture desert scenes, oases, and the teeming Arab cities with consummate skill. His portraits of his associates, his junior colleagues and his senior officers among the Allies, and his valued and capable friends among the Arabs are vivid word pictures. Lawrence had an eye for human qualities and human character, and he could record them memorably. As few Europeans have ever been able to do, Lawrence undertook to transform himself into an Arab, a member of the people he was working with, and the most understanding and intelligent of them realized this phenomenon and valued his efforts.

Perhaps the most puzzling and stimulating feature of this extraordinary book is almost coincidental: the picture of Lawrence himself that gradually emerges. Lawrence was an amazing person, capable of intense absorption in the task at hand, that of mounting a successful military operation to conquer the Turks. At the same time, he appreciated the stark beauties of barren lands and ancient cities; he evaluated human beings and their ways, judging, adapting their strength to the immediate purpose, and enjoying their companionship. He also subjected his own way of life and his own people to a very critical appraisal. In the end, he evidently found his institutions strangely lacking and disappointing. Hence, Lawrence apparently decided to refuse the honors heaped upon him, to cut himself off from the leaders of his own kind, and to submerge himself in obscurity. His was a lofty, powerful mind, honest but stern and implacable. When that mind could not reconcile itself to the English present, he simply chose anonymity. Like those of the fictional Gulliver, Lawrence's travels among strange peoples and regions left him far from satisfied with the ideals and practices in his homeland.

Further Reading

Allen, M. D. *The Medievalism of Lawrence of Arabia*. University Park: Pennsylvania State University Press, 1991. Describes *Seven Pillars of Wisdom* as a neomedieval romance; relates elements in it to medieval literary sources and analogues.

Calder, Angus. "T. E. Lawrence's *Seven Pillars of Wisdom*." In *Disasters and Heroes: On War, Memory, and Representation*. Cardiff: University of Wales Press, 2004. Calder examines how memories often transform the reality of war, analyzing how this process works in Lawrence's account of his experiences in World War I.

Meyers, Jeffrey. *The Wounded Spirit: A Study of "Seven Pillars of Wisdom."* London: Martin Brian and O'Keeffe, 1973. Meyers asserts that *Seven Pillars of Wisdom* is beautiful, insightful literature, and he views Lawrence as introspective and profound. Defines the book's style as mainly descriptive and narrative, but also comic, dramatic, emotive, epic, lyric, puerile, reflective, and technical.

_____, ed. *T. E. Lawrence: Soldier, Writer, Legend: New Essays*. New York: St. Martin's Press, 1989. Includes essays by Albert Cook on Lawrence's contrary roles in *Seven Pillars of Wisdom* as observant stranger, military ally, and autobiographical artist and by Eugene Goodheart on the clash of personal, patriotic, intellectual, and artistic motives in *Seven Pillars of Wisdom*. Goodheart's essay is reprinted in his own book *Novel Practices: Classic Modern Fiction* (2004).

Shāz, Rāshid. "T. E. Lawrence's *Seven Pillars of Wisdom*." In *In Pursuit of Arabia*. New Delhi: Milli, 2003. Analyzes Lawrence's book and other works that were written when the West started to doubt its age-old portrayal of Islam as a demonizing force.

Tabachnick, Stephen Ely. *T. E. Lawrence*. Rev. ed. New York: Twayne, 1997. Discusses *Seven Pillars of Wisdom* as the autobiography of an aesthete-hero and a dramatized version of the truth. Sees Lawrence as torn by British-Arab cultural and political diversities.

_____, ed. *The T. E. Lawrence Puzzle*. Athens: University of Georgia Press, 1984. Includes essays by Thomas J. O'Donnell on Lawrence's both asserting and denying his will in *Seven Pillars of Wisdom* and by Kenneth N. Hull on *Seven Pillars of Wisdom* as integrating documentary and personal material.

The Seven Who Were Hanged

Author: Leonid Andreyev (1871-1919)
First published: Rasskaz o semi poveshannykh, 1908
  (English translation, 1909)
Type of work: Novel
Type of plot: Social realism
Time of plot: Early twentieth century
Locale: Russia

Principal characters:
SERGEY GOLOVIN,
VASILY KASHIRIN,
TANYA KOVALCHUK,
MUSYA, and
WERNER, five revolutionists
IVAN YANSON and TSIGANOK GOLUBETS, two condemned men

The Story:

When the police inform a powerful minister that there is a plot to assassinate him, he is terrified. Nevertheless, the police assure him that he will be given ample protection; they know who the terrorists are, and they will arrest them.

As good as their word, the police seize three men and two women, young people ranging in age from nineteen to twenty-eight years old. A large amount of dynamite is also found. The evidence is so damaging that the prisoners know they will be sentenced to hang. The trial is swift, and the five revolutionists are imprisoned until the time of their execution, two days hence.

In the same prison are two other condemned men who have been waiting about two weeks for their execution. One is Ivan Yanson, a peasant workman. He is an Estonian who speaks Russian poorly and talks little. His ignorance makes him cruel. Since there are no humans on whom he can vent his rage, he regularly beats the animals under his care. He frequently drinks too much, and then his cruelty to animals is worse than usual. Once he tried to make love to another servant, but he is so repulsive-looking that she rejected him. One night, Yanson entered the room where his master was and stabbed him to death. He then tried to rape his mistress, but she escaped him. While attempting to flee with some money he stole, he was seized, tried, and sentenced to hang.

At first, he wants the time before his execution to pass quickly. Then, as the time grows shorter, he begins to tell his guards that he does not want to die, that he does not understand why he should be hanged. Yanson has no one to love or to believe in. Partly stupefied by fear, he is unable to take in much of what happened to him.

The other condemned man is Tsiganok Golubets, a robber and murderer who takes pride in his brutal accomplishments. At times, completely mad, he gets down on all fours and howls like a wolf. Then, for a time, he will be quiet. What little time remains of his life is meaningless to him, for he knows only how to rob and kill, and these pleasures are now taken away.

The five revolutionists each determine not to show fear. When Sergey Golovin's father and mother visit him in his cell, however, he can no longer be brave, and he cries. Sergey is young, and life is strong in him; he finds it hard to understand that he is soon to die.

Only Vasily Kashirin's mother comes to see him, for his father is not interested in seeing his son again. Vasily, who long ago lost respect for his parents, has no regrets about not seeing his father. Even his mother means little to him; there is really no one he hates to leave when he dies. While he waits for his execution, he shows no signs of fear.

It is not for herself but for her comrades that Tanya Kovalchuk worries. The fact that she, too, is to die has no meaning for her; she is concerned only for the discomfort and fears of her children, as she calls the others. She loves them all.

Musya knows that she will not completely die when she is hanged. She will join the martyrs whom she admires so much, and her name will live forever. She has only one regret; she did nothing significant enough to justify her martyrdom. She consoles herself with the thought that she was on the threshold of great deeds. She thinks that she conquered her captors, for the fact that they are going to kill her proves that they fear her. Musya eagerly awaits her execution.

The man called Werner long develops a contempt for humanity and is tired of life. There is no one he respects or ad-

mires; he is cold and superior even to his comrades. In his cell, however, he suddenly develops a love for humanity in his realization of human progress from an animal state. Loving and pitying other people, Werner feels more freedom in his prison cell than he ever knew outside. It is a long time since he felt sympathy for others; the feeling is a good one.

On the day of their execution, the five are allowed to talk together for a short time. They are almost afraid to look at one another, each not wanting to see fear in a comrade's face. Vasily cannot control his emotions. The others, particularly Tanya, urge him to be calm and not to allow their guards to see his fear.

When the time comes for the execution, Yanson and Golubets join them. Yanson is still babbling about not wanting to be hanged. Golubets retains his arrogance and makes a joke about dying. Transferred to a train, they are allowed to sit together until they reach their destination. Musya is happy to see that Werner loses his scorn for the others. As they draw nearer their final stop, she smiles; soon she will join those whom she admires so much.

On their arrival, Yanson has to be carried from the coach. Golubets wants to attack the guards. The night is cold, and often they slip in the snow as they march toward the scaffold. All refuse the services of a priest who is present. They all kiss one another good-bye and walk in pairs to the ropes. Sergey and Vasily go first, Vasily outwardly calm and in control of himself. At the last minute, Golubets is frightened and asks to go with one of the five brave ones. Musya takes his hand, kisses him, and they follow Sergey and Vasily. Musya's hand calms Golubets; he is arrogant again as he climbs the steps. Werner takes Yanson with him, but the peasant has to be carried most of the way. Tanya is the last, and she goes alone. Her children all went bravely. She is happy.

After Tanya's drop, there is silence for a moment in the wintry night. Then the bodies are taken back over the same road they traveled a short time before, but only their bodies— their souls are elsewhere.

Critical Evaluation:

In a 1908 letter to Herman Bernstein, his English translator, Leonid Andreyev stated that his task in *The Seven Who Were Hanged* "was to point out the horror and iniquity of capital punishment under any circumstances." That the author was effective in accomplishing this task seems clear, but for many decades criticism has been aware of something called the intentional fallacy, which holds that a work may offer meaning quite apart from what its creator intended. Late twentieth century critical theory puzzled over the instabilities of language, the tendency of literature to subvert its own apparent goal. Thus Andreyev's novel, while remaining an indictment of the death penalty and its execution, can be viewed as susceptible to a number of interpretations, not necessarily consistent with one another. There may be a bitter irony in linking selfless revolutionaries with common criminals, but then an argument may be made that people who visit death on others to achieve a political aim are themselves no better than common criminals. Feminist criticism might choose to look particularly at the two women among the seven who suffer the death penalty; here again, more than one reading is possible or even desirable. Reducing *The Seven Who Were Hanged* to Andreyev's declared intent or judging it by that intent alone is unwise.

At the same time, there is an advantage to knowing what the author regarded as his task, because it helps the reader to see how Andreyev, reacting to the increased use of the death penalty after the failed revolution of 1905, exercised his exceptional verbal facility to make vivid the brutality of any inflicted death. Andreyev may be seen as a kind of prose Acmeist, Acmeism being a movement in Russian poetry of about the same time that undertook to counter vague symbolism with language, vivid and concrete, that would convey true experience of the natural world. The mental and physical states of the seven who must die are sharply rendered, sometimes in metaphorical terms, as when the slender white arm of one young woman protrudes from the sleeve of a prisoner's coat like "a beautiful flower out of a coarse earthen jug," or when the newly executed prisoners lie "with blue, swollen tongues, looking like some unknown, terrible flowers between the lips." There is little superfluity in this novel, which is not much more than thirty thousand words in length. Of the twelve chapters that make up the book, the capital sentence is pronounced in the second and carried out in the twelfth. Everything in between treats the seven important characters (there are practically no others of consequence) as they prepare to die.

In the chapters in which they are developed, the doomed people have particularity and complexity, but they are not much realized as human beings. This seems to be true for two reasons. First, there is little dialogue. Most of the characters await execution in isolation (two receive brief visits from parents), and what readers know of them is given through the narrative voice. In addition, there is a measure of implausibility that may arise from Andreyev's having worked to create sharp impressions. The revolutionaries, where they are not sentimentalized, are idealized, and the common criminals, Yanson especially, are made so brutal as to be incongruent with ordinary experience, even of brutality. The horror of their predicament is clearly understood by the attentive

reader, but at the cost of seeing them as people one might encounter in everyday life.

The Seven Who Were Hanged is Andreyev's most successful work, even in its limitations. Andreyev was highly regarded in the first part of his career, but his standing among contemporaries dwindled even before he died. Early in his literary career, he was befriended by the writer Maxim Gorky, who helped give him a place among his literary peers, and the success of his fiction about capital punishment led some to think that, with Anton Chekhov and Leo Tolstoy, Andreyev might be one of the most important Russian writers of his time. It gradually became apparent that, although he was masterful with language, many of his productions were flawed. Andreyev further compromised his standing by building an opulent house in Finland with money made in Russia by his writing. He lost more sympathy, especially with the rising Soviets, by drifting to the right in politics and supporting Russia's active role in the earlier stages of World War I. His writing might not have been so closely scrutinized had he been more generally approved, but this was not the case, and with no sympathetic indulgence to help him along, the flaws showed through.

Whatever the flaws or limitations of *The Seven Who Were Hanged*, it remains a striking novel in a first encounter. If Andreyev had an avowed purpose in writing this story, he also had the good judgment to avoid leading the reader with direct moralizing, allowing his stark representation of two very different kinds of condemned people—political operatives and common felons—to make his point about the horror they must face. The clean, spare, concrete prose out of which Andreyev created his book gives the reader an impression of distinctly modern fiction. There are moments when Andreyev puts one in mind of writers of the generation that emerged after World War I—the American writer Ernest Hemingway would be an example. His most famous book also strongly resembles the slower, fuller fiction of Russian writers in the nineteenth century.

It is difficult, but not impossible, for a single work by a writer whose reputation has faded to hold its place among books that are sooner or later read. *The Seven Who Were Hanged*, although not an obligatory book, remains one that students of Russian literature should be expected to know well.

"Critical Evaluation" by John Higby

Further Reading

Connolly, Julian W. "The Russian Short Story, 1890-1917."
 In *The Russian Short Story: A Critical History*, edited by

Charles Moser. Boston: Twayne, 1986. Places *The Seven Who Were Hanged* in a historical framework of Andreyev's development. Emphasizes Andreyev's attention to the emotions of the convicted and terms *The Seven Who Were Hanged* his most famous political story.

Hutchings, Stephen. *A Semiotic Analysis of the Short Stories of Leonid Andreev, 1900-1909.* London: Modern Humanities Research Association, 1990. A semiotic study of Andreyev's short stories, placing them within the context of early twentieth century Russian literature and culture.

Kaun, Alexander. *Leonid Andreyev: A Critical Study.* New York: B. W. Huebsch, 1924. Standard critical biography of Andreyev, covering all aspects of his works. Labels *The Seven Who Were Hanged* a masterpiece in both technique and emotional power, because of its simplicity of style, keen psychological analysis, humane sympathy, and lasting effect.

Mihajlov, Mihajlo. *Russian Themes.* Translated by Marija Mihajlov. New York: Farrar, Straus & Giroux, 1968. Far-reaching treatment of Russian writers. Discusses the political aspect of *The Seven Who Were Hanged*, pointing out Andreyev's sympathies for the revolutionaries in their struggle with the czarist regime.

Newcombe, Josephine M. *Leonid Andreyev.* Letchworth, England: Bradda Books, 1972. Brief but pithy introduction to Andreyev, with a pertinent discussion of *The Seven Who Were Hanged* on pages 85-90.

Seventeen

Author: Booth Tarkington (1869-1946)
First published: 1916
Type of work: Novel
Type of plot: Comic realism
Time of plot: A summer in the early twentieth century
Locale: A small midwestern town

Principal characters:
WILLIAM SYLVANUS BAXTER, a seventeen-year-old
MRS. BAXTER, his mother
JANE BAXTER, his sister
MISS PRATT, a summer visitor

The Story:

William Sylvanus Baxter at last reaches the impressive age of seventeen, and as he emerges from the corner drugstore after indulging in two chocolate and strawberry sodas, he tries to impress the town with his lofty air of self-importance. No one notices him except his friend, Johnny Watson, who destroys William's hauteur in one breath by calling him "Silly Bill." At that moment, William sees a feminine vision in pink and white. A stranger in town, she carries her parasol and her little white dog with easy grace. William, not daring to speak, manages only an insincere yawn. The vision, taking no apparent notice of William, speaks in charming lisps to her little dog Flopit and disappears around the corner.

William goes home in a daze, hardly bothering to speak to his outrageous little sister, Jane, who greets him between mouthfuls of applesauce and bread. Scorning her, he goes up to his room, his heart full of the mystery of love, and composes a poem to his new and unknown lady. He is interrupted by his mother, who asks William to go with Genesis, the black handyman, to pick up some laundry tubs from the secondhand store. The errand, to William, is worse than being seen in public with a leper, for he looks on Genesis as a ragged, bedraggled, down-at-the-heels pariah, whose presence is an unwholesome reproach to the whole neighborhood.

Genesis is in reality a wise old philosopher, despite his seminudity and the ubiquitous presence of his mongrel dog, Clematis. However, William is in no mood to be tolerant. His worst fears are realized when, on the way home, he hears behind him the silvery voice of the fair stranger referring to Clematis as a nasty old dog. William is hidden by the laundry tub he carries over his head, but his invisibility in no way diminishes his growing horror at being taken for a companion of Genesis and the owner of the dreadful Clematis. Clematis, meanwhile, is fascinated by Flopit. When William hears the yips and barks of the two dogs, he runs away, still hidden under his protecting tub.

The young vision in pink and white is the summer visitor of May Parcher. Her name, William learns, is Miss Pratt. Soon the boys in the neighborhood collect on the Parcher porch and swarm around the adorable girl every evening after supper, much to the disgust of Mr. Parcher, who lies awake for hours in his room over the porch and listens reluctantly to the drivel of conversation below. William has an advantage over the other suitors, for he borrows his father's dress suit without his parents' knowledge and arrives each night in splendid attire.

During the day, William cannot escape his sister Jane, who insists on appearing in dirty summer sunsuits, her face smeared with her favorite repast of applesauce and bread, just at the moment when William would be walking by the house with Miss Pratt. His angry demands that his sister present a more ladylike appearance irritate Jane to a calm, smoldering intent to get even with William. She knows that William wears his father's dress suit every evening when he visits Miss Pratt. She also knows that Mr. Parcher is nearly crazy over the nightly sessions on his front porch. Putting these facts together, she coldly repeats to her mother some of Mr. Parcher's comments. Mrs. Baxter is horrified that William wore out his welcome at the Parchers', and when she discovers Mr. Baxter's dress suit under William's window seat, she takes it to a tailor and has it altered to fit only Mr. Baxter. William cannot go to see Miss Pratt without the dress suit. He is not among Miss Pratt's evening admirers thereafter.

As a reward to Jane, who immediately tells him of her part in decreasing by one the population of his front porch, Mr. Parcher sends her a five-pound box of candy, much to the amazement of the whole Baxter household. No one suspects Jane's perfidy.

Feeling herself to blame for William's gloomy moods, Mrs. Baxter decides to have a tea for some of her son's friends, with Miss Pratt as guest of honor. The great day arrives, swelteringly hot. Upstairs, William no sooner breaks his only collar button on his fifth and last white shirt than he has the misfortune to tear his white trousers. Another suit is splattered by Jane's paints. By the time he finds a heavy winter suit in a trunk in the attic, the guests are gone. Angry and miserable, William sits down on Jane's open, wet paint box.

The time comes for Miss Pratt to return home. As a farewell party, the relieved Parchers schedule a picnic in their guest's honor. To impress Miss Pratt, William buys a package of Cuban cigarettes, but coy Miss Pratt gives all her attention to George, a braggart who stuffs himself with food to impress the beauty with his gustatory prowess. Lunch over, William offers George his cigarettes. Before long, he has the satisfaction of seeing George disappear behind a woodpile. William is blissful once more.

When Miss Pratt unexpectedly grants the weary Parchers the privilege of her company for another week, they give a final farewell dance in her honor. Mrs. Baxter has her husband's dress suit again altered to fit William. Resplendent, but late as usual, William arrives at the dance to find all Miss Pratt's dances taken, and he is forced to spend the evening with a lonely wallflower. His dignity suffers another blow when Genesis, serving sandwiches, not only greets William with familiarity but also chides him about the dress suit. His evening is a dismal failure.

The next day, William goes down to the train to see Miss Pratt leave. Laden with candy and lush poetry, he finds her surrounded by her many admirers. He has the uncomfortable sensation that they are all laughing at him, for they are pointing derisively in his direction. Turning, he sees Jane, who deliberately comes to torment him in company with an equally disreputable female companion. The two pranksters are walking with a vulgar strut that William abhors. So flustered is he that he merely waves to Miss Pratt and goes sadly home, forgetting that he still carries under his arm the box of candy and the poem intended for the pink and white beauty who went out of his life forever.

Critical Evaluation:

Much of *Seventeen*'s charm for many readers will be found in the novel's quality as a period piece. It provides a solid sense of setting, character, and values as they were in the American Midwest in the first quarter of the twentieth century.

Although the novel's setting is not explicitly identified, Booth Tarkington's midwestern readers of 1916, and particularly his Indiana readers, would assume from the first sentence's reference to Washington Street and Central Avenue that the novel's action takes place in Indianapolis, Tarkington's hometown. The author's detailed descriptions of costume and customs of white middle-class Americans and his rendering of speech patterns and vocabulary not only are a source of his deliberate humor but also serve to ground the novel in a tangible realism.

Seventeen is, above all, a romantic comedy, a story that focuses mostly on lives that are divorced from any grim concerns of making a living, dealing with illness, or worrying about what evils may lurk in the city or in the hearts of its inhabitants. *Seventeen*'s midwestern setting is a place where there is no crime and little poverty, at least among the white middle-class characters who are the center of the author's attention.

As for the African Americans who appear in the novel, however, they are, socially and historically, only one step removed from slavery. Genesis, for example, is a servant and a worker of odd jobs, thoroughly accustomed to taking orders from his white employers and recognizing his secondary place in this society. Nevertheless, Genesis has his own ambitions, as the reader sees, when he enthusiastically works part-time as a waiter for catered affairs, a job he considers a definite step upward on the social ladder. Then, too, as an heir to the literary type of the kindly African American father figure, Genesis often looks with amusement and bemusement on the activities of white people, particularly the youngsters. In one notable scene, Genesis embarrasses William at a party, comically suggesting, as a relative of William might, that the boy surreptitiously dressed up in his father's evening clothes.

While Tarkington gives no evidence at all of social consciousness, it is also clear that his depictions of African Americans, like his characterizations of white people, are without deliberate malice. There is a naïve innocence in Tarkington's frequent exploitation of African American characters, customs, and speech mannerisms. In his narrator's poking fun at African American tastes in clothing and colors and his accounts of their attitudes toward white people, Tarkington is undoubtedly recalling his own midwestern milieu as he saw it.

Since *Seventeen*'s publication, generations of readers have considered the novel's characters to be familiar or easily imaginable. The Baxter and Parcher families represent a classic American ideal, one of those concepts that has been endorsed by literature and perhaps imitated in reality. William's family, for example, includes a breadwinner father and a mother whose life is defined by motherhood, by rearing her two children—boy and girl—and by maintaining the Baxter household. Both Mr. Baxter and Mr. Parcher are often strict and impatient with their youngsters, while their wives serve as intermediaries between the fathers and the children, softening paternal anger and edicts. In other words, *Seventeen*'s families are those that American popular literature, film, and television have perpetuated as "typical."

Critics, even in Tarkington's day, objected to the nature of William's obsession with Lola Pratt, the summer visitor in town who attracts the attention of several young men. William's pursuit of Miss Pratt is essentially that of dreamer after his dream, a pursuit uncomplicated by sexual passion. Indeed, Tarkington's descriptions of Miss Pratt's physical attributes have nothing to do with carnality, and William's behavior never indicates that his admiration of her is anything more than aesthetic.

In any case, it is Miss Pratt, the object of William's affections, who becomes the novel's chief comic interest. She is a caricature of femininity, evidently a young woman who has been convinced that the best way to get what she wants from male admirers is to emphasize vulnerability and childlike fragility.

Much of *Seventeen*'s success as comedy derives from Tarkington's third-person narrative style, whereby description and advancement of plot are usually expressed in very formal language, even though the events, characters, or motives described are amusing or even trivial. While dialogue is consistently colloquial, the narrator's authoritative, sometimes stilted tone provides a comic contrast that is always amusing. The novel's final, abbreviated, fairy-tale-like vision, in which it turns out that William is destined to marry Jane's new little friend and not Miss Pratt, is a logical development in a story that largely deals with dreams rather than with reality.

"Critical Evaluation" by Gordon Walters

Further Reading

Fennimore, Keith J. *Booth Tarkington*. New York: Twayne, 1974. A fine basic study of Tarkington and his work, although it lacks a sustained discussion of *Seventeen*. The author distinguishes *Seventeen* as a "juvenile" work, different from Tarkington's other novels.

Mallon, Thomas. "Hoosiers." *Atlantic Monthly* 293, no. 4 (May, 2004): 123-136. Takes a close look at Tarkington's oeuvre, finding that his few good works have been "suffocated" by the majority of the mediocre ones. Asks how the once ubiquitous Tarkington could "disappear so completely."

Mayberry, Susanah. *My Amiable Uncle: Recollections About Booth Tarkington*. West Lafayette, Ind.: Purdue University Press, 1983. Tarkington's niece recollects her personal experiences with the writer, providing an important contribution to Tarkington's biography. Includes family photographs.

Russo, Dorothy R., and Thelma L. Sullivan. *A Bibliography of Booth Tarkington*. Indianapolis, Ind.: Indianapolis Historical Society, Lakeside Press, 1949. Remains useful for anyone seriously interested in Tarkington, especially in the receptions his books received in the popular press.

Russo, Dorothy R., et al. "Additions to the Tarkington Bibliography." *Princeton University Library Chronicle* 15 (Winter, 1955): 89-94. An update of the previous entry.

Scott, John D. "Tarkington and the 1920's." *American Scholar* 26 (Spring, 1957): 181-194. Focuses on the social criticism in Tarkington's work.

Woodress, James. *Booth Tarkington: Gentleman from Indiana*. Philadelphia: J. B. Lippincott, 1955. Still one of the most thorough critical biographies of Tarkington, with an emphasis on chronological biography rather than on literary analysis.

Sexual Politics

Author: Kate Millett (1934-   )
First published: 1970
Type of work: Literary criticism

Kate Millett writes in the introduction to a revised edition of her feminist classic *Sexual Politics* that her purpose in writing the work was to

> restate and reestablish the fact of historical patriarchy in modern terms and for my generation, to see it as a controlling political institution built on status, temperament, and role, a socially conditioned belief system presenting itself as nature or necessity.

These goals exemplified the aims of the American feminist movement of the 1960's and early 1970's. The movement sought not only to examine but also to combat a pervasive, persistent, thoroughly institutionalized and internalized patriarchy in Western society, which silenced women's voices, distorted their lives, and universally treated their concerns as peripheral.

In the 1970's, the canon presented to students in American universities was overwhelmingly male and decidedly from a male viewpoint; this viewpoint was often touted as universal. Millett's *Sexual Politics* pioneered the field of feminist literary criticism through its systematic, evidence-based, and often in-depth examination of the work of many authors, illustrating through literary and cultural criticism that masculine viewpoints are not unbiased reflections of human nature, but rather support the patriarchal power structure that has existed since the beginnings of Western civilization.

Millett begins her study by dissecting descriptions of sexual intercourse written by men, specifically Henry Miller in his *Sexus* (1949) and Norman Mailer in his *An American Dream* (1965). Millett demonstrates how the language used in describing the sexual act speaks to the subjugation of women as persons, which in turn speaks to the larger issue of a patriarchal power structure. The politics of sexual activity—that is, the question of with whom and under what circumstances women are permitted to engage in sex—is an essential part of patriarchal power. In Millett's terms, in such a power structure, women are never their own agents; they are commodities silenced by the freedom of men to sexually possess them. The tacit or outward acquiescence of women, in turn, works to define their selves in terms of men.

Building on the evidence of sexual politics in literature, Millett describes next a theory of sexual politics, transitioning from an individual, intimate view of the sexual act to the broader scope of political reference. She clarifies the connection between the individual and society at large by outlining several areas in which patriarchy wields its influence.

The first area of influence Millett terms "ideological"; human personality is defined as strictly "masculine" or "feminine." A masculine personality shows "aggression, intelligence, force, and efficacy"; A feminine personality shows "passivity, ignorance, docility, 'virtue,' and ineffectuality." Millett further identifies the male/masculine role as typically involving leadership and ambition and the female/feminine role as involving domestic servitude and childbearing. Because masculine roles are valued over feminine roles, men are considered superior in status.

Following social conceptions of the masculine and the feminine, Millett next makes a distinction between "sex" and "gender," arguing that sex is based on anatomy and that gender is a social construct; what it means to be male and what it means to be female are learned behaviors. In describing the learned nature of gender roles, Millett explains that "patriarchy's chief institution is family"; it is the main area where gender roles are internalized and socially sanctioned. The husband/father is the head of the family and the wife/mother is the supporter, nurturer, and caregiver; these gender roles are consciously and subconsciously passed along to children. Millett also links the sociological sources of sexual politics to a discussion of what she terms "force," explaining that patriarchy sanctions the threat of force, if needed, to subjugate women.

In a discussion of class, education, and economics, Millett likens the sexism of males to racism before the Civil Rights movement, when even the poorest, uneducated white person could claim socially sanctioned superiority over any black person. Millett further describes the effect of denying women the same economic privileges as men; because marriage is a patriarchal institution, wealth has always typically followed men. In addition to suffering economic discrimination, women have had their roles defined for them by educational systems and are denied the same access to education as men.

Millett next discusses the origin and reflection of patriarchal values in myth and religion, citing such diverse examples of the nearly universal fear of women's menstrual cycles in primitive cultures and the idea of a woman's virginity as a prized commodity. Millett further examines the socially sanctioned fraternities of sports teams and the military, both of which have traditionally denied women access. She also examines the creation myth of Adam and Eve, in which knowledge is relatively synonymous with sex/gender, thus setting the stage for the subjugation of women in religion. Finally, Millett describes how these factors add up in the psychology of both men and women and result in a subtle, pervasive internalization that can be difficult to recognize and nearly impossible to change.

Millett next discusses the idea of sexual revolution, given the term's cultural currency at the time she wrote this book, and places it in context with her definition of sexual politics. She concludes that no sexual revolution, per se, has occurred. For a sexual revolution to occur, society would first have to realize the "end of traditional sexual inhibitions and taboos, particularly . . . homosexuality, 'illegitimacy,' [and] adolescent, pre- and extra-marriage sexuality." Any sexual revolution also would require a reassessment of what it means to be masculine or feminine.

Millett further notes that although there have been some major shifts in views of sexuality, none has led to a true revolution or to major shifts in patriarchal power. Her discussion also includes the Victorian era, the women's movement in the nineteenth and early twentieth centuries, woman suffrage in the United States, and the somewhat relaxed views on sexuality that emerged in the 1960's. In this section, too, Millett begins her examination of the responses to the sexual revolution in literature, examining writers and poets from diverse time periods, including the Brontë sisters, John Keats, Oscar Wilde, John Ruskin, George Eliot, and Alfred, Lord Tennyson. Millett concludes that the "sexual revolution" of 1830 to 1930 ultimately ended not in radical change but in slight reform. In turn, she argues, a counterrevolution emerged in about 1930 and remained until about 1960. Examples of this counterrevolution include, according to Millett, the rise of the hyperpatriarchal and hypermasculine Nazi regime and the rise of Freudian psychoanalysis.

In the final one-third of *Sexual Politics*, Millett examines in greater detail the works of D. H. Lawrence, Miller, Mailer, and Jean Genet. In Lawrence, she focuses especially on *Lady Chatterly's Lover* (1928). Although Lawrence's portrayal of women is not overly sexist, sexuality is described in entirely male terms. She concludes that the novel is essentially a narcissistic ode to the phallus, and women are mere vehicles

toward that narcissism. Lawrence, she argues, essentially manipulates the idea of sexual revolution to create a "new order of dependence and subordination."

Millett next argues that although many readers and critics believe Miller displays in his work the "sexual freedom" of his times, he instead articulates "the disgust, the contempt, the hostility, the violence, and the sense of filth with which our culture, or more specifically, masculine sensibility, surrounds sexuality." Millett also describes how Mailer's writing connects warfare and violence with sex, and she classifies his work as antigay. She concludes *Sexual Politics* with further discussion on the writing of Genet because of "the insight it affords into the arbitrary status content of sexual role." Genet's work directly counters the traditional gender roles Millett defines in such detail.

Alan C. Haslam

Further Reading

Clough, Patricia Ticineto. "The Hybrid Criticism of Patriarchy: Rereading Kate Millett's *Sexual Politics*." *Sociological Quarterly* 35, no. 3 (1994): 473-486. A rereading of *Sexual Politics* that illustrates how the development of feminist theory has depended on redefining the overlap between literary criticism and the social sciences.

Eddington, Ross Elliott. "Millett's Rationalist Error." *Hypatia* 18, no. 3 (Summer, 2003): 193-211. In this journal of feminist philosophy, Eddington argues against Millett's interpretation of critic John Ruskin's portrayal of women in his writing.

Lawson, Kate. "Imagining Eve: Charlotte Brontë, Kate Millett, Hélène Cixous." *Women's Studies: An Interdisciplinary Journal* 24 (Spring, 1995): 411-426. Discusses feminist interpretations of the Adam and Eve myth, including interpretations by Millett, novelist Charlotte Brontë, and writer-critic Hélène Cixous.

Mailer, Norman. *The Prisoner of Sex*. Boston: Little, Brown, 1971. Reprint. New York: Primus, 1985. Mailer, in this controversial book, argues against Millett's interpretations in *Sexual Politics* of his writings and the writings of D. H. Lawrence.

Poirot, Kristan. "Mediating a Movement, Authorizing Discourse: Kate Millett, *Sexual Politics*, and Feminism's Second Wave." *Women's Studies in Communication* 27, no. 2 (2004): 204-235. Examines the media's relationship with feminism in terms of its reportage on Millett and in terms of the popular reception of *Sexual Politics*.

Rivkin, Julie, and Michael Ryan. "Introduction: Feminist Paradigms." In *Contemporary Theory: An Anthology*. 2d ed. Malden, Mass.: Blackwell, 2004. Offers an overview of Millett's significance to feminist theory and links her work with the important feminist works of her contemporaries.

Stimson, Catharine, Alix Kates Shulman, and Kate Millett. "*Sexual Politics*: Twenty Years Later." *Women's Studies Quarterly* 19, no. 3 (1991): 30-40. An excellent examination by three noted feminists of the lasting contributions of *Sexual Politics* to the canon of feminist literary criticism.

Woolf, Mike. "Henry Miller and Kate Millett: Strange Bedfellows, Sexuality, and Introspection." *Dutch Quarterly Review of Anglo-American Letters* 15, no. 4 (1985): 278-292. Woolf defends Miller's fiction against Millett's criticism and argues that the work of both Miller and Millett transcend sexuality and politics.

Shadows on the Rock

Author: Willa Cather (1873-1947)
First published: 1931
Type of work: Novel
Type of plot: Historical
Time of plot: Late seventeenth century
Locale: Quebec, Canada

Principal characters:
EUCLIDE AUCLAIR, the apothecary in Quebec
CÉCILE AUCLAIR, his daughter
COUNT FRONTENAC, the governor of New France and Auclair's patron
PIERRE CHARRON, a Canadian woodsman

The Story:

Late in October of 1697, the last ship leaves Quebec to return to France, and the colony of New France is isolated from the world until the arrival of the fleet in June or July of the following year. One of those who watch as the last vessel passes out of sight down the St. Lawrence River is Euclide Auclair, the apothecary in Quebec.

Auclair lives on the street that winds up the slope and connects the Upper Town on the cliff with the Lower Town, which clusters along the shore of the river at the foot of the mountain. In his home behind his shop, Auclair and his daughter Cécile do their best to re-create the atmosphere they knew in France. So successful are they that many people come to the shop merely to visit and get a breath of the France they left behind.

Cécile is only twelve years old and her mother has been dead for several years. Although she is content to remain in Canada, her father seems to live only for the time when he can return to France with his patron, the governor of the colony, Count Frontenac. Auclair, who has served the count for many years, is a trusted friend of the governor as well as his apothecary.

A few weeks after the last ship departs, Cécile goes to see the count to ask his aid in obtaining some shoes for a little orphan boy. The governor is glad to see her, for too many of the people who come to him are anxious only to help themselves.

He says that when he makes his will he will leave the girl a bowl of glass fruit that she always admires.

The first days of December bring a heavy fall of snow that ushers in a reality of life in Canada, the long, dark winter. The snow also reminds Cécile of the boxes of Christmas presents that were sent to her by aunts in France the previous summer. On the twenty-fourth of December, the Auclairs bring the boxes out of their storage place. In one is a crèche to be set up in their living room. The crèche is the crowning point of Christmas for many of their friends, for the French colonists are, as a rule, very devout.

One day in March, Father Hector Saint-Cyr puts in his appearance. The priest spends several evenings recounting to the Auclairs stories of the missionaries, the Indians, and the hardships of backwoods life. When he leaves, Auclair wonders if, after all, the gifts of an educated man such as Father Saint-Cyr might not be going to waste in misplaced heroism among the Canadian missions to the Indians.

About the middle of March, the weather changes. There is a continuous downpour of rain that the snow soaks up as if it were a gigantic sponge. The ice in the St. Lawrence breaks up and floats downstream in huge gray blocks. It is a season of sickness, and the apothecary is busy from morning until night, acting as doctor to many of the inhabitants of the town. Cécile catches a cold and is in bed for several days.

One evening while Cécile is ill, Auclair has a strange visit with a misshapen hunchback who secures water and wood for the Auclairs in return for a bowl of soup and a small glass of brandy each evening. Blinker, as the hunchback is called, tells Auclair that as a boy he was an apprentice to his father, one of the king's torturers at Rouen. Blinker tortured an old woman into admitting that she murdered her son. Some months after her execution, the son returned. The shock of what he did was too great for the apprentice. He ran away, took ship, and went to Quebec to begin a new life. Nevertheless, visions of the old woman haunt him so that he cannot sleep. Filled with sympathy, the apothecary gives Blinker some laudanum so that he might have a little untroubled rest.

One day, while Cécile regains her strength, her father wraps her in a blanket and carries her to the door. There, outside the door, Cécile sees the first swallow hunting for its old nest in the wall of the cliff that rises sharply to the chateau above. Delighted at this sign, Cécile has her father inform old Bishop Laval of the bird's appearance. The old man kept a record of the changing seasons for thirty-eight years, and he always includes the date of the first swallow's arrival.

On the first day of June, the leaves begin to bud, and the hunters arrive from the woods with their loads of pelts. Among the first hunters to reach Quebec is Pierre Charron, an old friend of the apothecary and his daughter. Pierre, the son of a rich family in Montreal, was disappointed in love. His sweetheart decided to build a chapel with her dowry and enter the Church as a recluse. After she took her vows, Pierre became a hunter traveling through the wilderness as far as Michilimackinac and Lake Superior in his quest for furs and forgetfulness. During the spring, Pierre takes Cécile with him to visit some friends on the Isle d'Orleans, in the St. Lawrence four miles below Quebec. The squalid and primitive life there disgusts Cécile.

Early in July, the ships from France arrive. The count requested the king to recall him from Canada, and he promised that he would take the Auclairs back to France with him. As each ship arrives through the summer, the Auclairs wait for word of the governor's recall. When late October arrives, the count calls Auclair to the chateau to warn him that the king's request will never come. When the count offers to send the Auclairs back to France, Auclair refuses, assuring the count that he cannot leave while his patron is forced to remain in Quebec.

The last ship leaves Quebec in October. Shortly afterward, Count Frontenac becomes ill. Auclair knows that his patient cannot live through the winter. When the count dies, Auclair carries out his patron's last wish. He seals the count's heart in a lead box and sends it with a missionary priest to the English colonies in the south. From there, it is returned to France for burial.

The death of the count is a great blow to the Auclairs, for security seems to have gone from their lives. Thinking of returning to France that year, they did not even lay in a proper supply of food to last through the winter. Fortunately for them, Pierre arrives in Quebec with an offer of help. Later he marries Cécile. Pierre has not the authority of documents and seals that the count had to protect them, but he has his knowledge of the woods and the people, which is as good or better in the wilds of Canada. The future is safe.

Critical Evaluation:

To an extent, *Shadows on the Rock* stands apart from other Willa Cather novels because of its setting. Cather is known as a regionalist, one who writes of nineteenth and twentieth century Nebraska and the Southwest. In this novel, she not only does not write about the Midwest but also she does not write about the United States. Set in late seventeenth century Quebec, Canada, *Shadows on the Rock* shows the human spirit of a different type of pioneer than those Cather usually writes about. Typically, Cather's immigrants are Swedish, Bohemian, English, and Spanish, living on the plains or in the Southwest. In this novel, Cather deals with a French family living in an urban setting about two hundred years before the time of her other novels.

The plot revolves around twelve-year-old Cécile Auclair and her father Euclide, who settle in New France. Parts of the story are episodic; they are seemingly unrelated events that somehow connect to the lives of the Auclairs. For example, the Auclairs are visited by a hunchback known as Blinker, who tells how he tortured a woman into admitting she had killed her son. The woman was executed for her crime. Then her son returned. This is one of the memorable, haunting stories that appears in Cather's work. As a journalist, Cather often rewrote true stories she knew about into her fiction. She based her short story "Paul's Case," for example, on an incident she had read about in the newspaper.

Cather crafted *Shadows on the Rock* from a story she ran across at the Louvre in Paris. She happened upon the diary of an apothecary who worked for Count Frontenac in Quebec. She began to keep notes on the diary and then formulated a story about it. After the novel was published, a pharmacy company wrote Cather stating that her information was wrong; the drug she mentioned in *Shadows on the Rock* did not exist at that time. Cather produced her notes from the diary to prove she was right.

Cather also included biographical incidents in her book. For example, on Christmas Day, 1927, Cather was at the family home in Red Cloud, Nebraska. She was arranging her crèche, and her nephew Charles brought a toy cow with him. Cather thought maybe he might not want to give up his toy for the crèche, but Charles said he wanted to give it to Jesus.

Cather went to live in Quebec so she could better research this novel. The novel reflects the relationship between father and daughter, Cécile and Auclair. Like many of Cather's fictions, *Shadows on the Rock* tends to be autobiographical. She wrote the novel at a time of personal trauma and upheaval. Her father had died, and his death severely affected her. In addition, her mother had recently had a paralytic stroke. Cather's apartment, where she had happily lived for fourteen years, was being demolished, and she had to find somewhere to live. Her research into the history and culture of Quebec and her personal experiences with illness, death, and threats to the home all serve to enrich the novel.

Youth has always been a theme in Cather's works, and *Shadows on the Rock* is no exception. She felt her most important years were between nine and sixteen, and she would often try to recapture the qualities of those youthful years in her fiction. This is probably why Cécile is portrayed as a child and as a young woman. Part of Cécile's youth is a sense of the past, of the ancients. Quebec is filled with legends, and the Auclairs are also in contact with France, which also signifies centuries of culture, legend, and history. When Cécile and Pierre travel into the wilderness, they move into ageless, primitive situations. Cécile, the youth, is the past's ambassador to the future; she is the connection between the centuries of French culture and the open wilds of Canada.

Being a novel about youth, the novel is a maturation novel, a bildungsroman. Cécile's varied experiences at home and in the wilderness lead to her maturity. Specifically, after her trip into the wilderness, she is ready to grow up and marry Pierre. The wilderness is symbolic of alienation. In the novel, the wilderness is one of cold and vast areas of nothing. This makes the Harnois family symbolic of alienation; they are isolated on an island surrounded by wilderness.

The isolation and despair contrasts with the domestic life of the Auclairs. Cécile is concerned, much of the time, with cooking and cleaning. The Auclairs lead a simple life, yet their lives are as solid as the Rock of Quebec on which they live. Cather once related that she had, in Cécile's domesticity, caught something new. For Cather, it represented a kind of feeling about human life and fate that she could not accept, wholly, but that she could admire. Cather, personally, could not accept it; she chose a career over domesticity and chose the city over the prairie. She often wrote, however, about those like Cécile. The Auclairs, through their simple lives

and hard work, cast their shadows upon the rock of Quebec in this historical fiction.

"Critical Evaluation" by Mary C. Bagley

Further Reading

Carlin, Deborah. "Tales of Telling Fictions of History: Casting *Shadows on the Rock*." In *Cather, Canon, and the Politics of Reading*. Amherst: University of Massachusetts Press, 1992. Carlin reads the novel as a narrative instead of a history. She maintains that the novel is about the translation of French sensibility into Canadian character.

De Roche, Linda. *Student Companion to Willa Cather.* Westport, Conn.: Greenwood Press, 2006. An introductory overview of Cather's life and work aimed at high school and college students and the general reader. Discusses character development, themes, and plots of six novels, with chapter 9 focusing on *Shadows on the Rock.*

Harvey, Sally Peltier. *Redefining the American Dream: The Novels of Willa Cather.* Rutherford, N.J.: Fairleigh Dickinson University Press, 1995. Focuses on Cather's changing opinions of success and how she sought to redefine the American Dream in her novels. Includes analysis of *Shadows on the Rock.*

Jacobs, Wilbur R. "Willa Cather and Francis Parkman: Novelistic Portrayals of Colonial New France." In *Willa Cather: Family, Community and History*, edited by John J. Murphy. Provo, Utah: Humanities Publications Center, Brigham Young University, 1990. Traces the influence of nineteenth century Canadian historian Francis Parkman on Cather.

Lindermann, Marilee. *The Cambridge Companion to Willa Cather.* New York: Cambridge University Press, 2005. Thirteen essays, including some that examine Cather's politics, sexuality, modernism, and the theme of migration in her works.

Murphy, John J. "'Cécile' Fragment of Cather's *Shadows on the Rock*." In *Willa Cather: New Facts, New Glimpses, Revisions*, edited by Murphy and Merrill Maguire Skaggs. Madison, N.J.: Fairleigh Dickinson University Press, 2008. Murphy investigates an unpublished fragment of the novel, which many scholars have assumed to be an alternate ending.

Nelson, Robert James. *Willa Cather and France.* Champaign: University of Illinois Press, 1988. Discusses the fascination that Willa Cather had in writing about the French on both sides of the Atlantic. Deals with Cather's tour of France and what influenced her to write about the people and their customs.

The Shawl

Author: Cynthia Ozick (1928-   )
First published: 1989; includes "The Shawl," 1980;
　Rosa, 1983
Type of work: Short fiction
Type of plot: Psychological realism
Time of plot: Winter, 1942, and April, 1977
Locale: Poland and Miami

Principal characters:
ROSA LUBLIN, a Polish Holocaust survivor
STELLA, her niece, also a Holocaust survivor
MAGDA, Rosa's infant daughter, who is murdered in a
　concentration camp
SIMON PERSKY, a retiree and a friend of Rosa in Miami

The Story:

"The Shawl": Rosa Lublin is freezing and starving on a forced march to a Nazi concentration camp. She is carrying her infant daughter, Magda, wrapped up and hidden in a linen shawl. Rosa's teenage niece, Stella, walks alongside her and sometimes carries Magda, who sucks on a corner of the shawl when Rosa can no longer nurse her. She thinks about offering her daughter to one of the village women she passes along the way, but she also knows that if she steps out of line she will be shot.

Now at the camp, Magda is beginning to walk. Rosa hides her in the camp barracks by keeping her covered in the shawl. One day, Stella takes the shawl and falls asleep wrapped in it; Magda toddles outside into the sunlight, crying in her first attempt at speech. Rosa stops to find the shawl before running to catch Magda. She sees a German soldier in the distance, carrying Magda toward the electrified fence surrounding the camp. Rosa stuffs the shawl into her own mouth to keep from screaming, as the soldier throws Magda into the fence, killing her.

Rosa: Forty years later, Rosa, now fifty-eight years old, lives in a filthy one-room apartment in Miami. She had owned a second-hand shop in Brooklyn, New York, but vandalized it herself, using a hammer to destroy everything in it. Her niece, Stella, lives in New York and supports Rosa financially. The two women communicate in letters; Stella threatens Rosa with commitment to a mental institution, while Rosa thinks Stella is the crazy one. Rosa also receives letters from Dr. James W. Tree, a professor who hopes she will participate in his clinical study of Holocaust survivors.

Rosa writes long letters to Magda in Polish. In her mind, baby Magda is alive, a doctor or a professor of philosophy, and also married to a doctor. Rosa assures the blond and blue-eyed Magda that she is not the child of a German SS officer, as Stella says; Rosa admits she had been raped by a German but insists Magda's father was a respectable Polish man. Rosa also has persuaded Stella to send her the shawl from forty years ago, although Stella mocks her for treating it like a religious object. Rosa uses the shawl to help her imagine Magda as alive.

Rosa meets seventy-one-year-old Simon Persky, a retired button manufacturer who was born in Poland but left for the United States when he was fourteen years old. Persky's wife is in a mental hospital; he persists in flirting with Rosa even when she rejects him. Rosa insists they have nothing in common, even though he is from Warsaw as well. She thinks they share nothing because he is an immigrant who had left Europe before the Holocaust and she is a refugee. Also, Rosa is Polish, and Persky is a Yiddish-speaking Jew. He offers her simple comforts, such as hot tea, and tries gently to persuade her that her life is not over. After Persky helps her fold clothes at the Laundromat, Rosa notices she is missing a pair of underpants and walks the streets and beaches of Miami for hours in search of her lost underwear, suspecting all the while that Persky had kept them.

Rosa has her telephone reconnected and calls Stella, speaking disjointedly about being pursued by Dr. Tree and about her stolen underpants. Then she writes another long letter to Magda, but finds the effort tiring and her vision of Magda fading as her telephone rings. Persky has returned to visit Rosa, and even though his presence counteracts that of Magda, Rosa agrees to see him.

Critical Evaluation:

Cynthia Ozick is part of a generation of Jewish writers who did not experience the Holocaust directly and struggled with the ethics of writing fiction about actual atrocities. Upon publication, the short story "The Shawl" drew fire from critics and readers who felt it was immoral to fictionalize the Holocaust. Fiction writers also had to decide whether to set their stories in ghettos and concentration camps, or to write about characters only indirectly affected by the Holocaust. Having set "The Shawl" in a death camp, Ozick, in *Rosa*, explores the psychological aftermath of the Holocaust through the perceptions of one survivor.

Rosa's linen shawl keeps Magda alive by hiding her from soldiers, and it more magically allows Magda to suckle it. Stella indirectly causes Magda's death after taking the shawl from her, leading the toddler to be seen by a German soldier as she goes outside. When Magda is murdered, Rosa stifles her own scream with the shawl, knowing she could be killed if she attracts attention. Years later, Rosa uses the shawl to trigger her vivid fantasies—that Magda is alive. The shawl also could be linked to the traditional Jewish *tallit*, a prayer shawl worn as a symbol of faith.

In the two works, Ozick is showing her concern with the nature of Jewish literature and the responsibilities of Jews to carry on their culture and faith. *The Shawl*, as a collection, examines Jewish identity through Rosa, an assimilated woman who does not identify as a Jew. Rosa's parents had thought of themselves as middle- or upper-class Poles; Rosa's mother even had considered converting to Roman Catholicism. The family made a point of speaking Polish rather than the Yiddish typical among European Jews. Rosa takes pride in her beautiful, literary Polish, speaks no Yiddish and only broken English, and looks down on Simon Persky because he speaks and reads Yiddish. Rosa is actually prejudiced against Jews; as a young girl she thought observant Jews in Warsaw were superstitious and backward, and she could not understand why the Nazis counted her family among them. In spite of her horrific victimization as a Jew, she feels herself separate from them. At the same time, she cannot understand how her niece, Stella, and other Jews can be indifferent to or ignorant of the Holocaust, missing details of American life, such as barbed wire at the top of a fence around a private beach or a striped dress that reminds Rosa of the death-camp uniform.

Both stories convey Rosa's inner turmoil, contrasting language and images that signal life and death. She must protect Magda and so cannot acknowledge that the Nazi guards will inevitably discover her. Magda's first steps are taken in the death camp, and her first words attract the attention of the soldier who kills her. The camp is surrounded by fields and flowers, and Rosa sees Magda flying toward the electric fence as a butterfly, a symbol of life. For Rosa, the Miami sun recalls the sunlight that revealed Magda to the soldier who had killed her, as well as the heat of death-camp crematoria.

The Shawl is an example of Holocaust fiction written by women that focuses particularly on women's experiences. Rosa had been raped repeatedly; she conceived Magda while imprisoned (apparently in a brothel), tried in vain to protect her baby daughter, and witnessed the child's murder. Her psychological suffering decades later stems from her contin-

ued isolation; no one can share in the horror of losing a child as she did, no one wants to remember the Holocaust, and no one will let her speak about her past.

Maureen Puffer-Rothenberg

Further Reading

Cohen, Sarah Blacher. "*The Shawl*: The Tragicomedy of Revolt and Survival." In *Cynthia Ozick's Comic Art: From Levity to Liturgy*. Bloomington: Indiana University Press, 1994. Suggests that much of the language, dialogue, and activity in *Rosa* can be taken as the darkly humorous responses to the horrors of "The Shawl."

Franco, Dean J. "Rereading Cynthia Ozick: Pluralism, Postmodernism, and the Multicultural Encounter." *Contemporary Literature* 49, no. 1 (2008): 56-84. This scholarly study addresses Ozick's approach to human values in her fiction, including her short stories and novellas.

Jones, Billie J. "The Fabrics of Her Life: Cloth as Symbol in Cynthia Ozick's 'The Shawl.'" *Studies in American Jewish Literature* 21 (2002): 72-80. Details the magical roles Rosa assigns to the shawl, and how its power is diminished when she accepts Persky's friendship.

Kremer, S. Lillian. "The Holocaust and the Witnessing Imagination." In *Violence, Silence, and Anger: Women's Writing as Transgression*, edited by Deirdre Lashgari. Charlottesville: University Press of Virginia, 1995. Discussion of *The Shawl* and Norma Rosen's novel *Touching Evil* (1969) as examples of fiction written by women specifically to explore women's experiences of the Holocaust.

Langer, Lawrence L. "Two Holocaust Voices: Cynthia Ozick and Art Spiegelman." In *Preempting the Holocaust*. New Haven, Conn.: Yale University Press, 1998. Compares Ozick's *The Shawl* and Spiegelman's *Maus* (1986) and looks at the authors' strategies for telling Holocaust stories to an American readership.

Powers, Peter Kerry. "Disruptive Memories: Cynthia Ozick and the Invented Past." In *Recalling Religions: Resistance, Memory, and Cultural Revision in Ethnic Women's Literature*. Knoxville: University of Tennessee Press, 2001. This essay discusses the influence of Ozick's ethnic identity on her fiction. Part of a larger study on the intersection of literature, ethnicity, memory, and religion.

Scrafford, Barbara. "Nature's Silent Scream: A Commentary on Cynthia Ozick's 'The Shawl.'" *Critique* 31, no. 1 (Fall, 1989): 11-15. Pays particular attention to Stella in "The Shawl" as a threat to Magda and as representative of the other death-camp prisoners.

She

Author: H. Rider Haggard (1856-1925)
First published: 1887
Type of work: Novel
Type of plot: Adventure
Time of plot: Late nineteenth century
Locale: Africa

Principal characters:
LUDWIG HOLLY, a teacher
LEO VINCEY, his ward
SHE, a beautiful ageless woman
JOB, Holly's servant
USTANE, a woman of the Amahagger tribe
BILLALI, an old man of the Amahagger tribe

The Story:

Late one night in his room at Cambridge, Ludwig Holly receives an urgent visit from Vincey, a fellow student. Vincey is dying of a lung condition, and because he has no living relatives, he asks Holly to undertake the guardianship of his young son, Leo Vincey, after his death. Vincey explains that the boy would be the last representative of one of the oldest families in the world. He can trace his ancestry to the ancient Egyptians, to a priest of Isis named Kallikrates, who had broken his vows and fled the country with an Egyptian princess. Kallikrates had been murdered by the queen of a savage tribe, but his wife had escaped and given birth to a son, from whom Leo is descended.

Holly agrees to rear the boy. It is understood that he is to be tutored at home, where he will be taught Greek, mathematics, and Arabic. On his twenty-fifth birthday, he is to receive an iron box that Vincey will leave with Holly; at that time, he can decide whether he wants to act upon its contents. The following morning, Vincey is found dead in his room. Shortly afterward, five-year-old Leo begins living with his guardian.

Twenty years pass happily for Leo and for the man whom he calls his uncle. On the morning of the youth's twenty-fifth birthday, the iron chest is opened. Inside is an ebony box that, in turn, contains a silver chest. Within that chest is a potsherd inscribed by the wife of the ill-fated Kallikrates. A message to her son, it declares that the queen who had murdered Kallikrates had shown them both the Pillar of Life. The message ends by begging that some brave descendant should try to find the Pillar of Life and slay the evil queen.

In the inmost chest, there is also a letter to Leo from his father, who wrote that he had journeyed to Africa to find the land that his ancestors had visited but had reached no farther than the coast. There, suffering a shortage of provisions, he had been forced to turn back. Before he could plan another trip, he had been overcome by his fatal illness.

Leo at once determines that he will carry on from the point where his father had been forced to give up his quest.

Three months later, he, Holly, and their servant, Job, are on their way to Africa. Their destination is a rock shaped like a black man's head, a landmark on the eastern coast of Central Africa. As they draw near shore, the little party readies the whaleboat that they plan to use for travel inland. The boat is tied onto the large boat that carries them down the coast. Suddenly, a squall comes up, and huge waves wreck the boat. The three white men and an Arab named Mahomed manage to launch the small boat and reach the shore.

Holly and his companions find themselves at the mouth of a river with teeming marshy banks crowded with crocodiles. The little party rests for a while and then starts inland in the whaleboat. They travel without much difficulty for five days; then the river grows too shallow to continue farther, and they are forced to branch into another stream, which proves to be an ancient canal.

During the next four days, the trip becomes increasingly difficult, and because the canal is full of weeds, the boat has to be towed. The exhausted men are resting on the fourth evening when they are suddenly attacked by a party of about fifty tall, light-colored men who speak Arabic. They would have been slain on the spot had not the old man who is the leader of the natives ordered that their lives be spared. He explains that word had come from someone whom he calls She-who-must-be-obeyed that any white men who wander into the country are to be brought to her. The man, whose name the adventurers later learn is Billali, decrees that Mahomed's life also should be spared. The prisoners are carried in litters to a cave village of the Amahagger tribe. There, Billali leaves them with his people while he goes on to report to She-who-must-be-obeyed.

The next four days pass peacefully. The men are well treated, and Ustane, one of the Amahagger women, takes Leo for her husband by the simple ceremony of throwing her arms around him and kissing him.

On the fourth night, the three white men and Mahomed are invited to a party. The only refreshment being served is a fermented drink. After the brew has been passed around several times, a woman suddenly slips a rope around Mahomed's body. At the same time, some of the men reach into the fire around which they are seated, drag out a white-hot pot, and try to slip it on the Arab's head. Realizing that the natives are preparing to kill and eat Mahomed, Holly draws his gun and shoots the woman. The bullet passes through her body and kills the Arab as well. In the furious struggle that follows, Leo is seriously wounded in the side. The situation is growing desperate when Billali appears to restore order.

Three days later, with Leo's wound barely healed, the three white men, accompanied by Billali and Ustane, are taken to meet She in her hidden city of Kôr. The route leads through deep swamps that at last give way to spreading plains. The next day, the travelers reach a tunneled mountain. Their guides lead Holly and his friends, blindfolded, through the tunnel to a plain that had once been a lake. There, the blindfolds are removed, and the men are taken to dwellings cut into the solid rock.

After he has refreshed himself, Holly is taken to the apartments of the heavily veiled queen. She asks about the ancient Greeks and Egyptians and explains that she has been living in the mountain for the past two thousand years. Holly wonders at the strange power that has enabled She to live untouched by time or mortality. She declares that she stays with the Amahagger only to await the return of the man she had once loved, for he is destined to be born again. When Ayesha, as she asks Holly to call her, removes her veil, he sees that she is exceedingly beautiful.

That night, Holly cannot sleep because of the excitement. Wandering in the passages that lead off from his room, he sees Ayesha uttering curses over a fire. He discovers that they are directed against an Egyptian woman. Near the fire, on a stone shelf, lies a corpse covered with a shroud. Fearful for his own life if he is discovered, Holly creeps back to his room.

The next day, the savages who had plotted Mahomed's death are brought before Ayesha and condemned to death by torture. In the evening, Ayesha visits Leo, who is ill with a fever and near death. When she sees his face, the queen staggers back with a scream. Leo has the face of the dead Kallikrates. It is he whose arrival Ayesha has been waiting for. She gives Holly a life-giving fluid, which he forces down Leo's throat. In her jealousy, she would have killed Ustane if Holly had not reminded her of the suffering she bore for killing Kallikrates so long ago. Ustane is sentenced to leave the mountain.

On the following evening, the three white men are invited to attend a dance performed by natives dressed in animal skins. The caves are honeycombed by preserved human bodies, which are used to illuminate the proceedings; when a torch is applied to them they burn brightly. Ustane, who has not been able to bring herself to part from Leo, is one of the dancers. She reveals herself to Leo when he strolls to a dark corner of the room, but she is discovered by Ayesha before she can flee with him. When Ustane refuses to leave Leo's side, Ayesha kills her with a fierce look.

Ayesha leads Leo and Holly to the place where Holly had seen her uttering her incantations. Drawing back the shroud that covers the corpse, she discloses the body of Kallikrates. Then over it she pours some acid that destroys it quickly. With Leo present in the flesh, she explains, she has no more need for the body of the dead man.

Leo quickly falls under Ayesha's spell and forgets Ustane. Several days later, the queen and the white men begin their journey to the place where Leo is to bathe in the fire of the Pillar of Life and so be assured of thousands of years of existence. Traveling across the plain through the ruins of the ancient city of Kôr, the party reaches a steep mountain. At its foot, they leave the litter bearers in the charge of Billali, who had accompanied them, and begin the ascent. When, by difficult stages, they reach the top, they are forced to walk a plank across a deep chasm to reach the cave that holds the pillar of fire—the Pillar of Life.

When Leo hesitates to immerse himself in the spiraling flame, Ayesha, to show that there is nothing to fear, walks into it. As she stands in its rising flame, a sudden change comes over her. Her face and limbs begin to shrivel until, before the horrified onlookers, she shrinks into a little old monkeylike creature and dies. Whether her death was caused by some fatal quality that had crept into the flame or whether her earlier immersion in it had been neutralized, the men do not know. Shaken to their depths, Holly and Leo start back to Billali. They leave Job, who had died of shock, in the cave with Ayesha's remains.

Informed of Ayesha's fate, Billali hurries to lead the white men back through the swamps toward the coast before the Amahagger tribe learns that they need no longer fear their queen. Much the worse for wear, Holly and Leo manage to make their way to Delagoa Bay after leaving the old native at the edge of the swamp country. Although they had only spent three weeks in the interior, Leo's hair had turned white.

The two men eventually arrive in England and resume their old existence. As he sits alone at night, Holly frequently wonders what the next step in the drama he had witnessed will be, and what, some day, will be the role of the Egyptian princess whom Kallikrates had loved.

Critical Evaluation:

England in the 1880's and 1890's saw a great upsurge of interest and popularity in the historical adventure story, especially in the works of three vivid, skillful writers—Robert Louis Stevenson, Rudyard Kipling, and H. Rider Haggard. Although posterity has granted the greater artistic status to Stevenson and Kipling, the prolific Haggard was, in his own time, the most popular and immediately influential of the three. At his very best, as in *King Solomon's Mines* (1885) and *She*, Haggard's work is not unworthy of comparison with Stevenson and Kipling. In these two early works, Haggard established plot conventions and character types that became central to the jungle tale from the Victorian age to the present.

Like *King Solomon's Mines* and most adventure tales, *She* centers on a heroic quest. This one, however, is not for anything as mundane as hidden treasure but for something more mysterious and exotic—a white jungle queen who may or may not be a goddess. This shift in emphasis almost turns *She* from an adventure narrative to a dark fantasy. The object of the quest, She-who-must-be-obeyed, is discovered about halfway through the narrative, and thereafter the question, What will happen to the heroes? changes to Who or what is She? Where does She come from? What does She want? and What will happen to her?

Ayesha may never be completely believable, but her vivid, ambiguous presence dominates the book. She is, as American novelist Henry Miller once said, "*the* femme fatale." Haggard succeeds in conveying a sense of her physical perfection and sensuality by judiciously presenting only a few details, leaving her essentially an abstract, idealized vision of feminine beauty. Nevertheless, she is also depicted as very human, as a woman deeply in love who can be something of a coquette, even, for all her two thousand years, somewhat girlish. Ayesha is a determined, ruthless lover and ruler, a contradictory character who combines cynicism and innocence, weariness and eagerness, benign detachment and passionate involvement, generous good and vindictive evil in a single larger-than-life personality.

The scope and ferocity of Ayesha's character further suggest powers far beyond the merely mortal, although it is difficult to say exactly what she is supposed to stand for. She identifies herself with nature and yet in many ways seems to be supremely unnatural. She finds Kallikrates, the lover she once jealously murdered, reincarnated in Leo Vincey, and she plans a triumphant return to civilization and a use of her supernatural powers to create a magical paradise for humankind with herself and Leo as absolute monarchs. She destroys herself by returning a second time to the Pillar of Fire.

In short, Ayesha seems to embody the ultimate paganism, even Satanism, which denies the limits set on human beings by a providential divinity—that, at least, is the final interpretation Holly attaches to her disintegration. The ending of the book, however, strongly hints that, despite what readers have seen, she will somehow or other return to "finish" her story.

Such a bizarre, extreme character would be ridiculous if Haggard had not surrounded her with a wealth of images and details that reinforce the mysterious, primordial atmosphere of the novel: the mysterious artifacts and documents that Leo's dying father gives Holly to establish Leo's ancestry; the savage Amahagger cannibals with their "hot-pot" ceremonies; the strange, extinct Kingdom of Kôr, with its peculiar architecture and legends from human prehistory; and, most vivid of all, the incessant images of decay and death. The book abounds with such scenes and details, and they occur increasingly and in more extreme form as the novel develops. They include the killing and torturing of the natives; the tombs of Kôr, where the entombed sleep on burial slabs; the embalmed figures of long-dead Kôr aristocrats, including their greatest king; the great heap of bodies of the less favored; the wild native dance ritual where corpses are burned as torches; and finally, the image of Ayesha disintegrating before the eyes of her appalled comrades. The novel counterpoints and associates Ayesha's heroic sensuality with death and destruction—Eros and Thanatos—in a symbiotic relationship that gives the book much of its most disturbing emotional force.

This is not to say that *She* is a great novel. The plot is crude, the prose overblown, falsely ornate, and abstract. The secondary characters are weak; the natives are stereotypes, whereas the whites are bland, stiff, and trite. Although Holly's long rhetorical digressions are intended to expound the book's philosophical and religious themes, these passages are pompous, even somewhat embarrassing. In short, the novel teeters on the edge of absurdity. Nevertheless, it leaves a more lasting and powerful impression than many a more serious book. Perhaps *She* is one of a handful of novels—such as Mary Wollstonecraft Shelley's *Frankenstein* (1818) and Herman Melville's *Pierre* (1852)—that touch such vital centers and provoke such emotional responses in the reader that the flaws in their execution and the implausibility of their ideas become relatively unimportant.

"Critical Evaluation" by Keith Neilson

Further Reading

Barclay, Glen St. John. *Anatomy of Horror: The Masters of Occult Fiction.* New York: St. Martin's Press, 1979. In the chapter "Love After Death: Henry Rider Haggard," Barclay surveys the writer's supernatural fiction, focusing on *She* and its three sequels. Concludes that Haggard "found an ideal form of expression" in his African adventures, and ranks him above other writers of the supernatural, such as Bram Stoker and H. P. Lovecraft.

Haggard, H. Rider. *The Annotated "She": A Critical Edition of H. Rider Haggard's Victorian Romance*. Edited by Norman Etherington. Bloomington: Indiana University Press, 1991. Etherington's critical introduction is the single best source for the beginner. This annotated edition of *She* also includes a brief bibliography. Written especially for younger readers.

Higgins, D. S. *Rider Haggard: A Biography*. New York: Stein & Day, 1983. The most accessible and detailed survey of Haggard's life and works. Higgins discusses *She*'s sources and genesis, as well as the book's reincarnations on stage and screen. Includes a good bibliography.

Katz, Wendy R. *Rider Haggard and the Fiction of Empire: A Critical Study of British Imperial Fiction*. New York: Cambridge University Press, 1987. A study of Haggard's fiction writing as exemplary of British imperialist literature. Important for placing Haggard clearly in the psychological and sociological contexts of his times. Katz's final chapter, "A Negro Excepted," explores aspects of racism in Haggard's writing.

Monsman, Gerald Cornelius. *H. Rider Haggard on the Imperial Frontier: The Political and Literary Contexts of His African Romances*. Greensboro, N.C.: ELT Press, 2006. Monsman disagrees with other critics who consider Haggard an apologist for imperialism, demonstrating how his work subverts Victorian imperialist culture by celebrating African religion, autonomous female characters, and racial mixing. Chapter 3, "Romances of the Lakes Region: Tales of Terror and the Occult," focuses on *She*.

Moss, John G. "Three Motifs in Haggard's *She*." *English Literature in Transition, 1880-1920* 16, no. 1 (1973): 27-34. Moss summarizes but dismisses most critical interpretations of *She*, concluding that the novel "escapes definition or explanation." He also faults the novel's sequels for failing to maintain the enigmatic quality of the original work.

Murphy, Patricia. *Time Is of the Essence: Temporality, Gender, and the New Woman*. Albany: State University of New York Press, 2001. Examines how the Victorian obsession with time informed the late nineteenth century debate about women's rights, as reflected in five British novels, including Haggard's *She*.

Stiebel, Lindy. *Imagining Africa: Landscape in H. Rider Haggard's African Romances*. Westport, Conn.: Greenwood Press, 2001. Focuses on Haggard's depiction of land and landscapes in his African novels, including *She*. Stiebel argues that Haggard created an idealized Africa that reflected the fears and desires of late Victorian Britain.

She Stoops to Conquer
Or, The Mistakes of a Night

Author: Oliver Goldsmith (1728/1730-1774)
First produced: 1773; first published, 1773
Type of work: Drama
Type of plot: Comedy of manners
Time of plot: Eighteenth century
Locale: England

Principal characters:
MR. HARDCASTLE, an English gentleman
MRS. HARDCASTLE, his wife
TONY LUMPKIN, Mrs. Hardcastle's son
KATE HARDCASTLE, their daughter
CONSTANCE NEVILLE, Tony's cousin
MARLOW, Kate's reluctant suitor
HASTINGS, in love with Constance
SIR CHARLES MARLOW, Marlow's father

The Story:

Tony Lumpkin, son of Mrs. Hardcastle from a previous marriage, is a drinker and a prankster. Indeed, his pranks lead to confusions, mistaken identities, and false assumptions. His mother indulges him and hopes that her ward, Constance

Neville, will marry him. Mr. Hardcastle has little patience with his son.

Mr. Hardcastle makes his daughter, Kate, wear the clothes of a country girl, at least part of each day, hoping that doing so will make her overcome her wish to be a lady of importance. Thinking as well that she should marry, Mr. Hardcastle has asked his closest friend, Sir Charles Marlow, to send his son from London to meet Kate, who is pleased by her father's description of the young man in all features except one: She does not like that he is shy and retiring.

On the trip from London, the young Marlow has the company of his dear friend, Hastings, who has hopes of marrying Miss Neville. She is delighted that Hastings is coming, and she reveals to Kate that she knows the young Marlow. She describes him as being very shy with fashionable young ladies but quite a different character with young women of a lower class.

En route to the Hardcastle home, Hastings and Marlow lose their way and arrive at an alehouse, where Tony is carousing with friends. Recognizing the two men, Tony decides to play a trick on his stepfather. He tells Hastings and Marlow that they have gone way off course and that it would be wise to stop at an inn a short distance up the road. The inn is actually Mr. Hardcastle's home. Knowing nothing of Hastings and Marlow's misconception, Hardcastle treats them as guests, while they, in turn, treat him as an innkeeper. Each party thinks the other extremely rude. Hardcastle certainly sees no modesty in Marlow's brash behavior.

Hastings finally meets Constance, who quickly recognizes Tony's hand in the mischief, but they choose to keep the secret to themselves. Hastings explains to Marlow that the two young ladies had arrived at the inn after a long journey from the Hardcastle home. Then he takes Tony aside and expresses his desire to marry Constance, an arrangement quite satisfactory to the rascal Tony who has no wish to marry her himself. He promises to help the lovers and even to try to secure Constance's jewelry, presently in Mrs. Hardcastle's keeping. The bargain having been made, Tony goes to his mother's room, steals the gems, and gives them to Hastings. He then whispers to his mother that she should tell Constance they had been lost. Thinking it a capital plan for keeping Constance in her control, Mrs. Hardcastle complies with Tony's suggestion, only to discover later that the gems actually are missing. She screams about the loss with such distress that Tony congratulates her on her acting.

At their first meeting, Marlow and Kate engage in a stumbling, broken conversation. Marlow is so tongue tied and shy he cannot even bring himself to look at Kate. Later, Kate, according to her agreement with her father, puts on a simple peasant dress. She knows full well that Marlow thinks he is in an inn, and she decides to keep him in error. He believes that she is a serving-girl, and then reveals himself as a flirtatious dandy. As he tries to kiss her, Mr. Hardcastle enters the room,

and Marlow flees. Mr. Hardcastle asserts to Kate that she now has clear proof that Marlow is no modest young man. Kate vows she will convince her father that Marlow's personality could please them both. However, Marlow's continued impudence so angers Hardcastle that he orders him to leave his house, warning him that his father, Sir Charles, will soon be here. Marlow begins to realize that he may have made some mistake thinking this place an inn. Kate, still in the guise of a barmaid, tells Marlow about Tony's prank. She does so, but she alters her identity to a "poor relation" and Marlow finds himself more and more attracted to her, and she to him.

Hastings gives Marlow the jewels that Tony stole from Mrs. Hardcastle. To protect the valuables, Marlow sends them to Mrs. Hardcastle, supposing her to be the innkeeper's wife. The servants, under Tony's instructions, explain to the distraught lady that the jewels had been mislaid because of some confusion in the household. In the meantime, with Tony's help, Hastings and Constance are on the verge of eloping, fleeing into the night with fresh horses provided by Tony. Mrs. Hardcastle discovers the plan. Enraged, she decides to punish Constance by sending her to visit her aunt, Pedigree.

Tony drives the coach, apparently taking Mrs. Hardcastle and Constance to Aunt Pedigree; instead, he drives them around in circles for three hours until Mrs. Hardcastle believes they are lost a good forty miles from home. After hiding his terrified mother in the bushes, Tony takes Constance back to Hastings. Constance, however, is determined not to leave without her jewels. When Mrs. Hardcastle at last discovers Tony's trick, she is furious.

Sir Charles, on his arrival, is greatly amused by Hardcastle's account of Marlow's mistake. Hardcastle assures Sir Charles that Marlow loves Kate, but Marlow insists he has no interest in her. Kate promises the two fathers that she can prove Marlow loves her, and she tells them to hide while she talks with Marlow. Still under the impression that Kate is a serving-girl or a poor relation, the wretched young man tells her he loves her and wants to marry her. Sir Charles and Hardcastle emerge from their hiding place satisfied that the marriage would be arranged. Marlow is astounded that the young woman with whom he has behaved so freely is really Miss Hardcastle.

Mrs. Hardcastle reminds her husband that she has full control of Constance's fortune until she marries Tony when he comes of age. Only if he should refuse her would Constance be given control of her inheritance. Mr. Hardcastle then announces that Tony's real age had been hidden in the hope the lad would improve his character. Learning that he is already of age, Tony refuses to marry Constance. Sir Charles assures Mrs. Hardcastle that Hastings is a fine young man. Mrs. Hardcastle turns the jewels over to her ward, who may now openly marry Hastings. Marlow, the wiser for all the mistakes of the night, happily marries Kate.

Critical Evaluation:

A well-crafted play, Oliver Goldsmith's *She Stoops to Conquer* weaves several strands of action. Although the story transpires in not much more than one night, the play is densely packed with activity. This of course accounts for the play's subtitle, "Mistakes of a Night."

Two of the play's strands are of particular importance, both about bringing lovers together. There are two sets of lovers: One couple, Hastings and Constance Neville, have been in love for some time, but their hopes are thwarted by Mrs. Hardcastle's insistence that Constance marry her son, Tony Lumpkin. The only recourse appears to be eloping, a scheme that Tony happily aids and abets. The other couple, Marlow and Kate Hardcastle, is brought together by an arrangement between their respective fathers, Sir Charles and Mr. Hardcastle, as a way of confirming their friendship. Here, the problem is the awkward shyness of the young Marlow upon meeting ladies. Knowing that the shyness evaporates when he confronts a woman of lower station, Kate literally "stoops to conquer." Both strands of the play are thus deftly resolved: The elopement becomes unnecessary once Tony is revealed to be of age and free to reject Constance, and the marriage of Kate and Marlow can take place, now that Marlow's eyes are open to the truth.

All this might seem contrived were it not for the comic ironies and misunderstandings among the characters and the grace and wit with which Goldsmith portrays them. *She Stoops to Conquer* is very much a group play, as there is no protagonist in the usual sense. Tony provides most of the machinations that propel the plot. Kate brings Marlow to a crucial realization, and he suffers more than anyone from the mistaken identities and false assumptions. However, none of these characters is really central. Instead, together they draw parallels and contrasts between marriages, not only the two that come to pass but also the one of the Hardcastles and, for that matter, the fact of Tony's opting out of any marriage.

This charming play has entertained audiences since its first performance at Covent Garden in London in 1773, a time when sentimental comedies dominated the English stage, and had done so since Sir Richard Steele's *The Conscious Lovers* (pb. 1723) in 1722 had provided what its author called, "a pleasure too exquisite for laughter." These are plays calculated to inspire tears in the eyes of audiences as they witness love overcoming all obstacles. Goldsmith and

Sir Richard Brinsley Sheridan had declared war on such insipid drama, calling for a return to laughing comedy by producing pamphlets, articles, and plays, including some of the best comedies of the century: Sheridan's *The Rivals* (pr., pb. 1775) and *The School for Scandal* (pr. 1777, pb. 1780) and Goldsmith's *The Good Natured Man* (pr., pb. 1768) and *She Stoops to Conquer*.

Goldsmith died in 1774, one year after *She Stoops to Conquer* was first performed, thus leaving no other plays. Despite his position against sentimental comedy, *She Stoops to Conquer* has a gentle and amiable tone. It promotes the idea of honest humility and does so with humane good humor. These values, too, are typical of the eighteenth century, which exalted feeling and intuition and grace in opposition to the severe rationalism of the previous century.

Goldsmith was haunted by poverty and was irritable and envious; he also had a great wit, was generous, and had an essentially lovable nature—all of these contradictory characteristics are reflected in his writings. Hopelessly impractical, especially in money matters, he wrote with genius and Irish liveliness in many different forms and left a legacy of at least four masterpieces. He was forced to plod away as a literary hack, trying to survive in London's Grub Street literary world. He did editorial work for booksellers, wrote essays and criticism, and gradually gained a modest reputation. *The Citizen of the World* (1762; first published in *The Public Ledger*, 1760-1761), a collection of fictional letters, brought him even more recognition for their charm, grace, humor, and good sense.

Although this success somewhat eased the pinch of poverty, Goldsmith continued to find it necessary to write pamphlets and miscellaneous journalism. A philosophic poem, *The Traveller: Or, A Prospect of Society* (1764), brought high praise from Samuel Johnson, and the book of poems, *The Deserted Village* (1770), was a wide success. In 1766, *The Vicar of Wakefield*, written to pay the rent, brought Goldsmith fame as a novelist, but his money troubles continued. *She Stoops to Conquer*, Goldsmith's second comedy, received a flattering public response, but the financial returns paid off only a fraction of his huge debts.

Johnson saw this first performance and remarked, "I know of no comedy for many years that has answered so much the great end of comedy—making an audience merry." One may well agree and say that one or two comedies of the time might be considered superior, but none is merrier. Certainly, it reflects Goldsmith's own rich and genial personality.

"Critical Evaluation" by Bruce D. Reeves;
revised by Stanley Vincent Longman

Further Reading

Dixon, Peter. *Oliver Goldsmith Revisited*. Boston: Twayne, 1991. A solid introduction to Goldsmith's work in general and *She Stoops to Conquer* in particular. Details the biographical episode that inspired Goldsmith to write the comedy, and ties the play to Goldsmith's theories on dramatic writing.

Kiberd, Declan. "Radical Pastoral: Goldsmith's *She Stoops to Conquer*." In *Irish Classics*. Cambridge, Mass.: Harvard University Press, 2001. A discussion of the play within the context of classic Irish literature.

Quintana, Ricardo. *Oliver Goldsmith: A Georgian Study*. New York: Macmillan, 1967. An enthusiastic and graceful study of Goldsmith's work. Places less emphasis on the drama itself and more on the circumstances surrounding the play's production and theatrical success.

Sells, A. Lytton. *Oliver Goldsmith: His Life and Works*. New York: Barnes & Noble, 1974. Examines Goldsmith's life and offers a chapter on his writing of *She Stoops to Conquer* and on the problems he faced presenting it on the London stage. Offers two chapters on Goldsmith the dramatist and critically scrutinizes *She Stoops to Conquer*.

Swarbrick, Andrew, ed. *The Art of Oliver Goldsmith*. London: Vision Press, 1984. Ten essays touching on all aspects of Goldsmith's writings. Contains Bernard Harris's engaging "Goldsmith in the Theatre," examining Goldsmith's dramatic career, theater philosophy, and difficulties in staging *She Stoops to Conquer*.

Thomas, David, ed. *Four Georgian and Pre-Revolutionary Plays*. New York: St. Martin's Press, 1998. *She Stoops to Conquer* is one of the English, French, and German plays with themes of class and sex that are included in this volume. Thomas provides an introduction to the play, as well as introductory essays placing the play within the cultural and political context of eighteenth century England and the English theater of that period.

Worth, Katharine. *Sheridan and Goldsmith*. New York: St. Martin's Press, 1992. Intelligent investigation of the playwriting careers of Goldsmith and Richard Brinsley Sheridan, with special attention to Goldsmith's intense dislike of the prevailing sentimental comedy. Long chapter on *She Stoops to Conquer* is an excellent discussion of the boisterous play.

The Sheep Well

Author: Lope de Vega Carpio (1562-1635)
First published: Fuenteovejuna, 1619 (English translation, 1936)
Type of work: Drama
Type of plot: Social realism
Time of plot: 1476
Locale: Spain

Principal characters:
COMMANDER FERNÁN GÓMEZ DE GUZMÁN, a lustful tyrant
RODRIGO TÉLLEZ GIRÓN, youthful master of the Order of Calatrava
LAURENCIA, a peasant woman desired by the commander
FRONDOSO, a peasant youth in love with Laurencia
ESTEBAN, administrative officer of Fuenteovejuna and Laurencia's father
KING FERDINAND and QUEEN ISABELLA OF SPAIN

The Story:

In the troubled Spain of the 1470's, when King Ferdinand and Queen Isabella are trying to integrate their kingdom and preserve it from the depredations of Portugal, the grand mastership of the military and religious Order of Calatrava falls upon the shoulders of Rodrigo Téllez Girón, a young man scarcely out of boyhood. The new grand master's adviser is the lustful, tyrannical Commander Fernán Gómez de Guzmán, who takes women whenever and wherever he sees them and keeps his peasants in constant fear of himself and of his soldiers. The commander is not loyal to Ferdinand and Isabella, and so he counsels the young grand master to capture the Ciudad Real and hold it for Portugal, which is claiming sections of Spain because the Portuguese queen is Spanish. The grand master takes the commander's advice and captures the city.

When the commander returns to his lands, he continues his tyrannous ways with the peasants, especially the women. Among the unmarried peasants is a particularly pretty one named Laurencia, the daughter of Esteban, the administrative officer of the village. The commander sought her for more than a month, but she manages to elude his servants by staying in the fields as much as possible. Then the commander leaves to capture the city. He returns in triumph, and upon his arrival in the village of Fuenteovejuna he is praised and given two cartloads of foodstuffs as recognition of his military efforts. After receiving the gifts, he requests that the young women, including Laurencia, remain behind to amuse him. The women, however, refuse to stay. Ferdinand and Isabella, meanwhile, receive word of the treacherous action of the grand master of the Order of Calatrava and dispatch a force to retake Ciudad Real.

In Fuenteovejuna, Laurencia is wooed by a good-looking young peasant, Frondoso, but she refuses to accept him as her husband. One day, as she is working in the fields, the commander attempts to rape her. Frondoso, although a peasant, seizes the commander's crossbow and threatens to kill the knight unless he lets Laurencia go. The commander, having no choice, lets the woman go free but swears vengeance. Frondoso flees with the crossbow.

The commander later goes to the village, confronts Laurencia's father, and demands that he give up his daughter to him. Esteban refuses, and he and the other villagers leave the commander standing alone in the square. Some of the commander's servants appear and report that they think they killed Frondoso. As it turns out, they cut the throat of the wrong man. As they speak, a messenger comes to inform the commander that the grand master was besieged by the forces of Ferdinand and Isabella. The commander decides to rush to the grand master's aid.

As they ride away from the village, the commander and his servants try to force their attentions on several peasant women. The women flee until they reach one of the men of the village. When he tries to protect them, the commander has the man disarmed, bound to a tree, and flogged unmercifully with bridle reins. While that is done, the commander seizes one of the women, drags her into a thicket, and rapes her. The soldiers then proceed on their journey.

During the commander's absence, his subject peasants relax a bit. In the quiet interval, arrangements are made for the wedding of Laurencia and Frondoso, the young peasant who has become dear to her after he saved her from the commander's lust. On the day of the wedding, the commander returns and demands the woman for his own purposes. When her father again refuses, the commander has him beaten, and the wedding is broken up by the soldiers. Frondoso is imprisoned to await hanging; Laurencia is taken to the commander's citadel.

The next day, the town board assembles in the village hall to discuss what might be done to prevent further acts of violence by their wicked master. While they debate, Laurencia, who has escaped from the citadel, runs into the hall, where she rouses the men and women of the village to open revolt against the commander who treats them so brutally and ruthlessly. The people, spurred to action by their anger, storm the citadel. Once inside, they kill many of the soldiers and finally find the commander. They put him to death and return to the village with his head held high upon the point of a spear. Their plan is to leave the head in the village square as a symbol of the tyranny they broke. Not really rebels, the villagers hasten to raise the escutcheon of Ferdinand and Isabella in place of the commander's. Their plan is to place themselves at the mercy of the king and queen.

One of the commander's servants escapes and carries news of the uprising to the king and queen. The king, anxious to prevent revolt from spreading throughout Spain, dispatches soldiers and a judge to the village of Fuenteovejuna to investigate. When word arrives at the village that a judge is coming, the villagers meet and decide to stick together, even to hiding the murderers of the commander and his men. It is agreed that the entire village did the deed and that they will hang together, if need be.

The judge has the soldiers bring in villagers for questioning. When the villagers refuse to tell who were the leaders of the revolt or who actually killed the commander, the judge has them tortured. More than three hundred of the villagers are tortured, including small children, but not one breaks his or her vow to claim that the whole town is responsible for the deeds.

At last, the judge and the soldiers return to the court of Ferdinand and Isabella, where the judge reports that he made no decision, for in order to punish justly he would have to wipe out the entire village. He also reports to the king and queen the cruelties of which the commander was guilty. Villagers he brought with him to court plead with the king and the queen, pointing out that they did not rebel against the crown; they were forced to rid themselves of a tyrannous lord who threatened their lives and honor. The king, after hearing their stories, pardons the entire village of Fuenteovejuna and makes it a protectorate of the crown.

Critical Evaluation:

Lope de Vega Carpio was the central figure of the great dramatic movement in Spain during the sixteenth and seventeenth centuries. Acclaimed by many scholars as having created the *comedia* that provided the model for the Golden Age of Spanish theater in the seventeenth century, Vega Carpio received the honorary title of doctor of theology before terminating a career that produced hundreds of plays and extensive volumes of classical epics, lyric verse, one-acts, ballads, epistles, prose stories, and a novelized autobiography.

Vega Carpio was popular with the different levels of society; he was awarded the position of judge by the Spanish Inquisition, becoming an official censor. His popularity reflected his choice to represent the various social strata in his *comedia* instead of limiting his characters to the gentlemen of society. The best of his plays are those, such as *The Sheep Well*, that use peasants as heroes and heroines. Vega Carpio had a sympathy and feeling for those people, because they were of the same class from which he had come. *The Sheep Well*, because of its use of the entire population of a Spanish village as the hero, is sometimes referred to as the first proletarian drama, written some three hundred years before the flood of proletarian literature came out of the Great Depression in the United States.

Vega Carpio formulated concepts regarding the composition of the *comedia* toward the beginning of his career and, in *El arte nuevo de hacer comedias en este tiempo* (1609; *The New Art of Writing Plays*, 1914), read them to the Madrid literary society, who preferred the Aristotelian rules of dramatic composition. Vega Carpio rejected these classical rules in favor of popular dramatic style; his treatise in verse clarified two principal reasons for favoring this style: to give pleasure and to be true to life. In order to impart pleasure to the audience, Vega Carpio decided that comedy could be mixed with tragedy for variety and that the play, observing the unity of action, should be well constructed, with the denouement occurring in the last scene to sustain interest.

In the *comedia*, Vega Carpio portrays realism through natural speech that depicts the social class of the character and through the variety of verse forms that sets the mood of the characters. This treatise establishes Vega Carpio's main theatrical theme as honor, chosen to move people of any age or social class. Soon after Vega Carpio read his formula for composing *comedia*, he wrote *The Sheep Well*, which illustrates his contribution to the development of the Spanish *comedia*: the perspective of the society dedicated to the code of honor. *The Sheep Well* reflects this Spanish code that governs social relationships between king and subject, superior and inferior, friend and friend, and members of the same family.

The significance of the code resides in the correct ordering of social relationships. Since the social group is more important than individual integrity, honor stems from group esteem. The primary theme of *The Sheep Well* revolves around

honor; the main plot concerns the village of Fuenteovejuna (sheep well) representing the common group, and the commander, the villain, characterizing a superior social class. The two other subplots also involve honor and the commander: Ciudad Real versus the Order of Calatrava and the Spain of Ferdinand and Isabella versus the Portugal of Alfonso. The plot and subplots delineate an assault on the integrity of a societal faction by an exterior power, and this assault is assuaged and avenged. The commander participates in each plot or subplot, spreading his malevolent force to the village, the city, and the nation, until, overcome by his own evil, he is exterminated by the group.

The principal plot involving the commander and the inhabitants of Fuenteovejuna presents different social strata in a realistic manner. The commander reflects his military background through his frequent use of imperatives, hence, speaking with the authority of a conqueror. Upon entering the village in act 1, the soldier shows his excessive authoritarian posture by demanding to be told if the master knows he is in town. The commander then mistreats the girls, women, boys, men, and the town elders; he even asks them if they are his possessions. The commander acts contrary to a typical feudal lord, who protects his vassals and their property. If the feudal lord faithfully renders his service to his vassals, they will perform certain duties; however, the feudal lord's vassals are not unconditionally bound to him. The commander disregards this concept, because he associates the villagers with his stable horses or the wild animals of the forest. For example, he decides that a recalcitrant old man deserves the same castigation as he would give to an unruly horse. Another comparison with animals pertains to the soldier's pursuit of the village women: In addressing Esteban, the soldier shamelessly compares his pursuit of the latter's daughter to that of a greyhound stalking its game. The commander's cruel, obsessive behavior, therefore, severs the normal relationship between a lord and his vassals.

The commander's comparison of the villagers with animals such as horses, hares, and dogs transforms him into an animalistic brute. The peasants, who speak in a rustic dialect with copious homely expressions, recognize the irony and label him as a wild beast, a lynx, a wolf, and a tiger, finally envisioning him as a devil. In order to save themselves from the commander's tyranny, these country people realize that they will have to defend themselves. In act 1, Frondoso intervenes on behalf of Laurencia when he threatens to use the commander's crossbow to defend her from the leader's advances. In act 2, Mengo defies the commander in order to prevent two servants from taking Jacinta to their superior. Mengo's actions are heroic, because his only weapon is his arms. Although Mengo does not succeed in preventing Jacinta's seizure, Vega Carpio is preparing the denouement of the third act by revealing that individual heroic endeavors cannot curb the savage obsessions of the commander. Incited by Laurencia's speech, the villagers agree to end oppression and dishonor because of love. Esteban asserts that they experienced a sort of death when the commander stained their honor, so that their killing the commander is not an act of rebellion but of justice. The villagers prove their adherence to the established social order by going to the court of Ferdinand and Isabella, who acknowledge their bravery, hence establishing the concept of the just monarchs concerned with the honor code of their subjects.

The theme of honor portrayed by a convincing group protagonist composed of courageous individuals provides colorful, animated scenes, which give *The Sheep Well* its success in Vega Carpio's prolific production of *comedias*. It well illustrates Vega Carpio's purpose of creating realistic *comedias* to please the audience.

"Critical Evaluation" by Linda Prewett Davis

Further Reading

Cañadas, Ivan. *Public Theater in Golden Age Madrid and Tudor-Stuart London: Class, Gender. and Festive Community*. Burlington, Vt.: Ashgate, 2005. Compares English Tudor and Spanish Golden Age drama, focusing on theatrical conventions, social significance of the plays, and reception of audiences in London and Madrid. Part 5 is devoted to an examination of "Class, Gender, and Carnival: Communal Heroism in *Fuente Ovejuna*."

Crow, John A. *Spain: The Root and the Flower*. New York: Harper & Row, 1963. Chapters 6 through 9 contain a readable account of the history of Spain during the epoch of Vega Carpio.

Larson, Donald R. *The Honor Plays of Lope de Vega*. Cambridge, Mass.: Harvard University Press, 1977. Treats the concept of honor in Vega Carpio's *comedias*. Contains an informative section pertaining to *The Sheep Well* in the chapter titled "Plays of the Middle Period."

Northup, George Tyler. *An Introduction to Spanish Literature*. 3d rev. ed. Chicago: University of Chicago Press, 1960. A helpful presentation of the Spanish *comedia*. Includes a chapter devoted to Vega Carpio and his dramatic school.

Pring-Mill, R. D. F. "Sententiousness in *Fuenteovejuna (Sheep Well)*." *Tulane Drama Review* 7 (1962): 5-37. Relates the importance of maxims in *The Sheep Well*. The conclusions concerning the abundance of aphorisms in *The Sheep Well* can be applied to various *comedias* of the era.

Samson, Alexander, and Jonathan Thacker, eds. *A Companion to Lope de Vega*. Rochester, N.Y.: Tamesis, 2008. Twenty-one essays provide various interpretations of Vega Carpio's life and work. Includes discussions of Vega Carpio and the theater of Madrid, his religious drama, his chronicle memory plays, his comedies, and Vega Carpio as icon.

Wright, Elizabeth R. *Pilgrimage to Patronage: Lope de Vega and the Court of Philip III, 1598-1621*. Lewisburg, Pa.: Bucknell University Press, 2001. Chronicles how Vega Carpio used his publications and public appearances to win benefactors at the court of Philip III. Describes how his search for patrons shaped his literary work, and how the success of his plays altered the court's system of artistic patronage.

The Sheltered Life

Author: Ellen Glasgow (1873-1945)
First published: 1932
Type of work: Novel
Type of plot: Psychological realism
Time of plot: 1906-1914
Locale: Richmond, Virginia

Principal characters:
GENERAL DAVID ARCHBALD, an aged and aristocratic
    Southern patriarch
JENNY BLAIR ARCHBALD, his free-spirited granddaughter
AUNT ETTA, the general's neurotic spinster daughter
AUNT ISABELLA, the general's flirtatious daughter
EVA HOWARD BIRDSONG, an aristocratic, formerly
    celebrated beauty
GEORGE BIRDSONG, Eva's charming, philandering husband

The Story:

"I'm alive, alive, alive, and I'm Jenny Blair Archbald," exclaims the precocious nine-year-old Jenny, on having thrown aside as tedious Louisa Alcott's *Little Women* (1868). Jenny lives with three somewhat downtrodden females—her widowed mother and two aunts—in the household of her grandfather, General David Archbald. An aged, highly civilized man, the general seeks to maintain his aristocratic family amid declining fortunes in a once-elegant but rapidly failing Queenborough neighborhood. Jenny, like her mother, grandfather, and aunts, is an ardent admirer of the similarly circumstanced married couple who live nearby, Eva and George Birdsong, whose marriage is a subject of speculative discussion among the Archbald women.

Eva Birdsong, a queenly belle of the 1890's and still an acknowledged beauty as she approaches her forties, abandoned her social position as well as a planned singing career when she fell in love with George Birdsong. George, a barely successful attorney, is handsome, invariably charming and likable, and a consummate philanderer who recognizes Eva's worth but is unable to rise to it. Aware that her beauty and the social attentions that it commands are waning, Eva refuses to acknowledge even the most blatant evidences of George's adulteries.

Increasingly amoral and hedonistic, Jenny, even as a child, idolized Eva Birdsong for her regal beauty and character, neither of which, she realizes, lies within her reach. Jenny is also powerfully drawn to George, who has cultivated her affections since her childhood. Jenny, moreover, shares a secret with him: Having injured herself falling off roller skates one day in a poorer neighborhood, she was cared for, as it happened, by George and his black mistress. Over the years, Jenny is a frequent and favored visitor in the Birdsong household. Eva, as her fortunes worsen, begins to confide in Jenny, explaining how plans for her early career were jettisoned when, falling in love with George, she "stopped wanting anything else," and that a "great love doesn't leave room for anything else in a woman's life." At a grand party attended by all of the Archbalds and Birdsongs, George has an amorous encounter with a pretty young girl in a secluded garden. Eva, distraught, collapses, and even Jenny and other children present recognize her marital self-delusions.

Eight years later, old General Archbald muses over his life and the lives of his family and friends. Eva, whom the general reverences as the epitome of beautiful and courageous womanhood and thus as a symbol of his dying southern values, at the age of forty undergoes a maiming operation that is followed by a nervous collapse. Thereafter she is sickly and loses her striking beauty. Increasingly, she also recognizes the price exacted from her for a life of illusions. As General Archbald devotedly attends her, often in George's company, he pities Eva for this. While cognizant of the cause of her malaise, however, he still thinks George has the right to philander and that men's adulteries are irrelevant to their love relationships with their wives.

General Archbald also muses about his own youth and the destruction of his poetic talent by his father's callous insistence that he adhere to a traditional southern male role. The general realizes that his conventional marriage resulted from a mistaken obedience to outworn standards. He fell into the right pattern, as he phrases it, but the center of the pattern is missing.

As Eva passively awaits a further operation, it becomes clear that she is weary of a life of "exacting pretense" and that she wants to die. The operation strips her of her remaining beauty, and she succumbs to a postoperative breakdown. Nevertheless, she clings to a faith in her love, excusing George's philandering as a consequence of his kindness. Jenny, nearly eighteen, hopes to escape home and launch a career. She continues her idolatry of Eva, which Eva reciprocates by confiding her inner thoughts. Eva confesses to Jenny that for forty years she never really knew herself, and she warns Jenny that to surrender everything to love, as she did, is to become a slave to fear.

Despite Eva's soul-baring confidences, Jenny is nevertheless attracted to George. When Eva departs to convalesce, their opportunities for meeting increase. One day after Eva's return, Jenny and George, believing that she is upstairs, are locked in an embrace when Eva inadvertently discovers them. Terrified, Jenny flees into the ruins of Eva's garden. Shortly afterward, Eva fatally shoots George amid the blood of his recent kills. Rallying to Eva, General Archbald outfaces the law by describing the murder as an accident, thus continuing to preserve his sheltered life and the sheltered lives of his kin from an encounter with reality.

Critical Evaluation:

The Sheltered Life, the last of Ellen Glasgow's Queenborough novels, was appraised critically as one of her finest works and as a major American novel. Glasgow's tone throughout the work is ironic, at times satiric. The plot is tightly constructed, and the characters, notably General Archbald, Eva, George, and Jenny, are plausible, three-dimensional, and memorable. Glasgow uses deft metaphorical shadings and contrasts. Bright settings become darker and more somber as events proceed, and the encroachments of industrialism become progressively louder and more noxious. The waning of Eva's beauty and marriage are paralleled by her declining fortunes, dress, and gardens and by the steady erosion of her once-elegant neighborhood and her cherished delusions. The characters, too, are skillfully contrasted. The general and Eva are well-cast evocations of an old and dying order's values. By contrast, George and Jenny are less inhibited and more hedonistic, undisciplined, and vulgar in their vitality; neither is evil, however, and their actions, if not always commendable, are at least understandable. Similarly, General Archbald's daughters reflect a familiar range of feminine repressions: Etta, the homely spinster, neurotic and sexually starved, and Isabella drawn by her flirtations to blend into the commonplace.

Glasgow was one of many who were surprised that *The Sheltered Life* did not garner a Pulitzer Prize. The novel represented Glasgow's most intensive exploitation of themes she dealt with many times, chief among them her concern with evasive idealism, its subjective and cultural manifestations, and the consequences of its encounters with reality. This thematic exploration was informed by Glasgow's study of Darwinism and its emphasis on the biological imperatives that produced survivors. To satisfy her sexuality, Jenny is, for example, prepared to push others—even Eva, her idol—treacherously aside. Glasgow also drew her thematic material from her keen interest in psychology. Some of her psychological insights she discovered, for example, in the work of Russian novelists and of Virginia Woolf, authors who also analyzed the complex connections between people's mental states and emotional decay and the outward appearances they maintained.

In *The Sheltered Life*, Glasgow recounts that she employed two simultaneous yet related points of view that channeled her story like a stream in a narrow valley. One perspective is that of age: General Archbald's view of life as it was and might have been. The other is the perspective of youth as seen in the perceptions of troubled young Jenny. Both perspectives come to bear on the same events and personalities. However, through the workings of their different thoughts and emotions, each interprets reality differently.

An author whose feminist convictions placed her in advance of her times, Glasgow likewise sought to explore Eva, Jenny, and her other female characters as multidimensional people, not as mere symbols or metaphors for a male perception that predominated in literature, as in Western thought, long after the first decades of the twentieth century. In all of her writing, Glasgow reveals her disdain for sexual love, for homage to males, and for the glorification of a life of feminine sacrifice. Glasgow clearly sympathized with and in many regards admired Eva Birdsong, even to the point of

justifying Eva's murder of her husband. As critics have noted, however, Eva destroys herself by shooting George. Glasgow thus remains ambiguous about the desirable role for women's sexuality. This ambiguity is sharpened by her depiction of Jenny, socially and sexually a free spirit, as a shallow, treacherous person. What is not ambiguous is Glasgow's clear message that it is a mistake for women of any kind or at any time to derive their identities from their sexuality.

By choosing to end the story in 1914, the year in which not only the world of the Archbalds and the Birdsongs was in conspicuous decline but also Western civilization appeared headed for collapse, Glasgow reflected the questions and interests of her times. Serious philosophical issues were in debate about the hidden springs or motivations of human actions. Human thought and actions were increasingly being described as less the outcome of rationality than of obscure inner drives, primordial passions, and emotions. Human values were being depicted not as traditionally sanctified or divinely ordained but as relative and subject to changing biological and cultural interpretations. Human behavior, therefore, increasingly appeared to be a consequence of self-deception, illusion, or delusion.

Insofar as *The Sheltered Life* signals that not too much should be expected of life or of people—both are full of tricks and deceptions—and yet that love and compassion should not be abandoned, it is a wise book. It is all the wiser because Glasgow identifies courage as "the only virtue that has a lasting quality."

Clifton K. Yearley

Further Reading

Inge, Thomas M., ed. *Ellen Glasgow*. Charlottesville: University of Virginia Press, 1976. Excellent centennial essays on "Miss Ellen's" work, including pithy critical comments by Louis Rubin, Jr., on *The Sheltered Life*.

McDowell, Frederick P. W. *Ellen Glasgow and the Ironic Art of Fiction*. Madison: University of Wisconsin Press, 1960. Includes lucid analyses of *The Sheltered Life* in chapter 1, which provides fine background, and in chapter 11, which deals exclusively with this novel.

Patterson, Martha H. "Mary Johnston, Ellen Glasgow, and the Evolutionary Logic of Progressive Reform." In *Beyond the Gibson Girl: Reimagining the American New Woman, 1895-1915*. Urbana: University of Illinois Press, 2005. At the end of the nineteenth and beginning of the twentieth centuries, an image emerged of the "New Woman" who was well-educated, progressive, and white.

Patterson's book describes how Glasgow and other writers challenged this image, creating women characters who were African American, southern, and in other ways different from the popular conception of womanhood.

Raper, Julius Rowan. *From the Sunken Garden.* Baton Rouge: Louisiana State University Press, 1980. Fine survey of Glasgow's fiction between 1916 and 1945. Chapter 8 focuses on *The Sheltered Life* and places it in context with other Glasgow writings.

Scura, Dorothy M., ed. *Ellen Glasgow.* New York: Cambridge University Press, 1992. An immensely helpful and enlightening collection of contemporary reviews of Glasgow's writings, including an entire section devoted to *The Sheltered Life.*

Taylor, Welford Dunaway, and George C. Longest, eds. *Re-garding Ellen Glasgow: Essays for Contemporary Readers.* Richmond: Library of Virginia, 2001. This collection includes examinations of Glasgow and southern history, Glasgow and Calvinism, her depiction of southern women, and the feminist elements in her work. Includes chronology, bibliography, and index.

Thiebaux, Marcelle. *Ellen Glasgow.* New York: Frederick Ungar, 1982. A lucid and informative survey of Glasgow's novels. Includes an analysis of *The Sheltered Life* in chapter 7.

Wagner-Martin, Linda. "Glasgow's Time in *The Sheltered Life.*" In *Ellen Glasgow: New Perspectives,* edited by Dorothy M. Scura. Knoxville: University of Tennessee Press, 1995. Focuses on Glasgow's depiction of time in the novel.

The Sheltering Sky

Author: Paul Bowles (1910-1999)
First published: 1949
Type of work: Novel
Type of plot: Psychological realism
Time of plot: After World War II
Locale: Oran, Algeria; Sahara Desert; a remote Bedouin village

Principal characters:
PORT MORESBY, an American traveler
KIT MORESBY, his wife
TUNNER, their American companion
MRS. LYLE, an overbearing Englishwoman
ERIC LYLE, her adult son
BELQASSIM, a Bedouin who takes Kit into his harem

The Story:

Port Moresby wakes up unable to remember his dream. Later he sits with his wife, Kit Moresby, and their traveling companion, Tunner. They are three New Yorkers who find that North Africa is one of the few places to which they can get boat passage since the end of the war.

Port explains the difference between tourists and travelers. He is a traveler, a person who belongs to no place, who is not ruled by time, and who questions his own civilization. His wife, Kit, does not share Port's enthusiasm for maps and remote locations but is willing to accompany him.

Port then recalls his dream: He is on a speeding train, going ever faster. He is offered the chance to live his life over again, but he refuses. Kit leaves the table crying. Back at the hotel, Kit explains that the dream was too private to tell in front of Tunner, but Port feels that she is being too serious. He leaves on a walk.

He feels nervous, but he walks until the street lights are gone, and an Arab man asks what he wants. Port is offered a prostitute. The man leads him to a cliff and points to a tent in the valley. Port has sex with a beautiful young girl there, fantasizing that Kit looks on. When the girl attempts to steal his wallet, he pushes her and bolts from the tent. Several men pursue him.

That morning Kit reflects on her vanishing relationship with Port. Although she thinks Tunner is idiotic, she considers using him as an emotional tool that might force Port back to her. Tunner comes to wake her up. Then she notices that Port's bed is still made. Port arrives and is angry to find Tunner with Kit. She is angry at being accused. Kit and Tunner leave. In the hotel bar, Port meets Eric Lyle, a revolting character, and Eric's scolding mother. She is a travel writer, and they are touring Africa. Kit returns; she and Port argue briefly.

The argument over Port's whereabouts continues in the morning. Then Eric invites them to ride in his motorcar to avoid the long train ride to Boussif. Kit refuses to travel with the Lyles or to leave Tunner behind. She and Tunner will take the train. That evening, Tunner woos Kit over champagne.

Tunner and Kit get drunk in the compartment, riding toward Boussif. Kit leaves the train momentarily and boards a fourth-class carriage. She is frightened and soaked by rain when she makes it back. She misses having Port to lean on. Tunner takes this opportunity to seduce her. By lunchtime the three are reunited at a hotel in Boussif.

Kit and Port, somewhat reconciled, ride rented bikes out toward a cliff. They are finally relaxed and happy together. They climb and find themselves above the desert. Kit reflects sadly that although alike in feelings, they are hopelessly opposed in their aims. Port, gazing at the sky, says that he has the strange sensation that it is a solid thing protecting them from what lay behind. Kit shudders and begs him not to talk about it.

Port insists that they both are barely hanging on to life. Kit says that neither of them ever got into life. Kit feels guilty about Tunner, and she thinks that Port knows. After dinner, Port rents a bicycle and rides alone back to the gap. He can never tell Kit that he went there again.

Days later, their bus arrives in Ain Krorfa, accompanied by thousands of flies. Tunner, horrified, chooses to head to Messad. Afternoon tea leaves the couple snapping rather than amused, as Port had hoped. To make matters worse, he feels increasingly nervous, and Kit loses patience with the squalid hotel and the food. She vows that Port should have to work at getting them back together. Port comes to believe that the right time will present itself. Since they both regard time as nonexistent, they feel eventually everything will happen.

In Bou Noura, Port discovers that he lost his passport, and he blames Eric. Port grows even more distant. The next day Port and Kit leave for El Ga'a. On the bus Kit sees that Port is very ill. He is unable to move. The next day at El Ga'a, the hotel proprietor refuses to open the door when Kit screams that her husband is ill. They get a truck out of El Ga'a, a city infected with meningitis.

In Sbâ, a man named Captain Broussard gives Kit something for Port's fever. One can only wait with typhoid. They have a mattress in a small room. Port is unconscious. Once Port says blankly that he does not know whether he will come back. Back from a walk, Kit finds Port's fever higher and his speech fantastic. He insists that he always lived for her. Kit is revolted by his state; she is moved to violent sobs. He says that she is going away; she shouts that she is not. Kit runs outside into the star-filled landscape just as Port is approaching his death. Captain Broussard attends him and curses Kit's absence.

Then Kit finds herself reunited with Tunner, who tracked them from Bou Noura. He consoles her, until she feels guilty for leaving Port alone. Tunner scoffs at her concern. Back in the room, Port is alone with one image to accompany his final agony: spots of bright blood on the earth. He also feels the sensation of reaching out to pierce the sheltering sky. Kit tells Tunner that they can meet at eight that night; she then hastily returns. When she finds Port dead, she is calm. She kisses his forehead and packs her small valise.

Kit locks Port's body inside the room, then she escapes from the fort. She eludes the French soldiers. In the morning, when a caravan approaches her, she raises her arms to Belqassim, the younger of the two men in charge. He pulls her onto his camel. Kit travels with the caravan south into the desert. Each afternoon she submits to the sexual demands of Belqassim and his older companion. She grows feverishly attached to Belqassim.

At his village, Belqassim dresses her in boys' clothing, then he locks her inside a tiny room within his labyrinthine house. Each afternoon, he visits her for lovemaking.

The household women discover the deception. When Belqassim is away, the three wives descend on Kit and tear off her clothes. Belqassim arrives, shouting. The next day he holds a wedding ceremony. As his three humiliated wives look on, he drapes Kit with their gold jewelry. Kit cries and makes Belqassim angry. Then she is confined to the room again.

Kit is sentient only during her husband's fiery visits. She loses track of time. When he stops coming, she becomes desperate. She escapes the room and convinces the startled wives (with lipstick bribes and all of her gold jewelry) that they should let her outside. They agree. In the village, Kit tries to buy food with thousand-franc notes and draws a delighted crowd. A man who speaks French takes her to send a telegraph that says, "CANNOT GET BACK."

At a convent, Kit is prepared for a trip. She is flown, refusing food, hardly speaking, and with her arms tied down, north to the coast. Her caretakers agree that she is mad. The hotel people call Tunner to let him know that she will be there, awaiting passage to the United States. When the cab arrives at the hotel, she seems frozen into the seat. The proprietress runs for help, but before they return, Kit leaves. A crowded streetcar pulls past up the hill.

Critical Evaluation:

Paul Bowles first won recognition as a composer of modern and theater music. When his first novel, *The Sheltering Sky*, was published in 1949, it was a literary event. Readers of his unique and disturbing stories eagerly awaited his novel.

Living in Tangier, Morocco, with his wife, the writer Jane Bowles, Bowles was considered a literary outsider. The perception of his work as nihilistic and filled with horror and violence turned many critics away. Others have pointed out Bowles's great capacity for describing the wonder and the terror of life.

Many of Bowles's respected contemporaries, such as Tennessee Williams and Gore Vidal, championed the novel. The praise has been echoed by others. Most writers agree that Bowles is a master at depicting the essential separateness of each human psyche.

The Sheltering Sky is about two people who are emotionally estranged from each other. They are in love yet fundamentally separated by emotional impasses, fears, and inabilities. It is also a story about two cultures: the modern intellectual, time-driven American, and the timeless, sensual Saharan. As the story progresses, the American protagonists travel deeper into the desert and inward through many levels of consciousness. The farther south they travel, the less recognizable Kit and Port become to each other. They discard society's trappings and become more strongly impelled to search within themselves for understanding of their problems, their desires, and their estrangements.

The Sheltering Sky is a novel in three parts. In the first two, Port is the protagonist. His actions propel the novel, and events are filtered through his sensibilities. His melancholy sets the mood, which will grow darker, penetrated only by strained moments of gaiety. Kit's character serves the novel in the same way that she behaves; the reader watches her being propelled by the events Port and Tunner initiate, as if she were on a train she cannot stop. With her superstitions and system of omens, she is at the mercy of other people. She reacts to their signals and takes everything as a sign. Without others, she becomes inert. Tunner, handsome and empty-headed, is the classic foil; because of his attention to her, Kit must examine her loyalty to Port and deal with the consequences of her indecision.

Despite Port's emotional impenetrability, he needs Kit. She is the only person who can connect him to humanity, tenuous as this connection is. The chapters leading up to Port's death give several clues to the couple's mistakes. One fatal error is their fatalism, the belief that events will happen over which they would have no control. They give in to this belief and use it as a reason to avoid acting upon their desires to love each other once more. By the time they realize their mistake, it is too late.

The third section of the novel, after Port's death, is Kit's story. As the sexual slave of Belqassim, she finds freedom from responsibilities. She lives only for the times he comes to her chamber. She slips so far from active consciousness that her sudden return to civilization finds her unable to speak, completely mad. Like Port, Kit pierces the fabric of the sheltering sky and cannot deal with the emptiness on the other side. Bowles's literary reputation has grown steadily. Once neglected, *The Sheltering Sky* is now recognized as a masterpiece.

JoAnne Balingit

Further Reading

Bertens, Johannes. *The Fiction of Paul Bowles: The Soul Is the Weariest Part of the Body*. New York: Rodopi, 1979. Examines the work in light of Bowles's nihilism and attempts to connect the writer to a Calvinist tradition in American literature.

Bowles, Paul. *Conversations with Paul Bowles*. Edited by Gena Dagel Caponi. Jackson: University Press of Mississippi, 1993. Bowles discusses the genesis of *The Sheltering Sky*. Interesting background information for a study of the novel.

Caponi, Gena Dagel. *Paul Bowles*. New York: Twayne, 1998. Introductory overview of Bowles's life and work. Caponi analyzes all of his novels, describing *The Sheltering Sky* as the first American novel to express an existential philosophy. She also examines Bowles's other writings and musical compositions, interspersing her comments throughout the book with excerpts from her interviews with Bowles.

_____. *Paul Bowles: Romantic Savage*. Carbondale: Southern Illinois University Press, 1994. Interpretive biography examining the parts of Bowles's life that provide insight into his work. A section on *The Sheltering Sky* examines its influences, its critical reception, and the central characters' relationships. Includes bibliography and index.

Patteson, Richard F. *A World Outside: The Fiction of Paul Bowles*. Austin: University of Texas Press, 1987. Examines this novel and others through formal and thematic architectural concepts: the story as shelter, both necessary and fragile. Considered the most comprehensive of the full-length studies. Includes bibliography.

Pounds, Wayne. *Paul Bowles: The Inner Geography*. New York: Lang, 1985. Using psychological theories, the author compares *The Sheltering Sky* to Bowles's other works and to Edgar Allan Poe's *The Narrative of Arthur Gordon Pym* (1838).

Rawa, J. M. "*The Sheltering Sky*: Double Turns and Tea in the Sahara." In *The Imperial Quest and Modern Memory from Conrad to Greene*. New York: Routledge, 2005. A postcolonial analysis of the quest theme in several novels, including *The Sheltering Sky*. Demonstrates how Bowles's novel subverts Western ideas of imperialism.

The Shepheardes Calender

Author: Edmund Spenser (c. 1552-1599)
First published: 1579
Type of work: Poetry
Type of plot: Pastoral
Time of plot: Sixteenth century
Locale: England

Principal characters:
COLIN CLOUT, the greatest of the shepherd poets
HOBBINOL, his friend
THENOT, a wise old shepherd
CUDDIE, a young shepherd, an aspiring poet

The Poem:

January. Colin, forlorn and rejected by his beloved Rosalind, compares his mood with the wintry landscape:

> Thou barrein ground, whome winters wrath
>   hath wasted,
> Art made a mirror to behold my plight:
> Whilome thy fresh spring flowrd, and
>   after hasted
> Thy summer proud with daffadillies dight,
> And now is come thy winters stormy state,
> Thy mantle marred wherein thou maskedst late.

At the end of this poem, Colin breaks his shepherd's pipes and resolves to write no more poetry.

February. An impudent young shepherd, Cuddie, complains of the wintry blasts to the elderly Thenot, and he scorns the old man's philosophical view that one must learn to endure the long succession of misfortunes that this world brings and be concerned only with the safety of the flock. Tired of Cuddie's rudeness, Thenot tells the fable of an old oak and a proud briar bush. The briar persuades a farmer to cut down the tree to show off its own beauty. All is well until winter comes; the briar then dies without the protection of the oak against wind and frost. Cuddie is unmoved by this parable of youth and age and breaks it off abruptly.

March. Two young shepherds welcome spring as a time for love. They describe Thomalin's encounter with Cupid. Thomalin tells a friend how, while he was hunting on one shepherds' holiday, he heard a rustling in the bushes:

> With that sprung forth a naked swain
> With spotted wings like peacock's train,
> And laughing lope to a tree,
> His gylden quiver at his back,
> And silver bow, which was but slack,
> Which lightly he bent at me.

April. Thenot finds Hobbinol grieving over the sorrows of his friend Colin Clout and mourning that Colin's unrequited love deprived all the shepherds of his poems. Thenot asks Hobbinol to recite one of Colin's verses to while away the hours as their flocks graze, and he complies with an ode on "Fair Elisa, queen of shepherds all." Colin calls upon the muses, the graces, the sun, and the moon as he begins his praise of the daughter of Pan, the shepherds' god, and Syrinx. Then Colin describes Elisa's beauty:

> See, where she sits upon the grassie green,
>   (O seemly sight!)
> Yclad in scarlet, like a maiden queen
>   And ermines white.
> Upon her head a cremosin coronet,
> With damask leaves and daffadillies set:
>   Bayleaves between,
>   And primroses green,
> Embellish the sweet violet.

Thenot, convinced of Colin's gifts by this recitation, comments on the folly of giving in to love.

May. Piers and Palinode discuss the corruption of shepherds who neglect their sheep to seek their own profit (indirectly condemning the priests of the time). Palinode, who is discouraged because he cannot participate in the spring revels of other shepherds, asks why the good shepherd, the clergyman, should not have a right to the pleasures others enjoy. Piers, more serious than his companion, speaks at length about the responsibility of those who care for the flocks. They must, he argues, forsake worldly concerns and trust in God for their living if they are to set a good example for their sheep. He disagrees with Palinode's contention that there is no reason for shepherds to live less pleasantly than anyone else, and, to illustrate the dangers of association with the wicked, he tells the familiar fable of the innocent young kid who is duped and carried off by a smooth-talking fox.

June. Colin returns to admire the peaceful life his friend Hobbinol makes for himself in the fields. Hobbinol praises Colin's poetry, but the latter disavows the possession of any great talents: "But piping low in shade of lowly grove/ I play to please my self, all be it ill."

Colin is content to serve Pan, the god of shepherds; he makes no claims to be worthy of the patronage of the Muses. Because his poetic pleas are not powerful enough to pierce the heart of Rosalind, he is forever doomed. He entreats the "gentle shepherds": "Tell the lass, whose flower is woxe a weed,/ And faultless faith is turned to faithless fear,/ That she the truest shepherds heart made bleed/ That lives on earth, and loved her most dear."

July. Thomalin contrasts the simplicity and unpretentiousness of the life of the first shepherd, Christ, and "the brethren twelve that kept yfere the flocks of mighty Pan" with the lavish living of the purple-clad priests of his day. He was recently shocked to hear of their way of life:

> For Palinode (if thou him ken)
> Rode late on pilgrimage
> To Rome, (if such be Rome) and then
> He saw thilke misusage.
> For shepherds, said he, there doen lead,
> As lords done other where;
> Their sheep han crusts, and they the bread;
> The chips, and they the cheer.

August. Willy and Perigot contribute alternate lines to a rollicking love lyric, designed to cure Perigot of his melancholy mood, occasioned by an unhappy love affair. When they finish, Cuddie, their judge, recites for them one of Colin's doleful laments to his Rosalind.

September. Diggon Davie returns to the country with news of the miseries he experienced on his travels in the cities, where he found everything filled with greed and corruption. His language is harsh, and his mood is deeply pessimistic. When the shepherds sell their souls to the devil, he argues, their sheep inevitably suffer.

October. Cuddie questions the value of writing. Even when his work is good, it seems to bring him little reward. Piers, his older, wiser friend, answers, "The praise is better than the price." He has faith in the didactic effects of poetry: "O what an honor is it, to restrain/ The lust of lawless youth with good advice,/ Or prick them forth with pleasance of thy vein,/ Whereto thou list their trained wills entice!"

He counsels Cuddie to turn to epic, to sing of wars and of princes. This kind of poetry, the young man replies, might have been possible in Augustan Rome, where Vergil found willing patrons; in their age, however, there is no climate for poetry. Colin alone might soar toward the heavens in his verse, but he is the prisoner of love. Piers, a good Platonist, maintains that love, in fact, freed the poet, giving him wings to lift him up out of the "loathsome mire."

November. Colin presents a lament for Dido, a beautiful lady who died young. He speaks first out of deep distress, calling on the muses and all nature to mourn with him. Then the mood changes, and he rejoices to know that the lady "is installed now in heaven's height," where "lives she with the blessed gods in bliss."

December. Colin reminisces about the carefree days of his youth, the spring of his life, when he climbed trees in search of ravens' eggs and shook nuts from walnut trees and learned the art of song from the good, old shepherd Wrenock. His summer years brought the painful heat of love, which withered his promising poetic talents: "So now my year draws to his latter term,/ My spring is spent, my summer burnt up quite,/ My harvest hastes to stir up Winter stern,/ And bids him claim with rigorous rage his right." Colin finds himself old and ready to leave the world, and he concludes with a farewell to his art, his flocks, and his friends.

Critical Evaluation:

A new age in English poetry began with the anonymous publication in 1579 of *The Shepheardes Calender*, by Edmund Spenser. The work is a collection of twelve pastoral poems or eclogues, with themes familiar from the time of Vergil: the song contest, the elegy, the lament of the scorned lover, criticism of corruption in Church and state. Much of the lasting value of *The Shepheardes Calender* is in its language, the skillfully varied verse forms, the rich imagery of some parts and the direct rustic simplicity of others.

Renaissance Christian humanism generally makes use of the best of classical pagan literature and philosophy, reading it allegorically, or rewriting it as allegory, to teach Christian culture and morality. Spenser engages in this philosophical appropriation more thoroughly, skillfully, and audaciously than any other English poet. *The Shepheardes Calender*, although the work of a young poet just developing his art, startles readers with its political and personal verve and ambition. If Spenser aimed at reforming the state and the clergy with his satire, he also aimed at establishing his poetic reputation and gaining court patrons to support and protect him. That he succeeds in these two aims is one of the reasons *The Shepheardes Calender* remains a landmark in English literature.

Most of Spenser's poetry can be enjoyed for its beauty but exists for the allegory that shapes it. In emulation of Vergil,

Spenser begins with youthful pastoral poetry in preparation and anticipation of writing a national epic. *The Shepheardes Calender* contains in embryo many features of *The Faerie Queene* (1590, 1596): fulsome, calculated idealization and praise of Elizabeth; veiled criticism of some of the queen's policies; self-conscious construction of Spenser's own public identity as a poet-prophet; allegorical commentary on contemporary political issues; imitation of classical and continental poetic models; praise of the native English tradition of poetry and use of archaic language in imitation of Chaucer; love poetry with Petrarchan posturing; didactic purpose of moral reform of Church and state; and allegories of poetic identity and inspiration.

Many mysteries haunt the poem, chief among them the identity of the ubiquitous and prolix commentator, "E. K." Knowing E. K.'s identity might enable the reader to know whether E. K.'s frequent obtuseness is unintentional ignorance or a deliberate strategy to obscure some of Spenser's more dangerous criticism of Elizabeth. All that is known is that E. K. is a humanist scholar, a bit of a pedant, and eager to promote both Spenser and his friend Gabriel Harvey. Whether E. K. is Spenser or not, his presence is one of Spenser's tactics in an inventive, tireless campaign of self-promotion.

E. K.'s introductory epistle, headnote "arguments" (summaries), and "glosses" (commentary) on each eclogue add another layer in a text already rife with speaking personae. *The Shepheardes Calender* is typically Elizabethan in the complexity of the voices in the text. The allegory and the textual apparatus complicate these matters, but in deliberate and meaningful ways. Most twentieth and twenty-first century critics have read the shepherd speakers as instruments of Spenser's project to create a place for himself in court politics, hyperconscious of how Elizabeth and her powerful counselors and churchmen might react to his words.

The July eclogue provides an example of Spenser's simultaneous caution and audacity. It seems to begin with a debate between the Roman Catholic and Protestant views of holiness and sainthood, but it moves into a more specific and politically charged allegory of Archbishop Edward Grindal's fall from power. Queen Elizabeth ordered the suppression of Bible study meetings ("prophesyings") among the clergy, fearing they would become hotbeds of Puritan opposition to the official English Church. When Grindal defied Elizabeth's orders, she divested him of his power and sequestered him in his home for the remaining seven years of his life. The eclogue's tone and other sources provide strong evidence that Spenser admired Grindal's moral fortitude in standing up to the queen in a matter of conscience. Nevertheless,

Spenser shows considerable daring when he has the shepherd speaker Thomalin report that an eagle (symbol of imperial power) dropped a shell on the head of the gentle shepherd "Algrind," an anagram of Grindal's name.

Even more shocking is Spenser's insertion of his opinion into the fiery and perilous debate over Elizabeth's possible marriage to a French Catholic. Many Protestants feared the reestablishment of a Catholic regime, but it was dangerous to castigate the queen too directly for her attentions to her French suitor. A pamphleteer, aptly named Stubbs, lost his right hand as punishment for criticizing the proposed marriage too vehemently, and the pamphlet's printer, Hugh Singleton, narrowly escaped the same fate. The reader can only marvel at his and Spenser's courage when, a month after Stubbs's painful public humiliation, Singleton printed *The Shepheardes Calender*, which, in however veiled a way, also criticizes the potential marriage. This subtle criticism takes place in the April eclogue, where Hobbinol sings a gushing paean of praise to Eliza, queen of shepherds: Eliza is a goddess of divine descent; she is the fourth Grace; the abashed sun, unable to stand the comparison, retreats from her shining face below; and other Petrarchan conceits. In the middle of this overdone praise, he stresses her virginity and her marriage to England—an implicit denunciation of marriage to a foreign power. Perhaps it is too much to say that such allegorical fables participate in a sustained, underground resistance to Elizabeth's increasing chokehold on public discourse as her reign went on, but these strategies of covert commentary are, in some way, a response to censorship.

The metaphor of the shepherd and his flock points to another key dimension of the poem. In addition to being a commentary on the politics of Spenser's day, the poem may be read as a Christ-centered expression of personal commitment. The image of the Good Shepherd himself, sometimes in the figure of Pan, informs the text. Algrind, for example, in the July eclogue teaches humility, sacrifice, and self-denial and practices these in imitation of Jesus. If Spenser, in his poetry, acts as political reformer, he also acts as witness to what he sees as God's self-revelation in the person of the Christ.

"Critical Evaluation" by James David Schiavoni

Further Reading

Bouchard, Gary M. *Colin's Campus: Cambridge Life and the English Eclogue*. Selinsgrove, Pa.: Susquehanna University Press, 2000. Assesses the influence of Spenser's experiences at Cambridge University upon his pastoral poetry, including *The Shepheardes Calendar*.

Hadfield, Andrew, ed. *The Cambridge Companion to Spen-*

ser. New York: Cambridge University Press, 2001. Collection of essays providing an overview of Spenser's life and work. Some of the essays discuss the relevance of Spenser, his life and career, the historical contexts of his work, his use of language, and his literary influence. "Spenser's Pastorals: *The Shepheardes Calender* and *Colin Clout Come Home Again*" by Patrick Cheney examines these works.

Lethbridge, J. B., ed. *Edmund Spenser: New and Renewed Directions*. Madison, N.J.: Fairleigh Dickinson University Press, 2006. Reprints a collection of papers originally delivered at a conference about Spenser. Includes discussions of the Spenserian stanza, Spenser's relationship to Ireland, and the trend toward a new historical criticism of his work. "Pastoral Motivation in *The Shepheardes Calender*" by John Moore analyzes this poem.

McCabe, Richard A. *Spenser's Monstrous Regiment: Elizabethan Ireland and the Poetics of Difference*. New York: Oxford University Press, 2002. Analyzes how Spenser's experiences of living and writing in Ireland challenged his ideas about English nationhood. Assesses the influence of colonialism on the themes, imagery, language, and structure of his poetry.

Miller, David L. "Authorship, Anonymity, and *The Shepheardes Calender*." *Modern Language Quarterly* 40, no. 3 (September, 1979): 219-236. An early poststructuralist analysis of the poem and its ambitions. Argues that Spenser deliberately created a poem that would stake his claim as a major poet.

Nelson, William. *The Poetry of Edmund Spenser: A Study*. New York: Columbia University Press, 1963. A concise, insightful introduction to the poem and its place in Spenser's career and in English literary history.

Phillippy, Patricia Berrahou. *Love's Remedies: Recantation and Renaissance Lyric Poetry*. Lewisburg, Pa.: Bucknell University Press, 1995. Examines works by Spenser and other poets to analyze their use of the palinode, or an ode in which the poet retracts the opinion of an earlier poem. Discusses *The Shepheardes Calendar* and Spenser's other "palinodic pastorals."

Sacks, Peter J. *The English Elegy: Studies in the Genre from Spenser to Yeats*. Baltimore: Johns Hopkins University Press, 1985. Excellent analysis of Spenser's use of the elegy form in the context of the elegiac tradition in English poetry. Discusses the genre as a literary expression of the psychology of grief and consolation.

The Shining

Author: Stephen King (1947-   )
First published: 1977
Type of work: Novel
Type of novel: Horror
Time of plot: Early 1970's
Locale: Rocky Mountains, Boulder, and Denver, Colorado; St. Petersberg, Florida

Principal characters:
JACK TORRANCE, new winter caretaker at the Overlook Hotel
WENDY TORRANCE, his wife
DANNY, their five-year-old son
DICK HALLORANN, the Overlook's head chef
STUART ULLMAN, the hotel manager
AL SHOCKLEY, Jack's friend and a member of the Overlook's board of directors
WATSON, hotel maintenance person during open season
GHOST OF DELBERT GRADY

The Story:

Jack Torrance is chosen to be the winter caretaker of the lavish Rocky Mountain Overlook Hotel by an old friend from his drinking days, the wealthy Al Shockley. Nevertheless, Jack must sit through a humiliating interview with Stuart Ullman, the hotel manager, who does not believe he is right for the position. Jack has few options left. He was forced to resign from his last job as an English teacher at

Stovington Preparatory School in Vermont after he assaulted a student whom he caught slashing his tires. During his tour of the hotel, Jack meets Watson, a foul-mouthed maintenance person who warns him to release the pressure in the boiler every day because it steadily creeps up, creating a potentially disastrous situation.

Jack, his wife, Wendy, and their five-year-old son, Danny,

meet the Overlook's African American chef, Dick Hallorann, on closing day. Hallorann discovers that Danny possesses what Hallorann calls "the shining": telepathic and precognitive powers. Danny exerts this power through an invisible friend named Tony. Hallorann, who also has these powers but to a much lesser degree, tells Danny that nothing he sees in the hotel can hurt him. However, he also says that if there is trouble Danny should shout out to Hallorann with his mind, and Hallorann will come from Florida to help.

Jack and Wendy have had a strained marriage ever since a drunken Jack accidentally broke Danny's arm. They hope that spending the winter at the Overlook will bring them closer together and allow Jack to finish a play he has been writing. Danny has nebulous fears and horrific visions of the hotel, but he wants to stay for the sake of his parents' happiness.

Soon, unexplained things begin to happen. A wasps' nest supposedly destroyed by pesticide returns to life, and reanimated wasps sting Danny. Jack becomes increasingly fascinated with hotel memorabilia he uncovers in the basement. Though the hotel is devoid of liquor, Jack's old drinking habits return—he wipes his mouth and chews Excedrin—as does his temper, which he has struggled to control all his life.

Danny steals the passkey and enters room 217, where he is terrified to find the nude, bloated, decaying corpse of a woman in the bathroom coming to life. She attacks Danny before he can escape. Later, Jack's investigation of the room at first reveals nothing, but then he has the sense that something from the bathroom is coming for him. However, he tells Wendy and Danny that he found nothing in the room.

Jack smashes the hotel's citizens band (CB) radio while sleepwalking. He knows that Danny needs to get away from the hotel, but he also feels that he himself must stay. Struggling between the needs of himself and his son, Jack sabotages the hotel snowmobile. Snowed in, the Torrances are effectively cut off from the outside world.

The Torrance family soon realizes that they are living in a haunted hotel. Jack believes the Overlook wants him, but it soon becomes evident that the hotel wants Danny for his psychic abilities and is using Jack's weaknesses to achieve its aim. Jack and Danny each have separate, terrifying experiences in which the Overlook's topiary—hedges trimmed to look like animals—appears to come to life and attack them. All three have experiences that cannot be discounted as hallucinations or imagination.

Danny has continuously had visions of the seemingly nonsensical word "redrum." In one vision, the word is reflected in a mirror to read "murder." Terrified, Danny sends a psychic shout for help to Dick Hallorann in Florida. Hal-

lorann, knowing the danger the boy and his family must be in, immediately flies to Colorado.

Meanwhile, the Overlook's ghosts materialize, providing Jack with what he wants most—liquor. The ghost of Delbert Grady tells Jack that he must kill his wife and son. An inebriated Jack tries to strangle Wendy, who knocks him unconscious and locks him in the food pantry. However, Grady's ghost releases Jack from the pantry.

Possessed by the spirits of the hotel, Jack goes on a murderous rampage, viciously attacking Wendy on the stairs with a roque mallet and similarly assaulting Hallorann when he arrives. Both are severely injured but remain alive. Danny realizes that his imaginary friend Tony is actually himself, Daniel Anthony Torrance, ten years in the future. Jack then corners Danny, who saves his own life by reminding Jack that the pressure on the hotel's boiler has not been released that day, leading to an impending explosion. As Jack rushes to the basement to attend to the boiler, Hallorann, Wendy, and Danny make their way out of the Overlook to Hallorann's rented snowmobile.

Jack is too late, and the Overlook explodes, killing Jack. Wendy, Danny, and Hallorann escape via the snowmobile. Hallorann gets a new job in Maine, while Wendy accepts a job offer from Al Shockley in Maryland. The three agree to stay in touch, Hallorann once again promising that if Danny is ever in trouble, he will come if Danny calls.

Critical Evaluation:

Stephen King's *The Shining* fits neatly in the tradition of Shirley Jackson's *The Haunting of Hill House* (1959) and Richard Matheson's *Hell House* (1971): In all three novels, psychically sensitive individuals are placed in malefic houses with histories of horrors. King's novel is at once a haunted-house story, a ghost story, and a psychological horror story. It is also a rich study of the effects of alcoholism, rage, and child abuse, for the Torrances bring a history of family dysfunction with them to the Overlook. The novel could almost have been written without the supernatural elements; indeed, the reality of much of these elements is left to the characters' (and the readers') imaginations.

The Shining is generally considered by critics and King enthusiasts to be one of his best novels, along with *Carrie* (1974), *'Salem's Lot* (1975), and *The Stand* (1978). This recognition is ironic given that his early work was dismissed by critics and scholars when it was published; only in late mid-life did King gain literary acknowledgment (for example, he was invited to edit an edition of the annual publication *Best American Short Stories*). The novel has remained enduringly popular in part because of its strong characterization. While children with Danny's "shining" abilities are not exactly common, Wendy and Jack are solid, three-dimensional characters to whom readers can relate and with whom they can empathize. Thus, the terror that engulfs readers as the plot develops is a terror on behalf of the novel's characters.

King based Jack Torrance's alcoholic character on his own firsthand experiences. In *On Writing: A Memoir of the Craft* (2000), King reveals his own battles with alcoholism and other addictions, explaining that, in depicting Jack the alcoholic writer, he was writing about himself without realizing it. That is not to say that King depended on personal experience for his authorial voice, for the characters of Wendy, Danny, and Hallorann are just as well realized as Jack—and as characters in novels written during King's time of sobriety.

Emphasizing the character-driven nature of the novel should not minimize the work's horrific elements. *The Shining* is first and foremost a horror story. King uses every writerly tool available to him to frighten readers, including shock, suspense, terror, gore, parallel narration (especially when descriptions of Hallorann's journey to the Overlook alternate with scenes taking place within the hotel), and foreshadowing (evident in Ullman's tale of Grady's murder-suicide, Danny's visions brought on by Tony, and Watson's warnings about the boiler). In this respect, the novel reaches its apex during Wendy's nightmarish battle to escape a homicidal Jack on the staircase leading from the lobby to their apartment. Wendy is painfully battered by Jack with a roque mallet, suffering debilitating injuries, and must stab her own husband in the back with a kitchen knife in desperation and despair. To her horror, he continues to come after her. This scene is perhaps one of the most perfectly realized in all of King's fiction.

As King's third book, the novel does have its faults. When Jack accidentally uncovers a wasps' nest and is repeatedly stung, he explicitly identifies the incident as a symbol for all the things that have gone wrong in his life—as a husband, as a father, as a teacher, and as a writer. A more sophisticated approach would have been to retain the wasps' nest but allow readers to discern the symbolism for themselves.

The rare faux pas aside, the novel is a strong tale of horror, both realistic and supernatural. King makes excellent use of various horror techniques, such as isolation, fear of going mad, fear of being harmed by (or harming) a loved one, precognitive and telepathic powers, ghosts, and a malevolent building. King also plays subtly upon readers' phobias, including claustrophobia, fear of heights, fear of insects, fear of things that go bump in the night, and the very real fear of a marriage crumbling before a child's eyes. The novel's setting provides a place in which there is no escape from the terror. This winter horror contrasts to the summer grandeur of the Overlook. There is also sexual horror, both heterosexual and homosexual, as dead women compete for Jack's attention and the ghost of the bisexual Horace Derwent teases and torments a smitten gay lover in a dog costume.

Arguably the most terrifying element of the novel is the oscillation of Jack's relationship with Danny between love and homicidal abuse. This relationship is symbolic of the actual child abuse occurring in the United States. Painfully, Danny is torn between his love of Jack the good father and his fear of Jack the punishing father guided by the hotel. It is significant that Jack also had an abusive, alcoholic father. Wendy's mother is a cold, distant perfectionist, and Wendy therefore has no one to whom she feels she can safely escape from her husband. *The Shining*, then, can be read as a critique of America's dysfunctional family life, extended to extremes by its supernatural trappings.

In *The Shining*, King created a great horror novel and a literary classic. It features skillful characterization, a perfect setting, and finely wrought horror emanating from both real and supernatural sources. The novel is short enough to be accessible to most readers, unlike King's later, longer novels. It was adapted into a theatrical motion picture by Stanley Kubrick in 1980 and a television miniseries by Mick Garris in 1997.

Charles Lewis Avinger, Jr.

Further Reading

Alegre, Sara Martin. "Nightmares of Childhood: The Child and the Monster in Four Novels by Stephen King (*The Shining*; *Firestarter*; *It*; *Pet Sematary*)." *Atlantis* 23, no. 1 (June, 2001): 105+. An interesting article considering how King addresses the father-child relationship in American culture.

Holland-Toll, Linda J. "Bakhtin's Carnival Reversed: King's *The Shining* as Dark Carnival." *Journal of Popular Culture* 33, no. 2 (Fall, 1999): 131-146. Argues that *The Shining* is not affirmative of society's values, as critics of horror fiction and King himself typically claim.

King, Stephen. *Feast of Fear: Conversations with Stephen King*. Edited by Tim Underwood and Chuck Miller. New York: Carroll & Graf, 1992. A collection of interviews with King, conducted by a variety of people.

Magistrale, Tony, ed. *Discovering Stephen King's "The Shining": Essays on the Bestselling Novel by America's Premier Horror Writer*. I.O. Evans Studies in the Philosophy and Criticism of Literature 36. San Bernardino,

Calif.: Borgo Press, 1998. Collection of literary and philosophical essays analyzing the meaning and importance of King's novel, as well as its film adaptation.

Underwood, Tim, and Chuck Miller, eds. *Fear Itself: The Horror Fiction of Stephen King.* San Francisco: Underwood-Miller, 1982. A good collection of essays by various writers about King and his work.

Wiater, Stanley, Christopher Golden, and Hank Wagner. *The Complete Stephen King Universe: A Guide to the Worlds of Stephen King.* New York: St. Martin's Griffin, 2006. Examination of the various worlds and realities portrayed by King in his novels. Places *The Shining* in King's "prime reality" and explains the relationship of the novel to that world and to the other novels set within it.

Winter, Douglas E. *Stephen King: The Art of Darkness.* New York: NAL Books, 1984. A critical overview of King's early work, including a good chapter analyzing *The Shining.*

Ship of Fools

Author: Katherine Anne Porter (1890-1980)
First published: 1962
Type of work: Novel
Type of plot: Allegory
Time of plot: August 22-September 17, 1931
Locale: Aboard ship at sea

Principal characters:
JENNY BROWN, a young American painter
DAVID SCOTT, another painter, with whom Jenny lives
MARY TREADWELL, an American divorcé returning to Paris
DR. SCHUMANN, the ship's elderly doctor
LA CONDESA, a middle-aged déclassé noblewoman, formerly resident in Cuba
WILHELM FREYTAG, a young German businessman

The Story:

Many people of various nationalities wait in the heat of Veracruz, Mexico, on August 22, 1931, to board the North German Lloyd S.A. *Vera,* scheduled to arrive at Bremerhaven, Germany, on September 17. Some have urgent errands to perform before embarkation, while others simply kill the time. An elderly professor and his wife, the Huttens, share their lunch with their fat bulldog; a shrill, obnoxious young woman, Lizzi Spkenkieker, strides about with a little pig-snouted man, Siegfred Rieber; a solitary Swede, Arne Hansen, expresses indignation over the behavior of Mexican revolutionaries; a German couple, the Baumgartners, hush their young son, dressed in a hot leather riding costume; an American girl in slacks, Jenny Brown, strolls aimlessly with her boyfriend, David Scott; four pretty Spanish girls with their young men, a small *zarzuela* company, prowl through the streets and shops with disobedient six-year-old twins, Ric and Rac; a middle-aged American woman, Mrs. Treadwell, incredulously considers a painful bruise on her arm, inflicted in the street by a beggarwoman.

Aboard the *Vera* Dr. Schumann, the ship's elderly physician, watches passengers mount the gangplank: a hunchbacked dwarf, Herr Glocken, who sold his newsstand in Mexico City; a dying old man in a wheelchair, Herr Graf, pushed by his young nephew, Johann; a young Mexican woman with her baby and their Indian nurse; two Mexican priests; a Texan youth, William Denny, who continually leers at the Spanish girls; a German Jew, Herr Löwenthal, lugging a sample case containing Catholic religious articles; and a beautiful bride and groom on their honeymoon. When the combined freighter-and-passenger ship sets sail, the passengers examine the facilities and settle into their cramped cabins. Dinner at the captain's table that evening, presided over by Dr. Schumann, is served to a select German group, which includes the Huttens, Lizzi and Rieber, two elderly widows traveling alone, and Wilhelm Freytag, a presentable young German in the oil business. They eat and drink with pleasure and speak joyfully of their return to their fatherland.

During the first pleasantly monotonous days of the voyage, both friendly and hostile encounters occur among the passengers as they become acquainted. Jenny's discreet flirtation with Freytag angers David; Lizzi's loud vulgarity annoys her cabinmate, Mrs. Treadwell; the Huttens and their dog suffer from severe seasickness; Baumgartner embarrasses his family by failing to control or to hide his chronic alcoholism; Jenny befriends her cabinmate, an unattractive Swiss teenager returning home with her parents, hoping there to marry. Löwenthal, seated apart in the dining room, cautiously seeks amicable conversations with approachable Gentiles.

When the *Vera* docks in Havana, many disembark to amuse themselves on shore while new passengers are taken aboard. Deported from Cuba to their native lands because of a market failure, 876 Spanish sugarfield workers are crowded into steerage, where inadequate accommodations and inhumane conditions await them. Six Cuban students make themselves conspicuous by singing "La Cucaracha" endlessly. A mysterious Spanish countess, deported as a dangerous revolutionary by Cuban authorities, arouses considerable curiosity: About fifty, she remains beautiful, dresses elegantly, and adorns herself with jewels; Dr. Schumann treats her nervous disorder with drugs that she habitually uses.

As the *Vera* pursues its course toward Germany, the passengers discover more about each other's personal histories and private lives, and their early affinities and animosities deepen. Many of the Germans voice anti-Semitic attitudes; Freytag confides to Mrs. Treadwell that his wife is Jewish—a confidence she later betrays; Ric and Rac throw things overboard, including the Huttens's bulldog (a woodcarver in steerage loses his life saving it); the quarrels of Jenny and David threaten their already unstable relationship; Dr. Schumann and the countess resign themselves to the futility of the love that arises between them; and the young bride and groom float about the ship blissfully untouched by all these matters.

To celebrate the last night of the voyage, the *zarzuela* troupe organizes a fiesta designed to affront and insult the fundamental dignity of all the passengers. During this grotesque masquerade, not attended by Dr. Schumann, the dancers usurp the captain's table for themselves; Glocken sports a pink necktie bearing the words "Girls, follow me!"; and the drunken Baumgartner leads the children in a Nazi goose-stepping march. The guests disperse to seek their private pleasures and despairs in fights, amorous encounters, confrontations, or reconciliations. Johann loses his virginity to a Spanish prostitute, for a high price; Mrs. Treadwell, mistaken for a prostitute, hits a passenger in the face with the heel of her shoe. The next morning the passengers, behaving as if nothing unusual took place, face one another with indifferent and incommunicative faces, disembarking at Bremerhaven with their illusions apparently intact, fully expecting to create happiness for themselves by fashioning new lives in other countries.

Critical Evaluation:

For more than three decades, Katherine Anne Porter was renowned for her mastery of short narrative fiction, but only toward the end of her career did she direct her artistry toward the more extended form of the novel. Impressions she retained of a voyage from Veracruz to Bremerhaven in 1931 remained vivid in her mind and, in 1942, began to assume the shape of a complex and an intricate work that would reflect her perception of the general spiritual decay of Western civilization during the twentieth century. She formulated an appropriate design for her vision after reading Sebastian Brant's fifteenth century moral allegory *Das Narrenschiff* (1494). The writing progressed slowly, and the book was not completed until 1962. Her *Ship of Fools* enjoyed an immediate popular success and established her reputation firmly as a novelist of vision, of imagination, and of compelling virtuosity.

The theme of the work is stated in a short notice preceding the text, in which Porter explains that the *Vera* (meaning "truth") represents the ship of this world on its voyage to eternity, and the passengers include all humankind on its journey through life. *Ship of Fools* has no conventional plot or unfolding dramatic action; there is no "story" in the traditional sense. Instead, Porter devises nearly forty almost equally vivid and unforgettable characters, of different ages and nationalities, drawn from all walks of life, whose interactions during the voyage reveal truths about the nature of human beings and the human condition and whose behavior reflects common human responses in typical everyday situations.

Porter adopts an omniscient point of view as narrator, which permits her to look directly into her characters, overhear their thoughts, and understand their motivations, urges, and humiliations. Cultivating a classical style of remarkable purity comparable to that of the novelists Henry James and Gustave Flaubert, she employs plain and simple words to formulate sentences of striking rhetorical beauty, which either are concise and direct in their thrust or reveal their meaning gradually as they flow through a series of carefully balanced and modulated dependent clauses. She achieves an extraordinary blend of subtlety and intricacy of thought with simplicity and directness of expression, without ever sacrificing her long-trusted ideal of pristine clarity.

Porter paints a bleak picture of human nature in the book, for rarely does one find instances of kindness or of compassion aboard the *Vera*. Base inclinations and mean desires underlie the motivations of most of the characters most of the time. Many people are shown to be merely selfish, greedy, and unconsciously indifferent to their fellows; a few seem to be fundamentally evil at heart, taking pleasure in the suffering of others and occasionally wishing them still greater ill. Animal imagery, often referring to ugly, murderous, or repulsive activities, is appropriately applied to the characters throughout the book as metaphorical judgments upon their indifferent, inhuman, or brutal behavior.

Among the thirty-odd passengers closely observed aboard the *Vera*, a few are more intrinsically appealing than the others, less mean-spirited, more good-hearted and pleasant. Jenny Brown (a satirical self-portrait of Porter's own youth), entangled in a frustrating relationship with David Scott, seeks her identity as a person and as an artist, expecting new experiences to bring her closer to true spiritual fulfillment. Arrogant about his talent and maturity, David resents her rivalry, twisting their relationship, almost unwillingly, into one of mutual antagonism. Mary Treadwell (another self-caricature) is sensitive and compassionate but harbors an inner reticence that blocks the expression of her feelings for others and causes her to appear cold and aloof. Wilhelm Freytag, ostracized after his marriage to a Jewess is revealed, hides from truth behind a mask of politeness and genteel civility. Dr. Schumann, a deeply religious man threatened by a heart condition, is the most admirable person on the ship. His compassion, illustrated frequently during the voyage, suggests a possibility of hope for humankind's future. His love for La Condesa, expressed tentatively but unmistakably, reflects both tenderness and self-control; she, on the other hand, experiences her love for him as a deeply emotional, unrestrained and nonrational, passion.

Although Porter's sojourn in Germany in the early 1930's provided her with substantial material that she incorporated into the novel to expose the Nazi mentality during its formation, persons of other nationalities are represented as similarly guilty of moral irresponsibility and spiritual decay: Comparable nationalist attitudes, racial biases, and social prejudices are revealed among Americans as well as Germans. Those not actually committed to evil still contribute passively to its augmentation by their silent tolerance or calm indifference. They observe criminal behavior and do nothing, though they may condemn it privately in hushed whispers. The 876 deportees in steerage are looked upon with simple or contemptuous curiosity by those who deign to notice them at all. These representatives of all the suffering lower classes of the world accept their degradation with patience and stoical endurance, and it is a member of this class, a carver of small wooden figures, who performs the only heroic act during the voyage: He gives his life by leaping into the sea to rescue the Huttens's drowning bulldog. In Porter's view, all the passengers, whether through complacency or turpitude, share responsibility for the moral decadence which the entire book illustrates.

Raymond M. Archer

Further Reading

Bloom, Harold, ed. *Katherine Anne Porter.* New York: Chelsea House, 1986. Harold Moss's essay on *Ship of Fools* repeats the complaint that it has no novelistic tying up of loose ends. Robert B. Heilmann's essay on style compares Porter to Jane Austen and George Eliot, highlighting techniques, such as the use of series of nouns and participles, but claims that Porter evinces no trademark mannerisms. Joan Givner examines the Porter triangle of villain/victim/not-so-innocent hero or heroine and notes the consistency of Porter's description of evil characters.

DeMouy, Jane Krause. *Katherine Anne Porter's Women: The Eye of Her Fiction.* Austin: University of Texas Press, 1983. DeMouy categorizes Porter's women in three types: the Venus figures, the traditional mother and wife figures, and the unfeminine, androgynous figures. Like many other critics, DeMouy seizes upon the vignette witnessed by Jenny Brown—a man and woman locked in mortal combat—as an explication of Porter's pessimism about the possibility of love and her latter-day feeling that men, too, are victims.

Hendrick, George, and Willene Hendrick. *Katherine Anne Porter.* Rev. ed. Boston: Twayne, 1988. A thorough and well-written overview of Porter's life and fiction, with a chapter on *Ship of Fools.*

Liberman, M. M. *Katherine Anne Porter's Fiction.* Detroit, Mich.: Wayne State University Press, 1971. The first chapter makes a spirited defense of Porter's novel, analyzing some of the more common criticisms and making a case for *Ship of Fools* as an apologue.

Mooney, Harry John, Jr. *The Fiction and Criticism of Katherine Anne Porter.* Rev. ed. Pittsburgh, Pa.: University of Pittsburgh Press, 1962. Typical of some critical interpretations, this analysis uses some of the strengths of Porter's short stories to reflect on shortcomings of the novel and echoes other opinions that the novel's greatest fault is the absence of any possibility of human nobility.

Stout, Janis. *Katherine Anne Porter: A Sense of the Times.* Charlottesville: University Press of Virginia, 1995. An intellectual biography containing chapters on Porter's background in Texas, her view of politics and art in the 1920's, her writing and life between the two world wars, and her relationship with the southern agrarians. Includes notes and bibliography.

Titus, Mary. *The Ambivalent Art of Katherine Anne Porter.* Athens: University of Georgia Press, 2005. A look at the ways in which Porter confronted issues of gender in her work and her life, including a study of some of her unpublished papers.

Unrue, Darlene Harbour. *Katherine Anne Porter: The Life of an Artist.* Jackson: University Press of Mississippi, 2005. Comprehensive biography offering new insight into Porter's turbulent personal life and her writing.

_____. *Understanding Katherine Anne Porter.* Columbia: University of South Carolina Press, 1988. An excellent source for analysis of all Porter's major works. Clearly and simply written by an important scholar. Excellent annotated bibliography.

Warren, Robert Penn, ed. *Katherine Anne Porter: A Collection of Critical Essays.* Princeton, N.J.: Prentice-Hall, 1979. Contains an interview (1965) and seventeen essays, many of which deal with *Ship of Fools*.

The Shipping News

Author: E. Annie Proulx (1935-   )
First published: 1993
Type of work: Novel
Type of plot: Regional
Time of plot: Early 1990's
Locale: Mockingbird, New York; Killick-Claw, Newfoundland

Principal characters:
QUOYLE, a pathetic, middle-aged newspaperman and loving father, recently abandoned by his wife
AGNIS HAMM, Quoyle's aunt, a strong, resourceful woman who moves to Newfoundland with his family
BUNNY, Quoyle's elder daughter, a nervous and passionate child
SUNSHINE, Quoyle's younger daughter, a sweet and doting child
JACK BUGGIT, an avid fisherman and the editor of the Newfoundland newspaper *The Gammy Bird*
PETAL BEAR, Quoyle's philandering wife, who dies shortly after selling their daughters to a child molester
WAVEY PROWSE, Quoyle's love interest, a widow with a mentally handicapped son

The Story:

Quoyle is a thirty-six-year-old man with an ongoing history of mediocrity and failure stemming from his childhood. The awkwardness of Quoyle's formative years has never ceased, and in adulthood Quoyle continues to suffer torments that result from his low estimate of his own self-worth. His parents, never really loving or proud, commit suicide together after they are both diagnosed with cancer.

Shortly afterward, Quoyle comes home to find that his hateful, hyperphilandering wife Petal Bear has run off with another man and taken their two daughters with her. After selling Bunny and Sunshine to a pedophile, Petal and her lover are killed in a car accident. Fortunately, the girls are rescued and returned to their father without suffering any physical abuse. Quoyle's aunt, Agnis Hamm, arrives to claim her brother's ashes and convinces Quoyle to move with her and his girls to her childhood home in Newfoundland.

The employees of *The Gammy Bird*, the town newspaper in his new home of Killick-Claw, Newfoundland, rival Quoyle's flippant attitude concerning the news with their absurd brand of reporting. The staff includes Billy Pretty, an old fisherman who writes the Home News page and whose desk resembles a bazaar or flea-market display, and B. Beaufield Nutbeem, a British castaway who washed up in Killick-Claw and stayed. Nutbeem steals stories from the radio and then plagiarizes them for his foreign news section. Tert Card, the devilish managing editor, is notorious for his wildly nonsensical typographical errors.

Jack Buggit, a proud local, avid fisherman, and the founder and editor-in-chief of *The Gammy Bird*, has an odd set of standards for his newspaper. He considers Card's errors to be humorous additions, he allows Billy Pretty to publish more than three stories of sexual abuse per week, and he requires a front-page story of a car wreck every week—regardless of whether or not an accident actually occurs. Buggit assigns Quoyle the car wreck section of the paper, along with the task of writing the shipping news, which documents ships that have recently arrived in the harbor. In his introduction to *The Gammy Bird*, Quoyle is confronted with the major issues that haunt him: his lifelong fear of water, Petal's death in a car wreck, and his daughters' close call with a sexual predator.

Despite Quoyle's bland and uneventful personal history, he is quickly informed by several townspeople of the nature of his ancestors and their legacy in Killick-Claw. A source of both ire and entertainment for the community, the Quoyles were a notoriously uneducated and incestuous band of murderers and pirates. To escape their increasingly religious neighbors in the late 1800's, the Quoyles transported their house across the frozen sea and placed it on the high cliff on what would later become Quoyle's Point. The family house, still located on the cliff, rocks furiously in the gales of wind that blow off the sea. For many years, it has been anchored to the rock by iron cables.

The house, kept in place by such unnatural means, produces fears of the supernatural: Bunny has hysterics at the sightings of a big, white dog, and a mystery surrounds small knots that Quoyle continually finds throughout the house (placed there by Nolan, the last of the crazy Quoyle bloodline). The family and the home have an even darker past, which Agnis has kept secret all her life: In it, she suffered sexual abuse at the hands of her brother, Quoyle's father Gus.

Agnis's return to the family house and her plans to repair its years of neglect begin promisingly enough. However, she soon realizes the power the house holds over her, as painful childhood memories begin to resurface. Unable to stay in a place that represents such grief, Agnis moves to a neighboring town, while Quoyle and his daughters rent an apartment in Killick-Claw. The house's anchors eventually break in a storm, freeing it to tumble over the cliff onto the rocks below. It takes with it the legacy of the brutal Quoyle clan.

The intrusion of various outside people and forces into Killick-Claw alters the dynamic of the small fishing village. The seemingly normal instance of a quarreling couple (aboard a ship originally made for Hitler) turns into a grisly murder. Tert Card aligns himself with oil tankers and big industry, forsaking the natural world the town once represented. Quoyle becomes the new managing editor of *The Gammy Bird*, and Jack Buggit drowns and comes back to life at his own wake.

As the details surrounding these unusual events are uncovered, Quoyle finds himself playing a significant role in his new community. As he becomes increasingly comfortable in his skin and begins to value his existence, the women in his life—Bunny, Sunshine, Aunt Hamm, and Wavey Prowse—also work through their own sad and violent pasts. In time, Quoyle and his family come to find peace in the little town and achieve happiness among the eccentric townspeople. In essence, Quoyle's journey to Newfoundland teaches him, for the first time, "that love sometimes occurs without pain or misery."

Critical Evaluation:

E. Annie Proulx states in the introduction to *The Shipping News* that she was greatly influenced in writing the novel by *The Ashley Book of Knots*, which she purchased at a yard sale for a quarter. The novel's final chapter begins with an excerpt from *The Ashley Book of Knots* that mirrors Proulx's storytelling intent: "There are still old knots that are unrecorded, and so long as there are new purposes for rope, there will always be new knots to discover." *The Shipping News*, about a simple man in a seemingly simple town, has been met with critical acclaim since its debut, winning the National Book Award in 1993, and the Pulitzer Prize in fiction in 1994. Despite its humble origins, the novel's story warrants being told, and, like the inevitable discovery of new knots, there will always be new stories to tell.

Proulx's narrative style in *The Shipping News* is disjointed and fragmentary. This aspect of the novel has been viewed by some critics as a symptom of bad writing, rather than as a literary device intended to symbolize Quoyle's own fractured experience. Proulx introduces each chapter with an illustrated excerpt, the majority of which come from *The Ashley Book of Knots* and *The Mariner's Dictionary*. The novel begins with an explanation of the term "quoyle," which is a single, unknotted coil of rope. Quoyle's namesake is thus a metaphor for his own life and experiences. A quoyle has no knots to represent specific purposes—it simply sits, exposed and inactive.

As the story progresses and Quoyle begins to establish both familial and friendly bonds, the knots illustrated in the text come to represent the intertwining of the characters and their experiences. The extracts also provide readers with metaphors, commentaries, insights, and expectations of what is to come in the subsequent chapter. However, when read on their own, the introductions serve another purpose; they constitute a kind of instruction manual both for readers, in their literary journeys, and for Quoyle, in his search for meaning and self-value.

Quoyle excels neither physically or mentally, and, at the age of thirty-six, the closest thing he has to a career is an on-again, off-again position as a third-rate journalist. Quoyle admittedly (and ironically) takes no interest in the stories of war, famine, politics, and finance that fill the newspapers daily. His defeatist attitude consumes him, and he convinces himself that the stories in the news only affect those people who are out living their lives: As he feels that he has not yet begun to live, such topics do not concern him. In his hopelessly stagnant state, Quoyle withdraws further into his misery, dismissing the happenings of the outside world as irrelevant to his situation.

Quoyle's entrance into Killick-Claw provides an outsider perspective on the town's local color and the ways in which social and economic changes are affecting it. The town lives and dies by the water, and its residents are extremely proud of their independence and rugged individualism. However, when Quoyle is invited into a conversation between Billy Pretty and Tert Card regarding the bounteous McGonigle oil field, readers witness a disruption in the community's way of life. Billy bemoans the intrusion of big business and becomes nostalgic for the peaceful and remote way of life he sees coming to an end. Tert, however, has invested in McGonigle stock and eagerly awaits the monetary benefits of development: "We're all going to be rich. Jobs all over the place, dividends for stockholders, manufacturing, housing, and supplies. The biggest development project in the country. It's to be the golden days." It quickly becomes evident that Proulx's fictional community is grounded in a reality that is being threatened. Tert views "the golden days" as a financially booming era on the horizon, while Billy, in his love for the natural, simple life of his ancestors, sees "the golden days" being extinguished.

When Billy takes Quoyle to Gaze Island, the original settlement of the Quoyles before they relocated the house, Billy mentions an old adage his father used to recite: "There was four women in every man's heart. The Maid in the Meadow, the Demon Lover, the Stouthearted Woman, [and] the Tall and Quiet Woman." This passage is especially important, as it perfectly reflects the women in Quoyle's life. Bunny and Sunshine are the maids in the meadow, their mother Petal Bear is the demon lover, Aunt Agnis is the stouthearted woman, and Wavey Prowse is the tall and quiet woman. These women play significant roles in the narrative and aid Quoyle in his search for identity. Petal makes a cuckold of

him, yet he remains a devoted and loving father. He relies on Agnis's rationality and assertive strength to push him in the right direction—which leads him straight into the arms of Wavey Prowse.

Lydia E. Ferguson

Further Reading

Flavin, Louise. "Quoyle's Quest: Knots and Fragments as Tools of Narration in *The Shipping News*." *Critique: Studies in Contemporary Fiction* 40 (1999): 239-247. Addresses several critical reviews considering the narration and fragmented prose style of *The Shipping News*, which Flavin maintains is a thoughtful and meaningful reflection of Quoyle's own search for identity.

Hunt, Alex, ed. *The Geographical Imagination of Annie Proulx: Rethinking Regionalism.* Lanham, Md.: Lexington Books, 2009. A collection of essays discussing the unique qualities of Proulx's fiction, such as its use of geography, landscape, myth, caricature, community, and cultural hybridity.

Polack, Fiona. "Taking the Waters: Abjection and Homecoming in *The Shipping News* and *Death of a River Guide*." *Journal of Commonwealth Literature* 41 (2006): 93-109. A psychoanalytic reading using Sigmund Freud's theory of the uncanny (the uncomfortably strange) and Julia Kristeva's theory of abjection (degradation).

Seiffert, Rachel. "Inarticulacy, Identity, and Silence: Annie Proulx's *The Shipping News*." *Textual Practice* 16 (2002): 511-525. A feminist critical approach discussing the inarticulate yet empathic nature of Proulx's characters within the text's masculine landscape.

Varvogli, Aliki, *Annie Proulx's "The Shipping News": A Reader's Guide.* New York: Continuum, 2002. An accessible and comprehensive reader's guide to *The Shipping News*; discusses the author, the novel, and its reception and performance; suggests further reading and discussion questions.

Whalen, Tracy. "'Camping' with Annie Proulx: *The Shipping News* and *Tourist Desire*." *Essays on Canadian Writing* 82 (2004): 51-70. Addresses criticisms of Proulx's treatment of Newfoundland citizens, culture, language, and landscape.

Shirley

Author: Charlotte Brontë (1816-1855)
First published: 1849
Type of work: Novel
Type of plot: Comedy of manners
Time of plot: 1811-1812
Locale: Yorkshire, England

Principal characters:
SHIRLEY KEELDAR, a financially independent young
　woman
CAROLINE HELSTONE, a dependent young woman
MR. HELSTONE, rector of Briarfield, Caroline's uncle, and
　a High Tory
ROBERT MOORE, a textile manufacturer
LOUIS MOORE, Robert's brother, a tutor
HORTENSE MOORE, their sister
MR. HALL, vicar of Nunnely
MR. YORKE, gentleman of Briarmains, a radical
MRS. PRYOR, Caroline's long-lost mother
THE SYMPSONS, Caroline's aunt, uncle, and cousins
MR. DONNE,
MR. MALONE, and
MR. SWEETING, the curates

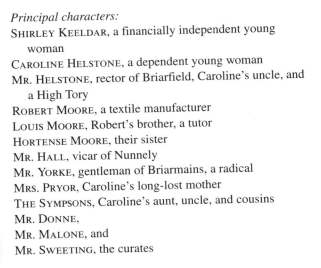

The Story:

Three self-centered Yorkshire curates are interrupted at dinner by Reverend Helstone, who is concerned about the dangers of sabotage. England is at war with Napoleonic France, and manufacturers have been confronted with the Orders in Council, developed by the British government to impose control and taxation on trade with Europe and America, greatly curtailing business. Moreover, the Industrial Revolution is well underway in England, resulting in the loss of jobs as machines make it possible to produce the same amount of goods with fewer laborers. Roving bands of men are destroying the machines they see threatening their way of life. Reverend Helstone, acting like a soldier, takes arms to protect a shipment of frames being delivered to Robert Moore's textile mill. He is unsuccessful, however, and the frames are destroyed.

Meanwhile, Caroline Helstone, an orphan, has been taken in by the reverend, her uncle. He provides for Caroline but shows her no affection. Caroline falls in love with Robert Moore, but he is so focused on making a success of his business that he cannot allow himself to love Caroline. Seeing this, Caroline resolves not to marry and to distract herself from grief by doing good works. The narrator comments on the "old maids" and the problem of what women can and cannot do while living in a "man's world."

Caroline, as is proper for a young woman, suffers in silence, but she knows she has to change her life. She tells her uncle that she wishes to leave his home and to earn a living since she herself is penniless. Caroline plans to become a governess, but her despair makes her ill. Distraction from her unhappiness is provided by Shirley Keeldar, a wealthy young woman who has just moved to Fieldhead, her property in Yorkshire. Both physically and emotionally, Shirley is Caroline's opposite, yet they become fast friends. Caroline also meets Mrs. Pryor, Shirley's former governess who still lives with her as a companion. Shirley owns Robert's mill, and she and Robert often consult about business. Seeing them together, Caroline resigns herself to the probability that they will marry.

Another attack on Robert's mill is repelled by Robert, Mr. Helstone, and a group of soldiers. Robert leaves the area to search out the rioters and bring them to justice. Caroline contracts a fever and becomes seriously ill; her illness is exacerbated by her hopeless love for Robert. Mrs. Pryor comes to nurse her and, in desperation because Caroline has no desire to live, tells her a secret: Mrs. Pryor is Caroline's long-lost mother. Her maternal love makes Caroline want to live, and she gradually gets better.

Shirley, who has been traveling with her uncle, aunt, and cousins, returns to Fieldhead, and her own secret is divulged: For some years, Shirley has been in love with Louis Moore, Robert's brother and her cousin Henry's tutor. Louis once tutored Shirley, and their relationship developed beyond that of teacher and student. However, because she was an heir while he was nothing more than an educated employee, they had to hide their feelings from society. Moreover, Louis's poverty and dependence upon Shirley's Uncle Sympson for his living affronts his pride and prevents him from loving Shirley. Meanwhile, Shirley's wealth has motivated other suitors for her hand. Shirley spurns them all, much to her uncle's disgust and anger. He feels that her independence is unwomanly and that she must be married.

When Robert returns, everyone assumes he will marry Shirley. He tells Mr. Yorke that he did propose to her, not because he loved her but because of her money; she turned him down. Because business is so bad, Robert plans to emigrate to America, but he is shot by someone who hates the mill owners. Robert survives and marries Caroline, and Shirley convinces Louis that money should not keep them apart. The English defeat Napoleon's army in Spain, and the repeal of the Orders in Council spurs a major growth in business. The double wedding of the Moore brothers with Caroline and Shirley concludes the novel.

Critical Evaluation:

Shirley is a complex novel. It has been variously classified as a comedy of manners, a historical romance, and a "condition of England" novel, focusing on social situations during that time. Originally written in three volumes, it includes two love stories, social history, and humor. Charlotte Brontë wrote *Shirley* after *Jane Eyre* (1847), at a time when she experienced the devastating losses of her brother Branwell and both her sisters, Emily and Anne. Following the success of *Jane Eyre*, Brontë struggled to complete *Shirley*, her third novel. She described writing the novel as her salvation, but the publication was not a success. Both readers and reviewers were disappointed with the novel. This attitude has persevered over the years. Part of the problem relates to the author's use of point of view. Unlike the earlier *Jane Eyre* and the later *Villette* (1853), *Shirley* is narrated in the third person. There is no sense of one person's ideas and reflections driving and unifying the story. The novel also includes a wealth of material concerning the times in England, both political issues and the impact of the Industrial Revolution on local communities. Consequently, rather than focusing on individuals, the novel shows how individuals are influenced by social forces.

The novel's structure also resists unity. *Shirley* begins with a satiric portrayal of three curates, who reappear throughout the narrative. The second chapter introduces a main character, Robert Moore, but chapters 3 and 4 concern Mr. Yorke, who is not a major character. It is not until chapter 6 that Caroline Helstone, a heroine, is introduced. The title character, a second heroine, is introduced in chapter 11, nearly one-third of the way through the novel and long after readers have become attached to Caroline. Shirley's love interest, Louis Moore, is not introduced until chapter 26 of the thirty-seven-chapter novel.

The novel includes a multitude of characters, who can be grouped into categories: churchmen, including the curates and their pastors; "old maids" and unmarried women; workers and the unemployed; those of no class in society, such as a governess and tutor; and landowners and businessmen. With the curates and their pastors, Brontë provides a commentary on a church that is basically insensible to the needs of the people. With the exception of Mr. Hall, Christianity appears absent from this Christian community. Generally, the male characters are seen as failures in their personal and professional relationships. Robert and Louis Moore, the two major male characters, are flawed. Robert is uncaring toward his workers and is blind to what constitutes true love; Louis exhibits an excessive pride in his poverty that will not allow him to love. The women characters, particularly those who are unmarried, are represented in a more positive light.

Unmarried women and their place in society is a major issue in the novel that is generally developed through the two heroines. Caroline and Shirley are complementary in more than their looks. The blonde Caroline is powerless; she is a dependent, duty-bound to her uncle, somewhat passive, and resigned to her "place" in society. The dark-haired Shirley is independent, empowered by her wealth, and bound to no one. Shirley is active and eager to embrace a traditionally masculine role in England's patriarchal society. With her name (which was then a male name) and her wealth, she jokes about being Captain Keedlar, fighting for her rights.

The two heroines become close friends, and they discover their similarities. Both believe that a woman can be more than an ornament in a man's home. When Robert's mill is threatened by the rioters, Caroline and Shirley sneak out of the house to help, and Shirley brings a pistol. Both women are in love, and neither can speak of her love publicly: Caroline cannot tell anyone of her love for Robert because she believes he does not love her as a result of her lack of fortune. Shirley cannot speak of her love for Louis because he is her cousin's tutor and, therefore, not a suitable match. However, both women work within the existing patriarchal system to get what they want.

The book is set in Brontë's home county of Yorkshire and has been described as a regional novel. The activities of small villages and their people and customs are portrayed against the background of increasing poverty and fear as new machines put people out of work. The attack on Robert's mill resembles actual attacks by Luddites in the newly developing mill towns. The conflict in England between the Liberals and the Tories is also portrayed among the novel's characters, such as Mr. Yorke (a Liberal who opposes the Church of England) and Reverend Helstone (a Tory churchman). The argument between Yorke and Helstone is enhanced by the larger issue of Napoleon's activities in Europe.

What is central to the novel is "the woman question": What is the position of women in a man's world? Victorians were concerned with single women. Those who did not marry usually remained dependent on their fathers or other male relatives, in a society whose economy was structured to distribute wealth through patriarchal familial structures. Unmarried women had few opportunities to be self-supporting; one was to become a governess. Brontë had described the role and fate of a governess in *Jane Eyre*.

In *Shirley*, Caroline wishes to be free of her uncle and to make her own way in the world. All she can expect, since she does not believe she will marry, is to become a governess, a household dependent wedged between the servant class and the family that employs her. She is both realistic and rebellious, not wanting to continue her dependence on her uncaring uncle, who dismisses her concerns for her future. When Caroline is told to go amuse herself, she caustically remarks to herself, "What with? My doll?" Caroline and the narrator, in a narrative aside, both speak of the necessity for single women to have something constructive to do with their lives. Shirley, because of her wealth, does not have to conform to the usual role for women, to marry, but she does. Despite her Uncle Sympson's insistence, she spurns a number of "suitable" men and, unlike many women, marries for love. Some critics have said that Shirley resigns her role as a strong woman when she chooses Louis, someone who can master her, but Shirley does not relinquish her strength or simply accept patriarchal norms. She convinces Louis to marry her, and her playfulness disguises an iron hand that will guide their future.

Marcia B. Dinneen

Further Reading

Craik, W. A. *The Brontë Novels*. London: Methuen, 1968. Sees *Shirley* as Brontë's "least successful novel." Discusses the failure of the male characters and the third-person point of view.

Edwards, Mike. *Charlotte Brontë: The Novels*. New York: St. Martin's Press, 1999. Part of the Analysing Texts series; different aspects of the novel are discussed, as well as their counterparts in Brontë's other novels. A particularly useful source for students.

Gilbert, Sandra M., and Susan Gubar. *The Madwoman in the Attic*. New Haven, Conn.: Yale University Press, 1979. In a chapter devoted to *Shirley*, the authors focus on Brontë's handling of women who are imprisoned and accepting of self-denial because of their gender.

Ingham, Patricia. *The Brontës*. New York: Oxford University Press, 2006. Part of Oxford's Authors in Context series; discusses how *Shirley* reflects concerns with social class as well as the governess "problem."

McLaughlin, Rebecca A. "'I Prefer a Master': Female Power in Charlotte Brontë's *Shirley*." *Brontë Studies* 29 (November, 2004): 217-222. Sees the novel as a subversive depiction of the power of women in a male-dominated world.

Torgerson, Beth. *Reading the Brontë Body: Disease, Desire, and the Constraints of Culture*. New York: Palgrave, 2005. Describes how Brontë uses disease and illness as a metaphor for issues of class and gender.

Shoeless Joe

Author: W. P. Kinsella (1935-   )
First published: 1982
Type of work: Novel
Type of plot: Fantasy
Time of plot: Late 1970's
Locale: Iowa, northern midwestern United States, and New England

Principal characters:
RAY KINSELLA, farmer, husband, and father
ANNIE KINSELLA, Ray's devoted wife
KARIN KINSELLA, their daughter
J. D. "JERRY" SALINGER, a famous American author
"SHOELESS" JOE JACKSON, deceased former Major League Baseball player

The Story:

Young Ray Kinsella gains a lifelong love for baseball from tales told by his father, including the story of disgraced former star "Shoeless" Joe Jackson. Ray leaves his native Montana to attend college in Iowa. One day, he overhears the daughter of his landlady vow that she will marry him when she grows up. Years later, that vow comes to pass. Suddenly a husband to Annie and a father to Karin, Ray begins selling life insurance, a job he detests. When local former ballplayer Eddie Scissons grows too elderly to maintain his farm, Annie talks Ray into buying it. Ray knows little about farming, but he is able to keep the farm afloat.

One evening, while sitting on his front porch, Ray hears a disembodied voice say, "If you build it, he will come." Ray somehow understands from this terse message that he is to plow away several acres of corn and build a baseball field, complete with outfield fences and lights. He also knows that, once complete, his field will be visited by the specter of Shoeless Joe. With Annie's blessing, Ray complies. It takes three seasons, but, finally, Annie spots a man dressed in old-fashioned baseball flannels standing in the outfield. It is indeed Shoeless Joe. He and several phantom teammates materialize regularly and play baseball on Ray's field. After each game, they vanish into the corn beyond the left-field fence.

Ray believes that he has accomplished his mission, until the voice revisits him and implores, "Ease his pain." Again, despite the brevity of the message, Ray perceives a full set of instructions. He is to travel to Windsor, Vermont, to the home of reclusive writer J. D. Salinger and take Salinger to a baseball game at Fenway Park in Boston. Ray sets out for Windsor and encounters the famous author in his Vermont driveway. Ray entreats Salinger to join him. Fearful of unduly agitating this strange visitor, Salinger accedes. On the way, Ray details the story of his magical baseball field in Iowa. Salinger does not understand, but he envies Ray's passion, and he relaxes enough to allow Ray to call him "Jerry."

At the game, Ray again hears the voice, urging him to "go the distance." Ray senses yet a third set of instructions: He must travel to Chisholm, Minnesota, and inquire after Archie "Moonlight" Graham, a ballplayer who appeared in a single game around the turn of the twentieth century but never got a turn at bat. To punctuate this directive, Graham's meager statistics appear on the Fenway Park scoreboard. Plainly, no one else in the crowd hears the voice or sees the record, and the game ends with no further incident. Afterward, back in Jerry's driveway, Ray is anxious to set out on this new quest. However, Jerry reveals that he, too, heard the voice and saw Graham's record on the scoreboard. The two set off for Minnesota.

In Chisholm, they learn that Archie Graham became a doctor. The local citizens bombard them with warm memories of "Doc" Graham, who died twenty years earlier. Ray and Jerry accumulate much information but remain uncertain of what to do with it. This uncertainty robs Ray of sleep, and late one night he slips out of his hotel room for a walk. He passes the building that once housed Graham's office. The door opens and an old man emerges. It is Doc Graham himself, alive and happy to talk. Graham explains how he came to be called Moonlight and divulges his greatest wish: To have come to bat in a Major League game. The next morning, Ray shares with Jerry the details of the encounter. The two have fulfilled their mission, and they decide to head for Iowa. Outside Chisholm, a young man stands beside the road, his thumb extended. His hair is slicked down, and he wears an old, featureless baseball uniform. Ray and Jerry pick him up. Their passenger's name comes as no surprise: it is Archie Moonlight Graham.

When they reach Iowa, Moonlight Graham joins the other players in their games, and Ray finds that he has a surprise visitor. His long-estranged twin brother, Richard, has arrived for an extended visit. As the family reunites, Archie slips away and joins Shoeless Joe's phantom team. Meanwhile, Annie's brother Mark has been plotting. Mark is a stern man who teaches at the University of Iowa and owns property. Like Richard, Mark has not been touched by whatever magic has pervaded everyone else; neither man can see the ballplayers. Mark simply believes that Ray has taken leave of his senses. He knows Ray has lost income because he replaced some of his crops with his baseball field, so Mark blackmails Eddie Scissons into selling him the mortgage on the farm. Mark and his business partner, Abner Bluestein, set a date for foreclosure.

Mark and Bluestein arrive at the field to serve papers. Karin, startled by the confrontation, falls awkwardly from the bleacher seats. The impact renders her unconscious, and she stops breathing. The nearest medical facility is twenty minutes away. Archie Graham approaches from the baseball field. As he draws closer, he changes from the young hitchhiker to the aged doctor whom Ray encountered in Chisholm. The magic finally strikes everyone present: Richard, Mark, and Bluestein all see him. Doc Graham declares that Karin is choking; he dislodges the obstruction, and Karin resumes breathing.

Karin will recover, but Doc has crossed a line: He can never again be Moonlight Graham. Ray and Annie are dismayed, but Doc has already fulfilled his wish by taking turns at bat during the phantom games. He contentedly strolls beyond the left-field fence and disappears. Mark and Bluestein, mortified by their role in Karin's mishap, withdraw.

Soon afterward, Ray overhears the phantom ballplayers inviting Jerry to accompany them into the cornfields after that night's game. Ray feels slighted. Jerry points out that Ray has a wife and a child, whereas Jerry's children are grown and he lives alone. Jerry promises Ray that he will write of their journey and of what it is like to realize a dream. Ray and Annie watch as Jerry and the players blend into the corn. They shut down the lights, and night falls.

Critical Evaluation:

W. P. Kinsella's *Shoeless Joe* is an epic fantasy in a contemporary setting. Such fantasy usually features a legend as background, and that role is fulfilled in *Shoeless Joe* by the infamous Black Sox scandal. In 1919, the Chicago White Sox was the best team in the major leagues, reaching the World Series. No player embodied the team's transcendent talent more than did Shoeless Joe Jackson. White Sox owner Charles Comiskey kept player salaries miserably low, and local gamblers proposed to the players a substantial share of their winnings if they deliberately lost, or "threw," the World Series. Jackson was allegedly one of eight players who participated in the conspiracy, and the White Sox indeed lost. The eight players were banned for life from Major League Baseball. Many claimed that Jackson was dimwitted and illiterate and could not have understood what he was agreeing to. Moreover, Jackson arguably played well during the series, batting .375 and recording twelve hits. Despite the outcry, Jackson never played Major League Baseball again. Thus, a legend launches the epic fantasy told in *Shoeless Joe.*

Shoeless Joe is suffused with the magic typical of epic fantasy. Like Frodo Baggins in *The Lord of the Rings* (1955; collective title for *The Fellowship of the Ring*, 1954; *The Two Towers*, 1954; *The Return of the King*, 1955), Ray Kinsella is an unremarkable figure who suddenly experiences magical events. Ray, an ordinary farmer from Iowa, repeatedly hears a voice from no discernible source. The voice says little; twice, it speaks but three words. Through magic, these terse communications implant in Ray's mind entire sets of instructions. The magic also touches Ray's wife, Annie. No one would blame Annie were she to express serious misgivings toward Ray's plans. The magic assures Annie that all will be well. Similarly, the character of J. D. Salinger somehow knows that if he accompanies Ray on his quest, good will result. *Shoeless Joe* offers many ordinary characters touched by something extraordinary.

The story supplies another integral ingredient of epic fan-

tasy: the quest, in which a hero leaves familiar territory and travels long distances to a hostile environment. The second message delivered by the disembodied voice directs Ray to leave home and drive more than halfway across the United States to the home of J. D. Salinger, a reclusive writer who consistently renounces his fame. Salinger reluctantly agrees to accompany Ray, first to a baseball game and then to Minnesota, before returning with Ray to Iowa. Salinger fulfills another role common to epic fantasy: the sage companion to the hero, one with perspective that the hero lacks.

Fantasy is also characterized by a conflict between opposing forces. In *Shoeless Joe*, love is the most pervasive benevolence besides magic. The most apparent love is shared by the two principle characters. Her love for Ray leads Annie to support Ray instead of disparaging him. She does not know the details of his quest, but her love is so sure that she trusts him beyond question. Annie believes in what he claims he must do, and she passionately wishes for his success. Furthermore, Ray genuinely loved his deceased father. Ray is far too young to have seen Shoeless Joe play baseball, but the athlete came to life for the young Ray through his father's wide-eyed tales of seeing Jackson play in amateur leagues after he was banned from the majors.

Love is expressed on other levels in *Shoeless Joe*. Ray repeatedly acknowledges his love for his adopted state of Iowa. Ray and Annie also frequently speak with love for the farm that they call home and through which the novel's opposing force comes into play. Annie's brother Mark represents greed and the lust for power. Mark is a genuine threat; he is not interested in why or where Ray has gone. He only knows that Ray could have been doing something to restore the income lost when he plowed under his corn and built an entirely frivolous baseball field.

Mark plots to seize control of the farm and exploit it for income. That his character represents greed is evident because he is deprived of the magic experienced by the other characters. Mark cannot see Shoeless Joe or any of the ballplayers. However, as is the case in much epic fantasy, the good forces ultimately prevail. As a result of confronting Ray, Mark sees his niece Karin tumble from the bleachers and nearly die. Mark feels genuine remorse. His business partner, Abner Bluestein, gives Ray his jacket to cover Karin after she falls. This momentary crack in their greedy natures allows them to see Doc Graham, who sacrifices his incarnation as ballplayer Moonlight Graham to minister to Karin until she recovers. Such selflessness compels Mark and Bluestein to withdraw their demands and vanish from the story.

Finally, epic fantasies often end with a character leaving

the world for a better one, as Frodo Baggins, for example, sails away from Middle-earth at the end of *The Lord of the Rings*. *Shoeless Joe* concludes with Ray and Karin fondly watching as J. D. Salinger accompanies the phantom ballplayers to wherever they go when they vanish amid the rows of corn. *Shoeless Joe* may feature numerous genuine settings and human characters, as opposed to elves and dwarves, but it has all the ingredients of epic fantasy. The overall impression at story's end is one of joy preserved, with a chance for more wonders yet to unfold.

Michael Kleeberg

Further Reading

Asinof, Eliot. *Eight Men Out*. New York: Pocket Books, 1979. A definitive account of the Black Sox scandal of 1919.

Dougherty, David. "Reviews: *Shoeless Joe Jackson Comes to Iowa: Stories*." *Studies in Short Fiction* 32, no. 1 (Winter, 1995). Takes a dim view of the sentimentality in *Shoeless Joe*, but provides useful commentary on a small variety of other works by Kinsella.

Fischer, David Marc. "Dreams, Magic, and Peerless Plotting: *Shoeless Joe*." *Writing* 22, no. 4 (January, 2000): 12-14. Lauds the plot structure of *Shoeless Joe*, finding much for other authors to emulate.

Jenkins, Clarence. "Kinsella's *Shoeless Joe*." *Explicator* 53, no. 3 (Spring, 1995): 179-180. Explores an interesting religious angle to the story of *Shoeless Joe*.

Kirtz, Mary. "Canadian Book, American Film: *Shoeless Joe* Transfigured on a *Field of Dreams*." *Literature Film Quarterly* 23, no. 1 (1995): 26-31. Discusses the making of the film adaptation *Field of Dreams* (1989); offers many worthwhile insights on the novel.

The Shoemaker's Holiday
Or, The Gentle Craft

Author: Thomas Dekker (c. 1572-1632)
First produced: 1600; first published, 1600
Type of work: Drama
Type of plot: Comedy
Time of plot: c. 1413-1422
Locale: London and the nearby village of Old Ford, England

Principal characters:
SIMON EYRE, a London shoemaker
HODGE,
FIRK, and
RAFE, his employees
SIR ROGER OTLEY, Lord Mayor of London
ROSE OTLEY, his daughter
SIR HUGH LACY, the earl of Lincoln
ROWLAND LACY, his nephew
MARGERY, Simon Eyre's wife
JANE, Rafe's wife

The Story:

Rose Otley, daughter of the Lord Mayor of London, Sir Roger Otley, and Rowland Lacey, nephew to Sir Hugh Lacy, the earl of Lincoln, are deeply in love. With evident irony, proud Sir Roger declares to Sir Hugh that he cannot presume to have his daughter marry above her station. With equal pride, Sir Hugh ironically counters that because of Rowland's dissolute ways it would be far better for Rose to marry a substantial young London businessman. Rowland, who toured Europe and learned the shoemaker's trade in Germany, is given a command in the army of King Henry V, who is preparing to invade France. Sir Hugh wants Rowland off to France as soon as possible, so that the youth might forget Rose.

Rowland has other ideas. Claiming pressing business in London, he turns his command over to his cousin, Askew, after promising that he will join his unit in Normandy, if not in Dover. When the troops assemble to leave London, Simon Eyre, a shoemaker, pleads to no avail with Rowland to allow Rafe Damport, his drafted journeyman, to stay home with his new bride, Jane. Rafe, resigned to going to the wars, gives Jane as a farewell gift, a pair of shoes that he made for her.

Meanwhile Rose, confined to her father's house at Old

Ford, a London suburb, sends her maid Sybil into the city to seek information about Rowland. Determined to win Rose, Rowland disguises himself as a German shoemaker. Singing a German drinking song, he seeks work at Simon's shop. When Simon refuses to consider hiring Rowland, Simon's workmen, charmed by Rowland's broken speech, threaten to leave. Rowland, as Hans Meulter, is taken on.

While hunting near Old Ford, Hammon and Warner, two London citizens, pursue a deer into the Lord Mayor's estate. There they encounter Rose and her maid. Hammon falls in love with Rose and Warner loses his heart to Sybil. Sir Roger, welcoming the young hunters, decides that Hammon is just the man to marry Rose.

Rowland, through his friendship with a German sea captain, speculates in a valuable unclaimed ship's cargo, to the enormous profit of Simon, his employer. As a result of this venture Simon is made an alderman, and the genial shoemaker seems destined for even greater city honors. Sir Hugh, meanwhile, learns from a servant that Rowland is not in France. Ashamed of his nephew, Sir Hugh sends the servant into the city to discover Rowland's whereabouts.

When Hammon confesses his love, Rose at first dismisses him coyly; finally she declares that she intends to remain single. Even though Sir Roger threatens to force Rose into the match, the offended and impatient Hammon returns to the city. In London, Sir Hugh's servant can learn nothing of Rowland's whereabouts, even though he inquires at the shop of Simon.

Simon, grown affluent and popular, continues to advance upward in political rank. To the amusement of Simon's journeymen, Firk and Hodge, his wife Margery assumes pretentious manners. Rafe, having been wounded in France, returns to London. Seeking his wife, he weeps to learn that Jane left the Eyre household, where she was a maid to Margery Eyre, and has not been seen since. The Eyres—Simon is now High Sheriff—visit Sir Roger at Old Ford, where Simon's employees, Rowland among them, perform a morris dance. Rose recognizes Rowland in spite of his disguise and drinks a toast to him.

Jane, also grown quite independent because of her ability as a seamstress, is courted by Hammon. In his desperate attempt to seduce her, he shows her, to her disbelief, Rafe's name on a casualty list from France. Sorrowfully, she promises Hammon that if she ever remarries she will accept his proposal. Rose, knowing of Rowland's presence in the city, returns to her father's town house and arranges to have Rowland see her on the pretext of fitting a pair of shoes. At the shoe shop, a servant brings in a shoe and orders that a pair of similar size be made in time for a wedding that is to occur

the next day. Rafe recognizes the shoe as Jane's; he learns from the servant where the ceremony is to take place.

Rowland, as a shoemaker, goes to see Rose and talks to her under the eyes of Sir Hugh, who is looking for his nephew, and Sir Roger, who declares to Sir Hugh that he did not see the young man. When Sybil reveals that Rose means to marry the German cobbler, Sir Hugh gloats, thinking that Rowland will never be able to marry this middle-class girl. Sir Roger, who secretly hoped that Rose would marry Sir Hugh's nephew, is furious. At the same time Firk delivers a pair of shoes for Rose and misleads the two men into believing that Rose and the German cobbler will marry the next day at the church where Hammon and Jane plan to be married. Sir Hugh, to his alarm, suddenly realizes that the cobbler must be his nephew Rowland.

Simon, now Lord Mayor but still his lusty, simple self, declares his gratitude because Rowland helped him to affluence and promises that he will help the young people to become husband and wife. The next day Dame Eyre accompanies the young couple to the Savoy, while Rafe and his fellow shoemakers, armed with cudgels, encounter Hammon and Jane in front of St. Faith's. Hammon resents the intrusion of the base craftsmen; Jane is filled with misgiving at the sight of Rafe, whom she believed dead. Hammon patronizingly offers Rafe twenty pounds to relinquish his claims to Jane. Rafe, insulted, would thrash Hammon, but he is prevented from doing so by his lameness. Expecting to apprehend Rose and Rowland, Sir Hugh and Sir Roger wait, too, in front of St. Faith's. Word reaches them there that Rose and Rowland were married at the Savoy.

The Lord Mayor gives a breakfast for all London apprentices; he himself is served by men of his own craft. The king pardons Rowland and blesses him and Rose. When Sir Hugh and Sir Roger protest the match, the king explains that love is not a respecter of blood. To crown the festivities of Simon's Lord Mayorship, the king grants the shoemakers the privilege of holding two market days a week in the newly built Leadenhall Market and accepts Simon's invitation to him to be the guest of honor at a banquet.

Critical Evaluation:

Thomas Dekker, an Englishman of probable Dutch descent, was a true son of London, as his plays, and especially *The Shoemaker's Holiday*, attest. Happy in its blending of quasi-history and ordinary London life, this plot contains young lovers, noblemen, solid merchants, artisans, and even a king. Surely the theme and treatment gave the play wide popularity in Dekker's own day. This drama, with its appeal to patriotic instincts, formed part of the Lord Admiral's

Men's answer to the popular history plays being written at the moment by William Shakespeare, who wrote for the Lord Chamberlain's Men. Dekker derived his plot from a prose tale, *The Gentle Craft* (c. 1597-1598) by Thomas Deloney.

The first performance of *The Shoemaker's Holiday* was given for Queen Elizabeth's court. At that time the drama scene in London was experiencing a state of transition; the earlier romantic style of Robert Greene and John Lyly now seemed superficial and escapist, but the darkly realistic comedies of Ben Jonson or the later Shakespeare had not yet been written. As comic drama, *The Shoemaker's Holiday* is an excellent example of the transitional period that produced it. Dekker possessed an uncanny talent for mingling realism and romanticism, and this, his first extant play, belongs to two strikingly contradictory literary currents. On the one hand, *The Shoemaker's Holiday* is probably the best illustration of romantic comedy that readers have. Yet, at the same time, subtle, but frequent, realistic touches make the play an effective tool for discussing the transition in English comedy from romance to realism that can be pinpointed as occurring roughly at the beginning of the seventeenth century.

The tone of exuberance—zest for life—that filters through *The Shoemaker's Holiday* may reflect the youthful Dekker who wrote the play. Though he lived for another generation, he never wrote anything better than this early comedy. A poet at heart, Dekker collaborated in writing more than thirty plays and was known as a hack. He was in and out of debtor's prison much of his life.

The play's realistic undercoating—found in the street scenes and whenever the shoemakers are onstage—suggests that even at an early age Dekker was already aware of the dramatic possibilities of realism in comedy. Realism became increasingly evident in his later plays, especially *The Honest Whore* (1604-1605).

The romantic essence of *The Shoemaker's Holiday* may well lie in the absence of a palpable evil, of really dangerous villains in the play. In terms of the genre, it exhibits all the motifs and thematic conventions of romantic comedy. The standard theme of "rival wooers," for example, is carried out through Rowland and Rose and, in the subplot, through Rafe and Jane. Dekker carries the theme through its conventional turns as the true love between these couples is blocked by disapproving and uncomprehending guardians or by circumstances beyond their control, and, finally, as they are each in turn separated and then joyfully reunited.

A second major convention is the gentility theme, the idea that true nobility is inborn, not simply inherited. The gentility theme weaves its way through all romantic comedy plots, and it is best displayed in *The Shoemaker's Holiday* by the

dignity and pride with which Simon approaches humble labor. The most succinct statement of the theme also belongs to Simon: "Prince am I none, yet nobly born." In act 5, King Henry, whose role is to rectify all the play's complications, makes the gentility theme rule supreme as he chides Lacy's uncle for thinking Rose not noble enough to marry Rowland: "Lincoln, no more. Dost thou not know that love respects no blood, Cares not for difference of birth or state? The maid is young, well born, fair, virtuous, A worthy bride for any gentleman."

Other stock features of romantic comedy in this play are the disguises (Rowland becomes Hans the shoemaker), the song and dance of the morris dancers, and the use of mythic machinery and folklore. Simon's blazingly quick rise to fortune and fame is perhaps the most romantic touch of all. Dekker's romantic plot is firmly wedded with realistic manners and scenes, a combination reminiscent of Geoffrey Chaucer. During the transition years of 1598 to 1603, comedies began catering to a rising interest in actual city types, and Dekker's choice of Simon as the central character of his play reflects an innovative turn. Although Simon is on stage during less than half the scenes, and although the action of his plot involves no conflict, it is his characterization that sets and to a large extent controls the mood of the play. His occupation as shoemaker is definitely a step away from the more aristocratic leanings of Greene and Lyly and reflects a growing bourgeois audience's increasing interest in itself.

More central to the success of Simon's characterization is its break from the traditional and the stereotyped, for he seems to be a living character. Perhaps the most memorable thing about the play is its brisk, workaday-morning mood of healthy, good-hearted, and not overly sensitive people. Simon's personality combines with that of his lively shoemakers, his shrewish wife, and Rowland and Rose, to present a copious picture of London life.

The extent of Dekker's realistic touches is indicated by the fact that the play refers specifically to thirty-five landmarks within a radius of three miles of the city. The references reveal that the playwright is mirroring the London of his own time, and not Simon's time of a hundred and fifty years earlier. Dekker is not careful to avoid anachronisms; but, if comic realism is defined as the frequent interjection of material familiar to the audience—bits of current speech, little natural touches of everyday environment, or references to well-known but ordinary people, Dekker's treatment is clearly realistic.

There is also evidence that the Rose-Rowland story has a parallel to real people and real situations contemporary to Dekker. Sir John Spencer, actual Lord Mayor of London, forbade his daughter to marry her chosen lover. He gained notoriety by hiding his daughter so she could not run away and by mistreating her so badly that the law was finally invoked to place her in the custody of an uncle. All of this happened in the months directly preceding the first performance of Dekker's play. Although the stingy Spencer is more an antithesis of the generous Simon, the comparison offers another intriguing parallel between the play and the time in which it was written.

Dekker's inveterate interest in dialect (Irish, Welsh, French, Spanish, thieves' Latin, and Dutch) may reflect a foreign background, and that may help explain the uncannily perceptive realistic touches imposed on the play. A partly foreign eye can sometimes pick out cultural characteristics that a native observer is blind to. Dekker's best scenes—early morning in Tower Street, Simon's election to the shrievalty, the party at Old Ford, Jane in the shop, Firk outwitting Otley and Lincoln, the "stir" outside St. Faith's, and the pancake feast at Leadenhall on Shrove Tuesday—demonstrate his ability to see continuity in London life throughout the ages, an ability by which he creates in *The Shoemaker's Holiday* an atmosphere of old and merry England at its jolliest.

"Critical Evaluation" by Jean G. Marlowe

Further Reading

Dekker, Thomas. *The Shoemaker's Holiday*. Edited by R. L. Smallwood and Stanley Wells. New York: Manchester University Press, 1979. Includes a comprehensive introduction that places the play in its biographical, historical, and literary context. Discusses Dekker's use of sources, analyzes the play, and reviews its stage history.

McLuskie, Kathleen. *Dekker and Heywood: Professional Dramatists*. New York: St. Martin's Press, 1994. Focuses on the performances of the two playwrights' works, examining the relationship between their plays and the cultural moment when these plays were produced

Price, George R. *Thomas Dekker*. Boston: Twayne, 1969. One of the few generally available biographical and critical book-length studies of Dekker's plays, including collaborations and nondramatic works. Especially useful is the discussion of Dekker's social attitudes and the concluding overall assessment of his achievements.

Smith, David L., Richard Strier, and David Bevington, eds. *The Theatrical City: Culture, Theatre and Politics in London, 1576-1649*. New York: Cambridge University Press, 1995. This examination of English Renaissance literature provides analyses of eight works, with an essay by a literary scholar and another essay by a historian discussing each of the works. *The Shoemaker's Holiday* is discussed in chapter 3, in the essays "The Artisanal World" by Paul S. Seaver and "Theatre as Holiday" by David Bevington.

Toliver, Harold E. "*The Shoemaker's Holiday*: Theme and Image." In *Shakespeare's Contemporaries*, edited by Max Bluestone and Norman Rabkin. 2d ed. Englewood Cliffs, N.J.: Prentice-Hall, 1970. An examination of how Dekker presents at once a realistic and romanticized view of London life. Shows how the playwright offers remedies for human faults that cause social deficiencies.

Wells, Stanley W. "Thomas Dekker and London." In *Shakespeare and Co.: Christopher Marlowe, Thomas Dekker, Ben Jonson, Thomas Middleton, John Fletcher, and the Other Players in His Story*. New York: Penguin Books, 2007. Wells examines the plays of William Shakespeare by placing them within the broader context of Elizabethan theater, discussing other playwrights of the period, including Dekker, the work of acting companies, and the staging of theatrical productions. The chapter on Dekker recounts his life, career, and collaborations and devotes several pages to *The Shoemaker's Holiday*.

The Shoes of the Fisherman

Author: Morris West (1916-1999)
First published: 1963
Type of work: Novel
Type of plot: Philosophical realism
Time of plot: Early 1960's
Locale: Vatican City and its environs

Principal characters:
CARDINAL LAKOTA, archbishop of Lviv, Ukraine, and future Pope Kiril I
CARDINAL RINALDI, a Roman Catholic official
KAMENEV, the Soviet premier
THE REVEREND JEAN TÉLÉMOND, a Jesuit scientist-theologian

The Story:

In the wake of the death of the pope, the sacred college of cardinals convenes in Rome to select a successor. Among the cardinals summoned to Rome is Cardinal Lakota of Ukraine, at age fifty the youngest cardinal and only recently freed from nearly seventeen years of harsh imprisonment in a Siberian labor camp for practicing his faith. Cardinal Lakota, handpicked by Cardinal Rinaldi to offer the sermon on the opening day of the conclave, moves the college with his earnestness, delivering impassioned remarks about the duty of the Papacy, to serve the forgotten souls of the Roman Catholic Church. The following day, the charismatic Cardinal Lakota is elected pope by acclamation on the first ballot. He takes the name Kiril I.

Determined to return the Church to its pastoral mission and to raise the spiritual life of the Church's despondent and indifferent millions, Kiril embarks on a historic call for change. There are crises everywhere—political turmoil in Africa, mass starvation in China, religious persecution in communist countries, global environmental pollution, escalating world population, financial crises in both Europe and the United States, and, supremely, the ever-escalating nuclear arms race. However, Kiril, writing of his spiritual agonies and the immense burdens of his elevation in his diary, sees the Church as made up of individuals needing to realize the hope of their faith. To that end, Kiril, wearing only the simple cassock of a parish priest, ventures out into the Roman streets. He shares coffee with some workers (he is embarrassed to discover he has brought no money), and in a tender moment he offers last rites for a man ravaged by tuberculosis and bonds with the spiritually troubled young woman who is the man's nurse.

Shortly after his elevation, Kiril is contacted through diplomatic back channels by Kamenev, the Soviet premier who years earlier was his jailer in the Siberian camps. Indeed, Kamenev, who had come to be impressed by the prisoner's unshakeable faith, had arranged for Kiril to escape. Now, Kamenev wants to secure the new pope's assistance in organizing a diplomatic initiative with the United States to avoid escalation of the nuclear arms race into catastrophe. Kiril, torn by concerns over the appropriate role of the Church in translating the word of Christ into Christian action, and wary of the possibility of the Vatican being used as a dupe, agrees after much soul-searching to use the cardinal of New York to communicate with the U.S. president.

Meanwhile, Father Jean Télémond, a world-renowned Jesuit paleontologist, is summoned to Rome. His incendiary writings challenging Church doctrine on special creation and original sin had caused him to be censured in a kind of virtual exile for twenty years in a variety of exotic outposts. Now, he is summoned to Rome to deliver the sermon at Rome's Gregorian University on the feast day of Saint Ignatius of Loyola, the founder of the Jesuit order. However, there is more at stake in this journey to Rome. In frail health, Télémond is seeking permission from the powerful Holy Office to at last publish the first volume of his controversial treatise. Its profoundly optimistic vision of humanity evolving inevitably toward an eventual union with Christ, seen less as divine and more as a cosmic force, had merged the argument of Darwinian evolution with the Christian doctrine of creation. Vatican opponents see Télémond's argument as a grave error. If creation evolved toward union with God, then creation was a necessary act, thus abrogating God's free will.

Bound by his Jesuit oath, Télémond cannot publish without the Church's imprimatur. Kiril, himself concerned by the pessimism in the Church and by the world's spiral toward nuclear apocalypse, is moved by Télémond's sermon and its luminous argument that humanity's long history of warfare would give way ultimately to the emergence of a species-wide consciousness, that humanity would perfect itself in a convergence with the energy of Christ. The pope invites the controversial cleric to the papal retreat at Castel Gandolfo. There the two share a lengthy discussion over the mystery of evil and the essence of hope itself—and Kiril is much moved. Despite the pope's sympathies, however, the Holy Office denies Télémond's request—crushed, the priest dies just days later. Pope Kiril, arguing that the Church must shred historical patterns, recommends that the Jesuit's writings be published in their entirety with appropriate annotations.

When the U.S. president agrees to meet the Soviet premier, Kiril confronts the challenge of putting into action his vision of a pastoral Church. With the endorsement of the Papal Curia, the pontiff agrees to go to Lourdes, the sacred Catholic shrine in France that commemorates the appearance of the Virgin Mary, despite centuries of the pope steadfastly maintaining his position in St. Peter's. Also, far more important, Kiril accepts the responsibility to begin to broker a historic summit between the Soviets and the Americans. The Church is prepared now to go out into the world. Pope Kiril, calm and ready, accepts what he knows in his soul will be a long and difficult pilgrimage.

Critical Evaluation:

It is difficult for a contemporary reader to appreciate the radical argument of Morris West's Vatican narrative, *The Shoes of the Fisherman*, decades after the pontificate of Pope

John Paul II (the first non-Italian pope in more than four centuries) and his visionary agenda to redefine the pastoral mission of the Papacy and to involve the Church in an aggressive global social-activist role. Much of West's achievement, the novel's international success, came from its timeliness.

In 1963, after considerable pressure from the Vatican, Soviet premier Nikita S. Khrushchev released Josyf Cardinal Slipyj, the head of the Ukrainian Greek Catholic Church, after close to twenty years in the Siberian gulag. Indeed, West had based the character of Pope Kiril I (Cardinal Lakota) on Slipyj. In addition, in 1963, East-West tensions were considerably heightened in the wake of several global events: the nuclear brinkmanship over Soviet missile installations in Cuba; the assassination of U.S. president John F. Kennedy, the United States' first Roman Catholic president; the convening of the historic Second Vatican Council, laying the groundwork for radical changes in Catholic protocols; and (on the very day *The Shoes of the Fisherman* was published) the death of the beloved pontiff John XXII. During the next several months the world's attention was riveted on the ritual of the elevation of Paul VI, who would himself undertake a decade-long effort to open the Papacy to an international congregation.

This timeliness, although it gave the premise of West's novel marketplace cachet and secured its position as the most discussed (and best-selling) novel of 1963, certainly compromises the significance of the novel in the twenty-first century—after all, the Cold War has long been over, and the Papacy is manifestly no longer an exclusively Italian appointment. The contemporary impact of the novel is further diminished by West's lengthy (and distracting) secondary plot concerning the efforts of an American correspondent to secure a Church annulment so that he might marry the estranged wife of a prominent Italian politician. The subplot reflects West's own considerable efforts to secure an annulment from his first wife, who had left him for years in a kind of limbo; he was a devout Catholic unable to participate in the sacraments. The lengths to which the reporter goes and the elaborate moral dilemmas suggested by relationships outside the Catholic sacrament of marriage do not hold up in the wake of the Church's own decades-long reassessment of its stand on divorce.

However, what distinguishes *The Shoes of the Fisherman* is not its plot, timely or not, but rather its invigorating play of ideas. That a novel of ideas would achieve the market prominence of West's novel testifies to his ability to make the interrogation of complex Catholic doctrine both dramatic and accessible to a large non-Catholic audience. Unlike Vatican narratives of the late 1990's—shadowy narratives rich with intrigue and mayhem—West's novel sees the leaders of the Catholic Church as caught up in profound questions that define the very nature of humanity's position in a spiritual universe. Certainly part of the narrative's achievement is West's meticulous re-creation of the Vatican backrooms and, particularly, the ritual of the papal elevation (the Church's most fiercely secretive rituals). This is a realism that reflects West's own long stint as a Vatican correspondent, but West is not impelled by a need to reveal Vatican secrets. He wants to explore Catholic theology and the relationship between the Church, its people, and its leaders.

Such a narrative risks reducing its characters to mouthpieces—less characters than positions in a debate, the sheer gravitas of which would inevitably compromise the reader's need for plot. However, such is not the case in this novel. Characters are given humanity, depth, and moral complexity. The powerful Cardinal Leone, for instance, after he leads the efforts to censure the Reverend Jean Télémond, makes a most agonizing confession to Kiril: that he had acted not so much out of concern for the Church as out of jealousy over Kiril's obvious love of the renegade Jesuit.

That said, the novel is given to lengthy theological passages in which characters sort through the implications of faith and obedience. The heartbreaking censure of the dying Jesuit gives West the opportunity to investigate the controversial arguments of the Jesuit paleontologist Pierre Teilhard de Chardin, whose teachings had raised intricate questions about the nature of humanity's evolution and the force and energy of God in that process. West's powerful interchapters, extracts from Kiril's private journal, give the narrative its dramatic heart. Kiril measures the risks of Christianity and its ancient demands to take its salvation message into places most hostile to it; he tests the logic of hope in a dark time in which humanity appears eager to execute its own extinction; and he assesses the troubling relationship between the institutional Church and the individual conscience and the burdens of obedience.

Finally, what defines West's achievement is Pope Kiril's character: introspective, haunted by his long imprisonment, compelled by his unflagging love of the people who struggle within a world whose mayhem and brutality sorely test any faith in a supreme and benevolent deity. Kiril is finally invigorated by his willingness to engage the forces of history itself in an effort to put into practice the Christian message of forgiveness and love on an individual as well as a global scale. Such depth and compassion humanize the pope. This is surely the enduring achievement of West's narrative.

Joseph Dewey

Further Reading

Confroy, Maryanne. *Morris West: Literary Maverick*. Milton, Qld.: John Wiley & Sons Australia, 2005. A literary biography of West, one of the rare book-length studies of the author. A slim sketch, but helpful to beginning students.

Gandalfo, Anita. *Testing the Faith: The New Catholic Fiction in America*. Westport, Conn.: Greenwood Press, 1992. An important assessment of Catholicism in the mainstream fiction of West's generation, which witnessed the groundbreaking theological events of the Second Vatican Council.

Lennan, Richard. *An Introduction to Catholic Theology*. Mahwah, N.J.: Paulist Press, 1998. A helpful guide for readers not familiar with West's theological argument. Outlines the basic tenets of Catholicism, the superstructure of the Vatican, and the Church's position on activism and the pastoral imperative.

Pelikan, Jaroslav Jan. *Confessor Between East and West: A Portrait of Ukrainian Cardinal Josyf Slipyj*. Grand Rapids, Mich.: Wm. B. Eerdmans, 1990. Still the most comprehensive biography of the religious figure upon whom West based Pope Kiril. Explains the long history of Soviet attempts to dismantle the Greek Catholic Church.

Savary, Louis M. *Teilhard de Chardin: The Divine Milieu Explained—A Spirituality for the Twenty-First Century*. Mahwah, N.J.: Paulist Press, 2007. A helpful explication of Pierre Teilhard de Chardin's complex theology, which is central to West's narrative. Reviews the nature of Teilhard de Chardin's concept of evolutionary humanity and shows how it conflicts with traditional Catholic doctrines of God's free will and the divine nature of Christ.

Shōgun
A Novel of Japan

Author: James Clavell (1924-1994)
First published: 1975
Type of work: Novel
Type of plot: Historical realism
Time of plot: Seventeenth century
Locale: Japan

Principal characters:
JOHN BLACKTHORNE, an English ship's pilot
LORD TORANAGA YOSHI, president of the Council of Regents who wants to be emperor
LADY MARIKO, Blackthorne's teacher and lover
YABU KASIGI, a feudal lord
VASCO RODRIGUES, a Portuguese ship's pilot
FATHER ALVITO, a Jesuit priest and an enemy of Blackthorne
FATHER DOMINGO, an anti-Jesuit Dominican priest
ISHIDO, Toranaga's archrival

The Story:

Elizabethan Englishman John Blackthorne has just shipwrecked off the coast of Japan after following sailing directions stolen from a Portuguese ship. He had hoped to sail to the island nation to help break the Jesuit/Portuguese monopoly on trade with Japan. With his crew, first welcomed by peasant villagers, he is tossed in a pit and humiliated by Yabu Kasigi, a feudal lord.

Some of Blackthorne's men suffer torture and horrifying deaths (such as being slowly burned alive in boiling water) before one of the aides of Lord Toranaga Yoshi, the president of the Council of Regents, intervenes for political purposes.

Toranaga then suggests that Lord Yabu have Portuguese captain Vasco Rodrigues transport the English sailors through high seas and storm to Osaka as a gift for Toranaga.

On the journey, Blackthorne is allowed to briefly steer the ship. One day, Captain Rodrigues goes overboard, and Blackthorne convinces Yabu to endanger his own life to save Rodrigues, given Yabu's feudal obligations. Likewise, Lord Toranaga endures confinement in the Osaka fortress because of his obligations as one of five regents to the prince. Blackthorne is thereby caught up in what he gradually discovers is a civilization full of greater intrigue than even the Elizabethan court. He soon becomes a tool of Toranaga, who uses him to break out of the trap of his archrival, Ishido, and to fulfill his own destiny as emperor, or shōgun.

Toranaga, who uses his underlings as chess pieces in his political intrigues, is quick in cleverly manipulating his pawn, Blackthorne, to exploit his knowledge of Westerners to prepare a strategy for expelling them from Japan. The first step is to break the hold of the Jesuits, including Father Alvito, as the only court translators. However, Toranaga must do so indirectly. His plan is to imprison Blackthorne in a hellhole that usually ends in prisoner crucifixion. He arranges for his protection, however. He also makes sure that Blackthorne connects with the anti-Jesuit father Domingo, who teaches Blackthorne the Japanese language and talks about Portuguese and Jesuit trade secrets. Toranaga hopes that these secrets will be passed to him by Blackthorne. When Blackthorne has learned enough, he is taken out of prison to what he expects to be death. Instead, he becomes part of the next stage in Toranaga's plan: to gain a refined education at the hands of the lovely Lady Mariko, who agrees to teach Blackthorne a more complex understanding of the Japanese language and culture.

Blackthorne's culture shock moves from initial delight to revulsion at practices he finds beyond the pale of human behavior. Gradually, however, he begins to accommodate himself to the new ways, such as baths and codes of honor, partly for the sake of survival and partly because he begins to understand the logic. He also begins to see his own men from a distanced and disdainful perspective. Lady Mariko is an essential part of this acculturation, for she enables Blackthorne (who falls in love with her) to see her world and to see his world through her eyes.

As he comes to admire the skill and courage of Japanese samurai and warlords, Blackthorne unknowingly becomes the "falcon" of the Japanese warlord Toranaga, who had saved his life with an ulterior motive and who tests Blackthorne's abilities and reliability. Blackthorne, in turn, saves Toranaga's life from Ishido's assassins and becomes a samurai. He plays the madman to help Toranaga leave Osaka disguised, misdirects the enemy to help him reach his forces, and then accepts a deal whereby the Jesuits will help Toranaga break through a harbor entrance barricade in exchange for Blackthorne. Blackthorne's excessive indulgence in European food and drink gives Captain Rodrigues the excuse to throw him overboard to a prearranged rescue, resulting in a sea chase.

Once free, Toranaga manipulates all who vie for power, promising alliances he has no intention of keeping and moving the pieces on his chessboard in a subtle game of misdirec-

tion. His willing queen, Lady Mariko, finds moments of love with Blackthorne, but her feelings for him do not overpower her sense of obligation and duty to Lord Toranaga. He enables her to regain her honor in return for helping Toranaga overcome conspiracies against him (an attack by ninjas, for example) and seize ultimate power in a war plan called Crimson Sky. Toranaga then sacrifices his queen for two of Ishido's castles.

Critical Evaluation:

James Clavell's historical adventure novels are studies of Western and Eastern minds in conflict over power, trade, and politics. *Shōgun* fits this pattern as well. However, *Shōgun* goes a step further because of the special circumstances that led Clavell to write the novel.

Shōgun is the product of Clavell's attempt to come to terms with terrible nightmares produced by the post-traumatic stress syndrome he experienced after surviving the horrors of a Japanese prisoner-of-war (POW) camp at Changi near Singapore, where only one in fifteen (10,000 of 150,000) prisoners survived. On the advice of his wife, he had forced himself to visit Japan and revisit the culture that had treated him and his fellow prisoners so inhumanely and to see if by reevaluating a culture and a people, he could put to rest the past that haunted him. *Shōgun* was the end result of this journey. As a consequence, Clavell seeks to do for his readers what he had sought for himself: discover the virtues of an "alien" people and make readers experience the extreme acculturation of one person—John Blackthorne. Clavell had Jonathan Swift's *Gulliver's Travels* (1726) in mind as he captured Blackthorne's psychological acculturation and immersion.

The novel is based loosely on real events: English captain William Adams did journey to Japan in the early seventeenth century, and his stay was manipulated by Ieyusu Tokugawa, a Japanese warlord, as a ploy against the Jesuits. However, Clavell added fictional events to make his plot serve his purposes. His strong stance against the clergy emerged because of his experiences at the POW camp. In *Shōgun*, the clergy he attacks as selfish, manipulative, and hypocritical are the Jesuits. As a POW, he also faced a Japanese sense of superiority that was expressed in their cruel treatment of outsiders and of those low on the class scale as subhuman, objects to be toyed with sadistically. Clavell aptly represents this cruelty in the novel's realistic descriptions of torture, prisons, and executions.

Nonetheless, Clavell's experiences in Japan after his imprisonment gave him the ability to capture one person's total immersion in and acculturation to the Japanese way of life.

Blackthorne came to see its virtues, he fell in love with a gentle and courageous Japanese woman, and he risked his life multiple times for a leader he had come to respect and admire. The Japanese virtues Clavell depicts include cleanliness, loyalty, courage, a strong sense of duty and obligation, a willingness for self-sacrifice for the sake of honor, an acceptance of suffering as part of the natural world that strengthens and educates, and a strong sense of community. Readers cannot help but share this shift of perspective as they see events through Blackthorne's new eyes. The novel's ending, however, remains shocking.

Blackthorne, like Lady Mariko, has been used as a tool by Toranaga, and he has developed a distorted view of the Japanese. Consequently, the Japanese dupe him and sacrifice him for their purposes; the readers are duped as well. Blackthorne is the English boy's adventure-story hero, the daring individualist who has traveled the high seas as a brave, bold sailor, more than competent at navigation and sailing. He has a strong sense of loyalty and gallantry. Still, he enables the expulsion from Japan of all Europeans and defends a power-seeking xenophobe, whose ways and means remain inscrutable.

Clavell carefully researched the period in which the novel is set by reading and studying British, Portuguese, Jesuit, and Japanese primary sources to develop a sense of the psychology of the times. He then skillfully interwove fact and fiction to create a world that readers could come to understand and, to some degree, appreciate. His method builds on a combination of parallels and contrasts in cultures—for example, the English and Japanese are both island peoples, dependent on the sea; and the sixteenth and seventeenth century English feared bathing, whereas the Japanese considered bathing a necessity for health and for social acceptance—and parallels and contrasts in characters—for example, Lady Mariko's illicit love for Blackthorne parallels that of Samurai Kungi Omi's love for courtesan Kiku yet contrasts with Toranaga's many brief and light-hearted affairs. The result is a panoramic vision of Japanese life that raises themes dear to Clavell's heart, including his strong interest in courageous entrepreneurship, his respect for seafarers and for technical competence, his appreciation of teachers (whether of languages, cultures, weapons, or good manners), his distrust of most clergy as selfish hypocrites with personal agendas, and his belief that Westerners need to encounter and come to understand other cultures if they are to survive in a modern world.

Experience taught Clavell that humans, though mostly similar, are not all alike, and that, for example, a community-centered culture has very different values and ways of thinking and acting than does an individual-centered culture; both cultures will have great difficulty understanding each other's psychology.

Gina Macdonald

Further Reading

Barreveld, Dirk J. *The Dutch Discovery of Japan: The True Story Behind James Clavell's Famous Novel "Shōgun."* San Jose, Calif.: Writers Club Press, 2001. A detailed historical account of the events fictionalized by Clavell in *Shōgun.* Tells the true story of the British captain William Adams—Clavell's John Blackthorne—and his command of the Dutch ship that reached Japan with a decimated crew.

Macdonald, Gina. *James Clavell: A Critical Companion.* Westport, Conn.: Greenwood Press, 1996. An overview of Clavell's life and work that includes a close analytical study of *Shōgun* and sections on plot development, structure, thematic issues, character development, genre conventions, and deconstruction as an alternative reading.

Smith, Henry. "Reading James Clavell's *Shōgun.*" *History Today* 31 (October, 1981): 39-42. An interesting study of the historicity of *Shōgun*, demonstrating how Clavell rearranged and refashioned events and historical figures in forming his novel.

Show Boat

Author: Edna Ferber (1885-1968)
First published: 1926
Type of work: Novel
Type of plot: Historical
Time of plot: 1870 to the 1890's
Locale: Chicago and Mississippi River region

Principal characters:
ANDY HAWKS, a steamboat captain and owner of the
   Cotton Blossom
PARTHENIA "PARTHY" HAWKS, his wife
MAGNOLIA "MAGGIE" RAVENAL, their daughter
GAYLORD RAVENAL, Magnolia's husband
KIM RAVENAL, their daughter

The Story:

Magnolia Ravenal is giving birth to her first child on a boat, the *Cotton Blossom*, on the Mississippi River in a storm. Her shrewish mother, Parthenia, or Parthy, Hawks is with her. Magnolia is the daughter of the boat's owner and captain, Andy Hawks, and, like her father, loves the theater, the river, and her husband, Gaylord Ravenal, who plays romantic leads opposite Magnolia in the showboat's troupe.

Magnolia's story goes back to the time when she had been growing up on the *Creole Belle* during the summers and in Massachusetts during the winters. Young Maggie, the story goes, hangs out in the pilothouse with Windy, the colorful old pilot. She is a sharp observer and imitator of the variety of passengers and troupe members who travel and work on the boat. Indeed, she is entranced by the "show people." She adores her father, the captain and king of the boat who knows every inch of the river, from St. Paul, Minnesota, to Baton Rouge, Louisiana; but she is rebellious toward her strict and overbearing mother.

Cap'n Andy, as the captain is also known, buys a new boat, the *Cotton Blossom*, and proposes to live on it year-round. However, Parthy refuses to travel on it, until young Maggie throws tantrums. Gradually, Parthy is seduced by the boat's well-equipped kitchen and consents to live on the boat when she sees the actresses flirting with her husband. She and Maggie spend more and more time afloat and soon get used to the lifestyle: the morning band-concerts ashore when Cap'n Andy hands out playbills; afternoon rehearsals and evening performances from the troupe's repertoire of melodramas; and talent shows, after which the cast and crew rehash the latest performance while eating a late supper. Young Maggie learns all the plays by heart, simply by listening.

One day, Julie Dozier, the troupe's star actress, becomes too ill to perform at a town in Mississippi. Her illness, it turns out, had been feigned: She had been trying to evade the local sheriff, who had come aboard the boat with a warrant to arrest Julie and her actor husband, Steve. It soon emerges that Julie is an octoroon, that is, a person of one-eighth black ancestry. She is married to a white man—a marriage in violation of Mississippi's antimiscegenation laws. This news sparks a frenzy of hate toward Julie from Elly Chipley, the other actress in the troupe. The sheriff orders Andy to clear his boat, and his "mixed-blood" cast, from town.

Julie and Steve leave the troupe at the next town. Shortly afterward, Elly runs off with a gambler, and her husband, Schultzy, the troupe's director, leaves as well to find her. Eighteen-year-old Maggie then steps in to fill the actresses' roles, playing ingenue leads.

Maggie's first performance is so realistic that a rube in the audience pulls a gun to shoot the actor playing the villain, which causes Andy to have to refund everyone's money. Maggie thrives on the acting life. The actor who plays the villains falls in love with her, so much so that he cannot act sufficiently evil while he is on stage with her. The need for a leading man to replace Steve leads Andy to pick up Gaylord Ravenal, an idle but elegant young man hanging around the wharf at New Orleans. He is set to play opposite Maggie and take Schultzy's place as director. Gaylord is an out-of-luck gambler on parole for murder; he had been looking for a way out of town. After he sees Magnolia, however, he accepts the acting-directing job.

Maggie's mother, Parthy, distrusts Gaylord and his claim that he belongs to an illustrious family, but he is adored by the showboat's audiences. Magnolia and Gaylord become famous stars along the river. Gaylord dresses exquisitely and shows Maggie New Orleans. The two fall in love despite Parthy's opposition and elope to a riverside church, where they are married.

Soon, Magnolia and Gaylord have a daughter, Kim, and she is fast growing up on the boat. After Kim's birth, her parents had stayed for a while with Parthy and Andy on the boat, but Cap'n Andy drowns suddenly in a spring flood. Parthy decides to continue on the boat as its captain and the head of the show company. Gaylord yearns to return to gambling and asks Magnolia to choose between him and her mother. Maggie decides on Gaylord. They secure Maggie's inheritance, leave the showboat, and move to Chicago.

In Chicago, they live a rags-to-riches-to-rags life that is dependent on Gaylord's luck at the card game faro. They live in posh hotels when they have money and have to pawn his cane and her jewelry for money when his luck turns. Maggie sees the seedy life of Chicago, with its gambling dens and prostitutes, and becomes nostalgic for the river and the indolent showboat life.

Maggie sings all the old African American river songs to Kim. When Kim becomes old enough, she is enrolled in a convent school and thrives on the orderly routine. Unlike Maggie, Kim is a serious child. Gaylord continues to dress elegantly and play the gentleman, and Maggie is still in love with him. In letters to her mother, she lies about not being poor, and so refuses to ask her for money. Maggie needs money, though, for Kim's future, and she asks her husband if she can return to acting. He derides her request, but at a rough party, Maggie sings for the guests; they love her river songs. She learns that the uncouth molls of Chicago's underworld are similar to the riverside farm girls she had known in her youth, and she believes she can succeed as a professional entertainer.

As time goes on, Chicago begins to reform its crude, vulgar image, and many of the gambling dens disappear, giving way to respectable businesses. The reformers spell hard times for gamblers, and Gaylord, who is no longer faithful to Magnolia, has reached bottom. One night he borrows one thousand dollars from a notorious madam. Magnolia soon returns it, recognizing the madam as Julie, the former showboat actress.

Determined to make some money legitimately, Maggie tries out for a vaudeville show. Then Gaylord disappears, leaving only a note and some cash. Maggie uses the money to buy a banjo and then begins to practice singing. She eventually becomes a successful singer in vaudeville and raises Kim alone. Kim grows up to marry a producer and becomes a famous New York actor herself.

Gaylord dies in San Francisco, and Parthy dies on the showboat at the age of eighty. Maggie returns to the South to attend her mother's funeral. Maggie, who soon discovers that Parthy had become locally famous for running the showboat, now realizes that her home is on the river. She inherits the *Cotton Blossom* and its company and decides to take over in her mother's place, giving her inheritance money to Kim to start a new American theater company.

Critical Evaluation:

Edna Ferber's novel *Show Boat* is reminiscent of poet Walt Whitman's work, in that it seeks uncritically to evoke and to celebrate a time, a place, a people, and a culture in American history. Like novelist Willa Cather, Ferber also explores the human roots of a region's culture and shows how lives intersect with and are shaped by the geographical realities of the land. Also like Cather, Ferber features strong women characters and traces their significance to the generations. *Show Boat* also shares affinities with writer Mark Twain's *Adventures of Huckleberry Finn* (1884) in its setting among the small Mississippi River towns in the latter part of the nineteenth century. In such ways, Ferber continues a tradition of American literature. *Show Boat*, however, is unique in focusing specifically on the phenomenon of the floating theater and how it had affected both actors and audiences.

In 1927, the year after Ferber published *Show Boat*, the novel was made into a musical play by Jerome Kern and Oscar Hammerstein II. The play was an immediate and lasting success, eclipsing the book to such an extent that virtually all critical commentary following the play's first production has been of the play, the films based on the play, and subsequent adaptations. The cultural impact of Ferber's work, which has been considerable, is therefore based on interpretive adaptations of her novel.

The play emphasizes and sensationalizes certain elements of the novel, distorting Ferber's original vision. The themes of miscegenation and feminism, for example, minor and only incidental in Ferber's novel, have been magnified in the various subsequent scripts and screenplays to add political currency to the original story. The play also has been harshly criticized by some for its "Uncle Tom" characters, who, incidentally, do not appear in Ferber's novel. It is thus important for readers to distinguish between the 1926 novel and the more dramatic (and melodramatic) 1927 play that made *Show Boat* most famous, or infamous.

In the novel, Ferber does not preach about or take sides regarding socioeconomic issues prominent at the time the novel is set. However, *Show Boat* does sympathetically contrast the careless vagabond life of the showboat players and the colorful people who knew and worked the rivers of the Mississippi basin with the repressed, Calvinist, and structured lifestyle of New England. The river itself is a metaphor for the life that surrounds it: easygoing, untamed, perennially variable, and uncritically tolerant. The showboat represents music, gaiety, and glamour to the pioneers in hamlets along the tributaries of the Mississippi and Ohio in the post-Civil War period: a form of escape not only to the local audiences but also to those who live and work on the boats. Ferber idealizes the warmth, enchantment, laughter, and music of the showboat, as well as the passion, lust, blood, and drama of the theater that continues even after the performance ends. She considers the showboat to be a form of medicine that alleviates the often-drab monotony and drudgery of everyday life for ordinary people.

The comedies and tragedies of human life aboard the showboat are seen in all their diversity in this novel, much as one would view the flotsam floating down the river during and after a flood. Objects humorous and horrific, poignant and reprehensible, are swept along in the flood to appear briefly; they then disappear in the muddy river. Similarly, readers are presented with characters who are variously appealing, distressing, or repellent; they emerge, catch reader interest, and then disappear. Like a passenger aboard a riverboat, the narrator uncritically observes the characters, describes them, and lets them be. Vignettes, too, appear and remain: the sunrise shimmers on the river; spittle displays itself on the pilothouse floor; catfish and mud settle on the bottom of a drinking barrel; and enraged bigots scream their coarse invectives. Loves and hates, strengths and weaknesses, beauties and horrors are equally of interest in *Show Boat*, all adding to the richness and variety of nineteenth century American life on the river.

Nostalgia for the showboat era continues in the latter part of the novel, when the expanding railroads have begun to encroach on the vitality of river-based enterprises and when the increasingly sophisticated theater arts have outgrown the naïve melodramas of showboat repertoires. Kim, Magnolia's daughter, goes to a New York theater school to learn acting; she participates in a critic-driven world of suave cosmopolites. Magnolia observes Kim's successful, civilized, and supposedly bloodless marriage and career and yearns for the passion, glamor, and heartbreak of the old days on the river with Gaylord, when audiences would swoon and sob and when the actors' lives were themselves filled with drama. Ferber compares Kim's personality and life with the Illinois River—well-behaved, clean, and manageable—to the muddy, volatile, and untamable Mississippi River. The Mississippi, in Ferber's mind, represents a far more exciting, diverse, and virile way of life, the real stuff of which true dramatic sensibility is made.

Sally B. Palmer

Further Reading

Batker, Carol. "Literary Reformers: Crossing Class and Ethnic Boundaries in Jewish Women's Fiction of the 1920's." *MELUS* 25, no. 1 (Spring, 2000): 81-104. Analyzes the work of Ferber, Fannie Hurst, and Anzia Yezierska, focusing on how Ferber depicts African American characters and class mobility.

Bloom, Harold, ed. *Jewish Women Fiction Writers*. New York: Chelsea House, 1998. Provides biographical information, a wide selection of critical excerpts, and bibliographies of Ferber and nine other female Jewish American writers. Designed for high school and undergraduate students.

Botshon, Lisa, and Meredith Goldsmith, eds. *Middlebrow Moderns: Popular American Women Writers of the 1920's*. Boston: Northeastern University Press, 2003. A collection of essays that examines the work of writers who were both critically acclaimed and commercially successful in the 1920's. Two chapters are devoted to Ferber.

Gilbert, Julie Goldsmith. *Ferber: Edna Ferber and Her Circle—A Biography*. New York: Applause, 1999. A well-researched biography that considers Ferber a romantic realist. Notes that although she was not opposed to working with the system, she created her own unique niche within it. Includes an index.

Meade, Marion. *Bobbed Hair and Bathtub Gin: Writers Running Wild in the Twenties*. New York: Nan A. Talese/Doubleday, 2004. Offers a nonscholarly, entertaining look at Ferber, Dorothy Parker, Edna St. Vincent Millay, and Zelda Fitzgerald, chronicling the lives of these writers in the Roaring Twenties.

Shaughnessy, Mary Rose. *Women and Success in American Society in the Works of Edna Ferber*. New York: Gordon Press, 1977. An examination of Ferber's life and work that provides an assessment of the author's place in the American women's movement.

Smyth, J. E. *Edna Ferber's Hollywood: American Fictions of Gender, Race, and History*. Austin: University of Texas Press, 2010. A look at the artistic and business partnership between Ferber and the Hollywood studios, who adapted her often controversial work into popular films. Explores the "research, writing, marketing, reception, and production histories of Hollywood's Ferber franchise."

Watts, Eileen. "Edna Ferber, Jewish American Writer: Who Knew?" In *Modern Jewish Women Writers in America*, edited by Evelyn Avery. New York: Palgrave Macmillan, 2007. An essay interpreting Ferber's work from the perspective of her Jewish heritage is included in this collection devoted to the discussion of American women writers whose lives and work have been influenced by Judaism.

A Shropshire Lad

Author: A. E. Housman (1859-1936)
First published: 1896
Type of work: Poetry

During his lifetime, A. E. Housman was the foremost classicist of Great Britain. He was a professor of Latin, first at the University of London and then at Cambridge University, until his death. During his tenure, he prepared celebrated scholarly editions of Manilius, Juvenal, and Lucan. He achieved these academic posts through his singular perseverance while working in the civil service, for he had failed his honors examinations at Oxford University. Normally, this failure would have disqualified him for an academic career. Some Housman biographers assert that the unrequited homosexual love he had for a fellow student caused a depression that had resulted in Housman's disappointing performance.

After his death, Housman's fame came to rest on two slim collections of poems, *A Shropshire Lad* and *Last Poems* (1922). Both collections deal with life's brevity and the indifference of nature and history to human tragedy. The Boer War (1899) and two world wars, as well as clues left by Housman's continual revisions of his poems, have encouraged an anti-imperial political reading of the poet's work, likely to a far greater degree than Housman himself intended when he wrote.

Housman's general pessimism and disillusionment locates his style closer to that of his contemporaries Thomas Hardy and Matthew Arnold than to Rudyard Kipling, and he is miles apart from the optimism of William Wordsworth and Alfred, Lord Tennyson. Within Housman's poetic domain—comprising themes of youth cut short by war, of love disallowed by history, and of peaceful landscapes threatened by turmoil—no poet can compete. The distinctive feature that underpins all of Housman's poetry is the resigned dispassion, quite distinct from cynicism, with which his narrator portrays his reaction to the human situation.

A Shropshire Lad comprises sixty-three poems. The introductory poem, "1887," is named for the fiftieth anniversary of Victoria's accession to the monarchy and introduces the political irony that critics have often assigned to the whole collection. Read superficially, it celebrates God's preservation of the queen, but it borrows its dominant image, that of the beacons that illuminate the landscape of the empire, from a Greek tragedy: Aeschylus's *Agamemnōn* (458 B.C.E.; *Agamemnon*, 1777). In that play, a series of signal fires extends across the Aegean from Troy to Argos to announce Troy's fall and Agamemnon's return. Paradoxically, the beacons parallel the flames of the hecatomb that Agamemnon's wife Clytemnestra offers to achieve success in her plan to murder him. Housman's narrator observes that when the flames go out "we" will remember "friends of ours/ who shared the work with God" of saving the queen. Proof of these friends' contributions exists on the tombstones of Asia and Africa that bear "Shropshire names."

"Loveliest of Trees" notes the cherry blossoms that appear at Easter. Humanity has a mere seventy years to witness this annual resurrection of life, and the narrator notes that twenty of his have already gone. The cherry is a medieval symbol of feminine love, and the narrator determines that since "fifty springs are little room" he must go about the woodlands immediately "to see the cherry hung with snow."

"The Recruit" describes a young soldier's departure from home. When he returns to Ludlow, whether on Sunday or on Monday, the chimes of its churches play "the conquering hero comes." This allusion to the coronation anthem George Frideric Handel wrote in 1727 for England's George II is rendered the more ironic when the narrator considers the possibility that the recruit might "come not home at all."

The untitled Poem XIII dispassionately continues the themes of youth and unrequited love. When the narrator was twenty-one, a wise man counseled him to pay any amount of material riches for love but never to give away his heart. At the age of twenty-two, having done just what the wise man advised against, the youth can only ruefully muse "'tis true, 'tis true."

The myth of Narcissus, the youth cursed to love his own reflection who dies as a result, is the primary allusion in Poem XV. The narrator advises his beloved not to look into his eyes: The beloved would see reflected in those eye a face he or she would love absolutely and would be as lost as the narrator himself. This poem, like Poem XIII, implies that total love ends with either self-absorption or the obliteration of death.

Housman frequently employs the language of sport in his most tragic poems. In "To an Athlete Dying Young," he parallels the victory celebration of an athlete carried on the shoulders of those celebrating to the funeral procession bearing that same athlete's coffin after he dies prematurely. The consolation, a combination of classical allusion and the influence of John Keats, is that the victor's laurel (the crown worn by victorious Greek and Roman athletes) "withers quicker than the rose," the symbol of love. The youth thus maintains his youth forever, like the lovers portrayed in Keats's "Ode on a Grecian Urn" (1820).

In Poem XXIII, young men come to Ludlow for a fair, seeking girls or drink. They derive from walks of life as diverse as Shropshire allows. Many, however, will adopt the life of a soldier, and some of these will not return from battle, nor "carry their looks or their truth to the grave." The narrator wishes there were "tokens to tell" those who will meet their end from those who will not. Then, at least, he could "wish them farewell/ and watch them depart on the way that they will not return." The consolation, such as it is, is that they will "carry back to the coiner the mintage of man" and another generation of handsome young men will arise.

Poem XXVII ironically merges the language of sport with that of the farm. The result approaches the bawdy, and it is from this humor that Housman derives the poem's irony. In the incrementally repetitive style of a folk ballad, the deceased narrator naively asks whether his team is plowing, then whether football is playing, then whether his girl is happy, and finally whether his friend is hearty. Following each stanza, the friend replies that his team still plows, that football goes on, that his girl is happy, and that the friend himself is quite well. One learns by the poem's end that the friend is cheering the dead man's sweetheart. The "team" refers variously to the dead narrator's friend and his girl, to his football chums, and to his field animals, and plowing assumes a sexual implication.

Poem XXXV describes a still, summer, Shropshire landscape. Though "sleepy with the flow of streams," the narrator hears the "steady drummer" and "soldiers marching, all to die." The bugles call, the fife replies, the scarlet files follow, and—as surely as he was born of woman—the narrator too will rise from his sleepy hill and follow.

Poem LIV marks the narrator's regret for his departed good friends, both "many a rose-lipt maiden/ and many a lightfoot lad." The boys lie where brooks are "too broad for leaping." The girls sleep in fields of faded roses.

In Poem LXII, Housman addresses himself as "Terence," after the Roman comic playwright Publius Terentius Afer.

Both poets treat the human comedy, and in this poem the narrator counsels that, just as a bit of poison taken daily brings immunity, so the lessons of serious poems, rather than drunken insensibility, do the soul good. Mithridates took his daily dose of poison and died old. So can readers profit from *A Shropshire Lad.*

Robert J. Forman

Further Reading

Bloom, Harold, ed. *A. E. Housman.* Philadelphia: Chelsea House, 2003. A short biography of Housman is followed by a selection of essays on his poetry and a discussion of homosexual subtext and "divided persona."

Efrati, Carol. *The Road of Danger, Guilt, and Shame: The Lonely Way of A. E. Housman.* Madison, N.J.: Fairleigh Dickinson University Press, 2002. Focuses on *A Shropshire Lad*, with particular attention to the homoerotic element in the work.

Graves, Richard Perceval. *A. E. Housman: The Scholar Poet.* New York: Charles Scribner's Sons, 1980. The standard biography. Examines Housman's career as a classical scholar and the allusive and metrical awareness this career brought to his poetry.

Leggett, B. J. *The Poetic Art of A. E. Housman: Theory and Practice.* Lincoln: University of Nebraska Press, 1978. A thorough examination of *A Shropshire Lad* with interesting citations to the critical essays of T. S. Eliot, Cecil Day Lewis, and Housman's own criticism.

Marlow, Norman. *A. E. Housman: Scholar and Poet.* Minneapolis: University of Minnesota Press, 1958. Remains the best source for Greek and Latin influences on Housman's poetry and draws parallels with classical English authors such as William Shakespeare and John Milton, as well as Victorian, Edwardian, and Pre-Raphaelite contemporaries.

Page, Norman. *A. E. Housman: A Critical Biography.* New York: Schocken, 1983. This useful examination of Housman's detachment concentrates on *A Shropshire Lad* as presenting a time and place that never really was. Argues that Housman continually adjusted much of his poetry to relate to ongoing events in his life.

Shroud for a Nightingale

Author: P. D. James (1920-   )
First published: 1971
Type of work: Novel
Type of plot: Detective and mystery
Time of plot: 1971
Locale: Heatheringfield, England

Principal characters:
MURIEL BEALE, inspector of nurse training schools for the General Nursing Council
SISTER ETHEL BRUMFETT, a plain nurse, second-in-command at Nightingale
MARY TAYLOR, matron of the Nightingale nursing school
ADAM DALGLIESH, chief superintendent, Scotland Yard
STEPHEN COURTNEY-BRIGGS, a wealthy surgeon-consultant
JOSEPHINE FALLON, an older student nurse
HEATHER PEARCE, a judgmental student nurse
SISTER MAVIS GEARING, a loquacious third senior nurse
CHARLES MASTERSON, a police inspector
THE BURT TWINS, student nurses
MORAG SMITH, a fearful maid at the school
MADELEINE GOODALE, a competent student nurse

The Story:

Miss Muriel Beale, the General Nursing Council's inspector of Nurse Training Schools, arrives at Nightingale House, a forbidding red-brick Victorian edifice. She is here to observe the third-year students' first teaching-session of the day, but instead she faces a murder. Authorities initially called the death a suicide, or a prank gone wrong.

Someone had substituted a cream-looking disinfectant for the warm milk used in a teaching session on feeding a patient by intragastric tube. Nurse Heather Pearce, the student subject, died a painful death. Sixteen days later, Josephine Fallon, the intended target of the deadly teaching session who had been excused that day because of influenza, is poisoned in her room after a quiet evening watching television. Again, the tightknit community would like to believe her death was a suicide, not a murder.

School surgeon-consultant Dr. Courtney-Briggs repeatedly troubles local police about the murders, so they call in an inspector, Adam Dalgliesh, and his team from Scotland Yard. Dalgliesh's method is to establish a work space in situ and begin interviewing witnesses, listening for lies, discovering relationships and discrepancies, checking motives and opportunity, and paying careful attention to time. A meticulous search uncovers the bottle of disinfectant that killed Nurse Pearce; it was found in the bushes near the nurses's apartments.

Police then discover that Sister Ethel Brumfett, present at neither death, had been called out the evening of the second death to help Courtney-Briggs with emergency surgery.

When she returned, the Burt twins were talking about taking Fallon some hot chocolate because her bedside light was on; they decided not to do so.

Courtney-Briggs remains reticent and actually misleads the police, claiming he had left the building immediately after surgery and had put a white scarf on a fallen tree to warn other pedestrians. Police also find out that Sister Mavis Gearing had invited Leonard Morris, the chief pharmacist of the hospital, to dinner; they had parted ways several minutes after midnight. Morris had seen Sister Brumfett leave the building, too, but testifies that at 12:17 A.M., he injured himself after stumbling over a fallen tree in the dark. Contrary to Courtney-Briggs's earlier claim, Morris had injured himself because the tree did not have a warning marker. A weakened pane of glass that had been blown out in the evening storm suggests an outside intruder, but the absence of other indicators turns the investigation on those who had been inside the building.

Later, a reenactment of the scene of the first murder shocks participants into recall, and Dalgliesh finds a discrepancy that narrows the window of opportunity for murder, suggesting who but not why: No one could have exchanged disinfectant for milk before a certain time. The housekeeper, Morag Smith, confesses to Dalgliesh that she had topped off the milk and added water to disguise her action. That bottle turned up in the nurses' refrigerator. The substitute bottle of disinfectant must have been left later, but before the teaching session. The Burt twins remembered during the reenactment that the bottle cap had indeed been different from the one on the bottle they had used earlier.

The next discovery is a bottle of nicotine that is used to control insects on rose bushes, a bottle that student nurse Madeleine Goodale, heir to Fallon's fortune, recalls joking about publicly in the past. Nicotine in a whiskey nightcap had killed Fallon, and the bottle had been hidden in the sand of a fire bucket.

The final pieces of the puzzle soon emerge. First, a patient Nurse Pearce had tended, Martin Dettinger, soon dies, but not before revealing, through feverish ramblings, that someone named Irmgard Grobel had been in his room. Second, Pearce had borrowed Fallon's library card to check out a book on war tribunals. Third, and finally, Sergeant Charles Masterson confirmed, by interviewing Dettinger's mother, that Grobel had been prosecuted but acquitted for war crimes. She also told Masterson of her connection to a hospital sister. The investigation leads to Dalgliesh nearly being killed by someone wielding a golf club; it also leads to a confession letter from Sister Brumfett, who ends up dead—her burned body found in a charred garden shed. Dalgliesh, however, had seen through the ruse and narrowed the investigation to two killers: Brumfett, who killed two women to protect her friend (Grobel) and to protect her power over that friend, and the nursing school's matron, Mary Taylor (also known as Irmgard Grobel), who killed her friend Brumfett to keep her own secret and win her own freedom.

With no evidence to provide a conviction for Brumfett's murderer and with little evidence that Brumfett had killed Pearce and Fallon, Dalgliesh cannot make any arrests. However, his pursuit eventually costs Mary her position and reputation, and her life. The next summer she kills herself with the same drug she had used to kill Brumfett.

Critical Evaluation:

The title *Shroud for a Nightingale*, seemingly suggestive of Florence Nightingale and the two dead student nurses of the novel, refers more particularly to Thomas Nightingale, the Victorian builder whose terrible abuse caused a servant girl to hang herself. Her suicide had been shrouded in secrecy for the modern students at the gothic Victorian structure Nightingale House. "Shroud" equally suggests burial garments and covering to protect, hide, or deceive. Thus, P. D. James evokes nursing, death, and dark secrets in a single phrase.

The novel has two chapters establishing two related murders, six chapters of investigation, and a ninth chapter, an epilogue, which sees justice finally complete. The story moves historically from Victorian evils to thirty-one victims of the Holocaust to modern murders, and it moves seasonally from the depths of winter to the warmth of summer.

As usual, James explores a closed community, the nursing world, which is claustrophobic, ingrown, and hierarchical, and a place of backbiting, gossip, secrets, bids for dominance, and pressures to conform. It also is a world of secret sexuality. Scotland Yard inspector Adam Dalgliesh finds the school's lack of privacy disturbing, as adult assignations (lovers brought in through back doors, movie theaters as "meeting" places) and private routines (a whiskey nightcap) are known to all. Thus, some purposefully use their sexuality to manipulate and control; Nurse Pearce lusts after proof of any level of wrongdoing to force others to confess and show repentance in ways she herself determines; Sister Brumfett revels in the secret power she holds over Matron Mary Taylor; and Dr. Courtney-Briggs seduces the young nurses he can dominate, and he misleads the police in hopes of blackmailing the matron to acquire the information only others seem to have.

Dalgliesh and his team painstakingly explore means, opportunity, and motive; and narrowing the time frame is vital. They conduct interviews and a stage a reenactment of the crimes. Adultery, abortion, homosexuality (female and male), and blackmail must be explored as well, and secrets must be exposed. Further searches reveal the means, with Dalgliesh intuiting that the missing library book Peirce had borrowed using Fallon's card, and the last patient she spent time with, will unravel the motive. However, the closer he comes to discovery, the greater the danger.

The great irony of James's novel is the similarity and attraction between Dalgliesh, who is compelled to justice, and Matron Mary, whose exemplary life cannot exonerate her cold-hearted decision to kill a woman who killed for her. Both the inspector and the matron lead restrained, self-controlled lives, dedicated to goals outside themselves. Dalgliesh finds Mary incredibly beautiful, her voice agreeable but authoritative, like his own. Readers enter her mind to some degree and hear her concern for the nurses whose welfare she protects. Even her war-crimes trial does not taint her, for she had been exonerated. James had created a certain sympathy for her as victim and survivor.

Mary and Dalgliesh are private people, bound by rules and obligations. She binds his wounds after Brumfett almost kills him. Even though Mary is aware that he thinks her guilty of murder, she insists that they are not so different. Their final conversation suggests the ambiguous nature of rules and of those who depend on rules ("We were only following orders," said the Nazis after World War II). Still, it is this close connection between the two that drives Dalgliesh to seek evidence where none exists; it makes him burn Mary's final letter of confession and suicide—the letter remains a private communication between them.

James does not provide easy answers to questions of evil and justice. Her characters are flawed, complicated human beings, well rounded and credible. She shows the high price of any criminal investigation on all involved, from maids to surgeons to high-ranking detectives. She details the medical examiner's ghoulish jokes and describes a lighted dead body—prepared by the police photographer—as a grotesque puppet, forcing readers to understand the desecration involved in any murder investigation. James looks with a cold, clinical eye on the realities of death, the pettiness of human behavior, and the closing of circles in tight communities.

Gina Macdonald and Andrew Macdonald

Further Reading

Barber, Lynn. "The Cautious Heart of P. D. James." *Vanity Fair*, March, 1993. Explores the then-seventy-year-old James as a titled, commercial literary success, a highly honored craftsperson who had extended the mystery genre.

Herbert, Rosemary. *The Fatal Art of Entertainment: Interviews with Mystery Writers*. New York: G. K. Hall, 1994. In this collection of interviews with writers of mystery fiction, James discusses her writing and personal habits, her choice of the mystery genre, and aspects of her private life.

Kotker, Joan G. "P. D. James's Adam Dalgliesh Series." In *In the Beginning: First Novels in Mystery Series*, edited by Mary Jean DeMarr. Bowling Green, Ohio: Bowling Green State University Popular Press, 1995. Kotker's analysis of the first novel in James's Dalgliesh series is important to understanding the entire series. Describes the evolution of the series from 1962 to the 1990's.

Macdonald, Andrew. "P. D. James." In *British Mystery and Thriller Writers Since 1960*, edited by Gina Macdonald. Farmington Hills, Mich.: Bruccoli Press, 2003. A thorough biographical study of James's life and works, including *Shroud for a Nightingale* and through *Death in Holy Orders*.

Priestman, Martin. "P. D. James and the Distinguished Thing." In *On Modern British Fiction*. New York: Oxford University Press, 2002. A lengthy essay placing James in the context of British literature. Argues that her undoubted skill is circumscribed by her genre choice.

Rowland, Susan. *From Agatha Christie to Ruth Rendell: British Women Writers in Detective and Crime Fiction*. New York: Palgrave Macmillan, 2003. A general study of detective and crime fiction written by women, with a section on the life and work of James. Also includes an interview with the novelist.

_____. "The Horror of Modernity and the Utopian Sublime: Gothic Villainy in P. D. James and Ruth Rendell." In *The Devil Himself: Villainy in Detective Fiction and Film*, edited by Stacy Gillis and Phillippa Gates. Westport, Conn.: Greenwood Press, 2002. Rowland focuses on several novels in the Dalgliesh series, including *Shroud for a Nightingale*, through the lens of the gothic. Provides a good introductory background to James.

The Sickness unto Death

Author: Søren Kierkegaard (1813-1855)
First published: Sygdommen til Døden: En christelig psychologisk Udvikling til Opbyggelse og Opvaekkelse, af Anti-Climacus, 1849 (English translation, 1941)
Type of work: Philosophy

Søren Kierkegaard gave *The Sickness unto Death* the subtitle "A Christian Psychological Exposition for Edification and Awakening," and he used the pseudonym Anti-Climacus when the book appeared. Walter Lowrie, in an introduction to his translation of this work, calls *The Sickness unto Death* "one of the most important productions of that most productive period" of Kierkegaard's life. The subtitle and the pseudonym reflect not the wit and eccentricity of a pedant but the conscience and intellect of a modest, though self-assured, philosopher in the service of God. The "sickness unto death" that Kierkegaard reveals in his psychological exposition—in so forceful a manner that the work has affected the course of modern philosophic thought—is the sickness of a self that wills to tear itself away from the Power that constituted it.

According to Kierkegaard, human beings are in despair, which they may not recognize, because they are always critically "sick unto death." For a spirit in such a condition, death is no escape; the sickness is "unto death" precisely because it is a despairing longing for death—not for extinction alone but for the experience of not being the self that one is. It is as if human beings were longing for the experience of death—an impossible experience because death, as death, is the end of all experience. Because the self is not content to be itself, because it is not content to relate itself to God, and because it cannot be satisfied with extinction, the result, in Kierkegaard's view, is "the sickness unto death."

Another way of understanding Kierkegaard's account of this dreadful malady of the spirit is through a consideration of what he means by health. Kierkegaard maintains that "to have a self, to be a self, is the greatest concession made to human beings, but at the same time it is eternity's demand upon them." Yet the self is a relation between the infinite and the finite, the temporal and the eternal, freedom and necessity—and as a relation, a synthesis, the self cannot exist before the synthesis is achieved. For that reason, there is some sense in which, as Kierkegaard claims at the outset, "human beings are not yet self": They have not achieved a synthesis with God, with the Power that constituted them. Sickness is this alienation; health is the elimination of despair, achieved when the self, recognizing its dependence on the Power that constituted it, wills itself to be itself.

Using language other than Kierkegaard's to explain the book's central thesis, it is possible to say that Kierkegaard is arguing that human beings, considered not as animal but as spirit, can realize themselves only by admitting that they become something worthy of the name "self" when they accept the whole of their condition. This acceptance of limitations, of opposing powers, even of God's eminence, is not resignation; it is a willingness to live "no matter what" and to be what human beings are in the world as it is.

It is tempting to make Kierkegaard's thesis broader than it is, to argue that the great Danish philosopher has more sense than to suppose that significant acts are possible only by relating the self to God. The term "God" is, however, not a convenient symbol for power; for Kierkegaard God is the power that relates itself to every spirit and makes possible, through the self's acknowledgment of that relation, the existence of every self.

Atheistic existentialists have found much that is helpful to them in Kierkegaard, but only by eliminating all references to God. Philosophers such as Jean-Paul Sartre are interested in arguing that in humans "existence precedes essence" and that only through action can human beings "make themselves" into some particular self. "Authentic" existence is not given to human beings, but they can create themselves through the lives they choose and live. For Kierkegaard also, health of the spirit is possible whenever people choose to be themselves—but only because to be themselves they must relate themselves to God. For Sartre, by contrast, health of the spirit consists not in relating to God but in recognizing the self's freedom from all such dependent relations. Sartre writes of the nausea and anguish that grip a human being who recognizes creative responsibility, but for Kierkegaard anguish is the condition of a self that is not yet a self, of a self that tries to escape from God and, consequently, from itself.

The despair that is the sickness unto death may take any one of three forms: It may be the despair of not being conscious of having a self, it may be the despair of not willing to be oneself, or it may be the despair of willing to be oneself. If human beings are in despair, how can they fail to be conscious of it? Kierkegaard asserts that those who are primarily sensuous can be in despair without being conscious of their condition. Those individuals "live in the sensuous categories agreeable/disagreeable, and say goodbye to truth." People who are sensuously happy will resent any attempt to take happiness from them; they refuse to acknowledge the despair that is deep within them. This form of despair—unconscious despair—is the most common. Since the sickness of not being willing to be oneself before God is sinful, it is important that all who are in the anguish of dread come to be conscious of that dread as the first step toward creating a self that is a synthesis. Kierkegaard defines sin as "before God, or with the conception of God, to be in despair at not willing to be oneself, or in despair at willing to be oneself." Both kinds of despair are eliminated by being willing, before God, to be oneself.

The formula that enables someone to escape the sin of dread is, at the same time, a definition of faith: "By relating itself to its own self and by willing to be itself, the self is grounded transparently in the Power that constituted it." The opposite of sin, according to Kierkegaard, is not virtue but faith.

To emphasize his conviction that the opposition of faith to sin is a Christian concept that is fundamental to all ethical concepts, Kierkegaard stresses the importance of the qualifying phrase "before God." Human beings come to have a reality, a self, "by existing directly in the sight of God," and because of this, their sin—not willing to be themselves before God—concerns God. Kierkegaard admits that the notion of people being invited to exist before God and of God's being concerned for them is unacceptable to many because it is both strange and demanding. Just as it would be puzzling and disturbing if an emperor were to invite a peasant to be his son-in-law, so it is puzzling and disturbing to suppose that God takes enough interest in individual people to wish to have them come to exist before him. Yet this is the Christian idea, Kierkegaard insists, and it is an idea that illuminates the entire area of ethical being and action.

The despair at not being willing to be oneself is called the despair of weakness, and the despair of willing to be oneself is called the despair of defiance. Such forms of despair result from a concern with self as if the self could exist by itself; this delusion is made possible by an absorption in matters that do not properly concern the spirit—matters of business or pleasure.

The sin of despair may give rise to new sins or to a continuation of sin. One may despair over one's sin, so concentrating attention on it as to make impossible the emergence of faith, or one may despair of being forgiven. In the latter case, sinners choose, out of weakness, to be sinners by rejecting the forgiveness that would enable them to be themselves before God. Finally, one may commit the sin of abandoning Christianity, of declaring it to be false. This sin is "offensive warfare," according to Kierkegaard, and it is a sin against the Holy Ghost.

Kierkegaard's conception of God is often difficult to grasp because he explains the relations between God and humanity in a dialectical way, claiming that one understands either God or humanity only by appreciating the subtle effects that the actions and attitudes of the one have on the other. An interesting feature of his account is his conception of God as a being who "can do no other" than make the possibility of human offense a part of the human condition. Dread must be possible for human beings because God is concerned to allow them the possibility of faith.

The influence of Kierkegaard in modern philosophy can be explained, paradoxically, by reference to the widespread loss of religious faith in later times. Dissatisfaction with unexamined creeds quickly leads to the rejection of those creeds. Human beings are then in anguish over the void they find before them, and the writers tell of "wastelands" and "lost generations." At such a time the existentialists are able to arouse interest by declaring that through action a person creates his or her self; the Christian existentialist turns to God as the factor to which a person must be related in order to be a self, while the atheistic existentialist makes virtues out of lucidity, courage, and action. Of the Christian existentialists, none has been more original and persuasive than Kierkegaard.

Further Reading

Caputo, John D. *How to Read Kierkegaard*. New York: W. W. Norton, 2008. Provides an accessible and concise overview of Kierkegaard's philosophy. Discusses the concepts in *The Sickness unto Death* and in the philosopher's other works.

Conway, Daniel W., and K. E. Gover, eds. *Søren Kierkegaard: Critical Assessments of Leading Philosophers*. New York: Routledge, 2002. Collection of sixty essays presents various interpretations of Kierkegaard's philosophy, including articles by philosophers Martin Buber, Emmanuel Levinas, and Jacques Derrida. Two essays focus on *The Sickness unto Death*: "Basic Despair in *The Sickness unto Death*," by Alastair Hannay, and "*The Sickness unto Death*: A Social Interpretation," by Stephen Crites.

Hannay, Alastair. *Kierkegaard and Philosophy: Selected Essays*. New York: Routledge, 2003. Collection of seventeen essays by Hannay, a leading Kierkegaard scholar, examining the ideas conveyed in Kierkegaard's philosophical works. Some of the essays also explore the ways in which other philosophers' ideas are related to those of Kierkegaard.

Heiss, Robert. *Hegel, Kierkegaard, Marx: Three Great Philosophers Whose Ideas Changed the Course of Civilization*. Translated by E. B. Garside. New York: Dell, 1975. Traces the development of dialectical thought and places Kierkegaard's perspective in that context. Provides an insightful discussion of *The Sickness unto Death* in the light of the dialectical philosophy.

Malantschuk, Gregor. *Kierkegaard's Thought*. Edited and translated by Howard V. Hong and Edna H. Hong. Princeton, N.J.: Princeton University Press, 1971. Informative work is helpful for understanding Kierkegaard's philosophical method, which is represented by *The Sickness unto Death*.

Mooney, Edward F., ed. *Ethics, Love, and Faith in Kierkegaard: Philosophical Engagements*. Bloomington: Indiana University Press, 2008. Collection of essays focuses on Kierkegaard's religious ideas, including discussions of his concepts of faith, love, melancholy and despair, personality and identity, and trust.

Sontag, Frederick. "Kierkegaard and the Search for a Self." In *Essays on Kierkegaard*, edited by Jerry H. Gill. Minneapolis: Burgess, 1969. Traces Kierkegaard's ideas regarding the relationship between the self and existence. Offers an interpretation of Kierkegaard's concept of the self that is particularly useful in understanding *The Sickness unto Death*.

Siddhartha

Author: Hermann Hesse (1877-1962)
First published: 1922 (English translation, 1951)
Type of work: Novel
Type of plot: Bildungsroman
Time of plot: 563?-483? B.C.E.
Locale: India

Principal characters:
SIDDHARTHA, the protagonist, son of a Brahmin
GOVINDA, Siddhartha's friend and follower
KAMALA, the courtesan
KAMASWAMI, the merchant
VASUDEVA, the ferryman
GOTAMA, the historical Buddha

The Story:

Siddhartha is a Brahmin's son. He grows up with his friend Govinda. Handsome, intelligent, and graceful, he is loved by everyone—his parents, friends, society, and especially Govinda. At an early age, he listens to the teachings of his learned father, masters the required Brahminical texts, performs all prescribed religious rites, and practices the art of meditation. Govinda admires his friend's superior intellect, strong determination, and high vocation. He knows that Siddhartha will be a great man someday, and he wants to be his friend and follower.

Siddhartha himself is, however, not happy. His soul is restless. Dissatisfied with what the scriptures tell him, he wants to experience knowledge himself. An inward voice compels him to leave the idyllic peace and harmony of his father's home and join the Samanas, a sect of ascetics who live a life of rigorous austerity in the forests. Govinda follows him like his shadow.

While living with the Samanas, Siddhartha learns many ways of losing the self. He learns how to mortify his flesh, to kill his senses, to suppress his ego, and to dwell at will in the bodies of dead birds and animals. He soon realizes that this flight from the self is only a temporary escape, not a permanent release from the life cycle. Still athirst for self-knowledge, he decides to leave the Samanas and goes with Govinda in search of Gotama Buddha.

Siddhartha meets Gotama Buddha in the Jetavana grove. He immediately recognizes that the Buddha attained the peace of Nirvana, which he is still seeking. He listens to Gotama's sermon on suffering, the cause of suffering, and the release from suffering through the Eightfold Path. He is impressed by Gotama's enlightened presence, but he is not convinced by his teachings. He concludes that, in order to find Nirvana, one must experience what the Buddha experienced. He therefore resolves to conquer his self, like the Buddha. Govinda becomes a follower of the Buddha, leaving Siddhartha to wander alone on his solitary path to self-conquest.

Carrying an indelible impression of Buddha's personal example in his mind, Siddhartha turns to himself and says, "I will learn from myself, be my own pupil; I will learn from myself the secret of Siddhartha." With this resolution, he experiences a new awakening and a sense of aloneness, for he decides to continue his quest alone and never to look back.

With this awakening, the world of appearance becomes palpable and real; it is no longer the veil of illusion that conceals the truth. Like a newborn child, he looks at the world with great wonder and curiosity. During the night, as he sleeps in a ferryman's hut beside the river, he has a strange dream in which he embraces and kisses Govinda, but Govinda turns into a woman. For the first time he feels the stirrings of sexual awakening.

He leaves the river and reaches a large town, where he falls in love with a famous courtesan, Kamala. Kamala tells him that he can gain her love only after he earns wealth, power, and prestige, and to help him acquire these things she introduces him to a rich merchant, Kamaswami. With Kamaswami as his instructor in acquiring wealth and Kamala as his teacher in the art of love, Siddhartha begins to live in excess and surrenders himself to the world of senses, immersing every cell of his being into desire and carnal pleasure.

One night Siddhartha has a dream that Kamala's rare songbird dies in its golden cage and that he takes it out and throws it away on the road. Suddenly, he feels sad, as if he threw away the most valuable thing in his life. The next day, he leaves Kamala and his life of sensual experience and disappears into the forest.

During his wanderings through the forest, he comes back to the river and yearns to be submerged in death. As he is about to commit suicide, suddenly he hears the holy sound "Om" coming from the depths of his inner being and he recognizes the folly of his action. The holy sound awakens his slumbering soul, and he remembers all that he forgot. Murmuring Om, he sinks into a deep sleep.

On awakening from his long sleep, he finds Govinda watching over him, and he feels happy once again. It seems to him that the river has a special message for him. He therefore wants to listen to the river and learn from it. To understand the river and its secrets, he decides to remain by the river and become the helper of the old ferryman, Vasudeva. Siddhartha learns deep secrets from the river. He learns that there is no such thing as time past or future. There is only the present, just as the water of the river is in a state of continuous flux and yet it is everywhere at the same time, at its source and in the ocean, always the same. The voice of the river is for him "the voice of life, the voice of Being, of perpetual Becoming."

Many years pass. One day Kamala arrives with some followers of the Buddha. She dies in Siddhartha's arms and leaves with him their son, who was born after his disappearance. Once again, Siddhartha experiences the pangs of love and loses his benign calm. He tries to win the boy's affection and to keep him, but the son runs away, rebelling against him as he himself rebelled against his father years before. Vasudeva consoles Siddhartha in his suffering, but the river seems to laugh at his pain. Vasudeva tells him to listen to the river and to absorb its lesson. Siddhartha tries to listen more intently and discovers the interconnectedness of all life. From Vasudeva, as from the river, he learns about the unity of all things. After Vasudeva's death, he becomes the ferryman, radiant and benign like his mentor, his face shining with the serenity of the inner awareness of the unity of all things.

Hearing about the old ferryman, Govinda comes to the river to see him. When he looks at the face of Siddhartha, he is reminded of the benign and peaceful smile of the Buddha. At Siddhartha's request, when Govinda kisses him on the forehead, he no longer sees the face of his friend Siddhartha. Instead he sees the multiplicity of all life-forms in various stages of development, even the gods, reflected in his unchanging countenance. He recognizes then that, like the Buddha, Siddhartha attained perfect enlightenment and wisdom. In great reverence and humility, Govinda bows his head before his old friend and tears trickle down his cheeks.

Critical Evaluation:

One of the major twentieth century writers and an important cultural and intellectual force, Hermann Hesse was awarded the Nobel Prize in Literature in 1946 for his achievement as a novelist, particularly for his masterpiece, *Das Glasperlenspiel: Versuch einer Lebensbeschreibung des Magister Ludi Josef Knecht samt Knechts hinterlassenen Schriften* (1943; *Magister Ludi*, 1949; also *The Glass Bead Game*, 1969). Hesse stated, "All the prose works of fiction I have written are biographies of souls." *Siddhartha*, his most widely read work of fiction, is a biography of the soul in the essential sense of the term. It evokes the magical realm of the spirit in exploring the protagonist's quest for self-knowledge and the unity of being.

Hesse called *Siddhartha* "an Indic Poem." Of all his fictional works, it is undoubtedly the one most impregnated with Indian religion and philosophy. Hesse himself unequivocally acknowledged his long-standing interest in India and his preoccupation with Hinduism, Buddhism, Vedanta, and Yoga. "More than half of my life," he stated, "I tried to come to an understanding of the Indian view of Life." India was his family's spiritual homeland for two generations, and he himself undertook a voyage to India in 1911 "to go back into that source of life where everything had begun and which signified the Oneness of all phenomenon." *Siddhartha* was an artistic expression of his understanding of the Indian view of life, modified by his own romantic vision.

Using the historical Buddha's life as a framework of his fictional narrative, Hesse appropriated Buddha's given name Siddhartha for his mythical hero and endowed him with many qualities of the Enlightened One. However, he presented them as two separate figures in the novel and used the encounter between them as a catalyst to reinforce his romantic concept of the bildungsroman. Hesse believed that all knowledge must come from personal experience rather than from formal training and doctrinaire teaching. Siddhartha's rejection of the teachings of Buddha served as a turning point in his quest, fortifying his conviction that, to attain the state of perfect enlightenment, he, too, must extinguish his ego and merge with the unity underlying the universe. That he attains his supreme destiny, Nirvana, through pure disinterested love and self-surrender is confirmed by the novel's conclusion.

Because *Siddhartha* deals with themes of initiation and search for the self and focuses on the emotional, intellectual, psychological, and spiritual development of the protagonist, it can be viewed as a bildungsroman, a novel of growth and education. All the major characters, episodes, and symbols in the novel serve as important milestones in Siddhartha's journey toward self-realization.

The predominant, all-inclusive symbol in the novel is the river. The river represents the continuum of life and time, the eternal process of being and becoming, and the constant flux in nature. It defines, divides, entwines, and merges the transitions in Siddhartha's journey and ultimately manifests the cosmic vision of totality and timelessness that he attains at the end of his quest. Siddhartha's vision on the riverbank leads to intuitive wisdom.

Though *Siddhartha*, like all great literature, has a timeless dimension, it had a profound impact on the youth culture in the United States from the 1950's to the 1970's. Its gospel of disinterested love appealed to the American flower children, as its emphasis on self-realization, integration, and wholeness attracted many alienated youth to Eastern religions and philosophies. Many Western youth were in rebellion against the institutionalization, growing materialism, and fragmented, scientific worldview of their own society. Written in a lucid, poetic, rhythmical, symbolic, and dignified style, *Siddhartha* presents the spiritual heritage of the East to the West. It came to be recognized as an important landmark in the history of East-West literary relations.

Chaman L. Sahni

Further Reading

Bishop, Paul. "Hermann Hesse and the Weimar Republic." In *German Novelists of the Weimar Republic: Intersections of Literature and Politics*, edited by Karl Leydecker. Rochester, N.Y.: Camden House, 2006. Hesse is one of the twelve German writers whose work is analyzed in this study of Weimar Republic literature. The essays focus on the authors' response to the political, social, and economic instability of the era.

Boulby, Mark. *Hermann Hesse: His Mind and Art*. Ithaca, N.Y.: Cornell University Press, 1967. Scholarly study of the major novels of Hesse. The chapter on *Siddhartha* provides illuminating information on Hesse's Orientalism. Discusses the work "in the context of Hesse's movement away from Buddhism" and views it as the culminating point of his art as a novelist.

Cornils, Ingo, ed. *A Companion to the Works of Hermann Hesse*. Rochester, N.Y.: Camden House, 2009. Collection of essays, including examinations of *Siddhartha*; Hesse's interest in psychoanalysis, music, and Eastern philosophy; the development of his political views; and the influence of painting on his writing.

Field, G. W. *Hermann Hesse*. Boston: Twayne, 1970. Contains a critical and analytical chapter on *Siddhartha*.

MacFarlane, Scott. "*Siddhartha* (1922): The Spiritual Quest." In *The Hippie Narrative: A Literary Perspective on the Counterculture*. Jefferson, N.C.: McFarland, 2007. A constructivist view of the novel, focusing on how it reflected the zeitgeist of the hippie counterculture.

Otten, Anna, ed. *Hesse Companion*. Albuquerque: University of New Mexico Press, 1977. Eight essays on Hesse's work by various scholars. Theodore Ziolkowski's essay, "*Siddhartha*: The Landscape of the Soul," gives an excellent critical analysis of the novel's Eastern background, plot structure, symbolism, and epiphany. Includes a useful glossary and a bibliography of secondary sources in English.

Timpe, Eugene E. "Hesse's *Siddhartha* and the *Bhagavad Gita*." *Comparative Literature* 10 (1969): 421-426. Demonstrates that Hesse was deeply influenced by the *Bhagavad Gita* (c. first or second century C.E.) when he wrote his book and that Siddhartha's quest for self-realization follows the path suggested by the *Bhagavad Gita*.

Tusken, Lewis W. *Understanding Hermann Hesse: The Man, His Myth, His Metaphor*. Columbia: University of South Carolina Press, 1998. Analyzes nine novels, including *Siddhartha*, pointing out their common themes, motifs, images, and how they incorporate events in Hesse's life and reflect his quest for self-discovery.

Zipes, Jack. "Hermann Hesse's Fairy Tales and the Pursuit of Home." In *When Dreams Came True: Classical Fairy Tales and Their Tradition*. 2d ed. New York: Routledge, 2007. Zipes examines how Hesse used the form of the fairy tale in his own writing, discussing some of the fantasy-like elements in Hesse's fiction.

The Siege of Rhodes

Author: Sir William Davenant (1606-1668)
First produced: Part 1, 1656; part 2, 1659; first published, 1663
Type of work: Drama
Type of plot: Historical
Time of plot: 1522
Locale: Fortress at Rhodes and the nearby coast of Caria

Principal characters:
SOLYMAN II, THE MAGNIFICENT, sultan of the Ottoman Empire
PIRRHUS, the general in charge of the Persian army before the arrival of Solyman
VILLERIUS, PHILIP VILLIERS DE L'ISLE ADAM, commander of the fortress at Rhodes
ALPHONSO, a Sicilian duke
IANTHE, Alphonso's wife
ROXOLANA, Solyman's wife

The Story:

In the fortress at Rhodes, seven bastions are maintained by eight Christian nations as united in opposition to the Turks as were the earlier Crusaders. Villerius, a Knight of St. John in supreme command of those forces, is successfully defending the fort from Solyman's assault. Alphonso, the most vigorous among those defending the Cross from the Crescent, considers this battle Christendom's last stand against the infidel. Ianthe, his bride of but a few months, first aids the war effort by sacrificing her jewels to buy arms, and then she decides to become one of history's termagants, or Amazons, and fight by the side of her husband. In her attempt to join him, she is captured by the Turks. Two days later she is released by order of the sultan as a mark of respect to her courage and her virtue.

In the battle that follows, Alphonso, mad with jealousy because he believes that his wife was unfaithful to him with the Turkish ruler, fights with the fierceness of many men. Roxolana, Solyman's wife, also becomes jealous, so highly is Ianthe praised by her husband. The battle is fought so ferociously, especially by the English, that the infidels are repulsed, forcing the sultan to resort to siege tactics. Honor is preserved in love and in battle by participants on the two sides of the fort.

Famine soon becomes a threat to the beleaguered garrison. While the leaders debate strategy, the populace demands that Ianthe sue for peace. Alphonso, recovered from his jealousy, refuses to allow Ianthe to be used as a hostage, but she, deciding otherwise in order to save her husband and the garrison from slow starvation, steals secretly away to the sultan's camp. Further misunderstanding ensues when Roxolana learns that Ianthe is in the sultan's tent. In her jealousy she sends a note to the aggrieved warrior-husband, word that causes the entire garrison to deplore the sacrifice of virtuous Ianthe to the supposed lust of Solyman. Ianthe's dis-

play of virtue, however, wins over the sultana, who is fearful only that her son will not succeed to the throne. Solyman declares that his intentions are always honorable, in love as well as in war.

As the palace of Villerius is set afire at the height of the siege, a last abortive attack is made by the Christians in order to rescue Ianthe. The two young lovers are secretly united by Roxolana. Her husband, moved as much by his wife's compassion for the young couple as by their own virtue and devotion, sends both back to Rhodes, leaving the terms of the surrender entirely to Ianthe's discretion. History has it that a general amnesty ensued and that all the Knights of St. John were allowed free egress from Rhodes.

Critical Evaluation:

The Siege of Rhodes was first performed in London in 1656, probably in early September, during the regime of Oliver Cromwell, the great Parliamentarian general who defeated the forces of King Charles I in the English civil war. Cromwell was said to have enjoyed stage plays, but his Puritan supporters most certainly did not. In fact, some years before Cromwell came to power, pressure from conservative religious factions led Parliament to pass an act closing London theaters and prohibiting the public performance of all "Spectacles of Pleasure." William Davenant was thus forced to present *The Siege of Rhodes* on a cramped, makeshift stage in the rear of Rutland House, the private home where he was living at the time. As a further means of avoiding government sanction, Davenant published his play a month before it was performed, with a title page announcing it as "A Representation by the Art of Prospective in Scenes, and the Story Sung in Recitative Music." Thus a drama was passed off as a type of dull recital, a spectacle, perhaps, but without pleasure. Davenant's strategy seems to have worked, for *The Siege of Rhodes* proved a popular success and performances continued without official interference.

Over the next seven years, which saw Cromwell's death and the restoration of monarchy in the person of Charles II, Davenant was an incredibly busy figure in the London theater world. During this period of intense activity, his best-known play underwent a series of complex, confusing, and seldom-discussed transformations, making it difficult even for scholars of the period to know exactly to which play the title *The Siege of Rhodes* refers in any given context.

These transformations began in 1659, when the original was reprinted (with several changes and additions) and was staged at the Cock-Pit Theatre together with a second play, a continuation of the first, titled *The Siege of Rhodes, Part II*. Following the Restoration in 1660, the ban on theatrical entertainments was completely lifted and Davenant became manager of the duke of York's acting company and owner-manager of the new playhouse in Lincoln's Inn Fields. On opening night in June of 1661, *The Siege of Rhodes, Part I* was revived and was presented in alternate performances for some eleven days with part 2. To add to the confusion, part 1 and part 2 were printed together in 1663, with yet more changes. Existing records indicate no performances of either play after 1677.

In spite of its confusing history, however, and in spite of the fact that it is a play that is seldom read and never performed, *The Siege of Rhodes* will always occupy an important place in any account of the Restoration theater. The reasons for this, oddly enough, have virtually nothing to do with the play's literary merits. *The Siege of Rhodes*, rather, will always be known as a play of "firsts": It was the first English play in which movable scenery was employed and the first English play in which a woman appeared on stage playing a female role. It was the first "heroic" play in English as well as England's first opera. The play's music has been lost and the question of which lines were sung in the manner of operatic arias and which recited remains open.

Davenant based the events of his play on the 1522 siege of Rhodes by the forces of Sulieman the Magnificent, sultan of the Ottoman Empire from 1520 to 1566. Davenant's principal source for these events was Richard Knolle's *The Generall Historie of the Turkes* (1603), which gives an inspiring account of the six-month siege in which five thousand Christian defenders (including an international force of six hundred Knights of St. John) heroically resisted a combined Turkish force numbering more than two hundred thousand before finally surrendering. Davenant seems also to have been influenced by several French writers, in particular Madeline de Scudéry. Her work was quite probably a source for both the romantic elements and the general heroic tone given character and action in the play.

Providing the dramatic cornerstone of both parts of *The Siege of Rhodes* is the story of Alphonso, a young Christian nobleman visiting Rhodes who remains to defend the city, and his wife of only a few months, Ianthe, who sails to Rhodes to join her husband. Ianthe's two vessels are captured by the Turkish fleet, and Ianthe is brought to Solyman. Duly impressed by Ianthe's beauty, courage, and virtue, the Turkish sultan orders the release of her ships and commands that she be safely escorted to Rhodes. In the revised version of part 1, the character of Roxolana, Solyman's wife, is introduced, allowing Davenant to develop the theme of jealousy. Part 1 ends somewhat inconclusively, with Alphonso and Ianthe reunited, but with a great battle raging in the background. As a result of the physical restrictions of the original Rutland House stage, the battle was suggested by a painted scene of a "general Assault" and probably—as indicated by stage directions in part 2—by a "Symphony expressing a Battail." In part 2, Davenant continues the essential action, with the siege again serving as background to the Alphonso-Ianthe love story, while bringing into sharper focus the conflict between love and honor that became typical of "heroic" drama. The role of Roxolana is greatly expanded, and she and Ianthe are brought together on stage, with Ianthe emerging even more dramatically as an example of the redemptive power of Christian virtue. Part 2 ends with the final reuniting of Alphonso and Ianthe and with Solyman's gracious and noble treatment of the defeated Christians.

Coming to any final judgment of *The Siege of Rhodes* is made difficult by time and circumstance. On the page, Davenant's language seems hopelessly turgid, even by seventeenth century standards, and his characters are at best one-dimensional contrivances. However, contemporary accounts make clear how thoroughly Restoration audiences enjoyed *The Siege of Rhodes*, and one can readily imagine how a modern audience might enjoy the pomp, spectacle, and music of Davenant's play. The play offers much theatrical entertainment.

"Critical Evaluation" by Michael Stuprich

Further Reading

Birchwood, Matthew. "Turning to the Turk: Collaboration and Conversion in William Davenant's *The Siege of Rhodes*." In *Staging Islam in England: Drama and Culture, 1640-1685*. Cambridge, Mass.: D. S. Brewer, 2007. Examines the representation of Islamic characters in *The*

Siege of Rhodes and other seventeenth century English dramas. Birchwood argues that during the period from 1640 to 1685, the depiction of "the Turk" evolved from an archetype of treachery to a more complex figure.

Bordinat, Philip, and Sophia B. Blaydes. *Sir William Davenant*. Boston: Twayne, 1981. One of the best places to begin a study of Davenant and his work. An account of Davenant's life and times is followed by discussions of his major works. Includes annotated bibliography.

Edmond, Mary. *Rare Sir William Davenant*. New York: St. Martin's Press, 1987. Besides playing a pivotal role in the re-establishment of the London theater following the English civil war, Davenant led a fascinating, multifaceted life. Edmond's biography, the first since the 1930's, provides a solid account of that life as well as a useful discussion of *The Siege of Rhodes*.

Hedback, Ann-Mari, ed. Introduction to *The Siege of Rhodes*, by Sir William Davenant. Uppsala, Sweden: University of Uppsala, 1973. A modern edition of *The Siege of Rhodes*. The textual scholarship is impeccably thorough, and the introduction provides the finest available discussion of the play.

Kroll, Richard. "William Davenant and John Dryden." In *A Companion to Restoration Drama*, edited by Susan J. Owen. Malden, Mass.: Blackwell, 2001. Kroll examines *The Siege of Rhodes* and other plays by Davenant. Other references to this play and to Davenant throughout this collection of essays on Restoration drama are listed in the index.

Powell, Jocelyn. *Restoration Theatre Production*. London: Routledge & Kegan Paul, 1984. A delightful study of Restoration drama. Contains a brief but very helpful discussion of *The Siege of Rhodes*.

Summers, Montague. *The Playhouse of Pepys*. London: Kegan Paul, Trench, Trubner, 1935. A chapter on Davenant includes a helpful account of *The Siege of Rhodes*.

The Sign in Sidney Brustein's Window

Author: Lorraine Hansberry (1930-1965)
First produced: 1964; first published, 1965
Type of work: Drama
Type of plot: Social realism and problem play
Time of plot: 1964
Locale: Greenwich Village, New York

Principal characters:
SIDNEY BRUSTEIN, a Jewish intellectual and the owner of a weekly newspaper
IRIS BRUSTEIN, his wife, a waitress and an aspiring actor
ALTON SCALES, his friend and part-time employee
MAVIS BRYSON, Iris's older sister
GLORIA PARODUS, Iris and Mavis's younger sister
DAVID RAGIN, a playwright and the Brustein's neighbor
WALLY O'HARA, a lawyer and a friend of Sidney

The Story:

Sidney Brustein and his friend Alton Scales are lugging wire racks with drinking glasses—salvage from the failure of Sidney's folk-music coffee house—around the Brustein's apartment—the site of Sidney's newspaper office. Later, Sidney argues with his wife, Iris, when he belatedly reveals to her his purchase on credit of a weekly local newspaper. The couple had earlier discussed Iris's continued desire to be an actor and her continuing psychoanalysis. Alton returns to the apartment with Wally O'Hara, a lawyer who is trying to persuade his friend Sidney to back his reformist campaign for office. Sidney, however, had earlier decided to withdraw from political concerns, so he rejects placing O'Hara's political poster in his apartment window; still, he is drawn to the poster, despite Iris's warning not to get involved.

The following week, Alton, Sidney, and a local artist are discussing the art and content for the front page of Sidney's weekly paper. The paper will now include political content as well. After the meeting, Alton and Sidney put up a banner for the reform party in the apartment window. Alton confirms news of his having asked Iris's sister Gloria to marry him. The news came to Iris in the form of a letter from Gloria, whom Sidney and Iris first identify as a traveling high-fashion model.

Sidney has a sharp exchange with Iris, which, as usual, belittles her intellect and her acting abilities. They also discuss the proposed front-page art for the newspaper. After Iris's set speech about the difficulty of an actress's life, her older sister, Mavis, unexpectedly arrives to deliver a fashionable dress she has bought for Iris. Mavis bemoans Gloria's life and lack of a husband. Sidney and Iris argue about sex in society—reminding themselves that Gloria is not a high-fashion model but a high-priced prostitute, as the rest of the family knows. Mavis is shocked that spousal prospects in Sidney's circle of friends include an African American (Alton) and a gay man (David Ragin).

David, a playwright and a neighbor of the Brusteins, comes to the Brustein apartment to ask for writing supplies. He then gets into an argument with Sidney about modern drama; Sidney thinks it is apolitical. David stays for dinner. Alton arrives with dinner extras then ends up exchanging insults with David. Alton is introduced for shock value to Mavis, who then leaves, justifiably criticizing the intellectual group's lack of compassion. What began as a communal dinner breaks up because Alton departs in antipathy to David. Then David departs because of Sidney's analysis of his previous argument with David. Iris warns that her arguments with Sidney have changed and now threaten the marriage; Sidney, too, leaves.

At dawn the next day, Sidney sits on a staircase landing above his apartment and is playing the banjo. He visualizes his fantasy of being with Iris in the mountains. Iris reminds him that she enjoys urban life and does not want to return to her rural roots, then tells Sidney to move the car because of the parking restrictions on Tuesdays.

Weeks later, Sidney and O'Hara are arriving at the apartment with campaign leaflets, optimistic about the unexpected upturn in O'Hara's election chances. David comes over with newspapers that praise him and his play. Sidney and Iris congratulate David, but Sidney again argues about the philosophy of disengagement in David's play and in modern drama generally. Iris complains to Sidney about all the political telephoning and election leaflets, while David expresses doubts about the worth of the efforts; he then leaves the apartment.

Iris reveals that she has arranged to attend, by herself, a party of shallow but successful theater folk, leading to another argument about Sidney's and Iris's interests. Sidney, too, has a jealous suspicion that Iris could have a romantic liaison with one of the partygoers. After Iris leaves, Sidney calls upstairs to David and, while David is meditating on his changed life through celebrity, asks the young dramatist to write a part in his next play for Iris. David is disgusted by the request to prostitute his art. He criticizes the childishness of Sidney and O'Hara's politics and then leaves after his personality and plays are insulted by O'Hara.

Sidney's problems with Iris lead to an ulcer attack, so Sidney asks O'Hara to get his tranquilizing medication. Sidney then contrasts the ancients' "sword" of righteousness—a yardstick Sidney has picked up—with the moderns' reliance on pills.

Several weeks later, Sidney exults in O'Hara's victory, his own newspaper's triumph over corrupt advertisers (one of whom he has just talked to on the telephone), and the nihilistic philosophy of David. However, Alton is bleak, having discovered that Iris and Sidney did not tell him the truth about Gloria, and he is angry, explaining that he is forced to reconsider his proposal of marriage to Gloria because of the shame among African Americans with the concept of commodity (Gloria, as a prostitute, is a sex commodity). He gives Sidney a note to give to Gloria, and leaves the apartment.

Mavis visits the apartment and congratulates Sidney on the election. She gives him a monetary reward. As the conversation proceeds, Mavis reveals a view of the sisters' father that is very different from that of Iris and is also far beyond stereotypically bourgeois. She recites from memory ancient Greek from Euripides' *Medea*, discloses the change of the family surname to reflect a component of ancient Greek drama, and reveals her years of struggle with the virtual bigamy of her husband, Fred, an apparent pillar of society. She then leaves.

Iris arrives home and mentions that Gloria is on her way over. She also defends her radically altered appearance, saying she has changed because of her acting career in television commercials. Though realizing the falsity of the advertising world, Iris notes that the election, too, is false, since O'Hara has been coopted by the opposing side's interests. She adds that Sidney's image of her is false as well. She leaves the apartment, but not before saying that she is leaving Sidney.

Hours later, Sidney is consuming alcohol, aggravating the pain of his ulcer. Gloria arrives at the apartment. Gloria asks him what is wrong, and Sidney sorrowfully answers that not only was the election a sham; he has lost Iris, too. David comes over to visit, and Sidney soon declares agreement with David's nihilism. Gloria is offended by David's remarks about prostitution, and his smug analysis of prostitutes. She then discusses the harsh realities of prostitution, including physical injury, but is optimistic about her rejection of drugs and her upcoming marriage with Alton. She rages when learning of Alton's decision not to marry her.

The three recite a kind of liturgy of nihilism and media criticism, and analyze the importance of a father's values for his children. As Sidney dozes, David makes an indecent proposal to Gloria, requesting that she make a voyeuristic threesome to sexually satisfy an aristocratic male friend waiting upstairs in David's apartment. Bitterly cynical, Gloria accepts and David leaves. However, she changes her mind on the stairs, looks meaningfully at the bottle of narcotic pills in her hand, and heads toward the bathroom to commit suicide, mentioning her father.

Early the next morning, in the aftermath of Gloria's suicide, a detective asks Iris and Sidney details about Gloria, including her occupation. The detective says that an inquest will be required. O'Hara comes to the apartment, briefly commiserates, and then attempts, with limited success, to justify being coopted by the corrupt opposition. Sidney assumes, and O'Hara confirms, that if Sidney's newspaper exposes the corruption, the newspaper will be shut down. O'Hara leaves, saying that he would like to send flowers for Gloria's funeral. He looks at the sign in Sidney's apartment window, which now has accumulated ironic meaning.

Later, Iris indicates some willingness to return home, presumably with changes in Sidney's ideas and behavior. Sidney says they can discuss it, but that in the meantime, they both need to yield to sorrow so that tomorrow they can make something strong out of it.

Critical Evaluation:

The banner remaining in the apartment window in Lorraine Hansberry's play *The Sign in Sidney Brustein's Window* symbolizes the conflicts between engagement and disengagement in social action and between appearances and realities in politics. Idealist Sidney Brustein cannot resist engaging in an attempt to better the world, but the banner in his window deceives because the politician it promotes is just another corrupt compromiser.

Furthermore, Sidney's yardstick-as-sword has multiple meanings: measuring people and deeds, the need for action in commitment, and the admirability of ancient heroes, such as the Maccabees in Sidney's Jewish heritage. His breaking of the yardstick indicates his symbolic acknowledgment of defeat.

Iris Brustein's dinner table symbolizes the gathering of segments of society often at odds with the Caucasian middle class—Jew, African American, gay, playwright, bookstore worker, waitress, intellectual. However, while temporarily united against the bourgeoisie, the group cannot cohere and dissolves in its own internal dissensions, including male versus female. Iris's name suggests the rainbow of not only her heritage but also of American society; she needs to work for unity and against selfish division. The rainbow of characters and concerns in the play makes its range even greater than it does in Hansberry's play *A Raisin in the Sun* (pr., pb. 1959).

The front-page art of the newspaper is one of several symbols for art that contribute a metapoetic element of ideas about art within an art work. The issue of whether art should, or does, deal with social and political issues connects this subject with the play's political content. Repeatedly, Sidney, Iris, Alton, David, and O'Hara allude to famous writers of world literature, from classic to contemporary. Even Mavis refers to and quotes Euripides and suggests the connection between the Parodus family and ancient Greek drama—members of the Chorus who comment on but rarely affect the plot. When referring to O'Hara as the deus ex machina, Sidney melds art and politics in a pun, because O'Hara is a minor god produced by a political machine, ironically paralleling an amoral supernatural force reaching down to the mortal world at the end of an ancient Greek play.

Women's concerns and romantic love are focused in the symbolism of Iris's hair (a motif to be found also in Hansberry's *A Raisin in the Sun*). Iris lets her hair grow long only to please Sidney, and she is vexed when he undoes it when it is pulled up, partly because of Sidney's pastoral dream forced on Iris. After her hair is cut, styled, and colored, Iris asserts herself; but she also is stained by the duplicity of commercialism and advertising. Whether Sidney and Iris can reunite remains open; certainly Sidney needs to be less of a demanding and demeaning father figure and more of an equal partner in the relationship.

Norman Prinsky

Further Reading

Adler, Thomas P. *American Drama, 1940-1960: A Critical History.* New York: Twayne, 1994. Chapter 9, on Hansberry and her work, focuses on the theme of art, especially literature, in *The Sign in Sidney Brustein's Window*.

Bigsby, C. W. E. *Confrontation and Commitment: A Study of Contemporary American Drama, 1959-1966.* Columbia: University of Missouri Press, 1968. Chapter 9 is an eighteen-page survey of Hansberry's plays, noting that *The Sign in Sidney Brustein's Window* examines issues of art as well as political liberalism.

Braine, John. "An Appreciation: Sidney Brustein—A 'Great Play'—No Other Word Is Possible." In *"A Raisin in the Sun" and "The Sign in Sidney Brustein's Window"* by Lorraine Hansberry. Edited by Robert Nemiroff. New York: New American Library, 1987. This expanded twenty-fifth anniversary edition of the drama argues that contemporary New York drama critics had missed the greatness of the play in its depth and range.

Carter, Steven R. *Hansberry's Drama: Commitment Amid Complexity.* New York: Meridian, 1993. Chapter 4 analyzes the play in detail, focusing on Hansberry's artistry in creating Sidney as a more complex character than found in *A Raisin in the Sun*.

Cheney, Anne. *Lorraine Hansberry*. Boston: Twayne, 1984. Chapter 2, which examines *The Sign in Sidney Brustein's Window*, is organized by analysis of the plot, major characters or character groups, the political content, and the stage history.

Effiong, Philip U. *In Search of a Model for African American Drama: A Study of Selected Plays by Lorraine Hansberry, Amiri Baraka, and Ntozake Shange*. Lanham, Md.: University Press of America, 2000. A study of the plays of three prominent African Americans, including Hansberry. Includes a bibliography and an index.

Leeson, Richard M. *Lorraine Hansberry: A Research and Production Sourcebook*. Westport, Conn.: Greenwood Press, 1997. This sourcebook includes a good listing with excerpts of the contemporary reviews of *The Sign in Sidney Brustein's Window*.

Scheader, Catherine. *Lorraine Hansberry: A Playwright and Voice of Justice*. Springfield, N.J.: Enslow, 1998. A biography that examines Hansberry's dual roles as civil rights advocate and dramatist. Includes a bibliography and an index.

Wilkerson, Margaret. "Lorraine Hansberry: Artist, Activist, Feminist." In *Women in American Theatre*, edited by Helen Krich Chinoy and Linda Walsh Jenkins. Rev. ed. New York: Theatre Communications Group, 2006. Hansberry's life and work are discussed as part of a collection of interviews and essays on women in American theater. Also examines topics such as actors and acting, playwrights and writing, nontraditional women's careers, and feminist theater.

The Sign of Four

Author: Sir Arthur Conan Doyle (1859-1930)
First published: 1890
Type of work: Novel
Type of plot: Mystery
Time of plot: 1888
Locale: London

Principal characters:
SHERLOCK HOLMES, a crime investigator
DR. JOHN WATSON, his friend
MARY MORSTAN, a client
THADDEUS SHOLTO, an art collector
JONATHAN SMALL, an escaped convict

The Story:

Miss Mary Morstan goes to Sherlock Holmes and Dr. Watson with something of a mystery. Her father, formerly an officer in an Indian regiment, sent her word from London that she was to meet him at a certain hotel. When she kept the appointment, her father failed to appear, and he has not been heard from in the ten years elapsed since that time. His only known friend in England was Major Sholto, a brother officer, but that gentleman disclaimed any knowledge of Morstan's presence in London. For the past six years, Mary has received one large and valuable pearl on a certain date each year. That morning, she received a note asking her to meet the writer at a certain spot near a theater. She is to bring two friends if she likes, but not the police. Apprehensive and puzzled, she turns to Holmes for help.

Holmes and Dr. Watson eagerly accept the assignment, Holmes from a need for excitement, and Dr. Watson from a newly kindled love for the young girl. When the three people keep the appointment at the theater, they are met by a coachman who drives them some distance and then deposits them in front of a house in a long row of new, dreary houses of the same design. Inside they are met by Dr. Thaddeus Sholto, the son of Major Sholto, who tells them a strange and frightening story that their father told him and his twin brother shortly before the major died.

In India, Morstan and Major Sholto came upon a large fortune that Sholto brought back to England. When Morstan arrived in London, where he planned to meet his daughter, he called on Major Sholto. In a disagreement over the division of the treasure, Morstan was stricken by a heart attack, fell, and struck his head a mortal blow. Fearing that he would be accused of murder, Major Sholto disposed of the body with the help of a servant. On his deathbed, Major Sholto wanted to make restitution to Morstan's daughter and called his twin sons to his side to tell them where the treasure was hidden. As he was about to reveal the hiding place, however, he saw a horrible face staring in the window, and he died before he could disclose his secret.

On the following morning, his sons found the room ransacked and on the dead man's chest a piece of paper bearing the words "The Sign of Four." The two brothers differ over their responsibility to Mary; Thaddeus wants to help her, and his twin wants to keep everything for themselves should the treasure be found. It is Thaddeus who sends her the pearl each year, their father having taken the pearls out of the treasure chest before he died.

The day before his meeting with Mary, Holmes, and Dr. Watson, Thaddeus learns that his brother found the treasure chest in a sealed-off portion of the attic in their father's house. Thaddeus declares his intention to take Mary and the two men to his brother and force him to give the girl her share of the wealth. When they arrive at the brother's house, however, they find him murdered and the treasure gone. It is a baffling case, for the door to his room is locked from the inside and the wall to the window impossible to scale. Nevertheless, Holmes finds certain clues that lead him to believe there were two accomplices, one of whom pulled the other up through a trapdoor in the roof. He also ascertains that one of the men had a wooden leg and the other had exceedingly small feet.

During the ten years since Morstan's death, various notes were found with the names of four men on them, the only English name being that of Jonathan Small. Many of the notes were signed "The Sign of Four," the words that were written on the paper left on the late Major Sholto's body. Using this clue and the evidence found in the murder room, Holmes goes to work. He believes that Small is the key to the mystery, and he tracks Small to a steam launch. After a harrowing chase on the river, Holmes catches up with him. Before Holmes can overtake Small, however, he has to kill the little man with the small feet. About to be taken, Small empties the treasure into the river. After his capture, he tells a story that unravels the mystery.

When he was a young man, Small fled from home because of trouble over a girl. He joined the army and went to India. Soon after his arrival there, he lost a leg to a crocodile. His accident necessitated a wooden leg, and he was discharged from the army. For a time, he worked on a plantation. When the natives staged an uprising, he accidentally came upon a treasure chest filled with precious jewels. Three natives, his partners in the discovery, swore loyalty to one another and called themselves The Four. After the uprising, the four men were imprisoned. In order to escape, they had entrusted their secret to Morstan and Major Sholto, and Major Sholto took charge of the treasure until the others could reach

safety. Major Sholto, however, tricked his confederates; his treachery resulted in Morstan's and his own conscience-stricken deaths. Holmes was right in assuming that Small left the paper with "The Sign of Four" written on it. Small escaped from prison and made his way back to England with a native companion, the man with the small feet. After Major Sholto's death, he waited until the son found the treasure. Small did not intend violence, but his companion murdered young Sholto with a poison splinter before Small could enter the locked room by means of a rope suspended through the trapdoor.

The rest of the story is known by Holmes. Small, attempting to escape the country with the treasure, dumped it into the river rather than part with it. To Dr. Watson, the loss is a happy circumstance, for he could now tell Mary of his love for her. He would not do this while he thought her an heir. Mary accepts his proposal, and the happy pair receive the good wishes of Holmes. As for Holmes, he prefers the stimulation of mystery to the stimulation of love.

Critical Evaluation:

Although considerable dispute exists as to the relative merits of the fifty-six short stories in the Sherlock Holmes series, there is a general agreement among most critics and fans as to the rating of the four Holmes novels. *The Sign of Four* is usually placed second to *The Hound of the Baskervilles* (1901-1902) and solidly ahead of *A Study in Scarlet* (1887, serial; 1888, book) and *The Valley of Fear* (1914-1915). *The Sign of Four* is praised for its picture of Holmes in action and the ingenuity of the initial puzzle for its evocation of the atmosphere of London in the 1880's, for its sharp delineation of character, and for its dramatic effectiveness. It is sometimes faulted, however, for a plot too closely reminiscent of Wilkie Collins's *The Moonstone* (1868), a solution that comes too early in the narrative, and for Jonathan Small's overly long confession. Critic Julian Symons is probably right in his opinion that the main problem in both *A Study in Scarlet* and *The Sign of Four* is that "they could have been condensed into short stories."

Although *The Sign of Four* may seem too long, it still contains some of Sir Arthur Conan Doyle's best writing as well as all the elements that make the Holmes stories so popular and entertaining. Indeed, the more leisurely structure of the novelette, if unnecessary for the substance of the events described, does allow for a fuller treatment of such "incidentals" as character development, general background, colorful digressions, and atmosphere—"peripheral" elements that are essential to the Holmes stories and that go a long way toward explaining their durability and universality.

One evident reason for this long-standing popularity lies in the characters of the principals and their unique relationship. Perhaps Doyle's most important contribution to the detective story was his "humanizing" of the detective. Edgar Allan Poe's C. Auguste Dupin is little more than a disembodied intellect. Collins's Sergeant Cuff is more personable but considerably less skillful. Émile Gaboriau's two early examples, Monsieur Lecoq and Père Tabaret, are ingenious detectives and amiable fellows, but they have almost no distinguishing personal traits. Holmes is both an extraordinary investigator and a sharply delineated character, and his relationship with Dr. Watson is the one of the first distinctive partnerships in novelistic crime fighting.

The most obvious characteristics of Holmes are his incredible powers of observation, deduction, and induction (despite what he says, most of Holmes's conclusions are arrived at by induction, not deduction; that is, he draws answers from a mass of small details). This talent is demonstrated again and again in unraveling the most exotic and obscure crimes. Holmes's procedures are always the same: first, his close examination; next, the set of conclusions; and, finally, the minute "elementary" explication. Usually, in the opening passages, Holmes "practices" on the client's superficial characteristics and then, as the substance of the story, he applies his extraordinary talents to the major problem of the narrative. In novels, such as *The Sign of Four*, there is usually a sequence of problems; as Holmes unscrambles one puzzle, the solution points to a new, more sinister one, and this continues until the entire problem is finally solved and the malefactor brought to justice.

Nevertheless, there is more to the Holmes stories than ingenious problem solving. If Collins originated the practice of "humanizing" his detective by giving him eccentric traits and hobbies (Sergeant Cuff grows roses), Doyle perfected the technique. He supplies Holmes with a wide range of sidelines and interests: beekeeping, violin playing, opera, boxing, toxicology, swordplay, food, theater, tobacco ash, and many others. Holmes, however, is no Renaissance man. He prides himself on large areas of total ignorance: art, philosophy, literature, astronomy, and politics, to name a few. The unifying factor is that all of Holmes's diverse knowledge and talent go into the solving of intricate problems. Holmes is, finally, a monomaniacal rationalist who feels lost without a challenging intellectual puzzle. That is why, he tells Watson near the beginning of *The Sign of Four*, when he is without a case, he must resort to drugs: "Hence the cocaine. I cannot live without brainwork. What else is there to live for? Stand at the window there. Was there ever such a dreary, dismal, unprofitable world? . . . What is the use of having powers, Doctor, when one has no field upon which to exert them?"

Thus, although Holmes is infinitely more interesting, he is, like Poe's Dupin, an intellectual freak. "You are an automaton," Watson tells him, "a calculating machine. . . . There is something positively inhuman in you at times." All in all, Holmes is a genius, detached from common society, even a Nietzschean "superman" who has chosen to use his extraordinary powers in the service of humankind, not so much from a sense of justice (although he has a strong one), but out of a need to use those abilities to fight the triviality and meaninglessness of everyday existence. Much of Holmes's long-term popularity comes from the fact that, as an "outsider," Holmes excites the popular imagination, but, as a defender of the status quo, he is ultimately reassuring.

Given the detective's one-sidedness, however, Holmes would be grotesque if he were presented alone. That which really humanizes Holmes is Dr. John Watson. If Holmes is the "superman" and "outsider," Dr. Watson is the ordinary professional man, astonished by his friend's capacities but aware of his human imperfections. Dr. Watson is neither a slavish worshiper of genius, like Dupin's narrator, nor an amiable drunk, like Father Absinthe, who assists Gaboriau's Lecoq. If Dr. Watson has little talent for deduction, he is not the blustering fool of many Holmes motion pictures. When Holmes says, "a client is to me a mere unit, a factor in a problem," Dr. Watson recoils. To Dr. Watson, clients are people to be helped, and it is through the good doctor that readers establish their own emotional connection to the characters. Doyle almost always centers his crime on a personal or family situation, and the fate of the people involved is as important as the solving of the puzzle. Because of this, Dr. Watson is every bit as important as Holmes.

This relationship is most evident in *The Sign of Four*, which is, in addition to a mystery, a love story in which Dr. Watson meets the client, Mary Morstan, falls in love, courts her, and, with the resolution of the problem, wins her. Doyle adroitly weaves this romance in and around the mystery story and deftly shows Dr. Watson's emotional reactions without distracting from the main line of detection. The fact that Dr. Watson pursues a bride while Holmes chases a criminal adds an extra dimension and flavor to the story as well as sharpening and deepening our picture of Watson as a man. Although his behavior, under the influence of his feelings for Mary, may occasionally be a bit foolish, his actions are admirable and resourceful. He never forgets the main problem, and he assists Holmes in his solution with considerable skill and courage. Readers must admire his resolute determination to rescue the fortune for Mary despite the fact that it will doom their romance. Therefore, when Jonathan Small throws the jewelry into the Thames, readers are glad, since it will enable Watson to realize his romantic ambition.

The Sign of Four has all the ingredients of the best Holmes puzzles: a peculiar situation, a tentative revelation that leads to further enigmas, a vivid London environment that leads to an exotic setting, and a spectacular and bizarre crime that can be explained only through the most elaborate and imaginative deductions. Mary's initial problem is strange enough to immediately seize a reader's attention, but it does not become truly threatening until readers are involved with the Sholto family and the sinister events that surround them.

The actual crime, the killing of Major Sholto, is a variation of the "locked room" murder situation so dear to the hearts of mystery story fans in general and "Sherlockians" in particular. The bizarre quality of the murder is further emphasized by the discovery of "a long dark thorn stuck in the skin just above the ear," the marks of a "wooden stump," and a set of footprints "half the size of an ordinary man."

As soon as these exotic clues are enumerated, however, they lead Holmes directly to Jonathan Small and Tonga, his dwarfish native accomplice. Unfortunately, the novel is at this point little over half-finished. The rest is divided between Holmes's pursuit of the malefactors and a long statement by the villain, Small, explaining the events leading up to the crime. The thwarted efforts of Holmes and Dr. Watson to track down Small and Tonga with a lumbering mixed-breed dog named Toby are amusing, Holmes's skill in accurately predicting Small's escape route and his strategy in tracing him are impressive, and the final boat chase on the Thames is exciting. Added to all of this is Small's confession, which gives the reader a fascinating villain who is both repulsive and sympathetic. Since the major mystery is already solved, however, all of this is anticlimactic. Once readers have seen Holmes's brilliant mind cut through the tangle of clues and ambiguities that surround Sholto's murder to identify the killers, their methods, and their motives, the other events are superfluous.

"Critical Evaluation" by Keith Neilson

Further Reading

Carr, John Dickson. *The Life of Sir Arthur Conan Doyle.* New York: Harper, 1949. Based on a thorough perusal of Doyle's private papers by one of the masters of the craft of mystery writing, this is considered the definitive biography.

Doyle, Arthur Conan. *Memoirs and Adventures.* Boston: Little, Brown, 1924. While this autobiography leaves many matters untouched and many questions unanswered, it does provide a valuable insight into the life and works of the author at the end of his career.

_____. *The New Annotated Sherlock Holmes.* 3 vols. Edited, with a foreword and notes by Leslie S. Klinger. New York: W. W. Norton, 2005-2006. Volume 3 in this three-volume set contains extensively annotated texts of *The Sign of Four* and three other novels, in which Klinger defines obscure terms and discusses various issues raised by each book. Additional information is provided in the appendixes that follow each novel.

Jaffe, Jacqueline A. *Arthur Conan Doyle.* Boston: Twayne, 1987. An excellent brief introduction to Doyle's life and especially to his works. Two chapters, "The Beginnings of a Modern Hero: Sherlock Holmes" and "The Return of Holmes," deal with Doyle's detective fiction. At the end of the work there is a short but useful bibliography.

Kestner, Joseph A. *Sherlock's Men: Masculinity, Conan Doyle, and Cultural History.* Brookfield, Vt.: Ashgate, 1997. Examines aspects of masculinity in the Sherlock Holmes novels and stories. Includes an analysis of *The Sign of Four.*

Lycett, Andrew. *The Man Who Created Sherlock Holmes: The Life and Times of Sir Arthur Conan Doyle.* New York: Free Press, 2007. Comprehensive and detailed biography, based in part on materials in Doyle's personal archive, which were not available to researchers until 1997. Lycett describes the events of the author's life and the variety of his writings, explaining how the author who created one of the world's most rational detectives was a believer in spiritualism and the supernatural.

McLaughlin, Joseph. "The Romance of Invasion: Cocaine and Cannibals in *The Sign of Four.*" In *Writing the Urban Jungle: Reading Empire in London from Doyle to Eliot.* Charlottesville: University Press of Virginia, 2000. Examines how Doyle and other British writers used words and images that defined the British Empire's colonies, particularly those in Africa, to describe life in metropolitan London.

The Significance of the Frontier in American History

Author: Frederick Jackson Turner (1861-1932)
First published: 1894; revised and enlarged, 1920, as
  The Frontier in American History
Type of work: History

On July 12, 1893, an annual meeting of the fledgling American Historical Association (AHA) was held in Chicago to coincide with the Columbia Exposition. The exposition celebrated the four hundredth anniversary of Christopher Columbus. Frederick Jackson Turner, from Wisconsin, got up to deliver a paper before the AHA. His paper, "The Significance of the Frontier in American History," permanently altered the study of American history in schools, colleges, and universities.

Turner's famous paper often was reprinted, but it was not until 1920 that he presented the first full statement of his theory of the frontier. Turner republished his original paper, with twelve supporting articles, in the book *The Frontier in American History*; the second and consequent part of his theory, *The Significance of Sections in American History*, was published in 1932, the year he died. His 1894 paper was preceded by his doctoral dissertation on the fur trade in Wisconsin and two articles on history and American history that show the development of his theory of the frontier.

Two events precipitated Turner's paper: First, the work of the Italian economist Achille Loria—who theorized that free land was the key to changes in human society—and of America as the best place in which to test this thesis, came to Turner's notice in the late 1880's. Loria's work influenced an earlier paper by Turner, "Problems in American History" (1892). The second event was the announcement of the superintendent of the 1890 census that insufficient free land existed in the United States for the frontier to feature in the census reports as it had done since the first census in 1790. Turner dramatized this fact in the beginning of his paper. In effect, he was directing his fellow historians away from political and diplomatic history, insisting that, no matter what happened in European capitals, American history was made in the hinterland, where the westward movement had been the most significant historical phenomenon for Americans. There was, for historians, a vast frontier of local history to investigate in whatever state they might be located. The dramatic setting and occasion for Turner's paper was not immediately appreciated, but it played its part in spreading his ideas rapidly.

The paper's expanded version, *The Frontier in American History*, is constructed in two parts, with an introduction. The first paragraph asserts that American history is the gradual settlement of the West, and this is followed by four paragraphs defining the frontier as a moving belt between settled and free land; it moved because of the force behind it. As an effect of the environment into which it moved, the frontier's chief characteristic is a process of reversion to savagery followed by a slow recovery of civilization that, because its chief influences are indigenous, cannot be an imitation of European life and must therefore be American alone. If the frontier is the maker of Americans, and they are the makers of their history, then the frontier holds the key to that history.

The first part of the book presents in rapid survey the different kinds of frontier in American history and the modes of advance from the time when it began as the frontier of Europe on the Atlantic seaboard in the early seventeenth century to its near completion in the 1880's. The changes in the frontier were determined by the different geographical boundaries or "barriers" to the westward advance— American Indians, farm land, salt supplies, and the like. Here, Turner draws several vivid sketches of the succession of different types of settlers who followed one another in any one settlement or who could be imaginatively plotted as a series of different kinds of frontier belts such as hunting, trading, nomadic, grazing, farming, and financing. These different types could be traced back eastward from the most advanced settlement at any given point in American history.

The second part of the book is a provocative summary of changes enforced by the frontier experience on the regions to the east and in Europe, from where the frontier impulse came. First, Turner proposes that the frontier is the real melting pot of immigrant nationalities, and without it the United States would resemble the nations of Europe. The next point is the success of the frontier. Although its rate of advance changed, it never faltered, and its increasing distance westward made Americans less dependent on England. Third, the power of the federal government stems from that granted to the U.S. Congress by the U.S. Constitution to dispose of the public domain and thus exert federal sway inside the state; without the frontier the federal government would have had little to legislate and less money with which to legislate. Fourth, the products of the frontier determined the development of the national economy, maintaining a rural influence over increasing industrialization in the East. Fifth, the egalitarianism of the frontier kept the states democratic. Last, in struggles with the economic, religious, and educational power of the East, the West came to have a character of its own, which determined that the federalist system would always be a duality of national and sectional interests.

Turner's essay is credited with causing a revolution in American historiography, but it would be truer to say that the 1893 paper was so completely in accord with the predilections of American historians in the decades that followed the paper that the work anticipated and supported what came to be the predominant social and economic interpretation of American history. This version of history came to be preferred to the dynastic version, or the succession-of-presidents version. This version helped to make possible a wholly economic explanation of the causes of the American Civil War, for instance, and it had the effect of determining Turner's life work. *The Frontier in American History* copes with his first task: to establish the historical outlines of his moving frontier and then to consider the unique character of postfrontier society, which Turner called the West. Turner's was first of all a new problem in historiography: how to explain that an "uninhabited" area could affect an inhabited area, a problem unknown in European historiography. He uses the term "frontier" as the area of overlap between two areas, and since the frontier was always moving westward, however irregularly, Turner conceived it imaginatively as altering the physical shape of the inhabited area behind it by leaving successive belts of postfrontier societies, each of which was a "West" and together formed "the West."

Before analyzing his "West," Turner outlined the westward or moving frontier from Massachusetts to the "Old West" to the "Middle West," where he expanded his outline to closer study of the Ohio and Mississippi valleys. "The Significance of the Mississippi Valley in American History" discusses the moving of the frontier and allows Turner to introduce "The Problem of the West," "Dominant Forces in Western Life," "Contributions of the West to American Democracy," "The West and American Ideals," and "Middle Western Democracy." This discussion leads him to the large claim that the West is democratic and that "democracy" is another name for "West." Thus, the whole meaning of American history is summed up in "the West." At this point, Turner becomes not a narrative historian but a social historian determined to explore "forces," "ideals," and "significances."

In his social history, Turner tends to conclude his work with perorations about the virtue of American democracy and that of the West in producing it. "The Significance of the Mississippi Valley in American History" concludes that the valley realized the American ideal of democracy and constitutes the heartland of America as almost an independent nation that has shed its light on the surrounding feebler nations of the South, the East, and the Far West. Turner developed these ideas during his long tenure at Harvard and modified them when he took up residence at the Huntington Library in San Marino, California. In turn, these ideas led him to his pioneer work on sections in American history and life.

Turner's methods are summarized in his presidential address to the AHA in 1910, "Social Forces in American History," the twelfth chapter of *The Frontier in American History*, in which he reviews statistics of American growth since 1890, arguing that the statistics provide evidence of the force behind the frontier. Turner summons his fellow historians to continue the work he began nearly two decades before by using statistics available from other disciplines, as he did in using the census bulletin in 1893. His embracing view forecasts the development of American studies, and the discipline he hinted at is given meaning by his insistence that the duty of historians is to engage themselves in the life of their nation by continually reinterpreting the immediate past in terms of the present, as he himself had done in Chicago in 1893. Turner's concluding chapter, "Middle Western Pioneer Democracy," presents his belief that pioneer life gave Americans a chance for a true democracy.

Further Reading

Billington, Ray Allen. *The Genesis of the Frontier Thesis: A Study in Historical Creativity*. San Marino, Calif.: Huntington Library, 1971. Traces the process by which Turner developed his frontier thesis through an examination of letters and documents that the historian used in framing his ideas. An important source for investigation of Turner's intellectual evolution, written by his foremost biographer.

Cronon, William. "Revisiting the Vanishing Frontier: The Legacy of Frederick Jackson Turner." *Western Historical Quarterly* 18 (April, 1987): 157-176. An examination of Turner's historical contributions by one of the New West scholars. A good overview of how Turner's reputation has progressed over time.

Etulain, Richard W., ed. *Does the Frontier Experience Make America Exceptional?* Boston: Bedford/St. Martin's, 1999. In addition to the entire text of *The Significance of the Frontier in American History*, this edition contains essays by modern historians who analyze Turner's ideas.

Three of the essays are by New West historians who discuss how the idea of the frontier shaped the American imagination, explore gender issues in Turner's work, and seek to answer the question, Whose frontier is it? Other essays examine the validity and meaning of Turner's ideas for the United States in the twenty-first century.

Jacobs, Wilbur R. *The Historical World of Frederick Jackson Turner: With Selections from His Correspondence*. New Haven, Conn.: Yale University Press, 1968. Uses Turner's letters and supplies editorial commentary to outline his emergence as a historian of the West. A fine source for Turner's own words about his historical theories.

Limerick, Patricia Nelson. *The Legacy of Conquest: The Unbroken Past of the American West*. New York: W. W. Norton, 1987. A history of Western settlement by one of the foremost modern exponents of the new Western history, which rejects Turner's thesis about the frontier as only a rationale for Anglo-American conquest of the West.

Nash, Gerald D. *Creating the West: Historical Interpretations, 1890-1990*. Albuquerque: University of New Mexico Press, 1991. An excellent survey of the various historical explanations of Western history that places the Turner thesis into context with other works about the region's development.

Turner, Frederick Jackson. *Rereading Frederick Jackson Turner: "The Significance of the Frontier in American History," and Other Essays*. 1994. Reprint. New Haven, Conn.: Yale University Press, 1998. A collection of ten of Turner's most significant essays, with scholarly commentary on each. A concluding essay examines later debates about Turner's legacy and his influence on Americans' understanding of their national character, freedom, and a free society for the individual.

Silas Marner
The Weaver of Raveloe

Author: George Eliot (1819-1880)
First published: 1861
Type of work: Novel
Type of plot: Domestic realism
Time of plot: Early nineteenth century
Locale: England

Principal characters:
SILAS MARNER, a weaver
EPPIE, his adopted daughter
AARON WINTHROP, the man whom Eppie marries
GODFREY CASS, Eppie's father
DUNSTAN CASS, his wastrel brother
NANCY LAMMETER, the woman whom Godfrey marries

The Story:

Silas Marner, the linen weaver, lives in the small community of Raveloe. Long years at his spinning wheel leave Silas extremely nearsighted so that his vision is limited to only those objects that are very bright or very close to him. Because of an unjust accusation of theft, Silas left his former home at Lantern Yard and became a recluse. For fifteen years, the lonely, shriveled man lives for no purpose but to hoard the money he receives in payment for his weaving. Night after night, he takes his golden hoard from its hiding place in the floor of his cottage and lets the shining pieces run through his fingers.

The leading man in Raveloe is Squire Cass, who has one fine son, Godfrey, and one wastrel son, Dunstan. It is said that Godfrey will marry Nancy Lammeter. Godfrey, however, becomes involved in Dunstan's gambling debts. He lends his spendthrift brother some of the squire's rent money, which Dunstan loses in gambling. Since neither brother can raise the money, they decide that Dunstan must sell Godfrey's favorite horse, Wildfire, at a nearby fair. Godfrey's one fear is that this affair will harm his reputation in the neighborhood and his chance with Nancy. Another thing that weighs on Godfrey's conscience and prevents his declaration to Nancy is the fact that he is already married. Once he was drunk in a tavern in a distant hamlet, and in that condition he married a woman of the lower class. Sober, he fled back to Raveloe and kept his marriage a secret.

Dunstan rides Wildfire across the fog-dimmed fields and cripples the animal on a high jump. With no means of raising the money, half-drunk and fear-driven, Dunstan comes to Silas's cottage. He knows through the neighborhood gossip that the weaver has a hidden hoard of gold. The cottage is empty, and instinct soon leads the drunken youth to the hiding place of the gold. Stealing out of the cabin with his prize and stumbling through the night, Dunstan falls into an abandoned quarry pit and dies.

The robbery of Silas's cottage furnishes gossip for the entire community. Another mystery is the disappearance of Dunstan. Godfrey is forced now to tell his father about the rent money he gave Dunstan and about the loss of the valuable horse, which was found dead. Silas begins to receive visitors from the neighborhood. One of his most frequent callers is Dolly Winthrop and her son Aaron, a charming little boy. Nevertheless, Silas cannot be persuaded to come out of his hermitage; he secretly mourns the loss of his gold.

On New Year's Eve, a destitute woman dies in the snow near Silas's cottage. She has with her a little yellow-haired girl who makes her way toward the light shining through the cottage window and enters the house. Returning from an errand, Silas sees a golden gleam in front of his fireplace, a gleam that he mistakes for his lost gold. On closer examination, he discovers a sleeping baby. He follows the child's tracks through the snow and discovers the body of the dead woman.

Godfrey is dancing happily with Nancy when Silas appears to say that he found a body. Godfrey goes with the others to the scene and sees to his horror that the dead woman is his estranged wife. He tells no one of her identity, and he does not have the courage to claim the baby for his own. Silas, with a confused association between the golden-haired child and his lost hoard, tenaciously clings to the child. After Dolly speaks up in favor of his proper attitude toward children, the villagers decide to leave the baby with the old weaver.

Years pass. Under the spell of the child who, in her baby language, calls herself Eppie instead of the biblical Hephzibah that Silas bestowed upon her, the cottage of the weaver of Raveloe takes on a new appearance. Lacy curtains decorate the once drab windows, and Silas outgrows his shell of reticence. Dolly brings her son to play with Eppie. Silas is happy. After many years, he even returns to Lantern Yard, taking Eppie. He searches his old neighborhood hopefully but can find no one who can clear his blighted past.

Godfrey marries Nancy, but it is a childless union. For sixteen years, Godfrey secretly carries with him the thought of his child growing up under the care of Silas. At last, the old stone quarry is drained, and workmen find a skeleton identified by Dunstan's watch and seals. Beside the skeleton is Silas's lost bag of gold, stolen on the night of Dunstan's disappearance. With this discovery, Godfrey's past reopens its sealed doors. He feels that the time comes to tell Nancy the truth. When he confesses the story of Eppie's birth, Nancy agrees with him that they should go to Silas and Eppie with their tale. After hearing this strange story of Eppie's parentage, the unselfish weaver opens the way for Eppie to take advantage of her wealthy heritage; but Eppie flees back to the man who was a father and a mother to her when no one else would claim her. There is one thing remaining to complete the weaver's happiness. Eppie marries Aaron Winthrop, her childhood playmate, while Silas beams happily on the scene of her wedding.

Critical Evaluation:

In four remarkable years, George Eliot published in succession *Scenes from Clerical Life* (1858), *Adam Bede* (1859), *The Mill on the Floss* (1860), and *Silas Marner*. The last, a short novel or novella, is unlike the other works, for its narrative combines elements of myth—some critics have called it a fairy tale—with the otherwise realistic details of English country life centering on the rustic village of Raveloe. Certainly the novel can be understood as a moral tale. Its message, however sentimental to a modern reader, is unambiguous: True wealth is love, not gold. As a myth of loss and redemption, the novel concerns the miser Silas Marner, who loses his material riches only to reclaim a greater treasure of contentment. Silas comes to learn that happiness is possible only for the pure and self-sacrificing. Because of his love for Eppie, he is transformed, as if by magic, from a narrow, selfish, bitter recluse into a truly human, spiritually fulfilled man.

The novel, however, has a dimension other than the moralistic. Eliot skillfully counterpoints the experiences of Silas with those of Godfrey Cass. Whereas Godfrey appears, when the reader first meets him, to be a fortunate man entirely the opposite of the sullen miser, his fortunes fail just as Silas's improve. The wealthy, genial Godfrey has a secret guilt: an unacknowledged marriage to a woman beneath him in social class and refinement. Silas, on the other hand, carries with him the smoldering resentment for a wrong that he suffered (and suffered innocently) from his friend William Dane. Godfrey's sense of guilt festers, especially after he learns about the terrible circumstances of the woman's death. Nevertheless, he remains silent, fearful of exposing his past. Eppie, the child of his brief union with the woman, becomes the miser's treasure and replaces the sterile gold stolen by Dunstan. Thereafter, the happiness of the old man is Godfrey's doom. His second wife, Nancy, is barren, and when he offers too late to adopt Eppie as his own child, she clings to her foster father. Silas's love earns what Godfrey's power fails to command.

By contrasting Silas's good fortune with Godfrey's disappointment, the author expands the mythic scope of her fiction. If some men—the pure and deserving—discover almost by accident the truths of happiness, others, maybe no less deserving, pass by their chances and endure misery. Silas is reformed not only spiritually but also psychologically. Once blasphemous, he returns to the Christian faith of his childhood, but his religious reaffirmation is not as important as the improvement of his psychological health. Freed of his neurotic resentment of past injustices, he becomes a friend to all, beloved of the village. For Godfrey, whose history is realistic rather than marvelous, quite the opposite fate happens. Without an heir, he shrinks within himself. He may endure his disgrace, even eventually make up to Eppie and her husband Aaron some of the material things he owes her; yet he cannot shake his sense of wrongdoing, appease his sorrow for betrayal, or make restitution for the evils of the past. Eliot, who once described her novel as "rather somber," balances her miraculous fable of rebirth for the favored Silas with another more common human story, that of the defeated Godfrey.

Further Reading

Beer, Gillian. *George Eliot*. Bloomington: Indiana University Press, 1986. A feminist approach to Eliot's novels that acknowledges her power to redefine issues relating to gender while remaining within the traditional canon of English literature. The chapter on *Silas Marner* focuses on Silas's weaving as a metaphor, with feminine associations, for the interconnections of circumstance that form Silas's destiny.

Bloom, Harold, ed. *George Eliot's "Silas Marner."* Philadelphia: Chelsea House, 2003. Essays analyzing various aspects of the novel, including Eliot's conception of sympathy, biblical realism in *Silas Marner*, a comparison of the novel with *Adam Bede*, and Silas Marner and the "anonymous heroism of parenthood."

Draper, R. P., ed. *George Eliot: "The Mill on the Floss" and "Silas Marner."* London: Macmillan, 1977. Casebook anthology, containing early reviews and nineteenth century and twentieth century criticism. David Carroll's "Reversing the Oracles of Religion" is an authoritative essay on Eliot's humanist religious views.

Ermarth, Elizabeth Deeds. *George Eliot*. Boston: Twayne, 1985. A compact literary biography that addresses various moral and philosophical aspects of Eliot's intellectual development. In the chapter on *Silas Marner*, Ermarth sees a central theme emerging from opposed realms of circumstance and moral order linked by the bonds of human sympathy and trust.

Hardy, Barbara. *George Eliot: A Critic's Biography*. London: Continuum, 2006. An examination of Eliot's life combined with an analysis of her works, which will prove useful to readers with some prior knowledge of her writings. Includes an outline of her works and the events in her life.

_____, ed. *Critical Essays on George Eliot*. New York: Barnes & Noble, 1970. This collection, edited by a pioneer in Eliot studies, helped interest critics in feminist analyses of her work. One of the essays is devoted to an analysis of *Silas Marner*.

Swinden, Patrick. *"Silas Marner": Memory and Salvation*. New York: Twayne, 1992. Critically sophisticated but readable book-length study that focuses on Eliot's narrative method. Offers a valuable analysis of the historical and societal contexts of the novel's two settings, Lantern Yard and Raveloe.

Uglow, Jennifer. *George Eliot*. New York: Pantheon, 1987. Explores the connections between Eliot's life and work, in particular the feminine values her work affirms. In the chapter on *Silas Marner*, Uglow sees imagery of rebirth and regeneration at the core of the novel's celebration of nurturing and maternal actions.

Wiesenfarth, Joseph. *George Eliot's Mythmaking*. Heidelberg, Germany: Winter, 1977. Wiesenfarth argues that Eliot's fiction in general embodies a mythology of fellow feeling that includes various folk, classical, and biblical sources. The chapter on *Silas Marner* explores the novel's fairy-tale analogues and influences and relates them to its form and themes.

Yousaf, Nahem, and Andrew Maunder, eds. *"The Mill on the Floss" and "Silas Marner": George Eliot*. New York: Palgrave, 2002. Collection of essays analyzing the two novels, including "*Silas Marner*: A Divided Eden" by Sally Shuttleworth and "The Miser's Two Bodies: *Silas Marner* and the Sexual Possibilities of the Commodity" by Jeff Nunokawa.

Silence

Author: Shūsaku Endō (1923-1996)
First published: Chimmoku, 1966 (English translation, 1969)
Type of work: Novel
Type of plot: Historical realism
Time of plot: 1632-1644
Locale: Japan

Principal characters:
SEBASTIAN RODRIGUES, a Portuguese Catholic missionary, later renamed Sanemon Okada
FRANCIS GARRPE, Rodrigues's religious associate and companion
CHRISTOVAO FERREIRA, a Jesuit priest who is renamed Sawano Chuan
KICHIGIRO, a weak Japanese convert to Christianity
INOUE, an infamous Japanese inquisitor

The Story:

Rumor has it that the respected Portuguese Jesuit missionary Christovao Ferreira, the leader of the small, underground Christian community in Japan, has renounced his faith under torture and has cooperated with Japanese officials to expose the faithful. As a result, seven priests (three of them Portuguese and former students of Ferreira) decide to enter Japan secretly in order to exonerate the hero who had inspired them. Juan de Santa Marta, Francis Garrpe, and Sebastian Rodrigues travel to Goa, India, where they meet a timid, hesitant Japanese named Kichigiro; they seek his help in entering Japan. Juan de Santa Marta contracts malaria, however, and has to be left behind.

After a sea voyage, Garrpe and Rodrigues are left at midnight in the fishing village of Tomogi, near Nagasaki. There Christian Japanese hide them, introduce them to Christians from nearby areas, and receive from them church rituals forbidden in Japan. Rodrigues, disturbed at the plight of priestless Japanese Christians, travels to Goshima to meet more of the faithful; upon his return, however, he learns that Japanese officials have discovered the presence of Christians and that he and Garrpe must hide. The Tomogi villagers deny their Christianity, but the guards take hostages anyway; Kichigiro is among them. The hostages stamp on the *fumie*, an engraving of the Virgin Mary, as proof that they are not Christians, but the guards notice their hesitation and make them also spit on a crucifix and call the Blessed Virgin a whore. Kichigiro does so, but two villagers (Mokichi and Ichizo) refuse and, consequently, are subjected to the water punishment and die as martyrs. The prolonged torture of their deaths, as the tides rise to drown them where they are staked, is not what the two young Portuguese priests had imagined martyrdom to be like.

A further search by guards forces Rodrigues and Garrpe to separate. During this period of hiding, Rodrigues begins to fear that God's silence means his nonexistence. Eventually, Kichigiro offers to lead Rodrigues to safety but instead turns him in. The discussions that Rodrigues has in jail with Japanese prisoners (Juan and Monica) reveal their misunderstanding of church doctrine, but when the Christian prisoners are transferred to Chizukano, Rodrigues has an opportunity to perform some humble religious rituals for them.

At Chizukano, Rodrigues is led before the infamous Japanese inquisitor Inoue, whose kindness and mildness defy expectations. Kichigiro is responsible for Rodrigues being in prison, yet Kichigiro begs Rodrigues's forgiveness for his betrayal. Rodrigues, expecting immediate torture and martyrdom, is lulled by the delay and is, therefore, caught unaware when the guards take him to a hill near the sea where he and Garrpe are told that three prisoners will be executed unless they renounce their faith. Rodrigues watches as the three prisoners are rolled up in mats, put on boats, and dumped into the sea to sink like stones. Garrpe runs into the sea screaming, "Lord, hear our prayer," and drowns while trying to rescue the victims.

Inoue continues to use subtle psychological torture to undermine Rodrigues's faith because Inoue is certain that Christianity is dangerous for Japan, and he believes that Christianity can be stamped out only if the European missionary priests can be exposed as unfaithful to their own teachings. He sends Rodrigues to the Saishoji temple to meet Ferreira, who has adopted the Japanese name Sawano Chuan, has accepted a Japanese wife, and is writing a book denouncing Christian teachings as erroneous. Ferreira explains that the Japanese Christian converts are simply confused because the Latin word *Deus* sounds to them like the Japanese word *Dainichi*, which refers to the ancient Japanese sun god. The ultimate test of Rodrigues's faith, however, comes when he hears a sound like snoring and learns that it is the moaning of Christians who are hanging upside down in manure pits, with slits behind their ears to allow blood to drain into their eyes and noses. At this point, Ferreira reveals his secret: His recanting of his faith was not because of personal suffering—he had been in such a pit—but because of the suffering of others for him. He argues that Christ, too, would have apostatized in such a situation. Finally, Rodrigues steps on the *fumie*, justifying his act by imagining Christ saying, "Trample! Trample! . . . It was to share men's pain that I carried my cross." As he does so, a cock crows, as it did when Peter betrayed Christ.

Later, in letters, Rodrigues is revealed as becoming more and more a tool of Inoue, taking a Japanese name and a Japanese wife and aiding the Japanese in their search for Christians and Christian symbols. Rodrigues's faith persists despite his repeated betrayals, however; like Kichigiro, he understands that the mystery of faith endures and that God's silence does not negate God's existence or mercy.

Critical Evaluation:

Silence, a short but powerfully realistic fictionalized history, reflects Japanese interest in the contacts between East and West and in the alien nature of Western religion. Just as James Clavell's *Shōgun* (1975) interprets the Japanese mind for Westerners, so Shūsaku Endō's *Silence*, set some forty years later, interprets the Western Christian mind for the Japanese. Through his Portuguese protagonist, Rodrigues, Endō captures the Western image of life and culture in order to help Japanese better understand Western attitudes.

In part, Endō's goal is to make Japanese rethink unexamined cultural perspectives and attitudes through a dramatized clash of worldviews. As Japan's most admired and widely read Christian writer, Endō is in a unique position to do so. His exploration of God's silence (the origin of the title) as proof of God's existence, with its paradoxical Zen implications, is meant to puzzle and intrigue Japanese, but his portrait of Japanese cruelties, the historically accurate, hideous tortures used to force captives to recant their faith, is intended to shock and disturb. Endō's description in his novel *Umi to dokuyaku* (1957; *The Sea and Poison*, 1972) of Japanese doctors vivisecting a captured American pilot during World War II criticized the Japanese for a lack of moral conscience; in *Silence* the criticism continues, as Endō contrasts the image of a compassionate Christ with the bland indifference and sadism of Japanese inquisitors. A Catholic educated in France, and the first Japanese to study abroad after World War II, Endō provides insights into another worldview and another mind-set. Endō is similar, in this respect, to Lafcadio Hearn, who introduced the culture and literature of Japan to the West.

The period in which *Silence* is set is highly significant for Japanese: It is the period following the Shimabara Rebellion. The Tokugawa Edicts expelling European Christians from Japan resulted in five thousand to six thousand Christians (both Japanese and Western) being martyred in Japan between 1614 and 1640. Shimabara, a longtime Christian stronghold dominated by Christian *ronin* (lordless samurai), was the center of a spontaneous, Japanese-inspired rebellion against oppression and persecution. This rebellion was a major historical event in which thirty-five thousand Japanese Christians were killed. In *Silence*, Rodrigues and Garrpe arrive in Japan shortly after this rebellion has been quelled, and this timing makes clear to Japanese why the inquisitor Inoue fears the effects of Western religious proselytizing on Japan.

Silence, the record of both a physical and a spiritual journey, consists of a series of letters and reports written by Westerners, both Portuguese and Dutch, about the Jesuit mission to Japan, the religious persecutions, and the Japanese enlisting of former priests in the Japanese antireligious campaign. These documents so closely echo the language and content of seventeenth century church documents that readers might well be convinced that they are reading genuine church records, and, to some degree, they are. Saint Francis Xavier, Alessandro Valignano, Father Christovao Ferreira, and Inouye Masashige are names from the pages of history, with the library of the Portuguese Institute for the Historical Study of Foreign Lands being Endō's proclaimed source for documentation. Ferreira was, in fact, the historical acting vice provincial of the Jesuits in Japan, but after six hours of being tightly bound and hung head downward from a gallows into a pit filled with excreta, his forehead and the flesh behind his ears slashed in order to vent the blood, Ferreira apostatized. Some time later, he actively helped persecute Christians when he was an assistant to Inouye Masashige, an apostate Japanese and the head of the Christian Inquisition Office. Masashige was commissioned to discover and to eliminate hidden Christians. Ferreira also helped Fabian Fukan, author of the virulent anti-Christian book *Ha-Deusu* (God destroyed), orchestrate an anti-Christian campaign.

Endō's descriptions of behavior, cultural interactions, methods of torture, and recanting are detailed and accurate and are in complete accord with the historical record; however, through the first-person narration of Sebastian Rodrigues, the dominant center of *Silence*, Endō personalizes history and brings to life both religious doubts and the mystery of faith, the compassionate care of the Portuguese missionaries for the peasants who sheltered them and gave their lives for them, and the Christians' self-sacrifice, even when the torture proved beyond imagining. Rodrigues was not one of the martyrs of recorded history, though his name echoes that of a real Jesuit, Joao Rodrigues, but Sebastian Rodrigues's fate is similar to that of a handful of daring missionaries who apostatized in order to save Japanese Christians.

The novel revolves around inexplicable religious mysteries: power in powerlessness, fullness in nothingness, faith in denial, God's silence and the trampling of the *fumie* as evidence of God's existence, the protagonist betraying his faith in order to practice it, and the Japanese attempts to stamp out Christianity assuring its transformation into something more solidly and irrevocably Japanese. The imagery of Japan as a "swamp" into which alien religions sink captures some of the paradox, for in that swamp, religions such as Christianity become diffused and mingle with the local elements until they become an inseparable part of them—another mystery of Christian syncretism.

The novel also depends on contrasts in interpretations and in values between Easterners and Westerners. For the Japanese in the novel, the group is most important, and individuals, particularly peasants, are a matter of indifference; for Westerners, however, the individual is more important than the group, and for this reason, the compassion of the priests for individual sufferers outweighs the priests' consideration of abstract values. Rodrigues's image of God changes because of his Japanese experience, however, and the image of God progresses from a distant, judgmental figure to a worn and care-ridden, humanized figure with whom Rodrigues can personally identify.

The novel also depends on irony, with the ultimate irony being that both Rodrigues and Inoue fail. Rodrigues fails to stand up for and propagate the faith of his fathers, but he does pass on the rituals of the church, and he does teach the Japanese faithful to set up their own religious forms. Inoue fails to stamp out Christianity and, in his persecution of it, inadvertently lends it a mystical strength that assures its endurance underground.

Gina Macdonald and Yasuko Honda

Further Reading

Bussie, Jacqueline Aileen. "Believing Apostates: Laughter in Shūsaku Endō's *Silence*." In *The Laughter of the Oppressed: Ethical and Theological Resistance in Wiesel, Morrison, and Endo.* New York: T&T Clark International, 2007. Focuses on the laughter of the persecuted Japanese Christians in the novel and asserts that their ability to find humor in their fate provides them with a means of resisting their oppression.

Higgins, Jean. "The Inner Agon of Endō Shūsaku." *Cross Currents* 34 (Winter, 1984-1985): 414-426. Discusses Endō's shift from Buddhist to Christian perceptions and his resultant identity crisis. Addresses *Silence* as the confrontation of Japanese and Western views, with the Japanese discovering their spiritual insensitivity and Westerners exchanging a patriarchal for a maternal image of God.

Hoekema, Alle G. "The 'Christology' of the Japanese Novelist Shūsaku Endō." *Exchange* 29, no. 3 (2000): 230-248. Examines Endō's life and several of his works, including *Silence*, within the context of his Catholicism.

Mase-Hasegawa, Emi. *Christ in Japanese Culture: Theological Themes in Shusaku Endo's Literary Works.* Boston: Brill, 2008. Analyzes *Silence* and some of Endō's other works from a theological perspective, demonstrating how Christian doctrine has been adapted by the Japanese. Charts the development of Endō's thoughts on this adaptation (or "inculturation") during his career.

Netland, John T. "From Resistance to Kenosis: Reconciling Cultural Difference in the Fiction of Shūsaku Endō." *Christianity and Literature* 48 (Winter, 1999): 177-194. Discusses Endō's translation of the polemics of cultural difference into art and argues that his works replace a simple binary postcolonial tension with a three-dimensional configuration of Christianity, Easter, and European perspectives.

Ribeiro, Jorge. "Shūsaku Endō: Japanese Catholic Novelist." *America* 152 (February 2, 1985): 87-89. Discusses the moral issues raised in Endō's canon and the conflicts between the interpretations and assumptions of Japanese and Western critics, with the Japanese missing the spiritual implications in *Silence* and Westerners projecting their own cultural values into the novel.

Williams, Mark. *Endō Shūsaku: A Literature of Reconciliation.* New York: Routledge, 1999. Interesting examination of Endō's fictive technique includes analysis of all of his major novels. Williams takes exception to the common characterization of Endō as the "Japanese Graham Greene" and locates the cultural and political contexts that differentiate Endō's work. Chapter 4 is devoted to an analysis of *Silence*.

Sinners in the Hands of an Angry God

Author: Jonathan Edwards (1703-1758)
First published: 1741
Type of work: Didactic literature

Jonathan Edwards, a descendant of four generations of Puritan ministers and the most renowned and influential of Puritan leaders, became active when Puritanism was already on the wane. The infamy of the Salem witchcraft trials in 1692, which sent twenty persons to their death and another 150 to prison, festered in the community for a generation as a tragic episode that exposed the excesses of misguided Puritan zeal. In the early part of the century, New Englanders enjoyed a rising level of affluence that induced a sense of both material and spiritual comfort and eventually led to the introduction of the Half-Way Covenant. Whereas full church membership was the privilege only of those and the children of those who could testify to a personal experience of conversion, the Half-Way Covenant extended such membership to the third generation of those who confessed an experiential faith. It was such creeping secularism and spiritual lethargy that Edwards sought to correct in the 1730's through a revival movement called the Great Awakening.

This revival movement stirred many to intensify their religious seriousness, not only in Edwards's own congregation of Northampton but also throughout New England. His sermons were intended as a wake-up call for those who underplayed the majesty of a holy God and overemphasized their own worthiness as decent, hard-working, successful citizens. Edwards believed strongly that only a genuine conversion experience should qualify a person for church membership. Revivalist preachers, therefore, sought not only to address the intellect but also to engage the emotions so as to convince the listeners of the seriousness of their sin and activate them to seek salvation from the punishment they could expect from a righteous God. The results were encouraging, but one congregation, that in Enfield, Connecticut, seemed to be immune to the call for radical conversion. Edwards was therefore invited to preach there. On July 8, 1741, at the height of the Great Awakening, he delivered a revival sermon in Enfield that became the most famous of its kind. He followed the traditional three-part sermon structure: a scripture text, which is the foundation for the sermon, and an exposition of its implications; discussion of the doctrine that is derived from the text; and the application of the doctrine to the personal situation of the listeners.

Edwards carefully selected the text for this occasion, for it was his single-minded intent to disturb profoundly the comfortable members of his audience. He found the words he wanted in Deuteronomy 32:35: "Their foot shall slide in due time." This short sentence was taken from a long passage, undoubtedly read in its entirety to the congregation, that enunciates God's anger toward the perversity and the unfaithfulness of the people of Israel. Edwards obviously wished to establish a close connection between those addressed in the biblical passage and those whom he addressed in his sermon.

He begins his sermon by pointing out four features of walking on a slippery slope: The threat of destruction is constant, the destruction is imminent, it is self-generated, and the delay of that destruction is due to God's restraining hand. He is clearly establishing here the foolhardiness of those who choose to walk in such slippery places and the fact that a fatal slide into the yawning abyss is an inescapable certainty. He speaks to both the head and the heart in leading his hearers to recognize the nature of such foolishness and to fear the consequences. The warning leads Edwards to his theme: "There is nothing that keeps wicked men, at any moment, out of Hell, but the mere pleasure of God."

In a ten-point elaboration that makes up one-third of the sermon, Edwards pursues his purpose of awakening the spiritually somnolent. Many of his points are interrelated, but cumulatively they persuade the hearers that God's power is terrifying, that his wrath burns hot against the wicked, that the wicked stand condemned by the law and are deserving of hell, and that nothing will save them from such eternal punishment except a saving faith in Christ. Edwards knows, of course, that a cognitive persuasion does not necessarily lead to action. True religion should be a matter of both head and heart, and the emotions, too, must be engaged and moved to reinforce the will to turn to God for mercy and to a spiritually transformed life.

What distinguishes this most famous example of Puritan revival sermons is its use of imagery so vivid that it left people in the pews trembling and weeping. The imagery in the first part of the sermon graphically underscores the theme of the lot of the unregenerated. They should not deceive themselves about their status or their strength. Their vaunted trust in their own wisdom, prudence, care, and caution is but a self-delusion and will not save them. Before God's almighty power, they are but "heaps of light chaff before the whirl-wind" and "dry stubble before devouring flames." They are like worms that crawl on the earth and are easily crushed underfoot; they are hanging as by a slender thread that is easily singed or cut. The glittering sword of justice is whetted and is brandished over their heads. The flames of the fiery pit below them rage and glow, hell's gaping mouth is ready to swallow them, the devils like hungry lions are straining to get at their prey, the arrows of death are poised at them. What Edwards tries to pound into his listeners is the notion of life's uncertainty: Death is always but a breath away. For the unconverted, therefore, and for the unredeemed sinner and those who have not embraced Christ as savior, perdition is but a breath away. They are "walking over the pit of hell on a rotten covering" that cannot be trusted to bear their weight. Only faith in Christ will bear them up. That may not save their life, for they are mortal still, but it will save their soul and awaken the deluded souls in their sinful condition to the wonders of divine grace. That is Edwards's sole concern.

The third part of the sermon, the application, makes up the largest and, to Edwards, the most important part. If up to this point he describes the plight of the unsaved in general, he now turns directly to the congregation of Enfield and to the unconverted persons before him. The use of the third person in the sermon's second part changes to the second person in the third part. All of the Bible's warnings about the fate of the unrepentant sinner apply to them, Edwards says: the "lake of burning brimstone, . . . Hell's gaping mouth, . . . the dreadful pit of glowing flames. . . ." He goes on to attack the reasoning of the unconverted, who try to persuade themselves that it is not God but their own care and caution that preserve their life. They may point to their religiosity, their ritual of family devotions and church attendance, and the uprightness of their moral life, but Edwards reminds them that unless they experience a "great change of heart by the power of the spirit of God" and unless they are made "new creatures" they are still sinners in the hands of an angry God, standing on the slippery slope of disaster, at any moment apt to be "swallowed up in everlasting destruction."

To break down the will's resistance and reinforce the notion of impending doom, Edwards unleashes a powerful arsenal of metaphorical weapons aimed at the emotions. Through metaphors and images, Edwards links the spiritual world to the physical world of the listeners. Images of weight and tension dominate. Sinners "heavy as lead" with their wickedness will "plunge into the bottomless gulf" as surely as a falling rock would plunge through a spider's web. The floods of God's wrath will sweep them off their feet with all the fierce power of a bursting dam. The "bow of God's wrath

is bent," the arrow of justice aims at the heart. The God whose hand is yet staying this ultimate doom is a righteous God of fury to all who reject him. In his sight such are like a loathsome insect that he holds over the fire of Hell, like a spider hanging by a slender thread above the leaping flames of the "great furnace of wrath."

Edwards wants to ensure that no one takes the wrath of this holy and infinite God lightly, and he frequently refers to biblical passages that support the point. He stresses that God's wrath is much more terrible than that of the fiercest human warrior, and that no one can endure it. Moreover, it will be inflicted without pity upon all who "remain in an unregenerate state." It is, however, Edwards's passion to lead the unregenerate to salvation. All of his dire warnings lead up to what now follows: the announcement of God's grace. Having mercilessly proclaimed the imminence of God's wrath without pity, Edwards now shifts dramatically to the theme that "Now God stands ready to pity you; this is a day of mercy." Woe to those who neglect this opportunity, however. God will show them both how excellent his love is and how terrible his wrath is; the God whose hand of wrath will destroy the wicked is the same God whose hand of mercy will save the repentant. In the concluding part of the sermon, Edwards addresses his invitation to receive salvation to everyone in the audience before him—the old, the young, and the children. This, says Edwards, is the time of God's gathering in, the pouring out of his spirit, and now is the time "to fly from the wrath to come" and to "hearken to the loud calls of God's word and providence." This emphasis on immediate response reflects Edwards's conviction that, though emotions can move the will to act, emotions are transient; therefore it is necessary to act before spiritual sloth returns and the door of mercy is forever shut.

This sermon is not typical of the preaching of Edwards, but it is typical of revivalist preaching during the Great Awakening. Such sermons were meant to appeal to the head and the heart and to destroy vain rationalization and to deter delay. According to historical sources, this sermon was not without the desired effect in Enfield. Nevertheless, the Great Awakening movement did not succeed finally in saving Puritanism.

Henry J. Baron

Further Reading

Adams, John C., and Stephen R. Yarbrough. "Jonathan Edwards, the Great Awakening and *Sinners in the Hands of an Angry God.*" In *Rhetoric, Religion, and the Roots of Identity in British Colonial America*, edited by James R.

Andrews. Vol. 1 in *The Rhetorical History of the United States*. East Lansing: Michigan State University Press, 2007. This analysis of Edwards's sermon is one of the theological treatises, sermons, and other examples of colonial rhetoric examined in this volume. The essays describe how this rhetoric helped create a new American identity.

Cady, Edwin H. "The Artistry of Jonathan Edwards." *Critical Essays on Jonathan Edwards*, edited by William J. Scheick. Boston: G. K. Hall, 1980. Analyzes the sermon as a genuine work of art by looking at its intellectual and literary structure and design.

Edwards, Jonathan. *The Sermons of Jonathan Edwards: A Reader*. Edited by Wilson H. Kimnach, Kenneth P. Minkema, and Douglas A. Sweeney. New Haven, Conn.: Yale University Press, 1999. Presents fourteen sermons, including five never before published, as well as *Sinners in the Hands of an Angry God*. The introduction places these sermons in their historical context and analyzes their literary structure; in addition, each sermon begins with a text from Scripture, a brief comment or interpretation and statement of doctrine, and a discussion of the uses and the applications of this doctrine.

Gura, Philip F. *Jonathan Edwards: America's Evangelical*. New York: Hill and Wang, 2005. Gura traces the central themes in Edwards's sermons and writings, which he maintains are the religious affections and the role of emotions in the personal religious experience. Makes numerous references to *Sinners in the Hands of an Angry God*.

Marsden, George M. *Jonathan Edwards: A Life*. New Haven, Conn.: Yale University Press, 2003. First critical biography of Edwards in sixty years, described by many critics as the definitive chronicle of his life and work. Marsden examines Edwards's life and explicates his sermons and other writings by placing the man and his work in the context of eighteenth century colonial America.

Munk, Linda. *The Devil's Mousetrap: Redemption and Colonial American Literature*. New York: Oxford University Press, 1997. Munk analyzes the writings of Edwards and two other New England Puritan ministers, Increase Mather and Edward Taylor, from the perspective of literary theory.

Pudaloff, Ross J. "'Sinners in the Hands of an Angry God': The Socio-Economic and Intellectual Matrices for Edwards' Sermon." *Mosaic: A Journal for the Interdisciplinary Study of Literature* 16 (Summer, 1983): 45-64. A helpful examination of the economic and social history of Enfield, the intellectual and philosophical aspects of Edwards's thought expressed in the sermon, and the rhetoric and metaphors shared by the sermon and the community.

Stein, Stephen J., ed. *The Cambridge Companion to Jonathan Edwards*. New York: Cambridge University Press, 2007. Collection of essays, including a biography, articles placing Edwards within the context of the Enlightenment and colonial New England, and analyses of Edwards in his roles as preacher, revivalist, theologian, philosopher, and missionary. Philip F. Gura discusses "Edwards and American Literature."

Yarbrough, Stephen R., and John C. Adams. *Delightful Conviction: Jonathan Edwards and the Rhetoric of Conversion*. Westport, Conn.: Greenwood Press, 1993. Includes an illuminating section that focuses on the experiential imagery of helplessness that points up the need for divine security.

Sir Charles Grandison

Author: Samuel Richardson (1689-1761)
First published: 1753-1754
Type of work: Novel
Type of plot: Fiction of manners
Time of plot: Eighteenth century
Locale: England

Principal characters:
SIR CHARLES GRANDISON, an English baronet of great virtue
HARRIET BYRON, a virtuous young Englishwoman
LADY CLEMENTINA DELLA PORRETTA, a young Italian woman in love with Sir Charles
SIR HARGRAVE POLLEXFEN, a libertine in love with Harriet Byron
CHARLOTTE GRANDISON, Sir Charles's younger sister
LADY L., Sir Charles's older sister
EMILY JERVOIS, Sir Charles's ward

The Story:

When Harriet Byron, a beautiful and virtuous young Englishwoman of modest expectations, departs her aunt's home in rural Northamptonshire to visit in London, she leaves three men who love her very much and various relatives who fear that the social life of the city might offer moral pitfalls unknown to a young and unsuspecting woman of virtue. Harriet spent all of her life in the country; living with an aunt after her parents' deaths, she is excited at the prospect of the London visit. She also goes with a happy heart, for she has no one, despite her many admirers, that she is interested in marrying; her suitors do not appeal strongly enough to her sentiments and mind despite their respectable, if ardent, attentions.

In London, Harriet has connections of a very respectable sort. She is invited to many homes and social events and meets many wealthy suitors. One of these is Sir Hargrave Pollexfen, who is determined not to accept a refusal. When told by Harriet that he does not suit her fancy, Sir Hargrave becomes enraged and vows he will have both Harriet and revenge. He lays a plot to abduct Harriet from a masquerade ball and force her to marry him.

Sir Hargrave's plot almost succeeds, and the experience is a horrible one for Harriet. Fortunately, however, Sir Charles Grandison hears her screams and rescues her from Sir Hargrave's clutches. Sir Charles takes Harriet to his country house, not far from London, where he and his sister invite Harriet to remain as a guest, almost a member of the family. Sir Hargrave sends a challenge to Sir Charles, but the latter refuses to fight a duel, insisting that no virtuous man, however brave and skilled, can become a duelist and retain his virtue.

Harriet soon falls in love with Sir Charles. She realizes that he is the very soul of honor and virtue, a man whose time is spent in carefully managing his own affairs and in doing good for others. When his father died, he had left his entire estate to Sir Charles with no provision for the two daughters of the family. When Sir Charles returned to England from the Continent to take over his estate, he treated his sisters with consideration and with devotion. The oldest receives his permission for her to marry Lord L., a suitor frowned upon by her father during his lifetime. Sir Charles also begins to improve his estates and their revenues so that he can set aside better marriage portions for both his sisters, something more than their father was willing to do. Sir Charles befriends everyone who will accept his kindnesses, and he always behaves wisely and with decorum. Even those persons who are prepared to dislike him find themselves won over by his sympathetic, friendly, and yet dignified ways. Even to his father's paramour, Mrs. Oldham, he behaves magnanimously, persuading the rest of the family to view her as a fellow human being.

Many women are in love with Sir Charles, including Harriet, but no one can ascertain if he has any inclinations toward any particular woman. Harriet, however, tries to hide her love for him and to subdue it, although many of Sir Charles's friends and relatives, including his sisters, favor the match. Sir Charles consistently refers to Harriet as a sister and behaves toward her with the same consideration he shows Charlotte and Lady L. Finally, it becomes known that two Italian women he met in his travels won some favor from him and have some claim to him and his affections. One is Lady Olivia and the other is Lady Clementina della Porretta, whom he met after saving her brother's life. Lady Clementina's family does not favor a marriage between their daughter and a Protestant Englishman, but the young woman is so enamored of Sir Charles that his departure from Italy unhinges her reason. Feeling a sense of responsibility to the lady and her family as the source of her misfortune, Sir Charles returns to Italy with English medical experts to try to effect a cure. Harriet believes that he would prefer Lady Clementina to her and begins to prepare herself for news of his marriage to the Italian woman.

After she recovers from her malady, however, Lady Clementina refuses to marry Sir Charles, despite the fact that her family and he were able to reach a compromise over religious differences. Lady Clementina, a devout Roman Catholic, fears that she will be tempted by her love for Sir Charles and his virtue to leave her faith to become a Protestant. She asks to be free not to marry at all, since she cannot marry him; her family hopes she will marry some other eligible man.

While he is still in Italy, an attempt is made on Sir Charles's life, almost certainly at the instigation of Lady Olivia, who previously struck at him with a poniard after he repulsed her addresses. After this incident, Sir Charles feels himself free to pay his court where he desires. He returns to England and immediately begins his suit for Harriet's hand, which he quickly wins. In the meantime, his sister Charlotte marries Lord G., and Harriet helps the impetuous and willful young woman to learn to bear properly the dignity of matrimony. Harriet's marriage to Sir Charles still faces some small obstacles. She has to learn to accept her suitor in new ways; she is shocked, for example, when he kisses her on the mouth instead of on the cheek. Furthermore, Harriet has to find a place in her heart for Emily Jervois, Sir Charles's young ward. The young girl loves her guardian, and Harriet, aware of the girl's feelings, has to help her accept Harriet's marriage to Sir Charles. Another disturbance is caused by a former suitor of Harriet, Mr. Greville, who tries, while emotionally deranged, to fight a duel with Sir Charles.

Harriet and Sir Charles are finally married. A short time later, they are visited by Lady Clementina, who ran away from her home in Italy because of her parents' insistence that she marry. Through a compromise, Sir Charles manages to arrange a satisfactory agreement between the young woman and her family. Word also comes of Sir Hargrave's death. Sir Hargrave, rescued in France by Sir Charles from the outraged relatives of a woman he attempted to seduce, discovered the evil of his ways. Wishing to make amends for the abduction and the attempted forced marriage to Harriet, Sir Hargrave leaves his fortune to her and her husband. Even the mother of Emily is influenced to become a respectable and virtuous woman. Encouraged by Sir Charles's magnanimity and financial generosity, she interests herself in religion. At one time, the unfortunate woman looked on Sir Charles as her enemy and she and Mr. O'Hara, her onetime paramour and second husband, attempted to force Emily into a degrading marriage with a rascal who promised to share with them the girl's fortune that Sir Charles holds in trust; now, however, they mend their dissolute ways and became sober, worthy persons.

Critical Evaluation:

Sir Charles Grandison provides, in a series of 182 familiar letters, the history of a hero who is as different as possible from Lovelace, the villain of Samuel Richardson's earlier novel, *Clarissa: Or, The History of a Young Lady* (1747-1748). Lovelace is many things, all of them bad: a libertine, an atheist, and a rapist, for example. He metamorphoses himself into whatever form of evildoer is needed to destroy whatever form of human decency and goodness might be within striking distance. Sir Charles Grandison, on the other hand, is always the same Christian gentleman, whatever he does. The letters in the novel, written by Sir Charles and the other characters in the novel, show him as a champion of right social order, compassionate benefactor of the unfortunate, doer of his duty toward his creator, defender of anyone—even a complete stranger—against injustice. He is especially a protector of women in need of protection.

Unlike Lovelace, who engages in no productive activity of any kind, instead spending his fortune and time entirely on furthering his sinister plans for seducing Clarissa, Sir Charles does work and all of it for good. He is seen on his estates caring for his tenants, repairing his buildings, and inspecting his fields. His good husbandry increases the wealth that makes his many charities possible. He makes friends easily. Instead of manipulating people for his own ends, he serves them by solving their problems or helping them to solve their difficulties by themselves.

Another quality of Sir Charles's gentlemanliness is his generosity in his relationships with women. He rescues his father's mistress from certain misery when her keeper dies. He forgives the Lady Olivia, whose unreturned love for him turns into hate, and he forgets the murderous assaults on his person committed by that lady and her accomplices. He assumes the guardianship of little Emily Jervois to preserve her from the bad influence of her immoral mother. He provides dowries for his penniless sisters to enable them to find suitable husbands. His tact helps his younger sister, Charlotte, whose flippancy almost ruins her marriage, to change her behavior so that she becomes a good wife.

His task with Lady Clementina, the delicate, mentally unstable Italian beauty to whom he was affianced, is more difficult. The English physicians he brings with him to Italy to restore her to health cannot deal with her dilemma. Although she loves Sir Charles, she refuses to marry him unless he abandons his Protestant religion—which he cannot do. Therefore, he must extricate himself from a fruitless involvement without causing ill feeling in her family, without precipitating a major breakdown on her part, and without losing her friendship. He carries out this difficult task with quiet discretion, totally unlike the secrecy with which Lovelace conducts his intrigues.

In the case of Harriet, Grandison's generous rescue and subsequent sheltering leads to love—a love that waits a long time for fruition. Harriet, the ideal mate for Sir Charles because she shares his sensitivity, sense of duty, and religion, soon recognizes in him the only man she can marry. Sir Charles must first retain her platonic affection because he cannot declare his love for her and ask her to be his wife until he frees himself from his obligations and entanglements in Italy.

Just as Sir Charles can be compared with Lovelace, Harriet can be compared with Clarissa. Harriet is a paragon, beautiful and sought after. She, too, refuses all proposals of marriage in favor of a perfect but still unfound spouse. Unlike the unfortunate Clarissa, who is cast off by her family and subsequently raped by Lovelace, Harriet finds herself rescued by Sir Charles from a rape attempt and then received into his family at Grandison Hall, where, in its warm and sympathetic atmosphere, she falls in love with her rescuer. When Sir Charles goes to Italy on his mission to the Lady Clementina, Harriet becomes ill of a strange malady that resembles the mysterious illness of which Clarissa dies after her rape. Harriet, however, is rescued again by Sir Charles— this time from death—and recovers to marry him and to live as his partner in earthly bliss.

Readers in Richardson's day were accustomed to the epistolary convention in novels. They enjoyed the feeling of intimacy and the thrill of reading other "people's" private correspondence. They reveled in the detail and realism of the letters, which chronicle the slow, circuitous way the union of the lovers becomes possible. They savored the psychological complexity of the action. They welcomed the opportunities to observe manners in good society and the ways these virtuous characters confronted and solved sexual, social, and ethical problems. To many of these readers who wanted to achieve perfect marriages for themselves, Harriet and Sir Charles provided models. Generations of young writers, among them Fanny Burney, Jane Austen, and Maria Edgeworth, also interested in the theme of good marriage, not only admired Richardson's *Sir Charles Grandison* but also imitated it in their own fiction.

Esteem for *Sir Charles Grandison*, once thought to be a novel far inferior to *Clarissa*, is growing. Several critics now credit the novel with advances in examining the relationship between the sexes, in developing the complexity of narrative, and in broadening the scope of fiction. These critics see *Sir Charles Grandison* as the predecessor not only of the novels by Fanny Burney, Maria Edgeworth, and Jane Austen, but also of the fiction of George Eliot and Henry James.

In many ways Richardson's *Sir Charles Grandison* is a more ambitious work than either *Pamela: Or, Virtue Rewarded* (1740-1741) or *Clarissa*. Its setting is not confined to countryside and town in England; the novel reaches to France and Italy. The range of public and private manners Richardson depicts covers not only those of England but also those of Italy. The sympathetic and tolerant account Richardson gives of Roman Catholic characters and ways is unusual in mid-eighteenth century English fiction. In addition, Richardson provides his letter writers in *Sir Charles Grandison* with a larger and more complicated cast of characters upon whom to exercise their pens. While the novel lacks the single-minded intensity of Richardson's earlier works, which concentrate on the fate of the main character, secondary characters in *Sir Charles Grandison* are granted lives of their own. The way their independent existences are connected one to another and the way their concerns are explored give *Sir Charles Grandison* dimension and realism that Richardson's other novels lack.

"Critical Evaluation" by Margaret Duggan

Further Reading

Blewitt, David, ed. *Passion and Virtue: Essays on the Novels of Samuel Richardson*. Toronto, Ont.: University of Toronto Press, 2001. A collection of essays examining various aspects of *Sir Charles Grandison* and Richardson's other novels. Includes discussions of the depiction of body and character, anxiety, and the dialectic of love in the novel.

Broome, Judith. "'Pronouncing Her Case to be Grief': Nostalgia and the Body in *Clarissa* and *Sir Charles Grandison*." In *Fictive Domains: Body, Landscape, and Nostalgia*. Lewisburg, Pa.: Bucknell University Press, 2007. Uses psychoanalytic, feminist, and other theories to analyze the depiction of bodies and landscape in the new nostalgic fiction of the eighteenth century, including Richardson's two novels.

Doody, Margaret Anne. *A Natural Passion: A Study of the Novels of Samuel Richardson*. Oxford, England: Clarendon Press, 1964. A sympathetic treatment, examining *Sir Charles Grandison* as comedy. Discusses the personalities of the women and the imagery in the novel.

Flynn, Carol Houlihan. *Samuel Richardson: A Man of Letters*. Princeton, N.J.: Princeton University Press, 1982. Includes brief discussions of various aspects of *Sir Charles Grandison*, such as the use of the epistolary method, the figure of the rake, sexual conflict, and the role of romance.

McKillop, Alan Dugald. "On *Sir Charles Grandison*." In *Samuel Richardson*, edited by John Carroll. Englewood Cliffs, N.J.: Prentice-Hall, 1969. Argues that *Sir Charles Grandison* excels in making readers feel "intimacy with a group of characters set in the framework of a familiar society." Suggests that the novel paved the way for later novels of manners.

Marks, Sylvia Kasey. "Man and God in Richardson's *Sir Charles Grandison*." In *Man, God, and Nature in the Enlightenment*, edited by Donald C. Mell et al. East Lansing, Mich.: Colleagues Press, 1988. Discusses the treatment of Christianity in *Sir Charles Grandison*. Examines Sir Charles's character in light of the Christian religion.

_____. *Sir Charles Grandison: The Compleat Conduct Book*. Cranbury, N.J.: Bucknell University Press, 1986. Examines *Sir Charles Grandison* in its social context. Discusses the novel as "the culmination of the conduct-book tradition."

Rivero, Albert J., ed. *New Essays on Samuel Richardson*. New York: St. Martin's Press, 1996. Includes three essays on *Sir Charles Grandison*: "Richardson's Girls: The Daughters of Patriarchy in *Pamela, Clarissa*, and *Sir Charles Grandison*" by Jerry C. Beasley, "*Sir Charles Grandison* and the Human Prospect" by Lois A. Chaber, and "Representing Clementina: 'Unnatural' Romance and the Ending of *Sir Charles Grandison*" by Albert J. Rivero.

Sir Gawain and the Green Knight

Author: Pearl-Poet (fl. latter half of the fourteenth century)
First transcribed: Fourteenth century
Type of work: Poetry
Type of plot: Arthurian romance
Time of plot: Sixth century
Locale: England

Principal characters:
SIR GAWAIN, a knight of the Round Table
SIR BERNLAK DE HAUTDESERT, the Green Knight

The Poem:

On Christmas Eve, many knights and fair ladies gather in King Arthur's banquet hall, there to feast and enjoy the holiday festivities. Suddenly a stranger enters the room. He is a giant, clad all in green armor, and with a green face, hair, and beard. He advances, gives his greetings, and then loudly issues his challenge. Is there a knight in the group who would dare to trade blows with the mighty Green Knight? He who accepts is to strike one blow with a battle-ax immediately. Then on New Year's morning, a year hence, the Green Knight is to repay the blow, at his own castle in a distant land. Arrogantly, the Green Knight waits for an answer. From King Arthur's ranks answers the voice of Sir Gawain, who accepts the challenge.

King Arthur and the other knights watch approvingly as Sir Gawain advances, ax in hand, to confront the Green Knight. The stranger kneels down, bares his neck, and waits for the blow. Sir Gawain strikes, sure and true, and the head of the Green Knight is severed from his body. While all gape in amazement, the Green Knight picks up his head in his hands, leaps upon his charger, and rides toward the gate. As he rides, the lips of the head shout defiance at Sir Gawain, reminding him of their forthcoming meeting at the Green Chapel on the coming New Year.

The months pass quickly. Noble deeds are legion at the Round Table, and an atmosphere of gaiety pervades King Arthur's castle. Then, when autumn comes, Sir Gawain departs on his promised quest, and with much concern the other knights see him set forth. Sir Gawain, riding his horse Gringalet, goes northward and at last arrives in Wirral, a wild and uncivilized region. On his way he was often in danger of death, for he faced fire-puffing dragons, fierce animals, and savage wild men in his search for the Knight of the Green Chapel. At last, on Christmas Eve, Sir Gawain sees a great castle in the middle of the wilderness. He enters it and is made welcome.

His host offers Sir Gawain the entire facilities of the castle. In the beautifully furnished chamber that he occupies, Sir Gawain is served the finest dishes and the best wines. The lady of the castle, a lady more beautiful even than Queen Guinevere, sits with him as he eats. The next day is Christmas, and the lord of the castle leads in the feasting. Expressing the wish that Sir Gawain will remain at the castle for a long time, the host assures the knight that the Green Chapel is only a short distance away, so that it will not be necessary for him to leave until New Year's Day. The lord of the castle also asks Sir Gawain to keep a covenant with him. During his stay Sir Gawain is to receive all the game that his host catches during the day's hunt. In return, Sir Gawain is to exchange any gifts he receives at the castle while the host is away.

On the first morning that the host hunts, Sir Gawain is awakened by the lady of the castle. She enters his chamber, seats herself on his couch, and speaks words of love to him. Sir Gawain resists temptation and takes nothing from the lady. That evening, when the host presents his bounty from the hunt, Sir Gawain answers truthfully that he received nothing that day. The second morning the same thing happens. Sir Gawain remains chaste in spite of the lady's conduct. On the third morning, however, the day before Sir Gawain is to depart, she gives him an embroidered silk girdle that she says will keep him safe from any mortal blow. Then she kisses him three times and departs. That evening Sir Gawain kisses his host three times, but he does not mention the silken girdle he received.

On New Year's morning, Sir Gawain sets forth from the castle and rides to the Green Chapel. He finds it without difficulty; as he approaches he hears the Green Knight sharpening his ax. When Sir Gawain announces that he is ready for the blow and bares his head, the Green Knight raises his ax high in the air in preparation for the stroke of death. Sir Gawain first involuntarily jumps aside as the ax descends. The second time, the Green Knight merely strikes at Sir Gawain, not touching him at all. With the third blow he wounds Sir Gawain in the neck, drawing a great deal of blood. Then Sir Gawain shouts that he fulfilled the covenant. The Green Knight laughs loudly at that and begins to praise Sir Gawain's courage.

To Sir Gawain's surprise, the Green Knight reveals himself as the host of the castle and explains the blows. On the first two blows Sir Gawain escaped injury, because for two days he faithfully kept the covenant. The third drew blood, however, because Sir Gawain failed to reveal the gift to Sir Bernlak de Hautdesert. Together with Morgain le Fay, King Arthur's half sister, the Green Knight planned this whole affair to test the strength and valor of King Arthur's knights. They devised the disguise of the Green Knight and persuaded Lady de Hautdesert to try tempting Sir Gawain. Sir Gawain withstands the test of temptation well, his only fault is the keeping of the girdle. The host forgives him for his act, however, because it is the love of life that motivated Sir Gawain.

The two knights return to the castle, and a few days later Sir Gawain journeys back to King Arthur's court. As he rides he gazes with shame at the girdle. It is to remain with Sir Gawain as a reminder of the moment when he yielded and succumbed to the weakness of the flesh. At King Arthur's castle all the knights and ladies listen to the tale of Sir Gawain and the Green Knight, and then, to show their love for the young knight, they all don silk girdles. This symbol became a traditional part of the costume of the Knights of the Round Table.

Critical Evaluation:

Sir Gawain and the Green Knight at first glance seems to be a conventional chivalric romance, featuring many of the standard trappings of Arthurian legend: A brave knight of the Round Table is challenged to a seemingly impossible task by a magical creature; on the way to meeting the challenge the knight fights fierce beasts and is charmed by a lovely lady; and he displays almost superhuman courage, skill, and chivalric courtesy to overcome his foe. The poem, however, is concerned with much more than these conventional features of courage and courtesy. In a conventional medieval romance, chivalric courtesy revolves around love, and adulterous love in particular. The "courteous" knight (in the medieval sense, a knight who is "courtly," and who understands and lives by the social rules of the court) is expected to be skilled in love and in romantic rhetoric and devoted to fulfilling the wishes of beautiful ladies. In temptation scenes with the wife of Bernlak, Gawain is forced to choose between this worldly, secular courtesy, which would require giving in to the lady's wishes, and a courtesy of a different sort: spiritual courtesy, which requires fidelity to a host as well as to chastity. To refuse the lady without giving offense requires all of Gawain's skill in courteous, roundabout rhetoric.

The wordplay between the seductive lady and the determined but courtly Gawain forms a game of sorts that the poet poses in direct contrast to the exchange-of-winnings game

Bernlak proposes as well as to Bernlak's own hunting exploits (for wild "game"). The exchange of ax blows between Gawain and the Green Knight is a game, too, and Gawain mistakenly believes that it is the game on which his life depends. Ultimately, readers realize that the Green Knight/ Bernlak enjoys a game of his own at Gawain's expense. Much of the poem's irony rests on the fact that Gawain and readers do not realize on which game Gawain's life depends until the end of the poem. The ironic interplay of these several kinds of games is central to the poem's meaning. By making a series of games into a matter of life and death, the poet offers a subtle criticism of the chivalric ideal of behavior, which places a higher value on honorably obeying the rules of a frivolous game than on saving one's life.

Gawain's failure to give up the girdle forms the central moral question of the poem. It seems clear that, according to chivalric principles, he should surrender the girdle. To do so is part of the game, and Gawain prides himself on his chivalrous qualities, which include keeping his promises. Readers can sympathize, however; after all, the Green Knight, who rides off holding his severed head under his arm, is using some kind of magic; why should Gawain not use what magic he might? The chivalric requirement that he give up the girdle seems ridiculous in the face of death. The reader is not surprised when Gawain conceals the magic girdle in order to save his life. Although Gawain later reproaches himself for covetousness in keeping the girdle, his only fault really is wanting to save his own life. This flaw, however, makes Gawain seem more real and thus makes it easier to admire his virtues of courage and knightly courtesy.

Much is made of the Green Knight as a symbol of wild nature, contrasted with the civilization of the court and the knightly ideals it admires and represents. This, however, is an incomplete view of the Green Knight. The elaborate description of the Green Knight at Arthur's court details how his green is lavishly embellished by gold embroidery and decoration. The gold can be seen as representing civilization imposed on nature and wildness. With the green-and-gold motif, the Green Knight represents a balance between nature and civilization; he is, after all, the same person as Bernlak, who is a perfect, courteous host. The Green Knight is the real, in contrast to Gawain, who represents the ideal. It does, after all, seem rather unnatural that Gawain should be willing to give up his life just to maintain a facade of civilization (that is, if he were to give up the girdle because it is the polite thing to do).

The theme of the poem is the attempt to achieve perfection (spiritual and secular) in the real world. Gawain's ideals for himself are shown to be unrealistic in the face of death. Although Gawain comes about as close to ideal behavior as a real person can expect to, his ideal of perfection is impossible to attain. In the end, he wears the green girdle back to the court of the Round Table as an emblem of his failure and shame. When Arthur's court laughs and congratulates him, paying little attention to his own notions of failure (just as the Green Knight did when he revealed himself as Bernlak), the reader is invited to join in the court's judgment. Gawain is not a two-dimensional embodiment of conventional knightly ideals but rather is a realistically drawn character facing a dilemma and demonstrating the compromises involved in putting an ideal standard of conduct into practice in the real world.

Sir Gawain and the Green Knight was first transcribed in the second half of the fourteenth century, the same era in which Geoffrey Chaucer wrote *The Canterbury Tales* (1387-1400) and other works in English. Unlike Chaucer, of whose life many details are known, very little is known about the author of *Sir Gawain and the Green Knight*. Only one original manuscript of the poem is known to exist, which is also the sole manuscript of three other poems. Although in terms of subject matter *Sir Gawain and the Green Knight* has little in common with the other poems of the manuscript, which are religious works, it is generally accepted that all four poems are by the same author. The dialect used in the poem suggests that the author was from the Midlands of England. Although the poet seems to have lived and written far from London and the court, his poem is as sophisticated and urbane as any of Chaucer's works. The author's emphasis on development of character, vivid descriptions, and use of naturalistic dialogue (a quality that, owing to the fact that his dialect has become obsolete, is not immediately recognizable) also mark a common ground with Chaucer. The complexity of the poem's themes, along with the poet's masterful use of irony and skillful artistry in weaving together the temptation game and the exchange-of-blows game, make *Sir Gawain and the Green Knight* one of the most important literary works of medieval England.

"Critical Evaluation" by Catherine Swanson

Further Reading

Anderson, J. J. *Language and Imagination in the Gawain-Poems.* New York: Palgrave, 2005. Examines *Sir Gawain and the Green Knight*, *Pearl*, and two other poems attributed to the Pearl-Poet. Anderson argues that all of the poems reflect the fourteenth century struggle between religious and secular forces for control of men's and women's minds.

Barron, W. R. J. *Trawthe and Treason: The Sin of Gawain Reconsidered.* New York: Manchester University Press, 1980. Examines Gawain's sin of deception, and the temptation and beheading games, in the context of medieval society and feudal law. Analyzes the parallels between the hunting and temptation scenes.

Benson, Larry D. *Art and Tradition in Sir Gawain and the Green Knight.* New Brunswick, N.J.: Rutgers University Press, 1965. Excellent background material and discussion of the sources, literary conventions, style, structure, and meaning of the poem.

Brewer, Derek, and Jonathan Gibson. *A Companion to the Gawain-Poet.* Rochester, N.Y.: D. S. Brewer, 1997. Collection of essays about the Pearl-Poet, including theories of authorship, the historical background of his work, and specific discussions of *Sir Gawain and the Green Knight*. Some of the pieces discuss the hunts, love, the color green, meter, stanza, vocabulary, and sources of *Sir Gawain* as well as novel, opera, and film adaptations of the poem.

Burrow, J. A. *The Gawain-Poet.* Tavistock, England: Northcote House/British Council, 2001. A concise analysis of the four poems written by the author of *Sir Gawain and the Green Knight*, an account of what little biographical information is known about the poet, and a discussion of the poems' history, rediscovery, and poetic techniques.

Fox, Denton, ed. *Twentieth Century Interpretations of Sir Gawain and the Green Knight.* Englewood Cliffs, N.J.: Prentice-Hall, 1968. A brief but useful collection of critical essays, which also includes brief writings on the poem by such noted critics as C. S. Lewis and A. C. Spearing.

Howard, Donald R., and Christian Zacker, eds. *Critical Studies of Sir Gawain and the Green Knight.* Notre Dame, Ind.: University of Notre Dame Press, 1968. Provides a thorough discussion of all major aspects of *Sir Gawain and the Green Knight*. Essays are grouped by subject and cover such topics as critical issues, style and technique, and characterization and setting.

Risden, E. L., ed. *"Sir Gawain" and the Classical Tradition: Essays on the Ancient Antecedents.* Jefferson, N.C.: McFarland, 2006. The essays examine how the anonymous author of *Sir Gawain and the Green Knight* uses elements of classical writings and past British tradition, as well as romantic adaptations of Trojan and British literature, to create his fourteenth century poems.

Waldron, R. A. Introduction to *Sir Gawain and the Green Knight.* London: Edward Arnold, 1970. Offers one of the best and most comprehensive overviews available of the poem's action, themes, and structure. Detailed annotation and an extensive glossary offer insights into the original text that are not found in most critical surveys. An excellent starting point.

The Sirens of Titan

Author: Kurt Vonnegut (1922-2007)
First published: 1959
Type of work: Novel
Type of plot: Science fiction
Time of plot: The Nightmare Ages, between World
War II and the Third Great Depression
Locale: Earth, Mars, Mercury, and the ninth moon of
Saturn (Titan)

Principal characters:
MALACHI CONSTANT, UNK, SPACE WANDERER, the victim
of a series of accidents
WINSTON NILES RUMFOORD, a space and time traveler
BEATRICE RUMFOORD, wife of Rumfoord, mate to Constant
CHRONO, son of Constant and Beatrice
BOAZ, a commander in the Martian army
SALO, a Tralfamadorian stranded on Titan

The Story:

Malachi Constant arrives at the Rumfoord estate to witness a materialization. Winston Niles Rumfoord, who is chrono-synclastic infundibula, scatters everywhere between the sun and Betelgeuse and appears various places sporadically. He is to materialize and Constant is invited to witness. Constant is a billionaire playboy who inherits his father Noel's estate.

Rumfoord materializes and tells Constant that he, Constant, will eventually go to Mars, Mercury, back to Earth, then to Titan. He and Beatrice, Rumfoord's wife, will have a child named Chrono. Chrono will pick up a good-luck piece on Mars and carry it to Titan. Beatrice and Constant are chary of their union. Constant sells the company that owns the only known transportation to Mars, which is a spaceship called *The Whale*, which Beatrice buys. This buying and selling, along with Constant's fifty-six-day party, which ends with him giving away all his oil wells, ruins Constant financially, and Beatrice is likewise ruined financially.

Upon losing all his money, Constant is open for options. Secret agents from Mars recruit him for the Martian army. Beatrice is surreptitiously recruited. On the spaceship to Mars, Constant rapes Beatrice. When on Mars, they are separated and their memories are erased from their brains.

Constant begins as an officer but after eight years he is made a private and is nicknamed Unk. His first act after having his memory cleared out for the seventh time is to execute his best friend Stony Stevenson in front of ten thousand Martian soldiers. Before Unk strangles Stevenson, Stevenson manages to tell him, "Blue stone . . . Barrack twelve . . . letter." Unk finds the stone and the letter. Written on it are things about Stevenson; about the antennas under the soldiers' skulls, which make them do whatever the commanders want; about Beatrice and Chrono; and about the Martian army and its plans to make war on Earth. It informs Unk that Boaz, a private first class in the army, does not have an antenna in his head and that he is the one who gives pain to everyone and controls everyone in Unk's squad. The letter is signed by Unk.

The war on Earth is a complete disaster from the Martian point of view. Before boarding the spaceship, Unk deserts the army and finds Beatrice and Chrono. They do not know him or care about him. Unk is returned to his unit, where he and Boaz are put on a spaceship designed by Rumfoord to go to Mercury instead of Earth and thus Unk and Boaz miss the war.

Unk and Boaz are stranded deep in a cavern on Mercury where there is no life except for harmoniums, small creatures that live by eating vibrations. Boaz is especially attached to the harmoniums. He plays music from the ship's tape collection, and he allows his favorite harmoniums to feed from his own pulse. Rumfoord occasionally arranges harmoniums on the walls of the caves to give Unk and Boaz messages. The final message is to turn the ship upside down and it will fly out. Boaz stays with the harmoniums and Unk travels on to Earth, where he is greeted as the Space Wanderer, the messiah of the Church of God the Utterly Indifferent. Rumfoord knows of many events that will transpire in future times and prophesied that Unk will arrive on Earth, exactly as he does, and that when he is asked what happened to him he will reply, "I was a victim of a series of accidents, as are we all." As Unk does exactly what was forecast, the religion Rumfoord set up becomes even stronger, as the only one on Earth in which predictions actually came to pass.

Rumfoord stages an elaborate ceremony in which Unk is told by Rumfoord that he strangled Stevenson. This is Unk's final blow, as he wished, since reading the message, to find his best friend. Rumfoord explains to Unk that he was Constant before becoming Unk and that Constant is the symbol of evil to the Church of God the Utterly Indifferent. With Beatrice and Chrono, Unk is martyred and sent away in exile to live out his life on Titan.

Upon arrival in Titan, Rumfoord informs Salo, the Tralfamadorian machine long stranded, that the replacement part for his spaceship is now there, in the form of Chrono's good-luck piece. Salo does not realize that the entire history of human life on Earth is for his sake. Human life is made to exist by the Tralfamadorians, who are working to get Salo the replacement part as quickly as they can.

Rumfoord disappears and Beatrice moves into his home on Titan. Salo self-destructs and Constant lives in Salo's spaceship. Chrono goes to live with the giant blue birds of Titan, the most noble creatures on the planet. Chrono's final gesture to Constant and Beatrice is to show appreciation for them having given him life.

Beatrice dies and Salo comes back to life. Salo gives Constant a ride to Earth, where he dies on a street corner. His last thought is a posthypnotic illusion, placed in his mind by Salo, that makes him believe that Stevenson comes to greet him and take him to paradise.

Critical Evaluation:

The book's disclaimer is a superbly creative and tongue-in-cheek way to begin. It reads: "All persons, places, and events in this book are real. . . . No names have been changed to protect the innocent since God Almighty protects the innocent as a matter of heavenly routine." *The Sirens of Titan*, Kurt Vonnegut's second novel, was originally published as pulp science fiction. There was no respectable hardcover edition. The book's satire and depth was not perceived until many years later, after Vonnegut had achieved fame through *Slaughterhouse-Five* (1969). *The Sirens of Titan* was written in less than two months; the plot line was determined over cocktails at a party. Vonnegut took the job writing it because the magazine market was not as good as the science fiction novel market, and he could make more money in two months on a novel. In *The Sirens of Titan*, Vonnegut fashioned several characters and scenes that were employed in his later novels. The invention of the planet Tralfamador is one of these. The Martian recruiters were characters he had used in a story for the *Saturday Evening Post*.

The theme of *The Sirens of Titan* is whether or not human history is meaningful. The answer and the moral, as often found in Vonnegut's books, are to love whoever is around to be loved, to abandon expectations, and to live fully in the moment at hand. In the caves of Mercury, Boaz states, "I don't know what's going on and I'm probably not smart enough to understand if somebody was to explain it to me. All I know is we're being tested somehow, by somebody or some thing a whole lot smarter than us, and all I can do is be friendly and keep calm and try to have a nice time till it's over."

Rumfoord is the most intricate character in this novel.

Vonnegut said that Rumfoord is based on Franklin Delano Roosevelt. Rumfoord's personal dilemma is that he is used by the Tralfamadorians, just as everyone else is used. Because he seems to have so much power and control, he thinks he should be allowed to determine his own fate and destiny. He is not, and his position is particularly obscure because he arranges the great suicide of the Martian army in order to do what he perceives to be a good thing, setting up a religion on Earth in which everyone is equal.

In this religion, people wear handicaps to limit whatever gifts or talents with which they are born. Strong people wear weights, beautiful women wear ugly makeup, people with good eyesight wear glasses to hamper their vision. All the people of Earth participate in this, under Rumfoord's supervision. Rumfoord thinks that, in causing a war and then presenting the world with a new and unified religion, he accomplishes a noble and decent act. He wants to think it is his own idea, that he is operating of his own free will.

In the end, Rumfoord is found to be no more in control of his destiny than any of the people he controls. He is made to stage the war and do everything he does by the Tralfamadorians. Vonnegut shows with Rumfoord that even those who appear to have the most power are just as baffled as to the meaning of life as everyone else is. Rumfoord is the only character who seems to be disgruntled with his lack of free will. Everyone else more or less accepts it.

Biblical references abound in the book. Constant adopts the name Jonah and owns a spaceship called *The Whale*. The fortune obtained by Noel Constant is accomplished by breaking the sentences of the book of Genesis into two-letter acronym combinations and finding company names that start with the two letters. The religion Rumfoord founds adopts the same God as is in the Bible, only this religion's God does not care about the plight of humans or the plight of anything else. Though Vonnegut claimed to be an atheist, he makes considerable use of the Bible in this and in many of his works.

With *The Sirens of Titan*, Vonnegut not only presents characters that he uses in later novels but also uses many themes that will later become Vonnegut hallmarks: middle-class virtues, decency, friendliness, respect, neighborliness, spiritual success through kindness and generosity. He asserts his theory of space and time through Rumfoord. Rumfoord says, "When I ran my spaceship into the chrono-synclastic infundibulum, it came to me in a flash that everything that ever has been always will be, and everything that ever will be always has been." This is as clear an explanation of Vonnegut's sense of fate as can be found.

Beaird Glover

Further Reading

Bloom, Harold, ed. *Kurt Vonnegut.* New ed. New York: Bloom's Literary Criticism, 2009. Collection of essays examining Vonnegut's works, including discussions of Vonnegut's melancholy, Vonnegut and postmodern humor, and "Kurt Vonnegut's *The Sirens of Titan*: Human Will in a Newtonian Narrative Gone Chaotic" by Mónica Calvo Pascual.

Davis, Todd F. *Kurt Vonnegut's Crusade: Or, How a Postmodern Harlequin Preached a New Kind of Humanism.* Albany: State University of New York Press, 2006. Examines the moral and philosophical foundations of Vonnegut's fiction, focusing on his belief that writing is an "act of good citizenship." Argues that in his desire to enact change by both critiquing and embracing humanity, Vonnegut created a new kind of literary humanism. The references to *The Sirens of Titan* are listed in the index.

Giannone, Richard. *Vonnegut: A Preface to His Novels.* Port Washington, N.Y.: Kennikat Press, 1977. Focuses on the method of Vonnegut's novels. The dignified and extensive treatment of *The Sirens of Titan* considers the chapters in small clusters, restating the plot and then discussing the implications from several angles.

Klinkowitz, Jerome. *Kurt Vonnegut.* New York: Methuen, 1982. Discusses *The Sirens of Titan* as a formula novel. Explains it as being like other novels by Vonnegut in adhering to the structures indicative of science fiction, as opposed to later, more experimental and personal novels.

McMahon, Gary. *Kurt Vonnegut and the Centrifugal Force of Fate.* Jefferson, N.C.: McFarland, 2009. Traces the development of Vonnegut's writing, analyzing his fiction and comparing his journalism to that of Hunter S. Thompson, Tom Wolfe, and other contemporaries. Chapter 4 is devoted to *The Sirens of Titan.*

Marvin, Thomas F. *Kurt Vonnegut: A Critical Companion.* Westport, Conn.: Greenwood Press, 2002. Uses a variety of critical approaches to examine Vonnegut's major works. Chapter 4 provides an analysis of *The Sirens of Titan*, discussing the novel's thematic issues and the development of its plot and characters. Offers information on Vonnegut's life and the literary contexts of his works.

Mayo, Clark. *Kurt Vonnegut: The Gospel from Outer Space (Or: Yes We Have No Nirvanas).* San Bernardino, Calif.: Borgo Press, 1977. A fairly short book adopting Vonnegut's style, voice, and satire while writing about Vonnegut. Discusses *The Sirens of Titan* in detail.

Morse, Donald E. *The Novels of Kurt Vonnegut: Imagining Being an American.* Westport, Conn.: Praeger, 2003. Examines all of Vonnegut's novels, demonstrating how they reflect the historical and social issues of the United States in the twentieth century, including the Great Depression, World War II, the atomic bomb, the Vietnam War, and the breakdown of marriage and the family. References to *The Sirens of Titan* are listed in the index.

Reed, Peter J. *Kurt Vonnegut, Jr.* New York: Thomas Y. Crowell, 1972. Considers the characteristic themes and fictional techniques of Vonnegut. The subhead to the thirty-page chapter on *The Sirens of Titan* is "Existential Science Fiction." Compares Vonnegut to classic and contemporary writers.

Schatt, Stanley. *Kurt Vonnegut, Jr.* Boston: Twayne, 1976. Extensive quotation and interpretation of *The Sirens of Titan* with attention to plot, structure, style, and technique. Includes a section on Vonnegut as a public figure.

Sister Carrie

Author: Theodore Dreiser (1871-1945)
First published: 1900
Type of work: Novel
Type of plot: Naturalism
Time of plot: 1889
Locale: Chicago and New York

Principal characters:
CARRIE MEEBER, a small-town young woman
CHARLES DROUET, her first lover
G. W. HURSTWOOD, Drouet's friend and Carrie's second lover

The Story:

When Carrie Meeber leaves her hometown in Wisconsin, she has nothing but a few dollars and a certain unspoiled beauty and charm. Young and inexperienced, she is going to Chicago to live with her sister and find work. While on the train, she meets Charles Drouet, a genial, flashy traveling salesman. Before the train pulls into the station, the two exchange addresses, and Drouet promises to call on Carrie at her sister's house.

When she arrives at her sister's home, Carrie discovers that her life there would be far from the happy, carefree existence of which she had dreamed. The Hansons are hardworking people, grim and penny-pinching; they allow themselves no pleasures and live a dull, conventional life. It is clear to Carrie that Drouet cannot possibly call there, not only because of the unattractive atmosphere but also because the Hansons are sure to object to him. She writes and tells him not to call, and that she will get in touch with him later.

Carrie goes job-hunting and finally finds work in a small shoe factory. Of her first wages, all but fifty cents goes to her sister and brother-in-law. When Carrie falls ill, she loses her job and again has to look for work. Day after day, she trudges the streets, without success. It seems as if she will have to go back to Wisconsin, and the Hansons encourage her to do so, since they do not want her if she cannot bring in money.

One day while looking for work, Carrie visits Drouet and tells him her troubles. He offers her money, and with reluctance, she accepts it. The money is for clothes she needs, but she does not know how to explain the source of the money to her sister. Drouet solves the problem by suggesting that he rent a room for her, where she can keep her clothing. A few days later, Carrie begins living with Drouet, who promises to marry her as soon as he completes a business deal.

In the meantime, Drouet introduces Carrie to a friend, G. W. Hurstwood. Hurstwood has a good job as the manager of a saloon and has a comfortable home, a wife, and two grown children. More than twice Carrie's age, he nevertheless accepts Drouet's suggestion that he look in on her while the salesman is out of town on one of his trips. Before long, Hurstwood is passionately in love with Carrie. When Drouet returns, he discovers from a chambermaid that Carrie and Hurstwood have been going out together frequently. Carrie is furious when Drouet tells her that Hurstwood is married. She blames Drouet for her folly, saying that he should have told her that Hurstwood is married.

Mrs. Hurstwood has meanwhile become suspicious of her husband. Drouet secures for Carrie a part in a theatrical entertainment presented by a local lodge. Hurstwood, hearing that Carrie is to appear, persuades many of his friends to go with him to the show. Mrs. Hurstwood learns of this and hears, too, that her husband had been seen riding with an unknown woman. She confronts Hurstwood and tells him that she intends to sue for divorce. Faced with social and financial ruin, Hurstwood is in despair. One night, he discovers that his employer's safe is open. He takes several thousand dollars from the safe and goes to Carrie's apartment. Drouet had just deserted her. Pretending that Drouet had been hurt, Hurstwood succeeds in getting Carrie on a train bound for Montreal. In Montreal, he is tracked down by an agent of his former employer, who urges him to return the money and settle the issue quietly. Hurstwood returns all but a relatively small sum and marries Carrie under the name of Wheeler. Carrie is under the impression that the ceremony was legal.

Hurstwood and Carrie then leave for New York, where Hurstwood looks for work but with no success. Finally, he buys a partnership in a small tavern, but when the partnership is dissolved, he loses all his money. Again he starts looking for work. Gradually he grows less eager for a job and begins staying at home all day. When bills pile up, he and Carrie move to a new apartment to escape their creditors.

Setting out to find work herself, Carrie manages to get a job as a chorus girl. With a friend, she gets an apartment and leaves Hurstwood to himself. Soon, Carrie becomes a well-known actor. A local hotel invites her to become a guest there, at a nominal expense. Carrie now has many friends and admirers, as well as money and all the comforts and luxuries that appeal to a small-town woman.

Hurstwood has not fared as well. He still has not found work. Once, during a labor strike, he worked as a scab, but he left that job because it was too hazardous. He begins to live in Bowery flophouses and to beg on the streets. One day, he visits Carrie, who gives him money, largely because she had seen Drouet and learned for the first time of Hurstwood's theft from the safe in Chicago. She believes that Hurstwood had kept his disgrace a secret to spare her feelings.

Although Carrie is a toast of the town and successful, she is not happy. She is invited to give performances abroad. Hurstwood dies and, unbeknownst to Carrie, is buried in the potter's field. As Carrie is sailing for London, Hurstwood's former wife, daughter, and son-in-law arrive in the city, eager for pleasure and social success, which had been made possible by the daughter's marriage and Hurstwood's divorce settlement, in which his family had received all of his property.

Critical Evaluation:

Sister Carrie, like most of Theodore Dreiser's novels, embodies Dreiser's belief that while humans are controlled and conditioned by heredity, instinct, and chance, a few extraordinary and usually unsophisticated individuals refuse to accept their fate wordlessly and instead strive, albeit unsuccessfully, to find meaning and purpose for their existence. Carrie, the title character, senses that she is merely a cipher in an uncaring world, yet she seeks to grasp the mysteries of life and satisfy her need to matter. In pointing out "how curious are the vagaries of fortune," Dreiser suggests that even when life is cruel, its enigmatic quality makes it all the more fascinating.

Despite its title, the novel is not a study of a family but of Carrie's strangely unemotional relationships with three men and of the resulting and unexpected changes that occur in her outlook and status. A "half-equipped little knight" with small talent, Carrie's "instinct" nevertheless raises her from a poor young woman to a successful actor. The novel traces the rise, through Carrie's increasing reliance on instinct, in three stages of development.

Initially, Carrie is at least partially ruled by reason, but by the end of the first phase of her rise—marked by her accidental second meeting with Drouet and her submission to his promises—she begins to abandon reason, since it has not served her well. During this second portion, her blossoming instinct pulls her to the material advantages offered by Drouet, and her life with him is evidence of her growing commitment to these instincts. However, it is her almost unconscious and unplanned switch to Hurstwood that reveals how totally she is now following her instincts. Hurstwood offers finer material possessions and more emotional rapport, and Carrie drifts easily into his orbit. Now fully and irrevocably tied to her instincts, Carrie throughout the rest of the novel considers it an obligation to self to let these impulses lead her where they will. When a stage career and her association with Ames replace the relationship with Hurstwood, she is merely proceeding further along that path. As a plant must turn toward the sun, Carrie must feed her unsatisfied urge for happiness.

Closely related to Dreiser's belief that instinct must prevail is his thesis that humans lack responsibility for their fate, a thesis suggested by all three main characters. Drouet leads Carrie to what some consider her moral downfall, but, as Dreiser states, "There was nothing evil in the fellow." His glands are to blame, not he. Neither is there any question of guilt in Hurstwood's case. Since he rarely makes a choice, he cannot be expected to answer for what happens to him. Chance, not conviction, makes him a thief. Hurstwood's wife, not he himself, ends their marriage. Even his attraction to Carrie is a thing of chance, for "He was merely floating those gossamer threads of thought which, like the spider's, he hoped would lay hold somewhere." Although merely a sham without true power or greatness (a fact Dreiser, dazzled by his own creation, seems to forget), Hurstwood, in his decline from partial prominence to degradation, reminds the reader that the forces that send Carrie to stardom can with equal ease reduce a person to nothing.

Dreiser presents his ideas through many symbolic images, most important of which are the city, the sea, and the rocking chair. The city, represented in the book by New York and Chicago, is a microcosm of Dreiser's universe. Nature is grim and unfeeling, as is the city. Unless a person is strong, productive, and fortunate, the world is indifferent, a state magnified in the city, where people are perhaps more isolated than elsewhere. When Hurstwood is dying, he is alone, even though Carrie is in a nearby apartment, Drouet is relatively close in a hotel, and his wife is arriving by train. No one knows, or cares, about his tragedy.

Dreiser's concept of an uncaring and ever-changing universe is equally conveyed by his use of the sea and the rocking chair. Again and again, Carrie is described as a "lone figure in a tossing, thoughtless sea." Like its counterpart, the city, the sea symbol suggests that only the strong or the lucky survive. The rocking chair hints at the futility of this constant flux, for a rocking chair is in continual motion but goes nowhere. Although Carrie's life would seem to improve, she is sitting miserably in a rocking chair not only at the novel's beginning but also its end. While this circular development suggests that Carrie has a small chance of becoming truly happy, her continued rocking symbolizes her never-ceasing aspiration.

Part of the book reflects events from Dreiser's own turbulent life. In 1886, L. A. Hopkins, a clerk in a Chicago saloon, took thirty-five hundred dollars from his employers and fled to New York with Emma Dreiser, one of the author's many troubled siblings. Dreiser modeled Carrie on his sister and used Hopkins for aspects of Hurstwood's personality. By the time Dreiser finished the novel in 1900, however, he had gone far beyond the cheap story of adultery and theft to create a work that presents complex questions of innocence and guilt.

The publication of Dreiser's first novel was surrounded by the kind of controversy and confusion that marked his entire career. Apparently, the novel was accepted by Doubleday during the absence of Frank Doubleday, the senior partner, who upon his return expressed doubt about its content and style. Refusing to release the firm from its unwritten commitment, however, Dreiser demanded that the book be published, and it appeared in 1900. Although it sold poorly (Dreiser earned only $68.40) and was not aggressively promoted by the publishers, stories relating Mrs. Doubleday's violent objections to its moral view and the resulting suppression of the novel are unverified legend. In his own typical confusion of fact and half-fact, Dreiser added to the myths by telling conflicting accounts of what had happened.

Reaction to the book was surprisingly widespread. While many critics attacked its philosophical premises as immoral, others said the novel was poorly written, wordy, and melodramatic; these same criticisms would greet each of Dreiser's later works. However, as Dreiser wrote book after book, exploring the yearning of the young for riches, position, and understanding—a yearning he himself experienced overwhelmingly, coming as he did from a poor and disturbed Indiana family in which he saw reflected much of the irony of the world. Readers were struck, however, by the sincerity, powerful detail, and massive impact of his work. Dreiser became especially known for *Jennie Gerhardt* (1911) and *An American Tragedy* (1925), which placed him securely among the most respected American writers of his time.

"Critical Evaluation" by Judith Bolch

Further Reading

Cassuto, Leonard, and Clare Virginia Eby, eds. *The Cambridge Companion to Theodore Dreiser.* New York: Cambridge University Press, 2004. A collection of twelve essays focusing on the novelist's examination of American conflicts between materialistic longings and traditional values. Includes essays on Dreiser's style and Dreiser and the ideology of upward mobility, and includes the essay "*Sister Carrie*, Race, and the World's Columbian Exposition."

Gerber, Philip. *Theodore Dreiser Revisited.* New York: Twayne, 1992. A biographical and thematic analysis of Dreiser's major works, which interprets *Sister Carrie* as a naturalistic novel in the tradition of Émile Zola in France and Stephen Crane and Frank Norris in the United States.

Gogol, Miriam, ed. *Theodore Dreiser: Beyond Naturalism.* New York: New York University Press, 1995. Ten essays examine Dreiser from the perspectives of new historicism, poststructuralism, psychoanalysis, feminism, and other points of view. Gogol's introduction advances the argument that Dreiser was much more than a naturalist and deserves to be treated as a major author.

Juras, Uwe. *Pleasing to the "I": The Culture of Personality and Its Representations in Theodore Dreiser and F. Scott Fitzgerald.* New York: Peter Lang, 2006. Juras examines how the two authors depict the then-emerging concept of personality, defined as the outward presentation of self. Includes a discussion of *Sister Carrie.*

Kaplan, Amy. "The Sentimental Revolt of *Sister Carrie.*" In *The Social Construction of American Realism.* Chicago: University of Chicago Press, 1988. Excellent discussion of the novel within the framework of American realism. Juxtaposes Dreiser's power as a realist, challenging moral and literary conventions, with his simultaneous reliance on sentimental codes. A second chapter, "Theodore Dreiser's Promotion of Authorship," explores Dreiser's conception of the realist within the literary marketplace.

Loving, Jerome. *The Last Titan: A Life of Theodore Dreiser.* Berkeley: University of California Press, 2005. This engrossing survey of the author's life and work is a welcome addition to Dreiser scholarship. Focuses on his works, including his journalism, discusses the writers who influenced him, and examines his place within American literature.

Pizer, Donald. *New Essays on "Sister Carrie."* New York: Cambridge University Press, 1991. In addition to Pizer's thorough discussion of the novel's historical and biographical background, this book contains four essays that explore Dreiser's naturalism, *Sister Carrie*'s narrative voice, and the relationship between the author and his heroine.

_____. *The Novels of Theodore Dreiser: A Critical Study.* Minneapolis: University of Minnesota Press, 1976. A classic treatment of Dreiser's novels by one of the most important Dreiser scholars. Discusses the composition history of *Sister Carrie* and its biographical and literary sources, and provides an excellent general introduction to the novel's themes.

Sasa, Ghada Suleiman. *The Femme Fatale in American Literature.* Amherst, N.Y.: Cambria Press, 2008. Analyzes the character of Carrie Meeber and other women in works of American naturalist literature. Argues that these women are femme fatales who deliberately use their femininity to overcome their trapping worlds.

Sloane, David E. E. "*Sister Carrie*": *Theodore Dreiser's Sociological Tragedy.* New York: Twayne, 1992. A book-length study of the novel that provides literary and historical context. Interprets the work as a sociological tragedy, focusing on plot, style, metaphor, symbol, and character. Includes an annotated bibliography of criticism.

Sister Philomène

Authors: Edmond de Goncourt (1822-1896) and Jules
de Goncourt (1830-1870)
First published: Sœur Philomène, 1861 (English
translation, 1890)
Type of work: Novel
Type of plot: Naturalism
Time of plot: Nineteenth century
Locale: Paris

Principal characters:
MARIE GAUCHER, later known as Philomène
CÉLINE, her friend
MADAME DE VIRY, the employer of Philomène's aunt
HENRI DE VIRY, Madame de Viry's son
BARNIER, a young doctor
MALIVOIRE, his friend and a doctor
ROMAINE, Barnier's former mistress

The Story:

In a hospital ward, two white-clad Sisters of St. Augustine are making their rounds. One of them, a novice, is Sister Philomène, whose name was originally Marie Gaucher. She is the daughter of a tailoress and a locksmith and was orphaned at the age of four, when she was adopted by an aunt who was a servant to the widowed Madame de Viry. In that pleasant household, the child began to thrive, and she soon assumed equal footing with Madame de Viry's son, Henri. Madame de Viry felt this situation to be dangerous and she sent the child, screaming, to a convent orphanage. To avoid confusion with another child there called Marie, the Sisters called her Philomène. Though she was miserable at first, she gradually lost her resentment as she became accustomed to convent routine, although she changed from a vivacious child into a quiet and a whining one. She was restless, living only for her aunt's monthly visit. One Sister, the ugly but good and kind Marguerite, paid special attention to Philomène.

At the age of ten, Philomène became the intimate friend of a newcomer, twelve-year-old Céline. Much of Céline's childhood was spent in reading the *Lives of the Saints* aloud to her infirm grandmother, and she developed a mystic temperament. She liked to deny herself pleasures, to fast, and to invent self-punishments, and she converted Philomène to a course of personal sacrifices. Philomène worked herself up to a state of religious agitation, habitually spending all of Sunday in church and looking forward to that prospect as she once did to her aunt's visits. She became sickly and irritable, and her thoughts were always on death. When her eyes began to give her trouble, the Sisters sent her with her aunt to see an eye doctor. On that occasion, Philomène visited Madame de Viry's house for the first time since she entered the orphanage.

Back in the convent, Philomène felt miserable and forlorn. She succeeded in maintaining her state of feverish piety for two years, but then her faith became automatic and unfelt.

Céline left the orphanage to become a nun; Sister Marguerite left for her health. The convent became unbearable to Philomène; she went into a decline and was so close to death that her aunt was permitted to take her away. Madame de Viry died, and Philomène became a servant to Monsieur Henri. Philomène longed to sacrifice herself for him, and she rejected the advances of a coarse groom who hoped eventually, by marrying her, to gain the management of Henri's house.

One night, Philomène overheard Henri telling her aunt that he would bring a woman home with him were it not for the presence of an unmarried girl in the house. When he suggested that Philomène marry the groom, she fainted. Later, though assured she would not be sent away, she decided to begin her novitiate to the Sisters of St. Augustine. With seven months of her novitiate to complete before taking her vows, she was sent to a hospital to replace her friend Céline, who died of typhoid.

The doctors agreed that Philomène was pretty, but Barnier, under whom she worked, said that he preferred the old ones, tried and true. Philomène's original horror of the hospital was relieved by its clean, peaceful atmosphere at first, but later the realization of death and disease tortured her. Midmorning breakfast was the happiest hour for her, for then, useful and busy feeding and cheering her patients, Philomène gained strength for the rest of the day. By the time she realized that she could do no more than relieve suffering, she was inured to the hospital. She was never hardened, however, and her patients loved her for her tenderness.

Philomène earned the respect of doctors and students alike by her courage and compassion. Soon she was all-powerful, softening hospital rules and lending courage to sufferers.

When one dying patient despaired for her little boy's future, Barnier generously proposed to send him to his mother in the country. Everyone admired his goodness, and he and Philomène became closer. Their chats were her one recreation, for Barnier told her about changes outside the hospital in Paris. She feared that she would be transferred, for the Sisters were not supposed to become attached to a ward, but she was pleased to learn that she was to remain. One day, Barnier, an unbeliever who often discussed religion with her, was silenced by her announcement that she just took her vows. Soon after, Philomène became ill and had to leave the hospital for a month. When she returned, she was very pale but seemed strong and active.

Malivoire told Barnier that he should have a more or less permanent mistress. Because a doctor's profession was so material, maintained Malivoire, the physician needed the illusions of love as well as the brutal fact of sex. Barnier was about to confess a love affair to Malivoire when they were interrupted. Barnier provided Philomène with laudanum to take for her neuralgic headaches. Her laudanum-provoked dream included the illusion of the touch of a kiss.

A new patient arrived. Barnier recognized her as the specter of Romaine, the woman he loved. They were happy lovers until she left him and began a life of dissipation resulting in a breast injury. When Barnier asked Philomène to prepare Romaine for the operation, Philomène spoke to the woman with unusual harshness. After the operation Romaine, raging in fever, alternately cursed Barnier and begged him not to let her die. As he was leaving, Barnier overheard Philomène say that women like her should not be admitted to the hospital. Romaine died, after a scene in which Philomène's prayers were broken by the woman's curses and singing. Returning, Barnier saw the coffin that was to carry her away.

At a drinking party, Barnier defended the Sisters against a cynic who said that they were tender only toward those who were religious and decent. A suggestion was made that Philomène loved Barnier. Drunk and aroused, he went to the ward and attempted to kiss her, but she slapped him. Sobered, he returned to his friends to say that he would fight anyone who suggested her impurity.

Miserable in his memories of Romaine, Barnier took to drinking absinthe. Intoxication became his real life. When he learned that the house surgeon's coveted medal would not be his, Barnier struggled to resist drink, but when sober he was haunted by thoughts of Romaine. Philomène was ill. After her laudanum dream she searched her heart for symptoms of attachment for Barnier and remembered her jealous reaction to Romaine. Resolving on a course of expiation, she punished herself by remaining in the hospital and suffering the torments of love. One day Barnier asked her forgiveness for the attempted kiss. Her heart too full to speak, she went silently to her closet.

Barnier's student period was soon to end. He told Mali-

voire that the subject of his thesis was to be death, that modern existence—a suicide more or less slow—does not use up but breaks life. Having deliberately scratched his hand while dissecting a diseased body, Barnier went to bed to await death.

Philomène went to a priest to have prayers said for Barnier by the Confraternity of Notre-Dame-des-Victoires, who were devoted to those who do not believe. Later, she knelt and prayed beside the dead Barnier. After she left, Malivoire was unable to find the lock of Barnier's hair that was to have been sent to his mother.

Critical Evaluation:

The brothers Edmond and Jules de Goncourt are considered to be both theorists and practitioners of the documentary novel in nineteenth century French fiction. They based their plots on newspaper articles, interviews, and personal investigation and, like Émile Zola and Fyodor Dostoevski, they described outrages to contemporary cultural convention. True to their mechanistic and analytical vision of the world, naturalist writers rejected myths of transcendence and brought tragedy into the sphere of everyday existence. Although their novels may have shocked middle-class readership, *Sister Philomène* also inspired sympathy for the poor and for reforms in hospitals and orphanages.

Sister Philomène is based on a firsthand account of a nun's unspoken love for an intern, which was told to the Goncourts by Gustave Flaubert. Initially, the story appealed to the brothers as a romantic tale. Their fictionalized version, however, is decidedly deterministic. The Goncourts believed that character is shaped by milieu, just as animals are formed by their habitat. They rejected realism as a flat imitation of reality and insisted on depicting the physiological causes of psychology. At the same time that they became interested in portraying the impact of the maternal instinct and nervous system on women, they also documented life in city hospitals. The Goncourts' fascination with the pathological and the deviant led them to investigate Paris hospitals, to follow doctors on rounds, and to interview interns. Their account of this social institution, while frequently ironic, seems authentic.

The Goncourts wished to show how a girl could become a nurse on the basis of temperament and upbringing. They also trace her search for identity, a search in which she has little choice. Marie Gaucher's life story follows the first chapter in the form of an extended flashback. After being orphaned at an early age, she is sheltered for a time in the household of Madame de Viry, where her aunt, a maid, cares for her. She acquires aristocratic tastes and falls in love with the young master, Henri. Unaware of the social mores that make it impossible to change class, she entertains the illusion that she is a true lady. When the adults realize her illusions, they send her to a Catholic orphanage.

Marie continues her struggle to define her identity at the orphanage, where her name is stripped away—from then on she is called Philomène—and she must rebuild her life. She alternates between acceptance of her new position and an inability to cope. The Church educates orphans on pious legends and miraculous apparitions. When one of her friends, Céline, becomes a mystic, Marie's religious yearnings are expressed by isolation, fasting, and the nervous irritation of constant prayer. The mystical teachings and First Communion coincide with her physical maturation. The Goncourts depict the emergence of her senses in detail as she approaches puberty. She really longs for marriage, but when she returns to Madame de Viry's home, Henri barely notices her. The destruction of her fantasy forces her to take up nursing as a substitute for motherhood.

Philomène has naïve and romantic views about her calling. The initial chapter, which shows the nurses making their rounds at night, emphasizes the hospital as a world apart. The moans of patients announce the themes of suffering and pessimism. After presenting this shadowy world of darkness and light, the Goncourts introduce the problem of the perception of reality. The nurses seem to comfort the patients, but they actually prolong the pain of life. The nurses' efforts cannot prevail against the inexorable progress of death. The Goncourts juxtapose the deaths of patients with the joyous cries of the maternity ward—but death always prevails. These scenes also show doctors without idealizing them. Philomène passes through various phases of training that offer more realistic visions of her profession. Trepidation gives way to security, then to overwhelming horror, and, finally, to pragmatism. The hospital must hide the reality of death to give the patients hope.

In the central episode, when Barnier, a young doctor, must operate on a woman who was once his mistress, all the plot lines are drawn together. Romaine, the mistress, who once symbolized youthful love, falls from virtue. Barnier's idealization of love and of his lover dies when he learns that her breast was damaged in an orgy. He thereupon declares that doctors need quick, brutal affairs, like animals. Meanwhile, Philomène is falling in love with Barnier. At first, he is impatient with her, but then he begins to indulge in shoptalk. Eventually, neither wishes to be transferred from the women's ward, where they meet daily. Each idealizes the other, and their friendship is deepened by Barnier's adoption of an orphaned child.

The strain of unspoken love takes its toll on Philomène's health. When Barnier gives her a drug to help her sleep, her repressed sexuality becomes apparent. The Goncourts portray her dream in an impressionistic style to reveal the psyche beyond the control of the conscious mind. The Goncourts, years ahead of the medicine of their time, recognized that psychological tensions and the will to live complicate physical medicine. Psychological strain affects Philomène's health, and Romaine's condition degenerates as she loses hope. Nevertheless, even though Romaine gives up, in her death throes she exhibits the animal desire to live. The constant presence of death leads to more searching religious questions for the characters, and Barnier's doubts regarding an afterlife heighten the horror of his suicide. His death is depicted as a retreat from the atrocities of reality, yet he dies with his illusions about Philomène in place.

The Goncourts try to unify Philomène's character, but the composite nature of her personality as a child, a nurse, and a Sister belies that effort. She is also presented in a vacuum; there are no friends, coworkers, teachers, or family. Although subtleties of plot and character are lacking, the Goncourts skillfully re-create the medical community of their time. In contrast to the Goncourts's usual stories of abject misery and failure, *Sister Philomène* portrays the possibility of independence and some fulfillment.

"Critical Evaluation" by Pamela Pavliscak

Further Reading

Ashley, Katherine. *Edmond de Goncourt and the Novel: Naturalism and Decadence.* New York: Rodopi, 2005. Ashley analyzes Edmond's four solo novels, arguing that these books deviated from the strict naturalistic style that characterized the novels he wrote with his brother. She places Edmond's work within the larger context of late nineteenth century fin de siècle literature.

Auerbach, Erich. *Mimesis: The Representation of Reality in Western Literature.* Translated by Willard Trask. New York: Doubleday, 1953. Considers the Goncourts as naturalist writers. Compares their novels with those of Émile Zola and classifies the Goncourts as second-tier writers.

Baldick, Robert. *The Goncourts.* London: Bowes, 1960. A very brief but excellent survey of the Goncourts' novels. Concentrates on biographical background to the novels. Includes some exploration of major themes and aspects of literary style. *Sister Philomène* is cited as their most positive and least sensational novel.

Billy, Andre. *The Goncourt Brothers.* Translated by Margaret Shaw. New York: Horizon Press, 1960. The standard biography of the Goncourts. Shows that their novels emerged from events in their lives. Traces the research efforts that contributed to *Sister Philomène*. Also furnishes contemporary reaction to their novels.

Grant, Richard B. *The Goncourt Brothers*. New York: Twayne, 1972. Surveys the lives and works of Jules and Edmond de Goncourt. Ordered chronologically, the book carefully integrates the lives of the authors with detailed stylistic and thematic analysis of their novels.

Nelson, Brian, ed. *Naturalism in the European Novel: New Critical Perspectives*. New York: Berg, 1992. Essays by prominent scholars of naturalism in England, France, Germany, and Spain. Includes several important discussions of the Goncourts' role in the development of social documentary as a literary genre.

Six Characters in Search of an Author

Author: Luigi Pirandello (1867-1936)
First produced: Sei personaggi in cerca d'autore: Commedia da fare, 1921; first published, 1921 (English translation, 1922)
Type of work: Drama
Type of plot: Comedy
Time of plot: Twentieth century
Locale: Stage of a theater

Principal characters:
THE FATHER
THE MOTHER
THE STEPDAUGHTER
THE SON
THE BOY
THE CHILD
MADAME PACE
THE MANAGER
LEADING LADY
LEADING MAN

The Story:

As a stage manager and a group of actors prepare to rehearse a Pirandello play, they are interrupted by the appearance of six characters: a man of about fifty, a woman, a young woman, a young man of twenty-two, a boy of fourteen, and a little girl. The man and the young woman are searching for an author who will put all six of them into a drama. They insist that they are already living characters but that they need an author to put their drama into suitable form for the stage. The manager, at first annoyed at the interruption of his rehearsal, finally listens with some interest to the rather confused story that the man and the young woman, who, it turns out, is his stepdaughter, try to tell him.

Years ago the father got rid of his wife, whom he found both boring and pitiable, by providing her with a lover, his former secretary, to whom she might go when she was rejected by her husband. Long afterward, the father visited Madame Pace's dress shop, a legitimate business that she operated as a cover for her procuring, and was provided with a pretty young woman whom he did not recognize as his stepdaughter until they were separated by the sudden appearance of his wife. When he learned that his wife was destitute, her lover having died two months before, he permitted her to return to his home with her daughter and two younger children, all illegitimate.

To forestall a refusal by the manager to act as vicar-author for the drama, the father assures him that he need not be bothered about the presence of the two children, for they will quickly disappear from the story. In fact, the daughter will also disappear, leaving only the three original members of the family. The manager dismisses his actors for a few minutes in order to hear more of the plot as it is outlined to him in his office.

Returning a few minutes later from the office conference, the manager sets about putting together the play, asking his prompter to take down the most important points in shorthand so that his actors might properly learn their parts later. At this point the father interrupts; the manager, he says, simply does not understand. This is not a play for the manager's professional actors; it belongs to the characters themselves. There is no need for actors when the manager already has six living characters at hand.

After hearing similar objections from the stepdaughter,

the manager consents to use the characters, as this is only a rehearsal, but he wonders who will play Madame Pace if they are going to do the dress shop scene. After borrowing hats and other clothes from several actors to hang on clothes pegs, the father arranges the set. Madame Pace suddenly appears to play her part, but when she finds that she is expected to play it in the presence of the mother, who will be watching the rehearsal from the side of the stage, she is scandalized at such impropriety and leaves in a rage.

The rehearsal continues, with the mother watching and listening intently, suffering all the while at the reenactment of the scene in which her husband, with honeyed words and actions, plans to purchase the favors of the pretty girl whom he does not recognize as his stepdaughter. The action is suddenly stopped and then repeated, this time with the parts of the father and the stepdaughter being taken by the leading man and the leading lady of the actors' company. The stepdaughter is unable to control her laughter at what seems to her the ludicrous performance of the leading lady, and the father objects to the way the leading man is portraying him. Again the scene is played with the original characters, this time up to the point where, after the girl reminds the father that she is wearing mourning, he suggests that she remove her dress. At that point the action is abruptly stopped by the entrance of the mother, who in horror pulls her daughter away from the father. The manager is well pleased with this action; it will, he decides, make a fine first-act ending for the drama.

Preparations begin for working up a second act, using a garden scene. The father engages in a lengthy discussion of the difference between reality and the mere illusion of reality to be found in conventional stage representations, or, for that matter, in life itself. The manager, the father says, must try to perceive what he so far missed: Ordinary people have illusions about themselves which they later discover are not the realities they thought them to be; the only reality the six characters have is that of a permanent, unchanging illusion, more real than any reality the manager himself might have.

The stepdaughter also enters the discussion, which is marked by the manager's increasing irritation and the father's persistence in following his argument through. She, her father, and the other characters were created by an author who then decided that he did not want to use them in one of his plays. Being created, however, they now have existence in drama which must be revealed. But, insists the manager, drama is action, not slow, dull philosophizing; let the talk stop and the action begin. The manager places the silent, fourteen-year-old boy behind a tree and some bushes in the garden and the little girl near a fountain. Then he prepares for a conversation between the legitimate son and his mother. There is no such scene in the garden, says the boy; what happened is that his mother comes into his room and he leaves, refusing to talk to her. The manager asks what happens then. The son replies that nothing happened, that he dislikes scenes and simply went away. He seems very unwilling to discuss the matter or to have anything to do with acting in the drama that his father and his half sister are trying to have presented.

When his father demands that he play his part, the son turns violently upon him, asking what madness makes him wish to expose the family shame before the world. If the son himself is in the theater, he explains to the confused manager, it is only because his father had dragged him there. However, the manager insists on knowing what happened after the son left his room. Reluctantly, the son answers that he merely walked in the garden. When the manager urges him to continue, he bursts out that it was horrible.

The manager, noting the mother's apprehensive look toward the fountain, partly comprehends, while the father explains that she was following her son. Then the son quickly tells that he found: the body of the little girl in the fountain pool and the brother staring insanely at it. At that moment a revolver shot sounds behind the stage bushes where the boy is hidden. Amid the resulting confusion the manager asks if the boy is wounded, and the actors disagree as to whether he is dead or merely pretending to be. The father cries that it is real. The manager, losing his temper, consigns the whole play and the characters to hell. He lost a whole day over them.

Critical Evaluation:

Six Characters in Search of an Author, Luigi Pirandello's best-known play, contrasts illusion and reality, as do several of the author's other works. It may also be thought of as a dramatic criticism of the popular but artificial "well-made" play of the nineteenth century. Instead of starting with a cleverly constructed drama, Pirandello begins with a group of characters and experiments with letting them—with some professional direction—try to fashion their story into an actable drama. Inexperience, clashes of opinion, interruptions, and above all a lack of poetic understanding defeat their purpose. Nevertheless, the attempt itself produces a drama of a sort, not the characters' but Pirandello's.

One of the greatest Italian playwrights of the twentieth century, Pirandello is now generally recognized as a classic figure of world literature. His stature was recognized when he received the Nobel Prize in 1934, two years before his death. First a poet, then a novelist and writer of short stories, finally a dramatist, Pirandello evolved gradually toward the forms and themes on which his international reputation is based. If his early work is realistic and naturalistic, much of his later, major work may be characterized by his description of *Six Characters in Search of an Author* as "a mixture of tragic and comic, fantastic and realistic." The basic ideas of his major plays are somber, even bitter: the idea that no one can penetrate or understand anyone else's world; the idea that the picture people have of themselves is different from the picture everyone else has of them; the idea that no mental image—about oneself or about others—can encompass the truth about life, which is always changing and always elusive. There is, therefore, no such thing as the Truth: There is simply truth "A" that one believes and truth "B" that another believes. However, they are both wrong. To themselves, however, they are always right. Or, to quote the title of one of Pirandello's plays: *Right You Are (If You Think So)*.

It is, of course, no wonder that these ideas should arise in the skeptical twentieth century. Pirandello was not alone among authors in thinking as he did, and a number of his attitudes may be traced to the French philosopher Henri Bergson (1859-1941). Pirandello had a personal reason for his reaction, however, a reason that made the concept that men cannot possibly understand one another become an obsession with him. He was for many years married to an insane woman who gave him no rest. Among other things, her insanity took the form of a violent, raging jealousy. Pirandello did everything he could to reassure his wife; he did not go out, he turned from his friends, he even yielded up his entire salary to her. Nevertheless, his wife's image of him remained the same, so that alongside his own picture of himself as a patient, resigned, pitying family man, there always hovered the image in his wife's mind of a loathsome being who gave her nothing but pain. As far as Pirandello was concerned, such conflicting images underlay even the most normal of human relations, though in insanity the problem is multiplied or at least seen more clearly.

Six Characters in Search of an Author deals with the problem of conflicting images and with the problem of reality in general, and it also deals with a special aspect of the same set of problems, for the playwright has a particularly difficult task. He must not only struggle to pin down the very elusive, ever-changing thing he calls reality but also he must work with the knowledge that he can never deal directly with his audience. Between him and the audience stand the actors and the directors; they give life to the script, but they can never give it quite the sort of life the author has in mind. Thus, an author may get Tallulah Bankhead's version of a character, or Helen Hayes's, or Meryl Streep's. Even if Shakespeare were alive today, audiences would not know exactly how he imagined Hamlet. Instead, audiences would know how

Laurence Olivier presented him, or John Gielgud, or Ralph Finnes: each with his own personality, his own background, his own voice. They can never have quite the personality, background, voice, or mannerisms that Shakespeare had in mind for Hamlet. No wonder, says one of Pirandello's characters, that a playwright may sometimes throw up his hands in despair and decide that the theater cannot present his situations and characters as he wants them presented.

That is what happens in *Six Characters in Search of an Author*. A playwright (Pirandello) gives up. He imagines six very tormented characters and a very sordid situation but decides not to go on with his play. As one of his characters puts it, "he abandoned us in a fit of depression, of disgust for the ordinary theater as the public knows it and likes it." However, once the characters are imagined they assume a life of their own. If the playwright refuses to look after them, they will look after themselves. Going to a theater where a play is in rehearsal, they insist that they have a play that must be produced. The story that the characters have to tell emerges in fits and starts. They are much too busy cursing or wrangling with one another to present a very coherent plot. For, as Pirandello insists, each character sees the central situation from his own point of view and each tries to justify himself from that vantage point.

The Father is a great talker and a great explainer. He insists that he put the Mother and his clerk out of his house together because he assumed that they were attached to each other and pitied them; indeed, he asserts that he tried to help them afterward. Still, the Mother, uneducated and nonverbal, insists that the Father threw her and the clerk out of the house and forced her on the clerk. The Stepdaughter refuses to believe that her Mother did not love the clerk initially; after all, the clerk (now dead) was the only father she knew. The Son—the legitimate son of the Father and the Mother—who feels that he was deserted by both father and mother, attempts to reject both. The Stepdaughter, consumed by a passionate hatred of the Son and the Father, passes up no opportunity to show her contempt and to remind the Father that, at a time when he did not recognize her, he almost had sexual relations with his own stepdaughter. No one is completely right, and no one is completely wrong—but none is able to understand that.

Act 2 develops the theme of mutual misunderstanding but modulates it into a different key. For now the characters learn, to their consternation, that they will not be able to play their parts themselves (that is, as they were realized by their creator). The actors will do it for them. Of course, the actors cannot possibly play the characters as the characters see themselves. As the Father explains,

It will be difficult to act me as I really am. The effect will be rather—apart from the make-up—according as to how he [the actor] supposes I am, as he senses me—if he does sense me—and not as I inside of myself feel myself to be.

Later the act moves to a general attack on the conventions of the theater and the limits of the theater. As the Manager points out, "Acting is our business here. Truth up to a certain point, but no further."

In the last act, the Father gives still another twist to the problem of reality and the artistic presentation of it. In a sense, he insists, the characters are more real than the actors are. For people change from day to day. What a person seems to be one day no longer exists the next day (though his image of himself may persist). The characters, on the other hand, will always remain the same. To turn the statement around, art, since it is static, can never deal with the fluid nature of reality. "All this present reality of yours," says the Father, "is fated to seem a mere illusion to you tomorrow . . . your reality is a mere transitory and fleeting illusion, taking this form today and that tomorrow."

Pirandello is a philosophical dramatist, the maker of a theater of ideas. Inevitably he has been attacked as an author who concerns himself more with concepts than with people and with action. He has also been stoutly defended as one who, immersed in certain basic, tragic facts of human existence, provides them with a hauntingly, overwhelmingly genuine dramatic substance.

"Critical Evaluation" by Max Halperen

Further Reading

Bassanese, Fiora A. *Understanding Luigi Pirandello*. Columbia: University of South Carolina Press, 1997. An introduction to Pirandello's work, focusing largely on his thought and the relationship of his life to his work. The numerous references to *Six Characters in Search of an Author* are listed in the index.

Bentley, Eric. *The Pirandello Commentaries*. Evanston, Ill.: Northwestern University Press, 1986. These essays include an erudite analysis of *Six Characters in Search of an Author*. Bentley explores the abstraction of time and space, the characterizations, and Pirandello's dialectical opposition of reality and illusion in the play.

Bloom, Harold, ed. *Luigi Pirandello*. Philadelphia: Chelsea House, 2003. Collection of critical essays on Pirandello's work, including analysis of *Six Characters in Search of an Author*.

DiGaetani, John Louis, ed. *A Companion to Pirandello Studies*. Westport, Conn.: Greenwood Press, 1991. This major source book features four studies on *Six Characters in Search of an Author* and two dozen essays on Pirandello's influence, life, and other works. Appendixes include the production history of *Six Characters in Search of an Author* and a bibliography.

Goffman, Erving. *Frame Analysis: An Essay on the Organization of Experience*. Cambridge, Mass.: Harvard University Press, 1974. An extraordinary sociological study, directly influenced by Pirandello, on the epistemological "frames" people use to make sense of the world. Goffman's discussion of the "theatrical frame" is essential for students who wish to understand more about Pirandello's violations of dramatic convention in *Six Characters in Search of an Author*.

Lorch, Jennifer. *Pirandello: "Six Characters in Search of an Author."* New York: Cambridge University Press, 2005. Production history discussing Pirandello's revisions of the play and interpretations by various directors. Chronicles the play's staging from its first production in Rome in 1921 through successive productions in London, Paris, New York, and Berlin.

Mariani, Umberto. "*Six Characters*: The Difficulty of Human Communication." In *Living Masks: The Achievement of Pirandello*. Toronto, Ont.: University of Toronto Press, 2008. An introduction to Pirandello's work, focusing on the fundamental themes of his plays and the aesthetic, technical, and critical problems associated with understanding and producing them.

Parilla, Catherine Arturi. *A Theory for Reading Dramatic Texts: Selected Plays by Pirandello and García Lorca*. New York: Peter Lang, 1995. Contrasts and compares plays by Pirandello and Federico García Lorca, focusing on Pirandello's *Six Characters in Search of an Author* and *Henry IV* and García Lorca's *Yerma* (1934; English translation, 1941) and *La casa de Bernarda Alba* (1945; *The House of Bernarda Alba*, 1947).

Pirandello, Luigi. "*Six Characters in Search of an Author*." In *Playwrights on Play Writing*, edited by Toby Cole. New York: Hill & Wang, 1960. Pirandello's personal account of his motivations for creating characters who, in turn, search for a dramatist to give them life.

Six Degrees of Separation

Author: John Guare (1938-   )
First produced: 1990; first published, 1990
Type of work: Drama
Type of plot: Tragicomedy
Time of plot: Early 1990's
Locale: New York City

Principal characters:
FLAN KITTREDGE, a New York art dealer
OUISA KITTREDGE, his wife
TESS, their daughter
WOODY, their son
PAUL, a young African American man
GEOFFREY, a South African investor and friend of the Kittredges
KITTY, a friend of the Kittredges
LARKIN, her husband
BEN, their son
DETECTIVE
DR. FINE
DOUG, Dr. Fine's son
TRENT CONWAY, a former schoolmate of Tess, Woody, Ben, and Doug
RICK, an aspiring actor from Utah
ELIZABETH, Rick's girlfriend, also an aspiring actor from Utah

The Story:

A two-sided painting by Wassily Kandinsky revolves over the stage, alternating between wild color and somber geometry. The painting provides the focus of an expensive Manhattan apartment near Central Park. The owners, Ouisa and Flan Kittredge, enter in nightclothes and speak directly to the audience, agitated over a recent traumatic incident. As they describe the previous evening, they begin to reenact it.

Flan and Ouisa are taking a wealthy South African friend, Geoffrey, out to dinner. Flan, an art dealer, hopes to persuade Geoffrey to invest two million dollars in an upcoming deal to purchase a painting by Paul Cézanne. The friends' banter over drinks is interrupted by the sudden arrival of a handsome young black man, Paul, who is bleeding and says he has been mugged. He describes himself as a college friend of the Kittredge children, Tess and Woody, who told him their parents were kind. Flattered, Ouisa and Flan offer first-aid and enjoy their conversation with the personable, articulate young man.

Paul eventually reveals that he is the son of the movie star Sidney Poitier, who is coming to New York the next day to cast the movie version of the musical *Cats* (pr. 1981). Ouisa, Flan, and Geoffrey are dazzled as Paul prepares a wonderful meal in the Kittredge kitchen and describes his thesis on J. D. Salinger's *The Catcher in the Rye* (1951). The Kittredges insist that Paul stay with them that night. Geoffrey quietly promises that he will invest in the upcoming deal. Ouisa and Flan celebrate their success and dream about art.

Early the next morning, Ouisa goes to wake Paul and discovers him in bed with a naked hustler, who menaces Ouisa and Flan before leaving. Distraught, they throw Paul out of the apartment and reenact the play's first scene, again articulating their distress.

A few days later, their friends Kitty and Larkin tell Ouisa and Flan a similar story of meeting the son of Sidney Poitier. All are appalled that they have been conned. A police detective shows no interest in the case, so the two couples investigate on their own. A third dupe emerges: A Dr. Fine treated Paul for a knife wound and then gave him the keys to his brownstone before discovering the hoax. The adults discover that Dr. Fine's son Doug, Kitty and Larkin's son Ben, and Tess and Woody Kittedge all attended boarding school together.

All four children are summoned from college to track down Paul using their boarding school connections. The children are resentful and hostile toward their parents, but they nonetheless discover the missing link in their former classmate, Trent Conway. Tess learns that Trent picked up Paul in Boston and Paul learned about Trent's address book. In exchange for sexual favors, Trent taught Paul to speak and behave like an upper-class young man. After three months,

Paul left with the address book, along with Trent's other possessions.

In a speech to the audience, Ouisa reflects on the idea of the play's title, that each person on Earth is separated from any other given person by only six relationships. Ouisa is simultaneously comforted by the idea of connection and tormented by the unknowable separations.

Flan's doorman spits at him, saying that he knows about Flan's secret Negro son. Meanwhile, Paul meets Rick and Elizabeth, a young couple who have recently moved to New York from Utah to become actors. Paul points out the apartment of his wealthy estranged "father," Flanders Kittredge, who abandoned his first wife and child and now refuses to see them. Rick and Elizabeth, horrified that Paul is living on the street, invite him to share their flat while he reconciles with his father.

Paul cons Rick out of the couple's savings and treats him to a romantic date and his first homosexual encounter before vanishing. Rick, sickened that he has squandered his future with Elizabeth, commits suicide by jumping out of his apartment window. Elizabeth contacts the police, who contact the Kittredges. The detective they spoke to earlier tells them that the police will now press charges against Paul.

While getting dressed for an auction at Sotheby's where Flan expects to make another important art deal, Ouisa receives an unexpected phone call from Paul. He has seen the newspaper story about Rick's death and asks Ouisa for help. Ouisa insists that he turn himself in, serve jail time, and make a fresh start. Paul asks Ouisa to intervene on his behalf with the police, referencing his race and class. He tells her that he dreams of staying with the Kittredges, of learning about art history, joining Flan's business, and becoming part of their family. Ouisa agrees and tells Paul that she loves him. Paul gives her his location at a movie theater, and Ouisa and Flan prepare to pick him up on their way to Sotheby's.

When the Kittredges arrive at the theater, Paul is not there. The box attendant tells them that the police have arrested a young man and taken him away, kicking and screaming. Ouisa and Flan try to find out what has happened, but they are repeatedly rebuffed, since they are not family members and do not know Paul's real name.

Ouisa, bereft, mourns losing Paul. While Flan moves forward with his lucrative trades, Ouisa wonders how to account for her life. She thinks of Paul and of the many colors in the Kandinsky, painted on two sides.

Critical Evaluation:

Six Degrees of Separation premiered at Lincoln Center in May, 1990, in a production directed by Jerry Zaks. It featured Stockard Channing as Ouisa, John Cunningham as Flan, and James McDaniel as Paul. The play was widely praised by critics and won the New York Drama Critics' Circle Award for best play of the 1990-1991 season. The play was also a hit in London, produced by the Royal Court Theatre, where it won the Olivier Award for Best Play for the 1992 season. In 1993, Metro-Goldwyn-Mayer (MGM) produced a film adaptation of *Six Degrees of Separation*, directed by Fred Schepisi. Subsequent revivals and critical studies of the play have made *Six Degrees of Separation* John Guare's best-known work.

The script begins with the description of a double-sided painting by Kandinsky that revolves over the stage, and the ambiguity of art—particularly the source of its value—is a central theme in the play. While private art dealer Flan Kittredge trades works by Cézanne and Henri Matisse in the booming art market, Paul tries to trade on his performance as "Paul Poitier" in the expensive apartments of Manhattan's East Side. Although Paul is quickly exposed as a fraud, Ouisa finds that he has given her a uniquely vital experience, one that she refuses to reduce to an anecdote. The minor characters of Trent and Rick seem likewise mesmerized by their intense connection with the elusive Paul.

Guare posits Ouisa's encounter with Paul in a distinctly postmodern universe, in which randomness overwhelms structure and imitation undermines any stable truth. Guare never reveals the "real" Paul, whose protean ability enables him to become whatever his audience wishes to see. Strangely, this mutability has extended beyond the stage into critical discussions of Guare's play. Just as Ouisa wants to see Paul as a loving surrogate son and Rick and Elizabeth want to see him as a romantic hero, so literary critics have chosen to use the ambiguous figure of Paul as a satirical scourge of racism, classism, and homophobia. The character is certainly transgressive, exposing the many degrees of separation drawn in American society.

While the wealthy, educated son of Sidney Poitier is welcome in the Kittredge home, the anonymous African American man enjoying gay sex is not. Once they realize they have been duped, the wealthy white characters quickly jump to racist, homophobic stereotypes, calling Paul a crack addict and wondering if he might have AIDS. Much critical attention has focused on the racial identities performed and assigned in the play and the hypocrisy of the liberal values that shrivel when confronted with an outsider. Guare's focus, however, is less on race relations than on the vacuous postmodern world of barren relationships in which the characters are starving for an authentic connection.

The play suggests that art and imagination are keys to unlocking authentic self-knowledge. As Paul remarks during his first scene,

> To face ourselves. That's the hard thing. The imagination. That's God's gift to make the act of self-examination bearable.

This kernel of wisdom lies inside Paul's fraudulent performance, but in Guare's bittersweet, ambiguous universe, even playacting can sometimes reveal truth.

Julia Matthews

Further Reading

Andreach, Robert J. *John Guare's Theatre: The Art of Connecting*. Newcastle, England: Cambridge Scholars, 2009. A full-length study of the recurring themes amid Guare's quirky, imaginative explorations of theatrical form.

Bouchard, Larry D. "Eliza and Rita, Paul and Luke: The Eclipse and Kenosis of Integrity in *Pygmalion, Educating Rita*, and *Six Degrees of Separation*." *Religion and Literature* 40, no. 2 (Summer, 2008): 25-60. A philosophical consideration of role-playing and role changing in terms of moral integrity and mutuality.

Curry, Jane Kathleen. *John Guare: A Research and Production Sourcebook*. Westport, Conn.: Greenwood Press, 2002. Provides summaries, production credits, and critical overviews of all of Guare's plays, along with a biographical essay and an extensive annotated bibliography.

Gillan, Jennifer. "Staging a Staged Crisis in Masculinity: Race and Masculinity in *Six Degrees of Separation*." *American Drama* 9, no. 2 (Spring, 2000): 50-73. Argues that the play demonstrates the hollowness of the American social contract: Despite Paul's persuasive performance of individual merit, Flan and the white upper-class hegemony exclude the "illegitimate" (black, gay) intruder from full participation in their dealings.

Plunka, Gene A. *The Black Comedy of John Guare*. Newark: University of Delaware Press, 2002. The first full-length study of Guare's work. Describes *Six Degrees of Separation* as Guare's finest achievement and analyzes its depiction of an alienated American society that substitutes superficial transactions and popular celebrity for authentic relationships.

Slethaug, Gordon E. "Chaotics and Many Degrees of Freedom in John Guare's *Six Degrees of Separation*." *American Drama* 11, no. 1 (Winter, 2002): 73-93. Using chaos theory, Slethaug describes the play's tensions between orderly systems and random turbulence, as well as the imagination's disruptive power to destabilize social patterns.

Zimmerman, David A. "Six Degrees of Distinction: Connection, Contagion, and the Aesthetics of Anything." *Arizona Quarterly* 55, no. 3 (Autumn, 1999): 107-133. Analyzes the play's economy of exchanges, in which signs are no longer tied to values and competition for social distinction leads to forgery and speculation.

The Skin of Our Teeth

Author: Thornton Wilder (1897-1975)
First produced: 1942; first published, 1942
Type of work: Drama
Type of plot: Phantasmagoric
Time of plot: All human history
Locale: Excelsior and the boardwalk at Atlantic City, New Jersey

Principal characters:
MR. ANTROBUS, a citizen of the world
MRS. ANTROBUS, his wife
GLADYS, their daughter
HENRY, their son
SABINA, their maid

The Story:

A great wall of ice is moving southward over the land, bringing with it an unprecedented cold spell in August. In Hartford they are burning pianos, and it is impossible to reach Boston by telegraph. The people do nothing but talk about the looming catastrophe. So far, only the extreme cold reaches Excelsior, New Jersey, where Mr. and Mrs. George Antrobus live in an attractive suburban residence. Their rather commonplace lives are to be greatly changed by the extreme form that the weather takes.

Mr. Antrobus is a fine man, a sterling example for his

community. He invented the wheel, the alphabet, and the multiplication table. Mrs. Antrobus is the picture of the middle-class mother, with the best interests of her children at heart. Their daughter Gladys is much like her mother, but their son is atypical. His name was Cain until an unfortunate accident occurred in which he hit his brother with a stone and killed him. As the result of that thoughtless action, his name was changed to Henry, and Mrs. Antrobus goes to some pains to keep his past history a secret. Members of the Antrobus household also include Sabina, the maid, a baby dinosaur, and a mammoth.

On this particular day in August, everyone is freezing and the dogs' paws are sticking to the sidewalk because it is so cold. Sabina is in an agitated state because nothing seems to be going properly. She milks the mammoth, but she let the only fire in the house go out. Her plight is doubly humiliating because her career in the Antrobus house began when Mr. Antrobus brought her back from the Sabine rape. He gave her a life of luxury until he tired of her; now she is relegated to the kitchen. She, however, is a canny and observant individual, an apex to an age-old triangle.

She is waiting nervously for the return of Mr. Antrobus when a domestic altercation with Mrs. Antrobus prompts her to give a two-week notice. Later a telegram announcing the arrival of Mr. Antrobus and some salvation from the cold causes her to change her mind for the time being. When he arrives, Mr. Antrobus brings news that most of the outside world is freezing and that there is probably nothing they can do to escape the same fate. When some tramps and refugees from the ice come to the house for warmth and food, Mrs. Antrobus is not in favor of admitting them, but Mr. Antrobus insists. Mrs. Antrobus agrees, but only after the dinosaur and the mammoth are evicted. The refugees include a judge, named Moses; a blind beggar with a guitar, named Homer; and the Misses E., T., and M. Muse. The Antrobus family attempts to keep up some semblance of hope as they gather around their small fire. When Henry, in another fit of hate, murders a neighbor with a stone, Mr. Antrobus stamps out the fire. However, he is cajoled into having faith in humanity again, and all, including the audience, are asked to burn their chairs in order to keep the fire going and save the human race from extinction.

That crisis over, Mr. and Mrs. Antrobus go to the Atlantic City convention of the Ancient and Honorable Order of Mammals, Subdivision Humans. Mr. Antrobus, just elected president of the society for the coming year, makes a speech of acceptance, which is followed by a few words from Mrs. Antrobus. During an interview immediately afterward, it is learned that Mr. and Mrs. Antrobus will soon celebrate their five thousandth wedding anniversary. Mr. Antrobus judges a beauty contest in which the winner is the former maid Sabina, now Miss Lily-Sabina Fairweather from the Boardwalk Bingo Parlor. She decides, as a result of her victory, to take Mr. Antrobus away from his wife. As soon as she can easily do so, she lures him into her beach cabana. During her father's sojourn in the cabana, Gladys buys herself a pair of red stockings and Henry becomes involved in an altercation with a boy, whom he hits with a stone. Mr. Antrobus is finally located, and he decides to leave his wife. Told of his intentions, she handles the situation very calmly and maneuvers him into staying with her. She is aided somewhat by a coming storm, which makes it necessary for the family and a large collection of animals to retreat to a boat in order to survive. Under the directions of a mysterious fortune teller, Mr. Antrobus takes them all, including Sabina, off to make a new world.

When the great war comes, much of the population of the world and most of Excelsior, New Jersey, are wiped out. The Antrobus household, including Sabina, manages to survive but not without considerable damage. Mrs. Antrobus and Gladys and Gladys's new baby hide in the basement. When the war ends, they come out into the world, which in a very short time begins to function very much as it did before the war occurred.

Sabina, dressed now as a Napoleonic camp follower, enjoys the war. She feels that everyone is at his or her best in wartime. Henry, following up his stone-throwing activities, progresses from a corporal's rank to the rank of a general; he becomes the picture of hate, the enemy of humankind. Mr. Antrobus orders that he never come into the house again or he will kill him. When Henry returns, he wants to kill his father, whom he hated all these years, and he brings a gun with which to shoot Mr. Antrobus. When Henry finally falls asleep from exhaustion, Mrs. Antrobus takes the revolver from him. Mr. Antrobus and Henry have an argument during which all the evil in the young man is revealed. Mr. Antrobus, in a fit of self-condemnation, admits that he would rather fight Henry than try to build a peace with him. His will to survive returns once again, however, and he asks Henry to try to live in peace. Henry agrees, provided he is given a freedom of his own will.

Mr. Antrobus, striving to regain his confidence in humanity, recalls the three things that always kept him going: the people, his home, and his books. In addition, he remembers the philosophies that he knew and through which he regains his hope for the future.

Critical Evaluation:

To American audiences who saw the original production of *The Skin of Our Teeth*, the play seemed mad and incomprehensible, but highly entertaining. Their reaction was understandable, for few American playwrights have employed such bizarre forms to convey serious content. "Dream plays," German expressionism, the comic strip, musical comedy—Thornton Wilder once listed these as his sources of dramaturgical inspiration. The play is, however, basically a parody of old-fashioned American stock-company productions and vaudeville. European audiences, for whom the play was performed in bomb-scarred churches and beer halls, had less difficulty in grasping Wilder's message. As the dramatist observed, the play "mostly comes alive under conditions of crisis." Since depressions, Ice Ages, and wars have hardly vanished from the scene, *The Skin of Our Teeth* promises to remain a vital part of the world's theater experience.

Despite their range and complexity, Wilder's main ideas can be briefly summarized. In Sabina's first direct address to the audience, Wilder does this. The play is, she says, "all about the troubles the human race has gone through." Such troubles are of two kinds: those caused by nature and those caused by people themselves. The Ice Age and the Flood are examples of the first type, although Wilder makes it plain that the real source of catastrophe in act 2 is not the weather but the disordered passions of the individual. Depression and war are clearly human creations. The human race is not, for Wilder, a disconnected assemblage of discrete cultures and generations. Rather, it is a being—a living person who experiences, remembers, and matures. The name Antrobus expresses this concept, being derived from the Greek word "for man."

As one learns from the closing philosophic quotations, humanity's best hope for "getting by" lies in the intellect. The first priority for the human race is to establish order in the individual by means of the discipline of reason. In doing so, humanity avails itself of a special energy that Aristotle considered divine. This holy energy is ultimately related to the force that created the heavens and the earth. The greatest threat to human survival is not merely the ego's unruly animal nature, which brings disorder to the soul. The more serious threat is an inclination toward evil, which infects the individual's rational faculties. To counter this threat, people may draw upon their capacity for love as well as upon the accumulated wisdom that history provides.

This set of ideas shapes all aspects of the drama. Mr. and Mrs. Antrobus stand for reason, which has masculine and feminine dimensions. Sabina, the maid, represents the passions, especially those seeking erotic pleasure and social power. Henry, their son, says Wilder, embodies "strong unreconciled evil." Like Sabina, he resists the rule of law in himself and society. His murderous nature reveals a far graver sort of wickedness. Like Cain, he despises God and

longs to overthrow his order. Wilder's characters are not merely allegorical types, however. Mr. Antrobus shows himself capable of homicidal intent, and because he loves his theories and machines too much, he is partly to blame for Henry's behavior. Sabina speaks for Wilder when she exclaims, "We're all just as wicked as we can be, and that's God's truth."

No single character symbolizes love in *The Skin of Our Teeth*. Rather this function is fulfilled by the Antrobus family as a whole. In act 1, they share their hearth with the refugees. In act 2, they refuse to enter the ship without Henry. In the final act they readmit Henry to their circle. Since the Antrobuses are a metaphor for humankind, their gestures have wider significance. The refugees are not strangers but relatives. So are members of the audience, a fact that the invitation to "Pass up your chairs, everybody" conveys. Wilder symbolizes this condition by making the father of Gladys's beloved baby an anonymous someone, an Everyman. The final acceptance of Henry is the most powerful moment in the play. Despite Henry's evil, Mr. Antrobus grudgingly must acknowledge that "Oh, you're related, all right." Thus Henry may take his place in a family where all belong.

If the human race is actually one, there is finally only one experience and one memory. Wilder dramatizes this concept in a variety of ingenious ways, all of which involve seeing time as an eternal present. Dinosaurs, biblical personages, and figures from Greek mythology crowd into the Antrobuses's living room. Each advance in technology requires a remembering of all previous discoveries, so Wilder has the invention of the alphabet "occur" during the era of telegraphic communication. Sabina is, simultaneously, a figure from classical history, a "Napoleonic camp follower," and a contemporary American. The constant interruptions of the action force the audience to dwell in a single time dimension—the present, in which are contained both past and future as well as "real" and "imaginary time."

By these means Wilder also reinforces the notion that the human race is what it is because of the experiences of its forebears. More exactly, human nature developed in certain ways because humanity inherited certain principles of interpretation. These principles are found in clearest form in the great books of history. Insofar as such principles shape human thought, the thinkers who expressed them live on. People can forget or ignore the education that history afforded them and become animals again. Books are instruments of humanization. In this sense, Mr. Antrobus is entirely correct when he says to the book-burning Henry, "You are my deadly enemy." Part of Wilder's optimism about humanity's future stems from the mere existence of books and libraries.

The seriousness and profundity of Wilder's themes tend, unfortunately, to escape most audiences. Indeed, the play's rapid pace and dramaturgical gimmicks draw attention away from its key symbols. Invited to participate on a superficial level, the typical viewer may feel puzzled and a bit resentful when, in the third act, the drama suddenly becomes very somber and too heavily philosophical.

"Critical Evaluation" by Leslie E. Gerber

Further Reading

Blank, Martin, Dalma Hunyadi Brunauer, and David Garrett Izzo, eds. *Thornton Wilder: New Essays.* West Cornwall, Conn.: Locust Hill Press, 1999. Collection of essays that discuss both the novels and the plays. Some of the essays examine Wilder's legacy and achievement, Wilder and the critics, his use of myth, and American Puritanism in his early plays and novels. Two of the essays focus on *The Skin of Our Teeth*: "*The Skin of Our Teeth*: A Psychoanalytic Perspective" by Jill Savege Scharff and "'Troubling the Waters': Visions of Apocalypse in Wilder's *The Skin of Our Teeth* and [Tony] Kushner's *Angels in America*" by James Fisher.

Bloom, Harold, ed. *Thornton Wilder.* Philadelphia: Chelsea House, 2003. Collection of critical essays by literary critic Edmund Wilson, director Tyrone Guthrie, and others who assess Wilder's contributions to American theater, the unique qualities of his work, the tragic features of his vision, and other elements of his plays. Contains a plot summary and list of characters for *The Skin of Our Teeth* and essays interpreting the play, including discussions of theatrical convention and nostalgia, Wilder as an actor in his own plays, a comparison of the play with Bertolt Brecht's *Mother Courage and Her Children*, and a summary of critical reaction to the drama.

Bryer, Jackson R., ed. *Conversations with Thornton Wilder.* Jackson: University Press of Mississippi, 1992. A collection of interviews with Wilder, providing interesting perspectives on the man and his literary works. Includes index.

Burbank, Rex J. *Thornton Wilder.* New York: Twayne, 1961. An excellent introduction to Wilder that emphasizes the humanism of his writings. Asserts that *The Skin of Our Teeth* succeeds in communicating its message about human survival, but that "the mixture of comedy and seriousness does not always come off successfully."

Castronovo, David. *Thornton Wilder.* New York: Frederick Ungar, 1986. An effective brief introduction to Wilder and his works. The section on *The Skin of Our Teeth* distills information about the play's writing and staging, interprets its themes, and evaluates its strengths and weaknesses.

Haberman, Donald. *The Plays of Thornton Wilder: A Critical Study.* Middletown, Conn.: Wesleyan University Press, 1967. Explores the philosophical, religious, and mythmaking dimensions of Wilder's dramas. Carefully defends Wilder against the plagiarism issues surrounding *The Skin of Our Teeth*.

Harrison, Gilbert A. *The Enthusiast: A Life of Thornton Wilder.* New York: Ticknor & Fields, 1983. A highly readable source, providing contextual details regarding Wilder's composition of *The Skin of Our Teeth* as well as information about the play's staging and reception.

Konkle, Lincoln. *Thornton Wilder and the Puritan Narrative Tradition.* Columbia: University of Missouri Press, 2006. Wilder was the descendent of Puritans, and Konkle argues that the writer inherited the Puritans' worldview, particularly the Calvinist aesthetic, and drew upon it to create his novels and plays. Includes chronology, bibliography, and index.

Lifton, Paul. *"Vast Encyclopedia": The Theatre of Thornton Wilder.* Westport, Conn.: Greenwood Press, 1995. A critical overview of Wilder's drama.

Slaughterhouse-Five
Or, The Children's Crusade, a Duty-Dance with Death

Author: Kurt Vonnegut (1922-2007)
First published: 1969
Type of work: Novel
Type of plot: Historical realism
Time of plot: 1922-1976
Locale: Dresden, Germany; Ilium, New York

Principal characters:
BILLY PILGRIM, foot soldier in World War II
VALENCIA, Pilgrim's wife
BARBARA, their daughter
ROBERT, their son
MONTANA WILDHACK, mate to Pilgrim on Tralfamadore
KURT VONNEGUT, author of *Slaughterhouse-Five*
BERNARD V. O'HARE, Vonnegut's friend

The Story:

Kurt Vonnegut and Bernard V. O'Hare go back to Dresden, Germany, on Guggenheim money in 1967. Before they leave, Vonnegut goes to O'Hare's house and meets his wife, Mary O'Hare. Mary is mad at Vonnegut; she knows he is going to write a book about World War II, and she is sure he is going to make war look glamorous and fun. Vonnegut insists that he is not going to write a book that makes war look good; he will even subtitle the book "The Children's Crusade." This makes her like him, and they start being friends.

While in Dresden, Vonnegut and O'Hare meet a taxi driver. He shows them around the city and shows them the slaughterhouse where they were prisoners during World War II.

When Vonnegut returns from the war, he thinks writing a book about Dresden will be easy. He expects a masterpiece that will make him a lot of money. The words, however, come very slowly and he becomes "an old fart with his memories and his Pall Malls," before he actually writes the book. He likes to call long-lost friends late at night when his wife is asleep and he is drunk, and he likes to listen to talk-radio programs from Boston or New York. He and O'Hare try to remember things about the war, and they have trouble. Vonnegut suggests the climax of his book will come when Edgar Derby is shot by a firing squad for taking a teapot out of the ruins in Dresden. O'Hare does not know where the climax is supposed to be.

Billy Pilgrim is born in Ilium, New York, in 1922. He is tall and weak as a child and becomes tall and weak as an adult. He dies in Chicago in 1976 and traveled back and forth through time frequently between his birth and his death. Pilgrim is in the infantry in Europe in World War II as a chaplain's assistant. He does not carry a weapon and does not have proper clothing for the climate, which is very cold. He is taken prisoner by the Germans. Before he goes to the war, he is on maneuvers in South Carolina, and he is given an emergency furlough home because his father died. While in the war, Pilgrim got lost behind German lines with three other soldiers; one is Roland Weary. Someone shoots at them and Pilgrim hears the bullet go by. Pilgrim lets the shooter try to hit him again. Weary hates everyone, including Pilgrim; Weary dies in a box car on the way to the concentration camp. He was about to kill or seriously maim Pilgrim when the Germans captured them.

Pilgrim's father throws Pilgrim into the deep end of a swimming pool when he is very young. Supposedly he will learn to swim, or he will drown. He would have drowned but someone saves him instead. In the concentration camp, Pilgrim time-travels often. He goes to the planet Tralfamadore, where the beings there teach him many things about the irrelevance of time and death. On Tralfamadore he is kept in a zoo. He mates with the beautiful Montana Wildhack, a pornography star who soon comes to love Pilgrim. They have a child together on Tralfamadore.

From the concentration camp, Pilgrim and his company are sent to Dresden, Germany, where they work in a factory that makes a vitamin-enriched malt syrup that is for pregnant women. Pilgrim and the other prisoners eat it as much as they can because they are malnourished. While Pilgrim is in Dresden, it is firebombed. One hundred and thirty-five thousand people die in the conflagration. No one suspected it would be bombed, because it has no armament factories, and almost no soldiers whatsoever. Pilgrim and the Americans with him are some of the only people in the entire city who survive. Vonnegut and O'Hare are with Pilgrim. They help to clean the wreckage of the city that was one of the most beautiful in the world and is now like the moon. American fighter planes fly over the city to see if anything is still moving and they see Pilgrim. They spray machine-gun fire at him but miss.

After the war, Pilgrim is back in Ilium. He finishes the optometry school that he began before the war, and he marries

Valencia Merble, the daughter of an optometrist and a very rich woman. She is also overweight and does not possess an astounding wit or intellect. They have two children, Robert and Barbara. Robert joins the Green Berets to fight in Vietnam. Barbara marries an optometrist and comes to see Pilgrim frequently after Pilgrim has brain surgery. Valencia dies trying to get to the hospital after Pilgrim is in a plane crash.

Pilgrim has the brain surgery shortly following the wreck of an airplane meant to carry a group of optometrists to a convention. The plane crashes into a mountain in Vermont, killing everyone except Pilgrim and the copilot. Barbara is very concerned about Pilgrim after the crash and the subsequent brain surgery because Pilgrim is writing letters to a newspaper, telling about Tralfamadore and his time-traveling experiences. He goes to New York, to be on a talk-radio program, on which he also tells about Tralfamadore.

Critical Evaluation:

Slaughterhouse-Five is Kurt Vonnegut's fifth novel; it was an overwhelming success and established him as one of the best fiction writers of his era. He wrote it while he was a writer-in-residence at the University of Iowa. With money from a Guggenheim Fellowship, he went to Dresden, Germany, to complete his research. Vonnegut appears in the first and last chapters, as a journalist reporting on the work at hand, and he appears three times during the narrative. Unique to this novel, this device is extremely effective. It was a great boon to experimental writing and was thought to be a progressive step in the evolution of literature and narrative stance. Vonnegut makes clear to the reader that he is not Billy Pilgrim. Vonnegut is a character in scenes with Pilgrim; he is watching Pilgrim, like the reader is watching them both. Vonnegut is telling an astounding truth, of the Dresden holocaust, that the allied forces managed to keep mostly unknown to Americans, while he tells the remarkably funny and moving tale of Pilgrim, who is helpless before the larger powers of the universe.

Vonnegut has the uncanny ability to implant suggestions in the mind of the reader and then work those suggestions into tangible forms in the text. For example, in the first chapter, Vonnegut says that when he is drinking he listens to talk-radio shows, then, as the novel proceeds, Pilgrim stumbles onto a radio program in which the topic is whether or not the novel, as a literary form, is dead. Also, after the firebombing of Dresden, innkeepers on the outskirts of town offer the soldiers their stable, as a place to sleep. Twenty pages later, Vonnegut reminds the reader of the book's epigraph, "The cattle are lowing,/ The Baby awakes./ But the little Lord Jesus/ No crying He makes." Biblical situations are considered

more and more often as the book draws to a close. These include discussion of the following: the friends who take Jesus down from the cross; the possibility that Jesus and his father, as carpenters, make crosses on which other people would be executed; and a time traveler who is the first to check on Jesus at the cross to make sure he is really dead before he is taken down. A new gospel is written in which Jesus is not made the Son of God until the very end, when he is on the cross. Until then he is a nobody. Vonnegut implies that if Jesus was the "wrong" person to kill, then there are necessarily "right" persons to kill, and this is inherently a bad idea.

All these examinations and refigurings are counter to orthodox Christianity, and they are couched in writing that makes extreme pleas for the kindness that people should show to other people. In the first chapter, Vonnegut calls this novel "short and jumbled and jangled . . . because there is nothing intelligent to say about a massacre." His critics have found fault in him and this novel for not taking serious matters more seriously, and for that reason his work was not highly acclaimed or accepted into the academic canon for many years. Vonnegut was categorized in the genre of science fiction, though he believed his work holds more depth than work in that genre usually has. With the eventual acceptance of *Slaughterhouse-Five*, he became classified as a satirist who seeks to make readers laugh, as did Mark Twain and Jonathan Swift before him.

In this book so conscious of time traveling, and postulating that all of one's life can be seen like an expanse of the Rocky Mountains rather than as a one-way train ride, how very fitting for the Pilgrim family car, in the year 1967, to have a bumper sticker on it that said, "Reagan for President." The book was published eleven years before Reagan became president of the United States in 1980. It was not something Pilgrim could have known about, dying as he did in 1976, but still it was an auspicious thing for Vonnegut to have slyly dropped into this book.

Beaird Glover

Further Reading

Bloom, Harold, ed. *Kurt Vonnegut's "Slaughterhouse-Five."* New York: Chelsea House, 2007. Provides a biographical sketch of Vonnegut, a summary and an analysis of the novel, and a list of characters as well as critical interpretations by several contributors. The critical essays include discussions of the novel's structure, the context of Dresden, Vonnegut's use of stream of consciousness and time, and a comparison of *Slaughterhouse-Five* with Joseph Heller's *Catch-22*.

Davis, Todd F. *Kurt Vonnegut's Crusade: Or, How a Postmodern Harlequin Preached a New Kind of Humanism.* Albany: State University of New York Press, 2006. Examines the moral and philosophical foundations of Vonnegut's fiction, focusing on his belief that writing is an "act of good citizenship." Argues that in his desire to enact change by both critiquing and embracing humanity, Vonnegut created a new kind of literary humanism. The references to *Slaughterhouse-Five* are listed in the index.

Giannone, Richard. *Vonnegut: A Preface to His Novels.* Port Washington, N.Y.: Kennikat Press, 1977. An astute reading of *Slaughterhouse-Five*, marking the biblical references and Vonnegut's personal testimony. Devotes similar attention to other novels by Vonnegut.

Klinkowitz, Jerome. *Kurt Vonnegut.* New York: Methuen, 1982. Defines *Slaughterhouse-Five* as one of Vonnegut's "personal" novels, as opposed to the earlier ones that adhere to the stricter forms of science fiction. Draws correlations among the Vonnegut novels.

_____. *Slaughterhouse-Five: Reforming the Novel and the World.* Boston: Twayne, 1990. A complete study of the novel. Criticism is taken from sources that reviewed *Slaughterhouse-Five* when it was published. Numerous passages of *Slaughterhouse-Five* are explained in depth as well as Vonnegut's philosophy as seen by the reviewers of his time.

McMahon, Gary. *Kurt Vonnegut and the Centrifugal Force of Fate.* Jefferson, N.C.: McFarland, 2009. Traces the development of Vonnegut's writing, analyzing his fiction and comparing his journalism to that of Hunter S. Thompson, Tom Wolfe, and other contemporaries. Chapter 10 is devoted to *Slaughterhouse-Five*.

Marvin, Thomas F. *Kurt Vonnegut: A Critical Companion.* Westport, Conn.: Greenwood Press, 2002. Uses a variety of critical approaches to examine Vonnegut's major works. Chapter 8 provides an analysis of *Slaughterhouse-Five*, discussing the novel's thematic issues, narrative technique, and the development of its plot and characters. Offers information on Vonnegut's life and the literary contexts of his works.

Mayo, Clark. *Kurt Vonnegut: The Gospel from Outer Space (Broch): Or, Yes We Have No Nirvanas).* San Bernardino, Calif.: Borgo Press, 1977. A short book with considerable insights into *Slaughterhouse-Five* and other novels by Vonnegut. The wit, sarcasm, and style of Vonnegut is prominent in the book's writing.

Morse, Donald E. *The Novels of Kurt Vonnegut: Imagining Being an American.* Westport, Conn.: Praeger, 2003. Examines all of Vonnegut's novels, discussing how they reflect the historical and social issues of the United States in the twentieth century, including the Great Depression, World War II, the atomic bomb, the Vietnam War, and the breakdown of marriage and the family. References to *Slaughterhouse-Five* are listed in the index.

Schatt, Stanley. *Kurt Vonnegut, Jr.* Boston: Twayne, 1976. Explores the construction, plot, and structure of *Slaughterhouse-Five* and considers Vonnegut's sense of aesthetic distance from the work. Discusses the contribution of *Slaughterhouse-Five* to the genre of science fiction and the Tralfamadorian philosophy.

The Sleepwalkers

Author: Hermann Broch (1886-1951)

First published: Die Schlafwandler, 1931-1932 (English translation, 1932); includes *Pasenow: Oder, Die Romantik-1888,* 1931 (*The Romantic,* 1932); *Esch: Oder, Die Anarchie-1903,* 1931 (*The Anarchist,* 1931); *Hugnenau: Oder, Die Sachlichkeit-1918,* 1932 (*The Realist,* 1932)

Type of work: Novel

Type of plot: Philosophical

Time of plot: 1888-1918

Locale: Germany

Principal characters:
JOACHIM VON PASENOW, a young lieutenant
HERR VON PASENOW, his father
BERTRAND, his friend
ESCH, a bookkeeper
FRAU HENTJEN, his wife
HUGUENAU, a businessman

The Story:

The Romantic. In 1888, Joachim von Pasenow is a lieutenant in the German army. Wearing a uniform for a long time, he looks on it as his natural dress. He believes a uniform hides a man's nakedness; unlike civilian clothes, it makes a man amount to something. His friend Bertrand left the army and now wears mufti all the time; it seems indecent. Joachim feels a little insecure about his honor, too. His brother Helmuth was killed in a duel, and his father makes much of Helmuth's unsullied honor.

Herr von Pasenow comes to Berlin to visit Joachim. He is a funny little man, rotund and intent, and his son is a bit ashamed of him. At a casino they meet Ruzena, a Bohemian girl. Von Pasenow strokes her familiarly and gives her money. She accepts the attentions easily, but when the old man jokes about marriage she goes into the lavatory to cry. Later, perhaps as a kind of penance, Joachim takes Ruzena as his mistress.

Bertrand, too, takes a friendly interest in Ruzena, and he helps her get on the stage. Ruzena is happy with Joachim, but she begins to distrust Bertrand. He lets slip the suggestion that she should leave the chorus and go into a notion shop. Joachim leaves Ruzena at times to visit his family, for his father is anxious that he should resign from the army and look after the family estate. He is also anxious that Joachim marry Elisabeth.

When Bertrand meets Elisabeth, he speaks to her eloquently of a love based on renunciation; the innocent girl is upset. Ruzena, convinced that Bertrand is the evil genius separating her from her lover, shoots him in the arm. She then leaves Joachim and goes back to work in a café. Joachim, also believing that Bertrand is a bad influence, settles money on Ruzena and proposes to Elisabeth. With this deed he breaks with his past, for he does not ask Bertrand's advice about the marriage.

Before accepting Joachim, Elisabeth visits Bertrand in the hospital. He declares his love for her but is resigned to her marriage with Joachim as inevitable. For a time after their marriage, Joachim thinks of Elisabeth as an unapproachable madonna. They do not have their first child for more than one year.

The Anarchist. In 1903, Esch is dismissed from his post as a bookkeeper at a shipping concern in Cologne. Martin, a crippled socialist, somehow learns of Esch's dismissal and tells him of a better job in Mannheim. They discuss the matter in Frau Hentjen's restaurant. Esch knows he will have to have a reference. He finally gets a good one by threatening to expose the crooked manager under whom he worked.

In Mannheim, he finds employment in a large firm owned by Bertrand. He makes friends with Korn, a customs inspector, and with Lohberg, a pallid tobacconist. In a short while, he goes to room with Korn and his sister Erna. Erna is unattractive but wants desperately to marry, and Korn hopes to acquire a brother-in-law in Esch. At last, Esch answers her provocations by going into her bedroom, but Erna reserves her favors until they are married.

By helping Gernerth, a theatrical manager, with his shipping, Esch receives passes to a show and takes Korn and Erna with him to the performance. The star attraction is Teltscher, a Hungarian knife thrower, and Ilona, his flashy blond target. Becoming acquainted with Korn and Esch, the actors visit them at Korn's house. For a while, Esch hopes to win Ilona, but she shows a preference for Korn; at last she sleeps with him openly.

Arriving in Mannheim during a strike, Martin is arrested at a workers' meeting. Esch is convinced that Bertrand hired baiters to trap Martin and that Bertrand should be imprisoned instead. Feeling restless, he accepts Teltscher's offer to join him in the theatrical business. They plan to operate in Cologne. Esch feels an odd responsibility to get Teltscher away from Ilona, because the knife-throwing act endangers Ilona's safety.

Back in Cologne, Esch spends much time with Frau Hentjen, and in time he overcomes her scruples against taking him as her lover. She does not like his new job, which is to hire lady wrestlers. Esch writes an article protesting against Martin's false imprisonment, but the socialist newspaper refuses to print it. During his wandering through the town, he stumbles on evidence that Bertrand is a sodomite, but again the paper refuses to print his story.

Driven by a vague compulsion, Esch goes to see Bertrand. On the way, he stops off to see the Korns and finds Erna engaged to marry Lohberg. Erna changed; she has no compunction about allowing Esch to sleep with her. Bertrand receives Esch kindly but is evasive on the subject of the strike. Bertrand dies soon after Esch returns to Cologne. For a while, Esch plans vaguely to go to America. After Frau Hentjen mortgages her restaurant to provide theatrical capital, she and Esch are married. Eventually they lose money, and Esch takes a good job in Luxembourg.

The Realist. Huguenau, a practical businessman, deserts from the army. By keeping an open countenance and refusing to skulk, he makes his way through Belgium to the Ardennes and back into the Moselle district. Since he is an Alsatian and knows both French and German, both sides of the Rhine are home to him. In Kur-Trier he spends enough of his carefully hoarded money to set himself up as a hotel keeper.

All about him others are questioning their beliefs during the last months of the war. Hanna, the lawyer's faithful wife, grows more and more virginal during her husband's absence. In Berlin, Marie the Salvation Army girl half-acknowledges her passion for a Talmudic Jew. The wounded in the hospitals have little spirit to live.

Huguenau, however, has no questions, no frustrations; he is intent only on business deals. He bluffs the military commandant, Major Joachim von Pasenow, into supporting him, and on the strength of that backing he persuades the local dignitaries to put up enough capital for him to buy control of a newspaper owned by Esch. He makes the deal easier by circulating rumors that Esch is subversive. Before long, Huguenau is editing the paper and eating Frau Esch's good meals without payment.

Having embraced the Protestant faith, Joachim finally becomes convinced that Esch is a malcontent and Huguenau a suspicious character. In November, 1918, the workers revolt and take over the town. Joachim is hurt and carried to the basement of Esch's printing house. Observing this, Huguenau takes advantage of the confusion and rapes Frau Esch. Then he follows Esch, who is returning to guard duty, catches up with him, and slips a bayonet into his back. After the war, Huguenau tricks Frau Esch by letter into returning the borrowed capital he invested in the paper. While he continues to amass more money, he prudently marries a German girl with a good dowry.

Critical Evaluation:

The Sleepwalkers is considered by many critics to be one of the major literary achievements of the twentieth century, ranking with James Joyce's *Ulysses* (1922), Thomas Mann's *Der Zauberberg* (1924; *The Magic Mountain*, 1927), and Marcel Proust's *À la recherche du temps perdu* (1913-1927; *Remembrance of Things Past*, 1922-1931, 1981). Hermann Broch's three-volume novel bears as little resemblance to any of these works as they do to one another; it stands alone, an uncompromising experiment in the art of fiction writing.

The Sleepwalkers consists of three short novels, *The Romantic*, *The Anarchist*, and *The Realist*, held together loosely by the reappearance of some of the characters. In structure, the work is hardly a novel, for the form is incidental. Using this technique, sometimes referred to as essayism, Hermann Broch examines the intellectual, psychological, and moral forces in Germany that culminated in World War I. The book presents an unsparing picture of the character traits and attitudes of the German people that resulted in the glorification of the militaristic personality. These traits are ex-

emplified in the rigid, proud personalities of the Pasenow family.

This carefully constructed novel builds slowly, but with great skill, its power deriving from the cumulative effect of the parts. The narrative relies not on melodrama or romance but on logical development to hold the reader's interest. Each incident serves to make an intellectual point, to symbolize an attitude, or to represent a psychological condition. Like somnambulists, the characters move rigidly and unavoidably to their fates, themselves becoming symbols in a world reduced to dehumanized symbols. Intellectual conversations and the discussion of philosophical and moral attitudes occupy much of the time of these characters, but often they repeat only platitudes and safe assumptions that will not disturb their world. More than anything else, *The Sleepwalkers* is an exploration of moral and ethical principles.

For its characters, correctness of conduct is all-important, regardless of the hypocrisy and of the deceit lying beneath the proper facade. Safety can be found behind elaborate manners and correct wardrobes and uniforms. Indeed, military uniforms assume symbolic proportions in the novel. When people cast off their uniforms, their true natures and their animal instincts are freed—for good and for evil. Joachim's and Bertrand's thoughts about military uniforms become an essay on the nature of uniforms in general. Much space is given to the significance of clothing of all kinds—any human covering becomes, in effect, a uniform, labeling the wearer. Women prefer men in uniform, and men feel more like men when in uniform; above all, men escape responsibility for being themselves when they are in uniform.

The military code overtakes all aspects of these people's lives, including their ability to love or experience grief. When Joachim is a boy, even the pastor calls him a "young warrior" and assumes that the boy will be happy attending the cadet school and devoting his life to military service. Hypocrisy, the narrator explains, is so ingrained in the attitudes of the people that they cannot recognize it in any form, but particularly in regard to any aspect of the military code of honor. When Joachim's brother Helmuth is killed in a duel, their father states, "He died for honor." They deceived themselves so long that they can no longer experience genuine grief. Yet, they still uphold the military code that not only makes duels possible but also considers them examples of noble conduct.

The novel moves slowly and, as in an underwater ballet, the characters forever circle around one another, striking dramatic but grotesque poses. The characters are presented in a stylized form; Broch does not attempt to render them as physical human beings, presenting them, instead, as representations of ideas. As such, they clash in an almost dream-like manner. Most of the characters sooner or later complain of boredom. Most people, Joachim and Bertrand agree, live in a state of vegetative indolence and inertia of feeling. Life, they repeat to each other, consists of compromises. Above all, however, one must protect one's name. Traditions and customs, habits and routines, are the first and last defense of these mediocre individuals. Even murder is permissible, if handled with the proper decorum. Their lives are lived in an aura of unreality, but Bertrand proclaims early in the book that the artificial is always superior to the real, just as play is the true reality of life.

The form of *The Sleepwalkers* is wedded to the content. Particularly in the third volume, readers find a dazzling range of technique, from the total objectivity of the abstract essay to the subjectivity of lyric poetry. The parallel plots of the novel and the interpolated essays serve to broaden the horizon of the narrative, to break out of the mold of the ordinary novel form, and to create new implications of meaning. Broch was striving in this novel to achieve an artistic detachment that would allow the work to stand separate and aloof, its many facets reflecting the reader's interpretation rather than that of the author. Perhaps only André Gide in *Les Faux-monnayeurs* (1925; *The Counterfeiters*, 1927) and Hermann Hesse in *Das Glasperlenspiel: Versuch einer Lebensbeschreibung des Magister Ludi Josef Knecht samt Knechts hinterlassenen Schriften* (1943; *Magister Ludi*, 1949; also known as *The Glass Bead Game*, 1969) attempted a similar experiment.

The progression of the three volumes is philosophic and aesthetic rather than narrative. In the first two books, Broch describes the deterioration of outmoded values in the Prussian Pasenow and the Rhineland proletarian mystic Esch; the final volume, which takes place in 1918, shows the triumph of Huguenau—symbol of the new, valueless society of postwar Germany—over the forces of the past. It is society that is on trial in this book, and Broch is a merciless judge.

Through the first two parts of Broch's trilogy, and well into the third, the reader is kept purposefully under the illusion that one is reading a story written by an objective third-person narrator (to be identified with Broch). In the middle of part 3, however, it becomes apparent that the narrator of all three parts is in reality the author of the essay "The Disintegration of Values," which is encapsulated into the fiction. At the close of the book, however, another shift takes place: The author of the essay turns out to be identical with the first-person narrator of one of the framework stories. The whole novel thus lives in a timeless state of suspension, an aesthetic whole with its own self-contained author and its own laws.

Broch takes a common narrative device, the unreliable narrator, and turns the device back upon itself, rendering the entire novel as a symbol of the chaos of the modern world. In *The Sleepwalkers*, as is often the case with twentieth and twenty-first century literature, the medium is, and must be, the message.

"Critical Evaluation" by Bruce D. Reeves

Further Reading

Bartram, Graham, and Philip Payne. "Apocalypse and Utopia in the Austrian Novel of the 1930's: Hermann Broch and Robert Musil." In *The Cambridge Companion to the Modern German Novel*, edited by Bartram. New York: Cambridge University Press, 2004. *The Sleepwalkers* and *The Death of Virgil* are analyzed and placed within the wider context of 1930's Austrian literature in this essay about novelists Broch and Robert Musil.

Broch de Rothermann, H. F. *Dear Mrs. Strigl: A Memoir of Hermann Broch*. Translated by John Hargraves. New Haven, Conn.: Beinecke Rare Book and Manuscript Library, Yale University, 2001. Broch's son recalls his father, focusing on the personal rather than on Broch's writing. Describes Broch's relationship with his father, his exile in the United States, and other aspects of his often difficult life. In both English and German.

Cohn, Dorrit. *"The Sleepwalkers": Elucidations of Hermann Broch's Trilogy*. The Hague, the Netherlands: Mouton, 1966. A close reading of Broch's novels. Describes the mechanics of the texts' structures and pays special attention to the importance and meaning of narrators in the novels.

Dowden, Stephen D., ed. *Hermann Broch: Literature, Philosophy, Politics: The Yale Broch Symposium 1986*. Columbia, S.C.: Camden House, 1988. *The Sleepwalkers* is specifically discussed in several articles, and each article is paired with a response.

Halsall, Robert. *The Problem of Autonomy in the Works of Hermann Broch*. New York: Peter Lang, 2000. Halsall argues that concerns about autonomy are central to understanding Broch's literature and philosophy and demonstrates how these concerns are evident in his major novels, including *The Sleepwalkers*.

Hargraves, John A. *Music in the Works of Broch, Mann, and Kafka*. Rochester, N.Y.: Camden House, 2001. Although Hargraves examines music as an element in the work of three German writers, this study concentrates on Broch because Hargraves maintains that, of the three, Broch was the most interested in expressing the primacy of music in his work. Includes essays discussing Broch's discursive writings on music and the musical elements in several of his novels.

Lützeler, Paul Michael, ed. *Hermann Broch, Visionary in Exile: The 2001 Yale Symposium*. Rochester, N.Y.: Camden House, 2003. Contains papers delivered at an international symposium that present a wide range of interpretations of Broch's work. Several papers analyze various elements of *The Sleepwalkers* and *The Death of Virgil*.

Schlant, Ernestine. *Hermann Broch*. Boston: Twayne, 1978. A basic and general introduction to Broch and his works that also provides a sound historical context for the nov-

els. The chapter on the "Mechanics and Metaphysics of Sleepwalking" presents a good introduction to Broch's philosophical and aesthetic project.

Ziolkowski, Theodore. "Hermann Broch: *The Sleepwalkers*." In *Dimensions of the Modern Novel*. Princeton, N.J.: Princeton University Press, 1969. Provides useful background on Broch's philosophical attitudes and how they are transformed into this theoretical and essayistic novel. Argues that Broch's novel, in its rigorous execution, is the logical end point of the modernist consciousness already put forward by Rainer Maria Rilke and Franz Kafka in their modernist novels.

Slouching Towards Bethlehem

Author: Joan Didion (1934-   )
First published: 1968
Type of work: Essays

Slouching Towards Bethlehem is a book of thematically connected essays, most of which were originally published in magazines between 1965 and 1967. Didion took her title from a poem by William Butler Yeats, "The Second Coming" (1920), and quotes it as an epigraph to the collection. Yeats's poem, written in the aftermath of World War I, draws on biblical imagery to depict a world that has become unmoored, a world falling into anarchy. In her preface, Didion says that lines from the poem kept coming to her as she wrote, and, while not every essay in *Slouching Towards Bethlehem* depicts a society falling apart, many of them do. Her title essay, in particular, depicts young people who have grown up without the centering influence of shared traditions and extended families, young people who are not so much rebellious as lost.

The collection is divided into three sections: "Life Styles in the Golden Land," "Personals," and "Seven Places of the Mind." Most of the essays in "Life Styles in the Golden Land" focus on California as a fallen frontier—the place where the land simply ran out, a place where people go to reinvent themselves or make one final try at the American Dream. Didion's California is more ominous than idyllic. Rather than a place of palm trees, pristine beaches, and sunny orange groves, her California is a world of dust-baked valleys, neglected tract houses, brush fires, and Santa Ana winds.

This ominous and oppressive atmosphere dominates the essay "Some Dreamers of the Golden Dream," Didion's profile of Lucille Miller, a middle-class housewife from San Bernardino, California, who may or may not have burned her husband alive in a Volkswagen on the way home from the all-night market. Despite the sensational subject matter, Didion's essay is more social commentary than true crime. She makes no judgment about Miller's guilt or innocence but is fascinated by the way Miller's story seems to echo 1940's film noir, such as *Double Indemnity* (1944). In contrast with the secondhand Hollywood drama of the Miller story, Didion's account is distanced and ironic, marked by strong visual images and unexpected juxtapositions. Her description of the funeral of Lucille's husband, Gordon Miller, details the casket and the sermon and the final hymn sung—then, almost offhandedly, Didion mentions that the service was tape-recorded so that Lucille could watch it from her prison cell.

Several essays in this section focus on well-known figures, but they are the antitheses of celebrity journalism. Didion's "John Wayne: A Love Song" was not written to promote the actor or to condemn him, but to examine what the myth of John Wayne and the legendary West associated with his films meant for Didion, as a young filmgoer, and for American culture. The essay shows a curious dissonance, as childhood dreams meet adult reality. Didion had met Wayne as he was shooting a film. Older and already diagnosed with cancer, he was, even with his human frailties, less real for Didion than was his heroic, tough film character. Similarly, her portrait of eccentric billionaire Howard Hughes is, as she frankly admits, not about the real Hughes (she had never met him) but about the idea of Howard Hughes and the stories people tell about him. For Didion, the essays in the section "Life Styles in the Golden Land" explore the gap between America's official heroes and the imperfect folk heroes who are truly, if secretly, admired.

"Slouching Towards Bethlehem," the long essay that concludes this section, is perhaps Didion's best-known essay. On the surface, it is about the hippie phenomenon, a look at the thousands of young people who flocked to San Francisco during the summer of 1967. Actually, the essay is an expression of Didion's mournful and ironic worldview, her sense that the "center" of things, as in Yeats's "The Second Coming," is no longer holding. This lack of a center is expressed even through the structure of the essay, which lacks a conventional beginning, middle, and end. Instead, Didion gives readers a series of vividly described moments, juxtaposed in seemingly random fashion: odd details such as graffiti on a wall or a snatch of song lyrics, overheard conversations, chance encounters, and unproductive interviews. Didion's one attempt at conventional journalism is a study in comic absurdity. After jotting down two words from a brief conversation she had with a police officer, she is told that she is not allowed to speak with anyone in the police department and that she must turn over her "notes." The people and incidents in Didion's essays all work as synecdoche, small parts that say a great deal about the whole.

Perhaps the most powerful images of the disordered culture Didion describes are the two images of children that conclude "Slouching Towards Bethlehem": a five-year-old child on acid and another small child who had started a fire, burned himself, and had been ignored by the adults around him who were preoccupied with retrieving some hashish that fell through some floorboards during the fire. In a style characteristic of her writing, Didion presents these scenes without commentary, letting the reader make the final judgment.

The essays in the section "Personals" are shorter and more focused on Didion's own life and opinions. (Labeling only this section "personal" is somewhat misleading.) For those writing as part of the New Journalism movement, which includes Didion, all writing is personal, even when it is "about" someone or something else. Still, it is true that the essays in "Personals" lack the journalistic framework of those in the first section. Didion talks about her writing in the essay "On Keeping a Notebook," analyzes Hollywood in "I

Can't Get That Monster out of My Mind," addresses the abstract concepts of self-respect and morality, and writes about her family in "On Going Home."

The final section, "Seven Places of the Mind," begins with the essay "Notes from a Native Daughter." Here, Didion writes about the California of her youth—Sacramento and the Central Valley—a California that traces its heritage to the wagon trains that survived the dangerous trip West. Didion writes with a note of melancholy that her California is receding a little more each year.

Didion also writes of other places she has lived or visited: Hawaii; Alcatraz Island; Newport, Rhode Island; Mexico; Los Angeles; New York City. Although the works are essays about place, they are not "travel writing" in the usual sense and are miles from anything that might promote tourism. Didion's view of most places is depressing. Outside Honolulu, for example, she is haunted by the World War II-era deaths at Pearl Harbor; in the marble halls of a Newport mansion, she can only imagine unhappy women retiring to their rooms with migraines. Taken as a whole, the essays in this section suggest that Didion's despair is not in the places she visits but in herself.

"Goodbye to All That," the final essay, is a perfect example of this tendency toward inner despair in her writing. Didion came to New York in her early twenties, a young woman so naïve that she shivered in her hotel room because she did not know how to turn down the air conditioning and was afraid to call someone to fix it because she did not know how much to tip that person. Whatever her struggles, Didion remembers her early years in New York as filled with a sense of expectation and endless possibilities. All mistakes could be mended, she believed, and something magical could happen at any moment. In her late twenties, and near the end of her stay in New York, a more jaded Didion felt that she could no longer bear to see the same people and places she had once found exciting. She describes her sense of having "stayed too long at the fair," a paralyzing inertia that she connects with the place New York, but which clearly comes from within herself.

One review of *Slouching Towards Bethlehem* suggests that aspiring writers could use the collection as a textbook; indeed, Didion's collection is frequently assigned in creative nonfiction and journalism courses. Quirky, pointedly honest, often melancholy, but sometimes mordantly funny, Didion's unique voice gives *Slouching Towards Bethlehem* a freshness that allows it to be rediscovered by new generations of readers born well after the decade it describes.

Kathryn Kulpa

Further Reading

Churchwell, Sarah B. "*Slouching Towards Bethlehem*." In *Cambridge Guide to Women's Writings in English*, edited by Lorna Sage, Germaine Greer, and Elaine Showalter. New York: Cambridge University Press, 1999. A brief overview of the work and its significance. This volume also includes a short biography of Didion and a summary of her literary contributions.

Felton, Sharon, ed. *The Critical Response to Joan Didion*. Westport, Conn.: Greenwood Press, 1994. A wide selection of both scholarly analyses and popular-press reviews of Didion's nonfiction and fiction. Includes an introduction, a time line of Didion's life and writings, and a bibliography.

Houston, Lynn Marie, and William V. Lombardi. *Reading Joan Didion*. Santa Barbara, Calif.: Greenwood Press, 2006. A close examination of Didion's works, including her essays in *Slouching Towards Bethlehem*. Also focuses on Didion as a critic and as a founder of New Journalism. A good place to start for readers new to Didion.

Muggli, Mark Z. "The Poetics of Joan Didion's Journalism." *American Literature* 59, no. 3 (October, 1987): 402-421. A critical article that examines Didion's little-studied "imagistic journalistic technique" as well as her narrative strategies in *Slouching Towards Bethlehem* and other works of nonfiction.

Weingarten, Marc. *The Gang That Wouldn't Write Straight: Wolfe, Thompson, Didion, Capote, and the New Journalism Revolution*. New York: Crown, 2005. This accessible study of 1960's New Journalism argues that Didion brought a deeply personal voice to narrative nonfiction.

Winchell, Mark Royden. *Joan Didion*. Rev. ed. Boston: Twayne, 1989. This collection of critical essays examines Didion's nonfiction and fiction and includes an analysis of *Slouching Towards Bethlehem*.

Slow Homecoming

Author: Peter Handke (1942-   )

First published: 1979-1981; includes *Langsame Heimkehr*, 1979 (*The Long Way Around*); *Die Lehre der Sainte-Victoire*, 1980 (*The Lesson of Mont-Sainte-Victoire*); *Kindergeschichte*, 1981 (*Child Story*); English translations in *Slow Homecoming*, 1985

Type of work: Novel

Type of plot: Philosophical realism

Time of plot: Late 1970's and early 1980's

Locale: United States, France, and Germany

Principal characters:

VALENTIN SORGER, a geologist

LAUFFER, Sorger's friend and fellow scientist

NATIVE AMERICAN WOMAN, Sorger's girlfriend

A FAMILY IN CALIFORNIA, Sorger's neighbors

A STRANGER IN NEW YORK, Sorger's traveling companion

A MAN

A WOMAN

THEIR DAUGHTER

NOVA, the goddess of Modern Times

GREGOR, a man returning home

HANS, Gregor's brother

SOPHIE, Gregor's sister

The Story:

The Long Way Around. The geologist Sorger is doing research in the vicinity of a small Indian village in Alaska. He knows few people there: his friend and fellow scientist Lauffer, and an Indian woman with whom he has a relationship. At first he and the woman keep their affair secret. However, they gradually allow their relationship to be apparent to others. The time Sorger has in Alaska is limited. He returns to his house in an unnamed university town in California. Sorger has a close relationship with a neighbor family. On his way eastward, Sorger stops in Denver to visit an old friend.

The discovery that this friend died makes Sorger rethink his relationship with his siblings. In New York, Sorger meets a man by chance who, despite all their differences, vaguely reminds Sorger of himself. Sorger's movement, both physically and emotionally, is toward Europe. At the end, Sorger's plane touches down onto European soil.

The Lesson of Mont-Sainte-Victoire. The narrator travels to the Provence area of France. Thanks to his appreciation of the paintings by Paul Cézanne, he views the highway, in all its banality, as pure color. He recalls other journeys, to

Yugoslavia and in Upper Austria. He travels to Mont-Sainte-Victoire, which Cézanne painted. Near Puyloubier he encounters a large mastiff, and the fear that this animal represents is enough to make him forget all color and form in the landscape. Elsewhere a man threatens his life, then they walk a short way together. In a café on the Cours Mirabeau he sees a scene with card players that is almost exactly like a Cézanne painting. His expedition to the mountain gives him the justification for writing *The Lesson of Mont-Sainte-Victoire*. He becomes fascinated with the unity of the "thing-image-script" as he learns about it through studying Cézanne. He recalls that his father is German and his mother of Slovenian stock, and that they lived in southern Austria. Recalling again his writing, he mentions that he transformed Sorger, the main character in *The Long Way Around*, into himself. The "lesson" is not to invent but to realize the world fully. He takes a second trip to Provence. He again wants to go to the mountain. He retraces his steps. The dog is gone. He climbs to the top. In a few months he will return to Austria. He is learning to see, really to see things.

Child Story. A daughter is born to a woman and a man. The family moves to Paris. While the child is still very young, the family moves to a country where their own language, German, is spoken. There they build a house. The mother decides to resume her career (acting) and drifts away from the man and child. When the child is three, she begins to play more with others and go to kindergarten. The father and the daughter move back to the "beloved foreign city" (Paris). There the girl begins school. The school is a Jewish school and this eventually leads to problems. Someone even threatens her life (because she represents the people who persecuted the Jews). She goes to another school. Over the next years she will attend several schools, changing because of age or dissatisfaction (hers or his). She prefers German to French, and he decides to send her back to her mother, who lives where German is spoken. He travels. After a year, he returns. She has her tenth birthday. Father and daughter go through a forest and paint over swastikas others drew there.

Über die Dörfer. Gregor is the oldest of three siblings. After the death of their parents, his brother, Hans, writes to him requesting that he come back home and settle some questions of inheritance. Gregor reflects upon the situation in the presence of the goddess Nova. She advises him to look beyond the villages; that is, he should look beyond the traditional way of thinking about his life and in particular avoid conflict, which seems inevitable, with his siblings. That conflict arises out of the fact that Hans and their sister Sophie want Gregor to relinquish his rights to their parents' house and

its lot. Sophie wants to use the property as collateral. With the borrowed money she plans to set up her own shop. Despite his doubts about Sophie's chances of financial success, Gregor eventually accedes to their wishes. The goddess Nova reappears at the end and repeats her counsel: Go beyond the villages.

Critical Evaluation:

The series in English translation consists of three works of prose that can be considered novels, with the first most closely fitting into that category. The *Slow Homecoming* series, however, is a tetralogy rather than a trilogy. The author, Peter Handke, has designated a play—or dramatic poem as he calls it—to be the fourth and final work in the series. The play, *Über die Dörfer* (beyond the villages), was not translated into English for the 1985 edition. The series was named for the first book's title, which in German means "slow homecoming."

Handke garnered international attention when he challenged a famous group of postwar German-language writers. According to Handke, the Group 47, named for the first year that they met, 1947, had become too much of an institution. Between 1969 and 1972, his daughter was born from his wife, and his mother committed suicide. From this point on, his writing slowly took on a different character: It became less openly rebellious and showed more self-reflection. It represents Handke's turn to a more subjective, introspective writing, which has been labeled, in reference to Handke and other writers, the New Sensibility.

The *Slow Homecoming* series chronicles Handke's gradual reconciliation with Austria, his home, and its history. In the series, Handke nevertheless maintains a critical attitude toward Austria. The slow trip "home" represents not only a trip back to Austria but also represents a trip back to Handke's poetics, or aesthetic of writing.

The main character in each work of the series may be read as a mask for Handke himself. In the first novel, *The Long Way Around*, the Handke mask is a geologist who decides to return to his home in Europe. Significantly, home is usually expressed as Europe. It is not until the final play, *Beyond the Villages*, that the main character is back in Austria.

The chronology of *Child Story* corresponds to the time in which Handke lived in West Germany (1965-1969 and 1971-1973) and in Paris (1969-1971). Handke then traveled in the United States, as does Sorger in *The Long Way Around*. The following year Handke traveled around Europe; some of this trip surfaces in *The Lesson of Mont-Sainte-Victoire*. Handke finally returned to Austria and settled in Salzburg, and *Beyond the Villages* takes place entirely in Austria. The homecoming, however, is fraught with family tension. Handke brings back to Austria a concept of home that explodes nationalism. Home is no longer a village; rather, the village (or city, or country) is part of the world. This is the message of *Über die Dörfer*, or "beyond the villages."

The tetralogy does more, however, than investigate the relationship of the personal to the historical. Description of landscape, objects, and the like takes up much of the tetralogy. In the first book, *The Long Way Around*, the world is seen in geographic—not just historical—time. The title of the second book informs the reader that there is a lesson, which seems to be primarily aesthetic, to be learned from viewing Mont-Sainte-Victoire. In *Child Story*, the narrator's daughter teaches him to appreciate color and to recognize form. He learns the "truth about the essence of beauty." From a sense of geologic time in the first work, to the artist Cézanne viewing nature in the second, to a child seeing things for the first time in the third book, the texts present the reader with a world that extends beyond the "village" of human history, activity, and perception.

Although the works are connected in terms of plot, one can speak more easily of theme as the unifying factor. Along with the slow homecoming, a recurrent theme is the art of writing.

Intimately connected to Handke's understanding of writing is his way of looking at the world. In *The Long Way Around*, Handke introduces the reader to his concern for underlying forms. Geologic formations, in their purity (in the sense of being what they are rather than representing something else) and their being what underlies visible, earthly forms, are, in a sense, touchstones for Handke's aesthetic of writing, which he explores in his writing. In his contemplation of the paintings by Cézanne and other artists, Handke seeks to recognize "the form that does not lament transience or the vicissitudes of history, but transmits an existence in peace." What follows from such a recognition is the problem that every artist faces: how to "communicate the essence of things."

Furthermore, the narrator in *Lesson of Mont-Sainte-Victoire* also needs a justification to write. The narrator finds it in his own self-critic. Rather than employing "celestial comparisons" in the face of beauty, he determines to look at and speak of the earth—where ever he might find himself. Throughout *Slow Homecoming*, Handke tries more to narrate nature rather than to tell a story. In his sense of pure narration, the separation of narrated and narration evaporates, and language should be transparent. This means that language should clearly refer to something, and not be a sign dangling outside meaning. At the same time, Handke tries to

create new mythic images that are as relevant and as gripping to the modern reader as the classical myths were to their audience.

Handke is known for experimenting with genres. That experimentation may be in part a result of Handke's looking for appropriate paradigms for his aesthetics. Handke, who has translated from the ancient Greek, is clearly reflecting, in *Slow Homecoming*, the influence of Plato's theory of forms. In summary, this theory posits that beyond this, the visible world, a world of ideal, eternal forms exists.

In addition, *Child Story* is clearly influenced by the Greek historian Thucydides, and the novel concludes with a motto from the sixth Olympic ode by Pindar. The dramatic poem *Über die Dörfer*, furthermore, is constructed along the lines of Greek drama.

Handke is difficult to read. He eschews story; he mixes and plays with genres; the act of writing is an important theme of his writing. Unlike many modern and postmodern writers, however, Handke strives for (and so, implicitly, believes in) a unity of language with the world it narrates. He looks for beauty and the essence, or form, of things.

Handke's attraction to form may be partly responsible for his interest in classical literature and philosophy. His fascination with classical literature, his concern for aesthetics, and his need to reimagine Austria are prominent themes of the *Slow Homecoming* tetralogy. At the end of *Über die Dörfer*, the goddess Nova challenges her listeners (onstage and, implicitly, those in the audience as well) to overcome the past and the crimes of their fathers. However, Handke does not want to heal old wounds by ignoring them. In *Child Story*, the narrator and his daughter make a special effort to paint over swastikas others had drawn in the forest. They protect nature—and by extension their home—from a far-too-present past. It is an ugly past that Austria needs to confront if it is ever to imagine itself into the future.

Scott G. Williams

Further Reading

Butler, Michael. "Identity and Authenticity in Swiss and Austrian Novels of the Postwar Era: Max Frisch and Peter Handke." In *The Cambridge Companion to the Modern German Novel*, edited by Graham Bartram. New York: Cambridge University Press, 2004. An overview of Handke's novels, including *Slow Homecoming*.

Coury, David N. *The Return of Storytelling in Contemporary German Literature and Film: Peter Handke and Wim Wenders*. Lewiston, N.Y.: Edwin Mellen Press, 2004. Discusses the origins and the definition of storytelling and describes how Handke has transformed the treatment of narration.

Coury, David N., and Frank Pilipp, eds. *The Works of Peter Handke: International Perspectives.* Riverside, Calif.: Ariadne Press, 2005. Fourteen essays examine the genres in which Handke has written and the themes of his work.

Firda, Richard Arthur. *Peter Handke.* New York: Twayne, 1993. Covers Handke's work through the tetralogy (chapter 5) and beyond. Annotated bibliography.

Klinkowitz, Jerome, and James Knowlton. *Peter Handke and the Postmodern Transformation: The Goalie's Journey Home.* Columbia: University of Missouri Press, 1983. Places Handke's work in the context of postmodern literature. Useful for understanding the themes of postmodern literature.

Konzett, Matthias. *The Rhetoric of National Dissent in Thomas Bernhard, Peter Handke, and Elfriede Jelinek.* New York: Camden House, 2000. Konzett analyzes how the three Austrian writers have created new literary strategies in order to expose and dismantle conventional ideas that impede the development of multicultural awareness and identity.

Parry, Christoph. *Peter Handke's Landscapes of Discourse: An Exploration of Narrative and Cultural Space.* Riverside, Calif.: Ariadne Press, 2003. Focuses on the landscapes in Handke's work. Parry maintains that Handke uses landscapes as a means of exploring the relationship between fiction and reality, and in the process the landscapes take on mythic and metaphorical qualities.

Wesche, Ulrich. "Peter Handke, Walker Percy, and the End of Modernity." *Essays in Literature* 19, no. 2 (Fall, 1992): 291-297. Establishes a link between the philosophies of Handke and Percy, two of whose books Handke has translated into German. Addresses the postmodernist crisis in language and Handke's desire for the transparency of words.

The Small House at Allington

Author: Anthony Trollope (1815-1882)
First published: serial, 1862-1864; book, 1864
Type of work: Novel
Type of plot: Domestic realism
Time of plot: Mid-nineteenth century
Locale: London and the county of Barsetshire, England

Principal characters:
CHRISTOPHER DALE, the squire of Allington
MRS. DALE, his widowed sister-in-law
LILIAN (LILY), her daughter
ISABELLA (BELL), another daughter
BERNARD DALE, the squire's nephew and heir
ADOLPHUS CROSBIE, Lily's suitor
JOHN EAMES, another suitor
LADY ALEXANDRINA DE COURCY, a young woman of fashion
DR. CROFTS, a man in love with Bell
LORD DE GUEST, Eames's benefactor

The Story:

There are two houses at Allington. The Great House is the residence of Squire Christopher Dale, an unmarried, plain, seemingly dour man whose ancestors were squires at Allington for generations. In the Small House nearby lives his sister-in-law, Mrs. Dale, and her two daughters, Bell and Lily. Mrs. Dale is the widow of the squire's youngest brother, who died young and left his family in modest circumstances. When the squire offered his brother's widow the Small House rent free, she immediately accepted his offer, not so much for her own sake as for that of her daughters.

The Dales are not the chief family of the neighborhood. Near the town of Guestwick stands Guestwick Manor, the home of Lord de Guest and his sister, Lady Julia. Although not intimate, the families have a tie by marriage. Years before, another of the squire's brothers, Colonel Orlando Dale, eloped with the earl's sister, Lady Fanny. The colonel did not make a career for himself and now lives with his wife in semiretirement at Torquay. Bernard Dale, their only son and a captain in the Engineers, is the squire's heir.

Mrs. Dale is a woman whose pride is as great as her means are small, and her brother-in-law's gruff manners did little to retain cordial relations between them during her ten years in the Small House. The uncle is kind to his nieces in his rather ungracious manner, however, so that they enjoy the social advantages if not the income of wealth. Bell is her uncle's favorite. It is his secret wish that she become Bernard's wife and thus mistress of the Great House. At one time, Mrs. Dale believed that Dr. Crofts, the Guestwick physician, would declare himself; but he did not speak, and now there seems little likelihood of that becoming a match.

One summer, Bernard arrives to visit his uncle, bringing with him his friend Adolphus Crosbie, a handsome, agreeable fellow who is a senior clerk in the General Committee Office at Whitehall. At first Crosbie makes the deeper impression on Bell, and Lily likes to tease her sister by calling him a swell because he is received in the drawing rooms of countesses and cabinet ministers. Crosbie himself is attracted to Lily. When the squire, more gracious than usual to his nephew's friend, invites him to return in September for the shooting, Crosbie gladly accepts the invitation.

Lily has another suitor in young John Eames of Guestwick, a clerk in the Income Tax office in London. Although he was hopelessly in love with Lily since boyhood, his meager income of a hundred pounds a year gives him no immediate prospect of marriage. Eames is awkward, callow, and susceptible. While professing adoration for Lily, he against his better judgment becomes entangled with Amelia Roper, the scheming daughter of Mrs. Lupex, his London landlady.

Crosbie returns to Allington in September; before long, neighborhood gossip is confirmed—a marriage is arranged between Lily and Crosbie. This is the news that greets Eames when he arrives in Guestwick to visit his mother in October. He is made even more wretched by the half-languishing, half-threatening letters he receives from Amelia during his stay. Lily's engagement makes Squire Dale more anxious than ever to see his own plans fulfilled for Bernard and Bell. Encouraged by his uncle, the young officer proposes but in such unconvincing terms that Bell refuses him immediately. Not even the settlement of eight hundred pounds a year promised by the squire tempts her to change her mind.

Crosbie made his choice, and he hopes that the squire would make a financial settlement on Lily, but when he brings up the matter, the squire declares that he feels under no obligation to provide for his niece's future. Crosbie is disappointed, but he consoles himself with the reflection that he is marrying for love and not for worldly advancement. That is the way matters stand when he receives from the Countess de Courcy an invitation to join a house party at Courcy Castle before returning to London.

The de Courcys entertain lavishly. One party guest is Lady Julia de Guest, a well-meaning busybody who spreads the news of Crosbie's engagement. The countess, who has some experience in getting daughters engaged and then seeing their engagements broken, says that nothing is likely to come of Crosbie's romance at Allington. She is right, for her campaign to secure the clerk for her own youngest daughter, Lady Alexandrina, is successful. Long before the end of his visit, Crosbie proposes and is accepted. He does not declare himself to Lady Alexandrina without severe twinges of conscience, it is true; after all, an earl's daughter will offer a better position in fashionable London life than would the penniless niece of a country squire. Hearing what happened, Lady Julia denounces him as a deceiver and a miserable wretch. Crosbie recognizes in her scorn the voice of public opinion; he wishes that he could blot out his visit to Courcy Castle.

Meanwhile, Squire Dale, told of Bell's refusal, goes to his sister-in-law to enlist her aid in furthering the match. He is greatly put out when she insists that Bell should be free to choose for herself. A short time later, the squire receives a letter from Lady Julia telling him of Crosbie's engagement to Lady Alexandrina. Hearing that Crosbie returned to London, the squire follows him there and tries to see the clerk at his club. Crosbie is conscience-stricken and refuses to meet the old gentleman; instead, he sends a disapproving but obliging friend to talk with the squire. The next day, Crosbie writes to Mrs. Dale and confesses that he broke his engagement to her daughter.

Shortly before the end of his vacation, Eames saves Lord de Guest from being attacked by a bull on his estate. Gratefully, the earl decides to take an interest in the young man's future, and he invites Eames to spend Christmas with him at Guestwick Manor.

The two months before Christmas pass with heavy slowness at Allington. Mrs. Dale can only hope that time will heal Lily's hurt. The squire feels that there should be some redress for the insult to his niece. Lord de Guest meets Eames in London and realizes the true state of the young man's feeling for Lily when Eames threatens physical punishment for Crosbie's deed. Meanwhile, Crosbie is preoccupied with financial arrangements for his marriage. Under the fostering hand of Mortimer Gagebee, his future brother-in-law and guardian of the de Courcy interests, he is induced to settle most of his income on Lady Alexandrina.

Crosbie goes to Courcy Castle for Christmas. Still involved with Amelia, Eames goes to Guestwick Manor. At a dinner, the earl announces his intention of settling some money on Lily and Eames if they marry. He asks the squire to do the same, but Lily's uncle refuses to commit himself. Returning to London on the same train with Crosbie, Eames is unable to restrain himself when they meet on the station platform. He thoroughly trounces Lily's faithless suitor.

Bernard renews his proposals to Bell and argues their uncle's wishes in the matter; but Bell tells him, as kindly as possible, that she can follow no wishes but her own. Stubborn in his desires, the squire becomes angry with his nephew and niece, and he decides to be angry with his sister-in-law as well if she refuses to reason with her daughter. After the exchange of heated words, Mrs. Dale decides that it might be better for all concerned if she and her daughters move away from the Small House.

A short time later, Lily becomes ill with scarlatina, and Dr. Crofts is called in. He comes daily, ostensibly to see his patient but actually to be near Bell. In the meantime, Mrs. Dale is preparing to move into a small cottage in Guestwick. During Lily's illness, Dr. Crofts declares his love to Bell. Taking her evasive answer for a refusal, he drives away in dejection. Lily, aware of Bell's true feelings, urges him to ask her sister again. Crosbie and Lady Alexandrina are married in London in February.

After Lily's illness, Lady Julia invites Mrs. Dale and her daughters to spend a week at Guestwick Manor. Eames is asked at the same time. Lily, however, sees through the scheme for bringing her and Eames together, especially after she learns that Squire Dale is to make another of the party, and she declines the invitation. The squire is so kind in his concern for Lily that Mrs. Dale begins to regret her decision to move into the village. In the midst of her perplexities, Dr. Crofts comes to tell her that Bell accepted him. While the doctor sits with the Dales beside the fire that night as if they are already one family, the anxious mother is almost able to believe that happiness returns to the Small House.

Eames, manfully escaping from the toils of Amelia, arrives at Guestwick Manor. He was recently made private secretary to the great Sir Raffle Buffle, largely through the earl's influence, and he is grateful. Since Lily did not come to the manor, it was decided that the squire and Bell should dine with the de Guests. On the next day, Eames is to call at Allington and declare himself to Lily. To his dismay, however, she will not have him. After his departure, Mrs. Dale adds her entreaties to his, but Lily remains firm. She is, she declares, like her mother, widowed; and so matters stand.

Mrs. Dale does not leave the Small House after all, for their family troubles bring her and the squire closer together, and he announces his intention of settling three thousand pounds on each of his nieces. When Bell marries Dr. Crofts in June, the squire throws open the Great House for the wedding. Bernard and Eames do not attend.

Crosbie's wedded life lasts only a few months. Lady Alexandrina becomes bored with the humdrum of a government clerk's life and goes off to join her mother at Baden Baden. Crosbie discovers too late that the settlements he made on his wife leave him a poor man, and he goes into cheap lodgings—happy at any price, however, to be free both of her nagging and her aristocratic relatives.

Critical Evaluation:

In *The Small House at Allington*, Anthony Trollope continues his investigation of the lives of men and women who inhabit the fictional district of Barsetshire, a country province modeled on those with which the author was familiar. The people of Trollope's imaginary countryside exhibit moral and social values that stand in contrast to those held by the more sophisticated but often more morally bankrupt men and women of London. In this novel, Trollope introduces a number of figures from the city into the lives of his countryfolk, so that the contrast is brought into sharp focus. Although *The Small House at Allington* can be read without reference to the other novels in the Barsetshire series, those familiar with works such as *The Warden* (1855), *Barsetshire Towers* (1857), *Doctor Thorne* (1858), or *Framley Parsonage* (1860-1861) will see how Trollope's vision of society is developed through his exploration of characters from a range of social classes and professions who share a common set of experiences and values. Characters who are featured in major roles in other novels in the series often make cameo appearances in this work, and Trollope introduces additional minor figures whose stories will form the central interest of novels in the author's Palliser series.

Like so many of Trollope's novels, *The Small House at Allington* is concerned with marriage, specifically with the choice to be made between marrying for love and marrying for money or social position. Although the novel contains many elements that resemble those of the romantic novels that achieved great popularity with Victorian audiences, Trollope undercuts the form at key points to highlight the dangers of adhering too closely to the romantic ideal. Instead of meeting his readers' demands for the expected happy ending, which should befall the heroine and hero regardless of how badly they behave, Trollope instead uses the familiar structural devices of the traditional romantic novel to explore a theme that intrigued him throughout his career: human perversity. Many of the characters in *The Small House at Allington* seem wilfully intent on making the wrong choices and avoiding the possibility for securing lasting happiness by opting for marriage partners or a single lifestyle that will bring them only unhappiness. To dramatize the universality of his theme, Trollope employs a structural pattern common in Victorian novels, that of multiple plotting. The central story of Lily Dale's unfortunate engagement to Adolphus Crosbie and her subsequent decision to reject Johnnie Eames and to remain a spinster is complemented by a series of similar love stories in which women and men face choices resembling the one Lily must make between her two lovers.

As he does in so many of his novels, Trollope lavishes a great deal of attention on characterization. Although he himself calls his heroine a "prig," she cannot be dismissed so glibly by serious readers. Lily represents a type of woman common in the Victorian era but not unknown in other times: the strong-willed, independent figure who is determined to make her own decisions but too proud to admit her mistakes, who remains perversely committed to a course of action even when that has been shown to be unwise. Certainly she shares affinities with that other, more famous jilted spinster, Miss Havisham of Charles Dickens's *Great Expectations* (1860-1861). By stubbornly adhering to the notion of constancy in love, she is led to reject the possibility of finding happiness in another romantic relationship. Readers who are disappointed that Trollope does not provide some means to rescue Lily from her self-induced intellectual blindness and have her marry Eames miss the point Trollope is making, that such idyllic resolutions are not plausible in the real world, and that individuals (men as well as women) who refuse to recognize their faults are doomed to a life of unwarranted loneliness. In effect, Lily gets what she deserves.

Eames suffers as well from Lily's haughty behavior, but Trollope is careful to show that the hero is not without flaws. His treatment of the unfortunate Amelia Roper demonstrates that he has flaws that may explain why Lily refuses to accept him, both before accepting Crosbie's proposal and later, after her engagement has been severed. In a similar fashion, the author introduces character traits in "villains" such as Crosbie that ameliorate, if they do not exonerate, their actions. A number of characters seem little more than stock figures, however: Lord de Guest and Squire Dale represent the pastoral tradition of the English countryside, whereas the de Courcys embody the false values of London gentry who find amusement in manipulating—and ruining—the lives of others. Trollope does offer readers one traditional "happy ending": that of Lily's sister, Bell, and Dr. Crofts. Like her sister, Bell is torn between two lovers, but she is shrewd enough to reject the dissolute Bernard Dale in favor of the emotionally more stable Dr. Crofts.

The vision of society presented in *The Small House at Allington* is noticeably darker than that of earlier novels in the Barsetshire series. Trollope seems less interested in making readers feel comfortable than in exposing human folly. No doubt that is why his contemporaries found the novel less appealing than some of his lighter works. Nevertheless, *The Small House at Allington* emerges as one of the finest in the extensive Trollope canon for illustrating the consequences that follow from the willful disregard of common sense and moderation in dealing with others and from the insistence on acting on ill-formed opinion or out of selfish motives.

"Critical Evaluation" by Laurence W. Mazzeno

Further Reading

Bridgham, Elizabeth A. *Spaces of the Sacred and Profane: Dickens, Trollope, and the Victorian Cathedral Town*. New York: Routledge, 2008. Describes how Trollope and Charles Dickens use the setting of Victorian cathedral towns to critique religious attitudes, business practices, aesthetic ideas, and other aspects of nineteenth century English life.

Bury, Laurent. *Seductive Strategies in the Novels of Anthony Trollope, 1815-1882*. Lewiston, N.Y.: Edwin Mellen Press, 2004. A study of seduction in all of Trollope's novels. Argues that seduction was a survival skill for both men and women in the Victorian era and demonstrates how Trollope depicted the era's sexual politics.

Hall, N. John. *Trollope: A Biography*. New York: Oxford University Press, 1991. Comprehensive scholarly biography of the novelist. Examines the composition and publication history of *The Small House at Allington* and a gives a brief analysis of the important characters in the novel, who also appear in subsequent works by Trollope.

Kincaid, James R. *The Novels of Anthony Trollope*. New York: Oxford University Press, 1977. Determines that *The Small House at Allington* is the darkest novel in the Barsetshire series, which is generally comic in tone. Claims that Trollope is intent on undermining the pastoral qualities that characterize earlier novels in the series.

MacDonald, Susan Peck. *Anthony Trollope*. Boston: Twayne, 1987. Discusses *The Small House at Allington* as one of the novels in which Trollope deals with the topic of love. Focuses on the perversity of the heroine, Lily Dale, and explains how Trollope achieves density and verisimilitude through the use of parallel plots.

McMaster, Juliet. "*The Small House at Allington*: The Moth and the Candle." In *Trollope's Palliser Novels: Theme and Pattern*. New York: Oxford University Press, 1978. Excellent analysis of the major themes of the novel: the "quest for truth among lies," and the prevalence of human perversity. Links the work to Trollope's Palliser series.

Markwick, Margaret. *New Men in Trollope's Novels: Rewriting the Victorian Male.* Burlington, Vt.: Ashgate, 2007. Examines Trollope's novels, tracing the development of his ideas about masculinity. Argues that Trollope's male characters are not the conventional Victorian patriarchs and demonstrates how his works promoted a "startlingly modern model of manhood."

_____. *Trollope and Women.* London: Hambledon Press, 1997. Examines how Trollope could simultaneously accept the conventional Victorian ideas about women while also sympathizing with women's difficult situations. Demonstrates the individuality of his female characters. Discusses his depiction of both happy and unhappy marriages, male-female relationships, bigamy, and scandal.

Mullen, Richard, and James Munson. *The Penguin Companion to Trollope.* New York: Penguin Books, 1996. A comprehensive guide, describing all of Trollope's novels, short stories, travel books, and other works; discusses plot, characters, background, tone, allusions, and contemporary references and places the works in their historical context.

Super, R. H. *The Chronicler of Barsetshire: A Life of Anthony Trollope.* Ann Arbor: University of Michigan Press, 1988. Critical biography of the novelist that provides excellent overview of his major works. Discusses the principal themes of *The Small House at Allington* and points out ways in which Trollope used it as a bridge between the Barsetshire and the Palliser series.

Smoke

Author: Ivan Turgenev (1818-1883)
First published: Dym, 1867 (English translation, 1868)
Type of work: Novel
Type of plot: Social realism
Time of plot: 1862-1865
Locale: Germany and Russia

Principal characters:
GRIGORY LITVINOFF, a serious young Russian man
TANYA SHESTOFF, his fiancé
KAPITOLINA SHESTOFF, Tanya's aunt
IRINA, a fashionable lady
GENERAL RATMIROFF, her husband
POTUGIN, a retired clerk

The Story:

At Baden, Grigory Litvinoff decides to enjoy a few days of vacation. The fashionable German watering place is full of Russians, and there, in a week or so, Litvinoff is to meet Tanya Shestoff, his fiancé, who is coming to Baden with her Aunt Kapitolina.

Litvinoff is poor, comparatively speaking. His father owns a large farm with forests, meadows, and a lake, but Russian farming is so unproductive that he can barely make ends meet. After his university days, Litvinoff decides to learn progressive farming, but, because Russia is so far behind in agriculture, he goes abroad to study. He goes to the Crimea, France, Switzerland, and England. Everywhere his keen mind absorbs the latest agricultural methods, and he is particularly impressed by the superiority of the few pieces of American machinery he sees. Full of ideas, his life is planned; he will make a model farm. First, however, he will marry Tanya.

Quite by chance, he runs into Bambaeff, a former acquaintance. Bambaeff is an ebullient person, filled with windy politics and intimate with the most advanced thinkers in Baden. When Bambaeff takes Litvinoff to meet Gubaryoff, the idol of the liberals, Litvinoff is repelled by the company he meets in Gubaryoff's rooms. They all talk long and loud in their assertions that Russia produces nothing good, that all virtue resides in Europe proper, that the emancipation of the serfs is a foolish step. He meets Bindasoff, a choleric boor who borrows a hundred rubles from him; he never repays the debt, although Litvinoff later watches him win four hundred rubles with the money. Only one man in the gathering is quiet; he sits unnoticed in a corner.

After leaving Gubaryoff's room, Litvinoff stops at a sidewalk café. The quiet man from Gubaryoff's rooms appears and presents himself at Litvinoff's table; he is Potugin, a former clerk in Moscow. They talk agreeably for a long time. Both men greatly dislike their compatriots who are so sure that nothing good comes out of Russia, and they both agree that by hard work Russia can advance. At last, as Potugin rises to go, he excuses himself by saying that he has a girl with him. Seeing Litvinoff's look of polite blankness, he explains that he is looking after a little child who has no parents.

After a short walk, Litvinoff returns to his hotel. He has a letter from Tanya to read; as he reads it, he was bothered by a heavy sweet smell. Looking around, he sees a bunch of fresh heliotrope in a glass. Here is a mystery. The servant says that a lady gave him money to get into the room. She must have left the flowers. Suddenly, he remembers Irina.

Ten years before, Litvinoff was a student in Moscow. He was poor, and he frequently visited another poor family, the Osinins. The family was of the real nobility, but for generations the Osinins declined, until they existed only on a small pension the father received from some obscure sinecures. Litvinoff was attracted greatly to Irina, the seventeen-year-old daughter of the household, but for a long time Irina paid little heed to the poor student. One day, her haughtiness suddenly changed. Pliant and cheerful, she talked eagerly with Litvinoff of his ambitions. When he declared his love, Irina was pleased and grateful. With no formal understanding, Litvinoff became her accepted suitor.

By a trick of fate, Prince Osinin, her father, received an invitation to the court ball. Now that Irina was grown, he decided to accept, to show his daughter in fine society. Litvinoff urged Irina to go to the ball. She repeated many times that she was going only at Litvinoff's insistence. On the night of the ball, Litvinoff brought her a bunch of heliotrope to wear. She took the flowers and kissed him passionately. The next day Irina had a headache and refused to see him. Two days after the ball Irina went to St. Petersburg with Count Reisenbach, a distant cousin of her mother. The explanation was brief and tragic. The count needed an ornament in his household. Grasping and ambitious as she was, Irina accepted and went to stay with her debauched cousin. Litvinoff put her out of his mind. He almost forgets the incident until the heliotrope appears mysteriously in his room.

Litvinoff wrestles with his conscience and decides not to see Irina again. He holds to his resolve until Potugin comes to him with a pressing invitation to visit the home of General Ratmiroff. At the party he meets Irina again, now the wife of General Ratmiroff, a vain, cruel aristocrat. Litvinoff is as much repelled by the empty smart set as he was by the empty liberals he met in Baden.

Irina will not let him ignore her. She begs her former suitor to love her again, and when she comes to his rooms he admits that his love never died.

Tanya and her Aunt Kapitolina appear. Even naïve Tanya sees at once that something happened to her fiancé; she is not wholly unprepared when he confesses his affair with Irina. Potugin tries his best to get Litvinoff to abandon Irina. He has good reason to do so. For love of Irina, he agreed to marry a friend of hers who was soon to bear an illegitimate child. Al-though the girl fell ill and the marriage never took place, Potugin is burdened with the care of the little girl. He acted because of his hopeless infatuation for Irina, and he warns Litvinoff that only evil consequences can come of leaving Tanya for the shallow aristocrat.

In his despair, Litvinoff makes a deal with Irina. He will not become her secret lover; she must go away with him and be his alone. He names the train on which he will leave. Irina is not at the station, and Litvinoff sadly takes his seat. Just then he sees Irina, dressed in her maid's costume, rush to the platform. He motions her to come aboard; she understands, but she refuses by gesture and motions him to dismount. She stands in a hopeless attitude on the platform as the train pulls out of the station.

Litvinoff recovers almost wholly from his hurt. He is too quiet for his years, but he is fairly happy. He finds his father's farm in bad shape, with insufficient income to keep up the house. His father is pathetically glad to see him and abandons the control of the estate to his son. That end accomplished, he dies content. For a long time there is no opportunity to introduce new methods; Litvinoff has all he can do to remain solvent.

After three years, he learns that Tanya lives on a farm a day's journey away. Resolved to mend his life, he decides to go to her and to ask her forgiveness. He finds Tanya ready to forget as well as to forgive, and she is even embarrassed by his penitence. They are soon married. Irina continues to attract admirers in St. Petersburg; despite her thirty years, she retains the freshness of youth. Although many gallants are in attendance upon her, she never singles out a special admirer. The society ladies all agree that Irina is not generally liked; she has such an ironic turn of mind.

Critical Evaluation:

When *Smoke* appeared in 1867, Ivan Turgenev had been publishing prose fiction for twenty years and was well past the midpoint in his literary career. He had learned most of what he was to know of his craft and had defined his themes, which could be summarized as the Russian question and how it affects, or is affected by, adult love entanglements. The Russian question is simply that of Russia's relation to the community of European nations and what might be done either to change that relation or to preserve it. Turgenev, who lived much in Western Europe and admired its values, saw that in science, industry, social attitudes, political institutions, and general progress, Russia was far behind Germany, France, and England, and he had little sympathy with conservative Slavophiles who felt that their native land was better off for being so. In his complicated relationship with Pauline Garcia Viardot, a highly successful French singer and actor who had both a husband and children, he saw further the impediment to purposeful action in men (or women) who were not secure or even fulfilled in love matters.

Although *Smoke* is set in Baden, a fashionable German spa, virtually all the characters are Russians, falling into three groups. First, there are nonentities such as the liberals Litvinoff meets in Gubaryoff's rooms, brittle and shallow people who pretend to liberalism and intellectuality though they lack the character and the purpose to serve their homeland well. Then there are the aristocrats, some of them military men, who have no interest in bringing about change in Russia, which suits them as it is. Finally, there is the novel's hero, Grigory Litvinoff, and a shadowy figure, Sozont Potugin, civilized and thoughtful, with whom Litvinoff becomes acquainted. Both these men seem to embody qualities of character and intelligence by which the condition of Russia and its people might be improved, but both are under the influence of Irina, who is now married to Ratmiroff, a brilliant young general and Russian aristocrat, whose social set Irina detests even as she is unwilling to leave a marriage that gives her power and a comfortable social place. Her brief liaison with Litvinoff seems motivated by genuine passion and true regard, but neither impulse is as strong as the tie that binds her to a world she does not admire but cannot forsake.

Turgenev seems to want his readers to be persuaded that the very people who have gifts that might lead Russia forward are, by virtue of their complete humanity, susceptible to passion, unrequited or impermanent, that effectively block sustained effort or real accomplishment, thereby guaranteeing that the Russian question will remain unanswered. Such a message would perhaps have been personally gratifying to the author, who believed himself enlightened to true progress as he believed he saw it in the West, but who was nevertheless attached to his own bewitching woman, Viardot, so that he was content to live in places such as Baden (Turgenev had large hereditary property in Russia) and fill his active life with literary pursuits. That Viardot seems to have been an honorable woman, who remained loyal in friendship to Turgenev even as she must have seen herself as a partial model for characters such as Irina, only emphasizes the degree to which Turgenev was captivated by someone stronger than himself. In youth, he had been considerably dominated by an imperious mother, and perhaps domination by a woman was something that he came to need.

It might be well to remember that, when Litvinoff arrives in Baden, he has been engaged in practical study that he hopes to take home to Russia with a view to improving his estate. He is betrothed to a lovely, innocent young woman, Tanya Shestoff, who suffers his adventure with Irina and accepts him back at the novel's conclusion. Turgenev was to take up the same story again in *Spring Torrents* (1871), but, in that novel, Sanin, the central male character, betrays Gemma, the young innocent, without redemption. After his encounter with Madame Polozova, he fails to return to Gemma, who marries another man and emigrates to America. By 1872, Turgenev was in his middle fifties, old enough to realize clearly that infatuation with an unattainable woman meant the loss of other possibilities in love relations and the conventional happiness (and potential contribution to ordinary Russian life) that might follow from that.

Even if *Smoke* has a happier ending than *Spring Torrents*, there is melancholy near its conclusion. When it becomes clear to Litvinoff that his brief affair with Irina will result in nothing permanent, he leaves Baden alone on a train whose smoke seems to illustrate "his own life, Russian life—everything human, especially everything Russian." He recalls his experiences among the fashionable and pretentious, he recalls the somewhat pessimistic sermonizing of his acquaintance Potugin, and he concludes his reflection with "a gesture of despair."

As happened on more than one occasion when a novel by Turgenev appeared, liberals in Russia were dissatisfied, even bitter, over *Smoke*, which they saw as their betrayal by a landed aristocrat living abroad, of whom they felt they had just cause to be suspicious. However, Turgenev did not feel that liberalism was the same thing as the ideological rigidities he sometimes found in the thinking of progressives among his own countrymen, rigidities that he believed could not result in anything purposeful. Indeed, Turgenev does not seem very hopeful about anything in *Smoke*, as the title implies. About the best thing Litvinoff can expect from life is marriage to Tanya, who has the good grace to take him back as the novel concludes.

"Critical Evaluation" by John Higby

Further Reading

Andrew, Joe, Derek Offord, and Robert Reid, eds. *Turgenev and Russian Culture: Essays to Honour Richard Peace*. New York: Rodopi, 2008. Some of the essays discuss the uses of poetry in Turgenev's prose, the dark side of the writer, and Turgenev and Russian culture. Michael Pursglove's essay provides an analysis of *Smoke*.

Bloom, Harold, ed. *Ivan Turgenev*. Philadelphia: Chelsea House, 2003. Collection of critical essays about Turgenev's work. Several essays discuss *Ottsy i deti* (1862; *Fa-*

thers and Sons*, 1867), while others compare Turgenev's works to those of Ernest Hemingway, Willa Cather, and Sherwood Anderson.

Dessaix, Robert. *Twilight of Love: Travels with Turgenev*. London: Scribner, 2005. Dessaix, an Australian writer and a scholar of Russian literature, traveled to Turgenev's homes and conducted research at the Moscow Library to locate the "soul" of the Russian writer. The resulting memoir provides insights into Turgenev's life, particularly the writer's experience of love.

Magarshack, David. *Turgenev: A Life*. London: Faber & Faber, 1954. An illustrated biography by Turgenev's translator describing Turgenev's life extensively and concentrating on the events shaping it, his relationships with Russian and foreign writers, and the factual circumstances surrounding his works, including *Smoke*.

Orwin, Donna Tussing. *Consequences of Consciousness: Turgenev, Dostoevsky, and Tolstoy*. Stanford, Calif.: Stanford University Press, 2007. A psychological analysis of the work of Turgenev and the two other great Russian realist novelists, examining how these writers depicted their characters' subjectivity. The references to *Smoke* are listed in the index.

Seeley, Frank Friedeberg. *Turgenev: A Reading of His Fiction*. New York: Cambridge University Press, 1991. Analyzes *Smoke* both as a novel and as an episode in Turgenev's fight with the critics and readers, seeing it as no less political than *Ottsy i deti* (1862; *Fathers and Sons*, 1867). Demonstrates how through the novel's main characters, Turgenev shows that personal and political life in Russia at that time were reduced to smoke.

Woodward, James B. *Metaphysical Conflict: A Study of the Major Novels of Ivan Turgenev*. Munich: Otto Sagner, 1990. A fine discussion of *Smoke*, especially of the ideas preoccupying Russians in the mid-nineteenth century as they are reflected in the relationships of the novel's characters.

Yarmolinsky, Avrahm. *Turgenev: The Man, His Art, and His Age*. New York: Orion Press, 1959. Sees *Smoke* primarily as a love story, but does not neglect the nonliterary components and the impact the novel has had in Russian society, primarily among the intellectuals and social activists.

The Snake Pit

Author: Sigrid Undset (1882-1949)
First published: Olav Audunssøn i Hestviken, 2
    volumes, 1925 (*The Axe*, 1928; *The Snake Pit*, 1929)
Type of work: Novel
Type of plot: Historical
Time of plot: Late thirteenth and early fourteenth
    centuries
Locale: Norway

Principal characters:
OLAV AUDUNSSON, the master of Hestviken
INGUNN STEINFINNSDATTER, his wife
CECILIA, their daughter
EIRIK, Ingunn's son by Teit
OLAV HALF-PRIEST, Olav's kinsman
TORHILD BJÖRNSDATTER, the housekeeper at Hestviken

The Story:

After Olav Audunsson receives his wife Ingunn from her kin, he returns with her to Hestviken to claim his inheritance. Lime trees are in blossom, and their scent brings back to him childhood memories of the manor that had not been his home since he was seven years old. Hestviken, on a ridge above Oslo fjord, was a place of chieftains. One of the heirlooms of Viking days is a wood carving showing legendary Gunnar surrounded by vipers in the pit where Atle threw him.

While Olav was growing up as Steinfinn's foster son at Frettastein and during his years of warring and outlawry, an aged kinsman lived at Hestviken. Old Olav, called Half-Priest because he studied for the Church before an accident crippled him, was more clerk than franklin. Under his stewardship the manor does not prosper, and young Olav has less wealth than he expects. Still, Hestviken is a rich homestead, and so he cheerfully sets about repairing the houses, increasing his herds, and outfitting boats to trade by sea. Besides, he likes Olav Half-Priest and spends many evenings listening to stories of his ancestors and their deeds in the old days.

Olav Half-Priest knew four generations of the Hestviken men, and his greatest wish, as he often tells Ingunn, is to see her son and Olav's before his death. The child Ingunn has the summer the old man dies lives only a few seconds. In the next four years she has three more children, all stillborn. During part of that time Olav is away on raids against the Danes, but when he is at home there is little cheer between them. Ingunn is fretful and sick, resentful of Signe and Una, Olav's distant cousins, impatient with her maids. Olav knows that she is thinking of the healthy son she had by Teit, the Icelander he killed to hide her shame, but there is no mention of the boy between them.

Olav's crime weighs heavily upon his own spirit. If he proclaimed it at the time, men would have found justice in Teit's slaying; his silence makes his deed secret murder. Unable to confess his guilt without bringing shame to Ingunn, whom he loves, he knows that he must live with the burdens of his sin. Perhaps, he thinks, the dead children are part of the chastisement he must suffer. He is always tender toward the useless wife whose misfortune he took, by violence, upon himself.

When Ingunn becomes really ill, Olav hires Torhild Bjönsdatter, whose mother was a serving woman at Hestviken, to keep his house for him. Afterward the manor is in better order, and for a time Ingunn's health improves, so that one spring she travels to see Tora, her widowed sister, at Frettastein. While there, she goes to see little Eirik, her son, at his foster mother's house. He is half-frightened of the richly dressed woman who gives him gifts and holds him so tightly. On her return to Hestviken, Olav asks her if she longs greatly for the boy. She says that Eirik is afraid of her.

Ingunn's brother Jon dies, and Olav rides north to collect her share of his goods. When he returns, he brings Eirik with him. In the neighborhood he lets it be known that the boy is his child and Ingunn's, born during his outlaw years and for that reason given to foster parents in the Upplands. Eirik likes Olav and follows him about; Ingunn sometimes grows fretful because the boy prefers her husband's company to her own. Then Olav, for the sake of peace, treats the child coldly. Often it seems that he is never to have ease because of the Icelander's brat.

After Ingunn gives birth to a son, Audun, Olav realizes how foolish his act was, for in claiming Eirik he defrauded his lawful son of his birthright. He becomes sharper in his manner toward Eirik, scolds him for childish lies, and to his own shame beats him for his boasting and loud ways. Sickly Audun dies the next winter.

One year Arnvid Finnsson, Ingunn's cousin and their true friend in the days of Olav's outlawry, comes to Hestviken. Arnvid says that he gave his manor to his oldest son; he himself is to enter the order of the Preaching Friars. Olav tells Arnvid the story of the guilt weighing so heavily upon him, saying it is as if God's wrath pursues him and gives him no peace, night or day. Arnvid, kind and good man though he is, can say little to comfort his friend.

Ingunn gives birth to her last child, a fair daughter christened Cecilia. From that time on, the mother seldom leaves her bed. Years before she lost the power of her limbs during an illness, and now her old sickness takes her again. Sometimes Olav looks at her, pale and wasted, and wonders how the sick woman could have been the beautiful girl he knew years before. He is not completely unhappy, however, in their last years together. He looks after Ingunn with patience and pity for the sad life she lives. Thinking she might become better if he were to make atonement for the slaying of Teit, he speaks to her one day of the matter, but she begs him to keep silent for her sake. Word comes that Arnvid died at Hamar. Olav feels that the only friend left from his youth is Ingunn, once so fair that he killed two men for her sake.

The two live so much to themselves at Hestviken that they are never popular with their neighbors. Consequently, there is much gossip when it becomes known that Olav fathered a child by his housekeeper. Feeling that his new sin goes back to the old one from which he can never be free and anxious to make amends to Torhild for the wrong, he gives her the farm at Auken for her own. Ingunn, who was always jealous of Torhild's strong, healthy body, says nothing. Eirik shows in every way his dislike for the stern, aloof man he calls father.

Torhild's child is a boy, Bjorn. On the day Torhild goes to Auken, Ingunn sends for her and asks to see him, a lusty child as fair as her own Cecilia. Afterward Eirik spits after Torhild and curses her son. Ingunn begs him never to speak so of any woman's child.

Olav is at the Oslo fair when a servant brings word that Ingunn is dying. Memories of the past, remorse, and the conviction that God will be merciful if he will only confess his guilt plague him as he rides homeward to be at her side. After her death, he intends to do as he planned on that night ride, confess and welcome his punishment, whether holy pilgrimage or headsman's ax, but he cannot, he realizes at last, because of Eirik and of Cecilia. Never can he abandon them to a kinsman's care or shame them by letting the world know their mother was wanton. Sometimes, in the slow, sleepless nights, he feels that he is Gunnar in the snake pit on the old carving—his hidden sin is the viper that pierces his heart.

Critical Evaluation:

The Snake Pit is one part of a multivolume novel. The characters in *The Snake Pit* are descendants of the fierce pagan Norsemen whose rough lives and deeds of valor form the substance of medieval sagas throughout the Scandinavian peninsula. The men and women in the novel can barely contain their emotions, and their lives are filled with hatreds and cravings for revenge and with unendurable remorse. Their family ties are as complicated as they are vital to their mode of existence. The work is filled with portrayals of superstitions, inarticulate fears, and blind religious convictions. Though Sigrid Undset is clearly intent on displaying the superiority of Christianity, especially Catholicism, over the pagan religious practices of her forebears, the people of Hestviken are still caught up in a form of worship that is inextricably tied to ancient terrors and dark legends. The author makes clear that her characters' lives are circumscribed by folk sayings and traditions that are ignored only at great risk, and that their hearts and minds bear a burden of ancient guilt.

The Snake Pit is both a historical picture of a grim age and a human testament of humankind's ability to survive. Undset's story centers on the tragedy of the trapped human lives of the men and women in thirteenth century Norway. While readers may be swept away by the action-filled saga, the novelist carefully crafts her story so that the moral dimensions are subtly reinforced by a series of symbols and allusions that transform the historically bound tale into one of more universal and timeless significance. The snake pit that gives the work its title is a symbol of considerable flexibility. It seems to Olav Audunsson to illustrate his own predicament, to readers it shows a further aspect of his situation, one that ultimately proves fatal to the protagonist's efforts to achieve salvation. When Olav first comes home to Hestviken, where he has not lived since he was a boy, he sees the ancient doorpost carved with the legendary figure of Gunnar in the snake pit. He applies it in his mind to the Hestvik people's historical propensity to disaster, often brought on by poor alliances or deliberate transgression of God's will. Later, seeing a parallel in his own situation, he congratulates himself for upholding the Hestvik tradition of dogged endurance under misfortune. Throughout his struggles, the heinous crime he committed—the murder of his wife's lover Teit—seems to him to be a serpent at the heart of his life with Ingunn.

In reality, however, the serpent in his bosom is pride. In that pride, he takes to himself all the guilt and suffering occasioned by Ingunn's fall. His intention in bringing her to Hestviken is to protect and to cherish her. At no time does he refer to his wife's liaison with Teit as a sin, or acknowledge her need for expiation, or show concern for the state of her soul. It is almost as though he does not consider her salvation of any importance; of course, he does not understand the nature of salvation, or the price one must pay to achieve it. That self-knowledge will come to him only after considerable struggle, which must include an acknowledgment of his insignificance in the face of God, whose plan transcends any individual's efforts to direct his own life. At this point, how-ever, when Olav is most ready to confess his own sin, he is thrown into confusion by the revelation that Ingunn, too, suffered, not for his sin but for her own. He realizes further that were he to confess his own guilt, he would bring shame on his wife and set her suffering at naught. Even her death does not free him from the need to maintain silence about their mutual transgressions, since he cannot bring himself to shame Ingunn before her children. At the close of the novel, Olav finds himself once more contemplating the carvings on the ancient lintel, perceiving himself a lost soul. At the midpoint of his life, and the midpoint of the saga, Undset's hero reaches the moral nadir on his quest for self-knowledge. His salvation is portrayed in the two volumes which follow, *In the Wilderness* and *The Son Avenger*, which reveal his acceptance of Christian principles of dependence on God and acceptance of his sinful nature.

Throughout this novel, Undset shows how blind human beings can be to the inner state of those nearest them and how selfish their apparent sacrifices are. Although set in the thirteenth century, *The Snake Pit* deals with the darker side of human passions of any age. The greatness of the work lies in the breadth of its vision and in the depth of its penetration of human nature.

Further Reading

Bayerschmidt, Carl. *Sigrid Undset*. New York: Twayne, 1970. Introductory overview of Undset's life and major works. A chapter devoted to Undset's novels of the Middle Ages provides commentary on *The Snake Pit*, focusing on the moral development of the hero.

Brunsdale, Mitzi. *Sigrid Undset: Chronicler of Norway*. Oxford, England: Berg, 1988. Summarizes Undset's achievement in *The Master of Hestviken* chronicle, of which *The Snake Pit* is the second part. Comments on the significance of the symbol of the snake. Discusses the hero's relationship with his demanding wife and his efforts to overcome his pride.

Gustafson, Alrik. *Six Scandinavian Novelists*. Minneapolis: University of Minnesota Press, 1968. Discussion of the four novels that make up *The Master of Hestviken* tetralogy. Describes Undset's concern with the moral development of her hero. Highlights her technique of using historical events to illuminate human concerns.

Maman, Marie. *Sigrid Undset in America: An Annotated Bibliography and Research Guide*. Lanham, Md.: Rowman and Littlefield, 2000. A useful resource for English-speaking students. Maman has compiled bibliographies of American publications featuring information about Undset, placing them into four categories: reviews and articles about Undset's novels set in the Middle Ages, materials about Undset's contemporary novels, other articles, and book chapters about the writer. Also includes a bibliography of autobiographical material found in Undset's own works.

Mishler, William. "The Epic Novelists: Undset, Duun, Uppdal, Falkberget." In *A History of Norwegian Literature*, edited by Harold S. Naess. Lincoln: University of Nebraska Press, in cooperation with the American-Scandinavian Foundation, 1993. Analyzes Undset's works and places them within the broader context of Norwegian epic fiction.

Whitehouse, J. C. "Sigrid Undset." In *Vertical Man: The Human Being in the Catholic Novels of Graham Greene, Sigrid Undset, and Georges Bernanos*. New York: Garland, 1990. Examines Undset's view of human nature as it emerges in her fiction. Comments on the scenes and characters from *The Snake Pit* are interwoven into a discussion highlighting Undset's generally optimistic vision of humanity.

Winsnes, A. H. *Sigrid Undset: A Study in Christian Realism*. Translated by P. G. Foote. New York: Sheed and Ward, 1953. A biography of Undset focusing on the development of Christian themes in her novels.

Snow Country

Author: Yasunari Kawabata (1899-1972)
First published: Yukiguni, 1935-1937, serial; 1947, book (English translation, 1956)
Type of work: Novel
Type of plot: Symbolic realism
Time of plot: 1930's
Locale: Mountains of northwest Japan

Principal characters:
SHIMAMURA, a writer from Tokyo
KOMAKO, a young geisha
YUKIO, the ill son of a music teacher
YOKO, a girl who takes care of Yukio

The Story:

Shimamura, a writer who lives in Tokyo with his wife and children, is on a train headed to a hot-springs spa in a mountainous area of northwest Japan, an area known for its heavy snows. Shimamura speculates about the nature of the relationship between an ill man and a girl seated across the aisle from him and becomes fascinated by the girl's image reflected in the mirrorlike window of the train. He sees her disembodied face against the background of the mountains and has a vision of her eye floating beautifully and transparently over the passing landscape of the mountains.

The girl and the man get off at the same stop as Shimamura, where a woman in a blue cape is waiting. Shimamura asks the stationmaster whether Komako, the girl who had lived with a music teacher and whom he had met the previous spring, is still in the area. The stationmaster informs him that the woman in the blue cape is the same girl he is trying to find. Shimamura checks in at the inn, a resort popular with visiting tourists. After his nightly bath he is startled to see Komako standing at the end of the corridor. They go to his room.

Shimamura remembers the first time he visited the inn and his first meeting with Komako: After returning to the inn after seven days of hiking in the mountains, he requests a geisha. No geishas are available, however, because of a celebration going on that evening. The maid suggests calling the girl who lives at the music teacher's house. The girl, Komako, is not a geisha, but she fills in when necessary to help at large parties.

Shimamura is struck by Komako's youth and purity. They talk at length, and he begins to feel uncomfortable asking for anything other than her friendship. He asks her to suggest the name of another geisha. After much hesitation, Komako sends for another girl, whom Shimamura finds distasteful and sends home. After the geisha leaves, Shimamura takes a short walk to the Shinto shrine near the inn, where he again briefly meets Komako, who has been watching him; he realizes that he is attracted to her. Later that evening, Komako bursts into Shimamura's room, drunk from a party at the inn. They make love, and she leaves early in the morning to avoid detection. Shimamura returns to Tokyo the same day.

Komako is now a geisha in snow country. She tells Shimamura that she has kept a diary of the events of her life. They again make love, and Komako leaves at daylight.

As Shimamura walks around the village the next day, he

comes upon a group of geishas, including Komako. He walks by, but is followed by Komako, who takes him to her home and shows him her room. Yukio, the ill man Shimamura had seen on the train, lives there as well; he is the son of the music teacher and is coming home to die from tuberculosis. Shimamura also sees the girl—Yoko—from the train and is struck by her voice and appearance. Later that day he hires a masseuse, who tells him that Yukio is Komako's fiancé and that Komako has become a geisha to pay his medical bills. Komako later refutes this. Shimamura and Komako again make love that evening.

The next day, Shimamura asks Komako to play the samisen, a traditional stringed instrument. Shimamura stays at the inn for a number of days, and their affair continues. Shimamura decides to leave, and Komako accompanies him to the station. While they are waiting for the train, Yoko informs Komako that Yukio is dying and has asked for her. Komako refuses to leave until she sees Shimamura off on the train. Shimamura leaves on the train, back home to Tokyo, disconcerted by his experience in the mountains.

Several months later, Shimamura again visits Komako. It is now fall, and the countryside is alive with insects, ripening grass, and fall foliage. Komako chastises Shimamura for not visiting her as promised last February. She informs him that Yukio and the music teacher are both dead, and that she is now living under contract as a geisha with a family in the village. She also tells him about Yoko, who is now working at the inn and who spends much of her time visiting the grave of Yukio. Shimamura continues to be confused and perplexed by Komako and puzzled over the relationship between her and Yoko, who appear to harbor hostile feelings for one another. Komako visits Shimamura at odd hours, often drunk as a result of the parties she attends as a geisha. In a random meeting, Yoko asks Shimamura to be good to Komako, and then asks him to help her move to Tokyo. He asks her about her dislike of Komako, and Yoko tells him that Komako fears that Yoko will go crazy.

Shimamura escapes from the village for a daylong outing to two neighboring villages in an area of the mountains known for its weaving of the prized Chijimi grass-linen. Young, unmarried women spend the entire snowed-in winter season producing the fabric. Shimamura makes a direct analogy between the fabric and Komako.

As Shimamura returns by taxi to the hot spring, he passes a group of geishas standing in the doorway of a restaurant. Among them is Komako, who desperately jumps onto the running board of the taxi as he goes by. She resents his leaving without her. Next, they all hear an alarm, alerting them of a fire in the cocoon warehouse in the village below. This old building, formerly used to store silkworm cocoons, is the site for a film screening for the community. The film has caught fire, and the building is ablaze. Shimamura is obsessed with the engulfing image of the Milky Way above his head. Yoko leaps from the balcony of the warehouse; Komako screams and rushes to carry the body of Yoko away from the fire.

Critical Evaluation:

In 1968, Yasunari Kawabata became the first Japanese writer to win the Nobel Prize in Literature, awarded in recognition of novels he published from 1925 to 1965, which had been brought to the attention of the West by his translator, Edward G. Seidensticker. Chief among Kawabata's works are *Izu no odoriko* (1926; *The Izu Dancer*, 1955), *Meijin* (1942-1954, serial; 1954, book; *The Master of Go*, 1972), *Nemureru bijo* (1960-1961, serial; 1961, book; *The House of the Sleeping Beauties*, 1969), and his universally acknowledged masterpiece, *Snow Country*.

In evocative prose that calls upon traditional Japanese culture and motifs but also incorporates elements of modernist imagism and symbolism, *Snow Country* tells the story of the relationships between the urbane Tokyo aesthete and dilettante Shimamura and the mountain hot-spring geisha Komako. Told over a period of less than two years, the short novel follows Shimamura's three visits to the hot-spring inn, told exclusively from Shimamura's point of view.

The novel opens with one of Kawabata's most celebrated scenes, the train ride bringing Shimamura to snow country. Shimamura observes a girl and an ill man sitting across the aisle. As he watches the image of the girl reflected in the window, her face becomes disembodied and floats across the passing snow-covered landscape and the night sky like a transparent mask, ultimately appearing as an abstracted eye fused with the landscape. In microcosm, this scene, conveyed in Kawabata's poetic, visionary prose, anticipates many of his images and themes.

Shimamura's stance as an observer in this scene reinforces his distance from human events. He sees the girl at second hand in the window, speculates about the nature of her relationship with the sick man, and transforms her from a real person with everyday concerns into an object of beautiful, but detached and symbolic, art. This detached aesthetic stance reappears throughout the novel, most strikingly in the final images of the story when Yoko jumps from the balcony of the burning cocoon warehouse. Shimamura transforms the image of the falling body into a slow-motion image of "an arrow figure against a red ground," floating horizontally and noiselessly to the ground. This image combines in

Shimamura's mind with the overpowering image of the stars of the Milky Way rushing into his body.

Central to the novel is the relationship of Shimamura and the geisha Komako, seen only through Shimamura's point of view. Her behavior, emotions, and apparent love for Shimamura are observed but not explained, and Shimamura seems incapable of understanding her feelings. The relationship is intense and claustrophobic, taking place as it does in enclosed rooms—the room at the inn, the baths, Komako's lodgings. Shimamura escapes the stifling environment by going alone into the mountains and on a day trip to the neighboring town. Contrasting images of heat/cold and light/dark permeate the novel. The white of the snowy landscape and the bleached Chijimi linen are offset by the warmth of the *kotatsu* stove and the redness of Komako's skin, which suggests her passion.

A sense of futility and sadness pervades the work. Shimamura refers to numerous instances of "wasted effort." His trips to the mountains result from his loss of "honesty with himself" and his need to escape a "life of idleness." He dabbles in Japanese dance, in writing, in collecting the prized Chijimi linen, and in his relationship with Komako. His only knowledge of Western dance (ballet) comes from books; he has never actually seen a performance.

The "wasted effort" of life, however, is most closely associated in the novel with women. Shimamura describes the production of Chijimi by mountain maidens, who waste away the entire winter producing the fabric, which is then "collected" by men like Shimamura. His knowledge of the process, again secondhand, comes from books. Shimamura compares the geisha, in the person of Komako, to the Chijimi linen, another beautiful item for him to collect. He sees Komako's life as "beautiful but wasted," even though he is the object of her love.

Shimamura observes life but finds himself on the periphery, keeping Komako's feelings and thoughts at arm's length and finding her desperate and pitiable. His isolation from her emotional life is highlighted by the cocoon-warehouse fire, where he is outside the arena of action, a detached observer. He is capable of intense emotion, but it is intense emotion occasioned only by an aesthetic appreciation of the natural world.

Ann M. Cameron

Further Reading

Carriere, Peter M. "Writing as Tea Ceremony: Kawabata's Geido Aesthetics." *International Fiction Review* 29, nos. 1/2 (2002): 52-61. Discusses *Snow Country* as representative of Japanese culture and aesthetics.

DeVere Brown, Sidney. "Yasunari Kawabata (1899-1972): Tradition Versus Modernity." *World Literature Today* 62, no. 3 (Summer, 1988): 375-379. Surveys Kawabata's six major novels and argues that Kawabata's work is autobiographical and only peripherally concerned with contemporary Japan.

Gessel, Van C. *Three Modern Novelists: Soseki, Tanizaki, Kawabata*. New York: Kodansha International, 1993. A significant biography of Kawabata with commentary on Japan's modernization and its increasing engagement with the world.

Keene, Donald. *Dawn to the West: Japanese Literature of the Modern Era*. New York: Holt, Rinehart and Winston, 1984. Keene, an eminent critic, scholar, and translator of Japanese fiction, devotes part of his discussion to Kawabata. Traces many of Kawabata's themes to his childhood experiences and describes the circumstances of publication and reception of his major works. Asserts that Kawabata's main preoccupations were Japanese landscapes, Japanese women, and Japanese art.

_____. *Five Modern Japanese Novelists*. New York: Columbia University Press, 2003. Presents brief portraits of five novelists Keene has known personally, with one chapter devoted to the life and work of Kawabata.

Matsugu, Miho. "In the Service of the Nation: Geisha and Kawabata Yasunari's *Snow Country*." In *The Courtesan's Arts: Cross-Cultural Perspectives*, edited by Martha Feldman and Bonnie Gordon. New York: Oxford University Press, 2006. This essay about the role of the geisha in Kawabata's *Snow Country* is included in a collection that explores the history of courtesan culture.

Miyoshi, Masao. *Accomplices of Silence: The Modern Japanese Novel*. Berkeley: University of California Press, 1974. A significant study of Kawabata within the larger context of the modern Japanese novel.

Mori, Masaki. "Kawabata's Mirrored Poetics." *Japan Studies Review* 8 (2004): 51-68. Explores Kawabata's light and dark imagery, mirror imagery, and the relationship to Shikibu Murasaki's *The Tale of Genji*.

_____. "Symbiotic Conflict in *Snow Country*." *Japan Studies Review* 11 (2007): 51-72. Explores the ambiguity, symbolism, and treatment of female characters in *Snow Country*.

Pollack, David. *Reading Against Culture: Ideology and Narrative in the Japanese Novel*. Ithaca, N.Y.: Cornell University Press, 1992. Examines *Snow Country* through the lens of culture, which constructs both a sense of identity and a sense of the exclusion of others from outside the culture.

Starrs, Roy. *Soundings in Time: The Fictive Art of Kawabata Yasunari.* Richmond, England: Japan Library, 1998. A thorough study of Kawabata's fiction that examines his practice as a novelist, his narrative techniques, and other characteristics of his work. Includes a lengthy discussion of *Snow Country.* The first full-length study of Kawabata's fiction.

Ueda, Makato. "The Virgin, the Wife, and the Nun: Kawabata's *Snow Country.*" In *Approaches to the Modern Japanese Novel*, edited by Kinya Tsuruta and Thomas E. Swann. Tokyo: Sophia University, 1976. An analysis of Kawabata's *Snow Country* is included in this collection of fifteen essays that focus on Japanese literature within a cultural and literary context.

Snow Falling on Cedars

Author: David Guterson (1956-   )
First published: 1994
Type of work: Novel
Type of plot: Psychological realism
Time of plot: Mid-1930's to 1954
Locale: San Piedro Island, Washington; Manzanar internment camp, California; Tarawa atoll, South Pacific

Principal characters:
ISHMAEL CHAMBERS, a local newspaper reporter and a war veteran
HATSUE MIYAMOTO, his former lover
CARL HEINE, a fisherman
KABUO MIYAMOTO, a fisherman, and Carl's accused murderer
ART MORAN, the county sheriff
NELS GUDMUNDSSON, a defense attorney

The Story:

San Piedro Island lies in the Straits of Juan de Fuca, north of Puget Sound and Seattle, Washington, and just south of the U.S.-Canada border. San Piedro is a small island with a population of about five thousand people, mostly farmers and fishermen. Its largest town is Amity Harbor, which houses a few businesses and is the center of the local government.

A substantial number of Japanese have lived on the island since 1883, when they began to settle in as growers, especially of strawberries, and as fishermen. The Japanese have since had a congenial but somewhat separate existence from the white population of the island. Their children, however, have attended the same schools, and their daughters routinely win the title of queen during the annual strawberry festival.

The bombing of Pearl Harbor in Hawaii by Japan, which brought the United States into World War II, and the subsequent panic along the West Coast of the United States, changed everything in the community. The relocation of the inhabitants of Japanese ancestry to Manzanar internment camp in California, and military service of the local men in the Pacific theater, fighting the forces of the Imperial Japanese military, further distanced the two groups. After the war, residual racism and prejudice against the local Japanese who had returned to San Piedro continued.

It is now 1954. Local fisherman Carl Heine is not on his boat, the *Susan Marie*, when it is found in the early morning, adrift in White Sand Bay with its lights on. Sheriff Art Moran and his deputy arrive to investigate. They subsequently find Carl, dead, when they haul in the boat's nets. Carl's body is tangled in the nets and has a bruise on its head. Adding to the mystery is how the boat had been found—with all of its lights on and carrying a wrong-sized battery in its hold—suggesting to Art that something is amiss.

Soon, Kabuo Miyamoto, a fisherman who was on the water the night or early morning that Carl died, is charged with Carl's death. Investigators discover that the two men earlier had been arguing about a seven-acre plot of land, a portion of a parcel owned by Carl, which Kabuo wanted to buy. The land was once nearly purchased by Kabuo's family, all of whom were removed from the area and taken to Manzanar before the purchase could be made. For his family's honor, and for the sake of owning property, Kabuo now wants to buy the same parcel of land. Owning land was once prohibited to the Japanese on the island.

Ishmael Chambers, the local newspaper reporter and a war veteran, was once in love with Hatsue Miyamoto, the wife of the defendant. Ishmael, the son of parents who were more tolerant than others in the community of the Japanese, had fallen in love with Hatsue when they were still children. For both, however, their affection for each other violated the cultural mores of their respective communities. Hatsue broke off their relationship when she and her family were sent to Manzanar, which crushed Ishmael's heart.

During the war, Ishmael had joined the U.S. Marine Corps. During the invasion of Tarawa Atoll, machine-gun fire had shattered his arm. He returned home an embittered, one-armed man, and after his father's death, he took over the *San Piedro Review*, as reporter, printer, and owner. Even living his father's life, Ishmael clearly did not feel that he was the man his father was. The great test of his life now arrives: He has uncovered information that could free Kabuo.

The trial plays out amid an increasingly severe snowstorm, which douses the lights and isolates people. Attorney Nels Gudmundsson's defense is convincing, as he teases out the truth from a string of prejudiced witnesses, including Carl's mother and the coroner. It appears that Kabuo, a decorated war veteran, might get a fair shake, but the community's prejudice and racism still hangs in the air as the trial goes to the jury.

At the last minute, Ishmael decides to reveal his evidence to the judge. He had discovered a report at the local U.S. Coast Guard facility that offers a more plausible explanation for Carl's death. The Coast Guard observers had recorded an off-course ship that had plowed through the fishing grounds in the fog the night in question. The ship's wake could have been responsible for Carl falling from his boat. Following the logic of the report, it now is probable that Carl had hit his head before falling into the water and getting tangled in his fishing nets. Kabuo is found "guilty" of having loaned Carl a battery and of having refused to show in his trial the expected emotion.

Critical Evaluation:

David Guterson's *Snow Falling on Cedars* contains a number of intersecting themes. First is the love theme between Ishmael Chambers and Hatsue Miyamoto that serves as both a bridge between the two cultural and racial groups and an example of how unbridgeable the gulf ultimately turns out to be. Second is the broader theme of community prejudice against the Japanese, which is brought to the surface by the entry of the United States into World War II. Third is the presence of a snowstorm, an event that underlies the tensions engendered by the trial of Kabuo Miyamoto.

The love affair between Ishmael and Hatsue complicates the narrative by creating a conflict of interest when Ishmael discovers the exculpating evidence. If he withholds it, and if Kabuo is convicted, then perhaps Ishmael will be able to re-

kindle his affection for Hatsue. Ishmael must overcome this rather pathetic state of mind to assume the mantle of his father. The love affair also provides an example of how children can transcend the prejudice of their parents. The affair also highlights differences that may prove insurmountable. In this case, Ishmael's immaturity and Hatsue's untenable situation—being confined at Manzanar—also play a part in the disillusion of their relationship. The love theme then works in multiple ways to inform the narrative.

Ishmael's problems are compounded by his disability caused by war. The loss of his arm makes him less of a man, both symbolically and psychologically. His name, too, takes on multiple meanings. The famous opening line of Herman Melville's novel *Moby Dick: Or, The Whale* (1851) is "Call me Ishmael." Ishmael is the survivor of the destruction of the *Pequod*; he is the one who tells the tale of the disaster at sea. Guterson's Ishmael is a teller of tales as well. He is a reporter.

The second large-scale theme of the novel is racial prejudice. Guterson's sympathies are against the prejudice inflicted on the local Japanese minority, a prejudice that has existed in the area since the late nineteenth century, when Asians worked on the West Coast as laborers. The attack on Pearl Harbor provides a catalyst that brings the racism to the surface.

The trial of Kabuo takes place in December, and Guterson uses a snowstorm to represent the upheaval the trial engenders. This use of the weather, as in William Shakespeare's *Macbeth* (pr. 1606, pb. 1623), in which the winds blow and the storm mounts as crimes multiply, symbolizes something bigger than a snowstorm: The blowing snow, which obliterates everything in its path, leads to the loss of electricity in town, including the courtroom. The snowstorm blinds justice, just as racial prejudice blinds the community and the courtroom. It is as if nature itself is angry that justice is being denied in the court.

Charles L. P. Silet

Further Reading

Bloom, Harold, ed. *David Guterson's "Snow Falling on Cedars."* Philadelphia: Chelsea House, 2004. A collection of essays covering multiple critical approaches to Guterson's popular novel *Snow Falling on Cedars*.

Brantley, Jenny. "Clorox the Dishes and Hide the Books: A Defense of *Snow Falling on Cedars*." In *Censored Books II: Critical Viewpoints, 1985-2000*, edited by Nicholas J. Karolides and Nat Hentoff. Lanham, Md.: Scarecrow Press, 2002. This chapter in a book on censorship and literature examines the representations of Japanese internment camps, Japanese Americans, racism, and censorship in *Snow Falling on Cedars*.

Haytock, Jennifer Anne. *David Guterson's "Snow Falling on Cedars": A Reader's Guide*. New York: Continuum, 2002. A general, helpful guide to Guterson's novel, including its characters, plots, and themes. A good place to start for readers new to the novel.

Lefkowitz, Daniel. "On the Relation Between Sound and Meaning in Hicks' *Snow Falling on Cedars*." *Semiotica* 155, nos. 1-4 (2005): 15-50. This essay explores the rela-

tionship between Guterson's novel and its adaptation to the screen. Also examines the film's and the book's dialogue and their use of memory.

Paul, Heike. "Old, New, and 'Neo' Immigrant Fictions in American Literature: The Immigrant Presence in David Guterson's *Snow Falling on Cedars* and T. C. Boyle's *The Tortilla Curtain*." *Amerikastudien/American Studies* 46, no. 2 (2001): 249-65. This comparative essay examines the treatment of immigrants in *Snow Falling on Cedars* and in *The Tortilla Curtain* by T. C. Boyle.

Snow White

Author: Donald Barthelme (1931-1989)
First published: 1965
Type of work: Novel
Type of plot: Sociopsychological fantasy and satire
Time of plot: Mid-twentieth century
Locale: A Euro-Asian country and a metropolitan city in the United States

Principal characters:
SNOW WHITE, an emotionally troubled young woman
BILL,
DAN,
KEVIN,
EDWARD,
HUBERT,
HENRY, and
CLEM, her seven "dwarfed" paramours
JANE VILLIERS DE L'ISLE-ADAMS, Snow White's friend
PAUL, an artist, and Snow White's admirer
HOGO DE BERGERAC, a Prussian huntsman who also admires Snow White

The Story:

Snow White wrestles with cognitive incongruence as she craves physical intimacy but also worries about her social reputation. She experiences episodic bouts of mental illness manifested by these conflicting emotions and repressed behaviors. During one such episode, she secretly scribes a four-page poem and speaks only the words from Chinese fortunes in an attempt to reconcile herself. She displays further cognitive incongruence with naïve innocence as she seeks a prince and a romantic happily ever after, yet, she lives in a perverse menagerie with characters who serve to appease her lust and distract her urges with abstract art and words she has not heard before.

These seven characters are "dwarfed" by Snow White, who equates all seven of them to only two whole men. Moreover, she does not consider them as men in the conjugal sense, even though they stimulate her in the shower and ac-

company her to bed at night as she dons black vinyl lingerie in the privacy of her boudoir. For the most part, the men respect and try to protect Snow White. They work and earn a sizable income cleaning buildings, making plastic buffalo humps, and tending vats of Chinese baby food (a recipe and legacy handed down by their father, of whom little is known). They worry about Snow White as they venture out in the red-light district to satisfy their own lust in a psychedelic sea of women. One of them feels twinges of guilt but justifies their behavior as betrayal not to Snow White but to the shower.

Bill is the leader of the seven, a strong personality who grows tired of and even sickened by Snow White's behavior. Her long black hair, which she hangs out the window to dry, triggers in Bill some repressed memories of childhood trauma involving scoutmasters who had threatened him. The scouts had told him the story of a black horse who would devour him in his sleep for disobeying their directives. (They had told Bill to use mud to clean the camp cookware.) Bill later confronts these tormentors in the streets of the United States with a six-pack of beer and is arrested for disrupting the peace. Bill's emotionally reactive behavior is justified by the court because of his youth; he is acquitted of the misdemeanor charge. However, he is subsequently convicted on the felonious charge of "vatricide" because he had neglected to tend the fires under the vats at the baby-food factory during his public outburst, causing the vats to die out.

Paul is supposedly a displaced prince of a fallen Eastern European monarchy and a friend of Snow White's family. Snow White travels to the United States to be with Paul, out of desire to end her life as a "horsewife" but also to remain linked with noble blood. Paul fancies himself an artist; however, he persists in the re-creation of a single hard-edged image that both he and Snow White agree seems to become increasingly more soft or weak each time. Paul admires Snow White but resists acting on his attraction for unknown reasons; he even tries to overcome his urges for her by joining a monastery, only to resort to voyeurism when he returns.

Jane Villiers de l'Isle-Adams is a lifelong friend and confidant of Snow White. Jane longs for the days when she had been considered the fairest of women and had been lusted after by men. As she ages she becomes bitter toward men and sets on a mission of randomly threatening them: She covertly replaces various phallic objects (for example, a Hermes rocket) with a predetermined number of increasingly irritating letters. Jane's only consolation in aging is her hold on Hogo de Bergerac, with whom she is engaged in a somewhat sadistic and masochistic sexual relationship. Hogo, a pedophile, had stolen Jane's childhood innocence; Jane's mother had forbidden her daughter from going to Hogo's home alone.

Hogo betrays his queen as he begins to fall in love with Snow White, who admits to being attracted to him. With his dark nature and large Prussian stature, she thinks she could freely submit to her wildest sexual fantasies. She ultimately rejects him, though, because he is not from the nobility. Jane becomes aware of Hogo's rejection of her in favor of Snow White, so Jane sets out to kill Snow White with poisoned vodka. Paul intercepts the drink meant for Snow White, and dies after drinking it. With Paul dead and Jane no longer his queen, Hogo moves in with Snow White, who is mourning the loss of her ideal dream (of being married to pure blood) by maintaining Paul's grave with flowers.

Bill's best friend, Dan, takes over and assumes the leadership role in the Chinese baby-food factory. Bill had been executed for his failures.

Critical Evaluation:

Donald Barthelme's rendition of *Snow White* is a twisted, incoherent version of the fairytale in episodic form. Barthelme's first novel, it contains fundamental elements of philosophy, psychology, and various forms of art and popular culture "abstracurately" (Barthelme's own wordplay) conveyed in his short stories. The work is, indeed, Joycean—a dark satire of human nature and a sociopolitical statement on postindustrial modern times.

Barthelme's innovative style entails the use of experimental literary devices to underline the effects of materialistic consumerism and sociopolitical repression on humans. The collage of words and concepts that precede each disjointed "chapter" are literary pieces of the puzzle meant to provide insight into the meanings being sought by the characters.

Snow White is a parody possessing the attitude typical of all of Barthelme's novels: A twisted, dark, humorous view of life in an irrational world. This work of experimental fiction displays nonsensical words, impeded dialects, inconsistent punctuation and person-tense, as well as varying writing styles. The novel's page layouts and fragmented quasi chapters are riddled with an intentional play on words in the form of puns and subtle literary symbolisms. Barthelme's manipulation of language targets the mass media's use of words promoting mindless consumerism. His stained veil of literary innuendo probes and punches the pulpit with blatant social judgments and political irony.

Snow White also presents a psychosocial diagnostic enigma of unsubstantiated childhood trauma, personality disorders, and a politically repressed society within a literary puzzle of suggestive images and loosely connected plots. Aspects of Snow White's dissociated identity appear to be projected in each of the seven men whom she "dwarfs" into two actual men; these men satisfy her lust as she indulges her sexual fantasies in the privacy of her shower and bedroom. The connection between Snow White's expressed disdain of being a horsewife defines her as a woman with strong urges for carnal knowledge; her disdain manifests in Bill's disgust for her long black hair, which he equates to a horse's tail, and in his withdrawal from wanting to be touched. Snow White represents the black mare whom he had feared would devour him in his sleep; to a degree, the mare does contribute to his demise.

Snow White reluctantly pursues Paul, whom she deems to be a well-integrated personality and, thus, representative of her own expectations. Paul wrestles with his own conflicts and constraints in his effort to keep his love for Snow White pure. His once hard-edged sculptures and paintings become weaker, as he retreats to a monastery only to resort to voyeurism when he returns. Although this may be a message of the faltering religious influence on youth, Paul does become the proverbial Knight in Shining Armor in his intercepting the poisoned drink meant for his beloved. Barthelme's use of vodka in the drink can be construed as part of the paranoia present in the Cold War between the United States and the Soviet Union.

Jane seems to disappear as Snow White unemotionally observes Paul's violent death and determines there may have been something wrong with the drink after all. Jane's disappearance supports the diagnosis of Snow White having an identity disorder—raising the question of whether Jane indeed was another part of Snow White. Nonetheless, Paul's convenient death gives reason for Snow White to reconsider Hogo's declaration of love for her, despite his not being of noble lineage.

Snow White is a covert parody filled with suggestive and sexually and graphically violent content against a backdrop of dark humor that twists the story into a psychological thrill ride. This "ride" includes the collective dinner discussion over killing Snow White's unidentified psychiatrist; Jane's mother's plan to exact revenge on Hogo for stealing her daughter's innocence; and Paul's grotesquely described death. In the end, Snow White's spiraling grasp on reality and reason descends as she succumbs to her primal urges and trades her idealistic white-picket-fence dreams for her hedonistic dark-horse fantasies.

Snow White's tragic realizations in her pursuit of the traditional American Dream are affirmations of how the black-and-white world of earlier generations is an illusion in the eyes of the disenfranchised youth of the modern era. Moreover, the inconclusive truths presented in the form of authority figures in the trial of Bill echoes the growing overall disillusionment with political processes; the average individual becomes increasingly aware of the absurdities that abound. Albeit a challenge to read and follow, Barthelme's *Snow White* draws and grasps the reader, who hopes to make sense of the eloquent absurdity.

Diana M. Merchant

Further Reading

Daugherty, Tracy. *Hiding Man: A Biography of Donald Barthelme*. New York: St. Martin's Press, 2009. Argues that Barthleme was writing in the modernist tradition of Samuel Beckett and James Joyce, and that he used advertisements, sentences from newspaper articles, instruction guides, and popular and commercial elements to make literature, not to subvert it.

Fleming, Bruce E. "*Snow White*." In *Magill's Survey of American Literature*. Rev. ed. Pasadena, Calif.: Salem Press, 2007. A review of *Snow White* that provides an excellent starting point for a more comprehensive psychological analysis of all characters in the novel. Examines, especially, the prototype fairytale version of the character Hogo.

Hudgens, Michael Thomas. *Donald Barthelme, Postmodernist American Writer*. Lewiston, N.Y.: Edwin Mellen Press, 2001. This volume in the series Studies in American Literature examines *Snow White* and some of Barthelme's other works. Includes bibliographical references and an index.

Trachtenberg, Stanley. *Understanding Donald Barthelme*. Columbia: University of South Carolina Press, 1990. A basic guide to Barthelme's body of work, including brief discussions of his biography and major writings. Includes an excellent annotated bibliography.

Snow-Bound
A Winter Idyl

Author: John Greenleaf Whittier (1807-1892)
First published: 1866
Type of work: Poetry
Type of plot: Idyll
Time of plot: Early nineteenth century
Locale: Haverhill, Massachusetts

Principal characters:
MEMBERS OF THE WHITTIER FAMILY
THE SCHOOLMASTER
A GUEST

The Poem:

One December day a wind from the east and a leaden sky forecast snow. As night came on, the members of the Whittier family brought in firewood, littered the cattle stalls with fresh straw, and fed the stock. All night the storm raged, and in the morning the Whittiers looked upon a world of fleecy snow. The elder Whittier, a man of action, ordered a path dug to the barn, and his sons merrily turned to the work, making a crystal-walled tunnel through the deepest drift. Although the snow no longer fell, all day a north wind drove bits of sleet against the windows of the house. Again, as night fell, wood was brought in for the great fireplace around which the family gathered. While the moon shone on the snow outside and the north wind battered the house, the family stayed snug and warm inside.

As the poet recalls this happy scene of long ago, he pauses a moment to think of the many changes that later took place. Only he and his brother now remain; death took all the others. His memory goes back to the old fireside, the stories told there, the puzzles and riddles solved, the poems recited. The elder Whittier told of adventures he had with the Indians, of fishing trips, and of the witches reputed to inhabit the land in olden days. The mother told of Indian raids and of the happy times she had as a girl. To these stories from her own life she added some that she read in books by famous and revered Quakers.

Next the poet calls to mind the tales of the world of nature told by his uncle, a man unschooled in a formal way but seemingly filled with a boundless knowledge of moons and tides, of weather signs, of birds and beasts. The memory of the poet's maiden aunt brings her also vividly before him. He remembers how she lived for others instead of bewailing her lonely maidenhood. He sees again his elder sister whose rich, full nature prompted many deeds of self-sacrifice. Tenderly he recalls his dearly loved younger sister, who was with him until a year ago, but whose body now lies with the others in the earth.

From the members of his family, the poet turns to the young schoolmaster, a boarder in the Whittier home. The son of a poor man, the schoolmaster as a boy learned independence. As a student he helped to pay his way through Dartmouth College by taking varied jobs. Later as a teacher he, when school was out, joined in schoolboy sports. In the schoolroom he was the earnest shaper of youthful minds. The poet prays that the cause of freedom might have many young apostles like him.

Another guest of the Whittier household on that night of long ago comes to the poet's mind. A strange woman, half feared, half welcome, she was as known for her violent temper as she was for her eccentric devotion to religion. Leaving her home, she later went to Europe and the Near East, prophesying everywhere the imminent second coming of Christ. The poet asks for God's mercy upon the poor woman whose mind seemed so odd to her neighbors.

As the hour grew late the group about the fire retired for the night. The next morning teamsters came to clear the snow-filled roads. The young folks played in the snowbanks. Later, along the cleared road came the neighborhood doctor on his rounds. A week passed before the mailman finally delivered a newspaper to tell of happenings beyond the Whittiers' snowbound world.

The poet shuts the covers of his book of memory upon these happy scenes of the past. He puts the book away with the hope that readers in the future might pause with him to view for a little while these Flemish pictures of old days.

Critical Evaluation:

Although John Greenleaf Whittier called *Snow-Bound* an "idyl," the term is not accurate in the sense of what that word means in classical literature. The poem centers on an admiring and pleasant depiction of simple country life, in the tradition of the pastoral, but it does not present that view of rustic life from a detached, aristocratic viewpoint. Rather, the speaker's perspective remains rooted in the values of the community he portrays, even as he acknowledges that the persons and scenes he describes are gone. Similarly, the poem's character as a pastoral elegy is qualified by the speaker's hope. Nostalgia for a former way of life pervades the poem, but the future, in particular the future after abolition of slavery, is imagined as a bright improvement on the past. Two major themes related to this optimistic mood figure in the poem. One of these is the image of an inner light encircled by darkness, and the other is a sense of continuity with the past.

The image of a circle of light within a dark surrounding ground recurs throughout the poem, as the speaker describes the family sitting around the household fire in the middle of winter darkness. The external darkness and the metamorphosis of the landscape under the heavy blanket of snow draw the family closer together. Their sense of fellowship and appreciation for one another grows as they form more intimate relationships through the stories they tell of their lives and experiences. A time of enforced inactivity and of restricted movement becomes an opportunity for reflection, insight, and enlightenment.

Whittier's conceptualization of the snowbound home as a place of spiritual and emotional enlightenment and of warmth and light in a dark world is in keeping with his Quaker background and his dedication to Quaker principles of nonaggressiveness, cooperation, and respect for the individual. Quakerism places great stress on individual enlightenment achieved through a process of meditation and reflection. Each person's inner light of understanding is respected and is sought as an island of light would be in a sea of darkness. The poet's lifelong, impassioned outcry in the cause of the abolition of slavery erupts in the last quarter of the poem: Slavery's degradation of black and white alike will be followed by an almost utopian era of peace, prosperity, education, and communication. The monstrous nature of slavery seems to prompt the poet to lay aside the Quaker principle of nonviolence and admire the schoolmaster's participation in the Civil War that has struck the chains from those in bondage. In keeping with Quaker emphasis on nonrational, intuitive spirituality, an almost mystical bond links the snowbound New Hampshire farmhouse and the newly freed South in a parallel and intimately felt process of enlightenment.

A major portion of *Snow-Bound* consists of the stories told by the various members of the household community: family, friends, and neighbors. The elders—father, mother, uncle, aunt—impress and entertain their listeners as they rehearse critical turning points in their own lives or retell stories from family and Quaker tradition. The poet dwells on the vividness with which family members, in particular his mother, re-create the scenes of their youth: the father's travels in the deep forests of French Canada, the mother's and her friends' clambakes on the New Hampshire shore, the uncle's hunting and gathering in the rich hills of New England. The poet's spiritual idealism and nostalgia emerge from a rich and almost sensual proliferation of sight, smell, sound, and texture evoked in these memories of far-off days, until they seem almost more tangible than the wintry present.

Storytelling unites the family members and creates their community, through the closeness of intimate and familiar revelation and through the construction of the community's history. The poet places himself and his poem at the end of the Civil War; the snowbound scene he reconstructs occurred many years before. The storytelling that went on in the snowbound farmhouse in turn related the listeners to an even more distant past, so that the historical continuity of the community stretches years back, beyond the memory of individuals long since passed away by the time the poet begins his work. The isolated farmhouse becomes an island in time as well as a beacon of light in space. The continuity of history is forged in the speaker's links with the past and past stories, and time is defeated in the liveliness of the telling, bringing the past more vividly to life almost than the present, where familiar elements of the landscape are obliterated by featureless drifts of snow. Day and night are rendered nearly indistinguishable by early darkness and the whirling blizzard. The snowbound farmhouse represents a paradox: transcendence of space and time is made possible through imagination and illumination in the most confining of circumstances.

The thematic emphasis on the construction of history emerges particularly in light of the author's prefatory note, prepared for the 1892 edition of the poem, some twenty-six years after first publication. In that note Whittier reaffirms that the characters depicted in the poem were actual members of his family and their neighbors, and he offers more information on their lives and personalities. The poem is documentary as well as imaginative. The opening material also emphasizes the poet's central image of a field of light within a darkened ground through the lines quoted from Cornelius Agrippa, linking angelic messengers of spiritual enlightenment with the physical light and warmth of fire. The embracing theme of *Snow-Bound* is that the lives of common, ordinary people—whether inhabitants of a rural New England farm or tormented slaves—are worthy and full of dignity and delight.

"Critical Evaluation" by Helen Jaskoski

Further Reading

Blue, Frederick J. "To Mitigate the Suffering of Our Countrymen: John Greenleaf Whittier, Abolitionist Poet." In *No Taint of Compromise: Crusaders in Antislavery Politics*. Baton Rouge: Louisiana State University Press, 2005. Chronicles Whittier's life and literary career, focusing on his political involvement in the abolitionist movement. Cites some of his antislavery poetry.

Kribbs, Jayne K., comp. *Critical Essays on John Greenleaf Whittier*. Boston: G. K. Hall, 1980. Includes early reviews and structuralist criticism. Discusses Whittier's Quaker principles. *Snow-Bound* is addressed in an early review and in an essay on imagistic and structural unity.

Leary, Lewis. *John Greenleaf Whittier*. New York: Twayne, 1961. Summarizes earlier views of *Snow-Bound* and offers lucid paraphrase of each part.

Pickard, John B. *John Greenleaf Whittier: An Introduction and Interpretation*. New York: Barnes & Noble, 1961. Focuses on the image of fire. *Snow-Bound* is discussed extensively in the chapter on genre poetry.

_____. *Memorabilia of John Greenleaf Whittier*. Hartford, Conn.: Emerson Society, 1968. Includes unpublished papers on Whittier and an extensive collection of photographs of the poet. Contains an essay on *Snow-Bound*.

Sorby, Angela. "Learning to Be White: John Greenleaf Whittier's *Snow-Bound*." In *Schoolroom Poets: Childhood, Performance, and the Place of American Poetry, 1865-1917*. Durham: University of New Hampshire Press, 2005. Focuses on the racial implications of the poem, arguing that it is about "whiteness"—the whiteness of the snow, of the family in the poem, and of Whittier himself. Maintains that this whiteness is questionable for Whittier, who initially depicts contrasts of black and white, but by the end of the poem presents shades of gray that reflect the potential for a multiracial America.

Wagenknecht, Edward. *John Greenleaf Whittier: A Portrait in Paradox*. New York: Oxford University Press, 1967. Considers Whittier in light of his philosophy, especially his Quaker principles of pacifism and enlightenment. Examines *Snow-Bound* in relation to these themes.

Wesley, Marilyn C. "'The Not Unfeared, Half-Welcome Guest': The Woman Traveler in John Greenleaf Whittier's *Snow-Bound*." In *Secret Journeys: The Trope of Women's Travel in American Literature*. Albany: State University of New York Press, 1999. Focuses on the appearance of the woman traveler in the poem, demonstrating how it reflects ideas about masculine identity and the depiction of women in male literature of the period.

The Snows of Kilimanjaro, and Other Stories

Author: Ernest Hemingway (1899-1961)
First published: 1961
Type of work: Short fiction
Type of plot: Impressionistic realism
Time of plot: Early twentieth century
Locale: Africa; Spain; Piggott, Arkansas; Hailey, Montana; Northern Michigan; Milan, Italy; Summit, Illinois; Fossalta di Piave, Italy; New Jersey; New York City

Principal characters:
NICK ADAMS, a writer and soldier
HARRY, a writer on safari
AN OLD WAITER
AN OLD MAN
SCHATZ, a sick young boy
CAYETANO, a gambler
MR. FRAZER, a writer
SISTER CECILIA, a nun
NICK'S SON
SIGNOR MAGGIORE, a major who has lost his wife
OLE ANDRESON, a boxer
JACK BRENNAN, a boxer
FRANCIS MACOMBER, a husband
MARGARET MACOMBER, Francis's wife
ROBERT WILSON, a professional hunter

The Stories:

"The Snows of Kilimanjaro" centers on the memories of a dying writer named Harry. On safari in Africa, he has been wounded and has developed an infection. Waiting around to die, he thinks about the past years of his life. He regrets that he did not accomplish more as a writer and realizes that he let himself get lazy. Part of Harry's reason for going on safari had been to discipline himself. Though he and his wife have been to many great places and have had wonderful experiences, Harry has been swept up in the empty world of the wealthy, forgetting that it was his experiences with poor and interesting people that first awakened his desire to write. Harry fights with his wife, recognizing that she drove him to a life of decadence. He dies, and his soul flies to the top of Mount Kilimanjaro, the House of God.

In "A Clean, Well-Lighted Place," two waiters (one old and one young) are at a café late at night, waiting on an old man who has recently attempted suicide. The young waiter wants to close up and get on with his night. He does not understand why the old man will not leave. The old waiter is kind to the old man and understands why he is there. He understands that the old man wants to avoid the darkness, that he needs the safety and security of a well-lit café.

"A Day's Wait" focuses on Schatz, a nine-year-old boy who has a fever of 102 degrees Fahrenheit. Confusing the Fahrenheit and Celsius temperature scales, the boy believes that he is going to die. He lives with the "knowledge" of his impending death all day, until his father tells him that he is merely sick and will survive.

"The Gambler, the Nun, and the Radio" centers on a Mexican gambler, a writer, and a nun who have come together in a Montana hospital. To ease the gambler's loneliness, Sister Cecilia, the nun, brings in three musicians. An intense conversation about revolution, religion, and music ensues.

Nick Adams is a writer and a soldier in World War I. In "In Another Country," Adams (who is unnamed in this story) is a member of the ambulance corps and is rehabilitating in a hospital in Milan during the war. He meets and befriends three soldiers, who dismiss him when they find out that he is an American who has received a distinguished medal for less than what they have had to suffer through. When Nick meets Signor Maggiore, who has just lost his wife, he is changed.

In "Fathers and Sons," an older Nick Adams takes his son back to his hometown. Nick remembers his relationship with his parents, especially with his father, and considers what life used to be like in the town. The story centers around Nick's relationship with his own son.

In "The Killers," a younger Nick Adams is at a diner in Summit, Illinois, when two gangsters come in looking for Ole Andreson, a boxer whom Nick knows. Nick admires Ole, who faces the situation with stoicism and grace under pressure. Finally, in "A Way You'll Never Be," Nick returns to the place that he was wounded during the war in Fossalta di Piave, Italy.

"Fifty Grand" concerns an aging boxer preparing for his final fight. He sees no chance to win and bets his life savings on his opponent. Two gamblers try to turn the fix around so he will lose of all his money, but he is shrewd and sharp and refuses to be taken.

In "The Short Happy Life of Francis Macomber," the title character makes an embarrassing display of cowardice after wounding a lion. His wife Margaret mocks him and sleeps with Robert Wilson, their guide. Later, on the hunt for water buffalo, Francis gains courage and does what he needs to do as a hunter, finally recognizing some sort of code of values. Wilson recognizes this change in him. In the final scene, Mrs. Macomber shoots her husband, as she believes he is about to be gored by the buffalo.

Critical Evaluation:

The ten stories included in *The Snows of Kilimanjaro, and Other Stories* are among Ernest Hemingway's best known. As occurs with any volume of selected stories, there are glaring omissions, but this book serves as a good introduction to Hemingway's mastery of the form. Containing stories previously published in *Men Without Women* (1927), *Winner Take Nothing* (1933), and *The Fifth Column and the First Forty-nine Stories* (1938), this collection highlights Hemingway's style. His prose is terse—not uncomplicated, not simple—and readers are made to feel more than they know.

Introduced to characters who exemplify the Hemingway code of values (the old man in "A Clean, Well-Lighted Place" and Signor Maggiore in "In Another Country," for example), a reader may become aware that Hemingway is a writer of manners and values as well as an observer of behavior. The stories display an intense animosity toward the wealthy, the undisciplined, and the lazy—toward people who do not live by a careful code of values. Hemingway's exemplary characters are men and women of action, and his antiexemplary characters are decadent phonies who have been consumed by greed and excess.

The stories collected in this volume are highly indicative of Hemingway's brilliantly difficult and dangerously complex art. They treat the major Hemingway themes and, as in all of his work, portray grace as both a possibility and a necessity. In a violent and meaningless world, this would not be so. Thus, although "A Clean, Well-Lighted Place" is often mistaken for a story about surviving in a violent and meaningless world, the story is clearly about "nothingness" in the mystical sense of the word. The old waiter knows that nothingness is not the absence of something but the presence of nothing.

In all of his stories, as in all of his novels, Hemingway's poise, control, and endurance are evident. Everything he does is carefully calculated. The sentences here are not merely simple, but sharpened to a point; they are not careless, but careful and exact.

William Boyle

Further Reading

Benson, Jackson J., ed. *New Critical Approaches to the Short Stories of Ernest Hemingway.* Durham, N.C.: Duke University Press, 1991. Identifies mastery of the short-story form as Hemingway's greatest literary accomplishment. Gives an overview of criticism written on Hemingway's short fiction from the mid-1970's to the late 1980's.

Broer, Lawrence, ed. *Hemingway and Women: Female Critics and the Female Voice.* Tuscaloosa: University of Alabama Press, 2004. Collection of essays that focus on—among other things—Hemingway's most important female characters, including several key figures from the ten stories collected in *The Snows of Kilimanjaro, and Other Stories.*

Flora, Joseph M. *Ernest Hemingway: A Study of the Short Fiction.* Boston: Twayne, 1989. A comprehensive overview of Hemingway's short fiction, including detailed analyses of every significant story. Includes interviews, essays, memoirs, and other biographical materials. Also includes a representative selection of critical responses, a comprehensive primary bibliography, and a selected bibliography of important criticism.

_____. *Reading Hemingway's "Men Without Women": Glossary and Commentary.* Kent, Ohio: Kent State University Press, 2008. Hemingway's *Men Without Women* features three of the stories—"The Killers," "Fifty Grand," and "In Another Country"—later collected in *The Snows of Kilimanjaro, and Other Stories.* Flora provides excellent, relevant commentary on these three stories.

Gajdusek, Robert E. "Purgation/Debridement as Therapy/Aesthetics." *Hemingway Review* 4, no. 2 (Spring, 1985): 12-17. Focuses on debriding and purging as thematic-stylistic devices in Hemingway's work. Considers art as a form of purgation and pays special attention to "The Snows of Kilimanjaro" as an exercise in psychic therapy.

Smith, Paul, ed. *New Essays on Hemingway's Short Fiction.* New York: Cambridge University Press, 1998. An overview of Hemingway's career as a short-story writer. Includes a selected bibliography designed to equip readers with the most valuable resources for the study of Hemingway's short fiction.

So Big

Author: Edna Ferber (1885-1968)
First published: 1924
Type of work: Novel
Type of plot: Social realism
Time of plot: Early twentieth century
Locale: Illinois

Principal characters:
SELINA PEAKE DEJONG, a woman of strong character and enterprise
PERVUS DEJONG, her husband
DIRK "SOBIG" DEJONG, her son
AUGUST HEMPEL, a Chicago capitalist and, later, Selina's friend
JULIE HEMPEL, August's daughter and Selina's old schoolfriend
SIMON PEAKE, Selina's father
ROELF POOL, Selina's protégé
MATTIE SCHWENGAUER, Dirk's former girlfriend
PAULA ARNOLD STORM, Julie's daughter
DALLAS O'MARA, an artist

The Story:

The first step in Selina's development is her life with her father. He is a man who lives by the whims of fortune; when his gambling goes well, he and his daughter live in the best hotels, and when it goes badly, they barely get by in cheap boardinghouses. No matter where they live, however, they live every moment, savoring life as a fine meal. This ability to live is, in fact, the true legacy that Simon Peake leaves his daughter, and it becomes her most important possession. Her other legacy, after Simon is brought back to the boarding-house dead from a bullet wound, is two diamonds and almost five hundred dollars in cash. With these, she is able to se-cure an education for herself and find the means of earning a living.

Simon's death forces Selina to step into the next phase of her life, one that is to give shape to her future. She takes a teaching position in the Dutch farming country of Illinois. In her new job, she moves into an environment as different from that of her life with Simon as the fine finishing school Selina attended in Chicago is different from the small country schoolhouse where she goes to teach. When Selina goes to live with the Pools, the family with whom she is to stay in Illi-nois, she sees a life that is not a game but an unending job. There is no time in the Pools's day for magic; every minute is spent making a livelihood from the soil: plowing and reap-ing, repairing farm tools, cooking, and mending clothes. The most striking aspect of life at the Pools', as far as Selina is concerned, is that there is no time for beauty. Up to this point, Selina spent her time only in the search for beauty; now she finds that she has to devote herself to the problems of farming life and to teaching children whose parents are more con-cerned with their children's ability in the fields than with their ability in the classroom.

Even in the midst of the drudgery of this life, however, Selina is able to find a source of beauty. Among the hard-working Pools there is an artist. Selina gives herself to the task of introducing young Roelf Pool to the magic that life can have. She nurtures his native talents at handiwork and treasures the chest that he builds and carves for her. The chest is the reminder that she keeps with her after Roelf leaves and goes to find his own life in the world outside Illinois. It is one of Selina's triumphs that Roelf ultimately becomes a fine and respected sculptor.

Selina's ability to find beauty even in the hard farm life becomes a guiding principle for her life. She marries a beau-tiful man, capable of beautiful acts. Pervus Dejong is the most unsuccessful farmer in the area, but he is a handsome man who recognizes the unusual beauty that marks Selina. When she is subjected to the embarrassment of having the "pretty" basket she prepares for the box supper mocked, Pervus bids a precious ten dollars for her box, turning the laughter to amazement. While Selina's life with Pervus is not marked by beauty, she found it a satisfying life. She becomes enamored of making things grow; her life becomes filled with "beautiful cabbages" and asparagus. When Pervus dies, she takes over the management of the farm and begins to build a future for her son.

With the aid of August Hempel, the rich father of Julie Hempel, one of Selina's former classmates at the finishing school, Selina is able to become a successful truck farmer, to send Dirk to good schools, and to give him the opportunity to find the life of magic and beauty of which she always dreamed. At this point, Selina's story becomes Dirk's story. The first test of whether Dirk will be able to grasp the chance to pursue beauty occurs when he is at the University of Chi-cago. There he meets Mattie Schwengauer, an Iowa farm girl who represents the innocent goodness of growing things. When Dirk rejects Mattie for the social life of the fraternities, where Mattie will not be accepted, Selina receives her first disappointment. Mattie represents the naïve appreciation of life that will be the first step toward discovering the magic that life can offer. Dirk's inability to continue his relationship with her is a foreshadowing of Dirk's future life.

After Dirk becomes an architect, he meets Paula Arnold Storm, Julie's daughter, whom he knew when they were chil-dren. She is now a bored, sophisticated woman married to a man old enough to be her father. It is her influence that leads Dirk to leave his career as an architect, to leave his dreams of building beautiful buildings, and to go into finance, where he is soon successful. To Selina's continuing disappointment, Dirk lives in a world of position and show. He takes a fashion-able apartment and acquires an Asian houseboy. He is, ac-cording to every conventional description, a success.

Then Dirk meets Dallas O'Mara, an artist who revels in life itself. For a time, it seems that she will be the force that will pull Dirk back to the course that Selina mapped for him. Dallas fascinates Dirk, and he is as puzzled as he is charmed by her blithe rejection of the social standards that Dirk comes to accept. A battle between the attractions of Paula's world and those of Dallas's world develops. The situation is brought to a crisis when Roelf returns to Chicago in the com-pany of a French celebrity. Suddenly, the Illinois farm boy and his friend are the toast of Chicago society. Paula goes to extreme lengths to entertain the celebrated pair, and Dirk is unpleasantly surprised when he discovers that they prefer the company of Dallas. His world is further shattered when he finds that the person Roelf most wants to see is Selina.

When Dirk sees Selina with Dallas and Roelf, all three laughing together, reveling in life, he realizes the emptiness of the life that Paula represents. He also realizes that he irrevocably committed himself to Paula's world. Ironically, Selina discovers that her own life holds the magic she always sought, for the magic lies in the seeking. Dirk, who earns his nickname by replying once to a question about how big he was that he was only "so big," discovers that there is not necessarily any magic in success.

Critical Evaluation:

Edna Ferber was awarded the Pulitzer Prize in fiction in 1925 for *So Big*, the first Jewish American woman writer to be so honored. Even though it is one of the earliest of her novels, most critics consider it her best. The decade prior to its appearance in 1924, Ferber was a newspaper reporter in Wisconsin and a writer of a popular series of magazine stories about businesswoman Emma McChesney. Later she went on to write other regional novels, such as *Cimmaron* (1930) and *Giant* (1952), and to collaborate with George S. Kaufman on stage plays, the most famous being the musical created from her novel *Show Boat* (1926). Working-class America, and particularly its women, provided her lifelong fascination. She was interested in the kind of life provided by the expanding industrial society, the values that controlled America's use of its great wealth, and the meaning of success. Lastly, although it is not an overt theme, but rather an underlying concern, she explored the role women were going to play in shaping America.

Ferber leaves no doubt as to her answers to these questions, opening herself to the frequent criticism of didacticism. Her biographer records that she claimed *So Big* was a book "whose purpose was to show the triumph of materialism over the spirit of America." Nevertheless, the characters she draws as vehicles for her ideas are strong enough, particularly in *So Big*, to carry their weight successfully. When her gambler father tells her that there are only two kinds of people in the world that really count, wheat and emeralds, Selina quickly understands that her two maiden aunts, wizened and fearful because they shied away from real life, are neither. Physical goods of real value to people, such as farm produce, and nonphysical entities of real value, such as beauty and quality—these are the wheat and the emeralds. Although, on the surface it seems possible to have either a "wheat" life or an "emerald" life, in a deeper psychological reality, Ferber reveals, they are related. If one has one without the other, as did High Prairie's Dutch farmers (wheat, through and through, impervious to the natural beauty of the land around them) or the glittering Chicago social set with their trappings

of art and music and leisure (shiny, attractive emeralds), one is only "so big." Selina's hard work saves Dirk the necessity of the grinding physical labor on the farm and of mixing with the lower elements in the Haymarket, freeing him for an artist's life dedicated, in his case, to making the ugly surroundings of Chicago beautiful. Instead, however, it becomes only too easy for him to fall into the trap of the empty rich life. He has emeralds, but, without wheat, they are of no value.

When Selina is emotionally at the lowest ebb after the death of Pervus, on her abortive trip to Haymarket in Chicago to sell his vegetables so that she and Dirk can survive, she seems to deny this philosophy of life. She comments then to August Hempel that she is wrong to think that if one just waits, living one's life as best one can, then beauty will come. She wants to save Dirk from making that same mistake. Hempel chides her gently that each person must live the life that is natural for him or her. Dirk must make his own mistakes. However, even if she does disavow her passionate belief in beauty (Dirk accuses her of that in the scene in which he informs her that he will never be an architect), her years of living avow it again and again. The two important artists in the book, Roelf Pool and Dallas O'Mara, both have a natural attraction to the old, mud-spattered farm woman, for they share the grand adventure of a life worth living, doing a work worth doing. Both wheat and emeralds, the three are successful Americans.

Ferber did not preach about the important role of women in shaping the American landscape as much as she preached about success. She did not need to do so. Her women protagonists prove it naturally. Selina herself towers above all the male characters in *So Big*. Her father may convey to her that life is an adventure, but he cannot provide consistently for his only child and is even killed by a bullet intended for someone else. Only Selina can see the beauty in the cabbage fields to which the Dutch farmers are blind. Pervus, her husband, does appreciate the beauty she creates in her boxed supper and the knowledge of figures she can give him with her teaching, but he cannot implement her excellent ideas to improve the farm, content to continue in his father's ways. Those ways kill him. In contrast, under Selina's control, the farm eventually flourishes with modern technology, producing even more beautiful products, ones that are sought after in the best eateries of Chicago. She goes into the marketing world, where women are not welcome, to achieve this success. Most important, Dirk, the son Selina loves above all else, though charming, intelligent, and successful by all worldly standards, causes her bitter disappointment when he deserts beauty for the false values of money and leisure with the idle rich.

It may not be that the female gender is necessarily the

stronger or better one for Ferber, although the pattern of a woman succeeding where a man has failed, as with Selina and Pervus, is common in the rest of her fiction. (Indeed, it is the pattern she observed in her own parents' marriage and business ventures.) After all, Roelf the artist exhibits the very success Selina desires for Dirk (how often she tells him so, enough so it must grate), but even Roelf could not escape High Prairie without her help. Then, too, there are the socialite women such as Paula who, like Dirk, refuse to live by true values. Nevertheless, the only conclusion to be drawn from *So Big* is that, if all Americans will work hard and think truly like Selina, an uncommon yet representative woman, the country will be truly great.

"Critical Evaluation" by Barbara J. Hampton

Further Reading

Bloom, Harold, ed. *American Women Fiction Writers*. Philadelphia: Chelsea House, 1997. Reprints critical extracts of Ferber's work.

Campbell, Donna. "Written with a Hard and Ruthless Purpose: Rose Wilder Lane, Edna Ferber and Middlebrow Regional Fiction." In *Middlebrow Moderns: Popular American Women Writers of the 1920's*. Boston: Northeastern University Press, 2003. Focuses on Ferber and other women writers who enjoyed both critical and commercial success but were dismissed as "middlebrow" for their efforts. Describes how these writers attracted a broad readership, bridging the gap between the economic, racial, ethnic, and religious differences of their audiences.

Gilbert, Julia Goldsmith. *Edna Ferber*. Garden City, N.Y.: Doubleday, 1978. Ferber's great-niece sets the context for Ferber's novels within her life and is not afraid to ask why the famous Americanist has gone into eclipse. This book later was reprinted as *Ferber: Edna Ferber and Her Circle, a Biography* (New York: Applause, 1999).

Meade, Marion. *Bobbed Hair and Bathtub Gin: Writers Running Wild in the Twenties*. New York: Nan A. Talese/Doubleday, 2004. Chronicles Ferber's life and career in the 1920's, when she was at the height of her commercial success. Places her career within the decade's free-spirited atmosphere.

Reed, Paula. "Edna Ferber." In *American Novelists, 1910-1945*. Vol. 9 in *Dictionary of Literary Biography*. Detroit, Mich.: Gale Research, 1981. Discusses Ferber's works within the context of her life. Concludes that Ferber's writings are significant for their "recognition of the contributions of women to the growth and development of America."

Shaughnessey, Mary Rose. *Women and Success in American Society in the Works of Edna Ferber*. New York: Gordon Press, 1977. This most thorough examination of Ferber's works claims that women and America are the novelist's two major themes. Ferber believed that "if women ever wake up to their potentialities . . . the world would be a better place."

Watts, Eileen. "Edna Ferber, Jewish American Writer: Who Knew?" In *Modern Jewish Women Writers in America*, edited by Evelyn Avery. New York: Palgrave Macmillan, 2007. This article and others in the book reevaluate the works of Jewish women writers, demonstrating that, despite assimilation and anti-Semitism, these writers' work continued to reflected their connections to Judaism.

The Social Contract

Author: Jean-Jacques Rousseau (1712-1778)
First published: Du contrat social: Ou, Principes du droit politique, 1762 (English translation, 1764)
Type of work: Philosophy

The Social Contract stands as one of the great classics of political philosophy. In three earlier works, Jean-Jacques Rousseau's basic theme had gradually emerged. Rousseau attacked the basic principles of Enlightenment thought, a philosophy that was dominant in eighteenth century Europe.

Enlightenment thinkers sought to free philosophy and religion from the superstitions of the past. They supported the use of reason and science as the foundation for all belief and conduct. In contrast, Rousseau maintained that human understanding is not the sole domain of reason, but is, as he stated, "greatly indebted to passions." Therefore, to understand one's relationship to society, it is necessary to return to a state of nature to search for a better political order.

Political philosophers before Rousseau, most notably the English philosopher Thomas Hobbes (1588-1679), believed that before people formed society, life was a perpetual state of war—"every man against every man." The only way for people to live together in peace, then, was to form a social contract in which the citizens establish a mutually agreed-upon form of social organization.

Rousseau's thinking about the social contract was the exact opposite of what was commonly accepted at the time. He argued that people are not evil and selfish in the state of nature as Hobbes claimed. In Rousseau's view, society breeds inequality and selfishness because society involves the acquisition of power and private property. Thus was born his famous concept of the noble savage, who existed in a time in which all people lived together in peace and harmony, free from the constraints of society.

The Social Contract revolves around the issue of political obligation. The issue is to find a form of association that will defend and protect a person with the united force of society but will allow each person the greatest possible measure of individual freedom. Unlike Rousseau's earlier works, *The Social Contract* recognizes the need for civil society, despite its depriving citizens of some of their freedoms. In the state of nature, people pursue their self-interest until they discover that the power to preserve themselves against the threats of others is not strong enough. In justifying the transition from the state of nature to civil society, Rousseau argues for a system of government that retains the best "instincts" that people had in the state of nature while incorporating the added values, such as stability and security, that a political organization can give. This is a radical departure from Rousseau's earlier writings, in which he was extremely suspicious of all forms of central authority. The task of *The Social Contract* is to find the basis for a legitimate compact between people and authority and then describe a legitimate form of government that will represent all people.

To begin, Rousseau first discounts some traditional forms of government that, he argues, can never be the basis of a just political order: the rule of the strongest, any government allowing slavery, and monarchy that claims the sanction of divine right. As for the first, the idea that might makes right has no place in Rousseau's political system. People yield to force out of necessity and fear not because they want to; there is no contract worthy of the name in such a society. Those who rule by force are not bound by any sense of morality, so Rousseau concludes that force does not create right. As for slavery,

Rousseau acknowledges that the Greeks and Romans had slaves, and they believed that slavery was natural for some people, but he argues that for people to surrender their rights to a master is incompatible with human nature, because people do not voluntarily enter into a condition of servitude. As for rule by divine right, Rousseau cannot see how one person could possibly preserve the rights of all of his (or her) subjects and at the same time protect his private interests. When the ruler dies, what most often happens is that his empire collapses as a result of the sudden lack of central authority and power. Such a collapse creates disorder and insecurity; the terms of the social contract are not, therefore, honored.

After rejecting each of these illegitimate forms of government, Rousseau turns to the idea of the social contract, and he uses it in a very different way than other seventeenth and eighteenth century political thinkers. Hobbes believed that after the contract is established, the people must surrender all of their authority to a sovereign, who alone would have the power to enforce it. The English philosopher John Locke (1632-1704) rejected Hobbes's conception and argued instead for a limited government in which the contract is formed to establish a market economy, set up a monetary system, and protect property rights. In Locke's government, power is exercised only to ensure safety and settle disputes. Rousseau takes the thinking of Hobbes and Locke a step further. Hobbes argued for a sovereign power, and Locke believed that the people should transfer their collective power to the agencies of government. Rousseau believed that sovereignty must always reside in the people. He states that a government needs executive and judicial functions but argues that their power must be completely subordinated to the power of the people.

The general will is the key concept in Rousseau's political philosophy. It sets him apart from Hobbes and Locke, who believed that the state was an artificial creation, made necessary by the fear and inequality present in the state of nature. In contrast, in book 2 Rousseau argues that government, established upon the idea of the general will, is a natural occurrence, and the state of nature teaches that the legitimacy of government must always rest on the consent of the governed. He further defines the general will by stating that it is determined by two elements: First, it always aims at the general good, and second, it applies to all. In saying this, Rousseau recognizes that unanimous consent in any government is impossible—the vote of the majority also binds the minority, but he does not see majority rule becoming a "tyranny of the majority." Those in the minority, he asserts, do not lose their freedom because they are bound to go along with the majority against their will. Instead, he claims that the minority merely does not recognize the general will; once the minority sees what their interests are, they will readily assent.

The problem of political representation lies at the heart of Rousseau's political philosophy, because if true sovereignty depends upon the power of the general will, then no elected legislative body could possibly serve the interests of every individual citizen. Thus, it becomes impossible to achieve a balance of liberty and authority. Rousseau believes that representative democracy is not truly democratic, because unless voters always have a direct voice in the laws enacted by the legislature, democracy is an illusion. However, Rousseau does not adequately solve the practical problem of ruling a large state. His idea of direct democracy may be workable in a small town, but it would not be practical in a country with millions of people. Some states may be too large for Rousseau's ideal government to be possible.

The second problem addressed in book 2 concerns itself with the role of law in a society. For Rousseau, the making of laws is simply another manifestation of the general will. Laws should be made for the benefit of all and not merely to protect private interests. Laws should never interfere with the individual liberty of citizens, because the laws reflect the citizens' wills.

In book 3, Rousseau gives the reader an idea of what his ideal government might look like. He understands that government is a balance between the general will of the people and sovereignty or power. In his system, government is merely the agent of the people and possesses no real power. The government administers and enforces the law, but it always remains accountable to the general will. This idea is radically different from the writings of previous political theorists. Classical political thinkers such as Plato and Aristotle believed that self-government must surrender itself to good government. Rousseau was the first political writer to attempt to combine good government and self-government through the concept of the general will. Many critics of Rousseau have argued that he does not clearly show how this is possible. For example, Rousseau would claim that the separation of powers found in both the American and British political systems is a denial of democracy and the will of the people. He might, in what for him would be an extreme conciliation to practical reality, place all political power in a supreme legislature that had little or no executive power. In addition, he believes that an ideal state should consist of no more than ten thousand citizens; anything larger would be too difficult to govern.

In surveying the various forms of government that have existed throughout history, Rousseau concludes that no one form of government is best. In looking at each form of government in turn, he sees strengths and weaknesses in each. To the practical question of what constitutes good government, Rousseau answers that the preservation and prosperity of the citizens is the ultimate aim, and any form of government that keeps this goal will, in general, be a good government.

In the fourth and final book, Rousseau talks about how a system of voting and elections should be established. He endorses the principle of majority rule, and argues, oddly enough, that in the small state mentioned earlier as his ideal, most votes would be close to unanimous. Critics have pointed out, however, that Rousseau does not consider that a majority could consist of as little as 51 percent, whose will would then prevail over the other 49 percent. In a time of extreme crisis, Rousseau says, a dictatorship and temporary suspension of civil liberties may even be necessary to ensure the survival of the general will. Rousseau does not say precisely how the likelihood for the invocation of the general will to become the basis for a totalitarian state can be avoided.

Rousseau also discusses the role of religion in society. Some religion, he thought, is indispensable to morality. He severely attacks Christianity, believing the Roman Catholic Church to be a disruptive force because it claimed to be above the political authority of the state. Thus, in times of war, Christians may find their loyalty divided between defending the state and defending their religious convictions. With this discussion Rousseau concludes *The Social Contract*.

Rousseau realized that within his discussion about the ideal political system he had omitted many important topics, such as foreign relations, treaties, and laws between nations. He hoped to return to such topics in the future, but did not. Still, the impact of Rousseau's thinking upon the French and American revolutions was enormous.

Raymond Frey

Further Reading

Cullen, Daniel E. *Freedom in Rousseau's Political Philosophy.* DeKalb: Northern Illinois University Press, 1993. An assessment of Rousseau's philosophy of freedom and its impact on his broader moral and political views.

Damrosch, Leo. *Jean-Jacques Rousseau: Restless Genius.* Boston: Houghton Mifflin, 2005. This one-volume biography is a useful addition to Rousseau scholarship, providing an incisive, accessible account of Rousseau's life and contributions to philosophy and literature. Includes illustrations, a time line, a bibliography, and an index.

Delaney, James. *Starting with Rousseau.* New York: Continuum, 2009. A comprehensive introduction to Rousseau's ideas, including his political philosophy as expounded in *The Social Contract*, his theories of human nature, his philosophy of education, and his social theory. Ideal for beginning students in philosophy, government, and other subjects.

Dent, N. J. H. *Rousseau.* New York: Routledge, 2005. An overview of the entire range of Rousseau's philosophy, paying particular attention to the theories of democracy and freedom outlined in *The Social Contract*. Explains Rousseau's concept of the general will.

_____. *Rousseau: An Introduction to His Psychological, Social, and Political Theory.* New York: Blackwell, 1988. A helpful analysis of Rousseau's views about education, human rights, community, and other social and political issues.

Grant, Ruth H. *Hypocrisy and Integrity: Machiavelli, Rousseau, and the Ethics of Politics.* Chicago: University of Chicago Press, 1997. An instructive comparative analysis of two important figures—Rousseau and Niccolò Machiavelli—in political philosophy.

Havens, George R. *Jean-Jacques Rousseau.* Boston: Twayne, 1978. A concise introductory account of Rousseau's life and career with analyses of his major works.

Hulliung, Mark. *The Autocritique of Enlightenment: Rousseau and the Philosophes.* Cambridge, Mass.: Harvard University Press, 1994. Shows how Rousseau both reflected and departed from main currents in Enlightenment philosophy.

Morgenstern, Mira. *Rousseau and the Politics of Ambiguity: Self, Culture, and Society.* University Park: Pennsylvania State University Press, 1996. Analyzes Rousseau's political theory and its historical context, showing how his thought introduced notes of ambiguity that remain in contemporary political life.

Wokler, Robert. *Rousseau.* New York: Oxford University Press, 1995. A concise and lucid introduction to Rousseau's life and thought.

Society and Solitude

Author: Ralph Waldo Emerson (1803-1882)
First published: 1870
Type of work: Essays

Society and Solitude is a collection of twelve essays previously delivered as lectures on various occasions and before varied audiences. Each essay is preceded by a few lines of original verse. The volume as a whole lacks the propagandistic fire of Ralph Waldo Emerson's earlier essays, although there is still a tendency to dwell upon humanity's better side, almost as though it had no other. Emerson continues also to see the world as filled with good for those who will receive what is offered. One of Emerson's biographers has called these late writings the cheeriest of Emerson's essays. Several are more discursive than necessary, but on many pages are the sparkle, wit, and happy phrasing that mark Emerson at his best.

In the title essay, Emerson makes clear that for humanity, both society and solitude are necessary. People differ in their need for these two opposites according to their personalities and their activities. Creative geniuses such as Sir Isaac Newton and Dante Alighieri needed isolation to accomplish their work. Emerson notes, however, that although now and then an ordinary person can and must live alone, "coop up most men and you undo them." A balance is needed. Humanity should not remain proudly alone nor let itself be vulgarized by too much society; one mood should reinforce the other.

"Civilization" may be considered an essay in definition since much of it is devoted to a description of what civilization is not and what it is. Emerson discusses both the civilized society and the civilized or cultured individual. Such a person is marked by the capacity for self-advancement, by the ability to associate and compare things with one another, and by the ability to move from one idea to another. The civilized society, says Emerson, is one that has progressed to agriculture from war, hunting, and pasturage. This society includes increased means of communication, a division of labor, a raising of the status of women, a diffusion of knowledge, a combining of antagonisms, and even a utilizing of evil so as to produce benefits.

Civilization results from highly complex organization. Climate is often a major force in producing it but, according to Emerson, any society with a high destiny must be moral. The wise person who would be civilized will use the powers of nature, which exist for the individual. The wise will hitch their wagon to a star and let the heavenly powers pull for them. They will work for the highest ends—justice, love, freedom, knowledge, utility. The test of the civilization in which the wise live will be the kind of people their country creates. In the civilized state all public action will be designed to secure the greatest good for the greatest number.

"Art" attempts to define both art and the artist. Emerson begins with the simple statement that art is the "conscious utterance of thought, by speech or action, to any end." It is the spirit's voluntary use and combination of things to serve its end; it is the spirit creative. Since this spirit aims at use or at beauty, there are the useful and the fine arts. The universal soul creates all works of art and uses the artist to bring them into being. Thus, all art complements nature. In the useful arts, nature is a tyrant over humanity, forcing humanity to use the tools that nature supplies and to learn which fit best. Turning to the fine arts, such as music, eloquence, poetry, painting, sculpture, and architecture, Emerson points out that each has a material basis that hinders the artist who works with it. Language must be converted into poetry, vibrations in the air into music, and stone into sculpture and architecture. The art resides, observes Emerson, in the model, the plan, and the harmonious arrangement of the material the artist uses. As with the useful arts, nature dominates the artist; the artist is the organ through which the universal mind acts. Believing in a moral universe, Emerson sees all great works of art as attuned to moral nature.

The reader may sense, regarding "Eloquence," that Emerson devoted more space than he needed to this theme. He seeks a distinction between the eloquent person and the mere speaker, and he describes the interrelationships between the speaker and the audience. Much that he says seems rather obvious, the sort of thing a public-speaking teacher might use to begin a course. The orator plays on the audience as a master pianist plays the piano. The audience influences the speaker by its reaction. The consummate speaker has, to begin with, a robust and radiant physical health. The speaker, Emerson states, is personally appealing, and the speaker's eloquence illustrates the magic of his or her ascendancy over the audience. The speaker must have the fact and know how to reveal it; reaching higher, however, the speaker must state the law above the fact and must be the means through which the moral law of the universe is revealed.

"Domestic Life" is one of the most pleasing essays in the volume, but one is inclined to wonder what Emerson's wife thought of the piece. It begins with an amusing picture of the infant despot for whom all services are performed. "All day," says Emerson, "between his three or four sleeps, he coos like a pigeon-house, sputters and spurs and puts on his faces of importance; and when he fasts, the little Pharisee fails not to sound his trumpet before him." The home belongs to the adults as well as the child. It must be managed by a wise economy that shall witness that human culture is its end. When visitors come, they shall not be simply fed and put in soft, warm beds; they shall see that here all deeds flow from truth and love, honor and courtesy. Although those who inhabit the home are not themselves divine, they should through their characters reveal that in each nature has laid foundations of a divine structure upon which the soul may build. Finally, the household should cherish the beautiful arts and the sentiment of veneration. It should not, however, attempt to be a museum but only a small work of art itself, nor a church but only an intimate sanctuary for those who dwell there and for their friends who come in.

"Farming" makes some pleasant statements about the occupation, but it is by a man who was better at talking about it than at being a farmer even on a half-acre scale. The farmer, says Emerson, lives by nature's schedule, because no person can speed nature up. The farmer is the trustee of health and wealth and is the progenitor of the city dwellers, who, in manufacture and trade, give to the world the products of the farm. The farmer is a continuous benefactor, a minder of nature, who provides not for one generation but for all. The farmer lives in the presence of nature and is ennobled by it.

"Works and Days" opens with a brief survey of the scientific and mechanical tools for labor and leisure newly available to the people of Emerson's day. Emerson observes that humanity, already having much, will have more of these tools; he even predicts, nearly a half century before World War I, that the next war would be fought in the air.

Emerson is more interested in people than in things, and it means much to him how people spend their days. As he says, "Works and days were offered us, and we took works." Several of the best sentences in the essay are a prose rendering of the famous sonnet "Days," which precedes the essay. Like his younger friend, Henry David Thoreau, Emerson laments that humanity wastes its days on trivia when it should write on its heart that every day is the best day in the year and is also doomsday. The measure of a person, says Emerson, is his or her "apprehension of a day."

"Books" was praised by Oliver Wendell Holmes in his biography of Emerson, but its appeal to later readers is limited. Much of it is devoted to recommending particular authors and books to be read, and these are drawn from Emerson's lifetime of reading. Memorable are Emerson's rules for choosing one's reading: "1. Never read any book that is not a year old. 2. Never read any but famed books. 3. Never read any but what you like."

"Clubs" has much about conversation but little about clubs, where conversation abounds, or should in Emerson's estimation. Emerson prizes conversation because it takes a person out of him- or herself and brings the person into relation with others. Each talker kindles the mind of another or others. Emerson cares little for those who must be masters of the group, the gladiators who must always win an argument, or the egotists who wish to be heard, not to listen. Emerson sees conversation as "the Olympic games whither every superior gift resorts to assert and approve itself . . . with the rest." He closes with the comment that when discourse rises highest and searches deepest, it is between two only.

In "Courage," Emerson observes that three qualities attract the wonder and reverence of humanity: disinterestedness, practical power, and courage. Courage is thought to be common, he says, but the immense esteem in which it is held proves it to be rare. Fear is based on ignorance, and knowledge is its antidote. The sailor loses fear when he can control sails and spars and steam; the frontiersman when he can aim surely with his rifle. Courage consists in being equal to whatever one faces, in the conviction that the opposition does not excel one in strength of resources or spirit. Each person has his or her own kind of courage, one a fury of onset, another a calm endurance. True courage does not show itself off, and it is a bond of union even between enemies who respect it in each other.

"Success" begins with comments on the multitudinous achievements of Americans and their smug self-satisfaction with what they have done. To show that this is the way of the world, Emerson cites the individual superiority of persons in other countries and other times. What rouses his hate is the American passion for quick and effortless success, and what rouses his scorn is the boasting when one has succeeded. Drop the brag and advertisement, says Emerson, and following Michelangelo's course in life, confide in yourself and be something of worth and value. Then, as if he were rephrasing a passage from his earlier "Self-Reliance," Emerson remarks,

Self-trust is the first secret of success, the belief that if you are here the authorities of the universe put you here, and for cause, or with some task strictly appointed you in your constitution, and so long as you work at that you are well and successful.

"Old Age," which closes Emerson's book, is one of the best essays in the collection. "The essence of age," he says, "is intellect," and experience ripens slowly. Elderly people have been honored in many lands and ages because of what they knew. Age has its benefits: It has weathered the capes and shoals of life's sea; it has the felicity of having found expression in living; it sets its house in order and finishes its works, and humanity is ready to be born again in this new and final home.

Further Reading

Allen, Gay Wilson. *Waldo Emerson: A Biography.* New York: Viking Press, 1981. Notes the reception to *Society and Solitude* by various critics. Provides an excerpt from the original manuscript that did not appear in the published work. Well-indexed. Features a chronology and comprehensive notes.

Buell, Lawrence. *Emerson.* Cambridge, Mass.: Belknap Press, 2003. This biographical account revisits the life and work of America's first public intellectual on the occasion of Emerson's two-hundredth birthday. The index lists the references to *Society and Solitude.*

Carpenter, Frederic Ives. *Emerson Handbook.* 1953. Reprint. New York: Hendricks House, 1967. A good research tool, providing background material to the ideas that shape Emerson's texts. Discusses Emerson's writing methods and style. Includes bibliographies.

Emerson, Ralph Waldo. *Journals of Ralph Waldo Emerson: 1820-24.* Vol. 1. Edited by Edward Waldo Emerson and Waldo Emerson Forbes. Boston: Houghton Mifflin, 1990. This volume of Emerson's journals is rich in comments on key notions found in *Society and Solitude.*

Lothstein, Arthur S., and Michael Brodrick, eds. *New Morning: Emerson in the Twenty-first Century.* Albany: State University of New York Press, 2008. Philosophers, poets, and literary critics, including Mark Strand, Gary Snyder, and Lawrence Buell, discuss how Emerson's ideas about the environment, race, politics, spirituality, and other areas remain relevant into the twenty-first century.

Porte, Joel. *Consciousness and Culture: Emerson and Thoreau Reviewed.* New Haven, Conn.: Yale University Press, 2004. Focuses on Emerson as a writer, analyzing the quality of his prose and the organization of his essays. References to *Society and Solitude* are listed in the index.

Porte, Joel, and Saundra Morris, eds. *The Cambridge Companion to Ralph Waldo Emerson.* New York: Cambridge University Press, 1999. Collection of essays in which contributors assess Emerson's writing, influence, and cultural significance. Chapter 4 examines Emerson as a lecturer.

Sohrab and Rustum

Author: Matthew Arnold (1822-1888)
First published: 1853, in *Poems*
Type of work: Poetry
Type of plot: Historical
Time of plot: Antiquity
Locale: Western Asia, along the Oxus River

Principal characters:
RUSTUM, a Persian chieftain
SOHRAB, a youth in the Tartar army
PERAN-WISA, the leader of the Tartars
FEROOD, the leader of the Persians
GUDURZ, another Persian chieftain

The Poem:

The two powerful armies of the Tartars and the Persians are encamped along the banks of the Oxus River. It is night, and the soldiers are asleep, but daylight will bring a great conflict between mighty forces. To one Tartar, rest refuses to come. In the grayness of the early dawn, he leaves his bed and makes his solitary way through the black tents of the great encampment to the quarters of Peran-Wisa, commander of the Tartar army. He is Sohrab, the youthful champion of the Tartars. Hardly more than a boy, he develops into the mightiest fighter of the Tartar host. Young in years and famous in arms, he is nevertheless restless and discontented. Above everything else, he wants to find the father he has never seen, the incomparable Rustum, invincible chieftain of the Persians.

Rustum does not even know that he has a son. He is told that a woman of Ader-baijan, after his departure from that place, bore him a child, but that was years earlier. Rustum gives the matter little thought because he believes the child to be a girl. After Sohrab is born, the fearful mother, hoping to prevent her son from being taken from her and reared for war, deceives Rustum with that report. Nevertheless, Sohrab becomes a warrior, and his mother's ruse avails nothing except to keep her son from a knowledge of his father.

Peran-Wisa awakens when Sohrab enters and asks an unusual favor of him: Sohrab wishes to challenge a leader of the Persians to single combat, the duel to occur as soon as arrangements can be made. He hopes that his fame as a fighter will thereby reach the ears of his father. Peran-Wisa urges patience and questions his wisdom in thus tempting fate, but at last he unwillingly agrees to Sohrab's request.

Thus challenged by their Tartar foe, the Persians are barely able to conceal their alarm. They have no champion to pit against the redoubtable young Sohrab except Rustum, and Rustum withdraws because of slights from the young Persian ruler. When the Persians appeal to him, cleverly implying that Rustum is hoarding his fame and becomes reluctant to risk combat with younger men, Rustum is aroused and grudgingly consents to meet the Tartar champion. He stipu-

lates, however, that he will fight unknown to the enemy and in plain armor, for he fears that his great name might otherwise daunt the brash young challenger at the outset. Now that his temper is aroused, Rustum is in no mood to give up the chance of another single combat.

Halfway between the waiting armies, Sohrab and Rustum come face-to-face. Before they fight, words pass between them, and a strange disquiet settles over their spirits. The moment passes, however, and the conflict begins. Sohrab's misgivings return; when his nimbleness gives him the initial advantage, he forebears to follow it up. Stung with anger and shame, Rustum gives him no second chance. With a shout of "Rustum" he renews his attack upon Sohrab, who, thunderstruck at the name, momentarily lowers his shield. Instantly he is transfixed by Rustum's spear and falls to the ground, mortally wounded.

As his life ebbs away, the young man reveals to his adversary the secret of his birth. Rustum, at first incredulous, is convinced when Sohrab bares his arm to reveal the sign of Rustum's own seal, pricked there soon after his birth. The unhappy Rustum, beset by extremes of agony and remorse, can barely be restrained from taking his own life and dying with his son. Broken by grief, he promises to bear the body of Sohrab far away, so that it might be in death where it was never in life, near the palace of snowheaded Zal, the boy's grandfather. There it will receive burial worthy of a son of Rustum. Thus ends Sohrab's quest for his father. Life passes from him; the day wanes; night comes on. The majestic river flows on into the frosty starlight, and campfires begin to twinkle through the fog. Rustum, grieving, remains on the river sands, alone with his son.

Critical Evaluation:

"Sohrab and Rustum" is based on a historical event that took place in Persia about 600 B.C.E. Matthew Arnold acknowledges his source to be Sir John Malcolm's *History of Persia* (1815) and states in his preface to the poem that he intends to "treat a noble action in a somewhat epic fashion." In preparing to compose the consciously Homeric poem, Arnold reread his beloved Homer with the great admiration which he expresses in such poems as "To a Friend" (1849) and such prose works as *On Translating Homer* (1861) and "The Study of Poetry" (1880).

Clearly based on a Homeric model are Arnold's elevated tone, ornate language, and elaborate extended similes, as well as the imposing stature he gives his two main figures, his use of an overriding fate working out their destiny, and his creation of a central dramatic episode of national significance. As an epic poem, "Sohrab and Rustum" is admired for its moving presentation of a dramatic conflict between father and son, its brilliance of language, and its richness of tone. In classical fashion, the poem involves one central action, which takes place in one day, and many critics have commented on the success of the poem's many epic similes and on other parallels.

The main critical interest of the poem lies in its allegorical presentation of the moral and intellectual conflict characterizing the Victorian age and in its dramatization of Arnold's personal dilemmas. The battlefield is Arnold's poetic landscape—the "darkling plain" of the poem "Dover Beach" (1867), "Swept with confused alarms of struggle and flight,/ Where ignorant armies clash by night." The characters Sohrab and Rustum may be seen as the personifications of the warring elements within the hearts and minds of all Victorian writers, who are as two-souled as the narrator of "Dipsychus" (1850) by Arthur Hugh Clough, Arnold's friend and rival for the admiration of his father, who died in 1842.

The single combat between the venerable father Rustum and his son has specifically personal parallels in the conflict between Matthew Arnold, the successful poet, and his father, Dr. Thomas Arnold, the renowned headmaster of Rugby school, who was known for instilling moral earnestness and devotion to duty in his pupils. In many ways, Thomas Arnold resembled the proud and invincible old warrior Rustum. Biographers have suggested that in a sense Arnold, like Sohrab, was engaged in the archetypal search for his father. From early boyhood, Arnold was both attracted to and repelled by his father's rigorous dedication to educational reform. As Arnold matured from the youthful poet into the mature prose writer, he took on the stoic nature and moral vigor of his father. The poet W. H. Auden suggested that the voice of Thomas Arnold kills the poet in the son Arnold just as Rustum kills Sohrab.

Arnold's rebellion against his father began during his school days at Rugby and was manifested for many years in a deliberately flamboyant lifestyle. While Arnold consciously played the part of the typical dandy, apparently as carefree as his "Strayed Reveller" (1849) wishes to be, his "Romantic" poetry portrayed a lonely and divided soul yearning for peace and unity. It is clear that in part the poet always wanted to embody the virtues he ascribed to his father in his tribute to him in the poem "Rugby Chapel" (1858), in which he described him as one of the "souls temper'd with fire,/ Fervent, heroic, and good,/ Helpers and friends of mankind." In his prose, Arnold deliberately embodies his father's admirable traits and his poetic self dies, as it were, in his father's arms. With the death of Sohrab, the conflict is resolved, but not without Rustum having to endure deep grief and lasting sorrow.

Even more specifically, the battle between Sohrab and Rustum embodies two aspects of Arnold's internal personal struggle during the 1850's and 1860's, when his poetic self challenged his prosaic self to single combat. That combat ended with the emergence of a sadder and wiser prosaic self. Though his youthful poetic self died in the 1860's, Arnold remains, along with Alfred, Lord Tennyson, and Robert Browning, one of the three great poets of the Victorian period.

Arnold began his transition from rebellious poet to social reformer in April, 1851. That same year, he was appointed to a position as inspector of schools, which he held for thirty-five years; in June he married and settled down to a life devoted to the dissemination of culture with the twenty-two volumes of prose that he wrote during the last thirty years of his life. After 1860, Arnold virtually willed his poetic self to death, and he replaced the writing of poetry with literary and social criticism and various types of religious and educational prose works.

In reading "Sohrab and Rustum" as an allegory of personal internal conflict, it is instructive to consider the very similar story told by William Butler Yeats in his drama *On Baillie's Stand* (1904), in which Cuchulain, the venerable old father character who symbolizes Irish nationalism, kills the young stranger who is his son. Yeats uses the single combat between father and son to define heroic identity in terms of the warring halves of the soul; the heroic self is formed through the dialectical opposition between the self and its opposite or antiself, just as the mature writer that Arnold becomes is formed through the opposition within his consciousness between his poetic self and its antiself.

In one interpretation of a specific image in Arnold's poem, the river Oxus, the chief river of central Asia, has been interpreted as an emblem of human destiny that runs through the desert wasting its energy in frustrations but at last reaching its tranquil goal in the starlit sea. At the beginning of the poem, the river Oxus is obscured by the fog in the gray dawn just as the course of Arnold's life was obscured, even from himself. As the poem ends, the stars emerge to shine on the tranquil waters of the united self of the mature Arnold.

"Critical Evaluation" by Constance M. Fulmer

Further Reading

Cervo, Nathan. "'Dover Beach,' 'Sohrab and Rustum,' 'Philomela,' and 'Stanzas from the Grande Chartreuse.'" *Arnoldian* 11, no. 1 (Winter, 1984): 24-31. Cervo discusses Arnold's use of sea and stone imagery as they are related to the Oedipus complex.

Frame, E. Frances. "Shaping the Self: Critical Perspective and Community in *Sohrab and Rustum.*" *Victorian Poetry* 45, no. 1 (Spring, 2007): 17-28. An explication of the poem, focusing on Arnold's metaphors. Frame argues that the theme of the poem is individuals' refusal to realize the limitations of their knowledge, a theme Arnold used in other works.

Gouws, John. "Matthew Arnold's 'Sohrab and Rustum.'" *Notes and Queries* 30 (August, 1983): 302. This note establishes Goethe as another author whom Matthew Arnold deeply admired. The way Arnold uses his sources demonstrates his practice of measuring his own poetry against "touchstones" from the great literature of the past.

Hamilton, Ian. A *Gift Imprisoned: The Poetic Life of Matthew Arnold*. London: Bloomsbury, 1998. A critical biography that explores the frustrations in Arnold's life, the tension between passion and repression in his poetry, and his decision to abandon poetry for prose writing.

Kline, Daniel. "'Unhackneyed Thoughts and Winged Words': Arnold, Locke, and the Similes of 'Sohrab and Rustum.'" *Victorian Poetry* 41, no. 2 (Summer, 2003): 173. Analyzes Arnold's use of similes in this and other poems and the persistent theme of human isolation and alienation in Arnold's work.

Pratt, Linda Ray. *Matthew Arnold Revisited*. New York: Twayne, 2000. An introductory overview of Arnold's life and literary career, with analysis of his work. Pratt also provides a postmodern interpretation of Arnold's work.

Roper, Alan. *Arnold's Poetic Landscapes*. Baltimore: Johns Hopkins University Press, 1969. Examines the degree to which Arnold achieves unity between human significance and literal landscape. In discussing "Sohrab and Rustum," Roper focuses on the tragically fateful dichotomy in Rustum between the individual fulfillment of finding a son of whom he can be proud and his public obligation to be a great warrior.

Thorpe, Michael. *Matthew Arnold*. New York: Arco, 1969. Contains a comprehensive treatment of the poem and of the manuscript. Also analyzes specific images and includes a comparison of "Sohrab and Rustum" with Arnold's other poems.

Solaris

Author: Stanisław Lem (1921-2006)
First published: 1961 (English translation, 1970)
Type of work: Novel
Type of plot: Science fiction
Time of plot: The future
Locale: A space station suspended above the oceanic surface of the planet Solaris

Principal characters:
KRIS KELVIN, a psychologist
DR. SNOW, an expert in cybernetics
DR. SARTORIUS, a physicist
RHEYA, a material apparition of Kelvin's dead wife

The Story:

Kris Kelvin arrives at the Solaris research station to find it in a state of utter confusion. Gibarian, one of the three scientists on staff at the station, has committed suicide. One of the others, Dr. Sartorius, has locked himself away. The third, Dr. Snow, is terrified to the point of madness. While trying to figure out what happened, Kelvin contemplates the mystery of

Solaris: a planet following an impossible orbit around a double sun, seemingly able to do so because the colloidal ocean that covers its entire surface is capable of making continual adjustments to the world's gravity to maintain its path. This living ocean undergoes ceaseless metamorphic transformations, producing many kinds of different structures with no discernible pattern; the Solarists studying the world produce many hypotheses to account for these transformations, but they are unable to confirm any of them.

After catching a brief glimpse of another person, Kelvin confronts Snow and demands to know who it is, but Snow refuses to tell him anything. Kelvin ascertains, however, that Sartorius, who is equally unhelpful, is not alone in his rooms. Later, Kelvin is visited in his own quarters by his dead wife Rheya, looking exactly as she did when he last saw her ten years before. Kelvin is horrified by the impossibility of Rheya's manifestation, while she is gradually possessed of an oddly passive anxiety as she realizes that she cannot understand or explain where she is or how she came to be at the station. Intent on getting rid of the unnatural visitor, Kelvin tricks her into entering a space capsule; he then blasts her into space.

Knowing that Kelvin might now be ready to believe him, Snow explains that all the station staff have been subject to such visitations. The manifestations invariably solidify guilty secrets of some kind—fetishes, obsessions, or unresolved psychological problems. Snow tells Kelvin that as a psychologist, Kelvin should be well aware that every man has such secrets, and Snow proposes that when men come to Solaris to confront the alien ocean, the ocean responds by confronting men with the discomfiting produce of their own inner selves. Snow suggests that if Kelvin wants explanations he might look at a book called *The Little Apocrypha*, a copy of which Kelvin already found. Kelvin begins to read it, finding it to be a speculative and pseudoscientific counterpart to the disciplined reports issued by the scientists sent to study Solaris.

Kelvin's studies are interrupted by Rheya's remanifestation. Accepting that he is unable to get rid of her for the time being, Kelvin begins to study her; slowly they begin to reconstitute their loving relationship. Sartorius helps him in the quest, explaining that the simulacra—which Sartorius labels "phi-beings"—are made of a different kind of matter.

With Snow's help, Sartorius tries to figure out a way to destroy the apparitions; he eventually succeeds in building a device that breaks down the matter of which the apparitions are composed. By the time the device is ready for experimental use, however, Kelvin's feelings are deeply ambivalent. Rheya, aware of her own unhumanness, has to trick Kelvin to be allowed to submit to Sartorius's experiment. It succeeds in destroying her—although the machine promptly breaks down—but no sooner is the simulacrum of Rheya banished than Kelvin begins wishing for her return.

There is nothing left for Kelvin to do but to try to derive some understanding of Solaris from the strange experience.

He suggests to Snow that they might imagine a sick and despairing god with the creative ocean of Solaris as a kind of "hermit of the cosmos" dimly reflecting that god's problematic creative power. Kelvin is able to simulate normality in his outward behavior, but inwardly he remains in turmoil, not knowing whether he could or ought to hope for Rheya's return. Were she to come back again, he feels, it will represent yet another imperfection of creation and of life, which ought not to repeat itself "like a hackneyed tune, or a record a drunkard keeps playing as he feeds coins into the jukebox." At the same time, he stubbornly persists in the belief that "the time of cruel miracles was not past."

Critical Evaluation:

Stanisław Lem's *Solaris* is science fiction in the purest possible sense, constituting an elaborate thought experiment in which imaginary science is employed to address fundamental questions of epistemology and human psychology in a disciplined fashion. *Solaris* is simultaneously preoccupied with the limits of humans' quest to understand the world in which they find themselves and the limits of their understanding. The ocean of Solaris is a hypothetical test case, bringing both these issues—and the bridge that inevitably connects them—into a dramatic focus that makes up in urgency and ambition what it lacks in clarity and conclusiveness. The English text of *Solaris* is two steps removed from the original, having been translated from the French rather than the original Polish, but it is unlikely that much has been lost, and there is a sense that the serial metamorphoses involved are appropriate to the substance of the plot.

The elaborate technical discourse employed to describe the peculiar behavior of the ocean of Solaris and the makeup of the phi-beings is itself a simulacrum, since most of its terms are imaginary and those borrowed from physics or biology are employed metaphorically. There is much more, however, in the discourse than mere jargon. The form is more important than the content, because the issue at stake is how people accumulate knowledge and how they test the accuracy of their conclusions. The physics may be fake, but its method is not, and *Solaris* is primarily concerned with the methods people employ in science and in their personal lives, and the problematic relationships between science and personal lives.

Scientific knowledge is supposed to be objective; its truths are supposed to exist independently of people's discovery of them. Physicists do, however, acknowledge the significance of Werner Heisenberg's uncertainty principle, which recognizes that the act of observing phenomena on the smallest scale must of necessity involve a disruptive interference with the phenomena in question. *Solaris* involves both a magnification and an inversion of this kind of interreaction; the vast living ocean responds to observation by disruptively interfering with its observers. The effect of this disruption is to force the observers to look at themselves as well as the ocean—indeed, to look into themselves, to look at awkward but revealing aspects of their own psychoses that have been suppressed or exorcised from the conscious narratives that compose their life histories and representations of themselves.

Kelvin, as a psychologist, is supposed to be able to bring the methods of science to bear on these kinds of phenomena. He is supposed to be able to catalog them and place them within tentative theoretical frameworks, exactly as the Solarists do with the ocean's problematic metamorphoses— but it is impossible to be objective in confronting the phenomena of the psyche, where every act of observation is a disruptive reconstruction. Significantly, neither Kelvin nor the reader is ever allowed to learn exactly what kind of manifestations haunt Snow and Sartorius because they refuse to submit their secrets to public scrutiny, not wanting their guilty secrets analyzed and understood by others. Kelvin can only wonder whether the ocean of Solaris is capable of understanding itself or others—and whether, if so, it has the least desire to be understood.

Andrei Tarkovsky's motion picture version of *Solaris* is better known than the book, but it is very different from it. The print medium is uniquely suited to the kind of technical discourse that forms the core of the project—and, for that matter, to the kind of pseudoscientific discourse that attempts to complicate the method of science and supplement its revelations, a haunting presence represented in the plot by *The Little Apocrypha*. In isolating and considerably elaborating the personal aspect of Kelvin's predicament, the film denudes his problems of their true context; the whole point of Kelvin's struggle to come to terms with his re-embodied wife is that the struggle is technical and personal at one and the same time—no separation of the two is possible. His painful ambivalence is not the result of mixed feelings about his dead wife—although the fact of the manifestation does, indeed, betray a harmful confusion—but, instead, his ambivalence is an inevitable consequence of a conflict between two very different strategies of understanding.

The dubious resolution of Kelvin's problem raises one of the central issues concerning the role of science in human affairs. Even an incomplete understanding can give rise to technologies that permit people limited but powerful control over the phenomena under consideration. Even in the absence of a sensible understanding of her production, Rheya

can still be obliterated. It is far easier to determine what she is made of than the reason for her existence. The same is true of scientific projects in general; it is possible to figure out what things are made of, but people are not sure that it even makes sense to ask why things exist at all.

Even if such questions are set aside in respect to the universe at large—discarding in the process Kelvin's speculations about the sickness and the despair of god as empty fantasies—these questions cannot be set aside in regard to people. People have to ask why they have chosen their ways of life, because they could be living some other way if they chose—and they could, like Gibarian, cease to live at all if they could find no reason to live. Kelvin can dispose of the phi-being version of Rheya, but he cannot dispose of the element in his own psyche that provoked her manifestation. That is why, even though he recognizes the folly and futility of endless repetition without transformation, he cannot avoid the hope that the cruel miracle of her return might be reenacted again, and again, and again.

Brian Stableford

Further Reading

Csisery-Ronay, Istvan. "The Book Is the Alien: On Certain and Uncertain Readings of Stanisław Lem's *Solaris*." *Science-Fiction Studies* 12, no. 1 (March, 1985): 6-21. A consideration of the "hermetic ambiguity" of a situation in which contact with the alien has been achieved and yet remains impossible.

Freedman, Carl. "Solaris: Stanisław Lem and the Structure of Cognition." In *Critical Theory and Science Fiction*. Hanover, N.H.: Wesleyan University Press, 2000. Freedman applies various critical theories to Lem's novel *Solaris* and works by four other science-fiction writers to demonstrate the affinity between contemporary literary criticism and the science-fiction genre.

Science-Fiction Studies 13, no. 3 (November, 1986). Entire issue devoted to consideration of Lem's work, including editorial materials and several papers that examine *Solaris*.

Suvin, Darko. "The Open-Ended Parables of Stanisław Lem and *Solaris*." In *Solaris* by Stanisław Lem, translated by Joanna Kilmartin and Steve Cox. New York: Walker, 1970. Suvin's afterword to this edition of the novel provides a general introduction to Lem's work, including an annotated bibliography. Relates *Solaris* to the main traditions of speculative fiction.

Swirski, Peter. *Between Literature and Science: Poe, Lem, and Explorations in Aesthetics, Cognitive Science, and*

Literary Knowledge. Montreal: McGill-Queen's University Press, 2000. A comparative study of Lem and Edgar Allan Poe that analyzes how the two authors use scientific concepts for fictional purposes. Includes bibliographical references and index.

_____. *A Stanislaw Lem Reader*. Evanston, Ill.: Northwestern University Press, 1997. A collection of various writings by and about Lem. Includes an introductory essay by Swirski, two lengthy interviews with Lem, and an essay by Lem. Also contains a complete bibliography of Lem's books in English and Polish, a list of Lem's essays and articles in English, and an extensive bibliography of critical sources on Lem in English.

_____, ed. *The Art and Science of Stanislaw Lem*. Montreal: McGill-Queen's University Press, 2006. A collection of essays analyzing *Solaris* and other works and examining some of the themes in Lem's fiction, such as social engineering, human violence, evolution, Freudianism, and virtual reality.

Yossef, Abraham. "Understanding Lem: *Solaris* Revisited." *Foundation*, no. 46 (Autumn, 1989): 51-57. Considers the significance of the names given to the characters and the relationship of certain ideas in the text to Judaic theology.

Ziegfeld, Richard E. *Stanisław Lem*. New York: Frederick Ungar, 1985. A general account of the philosophical themes in Lem's work.

The Solitudes

Author: Luis de Góngora y Argote (1561-1627)
First published: *Soledades*, 1627 (English translation, 1931)
Type of work: Poetry

Few writers have left so decisive a stamp upon the literature of their own and of successive ages as Luis de Góngora y Argote. Góngora is the embodiment of the Spanish baroque. His name also survives as a style, *gongorismo*, or Gongorism. Born in the city of Córdoba into a prosperous and cultivated family, he indifferently studied canon law at the University of Salamanca, although he is said to have led there the life of a dissolute poet rather than that of a student of theology. Returning to Córdoba, he took deacons's orders and in 1577 was made a prebendary of the cathedral. However, he seems to have remained incorrigibly devoted to the pursuit of pleasure, since, in 1589, he is recorded as having received a reprimand from his bishop for a disreputable lifestyle, which included too-frequent attendance at bullfights and consorting with actors of both genders.

By then, he had already attracted the notice and approbation of Miguel de Cervantes for his writing, but with the circulation of his *Romancero general* of 1600, his reputation as a poet was assured. In 1612, he left Córdoba for Madrid, seeking, like other Golden Age writers and artists, the fount of patronage at the royal court. He was appointed chaplain to Philip III, no discriminating judge of literature, and, following the latter's death, served Philip IV in the same capacity. The real source of patronage became the royal favorite, the count-duke of Olivares, who seems to have recognized Góngora's merits, but by whom the poet seems to have felt neglected in his last, rather unhappy years in the capital city, where he failed to acquire the material rewards he felt were his due.

Góngora's writing is generally opulent and baroque. He adopted the theory of *culteranismo*, first enunciated by the soldier, scholar, and poet Luis de Carrillo y Sotomayor. *Culteranismo*, as conceived by Carrillo, advocates the elevation of literature and especially of poetry. The hallmarks of *culteranismo* are excessive Latinization of the Castilian language, profound erudition, and learned allusion, that, together with deliberate obscurity, restrict comprehension to only the most learned readers. Perhaps no other Spanish poet has been so reviled, so praised, and so imitated. In approaching *The Solitudes*, it is important to be aware of *culteranismo* and *gongorismo*; the reader must work to understand Góngora's intricate, complex, and highly allusive work.

Góngora's years in Madrid, although less rewarding than he anticipated and leading eventually to decay of his physical and mental capacities, saw the composition of his most notable works. Góngora's writings circulated anonymously and were not published under his name until after his death, although everyone knew they were by him. *Fábula de Polifemo y Galatea* (1627; *Fable of Polyphemus and Galatea*, 1961) and *The Solitudes* began to circulate in 1613. Perhaps his greatest achievement, the "Fábula de Píramo y Tisbe," began to circulate in 1618. In these works, his pursuit of *culteranismo* was further honed by his adoption of the theory of *conceptismo*. *Conceptismo*, which originated with Alonso de Ledesma, and which at times is difficult to distinguish from *culteranismo*, seeks to achieve in prose, as much if not even more than in poetry, flashes of wit (*concepto*). Such flashes of wit are excessive and often of obscure subtlety. Again, they are aimed primarily for intellectual effect and addressed to a refined readership accustomed to epigram and wordplay. In *conceptismo*, it is the idea that is all-important, while in *culteranismo*, it is the use and play of language: figures of thought, it has been suggested, in contrast to figures of speech. *Conceptismo* appealed to many of the greatest writers of the Spanish Golden Age—for example, Francisco Gómez de Quevedo y Villegas, Baltasar Gracián y Morales, and Pedro Calderón de la Barca. *Conceptismo* also was a pervasive fascination for Góngora, whose many admirers and imitators applied the word *gongorismo* to his uniquely complex melding of *culteranismo* and *conceptismo*. Góngora's famous style is displayed conspicuously in *The Solitudes*. His complexity, obscurity, Latinizations, and neologisms were denounced by some contemporaries such as Quevedo, despite his use of his own version of *conceptismo*, and Lope de Vega Carpio. Vega Carpio, it should be acknowledged, sometimes emulates Góngora's style. For centuries, Góngora's writings have been mined by critics and commentators who, perhaps only in the first quarter of the twentieth century, began a consistent interpretation of his intentions.

Góngora's great aspiration was to so expand the possibilities of Spanish poetry that the Spanish language could reach the same state of "perfection and sublimity" he believed characteristic of Latin, and he believed that in *The Solitudes* he was accomplishing his goal. Indeed, he is said to be the particular voice that fully and finally changed Spanish literature at a time when the readership was demanding more from poetry. In Spanish poetry, one idiom had until Góngora's time prevailed—the Italianate, in accord with Renaissance poetic dictates. With the publication of *The Solitudes* and *Fábula de Polifemo y Galatea*, a new school of poetry was introduced, and few if any poets of Góngora's language have not since been influenced by his aristocratic, elevated poetic style.

The first modern edition of *The Solitudes* was brought out in 1927, the tercentenary of Góngora's death. In *The Solitudes*, a poem of about two thousand lines written in the *silva* meter (seven- and eleven-syllable lines in free pattern),

Góngora defies convention and takes as his subject matter the exact opposite of what was expected in Spanish letters in his time. Instead of using the highest level of poetic diction to praise the most heroic and noble of subjects, Góngora employs it to praise the beauties of nature and the virtues of the country and of natural life, while deprecating the artificiality and the vices of the court. The characters who speak with wisdom and live with integrity and nobility are the peasants, not the nobility.

It is a paradox of Góngora's art that, while his focus is on the rural and the natural as the authentic and the desirable, he expresses this vision in poetry of the most complex syntax and of allusively and metaphorically dense qualities accessible only to the intellectually trained reader of poetry, and certainly not accessible to the peasants whom he extols. *The Solitudes* describes rustic life in the most ornate diction.

Many commentators on Góngora, beginning with those in the seventeenth century, have said that *The Solitudes* was to have consisted of four parts, only two of which were written, and only one of which, the first, was completed. Although much has been written on *The Solitudes*, Góngora's critics have failed thus far to determine a thematic, narrative cohesion. It may be suggested, therefore, that the poem works in an associative manner rather than in a linear, narrative manner, and that this quality, along with that of the play of language for its own sake, may have made the poem attractive to the Spanish poets of the Generation of '27.

The Generation of '27 is so named for an important year, 1927, of that group's history. This year marks a high point in the careers of many of that generation, not the year of their birth. The key event in 1927 was the observation of the third centennial of Góngora's death. Góngora's influence may be seen in the work of such members of the Generation of '27 as Vicente Aleixandre and Gerardo Diego.

The first poem of *The Solitudes* begins with a dedication to the duke of Béjar, replete with images of the hunt. The first thirty-seven lines establish the tone and set the themes of loneliness and of the questionable status of humanity in relation to nature. The poet invokes the muse, acknowledging that some parts of his work, "lonely images," will be as evanescent as the "wandering pilgrim's" footprints on the sand, while others will "live inspired." In typical Renaissance fashion, the poet then dedicates his work to the immortality of his patron, expressing the notion that the arts can make mortals immortal because it is in art that people can live on.

The plot is one thing that is not very intricate. The reader should look to the brilliance of Góngora's prosody for inspiration. There is no cleverly developed plot or characterization in the modern sense of the word. The action opens with reference to spring and to "a pilgrim of love," a nobleman cast out of court life, rejected by a young and false woman, shipwrecked, and washed up on shore thorough the empathy of the "winds and waves." He is able to move a personified nature to sympathize with him and save him from drowning. This young pilgrim serves as the observer of the entire action of both of *The Solitudes*. This is not, however, a psychological narrative, and although readers see the world through his wanderings, he is not the focus of the story. Rather, readers should observe, through the voice of the poet and the vision of the young pilgrim, the life of rural beauty and of the state of unspoiled innocence that Góngora sets before the readers to admire. Góngora states that if the poem's difficulties engage the readers, the readers may then find the truth.

The pilgrim's initial action introduces a major motif of the poem: On shore, he wanders until he sees a light in the distance, and he cries out in hope. It is his task to wander until he finds some kind of metaphorical illumination of the primary truth of the universe. He follows the light to a cottage where a band of rustic goatherds welcome him. The "fortunate retreat" of the refrain is a "pastoral temple and a floral bower," a place where "Flattery's voice is banned,/ Siren of royal courts." He stays the night, and in the morning the goatherds show him the beauties of natural vistas. All that he sees, such as vines growing over a castle in ruin, reinforces the notion that nature is enduring while things of this world are fleeting. They observe "mountain maidens" playing "melodious strings" and ornamenting themselves with roses and lilies. A bucolic procession to a wedding feast follows.

An old shepherd, whose son drowned, invites the young pilgrim (also described as a youth) to the wedding and discourses on the dangers of the sea. Most likely, this is a personal, political interjection by Góngora to show that the sea can be literally as well as figuratively consuming in its providing venues for human greed. When the procession stops by a stream, there follow several lines of praise to the beauties of nature in spring. When finally the procession reaches a village by nightfall, the village is filled with lights. The wedding ensues, and the youth enjoys watching the festivities, the young women dancing and the young men engaging in athletics. A lovely epithalamium is sung, said by many to be the high point of *The Solitudes*. The first of *The Solitudes* ends with the bride and groom going off to their wedding night. The bride is compared to a phoenix ascending over the static works of humanity, and thus becomes emblematic of the capacity of life to regenerate itself eternally.

The second part of *The Solitudes* begins at daybreak, when many of the wedding guests leave on a boat and the youth joins two fishermen on another boat. Music still plays a large part in creating atmosphere. Overall, the tone changes from one of celebration to one of contemplation. In contrast to the youth's life-affirming attitude of the first part, he sings of the sadness of star-crossed love, of how he suffered in lonely wandering for five years, and of how he wants to be buried at sea. At the home of the fishermen, they are greeted by their father and six sisters, who garden and whom the father later characterizes as competent fishers also. Another bucolic scene follows, with the father introducing the youth to the beauties of their island home and with the daughters serving a dinner outdoors among the beauties of nature. They all are relaxed and refreshed by the sounds of birdsong and water. Grace after the meal is followed by the youth's imploring the father to be content with his life. Two of his daughters, Leucipe and Cloris, are beloved of two fishermen, named Lycidas and Micón, who bemoan in song the possibility of dying of love and of being entombed in their own boats.

A personified Night, along with Cupid, the daughters, and others, are moved by the mournful singing of the fishermen. At the youth's pleadings, the father agrees to allow his daughters to marry. Góngora interjects an authorial aside: The poet speaks to Cupid of the effects of his actions.

The next morning, the youth and the two fishermen depart on a boat, from which they hear the trumpet sounds announcing a hunt. There follows a description of the hunt, of a flycatcher who leads a flock of birds away from the hunters, but who is killed by a sparrowhawk. Ravens try to trick an owl into flying during the day by blocking the sunlight to make it think it is night. The ravens envy the owl the color of his eyes. One raven is killed by hawks, and the hunters, their horses, and birds find deserted shelters. The poem stops at this point.

Góngora's great editor and critic Dámaso Alonso has shown him to be the writer in whose works all the great strains of poetry of the Spanish Renaissance reach their artistic culmination. Difficult as *The Solitudes* is to read, it rewards perseverance, especially when the reader can reach that level that reveals Góngora's great "mysterious quality," as Góngora himself described it.

Donna Berliner

Further Reading

Chemris, Crystal Anne. *Góngora's "Soledades" and the Problem of Modernity*. New York: Tamesis, 2008. An in-depth look at *The Solitudes*, describing how it addresses issues of concern to the Baroque era while also serving as a precursor to Hispanic literary modernism.

Collins, Marsha S. *"The Soledades," Góngora's Masque of*

the Imagination. Columbia: University of Missouri Press, 2002. Collins likens *The Solitudes* to a court masque, a theatrical genre that combined a variety of cultural forms.

De Groot, Jack. *Intertextuality Through Obscurity: The Poetry of Federico García Lorca and Luis de Góngora.* New Orleans, La.: University Press of the South, 2002. Compares the two Spanish poets, describing how and why obscurity is an important element in their work. Includes analysis of *The Solitudes.*

Foster, David William, and Virginia Ramos Foster. *Luis de Góngora.* New York: Twayne, 1973. Includes a chapter on *The Solitudes* and a good annotated bibliography, which has entries for several studies in English.

Guillén, Jorge. "Poetic Language: Góngora." In *Language and Poetry: Some Poets of Spain.* Cambridge, Mass.: Harvard University Press, 1961. An essay on Góngora that Guillén, one of the great poets of the Generation of '27, delivered at Harvard University.

Jones, R. O. Introduction to *Poems,* by Luis de Góngora y Argote. New York: Cambridge University Press, 1966. This edition has an introduction by a noted expert on Spanish literature.

McCaw, Robert John. *The Transforming Text: A Study of Luis de Góngora's "Soledades."* Potomac, Md.: Scripta Humanistica, 2000. McCaw argues that *The Solitudes* conveys a well-defined message that is consistent with seventeenth century Counter-Reformation philosophy. He demonstrates how that message is one of change, of material and spiritual transformation, and of a code of personal conduct.

A Son of the Middle Border

Author: Hamlin Garland (1860-1940)
First published: 1917
Type of work: Autobiography

Principal personages:
HAMLIN GARLAND
BELLE GARLAND, his mother
RICHARD "DICK" GARLAND, his father
FRANKLIN "FRANK" GARLAND, his younger brother
HARRIET GARLAND, his older sister
JESSIE GARLAND, his younger sister
DAVID McCLINTOCK, his uncle
HUGH McCLINTOCK, his maternal grandfather
PROFESSOR BROWN, principal of the Boston School of Oratory
JOSEPH KIRKLAND, a writer who encouraged Garland in Chicago
B. O. FLOWER, editor of *Arena*
WILLIAM DEAN HOWELLS, the novelist and editor who encouraged Garland in Boston

A Son of the Middle Border begins with the same incident used in "The Return of a Private," probably Hamlin Garland's most popular short story, but more than twenty-six years separates the writing of the two versions. The discrepancies between the two may be caused by Garland's habit of squeezing as much publication out of his materials as possible or by Garland's tender age when his father returned from the Civil War. There is little doubt, however, about the main lines of his life from 1865 to 1893. The repetition of material chiefly shows that the two series of works for which Garland is best known begin with the earliest remembered dramatic incident in his life and that later reflection showed him some of the depths of meaning contained in that incident. Garland was four or five years old when his father returned from the war; he was thirty when he first published his short story and fifty-seven when he published *A Son of the Middle Border.* This was the first of four volumes of family history that won the Pulitzer Prize in 1921 and reestablished his career as a writer. The other three volumes are *A Daughter of the Middle Border* (1921), the story of his marriage and life until 1914;

Trail-Makers of the Middle Border (1926), the story of his family before 1865; and *Back-Trailers from the Middle Border* (1928), the history of the family after 1914.

Although the Middle Border is Minnesota, Wisconsin, Nebraska, and the Dakotas, the appeal and range of the volumes on this area is national in implication. The story of the Garlands and McClintocks, the two sides of Garland's immediate family, reaches back across the Atlantic to Scotland and forward to the coast of California. It is the American story of nineteenth century immigration and the moving frontier. Garland is a symbol of America at the turn of the century. Born in West Salem, Wisconsin, near the geographical center of the Middle Border, he moved with his parents farther west to Iowa and South Dakota. Then, obeying the attraction of the nation's cultural centers, he moved east to Boston and New York, eventually settling in Chicago in his middle years. In the last chapters of this volume he followed another attraction to California, where he was later to spend his last days. In three other aspects he was also typical: He broke with the land and became a white-collar worker; he left the country for the city; and he was a model son, spending his savings on the unheard-of luxury of taking his parents, pioneer farmers, to visit relations in California, "The End of the Sunset Trail," as Garland calls it. Finally he established "the Garland homestead" in a little house in the old home town of West Salem, Wisconsin.

In the typical Garland way, the story of his first thirty years is an unreconciled mixture of beauty and ugliness, of delight in the success resulting from unremitting hackwork and despair at the waste of the human soul in backbreaking labor. The saddest figure in the book is not grandfather Hugh McClintock, who saw his family break up and leave him, nor Belle Garland, the writer's mother, who like many frontier women worked till she dropped. It is his Uncle David McClintock, first seen as a tremendous physical giant, the hero of the boy Garland, and last as an exhausted wreck in California. One of the most moving scenes is that in which Uncle David plays his fiddle for the last time at the family reunion in California, and Garland realizes what a fine musician was ground down by toil and by chasing the pioneer's rainbow, the promise of ever better land to the west. David McClintock stands for the countless thousands who suffered to create the nation. Garland's own parents could have shared the same fate. His father, at the end of the war a physical wreck, could have perished while trying to revive his neglected holdings. That the story of his parents ends happily is a result of Garland's interference when his father wanted to make one more shift, the fifth, to some new land in the West. The book is thus a monument to the travail of "westering," to

the grim reality behind the song that runs through the book, "O'er the hills in legions, boys." Its central ritual is the "send-off," a surprise party for those moving on.

The memoir is in two roughly even halves, the first nineteen chapters being about life on the frontier in Wisconsin, Iowa, and South Dakota. The details are similar to those in local-color work elsewhere: plowing, reaping and threshing, the smell of horses and sweat rising above the aroma of fresh biscuits, bare one-room schools, dancing, skating, riding, reading, gatherings at the local store, the ever-present fear of crippling sickness, the tragedies of burnt barns, and death. Garland's sisters die on the frontier, leaving his mother and father alone when the boys depart. The break in the memoir comes near the end of Garland's schooling, when the family spent a year in the town of Osage, Iowa. After that, the family returned to the farm and then made a final move west to South Dakota. In the meantime, Garland was drawn back to the East. After a year spent with his brother Frank exploring Boston, New York, and Washington, D.C., living on odd jobs and on a teaching spell in Ohio, he returned to South Dakota to work his quarter-section. After his brother sold his holding and left for Chicago, Garland also sold out and went to Boston. The second part of the book tells an almost incredible story of hardship, self-education, and slow success, first as a "professor" at the Boston School of Oratory under Principal Brown, then as a writer encouraged by those interested in his local-color stories, such writers and editors as William Dean Howells, James Herne, Henry George, and B. O. Flower. Most of this section is Garland's straightforward autobiography and more germane to the study of how to achieve a career by passing through journalism to literature. As is, however, the case with Garland's first piece of writing, "The Western Corn Husking," which is intended to be typical of Middle Border life, so much of the personal detail is seen either by Garland or by the reader as illuminating the case history of the Middle Borderer. This effect springs from Garland's sense of duty not only to his parents—his first literary earnings are spent on his mother's first silk dress—but even more to his people, the sons and daughters of the Middle Border.

This realization of himself as a "son of the Middle Border" came only after his first return to the West, when he met Joseph Kirkland in Chicago and was told to write fiction because he was a farmer who could speak the truth about rural life. A second visit in 1889 confirmed this determination and provided material for the stories that make up his first book, *Main-Travelled Roads: Six Mississippi Valley Stories*, published in 1891.

In Garland's story, behind the moves of the family, the daily and seasonal activities on the farm, and the slow successes in the city, stand two figures: Dick Garland, ever westering, and Belle, following faithfully. It was the pathetic image of the latter that troubled Garland during his years in the eastern cities, and it was probably his realization of the cost wives and children paid in pioneering that precipitated his first fiction. Although the vogue for his work did not last, Garland was able to recapture his audience when late in life he began his memoirs of Middle Border life. That his real story was capable of a happy ending was due in part to his own persistence but more to the realization that pioneering was not a glamorous adventure, as many Americans have viewed it. Toward the end of the story, Garland's mother sings an old frontier song, the others joining in the chorus: "We'll stay on the farm and we'll suffer no loss/ For the stone that keeps rolling will gather no moss."

When Garland was thirty-three, he asked his mother what he could bring her from the city; she told him that the thing she wanted most was a daughter—and some grandchildren.

Further Reading

Browne, Ray B. "'Popular' and Folk Songs: Unifying Force in Garland's Autobiographical Works." In *Critical Essays on Hamlin Garland*, compiled by James Nagel. Boston: G. K. Hall, 1982. All four autobiographical works are discussed to show the importance of music in Garland's life. An unusual approach to understanding Garland's work.

Foote, Stephanie. "The Region of the Repressed and the Return of the Region: Hamlin Garland and Harold Frederic." In *Regional Fictions: Culture and Identity in Nineteenth-Century American Literature*. Madison: University of Wisconsin Press, 2001. Although this chapter focuses on *Main-Travelled Roads*, Foote also discusses *A Son of the Middle Border*, comparing it to other works of American regionalism. She argues that Americans' conceptions of local identity originated with Garland and other regional fiction writers of the late nineteenth and early twentieth centuries.

Howells, William D. "*A Son of the Middle Border*, by Hamlin Garland: An Appreciation." In *Critical Essays on Hamlin Garland*, compiled by James Nagel. Boston: G. K. Hall, 1982. Howells discusses Garland's style in his earlier fictional work and then his style in his autobiography. Examines Garland's depiction of prairie life as he lived it.

Nevins, Allan. "Hamlin Garland's Trilogy." In *Critical Essays on Hamlin Garland*, compiled by James Nagel. Boston: G. K. Hall, 1982. Garland's unorthodox autobiographical style is described, along with an analysis of *A Son of the Middle Border*. The trilogy, described as a "disjointed chronicle," was not published chronologically; this unusual approach gave each work more depth.

Newlin, Keith. *Hamlin Garland: A Life*. Lincoln: University of Nebraska Press, 2008. Newlin's biography of Garland, the first to be published in more than forty years, is based in part on newly available letters, manuscripts, and family memoirs. His book discusses Garland's contributions to literature and places Garland's work within the artistic context of its time. Chapter 17 focuses on *A Son of the Middle Border*.

Pizer, Donald. "Hamlin Garland's *A Son of the Middle Border*: An Appreciation." In *Critical Essays on Hamlin Garland*, compiled by James Nagel. Boston: G. K. Hall, 1982. Discusses the theme, style, and plot, providing a full plot summary.

_____. "Hamlin Garland's *A Son of the Middle Border*: Autobiography as Art." In *Essays in American Literature Presented to Bruce Robert McElderry, Jr.*, edited by Max F. Schulz with William D. Templeman and Charles R. Metzger. Athens: Ohio University Press, 1967. Shows that Garland's earlier fiction influenced the style and content of *A Son of the Middle Border*.

The Song of Hiawatha

Author: Henry Wadsworth Longfellow (1807-1882)
First published: 1855
Type of work: Poetry
Type of plot: Folklore
Time of plot: 1500's and 1600's
Locale: Southern shores of Lake Superior

Principal characters:
HIAWATHA, a hero of the Ojibway tribe
MINNEHAHA (LAUGHING WATER), a member of the Dacotah tribe; the wife of Hiawatha
NOKOMIS, the grandmother of Hiawatha and the daughter of the Moon
MUDJEKEEWIS, the West Wind and the father of Hiawatha
WENONAH, daughter of Nokomis; Hiawatha's mother, who dies in anguish at the desertion of Mudjekeewis
GITCHE MANITO, the Master of Life

The Poem:

Weary of the constant fighting of the people, Gitche Manito, the Master of Life, calls together all the Native American tribes to remind them of their foolish ways, to try to bring peace among them, and to smoke the peace pipe with them. Although Manito has provided fertile lands, abundant streams, and forests, the groups continue foolishly to feud, to quarrel, and to fight. The Master of Life promises to send a prophet to guide and to teach his people. Should they fail to follow the prophet's wise counsel, however, they will surely perish. Removing some of the minerals from the quarry and breaking them into pieces, Manito molds the red stone into peace pipes. He instructs the warriors to plunge themselves into the stream, to remove the war paint from their faces, and to cleanse the bloodstains from their hands.

One evening at twilight, the beautiful Nokomis falls to the earth from the full moon. There, among the ferns and mosses, she bears a daughter: Wenonah. As Wenonah grows tall and lovely, Nokomis fears for her daughter and warns her to beware of Mudjekeewis, the West Wind. Wenonah fails to heed the warning and succumbs to Mudjekeewis's wooing, bearing him a son, Hiawatha. Deserted by the false and faithless Mudjekeewis, Wenonah dies from grief.

Hiawatha grows up in the wigwam of Nokomis. Their home is near the shores of Gitche Gumee, by the shining Big-Sea-Water, and near the forest. From boyhood, Hiawatha masters the crafts of the hunt, of sports, and of other arts and labors. He is a master of speed and accuracy with a bow and arrow. He wears magic deerskin mittens that give him great physical power. On his feet, he wears magic moccasins that allow him to stride a mile with each step.

Angered by the story of his father's treachery, Hiawatha vows to visit Mudjekeewis and seek revenge. Nokomis, however, warns him of Mudjekeewis's magic and cunning; she asks Hiawatha not to go. Hiawatha does not listen. He

travels to the land of the West Wind, where he fights with Mudjekeewis for three days. At last, the West Wind admits that it will be impossible for Hiawatha to kill him because Mudjekeewis is immortal. Pleased, however, with the boy's courage, Mudjekeewis sends Hiawatha back to serve his tribe as the prophet and protector that Gitche Manito promised them.

On his long journey home to the shores of Gitche Gumee, Hiawatha stops in the land of the Dacotahs to purchase arrowheads from an old man. There, Hiawatha sees Minnehaha (Laughing Water), the arrow-maker's lovely daughter. She captivates Hiawatha.

When Hiawatha returns to his people, he builds a wigwam in the forest and goes there to fast and pray. On the fourth day of his fast, as he lies exhausted on his couch, Hiawatha sees a young stranger standing before him. The youth has green plumes over his forehead and wears green and yellow garments. He informs Hiawatha that, to have his prayers fulfilled, they must wrestle the next day, and Hiawatha must prevail in the struggle.

In spite of his weakness, Hiawatha refuses the food that Nokomis brings him during the night. He is still able, however, to struggle bravely with the young stranger the following morning. At last, the stranger yields to Hiawatha and asks Hiawatha to strip away his green and yellow garments and the green plumes, to bury him, and to guard the grave. The stranger vows to leap again into the sunshine. Hiawatha faithfully follows the stranger's command to bury his body. He guards the grave. Soon, he sees the green shoot of a plant, yellow silk, and finally a matured ear of corn; this crop becomes a vital food to nourish his people.

Hiawatha shapes a canoe from the birch tree. He and his strong friend Kwasind set out on the water to try to make the streams safe for the people; they clear the water of roots, sandbars, and dead trees. Later, Hiawatha rids the lake of its greatest menace: the sturgeon. After Hiawatha and Kwasind make the river safer, Nokomis asks Hiawatha to destroy Pearl-Feather (Megissogwon); this magician is responsible for fever, pestilence, and disease.

To reach Pearl-Feather, Hiawatha must first battle the dozen serpents that guard the entrance to the wizard's domain; only then can he gain entrance. As Hiawatha approaches the serpents, he kills them with his arrows. A woodpecker instructs Hiawatha in how to overcome the magician; Hiawatha must aim his arrows at the roots of the wizard's hair. After he conquers Megissogwon, Hiawatha rewards the woodpecker by dabbing the bird's tuft of feathers with the magician's blood. From then on, the woodpecker would wear this tuft of red.

When Hiawatha tells Nokomis that he intends to make Minnehaha his wife, Nokomis urges him not to marry a Dacotah but to marry a woman of their own tribe, the Ojibways. Hiawatha politely refuses her advice, however, and assures her that the marriage will unite the two tribes and encourage peace. He travels to the land of the Dacotah to retrieve his bride.

Upon the return of Minnehaha and Hiawatha, Nokomis honors the couple with a huge feast at the wedding ceremony. Hiawatha's friend Pau-Puk-Peewis honors the couple with a dance to the sound of many instruments. Chibiabos, Hiawatha's gentle friend, sings his famous love songs; Hiawatha's friend Iagoo relates his fanciful tales at the celebration. Hiawatha's people prosper in peace; their corn crops are abundant. To enable the tribes to keep a record of their history, Hiawatha invents picture writing for them.

Sadness arrives. Evil spirits attack and kill Chibiabos while he is on a hunting trip. Kwasind dies at the hands of the fairies and the pygmies. One winter, famine strikes Hiawatha's people. Snow covers the forests and lakes so deeply that it is impossible for hunters to seek food. Hiawatha's people are starving and dying of fever. When Minnehaha dies from fever, Hiawatha mourns her death for seven days. Finally, the warmth and fertility of spring return. Life begins anew in the earth.

Rumors begin to circulate that white men in large canoes with sails are coming. Hiawatha himself sees the white men in a vision and confirms the rumors. As a leader and peacemaker, Hiawatha urges his people to welcome the strangers. Hiawatha adds the admonishment that if the people ignore his counsel, the tribes will only destroy themselves.

As Hiawatha stands by the wigwam of Nokomis one evening, three white men approach; one of these men is a priest. Hiawatha welcomes them and invites his people to hear the stories the priest tells of the Virgin Mary and her Son. That night, as the white men lie sleeping, Hiawatha tells Nokomis that the time for him to leave has arrived. Having fulfilled his promises, he leaves to travel through the portals of the Sunset, to the Land of the Hereafter.

Critical Evaluation:

The commemorative poem *The Song of Hiawatha* is neither a historically accurate nor an exact chronological account of actual events among Native Americans in the southern Lake Superior area of the United States. Instead, Henry Wadsworth Longfellow bases the narrative in part on information about Native Americans from many areas and eras; he employs myths and folktales from many cultures. His main character, Hiawatha, combines features taken from the heroes of several different tribes, such as Tarenyawago of the Iroquois, a legendary chief named Hiawatha who may have helped form the Iroquois Confederacy, and the mythical Manabazho of the Algonquin or Chippewa tribe. In addition, Longfellow employs his own creativity.

Longfellow utilized some traditional myths in his poem, incorporating stories of the people that explain phenomena they do not understand. Thus, *The Song of Hiawatha* explains how the woodpecker got its red head, how the tribes acquired corn, how picture writing began, and how the peace pipe developed. In addition, the poet borrowed some characters (fairies and evil spirits) from traditional European tales and used some of his own imaginative storytelling as well to produce his episodic poem. Longfellow mentioned in his journals and diaries that one of his sources was *Algic Researches* (1836) by Henry Rowe Schoolcraft (a supporter of the finished work). The poet also utilized the travel logs of George Caitlin and the accounts of missionary John Heckewelder's experiences among the Delaware and Huron tribes. He wrote also of the inspiration he received from a young Harvard graduate who shared with him some stories from the West.

Longfellow drew on traditional literature, incorporating its three most popular themes into his work: the picaresque (journey) theme, the survival of the unfittest theme, and the reversal of fortune theme. The picaresque theme is one that Longfellow applied liberally in *The Song of Hiawatha*. Young Hiawatha travels to the land of the West Wind to find his father. He journeys also to the land of the Dacotahs; there, he sees and falls in love with Minnehaha. Other travelers— white men from a faraway place—arrive in the land of Hiawatha's people and receive welcome. To some readers, however, Longfellow presents a rather detached, benign view of the arrival of Europeans to the land of the Native

Americans. At the end of the poem, Hiawatha suggests another trip; he tells Nokomis that he must go on a journey to the "hereafter," perhaps a reference to heaven.

Longfellow uses the traditional theme of the survival of the unfittest in *The Song of Hiawatha*. As Hiawatha is enduring days of fasting, he encounters a stranger clad in green and yellow. This newcomer insists that Hiawatha must wrestle him the following morning. Hiawatha continues his fast and is still able to engage in the contest and conquer the stranger. This triumph of the weakened Hiawatha and the gift of corn suggest that the fittest do not always endure in literature.

The reversal of fortune figures prominently in *The Song of Hiawatha*. For example, as the result of his conquest of the stranger, Hiawatha is able to change the lives of his people. The starved members of the tribes receive the gift of the corn and will find plenty in their future crops—a reversal of their fortunes.

Longfellow uses symbolism abundantly in this quasi-epic. Gitche Manito creates pipes that symbolize peace for the tribes to smoke. He also instructs them to perform other explicitly symbolic acts of peace, such as cleansing their bodies of blood and war paint. The land of the hereafter to which Hiawatha tells Nokomis that he must journey is a heaven perhaps symbolic of the Christian Heaven.

Longfellow's studies of languages and literature after his 1925 graduation from Bowdoin and his travels in Europe (1926-1929) enabled him both to promote European literature in the United States and to share American folklore on the Continent. The publication of *The Song of Hiawatha* abroad and in the United States is an example of this cultural exchange.

The Song of Hiawatha employs the unrhymed, trochaic tetrameter; this structure is suggestive of that of the *Kalevala* (1835; English translation, 1888), by Finnish poet Elias Lönnrot, which Longfellow studied during his travels. In 1855, trochaic tetrameter represented a memorable departure from the then-usual form for serious English narrative poetry: iambic pentameter. Later, Robert Frost in his "The Road Not Taken" (1916) would also use trochaic tetrameter. "Tetrameter" means that the poem has four metrical feet per line. A trochee is a metrical foot composed of a long, or stressed, syllable followed by a short, or unstressed, syllable. Thus, although some variations may be necessary, there are usually eight beats—four stressed and four unstressed—for each line of poetry: "BY the SHORES of GITCHe GUmee/ BY the SHIning BIG-Sea-WAter." Longfellow noted in a letter that trochaic tetrameter was logical for *The Song of Hiawatha* because it mimicked somewhat the standard rhythm of the Indian tom-tom. The beat of four trochees is

much like the stereotypical "TUM tum TUM tum TUM tum TUM tum" of Native American drumming. Trochaic tetrameter also suggests light, quick movement.

Longfellow demonstrates great skill in his use of this unusual meter. His scheme, however, has encouraged parodies in subsequent years. Henry Eduard Legler observed in many articles and notes that the poem is among the most parodied poems in the English language; *Hiawatha's Photographing* (1857) by Lewis Carroll is one example of such a parody. Another is *Hiawatha's Rabbit Hunt* (1941), an Academy Award-nominated Warner Bros. cartoon starring Bugs Bunny. By contrast, the traditional iambic pentameter of Longfellow's day seems to convey some gravity and makes it a logical choice for poems on solemn subjects. Readers usually read iambic lines (each of whose feet begins with an unstressed syllable and ends with a stressed syllable) more slowly than they read trochaic lines.

Longfellow was a prolific author in a variety of literary forms. His translation of Dante's *La divina commedia* (c. 1320; *The Divine Comedy*, 1802) is still in print, but poetry remains his most popular style. Although sometimes receiving criticism for its moralizing, his literary work reflects high ideals; Longfellow's involvement with the abolition movement suggests his application of these values in his own life.

Many teachers of literature consider Longfellow's *The Song of Hiawatha* as a "children's poem" that creates little interest among more mature audiences. Other critics disagree. They note that Longfellow's poem makes use of some of the features of authentic epics, including supernatural intervention, the long journey, and heroic sacrifice. Because of these elements of serious literary content, they argue, it is not primarily children's literature. Rather, *The Song of Hiawatha* carries legitimate claim to be serious literature.

Revised by Anita Price Davis

Further Reading

Arvin, Newton. *Longfellow: His Life and Work*. Boston: Little, Brown, 1963. Discusses the significance of Longfellow's conscious use of American imagery in *The Song of Hiawatha*.

Calhoun, Charles C. *Longfellow: A Rediscovered Life*. Boston: Beacon Press, 2004. Comprehensive and sympathetic biography that seeks to rehabilitate Longfellow's reputation and document his contributions to American culture and literature.

Carr, Helen. "The Myth of Hiawatha." *Literature and History* 12, no. 1 (Spring, 1986): 58-78. Notes that Longfellow uses various source materials to fit his readers' expectations. Discusses Longfellow's use of the Finnish poem *Kalevala* as the source of both certain events in the poem and the poem's rhythm, which is similar to the standard rhythm of the Indian tom-tom.

Gale, Robert L. *A Henry Wadsworth Longfellow Companion*. Westport, Conn.: Greenwood Press, 2003. Includes several hundred alphabetically arranged entries about Longfellow's individual poems, other writings, family members, associates, and other aspects of his life and work. Includes an introductory essay and a chronology.

Gioia, Dana. "Longfellow in the Aftermath of Modernism." In *The Columbia History of American Poetry*, edited by Jay Parini. New York: Columbia University Press, 1993. Argues that Longfellow's poetry fell into critical disrepute because of the revision of the American poetic canon by modernist critics. Places *The Song of Hiawatha* in the foreground of American attempts to produce a national epic.

Lyons, Rosemary. *A Comparison of the Works of Antonine Maillet of the Acadian Tradition of New Brunswick, Canada, and Louise Erdrich of the Ojibwe of North America with the Poems of Longfellow*. Lewiston, N.Y.: Edwin Mellen Press, 2002. Compares Longfellow's poems about Native Americans, including *The Song of Hiawatha*, with Acadian Canadian and Native American writing.

Trachtenberg, Alan. *Shades of Hiawatha: Staging Indians, Making Americans, 1880-1930*. New York: Hill & Wang, 2004. Examines the images of Native Americans between 1880 and 1930; draws similarities with images of immigrants. Discusses *The Song of Hiawatha* and maintains that the work remains popular because it offers an image of "good," nonthreatening Native Americans.

Waggoner, Hyatt H. "Beginnings." In *American Poets from the Puritans to the Present*. Baton Rouge: Louisiana State University Press, 1984. Argues that *The Song of Hiawatha* romanticizes the life and culture of Native Americans without resorting to the sentimentality often found in other presentations.

The Song of Roland

Author: Unknown
First published: Chanson de Roland, twelfth century (English translation, 1880)
Type of work: Poetry
Type of plot: Romance
Time of plot: c. 800
Locale: Western Europe

Principal characters:
ROLAND, a prince in Charlemagne's court
OLIVER, his friend
CHARLEMAGNE, the Holy Roman Emperor
OGIER THE DANE, Roland's friend
GANELON, a wicked courtier
BERTHA, Roland's mother

The Story:

The boy Roland grows up far from his home country and lives with his penniless mother in a cave formerly occupied by a lonely monk. Nevertheless, his mother teaches him that someday he should be a brave hero like his father, Milon, and serve with the great army of Charlemagne. When he asks his mother to tell him the story of his birth, he learns that through his father he is descended from great heroes of old, Trojan Hector on one side and Wotan, king of the Norse gods, on the other. When his father, Milon, incurs the wrath of Charlemagne for taking the king's sister, the Princess Bertha, as his wife, he goes to Italy and dies there fighting pagans in single-handed combat.

One summer, when Roland is still only a lad, he meets his friend Oliver, the son of a local prince, and the two watch the coming of the great Charlemagne into Italy, where the king is to receive the blessing of the pope at Rome. Roland is impressed with the royal pageant but not overawed. That night, he walks into Charlemagne's banquet hall and demands his own and his mother's rights. Amused by the boy's daring, Charlemagne orders that Bertha be brought to him. When the emperor recognizes his long-lost sister, he rejoices and gives her and her son a place of honor in his court.

Roland's boyhood years pass quickly and with increasing honors. At first he is merely a page in the court—attending the ladies, carrying messages, and learning court etiquette. He is permitted to accompany the king's knights during war with the Saxons, and he is present when the swan knight, of the race of Lohengrin, appears at the court of Charlemagne.

When Roland is fourteen years old, he becomes a squire and makes the acquaintance of Ogier the Dane, the son of Duke Godfrey and a hostage prince at Charlemagne's court. The two boys become great friends. When, urged on by a new queen, Ogier's father plans a revolt against Charlemagne, the emperor in retaliation threatens to kill Ogier. Roland intervenes and saves his friend's life.

When barbarians attack Rome, Charlemagne, in an effort to save the pope, ignores the rebellion of the Danes and sets off to the south, taking Ogier with him as a prisoner. The great army is assisted on its passage across the Alps by a magnificent white stag that appears and leads the army through the mountain passes.

In the battles that follow, Charlemagne's army is divided. One force, led by the cowardly son of Charlemagne and the false knight Alory, attempts to retreat, thus placing the emperor's life in jeopardy. Roland and Ogier, aided by other squires, don the garments of the cowards and save the day. Charlemagne knights them on the battlefield.

One of the pagan knights proposes a personal combat. In this encounter, Ogier and a son of Charlemagne named Charlot meet two barbarians, Prince Sadone and Karaheut. The pagans trap Ogier and threaten to put him to death, but Charlot escapes. Karaheut, who was to have fought Ogier, rebels against the unchivalrous action of his pagan prince and surrenders to Charlemagne, to be treated exactly as Ogier would be treated. Reinforcements come to the pagans, among them the giant king of Maiolgre. In a dispute over the marriage of Glorianda, a Danish prisoner, Ogier fights for Glorianda and puts his enemy to rout. Charlemagne attacks at the same time, and as a result Ogier and Roland are reunited, and the pope is restored to his throne.

Roland is invested with royal arms. His sword is the famous Durandal; his battle horn is the horn of his grandfather, Charles the Hammer. None but Roland can blow that horn. His armor is the best in the kingdom.

A new war begins when Count Gerard refuses homage to the emperor. Oliver, grandson of the count, is among the knights opposed to Charlemagne. After the French besiege the fortress of Viana for seven months, it is decided to settle the war by encounter between a champion from each army. Roland is chosen to fight for Charlemagne. Unknown to him, his adversary is to be Oliver, his boyhood friend. When the two discover each other's identity, they embrace.

A few weeks later on a boar hunt near Viana, Charlemagne is captured by Count Gerard. The two leaders declare a truce, and Count Gerard agrees to be a faithful liege man of the emperor thereafter. Roland meets Oliver's sister, Alda, and becomes betrothed to her.

At Christmastime, the princess of Cathay arrives with her brothers at Charlemagne's court. She proposes a contest between a Christian knight and her brother Argalia. If one of Charlemagne's knights is the victor, he will have her hand in marriage. If the knight is defeated, he will become a hostage. Malagis, the wizard, discovers that the princess and her brothers really seek by sorcery to destroy Charlemagne. He visits the apartment of the foreigners but is discovered by them. They complain and Charlemagne, not understanding the wizard's desire to help him, sentences Malagis to be imprisoned in a hollow rock beneath the sea forever.

The jousts begin. After Argalia defeats the first knight, the fierce Moor Ferrau begins combat. Unhorsed, he fights Argalia on foot and overpowers him. Then the princess becomes invisible, and Argalia rides away, with Ferrau in pursuit. In the forest of Ardennes he discovers Argalia sleeping, kills him without honor, and seizes his wonderful helmet. Roland, having followed them, discovers the murder of Argalia and seeks Ferrau to punish him for his unknightly deed.

Reinold of Montalban finds the princess of Cathay in the forest after he drank from the waters of the fountain of Merlin, and the effect of this water is to make him see the princess as an ugly crone. She thinks him handsome, but he feels disgust and hurries away. Roland discovers Ferrau and challenges him to combat, but the Moor suddenly remembers that his liege lord in Spain is in need of his help and he does not remain to fight with Roland. When the princess of Cathay sees Ferrau wearing her brother's helmet, she knows a tragedy occurred, and she transports herself by magic to her father's kingdom.

Roland goes on a quest to the Far East in search of the complete armor of Trojan Hector. Whether by chance or by evil design, he comes to a fountain and there drinks the water of forgetfulness. He is rescued by the princess of Cathay and fights many battles for her sake, even though she is a pagan princess.

At last he comes to the castle of the fairy queen, Morgan le Fay, where the armor of Trojan Hector is said to be hidden. Overcome for the first time, he fails to gain the armor and is ordered to return to the court of Charlemagne. He arrives home in time to help the Danes resist an invasion of their country. When Ogier's father, Duke Godfrey, summons help, Ogier and Roland set out for Denmark. The invaders flee. Ogier's father dies, but Ogier, on the advice of Morgan the Fay, renounces his rights to his father's holdings in favor of his younger brother.

On his way back to France, Roland hears of a fierce orc said to be the property of Proteus. The orc is devouring one beautiful maiden every day until Roland overcomes it and is rewarded by Oberto, the king of Ireland, whose daughter he saves.

In the meantime Charlemagne's forces are being attacked by Saracens, and Roland sets out to help Charlemagne's knights. On the way he is trapped in a wizard's castle. He is released from his captivity by Bradamant, a warrior maiden. She wins a magic ring from the princess of Cathay and is able to overcome the wizard and release all the knights and ladies he is holding prisoner in his castle.

Ferrau, losing the helmet he stole from Argalia, vows he will never again wear a helmet until he acquires Roland's, which he succeeds in doing by trickery. Roland is set upon by Mandricardo, the fierce knight to whom fortune awarded the armor of Trojan Hector. They fight for the possession of Durandal, Roland's sword, the only part of Trojan Hector's equipment that Mandricardo does not possess. At last Mandricardo is forced to flee for his life.

Roland visits the forest where the princess of Cathay and Medoro, a Moorish prince, fell in love. Some declare it jealousy for the princess, but others declare it sheer exhaustion that causes Roland to lose his mind. He casts his armor away from him and wanders helplessly through the forest. Mandricardo seizes Durandal and makes Roland his prisoner.

Astolpho and Oliver set out from the court of Charlemagne to save Roland. Astolpho journeys on the back of a flying horse to the fabulous land of Prester John. Freeing Prester John from a flock of harpies, Astolpho journeys to the rim of the moon and there sees stored up all the things lost on earth. There he finds Roland's common sense, which he brings back with him and returns to Roland so that the knight becomes his former self.

In a battle against the Saracens the wicked Ganelon betrays the knights of Charlemagne. Greatly outnumbered, they fall one by one to their enemies. Roland, unwilling to call for help, refuses to use his famous horn to summon aid, and he dies last of all. Charlemagne, discovering the dead hero, declares a great day of mourning. Alda, the betrothed of Roland, falls dead and is buried with many honors. Then Charlemagne dies and is buried with great pomp. Only Ogier the Dane remains, and it is said that Morgan le Fay carried him to Avalon where he lives in company with Arthur of the Round Table. It is also said that Charlemagne dwells inside a vast mountain cave with all of his heroes gathered around him. There they wait for the day when they shall march out to avenge the wrongs of the world.

Critical Evaluation:

The Song of Roland is loosely associated with the chivalric romance literature—the adventure narratives—of medieval France. The romance is divided into three types on the basis of content. The first concerns matters of Britain and deals with Arthurian legend and Celtic lore. The second concerns matters of antiquity and takes its cue from the legends of Thebes, the legends of Troy (such as Geoffrey Chaucer's *Troilus and Criseyde*, c. 1382), and the legends about Alexander the Great. The third concerns France and focuses on stories of Charlemagne and his circle, as well as on stories of William of Orange, drawn from the *chansons de geste*. It is in this category that *The Song of Roland* is important, for it is, properly speaking, a "song of great deeds."

Chansons de geste are epic in nature, although the precise origins of the form are unknown. A popular literary form between the eleventh and thirteenth centuries, they were written in French verse, as were the early romances; late romances were written in prose, using first a ten-syllable, then a twelve-syllable (Alexandrine) line and assonance. Rhyme was substituted for assonance in the late *chansons*. The lines are grouped in stanzas—called *laisses* or *tirades*—of varying lengths, and series of *chansons* developed into story cycles dealing with a particular person, such as Charlemagne, or a particular theme, such as the conflict between Christians and Saracens. Like the classical epics, the *chansons de geste* concentrate, as the term implies, on battles, heroic feats, and knightly ideals. Little notice is paid to women or the theme of love. These tales furnished the material for the medieval romance, where, however, the emphasis shifts from the heroic to the chivalric, from war to love, and from tragic seriousness to lighthearted adventure. The *Song of Roland* is a narrative of knights in battle, but Lodovico Ariosto's sixteenth century *Orlando furioso* (1516, 1521, 1532; English translation, 1591) concerns a smitten Roland (Orlando) gone mad over his hopeless infatuation with the faithless Angelica, the princess of Cathay.

Some verification for the events narrated in *The Song of Roland* is provided in the *Annales regni Francorum* of Einhard (or Eginhard), Charlemagne's biographer and chronicler. On this basis, it is possible to pinpoint the essential Roland story as a Basque ambush, in 778, of the rear guard of Charlemagne's army during a retreat through the Pyrenees. One unusual aspect of the story is that it tells of a defeat; although defeat was not a total stranger in the epic world of *chansons de geste*, the heroic ambience that pervaded them precluded an emphasis on defeat. Among the scholars who have suggested explanations for the apparent anomaly, one traces the place names mentioned in the poem to the pilgrimage route to the shrine of St. James of Compostella; according to this theory, clerics on pilgrimage knitted the stories of Roland's defeat into an intrinsically Christian epic, in effect, an adaptation of history to a Christian poem. Another scholar construes the poem as a tribute to courage, loyalty, patriotism, and devotion in the face of overwhelming odds. However, a third scholar approaches the problem by way of the poem's purpose: If the poem were written to glorify Charlemagne and Christianity, then Roland dies a martyr's death and Charlemagne's vengeance redounds to his credit as a defender of the faith. Whatever their other merits, these theories suggest two recurring themes in any reading of *The Song of Roland*: the religious and the heroic, both of them major preoccupations of the high Middle Ages.

The religious theme pits Christians against Saracens, imbuing the story with a strong crusading spirit. Charlemagne and his peers display most, if not all, of the seven cardinal virtues. Even the proud Roland dies humble and contrite, and Charlemagne's early indecision is resolved later in the poem when he becomes a courageous leader. The pagans, on the other hand, embody the seven deadly sins. They are treacherous and greedy, and they fight for personal glory or material gain rather than for principle or faith. In this world of black-and-white morality, there are no good pagans, and the treasonous, deceitful Ganelon is severely punished for his perfidy. By contrast, the good Charlemagne is rewarded by the direct intervention of the archangel Gabriel, who deals the pagan Saracens a final defeat by slaying their leader, Baligant, while God makes the sun stand still. Divine intervention even affects the trial of Ganelon. The Christian cause is never questioned, nor is there any doubt about its justice. The forced baptism of the Saracen captives is described without qualm, just as is the battlefield bloodshed. If contradictions appear to later readers, they certainly did not occur to the medieval mind, for religious faith—by no means the least of the cardinal virtues—obliterated any inconsistencies between, for example, the virtue of temperance and the slaughter of pagans.

The heroic theme in *The Song of Roland* is closely linked to the religious, since most heroic deeds are performed in the name of religious principle. The hero's role, however, requires dedication to ideals that have only peripheral, if any, relationship to religious precepts. Loyalty and bravery are held in high esteem, but they are such basic heroic ideals that they are more implicit than explicit in the poem. Decision of major issues, or even of major battles by single combat, is another heroic ideal that often manifests itself in the poem. In addition, the motifs of victory and defeat, treason and vengeance, weigh heavily in the balance of heroic ideals. Still

another factor, which later readers might call team spirit, is the knightly obligation to subsume individual or personal honor and glory in furtherance of a cause. Thus Roland's early pride, especially his insistence on the use of force to subdue the Saracens and his subsequent refusal to blow his horn to summon Charlemagne's aid until all are dead or dying, is eventually brought low. Finally, Roland regrets his stubborn pride in a vivid demonstration of the need for that heroic ideal, teamwork. Not all is a self-evident exercise in primitive democracy. Charlemagne's word is still law, although the most powerful peers insist on having a voice in decision making; nor is there much attention paid to morality (as distinct from ethics) or to social courtesies. In fact, a pristine system of social and political justice characterizes Charlemagne's court as an essential ingredient in the heroic ideal, quite apart from religious considerations. Thus the unique features of the heroic ideal are distinguishable from religious precepts.

The Song of Roland is a remarkable panorama of medieval life and thought, imaginatively perceived. To those who would say that it is false history, one can answer only with the cliché that fiction is often truer than history, for that is certainly the case in *The Song of Roland*. The poem affords so vivid a picture of medieval reality that its historical accuracy is irrelevant; it presents psychological, emotional, and sociological realities that transcend factual data to reach a new plateau of reality, one reflecting the spirit of the times rather than the substance. In this sense, the *Song of Roland* is, despite its ethical simplicities and its literary primitiveness, remarkably successful as a document of the medieval spirit, a characteristic that may explain its enduring popularity.

"Critical Evaluation" by Joanne G. Kashdan

Further Reading

Ailes, Marianne J. *"The Song of Roland": On Absolutes and Relative Values*. Lewiston, N.Y.: Edwin Mellen Press, 2002. Examines the ethical and religious dimensions of *The Song of Roland*. Focuses on the characters of Roland, Ganelon, and Charlemagne within the context of their religious, feudal, and familial relationships. Discusses the concepts of human and divine justice as demonstrated by Ganelon's trial and Charlemagne's victory over the Saracens.

Burland, Margaret Jewett. *Strange Words: Retelling and Reception in the Medieval Roland Textual Tradition*. Notre Dame, Ind.: University of Notre Dame Press, 2007. Analyzes four medieval texts of *The Song of Roland* that are written in French and Occitan, with particular attention to the narrative function of the characters' speeches. Argues that the medieval authors of the poem and their audiences understood the battle of Roncevaux and the years following it as an appropriate story in which to include commentaries about contemporary issues.

Haidu, Peter. *The Subject of Violence: The "Song of Roland" and the Birth of the State.* Bloomington: Indiana University Press, 1993. Analyzes *The Song of Roland* as a "beginning moment" in the genealogy of Western culture, a time when Western subjectivity arose alongside a new image of the social body. Combines narrative semiotics and sociocultural history to explain how this change is reflected in the Roland text.

Kibler, William W., and Leslie Zarker Morgan, eds. *Approaches to Teaching "The Song of Roland."* New York: Modern Language Association of America, 2006. Provides background information about the epic, including its contexts, characters, language, and episodes. Accompanied by a compact disc with sung performances of the poem.

Reed, J. "The Passage of Time in *La Chanson de Roland*." *Modern Language Review* 87, no. 3 (July, 1992): 555-567. Analyzes the obvious and submerged references to the passage of time in *The Story of Roland* and concludes that the poem spans a period of thirteen days.

Short, Ian. *"La Chanson de Roland."* In *the New Oxford Companion to Literature in French*, edited by Peter France. New York: Oxford University Press, 1995. A thorough discussion and interpretation of the epic. Discusses the historical context for the work as well as describing variations among the extant sources.

Vance, Eugene. *Reading the "Song of Roland."* Englewood Cliffs, N.J.: Prentice-Hall, 1970. Analyzes Roland as a legendary character and discusses the work in the context of French epic poetry. Includes bibliography.

Song of Solomon

Author: Toni Morrison (1931-   )
First published: 1977
Type of work: Novel
Type of plot: Bildungsroman
Time of plot: 1869-1963
Locale: Detroit, Michigan

Principal characters:
MILKMAN DEAD, an African American man
MACON DEAD, his father
RUTH FOSTER DEAD, his mother
PILATE DEAD, his aunt
HAGAR, his second cousin
GUITAR BAINS, his closest friend
FIRST CORINTHIANS and LENA, his sisters

The Story:

Milkman Dead, so called because his lonely mother, Ruth Foster Dead, nursed him until he was six years old, grows up hating his family. His mother clings to her faded glory as the only daughter of Detroit's first black doctor. His father, Macon Dead, is a ruthless landlord who built a successful realty business by exploiting his black tenants in Southside (the black section of the city, also called the Blood Bank for its frequent eruptions of violence) and who abused his wife.

At age twelve, Milkman meets Guitar Bains. Guitar introduces him to Milkman's father's sister, Pilate, whom Milkman knows his father hates. Pilate supports herself, her illegitimate daughter Reba, and Reba's illegitimate daughter Hagar by making and selling bootleg wine. Milkman falls instantly in love with the beautiful Hagar, though she is five years older than he, and later maintains with her a sporadic affair that ends in tragedy.

Milkman's first visit to Pilate marks the beginning of his stumbling, almost inadvertent quest for identity. His father forbids him to visit Pilate and tries to explain his decision by telling Milkman what he can remember about his family and his own boyhood. He remembers that Milkman's grandfather, the first Macon Dead, was an illiterate slave freed at the end of the Civil War. He received his unusual name as a teenager in 1869, when a drunken Union army interviewer mistakenly combined his birthplace, Macon, and the status of his father, dead, in the space reserved for his name on his Freedmen's Bureau registration form. This first Macon Dead came north on a wagon filled with former slaves and, sometime before 1887, began building a profitable farm from nothing near the town of Danville, Pennsylvania. His son, the second Macon Dead, was born in 1891, and in 1895, his wife died giving birth to a daughter, Pilate. In 1903, the first Macon Dead was murdered by white landowners, who stole his farm. Milkman's father, then sixteen, and his aunt Pilate, then twelve, were hidden by Circe, a black cook, in her master's mansion until they could escape.

Milkman works for his father during the years of World War II, and the business prospers. During a dinner-table argument in 1953, Macon hits his wife and Milkman assaults his father. His father then explains to Milkman that he hates his wife because she and her father, the late Dr. Foster, carried on an incestuous affair. Milkman's mother denies the affair and tells Milkman that his own father, her husband, tried to abort him. Milkman's friend Guitar tells Milkman that he joined the Seven Days, a secret society that avenges murdered African Americans.

Disturbed by these revelations, Milkman begs his father to stake him to a new start, inadvertently mentioning a green bag, which Pilate calls her inheritance, hanging in Pilate's house. Startled, Macon tells Milkman how he and Pilate hid in a cave after the murder of their father, how he fought with and killed a white man also hiding in the cave, and how he and Pilate found a fortune in gold while hiding the body. Macon wanted to steal it, but Pilate stopped him. Macon suspected that the gold was in Pilate's bag, that she returned and stole the gold for herself. Milkman and Guitar, who plan to use his share of the gold to bankroll the Seven Days, steal the bag, but it contains nothing but bones, which Pilate says belong to the white man Macon killed in the cave. Haunted by guilt, she retrieved them months after the killing. Milkman then goes to Pennsylvania to recover the gold.

In Pennsylvania, Milkman finds the cave but not the gold and learns that his grandfather's body, buried in a shallow grave by his murderers, was washed out by the river and was later thrown into the cave, which means that the bones in Pilate's bag are actually her father's. Milkman then looks for the gold in the tiny hamlet of Shalimar, Virginia, where Pilate lived for a time after her father's death. Guitar, thinking Milkman is trying to cheat the Seven Days by keeping all the gold for himself, follows and tries to kill Milkman, but Milkman fights him off. In Shalimar, Milkman hears children singing a song that reminds him of a song he heard Pilate sing, except the children sing about "Solomon," and Pilate sang about "Sugarman." From local residents Milkman begins piecing together his lost family history and discovers that the children's song is that family history. The hero of the

song is an African named Solomon who can fly. Solomon tries to carry his twenty-first child, a boy named Jake, home to Africa, but drops the boy and goes on alone. That boy is Milkman's grandfather, Jake Solomon, renamed Macon Dead in 1869.

Milkman goes home, returning to Shalimar with Pilate and the bones of his grandfather, which they bury at Solomon's Leap, the spot from which legend claims Solomon had flown. The obsessed Guitar, hiding in the woods, fires a rifle at Milkman, but misses, killing Pilate instead. Milkman charges Guitar, and the story ends with the two locked in mortal combat.

Critical Evaluation:

The first African American to receive the Nobel Prize in Literature (1993), Toni Morrison has achieved a place in the first rank of American writers and is considered by many critics the greatest American novelist of the late twentieth and early twenty-first century. Born Chloe Anthony Wofford in 1931, Morrison earned a bachelor of arts degree from Howard University in 1953 and a master of arts degree from Cornell University in 1955, writing her master's thesis on the theme of suicide in the fiction of William Faulkner and Virginia Woolf, whose influence is apparent in her novels. She later taught at Howard and at the State University of New York at Purchase and served as a senior editor at Random House. She received a National Book Award nomination in 1975 for her second novel, *Sula* (1973), the National Book Critics Circle Award in 1977 for her fourth novel, *Song of Solomon*, and the Pulitzer Prize in 1988 for her fifth novel, *Beloved* (1987). Perhaps more than any other writer, Morrison is responsible for asserting the influence of African American literature and culture on American culture as a whole. She uses modernistic techniques such as multiple narrators, interior monologues, and discursive, nonchronological narration, so Morrison's fiction is highly complex, but because she possesses a rare skill in breathing life into settings and characters, her prose is also highly readable. *Song of Solomon* combines these qualities in a narrative that frequently employs the grotesque and occasionally the bizarre, yet seldom strains credulity. Telling the story of one man's quest for identity, the novel explores several important African American themes.

The primary theme of the novel is gaining identity through the recovery of a stolen and a forgotten past. Multiple narrators in *Song of Solomon* reveal the plot slowly, as Milkman learns his own story piecemeal from his father, his mother, Guitar, Pilate, and the people he meets in Pennsylvania and in Virginia on his search for the lost gold. In one sense these characters serve as guides on a journey in the long tradition of the epic quest in Western literature. In another sense, they are red herrings, tempting the reader to a misreading of the novel just as Western materialism tempts Milkman and his family to misread their own history, from which they are cut off by slavery, by the drunken Union Army officer's accidental renaming of Milkman's grandfather, and by their quest for a materialistic white lifestyle. Milkman's parents and sisters have little knowledge of their history. Like many African Americans, they derived their identities from absence rather than presence. They are, after all, the Deads, they live on Not Doctor Street, and their values are borrowed from the dominant white culture. Milkman's mother, Ruth Foster Dead, is known chiefly as Dr. Foster's daughter, and her family history seems to begin with her father. Milkman's father, Macon Dead, remembers very little of his heritage but, like his father, embraces the American values of rugged individualism and the relentless pursuit of profit. He disowns Pilate, evicts Guitar Bains's family from one of his rental properties because they owe four dollars in back rent, coldly demands that the deranged Porter pay his rent before committing suicide, and develops lakeshore vacation homes in which other middle-class black families isolate themselves from the African American community. Milkman's middle-aged, unmarried sisters, Corinthians and Lena, are defined chiefly by the absence of husbands. Milkman himself acquires his own identity from his mother's nursing and from his father's success in business. In seeking Pilate's gold, he seeks his own identity through the materialistic success valued by his father.

The gold, like the quest motif, is a red herring, one of many in the novel. Milkman finds no gold but instead discovers his own identity through a rite of passage in Shalimar, Virginia, where he becomes a warrior (he fights a local man with a broken bottle) and a hunter (the locals take him raccoon hunting, but they kill a fiercer animal, a bobcat). He becomes a part of a community (nearly everyone in Shalimar is surnamed Solomon, the real surname of Milkman's grandfather), and for the first time he gives and receives love. He also learns that the real gold in Shalimar is his African heritage, recovered through his rite of passage and through the song of the children. The novel's Old Testament title, *Song of Solomon*, is itself a red herring. It refers not to the Bible of the dominant white culture but to African American folklore. It allows the reader to experience vicariously Milkman's epiphany. Milkman's journey is not an epic quest in the Western tradition but a rediscovery of African roots.

Craig A. Milliman

Further Reading

Christian, Barbara. *Black Feminist Criticism: Perspectives on Black Women Writers*. New York: Pergamon Press, 1985. This compilation of criticism and commentary on literature by African American women addresses literature by Toni Morrison, Alice Walker, Gloria Naylor, and Gwendolyn Brooks. The book is composed of essays that include extensive analyses of individual works as well as examinations of common traits found in this literature. Each essay contains many explanatory notes and lists of sources.

Ferguson, Rebecca Hope. *Rewriting Black Identities: Transition and Exchange in the Novels of Toni Morrison*. Brussels, Belgium: Peter Lang, 2007. Examines Morrison's first eight novels, focusing on her depiction of the complex layers of African American identity. Analyzes these novels from the perspectives of feminism, poststructualism, and race-related theory. Includes a chapter on "Call and Response in *Song of Solomon*."

Furman, Jan, ed. *Toni Morrison's "Song of Solomon": A Casebook*. New York: Oxford University Press, 2003. Collection of essays analyzing various aspects of *Song of Solomon*, including discussions of the quest for and the discovery of identity in the novel, the depiction of the South, and the theme and tradition of naming in the book.

Gates, Henry Louis, Jr., and K. A. Appiah, eds. *Toni Morrison: Critical Perspectives Past and Present*. New York: Amistad Press, 1993. Includes Valerie Smith's argument that *Song of Solomon* invalidates Western concepts of identity and family, replacing those concepts with an African sense of community.

Harris, Trudier. *Fiction and Folklore: The Novels of Toni Morrison*. Knoxville: University of Tennessee Press, 1991. Harris argues that *Song of Solomon* relies on African American folklore rather than Western mythology for its meaning. Solomon's ability to fly, though it seems based on the story of Daedelus and Icarus, actually derives from African American myth.

McKay, Nellie Y., comp. *Critical Essays on Toni Morrison*. Boston: G. K. Hall, 1988. Includes three essays on *Song of Solomon*: Kathleen O'Shaughnessy traces the importance of community, Gary Brenner shows the novel's departures from Western literary traditions and from contemporary feminism, and Genevieve Fabre argues that the novel is a celebration of storytelling.

Morrison, Toni. Interview by Claudia Tate. In *Black Women Writers at Work*, edited by Claudia Tate. New York: Continuum, 1983. This interview serves as an excellent source of information about Morrison's writing habits and techniques. Morrison discusses the beliefs and biases that shape the presentation of her ideas.

Patraka, Vivian, and Louise A. Tilly, eds. *Feminist Re-Visions: What Has Been and Might Be.* Ann Arbor: Women's Studies Program, University of Michigan, 1983. This collection includes essays that compare narrative techniques. The critics discuss Morrison's use of naming, legend, and myth.

Pryse, Marjorie, and Hortense J. Spillers, eds. *Conjuring: Black Women, Fiction, and Literary Tradition.* Bloomington: Indiana University Press, 1985. The list of contributors to this collection of critical studies includes Claudia Tate, Gloria Hull, Bernard Bell, and others. They look at the literature of African American women, paying close attention to historical circumstances that control and limit the lives of the characters. Specifically, the contributors to this collection of essays discuss social conditions in the United States and the effects these conditions had on the writers and their works.

Samuels, Wilfred D., and Clenora Hudson-Weems. *Toni Morrison.* Boston: Twayne, 1990. Includes a brief biography and discussions of each of her first five novels, stressing *Song of Solomon*'s concern with self-affirmation as the key to identity.

Tally, Justine, ed. *The Cambridge Companion to Toni Morrison.* New York: Cambridge University Press, 2007. Collection of essays examining all aspects of Morrison's career. In addition to analyses of individual novels, including "*Song of Solomon* and *Tar Baby*: The Subversive Role of Language and the Carnivalesque" by Joyce Hope Scott, other essays provide more general discussions of the language and the narrative technique in her novels, the critical reception for her work, and her works of social and literary criticism.

The Song of the Lark

Author: Willa Cather (1873-1947)
First published: 1915
Type of work: Novel
Type of plot: Impressionistic realism
Time of plot: Late nineteenth and early twentieth centuries
Locale: Colorado, Chicago, and New York

Principal characters:
THEA KRONBORG, a young singer
DR. HOWARD ARCHIE, her friend and adviser
PROFESSOR WUNSCH, a music teacher
ANDOR HARSANYI, a concert pianist
FREDERICK OTTENBURG, a wealthy art patron
TILLY KRONBORG, Thea's aunt

The Story:

Thea Kronborg is the daughter of the Swedish Methodist pastor in the small town of Moonstone, Colorado. She is a tall, fair girl with grave, candid eyes, and her shy awkwardness hides restless depths of thought and feeling. Although she grows up in a lively household of brothers and sisters, she has no real friends among children her own age. Of her family, only her aunt, Tilly Kronborg, seems to understand her; but Tilly is so ridiculous in her speech and in her actions that neighbors only laugh when she tells them that the day is coming when Thea will make Moonstone sit up and take notice.

One of her few friends is Dr. Howard Archie, the town physician, who, when she was eleven, saved Thea's life during an attack of pneumonia. He is unhappily married to a mean-spirited woman who wants only three things in life: to have her cigar-smoking husband away from home as much as possible, to keep her house closed against dust, and to live on food from cans. Having no children of his own, Dr. Archie loves Thea in a fatherly way, and he often wonders what will become of a girl so passionate and determined.

Another friend of her childhood is gruff, disreputable old Professor Wunsch, her music teacher. A drunkard, but at one time a talented pianist, he drifted casually into Moonstone, and Fritz Kohler, the German tailor, pitied him and gave him a home. The two old men, both with memories of their younger years in Europe, become cronies. Fiercely resenting demands of family and school upon her time, he gives Thea her first glimpse of artistic endeavor, just as the Kohler house gives her a knowledge of true Old World simplicity and friendliness. Wunsch, unable to understand Thea's stubborn reserve, compares her to the yellow prickly pear blossoms of the desert.

Through these friends, she also knows Spanish Johnny from the Mexican settlement on the outskirts of town. He is another wanderer and drunkard, who always comes back to Moonstone and his patient wife to recover from his debauches. The neighbors are scandalized when the minister's daughter goes with the doctor and Wunsch to hear Spanish Johnny sing Mexican folk songs. Mrs. Kronborg, wiser than her husband, quietly allows Thea to go her own way. Still another man who takes great interest in Thea is Ray Kennedy, a railroad conductor on the Denver run. He is waiting until she grows up; then he intends to marry her. In his own way, he is the most protective of all.

Thea is fifteen years old when old Wunsch, in a drunken frenzy, smashes the furniture in the Kohler house and leaves town. After his departure, Thea takes over his pupils. A year later, Ray, injured in a wreck, dies, leaving Thea six hundred dollars in insurance. Dr. Archie advises her to take the money and study music for a winter in Chicago. After much discussion, the Kronborgs agree, if the doctor will take her there and get her settled.

In Chicago, living in cheap rooms and earning extra money by singing in a church choir, Thea is homesick for the sand dunes and deep, silent snows of Moonstone. She hates the city, but she works hard for Andor Harsanyi, under whom she studies. Like Wunsch, the brilliant young musician is baffled by qualities of Thea's imagination and will. He is almost in despair over her when he discovered that her real talent is in voice. Relieved yet sorry, he tells her that she will never make a great pianist. She might, however, become a great singer.

The next summer, Thea goes back to Moonstone. There she disturbs her family by refusing to sing at the funeral of Maggie Evans, a neighbor. Persuaded by her mother, she finally consents. Later, she shocks the town and disgusts her brothers and sisters by going to a party in the Mexican village and singing with Spanish Johnny and his friends. Returning to Chicago, she studies under Madison Bowers, a teacher whom she both admires and dislikes. At his studio, she meets for the first time Fred Ottenburg, son of a rich brewer and an amateur musician. Bowers is cynically amused that the wealthy young man is attracted to the strange girl from the West. Through Ottenburg's influence, Thea is given singing engagements at the parties of his fashionable friends.

That winter, Thea catches a severe cold. Her convalescence is slow, and she feels weak and dispirited. Ottenburg, concerned for her welfare, urges her to go away for a rest at his father's ranch in Arizona. There Thea discovers a West different from the crude, vulgar Moonstone she knows. Prowling among the cliff dwellers' ruins in Panther Canyon,

she feels herself part of an older West, a land closer to the everyday simplicities of sun, wind, and water. Thoughts of those primitive people arouse her own half-awakened nature; the desert country, ancient but filled with relics of human endeavor, give her a realization of art as form given to hope and experience.

Rested, and grateful to Ottenburg, she accepts his proposal of marriage when he arrives at the ranch. On the way to Mexico, however, she learns that he already has a neurotic, disabled wife. Hurt and shocked, she refuses his offers of assistance, borrows money from Dr. Archie, and goes to Germany for further study.

Years pass. By that time, Dr. Archie is a widower, his wife having been killed when some cleaning fluid exploded. He moved to Denver to take charge of some mining investments that prospered. From time to time, reports reach him of Thea's progress abroad, and he is pleased when Ottenburg brings word that she sang Elisabeth at the Dresden Opera. He alone understands why Thea, at a critical point in her career, is unable to return to Moonstone for her mother's funeral.

He is in New York on that great night when the sudden illness of a famous singer gave Thea her chance to sing Sieglinde in *Die Walküre* (1856) at the Metropolitan Opera House. He and Ottenburg, whom Thea forgives, hear the performance together, both pleased and proud because they are the two men who meant most in her career.

By 1909, Tilly is the last Kronborg in Moonstone. She never tires of boasting to her neighbors about Thea's successes and her marriage to wealthy Ottenburg after his wife's death. Best of all, she likes to remind the townspeople that Thea once sang in Moonstone at Maggie Evans's funeral.

Critical Evaluation:

The West and the past—one is the physical background of Willa Cather's writing, the other is its spiritual climate. Against her chosen backgrounds, she projects her stories of pioneers and artists, men and women of simple passions and creative energies. The very nature of her material determines her own values as an artist: to find in the people of her creation those realities of the spirit that are almost overwhelmed in the complexity and confusion of the present. *The Song of the Lark*, which carries Thea Kronborg from an obscure Colorado town to the concert and opera stage, is a novel rich and sustaining in homely realism. The character of Thea is drawn in part from Olive Fremstad, a Swedish American opera singer, but there is much of Cather's own story in the experiences of her heroine. Like Thea, she made common things and disciplined effort the shaping influences of her art. The story of the artist in America is usually sentimentalized or idealized. This novel is a notable exception.

Though it never shared the success of some of Cather's other works, *The Song of the Lark* is nevertheless a rewarding and significant part of the Cather canon. The novel has been criticized, and perhaps justly so, for its unselective use of detail and episode in developing Thea's story; yet such thoroughness is also what has allowed Cather to convey so fully to the reader Thea's passionate spirit for living. Thea's growth as an artist is shown in the context of two themes that run throughout Cather's works: the invigorating, spiritual significance of the Southwest and its history, and the alienation of the artistic temperament from conventional life and values. *The Song of the Lark* is essentially a chronicle of the delicate awakening of the artistic sensibility and its consequent struggle to escape the limitations of a commonplace environment.

This theme is introduced in the novel through Thea's early opposition to the standards and values of Moonstone. The young girl's friends are those who, like Thea herself, display a quality of mind and spirit for life that Moonstone conventionality interprets as either wild and eccentric or blatantly selfish. The lifestyles of Dr. Archie, old Wunsch, Ray Kennedy, and Spanish Johnny are in marked contrast to the provincial conformity and petty materialism embodied in the likes of Mrs. "Livery" Johnson or the community's endorsement of Thea's less talented rival, Lily Fisher. Although Thea's talent and ardent nature set her apart from the rest of her community, she finds happiness and fulfillment in expanding her awareness of things. Visiting the countryside with Dr. Archie, learning German from Wunsch, or singing songs with Spanish Johnny, she is progressively introduced to a broader sense of values and culture than the narrow environment of Moonstone can supply. Her later experience with the ancient pottery at the cliff dwellings in Arizona only makes Thea more conscious of the immense aspirations and possibilities within her own spirit and the human spirit in general.

Seeking to develop her own aspirations to their fullest, Thea becomes more and more dedicated to the disciplines of her art. By the end of the novel, her commitment leaves almost no time in her life for other people, but she fulfills the artistic impulse that drove her beyond the limitations of a small-town environment and into a world of intense, rapturous feeling for the quality of life. Her disciplined, self-imposed isolation from the conventional world is the price the serious artist must pay for his expansive spirit.

When *The Song of the Lark* was reissued in 1932, Cather revised the novel rather heavily in an attempt to reduce wordage and tighten its style. Most of the changes occurred in the later parts of the book, where the author felt that, because Thea's struggle was now over, the dramatic pull of the story necessarily lagged into the anticlimactic. None of these changes, however, appreciably affect the novel's content or thematic statement.

Further Reading

Bender, Bert. "Sex and Evolution in Willa Cather's *O Pioneers!* and *The Song of the Lark.*" In *Evolution and "the Sex Problem": American Narratives During the Eclipse of Darwinism.* Kent, Ohio: Kent State University Press, 2004. Examines how Darwinian theories about the emotions and about social and sexual selection were an essential part of American fiction—including the work of Cather—from the late nineteenth century through the 1950's.

De Roche, Linda. *Student Companion to Willa Cather.* Westport, Conn.: Greenwood Press, 2006. An introductory overview of Cather's life and work aimed at high school and college students and the general reader. Discusses character development, themes, and plots in six novels, with chapter 5 focusing on *Song of the Lark.*

Funda, Evelyn I. *Reading Willa Cather's "The Song of the Lark."* Boise, Idaho: Boise State University Press, 1999. Provides a concise interpretation of the book. Includes bibliography.

Giannone, Richard. "The Lyric Artist." In *Critical Essays on Willa Cather,* edited by John J. Murphy. Boston: G. K. Hall, 1984. Guides the reader through *The Song of the Lark* with short, well-chosen quotations and unifying interpretation. The chapter is preceded by an interesting, anonymous *New Republic* review published in 1915.

Middleton, Jo Ann. *Willa Cather's Modernism: A Study of Style and Technique.* Madison, N.J.: Fairleigh Dickinson University Press, 1990. Middleton's discussion of Cather's deceptively simple style uses *The Song of the Lark* repeatedly as an example. Careful indexing allows the reader to locate these references.

Monroe, Stephen. "Shame and Rage: A Generative Pairing in Willa Cather's *The Song of the Lark.*" In *Violence, the Arts, and Willa Cather,* edited by Joseph R. Urgo and Merrill Maguire Skaggs. Madison, N.J.: Fairleigh Dickinson University Press, 2007. Monroe's paper originally was delivered at the Tenth Annual Willa Cather International Seminar in 2005. Seminar participants examined Cather's representation of violence in her depictions of war, suicide, sexual trauma, shame, and rage.

Rosowski, Susan J. *The Voyage Perilous: Willa Cather's Romanticism.* Lincoln: University of Nebraska Press, 1986.

Gives a good sense of how *The Song of the Lark* fits into Cather's canon. Rosowski devotes much of one chapter to the novel.

Schwind, Jean. "Fine and Folk Art in *The Song of the Lark*." In *Cather Studies*. Vol. 1, edited by Susan J. Rosowski. Lincoln: University of Nebraska Press, 1990. Investigates the artistic forces at work in the novel. Focuses on the meaning of the title and importance of the epilogue.

Thomas, Susie. *Willa Cather.* New York: Barnes & Noble, 1990. Devotes much of chapter 2 to her analysis of *The Song of the Lark* as the most overtly Wagnerian of all of Cather's novels.

The Song of the World

Author: Jean Giono (1895-1970)
First published: Le Chant du monde, 1934 (English translation, 1937)
Type of work: Novel
Type of plot: Impressionistic realism
Time of plot: Early twentieth century
Locale: Basses-Alpes region, France

Principal characters:
ANTONIO, a man of the river
SAILOR, a woodcutter
JUNIE, his wife
DANIS, their son
MAUDRU, a wealthy ox tamer
GINA, his daughter
CLARA, a blind woman
JÉRÔME or MONSIEUR TOUSSAINT, Junie's brother

The Story:

For years the man called Sailor lives with his wife Junie and their twin sons in a woodcutters' camp in the forest beyond Christol's Pass. Shortly after one of the twins, who was married and had a child, is killed by a landslide in a clay pit, the other red-haired twin goes north into the Rebeillard country to cut fir trees and raft them down the river. When he fails to return two months later, Junie becomes alarmed and sends her husband to ask help of Antonio, who lives on the isle of jays.

Antonio is a fisherman, a fierce, hardy, yet strangely compassionate fellow, wise in the ways of streams and the weather. He carries three scars on his body—a knife wound, a man's bite, and the slash of a billhook—for he is as reckless in a fight as he is daring in making love to the maidens and wives of the river villages. Men call him Goldenmouth. He promises to help Sailor search the river and creeks for some sign of Danis, the red-haired twin.

The men start early the next morning, Antonio on one side of the stream, Sailor on the other. Both are armed, for the Rebeillard region is wild country beyond the gorges. There Maudru, the ox tamer, keeps his great herds, and his word is the only law. The wind blowing from the north is chill with frost as the two men work their way up the river. Although they find no sign of Danis or his logs, they see some of Maudru's drovers and hear their horns, which seem to signal the coming of strangers into the district. Antonio wonders why Maudru's men are on watch.

At nightfall, he swims across the river to join Sailor. While they sit by a fire that they build to warm themselves and to cook their food, they hear the moaning of a creature in pain. Investigating, they find a young woman suffering in childbirth. Following the directions of a drover who was spying on their fire, they carry her and her newborn child to the house of a peasant woman called the mother of the road. The next morning Antonio learns that the woman he helped is unmarried, blind, and named Clara. When he sees her for the first time in the daylight, he loves her. That day, over the protests of Maudru's men, he kills a wild boar to provide meat for the house. Four drovers come to the house at twilight. They are sent to the fields near the river gorges to keep two travelers from leaving the country. Because Antonio and Sailor came into the district, the watchers are uneasy. While Antonio and Sailor wait to see whether the drovers will make a fight of the matter, signal beacons flash on the northern hills. From what is said, Antonio realizes that the red-haired twin, for whom the whole country is searching, was sighted or captured.

Antonio asks the mother of the road to keep the blind woman for him while he and Sailor travel on toward Villevielle, where they hope to have some word of Danis' doings from Junie's brother Jérôme, the almanac vendor and healer. On the way, they overtake a cart carrying Mederic, Maudru's wounded nephew. Danis shot him, Antonio learns from a drover, and the young herder is likely to die. For that reason, beacons are burned on the hills.

Years before, Maudru's sister, Gina, ran away from her brother's farm at Puberclaire with twenty-three of his drovers and took the Maladrerie estate as her own. There she ruled her fields and her bed, and she bred her sons as she did her bulls. Mederic is the last of her children. Maudru married and had a daughter, Gina. It is planned that the cousins should marry, but Danis shot old Gina's son and carried off her namesake. While Maudru's men are searching for the fugitives, the wounded man is being carried to Puberclaire to die.

Saying they wish to visit the healer of Villevielle, Antonio and Sailor enter the old medieval town and find the house of Jérôme, a hunchback whom the Rebeillard folk call Monsieur Toussaint. Danis and young Gina are hiding in his house. The twin cut his trees and hid the raft in Villevielle creek, where it remains. Then he stole Gina, but Maudru sent out an alarm before Danis and Gina could escape down the river. Now men watch the river and every hamlet and road. The lovers are trapped.

Winter comes early in the Rebeillard country. After the first snows, Jérôme sends a messenger to tell Junie that Danis and Sailor still live. Since they are unknown in the town, Antonio and Sailor visit the wine shops from time to time and hear the news. Gina grows fretful. Sometimes she treats Danis with great tenderness; sometimes she mocks him because he is not stronger and more clever than her father or complains because they live like cuckoos in another's house. In spite of Jérôme's efforts, Mederic dies. Antonio goes to the burial at Maladrerie and meets Maudru, a powerful, slow-spoken man. One day, Danis goes out on skis to inspect his raft and is almost captured. A short time later, three of Maudru's men, pretending to be sick, came to Jérôme's house. The inmates realize then that the fugitives are located. When he ventures out thereafter, Antonio comes and goes through passages connecting the cellars of the old houses.

One day, when there is a touch of spring in the air, Antonio and Sailor go out through the cellars and drink at an inn. Both become drunk. Antonio pursues a woman whom he mistakes for Clara and leaves Sailor alone. Sailor is confused by the brandy; it seems to him that he is young again and about to embark on a long sea voyage. Forgetting to be cautious, he never hears the two drovers who creep up behind him and stab him in the back.

Antonio returns home and discovers that Clara arrived with Jérôme's messenger. Her child died, and she no longer wishes to be alone. In his joy at seeing her, Antonio completely forgets Sailor, until Jérôme becomes alarmed by his absence. Then, with Clara's keen sense of hearing to tell them where danger might lurk in the darkened streets, Antonio and the healer search for the old man. When they find him, they carry his body back to the house and call Danis to look at his dead father. Danis is enraged. That night, he and Antonio go to Puberclaire and set fire to Maudru's barns and house. Many of his prize bulls and tame oxen die in the blaze as the great bull farm is destroyed.

The light of the burning draws off Maudru's watchers; under cover of the confusion, Danis, Gina, Clara, and Antonio start off down the flooded stream on the log raft. Below the gorges they see green on the trees; spring arrived. Danis is planning the house he will build for Gina. Antonio thinks of his life with Clara on the isle of jays. None of the travelers sees Maudru, alone on horseback, as he watches from a high peak the raft passing below him and out of sight toward the south.

Critical Evaluation:

Jean Giono's novels achieve a quality of timelessness because, in most of his work, he deliberately ignores the discoveries of modern science and mechanical inventions. Instead, he presents in his books pictures of semiprimitive and pastoral life such as survived until the mid-twentieth century in his remote region of France. Giono's feeling for nature is deeply mystical, and he attempts to bridge the worlds of inner and outer reality by the use of poetic images and metaphors. His style is vigorous and sensuous. Nowhere does he show himself a lyric novelist of the soil better than he does in *The Song of the World*, a novel that is both an exciting adventure story and a paean in praise of nature and the simple, rustic life.

Giono successfully combines his interests in the pastoral, simple life of the French peasant with the sociological issue of one's active response to human interaction and strife. Perhaps because of its theme of the maturing of the individual through social growth, *The Song of the World* is the best known of Giono's novels. His first two novels concentrated only on the individual without community; this, his third novel, expresses his love of the peasantry's commitment to preserving the family and its traditional ways, as well as his strong aversion to bloodshed and war. Giono became a pacifist after participating in the Battle of Verdun during World War I.

The Song of the World is an appropriate title for this work, which recounts the myth patterns of the great epics. Giono, in fact, was a great lover of the Latin and Greek epic forms; his favorite was Homer's *Odyssey* (c. 725 B.C.E.; English translation, 1614), which greatly influenced his writing. The obvious structural correlation is the journey motif. The journey is not only the basic pattern of myth but also the form of the epic; in this novel, all the elements of the journey theme are employed. First, there is a call to the hero, Antonio, who is widely known as Goldenmouth, to help his friend, Sailor, find a lost son. The hero accepts the call and sets forth on a journey of physical as well as spiritual trials. He is risking his life to preserve life in the sacrificial pattern associated with heroic travels. Symbolically, one of Antonio and Sailor's first encounters is with a woman giving birth to a son. They save the woman and thus the child. She is eventually the hero's prize; her love is his reward for the risk he takes to find and save her. Later, great risk is involved in saving his friend's son.

Another familiar element of the epic is the helper motif. This is present in the guise of the barmaid and, more important, in Monsieur Toussaint. As is often the case with the "helper person" in an epic, Toussaint is a hunchback, a philosopher, and a magician doctor of sorts. Although seemingly unchanged by the events in his house, he is the catalyst for change for all those involved with him.

Antonio's goal is to rescue Sailor's red-haired son. The boy marries the daughter of wealthy and powerful Maudru, who controls the whole region. Besides marrying her secretly, in wooing and winning her he slays her other suitor, the son of Maudru's sister. It is the hero's responsibility to free the boy and his bride from the domination of her father. The goal of the saga is to restore the boy to his homeland so that he may begin living as a man.

The son experiences the initiation rite essential to his developing manhood. During the course of this process, his father realizes he is dying. Giono employs Sailor's death symbolically as a commentary upon the growth of the son. It is at the death of the father that the son is finally free to act on his own behalf—free in will and bursting with power—against the obstacle to his happiness, Maudru. The son boldly risks his life to right the wrong done to his father and thus to himself. He burns all that made Maudru wealthy and leaves the man so much the poorer for his jealousy and vengefulness.

The novel comes full circle when Maudru, on the hill overlooking the river, watches the entourage of his daughter and son-in-law, and Antonio and his new bride drift down the river, just as, when Maudru was powerful, his man watched Antonio and Sailor come into the territory. This river provides life to the foursome and a renewal or rebirth of spirit as well as a socialization through marriage. The hero, formerly one who lived in a hut in the woods, dreams of creating a home

for his bride. The son, now a man, prepares to build a home for his young wife and to care for his newly widowed mother.

The style of *The Song of the World* complements its epic content. The vivid detail and economy of language provide it with a fluidity and a rhythmic tempo. Passages describing Antonio and his activities are mainly short, declarative sentences, reflecting the hero's simple, pastoral personality. Antonio's dialogue, however, reflects an eloquence and a sensitivity more lofty than is characteristic of a simple peasant. From the first, he is presented as a superior man.

The use of the three-part structural form divides the novel not only by seasons—spring, winter, and spring again—but by location, the setting forth from, absence from, and return to the homeland. Thus, the title is meaningful, not only mythically but also seasonally. One is inextricably tied to the other, as it is the seasons that evoke birth, death, and renewal.

Giono's novel urges the idea that action and risk are the price of freedom. Maudru, clinging to severity and power with an iron hand, loses the people and things he loves because he is unable to accept and respect his daughter's freedom. Giono is searching for those modes of living in which people are free to be themselves and are reunited harmoniously with nature and society.

"Critical Evaluation" by Gayle Steck

Further Reading

Badr, Ibrahim H. *Jean Giono: L'Esthétique de la violence.* New York: Peter Lang, 1998. An examination, in English, of violence in Giono's work, particularly the horror and psychological effects of war. Explains how Giono, a pacifist, used war and other forms of violence as literary motifs.

Brée, Germaine, and Margaret Guiton. *An Age of Fiction: The French Novel from Gide to Camus.* New Brunswick, N.J.: Rutgers University Press, 1957. Describes Giono as a novelist who creates private worlds to stand apart from contemporary public issues. Reads *The Song of the World* as a novel concerned chiefly with problems of love and of death.

Ford, Edward. *Jean Giono's Hidden Reality.* Lewiston, N.Y.: E. Mellen Press, 2004. An analysis of Giono's novels, in which Ford argues that the quest for faith is a continual theme. Ford also defends the works Giono wrote during World War II, arguing that he did not collaborate with the Vichy government and the Nazis, as other critics have charged.

Golsan, Richard Joseph. "Jean Giono: Pacifism and the Place of the 'Poet.'" In *French Writers and the Politics of Com-*

plicity: *Crises of Democracy in the 1940's and 1990's.* Baltimore: Johns Hopkins University Press, 2006. Golsan, who has written journal articles about Giono's collaboration with the Nazis during the German Occupation, discusses that complicity in this chapter of his book. Golsan argues that for Giono and two other French writers of the period, cooperation with the Nazis often arose from "nonpolitical" motives, such as sexual orientation, antimodern aesthetics, and distorted religious beliefs.

Goodrich, Norma L. *Giono: Master of Fictional Modes.* Princeton, N.J.: Princeton University Press, 1973. Scholarly study focusing on Giono's creative abilities and diversity of expression. Goodrich labels Giono a major figure in twentieth century fiction. She places *The Song of the World* among the significant accomplishments Giono completed during the first phase of his career.

Peyre, Henri. *French Novelists of Today.* New York: Oxford University Press, 1967. One chapter outlines Giono's literary achievements, briefly explicating the plot of *The Song of the World.* Peyre asserts that Giono uses his characters to represent forces of nature.

Redfern, W. D. *The Private World of Jean Giono.* Durham, N.C.: Duke University Press, 1967. Surveys Giono's major works, including a section on *The Song of the World.* Redfern classifies this book as a peasant novel and calls it idealistic in tone and uncluttered in plot and in style; he believes Giono intended this work to be a private epic.

Smith, Maxwell. *Jean Giono.* New York: Twayne, 1966. Discusses *The Song of the World* in a chapter devoted to Giono's epic novels. Describes ways in which the novelist achieves unity in a work of great scope and diversity.

Songs of Innocence and of Experience

Author: William Blake (1757-1827)
First published: Songs of Innocence (1789) and *Songs of Innocence and of Experience* (1794)
Type of work: Poetry

Songs of Innocence and of Experience is the foundation of the work of one of the greatest English poets and artists. The two sets of poems reveal what William Blake calls "the two contrary states of the human soul." The presentation of these states is deceptively simple, literally childlike in the "Innocence" poems. In both series, he offers clues to deeper meanings and suggests ways out of the apparent trap of selfhood, so that each reading provides greater insight and understanding, not only to the poems but also to human life.

The first poem in the "Innocence" series, "Introduction," establishes the pastoral background of most of the poems. The speaker in the poem (not Blake) has been playing tunes on a pipe in a pleasant valley when he or she is stopped by a vision of a child on a cloud, perhaps an angel, who functions as an encouraging muse. The child asks the pipe player to pipe a song about a lamb, then asks that the song be repeated and weeps. The child asks the speaker to sing a song, then asks that the songs be written "In a book, that all may read." The child disappears, and the speaker makes a pen from a reed, makes ink by staining water, and writes "happy songs/ Every child may joy to hear."

The last lines establish the apparent audience of *Songs of Innocence*: children. The poems in this series have a simple vocabulary and meter and can be read, and at least partly understood, by small children. This collection is not aimed exclusively at children, however. The child on the cloud tells the speaker to write so that "all may read"; it is the speaker who assumes that "every child may joy to hear" and restricts his or her audience to children. Perhaps "child" does not mean children but everyone, in the sense that all are children of God. Thus, in the first poem, the apparently simple vocabulary leads to complex interpretations.

"Introduction" also describes and wryly comments on Blake's technique. At first, the speaker is playing music, an evanescent expression that only the speaker and the child on the cloud hear. The child asks the speaker to sing songs that can be recorded in a book, specifically a book written and decorated with natural colors. The child, who acts as inspiration, vanishes when the hard work of composing and painting the volumes begins. Also, music strikes the senses directly, but the use of words restricts the audience to those who know and can understand a particular language. *Songs of Innocence*, which appears to be addressed to innocent children, actually requires some sophistication to be read, much less understood.

The next two poems, "The Shepherd" and "The Ecchoing Green," continue the pastoral atmosphere established by the first poem, but there is an ominous element at the end of the second poem. An old man has been watching the children at play, and they note that he and the other older people remember that they used to play like that in their youth. In the last line, the area is no longer "ecchoing" but "darkening."

The light apparently returns again in "The Lamb," which returns to the biblical idea of the good shepherd of "The Shepherd." A child asks a lamb if the lamb knows who made it, then informs the lamb that "He is called by thy name/ For he calls himself a Lamb./ He is meek, & he is mild./ He became a little child." The child is referring to Jesus, but does not explain why Jesus is called a lamb. Adults know that Jesus was the sacrificial lamb of God, who paid for the sins of humanity with death, like those of the animal sacrifices of the Old Testament.

The source of the description becomes clear in the next poem, in which "The Little Black Boy" cries that "White as an angel is the English child:/ But I am black, as if bereav'd of light." Instead of telling the child that he should be proud of who he is, the boy's mother tells him that this physical life is a trial and preparation for the next, spiritual, world. The little boy then imagines a life after death in which the white child will accept him.

A child's acceptance of a cruel fate because society demands it is also present in "The Chimney Sweeper," the first poem with an urban setting. In the late eighteenth and early nineteenth centuries, small boys, with their heads shaven for streamlining, swept chimneys, their lungs filling with soot, doing a job that often led to an early death. In this poem, Tom Dacre, whose head "that curl'd like a lambs back" was shaved like an animal being prepared for slaughter, has a dream in which an angel frees the sweepers from their "coffins of black," another suggestion that only death will bring freedom from life's suffering. The speaker urges the other boys to continue with their work, "So if all do their duty, they need not fear harm."

The idea that God will somehow take care of everyone is reinforced by "The Little Boy Lost" and "The Little Boy Found," in which God miraculously appears to a fatherless boy, lost in a dark swamp, and returns him to his grieving mother. In "A Cradle Song," "Nurse's Song," and "Infant Joy," loving parents or servants watch over helpless babies and playing children. In "Holy Thursday," a description of a religious ceremony in St. Paul's Cathedral, even the orphans of London receive help from "wise guardians of the poor," and the audience of the poem is urged to "cherish pity, lest you drive an angel from your door."

The speaker in "Holy Thursday" is clearly an adult, since he or she has a more sophisticated vocabulary than the speakers in the other poems. The adult viewpoint also appears in "The Divine Image," in which the speaker describes God and the virtues of "Mercy Pity Peace and Love" as dwelling in living human beings, all of whom are entitled to respect and love, no matter what their religion.

Songs of Experience reveals that this acceptance of society as it is and belief in a caring God is naïve. This series does not begin with joy in a pastoral landscape, as does *Songs of Innocence*, but instead the "Introduction" is spoken with "the voice of the Bard . . . Who Present, Past, & Future, sees" and who describes a fallen world with a "lapsed Soul . . . weeping in the evening dew." In the next poem, "Earth's Answer," the earth itself asks to be released from the chains of jealousy and fear. "The Clod and the Pebble" presents two views of love, the clod finding the experience selfless and giving, the pebble stating that love is selfish and restricting.

These poems remind the reader that there is more than one way to view the same experience, a point further underscored by several other poems in *Songs of Experience* that are answers or companions to poems in *Songs of Innocence*, some even bearing the same name. In the "experience" version of "Holy Thursday," the speaker is appalled by the presence of poverty in such a rich country as England. If people lived in a right relationship with each other and nature, the speaker suggests, hunger and poverty would not exist. In the second "Nurse's Song," the nurse urges the children to come in from their wasteful play, in which she finds no happiness. The "experience" version of "The Chimney Sweeper" makes clear how both a world of misery and the attitude of hopefulness presented in *Songs of Innocence* can exist side by side. A person asks a forlorn chimney sweeper where his parents are, and the child replies that they have gone to church "to praise God & his Priest & King,/ Who make up a heaven of our misery." The society's failings are supported and excused away by the institutions of religion and government, which manage to persuade many that all will somehow be all right, perhaps after death, the same point that is made in "London."

The child in "London" has parents, but is more bitter than the orphan of the "innocence" "Chimney Sweeper," because he is intelligent enough to recognize what is being done to him. His response, coupled with that of the accepting adult in the "innocence" version of "Holy Thursday," show that the sour viewpoint of the "experience" poems is not a result of obtaining wisdom by growing older. Some children are able to see the larger truth; some adults never perceive it. Intelligence and circumstance cause the difference, not age.

The companion poem to "The Divine Image" is "A Divine Image," which points out that cruelty, jealousy, terror, and secrecy are also human properties, and if people are created from God's image, those qualities must belong to God also. In "Infant Sorrow," the baby is unhappy to be born into a dangerous and sorrowful world, unlike the child of "Infant Joy." The companion poem to "The Lamb" is the famous "The Tyger," in which the speaker notes that the same God created the defenseless lamb and the fierce tiger, although he or she seems incredulous: "Did he who made the Lamb make thee?" In the "experience" poems, Blake presents the shock and dismay that arise from the contemplation of the theological problem of evil: If God created everything, God is ultimately responsible for everything, and if God is good, why does evil exist?

There are many answers to this question, including those given in the "innocence" poems, such as the little black boy's mother's contention that this life is a test and those who behave as God or the society directs (as in the "innocence" "Chimney Sweeper") will receive rewards after death, but these answers are emotionally and spiritually unsatisfying for the speakers in the "experience" poems. Nature itself is tainted in such poems as "The Sick Rose," in which the rose is destroyed by a worm—innocence and beauty give way to sin and corruption. In "Ah! Sun-flower" the flower is rooted to its spot and cannot go where repressed youths and virgins go for fulfillment in the next world. In "The Garden of Love," a chapel dedicated to negative commandments, sin, and death has been placed in the middle of what once was a refreshing garden. Now it is clear why the child on the cloud in the "innocence" introduction had wept to hear the song piped a second time.

If "innocence" is a naïve viewpoint, Blake shows in the rest of his work that "experience" is also, being fixated on sin and corruption when there is a fuller, genuinely spiritual world at hand. In "The Voice of the Ancient Bard," the speaker urges the reader to "see the opening morn,/ Image of truth new born."

Jim Baird

Further Reading

Adams, Hazard. *William Blake: A Reading of the Shorter Poems*. 1963. Reprint. Folcroft, Pa.: Folcroft Library Editions, 1980. Adams, a well-known literary critic, interprets *Songs of Innocence and of Experience* from symbolic and archetypal perspectives.

Bentley, G. E., Jr. *The Stranger from Paradise: A Biography of William Blake*. New Haven, Conn.: Yale University Press, 2001. Bentley, a veteran Blake scholar, has compiled a meticulously researched and comprehensive account of Blake's life and work, illustrated with 170 black-and-white and color reproductions of Blake's artwork. Published for the Paul Mellon Centre for Studies in British Art.

Eaves, Morris, ed. *The Cambridge Companion to William Blake*. New York: Cambridge University Press, 2003. Collection of essays that covers the entire range of Blake's works and includes discussions of his language, painting, political opinions, and ideas about history. The book also features a chronology, a guide to further reading, and a glossary.

Hirsch, E. D., Jr. *Innocence and Experience: An Introduction to Blake*. 2d ed. Chicago: University of Chicago Press, 1975. Analyzes *Songs of Innocence and of Experience* based on perceived changes in Blake's philosophical and religious ideas while he wrote them.

Leader, Zachary. *Reading Blake's Songs*. London: Routledge & Kegan Paul, 1981. Shows the relation between *Songs of Innocence and of Experience* and Blake's possible models—contemporary children's educational books.

Phillips, Michael. *William Blake: The Creation of the "Songs," from Manuscript to Illuminated Printing*. Princeton, N.J.: Princeton University Press, 2000. A scholarly presentation of the *Songs of Innocence and of Experience*. Colorfully illustrated, with transcriptions of the text and subsequent revisions.

Roberts, Jonathan. *William Blake's Poetry: A Reader's Guide*. London: Continuum, 2007. Concise introduction to Blake's poetry and philosophical ideas. Includes a discussion of the social and intellectual contexts of *Songs of Innocence and of Experience*.

Williams, Nicholas M., ed. *Palgrave Advances in William Blake Studies*. New York: Palgrave Macmillan, 2006. Collection of essays that apply modern critical perspectives to analyze Blake's works. Includes discussions of Blake and language, gender, the Bible, psychology, the communist tradition, and postmodernism.

Sonnets for Helen

Author: Pierre de Ronsard (1524-1585)
First published: Sonnets pour Hélène, 1578 (English
    translation, 1932)
Type of work: Poetry

Hélène de Surgères was the third woman to provide major in-spiration for Pierre de Ronsard's poetry. His first poetic love, Cassandre Saviati, whom he met when he was twenty and she only thirteen, married someone else soon after. Marie Dupin, the peasant girl who was the love of his middle years, was separated from him by death. In his late forties, Ronsard took Hélène as his muse. Much younger than the poet, she was a member of the court of Catherine de Médicis (1519-1589). Hélène's fiancé was killed at war in 1570, so Ronsard addressed his poems to her in order to comfort her as well as to tell her of his love.

A dualism of the personal and the conventional pervades the poetry. Ronsard expresses passionate emotions to Hé-lène, but he writes in the newly popular sonnet form, which he and his fellow poets of the Pléiade established as a major French verse form. The Petrarchan sonnet, following the model established by Francesco Petrarca, regularly divides its fourteen lines into an introductory octave and a conclud-ing sestet on distinct but complementary themes. Sonnets were frequently composed in sequences devoted to a single subject. In a sense the entire work may be seen as a sonnet se-quence, extremely varied in its details but drawn together by the overriding theme of Ronsard's passion.

The collection is divided into two books that show little progression or distinction between them. There are approxi-mately 130 poems, all sonnets except for an occasional song or elegy (the exact number of poems varies among modern editions). Ronsard varies his subject matter but provides an overall thematic continuity by frequent returns to favored subjects.

The opening sonnet, "Le premier jour de mai, Helene, je vous jure" (The first day of May, Hélène, I swear to you), be-gins with the appropriate declaration of love on the first of May, a day linked with amorous endeavors. Ronsard swears not only by the vines, the elm trees, and the verdant woods but also by Castor and Pollux, mythological brothers who ac-cording to legend became the constellation Gemini. While the June constellation of the zodiac nearly coincides with the springtime setting, Ronsard more likely invokes the brothers because they are also related to the classical Helen of Troy. In appropriate Renaissance tradition, Ronsard invokes the

heroes and gods of antiquity, and especially those of Troy be-cause of the analogy of Helen's name. The idea to which Ronsard swears in the octave—his love for Hélène—remains dominated by the images of nature and spring. The sestet turns specifically to his love with another major theme of the work, that of fate. Ronsard calls himself here author of his own fate because he willingly accepts love's dominion.

The second sonnet, "Quand à longs traits je boy l'amoureuse etincelle" (When I drink deeply of the spark of love), continues the documentation of love's effects on the lover in conventionally physical terms. The first focus is on Hélène's eyes, whose light dazzles Ronsard and troubles his reason so that he staggers as if drunk with love. His heart beats so hard that he fears the experience will kill him, but Hélène remains aloof, unaware of the pain she causes him. The themes of physical enumeration of love's effects and of the lover's suffering, both common in poetry of the time, re-cur throughout the work.

The third sonnet, "Ma douce Hélène, non, mais bien ma douce haleine" (My sweet Hélène, no, but rather my sweet breath), combines the poet's suffering with the legend of Troy. Ronsard finds himself fortunate to suffer the pains of love for one with such a name of destiny. She is both his Penelope and his Helen, combining the virtue of Ulysses' faithful wife with the fascination Helen exerts on all the men around her.

Ronsard reinforces the link between classical precedents and his modern love in "Amour, abandonant les vergers de Cytheres" (Cupid, abandoning the orchards of Cythera), in which Cupid comes personally to France to strike him with his light wings so as to implant the feverish need in his heart. The need is that of the poet as much as that of the lover. Ronsard must sing of Hélène's beauty, and when he protests his inability to treat such a heavenly subject, Cupid assures him that he will have exceptional and divine inspiration. The theme of the poet's vocation enters the work, a theme that will recur, especially in the second book, as a gift that love bestows upon the poet and also as a form of immortality with which that poet promises to reward his beloved if she will share his passion.

Just as Cupid's visit drew Ronsard into the classical tradition of poetry, Hélène's beauty links her to classical goddesses. "Deux Venus en avril, puissante Deité" (Two Venuses in April, powerful goddess) compares two figures of Venus, one from Cyprus and the other from the Saintonge region of southwestern France where Hélène was born. Ronsard describes both as born in April but finds the French Venus to be truer than the "Greek lie" that can no longer equal her. He feels fortunate to live at the time of his true Venus, even though she imprisons his spirit as one might catch a fish.

Many devices throughout the poems vary the similarities and contrasts that depict the richness of love. Just as the haughty figure of Venus may trap her admirer with an everyday image of fishing, parallel structures bracket opposing feelings. "Tant de fois s'appointer, tant de fois se fascher" (So often drawn to each other, so often angry with each other) lists the stark contrasts of lovers' emotions. They break up only to reconcile, blame love but then praise it, flee each other but then seek each other again. Each of these pairings contains in a single poetic line echoes of the frenzied activities leading nowhere from which the lover seems incapable of escape. Thus Ronsard concludes with a wry paradox that inconstancy becomes the sign of constant love.

Toward the end of the first volume, however, Ronsard worries that, even though his love for Hélène persists, she is turning away from him. In "Ma fiéve croist tousjours, la vostre diminue" (My fever still grows, yours diminishes) Ronsard underlines this contrast and continues his use of parallelism when he writes that Hélène "remains cold leaving the heat" to him. Passion is still portrayed in physical terms, and the lovers are still linked by parallel language, but the emotions reflect their separation. Now Cupid takes on the role of fate. Ronsard says that he can never free himself from Hélène's domination because Cupid's arrows engraved her portrait on his heart.

The final sonnet of the first book, "Si j'ay bien ou mal dit en ces Sonnets, Madame" (If I have spoken well or poorly in these sonnets, my lady), abandons the idea of abstract fate to say that neither it nor Ronsard can be fully responsible for the love his poetry expresses. Hélène is his inspiration, and his voice becomes mournful or joyful as she rejects or accepts his love. Ronsard concludes with an image unusual for an author to whom poetic creativity is so important. He is, he says, like a mirror that "always represents what is shown in front of it." This may be true, of course, in the alternations of happy and of sad love, without denying the importance of the poet's artistic skill.

The poet's special vocation gains importance in the second book. The opening sonnet, "Soit qu'un sage amoureux

ou soit qu'un sot me lise" (Whether a wise lover or a foolish one reads me), links it to Ronsard's preoccupation with his advanced age. The reader, he says, may be astonished by the passion that remains beneath his gray hair as a spark remains under ashes. He notes, however, that dry wood burns more readily than that which is too young and green. Still, Ronsard cautions that he must avoid being like Icarus or Phaeton, two classical figures linked to inappropriate and unsuccessful attempts to rise to heaven.

Images of death multiply as Ronsard expresses fears of his own advancing years and of the possible end of his love. After a sonnet depicting Hélène surrounded by the gaiety of carnival, "N'oubliez, mon Hélène, aujourd'huy qu'il faut prendre" (Don't forget, my Hélène, that today one must take) focuses on Ash Wednesday, a day when she should make atonement for killing him with her eyes. Amid despair, positive images always offer new hope for happiness. In "Laisse de Pharaon la terre Egyptienne" (Leave the Egyptian land of Pharoah) Ronsard returns to a classical analogy to suggest that they leave Egypt, a land emblematic of the life of the court, to take refuge in the more bucolic lands on the banks of the Jordan where "I will be your Orpheus, and you my Euridice."

The invocation of Orpheus, whose musical skills offered him the possibility of saving Euridice from hell, leads to what is probably Ronsard's most famous sonnet, "Quand vous serez bien vieille, au soir à la chandelle" (When you are very old, in the evening by candle light). This poem, on which William Butler Yeats (1865-1939) based his adaptation "When You are Old" (1892), combines the ideas of age and death with those of immortality and the power of both love and poetry. Here not only Ronsard but also Hélène becomes old. Even though he may be long dead, Ronsard flourishes in a classical paradise among myrtle bushes while Hélène remains an "old woman stooped" by the fireside. The reversal underlines the importance of their roles, for it is through Ronsard that both will attain immortality. At this future time, both will be remembered because of the beauty of Ronsard's art.

The graceful moral Ronsard attaches to this poem leaves intact Hélène's superiority. In the usual tone of the Renaissance *carpe diem*, he urges her to love him in the present lest she be sad in the future that she has not taken advantage of this possibility. The poet retains the capacity to create immortality but, because of his deference to the woman he loves, he lays his talent at her disposal and allows her to control their actual fate. This appropriately sums up Ronsard's diverse sonnets for Hélène. He offers her the varied aspects of love, from the physical suffering through the immortality of lovers, and allows her to accept what she will in accepting him.

Dorothy M. Betz

Further Reading

Bishop, Morris. *Ronsard: Prince of Poets.* Ann Arbor: University of Michigan Press, 1959. A general biography of Ronsard. Chapter 12, "Hélène," gives a detailed description of Hélène de Surgères, the circumstances in which Ronsard met her, and the surrounding atmosphere of court intrigue. Includes limited references to the sonnets.

Cave, Terence, ed. *Ronsard the Poet.* London: Methuen, 1973. Contains eight essays by various authors presenting a largely thematic approach to Ronsard's work. In chapter 2, Grahame Castor discusses Petrarchism and the quest for beauty in the *Sonnets pour Hélène*; chapter 7, by Odette de Mourgues, on Ronsard's later poetry, contains references to Hélène. The index lists references in other essays.

Fallon, Jean M. *Voice and Vision in Ronsard's "Les Sonnets pour Helene."* New York: Peter Lang, 1993. Examines the 1584 edition of the sonnets, the last edition published in Ronsard's lifetime. Analyzes the work as a text about poetry rather than about love, describing its duality between the voices of the lover and the poet. Points out other unifying elements in the work as a whole

Jones, K. R. W. *Pierre de Ronsard.* New York: Twayne, 1970. This standard introductory overview to Ronsard's life and work discusses Hélène chiefly in chapter 9, "Ronsard's Private World."

Lewis, D. B. Wyndham. *Ronsard.* New York: Sheed and Ward, 1944. Chapter 9, "Hélène," begins with a description of Hélène as Ronsard saw her. A subsequent analysis takes a thematic approach and quotes extensively from the sonnets.

Lewis, John. "Helen on Lesbos: A Sapphic Echo in Ronsard's *Sonnets Pour Helene?*" *French Studies* 48, no. 1 (January, 1994): 4. Discusses Ronsard's interest in the Greek poet Sappho and points out similarities between Sappho's poetry and Ronsard's *Sonnets for Helen.* Describes how fragments of Sappho's poetry are adapted to Ronsard's images and how the work of both poets confers immortality on the poets and their subjects.

Ronsard, Pierre de. *Sonnets for Helen.* Translated by Humbert Wolfe. London: Allen and Unwin, 1972. Provides both English and French texts for a majority of the sonnets. An introductory essay details the circumstances in which the poems were written and their importance to Ronsard's literary reputation.

Sonnets from the Portuguese

Author: Elizabeth Barrett Browning (1806-1861)
First published: 1850
Type of work: Poetry

Whenever English love poetry is discussed, almost invariably the opening of Elizabeth Barrett Browning's penultimate poem of *Sonnets from the Portuguese* is quoted: "How do I love thee? Let me count the ways." The collection represents, variously, depending on the quoter's prejudice, a gem of lyrical eloquence, an oversentimental extravagance, or a tired cliché. Browning's masterpiece, *Sonnets from the Portuguese,* went through a complete cycle of literary reception, first being overpraised as "the noblest [sonnets] ever written," then undervalued as overly emotional effusions, and eventually accepted as a major work. Despite minor cavils, Browning's *Sonnets from the Portuguese* is assured a permanent reputation as one of the foremost collections of love poetry in the English language.

The recurring criticism of sentimentalism has some validity, but the charge may be met on several grounds. Elizabeth Barrett wrote *Sonnets from the Portuguese* during her passionate courtship with Robert Browning. They record the emotions of that time, and emotions are not always "recollected in tranquility" as William Wordsworth suggested poetry should be. Moreover, the poet never intended them for publication. Then, too, she was writing in a culture whose strictures against poetic display of emotion were less narrow than those of later times; indeed, compared to the other popular love lyrics of her time, *Sonnets from the Portuguese* are less sentimental, as an 1860 review in *The Southern Literary Messenger* attests. Finally, the sonnets were written by a poet to a poet, which makes them unique among love sonnets and allows for a freedom of emotional language that could be relied upon to be understood.

Browning did not, however, show the poems to her husband until three years after their marriage. When she did, he insisted that she publish the sonnets, which he reportedly deemed the best since William Shakespeare's, in her 1850 volume of collected poems. He suggested the title "Sonnets from the Portuguese" to disguise the work as a translation. Neither of the Brownings believed that it would be in good taste to publicize their private relationship. Robert had admired Elizabeth's early poem "Catarina to Camoëns," which suggested the title, since Luis Vaz de Camoëns was a Portuguese poet.

Although individual sonnets were written in English since their vogue in the 1590's (except for a 150-year hiatus between the sonnets of John Milton and those of Wordsworth), Browning's *Sonnets from the Portuguese* represented the first true sonnet sequence in English since the Elizabethans. Since Shakespeare's time, sonnets in English tended to follow the pattern established by Shakespeare's sonnets: three sets of four lines (quatrains) concluding with a couplet. The sonnets Elizabeth Barrett wrote before *Sonnets from the Portuguese* followed this Shakespearean or "English" sonnet form. In her sonnet sequence, however, she followed the much more demanding Petrarchan or Italian form, where the first two quatrains share rhyme pairs and form a single unit (the octave) that rhymes *abba abba*. The remaining six lines, instead of breaking into quatrain and couplet, are similarly unified; the Italian form allows many variations, but the scheme Elizabeth Barrett settled on was invariably *cdcdcd*. This means that in the entire fourteen lines of each sonnet there are only four rhyme sounds, an unparalleled economy of rhyme.

The opening sonnet of the sequence introduces the biographical element that has always been at least part of the attraction of these love sonnets. In 1845, as she wrote these lines, Elizabeth Barrett was nearing forty, still living with a domineering father who had forbidden her to marry but encouraged her writing and her scholarship. The "antique tongue" represents the ancient Greek in which she was fluent and from which she had translated many classical works. A childhood accident had left her disabled and doubtful of her prospects for marriage even if her father's ban had been lifted. No wonder, then, that a meditation on her "wished for years" were not just "sweet," like those of the Greek pastoral poet Theocritus (third century B.C.E.) but "sweet, sad" and "melancholy," and "had flung/ A shadow across" the poet.

In the early poems of the sequence, this ambivalence of emotion is traced through the speaker's expectation of Death rather than of Love and through skepticism about love. In fact, "Love," the last word of the opening sonnet, comes as a surprise to the speaker just as it surprised Elizabeth when Robert proposed to her in the summer of 1845. In the second sonnet, the speaker protests that to accept the gentleman's proposal would be to go against God's will. In the third, the objection is to the many differences between them (a letter to Robert, dated March 20, 1845, strikes the same theme), and again the last lines refer to Death as her only expectation: "The chrism is on thine head,—on mine the dew,—/ And Death must dig the level where these agree." Robert was a young poet, six years younger than Elizabeth, and full of vitality. Elizabeth saw herself as an aging poet, resigned to death and to the idea of living alone. The earliest sonnets of the sequence reflect this harsh perception of reality; they are far from being idealizations of love.

In sonnet 4, the poet evokes the image of solitude that she saw as her fate. Depicting her suitor as a medieval troubadour, she urges him to sing at a balcony less run-down and deserted, images of the isolation brought on by her injury and her consequent opium addiction. She continues to ask the suitor to leave for his own good: If he stays merely to stamp out the "red wild sparkles" of her grief, she says in sonnet 5, he better beware that they do not burst into flame. Sonnet 6, one of her most anthologized poems, begins with the same theme, "Go from me," and is no less insistent, yet she is clearly beginning to feel, not a softening of her conviction that the love is wrong, but a resignation to the inevitability of the suitor's presence in her life. "Yet I feel that I shall stand/ Henceforth in thy shadow." The image of solitude in sonnet 4 dissolves into the two-in-one paradox of love: "Nevermore/ Alone," "pulses that beat double," "within my eyes, the tears of two." Sonnet 6 is a major transition in the sequence, the first to acknowledge the change in her life.

That change is the focus of sonnet 7, which opens "The face of all the world is changed." The speaker does not deny the earlier vision of Death but merely presents the suitor's figure as standing between her and death (now lowercased). The suitor changes her expectations from "obvious death" to life with a vital young man. That poses a problem, however, in the next five sonnets, 8 to 12. In giving her life, the suitor gives her more than she can ever return, "For frequent tears have run/ the colours from my life" (8), leaving her nothing to offer him. She does not quite return to the plea for the lover to go—she knows since sonnet 6 that he is in her heart to stay—but she tells him to "Go farther" than using her life as a pillow for his head; he is to "let it serve to trample on," the total self-giving of love. However, this image also suggests the lack of self-esteem that is the bane of love. This continues in sonnet 9, where the poet emphasizes the disparity in the exchange of "gifts," but in sonnet 10 the speaker comes to realize that love itself is "beautiful indeed/ And worthy of acceptation" and she can finally say, *"I love thee!"* with confidence. "I am not all unworthy," she observes in sonnet 11. "Indeed, this very love," claims the next sonnet, "Doth crown me with a ruby."

Sonnet 14, a justly famous poem, examines the psychology of love and warns against the danger of focusing love on any one quality of the beloved: "If thou must love me"—even beginning with that "if" reveals how tentative her approach is to this unlooked-for situation—"let it be for nought but love's sake only." Sonnets 13 and 15 respond to the suitor's apparent concern over the fact that she does not put her love into words; sonnet 21 reminds her wordier lover "To love me also in silence, with thy soul."

As the sequence progresses, the speaker grows more confident in her love, yet she is aware of the dangers of idealizing love. In sonnet 22 she imagines her soul "erect and strong" with her lover's and contrasts that with her bedridden body; yet she ends the poem preferring earthly love. "The world's sharpness," which before threatened her, is now more like "a clasping knife" closing harmlessly (sonnet 14). Love is now "as strong as Death" (sonnet 27). There are occasional moments of tears still (sonnet 30), for love does not mean an end to sadness. She is now confident enough to ask him to call her pet names (sonnet 33), and their love is now established enough for her to look back with wonder at its beginning (sonnet 32) and their first kiss (sonnet 38).

The series concludes with three sonnets of hopeful anticipation of life with the beloved: "My future will not copy fair my past" (sonnet 17, originally published separately). The metaphors of a "fair copy" of a manuscript, an impeccable final draft that corrects the false starts and errors of the first, is proper to a poet. Instead of fixing the past, she looks for a new future. Sonnet 48 is the famous "How do I love thee?" As critic William Going first pointed out in 1953, the poem is abstract and enumerative. Its intention is to conclude and summarize the whole sequence, and each of the eight ways of loving echoes a previous sonnet. Though long beloved as an individual sonnet, it gains even more luster as the capstone of the entire series.

John R. Holmes

Further Reading

Avery, Simon, and Rebecca Stott. *Elizabeth Barrett Browning.* London: Longman, 2003. A biography and critical assessment of Browning's poetry and her influence on later poets. Dispels the myth that Browning was reclusive and disabled, depicting her as one of the great intellectuals of her time.

Billone, Amy Christine. *Little Songs: Women, Silence, and the Nineteenth-Century Sonnet.* Columbus: Ohio State University Press, 2007. A study of Browning and other women poets who revived the sonnet form in the nineteenth century. Billone focuses on the poets' use of lyric volubility and silence in the themes and styles of their works.

Bloom, Harold, ed. *Elizabeth Barrett Browning.* Philadelphia: Chelsea House, 2002. Collection of essays by scholars and literary critics that interpret Browning's work and literary influence, including analyses of *Sonnets from the Portuguese* by Jerome Mazzaro, Dorothy Mermin, and Margaret Reynolds.

Cooper, Helen. *Elizabeth Barrett Browning: Woman and Artist.* Chapel Hill: University of North Carolina Press, 1988. An excellent study of Browning's poetics, relating them to the conflicting roles of women in the Victorian era.

Forster, Margaret. *Elizabeth Barrett Browning: A Biography.* New York: Doubleday, 1989. Shows Mary Barrett, Browning's mother, to have been the shaping influence in her education. Revises the myth of Browning's father as the tyrant of Wimpole Street.

Leighton, Angela. *Elizabeth Barrett Browning.* Bloomington: Indiana University Press, 1986. A feminist reevaluation of Browning's life and works that also examines the Browning myth. Discusses the poet in relation to her male predecessors.

Lupton, Mary Jane. *Elizabeth Barrett Browning.* Long Island, N.Y.: Feminist Press, 1972. A general study of Barrett Browning combining criticism and biography, this book includes a generous section on the *Sonnets from the Portuguese*, which emphasizes Browning's unusual, for 1850, feminine point of view in love sonnets yet notes the irony of that point of view expressing dependence and weakness.

Mermin, Dorothy. *Elizabeth Barrett Browning: The Origins of a New Poetry.* Chicago: University of Chicago Press, 1989. Mermin claims that Browning originated a female tradition in Victorian poetry. She draws heavily on Browning's earlier diary and numerous letters. Extensive notes and bibliography.

Radley, Virginia L. *Elizabeth Barrett Browning.* New York: Twayne, 1972. A good starting point for the study of Browning, this volume opens with a brief biography and goes on to analyze Browning's works. The chapter on the

Sonnets from the Portuguese gives background on their composition, analyzes them sequentially, and relates them to the Brownings' love letters.

Stephenson, Glennis. *Elizabeth Barrett Browning and the Poetry of Love*. Ann Arbor, Mich.: UMI Research Press, 1989. Begins by discussing Browning's immediate predecessors, then examines her early ballads and lyrics,

Lady Geraldine's Courtship, *Sonnets from the Portuguese*, *Aurora Leigh*, and *Last Poems*. Discussion of the sonnets considers how the female poet enters into a male poetic tradition, specifically examining the role of distance in the sonnet tradition and Browning's use of it as well as Browning's replacement of predominantly visual images with predominantly "tactual" images.

Sonnets of Michelangelo

Author: Michelangelo (1475-1564)
First published: Rime di Michelagnolo Buonarroti,
1623 (English translation, 1878)
Type of work: Poetry

The fame of Michelangelo Buonarroti as a painter and a sculptor far outdistances his reputation as a poet. This is unfortunate, for while it is open to question whether Michelangelo could have ever developed into a poet of a stature equivalent to his stature in the plastic arts, his reputation as a poet is less than it should be. Modern critics have discovered that he is an important Renaissance Italian poet, and he is considered by many the best Italian lyric poet of the sixteenth century.

The reasons for the slow growth of Michelangelo's poetic reputation are easy to identify. First, even in his own day, while his poetry was extravagantly praised by a circle of friends, it was Michelangelo's painting and sculpture that drew the eyes of the world at large. Moreover, his poetry was not published until 1623, fifty-nine years after his death, and then only in an incomplete, much-edited, and censored edition. By that time the Renaissance style of writing was being replaced by the neoclassical style throughout Europe, and the poems did not attract major attention. It was not until the early nineteenth century, when the Romantics were rediscovering the Middle Ages and the Renaissance, that complete and well-edited editions of the poetry began to appear. Only in the twentieth century were completely authoritative editions published.

Even Michelangelo never took his poetry seriously enough to collect, revise, or preserve the whole of it. While he considered himself a professional painter and sculptor, he, like almost every poet of the Renaissance, thought of himself as an amateur as a poet. Poetry, after all, was never much of a way to earn a living; in Michelangelo's age poetry was valued as a social pastime and a gentleman's skill. Even if a man

did think of himself as a professional poet, it was bad form to act as if he did. This Renaissance attitude has given scholars much trouble, and only after much searching have they managed to locate in various places 343 separate poems and poetic fragments (and many variants) by Michelangelo. Most of these were composed after 1530.

Although the poetry is sometimes written in the traditional Petrarchan manner, and although the conventions of neo-Platonism are also important in the work, the best poems are characterized by Michelangelo's unique style. The structure, syntax, and even the grammar are twisted and full of tension; the poems are often obscure, and the poet sometimes seems to pay scant attention to such relatively simple things as rhyme and metrical regularity. The overall impression of the verse, as critics like to point out, is as if Michelangelo in writing was struggling to shape his complex thoughts into hard, unmalleable language the way a sculptor struggles with marble or granite.

The poems fall into several categories. First in importance are the pieces written to Vittoria Colonna, either proclaiming Michelangelo's platonic love for her (he met her when he was sixty-three) or lamenting her death, as in this sonnet:

So that I might at least be less unworthy,
Lady, of your huge high beneficence,
To balance it, my poor wits at first
Took to plying my own wholeheartedly.
But then, seeing in me no potency
To clear the way to grasp that goal exists,
My evil fault for its forgiveness asks,

And the sin makes me wiser constantly.
And well I see how anyone would stray
Who thought my flimsy, transient work could equal
The grace pouring from you, which is divine.
For wit and art and memory give way;
In a thousand attempts none who is mortal
Can pay for Heaven's gift out of his own.

Vittoria was herself a poet of some note and a patron of the arts, and she inspired several notable men of her day to the composition of verse. Generally speaking, there are three levels of love spoken of in Michelangelo's poetry: human, fleshly love, which takes the Petrarchan convention; honest love, a transcendental emotion that takes the neo-Platonic convention; and good love, the spiritual love of God. Good love is the subject of the greater number of Michelangelo's poems, but honest love is the dominant theme in the best of his love poems, most of which are written to Vittoria. Human love is a theme in these poems, too, but as an antagonist to honest love. In a typical poem to Vittoria, for example, the poet describes how honest love has come to him forbidding corrupt desire (human love) and raising him to the level of the spirit. This is a conventional, neo-Platonic theme, yet Michelangelo's energetic expression of it reanimates the convention and produces a remarkably unconventional poetry:

I want to want, Lord, what I do not want,
An icy veil hides between heart and fire
And damps the fire, making my page a liar,
Since my pen and my conduct do not fit.
I love you with my tongue, then I lament
Love does not reach the heart, and can't tell where
To open the door to grace so it can enter
And thrust all ruthless pride out of my heart.
Tear the veil thou, O break that wall, my Lord,
Which with its hardness keeps in check the sun
Of your own light; on earth it is put out.
Send that same ray of light to your fair bride
Which we are then to have, so I may burn,
And my heart feel you only with no doubt.

The poems concerning the good love of God are next in importance after the poems to Vittoria. Michelangelo was seriously dedicated to the Christian ideal, and the religious poems are full of his deep, though often agonized love for Christ. Many of them are tortured, self-debasing confessions. Among the most frequent themes in these poems are fear of the judgment day, fear for salvation, the feeling of moral inadequacy, and prayer and supplication: "I live on my own death; if I see right,/ My life with an unhappy lot is happy;/ If ignorant how to live on death and worry,/ Enter this fire, where I'm destroyed and burnt."

Tommaso Cavaliere was a young Roman aristocrat to whom Michelangelo was strongly attracted; a significant group of the poems are dedicated to the poet's admiration and love of that youth. He saw in Tommaso a model of elegance and grace, a man with manners and a social style the opposite of that of Michelangelo himself. The main burden of this group is Michelangelo's statement of admiration of the young man, and the poet's offer of friendship:

I feel how a cold face that fire has lit
Burns me from far, and turns itself to ice;
Two lovely arms submit me to a force
That does not move, but moves all other weight;
Unique, and grasped by me alone, a spirit
That has no death, but others' death can compass,
I see and meet, that binds my heart, being loose;
From one who helps I feel the only spite.
Lord, from a beautiful face how can it be
Effects so far opposed are borne on mine?
It's hard to give to men what you have not.
As for the happy life he's snatched from me,
He may, if you're not kind, act as the sun,
Which heats the world although it is not hot.

Michelangelo's overtures were, apparently, coolly received. All in all, these poems speak of a platonic kind of love very similar to the kind of affection for a young man readers may be familiar with in William Shakespeare's sonnets. Much different are the forty-eight quatrains to Cecchino Bracci, who died at the age of fifteen in 1544. His uncle, Luigi del Riccio, requested of Michelangelo a tomb design and an epitaph for his nephew. Michelangelo had seen very little of Cecchino, and the moods of the poems represent those of the uncle, not of Michelangelo.

Naturally enough, a group of Michelangelo's poems is concerned with art in general and some of his own works in particular. One interesting piece describes the physical difficulties he endured painting the Sistine Chapel ceiling. Two poems are written as speeches for two of the statues (*Night* and *Day*) that Michelangelo made for the tomb in Florence of the young Duke Giuliano de Medici. A number of the poems use metaphoric structures drawn from aspects of the practice of various arts, painting and sculpture in particular. Among these is Michelangelo's perhaps best-known poem, the sonnet "Non ha l'ottimo artista alcun concetto" ("No conception the greatest artist can have"). Written between 1538 and

1544, the first four lines of this platonic love poem became famous immediately. Within a few years they were known in Spain and elsewhere, and they were translated into French by Phillipe Desportes, the only verses of Michelangelo translated into French before the nineteenth century. In these four lines is condensed Michelangelo's idea of art. They can be roughly paraphrased as follows: "No conception the greatest artist can have is not imprisoned in the rough marble block; to break away the excess stone to reveal it is all the mind-guided hand can do." This idea of sculpture (and by extension the other arts as well) as the achievement by skill of the artist's intellectual conception was not entirely new, but Michelangelo's unique and authoritative expression of it became, and still is, a touchstone for critics of his art.

Another group of poems is concerned with messages to acquaintances, patrons, and friends and with the pronouncement of opinion, praise, and condemnations. A friend is lectured on ingratitude; Giorgio Vasari, the great biographer of artists, is praised for his preservation of the reputations of painters; Pope Julius II is angrily denounced; and the deaths of friends and relatives are eloquently regretted. Some of these poems are cautiously political and complain or condemn the actions of powerful contemporaries of the poet. The best-known of this class of poems is Michelangelo's poem in which his statue *Night*, on the Florentine tomb of Duke Giuliano de Medici, speaks. Another poet, Giovanni Strozzi, had praised the statue, carved in the shape of a sleeping young woman. Strozzi suggests that since she is so much alive in art she be awakened. In reply, Michelangelo condemns the excesses of contemporary Medici politics in his native Florence. (Michelangelo, who to some extent identified himself with the exile Dante Alighieri, lived in Rome in self-imposed exile.) He has his statue answer that she would rather sleep than endure the vile corruption that she would witness around her if she were awakened.

The poems that do not fall into any one or more of these major groups cannot be easily classified. Michelangelo wrote in an unsystematic way and, apparently, as the spirit moved him. Many of his poems, for example, have been found jotted down on the back of prints or in the margins of letters or notebooks. It was only in his later years that he wrote consistent groups of poems. Among the unclassified poems are pieces on such various subjects as fire, night, the rustic life, death (he was already writing of his "approaching death" fifty years before he died), cities he had visited, and the manners and morals of his times. Not a few of this last type of poem are satirical burlesques, some full of the earthy language that has always upset censors and self-appointed guardians of public morality.

Further Reading

Brandes, Georg. *Michelangelo: His Life, His Times, His Era.* Translated with a foreword by Heinz Norden. New York: Frederick Ungar, 1963. Highly readable interpretive biography by a great Danish scholar. Cites more than twenty poems, with an evaluation of Michelangelo as "in many ways . . . the most compelling poet Italy ever produced." Demonstrates the self-mockery, the satire, even the *buffo* quality of some of the poetry.

Bull, George, ed. *Michelangelo: Life, Letters, and Poetry.* Poems translated by George Bull and Peter Porter. New York: Oxford University Press, 1987. Accessible collection of writings by and about Michelangelo. Includes Condivi's affectionate biography of his teacher, one of the earliest sources for Michelangelo's life, along with selected translations of the master's poems and letters, a fine introduction, and other study aids.

Clements, Robert J. *Michelangelo's Theory of Art.* New York: New York University Press, 1961. An intense and thorough exploration of Michelangelo's formative influences. Devotes attention to the relationship between his writing and other forms of artistic expression.

_____. *The Poetry of Michelangelo.* New York: New York University Press, 1965. Thorough analysis of the poetry in terms of its relation to Italian and broader European literary traditions. Documented discussion of the poetry as a reflection of the life of the artist. Best study in English of Michelangelo's writing.

Pater, Walter. "The Poetry of Michelangelo." In *Michelangelo: Selected Readings*, edited by William E. Wallace. New York: Garland, 1999. An evaluation of Michelangelo's poetry by an eminent Victorian literary critic.

Ryan, Christopher. *The Poetry of Michelangelo: An Introduction.* Madison, N.J.: Fairleigh Dickinson University Press, 1998. Analyzes the chronological development of Michelangelo's poetry, explaining the meaning and technique of his work. Cites quotations from his poetry in both Italian and English translation.

Sonnets of Shakespeare

Author: William Shakespeare (1564-1616)
First published: 1609, as *Sonnets*
Type of work: Poetry

Although William Shakespeare's sonnets are generally considered to be among the most beautiful and most powerful poems in English literature, the attention of readers and scholars has more often centered on their possible biographical significance than on the literary qualities that give them their greatness. So little is known of the inner life of the poet, so little that helps to explain his genius, that it is not surprising to find critics minutely examining these lyrics that seem to reveal something of Shakespeare the man.

The sonnet sequence was one of the most popular poetic forms in the early 1590's; modeled originally on works by Dante Alighieri and Petrarch, the genre developed in sixteenth century France and Italy and quickly reached England. Sir Philip Sidney's *Astrophel and Stella* (1591), written a few years before the poet's death in 1586, is a demonstration of how quickly the sonnet cycle achieved excellence in English. Edmund Spenser, Samuel Daniel, Michael Drayton, and many other well-known Elizabethan men of letters followed Sidney's example, paying tribute to the idealized ladies who inspired their almost religious devotion.

Shakespeare's poems, probably composed at intervals during the decade between 1590 and 1600, differ radically from the sonnets of his contemporaries in several ways. They are not based on the traditional Petrarchan theme of a proud, virtuous lady and an abject, scorned lover, and there is in them relatively little of the platonic idealism that fills such works as Spenser's *Amoretti* (1595), in which the poet's love for his lady lifts him above human weakness to contemplation of the divine. Shakespeare records a strangely ambiguous, tortured affection for a young nobleman; the emotions he expresses in his sonnets have a depth and complexity, an intensity, that can be encountered elsewhere only in the speeches of some of his greatest dramatic creations.

The narrative of Shakespeare's sequence is exceedingly sketchy. Scholars have, in fact, rearranged the poems many times in an attempt to produce a more coherent "plot" than appeared in the volume published, without the author's supervision, in 1609. It seems likely that the work as it now stands contains at least a few poems that were written as independent pieces, sonnets on popular Renaissance themes that have no real bearing on the subject of the sequence itself.

Three shadowy figures move through the reflections of the poet as he speaks in his sonnets. The most important is the "fair youth," the young nobleman. The fervor of the language with which Shakespeare speaks of his feelings for the youth has led to considerable discussion of the precise nature of the relationship. It must be remembered that the Renaissance regarded the friendship of man and man as the highest form of human affection, for within this relationship there could be complete spiritual and intellectual communication, unmarred by erotic entanglements.

The nobleman is initially idealized in much the same way that most poets envision their ladies, as the embodiment of beauty and virtue. Unlike the typical lady of more conventional sonnets, however, he proves to be false and deceptive, shifting his attention to a rival poet, whose identity has been the subject of much speculation. The sequence records the narrator-poet's despair at this betrayal and at the nobleman's affair with the "dark lady," the poet's mistress, who is, in a sense, his evil genius. It is not the loss of the lady he regrets, for he knows her character all too well, but that his friend has yielded to her corruption. Throughout the sonnets the reader feels the poet's agonized sense that there is nothing lastingly beautiful or virtuous.

While it is customary to speak of the "I" of the sonnets as Shakespeare, it is dangerously misleading to overlook the possibility that these poems are dramatic, that "I" is as vividly conceived a creature of Shakespeare's mind as Hamlet, and that the poet is projecting himself into an imagined situation rather than describing a personal experience. Whether the speaker of the sonnets is Shakespeare or not, it does not alter the essential value of the poems themselves.

The greatness of the sonnets lies in their intellectual and emotional power, in Shakespeare's ability to find exactly the right images to convey a particular idea or feeling and in his magnificent gift for shaping the diction and rhythms of ordinary human speech into expressions of the subtlest and deepest human perceptions. He also developed his own sonnet form, the Shakespearean sonnet form, with which Thomas Wyatt and Henry Howard Surrey experimented earlier in the century. Almost all of Shakespeare's sonnets are divided into three quatrains, each with alternately rhyming lines, followed by a concluding couplet. This form is technically less complex than the Italian pattern, in which the first eight lines are built around two rhymes, rather than four. The technical requirements of the two forms determine to a degree their organization. The Italian sonnet generally breaks down into two sections, with the statement of a problem in the octave and its solution in the sestet, while the form used by Shakespeare lends itself to a tripartite exposition followed by a brief conclusion in the couplet. Shakespeare was, however, capable of varying his development of his subject in many different ways; a thought may run through twelve lines with a surprise conclusion or shift of emphasis in the couplet; it may break into the eight-line, six-line division of the Italian sonnet; or it may follow one of many other patterns.

The organization of the sequence seems somewhat haphazard. Within it are several groups of poems that clearly belong together, but they do not form an entirely satisfying narrative. Shakespeare uses his half-untold story as a basis for poems upon many familiar Renaissance themes: love, time, mutability, the conflict of body and soul, passion and reason. The first eighteen poems, all addressed to the nobleman, are variations on the theme of the transience of youth and beauty and the need for the youth to marry and beget children in order to preserve his virtues of face and mind in them. Shakespeare draws upon nature for images to convey his sense of the destruction that awaits all beauty, referring to "the violet past prime," "winter's ragged hand," "summer's green all girded up in sheaves." Youth becomes more precious and the preservation of beauty more important still when the poet considers that "everything that grows holds in perfection but a little moment."

Shakespeare's sense of the ravages of time leads him to a second important theme: Poetry, as well as heirs, can confer immortality. Sonnet 18 is one of the most beautiful and clearest expressions of this idea:

> Shall I compare thee to a summer's day?
> Thou are more lovely and more temperate:
> Rough winds do shake the darling buds of May,
> And summer's lease hath all too short a date;
> Sometime too hot the eye of heaven shines,
> And often is his gold complexion dimm'd;
> And every fair from fair sometime declines,
> By chance, or nature's changing course, untrimm'd:
> But thy eternal summer shall not fade
> Nor lose possession of that fair thou ow'st;
> Nor shall Death brag thou wander'st in his shade,
> When in eternal lines to time thou grow'st;
> So long as men can breathe or eyes can see,
> So long lives this, and this gives life to thee.

The same idea forms the basis for another well-known sonnet, "Not marble nor the gilded monuments of princes," in which Shakespeare affirms the power of his verse to withstand the assaults of war, fire, and death. The sonnets making up the middle of the sequence deal with many aspects of the poet's feeling for the nobleman. Their tone is almost universally melancholy; the haunting language and clear visual images of Sonnet 73 make it perhaps the finest expression of this dominant mood:

> That time of year thou mayst in me behold
> When yellow leaves, or none, or few, do hang
> Upon those boughs which shake against the cold,
> Bare [ruin'd] choirs where late the sweet birds sang.
> In me thou see'st the twilight of such day
> As after sunset fadeth in the west,
> Which by and by black night doth take away,
> Death's second self, that seals up all in rest.
> In me thou see'st the glowing of such fire
> That on the ashes of his youth doth lie,
> As the death-bed whereon it must expire,
> Consum'd with that which it was nourish'd by.
> This thou perceiv'st, which makes thy love more strong,
> To love that well which thou must leave ere long.

The speaker pictures himself as a man aging, unworthy, despairing. Initially his friendship with the young nobleman provides his one comfort against the frustrations of his worldly state. At those moments, as in Sonnet 29, when he is most wretched,

> Haply I think on thee; and then my state,
> Like to the lark at break of day arising
> From sullen earth, sings hymns at heaven's gate.
> For thy sweet love remember'd such wealth brings
> That then I scorn to change my state with kings.

A brilliantly conceived image, in Sonnet 33, communicates the impact of the poet's loss of confidence in the youth when the youth turns to the rival poet.

> Full many a glorious morning have I seen
> Flatter the mountain tops with sovereign eye,
> Kissing with golden face the meadows green,
> Gilding pale streams with heavenly alchemy;
> Anon permit the basest clouds to ride
> With ugly rack on his celestial face,
> And from the forlorn world his visage hide,
> Stealing unseen to west with this disgrace:

> Even so my son one early morn did shine
> With all triumphant splendour on my brow;
> But out, alack! he was but one hour mine,
> The region cloud hath mask'd him from me now.
> Yet him for this my love no whit disdaineth;
> Suns of the world may stain when heaven's sun staineth.

Many of the poems show the poet's attempts to accept the faithlessness, the fall from virtue, of the youth. While his betrayal cannot destroy the poet's affection ("Love is not love which alters when it alteration finds"), it represents the decay of all good, leaving the speaker filled with despair.

There are, toward the end of the sequence, approximately thirty poems addressed to or speaking of the "dark lady." The lighter of these lyrics are witty commentaries on her brunette beauty—in the sonnet tradition, the lady is fair: "Thine eyes I love, and they as pitying me,/ Knowing thy heart torment me with disdain,/ Have put on black, and loving mourners be,/ Looking with pretty ruth upon my pain."

The overworked Petrarchan metaphors about the charms of the sonneteer's mistress are parodied in another well-known poem.

> My mistress' eyes are nothing like the sun;
> Coral is far more red than her lips' red;
> If snow be white, why then her breasts are dun;
> If hairs be wires, black wires grow on her head.

Surrounding these relatively happy pieces are verses revealing the pain and conflict in the relationship between the poet and the lady. He knows that his feeling for her is primarily lustful and destructive; yet, as he says in Sonnet 129, he cannot free himself from her: "All this the world well knows; yet none knows well/ To shun the heaven that leads men to this hell."

Irony pervades the sonnets in which Shakespeare declares his full knowledge of her vices and her deceptions both of her husband and of him: "When my love swears that she is made of truth,/ I do believe her, though I know she lies." The poet's conflict is intensified by the lady's affair with the nobleman, and he tries to explain his reaction in the little morality play of Sonnet 144.

> Two loves I have of comfort and despair,
> Which like two spirits do suggest me still:
> The better angel is a man right fair,
> The worser spirit a woman colour'd ill.
> To win me soon to hell, my female evil
> Tempteth my better angel from my [side],

> And would corrupt my saint to be a devil,
> Wooing his purity with her foul pride.
> And whether that my angel be turn'd fiend,
> Suspect I may, yet not directly tell;
> But being both from me, both to each friend,
> I guess one angel in another's hell.
> Yet this shall I ne'er know, but live in doubt,
> Till my bad angel fire my good one out.

The tremendous appeal of Shakespeare's sonnets through the centuries rests essentially on the same qualities that have made his plays immortal, his phenomenal understanding of the workings of the mind and his incredible ability to distill many aspects of human experience into a few lines. The sonnets are, in many ways, dramatic poetry; the reader is constantly aware of the presence of the poet, the "I" of the sequence, who addresses the nobleman and the dark lady forcefully and directly, not as if he were musing in his study. A brief perusal of the opening lines of the sonnets shows a remarkable number of questions and commands that heighten the reader's sense of a dramatic situation:

> That thou hast her, it is not all my grief,
> And yet it may be said I lov'd her dearly . . .
> Being your slave, what should I do but tend
> Upon the hours and times of your desire?
> Farewell! thou art too dear for my possessing,
> And like enough thou know'st thy estimate.

The compression of language; the vivid images drawn from nature, commerce, the theater, and many other aspects of life; the wordplay; and the flexibility of rhythms of speech that characterize Shakespeare's blank verse—all contribute to the greatness of the sonnets as well. In these poems, as in his plays, he was able to transform traditional forms and raise them to new heights.

Further Reading

Blades, John. *Shakespeare: The Sonnets*. New York: Palgrave Macmillan, 2007. An introduction to the *Sonnets*, providing textual analysis, discussion of themes, and critical history of these poems. Examines the development and characteristics of the sonnet form, Humanist themes, and early modern print culture.

Callaghan, Dympna. *Shakespeare's "Sonnets."* Malden, Mass.: Blackwell, 2007. Comprehensive introduction, discussing the poems' structure, images, and themes of identity, beauty, love, numbers, and time. An appendix provides a summary of each sonnet with descriptions of their key literary figures.

Cheney, Patrick, ed. *The Cambridge Companion to Shakespeare's Poetry*. New York: Cambridge University Press, 2007. Includes essays discussing Shakespeare and the development of English poetry; rhetoric, style, and form in his verse; the poetry in his plays; his poetry as viewed from a twenty-first century perspective; and "The *Sonnets*" by Michael Shoenfeldt.

Cousins, A. D. *Shakespeare's Sonnets and Narrative Poems*. New York: Longman, 2000. Divides the *Sonnets* into three parts, devoting a chapter to each and focusing on a particular aspect of each part. The discussion of *Sonnets 1-19* is described as "The Young Man, the Poet, and Father Time"; *Sonnets 20-126* are summarized as "The Poet, the Young Man, Androgyny, and Friendship"; and *Sonnets 127-154* center on "The Poet, the Dark Lady, and the Young Man."

Green, Martin. *Wriothesley's Roses: In Shakespeare's Sonnets, Poems, and Plays*. Baltimore: Clevendon Books, 1993. Links historical records with poetic context in various sonnets in an interesting attempt to establish the identities of Shakespeare's fair young man and of the rival poet who seems to compete with Shakespeare's speaker for the affections of the dark lady. Provides a good historical background.

Hyland, Peter. *An Introduction to Shakespeare's Poems*. New York: Palgrave Macmillan, 2003. Discusses the characteristics of the Elizabethan sonnet and Shakespeare's contributions to this genre. Provides interpretative readings of the *Sonnets*. Places Shakespeare's poetry within the context of the politics, values, and tastes of Elizabethan England, arguing that he was a skeptical voice during this socially turbulent era.

Matz, Robert. *The World of Shakespeare's "Sonnets": An Introduction*. Jefferson, N.C.: McFarland, 2008. Focuses on the social and cultural world in which Shakespeare lived and how this environment shaped his sonnets. Describes the sonnets as "brilliant, edgy expressions" of English Renaissance culture.

Ramsey, Paul. *The Fickle Glass: A Study of Shakespeare's Sonnets*. New York: AMS Press, 1979. A clearly written scholarly examination of critical problems, poetic techniques, and meaning in the sonnets. Explores questions of authorship, order, and date of composition. Excellent discussion of metrical rules and Elizabethan rhetoric in the sonnets.

Smith, Hallet. *The Tension of the Lyre: Poetry in Shakespeare's Sonnets*. San Marino, Calif.: Huntington Library, 1981. General discussion of the sonnets, beginning with an exploration of poetic voice and audience, and including an overview of Shakespeare's world as it is reflected in the sonnets.

Weiser, David K. *Mind in Character: Shakespeare's Speaker in the Sonnets*. Columbia: University of Missouri Press, 1987. Thorough explication of the sonnets. Useful appendix classifies the sonnets by modes of address.

Sonnets to Orpheus

Author: Rainer Maria Rilke (1875-1926)
First published: Die Sonette an Orpheus, 1923 (English translation, 1936)
Type of work: Poetry

Rainer Maria Rilke, one of the great lyric poets of the twentieth century, wrote *Sonnets to Orpheus* in memory of Vera Ouckama Knoop, the nineteen-year-old daughter of a Dutch friend. When she was about seventeen, the girl was stricken with an incurable glandular disease. As her body became heavier and more massive, she stopped dancing and began to play music, and when her body became still heavier, she began to draw. Although Rilke barely knew the girl, he was touched by her story and shaken by the news of her death. At the time *Sonnets to Orpheus* were written, Rilke was staying at a château in Muzot, Switzerland, where he took refuge during several periods in his life after World War I and where he found the solitude he needed to work. It was here that in 1923 Rilke, in a burst of creative genius unlike any that he had ever before experienced, completed *Duineser Elegien* (1923; *Duino Elegies*, 1931) and *Sonnets to Orpheus* (a complement to the *Duino Elegies*).

In Greek mythology, Orpheus, the son of Apollo, was the

master magician, able to animate nature with his song. When his wife Eurydice died, he obtained her release from the underworld on the condition that he would not look at her until they reached the upper world, but he could not resist glancing back at her at the last moment. Legend had it that he was subsequently dismembered by Thracian women and scattered throughout the universe until all of nature became his song. This introduced a second phase, during which Orpheus became the religious center of a Dionysian sect (Dionysus was the god of uninhibited desire, vegetation, and wine) and presided in his magical divinity over the ancient religious mysteries of Greece. *Sonnets to Orpheus* incorporates this second, magical, aspect of the god.

Rilke's Orpheus symbol is the culmination of a number of themes and motifs dating back to the poet's earliest writing, which coalesce into the figure of the singing god who redeems out of time into space. His function links him with *Duino Elegies* through the principle of transformation. Orpheus is also equated with the poet, and by alluding to his special role as a singer of both realms, Rilke reiterates the need to unite life and death through song and praise. Orpheus literally sings among the dead. The mortal poet is to do the same.

The two main attributes of the Orpheus symbol are openness toward all experience—a fullness that includes both life and death—to an extent that Rilke refers to as an "overflowing"; and the ordering or forming of this experience through music, that is, art or poetry. The elevation of music as the final court of appeal, after suffering, love, and death have individually failed to reveal their secret, is declared in sonnet 1.

Sonnets to Orpheus speaks of "we," "you," and "I" interchangeably and is thus directed toward no particular person but to humanity in general (the exceptions are the two Knoop sonnets and the one addressed to a friend of Knoop). Rilke maintains a certain distance by the sparing use of the first-person pronoun. Although the poems cannot be arranged in any unified metrical scheme, Rilke adheres to a thoroughly symmetrical sonnet composition, with divisions into quatrains and tercets; the individual metrics are flexibly varied. He seems to have set himself the challenge of modifying the sonnet form while at the same time not destroying it altogether.

A kind of metaphorical primitivism may account for the simplicity, grammatical and otherwise, of most of *Sonnets to Orpheus*. In Rilke's later poetry, words are used as signs, and images become "points" or "cosmic configurations." Only in such a pattern, endorsed by Orpheus, can the totality of forms be preserved, a totality no longer viewed in isolation but adapted to the requirements of a universal myth.

Both part 1, which consists of twenty-six sonnets, and part 2, with its twenty-nine sonnets, form a cycle. Rather than forming thematic or chronological groups, the poems may be loosely characterized as the Orpheus sonnets, the sonnets incorporating poetic memories, and the sonnets of a didactic, reflective nature. Twelve poems (all but one in part 1) deal with the Orphic legend. Sonnets, 1, 7, and 26 in part 1 contain the main elements of the Orpheus theme, which opens the series and, as the circle widens to include other motifs, gradually disappears, to resurface finally in part 2, sonnet 26. The initial sonnet of part 1 is pure myth making: At the beginning of the world (or of the poet's art consciousness) stands Orpheus, whose music instills life into trees and stones, breaking down the rigid forms of nature and lending them new rhythms and dimensions. As the archetypal poet, Orpheus does not sing about a tree, he sings a tree, and as he sings the visible ascends into invisibility, while a temple to receive it rises in the ear. Here, as elsewhere, Rilke interchanges acoustic and visual imagery.

The functions of Orpheus in relation to the poet's world are expressed in part 1 in the key sonnet 7. Orpheus is the poet's surrogate, alone able to cross the threshold and, by virtue of his adherence to both the realms of the living and of the dead, to praise the things of earth before the dead. In fact, the poet identifies himself with his symbol, and they unite. The creative process operates within the paradox of silence and song, perishable and imperishable. It is visualized in the landscape and in the warm vineyards of the south, for whose infinite wine the poet's heart is the perishable wine press.

Praise is only one function of Orpheus's song; the chord of lamentation is its complement. In sonnet 8 in part 1, lamentation is personified and acted out. Sorrow is the youngest sister of Rejoicing, who knows, and Longing, who confesses. Sorrow is still young enough to learn from grief-stricken nights and yet, in abrupt reversal and by virtue of that very experience, is able to represent mortality among the constellations.

Part 1 further defines the Orphic double nature with the aid of nature symbols. In the second quartet of sonnet 6, Rilke draws effectively on folklore and superstitions about the spirits of the dead. To these primitive superstitions, Rilke opposes the gentle knowledge and memory of the dead. Only those who eat poppies with the dead (sonnet 9) can register the full scale of Orphic praise. Sonnet 3 contrasts the divine art of the god with human inadequacy resulting from humanity's divided nature. The phrase "Song is being" balances non-Being, humanity's unrelatedness to earth and stars. After the antithesis, the real definition of poetry, its stability and inevitability, provides the final lines. That leads logically to sonnet 4, which introduces the theme of the lovers to whom the Orphic attributes are applied.

Once Rilke establishes the basic Orphic myth, about twenty-eight sonnets incorporating poetic memories explore the varied material of the poet's artistic world. Roses, mirrors, dancing, and breathing are transformed into legend. The greatness of Rilke's best poetry lies in the insight offered by individual subjects or themes, even though they seem to possess only aesthetic implications. The underlying tensions in Rilke's poetry are between art and life, permanence and change, the formed and the formless. His problem is essentially linguistic rather than metaphysical, and it is to be solved by the transformation of the idea through language. The work's Orphic music is the very element calculated to activate inert space, for it is dynamic. In the "dancer" sonnet in part 2, Rilke fuses the dancer and the dance, the transient motion and the permanent form. The dance actually grows, step by step, out of the functions of language. Rilke perpetuates the movement of the final whirl by projecting the dancer into art forms.

The third type of Rilke's *Sonnets to Orpheus*—the didactic, reflective ones—are among his best. In them, the Orphic lyre conjures up the problems of a machine age and the metaphysical problems of time and eternity, God, and the possibilities of regeneration. Time is present in all of Rilke's poetry, and this is particularly true of these sonnets. Time enters into the unfolding of the machine motif, into the conception of historical and cultural evolution—those "splendid excesses of our own existence"—and into modes of belief. The genetic evolution of human beings, who create their own gods that fate destroys, is a hopeful projection, for eternity still lies before them. This is the timeless Orphic realm of spatial fullness.

Six sonnets deal directly with the role of the machine in the modern age, in the context of aimless motion versus contained repose. In Rilke's view, technology has its function as a means but not as an end. Many sonnets deal negatively with the acoustic unpleasantness of a mechanistic age, the "droning and drumming" of machines. The spiritual impasse invoked by the machine is described in sonnet 24 of part 1, in which humanity loses the "primeval friends of ours, the unfated,/ ever unsuing gods."

Escape from time, the destroyer, is possible through transformation in Orpheus. Some of Rilke's finest sonnets are concerned with this theme, but none so profoundly as the final ones of part 2, which make up a small cycle of their own. Sonnet 12 urges the readers to be prepared for transformation, like a flame altering all things that slip from their grasp. The theme ends in a mythological figure: Daphne in laurel can desire only that her lover transform himself into the wind that blows through her leaves. Two sonnets describe the inner landscape of transformation, the summer dreamworld with continuously watered gardens. These gardens of oriental profusion have symbolic reality for those who, with Orpheus, have advanced into another dimension of experience.

Sonnet 13 in part 2 is also concerned with the transformation theme. It is didactic and contains at least six categorical commands to the reader. The full scope of the transformation process is contained in the first verse, its stoic implications in verses 2 and 5: To anticipate departure is to be ever ready for the transformation into new forms. Whatever ultimate moment of experience this may mean, readers are to look forward to it as they look backward at the winter, "almost gone." The poet then moves from the human to the mythical plane in the command to be "ever dead in Eurydice." The poet-god may overcome love that vanished into the shades by transforming it into art. The conquest of loss restores the individual or the artist to the pure relationship that encloses that more adequate and inviolate world people create in themselves. This world is a declining one, and the realization and full acceptance of this fact is the highest possible accomplishment. Submission to this twofold act of Being and at the same time non-Being, of life and death, raises human beings above themselves, completing the spiral of life. Thus time and destiny can be overcome, and the circle of fullness can be completed.

Beyond exemplifying brilliant structure and innovative use of tradition, *Sonnets to Orpheus* brings the physical and the spiritual together and interchanges their qualities and meanings. The marriage of human being and god, and of concrete and abstract, of grief and celebration, of changelessness and change makes reading *Sonnets to Orpheus* a challenging and uplifting experience.

Genevieve Slomski

Further Reading

Casey, Timothy J. *A Reader's Guide to Rilke's "Sonnets to Orpheus."* Galway, Ireland: Arlen House, 2001. An accessible explanation of the poems written by a Rilke scholar.

Mandel, Siegfried. *Rainer Maria Rilke: The Poetic Instinct.* Carbondale: Southern Illinois University Press, 1965. Reflects a thorough knowledge of Rilke's craftsmanship and discusses the deeper reality expressed in his works. Includes a bibliography.

Metzger, Erika A., and Michael M. Metzger, eds. *A Companion to the Works of Rainer Maria Rilke.* Rochester, N.Y.: Camden House, 2001. Collection of essays discussing

Rilke's life and analyzing specific works. Alan Keele's piece, "Poesis and the Great Tree of Being: A Holistic Reading of Rilke's *Sonette an Orpheus*," analyzes the sonnets.

Nelson, Erika M. *Reading Rilke's Orphic Identity*. New York: Peter Lang, 2005. Analyzes Rilke's poetry within the context of fin-de-siècle literature and as a precursor of modernism and postmodernism. Focuses on Rilke's preoccupation with identity and how he reinterpreted the myth of Orpheus in modern psychological and poetic terms.

Peters, H. F. *Rainer Maria Rilke: Masks and the Man*. Seattle: University of Washington Press, 1960. Shows Rilke's impact on modern poetry and concludes that the poet consciously tried to express the human predicament of his age by creating new forms, styles, and myths. Contains a chronology of Rilke's life.

Pollock-Brodsky, Patricia. *Rainer Maria Rilke*. Boston: Twayne, 1988. Excellent introductory analysis to the poet's life and work. Focuses on Rilke's sensitivity to art, his position as a cosmopolitan within the international culture of Europe at the turn of the century, and the contradictory nature of many aspects of his work and life.

Ryan, Judith. *Rilke, Modernism, and Poetic Tradition*. New York: Cambridge University Press, 1999. Traces Rilke's poetic development from his early aestheticism to his later modernism. Argues that he is not a "solitary genius" but a poet whose work was deeply influenced by the culture of his time.

Wood, Frank. *Rainer Maria Rilke: The Ring of Forms*. New York: Octagon Books, 1970. Detailed discussion of the growth and structure of Rilke's later poetry. Describes Rilke's "inverted Christianity."

Sons and Lovers

Author: D. H. Lawrence (1885-1930)
First published: 1913
Type of work: Novel
Type of plot: Psychological realism
Time of plot: Late nineteenth century
Locale: England

Principal characters:
GERTRUDE MOREL, a devoted mother
WALTER MOREL, her husband and a coal miner
WILLIAM, her oldest son
ANNIE, her daughter
PAUL, her favorite son
ARTHUR, another son
MIRIAM LEIVERS, Paul's sweetheart
CLARA DAWES, Paul's mistress
BAXTER DAWES, Clara's husband

The Story:

Walter Morel, a coal miner, was a handsome, dashing young man when Gertrude married him. After a few years of marriage, however, he proves to be an irresponsible breadwinner and a drunkard, and his wife hates him for what he once meant to her and for what he is now. Her only solace lies in her children—William, Annie, Paul, and Arthur—for she leans heavily upon them for companionship and lives in their happiness. She is a good parent, and her children love her. The oldest son, William, is successful in his work, but he longs to go to London, where he has promise of a better job. After he leaves, Mrs. Morel turns to Paul for the companionship and love she found in William.

Paul, who likes to paint, is more sensitive than his brothers and sister and is closer to Mrs. Morel than any of the others. William brings a young woman named Lily home to visit, but it is apparent that she is not the right kind of woman for him; she is too shallow and self-centered. Before long, William becomes aware of that fact, but he resigns himself to keeping the promise he made to his fiancé.

When William becomes ill, Mrs. Morel goes to London to nurse her son and is with him there when he dies. Home once more after burying her first son, Mrs. Morel cannot bring herself out of her sorrow. Not until Paul becomes sick does she realize that her duty lies with the living rather than with the dead. After this realization, she centers all of her attention upon Paul. The two other children are capable of carrying on their affairs without the constant attention that Paul demands.

At sixteen years of age, Paul goes to visit some friends of Mrs. Morel. The Leiverses are a warmhearted family, and Paul easily gains the friendship of the Leivers children. Fifteen-year-old Miriam Leivers is a strange girl, but her inner charm attracts Paul. Mrs. Morel, like many others, does not care for Miriam. Paul goes to work at a stocking mill, where he is successful in his social relationships and in his work. He continues to draw. Miriam watches over his work and, with quiet understanding, offers judgment concerning his success or failure. Mrs. Morel senses that someday her son will become famous for his art.

By the time Miriam and Paul grow into their twenties, Paul realizes that Miriam loves him deeply and that he loves her; for some reason, however, he cannot bring himself to touch her. Through Miriam, he meets Clara Dawes. For a long while, Mrs. Morel was urging him to give up Miriam, and Paul tries to tell Miriam that it is over between them. He does not want to marry her, but he feels that he does belong to her. He cannot make up his mind.

Clara is separated from her husband, Baxter Dawes. Although she is five years Paul's senior, Clara is a beautiful woman whose loveliness charms him. Although she becomes his mistress, she refuses to divorce her husband and marry Paul. Sometimes Paul wonders whether he could bring himself to marry Clara if she were free. She is not what he wants. His mother is the only woman to whom he can turn for complete understanding and love, for Miriam tries to possess him and Clara maintains a barrier against him. Paul continues to devote much of his time and attention to making his mother happy. Annie marries and goes to live with her husband near the Morel home, and Arthur marries a childhood friend; the couple has a son six months after their wedding.

Baxter resents Paul's relationship with his wife. Once he accosts Paul in a tavern and threatens him. Paul knows that he cannot fight with Baxter, but he continues to see Clara.

Paul enters pictures in local exhibits and wins four prizes. With encouragement from Mrs. Morel, he continues to paint. He wants to go abroad, but he cannot leave his mother. He begins to see Miriam again. When she yields herself to him, his passion is ruthless and savage. Their relationship, however, is still unsatisfactory, and he turns again to Clara.

Miriam knows about his love affair with Clara, but Miriam feels that Paul will tire of his mistress and come back to her. Paul stays with Clara, however, because he finds in her an outlet for his unknown desires. His life is in great conflict. Meanwhile, Paul is earning enough money to give his mother the material possessions her husband failed to provide. Mr. Morel stays on with his wife and son, but he is no longer accepted as a father or a husband.

One day, it is revealed that Mrs. Morel has cancer and is beyond any help except that of morphine and then death. During the following months, Mrs. Morel declines rapidly. Paul is tortured by his mother's pain. Annie and Paul marvel at her resistance to death and wish that it would come, to end her suffering. Paul dreads such a catastrophe in his life, although he knows it must come eventually. He turns to Clara for comfort, but she fails to make him forget his misery. While visiting his mother at the hospital, Paul finds Baxter recovering from an attack of typhoid fever. For a long time, Paul sensed that Clara wants to return to Dawes, and now, out of pity for Baxter, he brings about a reconciliation between the husband and wife.

When Mrs. Morel's suffering mounts to a torturing degree, Annie and Paul decide that anything would be better than to let her live in agony. One night, Paul gives her an overdose of morphine, and Mrs. Morel dies the next day.

Left alone, Paul is lost. He feels that his own life ended with the death of his mother. Clara, to whom he turned before, returned to Dawes. Because they cannot bear to stay in the house without Mrs. Morel, Paul and his father part and each takes different lodgings.

For a while, Paul wanders helplessly, trying to find some purpose in his life. Then he thinks of Miriam, to whom he once belonged. He returns to her, but with the renewed association, he realizes more than ever that she is not what he wants. Once he thought of going abroad; now he wants to join his mother in death. Leaving Miriam for the last time, he feels trapped and lost in his own indecision, but he also feels that he is free from Miriam after many years of passion and regret.

His mother's death is too great a sorrow for Paul to cast off immediately. After a lengthy inner struggle, he is able to see that she will always be with him and that he does not need to die to join her. With his newfound courage, he sets out to make his own life anew.

Critical Evaluation:

Although Sigmund Freud was the first to provide a systematic analysis of the Oedipal relationship, this instinct has been a part of the human unconscious from the earliest beginnings of humans as social animals. The establishment of the taboo against a son's murdering his father and having sexual relationships with his mother was, one may argue, an initial step in the creation of civilization, because, according to Freud, this psychic drive lies deep in every man's subconscious, or id, as a reservoir of anarchistic energy. If a male fails to acknowledge this biological compulsion and to incorporate its prohibition into his own ego, he invites annihilation: specifically, in the form of castration by the father; generally, in the loss of freedom and power.

One of the earliest and best-known dramatizations of this drive is Sophocles' play, *Oedipus Tyrannus* (c. 429 B.C.E.; *Oedipus Tyrannus*, 1715). Without foreknowledge and culpable guilt, Oedipus murders his father and marries his mother. Since he has transgressed, however, he must be punished; he blinds himself, a form of castration. William Shakespeare's *Hamlet, Prince of Denmark* (pr. c. 1600-1601, pb. 1603) has also been explored and explicated, most notably by Ernest Jones, as a reenactment of the Oedipal myth. *Sons and Lovers*, based directly on D. H. Lawrence's own childhood experiences, is the most significant post-Freudian novel dealing with a young man's murderous feelings toward his father and his erotic attraction to his mother.

Although it would be overly simplistic to explain *Sons and Lovers* as a mere gloss on a psychological concept, Freud's complex does offer a convenient way to begin understanding the character and cultural situation of Lawrence's hero, Paul Morel. He is the youngest and adored son of a mother who married beneath herself. A member of the failed middle class, she is educated to a degree, refined with pretensions toward the higher matters of life. As a girl, she is attracted to Walter Morel, a miner who possesses a passionate exuberance she missed on the frayed edges of the middle class. Their marriage, however, soon disintegrates under the pressures of poverty and unfulfilled expectations. As the father and mother grow apart and the older children leave home, Mrs. Morel turns toward her youngest child, mapping out his life and intending to free him from the ignominy of the working class. Her ambitions for Paul are not untainted by her own frustrations, and it becomes clear that she wishes to live out her life through him.

Sensitive and frail, Paul finds his father's drunkenness and rough-edged masculinity repellent. Reared by his mother as if he were a fragile hothouse plant, he is further alienated by his father's vulgar habits and degrading job. Without sympathy or understanding of his father's suffering or his hard and abrupt love for him, Paul withdraws and joins his mother in the domestic battle. Morel becomes enraged and disappointed by the loss of his son and wife and withdraws into self-pity and alcohol.

Bereft of his father's influence, Paul finds his life dominated by his mother. Smothered by her warm maternity, cut off from the real world, he returns her ardent affection, and they form a relationship designed to hold off the horrors of reality. As he grows up, however, he discovers that he traded his self for security. His mother's protectiveness costs him the power and freedom to relate to others. Every relationship

he tries to create is inhibited by her jealousy and demands for his entire attention. Indeed, he comes to feel that every relationship he attempts to pursue is in some way a denial of her.

Paul's attraction to Miriam Leivers, which gradually develops into a love affair, is, ironically, both a rejection and a reaffirmation of his mother. Their immature love, which Mrs. Morel rightfully sees as a threat, is in some ways an acting out of the sexual implications of the mother-son relationship. In her passive dominance, Miriam unconsciously assumes for Paul the figure of his mother. If their love manages to remove him temporarily from his mother's sway, it also reinforces it. Both relationships are symbiotic; Paul draws sustenance from the women but loses the power of self-propulsion. That Paul does not completely acquiesce in the symbiosis is evident both in his brutal sexual treatment of Miriam and in his sexual ambivalence toward his mother.

Paul's connection with Clara and Baxter Dawes is much more interesting and complex. Clara provides him with an adult sexual experience unlike that which he has with Miriam. She is neither dominating nor submissive, but she demands that he meet her as an equal. He therefore must remain emotionally on his own; he is expected to give affection as well as to receive it. Unfortunately, Paul cannot maintain such independence, and this fact undermines their love. He cannot exist as a self-sufficient entity, and Clara will not tolerate an invasion of her self. Paul, however, does not understand this about their relationship until after Mrs. Morel's death. His subsequently successful attempt to reunite her with Baxter thus becomes his first sign of health; it is not only an admission that their romance is impossible but also a reparation for having alienated her from Baxter.

Paul's act of reparation is also symbolic. Released from his mother's dominance by her death, he must continue his growth toward freedom and power by making peace with his father. Unable to confront his father directly, Paul's bringing together Clara and Baxter is an admission of the higher moral demands of marital love, a love he helped to destroy—although in the innocence of childhood—between his father and mother. In this act, moreover, he negates the child in himself and salutes the reality of the father and husband.

"Critical Evaluation" by David L. Kubal

Further Reading

Balbert, Peter, and Phillip L. Marcus, eds. *D. H. Lawrence: A Centenary Consideration*. Ithaca, N.Y.: Cornell University Press, 1985. Contains eleven essays on Lawrence and his novels. Two essays pertain to *Sons and Lovers*: Mark Spilka's "For Mark Schorer with Combative Love:

The *Sons and Lovers* Manuscript" and feminist critic Sandra M. Gilbert's masterful "Potent Griselda: 'The Ladybird' and the Great Mother."

Cushman, Keith, and Earl G. Ingersoll, eds. *D. H. Lawrence: New Worlds.* Madison, N.J.: Fairleigh Dickinson University Press, 2003. Collection of essays that seek to reinterpret Lawrence's work. Includes discussions of his influence on British fiction, debates over his national identity, and the chapter "The Life of the Son/Sun and the Death of the Mother in *Sons and Lovers*" by Gavriel Reisner.

Fernihough, Anne, ed. *The Cambridge Companion to D. H. Lawrence.* New York: Cambridge University Press, 2001. Collection of essays interpreting Lawrence's work from various perspectives, including discussions of Lawrence and modernism, psychoanalysis, and sexual politics and an assessment of Lawrence's critical and cultural legacy.

Gilbert, Sandra. *D. H. Lawrence's "Sons and Lovers" and Other Works: "The Rainbow," "Women in Love," "The Plumed Serpent."* New York: Simon & Schuster, 1965. Provides introductory biography and information on people behind the fictional characters in this autobiographical novel. Includes Lawrence's plan for the novel, Freudian influences, chapter-by-chapter summary with explication, character descriptions, and critical commentary. A gold mine for researchers.

Kazin, Alfred. Introduction to *Sons and Lovers*, by D. H. Lawrence. New York: Modern Library, 1962. Kazin, a prominent literary critic, provides pertinent background information on *Sons and Lovers* as autobiographical fiction, discusses crucial concerns of the content, and analyzes style and Freudian elements in the novel.

Rylance, Rick, ed. *Sons and Lovers.* New York: St. Martin's Press, 1996. Collection of essays providing critical interpretations of *Sons and Lovers*, including discussions of psychoanalysis and society, sexual politics, feminism, and individuality and society in the novel.

Salgado, Gamini, ed. *D. H. Lawrence, "Sons and Lovers": A Casebook.* Nashville, Tenn.: Aurora, 1970. An excellent collection of materials for researchers of *Sons and Lovers*. Includes the original foreword from the novel, original reviews, criticism, questions, bibliography, and index.

Worthen, John. *D. H. Lawrence: The Life of an Outsider.* New York: Counterpoint, 2005. Written by a distinguished Lawrence scholar, this compelling, readable biography is accompanied by several photographs.

Worthen, John, and Andrew Harrison, eds. *D. H. Lawrence's "Sons and Lovers": A Casebook.* New York: Oxford University Press, 2005. Collection of essays approaching *Sons and Lovers* from various perspectives, including discussions of narrative structure, relationship and class, and images of women in the novel. Also includes excerpts of Lawrence's letters.

Sophie's Choice

Author: William Styron (1925-2006)
First published: 1979
Type of work: Novel
Type of plot: Psychological realism
Time of plot: 1947
Locale: Brooklyn, New York

Principal characters:
STINGO, the narrator, would-be writer of the Great American novel
SOPHIE ZAWATOWSKA, a displaced concentration camp survivor
NATHAN LANDAU, a brilliant madman, Sophie's lover
STINGO'S FATHER, a southern, liberal gentleman

The Story:

Stingo, an aspiring southern novelist in his early twenties, resigns an unrewarding editorship with a major New York publishing firm and moves into economical lodgings in a Brooklyn rooming house to devote all of his energies to his writing. Stingo's father sends him five hundred dollars from a recent discovery of old gold pieces that were obtained by his great-grandfather for the sale of a slave, Artiste. Although embarrassed by the source of this windfall, Stingo uses the money to live on while he creates his first literary masterpiece, a novel about Maria Hunt, a high school friend whose suicide Stingo's father relates to him as of possible interest. His father writes him regularly and once comes to visit him to try to persuade Stingo to return to his roots in the South. Stingo refuses to leave New York, but he often reconsiders that decision.

Soon Stingo is deeply involved in the lives of Nathan Landau, one of several Jewish boarders, and Nathan's passionate lover, the beautiful Polish, former Catholic refugee, Sophie Zawatowska. Stingo falls in love at first sight with Sophie but has too much respect for Nathan's prior claim to woo her. He befriends the couple and retells Sophie's story as she gradually unfolds it to him. Sophie was raised in Cracow. Her professor father provided Sophie a strict, oppressive upbringing, while her passive but refined mother taught her a love for classical music that became her only consolation in the madness of Auschwitz and of the postwar United States.

At first, Stingo idealizes the brilliant, talkative, and volatile Nathan, whose claim to be a cellular biologist Stingo accepts at face value. It soon becomes clear that Nathan indulges in brutally abusive moods, exacerbated by drug use, ending in gun-waving, threats to kill, in physical and verbal abuse, and in sexual violence for Sophie. Stingo's perplexity about Sophie's enduring attachment to this disastrously destructive relationship is only partially satisfied when he learns Sophie's story. She inherits guilt for her professor-father's fascist political beliefs, his anti-Semitism, his foreshadowing the Holocaust through a monograph he wrote calling for the extermination of Jews, his demand that Sophie distribute the monograph, and his death as the Nazis shot him and Sophie's husband because they were professors and Polish. Sophie's most terrifying burden arises from the first few horrifying moments when she arrived at Auschwitz with her two children, a boy and a girl, and a drunken German physician demanded that she decide which of her two children should be sent to the gas chambers. Such was Sophie's choice.

Her boy lived, and Sophie obtained a clerical position with the camp commandant, Rudolph Hoss. Sophie tried to seduce Hoss, kissed his boots, and begged to see her child—all to no effect. She never saw her son again.

Only her love for Nathan and classical music fuel Sophie's will to live. She constantly fills the neighborhood with strains from Wolfgang Amadeus Mozart, Johann Sebastian Bach, and Ludwig van Beethoven, played on Nathan's gramophone. Stingo learns from Nathan's brother Larry, a wealthy physician, that Nathan suffers chronic mental illness, is not employed as a scientist or anything else, and, between bouts in mental hospitals, occupies the boardinghouse room paid for by his family, on whose patronage he is completely dependent. Now convinced that Nathan might well be homicidal, Stingo offers Sophie an escape, a new life married to him, living on the small Virginia farm his father offers for his use—ironically, inherited from a man of offensively rightist ideology, whom his father tolerates and befriends in traditional liberal American style.

Once again, Sophie becomes a refugee, on a train bound this time for Virginia, where former slave territory now offers possible liberation, healing, and life accompanied by Stingo, the gallant lover nearly twenty years younger than she. After a stopover in Washington, D.C., so Sophie can have a tourist's introduction to America's political heart, Stingo and Sophie spend a passionate night together. Stingo then awakens to find himself alone. Grieved, Stingo wavers between continuing on toward his life as a southern gentleman-farmer and writer or returning to New York. At last, his illusions nearly all dispelled, and realizing Sophie's latest choice entails her death, Stingo frantically returns to the boardinghouse to discover officials removing the bodies of Nathan and Sophie, who fulfilled their suicide pact.

Critical Evaluation:

Judging by the large body of critical attention given to William Styron, he quickly earned major status among American writers. Many critics consider his fourth novel, *Sophie's Choice*, to be his best achievement.

In *Sophie's Choice*, Styron introduces a theme new to his novels, the Holocaust, and revisits an old theme, the suicide of a woman. *Sophie's Choice* is a memoir narrated by Stingo twenty years after the events it records. As is usual in Styron's fiction, it attempts to connect major themes of recent Western history to a confessional type of story. The parallels between the facts of Stingo's experiences at the rooming house are so consistent with Styron's own life at that age that readers should interpret Stingo as a persona tied extremely closely to Styron himself. Styron did live in such a boardinghouse in order to write and did know such a woman as Sophie, "beautiful but ravaged." He knew her, however, only slightly. This gives an authenticity to the narrative voice, yet allows a freedom to the artist to realize a personal vision. Through Stingo, Styron unifies a complex variety of themes, two of which are central: the difficulty of keeping faith with God, religion, and human nature in view of the Nazi atrocities; and the difficulty of becoming a literary artist, in view of those atrocities as well as in view of the decline of southern regional writing. As Nathan observes to Stingo, Southern literature is a dying tradition; the difficulty of creating in the wake of such notables as Lillian Hellman, William Faulkner, Robert Penn Warren, and Carson McCullers is Styron's great challenge. A major theme of *Sophie's Choice* is Styron's focus on this challenge, and he responds by creating a South contextualized in the colorful mixture of many ethnicities and backgrounds. As Stingo notes, the Brooklyn rooming house is a microcosm of American heterogenous types. By placing his South in such a broad context Styron is able to make his point that suffering is universal for human beings, and even the Holocaust may be integrated into a larger picture of human tragedy. The risk is in proposing such a morally ambiguous world and such a pessimistic vision of life that creativity becomes wholly arbitrary and useless. Styron seems to find a sufficient balance and some rays of convincing hope, but only as Stingo overcomes his youthful naïveté and exercises self-control in his relationships with others. The South of his youth and the European past are as sweet, as innocent, and as irrecoverable as Sophie's own childhood in Gothic Cracow, resounding with the divine music of the classic composers Wolfgang Amadeus Mozart, George Frideric Handel, Johann Sebastian Bach, and Johannes Brahms. The past is not altogether obsolete and archaic, however, nor are the obstacles to happiness the only powers at work. Joy visits at unexpected moments. Whether readers find in these moments sufficient recompense for pain or little more than an interruption of pain will determine the degree to which they find Styron's tragedies absolute. The joy is, in any case, real in Nathan's brilliant conversation, in the progress of Stingo's first novel, in Sophie's friendship, uninhibited sexuality, and beauty. Joy is there even in his father's idealism and old-fashioned manners, his solicitous love for and faith in his son. It is present in Sophie's quasi-mythical youth in prewar Poland; in her struggles to help others and make the best of her imprisonment in the concentration camp at Auschwitz; and in her efforts to regain her health, to love faithfully, and to rebuild her life in the United States, although she is haunted by memories, especially guilt over her choice.

Structurally, *Sophie's Choice* is a complex achievement. Styron structures the novel on stated and implied parallels—between Poland and the American South, between Nathan's sadistic moods and the Nazi persecution of his race, between Stingo's and Sophie's inability to find permanent happiness through love. Styron's literary output is not large, but it benefits from careful craftsmanship and such deeply considered relationships. Its only serious narrative weakness comes when Stingo gives over his storytelling persona in order to summarize historians' recent scholarship concerning Rudolf Hess's involvement in the Nazi movement, an interruption in the fictional world that jars readers' sensibilities. While critics have rightly observed that Nathan is weak because he is too improbable, Styron's strength rests with his recurring thematic emphasis on tragic women trapped between their need for self-realization and their dependence on unstable and neurotic men. He writes with great sensitivity about traditional women's roles and offers convincing psychological insights into the major dilemmas of feminine existence.

While recent history and Styron's autobiography provide a realistic atmosphere, the female character, presented with extraordinary sensitivity and intimacy, is an archetype synthesized in Styron's imagination, the femme fatale become voluntary sacrifice, in a ritual of recompense as old as humanity, a self-assigned offering necessary to balance the scales against man's terrible inhumanity to man.

Men are not immune from pain or victimhood, as the tragicomic adventures during which Stingo tries unsuccessfully to lose his virginity remind us. In Styron's fictional world, no one group, ideology, religion, race, or gender owns exclusive rights to suffering or claims to the superiority of their sufferings. Nor are victims merely passive objects of sadism. Tragedy is defined by the complicity of victims in their suffering, whose commitment to life and goodness ironically traps them as accessories to the evils that befall them. Sophie's choice illustrates the point precisely. One's acceptance of this burden of responsibility restores some dignity to human life, and this theme redeems Styron's literary vision from absolute darkness.

Diane Brotemarkle

Further Reading

Bloom, Harold, ed. *William Styron's "Sophie's Choice."* Philadelphia: Chelsea House, 2002. A collection of critical essays about *Sophie's Choice*, including discussions of the problem of egotism, the speakable and the unspeakable, narrative technique, and sound in the novel. Includes a conversation with Styron.

Casciato, Arthur D., and James L. W. West III, eds. *Critical Essays on William Styron*. Boston: G. K. Hall, 1982. A cross-section of reviews of Styron's fiction, including essays on *Sophie's Choice*.

Coale, Samuel. *William Styron Revisited*. Boston: Twayne, 1991. Chapter 7 provides an insightful analysis of the characters in this novel.

Cologne-Brookes, Gavin. *The Novels of William Styron: From Harmony to History*. Baton Rouge: Louisiana State University Press, 1995. Examines the influence of the modernist movement on Styron's novels, exploring his psychological themes and analyzing his shifting patterns of discourse. Chapter 5 focuses on *Sophie's Choice*.

Hadaller, David. *Gynicide: Women in the Novels of William Styron*. Madison, N.J.: Fairleigh Dickinson University Press, 1996. Explores the treatment of women in Styron's fiction, with special emphasis on his handling of women's deaths and the meaning of these deaths. Argues that Styron's depictions force readers to question a society that victimizes women. Chapter 5 focuses on *Sophie's Choice*.

Karl, Frederick. *American Fictions, 1940-1980*. New York: Harper & Row, 1983. Contains especially high praise for *Sophie's Choice* as Styron's best novel.

Ross, Daniel W., ed. *The Critical Response to William Styron*. Westport, Conn.: Greenwood Press, 1995. A collection of previously printed reviews, articles, and original essays that chronologically trace the critical reception of Styron's novels.

Sirlin, Rhoda, and James L. W. West III, eds. *"Sophie's Choice": A Contemporary Casebook*. Newcastle, England: Cambridge Scholars, 2007. Collection of essays that interpret and react to the novel. Focuses on the themes of sexual politics, anti-Semitism and the Holocaust, and silence. Contributors include Gloria Steinem, Cynthia Ozick, and Elie Wiesel.

West, James L. W., III, ed. *William Styron: A Life*. New York: Random House, 1998. A comprehensive biography that lucidly and cogently connects events in Styron's life to his fiction. An essential work for anyone who wishes to understand Styron and his writing.

The Sorrows of Young Werther

Author: Johann Wolfgang von Goethe (1749-1832)
First published: Die Leiden des jungen Werthers, 1774 (English translation, 1779)
Type of work: Novel
Type of plot: Bildungsroman
Time of plot: Mid-eighteenth century
Locale: Germany

Principal characters:
WERTHER, a young man
CHARLOTTE (LOTTE), a young woman with whom he falls in love
ALBERT, Charlotte's fiancé

The Story:

Young Werther, leaving home, writes to his friend Wilhelm to describe the secluded region where he went to forget the unhappiness of his earlier years. He discovered a pleasant cottage surrounded by a lovely garden, and he felt that in this peaceful retreat he could live in happy solitude forever. A few days later, he reports that his soul recovered in his rustic surroundings. He does not want books or the companionship of his old friends, for he is transported into a new world of kinship with nature. He mentions a nearby hamlet, Walheim, and the village inn where he can drink good coffee, sit in solitude, and read the works of Homer. Several letters to Wilhelm continue describing Werther's simple life among scenes of natural beauty.

Suddenly there is a break in his letters, followed by the announcement that he met an angel. At a ball, he was introduced to Charlotte S., the daughter of a judge who retired to a hunting lodge not far from Walheim. Charlotte is a beautiful and charming girl, and despite her being betrothed to another young man, who was not present at the ball, Werther fell deeply in love with her at first sight.

Perhaps his passion became all the deeper because he was warned not to fall in love with her. At the dance, Werther demanded much of her attention, and he began to ask her about Albert, her fiancé, when a storm suddenly interrupted the dance. The host led the guests into a room protected by curtains and shutters. There they played a game called counting. Once Werther kissed Charlotte's hands. When the party broke up at sunrise, he took her to her home through a dazzling world of raindrops and morning sun. From that time on, he called every day on Lotte, as he refers to her in his letters. He grieved over their separation when she went to attend a sick woman. One day, he went with her to visit an old pastor; he noted that her youthful presence seemed to bring new life to the old man.

Because he could not bear to have her out of his sight, Werther began to object to the time Lotte gave to sick friends and other acquaintances. A glimpse of her as she rode away on some errand was enough to set his head spinning and his heart beating wildly. If her finger accidentally touched his, the blood pounded through his veins. He confesses to his friend that he did little of the painting he had intended; all of his time is consumed with his love for Charlotte.

After he receives Wilhelm's advice either to press his suit with Lotte or to relinquish his hopeless passion, Werther decides to see the girl less frequently. His decision is further strengthened by Albert's return to Walheim. Werther is jealous of Albert but writes that he nevertheless admires his rival's fine character. In answer to further urging from Wilhelm, Werther replies that he can neither give up Lotte nor hope to win her from Albert. That being so, Werther grows more and more melancholy. Because he can possess Lotte only in his dreams, he succumbs to gloom and despair. At last, deciding that he must leave Walheim, he asks Wilhelm to secure a government post for him. When Wilhelm suggests a post with an ambassador, Werther postpones his acceptance or refusal of the position. Wilhelm, however, obtains the appointment without waiting to hear from his friend, so Werther's course is decided for him. During the two last hours he spends with Lotte and Albert, he pretends that he is not going away, feeling that their farewells will be more than he can bear.

At first, the official duties of his new position keep Werther from brooding over his sorrows, but as time passes he begins to dislike the ambassador for whom he works. No longer interested in government affairs, he reproaches Wilhelm for securing the appointment. He chafes under the responsibilities he is forced to assume. Finally, he writes to Lotte. Albert writes in reply, informing him that the two were married some time earlier.

Werther resigns his position at court. Failing in his attempt to enter the army, he accepts the offer of a young prince to spend the summer on his estate. When he fails to find in the nobleman's household the peace and calm for which he hoped, he decides to return to Walheim to be near Lotte. However, his first encounter with Albert and Lotte throws him into such a state that his letter to Wilhelm is almost incoherent. He cannot understand why Albert does not look more distractedly happy. Although Lotte pities Werther and Albert sympathizes with him, they are unable to help him. At the same time, Werther is concerned with the fate of a peasant who was convicted of murder. Failing to save the man from his fate, Werther is more wretched than ever. At last, following her husband's suggestion, Lotte suggests that Werther visit her house less frequently. In despair, he writes that when he can bear his sorrows no longer he intends to end his life.

The rest of his story is told by others. One night, while Albert was away from home, Werther went to Lotte's house. Frightened by his speech and appearance, she asked him to read aloud some passages from Ossian. After he seized her in a wild embrace, she fled and locked herself in her room. He stood outside the door and begged her to speak so that he could hear her voice for the last time.

The next day, he sent a servant to Albert and asked for the loan of a brace of pistols to take with him on an unexpected journey. He shot himself that night, but he was not quite dead when his servant found him the next morning. He died at noon without regaining consciousness. Hearing of his death, Charlotte fell into a swoon so deep that it threatened her life. Workmen of the village carried Werther's body to its resting place under the lime trees at Walheim.

Critical Evaluation:

Johann Wolfgang von Goethe wrote *The Sorrows of Young Werther* in the space of a few weeks in 1774, in a burst of creative energy that charged the whole work with a rare intensity. He drew upon his own experiences, and much of the work is autobiographical. Perhaps because of this, it captured a mood of the times and was greeted with great admiration and enthusiasm by the public. It was the one work that can be said to have made Goethe's reputation; to the end of his life, he was for many readers primarily "the author of *Werther.*" At the same time, it was a turning point in his career, for it marked the end of his "storm and stress" period. The outburst of all-consuming emotion was followed by a quieter period, which led to his classical style of the 1780's. Goethe himself later regarded *The Sorrows of Young Werther* as a kind of therapeutic expression of a dangerous side of his own personality, one that he overcame and controlled. He was appalled to find that Werther became regarded as a model of behavior, influencing men's fashion (blue coat with yellow vest and trousers; long, unpowdered hair) and inspiring a rash of suicides all over Europe.

The immediacy of the work is, in large part, the result of its epistolary form. After a brief foreword by the fictional editor, the reader plunges straight into the world of Werther's mind, and the style of his letters, full of exclamations, broken sentences, and impassioned flights of imagination, expresses his personality better than could any description. Throughout the novel, Werther moves from peak to peak of emotion, and the letters pick out the high points of his life. When he finally becomes too incoherent to write, the editor enters, which creates a chilling effect. The editor observes events from a distance, and his observing Werther with a sympathetic but dispassionate eye retards the headlong rush of the story. The novel possessed a further immediacy for its first readers in that it was set in their own contemporary world. The first letter is dated May 4, 1771, and from there Goethe leads the reader through that year's summer, fall, and winter into the next year with its new hope in the spring and the final tragedy at the end of the year in midwinter. Werther shares the interests of his generation: He reads Homer, Friedrich Gottlieb Klopstock, and Ossian; loves nature and the simple folk in the fashion of Jean-Jacques Rousseau; and chafes against the conventions and the fashions of aristocratic eighteenth century society.

Aside from some secondary plot elements that mirror Werther's own predicament, especially the story of the peasant who commits murder out of frustrated love, the work is developed entirely around three characters: Werther, Lotte, and Albert. Lotte is in many ways the pivotal character, since she is placed between the two men, who are almost opposites. She is attracted to both, perhaps more to Werther than to Albert, since Werther appeals to her romantic side and she shares with him a capacity for passionate emotion that Albert lacks. When Goethe first introduces her into the narrative, she is caring for her younger brothers and sisters, the very image of responsibility and self-sacrifice. Her mother is dead, and she has taken over her duties in the family. At the party in the storm, she takes over and organizes games to quiet the fears of her companions. However poetic she may be, she has a calm head and understands that Werther is hopelessly impractical in his emotion-centered life. Albert is a good husband and father, a bit dry perhaps and overly rational, but dependable, devoted, and clearheaded. Lotte, a complex character, would like to have both men in her life. While Werther is certainly the most directly autobiographical of the characters, Lotte is perhaps closer to Goethe's own personality, combining the practical, responsible traits that would find expression in his official activities in Weimar with the poetic imagination that constantly drew him back into the world of literature. This union of opposites is a common feature of Goethe's work, from *Faust: Eine Tragödie* (1808; *The Tragedy of Faust*, 1823)—"two souls dwell, alas, within my breast"—to Wilhelm, who wants to be an actor but becomes a doctor instead.

From the very beginning, Goethe distinguished his own character from that of Werther. Indeed, *The Sorrows of Young Werther* is more a judgment on the dangers of emotion than an incitement to emulation. The novel is, in fact, a tragedy of character, for the unhappy romance is not the cause of Werther's tragedy. From the very beginning, as Werther exclaims "what a thing is the heart of man," his situation is clear. Werther is important as one of the first modern tragic figures for whom his own personality, not events, is the tragedy. The conflict rests within him, and the world merely provides the occasion for his inner conflict to express itself. He embodies a life-spirit that strives for the absolute and the unconditional, which is carried forward by a stream of emotion that seizes on life and constantly transforms it into an inner experience of great intensity. His life is centered on his own emotions and drawn inward as in a whirlpool. There is no

compensating outward flow in the form of activity or other-directedness, no objective pole that can counter the all-transforming subjectivity. It is the spirit of Faust, or of Goethe's tragic poet-figure Torquato Tasso. It is the spirit that he sees as the inevitable consequence of the emotion-centered Sturm und Drang, or "storm and stress," writers, not a few of whom ended in madness or in suicide. In Werther, Goethe created perhaps the most memorable representative of this tragic type, the embodiment of one extreme of the human personality. In his subsequent work, Goethe continued to keep this aspect of himself alive, to provide the motive force for a series of masterpieces. *The Sorrows of Young Werther* itself became the inspiration for a host of Romantic writers in Germany, England, and France, and thus represents a landmark in European literature.

"Critical Evaluation" by Steven C. Schaber

Further Reading

Armstrong, John. *Love, Life, Goethe: Lessons of the Imagination from the Great German Poet*. New York: Farrar, Straus and Giroux, 2007. Goethe's works are analyzed and his life examined in this comprehensive volume. Armstrong discusses a wide range of Goethe's writings, including his lesser known works, and gives a close study of his personal life. Knowing German and English, he provides translations of several key passages, while keeping his writing style plain and clear. This volume offers readers a better understanding of Goethe's writing and the circumstances that inspired it.

Dieckmann, Liselotte. *Johann Wolfgang Goethe*. New York: Twayne, 1974. Discusses the versatility Goethe has displayed in his poetry, drama, novels, and tales. Places the writer's oeuvre within its historical framework, particularly with regard to the impact of the French Revolution and the influence of Goethe's friendship with Friedrich Schiller.

Duncan, Bruce. *Goethe's "Werther" and the Critics*. Rochester, N.Y.: Camden House, 2005. Traces the critical reception of the novel over 230 years, from the sensation it caused when first released in 1774 through analyses in the nineteenth and twentieth centuries. Duncan demonstrates how the changing critical reaction to the book mirrors the history of literary criticism from the late eighteenth through the late twentieth centuries.

Hatfield, Henry. *Goethe: A Critical Introduction*. New York: New Directions, 1963. Focuses on the epistolary novel and the sociological impact of *The Sorrows of Young Werther*. Discusses Goethe's influence on later writers.

Hutchinson, Peter, ed. *Landmarks in the German Novel.* New York: Peter Lang, 2007. Traces the development of the German novel from the eighteenth century until 1959 by analyzing thirteen milestone works, including separate essays discussing Goethe's *The Sorrows of Youth Werther, Elective Affinities,* and *Wilhelm Meister's Apprenticeship.*

Reiss, Hans. *Goethe's Novels.* Coral Gables, Fla.: University of Miami Press, 1969. In-depth review of Goethe's earlier novels, with a comprehensive discussion of *The Sorrows of Young Werther* as being representative of Goethe's involvement in the storm and stress movement. Compares the novels thematically.

Sharpe, Lesley, ed. *The Cambridge Companion to Goethe.* New York: Cambridge University Press, 2002. Collection of newly commissioned essays analyzing Goethe's prose fiction, drama, and poetry; Goethe and gender, philosophy, and religion; and Goethe's critical reception, among other topics. Includes bibliography and index.

Swales, Martin, and Erika Swales. *Reading Goethe: A Critical Introduction to the Literary Work.* Rochester, N.Y.: Camden House, 2002. A comprehensive critical analysis of Goethe's literary output, which argues that the writer is an essential figure in German modernity. Chapter 3, "Narrative Fiction," focuses on Goethe's novels. Includes bibliography and index.

Trevelyan, Humphrey. *Goethe and the Greeks.* New York: Octagon, 1972. Reveals the enormous influence of classical and neoclassical thought and mythology on the work of Goethe. Includes in particular a discussion of the importance of Homer's work for the character of Werther.

The Sot-Weed Factor

Author: John Barth (1930-   )
First published: 1960
Type of work: Novel
Type of plot: Picaresque
Time of plot: Late seventeenth and early eighteenth centuries
Locale: Maryland

Principal characters:
EBENEZER or EBEN COOKE, son of Andrew Cooke, owner of a tobacco plantation
ANNA COOKE, his twin sister
HENRY BURLINGAME, their tutor in youth and associate in later life
JOAN TOAST, a prostitute who becomes Eben's ideal love and later his wife
JOHN McEVOY, her pimp

The Story:

Ebenezer, or Eben, Cooke and his twin sister, Anna, are born in 1666 to Andrew Cooke on a tobacco, or sot-weed, plantation at Cooke's Point in the colony of Maryland. Their mother dies giving birth and their father returns to England, hiring eventually as his children's tutor a young man who had been found floating in Chesapeake Bay with the name Henry Burlingame III pinned to his chest. Burlingame hopes to find the secret journal of Captain John Smith. Burlingame had an ancestor who had served with the famous explorer and thought that the secret of his birth might be found in the journal.

Eben goes to Cambridge for his formal education. After a period of indecision and carousal with his friends, he finally determines that he wants to be a poet. Burlingame also reappears to assist Eben during this period. Andrew Cooke asks him to return to Maryland to take over the operation of the family plantation. Two events then occur to shape Eben's future.

On a dare, Eben meets a prostitute named Joan Toast, and he is taken by her beauty and personality. Instead of having sex with her, he vows eternal devotion to her and to preserve his virginity eternally. John McEvoy, Joan's pimp, wants Eben to pay for the time he spent with her even though there had been no sex. Eben gains an enemy. The second important event is Eben's interview with Charles Calvert, Lord Baltimore and former governor of Maryland, who appoints Eben poet laureate of Maryland and urges the astonished young man to help Calvert regain the governorship of Maryland, which had been wrested from him by a host of villains headed by Jonathan Coode. Calvert had no authority to name Eben to any position because Calvert is no longer governor of Maryland. In fact, Calvert is not Calvert; he is Burlingame, in the first of many disguises.

Eben, Bertrand (Eben's servant), and Burlingame head for a seaport to begin their voyage to Maryland, but brigands set upon Eben, thinking that he will cause trouble for Coode's side of the Maryland conspiracy. Burlingame is separated from the others. Eben and Bertrand exchange identities to confuse those who are after Eben. Bertrand, pretending to be Eben, gets a coquettish daughter of a landowner pregnant and gambles away part of Eben's estate. The ship they are on is attacked by pirates and they are taken prisoner. The pirate ship encounters a ship carrying prostitutes headed for the New World; the pirates rape the women. Even Eben is so caught up in the mood that he almost rapes a woman who later turns out to be his ideal love, Joan Toast.

The pirates cast Eben and Bertrand overboard. The two make their way to land, which turns out to be Maryland. There they make friends with an Indian chief and eventually make their way to Cambridge, where an open-air court is in session. Eben, thinking that an injustice is about to be done, insists on making the court's judgment himself, giving some land to the plaintiff. The land turns out to be his own estate. He had given his land to Henry Warren, a blackguard who had turned Eben's land into an opium farm. Eben is forced to work as a servant on the land that had been his. During this time of servitude he again meets Joan Toast, now known as Susan Warren and suffering from smallpox. He is so disillusioned by the course his life has taken that he abandons his idea of writing an epic about Maryland and instead writes a bitter satire, "The Sot-Weed Factor."

John McEvoy has reappeared, and he, Bertrand, and Eben are captured by local Indians. Eben is able to use his relationship with the Indian chief he had befriended earlier to free himself and his companions. This episode also produces the solution to the mystery of Burlingame's parentage. He is one of three brothers descended from a martyred priest and an Indian maiden. One of his brothers is the consort of Anna Cooke, who had followed her brother to the New World.

The governor of Maryland convenes a special court to settle the claims to Malden, the manor-house on Eben's family estate, which are finally resolved in Eben's favor. To reclaim his estate, however, Eben is forced to marry, and have sex with, the no-longer-beautiful, pox-ridden Joan Toast. Burlingame is reunited with Anna, who had loved him when they were in England. She gives birth to a boy, Andrew. At the end of the novel, Eben settles down to run the plantation and take care of his wife, sister, nephew, and servants. Burlingame, who finally discovers who he really is, disappears from the novel.

Critical Evaluation:

A real Ebenezer Cooke lived in colonial Maryland and wrote a satirical poem entitled "The Sot-Weed Factor" (1708). Very little is known of the historical Cooke, so John Barth, who was born in Maryland and spent his early life there, set out to write a novel in the style of the time in which Cooke lived. The novel creates the experiences that might have brought Cooke to write such a poem. Barth's novel *The Sot-Weed Factor* is a long, hilarious, complex work that has echoes not only of eighteenth century novels but also of the other literary models that the eighteenth century novelists used. The ideological viewpoint of the novel, however, reflects its twentieth century origins. Its language and humor are of the eighteenth century; its themes and philosophical implications are of the twentieth.

Barth's most obvious eighteenth century model is Henry Fielding's *Tom Jones* (1749), which Fielding described as a "comic epic in prose." *The Sot-Weed Factor* is comic in the ordinary and dramatic senses; it is filled with jokes of which Eben is usually the target, yet all is finally resolved in Eben's favor. *The Sot-Weed Factor* also has elements of the epic. An epic is about a heroic figure who fights through difficulties to do good not only for him- or herself but also for his or her people. Eben finally does help to establish a peaceful and prosperous Maryland after being captured by pirates and Indians, reduced to servitude, and physically attacked and threatened with death numerous times. Eben is an ironic, comic hero, and instead of confronting all these dangers and emerging victorious through his own efforts, he frequently escapes through luck or the intervention of others, particularly Burlingame, who reappears in a bewildering number of identities and disguises.

An epic also involves a complex series of events, and Fielding set out in *Tom Jones* to construct a plot so complicated that no one would doubt its epic claims. Barth wanted to write a novel with a plot more convoluted than that of Fielding, and he succeeded. A plot twist exists on almost every page of *The Sot-Weed Factor*, and the novel features dozens of characters, subplots, and interpolated stories.

Earthy, physical, and sexual humor is also a distinguishing feature of eighteenth century novels such as those of Tobias Smollett, John Cleland, and Daniel Defoe. *The Sot-Weed Factor* is full of such comedy. Eben is often so frightened that he vomits or loses control of his bowels and bladder. Barth's Joan Toast, like Moll Flanders, is a prostitute who journeys to the New World. This similarity makes *The Sot-Weed Factor* an imitation of yet another eighteenth century genre, the travel novel. Another of Defoe's novels, *Robinson Crusoe* (1719), and Jonathan Swift's satire *Gulliver's Travels* (1726) are originals in this category. Most people in the eighteenth century had no chance to travel but loved to read of the new lands visited by explorers and colonists. Many of these original travel novels romanticized, idealized, or simply lied about the places they described. In Barth's ironic novel, Eben's naïve view of Maryland as a blissful paradise is shattered when he finds that it is instead a wilderness filled with dangers.

Finally, *The Sot-Weed Factor* is a twentieth century novel that masquerades as an eighteenth century novel. Barth has described his first three novels (*The Floating Opera*, 1956; *The End of the Road*, 1958; and *The Sot-Weed Factor*) as examinations of philosophical nihilism, the theory that there is no ultimate meaning to life or existence. In the first two novels, characters announce their nihilistic attitudes as a result of their philosophical speculations. In *The Sot-Weed Factor*, a nihilistic world is something that happens to the main character, Eben. He begins life with certain received notions about truth, value, and human relationships. All of his assumptions are left in tatters; he finds that they cannot help him make his way in a world in which nothing is what it appears to be.

Eben thinks that the artificial ideals he has gleaned from his voracious reading will be a guide for behavior in the world. Instead, he finds a society devoted to greed, power, and the satiation of every base appetite. Moreover, the world is so confusing that no one can hope to understand it. For example, Lord Baltimore tells Eben to beware of the evil machinations of Jonathan Coode. Later, Eben discovers that Baltimore is considered by some to be just as evil as Coode, and he is further perplexed when he finds that the Baltimore who urged him to watch out for Coode was really his friend, Burlingame. Eben's world turns upside down so many times that, in a memorable episode, as he rides along listening to one of Burlingame's typically sophistic discourses, he wonders why he and the horse he is riding on do not tumble off a whirling, topsy-turvy planet.

The Sot-Weed Factor is not merely a hilarious novel offering no values. In the end, Eben abandons his dreams, and he is not bitter. He finds a new sense of value in his commitments to his friends and family. He becomes interested in people, not solely in ideas.

Jim Baird

Further Reading

Bowen, Zack. *A Reader's Guide to John Barth*. Westport, Conn.: Greenwood Press, 1994. The chapter on *The Sot-Weed Factor* treats the book both as a parody of earlier forms and as a contemporary novel. Includes an extensive bibliography on *The Sot-Weed Factor*.

Clavier, Berndt. *John Barth and Postmodernism: Spatiality, Travel, Montage*. New York: Peter Lang, 2007. Clavier analyzes Barth's work from the perspective of postmodernism and metafiction, focusing on theories of space and subjectivity. He argues that the form of montage is a possible model for understanding Barth's fiction.

Elias, Amy J. "Coda: *The Sot-Weed Factor* and *Mason and Dixon*." In *Sublime Desire: History and Post-1960's Fiction*. Baltimore: Johns Hopkins University Press, 2001. Elias's study of postmodern historical fiction includes analyses of *The Sot-Weed Factor* and of Thomas Pynchon's *Mason and Dixon*. Argues that historical fiction written after 1960 reflects society's conflicting desire to both acknowledge and escape from the violence of the twentieth century.

Morrell, David. *John Barth: An Introduction*. University Park: Pennsylvania State University Press, 1976. An overview of all of Barth's work to 1976, with two chapters analyzing *The Sot-Weed Factor* as a contemporary novel.

Walkiewicz, E. P. *John Barth*. Boston: Twayne, 1986. An excellent short introduction to Barth's work, with numerous comments on *The Sot-Weed Factor*. Includes a bibliography.

Soul Mountain

Author: Gao Xingjian (1940-   )
First published: Ling shan, 1990 (English translation, 2000)
Type of work: Novel
Type of plot: Magical Realism
Time of plot: 1980's
Locale: Yangzi Valley, China

Principal characters:
UNNAMED MALE NARRATOR, referred to as "I"
UNNAMED MALE, referred to as "You"
UNNAMED WOMAN, referred to as "She"

The Story:

The narrator is misdiagnosed with lung cancer, the same disease that killed his father. He is panicked, but a second set of X rays convinces his doctors that he is healthy and will live for many years. The narrator leaves Beijing to travel among ethnic minority peoples living along the Yangzi River. He begins in the west and moves eastward toward the East China Sea. Early in his wanderings, he hears of Soul Mountain (Ling shan). He is intrigued and tries to locate the place.

The narrator wanders through remote parts of southern Sichuan, through rugged Guizhou, and farther east to Hunan Province. Much of his time is spent in forests or natural reserves, where he talks with forest rangers, archeologists, and local residents, most of whom are members of ethnic minority groups. He delights in meeting and talking with elders in minority communities. The narrator records detailed explanations of the flora and fauna he encounters, as well as a series of strange and marvelous stories from the people he meets.

The narrator's wanderings lead him to Jiangxi, his home province. The homecoming stirs up memories of his dead mother and grandmother. From Jiangxi, he proceeds eastward to Zhejiang Province, where he continues to visit remote wilderness areas. He stays away from cities, but on occasional visits he finds city people who are aware of his published writing and eager to meet him. For short periods, he enjoys their company.

Interspersed through the novel are chapters involving a woman identified as "she" who interacts with a person called "you." "She" is frequently identified as a nurse and expresses great fears, despondency, and anger toward "you." At times, "she" appears to be a composite of more than one woman.

The novel ends in the late 1980's in Beijing, where various people seek out the narrator looking for assistance. The narrator remains an observer, however, and offers no help to his visitors. In a closing chapter, he realizes that he does not yet want to find Taoist enlightenment but rather wants to continue to live in the puzzling, confusing, and cruel human world. The novel closes with a short chapter expressing the narrator's lack of understanding of the meaning of existence.

Critical Evaluation:

Gao Xingjian was born in 1940 in the province of Jiangxi, where he spent his childhood. In 1962, he graduated as a French language specialist from the Beijing Foreign Language Institute. He joined the Foreign Languages Press, where he worked as a translator of French until he was swept up in the Cultural Revolution (1966-1976). During these years, Gao was initially a member of the pro-Maoist Red Guards, but he later was sent to the countryside to be "reeducated" through hard labor. Following Deng Xiaoping's reemergence in politics as China's most powerful leader, many formerly banished intellectuals, including Gao, were rehabilitated around 1980. Gao began to write about French contemporary literary theory and to produce plays in the style of the Theater of the Absurd associated with Samuel Beckett (1906-1989) and Eugène Ionesco (1909-1994). Gao's best-known play is *Chezhan* (pr. 1983; *The Bus Stop*, 1996), in which a group of people wait for a bus that never comes. It is derivative of Beckett's *En attendant Godot* (pb. 1952, pr. 1953; *Waiting for Godot*, 1954).

Soul Mountain is an ambitious and original work influenced by the Soviet Russian literary theorist Mikhail Bakhtin (1895-1975). The form of the novel echoes Bakhtin's concept of the self emerging out of a dialogue with others. The narrator is an autobiographical figure, and the novel shows him interacting with other people and discourses in ways that shape his own self and writing. Most chapters contain two or more stories that have been relayed to the narrator by the people he has met on his travels. This interweaving of disparate narratives enacts Bakhtin's theory of the novel as a dialogic text.

The most difficult aspect of *Soul Mountain* is Gao's use of the pronouns "I," "You," "She," and later "He" to carry all the action. The narrator reveals in chapter 42 that "She" is a fantasy invoked by the character "I." Further, "You" is revealed to be an aspect of "I."

Gao's characters represent his own interpretation of Bakhtin's theories. Bakhtin is a puzzling figure himself whose ideas challenged Marxist materialism but nonetheless became widely influential among neo-Marxists in Europe after his death. Bakhtin lived in obscurity most of his life, and few of his works survive in complete form. He argued that the self is realized only in relationship to others, and Gao borrows Bakhtin's conception of the self as being composed of "I," "I in relation to others," and "others in relation to me" to portray the autobiographical narrator of *Soul Mountain*. Gao must have been aware of Bakhtin's growing reputation in French intellectual life, but *Soul Mountain* does not reflect a deep study of Bakhtin's ideas, which became influential in European and American literary theory during the 1980's and 1990's.

Seen in the context of Chinese literary ideas, Gao's concern with the self is a major departure from China's mainstream socialist realism, in which the narrative centers on individuals whose life purpose is to advance socialism in China. Fulfillment of ideological goals is everything in socialist realism, but Gao rejects collectivist ideology and politics to emphasize the experiences and fantasies of a particular individual.

Gao was an avant-garde figure, but his absurdist plays and his pamphlet *Xiandai xiaoshuo jiqian chutan* (1981; discussion of the techniques of modern fiction) played only a minor role in post-1980 Chinese circles. In that pamphlet, Gao sought to influence his contemporaries by introducing literary concepts from French and European writers to China. During the 1980's, Chinese intellectual life went through a zigzag pattern of liberalization followed by conservative Marxist repression. As an advocate of Western literary theory, Gao became an obvious target during the recurrent periods when bourgeois liberalism drew the ire of China's Marxist old guard bent on upholding class struggle. The old guard produced stinging criticism of Gao and his work as reflecting decadent bourgeois ideas. Fearful of once again becoming a target in ideological campaigns, Gao withdrew from public life and undertook the journeys described in *Soul Mountain*.

Gao left China in 1987 and settled in France, where he became a French citizen. *Soul Mountain* was first published in Chinese in Taiwan in 1990 and was later translated into French and English. Gao's works have been banned in the People's Republic of China since 1989, so they circulate there only clandestinely. Because of this prohibition, Gao

has never been prominent in China but rather is much better known in French- and English-speaking worlds.

Mabel Lee, an Australian, published the English translation of *Soul Mountain* in 2000. Gao was awarded the Nobel Prize in Literature in 2000, becoming the first Chinese author to win this award. It is ironic that, like Beckett, Ionesco, and Bakhtin, Gao can be seen as a representative of the Francophone literary world, rather than a widely appreciated author in his native land.

Much of *Soul Mountain* consists of realist accounts of travels heightened by magical feelings that come from the wandering writer's efforts to understand existence. These more straightforward accounts contain a host of references to themes and stories from Chinese culture that may seem fanciful, exotic, or simply puzzling to Western readers but would not be strange to Chinese readers. At the same time, Chinese readers may be repelled by Gao's complete abandonment of narrative conventions. Gao's idiosyncratic use of Bakhtinian notions of dialogue is likely to puzzle most readers in any language. In chapter 72, Gao Xingjian provides a defense of his writing that helps clarify his intent.

The novel has qualities of a Zen *koan*, a brief puzzling or paradoxical story intended to awaken the Buddhist adept to the possibility of enlightenment through meditation. A deep sense of existential sadness underlies the novel's tone and moods. Many of the narrator's adventures involve Taoists and Taoist principles. These Taoist themes include both references to philosophical Taoism represented by the collection known as *Zhuangzi* (c. third century B.C.E.) and to Taoism used as a general category for popular religious beliefs and practices in China.

Gao, before winning the Nobel Prize, was also well known as a painter working in the traditional medium of black ink on white paper. His work typically is abstract and sometimes portrays loosely defined human figures in a vague landscape. Chapter 70 of *Soul Mountain* discusses a famous seventeenth century eccentric painter, Gong Xian (1618-1689). Gong remained loyal to the Ming Dynasty after its fall in 1644 and, during the ensuing Qing Dynasty, was shunned for his continuing loyalty to the Ming. Gong eked out a living as a struggling painter, but in later times his works became highly prized. Gao invokes Gong's model and, in a revealing remark, Gong is said to have worked "not for money, painting itself was an expression of his heart." This should be read as Gao's conception of his own writing and painting. There also is a parallel between this story and Bakhtin's life in the Soviet Union.

Gao's most striking theme is that life has no goal but is only to be lived, and individuals have little or no control over what happens in their lives. Fate rules in Gao's world. Another theme is Gao's insight that humans have insatiable desires, while men and women have different ways of manifesting this principle.

Gao sees individuals as living in relative isolation from others and so finding themselves plagued by loneliness. This aspect of Gao's fiction resembles the work of Samuel Beckett, yet, unlike Beckett's texts, in which characters seem to live in a cultural vacuum, Gao's work is steeped in Chinese culture, both past and present. Interestingly, Gao's strong sense of China's unique identity is found in the remote and rural China and equally among the Han majority and the nation's ethnic minority peoples, who he believes are moored to places and to their history. Urban Chinese are depicted as having lost many of these qualities. *Soul Mountain* abounds with descriptions of minority peoples, rare flora and fauna seen during the writer's travels, and all sorts of retold histories and fairy tales. The purpose of these descriptive asides is seldom obvious, yet all reinforce that the novel is rooted in twentieth century China.

Some critics have identified *Soul Mountain* as a modern Zen-inspired novel. The work, however, has a strong Taoist flavor, in addition to its Buddhist notions. There is no need to disentangle the Buddhist and Taoist influences in the novel, for Gao apparently is comfortable with their mixture. His understanding that life has no goal leads him not to a general sense of despair, but rather to a willingness to savor both the joy and the suffering of life's journey.

David D. Buck

Further Reading

Gao Xingjian. *The Case for Literature.* New Haven, Conn.: Yale University Press, 2008. Contains several important essays, including Gao's Nobel Prize lecture, plus "Literature and Metaphysics: About *Soul Mountain*" and "The Necessity of Loneliness." Gao explains his purposes and techniques.

_____. "Living Without 'isms.'" Interview by Maya Jaggi. *The Guardian*, August 2, 2008. Gao advocates "cold literature" that is detached from politics and consumerism. He denounces both Marxism-Leninism as it was practiced in China and contemporary capitalism as it exists in China and elsewhere.

Lee, Mabel. "Gao Xingjian's Fiction in the Context of Chinese Intellectual and Literary History." *Literature and Aesthetics: Journal of the Sydney Society of Literature and Aesthetics* 16, no. 1 (2008): 7-20. Mabel Lee is the principal translator of Gao's works into English. Here, she attempts to place his work in the context of Chinese literature.

Link, E. Perry. *The Uses of Literature: Life in the Socialist Chinese Literature System.* Princeton, N.J.: Princeton University Press, 2000. This definitive account of literary life in the People's Republic of China does not mention Gao as an important writer, but it is useful for understanding the literary institutions that helped shape his work and his understanding of literature.

Pearce, Lynne. "Bakhtin and the Dialogic Principle." In *Literary Theory and Criticism: An Oxford Guide*, edited by Patricia Waugh. New York: Oxford University Press, 2006. A short introduction to Bakhtin's literary ideas, which Gao appropriated in his own writing.

Silbergeld, Jerome. "Kung Hsien: A Professional Chinese Artist and His Patronage." *The Burlington Magazine* 123 (July, 1981): 400-410. A brief survey of Gong Xian and his work.

Taylor, John. "Three Francophone Writers: Francois Cheng, Dai Suie, Gao Xingjian." *Michigan Quarterly Review* 2 (September, 2008): 369-379. Reveals how Gao has been shaped by French literature and literary theory even though he writes in Chinese about China.

The Souls of Black Folk
Essays and Sketches

Author: W. E. B. Du Bois (1868-1963)
First published: 1903
Type of work: Autobiography

The Souls of Black Folk is a passionate and eloquent auto-biography. It tells the life story of an individual, W. E. B. Du Bois, and of a group, African Americans. In the process of telling his personal autobiography, Du Bois shows how he is shaped by his community's story. Du Bois inhabits a world in which a color line divides all life into two parts. One part is privileged and white, and it exploits the other part that is con-strained and black.

As an author reflecting on his life, Du Bois could not sep-arate himself from "what was then called the Negro prob-lem." Even his consciousness is divided into two parts, be-coming a double consciousness. He calls the experience generated by the color line "the Veil." As a man living behind the Veil, part of his being is hidden. One part of his con-sciousness belongs to the human race, and the other con-sciousness is shrouded behind the Veil. Du Bois allows his readers to look behind the Veil, to share his pain and humilia-tion and to celebrate a world populated by heroes and by joy. The souls of black folk are the flame of hope and life in a world where hatred diminishes and kills the body and the spirit.

The triumph of African American culture is revealed through the songs of sorrow that introduce each chapter. In the hymns, both suffering from enslavement and surviving through hope are conveyed simultaneously. Although the book is often based on facts, the spirituals connect the infor-mation to the heart and the soul. The result is a moving story of a race and a man. Spiritual striving shapes the lives of Afri-can Americans who search for freedom and fulfillment.

The second chapter begins with one of the most famous lines in this book: "The problem of the twentieth century is the problem of the color line." These prophetic words tell the story of American slaves and their descendants who continue to search for freedom in America and throughout the world. The international dimensions of the color line are rooted in the economy and in the politics of a worldwide struggle.

One way to address these issues is to work for gradual change. This position was held by Booker T. Washington, the most powerful African American leader in the United States when Du Bois wrote this book. Although Du Bois respected Washington's rise from slavery, Du Bois was opposed to any position that accepted the limitations of African Americans' rights. Washington represented adjustment and submission to an intolerable injustice. The training of the most talented members of the community was central to changing the com-munity, but Washington stressed manual and vocational training at the expense of the gifted. Du Bois's unflinching criticism of Washington created a public debate about how to fight against discrimination and the reason for engaging in the struggle.

Du Bois tells his personal story of entering Fisk Univer-sity in Nashville, Tennessee, in 1884. He experiences the Jim Crow world of the South and teaches children who are lim-ited by its cruelty. Their life behind the Veil makes a mockery of the idea of progress and constrains his life as a school-teacher. Du Bois moves out of the elementary school and on to higher education.

Before leaving the South, he takes the reader on a journey through the black belt. Georgia is the heart of this region where African Americans live behind a color line. Jim Crow railway cars physically and socially segregate black and white passengers. The railroads enforce this segregation throughout the South. Plantations dot the landscape, echoing the slavery that maintained them and continued their legacy years after emancipation was proclaimed but not realized. Churches, however, sustain the souls of black folk, who are isolated behind the Veil.

Du Bois discusses the continuation of the plantation sys-tem through tenant farming. The struggle for freedom from economic and from political slavery is like the quest for the golden fleece, a journey of epic proportions. Even off the land, segregation is enforced in housing, the economy, poli-tics, and social customs. The vote creates the possibility to fight back, but political corruption subverts this power. Crime and poor public education further weaken the commu-nity and sap the strength needed to resist. Sympathy and co-operation, not charity, are necessary to improve the situation.

Faith in God, the community, family, and one another sus-tains African Americans. Du Bois reveals how the "faith of our fathers" is a communal heritage. The souls of black folk contain a deep religious feeling, a powerful heart nourished by dynamic vigor. The sorrow songs that introduce each chapter are part of the community and its continuing faith. Music, song, and lyrics combine to make a heritage from the past that lives in the present.

The death of Du Bois's first (and only) son, Burghardt, occurs because medical caretakers refuse to aid the dying African American infant. Despair and rage at the Veil cause Du Bois to be darkly and perversely glad that his son escaped its ravages. His baby is beyond the Veil in the valley of death. His keening cry against the evil that murdered his baby is a heart-wrenching paean to lost hope and love.

People are able, nevertheless, to triumph behind the Veil, and the African American leader is the key to ending the despair and the suffering behind the color line. Alexander Crummell, a friend and mentor of Du Bois, is such a hero. He survives the temptations to hate, to despair, and to doubt the goodness of life. After Crummell is denied entry into the ministry because of the color line, he continues to serve others as a witness to the spirit. He fights against the wickedness of the color line and triumphs through his love and generosity until his death after a life of righteousness.

Ordinary people also have the ability to be extraordinary. Their path may be hard to find and filled with stumbling blocks caused by the Veil, but the triumph of the soul is a cause for joy and for celebration even in the midst of darkness. This book is a literary masterpiece because it articulates the cost of hatred and celebrates the power to resist it. Although it was never out of print since its publication in 1903, it assumed an especially important role in the 1960's. It then became a rallying voice and inspiration for the American civil rights struggle. Du Bois's life story is the story of a people: It reaches the soul of all its readers while revealing the souls of black folks. Du Bois forges a new autobiographical form in this book, revealing the contours of his life as rooted in black culture. His essay on Booker T. Washington turns his personal struggle with the man and what he stood for into a national political statement about the nature of civil rights. Du Bois calls for an active demand for social justice that will compromise with nothing less than full equality. Similarly, his grief at his baby son's death becomes a eulogy for all the African American children slaughtered by white people's hatred.

This technique of telling his life story while he tells the story of a people was used by Du Bois during the rest of his long and productive life. Thus, other Du Bois autobiographies tell of friends, struggles, and humiliations over the next sixty years; they do not reach the heights of this first one. *The Souls of Black Folk* is unique in its passion and eloquence. His phrases soar with anguish and anger, reflecting his pain and that of others. His language captures the imagination so dramatically that Du Bois's book reaches out to all people who resist hatred. It offers hope for the triumph of the spirit and the possibility of social justice. Du Bois rose above the Veil.

Mary Jo Deegan

Further Reading

Blum, Edward J. *W. E. B. Du Bois: American Prophet*. Philadelphia: University of Pennsylvania Press, 2007. Focuses on Du Bois's spiritual ideas and temperament, tracing the religious meanings and biblical references in his writing. Chapter 2, "Race as Cosmic Sight in *The Souls of Black Folk*," analyzes that work.

Byerman, Keith E. *Seizing the Word: History, Art, and Self in the Work of W. E. B. Du Bois*. Athens: University of Georgia Press, 1994. Examines Du Bois in terms of contemporary literary and cultural theory. Discusses the work of Du Bois and its influence on nineteenth and twentieth century America.

Crouch, Stanley, and Playthell Benjamin. *Reconsidering "The Souls of Black Folk": Thoughts on the Groundbreaking Classic Work of W. E. B. DuBois*. Philadelphia: Running Press, 2002. A dialogue between two black intellectuals in which they assess Du Bois's ideas and the legacy of this book.

Horne, Gerald, and Mary Young, eds. *W. E. B. Du Bois: An Encyclopedia*. New York: Greenwood Press, 2001. A guide to Du Bois's life and work.

Hubbard, Dolan, ed. *"The Souls of Black Folk": One Hundred Years Later*. Columbia: University of Missouri Press, 2003. Collection of essays examining the work from a variety of perspectives. Includes reviews of the book, a comparison of it to works by Frederick Douglass and Richard Wright, and a discussion of Du Bois and the "construction of whiteness."

Lewis, David Levering. *W. E. B. Du Bois: Biography of a Race, 1868-1919*. New York: H. Holt, 1993. This 1994 Pulitzer Prize-winning book chronicles the major impact of Du Bois's controversial thinking on the United States. It focuses on a crucial fifty-year period in Du Bois's life and in the nation's civil rights struggle.

_____. *W. E. B. Du Bois: The Fight for Equality and the American Century, 1919-1963*. New York: Henry Holt, 2000. This second volume in Lewis's massive biography of Du Bois focuses on the last forty-four years of his life.

Rampersad, Arnold. *The Art and Imagination of W. E. B. Du Bois*. Cambridge, Mass.: Harvard University Press, 1976.

One of the few good treatments of Du Bois's creative genius. Essentially a biography, this work traces Du Bois's life from his New England beginnings to his last years in Ghana. Not so much concerned with controversies and rivalries as with his literary accomplishments, especially his fiction. Du Bois comes through as a concerned man, not a self-styled propagandist.

Rudwick, Elliott M. *W. E. B. Du Bois: Voice of the Black Protest Movement*. Champaign: University of Illinois Press, 1982. A well-documented study; covers the full sweep of Du Bois's career from his youth to his later involvements in pan-Africanism and peace promotion. Presents Du Bois as both a realist and an idealist, a skilled propagandist, and a devoted believer in equality. Rudwick suggests that although Du Bois erred in predicting socialism as the answer to the needs of African Americans, he accurately forecast the strong African orientation of contemporary black culture.

The Sound and the Fury

Author: William Faulkner (1897-1962)
First published: 1929
Type of work: Novel
Type of plot: Stream of consciousness
Time of plot: 1900-1928
Locale: Mississippi

Principal characters:
JASON COMPSON, a retired lawyer, the Compson family patriarch
CAROLINE COMPSON, his wife
CANDACE "CADDY" COMPSON,
QUENTIN COMPSON,
BENJAMIN COMPSON, and
JASON COMPSON, their children
QUENTIN COMPSON, Candace's daughter
DILSEY, the Compsons' maid
LUSTER, Dilsey's grandson

The Story:

The Compsons, a once-prominent Mississippi family, are in decline. The land that was once their sprawling plantation has been sold and turned into a golf course, and their once-splendid mansion is badly dilapidated. At the head of the family are Mr. Jason Compson, a retired lawyer taken to drink, and his wife, Caroline, a hypochondriac who spends most of her days in bed.

Benjamin, the Compsons' youngest child, a developmentally disabled man, begins to tell the story of his life. On April 7, 1928, his thirty-third birthday, while he walks along the golf course with Luster, his caretaker, Benjy begins to reminisce about his childhood years. His mind jumps from event to event, covering more than a dozen events in all.

Several of Benjy's flashbacks concern his older sister, Caddy, to whom Benjy is quite attached. In his childhood memories she cares for him and plays with him and lies next to him in bed until he falls asleep. Benjy also remembers Caddy's wedding and her subsequent departure from the Compson household, which disturbs Benjy profoundly.

Many of Benjy's memories are painful. They include the death of his grandmother, whose wake takes place while the Compson children play in a stream, and his brother's death. He recalls a day during his teenage years when he embraces and fondles a local schoolgirl, thinking she is his sister, Caddy. Benjy is castrated for that offense.

At the end of his narrative, Benjy returns to the present. He and Luster look out his bedroom window and watch his niece, Quentin, climb out the window of her bedroom and run off into the night.

In the second chapter, dated June 2, 1910, Quentin, the Compsons' oldest son, tells of the events leading to his suicide. He is a Harvard University student, and he spends the final day of his life getting his affairs in order—delivering suicide notes to his roommate and father and packing his trunk. As he takes one last trolley ride around Cambridge, his mind flashes back to the troublesome events that have led him to suicide. He has been particularly upset by his sister Caddy's romantic affairs. The night that she lost her virginity was especially traumatic for Quentin, as was her marriage the following year. (Caddy married because she was pregnant.) Quentin has been jealous of his sister's lovers.

While he wanders around Cambridge, he observes some local boys fishing, and he befriends a young immigrant girl whom he meets in a bakery. Late in the day, he meets some schoolmates and attends a party that ends abruptly when Quentin inexplicably picks a fight with the hosts' son. In his own mind, Quentin is lashing out at one of Caddy's lovers.

Quentin eventually returns to his room, puts on a fresh collar, brushes off his clothes, packs a few more articles in his trunk, and departs to take his own life. Quentin's brother Jason later reveals that Quentin drowned himself.

In the third chapter, Jason (along with Benjy) relates the events of April 6, 1928. He argues with his teenage niece, also named Quentin, before she leaves for school, accusing her of cutting classes and chastising her for wearing revealing clothing and excessive makeup. He then goes to work at the local hardware store and argues with his boss. Throughout his narrative Jason makes disparaging remarks about Jews, African Americans, women, and the members of his own family.

Jason reveals that Caddy, rejected by her husband, has been expelled from the Compson household, though her daughter, Quentin, remains. Jason explains that he receives and cashes Caddy's child-support checks, then delivers phony checks to his mother, which she burns because she will not accept Caddy's money.

On his lunch break, Jason spots his niece driving around town with a man wearing a red tie. He pursues them but loses their trail after they clandestinely flatten one of his tires.

The events of the final chapter took place on April 8, 1928, Easter Sunday. Dilsey, the Compsons' elderly African American maid, prepares breakfast shortly after daybreak. She feeds Luster and Benjy, then waits for Jason, Quentin, and Mrs. Compson to come to breakfast. When Jason appears, he announces that he has been robbed; the window to his room has been broken and his strongbox pried open. When he finds out that his niece Quentin is not in her room, he correctly assumes that she has stolen his savings (which consist mainly of Caddy's child-support payments). He notifies the police and embarks on a long, fruitless drive to find Quentin and the man wearing the red tie.

While Jason tries to track Quentin, Dilsey, her family, and Benjy attend Easter services. Dilsey feels the pain that the Compson family has endured over the years and weeps, claiming that she has done her best to raise the Compson children properly.

After church, Luster drives Mrs. Compson and Benjy in a surrey to the cemetery. When Luster takes a wrong turn at the town square, Benjy breaks into hysterics. With the help of Jason, who has returned to town following his futile search, Luster regains control and heads the vehicle home.

Critical Evaluation:

The Sound and the Fury is William Faulkner's first masterpiece. His initial two novels, *Soldiers' Pay* (1926) and *Mosquitoes* (1927), were apprentice efforts. His third novel, *Sartoris* (1929), was the first set in his fictional Yoknapatawpha County, a territory in northern Mississippi that would serve as the setting for most of his subsequent novels and short stories. In telling the Yoknapatawpha County saga, Faulkner created a fictional history of the entire American South.

What separates *The Sound and the Fury* from his three earlier novels is its technique. Faulkner's first novels are, for the most part, narrated chronologically by an omniscient narrator. *The Sound and the Fury* breaks that pattern. Each of the novel's four chapters is told by a different narrator. The first chapter is told by Benjy, the second by Quentin, the third by Jason, and the fourth by an omniscient narrator. Faulkner was one of the first American writers to employ such a complex narrative strategy, though modernist British novelists such as Joseph Conrad, James Joyce, and Virginia Woolf had earlier published works using such strategies.

Through the use of multiple narrators, Faulkner is able to relate the Compson family saga from four separate viewpoints. Each of the three Compson sons brings to the story a different set of perspectives and prejudices. Benjy, whose narrative covers about twenty-five years of Compson family history, is the most honest of the novel's narrators. Mentally incapable of making critical judgments, Benjy simply narrates events as he saw them. Moaning and weeping, Benjy registers the painful episodes in this family's tragic history.

Opening the novel with Benjy's narrative was risky for Faulkner. Benjy's mind is unable to focus on a single event for more than a few pages; he skips arbitrarily from event to event, rendering his tale meaningless to anyone who does not read it very carefully. Faulkner's decision to let Benjy speak first was a brilliant one, for it suggests the themes to which the author would return again and again. For Faulkner, a southerner with a keen sense of his region's tragic past, history was not the linear story of humanity's accomplishments but rather a jumbled tale of pain. The title of *The Sound and the Fury* comes from lines in William Shakespeare's *Macbeth* (pr. 1606, pb. 1623): "Life . . . is a tale/ Told by an idiot, full of sound and fury,/ Signifying nothing." Benjy's rendering of Compson history is, indeed, the anguished tale of an idiot, full of sound and fury.

Quentin's narrative also features time shifts and stream-of-consciousness narration, techniques that Faulkner borrowed from James Joyce and used brilliantly in *The Sound and the Fury* and future novels. Quentin can function better than Benjy in the present, but, like his developmentally disabled brother, he is unable to keep past events from dominating his present life. He is traumatized and emotionally paralyzed by his sister's sexual promiscuity; he cannot forget these past events and move on with his life. Tormented by the past, and guilty over his own incestuous desire for Caddy, Quentin finds no escape other than suicide. His tragic end suggests Faulkner's view that the past is inescapable; it continues to affect and shape the present and future.

Jason's narrative is, for the most part, chronological, yet he, like his brothers, is unable to escape the traumas of the past. He is an angry man, and his bitterness is rooted in events from the past—his family's willingness to offer Quentin a Harvard education while Jason was not even able to attend the state university and Caddy's failure to arrange a banking career for him through her husband. Though Jason holds a job and functions normally, he is a man on the verge of a nervous breakdown, obsessed with past events. Jason is also a greedy man, and his preoccupation with money reflects the drift toward commercialism in the South as the plantation society faded in the post-Civil War period.

The novel's final chapter is told by an omniscient narrator, an attempt by Faulkner to allow an objective speaker to tell the Compsons' story. This chapter focuses on Dilsey, who is depicted sensitively by neither Benjy nor Jason. With Faulkner narrating, Dilsey emerges as something of a heroine, a woman who has attempted to hold the Compson family together through decades of tragedy.

Though each of her three brothers assumes the role of narrator, Caddy is never allowed to tell her story in the first person. Faulkner once stated that he decided not to use Caddy as a narrator because she was "too beautiful and too moving to reduce her to telling what was going on, that it would be more passionate to see her through somebody else's eyes." As Faulkner suggests, Caddy becomes a symbol of lost innocence. Benjy narrates an episode in which Caddy muddies her drawers in the stream (on the evening of their grandmother's funeral), and Caddy's soiled undergarments foreshadow her fall from innocence. Finding little compassion and love in the Compson household, she seeks it through sexual encounters, which ultimately leave her pregnant and, later, rejected by her husband and family. She becomes a focal point in all her brothers' narratives and the major cause of their anger.

Told chronologically, *The Sound and the Fury* is the saga of a southern family in decline. Faulkner's portrait of the once-prominent Compson clan shows two dysfunctional parents, a suicidal son, a fallen daughter, a developmentally disabled son, and a son racked with bitterness. For Faulkner, the Compsons represent the collapse of the South's social order in the decades following the Civil War. Faulkner would elaborate on this compelling theme in future works and, in novels such as *As I Lay Dying* (1930) and *Absalom, Absalom!* (1936), perfect the daring narrative strategies he first employed in *The Sound and the Fury*.

James Tackach

Further Reading

Bloom, Harold, ed. *Caddy Compson*. New York: Chelsea House, 1990. Collection of critical essays focuses on the character of Caddy Compson.

————. *William Faulkner's "The Sound and the Fury."* New York: Bloom's Literary Criticism, 2008. Compilation of essays offers various interpretations of the novel, including examination of its composition and themes. Topics addressed include the Reverend Shegog and the dynamics of alcoholism in the work.

Gandal, Keith. "*The Sound and the Fury* and Military Rejects: The Feebleminded and the Postmobilization Erotic Triangle." In *The Gun and the Pen: Hemingway, Fitzgerald, Faulkner, and the Fiction of Mobilization*. New York: Oxford University Press, 2008. Chapter focusing on *The Sound and the Fury* is part of a larger examination of how Faulkner, Ernest Hemingway, and F. Scott Fitzgerald, who were all deemed unsuitable for military service or command in World War I, felt emasculated by this failure and how their works of the 1920's reflect this frustration.

Karl, Frederick R. *William Faulkner: American Writer*. New York: Weidenfeld & Nicolson, 1989. Comprehensive biography provides insightful critical analyses of Faulkner's major works. Offers a particularly illuminating discussion of how Faulkner wove together the complex parts of *The Sound and the Fury*.

Marius, Richard. *Reading Faulkner: Introduction to the First Thirteen Novels*. Compiled and edited by Nancy Grisham Anderson. Knoxville: University of Tennessee Press, 2006. Collection of the lectures that Marius, a novelist, biographer, and Faulkner scholar, presented during an undergraduate course. Provides a friendly and approachable introduction to Faulkner. Includes a chapter on *The Sound and the Fury*.

Matthews, John T. *"The Sound and the Fury": Faulkner and the Lost Cause*. Boston: Twayne, 1991. Brief but insightful study of the novel includes chapters devoted to its importance in Faulkner's canon and its composition, critical reception, characterization, setting, and narrative technique.

Porter, Carolyn. *William Faulkner.* New York: Oxford University Press, 2007. Concise and informative, this resource spans Faulkner's entire life but focuses on his most prolific period, from 1929 to 1940. Examines his childhood and personal struggles and offers insightful analysis of his major works. Includes discussion of *The Sound and the Fury.*

Towner, Theresa M. *The Cambridge Introduction to William Faulkner.* New York: Cambridge University Press, 2008. Accessible resource, aimed at students and general readers, focuses on Faulkner's writings. Provides detailed analyses of his nineteen novels, discussion of his other works, and information about the critical reception of his fiction.

Tredell, Nicholas. *William Faulkner: "The Sound and the Fury," "As I Lay Dying."* Cambridge, England: Icon Books, 1999. Traces and explains the changing critical reception of both novels from 1929 through the 1990's. An informative introduction places the novels within the context of Faulkner's life and work.

Vickery, Olga W. *The Novels of William Faulkner.* Baton Rouge: Louisiana State University Press, 1959. One of the first, and still among the most useful, book-length studies of the Faulkner canon. Offers a discussion of *The Sound and the Fury* that focuses on the narratives of the Compson brothers.

The Sound of Waves

Author: Yukio Mishima (1925-1970)
First published: Shiosai, 1954 (English translation, 1956)
Type of work: Novel
Type of plot: Idyll
Time of plot: 1950's
Locale: Uta-jima (Song Island), Japan

Principal characters:
SHINJI KUBO, a young Japanese fisherman
MISTRESS KUBO, his mother
HIROSHI, his younger brother
HATSUE MIYATA, a woman loved by Shinji
TERUKICHI MIYATA, her father and a wealthy boat owner
YASUO KAWAMOTO, a suitor for Hatsue's hand
CHIYOKO, a student at Tokyo University who betrays the lovers
JUKICHI OYAMA, a master fisherman who befriends Shinji

The Story:

Shinji Kubo, a young fisherman who is strong beyond his eighteen years, is the provider for his younger schoolboy brother Hiroshi and his widowed mother, formerly the best abalone diver on Uta-jima. One day, returning from his day's work with Jukichi Oyama, a master fisherman and his good friend, Shinji sees an unfamiliar, hauntingly beautiful face among the women helping to beach the fishing boats. The woman is Hatsue Miyata, daughter of the owner of two oceangoing freighters, who has been living with adoptive parents on another island. The boy cannot get her image out of his mind. The next night, he visits the beautiful Yashiro Shrine, dedicated to the god of the sea and within sound of the never-ceasing waves, and prays that the god would in time make him a fisherman among fishermen, worthy of a bride such as Hatsue, the beautiful daughter of Terukichi Miyata, the shipowner.

Shinji's prayer is to come true, but not without many trials for the young lovers. On a day when the weather is too stormy for fishing, they arrange to meet in an old ruined tower. Shinji, soaked with the rain, arrives first, builds a fire, and falls asleep. He awakens to see Hatsue, unclothed, standing nearby. Innocently, she had decided to dry her wet clothes before the fire while he slept. The tender love scene that follows is as natural, innocent, and idyllic as her act, for Hatsue decides that since they are to be married as soon as her father gives his permission, both have to remain virtuous.

Shinji and Hatsue, however, had been spied on by Chiyoko, daughter of the lighthouse keeper. She, unlike the naïve, wholesome, and unlearned young couple, had "spoiled" her good nature by too much introspection and by acquiring a veneer of learning at Tokyo University. Without an inherent sense of honor, she tells Yasuo Kawamoto, Hatsue's more acceptable suitor, what she suspects. Yasuo had also been spoiled by the gloss of culture. The whispering campaign that results has to be stoically withstood by the lovers, who can no longer be together; even their innocent letters are intercepted.

Terukichi is stern and proud, but not unjust, and he is sufficiently moved by his daughter's devotion to Shinji to try a plan proposed by Jukichi. Shinji and Yasuo are of an age to serve an apprenticeship at sea, so they are signed on one of Terukichi's freighters; the one who shows better character will marry Hatsue. Yasuo, good-natured but lazy, allows Shinji to do part of his work for him. Neither knows he is being watched. Then, in a heavy storm off Okinawa, when a broken cable threatens to set the ship adrift from its mooring buoy, Shinji swims through the rough seas to secure the vessel from disaster. Young Shinji proves himself, and Terukichi accepts him as his future son-in-law.

Critical Evaluation:

Yukio Mishima's artistic accomplishment includes a wide range of genres. For example, he adapted ancient No dramas, science fiction, modern plays, and stories from Japanese history. In addition, *The Sound of Waves* is an idyllic romance, unlike any of the writer's other novels. It is limited in scope and in ambition, showing none of the tedious intellectual debate, emotional strain, or sardonic tone that characterize much of his other work. Also, evil and perverted love are conspicuous by their absence.

What evil there is in the story remains basically peripheral, for the pure love of Shinji and Hatsue cannot be corrupted. It is the most normal and healthy of his works. *The Sound of Waves* is lyrical, simple, and satisfying, so much so that some have criticized it as being sentimental. While the setting is exotic, it is not exotic in a negative sense. Furthermore, it is the least obscure, and it reads in English as the least "foreign" of his novels, for it is intentionally unsophisticated and uses simple pastoral elements to tell a story that is concerned with human relationships that are as timeless as the sea that surrounds the island on which the events of the tale occur.

In *The Sound of Waves*, Mishima appears determined to demonstrate to himself that he could create in his writing a world totally different from his own, but even more than that, to show that he could have a place in that world. Several years after the novel was written, Mishima is said to have commented that at about the time of its writing, he had felt a desire to try to turn himself into his own opposite.

Mishima long entertained a hope to visit Greece, and on a voyage around the world in the early 1950's, he found that Greece was even more wonderful than he had imagined. On this voyage, he began to realize that many of the pictures he had painted of human life in the past were highly incomplete; they dwelled only on the dark side of life. Thus was born the idea of writing an idyllic story that would be based on a classical Greek myth, that of Daphnis and Chloë. It would provide an idyll of a boy and a girl and the sea and would include a fairy-tale-like series of trials that the fisher boy would have to overcome to gain the hand of his "princess." In terms of Mishima's own artistic development, writing this novel based on classical literature demonstrated that, whether that classical background was Japanese or Western, it could serve as an effective substitute for personal experience. Mishima secured some help in locating the kind of island he envisioned for the setting of the story, Kamijima, off the coast of Izu. He spent about ten days on the island, becoming familiar with it. Completed in 1954, the novel became Mishima's best-selling novel up to that time, with some 106,000 copies sold immediately and more than 100,000 copies sold annually thereafter for some years. Soon, major Japanese film companies were in competition with one another for rights. After a film version was released a few months later, Mishima received the first Shinchosha Literary Prize for the novel.

The Sound of Waves makes use of a number of important images, not the least of which is the human body, especially the male body. In this respect, it is not unlike other Mishima works. In *The Sound of Waves*, the major characters embody the fullness of life through their physical strength. Mishima notes the healthy skin and rosy cheeks of Hatsue and Chiyoko, and he details the sunburned skin of most of the characters. It is Shinji's body that is especially important. When he stands against the firelight, he is "like a piece of heroic sculpture," underscoring the classical source of the story. It is the physical strength of that body that is the most important, however, for without superior strength, even Shinji's courage would have been insufficient to win the final test of his fitness during a typhoon at sea, an event that turns the tide for him in gaining the approval of Hatsue's father.

As suggested by the title of the novel, the sea is critical to the story. Even though Japan is an island nation, the sea has not played an especially prominent role in Japanese literature. *The Sound of Waves* is an exception. Early in the novel, the reader finds that "Yashiro Shrine is dedicated to Watatsumu-no-mikoto, god of the sea," making it clear that the fishermen of this island are devout worshipers of this god. Frequently, the islanders pray for calm seas, and if one is rescued from some peril at sea, a votive offering at the sea-god's shrine is made immediately. Hatsue writes to Shinji, when he gets a job on the *Kamikaze-maru*, and tells him that she will go daily to Yashiro Shrine to pray for his safety. The sense that the island is favored by the gods foreshadows the happy ending that Shinji and Hatsue enjoy. Very near the end of the novel, Shinji reflects that the blessing of the gods on the little island of Uta-jima had protected their happiness and "brought their love to fulfillment."

Furthermore, Mishima uses the sea in characterizing the lovers: Shinji's clear eyes are a gift that the sea makes to those who make their livelihood upon it. Elsewhere, Shinji is said to feel no lack of music in his life because nature itself, the sea, satisfies that need for him. Hatsue's association with the sea as a pearl diver enhances her beauty as it stretches the skin smooth. In the last major scene of the novel, Shinji acts valorously in the sea near Okinawa when he secures the ship to a buoy during a typhoon, putting his own life at great risk, but also enabling him to prove himself to Hatsue's father.

"Critical Evaluation" by Victoria Price

Further Reading

Keene, Donald. *Five Modern Japanese Novelists.* New York: Columbia University Press, 2003. Keene, a well-known scholar of Japanese literature, devotes a chapter to Mishima in his examination of five Japanese novelists with whom he was acquainted. Provides his personal recollections of the writers, as well as literary and cultural analyses of their works.

Napier, Susan J. *Escape from the Wasteland: Romanticism and Realism in the Fiction of Mishima Yukio and Ōe Kenzaburō.* Cambridge, Mass.: Council on East Asian Studies, Harvard University, 1991. Declaring *The Sound of Waves* devoid of realism, Napier explores the romantic, idyllic quality of the novel. Emphasizes the story's purity and simplicity.

Nathan, John. *Mishima: A Biography.* Boston: Little, Brown, 1974. Reprint. Cambridge, Mass.: Da Capo Press, 2000. This classic biography establishes the background and context for *The Sound of Waves*, and identifies the inspiration for the novel in the myth of Daphnis and Chloë. Includes a new preface.

Petersen, Gwenn Boardman. *The Moon in the Water: Understanding Tanizaki, Kawabata, and Mishima.* Honolulu: University Press of Hawaii, 1979. Sees the classical male body as a dominant figure in all of Mishima's works, including *The Sound of Waves*. Notes associations of fire and desire in the novel.

Piven, Jerry S. *The Madness and Perversion of Yukio Mishima.* Westport, Conn.: Praeger, 2004. A psychological study of Mishima. Piven traces the events of Mishima's life—most notably his early childhood, spent largely in his grandmother's sick room—to provide a better understanding of the author and his works.

Scott-Stokes, Henry. *The Life and Death of Yukio Mishima.* New York: Farrar, Straus and Giroux, 1974. A brief section on *The Sound of Waves* discusses Mishima's visit to Greece as inspiration for the novel. Explains the widespread popular acclaim given the novel in Japan, unmatched by its critical attention.

Starrs, Roy. *Deadly Dialectics: Sex, Violence, and Nihilism in the World of Yukio Mishima.* Honolulu: University of Hawaii Press, 1994. Starrs provides a critical and interpretive look at Mishima's work. Examines Mishima's intellectual background, including the influences of Thomas Mann and Friedrich Nietzsche, and describes the quality of Mishima's thought. Includes a bibliography and an index

Viglielmo, Valdo H. "The Sea as Metaphor: An Aspect of the Modern Japanese Novel." In *Poetics of the Elements in the Human Condition*, edited by Anna-Teresa Tymieniecka. Boston: D. Reidel, 1985. This scholarly essay argues that unlike Mishima's other novels, *The Sound of Waves* is exceptionally positive and even idyllic. Identifies Shinji and Hatsue as creatures of the sea.

South Wind

Author: Norman Douglas (1868-1952)
First published: 1917
Type of work: Novel
Type of plot: Social satire
Time of plot: Early twentieth century
Locale: Island of Nepenthe

Principal characters:
BISHOP HEARD OF BAMPOPO, an Anglican clergyman
MRS. MEADOWS, his cousin
DON FRANCESCO, a Catholic priest
MR. VAN KOPPEN, an American millionaire
FREDDY PARKER, the proprietor of a drinking club
MR. KEITH, a hedonist
MR. EAMES, an elderly scholar
COUNT CALOVEGLIA, an antiquarian
DENIS PHIPPS, a student
RETLOW (alias MUHLEN), a blackguard

The Story:

Bishop Heard goes to Nepenthe to meet his cousin, Mrs. Meadows. Since her second husband was unable to leave his post in India, the bishop is to escort Mrs. Meadows and her child to England. The bishop himself is returning from ecclesiastical labors in Bampopo, Africa. The bishop is introduced to Nepenthe society by Don Francesco, a priest he met on the boat. The social leader is the American-born duchess of San Martino, who is about to join the Church through Don Francesco's influence. Other figures are Mr. Keith, a wealthy hedonist; Denis Phipps, a frustrated college student; Mr. Eames, a faithful compiler of material for an annotated edition of a forgotten work on the *Antiquities* of Nepenthe; Count Caloveglia, an antiquarian interested in the Golden Age of Greece; and Freddy Parker, proprietor of a drinking club that serves a strange brand of whiskey bottled by his stepsister.

There is also much talk of some religious fanatics, disciples of an unwashed Russian mystic named Bazhakuloff. Because of a virile apostle, Peter, the group is favored by Madame Steynlin and has access to her villa by the sea. One of the few Englishwomen on the island is Miss Wilberforce, who frequently drinks to excess and undresses in the streets at odd times of the day and night. Fortunately, the bishop developed a tolerant point of view while living among African natives, and he is able to accept these strange characters as he finds them. Except for a festival in honor of Saint Dodekanus and a visit with his cousin, who does not seem pleased to see him, the first days of the bishop's stay are uneventful. Then one of the old springs on the island suddenly dries up, and the natives report several unusual births. Next, Mr. Parker's stepsister is bitten by a strange insect. She dies swiftly and would be as swiftly buried if the volcano did not erupt at the same time.

Mr. Parker watches ashes falling over the city and is saddened both by his stepsister's death and by news that a cabinet minister of Nicaragua was removed from office. Since the minister made Parker the Nicaraguan finance commissioner for southeastern Europe, the proprietor fears that he is about to lose his pretentious but empty title. Hoping that the Vatican will intercede for him if he were to become a Catholic, he consults the parish priest and suggests a procession in honor of the island's patron saint to bring an end to the eruption. The priest is delighted to hear such a pious suggestion from a non-Catholic, and before long, the holy procession is winding through the ashy streets. Miraculously enough, the ashes stop falling and rain that follows washes away all traces of nature's upheaval.

The eruption ends, and life goes on as usual. Several parties are given for Mr. Van Koppen, an American millionaire who visits the island every year. At these parties, the bishop hears more about the life of the colony. He talks with Denis and learns about his problems. He hears with amusement of Van Koppen's promise to contribute liberally toward a clinic for Miss Wilberforce, if Mr. Keith will give a like sum. Van Koppen knows that Keith believes people should be allowed to do what they like with their lives, and he thus knows that Keith will never part with the amount he promised.

One day the bishop, visiting Count Caloveglia, finds him about to sell the American a small bronze statue of wonderful antique Greek workmanship. To authenticate the statue, which was unearthed on the count's property, Van Koppen calls in an English art expert. Although the expert declares the piece a real masterpiece and a rare find, Van Koppen knows that the work is a fake. He is willing to pay the price, however, as a compliment to the count's ability to deceive the expert.

The next day, the bishop goes for a walk along the cliffs with Denis, who is still perturbed about his problem of where to go and what to do. While they rest, the bishop sees that they are in sight of his cousin's villa. As he watches, he sees Mrs. Meadows come out of her house and walk along the cliff with a man who called himself Muhlen when the bishop met him on the boat. Later, he hears that the man is a blackmailer whose real name is Retlow. He wonders what his cousin is doing with such a person. Suddenly, the man disappears, and Mrs. Meadows walks briskly back to her house. The bishop just watched a murder.

Suddenly he remembers where he heard the name Retlow before; it was the name of his cousin's first husband. Doubtless he is blackmailing her. As far as the bishop can see, she was justified in killing him. He remembers that on the boat Retlow said a particularly annoying child ought to be thrown overboard. The bishop decides that Retlow's own end is consistent with his ideas.

Unfortunately, a gold piece that belonged to Retlow comes to light in the possession of a native boy. When the boy is accused of murder, the case becomes a battle of rival factions. The boy is a cousin of the village priest, and Signor Malipizzo, the magistrate, is a Freemason who hopes to discredit the Church through that relationship. To defend the boy, the priest calls in Commendatore Morena, a lawyer who rose to fame and to power through his membership in the Black Hand. At the trial, the boy is judged innocent, chiefly because of Morena's eloquence. He first calls the jurors' attention to the crime they will commit if they remove the boy from his mother, a relationship that was important to so many famous men. Then, learning that the boy is an orphan, he shifts his argument to show what an injustice they will commit if they convict an innocent boy. The accused goes free. Under the circumstances, the bishop resolves to say nothing of Mrs. Meadows's guilt. With her fears of blackmail removed, she seems a different woman. Nobody suffers from the murder but Retlow, who deserved his fate.

Denis finally becomes angry at Mr. Keith's drunken meddling, and he tells the old hedonist to shut up. It is the first time Denis ever makes a decision for himself and carries it through. His visit to Nepenthe starts him on the road to manhood. On the whole, reflects the bishop, most matters affecting the people of Nepenthe turn out well in the end.

Critical Evaluation:

Commentators on Norman Douglas's work frequently noted that he never wasted material. He not only recycled articles and essays but also viewed his books as opportunities to expound upon the myriad subjects on which he was an expert or at least had strong opinions. *South Wind* is a kind of grab bag of lectures and observations on various, often obscure, aspects of geology, climatology, history, morality, religion, and folklore, among other topics. Douglas's use of articulate characters confined to a restricted setting allows for ample airing of views and recalls the methods of English novelist Thomas Love Peacock, whose country house novels were once very popular.

South Wind's setting itself is a good example of Douglas's methods. Nepenthe is not to be found on a map, but critics have generally related it to the island of Capri, about which Douglas wrote a series of scholarly pamphlets and upon which he was living when he completed *South Wind*. Douglas did not deny his novel's debt to a real location but insisted that Ischia, Ponza, and the Lipari Islands (all lying off the southwest coast of Italy) were the actual sources for Nepenthe's natural scenery. Douglas even incorporated a version of his observations regarding the pumice stone industry of the Lipari Islands, the subject of one of his first publications. Douglas's creation had deep roots in his own experience—the details of which he drew upon heavily.

The novel's characters are the result of much the same process, which represents a central weakness of *South Wind*. One or two seem to be based on historically obscure acquaintances of Douglas, but others are little more than personifications of facets of their author's own personality. The voluble Mr. Keith is clearly a spokesman for Douglas's hedonistic views, and Mr. Eames and Count Caloveglia represent Douglas's scholarly and antiquarian interests. All are perfectly adequate mouthpieces, but none emerges as rounded or particularly memorable.

While Douglas had difficulty in creating complex characters, he also experienced problems in plotting. When this deficiency was pointed out in reviews, Douglas retorted that *South Wind* was "nothing but plot" and went on to describe that plot as "how to make murder palatable to a bishop." Readers may be forgiven for thinking that Douglas was protesting too much, because few of them turn the pages of *South Wind* to find out what happens next. Instead, readers continue with the book because they are captivated by Douglas's attractive personality and entranced by the sunny mood he captures.

Douglas spent most of his adult life near the shores of the Mediterranean, and he championed the region's values as his own. He prized the Mediterranean's temperate climate (and put his ideas about the relationship between climate and culture into the mouth of Count Caloveglia), its historical associations, and the moderation it seemed to induce in matters of religion, philosophy, and morals. Indeed, *South Wind* might be read as an account of the adjustment of Bishop Heard to the Mediterranean.

South Wind appeared at the height of World War I, and its gaiety contrasts sharply with the bleak, somber mood prevalent throughout Europe and the United States at that time. It also appeared at a time when urbanization and mass production seemed to threaten the individualistic way of life Douglas enjoyed and celebrated. These factors contributed to the book's enormous popularity, and it became the sort of book that anyone with a claim to sophistication read. As British novelist Graham Greene wrote in his introduction to Douglas's last book, "My generation was brought up on *South Wind*."

Indeed, several British writers of Greene's generation were directly influenced by Douglas in general and by *South Wind* in particular. Aldous Huxley's satirical novels *Crome Yellow* (1921, in which Douglas appears as the character Scrogan), *Antic Hay* (1923), and *Point Counter Point* (1928) bear its stamp. Greene himself generally wrote books of a darker character, but his humorous novel *Travels with My Aunt* (1969) bears similarities to *South Wind* and was received with some of the criticisms that greeted Douglas's work. Among later British writers, Lawrence Durrell owes a debt to Douglas. Several of Durrell's early novels and Greek travel books exhibit Douglas's hedonistic attitude, his kaleidoscopic interests, and his erudite style.

Among readers, the key to *South Wind*'s enduring popularity may be that it is greater than the sum of its parts. Just as the sirocco, the south wind of Douglas's title, works its magic on Nepenthe's visitors, so Douglas's infectious good humor transforms what might under other circumstances be indifferent material. *South Wind* is one of the most enjoyable satires in the English language. Douglas's attitudes hardened later in life, but when he wrote his first novel he was content to poke gentle fun at the targets of his satire, and he did not hesitate to include himself. For example, Denis asserts his independence by turning on the drunken and garrulous Mr. Keith, Douglas's most obvious alter ego. Concepts of sophistication have changed since *South Wind* appeared, but many of Douglas's concerns remain as important to contemporary readers as they were in 1917. Under these circumstances, Douglas's laughter and his healthy scorn are still important.

"Critical Evaluation" by Grove Koger

Further Reading

Brothers, Barbara, and Julia M. Gergits, eds. *British Travel Writers, 1910-1939*. Vol. 195 in *Dictionary of Literary Biography*. Detroit, Mich.: Gale Research, 1998. Includes an article about Douglas, providing biographical information and critical analysis.

Greenlees, Ian. *Norman Douglas*. Harlow, England: Longman, 1971. A pamphlet-length survey by a man who knew and traveled with Douglas. *South Wind* receives careful attention.

Holloway, Mark. *Norman Douglas: A Biography*. London: Martin Secker & Warburg, 1976. Comprehensive, judicious consideration by a man who admits to enjoying Douglas's work "almost without reservation." Contains a thorough investigation of *South Wind*'s origin, composition, and influence.

Leary, Lewis. *Norman Douglas*. New York: Columbia University Press, 1968. A brief survey that treats *South Wind* prominently. Concludes that the novel remains as fresh as when it first appeared.

Lindeman, Ralph D. *Norman Douglas*. Boston: Twayne, 1965. Easily one of the best book-length introductions to Douglas and his writings. *South Wind* receives specific treatment. Includes bibliography.

Matthews, Jack. "Jack Matthews on Norman Douglas's *South Wind*." In *Rediscoveries: Informal Essays in Which Well-Known Novelists Rediscover Neglected Works of Fiction by One of Their Favorite Authors*, edited by David Madden. New York: Crown, 1971. A genial appreciation stressing the novel's intelligence, compassion, and humor. Matthews wonders at the book's neglect. A good starting place for research.

Spain, Take This Cup from Me

Author: César Vallejo (1892-1938)
First published: España, aparta de mí este calíz, 1939
(English translation, 1974)
Type of work: Poetry

For the reader who must rely on the English translation of the poetry of César Vallejo, there will always be some sense of distance from the original Spanish. This is all the more the case as Vallejo, like the Irish writer James Joyce, often played with his native language in his poetry, and wordplay is nearly always untranslatable.

Vallejo, who was born in Santiago de Chuco, a tiny town nestling in the Peruvian Andes, and who died in Paris, is considered by many to be the finest of all Latin America's poets of the twentieth century. He wrote essays, short stories, a novel, literary criticism, and drama, but he is remembered mainly for his poetry. Vallejo's work falls into five main stages: 1915-1918, *Modernismo*; 1919-1926, the avant-garde; 1927-1931, Marxism (Trotskyism gradually transformed into Stalinism); 1932-1935, political disillusionment; and 1936-1938, Christian Marxism. *Spain, Take This Cup from Me* belongs to the culminating phase of Vallejo's work, the Christian Marxist phase. This collection of poems was written during the first two years of the Spanish Civil War (1936-1938). Vallejo died on Good Friday, 1938, after which the war dragged on for another year. *Spain, Take This Cup from Me* was inspired by the events of the war, about which Vallejo read in newspaper reports. (He used to wait in the railway station in Paris for news from Spain.) Vallejo also drew on his experiences during two visits he made to Spain, one as a reporter in the winter of 1936, the other as the Peruvian delegate at the International Writers' Conference held in Madrid and Valencia in the summer of 1937.

Vallejo was not alone in writing poems about the Spanish Civil War. Others, among them the English poet Stephen Spender, the French poet Louis Aragon, the Chilean Pablo Neruda, the Cuban Nicolás Guillén, and the Spanish poets Miguel Hernández and Rafael Alberti, also used the war as a theme of their work. Vallejo's poetry is unique, however, in that it expresses a political faith in the Republican cause through the motif of Christian resurrection, a rather unusual choice given the proletarian and often anticlerical bias of the Republicans and especially the communists who supported the Republican war effort. It was thought for many years that *Spain, Take This Cup from Me* had never been published. The 1939 publication had appeared just before Francisco Franco's troops invaded Barcelona, and copies were secretly hidden in the monastery at Montserrat to prevent the work's being destroyed; the copies were not unearthed until 1981.

Spain, Take This Cup from Me consists of fifteen poems of varying lengths. The opening poem, "Hymn to the Volunteers for the Republic" (176 lines), which is addressed to the Republican militiamen, imagines a world in which the Republicans have already won the war; it is a utopian world of harmony similar to that envisioned in the prophecies of Isaiah. "Battles" (144 lines) is dedicated to the people of Estremadura, a poor region of Spain on the west near the Portuguese border, which took the brunt of the war effort early on; Franco's troops first landed in southern Spain from the Canary Islands and Morocco and then moved northward.

Poem 3, "He used to write with his big finger in the air . . ." (45 lines), is based on the death of an imaginary railwayman named Pedro Rojas. Both parts of his name have symbolic connotations, Pedro referring to Peter, the founder of the Christian church, and Rojas to the symbolic color of communism, red. Pedro Rojas therefore stands as a fusion of Christianity and communism. Most striking about the poem is its use of the myth of Prometheus, who was tied to a rock and had his liver eaten by an eagle every day as punishment for having given fire to humankind. In Vallejo's use of the myth, the animal exacting the punishment becomes a vulture to underline the earthiness of the pain of warfare. Vallejo also alludes to the betacism (sound change) of the Spanish language, that the letters "b" and "v" sound the same in Spanish, to emphasize his allegiance with the lower classes, who often misspell words with a "b" instead of a "v." Vallejo reflects the illiteracy of the uneducated classes not to ridicule them but to express his political solidarity with them.

Poem 4, "The beggars fight for Spain . . ." (25 lines), portrays the struggle for the city of Santander on the northern coast of Spain. Here Vallejo expresses the powerlessness of the have-nots of this world through the image of the beggar. The sinister poem 5, "Spanish Image of Death" (45 lines), describes death, here personified and walking around the field of battle. In conclusion, the poet seems to be welcoming the person of death into his own life, as if expressing a suicidal desire. "Cortege after the Capture of Bilbao" (dated

September 13, 1937; 28 lines) is based on the final procession of Republicans killed by the assault on the northern Basque town of Bilbao, which fell to the Nationalists on June 18, 1937.

Poem 7, "For several days the air, companions" (dated November 5, 1937; 26 lines), portrays the movement backward and forward of enemy lines during the struggle for the city of Gijón in the north of Spain; Gijón was finally invaded by Nationalist forces on October 21, 1937. To stress that Franco's troops are the foreign invaders in this war, Vallejo suggests that the land "is Spanish" when it is still loyal to the Republicans. He refutes the legitimacy of Franco's war effort, which was called a "crusade" by the Nationalists, including the Catholic Church.

Poem 8, "Here . . ." (dated September 10, 1937; 38 lines), is devoted to a mythical Republican militiaman, Ramón Collar, who is explicitly compared with Christ. The eleventh poem, "Short Prayer for a Loyalist Hero" (dated September 10, 1937; 22 lines), refers to a militiaman who fell at the battle of Toledo. The opening stanzas of the poem refer to the image at the beginning of the Gospel of St. John, where Christ is referred to as the "Word made flesh." In his poem, Vallejo describes—in surrealist terms—a book as emerging from the dead body of a militiaman. This image also alludes by implication to the poet's verse, which is produced from and transcends death.

"Winter During the Battle for Teruel" (33 lines), the tenth poem, is based on the ferocious battle for the city of Teruel in eastern Spain. That battle went on from December 15, 1937, until February 22, 1938, and was interrupted by some of the coldest winter weather ever experienced in that region. In this poem, Vallejo concentrates on the vicarious pain he experiences at witnessing the soldiers' misery. The eleventh poem, "I looked at the corpse, at his visible swift order . . ." (dated September 3, 1937; 14 lines), refers to the way a dead militiaman seemed momentarily to come back to life but was confirmed dead. When the soldiers listened to his heart, they heard nothing but "dates."

"Mass" (dated November 10, 1937; 17 lines) is perhaps Vallejo's most famous poem; it depicts the imaginary moment on the battlefield in which a dead Republican militiaman, like Lazarus, rises and begins to walk. It is not Christ who resurrects the dead militiaman, however, but the combined love of all the inhabitants of the world. This poem is a humanist rewriting of the Lazarus story from the Synoptic Gospels; in essence it fuses the transcendent Christian belief in eternal life with the human solidarity of socialism.

"Funeral Drumroll for the Ruins of Durango" (30 lines) is based on the bombing of the city of Durango, which was destroyed on April 26, 1937. A rewriting of the Lord's Prayer, this poem in effect sanctifies the dust and destruction that is all that is left of Durango.

"Beware, Spain, of your own Spain! . . ." (22 lines) is one of the most confessional of all of the poems in *Spain, Take This Cup from Me*. At the time of the Spanish Civil War, worldwide communism was split between two options: the Stalinist option, which favored "socialism in one country," and the Trotskyist option, which favored revolutionary internationalism—that is, the spreading of the doctrine of communism throughout the world. Vallejo's poem refers to the purges taking place in the Republican zone, which the English writer George Orwell described magnificently in his *Homage to Catalonia* (1938). At this time, the Stalinists were rooting out the Trotskyists and murdering them; in fact, Trotsky would himself be murdered by a Stalinist henchman, though not in Spain but in Mexico. Thus the reference in line 2 to the "sickle without the hammer" should be understood to mean an incomplete communism, a doctrine, such as Stalinism, that is missing an important ingredient. The phrase "Beware of the one hundred percent loyal" (line 15) is a reference to overzealous communist doctrinarians who are prepared to sacrifice their friends to the cause of communism.

Finally, "Spain, Take This Cup from Me" (51 lines), the fifteenth poem, from which the title of the collection is taken, describes the possibility that Spain may actually fall to its enemy; this is in fact what did happen, though Vallejo did not live to see the day. Spain, in this poem, becomes a motherlike figure, symbolizing nature (she holds the energy of the earth within her) and culture (she is compared to a schoolteacher who teaches her children how to read and write). As a mother figure, Spain stands as a mother not only for all the citizens of Spain but also for the citizens of the Spanish-speaking Latin American countries, where Spain is commonly known as *la madre patria*, the mother country. The poem concludes by declaring that, should Spain fall, the whole world must go out and search for Spain. This poem, like the fourteen others in *Spain, Take This Cup from Me*, is a gesture of anguished solidarity with Spain and the Republican militiamen who lost their lives fighting for their homeland.

Stephen M. Hart

Further Reading

Brotherston, Gordon. *Latin American Poetry: Origins and Presence*. New York: Cambridge University Press, 1975. Includes a discussion of Vallejo's work that shows how he uses images from the Bible to describe the apocalyptic nature of the Spanish Civil War.

Franco, Jean. *César Vallejo: The Dialectics of Poetry and Silence*. New York: Cambridge University Press, 1976. Chapter 9 concentrates on *Spain, Take This Cup from Me* and discusses the use of certain images throughout the poem, such as fire and water, which signify salvation and purification.

Hart, Stephen M. *Stumbling Between Forty-six Stars: Essays on César Vallejo*. London: Centre of César Vallejo Studies, 2007. Examines Vallejo's life and work, including discussions of Vallejo the man, Vallejo and politics, his language revolution, and his relations to cinema and music. Print volume is accompanied by a DVD, "Traspié entre 46 estrellas," a docudrama about Vallejo's life and poetry.

_____. "The World Upside-Down in the Work of César Vallejo." *Bulletin of Hispanic Studies* 62, no. 2 (April, 1985): 163-177. The section on *Spain, Take This Cup from Me* shows how Vallejo uses the image from the book of Isaiah of the prophecy of world peace and harmony to portray his vision of a Republican utopia.

Higgins, James. *The Poet in Peru*. Liverpool, England: Francis Cairns, 1982. Offers a good overview of Vallejo's work, including discussion of his poetry published posthumously. Analyzes the interplay of the visionary and the socially committed sides of Vallejo's poetic personality.

Vallejo, César. *The Complete Poetry: A Bilingual Edition*. Edited and translated by Clayton Eshleman. Berkeley: University of California Press, 2007. Anthology contains the original Spanish and the translated English versions of *Spain, Take This Cup from Me*. Efraín Kristal, a professor and author of several books on Latin American literature, provides an informative introduction, and Peruvian author Mario Vargas Llosa contributes a foreword.

The Spanish Friar
Or, The Double Discovery

Author: John Dryden (1631-1700)
First produced: 1680; first published, 1681
Type of work: Drama
Type of plot: Tragicomedy
Time of plot: Fifteenth century
Locale: Aragon, Spain

Principal characters:
TORRISMOND, son of Sancho, the deposed king, and defender of Aragon against the Moors
LEONORA, queen of Aragon, the daughter of the usurper, and engaged to Bertran
BERTRAN, made a duke by Leonora's father, now in military disgrace
RAYMOND, foster father of Torrismond
DOMINIC, a licentious friar
LORENZO, a young gallant and soldier
GOMEZ, an elderly usurer
ELVIRA, his young wife

The Story:

Aragon is in a state of siege because the usurper king, lately dead, refused to acknowledge and reward the services of the Moors in gaining the kingdom for him. Queen Leonora, promised on her father's deathbed to Duke Bertran, regrets this alliance as well as the fact that she holds in a dungeon the deposed King Sancho, a righteous and beloved ruler. Bertran's forces were routed three times by the Moors before Torrismond, supposed son of Raymond, one of the leading nobles, rallied the scattered Christians and saved the kingdom from the infidels.

Young Lorenzo, a valiant colonel in Torrismond's army, brings news of the victory and confides to his friends his desire to celebrate with the first prostitute available. He boasts that he robbed his Moorish victims of gold and jewels. Elvira, the young wife of a jealous old moneylender named Gomez, makes advances to the handsome soldier, but her husband immediately thwarts plans for the assignation that was put in motion by Friar Dominic.

Upon his triumphal return, Torrismond offends Bertran by openly ridiculing him for ineptness. He also naïvely declares his love for the queen, who, in turn, is smitten with love for the young hero. Bertran vows vengeance and agrees to her suggestion to kill King Sancho because he thinks that will hasten the marriage. Leonora makes the suggestion with the intention of thereby making Torrismond her king-husband. Torrismond, however, remains loyal to the old king and to Raymond.

Despite all efforts to the contrary, clandestine love prevails in the palace, though not in Gomez's mansion. Friar Dominic, ghostly father to Elvira, makes a series of arrangements for the young wife and her hopeful gallant to meet, but each meeting is discovered by the near-cuckolded husband. Bertran, too, does his best to keep Leonora and Torrismond apart by testing the reaction of the populace to the supposed murder of King Sancho.

Raymond, incensed by such intrigues, admits that in the troublesome days of the Moorish invasion King Sancho entrusted to him his son Torrismond. Raymond urges Torrismond to take over the kingdom and to avenge the old king's death by deposing or by killing the usurpers. Torn between his love for Leonora and his filial duty to his foster father and real father, Torrismond is unable to commit so bloody a deed. He declares his belief that Leonora's repentance and his own attempt to thwart the regicide settled that score. After learning Torrismond's decision, Raymond, though he is moved to compassion over his adopted son's predicament, departs to rouse the citizens.

The intrigue involving Elvira and Lorenzo comes to nothing; no amount of bribery, blackmail, or disguise can bring the two together, despite the fact that Friar Dominic is a master of trickery and knavery. The friar is finally exposed when Lorenzo's father reveals that Elvira is his daughter, married to Gomez the usurer in order to prevent her suffering a worse fate in those troubled times. Thus the affection Elvira and Lorenzo feel for each other is based on the family relationship of brother and sister.

To this double discovery of the true parentage of Torrismond and Elvira comes a third: King Sancho is not dead. Bertran, suspicious of the queen's motives and aware of the people's loyalty to the old king, merely spread the rumor of King Sancho's death. Knowing also that the queen is devoted to Torrismond rather than to himself, Bertran begs forgiveness for his part in the many sad events that occurred in the kingdom. Leonora, much relieved, wishes only for King Sancho's permission for her marriage to his son. Torrismond assures her that the good king, quick to forgive, will grant such a boon.

Critical Evaluation:

The Spanish Friar is a modified form of John Dryden's earlier heroic drama. Features in this play common to the mode are a noble hero of great ability and renown, violently torn between his love for a lady and his honor, which impels

him to give her up; an exaggerated, often bombastic style of language; an intricate (and often barely credible) plot, sometimes with a comic, dramatically parallel subplot; and a dramatic movement that threatens to, even if it does not actually, end in tragedy. *The Spanish Friar* is a considerably more controlled example of the genre than Dryden's *The Conquest of Granada by the Spaniards* (1670-1671), but the resemblance is clear.

It is easy enough to ridicule the fantastic plot complications of heroic drama, and the often extravagant language in which the heroes and heroines express themselves—as in the line "Despair, Death, Hell, have seized my tortured soul . . ."—but it must be remembered that these plays were designed primarily as entertainment, not as historical dramas or as studies of character. "'Tis my interest to please my audience," Dryden noted in his preface. The final revelation that old King Sancho is really alive, saved by Bertran's better nature, tends to render nonsensical Torrismond's earlier anguish over whether or not he must turn against Leonora, and the queen's own painful resolve to renounce her husband and retire to a convent. Nevertheless, the earlier dramatic action that leads to this crisis is no less fanciful than the conclusion.

Apart from the unlikely plot twists and the larger-than-life characters, it is apparent how skillfully Dryden, largely through brilliant dialogue, manipulates the intellectual and emotional sympathies of his audiences so that they see the issues of the play from the same points of view as the participants. No one character is either fully unsympathetic or fully sympathetic. Leonora is to be condemned for her crime and for her evasion of responsibility but pitied in her plight ("to lose a crown and a lover in a day"); the reader may wish to see justice done but not at the expense of her life or happiness. Similarly, Torrismond is to be admired for his love and devotion, but it is easy enough to see the "womanish" quality in him that makes Raymond despise him for his lethargy in love. The audience—not just the hero—is torn by conflicting sympathies, and Dryden's dramatic prowess in creating and modulating this audience involvement is never more apparent than in the exciting exchange between Torrismond and Raymond at the end of act 4, in which the conflict between love and honor becomes the focal point.

Dryden, author of the stinging lampoon *Mac Flecknoe* (1682), had a sure hand for comedy, and the comic subplot that gives the play its title is a rollicking one. Friar Dominic is a splendid compendium of all the avaricious, hypocritical, debauched friars who populated English literature since the Middle Ages. Here again, however, Dryden's dramatic portrait is not purely vitriolic but also sympathetic, even half-admiring; certainly it is difficult to take the part of the near-cuckold Gomez over that of the witty and exuberant "old gouty friar."

In addition to his anti-Catholicism, many other of the playwright's sentiments are apparent in *The Spanish Friar*. Possibly most objectionable is the strain of misogyny (another long-established literary tradition) that characterizes women as the weak, lustful, seductive, and inferior sex: "That toy a woman," says Raymond, "made from the dross and refuse of a man." Finally, Dryden's essential political and religious conservatism, his deeply rooted mistrust of the popular will, and his dread of any kind of rebellion against legitimate power are everywhere apparent here. Even in a work devoted primarily to thrills and laughter, Dryden's implication is clear: Without the guides of established political and religious authority, morality becomes relative and behavior mechanical, as Leonora realizes when she allows Bertran to perpetrate the murder of the lawful king.

Further Reading

Eliot, T. S. *John Dryden: The Poet, the Dramatist, the Critic*. 1932. Reprint. New York: Haskell House, 1966. Eliot's discussion helped introduce Dryden to twentieth century audiences and still serves as a starting point for other critiques. Although very generalized, it highlights reasons why Dryden's plays continue to fascinate critics and students.

Hammond, Paul, and David Hopkins, eds. *John Dryden: Tercentenary Essays*. New York: Oxford University Press, 2000. This collection, published during the tercentenary of Dryden's death, examines some of Dryden's individual works, as well as more general characteristics of his writing. Some of the essays question if Dryden is a classic, explore Dryden and the "staging of popular politics," and describe the dissolution evident in his later writing.

Hopkins, David. *John Dryden*. New York: Cambridge University Press, 1986. Within this updated assessment of Dryden's place among English writers, Hopkins provides an introduction to *The Spanish Friar* for new readers. He includes a plot summary and focuses on Dryden's preface.

_____. *John Dryden*. Tavistock, England: Northcote House/British Council, 2004. Concise and up-to-date overview of Dryden's life and work. Hopkins demon-strates that Dryden not only was a man of his times but also continues to have significant ideas to express to a twenty-first century audience.

Lewis, Jayne, and Maximillian E. Novak, eds. *Enchanted Ground: Reimagining John Dryden*. Toronto, Ont.: University of Toronto Press, 2004. Collection of essays that apply twenty-first century critical perspectives to Dryden's work. The first section focuses on Dryden's role as a public poet and the voice of the Stuart court during Restoration; the second explores his relationship to drama and to music.

Loftis, John. "Chapter Two: Dryden's Comedies." In *Writers and Their Background: John Dryden*, edited by Earl Miner. Athens: Ohio University Press, 1972. Carefully differentiating between the play's comic and serious plots, this discussion calls attention to the English political context, especially the anti-Catholic bias and the Exclusion Controversy.

Rawson, Claude, and Aaron Santesso, eds. *John Dryden, 1631-1700: His Politics, His Plays, and His Poets*. Newark: University of Delaware Press, 2004. Contains papers presented at a Yale University conference held in 2000 to commemorate the tercentenary of Dryden's death. The essays focus on the politics of Dryden's plays and how his poetry was poised between ancient and modern influences.

Ward, Charles E. *The Life of John Dryden*. Chapel Hill: University of North Carolina Press, 1961. This biography puts the play in the context of Dryden's career and details the play's political background, performances, and audience. Ward interprets the main character, Friar Dominic, as a satirization of Catholicism rather than of the clergy.

Wasserman, George R. *John Dryden*. New York: Twayne, 1964. Wasserman gives an overview of Dryden's life and works. He fits *The Spanish Friar* among the tragicomedies and draws heavily on Dryden's interest in Ben Jonson's comedy of humours prototype in discussing style and theatrical context.

Zwicker, Steven N., ed. *The Cambridge Companion to John Dryden*. New York: Cambridge University Press, 2004. Among these seventeen essays are discussions of Dryden and the theatrical imagination, the invention of Augustan culture, patronage, and Dryden's London and the "passion of politics" in his theater.

The Spanish Tragedy

Author: Thomas Kyd (1558-1594)
First produced: c. 1585-1589; first published, c. 1594
Type of work: Drama
Type of plot: Tragedy
Time of plot: Sixteenth century
Locale: Spanish and Portuguese royal courts

Principal characters:
DON ANDREA, a murdered Spanish nobleman
BALTHAZAR, prince of Portugal
LORENZO, a Spanish nobleman
BEL-IMPERIA, fiancé of Don Andrea before his death
HIERONIMO, a Spanish general
HORATIO, Don Andrea's friend and Hieronimo's son
ALEXANDRO and VILLUPPO, Portuguese noblemen

The Story:

Don Andrea, a Spanish nobleman, has been killed in battle with the Portuguese. After his soul arrives in the underworld, Pluto sends it and the Spirit of Revenge back to the world of the living to learn what happened after Don Andrea's death. At the Spanish court, Don Andrea's ghost hears that the Portuguese have been defeated in war and that Balthazar, prince of Portugal, has been taken prisoner. Balthazar, Don Andrea learns, is the man who killed him. A quarrel has developed between Lorenzo and Horatio, each claiming the honor of capturing Balthazar.

Meanwhile, at the Portuguese court, Villuppo tells the viceroy that his son, Balthazar, is dead, having been killed by the traitorous Alexandro. Alexandro is then sentenced to death.

Balthazar, while a prisoner, falls in love with Bel-Imperia, as does Horatio. Bel-Imperia, who had been the fiancé of the slain Don Andrea, falls in love with Horatio. Plans are proposed for a treaty of peace between Spain and Portugal. These events are all distasteful to Don Andrea's ghost. He is comforted, however, by the Spirit of Revenge's promise that grim fate will overtake all concerned.

Balthazar, aided by Lorenzo, plans to win the love of Bel-Imperia. Lorenzo sends a servant to spy on Bel-Imperia and to discover whom she loves. When the servant returns to tell his master that Bel-Imperia is in love with Horatio, Lorenzo and Balthazar plot Horatio's death.

The king of Spain plans to make diplomatic use of Bel-Imperia, who is his niece, by marrying her to the Portuguese prince, Balthazar, thus cementing the friendship of the two countries. The king warns her that she must do as he commands. One night, when Bel-Imperia and Horatio meet in the garden, Horatio is set upon by Balthazar and Lorenzo; they kill Horatio by hanging and then take Bel-Imperia away. When Horatio's body is discovered, Hieronimo, Horatio's father, goes mad, as does his wife. Seeing these events, Don Andrea's ghost becomes even more bitter, but the Spirit of Revenge tells him to be patient.

The ambassador to Spain, returning to the Portuguese court, arrives in time to prevent the death of Alexandro, because the ambassador brings word that Balthazar still lives. Villuppo, who had plotted Alexandro's death in the hope that he could gain advancement from it, is sentenced to die.

In Spain, Hieronimo, partly recovered from his madness, plots to avenge his son's murder. Afraid of Hieronimo, Lorenzo and Balthazar plan to murder one of their accomplices, lest he give away their secrets. They have him slain by another of their accomplices. When the murderer is arrested and sentenced to hang, they tell him that he will be saved with a pardon. The man goes to his death in silence, or so Lorenzo and Balthazar believe. Before his execution, however, he writes a confession in which he tells the true story of Horatio's death, and he sends the document to Hieronimo.

Meanwhile, Lorenzo and Balthazar imprison Bel-Imperia in the hope of forcing her to marry Balthazar. She, bewildered by all that has happened, finally believes Lorenzo's statement that she will suffer her father's and the king's anger if she fails to marry Balthazar willingly.

Balthazar and Lorenzo enlist Hieronimo's aid in presenting an entertainment for the Spanish court and the Portuguese viceroy, who has arrived to swear fealty to the king of Spain. Hieronimo suggests that they do a play that he has written; when they protest, he silences them with the observation that even Nero did not consider it beneath his dignity to act in a play. The play, Hieronimo tells them, is a tragedy befitting royal actors and a royal audience.

In the meantime, Hieronimo's mad wife, still lamenting the death of her son, cuts down the arbor where he was hanged by his assailants and then stabs herself. Hers is the fourth death in the action watched by Don Andrea's ghost and the Spirit of Revenge.

That evening, the royal party gathers to watch the play that Hieronimo and the others are to present. When the members of the party arrive, Hieronimo insists that they all enter a gallery, lock the door, and throw the key down to him. The king, thinking nothing amiss, agrees to do so. Thus the stage is set for Hieronimo to avenge the murder of his son.

In Hieronimo's play, Balthazar has the role of the Muslim emperor Soliman, Lorenzo plays a knight, and Bel-Imperia plays a Christian woman captured and given to Soliman. While Soliman and the knight argue over the captured woman, a Muslim nobleman, acted by Hieronimo, enters and kills the knight, and the captured Christian woman kills the stage emperor. Then, stopping the audience's applause for the fine performance, Hieronimo introduces the body of his dead son and assures those present that the killings they have watched are real. Then he runs to hang himself before the royal party can break out of the locked gallery.

Overtaken by courtiers before he can kill himself, Hieronimo bites out his own tongue to prevent a confession. Told that he must confess in writing, he gestures for a knife to sharpen the point of his pen. With that weapon he stabs the king's brother and himself, thus bringing the number of deaths to eight.

At the end, Don Andrea's ghost, who has been watching all the while, announces to the Spirit of Revenge that he is satisfied; all his enemies have received their just deserts. The Spirit of Revenge tells him that they will return to the underworld, where Don Andrea can watch his enemies in their torment and consort happily with his friends.

Critical Evaluation:

The Spanish Tragedy, one of the most popular English plays of the sixteenth century, marked a change from the earlier, stilted English drama. Thomas Kyd built his plot on a foundation of three conventional devices found in the Roman tragedies of Seneca. One is a ghost, the second is revenge for a murdered relative, and the third is a liberal use of bombast and soliloquy in the dialogue. To these he added strange characters with perverse psychological twists: madmen, murderers, suicides. He also employed the device of a play-within-a-play, public hanging, and other items new to English drama. Kyd upstaged all his contemporaries in his ability to devise thrilling stage tricks. As a pioneering playwright, Kyd, in this play, pointed the way to the lurid, bloodthirsty revenge plays of the Jacobean and Caroline stage. The popularity of *The Spanish Tragedy* is evidenced by the fact that it is known to have gone through at least ten editions by 1634.

The play defines Elizabethan revenge tragedy. The major stock features are all to be found in it, including revenge directed by either a father or a son for the sake of the other; a ghost, outside the action of the play, who aids the revenger;

hesitation of the hero or revenger (the hero often is contaminated by his passion and becomes, because of the delay, Machiavellian); real or pretended insanity; and the presence of suicides, intrigues, scheming villains, and other various horrors.

Comparison between *The Spanish Tragedy* and William Shakespeare's *Hamlet, Prince of Denmark* (pr. c. 1600-1601, pb. 1603), written about fifteen years later, is provocative. Both plays have an amiable Horatio, ghosts returning from the dead, father-son vengeance themes, justice delayed because of the mental state of the avenger, a dumb show, a play-within-a-play, and profound sensationalism. There is no doubt that Kyd's play in some ways helped to shape *Hamlet*. Kyd is in fact attributed as author of the lost play that is probably an earlier version of the Hamlet story.

The Spanish Tragedy withstands the test of critical analysis. Its multiple-subplot construction produces some interesting and sophisticated critical questions. As a result of the liveliness of his play, Kyd is not always regarded as a careful playwright. The revenge motif, for example, plays itself out through three characters: Don Andrea, Bel-Imperia, and Hieronimo. Furthermore, in addition to the audience of the play, there are two other onstage audiences. One is the ghost of Don Andrea and the Spirit of Revenge. The other is the Spanish court, which witnesses the dumb show.

A major critical issue regarding *The Spanish Tragedy* is the question of audience response to Hieronimo. Is he a hero or a villain? Ambiguously, he is both. Judged by Elizabethan ethical and legal standards of behavior, Hieronimo becomes a wholly despicable Machiavellian villain when he decides to effect his revenge through secret—private, rather than public—means. In terms of revenge tragedy, the development in Hieronimo's character from public avenger-hero to private avenger-villain is evidence that Kyd is deliberately turning his audience's sympathy against the revengeful father.

In the play's famous *vindicta mihi* passage, Hieronimo concludes that he will act out private vengeance for his son's death:

> And to conclude, I will revenge his death.
> But how? Not as the vulgar wits of men,
> With open, but inevitable ills,
> As by a secret, yet a certain mean,
> Which under kindship will be cloaked best.

Hieronimo chooses his secret plan over the publicly acceptable alternative of open duel or, better yet, due process of law. Moreover, his final atrocity of killing the innocent duke of

Castile, brother to the king, marks him as total villain. By this deed he departs so far from the English sense of justice that all sympathy is withdrawn. Hieronimo's suicide is then forced by the audience's demand that the villain be properly punished. His death satisfies the stern Elizabethan doctrine that murder by private individuals, no matter what the motive, must not be tolerated.

One may argue that Hieronimo has no choice but to act as he does. His reversal is forced by events in the play. He is the chief magistrate of Spain, and his life has been devoted to administering the law. He believes in public justice and wants compensation for wrongs by due process. Hieronimo, in fact, is the only character in the play who attempts to circumvent disaster by appeals to public law. His appeal to the king, however, is blocked. The king is busy when Hieronimo approaches him, and Hieronimo is hit by another fit of distraction at the moment when he most needs to be in complete control of his faculties. Believing that Horatio's murderer must not go unpunished, and believing that no recourse to public vengeance is left open, Hieronimo assumes that he, the next of kin, must be the appointed avenger, and he becomes a scourge of God, attempting to mete out justice on his own terms. Only if the play is read as a treatise on the nature of divine justice operating on the human level can Hieronimo's character be interpreted as heroic.

Kyd manipulates his audience to feel satisfaction and horror at the catastrophe of the play by using his two onstage audiences to guide the responses of the real audience. The Spirit of Revenge's promise of revenge to Don Andrea sets up a pattern of anticipation for the audience. This response may be described as aesthetic, and Revenge becomes a mouthpiece for the playwright's intent. Revenge says in effect that he is making it all up, that the play is a work of art rather than a piece of reality.

The audience of Hieronimo's dumb show, however, sees not a fiction but a story with clear ties to reality. Only at the end of his show does Hieronimo reveal that the actors in his play have not been feigning but, instead, have stabbed in earnest. The audience's response is, understandably, horror. The line between art and reality is blurred. Rather than responding to a play, the members of the Spanish court audience find themselves suddenly responding to a real and immediate experience. Kyd's audience is manipulated by this second level of response, so that the general audience sees the play through the eyes of the onstage audience. The real audience, however, is informed, as the onstage audience is not, of the "fiction" that Revenge has created.

Viewers of *The Spanish Tragedy* leave the theater with a sense—conscious or not—of having witnessed a play with implications for their everyday lives. Audience response on this level is necessary for any good drama. Kyd seems to have built into the play, on a structural level, a sense of relevance that makes the play more than the sensational bloodbath it is often labeled.

Jean G. Marlowe

Further Reading

Ardolino, Frank R. *Apocalypse and Armada in Kyd's "Spanish Tragedy."* Kirksville: Sixteenth Century Journal Publishers, Northeast Missouri State University, 1995. Compares the play to the apocalyptic visions in the biblical books of Daniel and Revelation and then places the work within the historical context of England's victory over the Spanish Armada in 1588, describing the play as a triumph of English revenge.

_____. *Thomas Kyd's Mystery Play: Myth and Ritual in "The Spanish Tragedy."* New York: Peter Lang, 1985. Argues that the play is a combination of murder mystery, allegory, and religious ritual. Notes that Hieronimo chooses pagan vengeance over Christian forgiveness because the latter does not seem to offer justice.

Barber, C. L. *Creating Elizabethan Tragedy: The Theater of Marlowe and Kyd.* Edited by Richard P. Wheeler. Chicago: University of Chicago Press, 1988. Discussion of *The Spanish Tragedy* asserts that Lorenzo's murder of Horatio violates the social order and disrupts Hieronimo's belief in an ordered universe. Hieronimo's violence is at first improperly directed but finds a proper focus at the end of the play.

Bowers, Fredson T. *Elizabethan Revenge Tragedy, 1587-1642.* Princeton, N.J.: Princeton University Press, 1940. Traces the origins of revenge tragedy to Senecan drama. Shows how *The Spanish Tragedy* follows Senecan patterns closely.

Braunmuller, A. R., and Michael Hattaway, eds. *The Cambridge Companion to English Renaissance Drama.* 2d ed. New York: Cambridge University Press, 2003. Collection of essays devoted to Renaissance drama includes discussion of Kyd and *The Spanish Tragedy*.

Edwards, Philip. *Thomas Kyd and Early Elizabethan Tragedy.* Edited by Ian Scott-Kilvert. 1966. Reprint. New York: Longman, 1977. Analyzes Elizabethan tragedy from the 1560's to the 1580's. Offers a brief biography of Kyd.

Erne, Lukas. *Beyond "The Spanish Tragedy": A Study of the Works of Thomas Kyd.* New York: Manchester University Press, 2001. Presents a broad critical overview of all of

Kyd's work, with several chapters devoted to *The Spanish Tragedy*. Discusses the play's origins and its framing of revenge. Chronicles the additions and adaptations to the drama that have been made over the years, as well as the play's twentieth century production history.

Murray, Peter B. *Thomas Kyd*. New York: Twayne, 1969. Places *The Spanish Tragedy* in the context of the times in which it was written and also explores the play's influence on later authors. Examines the play sequentially and explains how its central theme is the corruption of love.

The Spectator

Authors: Joseph Addison (1672-1719) and Sir Richard
    Steele (1672-1729)
First published: 1711-1712, 1714
Type of work: Essays

Joseph Addison and Richard Steele's *The Spectator* was among the most popular and influential literary periodicals in England in the eighteenth century. Begun on March 1, 1711, this one-page essay sheet was published six days a week, Monday through Saturday, and reached 555 issues by its last issue on December 6, 1712. Each issue was numbered, the articles were unsigned, and many had mottoes from classical authors. *The Spectator*'s end was brought about by a combination of the other interests of its authors and by a rate increase in the taxes that were levied on paper. In 1714, *The Spectator* was revived from June through December by Addison and two other writers, who had occasionally contributed to the original publication. Reading *The Spectator* yields a vivid portrait of London life in the first decades of the eighteenth century.

The Spectator, like its equally famous predecessor, *The Tatler* (1709 to 1712), was the creation of Sir Richard Steele, who combined a life of politics with a writing career as a poet, a playwright, and a literary journalist. Steele became a member of Parliament, was knighted by King George I in 1715, and achieved success as a dramatist with his play *The Conscious Lovers* in 1722. Using the pseudonym of Isaac Bickerstaff, Steele provided lively stories and reports on London society through *The Tatler*, which attracted male and female readers. Addison, already popular as poet, was also a playwright and a writer on miscellaneous topics who held a series of government appointments. He contributed material to *The Tatler* and then formed a collaborative relationship with Steele to write for *The Spectator*. While *The Tatler* featured both news and short essays on topical matters, *The Spectator*, with the established readers of *The Tatler* as its pri-

mary buyers, was composed of one long essay on the social scene or a group of fictive letters to the editor that gave Addison and Steele a forum for moral or intellectual commentary. This was presented in the periodical by the specially created, fictional social observer, "Mr. Spectator."

To give the essays structure, Steele created the Spectator Club and presented the character of Sir Roger De Coverly, a fifty-six-year-old bachelor and country gentleman, as its central spokesman. Other members of this fictional group included a merchant, Sir Andrew Freeport, a lawyer, a soldier, a clergyman, and a socialite, Will Honeycomb, who contributed gossip and interesting examples of social behavior to Mr. Spectator. Although Steele ultimately did not use the Spectator Club as a device as often as he apparently anticipated, the De Coverly essays were the best recognized and most popular section of *The Spectator*. In later literature of the century, characters similar to those created by Steele for the club appeared in novels and political periodicals. Through De Coverly and Freeport, Addison and Steele are able to contrast the political views of the Tory and Whig parties and, through Honeycomb, to satirize the ill effects of an overly social life on personal morality and good judgment.

The first number of *The Spectator* begins with Addison's general introduction of Mr. Spectator to his readers. As Mr. Spectator explains, readers want to know something about an author, even if the information is general:

Thus I live in the World, rather as a Spectator of Mankind, than as one of the Species . . . as a Looker-on, which is the Character I intend to preserve in this Paper.

As for keeping some personal details to himself, Mr. Spectator notes that knowing his real name, his age, and his place of residence would spoil his ability to act as a nonpartisan observer. By issue 10 (written by Addison), Mr. Spectator reports to his readers that the periodical has a daily circulation of three thousand papers, and, by its height in 1712, nine thousand issues of it are sold daily in London. In addition to essays on a single theme, some issues used letters from readers (written by friends of Addison and Steele), which created the impression of a widespread circulation while offering a means for Mr. Spectator to address specific social problems. Issue 20, for example, written by Steele, is based on a young lady's note about men who stare at women in church. Mr. Spectator gives a detailed and courteous reply that contrasts "male impudence," as he labels it, among the English, the Irish, and the Scots. Several subsequent issues, such as 48 and 53, are composed entirely of these sorts of letters, which become a typical way for the authors to discuss male and female social behavior and, usually, female fashion. The importance of conversation in society is profiled in issue 49, also by Steele, on the role of the coffeehouse as "the Place of Rendezvous to all that live near it, who are thus turned to relish calm and ordinary life." Besides moral and amusing accounts, *The Spectator* featured short pieces of prose fiction with developed characters, plots, dialogue in some cases, and themes specific to the story itself. In issue 50, Addison reworks an idea about cultural encounters that was originally proposed by Jonathan Swift for *The Tatler* in his story of the Indian kings. Earlier, in issue 11, Steele tells the tale of Inkle and Yarico. This story concerns an Indian girl, Yarico, who unwisely, though sincerely, befriends an English merchant, Thomas Inkle, who is more interested in commercial gain than in friendship and love.

Issues 106 to 131, which cover June and July, 1711, form the De Coverly papers of the periodical to which both Addison and Steele are contributors. Since they both created Sir Roger daily, his character evolves into something slightly different from Steele's original portrait in issue 2, as the gentleman's eccentricities and unworldliness make him a comic contribution to literature on the scale of Miguel de Cervantes' Don Quixote. In issue 106, Mr. Spectator accepts Sir Roger's invitation to spend a month with him in the country. Once there, Mr. Spectator is impressed by the freedoms of unstructured country life and the many amusements available to pass each day. Over the course of these letters, Mr. Spectator meets Sir Roger's loyal servants, his chaplain, and an assortment of rural neighbors.

The broad outlines of country life sketched by Mr. Spectator would have been familiar to the London readers as many had country homes of their own, relatives outside London, and opportunities to travel into the cooler northern climates in the summer months. There is more to these lively, pictorial entertainments, however. Through Mr. Spectator, Addison and Steele are able to comment on the positive effects of good household management, the shortcomings of the aristocracy, the benefits of commerce, the landed gentry's role in maintaining social order, the differences between the fear and the shame of poverty, the signs of good breeding—behavior, conversation, and dress—as they are found in the country, and the reach of party politics outside London. The brief accounts of Sir Roger's unrequited love for a "perverse country widow" allow Steele, who wrote issues 113 and 118, to continue his conversation on love and marriage initiated in *The Tatler* and carried on in *The Spectator*. Issue 116, contributed by Eustace Budgell, who later wrote with Addison on the continuation of the paper, offers an amusing and detailed story of Sir Roger's hunt and an opportunity for Mr. Spectator to consider the fickleness of human compassion. At the end of the chase, Sir Roger directs that the hunted rabbit be freed to live its life in its garden as it gave them all good sport. In issue 117, written by Addison, Mr. Spectator relates the story of Moll White, an insensible old woman believed by many, including Sir Roger, to be a witch. The lack of understanding of the plight of the elderly, abandoned poor is the theme of this more serious essay. Placed back to back as these stories are, the reader quickly sees the contradictions in Sir Roger's attitude toward humans and his attitude toward animals, which sounds a cautionary note to the audience. To complete the cycle, issue 131 announces Mr. Spectator's departure, and issue 132 describes his memorable journey back to London. The entire story of Sir Roger includes four papers on his visit to the sights of London (issues 269, 329, 335, and 383) and one on his death (issue 517) on October 23, 1712. Addison did not want the character to be imitated by other, later periodical writers.

In all, the De Coverly papers are representative of the themes, scope, and treatment of the subjects of *The Spectator* as a whole. These essays also show the balanced style of *The Spectator*, which is maintained through the careful craftsmanship of Addison and of Steele. Neither writer concentrates solely on writing either topical or moral essays; they write both with equal facility and in complementary styles.

Since the purpose of *The Spectator* is to allow its readers to observe all parts of life, there are a great many topics covered to different degrees in the periodical. One important subject is literary criticism, treated in essays on tragedy (issues 39, 40, 42, and 44), on poetry (issues 70 and 74), on comedy and wit (issues 23, 28, 59-63, 65, 270, and 446), and, interspersed between issues 267 and 463, concerning extended analyses of the writing of John Milton. *The Spectator*'s essays on literature, popular entertainment, and refinement set the standards of taste for the readers, while providing prose composition models and examples of methods of characterization suggestive to other writers. Another series of essays is written in praise of scientific discovery and in response to popular pseudoscientific ideas on animal intelligence and on the supernatural. Addison, who composed many of the issues on science, is careful to balance his arguments for the power of science with references to the power of God, as shown in issue 420, in which he discusses the advances in knowledge offered by the microscope and the way that scientific information can be used to heighten faith.

Personal and public morality is also a theme of great import in *The Spectator*. For example, Steele writes on lewd conduct in issues 155, 266, and 274 and on the dangers of plays with situations in which immoral behavior is rewarded in issues 51 and 208. He also uses the paper to stress the need for parental responsibility (issues 192, 320, 437, and 479) and for marital fidelity. Addison also writes on religious and philosophical topics with his five hymns, which appear in issues 441, 453, 465, 489, and 513, reminding readers of his popularity as a poet.

There are, of course, many papers celebrating the diverse characteristics of human nature and numerous portraits of individuals with distinctive traits found throughout *The Spectator*. An interest in and curiosity about people as individuals are hallmarks of the eighteenth century, which emphasized, through the philosophy of Enlightenment, the social roles of humans in their societies.

Issue 555, written by Steele and published on December 6, 1712, brought *The Spectator* to a close. In this issue, Mr. Spectator acknowledges the contribution of Addison to the success and variety of the papers in an indirect way and names seven other writers who he claims contributed the letters that enlivened the conversations in its pages. He also announces the impending publication of *The Spectator* in seven volumes, and he clearly blames the higher taxes for driving the paper out of business. In the summer of 1714, Addison, with Budgell and Thomas Tickell, revived *The Spectator* and published issues through issue 635. These additional essays were collected for volume 8 of the complete *Spectator*, published in September, 1715. Steele, after *The Spectator* ended, started a political essay periodical, *The Guardian*, in March, 1713, which was succeeded by *The Englishman* in October, 1713. It went into a second series before its end in November, 1715. Donald F. Bond edited the standard edition of *The Spectator* (1965), which has an extensive introduction and identifications of the issues written by Steele, Addison, and the other contributors.

The Spectator was frequently republished throughout the nineteenth century and could be found in many home libraries after 1712. It was an unparalleled accomplishment in eighteenth century periodical journalism and was highly influential on many later English writers. The congenial eye of Mr. Spectator touched on all parts of ordinary life; *The Spectator* compares to Samuel Pepys's *Diary* (1825) and James Boswell's *Life of Samuel Johnson, LL. D.* (1791) as a work representative of the eighteenth century within cultural history.

Beverly E. Schneller

Further Reading

Bloom, Edward, and Lillian Bloom. *Educating the Audience: Addison, Steele, and Eighteenth-Century Culture.* Los Angeles: William Clark Andrews Memorial Library, University of California, 1984. A study of *The Spectator* providing a detailed perspective on the readers of the periodical and how the authors appealed to them.

Bond, Richmond P., ed. *Studies in the Early English Periodical.* Chapel Hill: University of North Carolina, 1957. This indispensable history of the eighteenth century periodical provides the terminology currently in use to describe literary essays and magazines.

Dammer, Richard H. *Richard Steele.* Boston: Twayne, 1982. This biography in the Twayne's English Authors series argues that Steele used themes from an earlier moral tract, *The Christian Hero* (1701), as a unifying feature in his essays for *The Spectator.*

Ketcham, Michael D. *Transparent Designs: Reading, Performance, and Form in "The Spectator" Papers.* Athens: University of Georgia Press, 1985. A significant and careful study of Addison's and Steele's literary styles.

Mackie, Erin Skye. *Market à la Mode: Fashion, Commodity, and Gender in the "Tatler" and the "Spectator."* Baltimore: Johns Hopkins University Press, 1997. Mackie examines both of the periodicals edited by Addison and Steele, focusing on how they covered fashion in their role as arbiters of eighteenth century English taste. Places the periodicals within the commercial context of publishing and describes how their fashion reportage expressed contemporary ideas about gender identity and cultural standards.

Newman, Donald J., ed. *"The Spectator": Emerging Discourses.* Newark: University of Delaware Press, 2005.

Examines how *The Spectator* served as a manual to help the emerging middle class organize its life. The essays discuss the periodical's ideas about children, literature, education, femininity, death, and other topics.

Winton, Calhoun. *Captain Steele: The Early Career of Rich-* *ard Steele.* Baltimore: Johns Hopkins University Press, 1964. The first of Winton's two-book biography of Steele, covering his early career between 1690 and 1714. Half of this volume is on Steele's periodical journalism and *The Spectator.*

Speculations About Jakob

Author: Uwe Johnson (1934-1984)
First published: Mutmassungen über Jakob, 1959
(English translation, 1963)
Type of work: Novel
Type of plot: Psychological realism
Time of plot: Mid-1950's
Locale: East Germany

Principal characters:
JAKOB ABS, a railroad dispatcher in East Germany
GESINE CRESSPAHL, a worker for NATO in West Germany and lover of Jakob
HERR ROHLFS, an agent of the East German secret service
JONAS BLACH, an assistant in the English department at the university in East Berlin, in love with Gesine
HEINRICH CRESSPAHL, a cabinetmaker in East Germany, Gesine's father and a father figure to Jakob

The Story:

Jakob Abs is killed crossing the railroad tracks, tracks he has crossed many times in the past. His death leads several people to recall what they know of his life and to speculate about his death.

Rohlfs, an East German secret agent, is observing Heinrich Cresspahl in the small northeastern town of Jerichow because Cresspahl's daughter, Gesine Cresspahl, works for the North Atlantic Treaty Organization (NATO) in West Germany. Gesine met Jakob Abs when he and his mother arrived in Jerichow as refugees from Pomerania at the end of World War II. She was thirteen and he eighteen at the time. They soon developed a brother-sister relationship, which they have continued through her university years and his time working at a railroad job in another town. Gesine finally decided to leave Communist East Germany and move to West Germany.

Rohlfs talks to Jakob's mother about the goals of socialism; she asks Heinrich Cresspahl to carry two suitcases for her to the train station, which causes the rumor that Cresspahl has left for West Germany. Jakob, who works as a dispatcher for the state-owned East German railroad, is contacted by Rohlfs and receives a telegram from Cresspahl, saying that his mother has gone to the West.

Jonas Blach leaves East Berlin, where he teaches English at the university; he meets Gesine in the street when she is walking with American officers to their car. In Jerichow, he is

introduced to Jakob at Cresspahl's house, where Jakob has gone because his mother has left. Some time before he traveled to Jerichow, Jakob broke up with his girlfriend, Sabine. As usual, Rohlfs is keeping them all under surveillance. Jakob puts his mother's things in order; to him it feels as though she has died. Jonas, who is involved in a group critical of the Communist government, tells Jakob and Cresspahl about the group.

When Cresspahl calls Gesine to tell her about Jakob's death, she has already heard about it. She remembers how she, on a surprise visit from West Germany, had run into Rohlfs, whom she did not know at the time. She had sat in a restaurant, waiting, and as Jakob walked in, he recognized Rohlfs. Jakob denied Gesine's identity while establishing eye contact with her to let her know he would meet her later. He then left with Rohlfs to talk about his mother. When Jakob met Gesine outside, they took a cab to another city to catch the train to Jerichow. After an escapelike trip that involved changing trains, long after midnight they ended up at Cresspahl's house, where Jonas still waited. Rohlfs met them all there later, and they discussed the political situation, especially the rebellion in Hungary. Rohlfs allowed Gesine to return to West Germany.

Jonas returns to East Berlin; Gesine sends a telegram from the first post office on the West German side. Coming to his office, Rohlfs discovers that Jakob disappeared Tuesday evening. Jonas, who has lost his job at the university, visits Jakob that Tuesday, October 30. It is the day when Jakob has to decide for himself whether to use his job at the railroad to delay a troop transport with tanks under way to end the rebellion in Hungary; he lets it pass through because he understands that a delay of ten minutes or even a day will not make any difference. In their conversation, Jonas also realizes that Gesine has not told Jakob about her love for Jakob.

The next day, Jakob makes his trip to the West, officially to see his mother, which Rohlfs has cleared with the authorities. Jakob calls Gesine from his hotel, and they spend time together over the next few days. Coming from a visit to the refugee camp, they hear on the radio about the suppression of the Hungarian rebellion by the Soviets and the imminent military action by the West in the Suez Crisis. On their last night together, Gesine asks Jakob to stay in the West, while he asks her to come with him to the East. She takes him to the local train station, and he leaves alone. The next morning, he is very tired, and, as he crosses the railroad tracks on his way to his job, he is struck by a train. He dies shortly afterward during surgery. Sabine and Jonas, who have in the meantime been staying with friends and visited a literature class at another university, notify Cresspahl. Cresspahl arrives in the early afternoon, and Jonas takes a train to Jerichow. The next morning, however, Jonas turns himself in to Rohlfs, who arrests him. Gesine meets with Rohlfs in West Berlin to talk about what has happened.

Critical Evaluation:

Uwe Johnson is counted among the most important German novelists in the period following World War II. In 1959, three German novels contributed to reestablishing German literature as world literature. The best known of these is Günter Grass's *Die Blechtrommel* (*The Tin Drum*, 1961), with its grotesque allegories. *Billard um halbzehn* (*Billiards at Half-Past Nine*, 1962), by Heinrich Böll, who later received the Nobel Prize in Literature, is the most traditional of these three novels. *Speculations About Jakob* stands out among them as the most experimental novel and the one that focuses on the East-West conflict rather than on the Nazi legacy.

Speculations About Jakob invites readers to form their own opinions based on the speculations they encounter among the book's characters. Reader participation is required, which makes the novel challenging as well as rewarding. The information is presented in three distinct, although at times intertwined, modes: interior monologue, dialogue, and third-person narration. The interior monologues, which are by Rohlfs, Jonas, and Gesine, are scattered throughout

the book, but they are easy to recognize because they are in italics. (In contrast to the German original, the English translation identifies the speaker at the beginning of each section of monologue.) The dialogues, also spread throughout the novel, are marked by dashes, while the contributions by the narrator, which provide the transitions and background information to hold the novel together, are regular text.

It has been pointed out that Johnson's novel is not speculation itself; rather, it portrays speculation. The technique of flashback dominates the flow of the story, and the story line as it is summarized above unfolds in a fragmented manner within five main divisions covering a period of about one month. Each character describes Jakob in a different manner because Jakob means something different to each one; therefore, readers have to consider the issues of the individual characters' reliability and their points of view in interpreting what they say.

Johnson's narrative technique owes much to the experimental tradition of the twentieth century, especially to the American writer William Faulkner. Faulkner was a master of the abandonment of the omniscient narrator for the sake of multiperspectivism. On the level of vocabulary and syntax Johnson is also innovative; for instance, he mixes various kinds of idioms. Some of this, however, is lost in the translation. For example, Gesine tells Jonas about her love for Jakob in biblical language: A literal translation of the German is "It is my soul which loveth Jakob"; however, the translation of this line in the English edition reads prosaically, "I happen to love Jakob."

The narrative structure of the novel is designed to challenge the reader to piece information together as a detective would. Some of the facts are not quite clear. Jerichow, for example, is Johnson's invention, but it bears resemblances to cities in the actual German region of Mecklenburg. Real places, in contrast, are often only alluded to; the name of Dresden, for instance, is given only toward the end of the novel, with the implication that Jakob works there, but the description of the city does not match the actual Dresden. Furthermore, the name of the West German town where Gesine works is never given. In addition, the true nature of the love relationship between Gesine and Jakob does not become clear except in later works by Johnson. Also, the question of whether Jakob's death was an accident or suicide remains unanswered. Readers are challenged to make sense of these and similar uncertainties.

All of this ties in with the novel's overriding issues of identity and reality. Such issues were especially pressing during the Cold War in the divided Germany of the 1950's. Germany provides a focal point for the conflict between these two social systems, as the country was divided into capitalist West Germany and Communist East Germany. Johnson, who left East Berlin for West Berlin on the day the manuscript of *Speculations About Jakob* was sent to its West German printer, has been called the writer of the two Germanies.

Characters are represented in terms of what the novel considers most important; there is no simple right or wrong in regard to the social systems. Gesine and Jakob's love is complicated by their mutually exclusive decisions regarding systems. Their decisions are not easy: Just as Jakob struggles to make the Soviet intervention in Hungary fit into his value system, Gesine is disgusted by the military solution to the Suez Crisis by the West. As a consequence, she decides to quit her job with NATO.

The issues of problematic identity and reality also are addressed in the plot, which is in conflict with the demands of Socialist Realism, the typical elements of which include an idealistic communist (Rohlfs), a wavering intellectual (Jonas), a citizen who is seduced by the West (Gesine), and another citizen who resists this seduction (Jakob). Jakob, however, dies under mysterious circumstances, and the psychological approach to the novel's issues runs counter to a party-line interpretation of the characters.

Interpretation of *Speculations About Jakob*, then, lies in understanding that there is no clear-cut truth; what is more, it has been argued that such an objective truth cannot exist in a country in which truth is a commodity and a construct of the propaganda machine. Consequently, Jakob's death can be seen as symbolic of the political situation of the Cold War. Caught between the two social systems in West and East Germany, Jakob cannot develop or live his true identity and is therefore destroyed. It is not possible for an individual to find his or her own place somewhat independently, so to speak— one is either independent or one is not. Jakob is successful at cutting across the tracks of the social systems only for so long. The shocking insight that cutting across the tracks is ultimately impossible, although some people may do it for a short time, is expressed in the first sentence of the novel. Voicing disbelief at the news of Jakob's death, it is one of the famous first sentences in German literature: "But Jakob always cut across the tracks."

Ingo R. Stoehr

Further Reading

Baker, Gary Lee. *Understanding Uwe Johnson*. Columbia: University of South Carolina Press, 1999. Presents examination of Johnson's five novels, with chapter 4 devoted to an analysis of *Speculations About Jakob*. Another chapter discusses Johnson's approach to narrative and storytelling.

Boulby, Mark. *Uwe Johnson*. New York: Frederick Ungar, 1974. Places *Speculations About Jakob* within the context of world literature and German literature. Provides plot summary and character analysis for this intricate novel, with English translations for all quotations.

Demetz, Peter. *After the Fires: Recent Writing in the Germanies, Austria, and Switzerland*. 1986. Reprint. San Diego, Calif.: Harcourt Brace Jovanovich, 1992. Presents concise discussion of Johnson's complete works that is useful for understanding *Speculations About Jakob*.

Fickert, Kurt J. *Dialogue with the Reader: The Narrative Stance in Uwe Johnson's Fiction*. Columbia, S.C.: Camden House, 1996. Focuses on Johnson's innovative narrative techniques, through which the author seeks to involve his readers in creating the structure of his novels. Chapter 1 examines *Speculations About Jakob*.

Hirsch, Marianne. *Beyond the Single Vision: Henry James, Michel Butor, Uwe Johnson*. York, S.C.: French Literature Publications, 1981. Offers interpretation of *Speculations About Jakob* as well as character analysis, including discussion of each character's function as narrator. Presents all quotations in the original German and in English.

Johnson, Uwe. "'Unacknowledged Humorist': An Interview with Uwe Johnson." Interview by Leslie A. Wilson. *Dimension* 15, no. 3 (1982): 398-413. Johnson answers several questions directly pertaining to *Speculations About Jakob*.

Taberner, Stuart. *Distorted Reflections: The Public and Private Uses of the Author in the Work of Uwe Johnson, Günter Grass, and Martin Walser, 1965-1975*. Atlanta: Rodopi, 1998. Examines the fiction of the three writers and public intellectuals who lived in the former West Germany to determine their involvement in political activities. Demonstrates how Johnson's fiction portrays intellectuals who acknowledge their impotence and retreat from political engagement.

The Spirit of the Laws

Author: Montesquieu (1689-1755)
First published: De l'ésprit des loix: Ou, Du rapport que les loix doivent avoir avec La Constitution de chaque gouvernement les mouers, le climat, la religion, le comerce . . . , 1748 (English translation, 1750)
Type of work: Politics

In terms of its practical effect, *The Spirit of the Laws* is one of the most important political science books. It was one of the primary sources of the United States Constitution and, through that document, one of the major influences on the development of democratic institutions in Europe during and after the French Revolution. All this is out of proportion to Montesquieu's objectives in writing the book, which were to analyze the various types of political institutions known throughout the world throughout history. Montesquieu also aims, in his book, to denounce the abuses of the French monarchical system and to encourage a liberal and more equitable monarchical government for France.

In setting out to write his book, Montesquieu's major inspirations were the works of René Descartes, Nicholas de Malebranche, and Niccolò Machiavelli, all of which he viewed with the kind of healthy skepticism typical of Michel Eyquem de Montaigne. This inspiration did not give him his conclusions, but it gave him his method: a rational, descriptive, and analytic approach to the problem of the nature of the good constitution of society. Montesquieu, like most early political thinkers after Machiavelli, was essentially concerned with the problem of the relationship of right and might, of law and power. Many of these thinkers, however, especially those opposed to what they considered the evil in Machiavelli's realistic approach to politics, tried to theorize on a moral base. They sought to find the basis for the right constitution of society in a consideration of right and wrong and in a natural law of right and wrong. Such an approach was alien to Montesquieu. Political society, for him, had to be based on civil law. Law should reflect what individuals consider right or wrong, but subjective morals and objective law are two different things. Morals, like law, are relative; what one society might consider both right and legal, another might well consider both wrong and illegal.

In considering the problem of adjusting right and might, law and power, Montesquieu did not attempt to solve the problem. He was convinced the problem could not be solved but only understood and dealt with in more rational and equitable ways than societies had used in the past. Thus, he was no more a political moralist than he was a political utopian. Montesquieu's political theory rested on the following assumptions: First, there is no universal solution to the problems of politically structuring a society, because there are only kinds of solutions; second, different cultures require different solutions; third, whatever the solution in a given society, it cannot be arbitrary and will not be accidental—it will depend on the cultural tradition and factors of history and geography; fourth, there is no ideal solution for any culture, only better and worse solutions; fifth, no solution is permanent but is subject to change by conscious or unconscious action and corruption; and, sixth, any workable solution must be the result of rational analysis of objective factors.

The book itself is vast in terms of both the ground it covers and the ideas it generates. Nevertheless, it does not, and could not, achieve the objectives set for it. The scope is too large for the author's abilities and resources. The evidence is often incorrect because techniques for gathering information were still undeveloped. Often Montesquieu's interpretation of valid evidence is not logical or warranted by the facts. The excellence of the book, however, far outweighs its relatively minor defects, and it will continue to be read if only for the sake of its most important contribution to political thought: Montesquieu's discovery of the principle of the separation of powers as a method of securing justice and continuing political liberty.

As a result of the great amount of information incorporated into the book, the great number of subjects considered, and the great number of ideas presented in the course of Montesquieu's analysis, *The Spirit of the Laws* has a structure that is random and difficult to perceive. It is not a formless book by any means, but it does not lend itself to a precise analytic outline. The only principle of organization that seems to hold up under examination is one based on the path of the meandering but directed argument. One widely accepted idea of the arrangement is as follows: Books 1 to 13 are concerned with the concept of government as such, and its specific and general functions. Within this larger division are subdivisions. Books 1 through 8 outline the various types of governments, their essential natures, their structures, and the ways their structures are maintained and corrupted. Books 9 through 13 discuss the functions and the purposes of governments; more specifically, books 9 and 10 discuss the army as the protective agency of the state and the problem of war; book 11 discusses ways to protect the citizen and the meaning of political liberty, and considers the accomplishments of Great Britain in this area; and book 12 is concerned with problems of individual security, the rights of property, the availability of justice, and the function of legal tribunals. Taxes and taxation are the subjects of book 13.

Books 14 through 19 make up the second large section of *The Spirit of the Laws* and, in general, are concerned with the effect of climate, which is seen as a function of geography on various political considerations: book 14, the relation of law and climate; book 15, civil servitude and climate; book 16, domestic servitude and climate; book 17, the relation of political servitude and despotism to climate. Book 18 is concerned with the effect of geographical situation and the nature of the soil on the development of law and of government, and book 19 discusses the morals and customs of a nation and the relation of law to the national spirit.

Books 20 through 25 are generally concerned with economics and religion. Book 20 presents a general theory of the organic interrelation of commerce, morals, poverty, and system of government. Book 21 examines the relation of law and commerce and historical change, and book 22 comments on law and its relation to the use of money. Book 23 examines the relation of population density and the development of law. Book 24 discusses the effect of religion qua faith, doctrine, and belief on law; and book 25 considers the effect of religion qua institution and establishment on law.

Books 26 through 31 are difficult to consider in numerical order. Books 26 and 29, although separated numerically, concern the theory of law and legislative practice; the former discusses kinds of law—positive, natural, canon, and civil; the latter considers the manner of composing laws. Books 27 and 28 are more or less fragmentary considerations of various matters: Book 27 discusses the effect of time on political institutions, and the Roman law of succession; book 28 discusses the origin and evolution of French civil law and the conflict between Germanic and Roman law. Books 30 and 31 examine the development of French feudal laws and institutions: Book 30 is particularly concerned with laws and institutions as they evolved during the period of the establishment of the French monarchy, and book 31 is concerned with feu-

dal law and institutions in relation to the evolution of the monarchy.

One of the most interesting and important sections of *The Spirit of the Laws* is book 2. Here Montesquieu discusses his most famous idea, the separation of powers in the state. Basing his observations on an examination of the English constitution, which he and many other political scientists of the period considered the most advanced and just in history, Montesquieu points out that government has three general functions: the legislative, the judicial, and the executive. If political liberty is to be preserved for the individual, he says, no one man or body in the state should have control of more than one of these functions. Montesquieu's definition of political liberty is as practical and objective as his method of analysis: It is not a moral or philosophical abstraction, but a simple, relativistic statement. Political liberty—which is not the same thing as independence—is simply the right to do what the law permits. This right, the author demonstrates by reference to history and the contemporary state of affairs in Europe, inevitably is abridged when any person or governmental body falls into control of more than one of the three basic functions of government. Thus, the good constitution should be constructed so as to prevent usurpation of power. The framers of the United States Constitution accepted this observation, as they did many of Montesquieu's other positions, and the result has been manifest in history.

Further Reading

Carrithers, David W., Michael A. Mosher, and Paul A. Rahe, eds. *Montesquieu's Science of Politics: Essays on "The Spirit of the Laws."* Lanham, Md.: Rowman & Littlefield, 2001. Collection of essays providing various interpretations of the book's philosophy and influence, including an introductory appreciation by Carrithers and discussions of Montesquieu and natural law, despotism in *The Spirit of the Laws*, and Montesquieu and English liberty.

Cohler, Anne M. *Montesquieu's Comparative Politics and the Spirit of American Constitutionalism.* Lawrence: University Press of Kansas, 1988. Scholarly but accessible work for advanced students. Discusses the narrative content of *The Spirit of the Laws* and explores Montesquieu's conceptualization of liberty, legislation, democracy, and other themes.

Dijn, Annelien de. *French Political Thought from Montesquieu to Tocqueville: Liberty in a Levelled Society?* New York: Cambridge University Press, 2008. Describes Montesquieu's concept of "aristocratic liberalism," which held that a corps of aristocrats was needed to preserve freedom in a monarchy. Demonstrates how this idea had a continued impact on France's politics and society after the French Revolution.

Durkheim, Émile. *Montesquieu and Rousseau: Forerunners of Sociology*. Ann Arbor: University of Michigan Press, 1960. Durkheim, a major contributor to the theoretical foundations of sociology, argues that *The Spirit of the Laws* lays down the principles of the then-emerging science of sociology. Outlines and critiques Montesquieu's methodological logic from a classic social scientific standpoint.

Kingston, Rebecca E., ed. *Montesquieu and His Legacy*. Albany: State University of New York Press, 2009. Collection of essays analyzing the significance of Montesquieu's ideas in the development of Western political theory and institutions. Includes discussions of *The Spirit of the Laws* and the Chinese empire, free speech and *The Spirit of the Laws* in Canada and the United States, and a comparison of the political philosophies of Montesquieu and Alexis de Tocqueville.

Levin, Lawrence Meyer. *The Political Doctrine of Montesquieu's "Esprit des lois": Its Classical Background*. New York: Columbia University Press, 1936. A voluminous but straightforward examination of Montesquieu's reliance on Greek, Roman, and other ancient texts as intellectual sources. Includes a large bibliography of studies, predominantly in French, on Montesquieu.

Shackleton, Robert. *Montesquieu: A Critical Biography*. New York: Oxford University Press, 1961. Devotes eight lucid chapters to the writing of and concepts in *The Spirit of the Laws*. A useful introductory survey of the work.

The Spoils of Poynton

Author: Henry James (1843-1916)
First published: 1897
Type of work: Novel
Type of plot: Social realism
Time of plot: Late nineteenth century
Locale: England

Principal characters:
MRS. GERETH, the mistress of Poynton
FLEDA VETCH, her companion
OWEN GERETH, her son
MONA BRIGSTOCK, Owen's fiancé

The Story:

While visiting one weekend at Waterbath, the country house of the Brigstock family, Mrs. Gereth meets and is immediately drawn to a young woman named Fleda Vetch. The basis of the attraction is a mutual sensitiveness to beautiful things; each guesses that the other possesses such a feeling when they meet one morning while obviously trying to escape the house and the rest of the party. Their aversion emerges not because Waterbath is exceptionally ugly, but rather because it is so very ordinary while pretending to be lovely. The house and the garden might have been quite attractive, and should have been so, but the Brigstocks, people without even a hint of feeling or taste, had had everything done over to fit the very latest fashion. It is this air of fashionable conformity to which Fleda and Mrs. Gereth object. They recognize what the estate would have been naturally, and they can only be repulsed by what it has become.

Mrs. Gereth's horror of Waterbath is particularly acute because of the comparison she inevitably makes between it and her own home at Poynton. Everything at Poynton is exquisite. She and her late husband had gradually furnished it after years of scraping and saving so that they might have the best. Every article in the house had been carefully chosen during their travels in various parts of the world, and she rightly considers their home the most beautiful place in England. Unfortunately, the estate had been left to her son Owen, and she knows that she will have to give it up, along with her beloved treasures, when he marries. Her secret dread is that he will marry a woman with as little a sense of the beautiful as he himself has. She therefore spends much of her time at Waterbath trying to turn his attention from Mona Brigstock, who personifies everything she dreads, to Fleda Vetch, the one person of her acquaintance who would appreciate and preserve Poynton as it is.

When Mrs. Gereth, with somewhat ulterior motives, invites Fleda to come to Poynton as a friend and permanent companion, Fleda, who has no real home of her own, readily accepts. To the chagrin of both women, Owen soon writes that he is planning to marry Mona and that he is bringing her within a week to see the estate. Mona, of course, approves of the home. Although she fails to appreciate its beauty and immediately begins planning certain changes, she does realize that every article in the house has some value, and she insists that Mrs. Gereth leave all but her personal belongings as they are. Mrs. Gereth is to be given the smaller, but still charming, estate called Ricks.

At first, Mrs. Gereth refuses to be moved, but she finally agrees to make the change when it is decided that she can take with her a few of her prized objects. Owen, who is very much disturbed at being pushed by Mona to the point of having a serious conflict with his mother, solicits Fleda's aid in getting his mother to make the move quickly. This request only complicates matters, however, for Fleda soon falls in love with Owen and cannot really be effective as an agent for both parties in the controversy. She encourages Mrs. Gereth to move quickly and quietly, leaving Poynton essentially as it is, but, because of her feelings toward both her friend and the estate, she also encourages Owen to give his mother more time.

During these negotiations, it becomes necessary for Fleda to go to London to see her father. While she is gone, Mrs. Gereth leaves Poynton. Her moving is quick and quiet. When Fleda rejoins her at Ricks, she finds that the woman has moved virtually all of the furnishings from Poynton. Owen and Mona are less than pleased. In fact, Mona postpones the wedding; she refuses to marry Owen until Poynton again holds its rightful belongings. Again, Mrs. Gereth is stubborn, and more negotiations ensue, with both sides once more depending on Fleda for aid.

This time it is Owen's turn to fall in love. His strained relations with Mona, which cause a rather close relationship with Fleda, leave him emotionally unstable. He had also lately come to realize how much Poynton, as he had always known it, means to him and to appreciate anyone who understands its beauty and value as Fleda does. He knows that his life would be much more satisfactory if he were about to marry Fleda instead of Mona. Mrs. Gereth, who had always been willing to give up Poynton to anyone who could love it as she does, says that she will gladly send back everything for Fleda. A realization of this fact finally causes Owen to declare his love for Fleda and to ask her to marry him.

Fleda, although she acknowledges her own feelings, will make no move until Owen has completely broken with Mona, and it is to this end that she sends him away. When Mrs. Gereth hears of these developments, she thinks that the situation has finally worked out to her liking, and she immediately sends everything back to Poynton. This act proves a mistake, however, for as soon as Mona hears that the furnish-ings have been returned, she immediately becomes her former charming self and again captivates Owen. Unfortunately, because of his honor as a gentleman, Owen cannot break the engagement unless the lady demonstrates that she wishes to do so; Mona now makes it clear that she does not wish to end the engagement. She quickly marries him and moves at once to Poynton to acknowledge and secure her possession of the house and its contents. Soon, the couple begins an extended tour of the Continent.

Fleda and Mrs. Gereth again take up residence at Ricks and succeed in making a charming place out of it, in spite of having little to work with and of having to do it with broken hearts. Some time later, Fleda receives a letter from Owen asking her to go to Poynton and take whatever object she most prizes; because of her love both for Owen and for the estate, she resolves to do so. When she arrives at the station, still more than a mile from Poynton, she sees great billows of smoke rising from that direction. It is a porter who tells her that everything is lost. Poynton and all of its beautiful furnishings are destroyed in a fire, which was probably caused by a faulty lamp, aided tremendously by a strong wind.

Critical Evaluation:

According to Henry James in his preface to *The Spoils of Poynton*, he perceived the germ of the short novel in a friend's casual mention of an acrimonious conflict between a mother and her son over the disposition of the family furniture following the death of the father. "There had been but ten words, yet I recognized in them, as in a flash, all the possibilities of the little drama of my 'Spoils.'" He continues,

> On the face of it, the "things" themselves would form the very center of such a crisis; these grouped objects, all conscious of their eminence and their price, would enjoy, in any picture of a conflict, the heroic importance.

The "things" alone, however, must not have been enough to provoke James to immediate creation, since he left the idea unused for almost two years. In 1895, however, needing a story to fulfill an obligation to the *Atlantic Monthly*, James returned to the "spoils" idea and added the necessary missing ingredient, the central character.

Thus, James found the two lines of action that give the story its final shape: the conflict between Mrs. Gereth and her son, goaded on by Mona Brigstock, over the furnishings of Poynton, and the romance between Owen Gereth and Fleda Vetch. The problem of who is to get the spoils dominates the first third of the book, but by chapter 8, the center of interest has shifted to the question of who will marry Owen.

The two issues are completely intertwined since Owen is actually one of the spoils himself, and his marital decision also determines the disposition of the things.

The dispute over the spoils is really a trial between two strong-willed, determined women, Mona and Mrs. Gereth, who direct their strategies through Owen and Fleda. The contest becomes ambiguous and the outcome doubtful because the "agents" prove unreliable: Owen's emotional involvement with Fleda upsets Mona's calculations, and Fleda's ambivalent reactions threaten Mrs. Gereth's design.

It is unlikely that Mona cares much for the things of Poynton for themselves. After she finally wins Owen and Poynton, she flaunts her indifference to the house by not even living there. Her tenacity in seeking the spoils is a matter of willful pride. "Mona," wrote James, "is all will." She insists on the furniture because it "goes with the house"—and the house goes with Owen. In addition, it is probable that Mona sees the dispute as a "test" of Owen or, rather, of her ability to control him. If she can force him to act against his mother's deepest wishes, then she can be confident of dominance in their marriage.

Even though Mrs. Gereth is no less strong-willed and ruthless in her passion to keep control of the artifacts of Poynton, she is a considerably more sympathetic figure. If her attitude toward Poynton reveals her to be a thorough materialist, she is at least a materialist with taste; Poynton, the fruit of her labors, is a fine artistic product, and her devotion to it is passionate and complete. If she is a snob, judging people solely in terms of their taste and "cleverness," she seems accurate in her judgments: Mona is vulgar, Owen is stupid, and Fleda is superior. If Mrs. Gereth's actions are arrogant and extreme, they are mitigated by her situation; the English law that grants all inheritance rights directly to the son, regardless of the wife and mother's needs, is an unjust one and, if she "collected" Fleda to use as part of a scheme to regain Poynton, she does, in the end, show genuine feeling and concern toward the girl as a person, not just a "piece of furniture."

The most sympathetic and interesting person in the story, however, is Fleda. In his preface, James identifies her as the only real character in the story, that is, the one figure of feeling and intelligence who is capable of development and change. It is through her perception and sensibility that the reader experiences the story and, in James's words, "the progress and march of my tale became and remained that of her understanding."

Not surprisingly, Fleda is the most complex and puzzling character in the book. Although her intelligence and moral superiority are evident throughout, her behavior frequently seems contradictory and self-defeating. Critics have disputed the motivations behind many of her actions and especially those during the crucial scenes that determine the outcome of her romance with Owen. The primary question is this: At the point where Owen says he loves her and wants to marry her, why does she send him straight back to Mona with "conditions" that virtually guarantee losing him? Or, to put it more generally, why does she throw away her one chance for happiness at the very time she seems to have it within her grasp?

In attempting to answer this question, three variables must be kept in mind: Fleda's relationship with Mrs. Gereth, her relationship with Owen, and her own aesthetic and moral values. From the beginning, Fleda is flattered and awed by Mrs. Gereth's attentions and compliments. The older woman sees in Fleda the perfect protégé, a girl gifted with intelligence and intuitive good taste, but with little background experience, who can be influenced, even molded, by an astute mentor. Thus, Mrs. Gereth grooms a replacement for herself who can not only keep Poynton out of Mona's grasp but also minister to its treasures long after she, Mrs. Gereth, is gone. In matters of artistic taste, Mrs. Gereth probably has her way with Fleda, but after Owen becomes a factor, her control over the girl becomes doubtful. In addition, as the book progresses, Fleda becomes increasingly aware of being manipulated by Mrs. Gereth and, while she may not personally object to being a "piece of furniture," she does feel quite guilty about being used as bait in a trap for Owen.

Fleda's relations with Owen are equally problematic. At first, she rejects him on the grounds that he is "too stupid," but even from the beginning, his amiable personality and physical desirability make a strong impression on her. As their relationship grows, Fleda's view of him becomes more and more clouded by self-deception. Her first impressions of him as stupid and weak are accurate, but, as she falls in love with him, she suppresses these obvious insights or rationalizes them into strengths. She insists that he act with independence and maturity, yet, like Mona, she fully expects to dominate him after marriage, as can be seen when she says, "It's because he's so weak that he needs me."

Fleda feels strongly attracted and obligated to both people, so she gives each of them the impression that she favors their cause. From these contending loyalties come such self-defeating acts as her persistent claim to Owen that she is winning his mother over and her lies to Mrs. Gereth regarding her emotions toward Owen and his toward her.

Thus, conflicting impulses probably determine her final self-defeating act. Because of her innate morality and her Victorian upbringing, Fleda is unable to accept the idea of winning a previously committed man away from his intended; she cannot act the part of the "designing woman"—especially in someone else's design. Given her tendency to self-deception, she probably convinces herself that Owen can, in fact, meet the conditions she imposes; unfortunately, "her Owen" is largely imaginary, and the real Owen cannot resist a captivating Mona. Fleda seems to lack the emotional capacity, as Mrs. Gereth puts it, to "let go." These speculations, however, do not answer the central question about Fleda: Does her final act represent a failure of nerve, a running away from life and experience? Or, does it represent the moral victory of a woman too proud to jeopardize her ethics in return for a chance at happiness? Both views, and most positions in between, have been argued by the critics with little consensus.

If Fleda's actions cost her a life with Owen, however, her reaction to that loss demonstrates her strength of character and her mature appreciation of life. It is she who senses the meaning of Ricks and brings a measure of solace to the defeated Mrs. Gereth. It is here that readers come to understand Fleda's aesthetic sensibility; to her, objects have moral qualities and their beauty is a product of the human experience they reflect. If she can succeed in impressing that view on her companion, a mellowed Mrs. Gereth may find a measure of happiness at Ricks—even after the accidental fire that resolves forever the fate of the spoils of Poynton.

This novel, written in the middle period of James's career, shows the detailed character analysis, careful development, and acute insight into human affairs for which he has become famous. Here, one has a kind of tragedy, but not one in the classical sense. This novel is tragic first because many beautiful things are unavoidably given up to one who has no appreciation of them and, second, because these same objects are completely destroyed in a freak accident. The human emotions involved are seen to be somewhat mean in spite of the grandeur of the objects with which they are connected and, throughout the novel, readers have James's astute comments on, and impressions of, the society in which these emotions and events take place.

"Critical Evaluation" by Keith Neilson

Further Reading

Cargill, Oscar. *The Novels of Henry James.* New York: Macmillan, 1961. Explores the evolution of *The Spoils of Poynton*, with careful consideration of James's comments, and provides an excellent summary of the major contradictory criticisms of the novel.

Clair, J. A. *The Ironic Dimension in the Fiction of Henry James.* Pittsburgh, Pa.: Duquesne University Press, 1965. An excellent study of the irony in *The Spoils of Poynton.* Clair sees Fleda Vetch as the center of action and examines her motives and her relationship with other characters in the novel.

Coulson, Victoria. *Henry James, Women, and Realism.* New York: Cambridge University Press, 2007. Examines James's important friendships with three women: his sister Alice James and the novelists Constance Fenimore Woolson and Edith Wharton. These three women writers and James shared what Coulson describes as an "ambivalent realism," or a cultural ambivalence about gender identity, and she examines how this idea is manifest in James's works, including *The Spoils of Poynton.*

Freedman, Jonathan, ed. *The Cambridge Companion to Henry James.* New York: Cambridge University Press, 1998. A collection of essays that provides extensive information on James's life and literary influences and describes his works and the characters in them.

Graham, Kenneth. "The Passion of Fleda Vetch." In *Henry James: The Drama of Fulfillment, an Approach to the Novels.* New York: Oxford University Press, 1975. Graham views the novel as a story of the conflicting passions of Fleda Vetch. He examines James's narrative mode, provides a detailed study of character relationships, and justifies the conclusion of the novel.

Hoffmann, Charles G. *The Short Novels of Henry James.* New York: Bookman, 1957. A good introduction to the novel which argues that the work achieves its dramatic depth from James's decision to emphasize character portrayal and, through that, to focus on possessions. Hoffmann views Fleda's actions as heroic and based on a code of high conduct but finds the conclusion of the novel unsatisfactory.

Otten, Thomas J. *A Superficial Reading of Henry James: Preoccupations with the Material World.* Columbus: Ohio State University Press, 2006. Otten argues that physical surfaces—such as items of clothing and furniture—are a significant element in James's work, making it impossible to determine "what counts as thematic depth and what counts as physical surface." Chapter 3 provides an analysis of *The Spoils of Poynton.*

Sharp, Corona. *The Confidante in Henry James: Evolution and Moral Value of a Fictive Character.* Notre Dame, Ind.: University of Notre Dame Press, 1963. Explores the unusual role of Fleda Vetch as simultaneously the center of consciousness for the novel and the confidant.

Spoon River Anthology

Author: Edgar Lee Masters (1868-1950)
First published: 1915
Type of work: Poetry

Edgar Lee Masters is a rarity among writers: He established his reputation on the basis of one work, *Spoon River Anthology*. Masters was a prolific writer, producing many volumes of verse, several plays, an autobiography, several biographies, essays, novels, and an attempt to recapture his great success in a sequel, *The New Spoon River*. Except for a handful of individual poems from the other volumes, however, he will be remembered as the re-creator of a small midwestern town that he calls Spoon River. Spoon River is probably Lewiston, Illinois, where he studied law in his father's office and practiced for a year before moving on to Chicago.

In form and style, *Spoon River Anthology* is not a work that sprang wholly out of Masters's imagination; it is modeled on *The Greek Anthology* (dating from the seventh century B.C.E.), and the style of the character sketches owes a considerable debt to the English poet Robert Browning. Masters wrote his book with such an effortless brilliance and freshness that nearly a century after its first publication it retains a startling inevitability, as if this were the best and the only way to present people in poetry. From their graveyard on the hill, Masters lets more than two hundred of the dead citizens of Spoon River tell the truth about themselves, each person writing what might be his or her own epitaph. The secrets they reveal are sometimes shocking—stories of intrigue, corruption, frustration, adultery. On the other hand, the speakers tell their stories with a calmness and a simplicity that induce a sense of calmness and simplicity in the reader. As a result of its frankness, *Spoon River Anthology* provoked protest from readers who felt that the book presents too sordid a picture of American small-town life. While many of the poems are interrelated and a certain amount of suspense is created by having one character mention a person or incident to be further developed, the anthology is not centered on a unifying theme. About the closest approach to such a theme is the tragic failure of the town's bank, chiefly attributed to Thomas Rhodes, its president, and his son Ralph, who confesses from the grave:

> All they said was true:
> I wrecked my father's bank with my loans
> To dabble in wheat; but this was true—
> I was buying wheat for him as well,

Who couldn't margin the deal in his name
Because of his church relationship.

Many people suffer from the bank's collapse, including the cashier, who has the blame placed on him and serves a term in prison; but a far more corroding effect is the cynicism generated in the citizens when they find that their leaders, the "stalwarts," are weak and culpable.

Masters pictures many vivid characters in *Spoon River Anthology*. They range from Daisy Fraser, the town harlot, who "Never was taken before Justice Arnett/ Without contributing ten dollars and costs/ To the school fund of Spoon River!"

to Lucinda Matlock, who

> Rambled over the fields where sang the larks,
> And by Spoon River gathering many a shell,
> And many a flower and medicinal weed—
> Shouting to the wooded hills, singing to the
>   green valleys.
> At ninety-six I had lived enough, that is all,
> And passed to a sweet repose.

Others are the town physicians, Doc Hill and Doc Myers, both of whose lives are scarred; Petit, the Poet, whose "faint iambics" rattle on "while Homer and Whitman roared in the pines"; Ann Rutledge, from whose dead bosom the Republic blooms forever; Russian Sonia, a dancer who meets old Patrick Hummer, of Spoon River, and goes back with him to the town, where the couple live twenty years in unmarried content; and Chase Henry, the town drunkard, a Catholic who is denied burial in consecrated ground but who wins some measure of honor when the Protestants acquire the land where he is buried and inter banker Nicholas and wife beside the old reprobate.

Spoon River Anthology is weighted so heavily on the sordid side—abortions, suicides, adulteries—that the more cheerful and "normal" epitaphs come almost as a relief. Lucinda and Ann fit this category; others are Hare Drummer, who delights in the memory of a happy childhood; Conrad Siever, content in his grave under an apple tree he planted, pruned, and tended; and Fiddler Jones, who never can stick to farming and who ends up with "a broken laugh, and a thousand memories,/ And not a single regret."

One especially effective device that Masters makes use of in his collection is the pairing of poems so that the reader gets a startling jolt of irony. For example, Elsa Wertman, a peasant woman from Germany, confesses that her employer, Thomas Greene, fathered her child and then raised it as his and Mrs. Greene's. In the next poem, Hamilton, the son, attributes his great success as a politician to the "honorable blood" he inherits from Mr. and Mrs. Greene. There is also Roscoe Purkapile, who runs away from his wife for a year, telling her when he comes back that he was captured by pirates while he was rowing a boat on Lake Michigan. After he tells her the story, "She cried and kissed me, and said it was cruel,/ Outrageous, inhuman!" When Mrs. Purkapile has her say in the next poem, she makes it known that she is not taken in by his cock-and-bull story, that she knows he was trysting in the city with Mrs. Williams, the milliner, and that she refuses to be drawn into a divorce by a husband "who had merely grown tired of his marital vow and duty."

Masters displays an amazing variety of effects in these short poems. His use of free verse undoubtedly helps to achieve this variety, for a stricter form or forms might make the poems seem too pat, too artificial. Sometimes Masters lets his characters' only remembrance of life be a simple, vivid description, as when Bert Kessler tells how he met his death. Out hunting one day, Bert kills a quail, and when he reaches down by a stump to pick it up, he feels something sting his hand, like the prick of a brier: "And then, in a second, I spied the rattler—/ The shutters wide in his yellow eyes . . ./ I stood like a stone as he shrank and uncoiled/ And started to crawl beneath the stump,/ When I fell limp in the grass."

Bert tells of his death without comment, but when Harry Williams describes how he was deluded into joining the army to fight in the Spanish-American War, in which he is killed, the poem is full of bitterness, horror, and brutal irony.

To say that every poem in this volume is successful would be as foolish as to contend that each entry in William Shakespeare's sonnet sequence is a masterpiece. Masters frequently strains for an effect; for instance, "Sexsmith the Dentist" seems to have been created so that Sexsmith may remark, at the end, that what people consider truth may be a hollow tooth "which must be propped with gold"; and Mrs. Kessler, a washerwoman, is probably included so that she might observe that the face of a dead person always looks to her "like something washed and ironed." There are other poems in which the speakers do not, so to speak, come alive.

One suspects that the poet wrote a number of philosophical lyrics, some of them marred by clichés and cloying rhetoric, and then titled them with names selected at random.

In the main, however, Masters does a remarkable job in *Spoon River Anthology*. Anyone may recognize in these poems the people one sees every day, and, though one may not like to admit it, when these people die they may carry to the grave secrets as startling as those revealed by many of the dead of Spoon River.

Further Reading

Flanagan, John T. *Edgar Lee Masters: The Spoon River Poet and His Critics*. Metuchen, N.J.: Scarecrow Press, 1974. Examines critical reaction over several decades and discusses attitudes toward *Spoon River Anthology*. Evaluates subject matter and poetic form. Includes descriptions of theatrical presentations.

Hallwas, John E., ed. Introduction and annotations to *Spoon River Anthology*, by Edgar Lee Masters. Champaign: University of Illinois Press, 1992. An excellent starting point. Hallwas's introduction evaluates style, rhythm, meter, and literary influences; discusses social attitudes, focusing on the influence of American myths and democratic ideals on characterization. Notes and annotations include textual variations and provide real-life counterparts and explanations of period names and information. Includes an annotated bibliography.

Hollander, John. "*Spoon River Anthology*: A Late Appreciation." In *The Work of Poetry*. New York: Columbia University Press, 1997. Hollander, a prize-winning poet, has compiled a collection of essays in which he expresses his opinions about what constitutes "good" poetry. Includes an analysis of *Spoon River Anthology*.

Masters, Edgar Lee. *Across Spoon River: An Autobiography*. New York: Farrar & Rinehart, 1936. Masters's autobiography begins with his early years in Petersburg and Lewiston, Illinois, and reveals incidents that are recreated in *Spoon River Anthology*. He compares and contrasts his legal and writing careers and discusses literary influences and his relationships with other writers, such as Carl Sandburg and Theodore Dreiser.

Primeau, Ronald. *Beyond Spoon River: The Legacy of Edgar Lee Masters*. Austin: University of Texas Press, 1981. Detailed exploration of literary influences, from classical literature to Ralph Waldo Emerson and Walt Whitman. Analyzes style, comparing Masters's poems with those of earlier writers. Discusses unusual blend of regionalism and unsentimental realism.

Russell, Herbert K. *Edgar Lee Masters: A Biography*. Urbana: University of Illinois Press, 2001. Comprehensive biography, in which Russell provides a multidimensional portrait of Masters the man and the writer.

Stanford, Michael. "The Cyclopean Eye, the Courtly Game, Admissions Against Interest: Five Modern American Lawyer Poets." *Legal Studies Forum* 30, nos. 1-2 (2006): 9-45. Examines the legal careers and poetry of Masters and four other lawyer-poets to determine how the law, the legal system, and the lives of lawyers are reflected in twentieth century American poetry.

Wrenn, John H., and Margaret M. Wrenn. *Edgar Lee Masters*. Boston: Twayne, 1983. A good critical source, providing biographical information and tracing literary influences. Discusses organization, style, and language. Explores relationships between characters, stressing realistic portrayals of social repression and sexuality.

The Sport of the Gods

Author: Paul Laurence Dunbar (1872-1906)
First published: 1901, serial; 1902, book
Type of work: Novel
Type of plot: Naturalism
Time of plot: Late nineteenth century
Locale: Southern United States and New York City

Principal characters:
BERRY HAMILTON, an African American servant
FANNIE, his wife
JOE, his son
KITTY, his daughter
MAURICE OAKLEY, his employer
FRANK, his employer's half brother
HATTIE STERLING, an African American performer

The Story:

After the Civil War, Maurice Oakley, a southern businessman, was able to recover his fortune quickly because of his prudence. Maurice is more than generous in supporting his younger half brother, Frank, who is studying art in Paris; he is also generous to his African American servant, Berry Hamilton.

On the last night of one of Frank's brief visits home, a jolly going-away party is held, but the party is spoiled for the brothers when Frank discovers that the money for his trip has been stolen; he had left the money, $986, in his room. Maurice says that the crime does not embarrass him financially—he can resupply Frank with funds—but he is hurt by the fact that a friend or employee would steal from his house. Suspicion falls on Berry, who is the only person other than Frank who had been alone in the room. When it is discovered that Berry deposited a large sum in the bank on the day after the theft, Maurice and the police feel that the case against Berry is proved. Although Berry's years of loyal service show that such stealing is very out of character for him, the servant receives a ten-year prison sentence.

Among the town's whites, Berry's alleged criminal behavior confirms their belief in the natural depravity of blacks. Ironically, the town's African Americans are almost as prejudiced against Berry as are the whites. Berry's son,

Joe, is fired from his barbershop job, and no one else will hire him because of the family disgrace. For the same reason, no fellow African American will rent rooms to Berry's wife, Fannie, when she needs quarters. Berry's family members make the momentous decision to relocate to New York City. Although Fannie is afraid that her children might succumb to the temptations of urban life, the family has to start anew in order to survive.

Fannie's fears prove all too justified. Joe is the first to fall. As a first-class barber in a whites-only establishment in the South, he had listened enviously as the town's young blades had recounted their high-living exploits. In New York, he finds that even African Americans can aspire to such aristocratic dissipation. Becoming friends with the sporting character William Thomas, Joe is quickly initiated into the wild goings-on in cabarets, gambling dens, and cheap saloons. He meets and falls for the aging, hardened showgirl Hattie Sterling, who, charmed by his youth and, particularly, by the good money he makes as a barber, becomes his mistress.

Meanwhile, Fannie and her daughter, Kitty, maintain their respectability by working in a factory. Their humdrum life is shattered, however, when Minty, a hometown acquaintance, arrives and spreads the story of Berry's imprisonment. As a result of the scandal, Fannie and Kitty lose their apartment and their jobs. Lacking other economic prospects, Kitty auditions for a job as a vaudeville singer. Once hired, she soon follows her brother into blind devotion to the sensations of the moment.

Concurrently, at the Oakley mansion, an equally somber story is unfolding. Maurice receives a revelatory letter from his brother in which Frank confesses that the money had never been stolen; he had gambled it away and had been ashamed to admit it. Stunned by this admission, Maurice becomes a changed man. Rather than damage his family honor, he refuses to divulge the secret, thereby leaving Berry in prison. Growing almost psychotically fearful of exposure, Maurice changes from an affable man-about-town into a reclusive misanthrope; he keeps the letter with him at all times, in a hidden breast pocket.

Five years pass. The New York Hamiltons having gone further down the road to ruin, the despairing Fannie has been talked into marrying a racetrack character, Gibson, who has convinced her that her first marriage is void. Now, however, Berry's fortunes, at least, change for the better. A white newspaper reporter named Skaggs is interested in Joe Hamilton's story of how his father was railroaded into jail. His curiosity piqued, Skaggs travels to the Hamiltons' hometown. Posing as a friend of Frank, he tricks the half-mad Maurice into handing him Frank's letter, which he then publishes in his New York newspaper. Public outcry over this miscarriage of justice forces Berry's pardon, and the paper sponsors his trip to New York.

While these events are going on, Joe is being driven to despair by Hattie's repeated rejections; eventually he strangles her. He goes on trial for her murder, and Kitty is so estranged from her family that she pays no attention to her brother's problems. When Berry at last reaches his wife's home, he finds her married to another man and his children jailed or out of touch.

Berry has nothing left but one desire: to kill the man who has taken his wife. For a second time, however, fortune smiles. When Berry has worked up the courage to confront Gibson, he discovers the man's house in mourning. Gibson has been killed in a brawl, and Fannie is ready to reunite with Berry. The couple return to their old cottage on the Oakley place, where they are welcomed back by Maurice's repentant wife. Maurice himself has gone insane, and Berry and Fannie occasionally hear his ravings as they go about living their simple life.

Critical Evaluation:

Readers of Paul Laurence Dunbar's first three novels, which were light, sentimental potboilers, were surprised by the vehemence and darkness of his last one, *The Sport of the Gods*. Dunbar had already proven himself as one of the first African American writers of the period to break into polite letters. His facile magazine verse showed him the equal of his fashionable peers. In his last novel, however, under the threat of death from the tuberculosis that would eventually kill him, he turned from his popular vein to compose a work of naturalism.

The literary movement known as naturalism began in the United States in the 1890's. Naturalism is a child of realism, but it differs from its parent in some points of content and attitude. American realism emphasizes everyday situations, whereas naturalism focuses on the out of the ordinary, such as portraits of killers, prostitutes, and showgirls. Whereas the psychology and sociology that form the background of realist fiction is a reworked and clarified common sense, naturalism tends to draw on "scientific" doctrines, such as those concerning genetic inheritance, for its conceptual framework. As a consequence, whereas realism, like common sense, posits human beings with free will and shows its characters fighting and often overcoming obstacles, naturalism stresses the inexorability of scientific laws and gives all the power to the obstacles. Naturalism's characters fall prey to forces that they cannot effectively combat. Although Dunbar differs in a few respects from other naturalists, he shares with them an interest in seamy subjects (as indicated by his fascination with drunks and chiselers) and a belief in the overwhelming strength of circumstances.

A typical naturalist way of stressing the power that events and milieu exert on personality is to depict an innocent being sucked down by the whirlpools of vice in a big city. In Theodore Dreiser's *Sister Carrie* (1900), for example, the heroine, after moving from a small town to Chicago, is so dazzled by department-store displays that she quickly drops her factory job and her morals so that she can indulge her taste for splendor; she becomes the mistress of a well-off salesman. Dunbar provides a male version of this story. As is usual in naturalism, it is a lover—in this case, Hattie Sterling—who starts the protagonist on a downward spiral. Joe sinks from degradation to degradation until he ends as an unrepentant murderer.

Dunbar's refusal to abide by strictly naturalist tenets is seen, however, in his use of a background conceptual network. As his novel's title indicates, the author blames his characters' misfortunes on a mischievous fate rather than on the effects of a powerfully stimulating environment on weak personalities. Dunbar indicates this feeling in many explicit statements, such as "One might find it in him to feel sorry for this small-souled, warped being," Joe, "for he was so evidently the jest of Fate." Although such invocation of supernatural entities hardly fits in with the prosaic tone dominating much naturalism, in Dunbar's text it does work well to tie together his mixed discourse in which fantastic coincidences of one genre meet the gritty actualities of another. Dunbar's fate can mediate between these worlds because while fate is held accountable for unusual events (such as Berry's unlucky depositing of his savings on the day after the robbery), such accidents result in effects (such as the imprisonment of an African American on flimsy evidence) that are in keeping with the everyday realities of the time.

In fact, what is special about Dunbar is that he pioneered in describing the important but unexplored post-Civil War migration of African Americans from rural areas to the cities. Although *The Sport of the Gods* is marred by Dunbar's moralizing and by his inclusion of trite, melodramatic elements, it is valuable in that it broke new ground in its portrayal of the kind of uprooting that would take place more often later in the century and that would be redescribed in such major novels as Ralph Ellison's *Invisible Man* (1952). Moreover, in many of its city passages, Dunbar's book rises to creative heights in its depictions of human interactions. In Hattie's first meeting with Joe, for example, Dunbar displays great skill in picturing simultaneously the charm and the implicit threat in her response to his overtures. In such passages, Dunbar moves beyond professional facility to achieve a refined and moving execution.

James Feast

Further Reading

Alexander, Eleanor. *Lyrics of Sunshine and Shadow: The Tragic Courtship and Marriage of Paul Laurence Dunbar and Alice Ruth Moore—A History of Love and Violence Among the African American Elite.* New York: New York University Press, 2001. Biographical work focuses on the couple's six years of courtship and marriage, which began happily but ended in despair.

Best, Felton O. "Paul Laurence Dunbar's Protest Literature: The Final Years." *Western Journal of Black Studies* 17 (Spring, 1993): 54-64. Argues that Dunbar uses plantation settings to counteract the plantation myth that was prevalent at the start of the twentieth century. Maintains that Dunbar was more active as a writer of protest literature than some critics have asserted.

Brawley, Benjamin. *Paul Laurence Dunbar: Poet of His People.* 1936. Reprint. Port Washington, N.Y.: Kennikat Press, 1967. Biographical work provides context for Dunbar's fiction. Discusses how the emotional roots of *The Sport of the Gods* are to be found in Dunbar's feelings after the breakup of his marriage, and argues that Dunbar's verse is superior to his prose.

Dowling, Robert M. "Marginal Men in Black Bohemia: Paul Laurence Dunbar and James Weldon Johnson in the Tenderloin." In *Slumming in New York: From the Waterfront to Mythic Harlem.* Urbana: University of Illinois Press, 2007. Examines how "mainstream outsiders" such as Dunbar and Johnson wrote slum narratives about "marginalized urban insiders."

Gayle, Addison, Jr. *Oak and Ivy: A Biography of Paul Laurence Dunbar.* Garden City, N.Y.: Doubleday, 1971. Critical biography deals equally with Dunbar's life and his works. Presents extensive discussion of the tragic results of Dunbar's efforts to free his work from racial stereotypes while dealing with powerful white publishing firms.

Revell, Peter. *Paul Laurence Dunbar.* Boston: Twayne, 1979. Critical biography covers all of Dunbar's poetic and fictional works. Emphasizes the naturalistic elements of Dunbar's fiction and discusses Dunbar's work in relation to French naturalism. States that *The Sport of the Gods* is Dunbar's most successful novel and places it at the center of the African American tradition of novel writing.

Rusk, Nancy Von. "Coon Shows, Ragtime, and the Blues: Race, Urban Culture, and the Naturalist Vision in Paul Laurence Dunbar's *The Sport of the Gods*." In *Twisted from the Ordinary: Essays on American Literary Naturalism*, edited by Mary E. Papke. Knoxville: University of Tennessee Press, 2003. Essay devoted to Dunbar's novel is part of a collection focusing on redefining American literary naturalism. Demonstrates how Dunbar's novel can be classified as a work of this genre.

Thomas, Lorenzo. "Dunbar and Degradation: *The Sport of the Gods* in Context." In *Complexions of Race: The African Atlantic*, edited by Fritz Gysin and Cynthia S. Hamilton. Munich, Germany: Lit, 2005. Essay on *The Sport of the Gods* is included in a collection of pieces that examine how concepts of race have informed readings of the African American experience.

The Sportswriter

Author: Richard Ford (1944-   )
First published: 1986
Type of work: Novel
Type of plot: Psychological realism
Time of plot: April, 1984
Locale: Haddam, New Jersey; Detroit and Walled Lake, Michigan; New York City; Florida

Principal characters:
FRANK BASCOMBE, a sportswriter
X, his former wife
RALPH, their dead child
PAUL and CLARISSA, their other children
VICKI ARCENAULT, Bascombe's girlfriend, a nurse
HERB WALLAGHER, a former professional football player
WALTER LUCKETT, a member of the Divorced Men's Club

The Story:

It is early on Good Friday morning, and Frank Bascombe is waiting for the arrival of his former wife, whom he refers to as X. Today is the anniversary of the death of their oldest son, Ralph. Bascombe and X try to mark the sad date, but X does not want to hear the poem that Bascombe brought with him to read today. Bascombe recalls an event that signaled the end of their marriage—a small fire his wife used to burn letters he had received from a woman in Kansas. He reflects on the changes he has seen in his former wife over the four years since their son's death and the two years since their divorce.

Later this morning, Bascombe meets up with Vicki Arcenault, his girlfriend. She is set to accompany him on his sportswriting assignment, which is to fly to Detroit, Michigan, and interview Herb Wallagher, a former professional football player who lives at Walled Lake. He had been an offensive lineman, and he was paralyzed in a boating accident after he had retired from football. Bascombe hopes to write an inspirational story about Wallagher, who is planning to start law school. Following the quick trip, the couple plan an Easter dinner with Arcenault's father and stepmother.

During the flight, Bascombe is troubled by events of the previous day. The local Divorced Men's Club, to which he belongs, had gone on a fishing trip. As Bascombe had tried to leave, fellow member Walter Luckett persuaded him to have a drink first. They had an odd conversation, as Luckett hinted at and then avoided discussing what bothered him. Luckett asked Bascombe if Bascombe had anyone to confide in. After Luckett noted that Bascombe has problems with confession, Luckett revealed that he had had a sexual encounter with a married man the night before. Though Luckett wanted someone to talk to, Bascombe hurried off to watch the house of his former wife and children from his car in the dark. While there he had a conversation with his ten-year-old son, Paul, who was launching a pigeon with a mission to speak to Paul's dead older brother, Ralph.

Things do not go well in Detroit, either. Bascombe's in-terview with Wallagher fails. Though the plan was to write an optimistic feature story about a man triumphing over the physical challenges of his disabilities, including using a wheelchair, Bascombe finds Wallagher angry and having thoughts of violence. His moods swing from deep sadness to anger, relating dreams of strangling people. He insults Bascombe after the writer suggests that his feature is to be a story about cheerfully overcoming life's challenges; Bascombe never gets a chance to interview him, and he just escapes his wrath.

Bascombe also upsets his girlfriend. Deep in the night, while she is asleep, he searches through her handbag and fixates on a photograph he finds in the purse. He assumes the picture is of her former husband, indicating hidden emotions, but she angrily reveals the photo is of her dead stepbrother-in-law. She and Bascombe talk about marriage, but she is beginning to have serious doubts.

Bascombe returns to his house in Haddam and finds Luckett inside, waiting for him. Luckett is miserably unhappy about his divorce, his recent actions, and his out-of-control life. He kisses Bascombe, who then throws him out of the house and unplugs his phone.

On Easter, Bascombe drives to the home of Vicki's father and stepmother for dinner. He immediately makes friends with her family, but everyone knows something is troubling Vicki. Bascombe, almost offhandedly, suggests that the two of them marry. She laughs him off, saying she does not love him enough. He even gets on his knees in a mock proposal; then the phone rings. It is a call for Bascombe: Luckett has committed suicide and left a note, addressed to Bascombe. As he readies to leave, he again talks to Vicki about the permanence of their relationship. She tells him no, and when he attempts to pull her toward him, she punches him in the mouth.

The drive back to Haddam to meet with police goes badly. Though Bascombe has pledged undying love to Vicki, he stops at a phone booth to call an old lover. While in the booth, he sees a car strike a grocery cart; the cart then flies against the booth, and Bascombe. A teenage girl, working at the hamburger booth nearby, rushes over to check on him. For the slightest moment, he thinks about the possibilities of a relationship with her.

Bascombe checks in with the police to discuss Luckett's suicide. All he thinks of is his son Ralph's death. Bascombe's former wife meets up with him later, and the two of them visit Luckett's house. There, X notes how miserable Bascombe appears. He proposes they get into Luckett's bed to make love, and she responds by telling him that he has become a terrible person.

Bascombe goes to the train station to pick up one of Luckett's family members, who is coming into town from Ohio. Bascombe sees someone he imagines is Luckett's sister, but instead of meeting her, he enters the train and rides to New York City. On the train, he reads Luckett's last letter, which angers him. Given so many possibilities in life, Bascombe sees no sense in suicide. He goes to his office in the city and begins a conversation with a young female intern named Catherine Flaherty. She talks about her uncertainly about her own future, including whether or not she should continue with the pre-med program in college. Bascombe realizes how easy it would be to invite her for a meal. For a moment he ponders life, thinking about how in the matter of one day he has gone from thinking that everything is wrong to living a moment of sweet anticipation of the future.

Bascombe had earlier gone to Florida to search for Luckett's daughter. There, he had looked up some distant family members and even got to know them. Now, he waits to hear from Vicki, but also has kept in touch with Catherine, who is planning to visit. He feels total happiness now, but also recognizes the ephemeral nature of sensation.

Critical Evaluation:

Richard Ford's *The Sportswriter* is the first of three books—including *Independence Day* (1995) and *The Lay of the Land* (2006)—about the life of real estate agent Frank Bascombe. Ford's popular notice as a novelist came with the release of *The Sportswriter*, soon followed by the release of a short-story collection. He won the Rhea Award for short fiction and received both the PEN/Faulkner Award and a Pulitzer Prize in fiction for *Independence Day*.

With the creation of Bascombe, Ford has developed an Everyman figure, similar to novelist John Updike's character Rabbit Angstrom. In interviews, Ford tries to soften this view of his character as representative of the ordinary person, suggesting Bascombe offers only one view among many. Much of the novel focuses on the central character's views on life, love, and happiness.

Similar to Updike, in his quartet of novels about Angstrom, Ford uses the present tense to give a sense of immediacy and uncertainly to *The Sportswriter*. The choice of tense suggests the unknowability and uncertainty of the future. Unlike Updike's novels, though, Ford chooses to use a first-person presentation for Bascombe. Therefore, as the events of the novel unfold, the reader feels a sense of eavesdropping on Bascombe's inner thoughts, as he goes through this challenging weekend.

The choice of first-person narrative also raises a challenging question about whether or not Bascombe understands himself. As critics have noted, the degree of irony with which Bascombe should be read is difficult to determine. Certainly, the character is slow to reveal events that place him in a negative light. For instance, early in the novel, it is suggested that the death of their son, Ralph, led to their divorce. Then the reader learns that Bascombe has carried on a secret correspondence with another woman. Finally, an acknowledgment of one affair becomes an acknowledgment of affairs with eighteen women in two years. Bascombe pledges his love to Vicki, but he also notes he has never stopped loving his former wife, X. When his relationship with Vicki comes to an end, he quickly turns to other women.

While he is able to make friends and appears to accept people as they are, Bascombe can be suspicious and often expects the worst of others. When he searches Vicki's purse, late at night, he is certain the photo he finds is that of her former husband, a horrible man she shows no sign of missing. When he visits her parents, he assumes her father is ignoring him, while Vicki knows her father is just a private man, happy working on his car in his basement.

In interviews, Ford has suggested that he sees Bascombe as a happy man. While it becomes easier to see this view in the later novels, the question of happiness in *The Sportswriter* remains. Bascombe considers himself happy, but he also acknowledges a sense of "dreaminess" in his life that he uses to explain much of his behavior. He finds it difficult to accept responsibility for his past actions, noting that in many ways he just does not really remember what his marriage was like. Bascombe says he has no one to confide in, and that he is okay with this. His relationship with Vicki begins to falter after she realizes that his major concern is his own happiness. He does not want to listen to anyone else's problems and believes that they would be happier, too, if they stopped dwelling on themselves so much.

Bascombe became a sportswriter for just these reasons. He had published a serious work of fiction, but he is drawn to sportswriting. He prefers working with athletes because he considers them to be nonreflective people who live in the physical moment; they consider how each moment will, in the future, offer many choices rather than ponder the rightness or correctness of past choices. Bascombe is happy, if happiness is this ephemeral moment. As the concluding words of the book note, the goal is to escape the "skin" that life builds up; happiness is being free of that skin of life.

Brian L. Olson

Further Reading

Flora, Joseph M., Amber Vogel, and Bryan Albin Giemza, eds. *Southern Writers: A New Biographical Dictionary*. Baton Rouge: Louisiana State University Press, 2006. Ford is included in this literary dictionary of authors with a significant connection to the American South. Provides information about Ford's birthplace, his upbringing in the South, and his use of the South as a setting for his writings.

Ford, Richard. "Nobody's Everyman." *Book Forum*, April/May, 2009. Ford writes about his protagonist Bascombe as an Everyman figure. A brief article.

Guagliardo, Huey, ed. *Conversations with Richard Ford*. Jackson: University Press of Mississippi, 2001. A collection of personal interviews with Ford.

_____. *Perspectives on Richard Ford*. Jackson: University Press of Mississippi, 2000. A collection of critical essays on Ford's work, with essays specific to *The Sportswriter*.

Guinn, Matthew. *After Southern Modernism: Fiction of the Contemporary South*. Jackson: University Press of Mississippi, 2000. Ford is one of several authors whose works are analyzed in this study, which attempts to engage Southern fiction on its own terms rather than as a provincial or second-class genre.

_____. "Into the Suburbs: Richard Ford's Sportswriter Novels and the Place of Southern Fiction." In *South to a New Place: Region, Literature, Culture*, edited by Suzanne W. Jones and Sharon Monteith. Baton Rouge: Louisiana State University Press, 2002. Discusses *The Sportswriter* and *Independence Day* with reference to Ford's place in southern literature, the place of the South in Ford's identity as a novelist, and Ford's status as a southern novelist.

Hogan, Phil. "To Be Frank." *The Guardian*, September 24, 2006. A reflective piece on the Bascombe trilogy, written upon the publication of *The Lay of the Land*, the third book in the series that includes *The Sportswriter* and *Independence Day*.

Walker, Elinor Ann. *Richard Ford*. New York: Twayne, 2000. Examines Ford's career, provides readings of individual novels that address his dominant themes, and discusses his connection to trends in American and southern literature.

Spring Awakening
A Children's Tragedy

Author: Frank Wedekind (1864-1918)
First published: Frühlings Erwachen, 1891; first produced, 1906 (English translation, as *The Awakening of Spring*, 1909)
Type of work: Drama
Type of plot: Psychological
Time of plot: Late nineteenth century
Locale: Germany

Principal characters:
MELCHIOR GABOR, an intelligent high school boy
MORITZ STIEFEL, his friend
WENDLA BERGMANN, a schoolgirl, age fourteen
MRS. BERGMANN, her mother
MR. GABOR and MRS. GABOR, Melchior's parents
MARTHA and THEA, schoolgirls
ILSE, a young prostitute and model
RENTIER STIEFEL, Moritz's father
THE MASKED MAN

The Story:

Wendla places in the closet the long, grown-up dress that her mother has just finished making for her, protesting that she does not see why next year would not be soon enough to put on such a penitential garment. Mrs. Bergmann acquiesces with motherly affection to her daughter's wish to continue wearing, for the present, the freer, familiar clothes of childhood, remarking at the same time on the fact that Wendla has retained her childhood grace without a trace of the gawkiness usual to her age. Mrs. Bergmann is not without misgivings, even while she cherishes that appearance of innocence and grace, and she expresses her uneasiness in various equivocating substitutes for her real fears.

Melchior Gabor, Moritz Stiefel, and their classmates end their games to attend to their homework. Moritz and Melchior, walking home in the spring night, discuss the meaninglessness of the exam system and the sexual phenomena of adolescence that they are beginning to experience. For Moritz, the mysterious sexual pressures are a great burden, partly because they hinder his already desperate attempts to meet the demands of school and parents. Although he is a poor student and excessively timid, he possesses an acute sensitivity that is unrecognized by all but Melchior, who is his closest friend and, unlike Moritz, an extremely promising student. The ease with which Melchior deals with his schoolwork leaves him time not only for metaphysical speculation but also for the scholarly acquisition of the facts of reproduction, which he now offers to impart. Moritz accepts Melchior's offer on the condition that the facts be in written form and slipped into his books, where he can come upon them later as if by chance.

On a blustery spring day not long afterward, Wendla, Thea, and Martha exchange confidences on the subjects of parental tyranny, love, marriage, and children. The talk turns to boys of their own age and to the peculiar behavior they sometimes exhibit. Wendla discloses that Melchior once told her he believes in nothing. Mention of the spring floods reminds the girls that Melchior once came near drowning in one of the swollen streams but had been saved by his ability as a swimmer.

Moritz illicitly enters the school's staff common room (repository of all records), driven by the need to know whether he is to be promoted. When he comes out of the room, dazed by his own boldness but relieved by the knowledge of a provisional remove, he is taunted by the other boys for having said that he would shoot himself if he were not being promoted.

Melchior and Wendla meet by chance in the woods, where Wendla has gone to gather woodruff for her mother and has stopped to daydream by a brook. Melchior persuades her to sit down and asks if she enjoys going among the poor to take them food and money, errands on which her mother often sends her. Wendla's answer, that doing so gives her pleasure, begins an argument on the reality of virtue and selflessness.

Wendla also confesses that she daydreams of being a poor beggar child, beaten by a cruel father, although she herself has never been beaten. She picks up a stick to use as a switch and begs Melchior to strike her with it, to show her how such punishment feels. The boy at first refuses; then, as she persists in her request, he throws the stick aside and pummels her with his fists before he runs away into the woods, crying in anguish.

Moritz finds himself again on the verge of school failure. While reading Johann Wolfgang Goethe's *Faust* (1790) with Melchior, he relates his grandmother's story of the headless queen, a tale that has long haunted him. It tells of a beautiful queen born without a head who is one day conquered by a king who happens to be provided with two heads that argue constantly. The court wizard gives one of the king's heads to the queen, on whom it proves very becoming, and the two are married with great joy, the heads now being on the best of terms. Mrs. Gabor, Melchior's mother, enters with tea and words of encouragement for Moritz. Noticing the copy of *Faust*, she wonders if they ought to be reading it, saying elliptically that she prefers to place her trust in Melchior rather than in pedagogical principles. Realizing that she is thinking of the Gretchen episode in Goethe's play, they become annoyed, Melchior because everyone insists on acting as if the world turns on nothing but obscenities, Moritz because he has begun to fear that it actually does. He has received Melchior's essay on sex, which has affected him like a series of dim recollections. He is disposed to exalt the satisfaction experienced by the woman and to regard that of the man as insipid.

Meanwhile, Wendla persistently interrogates her mother on the subject of her sister's latest baby. She mocks her mother's silly fairy tales about how babies are made by pretending to see a ridiculous vision outside the window. At Wendla's insistence, Mrs. Bergmann is forced to begin telling her daughter the truth, but she manages to evade the issue by saying that the things required to make a baby are marriage and a capacity for love that Wendla is too young to comprehend. A short time later, Wendla goes looking for Melchior and, swayed by his intensity and his tortured insistence that there is no such thing as love, she remains with him in the hayloft, where they have sex and she conceives a child.

Moritz finally reaches the end of his resources and, at the brink of suicide over the realization that he is about to fail at school, writes to Mrs. Gabor to ask for a loan that will enable him to leave home. She considers it her duty to refuse; she attempts to appeal to his common sense and better nature. At dusk, in a parting soliloquy pervaded by his unfailing wry humor mixed with self-pity, he concludes that life is not his responsibility. The headless queen beckons. Life is a matter of taste. His only regret is that he has not known sexual fulfillment, the most human experience of all. When Ilse, a young model with an insatiable appetite for life, appears and tempts him with tales of her warm, carefree, animal existence, he wavers, but then he rejects the opportunity she offers. Moritz shoots himself and dies. Later, Ilse discovers the pistol he used and conceals it.

Moritz's suicide precipitates an investigation by school officials. Melchior, charged with indecency on the basis of the notes on sex he had written, which are discovered among Moritz's books, becomes the scapegoat. At the funeral service, the adults condemn Moritz for his crime against humanity and God. Rentier Stiefel, Moritz's father, comforts himself by repeating that he never cared for the boy; he was no son of his. With consummate coarseness, the pastor urges Stiefel to seek comfort in the arms of his wife. While the reaction of the schoolboys at the funeral is largely one of curiosity as to the exact manner of the suicide, Martha and Ilse bring a profusion of flowers to the grave.

Mrs. Gabor indignantly opposes her husband's decision to send Melchior to the reformatory. She defies anyone to perceive moral corruption in what the boy had written, but she is unable to stand up to the discovery that Melchior is responsible for Wendla's pregnancy. After undergoing various treatments concocted by Dr. Von Brausepulver and mother Schmidt for inducing abortion, Wendla dies. After her death, Melchior, hounded by society and by his own self-contempt, manages to return to look at her grave. As he wanders enviously in the cemetery, he encounters Moritz Stiefel, his head tucked under his arm. Moritz attempts to persuade Melchior to join him in his life among the dead, which he depicts as a fabulous if grotesque freedom. While Melchior hesitates, a masked man appears to take Moritz to task for his attempt, his lack of a head, and his general crumbling condition. The masked man accuses Moritz of charlatanism and asks Melchior to submit himself to his care. Melchior, contending that he cannot entrust himself to a masked unknown, interrogates the man regarding his moral position. Moritz admits that he has been boasting and urges Melchior to accompany the gentleman, who is, in any event, alive. The two living beings withdraw together while Moritz returns to warm himself with putrefaction.

Critical Evaluation:

Frank Wedekind's *Spring Awakening*, subtitled *A Children's Tragedy*, was his first major work and the one that made him famous—and infamous. When the play was first produced, many regarded it as pornographic; riots broke out at performances, and the work was subjected to repeated censorship. The play, however, avoids the explicit and obscene,

and later generations have come to see it as a powerful creation shaped out of inner experience.

The world of anxiety in which students live and suffer was familiar to Wedekind from his own school years. He shaped *Spring Awakening* not as a documentary, however; rather, it takes the form of a bizarre fantasy charged with irony. The adults, especially the teachers and the pastor, are grotesque parodies. Even their names resemble the sorts of mocking epithets students might invent. Scenes such as that in which Melchior is interrogated by the faculty and that of Moritz's funeral are bitter parodies of the cruelty inflicted on children by adults as that cruelty is perceived by the children.

Indeed, Wedekind places all the lyricism and humanity in the play in the world of the young, perhaps for the first time on the German stage giving expression to the experience of this age group. Using naturalist techniques, Wedekind accurately captures the speech patterns and behaviors of young people while lifting them beyond the level of mere naturalism. That the play is allied more with the Symbolist school is evident from the fantasy of the final scenes: the temptation of Melchior by Moritz and his rescue by the "masked man." Wedekind dedicated the play to this mysterious figure, who clearly represents the life force, perhaps within Melchior himself, which enables him to reject death and return to the world of the living, grotesque though it may be, to experience the fullness of life, of which Moritz, by his suicide, has robbed himself.

Many have considered Wedekind a precursor of German literary expressionism, and Bertolt Brecht considered him to be one of the principal influences on his own political and experimental plays. *Spring Awakening* cannot be considered an example of pure expressionism, but Wedekind does anticipate expressionism in his concern with authority and rebellion, his portrayal of youthful experimentation, his virtually plotless method of storytelling (particularly in scenes that are sprung on an unprepared audience, as, for example, scenes of homosexual love and of masturbation), and his use of the ambiguous masked man (a role played by Wedekind himself in the play's original production). In portraying the adult world, Wedekind projects the children's subjective and innocent interpretations of the world of experience onto the authority figures.

As the adults in *Spring Awakening* clearly show, bourgeois society is incapable of accepting sexuality as natural. Wendla's mother, by constructing motherhood as a secret world, prepares the way for her daughter's downfall. Almost all the tragic events that happen to the children are the result of adult interference or neglect. The schoolteachers refuse to consider Melchior's humanity when they indict him for describing reproduction, for they cannot accept their own sexual—or, in other words, human—natures. When the masked man appears, he offers a kind of salvation for Melchior from conventional society. As long as the Melchiors of the world—in Wedekind's world, Melchior is the hero—survive, there is a glimmer of hope that the human instinct can be explored and celebrated.

Ironically, organized religion cannot cope with human nature because it has constructed a false set of ideals that are unattainable. With the approval of the Church, Moritz's father condemns his son to an eternity in hell and takes no responsibility for having driven him to his death. Moritz, who is modeled on one of Wedekind's friends, can no longer face the pressures of trying to conform to adult expectations. Rather than teach the children what they need to know, adults fill children's heads with trivial details and the histories of dead cultures. Rather than teach children to think for themselves, as Mrs. Gabor, the most redeemable of the adult characters, has taught Melchior, the adults fear questions and resent children when they do not conform.

Wedekind's indictment of the adult world is reflected in his language. When the children speak, they often do so in lofty, lyrical, highly subjective language, whereas the adults use the rhetoric of avoidance and noncommunication. When the teachers speak, their words are full of the language of oppression, power, and control over the imagination and the emotions.

The greatest victims of adult oppression in the play are Moritz and Wendla, both of whom die as a direct result of adult intervention (Moritz from suicide and Wendla from a botched abortion). Adults' unwillingness to accept their own humanity as well as the humanity of children often brings about such devastating results. The masked man represents an affirmation of life and offers the only possibility for hope. By rejecting social definitions of morality (which Melchior claims are nothing more than social constructs) and by refusing to give in to society's narrow definitions of normality and reality, Melchior illustrates Wedekind's youthful optimism. To reform society, the individual must risk social rejection and even life itself.

"Critical Evaluation" by D. Dean Shackelford

Further Reading

Boa, Elizabeth. *The Sexual Circus: Wedekind's Theatre of Subversion*. New York: Blackwell, 1987. Provides an excellent exploration of Wedekind's primary and subversive purpose in attacking bourgeois authoritarianism and speaking out for the rights of the individual. Offers a useful interpretation of *Spring Awakening* as a critique of social roles and an examination of moral authority.

Bond-Pable, Elizabeth. Introduction to *Spring Awakening*. Translated by Edward Bond. London: Methuen, 1980. Gives a brief biographical introduction to Wedekind's life and career and points out central themes in the play. The volume also includes Edward Bond's "A Note on the Play," in which he concludes that the play is about "the misuse of authority" and shows the effects of the state on the individual.

Del Caro, Adrian. "The Beast, the Bad, and the Body: Moral Entanglement in Wedekind's *Frühlings Erwachen*." *Colloquia-Germanica* 24, no. 1 (1991): 1-12. Focuses on the influence on Wedekind of Georg Büchner and Friedrich Nietzsche and on the difficulty of integrating morality, humanity, and nature. Describes how Wedekind criticized society's attempts to expunge the natural from human existence.

Gittleman, Sol. *Frank Wedekind*. New York: Twayne, 1969. Useful general introduction to Wedekind's life and work includes analysis of *Spring Awakening* that focuses on the tragic effects of society's failure to teach children about their instincts. Concludes that the play blends tragedy, absurdism, allegory, surrealism, and morality.

Izenberg, Gerald N. "Frank Wedekind and the Femininity of Freedom." In *Modernism and Masculinity: Mann, Wedekind, Kandinsky Through World War I*. Chicago: University of Chicago Press, 2000. Examination of Wedekind's work is part of a larger study of the creations of Wedekind, writer Thomas Mann, and painter Wasily Kandinsky. Argues that these artists all experienced a "crisis of masculinity" and turned to a feminine aesthetic as a means of criticizing industrialism and materialism.

Jelavich, Peter. "Wedekind's *Spring Awakening*: The Path to Expressionist Drama." In *Passion and Rebellion: The Expressionist Heritage*, edited by Stephen Eric Bronner and Douglas Kellner. New York: Universe Books, 1983. Presents an excellent analysis of the play's central themes as well as discussion of the connections among Wedekind, expressionism, and playwright Bertolt Brecht.

Lewis, Ward B. *The Ironic Dissident: Frank Wedekind in the View of His Critics*. Columbia, S.C.: Camden House, 1997. Chronological survey addresses the critical reception of Wedekind's plays and his works in other genres. Charts the changes in Wedekind's critical reputation from the late nineteenth through the late twentieth centuries. Chapter 2 discusses *Spring Awakening*.

Shaw, Leroy R. "Frank Wedekind's *Spring Awakening*." In *Alogical Modern Drama*, edited by Kenneth S. White.

New York: Rodopi, 1982. Offers an informative general analysis of the play. Describes the work as a critique of rationalism and suggests that it is an alogical and amoral indictment of bourgeois Christianity.

Whalley, Fred. "The Rejection of Christianity: *Elins Erweckung* and *Frühlings Erwachen*." In *The Elusive Transcendent: The Role of Religion in the Plays of Frank Wedekind*. New York: Peter Lang, 2002. Notes that Wedekind was strongly influenced by nineteenth century concepts of religion and philosophy. Demonstrates how the characters in his plays transgress moral boundaries in a fruitless search for transcendent value.

The Spy
A Tale of the Neutral Ground

Author: James Fenimore Cooper (1789-1851)
First published: 1821
Type of work: Novel
Type of plot: Historical
Time of plot: Late eighteenth and early nineteenth centuries
Locale: New York

Principal characters:
HARVEY BIRCH, a peddler
MR. HARPER, General George Washington
MR. WHARTON, a Loyalist sympathizer
FRANCES and SARAH, his daughters
HENRY, his son
MAJOR PEYTON DUNWOODIE, an American officer
CAPTAIN LAWTON, another American officer
COLONEL WELLMERE, a British officer

The Story:

At the beginning of the Revolutionary War, Harvey Birch, a peddler, becomes a spy for the American side. Because of the extremely secret nature of Birch's work, few Americans are aware of his true mission. As a matter of fact, they suspect that he is a British spy. At the time, Westchester County in New York is considered common ground for both the rebels and the Loyalists, and the inhabitants of the county pretend to possess a neutrality they do not feel. This is the case of Mr. Wharton, a British sympathizer, who at the outbreak of hostilities retires to his country estate with his two daughters, Sarah and Frances, and their aunt, Miss Jeanette Peyton.

One evening, as a storm approaches, a horseman rides up to the Wharton house, The Locusts. He is a tall man of powerful frame, military in his bearing but plain in his dress. After being let into the house by the Whartons' servant, Caesar Thompson, the traveler introduces himself as Mr. Harper and asks for shelter from the storm. Mr. Wharton courteously grants the traveler's request, and the two men are soon engaged in conversation concerning the progress of the war. Mr. Wharton expresses his views cautiously in order to determine Mr. Harper's sentiments, but the stranger remains uncommunicative in his replies.

The conversation between the two men is interrupted by the arrival of Henry Wharton, Mr. Wharton's son and a captain in the British army. The young man wears a disguise in order to cross the American lines safely, but Mr. Harper recognizes him. Later, Birch, the peddler believed by all to be a Loyalist spy, comes to the Wharton home, bringing supplies and news of the war. During Birch's visit, Caesar remarks to his master that he heard voices in Mr. Harper's room.

With the return of fair weather, Mr. Harper says good-bye to his host. Before he departs, he promises to help Henry, if he ever needs help, in return for Mr. Wharton's hospitality. Shortly after Mr. Harper leaves, the Wharton home is surrounded by a troop of Virginia cavalry looking for a man answering Mr. Harper's description. When the American soldiers enter Mr. Wharton's house, they discover Henry. Captain Lawton, in command of the troop, sees through Henry's disguise. The captain is certain that Henry is a spy because he knows that Birch recently visited the Whartons. Not certain what to do, Captain Lawton consults his superior, Major Peyton Dunwoodie, who is interested not only in Henry but also in Henry's sister, Frances. She pleads with her lover for Henry's release, but, when Henry is found to have a pass signed by General Washington, Major Dunwoodie thinks that the case warrants Henry's arrest.

Further investigation into the matter by Major Dunwoodie is halted by a report that British troops are in the neighborhood. The major rushes to his command. In the confusion, Henry escapes. He reports to his superior, Colonel Wellmere, leader of the advancing British troops, who professes to be in love with Sarah Wharton. When Henry advises the colonel to be wary of Major Dunwoodie and his Americans, Wellmere scorns the advice and determines to force a fight with the rebels. In the brief engagement that follows, the British are routed, and Captain Lawton succeeds in recapturing Henry, who is returned under guard to his father's home. Colonel Wellmere, also taken prisoner, is slightly wounded in the action.

Birch is watching Major Dunwoodie's success from a distant hill when he is sighted by Captain Lawton. In the pursuit, Captain Lawton overtakes Birch, but he falls from his horse and finds himself at the peddler's mercy. Birch, however, spares Captain Lawton's life, and for that act of magnanimity, the captain will not allow his men to overtake the peddler.

A price is put on Birch's head. One night, his house is ransacked and burned by a band of lawless men called Skinners. They then deliver Birch to Captain Lawton and claim their reward. Major Dunwoodie, who is also present when the peddler is brought in, accuses him of treason. Although Birch possesses a paper that would clear him of the charge, he swallows it rather than betray the confidence of his secret employer. Birch is put in jail, but that night he escapes in the guise of a washerwoman who visits his cell. The next morning, on the outskirts of the American camp, he confronts Major Dunwoodie again. With a gun pointed at the officer, to prevent recapture, the peddler warns him to be on guard against danger to the Whartons. Major Dunwoodie is alarmed by the thought of danger threatening Frances. He is also disturbed because he feels that he can never win Frances if her brother is executed as a spy. Major Dunwoodie's troubles are magnified when, after assuring Frances that he will try to get General Washington's help for her brother, she turns from him coldly because she believes that he is in love with Isabella Singleton, the sister of an American officer recuperating at The Locusts from injuries sustained in the battle.

Meanwhile, Sarah accepts Colonel Wellmere's proposal of marriage, and the date for the wedding is set. Major Dunwoodie and Captain Lawton are among the guests during the truce arranged for the exchange and the wedding. The ceremony is suddenly interrupted, however, by the appearance of Birch. Sarah faints when Birch tells the colonel that his wife, Mrs. Wellmere, crossed the ocean to find him. Captain Lawton challenges Colonel Wellmere to a duel. The Englishman misses his mark, but Captain Lawton is prevented from killing his adversary when the Skinners over-

power him. Colonel Wellmere flees the scene, and Captain Lawton is able to escape his enemies only after a fierce struggle.

The Skinners then burn Mr. Wharton's house. Captain Lawton returns to the scene with troops he met on the road, and, after routing the Skinners, he rescues Frances from the blazing house. Birch rescues Sarah, and, again, Captain Lawton permits the peddler to escape. A bullet fired at Captain Lawton from the darkness strikes Isabella. On her deathbed, she confesses that Major Dunwoodie thinks of her only as a friend.

At his trial, Henry admits that he used a disguise in order to pass through the American lines, but he insists that he did so only in order to visit his family, especially his aged father. Major Dunwoodie himself vouches for Henry's character. Frances, however, ruins her brother's chances for acquittal when she admits that Henry had dealings with Birch. Henry is found guilty and sentenced to be hanged on the following day. Major Dunwoodie makes an appeal to General Washington for the life of his friend but is unsuccessful, for the commander-in-chief is not at his headquarters.

Soon afterward a tall, gaunt man in clerical dress appears and announces himself as a minister from a nearby village who comes to offer spiritual comfort to the condemned man. Admitted to Henry's cell, he reveals himself as Harvey Birch. He helps Henry to disguise himself as Caesar Thompson, the faithful servant of the Whartons, and leads the young officer past the unsuspecting sentinel. Frances, hearing of the escape, thinks that her brother and the peddler will probably hide in a nearby cabin. Stealing away, she sets out to join them, but she finds the cabin occupied by Mr. Harper. Recalling his promise to help her brother, she tells him the whole story. He reassures her that all will be well and tells her to return to headquarters to await Major Dunwoodie.

Orders from General Washington arrive in time to relieve Major Dunwoodie of the necessity of finding Henry. Several days later, Birch sees him safely aboard a British man-of-war in New York harbor. Frances and Major Dunwoodie decide to be married immediately. Within a short time, however, their bliss is tempered by the news that Captain Lawton fell in battle with the British.

Some time later, Birch appears at the headquarters of the army in a New Jersey town. There he has a long interview with a grave and noble man whom the Whartons would have recognized as Mr. Harper; he is also known as General Washington. During their talk, the general attempts to reward his faithful spy by giving him money. The peddler refuses to accept payment for his services to his country, but he does welcome a letter of approbation from his commander-in-chief. It is agreed that the peddler's real mission as an American spy should remain a secret that only they will share.

Thirty-two years later, in the War of 1812, a gaunt old peddler appears on the Canadian border and carries word of British troop movements to the American lines. There he meets Captain Wharton Dunwoodie, the son of Major Peyton Dunwoodie and his wife Frances. To him, the peddler acknowledges his earlier acquaintanceship with the young officer's parents. A few days later, during a battle, the old peddler throws away his pack and rushes into the fight with a musket seized from a fallen soldier. After the battle, Captain Dunwoodie finds the old man's body and on his person a letter, signed by George Washington, that reveals Harvey Birch to be not a despicable spy but a loyal, heroic, and long-suffering patriot.

Critical Evaluation:

Judged by contemporary standards, *The Spy: A Tale of the Neutral Ground* is still a satisfactory historical novel. As James Fenimore Cooper remarked in the introduction to his novel, however, his purpose in *The Spy* is frankly patriotic. If one bears this fact in mind, one can see that Peyton Dunwoodie represents the ideal American soldier and officer; Frances Wharton, the ideal of American womanhood; and George Washington, the ideal father of his country, combining Roman strength and vigor with American humanity and humility. This understanding will help the reader to appreciate Cooper's point of view. The great historical novelist of the early nineteenth century was an intensely nationalistic individual who, conscious of the past achievements and potentialities of his country, eagerly looked forward to the development of a great nation.

The Spy is an important novel both in Cooper's career and in the history of American literature. For Cooper, *The Spy* represented a first success in a literary career that was to include thirty-three fictional works as well as a number of other writings over a period of thirty-one years. *The Spy*, however, also signifies the establishment of an independent American literature, one based on American life and American characters, and set in an American landscape. It is significant, then, that the novel that declared "independence" from European, and especially English, literature should take for its subject the American War of Independence.

In his preface to *The Spy*, Cooper showed that he was acutely conscious of being an American writer and of writing about American subjects. Still, there is no doubt that he was influenced by the major currents in literature written abroad, and, though in his preface Cooper offers a tongue-in-cheek apology for not including castles and nobles as Sir Walter

Scott had done in his works, it is certain that Scott influenced Cooper in *The Spy* and in his later career as well. Scott was a great pioneer in the art of the historical novel, and *The Spy* shows that Cooper learned much from Scott.

An important aspect of the historical novel is authenticity of historical types, characters who live in a specific historical period and in a particular place. One of the key differences between an authentic historical novel and a contemporary novel in a historical setting is characterization. Though one may argue that people are, in a sense, the same everywhere and at all times, it is apparent that the differences cannot be overlooked if one is mainly interested in accurately portraying a specific era. Thus, to capture a particular place at a particular time, the novelist must do more than merely dress his or her contemporaries in the clothing of days past: He or she must have a grasp of those human features and aspects that a historical period typically requires of men and women.

The Spy is full of historically typical men. The spy himself is a courageous and ingenious man able to affect the times in which he lives and also permitted (and encouraged) by those times to display such qualities. Thus, another difference between an ordinary novel in a historical setting and a historical novel as such is that the characters help fashion history as they are fashioned by it. The novel, set during the American Revolutionary War, is fought on political as well as military grounds, involves civilians to a great extent, and always poses the problem of divided loyalties. Cooper's choice of a spy is especially effective too. The spy is more than a soldier in a war; he must have a grasp of politics (and of theater) as well.

Cooper discovered another advantage in the use of a spy as a central character. This advantage is connected to the subtitle of the novel, *A Tale of the Neutral Ground*. Effective historical novels tend to focus on periods in which significant conflicts occur. Such conflicts as the American Revolution not only provide good dramatic material for the novelist but also offer later readers an insight into their own condition, since significant conflicts in the past have shaped their lives.

There is, however, an artistic problem in portraying such conflicts. To give a full picture of the clash of forces, an author must describe both sides in the fight (in Cooper's case, both the British and the Americans). Describing only one side tends to rob the novel of drama—but how is the novelist to show both and, at the same time, focus these forces on a single, central character?

Scott solves this problem by using figures of secondary historical interest as his primary focus of dramatic action. These secondary figures are able to move from one side to another as negotiators, go-betweens, and messengers. This movement back and forth allows scope for the novelist to show both sides of the conflict in a specific, concrete fashion.

Cooper does this in *The Spy*. Instead of choosing Washington as a central character, Cooper chooses a spy, a man able (and required) to move from one side to the other and yet a man who remains in the thick of the dramatic action. The "Neutral Ground," the space between opposing forces that Birch must cross and recross in his missions, the seam between the opponents, also reflects the need for an effective historical novel to move from one side to the other.

Other aspects of the historical novel are also significant. Besides the presence of other, minor "type" characters (the doctor, the housekeeper, the servant), there are the details of the warfare—the names, dates, places, and historical facts—that Cooper makes a conscious effort to use; *The Spy* reflects a degree of historical accuracy and fidelity to the facts that, despite moments of highly imaginative drama and humor, lend an air of reality to the action of the book as a whole.

Additionally, Cooper expends much prose and dialogue on the arguments for and against the American Revolution. The revolutionaries argue with the counterrevolutionaries. Because he is able to show both sides dramatically, in real life, Cooper is able to describe the intellectual and political conflict of the era. In this way, Cooper avoids the trap of turning a historical novel into a mere adventure story; for in the course of history, and certainly in the course of the Revolutionary War, the battle of ideas deeply influences the physical battles. If Cooper is less successful in showing how arguments change individuals, he is still able to give a richer sense of the times and of the war than if he had concentrated entirely on physical action and adventure.

There are obvious weaknesses in Cooper's work. Cooper was, apart from being an opinionated man, one who shared many of the prejudices and preconceptions of his day. These views naturally affect the quality of his work. One problem, for example, is that he seems unable to characterize certain types of people in much depth. His attitude toward women and African Americans specifically is condescending. As a result, his portrayal of these figures is frequently superficial. Cooper also has a tendency to use a rather heavy-handed ironic tone. In *The Spy*, Cooper follows a long tradition in English literature by making his comic characters members of the lower class. One senses that the class characteristics of those below him were humorous to Cooper. Corresponding to this general characterization of the lower orders (not true in every case, to be sure) is a general deference to those of higher rank.

Thus, in fully evaluating *The Spy* as literature, the reader is drawn to a central contradiction. On one hand, Cooper clearly supports the American side of the Revolutionary War and agrees with the arguments for independence, especially those arguments based on equality. In Cooper's mind, people are equal before God. At the same time, Cooper himself is a creature of his own time and upbringing. For him, though people may be equal under God, they are by no means equal to one another.

The conflict between ideals and reality is an old one in the United States, and it is no surprise that Cooper, declaring himself an authentic American novelist, should exhibit that conflict. Thus, *The Spy* is an informative historical novel both because it reflects a basic conflict in the history of a nation and because, as a work of art, it contains a basic conflict in human nature.

"Critical Evaluation" by Howard Lee Hertz

Further Reading

Darnell, Donald. *James Fenimore Cooper: Novelist of Manners*. Newark: University of Delaware Press, 1993. A close analysis presenting manners as Cooper's method of introducing his views on society, humor, and social mores. Chapter 3 is especially insightful concerning *The Spy*.

Fields, Wayne, ed. *James Fenimore Cooper: A Collection of Critical Essays*. Englewood Cliffs, N.J.: Prentice-Hall, 1979. This useful volume offers lengthy biographical, historical, and critical studies of Cooper as the representative American author. The volume is particularly well edited.

Long, Robert Emmet. *James Fenimore Cooper*. New York: Continuum Books, 1990. This lively text offers a colorful introduction to Cooper the man and insightful comparisons to his contemporaries. Chapter 2 provides a concise summary of *The Spy*.

Person, Leland S., ed. *A Historical Guide to James Fenimore Cooper*. New York: Oxford University Press, 2007. Collection of essays, including a brief biography by Cooper biographer Wayne Franklin and a survey of Cooper scholarship and criticism. *The Spy* is discussed in "'More than a Woman's Enterprise': Cooper's Revolutionary Heroines and the Compromise of Domesticity" by John P. McWilliams. Features an illustrated chronology of Cooper's life and important nineteenth century historical events.

Reid, Margaret. "Imagining Cultural Origins in James Fenimore Cooper's *The Spy*." In *Cultural Secrets as Narrative Form: Storytelling in Nineteenth-Century America*. Columbus: Ohio State University Press, 2004. An analysis of nineteenth century literature, in which Reid explores how the Puritan legacy, the Revolutionary War, and the Western frontier acquired the status of American myth. The sixty-eight-page section on *The Spy* discusses how Cooper's representation of the American Revolution contributed to this mythmaking process.

Ringe, Donald. *James Fenimore Cooper.* New York: Twayne, 1962. Contains an excellent chronology, bibliography, and cogent biographical sketch. *The Spy* is referenced in Cooper's canon.

Rosenberg, Bruce A. *The Neutral Ground: The André Affair and the Background of Cooper's "The Spy."* Westport, Conn.: Greenwood Press, 1994. In 1790, John André, an American, was captured outside British lines and hanged as a spy. Rosenberg argues that Cooper's novel is based upon the André affair and that it examines the morality of deceit and concealed intentions in both normal life and wartime. He further maintains that Cooper is the first spy novelist.

Spiller, Robert E., and Philip C. Blackburn. *A Descriptive Bibliography of the Writings of James Fenimore Cooper.* New York: B. Franklin, 1968. An outstanding and essential tool for a study of Cooper.

The Spy Who Came in from the Cold

Author: John le Carré (1931-   )
First published: 1963
Type of work: Novel
Type of plot: Espionage
Time of plot: c. 1960
Locale: England, especially London and environs; the Netherlands; Berlin, East Germany

Principal characters:
ALEC LEAMAS, career British espionage officer
KARL RIEMECK, British-run German agent
GEORGE SMILEY, retired British spymaster
ELIZABETH "LIZ" GOLD, library worker, member of the British Communist party, and friend and lover of Alec Leamas
BILL ASHE, recruiter for East German intelligence
COMRADE FIEDLER, Jewish deputy head of East Germany's Abteilung (espionage agency)
HANS-DIETER MUNDT, head of the Abteilung

The Story:

Alec Leamas is a burned-out British espionage officer who has been in charge of running spies in the German Democratic Republic (GDR). When his last agent, Karl Riemeck, is shot down in front of him at a border crossing, it signals the end of his network: The group of agents he has been running has been exposed by the head of the Abteilung (the East German counterespionage agency), and Leamas is sent back to England for reassignment.

The shock of Riemeck's death and the demise of Leamas's network appear to indicate the close of his career as a field officer, so Leamas believes that he will finally be allowed to abandon field work ("be brought in from the cold," in the parlance of the British Secret Intelligence Service). Leamas returns to the headquarters of the Secret Intelligence Service, nicknamed the Circus, because its headquarters is located in Cambridge Circus, London. The head of the Circus, a man known only as Control, informs Leamas that, if he is not ready for a desk job, there is another field position that

may be open to him. With the collaboration of Control and the retired spymaster George Smiley, Leamas participates in a counterespionage plan to destroy the East German spies who broke apart the British network.

The plan begins when Leamas sets up an elaborate charade in which he pretends to be disgruntled with the Circus. Amid bitter recriminations, he quits his desk job, claiming that it represented an undeserved demotion. Then, his life apparently spirals out of control. He circulates through a series of jobs, drinks too much, and lives a rough lifestyle. Finally, he secures a job in the Bayswater Library for Psychic Research, where he does menial work for little cash under the eye of the librarian Miss Crail, who seems to spend much of her day complaining about Leamas to her mother over the phone.

The one bright spot in Leamas's new existence is that he meets a young fellow worker, Liz Gold, who befriends him; the two become lovers. Although he genuinely begins to have feelings for Liz, Leamas continues to play the dissolute former spy, alcoholic and angry. He becomes violent with his local grocer, is arrested, and is sentenced to jail.

The payoff for this deception occurs upon Leamas's release from prison, when he is befriended by an odd little man named Bill Ashe. Ashe buys him food and drinks and gives him some cash, even putting Leamas up in his apartment for a few days. Ashe is a contact for East German intelligence, and he eventually passes Leamas off to another contact, who supplies him with false identity papers, some money, and booze and sneaks him out of the country. In Holland, another agent, apparently Russian, intensively interrogates Leamas. Meanwhile, a notice appears in the British newspapers reporting his defection and implying that he has betrayed his country. Leamas is now fully committed as a defector, providing British intelligence to a foreign power for money and a berth in a neutral country.

Leamas is next transported to communist Berlin and then farther east to some sort of prison or interrogation center. There, he is questioned at some length by Fiedler, the deputy head of the Abteilung. During their sessions, the men not only discuss the secrets Leamas is supposedly selling to East Germany but also engage in philosophizing about why they do what they do. Fiedler is shocked that Leamas has no overarching belief in anything, thus echoing Liz's similar earlier confusion. Fiedler also makes known his dislike and distrust of his superior, Mundt, and it becomes clear that he is looking for a way to implicate Mundt with British intelligence.

Mundt himself arrives, radically changing the situation. Fiedler disappears; Leamas is imprisoned, harshly interrogated, and charged with crimes against the state. He next appears in court, and during the trial it becomes apparent that Fiedler and Mundt are jockeying for power. At first Fiedler appears to be successful in using Leamas's information against Mundt and to be winning the sympathy of the court. Mundt turns the tables on Fiedler, however, by producing Liz Gold as a witness and using her testimony against Fiedler.

It is revealed that, while Fiedler was interrogating Leamas in East Germany, Liz was offered a chance by her local Communist Party cell to visit East Germany as part of a cultural exchange program. Liz is thus in the country when Leamas is put on trial. It becomes clear that Mundt and perhaps some other unknown agency have colluded in setting up Fiedler. After the trial, Liz and Leamas appear to be in for long prison sentences, trapped behind the Iron Curtain. They are surprised, however, when an escape to the West unfolds, and they are whisked into a car and told to drive to a certain point along the Berlin Wall.

During the drive, Leamas explains to Liz what has transpired. It is now clear that British Intelligence is involved in the events that have transpired: Mundt is actually a double agent working for the British, and the Circus has grown concerned that Fiedler is getting too close to discovering the truth about his boss. Mundt's exposure would compromise whatever is left of the British spy network in the East. The real purpose of Leamas's mission, kept a secret from Leamas himself, was to provide Mundt with a means of discrediting Fiedler, thereby eliminating the threat to him and preserving an extremely valuable source of intelligence.

The fleeing couple is given precise instructions about how to scale the wall without detection by avoiding the searchlight and the guards. Leamas is to go first and then pull Liz after him. During the escape, however, everything goes wrong: It appears as though Liz is to be sacrificed, and only Leamas will be allowed to escape. Unable or unwilling to flee alone, Leamas crosses back onto the East German side of the wall, where he too is killed.

Critical Evaluation:

In the early 1960's, there were two main types of spy fiction. One, exemplified by Ian Fleming's James Bond novels, concerned glamorous action and adventure. Indeed, by 1963, the Bond novels—and increasingly the film adaptations based on them—were dominating spy fiction. The second type of spy novel is exemplified by the work of John le Carré, who was himself a former spy. This tradition focused more on the mundane aspects of espionage and featured not larger-than-life super-spies, but the often tired and burned-out, mendacious little men who conduct real spying.

Intelligence organizations gather information; they play individuals against one another, along with their countries. Espionage is all about playing games, using disguises, and assuming roles. The spy observes but may not necessarily participate in events, subsuming his or her personal feelings to the operation and assuming whatever persona will help the cause.

Alec Leamas is a casualty of the Cold War, a used-up spy who has been out in the cold too long. With his Berlin-based network in shambles, apparently because of the effective counterespionage work of the East German Abteilung, he is adrift when he is recalled to headquarters in London. With this opening, le Carré sets up his breakthrough spy novel and establishes the approach he would follow in his subsequent novels that examine the moral parameters of the Cold War and its aftermath.

Leamas has been doing his country's bidding so long that he has stopped asking the reasons or questioning the morality of his actions. He believes in nothing more than doing the job. Le Carré portrays events that force Leamas to confront not only his basic cynicism but also his detachment from other human beings. This confrontation is brought about through his relationship with the young and vulnerable Liz Gold and through his philosophical discussions with Fiedler, his East German adversary.

Liz, Leamas's fellow worker at the library, immediately exhibits a concern for him when he first comes to work. She offers him part of her lunch and later entertains him at her flat and cooks him meals. When he becomes quite ill, she nurses him at his rooms and buys him costly foods and medicines. She even takes him into her bed. Throughout their relationship, Leamas seemingly remains detached and within the role he is playing for the Circus. He rarely talks to her and mocks her commitment to communism. He is astounded that she should be so naïve; she is equally astounded that he is so cynical.

Leamas's discussions while a prisoner of the Abteilung with Fiedler further introduce this issue of moral commitment, or lack of it, on Leamas's part. Fiedler is shocked that Leamas has no overriding philosophical purpose that guides his life. The communist East German finds this a sign of the decadence of the West.

Leamas, as a representative of Western values, especially of the intelligence services, does seem morally bankrupt. In the novel, espionage—and all of the lives, money, and values that it wastes playing an essentially unwinnable game—reveals the essential similarity of both sides of the Cold War, each equally corrupt and equally futile in its actions. Leamas represents the degradation to which the idealism and heroism of World War II have sunk.

With a solid record in both Holland and Norway during the war, Leamas is close to devolving into a home-office manipulator, but he cannot quite go that far. Hidden under layers of alcohol, anger, and frustration, there is still a remnant of something that demands that he avenge his lost network by getting Mundt. When it becomes apparent that he, and particularly Liz, has been manipulated by his superiors, Leamas does the right thing by surrendering his own life. It is a gesture, largely gratuitous, that nevertheless provides a measure of redemption on his part. Perhaps in the end, Fiedler and—more so—Liz have penetrated his thick skin of professional indifference to reach something basic underneath, and Alec Leamas becomes in his death a human being once more.

Charles L. P. Silet

Further Reading

Aronoff, Myron J. *The Spy Novels of John le Carré: Balancing Ethics and Politics*. New York: St. Martin's Press, 1998. This study focuses on the ethical dilemmas faced by citizens when they become engaged in espionage.

Barley, Tony. *Taking Sides: The Fiction of John le Carré*. Philadelphia: Open University Press, 1986. Study of le Carré's work, novel by novel, from *The Spy Who Came in from the Cold* to *The Little Drummer Girl* (1983).

Bloom, Clive, ed. *Spy Thrillers: From Buchan to le Carré*. New York: Macmillan, 1990. Overview of the history of the modern spy novel, placing le Carré in the context of the traditions of the genre.

Bold, Alan, ed. *The Quest for le Carré*. New York: St. Martin's Press, 1988. This collection of essays covers a breadth of topics regarding le Carré's novels; includes a chapter on narrative techniques in *The Spy Who Came in from the Cold*.

Cobbs, John L. *Understanding John le Carré*. Columbia: University of South Carolina Press, 1998. Series book that provides an explication of le Carré's novels.

Hoffman, Tod. *Le Carré's Landscape*. Montreal: McGill-Queen's University Press, 2001. Explores the relationship between writers and spies, the reality of espionage, and its mythology.

Le Carré, John. *Conversations with John le Carré*. Edited by Mathew J. Bruccoli and Judith S. Baughman. Jackson: University Press of Mississippi, 2004. A series of interviews with le Carré that casts light on his writing style and background.

Lewis, Peter. *John le Carré*. New York: Frederick Ungar, 1985. Good, short overview of le Carré's fiction.

Monaghan, David. *The Novels of John le Carré: The Art of Survival*. New York: Basil Blackwell, 1985. Attempts to tie together the various novels of le Carré through a unifying and consistent imagination.

_____. *Smiley's Circus: A Guide to the Secret World of John le Carré*. London: Orbis, 1986. This encyclopedia-style book lists the various places, terms, and characters in the novels. Maps and photos included.

Sauerberg, Lars Ole. *Secret Agents in Fiction: Ian Fleming, John le Carré, and Len Deighton*. New York: Macmillan, 1984. Comparative study of the three most significant writers of espionage fiction of the mid-twentieth century.

Wolfe, Peter. *Corridors of Deceit: The World of John le Carré*. Bowling Green, Ohio: Bowling Green State University Popular Press, 1987. A topical study of the spy novels.

The Stand

Author: Stephen King (1947-   )
First published: 1978
Type of work: Novel
Type of plot: Fantasy
Time of plot: June 13, 1980, and after
Locale: North America, principally the United States

Principal characters:

STUART REDMAN, an easygoing Texan in his mid-thirties
FRANCES GOLDSMITH, a pregnant college student from Maine in her early twenties
HAROLD LAUDER, a social outcast teenager from the same town as Goldsmith
"MOTHER" ABAGAIL FREEMANTLE, an elderly African American from Nebraska, who gathers the forces of good in Boulder, Colorado
RANDALL FLAGG, an ageless demoniac being who gathers the forces of evil in Las Vegas, Nevada
CHARLIE D. CAMPION, the original carrier of the superflu
NADINE CROSS, a virginal teacher from Vermont destined to become the wife of Randall Flagg
GLEN BATEMAN, a retired sociology professor from New Hampshire
KOJAK, an Irish setter who, after his owner dies, stays with Bateman
NICK ANDROS, a deaf-mute drifter from Arkansas
TOM CULLEN, a mildly retarded, illiterate man in his thirties from Oklahoma
RALPH BRENTNER, a midwestern farmer in his forties who is skilled with tools and machinery
DONALD MERWIN ELBERT (TRASHCAN MAN), an Indiana pyromaniac and schizophrenic who has a savant talent for destruction and destructive devices
LLOYD HENREID, a petty criminal in his thirties from Nevada who becomes Flagg's second-in-command
PETER GOLDSMITH-REDMAN, infant son of Frances Goldsmith, the first living human being to contract the virus and survive

The Story:

Charles D. Campion, a soldier working in a military biological weapons facility, discovers that the containment measures securing one of the base's weapons have been breached. Campion narrowly eludes the lockdown that follows and escapes the base, where people are already dying of the plague they have unleashed, an augmented strain of influenza known as superflu or Captain Trips. Campion flees home to pick up his wife and daughter and drives them east from California. He does not realize that he was infected by the superflu before he managed to flee the base.

Campion travels across the country, infecting many people. Roughly 99.4 percent of the human population is suscep-

tible to the virus, and everyone infected by it dies. The other 0.6 percent are completely immune; on them, the virus has no effect. Finally, after stops in many states, Campion crashes his car into a gas station in a small town in Texas. He dies on the way to the hospital.

The medical examiner cannot determine what killed Campion and calls the Centers for Disease Control (CDC) in Atlanta, Georgia. Federal officials quarantine the small town of Arnett, Texas, while the military escorts the survivors to the CDC in Atlanta. Stuart Redman, an East Texas plant worker, ends up quarantined in Stovington, Vermont, after a brief stay in Atlanta. He is one of those who are immune to the disease. Doctors try to determine why he is immune in the hope of making a vaccine. After days of tests, the lone survivor at the CDC facility in Vermont is Redman.

Leaving the CDC, Redman roams New England, meeting Glen Bateman (a retired New Hampshire sociology professor) and Kojak, an Irish setter. The three travel together toward a farmhouse in Nebraska to which they are drawn by dreams of an old woman (Mother Abagail) sitting on her front porch. About half of the survivors of Captain Trips are having these dreams of the old woman. They travel toward Nebraska and the farmhouse from all over the United States. The travelers begin to find each other on the road, and they form groups to travel together safely. Redman, Bateman, and Kojak join Harold Lauder—a teenage social outcast—and Frances Goldsmith—a pregnant young lady in her early twenties. Harold and Frances are the only survivors from Ogunquit, Maine.

In New York City, Larry Underwood, a singer, meets Rita Blakemoor, a wealthy socialite and cocaine addict. They decide to travel together, but Blakemoor dies from a drug overdose, leaving Underwood alone. Underwood makes his way to Maine, where he meets Nadine Cross, a virginal teacher destined to become the wife of Randall Flagg, and a young boy she calls Joe. Before leaving Ogunquit, they see signs that Lauder has painted indicating that he and Goldsmith are going to Stovington. On the way to Vermont, the party of three meets others traveling toward what they hope is a place of sanctity.

Meanwhile, Nick Andros (a deaf-mute drifter from Arkansas on his way to Nebraska) finds Tom Cullen, a mildly retarded man, in Oklahoma. Later, the two men find Ralph Brentner, a farmer who seems to understand tools and machinery, on a stretch of highway somewhere between Oklahoma and Nebraska. These three travelers meet others who eventually become what Andros perceives as his family. Andros leads his group to Nebraska and Mother Abagail. Together, the parties of Redman, Andros, Underwood, and many others then set out for Boulder, Colorado, led by Mother Abagail.

While these groups are gravitating toward Mother Abagail and Boulder, other groups are traveling toward Randall Flagg and Las Vegas. Flagg, known by many names, is the counterpart of Mother Abagail, a beacon who appears in the dreams of the other half of the survivors. The people who are drawn toward Flagg are not pure in thought, deed, or heart; they crave power and destruction. One of them is Donald Merwin Elbert, a pyromaniac and schizophrenic who has a savant talent for sowing destruction and creating destructive devices. Known as the Trashcan Man, Elbert sets fire to oil

tanks and cities just because he can. When he arrives in Las Vegas, Elbert receives a black stone with a red flaw, to symbolize his allegiance to Flagg. Flagg instructs Elbert to search the desert for weapons and to assist in arming fighter jets at a nearby military base.

While the Trashcan Man makes his way to Las Vegas, Flagg rescues Lloyd Henreid from a Phoenix jail cell. Henreid, along with a partner, is responsible for a series of murders across three states. Police captured Henreid and fatally shot his partner. The superflu has killed everyone in the jail, and Heinreid is slowly starving to death and desperate to escape. Flagg makes Henreid his second-in-command and gives him a black stone with a red flaw. Henreid oversees the day-to-day operations that Flagg plans. He is privy to the knowledge that there is a day of reckoning coming between the people in Las Vegas and the ones in Boulder. The survivors in Boulder are striving to rebuild society as it existed, and the survivors in Las Vegas seek to destroy them.

In Boulder, the followers of Mother Abagail form the Free Zone Committee. Mother Abagail says that Bateman, Brentner, Redman, and Underwood must go to Las Vegas to confront Flagg. Kojak decides to go with the four men. Along the way, Redman breaks his leg and must stay behind, while the others continue to Las Vegas; Kojak stays behind with Redman. He hunts small animals for Redman to eat. The three others continue, then meet forces of Flagg who take them into Las Vegas. The captured men have a choice: serve Flagg and live, or deny Flagg and die. Bateman dies by a single bullet fired by Henreid at Flagg's insistence.

The Trashcan Man, in the meantime, has a schizophrenic episode and destroys almost everything and everyone at the military base, including the pilots. When he realizes what he has done, he goes into the desert to find something very special to bring back to Flagg to make up for it. He finds a nuclear bomb, which he attaches to his all-terrain vehicle (ATV). He travels back toward Las Vegas with the nuclear weapon in tow, but he contracts radiation sickness from his proximity to it. Out of his mind with the sickness and overjoyed at the prospect at how happy Flagg will be at his discovery, Elbert drives the bomb into the heart of the city. Everyone has gathered in front of a casino, at the behest of Flagg, to watch the executions of the two men from Boulder.

At that precise moment, everyone in the crowd sees what appears to be a giant hand forming in the sky—the Hand of God. As they watch, the Hand descends and activates the warhead. Everything is destroyed, with one exception: the embodiment of evil, Randall Flagg. In Boulder, everyone sees the giant mushroom cloud as it ascends into the sky.

Redman and Kojak see it as well. Tom Cullen, who had been a spy in Las Vegas with a posthypnotic suggestion to leave at a certain time, was on his way back to Boulder when he saw the cloud.

Cullen finds Redman and Kojak on the road toward home; Redman has a high fever. They spend much of the winter holed up in a lodge while Cullen nurses Redman back to health. After many hardships, they end up walking the last few miles into Boulder. In Boulder, Redman finds out that Goldsmith has given birth to a boy she named Peter Goldsmith-Redman; he contracts the superflu but survives, indicating that he has partial immunity. Boulder has become what Redman sees as an organized civilization, much like what was wiped out during the epidemic; he wants no part of it.

When winter is over, some of Redman's friends have decided to travel to Mexico, maybe farther, to see if any people survive in that area of the world. Goldsmith wants to go home to Maine to raise her son, so she and Redman begin the journey back to Maine, stopping at the farmhouse in Nebraska for a while. They ponder the question of whether or not humankind will repeat the same colossal mistakes that destroyed the world as they knew it; no answer is forthcoming.

Critical Evaluation:

Stephen King has been nominated for and won numerous awards from around the world. *The Stand* was nominated for the 1979 Gandalf Award for Book-Length Fantasy, the 1979 Locus Award for Best Novel, and the 1979 World Fantasy Award for Best Novel. Although it did not win any of these awards, it is still a masterful telling of the timeless battle between good and evil. Personifying good and evil in the guise of human beings is not a new idea. Personifying good as a century-old woman living in Nebraska and evil as a man, seemingly ageless and from no place in particular, King takes the concept and weaves this story into a classic tale.

With his complex plots, intense and complicated characters, skillful use of narrative point of view, and ability to create a believable future world, King portrays people who do not learn from their mistakes and, therefore, are destined to make them again. These characters find themselves in an epic novel in which King has said he was explicitly attempting to create a tale of the same scope and power of J. R. R.

Tolkien's *The Lord of the Rings* (1955), but set in the United States rather than in a fantasy world. The plot is also reminiscent of Christian narratives of the Ecstasy, in which many people will be "taken" from Earth and those left behind will be charged with fighting the last, apocalyptic battle between good and evil.

Melinda Madden

Further Reading

Beahm, George. *Stephen King: From A to Z—An Encyclopedia of His Life and Work*. Kansas City, Mo.: Andrews McMeel, 1998. Examines King's life as a publishing marvel who has published more than forty books. Complete with photos.

Bloom, Harold, ed. *Stephen King*. New York: Chelsea House, 1998. Collection of essays by scholars in the field, who examines most of King's works from a variety of critical perspectives.

Hoppenstand, Gary, and Ray B. Browne, eds. *Gothic World of Stephen King: Landscape of Nightmares*. Madison, Wis.: Popular Press, 1987. Analyzes King's interpretations and his mastery of popular literature.

Magistrale, Tony. *A Casebook on "The Stand."* Mercer Island, Wash.: Starmont House, 1992. Collects scholarly essays on issues raised by *The Stand*; includes political, theological, and philosophical readings of the text.

Russell, Sharon A. *Stephen King: A Critical Companion*. Westport, Conn.: Greenwood Press, 1996. Interpretive overview of King's oeuvre. Includes a complete bibliography of all King's work, critical sources, and a listing of reviews of the novels examined in depth.

Spignesi, Stephen J. *Shape Under the Sheet: The Complete Stephen King Encyclopedia*. Ann Arbor, Mich.: Popular Culture, Ink, 1991. Includes an eighteen-thousand-entry concordance to every character, location, and physical object mentioned in King's novels and short stories.

Wiater, Stan, Christopher Golden, and Hank Wagner. *The Complete Stephen King Universe: A Guide to the Worlds of Stephen King*. New York: St. Martin's Griffin, 2006. Details the scope and interconnections of King's various realities. Begins with the worlds of *The Stand* and *The Dark Tower* (1982-2004).

The Star of Seville

Author: Unknown
First produced: La estrella de Sevilla, c. 1617 (English
  translation, 1837)
Type of work: Drama
Type of plot: Tragedy
Time of plot: Thirteenth century
Locale: Seville

Principal characters:
KING SANCHO IV, THE BRAVE, the ruler of Castile
ESTRELLA TABERA, the Star of Seville
DON BUSTOS TABERA, her brother
DON ARIAS, the king's confidant
DON PEDRO DE GUZMÁN and DON FARFÁN DE RIVIERA,
  alcaldes of Seville
DON SANCHO ORTIZ, a nobleman of Seville
CLARINDO, Don Sancho's servant

The Story:

Sancho IV, king of Castile, is delighted with his welcome to Seville, and he is especially charmed by a black-haired beauty he catches sight of on a balcony. The alcaldes of the city identify her as Estrella Tabera, the Star of Seville. King Sancho whispers orders to his confidant, Arias, telling him to arrange for the monarch to visit Estrella the next evening. He also sends for Estrella's brother, Don Bustos Tabera, in the hope of winning his agreement to the royal suit.

When Don Bustos is offered the command of the military post at Archidona, already sought by two veteran soldiers, the nobleman amazes the king by refusing the honor and by accepting with obvious reluctance other friendly gestures; his excuse is that he does not deserve them. At home, Don Bustos finds his sister and Don Sancho Ortiz planning their marriage. Before long the disguised king appears, but Don Bustos, pleading a house in disorder and foreseeing the possibility of a scandal, does not invite him in. Arias does succeed in entering the house, however. When he reveals his errand, Estrella indignantly refuses his request that she be kind to the king. Arias has better luck when he tries to bribe Matilde, the maid, who promises to admit the king to the house after dark.

That night, after the king has been admitted, Don Bustos returns home unexpectedly and finds the monarch there. Pretending not to believe that the intruder is the king, since a noble and just ruler would not stoop to dishonor, Don Bustos insults him as a masquerader. The angry king, with no legal way to get revenge for the insults he has endured, sends for Don Sancho Ortiz and offers to arrange the young nobleman's marriage to anyone he chooses, in return for ridding the king of an enemy. Don Sancho is given a paper on which is written the name of the man he is supposed to kill.

In the meantime, Don Bustos, having forced Matilde to confess her treachery, hangs her from the king's balcony.

Then he instructs Estrella to arrange for her marriage to Don Sancho at once, and she sends her lover a message informing him of the plan and asking him to come to her. Don Sancho is faced with a conflict between duty and inclination. He loves Estrella, but he has sworn to serve the king faithfully; thus, when he meets Don Bustos, he picks a quarrel with his sweetheart's brother and kills him in a duel. Afterward he stubbornly refuses to give any explanation of his deed and is taken, under arrest, to the Triana prison.

Estrella, awaiting the arrival of Don Sancho, receives instead the body of her dead brother. When she learns the name of his killer, she decides to go at once to the king to demand vengeance. Before her arrival at the palace, the king has already been assured that Don Sancho is loyally keeping silent about the king's part in the death of Don Bustos. Since justice is expected, however, the king is forced to order the execution of Don Sancho. Speaking to Arias, the king marvels at the honor and dignity of the citizens of Seville.

When Estrella appears, the king delegates to her the power to pass sentence on the murderer of her brother and sends her, with his ring, to the Triana prison. Alone, he soliloquizes on the tragic results of his unbridled passion. Meanwhile, in the prison, loyal Clarindo is trying to amuse Don Sancho, who seems to be out of his mind. The alcaldes cannot understand his ravings or his refusal to explain his crime. He keeps telling them that he has acted as a king, and that it is the duty of someone else to confess. As they are about to order his execution, Estrella appears, veiled. By now her love has conquered her anger, and she orders the release of the prisoner.

At the palace, Arias keeps insisting that Don Sancho deserves to be saved. On the other hand, if the king were to confess, his action might cost him his throne. At last the king sends Arias to smooth things over, and in private Arias urges each alcalde to spare Don Sancho's life. They, however, consider a pardon incompatible with their concepts of honor and royal dignity, and in spite of both Estrella and the king they order Don Sancho's execution.

With such examples of honor confronting him, the king is moved by his own conscience to confess that he instigated the assassination. Since a king can do no wrong, he goes unpunished, and Don Sancho is set free. Don Sancho and Estrella refuse to obey the king's order that they marry—the blood of Estrella's slain brother separates them forever.

Critical Evaluation:

With the reasoning that *The Star of Seville* is an excellent play and Lope de Vega Carpio was an excellent playwright, people have believed for centuries that the play is the work of Vega Carpio; however, modern scholars have taken a closer look at the two extant versions and have begun to doubt his authorship. The play is unlike dramas that Vega Carpio is known to have written. Whoever the author may have been, he produced a masterpiece of the Spanish Golden Age.

The Star of Seville is frequently cited as the best example of the Spanish honor play, a form popular during that country's Golden Age of drama and related to similar productions in France and England during the sixteenth and seventeenth centuries. It is no surprise that *The Star of Seville* was long thought to be the work of Vega Carpio, since that popular and prolific playwright wrote a number of dramas characteristic of the genre. The interest in grand themes and in characters whose actions could determine the fate of a city, a kingdom, or an empire seems to have gripped audiences throughout Europe.

No audience or reader of *The Star of Seville* can appreciate the play without a sound understanding of the importance of honor in sixteenth and seventeenth century Spain. The term "honor" had both private and public meanings, and Don Sancho's predicament is a perfect example of the problems that arise from the demands of private and public honor. Honor regulated all social relationships: those between king and subject, between superior and inferior, between friend and friend, and between family members. It lay at the root of all personal transactions and established a foundation for social interactions. Upholding one's honor took precedence over personal satisfaction and over other commitments one might make. Such an attitude may seem extreme to succeeding generations, but it served as the informing principle of the society depicted in *The Star of Seville*.

Similarly, for the first audiences who viewed this play, the king remained a figure of paramount importance in their lives, and people believed in the special privileges of monarchs, who, when acting as heads of state, were not subject to the laws that governed ordinary individuals. That idea, coupled with the belief that the sovereign was protected by God and enjoyed special favors from God, made it possible for Sancho the Brave to act with impunity. The assumption was that the king would always act in accord with the dictates of honor. When he did not, the potential for chaos hovered over society and served as the breeding ground for tragedy. Such is the situation that the author of *The Star of Seville* dramatizes in his play.

The admirable male characters in the play, Bustos Tabera and Sancho Ortiz, believe in honor as a quality inherent in the individual and earned through deeds. Not surprisingly, their adherence to this demanding code of behavior leads them into conflict with the king, who has a very different sense of how his subjects should behave. Hence, when Sancho offers Bustos a key military appointment, Bustos refuses because he is not worthy, making it impossible for the king to use the commission as a bribe for Bustos's cooperation in the king's seduction of Estrella. Sancho is forced to use other means to gain his evil end. Similarly, Don Sancho is quick to agree to be the king's emissary in eliminating the purported traitor; he never questions the king's motives, and even though he is distraught at having to kill the brother of his betrothed, he carries out his promise rather than stain his honor. The king refuses to come to Don Sancho's aid when the citizens of Seville demand the killer's execution, so Sancho nearly loses his life for a deed he committed as a matter of honor.

The king and his confidant Don Arias possess a different notion of honor. For the king, the blind allegiance of his subjects to this code of behavior permits him to use them for his personal pleasure. Don Arias, ever present with words of advice, urges the king on in his plot to satisfy his passion for Estrella by taking advantage of the high-minded notions of men such as Don Bustos and Don Sancho. One of the great ironies of the drama is that the king makes glib promises, often in writing, to a number of people who fail to benefit from them because the king is unwilling to admit his evildoing when these individuals face punishment and death. For the king, as it is for William Shakespeare's Falstaff, honor is but a word.

In *The Star of Seville*, the concept of honor is saved by the citizens of Seville, who force the king to admit publicly his role in the murder of Don Bustos, thereby halting the execution of Don Sancho. Through the heroic stance of the mayor and city elders, who defy the king's efforts to bribe them to set Sancho free, the king is made to act in accordance with the principles that should govern the behavior of rulers and admit his role in the murder. It is not clear that the king is actually changed by his actions, but at least Sancho is spared and the citizenry reassured that social justice is still possible in their city.

Modern audiences may have difficulty with the way in which women are portrayed in *The Star of Seville*. Estrella is little more than an object to be bargained for. She enters into the action of the play only rarely, most notably in the scene in which she pardons Don Sancho for killing her brother. As a symbol of constancy and an object for evoking sympathy, she is well drawn. She remains, however, little more than an appendage to the central moral action, which involves the male figures only.

At the time of the play's writing, Spain was the most powerful nation on earth. Despite this power, the country was still under the influence of medieval superstitions and customs. The Spanish Inquisition had purged the land of heretics and infidels. Silver was pouring into the king's coffers. The war with the Moors was still fresh in the memory of the people. Duels were fought every day. *The Star of Seville* is a reflection of the ethical and moral concerns of the time. Abstractions such as honor and corruption presented themselves to the people of the time with an immediacy like that seen in the play.

The theme of fatalism is also central to the play. The thinking of the time was, in comparison to modern times, very religious. It was widely accepted that God is supreme and the ultimate reality. God allows evil and mischance to enter one's life, but nothing is hopeless because God is the rewarder of the faithful. Miraculous and accidental events govern people's lives and circumstances. Given this condition, one must be resigned to fate.

In *The Star of Seville*, stars are an important metaphor for fate. The play refers to the stars many times and dramatically portrays the intervention of the stars in people's lives. Estrella (whose name is Spanish for "star") denies the influence of the stars in her life as long as things appear to be going in the direction that she desires. As soon as her wishes are thwarted, by the killing of her brother by her lover, she gives vent to her grief and declares that her star is on the decline. Estrella, known as the Star of Seville, is so beautiful and bright that her influence is enough to change the lives of all the men who love or desire her—her brother, her lover, and even the king.

The king further portrays the belief that ultimately all things are in God's hands. Monarchs are appointed by God and are accountable only to God. The duty and responsibility of any loyal subject is to obey the king. One of the king's men reminds him that the staves of his office point to God and signify the king's accountability to God, but if the staves are bent, they point to humanity. Herein lies the king's dilemma: He cannot be true to God and also achieve his heart's desire.

In the character of Don Sancho Ortiz the audience sees the terrible consequences of loyalty and obedience to the king. Don Sancho knows he must kill his friend or disobey his monarch. He struggles with his conscience until he finally rationalizes that the king is accountable to God alone and he, Don Sancho, is accountable to the king. In this way he resolves the conflict and does the king's bidding.

The people of Seville believe they are like pawns in a giant chess game, with outside forces moving them to and fro, without malice, wreaking havoc in their lives. Morbid humor is displayed in several scenes, notably in the third act, in which the disguised king tries to break into Estrella and Don Bustos's house and is caught. Another humorous scene occurs when Don Sancho and Clarindo debate upon hell, or "the other world," where all professions are represented except lawyers. Don Sancho asks why there are no lawyers and is told it is because they would bring lawsuits if they were there. He then says, "If there are no lawsuits . . . hell's not so bad."

"Critical Evaluation" by V. Addington;
revised by Laurence W. Mazzeno

Further Reading

Bergmann, Emilie. "Reading and Writing in the *Comedia*." In *The Golden Age Comedia: Text, Theory, and Performance*, edited by Charles Ganelon and Howard Manning. West Lafayette, Ind.: Purdue University Press, 1994. Discusses the ways that reading and writing define women's roles in *The Star of Seville*. Compares the treatment of women in this play with the depiction of women in another contemporary drama.

Oriel, Charles. *Writing and Inscription in Golden Age Drama*. West Lafayette, Ind.: Purdue University Press, 1992. A chapter on *The Star of Seville* focuses on the written texts, such as letters, that appear in the play and explores their function in illuminating the code of honor.

Samson, Alexander, and Jonathan Thacker, eds. *A Companion to Lope de Vega*. Rochester, N.Y.: Tamesis, 2008. Twenty-one essays provide various interpretations of Vega Carpio's life and work. Includes discussions of Vega Carpio and the theater of Madrid, his religious drama, his chronicle memory plays, his comedies, and Vega Carpio as icon.

Thomas, Henry. Introduction to *The Star of Seville*. New York: Oxford University Press, 1950. Calls the work one of the greatest plays of the Golden Age of Spanish drama.

Analyzes the development of the king, Don Sancho, and Don Busto, whose varying understandings of the concept of honor lie at the heart of the drama.

Wright, Elizabeth R. *Pilgrimage to Patronage: Lope de Vega and the Court of Philip III, 1598-1621*. Lewisburg, Pa.: Bucknell University Press, 2001. Chronicles how Vega Carpio used his publications and public appearances to win benefactors at the court of Philip III. Describes how his search for patrons shaped his literary work and how the success of his plays altered the court's system of artistic patronage.

Ziomek, Henryk. *A History of Spanish Golden Age Drama*. Lexington: University Press of Kentucky, 1984. Briefly sketches the dramatic conflict of *The Star of Seville*, discusses the theme of loyalty, and comments on historical parallels.

Steppenwolf

Author: Hermann Hesse (1877-1962)
First published: 1927 (English translation, 1929)
Type of work: Novel
Type of plot: Psychological
Time of plot: 1920's
Locale: Germany

Principal characters:
HARRY HALLER, the steppenwolf
HERMINE, a friend
PABLO, a saxophonist
MARIA, a demimondaine

The Story:

The aunt, who keeps a spotless bourgeois house, is attracted to Harry Haller, the new lodger who rents her attic, but her nephew's suspicions are aroused when the lodger asks them not to report his domicile to the police. Haller explains that he has a repugnance for official contacts. His room is always in disorder; cigar ends and ashes, wine and brandy, pictures and books litter the apartment.

Haller is about fifty years old, sometimes in poor health and addicted to painkillers. He arises very late and becomes active only at night. He is invariably polite but remote. Once the nephew finds him sitting on the stairs near a landing. Haller explains that the landing, which smells of wax and turpentine and is decorated with washed plants, seems to him the epitome of bourgeois order. Occasionally a pretty girl comes to see Haller for brief visits, but her final visit ends in a bitter quarrel.

One day, Haller disappears, after meticulously paying his accounts. He leaves behind a manuscript, written during his stay, which tells the story of a steppenwolf. The nephew, sure that Haller is not dead, makes the account public.

Haller suffered a series of blows. His wife became mad and chased him from the house. His profession was closed to him. Living a solitary life, he became a divided personality, one part of him a neat, calm bourgeois, the other, a wolf from the steppes. When he acted politely and genteelly, the world mocked his respectability. When he snarled and withdrew from society, he shocked his bourgeois self. He seemed to be a true steppenwolf.

On a solitary night ramble, he thought he saw an electric sign over a Gothic door in an old wall. The words, which he could barely discern, told of a magic show only for madmen. A little later, he saw a peddler with a similar sign. From a hawker he bought a treatise on the steppenwolf and read it avidly.

The treatise explained the popular concept of a steppenwolf, a creature that is half wolf and half human being as a result of mischance or spell. This was an oversimplified concept, however, for everyone is actually composed not of two but of many selves. The great bulk of the populace is held to one self through the rigid patterns of the sheeplike bourgeoisie; only a few individuals, ostensibly complying, are not really part of the pattern. They act like the lone wolf and are the leaders in all fields. Meditating on this philosophy, Haller understood his own nature a little more clearly, but it was difficult to think of himself as containing many selves.

An old acquaintance, a professor, met him and insisted on inviting him to dinner. The occasion was not a happy one. The professor and his wife were naïvely jingoistic and approved a vicious newspaper attack on a writer who advanced the opinion that perhaps the Germans shared the guilt for World War I. The professor did not realize that the writer was his guest. Haller, for his part, ridiculed a pompous painting of

Johann Wolfgang von Goethe that turned out to be greatly prized by the professor's wife.

Feeling the wolf in him gain ascendancy, Haller dropped in at the Black Eagle Tavern, where merriment reigned. At the bar, he encountered a young girl whom he thought sympathetic. He told her his long tale of woe, including the professor's dinner and his mad wife, Erica, whom he saw only every few months and with whom he quarreled. The girl, who refused to give her name, good-naturedly ridiculed his preoccupation with Wolfgang Amadeus Mozart and Indian myths when he did not even know how to dance. She seemed almost motherly in her concern for him; when he confessed he was afraid to go back to his lodging, she sent him upstairs to sleep. Before they parted, Haller made a dinner date with her.

At their next meeting, the girl, who said that her name was Hermine, set out to change Haller. She would help him for friendship's sake, so that in the end Haller would love her enough to kill her. Haller himself had thought of death; in fact, he was seriously contemplating committing suicide on his fiftieth birthday. Perhaps that was why he did not think Hermine's plan strange.

Hermine began her campaign. First she took him shopping for a gramophone, whereupon he took dancing lessons in his cluttered room. Although he was stiff, he learned the steps of the foxtrot. Then she took him to a tavern to dance. At her urging, he asked the most beautiful girl there, Maria, to be his partner. To his amazement, she accepted, and they danced well together. Hermine complimented him on his progress.

Late one night, as Haller returned quietly to his bedroom, he found Maria in his bed. Thinking he was too old for her, Haller hesitated; Maria was so sympathetic, however, that he lost his reluctance. He met Maria frequently in another room he rented nearby. Haller was grateful to Hermine, who arranged it all. She kept track of his progress in love. After some time Haller realized that only through a lesbian relation could Hermine have known Maria's technique so well.

Another new acquaintance was Pablo, a gentle, accommodating saxophonist. He agreed readily with Haller's criticisms of modern jazz and with his preference for Mozart. Nevertheless, Pablo felt that music was not something to criticize; it was something for listeners and dancers to enjoy. Part of Pablo's great popularity came from his ability to provide drugs for jaded profligates. One night, Pablo invited Haller and Maria to his room and proposed a love episode for three. Haller refused abruptly, but Maria would have liked to accept.

On several occasions, Hermine hinted that she was more unhappy than Haller. He was learning other sides of life, but she knew only a life of pleasure and the senses. She was hoping that Haller would come to love her, because at the coming masquerade ball she would give her last command.

At the ball, Hermine was dressed as a man, reminding Haller of his friend Hermann. They danced with many different women. When Hermine finally changed into women's clothes, Haller knew that he loved her. After the ball, Pablo took them up to his Magic Theater. In a hall of mirrors, Haller saw his many selves; in the various booths, he lived his many lives. In one booth, he killed automobile drivers recklessly. In another, he met all the girls he had ever loved. Toward the end, he was Mozart, a laughing, reckless Mozart who played Handel on a radio. The whirling came to an end. In the last booth, he saw Hermine and Pablo naked on a rug. They were asleep, sated with love. Haller stabbed Hermine. In the court, Mozart was his friend and comforted him when the judges sentenced him to eternal life; he was to be laughed out of court. Mozart turned into Pablo, who picked up Hermine's body, shrank it to figurine size, and put it in his pocket.

Critical Evaluation:

Hermann Hesse, one of the most influential German writers of the twentieth century, traveled widely and lived for a time in Italy and India. Following his journey to the East, he settled in Switzerland, where he spent the remainder of his life. He began writing at the turn of the century and published short stories, essays, and poems as well as several novels. In 1946, he was awarded the Nobel Prize in Literature.

Hesse called *Steppenwolf*, which fell in the middle of his literary career, his most misunderstood novel. The work is complex and confusing because it is never clear whether the narrator, Harry Haller, is sane or not. There is ample evidence to indicate that Haller is schizophrenic, but to dismiss his account as the vision of a madman is to ignore the basic conflict of the novel. The safe, middle-class reaction that sees Haller as mad is precisely the type of reaction that Hesse and Haller find most despicable. As Hesse said, "You cannot be a vagabond and an artist and at the same time a respectable, healthy, bourgeois person. You want the ecstasy so you have to take the hangover." Hesse's attitude is basically Romantic, and this work is a Romantic statement.

The most dangerous way of misreading the novel is to see Haller/steppenwolf as a hero. He sees himself that way, but by the final scene it is clear that Haller is a failure. Despite the temptation to interpret the character of the steppenwolf as that of the intellectual outsider at war with the middle class, Haller, when put to the final test in the Magic Theater, suddenly finds himself responding with the middle-class values he hates. Faced with Hermine's hallucination while she is in Pablo's arms, Haller reacts like any bourgeois husband and stabs, or believes he stabs, the unfaithful lover. With that, it becomes clear that he did not learn how to laugh and thus that he did not become one of the Immortals, the original purpose of his quest. He tells the reader: "One day I would be a better hand at the game. One day I would learn how to laugh." Haller himself is aware of his failure.

Mirrors have an important function throughout the novel. The doubling effect of a mirror is indicative of the split that Haller sees in himself. The act of doubling abounds: Streetlights reflect on wet pavement; Haller sees himself in Hermine's eyes; Hermine herself is a double at the ball, appearing first in the costume of a male and then in that of a female. As a male, she reminds Haller of a high-school male friend. Mirrors in the novel range from Hermine's pocket mirror to Pablo's magic hall of mirrors, and the reader is reminded of the standard magician's reply: "It was done with mirrors." Pablo is the magician who shows Haller that magic is the creative will of the imagination. Human beings are not singular or even double; each is filled with infinite possibilities, all of which can be realized if people will only open themselves to the experience.

The novel is a definition of the moral and intellectual condition of Western culture in the early twentieth century, more particularly of Germany in the 1920's. The setting is a large, modern city filled with electric lights, signs, bars, movies, music, and impersonal streets. The culture depicted is essentially humorless, just as Haller lacks humor. Throughout the novel, Haller and the reader are told that they must learn to laugh, that is, to laugh at themselves and at their condition. They must achieve detachment. When readers first see Haller, he is taking himself far too seriously. At the age of forty-eight, he promises himself the dramatic gesture of suicide at fifty.

The novel falls into three general sections: the introduction of Haller, the education of Haller, and the test of Haller. The introduction is divided into three parts. There is the burgher's view of Haller; Haller's own view of himself as a split personality, both middle class and steppenwolf; and the view represented by the treatise. Whereas the burgher's view is superficial and Haller's view is subjective, the treatise is the objective observation of a higher intelligence. Haller sees only the conflict between his steppenwolf character and the middle class, but the treatise distinguishes three types of individuals: saints, middle class, and sinners. The burgher must resist the temptation to either extreme. It is with this burgher mentality that Haller is at odds. The treatise points out that this is the wrong battle. Haller is pulled in all three directions:

He wants to be burgher yet hates it; he enjoys the role of steppenwolf yet loathes it; and he desires to be an immortal but does not have the humor to achieve that level. The introduction gives an exposition, development, and a recapitulation, the same structure as that of sonata allegro form in music.

Music is central to much of Hesse's writing. He played the violin, and his first wife was a gifted pianist. In *Gertrud* (1910; *Gertrude*, 1955), Hesse tells the story of a composer; in *Die Morgenlandfahrt* (1932; *The Journey to the East*, 1956) he writes of a violinist; and in *Das Glasperlenspiel: Versuch einer Lebensbeschreibung des Magister Ludi Josef Knecht samt Knechts hinterlassenen Schriften* (1943; *The Glass Bead Game*, 1969), there is a pianist and a musical theorist. In *Steppenwolf*, too, music plays an important role. Pablo is a jazz musician, and the music of Wolfgang Amadeus Mozart epitomizes the level of the immortal. Music becomes the synthesis of opposites, harmony within dissonance. Music, for Hesse, is the ideal abstract statement of harmony: It is written, heard, and felt. Moreover, it is timeless or outside time at a level that language can never achieve.

During the middle section of the novel—the education of Haller—the narrator, on the verge of mental collapse, discovers his initiator to self-understanding to be a strange young girl named Hermine. Under her tutelage, Haller must first learn to dance; that is, to experience the sensual side of his nature without disgust. Following the direction of Hermine and her friends, Maria and Pablo, Haller is forced to realize that the self has infinite possibilities. By experiencing the sensual, Haller is following the downward path to wisdom and sainthood. The trip is essentially a mystical one, and Haller experiences what so many mystics before him discovered. Many of the Christian saints were first profligates who rose from sinner to saint. Other mystics, such as Walt Whitman, relate that salvation is through indulgence of the flesh, not through denial of it. As T. S. Eliot discovered in the *Four Quartets* (1943), the way down and the way up are one and the same. In learning to dance, Haller learns to divest himself of his ego. On his way to the intuitive mystic vision that all Romantics eventually achieve, he experiences dance, drink, music, sex, and drugs. Haller is flawed, however. Like the quester in Eliot's *The Waste Land* (1922), Haller, when put to the final test, fails.

In Pablo's Magic Theater, Haller, on a hallucinatory drug trip, experiences the recapitulation of the first two sections of the novel and sees his personality in all of its aspects. Pablo tells him: "I help you make your own world visible, that's all." From the Magic Mirror spring two versions of himself, one of which goes off with Pablo, implying the homosexual side of Haller that Sigmund Freud insisted exists in all men. During the Great Automobile Hunt, Haller, the pacifist, learns that he loves to kill. All things contain their opposites. In his third vision—The Marvels of Steppenwolf Training—Haller sees a surrealistic presentation of the main metaphor of the novel that reappears from the introduction. It is with the final vision of Hermine being unfaithful to him that he is unable to cope. In the hallucination, he stabs her, but Pablo cannot take it seriously, just as Haller cannot laugh at it. Because Haller cannot let his ego dissolve, he cannot join the universal flow of things.

"Critical Evaluation" by Michael S. Reynolds

Further Reading

Bishop, Paul. "Hermann Hesse and the Weimar Republic." In *German Novelists of the Weimar Republic: Intersections of Literature and Politics*, edited by Karl Leydecker. Rochester, N.Y.: Camden House, 2006. Hesse is one of the twelve German writers whose work is analyzed in this study of Weimar Republic literature. The essays focus on the authors' response to the political, social, and economic instability of the era.

Boulby, Mark. *"The Steppenwolf."* In *Hermann Hesse: His Mind and Art*. Ithaca, N.Y.: Cornell University Press, 1967. Compares the structure and motifs of *Steppenwolf* with those of Hesse's other novels. Discusses how depersonalization becomes an essential element in the solution of Harry Haller's dilemma.

Casebeer, Edwin F. *"Steppenwolf:* Siddhartha Today." In *Hermann Hesse*. New York: Warner Paperback Library, 1972. A Jungian interpretation of *Steppenwolf*. Sees Hermine as the anima and Pablo/Mozart as the Self of Harry Haller, especially in the Magic Theater dream world that the Self creates to discover its real nature.

Cornils, Ingo, ed. *A Companion to the Works of Hermann Hesse*. Rochester, N.Y.: Camden House, 2009. Collection of essays, including examinations of *Steppenwolf*; Hesse's interest in psychoanalysis, music, and Eastern philosophy; the development of his political views; and the influence of painting on his writing.

Field, George Wallis. *"Der Steppenwolf:* Crisis and Recovery." In *Hermann Hesse*. Boston: Twayne, 1970. Traces the autobiographical element and the development of the theme of humor from Hesse's earlier works into *Steppenwolf*. Discusses the themes of sexuality, cultural criticism, music, and the transcendence of reality.

Richards, David G. *Exploring the Divided Self: Hermann Hesse's "Steppenwolf" and Its Critics*. Columbia, S.C.: Camden House, 1996. Richards traces the critical writing about *Steppenwolf* from the book's initial publication through the 1990's; the novel was a disappointment to many when it first appeared, but it is now considered one of Hesse's finest achievements. Includes bibliographical references and an index.

Robertson, Ritchie. "Gender Anxiety and the Shaping of the Self in Some Modernist Writers: Musil, Hesse, Hoffmannsthal, Jahnn." In *The Cambridge Companion to the Modern German Novel*, edited by Graham Bartram. New York: Cambridge University Press, 2004. Hesse's novels are among the works examined in this introductory survey of German-language novels from the late nineteenth and early twentieth centuries. Includes chronology and bibliography.

Tusken, Lewis W. *Understanding Hermann Hesse: The Man, His Myth, His Metaphor*. Columbia: University of South Carolina Press, 1998. Analyzes nine novels, including *Siddhartha*, pointing out their common themes, motifs, images, and how they incorporate events in Hesse's life and reflect his quest for self-discovery.

Ziolkowski, Theodore. *"The Steppenwolf:* A Sonata in Prose." In *The Novels of Hermann Hesse: A Study in Theme and Structure*. Princeton, N.J.: Princeton University Press, 1965. Focuses on the technical problems of the novel's structure and explains how Hesse used the musical sonata form to shape *Steppenwolf*.

Zipes, Jack. "Hermann Hesse's Fairy Tales and the Pursuit of Home." In *When Dreams Came True: Classical Fairy Tales and Their Tradition*. 2d ed. New York: Routledge, 2007. Zipes examines how Hesse used the form of the fairy tale in his own writing, discussing some of the fantasylike elements in Hesse's fiction.

Steps

Author: Jerzy Kosinski (Josek Lewinkopf, 1933-1991)
First published: 1968
Type of work: Novel
Type of plot: Existentialism
Time of plot: Indeterminate
Locale: Unnamed

Principal characters:
THE NARRATOR, the protagonist
A WOMAN, his wife or mistress
THE READER, a participant

The Story:

The narrator is a young man who travels from place to place experiencing life in its rawest form. In a small village, he shows his credit cards to a young orphaned woman who washes and mends his clothes and tells her that she will never need money again if she comes with him. She follows him to the city to find a better life for herself and trades sex with him for money. The situation is reversed when he finds himself in a strange city without money and has to trade sex for food.

As a ski instructor in an area close to a tuberculosis sanatorium, he makes love to a woman patient through mirrors; the two never touch. An encounter with a woman at a zoo leads to the narrator's picking up another woman, who turns out to be a male transvestite. A waiter at a train-station restaurant arranges for the narrator to attend a show where a woman and a large unidentified animal copulate while observers place bets as to the depth of penetration.

A grouping of anecdotes about the army includes stories in which two civilians are killed by a sniper, a group of soccer players disappear when they drive across an artillery practice field, and soldiers play a macho gambling game for entertainment. Punishment for a man who cheats in the game is to have his genitals crushed to a pulp between rocks.

The narrator remembers events that occurred during World War II but were not army experiences. As a boy, he was boarded out with farmers who mistreated him. He got revenge by enticing their children to swallow concealed fishhooks and broken glass, which killed them. A cemetery caretaker he knew had been a boxer before being put into a Nazi concentration camp; his captors let him survive so that he could entertain them by fighting with professionals, but the rules were such that no one wanted to fight against him.

When the narrator was a student at the university, he heard about a scientist who at a Communist Party reception pinned gold condoms on every guest instead of medals. At one time the narrator was banished to an agricultural settlement, where he met a circus contortionist who could do sexy things with her body. As editor of the university newspaper, he was assisted by a girl who took pictures of herself nude. He stole some of the pictures and showed them to people. When the girl died a natural death, everyone assumed that she had committed suicide in shame because he had displayed lewd pictures of her.

Among the narrator's stories about sexual force being used against women are descriptions of a gang rape in a city park; of farmers in a village who keep an enslaved woman in a cage high up in a barn, and men who want to use her lower the cage with a rope; and of a friend whom the narrator enlists to help him have sex with a woman who has spurned him.

The narrator tells of senseless killings. Butterflies in a jar are killed slowly as their supply of oxygen is exhausted with burning matches. Empty beer bottles murder a factory watchman. An innocent bystander is beheaded in a "book-knock-off" driving game, in which cars drive close to parked cars that have books attached to them.

When the narrator leaves his original country, he wears a silvery Siberian wolf coat that is totally unsuitable for his new life. Unemployed and destitute, he gets a job chipping paint and rust from a ship, but his fur coat becomes stiff and heavy with paint, and at night the fumes nauseate him. He is fired from the job and takes another parking cars in a parking lot. He becomes involved in a protection racket that victimizes his fellow immigrants. From there he goes into truck driving.

As he tries to adjust to his new city, he sees black people living in poor areas where there is no future, but he envies them their freedom. He wishes that he could make his own skin dark so that he could not be seen at night. Then he could kill the rich, destroy the city, and put bent nails on highways to crash cars. That might destroy his dream of having material things, and it might drive away the image of what he has been so that he can live in peace with no fear of failure. He plays at being deaf and mute for a while before flying to another country to join a revolution. There, he finds himself forced to behead a man with a knife.

Without warning, the narrator leaves a woman with whom he has been living. After the hotel clerk delivers a message to her from the narrator, saying that he will not return, she dives deep into the ocean. On the seaweed covering the ocean floor is a moving shadow, cast there by a tiny rotten leaf that is floating slowly on the surface above.

Critical Evaluation:

Jerzy Kosinski stated that he preferred *Steps* to all his other writings. It has been translated into more than twenty-five languages, and it received both the National Institute of Arts and Letters Award for Literature and the National Book Award. *Steps* is experimental fiction belonging to the "new wave" school led by the French author Alain Robbe-Grillet. Events dominate, and readers must participate in the action if they are to find meaning in the work. Its unusual, brilliant tone and technique sets *Steps* apart from other fiction of its time.

In 1967, Jerzy Kosinski received a Guggenheim Fellowship to write the novel. His purpose, as he explained it, was to discover the self through incidents that were symbolic of the world. He said that the book's characters and their relationships exist in a fissure of time between past and present.

The novel proceeds in short sentences; it is told in the first person except for the last incident, which is in the third person. Place-names are not given. Poland may be the setting for some of the incidents; others may take place in the United States (the author lived in both places). There is no unifying plot, no order to time in the work. The characters are like stick figures, stripped to their bare bones. They have no personalities and are nameless. Only the women are allowed admirable traits.

The narrator is a man trying to discover who he is in a world he considers hostile. Having come from a Communist country where human beings are externally controlled, he is surprised to find that there are collective forces in the new country that prevent the self from being free. Both society and religion exert control over people.

Much of Kosinski's writing is autobiographical. He spews the horrors he encountered in Communist Poland out onto his pages in graphic form, colored dramatically by his vivid imagination. The jobs held by his narrator are jobs that Kosinski, too, held at various times. An outgrowth of his first novel, *The Painted Bird* (1965), in which he was a child, *Steps* shows the author as a young man. The incidents seem disconnected, like a mirror that has been broken and the fragments scattered. If the protagonist could only find the pieces and put them together again, perhaps he could look into the reflective surface and see himself clearly. His self is shattered

like the narrative, and the chaotic society in which he lives seems shattered as well. A former photographer, Kosinski records each event in visual detail as a camera would see it. He uses sight to achieve neutrality. The book is almost totally without emotion.

The significance of the title is elusive. Steps should go somewhere, but these steps seem only to travel between experiences. Some readers see the steps as a moral descent into hell, but it is certain that the author hoped that the steps would be his narrator's progression toward self-discovery.

As in other novels of its time, in *Steps* disease is used to symbolize the sick modern world. The disease in this case is tuberculosis, which is introduced when a ski instructor gets involved with a woman in a European sanatorium. Many of the book's incidents are about people consumed by their desires. In one story an octopus consumes itself. The narrator preys on and consumes women.

Interspersed with thirty-five anecdotes in the past tense are fifteen italicized dialogues with a woman told in the present tense. Most of them concern personal feelings about sexual subjects: circumcision, menstruation, fellatio, jealousy, infidelity, and prostitution. *Steps* is strongly sexual, and these dialogues take place during or after sex. The narrator tells the woman two stories. One is about an architect who designed funeral parlors and concentration camps, the latter because certain humans, like rats, had to be exterminated. In the second, he reminisces about a student at his university who spent time in lavatory cubicles that he called his temples. When he got into trouble over a political mistake, he killed himself in one of the "temples."

Reality and fantasy are so entwined in the novel that it is hard to distinguish one from the other. Every awful thing that humans can do to each other seems to have been included. As Kosinski said of his protagonist, "To him the most meaningful and fulfilling gesture is negative." The theme of the book may be that brutality and violence are so destructive that they make life meaningless. Human beings are no freer in a free society than they are in a politically controlled society. The work displays an anticollectivist bias and a detached, objective viewpoint. Dispassionate acceptance of crude, degrading acts in an uncaring world gives tremendous power to the narrative.

Distinguished by its commanding structure and poetic prose as well as by—despite its portrayal of depravity—its underlying morality, *Steps* has been called existentialist. Its epigraph from the ancient Hindu scripture the Bhagavad Gita indicates that the author hoped for peace and happiness to be restored to human life. That cannot occur if manipulative sex and brutal violence are the sum total of an individual's experience. The stark reality of this powerful novel is an admonition to modern society that bizarre relationships and fragmented experiences are capable of destroying the self.

Josephine Raburn

Further Reading

Cahill, David. "Jerzy Kosinski: Retreat from Violence." *Twentieth Century Literature* 18, no. 2 (April, 1972): 121-132. Discusses Kosinski's belief that incessant violence can destroy the power of humans to create a moral society and describes *Steps* as the author's plea for people to turn away from that violence.

Coale, Samuel. "The Quest for the Elusive Self: The Fiction of Jerzy Kosinski." *Critique: Studies in Modern Fiction* 14, no. 3 (1973): 25-37. Discusses the use in *Steps* of detailed, concrete impressions to simulate external reality. Compares the radical and secular art with which Kosinski tries to depict the human struggle toward personal identity in the modern world with techniques used by Franz Kafka.

Gladsky, Thomas. "Jerzy Kosinski: A Polish Immigrant." In *Living in Translation: Polish Writers in America*, edited by Halina Stephan. New York: Rodopi, 2003. Focuses on Kosinski's acculturation to U.S. society and how his writing was influenced by his having lived in two very different countries—the democratic United States and totalitarian Poland.

Howe, Irving. "From the Other Side of the Moon." *Harper's*, March, 1969, 102-105. Detailed critical review concludes that *Steps* is the hallucinatory self-displacement of a man looking too closely at his own experience.

Lazar, Mary. *Through Kosinski's Lenses: Identity, Sex, and Violence*. Lanham, Md.: University Press of America, 2007. Draws on interviews with scholars and friends of Kosinski in examining the themes of identity, sex, and violence in his work.

Lupak, Barbara. *Plays of Passion, Games of Chance: Jerzy Kosinski and His Fiction*. Bristol, Ind.: Wyndham Hall Press, 1988. Examines all of Kosinski's work, including *Steps*. Includes a discussion of the ways in which the author's life affected his work and points out how his novels differ from other twentieth century novels.

_____, ed. *Critical Essays on Jerzy Kosinski*. New York: G. K. Hall, 1998. Collection of reviews of Kosinski's novels includes Hugh Kenner's and Stanley Kauffman's reviews of *Steps* as well as essays interpreting Kosinski's writings.

Steps to the Temple

Author: Richard Crashaw (c. 1612-1649)
First published: 1646; revised, 1648
Type of work: Poetry

The 1646 edition of Richard Crashaw's *Steps to the Temple*, apparently edited by the anonymous author of the preface, also includes a section of secular poems called "The Delights of the Muses," equivalent to another volume. The 1648 edition contains revisions of some of the originals and many new poems, including "The Flaming Heart," a famous poem about Saint Teresa of Ávila in Spain and her mystical religious ecstasy. This discussion will focus on the sacred poems composing the first edition.

The central, unifying metaphor of the title was based on a collection of poems called *The Temple* (1633) by Welsh poet George Herbert. Crashaw's modification of Herbert's title invites comparison between the two poets; indeed, Crashaw included in his volume the poem "On Mr George Herbert's Book entitled 'The Temple of Sacred Poems.'" In this poem, Crashaw poses as a donor of Herbert's book to a lovely, pious woman. The poem tells the lady reader that she will, by reading the lines, kindle in herself the fire that lies in the words of the meditational poems. Unlocking the secrets of the poems will be like finding an angel and grasping its wings. This angel will transport the perceptive reader daily to heaven, where she can become acquainted with the glories that await her among the gentle souls residing there.

The simple eighteen-line poem, written in rhymed iambic tetrameter couplets, ends with a strange act of appropriation: Crashaw says that the poems in the book, as he gives them to the lady, actually belong to him rather than to Herbert, under whose name they appear. This paradox combines many of the tensions that appear throughout the poetry of Crashaw's entire career. It merges the heavenly and the inspirational with the earthly and the physical. His earthly admiration of the lady, a kind of love, finds its high fulfillment in his homage to her spirit and his attempt to help it strive toward ultimate bliss. The paradox also allows Crashaw to place himself in a tradition of meditative poetry and to choose his own literary precursor.

Even though the subject matter of Herbert's and Crashaw's poems was similar, the two were well distinguished in their styles. Herbert's faith was filled with daily drama and grounded in concrete, mundane experience. In a tone of intimacy, he spoke directly and honestly with his God, trying to discover God's will. Crashaw's poetry, at the other extreme, was lofty, elevated, and elaborate in diction and in situation.

Some of the difference may stem from religious influence. Although both were associated with Little Gidding, a High Church Anglican place of retreat, Herbert was famous as a country minister, having taken orders in the Church of England in 1630. Crashaw, while raised by a staunch Protestant father, was drawn to the ritual, color, and tradition of Roman Catholicism and converted, probably by 1645, after also having taken orders in the Church of England seven years earlier (1638). During his stays in Paris and Rome, after leaving Cambridge shortly before it was visited by Cromwellian anti-Royalist forces, Crashaw also became influenced by a continental and anti-Reformationist strain of thought and art. The qualities of Roman Catholic meaning and matter in his poetry and his tie to continental style mark Crashaw's poetry as unique in England during this period.

The anonymous writer of the preface to the sacred poems of Crashaw indicates that they are the document of an extraordinary man. The title is apt, this writer maintains, because Crashaw lived his life literally and metaphorically on the steps to the temple. The poems are presented as a key to Crashaw's own holy life and as a link whereby the reader might achieve a similar intensity of religious devotion. Crashaw is to lead the reader up the steps to the temple; his poems are to participate in the spirit of Scripture. They are to be as inspiring in their turn as the Psalms and other meditational matters that they translate or emulate.

Although Crashaw's style is unique, he also synthesizes many of the poetic trends of the seventeenth century. At various times he is master equally of the plain style, the classical imitation, and the metaphysical mode, which he inherited from poets such as John Donne. Crashaw, like the metaphysical poets, employs the poem as a form of creation; within its lines, paradoxes, or mutually exclusive realities, can be

proven true. However, Crashaw exhibits little of the cynicism of his predecessors; his poems often strive for a mystical transformation, of unity with God through the medium of the poem. As vehicles of meditative transformation, the poems draw from a tradition of contemplation of a sacred image for inspiration.

This guise of imagistic contemplation has several effects. First, Crashaw's poems do not resist flowery and extended description as a way of achieving the sensory intensity of the image. Because Crashaw seems to have a propensity for using the physical details of the body's experience of holiness, these poems are packed with tears, blood, wounds, milk, water, and wine. This exuberance of detail led some to term Crashaw's poetry baroque, ornate, rococo, and excessive. Because it is possible to discover actual paintings and sculptures upon which certain of his poems were based, critics also began to use the vocabulary of the plastic arts to describe Crashaw's poetic artistry. His imagistic intensity led many to compare his poetry to painting, sculpture, and music and label it with terms by which these arts are categorized, such as "mannerist." Crashaw's complexity has been contextualized richly in the light of the artistic movements of his time.

Steps to the Temple begins with a translation of a portion of a long poem by Neapolitan Giambattista Marino called "Sospetto d'Herode" ("The Suspicion of Herod"). In Crashaw's translation, this poem appears to be a hybrid of Dante Alighieri's inferno (from the early Renaissance in Italy) and John Milton's *Paradise Lost* (1667, 1674). In Crashaw's poem, Satan, knowing that the birth of Christ will conquer Death, sends Alecto, one of the classical Furies, to stir Herod Antipas, ruler of Galilee, into a frenzy in order to vex if not to hinder the birth of Jesus under his jurisdiction. The eight-line narrative stanzas are in iambic pentameter with an *abababcc* rhyme scheme.

Most notable about this translation is the vivid picture painted of Satan. Stanza after stanza visualizes his situation, while Crashaw enlivens his portrait with an interior monologue, giving the reader a glimpse of the psychological and cognitive processes of the Devil. Snakes, flames, horns, chains, red eyes, black nostrils, blue lips, spacious dark wings, groans, stench, gnashing of teeth, lashing of tail—these physical manifestations set the scene for his mental pondering of God's planned benevolent pattern of history and Lucifer's ultimately insignificant role as a character in that plan.

Lucifer is cast in semiheroic terms, as one who exhibits an individualistic will to strive and to dare. He feels himself in painful conflict with God, a regent of a rival kingdom. His thoughts stimulate him to act against the impending birth of Christ, for he feels he will lose even the pale prize he earned after his rebellion in heaven, the rule over his own nether world, for Christ will render Death an impermanent state through his capacity to save and to redeem the souls of humanity. The translation of book 1 of this poem ends with a stunning irony, that the power of Christ is cloaked in humility, in the modesty of the human form, and with the homage of rude stable beasts.

Other translations in the collection include the famous Twenty-third Psalm, which begins with the words "The Lord is my Shepherd." Crashaw recasts this song as rhymed iambic tetrameter couplets filled with rich sensory images. He animates the pastoral landscape by personifying spring and death and by having the elements of the natural scene partake of human qualities and actions, such as weeping, sweating, and breathing. By the end of the poem, Crashaw turns dying into an act of loving. Rather than a goal of simply to "dwell in the house of the Lord forever," the speaker in this translation will merge with Death as with a lover, after sating on balm and nectar specifically rather than the more traditional image of the brimming cup.

Psalm 137 is also translated, and the collection has a long section of epigrams based on Scripture and on events in the life of Christ. These epigrams range from two-lined rhymed couplets in iambic pentameter to a twenty-six-line sequence of rhymed iambic tetrameter couplets, Crashaw's preferred meter, meditating on Matthew 22:46.

The best and most famous poem among the epigrams is "On the Wounds of Our Crucified Lord." This poem is typical of Crashaw, simultaneously metaphysical and baroque. The metaphysical element consists of the elaborate conceit (or metaphorical "concept"), evidenced by the many levels on which the wounds of Christ are interpreted as eyes or as mouths, resulting in an impossible transformational truth: "This foot hath got a mouth and lips, . . . [and]/ To pay thy tears, an eye that weeps." By the end of the poem, the worshiper who weeps pearly, watery tears for the suffering of Christ is repaid by Christ with reciprocal tears from the wounded foot, tears of saving blood called ruby drops. The baroque quality of this poem is its almost unsavory, excessive dwelling on the physicality of the conceit. That the metaphor is unusual and far-fetched is metaphysical, but that it is extended beyond all predictable limits is baroque.

"On a Treatise of Charity" is a poem that tries to reclaim the original state of the true religion. It is, in fact, addressed to religion personified as a beautiful maiden. The poet entreats the maiden to brush away the dust of human perception that dims and alters her true beauty and to take her place as queen served by the handmaiden Charity (used in the sense of the Latin root, *caritas*, or love). The middle of the poem changes

abruptly in tone, becoming a call to action and transforming the poem into a treatise considering the relative merits of the primacy of individual faith, as the Protestant Reformation proposed, as opposed to the Catholic and Anglican stress on the primacy of good works, bolstered by faith. Archbishop Laud led the latter faction, advocating both love and social works, to animate charity by redeeming "virtue to action." Crashaw ends this poem with an atypically sarcastic comment, that the definition of a Protestant is simply a person who hates the pope. This movement toward a return to Catholic ways marks the biographical path of Crashaw's life and testifies to his poetry as indeed the literary and the spiritual document of an extraordinary Englishman.

Sandra K. Fischer

Further Reading

Bertonasco, Marc F. *Crashaw and the Baroque*. Tuscaloosa: University of Alabama Press, 1971. Considers meditative exercises and the baroque style. Includes a helpful bibliographical essay surveying twentieth century criticism of Crashaw.

Bloom, Harold, ed. *John Donne and the Metaphysical Poets*. New York: Bloom's Literary Criticism, 2008. Contains criticism written from the seventeenth through twentieth centuries about the work of Crashaw and four other Metaphysical poets.

Low, Anthony. "Richard Crashaw." *The Cambridge Companion to English Poetry, Donne to Marvell*, edited by Thomas N. Corns. New York: Cambridge University Press, 1993. Most of the fourteen essays focus on the work of individual poets, including Low's article about Crashaw. Other essays provide context for these poets' work by discussing politics, religion, gender politics, genre, and tradition in the early seventeenth century.

Parrish, Paul A. *Richard Crashaw*. Boston: Twayne, 1980. One of the best places to begin a study of Crashaw. Surveys Crashaw's life and the historical and cultural context of his poetry, provides close readings of his poems, and includes a thorough bibliography.

Reid, David. *The Metaphysical Poets*. Harlow, England: Longman, 2000. Chapter 3 focuses on Crashaw, discussing his life and his poetry and interpreting his work from the perspective of metaphysical poetry.

Roberts, Lorraine M. "Crashaw's Sacred Voice: 'A Commerce of Contrary Powers.'" In *New Perspectives on the Life and Art of Richard Crashaw*, edited by John R. Roberts. Columbia: University of Missouri Press, 1990. Argues that the sacred poems are not personal or mystical;

instead, Crashaw creates an objectified voice that can witness artistic renderings of religious events.

Roberts, Lorraine M., and John R. Roberts. "Crashavian Criticism: A Brief Interpretive History." In *New Perspectives on the Life and Art of Richard Crashaw*, edited by John R. Roberts. Columbia: University of Missouri Press, 1990. A valuable outline and evaluation of criticism of Crashaw's work, beginning in the seventeenth century. Types of criticism are helpfully grouped together.

Sabine, Maureen. *Feminine Engendered Faith: The Poetry of John Donne and Richard Crashaw*. London: Macmillan Academic and Professional, 1992. Sabine argues that devotion to the Virgin Mary is an important link between the two poets. She analyzes the poems they wrote to and about women to find evidence of their common devotion.

Young, R. V. *Doctrine and Devotion in Seventeenth-Century Poetry: Studies in Donne, Herbert, Crashaw, and Vaughan*. Rochester, N.Y.: D. S. Brewer, 2000. Interprets the poetry of Crashaw and the other writers from the perspective of continental Catholic devotional literature and theology, arguing that these British poets' work is not rigidly Protestant.

The Stone Angel

Author: Margaret Laurence (1926-1987)
First published: 1964
Type of work: Novel
Type of plot: Psychological realism
Time of plot: 1870's to early 1960's
Locale: Manawaka, Vancouver, and Shadow Point, Canada

Principal characters:
HAGAR SHIPLEY, a ninety-year-old woman
BRAMPTON SHIPLEY, her husband, an unsuccessful farmer
MARVIN SHIPLEY, their older son, a paint salesperson
JOHN SHIPLEY, their younger son, an alcoholic and a wastrel
DORIS SHIPLEY, Marvin's wife and Hagar's primary caretaker
ARLENE SIMMONS, the woman John wants to marry
JASON CURRIE, Hagar's father, a prosperous merchant
MATTHEW CURRIE, his older son
DANIEL CURRIE, Jason's younger son
LOTTIE DRIESER SIMMONS, Arlene's mother

The Story:

Ninety-year-old Hagar Shipley describes the imposing marble angel that her father had erected to mark her mother's grave; she recalls visiting the cemetery as a child. Hagar still has two pleasures: smoking cigarettes and annoying her son, Marvin (Marv), and his wife, Doris, who live with Hagar. Often, too, Hagar revisits the past.

Hagar reminisces about being six years old. She is proud to be the daughter of Jason Currie, a Manawaka merchant who favors Hagar because she is more like him than are her two older brothers, Matthew (Matt) and Daniel (Dan). At school, Hagar's best friend is the doctor's daughter, and she looks down on Telford Simmons, the undertaker's son, and on Lottie Drieser, a poor, illegitimate child. One winter, Dan falls into the river and becomes desperately ill. Hagar refuses to put on a shawl and sit by Dan and pretend to be his mother.

Instead, Matt does so, and he sits with his brother until he dies.

The elderly Hagar falls again. At tea, Marv broaches the subject of selling the house, but Hagar points out angrily that the house is hers, not theirs. To mollify Doris, Hagar agrees to a visit from her minister, Mr. Troy. When Mr. Troy calls, Hagar mentions that though her father had died a rich man, he left her nothing. She remembers being sent by him to finishing school in Toronto and then being kept by him from teaching. Hagar had begun to see Brampton (Bram) Shipley, whom even Lottie calls common. When Hagar's father points out that Bram is a nobody, Hagar marries him anyway and moves out to his farm. Her father never communicates with her again.

After finding a newspaper with a marked advertisement

for Silverthreads, a nursing home, Hagar again announces that she will not move from her home. She remembers hearing of her brother, Matt's, death from influenza. She also recalls being so embarrassed by Bram's vulgarity that she will no longer go into Manawaka with him. Marv and Doris keep insisting that the nursing home is an ideal solution for their problems, but Hagar is too busy remembering the pleasures of lovemaking to pay much attention to the two.

While she waits to see her doctor, Hagar remembers having sympathized with Bram after he had lost his favorite horse. In the evening, Marv and Doris take Hagar to visit Silverthreads, and Hagar relives the birth of Marv, the son she never really loved. She undergoes a battery of tests, but Marv is secretive about the results. Hagar then remembers John's birth, his wildness as a child, and her hopes for him. She also recalls being so poor that she had to peddle eggs in Manawaka and sell her prized possessions to Lottie, whose husband, Telford, is now a bank manager.

After Hagar learns from Marv that she is to enter the nursing home in a week, she decides to run away. She remembers having run away to Vancouver with John. This time, she will go to Shadow Point, a quiet place on the sea. After cashing her pension check, she takes two different buses and finally arrives at Shadow Point, where, with some snacks she has bought, she makes her way down some stairs and moves into a deserted house. She thinks about her days working as a housekeeper for Mr. Oatley and about John lying to her about having friends and later pretending to be Mr. Oatley's nephew.

Hagar is cold, afraid, and confused at Shadow Point. She remembers losing her savings in the stock-market crash and John returning to the farm. She remembers hearing that Bram had been dying. Hagar had dutifully returned to her husband, who could no longer recognize her. She discovered that under the influence of Lottie's daughter, Arlene, John had cut down his drinking. After Bram died, Hagar had him buried in the Currie family plot.

The summer after Bram's death, Hagar had returned to the farm. After learning that John and Arlene, though both unemployed, plan to marry, Hagar persuades Lottie to send Arlene away.

At Shadow Point, realizing that she cannot climb back to the house after falling once again, Hagar moves into the nearby cannery. There she meets Murray Lees, an insurance salesperson, who tells her about the death of his young son in a house fire, prompting Hagar to tell him about the death of her son, John. After having learned that Arlene was leaving him, John had gotten drunk and driven onto a railroad trestle. The car had been hit by a train, killing both John and Arlene.

Hagar then had returned to Vancouver, and with an inheritance from Mr. Oatley, she had bought her house.

Lees covers Hagar with his coat, and she falls asleep. When she wakes up, Marv and Doris are with her. Marv tells his mother what her X rays reveal and then takes her to the hospital. She is her usual defiant self, infuriating the nurses. To her surprise, however, she finds herself making friends with the other patients. Hagar gives Doris a sapphire ring for her granddaughter, Tina, and when her grandson, Steven, comes to visit, she tells him that he has the good looks of his grandfather Shipley. Hagar even tells Marv that he has been a better son than John, trusting that she will be forgiven for the lie. In one last triumphant act, Hagar snatches a drink being held by Doris, and then dies.

Critical Evaluation:

Margaret Laurence published three books before *The Stone Angel*, all three set in Africa; *The Stone Angel* is the first of her works set in Canada. This novel was followed by three more and a collection of fiction, also set in and around Manawaka, a fictional place based on the real town of Neepawa, where Laurence's family had long been established and where the author herself lived as a young child and teenager.

Two of the Manawaka books, *A Jest of God* (1966) and *The Diviners* (1974), won the Governor General's Award for fiction, and *A Jest of God* was adapted for film (*Rachel, Rachel*, 1968). A film version of *The Stone Angel* was released in 2008. Laurence's Manawaka books are considered her highest achievements, works of a writer who is often ranked as the finest Canadian novelist of her generation.

According to the letters quoted by Adele Wiseman in her afterword to *The Stone Angel*, as early as 1957, Laurence had been considering making an old woman the subject of a novel. However, after she began to write the work, she could see that it was hopelessly dull. Four years later, after an obnoxious old lady invaded her imagination, she found herself able to proceed. Laurence said that initially, she simply let her testy character tell her own story. Also, she had finished writing half the novel before realizing its structure and theme.

Laurence's decision about the structure of *The Stone Angel* proved to be brilliant. Instead of making the novel a collection of memories, presented either in a random fashion or in some psychological pattern, she organized it as two narratives, each written in chronological order, with spaces to indicate clearly each movement between the present and the past. Laurence's artistry is also evident in her strong character Hagar Shipley, who dominates the novel. Hagar provides the excitement in what could have been simply a sentimental story about a dying old lady. Her defiance of life and death alone makes her a heroic figure.

Along with her heroic qualities, however, Hagar does have serious flaws. Because she views any opposition as a challenge, she makes some disastrous decisions. As she later comes to realize, Lottie Drieser's denigrating comment about Hagar's future husband, Bram, makes Hagar even more determined to marry him. Moreover, she eventually admits to herself that her capacity for empathy is limited. Even though she knows her brother Dan is dying, she cannot bring herself to sit by him in their dead mother's shawl. Though she knows how much her brother Matt wants to go to college, she makes only a halfhearted attempt to persuade her father to send him; when her father disagrees with her, she quickly drops the subject and waltzes off to Toronto.

As she relives her years with Bram, Hagar moves from remembering how vulgar he had been to focusing on her own deficiencies. She later recalls how often she had criticized him and how seldom she had said anything kind to him. Now she can understand why he is so surprised when she says she is sorry that his favorite horse has died. Remembering Bram's awkward apologies after they had made love, Hagar asks herself why she had never told him how much she enjoyed their nights together. She does, however, eventually display empathy for Murray Lees and for her fellow patients in the hospital, and she even tells her son Marv a charitable lie.

Laurence is too fine an artist to destroy the feisty old woman she has created by making her cower before death or before God, and certainly not before her daughter-in-law Doris. Though at the end of the novel Hagar is no longer as blind or as unfeeling as the stone angel marking her mother's grave, she dies heroically, holding her own glass.

Rosemary M. Canfield Reisman

Further Reading

Coger, Greta M. K. McCormick, ed. *New Perspectives on Margaret Laurence: Poetic Narrative, Multiculturalism, and Feminism.* Westport, Conn.: Greenwood Press, 1996. Eighteen original essays, predominantly by American writers, covering topics thought to be overlooked. In a group of essays on the topic "Language, Theme, and Image," the techniques of poetic analysis are applied to Laurence's highly poetic prose.

Comeau, Paul. *Margaret Laurence's Epic Imagination.* Edmonton: University of Alberta Press, 2005. Demonstrates how Laurence was influenced by the great epics of the past in developing her own fiction. *The Stone Angel* is cited as one of the works in which she utilizes the epic format for her story and focuses on the epic qualities of her heroine.

DeFalco, Amelia. "'And then—': Narrative Identity and Uncanny Aging in *The Stone Angel.*" *Canadian Literature* 198 (Autumn, 2008): 75-89. Discusses various theories about how people search for their identities through time, focusing especially on "late-life review," the process dramatized in *The Stone Angel.*

King, James. *The Life of Margaret Laurence.* 1997. Reprint. Toronto, Ont.: Random House Canada, 2002. This biography presents a compassionate account of the events of Laurence's life and discusses how these events and the author's personality influenced her fiction. Includes bibliographical references and an index.

Powers, Lyall. *Alien Heart: The Life and Work of Margaret Laurence.* East Lansing: Michigan State University Press, 2003. In a scholarly but highly readable work, a lifelong friend of Laurence applies her personal knowledge of the author to an analysis of her fiction. Includes a bibliography and an index.

Stoval, Nora Foster. *Divining Margaret Laurence: A Study of Her Complete Writings.* Montreal: McGill-Queen's University Press, 2008. The first comprehensive study of all Laurence's writings, including a manuscript that was left unfinished at her death. An invaluable addition to Laurence criticism. Includes bibliographical references and an index.

Wiseman, Adele. "Afterword." In *Margaret Laurence: "The Stone Angel."* Toronto, Ont.: McClelland & Stewart, 1988. A close friend of Laurence recalls her conversations with Laurence about the possibility of writing a novel about an elderly woman. Quotes letters in which Laurence describes the genesis of *The Stone Angel.*

Woodcock, George. *Introducing Margaret Laurence's "The Stone Angel": A Reader's Guide.* Toronto, Ont.: ECS Press, 1989. Written by one of Canada's most respected critics, this short work is an ideal starting point for the study of Laurence's novel. Includes bibliographical references.

Xiques, Donez. *Margaret Laurence: The Making of a Writer.* Toronto, Ont.: Dundurn Press, 2005. A thoroughly researched account of the first thirty-eight years of Laurence's life, when she had been serving the literary apprenticeship that ended with the publication of *The Stone Angel.* Includes a bibliography and an index.

The Stone Diaries

Author: Carol Shields (1935-2003)
First published: 1993
Type of work: Novel
Type of plot: Narrative
Time of plot: 1905 to the early 1990's
Locale: Tyndall, Winnipeg, and Ottawa, Canada;
   Bloomington, Indiana; Sarasota, Florida

Principal characters:
DAISY GOODWILL FLETT, a writer
CUYLER GOODWILL, her father
BARKER FLETT, her husband
CLARENTINE BARKER FLETT, Barker's mother
MAGNUS FLETT, Clarentine's husband
MERCY STONE GOODWILL, Daisy's mother
JAY DUDLEY, a newspaper editor, and Daisy's boss

The Story:

Daisy Goodwill is born to Mercy Stone Goodwill, a large woman who had not realized she was pregnant until she was giving birth. Mercy dies in childbirth, and her devastated husband, Cuyler, leaves Daisy in the care of a neighbor, Clarentine Flett.

Clarentine soon leaves her husband and moves with Daisy to Winnipeg, where the two live with Clarentine's botanist son, Barker. Clarentine begins a flower business. Cuyler remains in Tyndall, building a massive stone monument to his late wife; the monument is known as the Goodwill Tower. People come from all over to view it, not realizing that it actually obscures Mercy's headstone.

Daisy is now eleven years old. After surviving a bout of measles followed by pneumonia, her guardian, Clarentine, dies in an accident. Cuyler, thanks to the attention he received from the Goodwill Tower, has gotten a lucrative job offer in Bloomington, Indiana. He comes to Tyndall to claim Daisy.

Eleven years later, Daisy is engaged to be married. Her fiancé is an alcoholic who dies on their honeymoon, leaving the marriage unconsummated. Magnus Flett, Barker's father, has been so affected by his wife's abandonment that he returns to his home on the Orkney Islands and memorizes his wife's copy of Charlotte Brontë's novel *Jane Eyre*. After Daisy's first husband dies, she spends the next nine years living at home with her father, who is now remarried. Thanks to some money she receives from the proceeds of Clarentine's business, Daisy is able to take a two-week vacation to Niagara Falls and Ontario. While in Ottawa, she meets Barker, and the two quickly get married.

Eleven years later, Daisy is the mother of three children, two girls and a boy. Barker is nearly sixty-five years old and is about to retire. Daisy explains sex to her eldest daughter, and deals with an unwelcome visit from Barker's niece and from her old friend, Fraidy Hoyt. Daisy's father, who has remarried, is building a new stone pyramid at his home in Bloomington. Alongside the pyramid, he buries his first

wife's wedding ring, something he had promised Daisy he would do. Daisy feels this slight bitterly because she does not own anything that had belonged to her mother.

Daisy's love of gardening helps her through Barker's death. She gets a job as the writer of the column "Mrs. Green Thumb" in the *Ottawa Recorder*. Daisy enters into a relationship with her editor, Jay Dudley, who then panics over the relationship and fires her over the phone. She loses her column, leading to a period of depression for Daisy. Her children, her niece, Fraidy, Jay, and others try to figure out why she is depressed, and they come up with many theories.

Twelve years later, in 1977, Daisy has shaken off her major depression. She lives in Sarasota, Florida. She accompanies her grandniece, Victoria, on a trip to the Orkney Islands, where she looks up the 115-year-old Magnus Flett, Clarentine's surviving husband. Magnus is so old and senile that Daisy feels happy and young in comparison, and she lives eight more happy years playing bridge and gardening in Florida. Illness eventually overtakes Daisy, however, and she can no longer live on her own and must settle into a nursing home.

At her death sometime in the 1990's, Daisy had been thinking about her life. Remembering snippets of family conversations, her bridal lingerie, and old recipes, her final thoughts are that she is not at peace with her life.

Critical Evaluation:

The question of the narrator or narrators in *The Stone Diaries* is an important one. Who is telling Daisy's story? Is it Daisy, or someone else, or both? As Penelope Fitzgerald notes in a 1993 review of *The Stone Diaries*, the novel is, "among other things, about the limitations of autobiography." Throughout the work, Carol Shields makes use of ephemera such as photographs, letters, diary entries, a detailed family tree, and newspaper clippings to tell Daisy's story; she also uses first- and third-person narrative.

Fitzgerald is just one of many critics to note that the novel, through its structure, comments on the blurring of autobiography and fiction. In the story, Daisy tells of things that she could not possibly know, such as her mother's thoughts and feelings in the moments leading up to Daisy's birth, and her father's dying thoughts fifty years later.

Although parts of the novel read like a standard autobiography—Daisy's life is told from birth to death, but with significant gaps—it differs in that her story is told not from her point of view alone. After Daisy shares the events leading up to her birth, the story switches to third-person narration; this narrative change and the telling of Daisy's story through the people around her lead to questions about the level of control people have of their own life stories—does anyone really know anyone else?

Daisy seems to disappear many times in the story, as other characters take on a more prominent role; two examples are the stories of Magnus Flett and of her father's building of the Goodwill Tower. Even when the narrative deals directly with Daisy's life—points in the text where her voice would be expected, such as the descriptions of personal letters—her voice is not heard. In fact, none of her personal letters has been kept. Aside from points in the novel where Daisy is the first-person narrator, her voice is absent, although it can be argued that Daisy's voice comes through in the third-person narration. In the section of the novel showing photographs of Daisy's family and friends (a similar feature in most autobiographies and biographies), Daisy's photograph is not included. The only clues to what she looks like come from others' descriptions of her at various points in the novel.

Daisy's tendency to be hidden begins from the time of her birth; her mother had no idea she was pregnant with her. Daisy is then almost immediately taken to Winnipeg by Clarentine Flett and does not see her father for eleven years. The question of the identity of the third-person narrator reemerges: If it is Daisy, why does she choose to imagine such stories for these people? In some ways, even as readers are getting an incomplete and variously biased account of Daisy through the letters and theories of others, readers are also getting an unreliable account of key characters from Daisy's narration. For example, although Daisy's mother is obese, the photo included of her shows that she is not morbidly so, as Daisy describes her. The third-person narrator makes note of Daisy's inadequate description: "Maybe now is the time to tell you that Daisy Goodwill has a little trouble with getting things straight; with the truth, that is."

The narrator goes on to note that Daisy's tendency to exaggerate can be seen in her reminiscences of her childhood and especially of her first mother-in-law, Mrs. Hoad. However, the narrator also notes that as the teller of her story,

Daisy has the power to do as she pleases: "Still, hers is the only account there is, written on air, written with imagination's invisible ink."

In interviews, Shields, who won the 1995 Pulitzer Prize in fiction for the novel, noted that she had always had a strong interest in biography. Having studied biographer Susanna Moodie in graduate school, she incorporates elements of biography and autobiography in her own fictional works. In 1996, Shields shared a part of her fascination with personal narratives: "You've always got an unreliable narrator, so much gets enhanced, so much gets erased, so much has to be imagined." Creating one's own story is, in the end, not always a job for the person attempting to tell her life story—in this case, the protagonist of *The Stone Diaries*, Daisy; the impressions of others also make up much of a person's life. As Shields notes, Daisy

continues to revise herself . . . and that's an issue that autobiography raises: how much can we alter, revise, subtract? She's made up of all these people's impressions, so her real identity is a big question mark in her head.

In the end, *The Stone Diaries* is the story of an incomplete and frustrating attempt by a woman trying to reconstruct her long life. Daisy's final lucid thought, "I am not at peace," shows her frustrations in trying to find a way to share her life story. She finds only "the deep, shared common distress of men and women, and how little, finally, they are allowed to say."

Julie Elliott

Further Reading

Atwood, Margaret. "A Soap Bubble Floating over the Void." *Virginia Quarterly Review* 81, no. 1 (Winter, 2005): 139-142. A tribute to Shields by Canadian novelist Atwood that characterizes her as intelligent, witty, and observant, a writer equally capable of creating images of intense joy and images of despair.

Bell, Karen. "Carol Shields: All These Years Later, Still Digging." *Performing Arts and Entertainment in Canada* 31, no. 3 (Winter, 1998): 4-7. This interview with Shields provides an overview of her works and reveals her interest in strong narratives in fiction.

Fitzgerald, Penelope. "Sunny Side Up." *London Review of Books*, September 9, 1993. A good introductory overview, in which Fitzgerald examines *The Stone Diaries* and its themes. A brief, readable article.

Mellor, Winifred M. "'The Simple Container of Our Existence': Narrative Ambiguity in Carol Shields's *The Stone Diaries*." *Studies in Canadian Literature* 20, no. 2 (March, 1996): 96-110. Mellor examines themes of identity, narration, and autobiography in the novel, including the use of letters and other forms of female biography as a means of expression.

Weese, Katherine. "The 'Invisible Woman': Narrative Strategies in *The Stone Diaries*." *Journal of Narrative Theory* 36, no. 1 (Winter, 2006): 90-120. Applies feminist theories to the complex narrative techniques used in *The Stone Diaries* to reveal a main character who is simultaneously central to and distant from her own story.

Roy, Wendy. "Autobiography as Critical Practice in *The Stone Diaries*." In *Carol Shields, Narrative Hunger, and the Possibilities of Fiction*, edited by Edward Eden and Dee Goertz. Toronto, Ont.: University of Toronto Press, 2003. Examines the argument that the novel is a commentary on autobiographies, as other critics have noted, but specifically on the genre of women's "life writing," another term for autobiography or memoir.

Werlock, Abby. *Carol Shields's "The Stone Diaries": A Reader's Guide*. New York: Continuum, 2001. Provides an excellent overview of the novel, its characters, and its setting. Also includes critical responses, a biography, lengthy quotations from an interview with Shields, and a list of further introductory readings.

The Stones of Venice

Author: John Ruskin (1819-1900)
First published: 1851-1853
Type of work: Art history

The Stones of Venice has been called not only a great work of scholarship but also a great work of art. It is not merely a catalog of architectural accomplishments; it is a work of cultural history and a commentary on human character. For John Ruskin, the relationship between a nation's buildings and its morality were inseparable, and his three-volume treatise on the edifices of Venice, Italy, ranges widely to tell the story of the city he sees as the midpoint, both literally and figuratively, between the cultures of East and West. In *The Stones of Venice*, Ruskin praises the accomplishments not only of the great leaders of Venice, but also of the countless numbers of common workers who toiled with skill, patience, and reverence on the great Gothic structures of medieval Europe.

For Ruskin, the polish of the Renaissance was anathema. The exquisite finish of Renaissance architecture values perfection in a limited sphere, and slavish copying of idealized form counts more than attempts to re-create human emotions in art. By contrast, the workers who constructed Gothic buildings were given greater freedom to express themselves. Although their work may appear rougher, even unfinished, it is the consequence of each person's struggle to make something unique; the value of the work lies in the effort of the worker, not in the perfection of the work itself. In Ruskin's view, Renaissance artisans built to please others and to gain glory for themselves, but Gothic workers built to celebrate life and praise God. Small wonder that, for Ruskin, the persistence of Renaissance values indicated a decline in moral stature for humankind.

Ruskin stands with his contemporary, the architect A. W. Pugin, as one of the premier exponents of the Gothic movement of the time. His influence on Victorian sensibility should not be underestimated. In addition to supporting the movement that led to the construction of a number of nineteenth century buildings in the Gothic style, his writings on the Gothic, particularly his celebration of Gothic qualities in *The Stones of Venice* and his praise of painters and sculptors of the medieval and early Renaissance periods, had a significant impact on a younger generation of artists who eventually dubbed themselves Pre-Raphaelites. Poets and painters such as Dante Gabriel Rossetti, William Holman Hunt, and William Morris found Ruskin's works inspirational. Additionally, the tenets of architecture expressed so gracefully and in such detail in *The Stones of Venice* were among the first to make an impression on one of the most important architects of the twentieth century, Frank Lloyd Wright. *The Stones of Venice* was the first book on architecture that Wright read, and its influence can be seen not only in his designs but, more important, in his constant assertion of the value of architecture in reflecting the aspirations of a society.

In the three volumes of *The Stones of Venice*, Ruskin

traces the development, apex, and decline of three architectural expressions: Byzantine, Gothic, and Renaissance. Ruskin relates their growth and deterioration to the rise and fall of the Venetian state. He shows that the virtue and piety that marked Venice at its flourishing found expression in Gothic architecture and that as this faith declined, Venice's corruption was expressed in Renaissance architecture. The architecture expressed not only the morality of the state but also the morality of the individual architect and common workers who designed the buildings and did the labor. Ruskin believes that the artistic expression of any nation is clear and direct evidence of its moral and spiritual condition; thus, when Ruskin states that since the fading of the Gothic tradition there has been no architectural growth in all of Europe, he is also commenting on the spiritual poverty of his own time.

In the first volume, *The Foundations*, Ruskin traces the history of Venice. For nine hundred years the Venetians had struggled to bring power and order out of anarchy. They succeeded in doing so largely because they possessed a childlike religious spirit that dignified even their business transactions and brought them peace, energy, and, whenever necessary, heroes. The geographical location of the city and the nature of its maritime activities were crucial. In Venice, the three preeminent architectures of the world—Roman, Lombardic, and Arabian, each expressing a different religious view— flourished separately and blended into one another. For this reason, Ruskin calls the Ducal Palace the central building of the world.

According to Ruskin, to appreciate or judge any architecture, one must first establish canons of judgment. To do so, one must understand the basic requirements and structure of any building. When speaking of buildings, parts of buildings, or decorations, Ruskin consistently uses words such as moral, immoral, virtuous, and corrupt, terms that normally are applied to people or actions. His descriptions are such that he makes buildings come alive, as indeed they were to him, visible manifestations of the souls of their builders. As a result he speaks of the three virtues required of a building as being: to act well, or do properly what was intended; to speak well, that is, record fact, feelings, and history; to look well, presenting a pleasing appearance. He feels that the second virtue is an individual matter, depending on the character of the observer and his or her mood, but that the first and third are matters that can be weighed and judged according to a known standard. People should admire in architectural construction an admirable human intelligence whose work may be imperfect, but whose feelings are deep and true and honest and show delight in God's work.

Ruskin then describes brilliantly the construction of the parts of a building—foundation, wall veil, cornice, roof, and apertures—and explains with great clarity not only how a part is constructed but also, more important, why. The why involves not only logical, practical considerations, but geographical, moral, and spiritual ones as well; all these observations testify to the wide scope of Ruskin's perception and historical sense. After describing the practical construction of a building, he considers the decoration. To judge decoration, one must determine the rightness of the material in terms of function and treatment and its placement with regard to the whole. Ornament should not take for its subject human work, such as figures taken from agriculture, sailing, or manufacture, for that is too self-centered. Ornament should express delight in God's work; thus, architects may use the abstract lines in nature, moving from the lower to the higher through the whole range of systematized inorganic and organic forms: earth, water, fire, air, animal organisms, and humanity. An ornament should be so fitted to its place and service that if it were lifted out and placed elsewhere, it would not be satisfactory or complete. The architect must govern the ornament and design it so that workers can accomplish the architect's intention. It is the architect's duty not to try to improve upon nature but to explain it and express his or her own soul.

In the second volume, *Sea-Stories*, Ruskin describes the Byzantine period and the Gothic, and he concludes with a careful, elaborate detailing of the Ducal Palace. He describes three churches, Torcello, Murano, and St. Marks. Torcello lies to the northeast of Venice, in the marshes. It was an early church built by people fleeing their pillaged homeland. Thus it was built in haste but with effective simplicity, expressive, Ruskin feels, of the great faith they placed in God. It admits an unusual amount of sun and light for such a building, a psychological need, Ruskin points out, in a people fleeing the darkness of oppression. The pulpit is built with simplicity but is sturdy and functional, and Ruskin ponders the effect of the pulpit on congregations. Such a pulpit inspires confidence, whereas many modern pulpits distract the congregations by being too ornate or raising fears that the entire structure will soon collapse.

Murano, built in the tenth century, furnishes a particularly fine study in proportion and the use of color. The apse is heptagonal on the outside and constructed with mathematical precision. Inside, the placement of the shafts with respect to one another, to the nave and the aisles, reflects subtle, true harmony.

St. Marks was constructed in the Byzantine style during the eleventh century and underwent Gothic additions during the fourteenth century. Its peculiarity is adroit incrustation, brick covered with precious materials. This practice saved materials, expense, and weight, and it required that cutting must be shallow, so that the ornamentation had to be done with care and simplicity rather than with crude force. Also, shallow design permitted delicate shading of color. Beauty, Ruskin believes, is a legitimate offering to God, and the entirety of St. Marks, with its rich colors, mosaics, paintings, and inscriptions, is one great book of Common Prayer, a poor person's Bible. Color is one of God's most divine gifts and one that the most thoughtful value highly; thus, Venice was most colorful during the time of its early, earnest religion. Ruskin says that no style of architecture can be exclusively ecclesiastical. Wherever Christian church architecture has been good and lovely, it has been the perfect development of the common dwelling-house architecture of the period. A style fit for a church, he felt, is no less fit for a dwelling, and no form was ever brought to perfection where it was not used for both purposes. Once St. Marks has been judged as a work of art, it must be judged for its fitness as a place of worship. If a church is too beautiful, it will divert the attention of intelligent persons from religion to admiration. Thus, Ruskin believed that effective religious art lies between barbarous idol-fashioning on one side and magnificent craftsmanship on the other.

Ruskin lists six moral elements of the Gothic style: savageness or rudeness, love of nature, love of change, disturbed imagination, obstinacy, and generosity. Gothic is the most rational of forms in that it can fit itself to all services; it is also restless, unquiet, tender, and reverent. Its most striking outward feature is the pointed arch. The Ducal Palace, originally Byzantine, was superseded by Gothic, begun in 1301, and later united with Renaissance in 1423, the year in which Venice and its architecture began to decline.

In the third volume, *The Fall*, Ruskin discusses the moral nature of the central Renaissance, which is corrupt, its two main immoral elements being pride and infidelity. It is a cold, inhuman form. It is highly trained and erudite and meant only for the act of worship, not, as was the Gothic, for humanity or for the praise of God. Ruskin stresses again forcefully his belief that a fault in feeling induces a fault in style. It was a self-centered, pleasure-seeking, and hypocritical age in that it named one god but dreamed about pagan gods, meanwhile dreading none.

Ruskin deplored machinelike work. He thought one should never encourage the production of anything in which invention has no major share. Imitation or copying should be done only for the sake of preservation. He believed that a truly religious painter or architect would more often than not

be rude and simple. The work of such an artist, Ruskin argues, should not be scorned for lack of perfection; the demand for perfection implies a complete misunderstanding of the ends of art. No one, says Ruskin, ever stops until one has reached a point of failure, and so imperfection is essential; it is a sign of life, of change and progress. One of the chief elements of power in all good architecture is the acceptance of rude and uncultivated energy in the workers. Ruskin believed that many people possess, even unsuspected by themselves, talent that is wasted from lack of use. Ruskin hoped, through the work of common people, for a rebirth of true and expressive art throughout Europe.

Revised by Laurence W. Mazzeno

Further Reading

Cate, George Allan. *John Ruskin: A Reference Guide—A Selective Guide to Significant and Representative Works About Him*. Boston: G. K. Hall, 1988. Surveys Ruskin's literary career and responses to his work. The bibliography covers the years 1843 to 1987, with detailed annotations.

Connelly, Frances S. "*The Stones of Venice*: John Ruskin's Grotesque History of Art." In *Modern Art and the Grotesque*, edited by Frances S. Connelly. New York: Cambridge University Press, 2003. Focuses on elements of the grotesque in Ruskin's work; examines how concepts of the grotesque influenced the history, theory, and practice of nineteenth and twentieth century art by encouraging artists to push beyond established boundaries and challenge the status quo.

Conner, Patrick. *Savage Ruskin*. Detroit, Mich.: Wayne State University Press, 1979. Examines Ruskin's art criticism, its nature and significance, and its flaws and virtues. Analysis of *The Stones of Venice* concludes that the second volume of the work is Ruskin's masterpiece. Includes a helpful bibliography listing pertinent texts from the eighteenth century to the 1970's.

Kirchhoff, Frederick. *John Ruskin*. Boston: Twayne, 1984. Detailed analysis of *The Stones of Venice*. Includes a selected bibliography with brief annotations.

Read, Richard. *Ruskin in Perspective: Contemporary Essays*, edited by Carmen Casaliggi and Paul March-Russell. Newcastle, England: Cambridge Scholars, 2007. Includes two discussions of *The Stones of Venice*: "Anglo-Italian Contrasts in *The Stones of Venice*" by Richard Read and "Lessons of Multiple Perspective: Ruskin, Turner, and the Inspiration of Venice" by Carmen Casaliggi.

Rosenberg, John D. *The Darkening Glass: A Portrait of Ruskin's Genius*. 1961. New ed. New York: Columbia University Press, 1986. An influential biography of Ruskin that gives considerable attention to defining the character of *The Stones of Venice* and its thesis.

_____, ed. *The Genius of John Ruskin: Selections from His Writings*. 1963. New ed. Charlottesville: University Press of Virginia, 2000. Presents a number of Ruskin's works, including excerpts from *The Stones of Venice*. Each section introduction illustrates how his works relate to each other and to the development of Ruskin's thought. In-

cludes a bibliography, updated by the editor, and a new foreword.

Siegel, Jonah. "Vast Knowledge/Narrow Space: *The Stones of Venice*." In *Desire and Excess: The Nineteenth-Century Culture of Art*. Princeton, N.J.: Princeton University Press, 2000. Discusses Ruskin's contributions to the aesthetic developments of the nineteenth century. The book as a whole examines the rise of new ideas about art and artists that arose in the nineteenth century, along with the emergence of professional art critics.

The Story of an African Farm

Author: Olive Schreiner (1855-1920)
First published: 1883
Type of work: Novel
Type of plot: Social realism
Time of plot: 1880's
Locale: South Africa

Principal characters:
TANT' SANNIE, a Boer farm woman
LYNDALL, her stepdaughter
EM, Lyndall's cousin
WALDO, the son of a German overseer
BONAPARTE BLENKINS, a hypocrite
GREGORY ROSE, a young Englishman

The Story:

Shortly before the Englishman dies, he marries Tant' Sannie, so that there will be someone to take care of his farm and his motherless daughter, Lyndall. Tant' Sannie, a heavy, slow, and simple Boer woman, takes over the farm and the care of Lyndall and her cousin, Em. Most of the hard work is done by an old German, who lives with his young son in a small house nearby. The boy, Waldo, watches over the sheep and helps his father take charge of the black natives who do the heaviest work.

The farm lies in a dreary flat plain of red sand sparsely dotted with pale bushes. The sun always glitters in a blinding way on the zinc roofs of the buildings and on the stone walls of the enclosures for the animals. Life is monotonous and deadly. Tant' Sannie sits in the farmhouse drinking coffee; the children play in a halfhearted way; young Waldo does his chores; and the German goes about seeing that things are as they should be.

Tant' Sannie is asked by the Englishman to see that the two girls are educated, but she, believing only in the Bible, pays no attention to their demands for books. The two girls and Waldo find some old histories and study them when they can. Lyndall learns rapidly, for she is a quick, serious girl,

fascinated especially by the story of Napoleon. Em is more quiet and reserved. Waldo is the strangest of the three. His father is deeply devout, with an innocent faith in the goodness of man and the mercy of God. He fills the boy's head with frightening and overpowering ideas.

One day a visitor comes to the farm and asks for a night's lodging. He introduces himself as Bonaparte Blenkins. Tant' Sannie will have nothing to do with him, because he is English-speaking. The old German intercedes for the visitor, however, and finally wins Tant' Sannie's grudging permission for him to spend the night. The German cannot bear to pass up an opportunity to practice Christian charity.

Blenkins soon wins the German over completely with his fantastic tales of adventure and travel, and he even conquers Tant' Sannie by the wonderful way he reads and preaches the service on Sunday. The children, however, are not fooled. Lyndall knows that the man is lying when he talks and that his religion is all hypocrisy. Nevertheless, Blenkins is soon installed on the farm as tutor to the children. After a few days, Lyndall walks out of class and refuses to return.

Blenkins slowly gains Tant' Sannie's esteem, until he feels that it is safe to try to get rid of the German and take over his job. With a trumped-up charge, he accuses the overseer to his mistress and stands by happily as the old German is ordered off the farm. Shocked the more deeply because of the support he gave Blenkins, the German goes to his house to pack up and leave. It is not in his nature to argue or to fight for his rights; what God sends must be accepted. In his grief he dies that night.

Blenkins takes over the farm. Like his namesake, he loves power and takes advantage of his new position. He orders Waldo about, beats him, and destroys the model for a sheep-shearing machine the boy made. None of these matters makes any impression on Tant' Sannie. She thinks that Blenkins has a wonderful sense of humor, and daily he grows more and more valuable to her. She hopes someday to be his wife.

A visit by one of Tant' Sannie's nieces disillusions her. The niece is young, only a little overweight, and wealthy. One day Tant' Sannie climbs up to the loft to see if everything there is neat, and she lets her maid take the ladder away. While she is there, Blenkins comes into the room below with the niece and begins to make love to her. Furious at Blenkins's deception, Tant' Sannie drops a barrel of salt meat on his head, almost knocking him out, and drenching him with pickle water. His stay on the farm is over.

When the children grow up, Lyndall has her way about going to the city to work and to study. Waldo begins to doubt the God he so terribly feared in his childhood, and Em grows to attractive, if not beautiful, womanhood. Tant' Sannie rents part of the farm to a young Englishman named Gregory Rose, who soon falls in love with Em. It is the first time anyone pays much attention to the girl, and she is enraptured at the prospect of marriage. Tant' Sannie thinks she herself might as well marry again, and she sends out word to the surrounding farms that she is looking for a husband.

Waldo eagerly awaits Lyndall's return from the city. He wants to know what she discovered about the world and to tell her of his own problems. He learned wood carving. One day, while he was watching the sheep, a stranger approached to talk with him. After looking at one of Waldo's carvings, the traveler told the boy a story of a man who searched for truth but found merely a creed until, just before his death, he caught a glimpse of his goal. The meeting was short but unforgettable. Waldo wants to go out into the world, to find the man again, to learn more about the search for truth.

When Lyndall returns, she is a different person. Waldo finds that he cannot talk with her as he did before. She learns the problems a woman faces in the world, and she refuses to be held down by the laws and restrictions that bind her. Neither Em nor Gregory Rose, her fiancé, can understand Lyndall. Gregory dislikes her at first, but he becomes more attracted to her as time passes. At Tant' Sannie's wedding feast—for she finds a widower who wants to marry again—Em discovers that she does not really love Gregory, and she asks him to forget the plans they made.

When Lyndall asks him to marry her—just to give her his name—Gregory consents. It is a long time before he discovers the reason. Lyndall made a friend in the city, a man who wants her to marry him, but she cannot stand the idea of being tied down by legal marriage. She wants freedom, not bondage. She feels that if she can threaten her lover with marriage to another man, she can get what she wants from him. Her plan works. When he receives a letter telling of her plans, he sets out at once to see her. Lyndall meets her friend secretly at the farm and goes away to live with him, but not as his wife.

Since Waldo, too, goes off to seek his way in the world, the farm is quiet for a time. Gregory does not know what to do about Lyndall's disappearance. The longer she is away, the more he feels he loves her. At last he starts out to learn what became of her. As Gregory tracks Lyndall from town to town, he learns the story of a slowly fading love between the two people he is following. In time he finds Lyndall, lying sick in a hotel room, deserted by her lover. She had a child, but it died shortly after birth. Seeing her so weak and sick, Gregory wants to be near her, to care for her. Dressed as a woman, he is hired as Lyndall's nurse. When she dies, he takes her body back to the farm for burial.

One night Em is startled by a knock on the door. Waldo has returned. He traveled much but learned little. Once he saw the stranger who talked to him so wonderfully about truth, but the man, not recognizing him, turned away. The first thing Waldo does is to sit down and begin a letter to Lyndall. When Em learns what he is doing, she tells him that Lyndall is dead.

Gregory still thinks of Lyndall and keeps as his greatest treasure the one letter he received from her, a letter that advised him to marry Em. In time, he asks Em again to be his wife, and she accepts. Waldo knows that Em feels she will have only half a husband, but he also knows that she never learned to hope for much, as he and Lyndall did. Waldo keeps one of Lyndall's dancing shoes in his shirt. He spends much of his time wandering about the farm watching the insects and looking at the flowers. He wants to be like them, to die, to sleep in the same earth with Lyndall. One day, lying in the warm sunshine, he dies.

Critical Evaluation:

The Story of an African Farm is one of the first post-colonial novels in English. Olive Schreiner's South African setting is not just an exotic local-color background. It is inextricable from the novel's significance. Schreiner explores the transplantation of European culture and ideals to a new landscape. In chronicling the personal, spiritual, and intellectual evolution of Lyndall and Waldo from childhood to adulthood, she explores the effect this transplantation has on individuals who, though of European background, have never known Europe itself.

Schreiner has been criticized for seeming to depict a depopulated landscape, for effacing the presence of native Africans from the lands colonized by English and Boers. However, Schreiner, who concerns herself explicitly with issues of racism and colonization in later works, such as "Trooper Peter Halket of Mashonaland," even in *The Story of an African Farm* makes clear how foreign and how estranged from the land the European colonizers feel themselves to be.

Lyndall is perhaps the most beloved character in all of South African literature. Many generations of women, in South Africa and elsewhere, have been named Lyndall after Schreiner's heroine. Although Lyndall derives much of her character and outlook from the environment—Tant' Sannie's ostrich farm in which she spends her youth—her sensibility is always roving; it strives to go outside the bounds of locality and circumstance in which it is constrained. As opposed to the more domesticated Em, Lyndall finds the straitjacketing effects of Victorian definitions of womanhood exacerbated by the cultural impoverishment of her colonial setting. Lyndall knows that the lover she takes is unworthy of her, but she can think of no other option to escape her situation. There is a vast gulf between the level of Lyndall's personal aspirations and the practical steps she can take to fulfill them. That she is never able to return the love of the two men who truly love her, Waldo and Gregory Rose, is an indication of the unfulfilled quality of Lyndall's life. For all her energy and ambition, her character is not able to take root in African soil, to establish itself as a spirit and a presence capable of taking on the dominating circumstances of life in that place and time.

Waldo, weak and sensitive, is in a way even more vulnerable than Lyndall, lacking her drive and willpower. Nevertheless, he has an outlet unavailable to the young girl: his penchant for speculating and philosophizing. Untalented in any aspect of life but the mental one, Waldo is a rare soul, somebody whose mixture of simple belief in God and complex intellectual musings would make him unusual in any setting, but especially that of colonial South Africa. The peak of Waldo's introspection is achieved when he encounters the stranger who tells the story of the man who searches for truth. The feather that is the only material vestige of this search becomes Waldo's symbol. The feather does not represent the truth itself, but rather the small specimen of art or experience that is left when the search for truth inevitably fails to achieve its goal. The feather, however, is enough for the man in the stranger's story, and, inferentially, for Waldo. Art, as represented by Waldo's carvings, has the power to express an otherwise elusive truth.

Despite Waldo's mental strength, he is too weak in character to withstand the devastating blow of Lyndall's early death. The understated scene at the end of the book in which Waldo dies as the chickens go on living in their instinctual way (a death scene so understated that readers often do not immediately understand what has happened) shows that without the spark of Lyndall to animate him, Waldo recedes and yields to the land, not able to sustain the mental and physical energy necessary to keep himself alive. Lyndall's other oddly passive male admirer, Gregory, is similarly lost without Lyndall and unable to help her, despite the enormity of his admiration for her. Gregory's willingness to dress up as a woman in order to comfort Lyndall after her tragic childbirth indicates his willingness to discard Victorian gender stereotypes and to respect the vigor of Lyndall's self-assertion. In casting an androgynous haze over his sexual identity, however, the act implies that Gregory is not strong enough to be the kind of man Lyndall needs as her soulmate.

The other characters in the book are largely foils to the tragically doomed ambition and spirit of Lyndall and Waldo. The spiritual differences between the two main characters and figures such as Tant' Sannie and Em are so vast as to make the situation almost ridiculous. That Tant' Sannie and Em should both be hoodwinked by an opportunistic buffoon such as Bonaparte Blenkins even as Waldo is working out his own inner destiny is almost pathetically incongruous. However, Tant' Sannie and Em do provide a loving and supportive environment for the youngsters to grow up in. In addition, Em's marriage to Gregory at the end of the book is a signal that, despite the deaths of the two main characters, life in the farm will go on and that Lyndall and Waldo will not be forgotten.

In *The Story of an African Farm*, Schreiner combines the philosophical inclinations of a novelist such as George Eliot with the concern about practical issues of women's self-definition raised by novelists of the 1890's such as George Egerton, Mona Caird, and Mary Cholmondeley. Schreiner's book is not, however, only a Victorian woman's novel; it is an exploration of the colonial experience. Without Schreiner, later South African novelists such as Pauline Smith, Sarah Gertrude Millin, and Nadine Gordimer would have lacked a crucial precedent and reference point for their work. Schreiner explores social and cultural issues that are still resonant. That she does this while writing a novel of striking originality and imagination is a tribute to her power as a novelist.

"Critical Evaluation" by Margaret Boe Birns

Further Reading

Berkman, Joyce Avrech. *The Healing Imagination of Olive Schreiner: Beyond South African Colonialism*. Amherst: University of Massachusetts Press, 1989. Stresses Schreiner's humanistic and progressive sociological views and discusses how they are represented in her fiction.

Burdett, Carolyn. *Olive Schreiner and the Progress of Feminism: Evolution, Gender, Empire*. New York: Palgrave, 2001. Analyzes Schreiner's work within the context of political events in South Africa in the 1890's and the English feminist movement of the late nineteenth century.

Chrisman, Laura. "Empire, Race, and Feminism at the Fin de Siècle: The Works of George Egerton and Olive Schreiner." In *Cultural Politics at the Fin de Siècle*, edited by Sally Ledger and Scott McCracken. New York: Cambridge University Press, 1995. Examines Schreiner's work in the light of the New Woman movement of the 1890's and its contributions concerning gender and imperialism.

Clayton, Cherry. *Olive Schreiner*. New York: Twayne, 1997. Examination of Schreiner's life and work, pointing out autobiographical elements in her fiction. Chronicles the development of her feminism and anticolonialism. Analyzes *The Story of an African Farm* and other works of fiction and nonfiction.

First, Ruth, with Ann Scott. *Olive Schreiner*. London: André Deutsch, 1980. Authoritative chronicle of Schreiner's life and times, cowritten by an African National Congress activist, explores the relationship of Schreiner's life to the history of her troubled nation.

Heilman, Ann. "Transitions and Transfigurations: *Dreams* (1890), *The Story of an African Farm* (1883), and *From Man to Man* (1926)." In *New Woman Strategies: Sarah Grand, Olive Schreiner, Mona Caird*. New York: Manchester University Press, 2004. Feminist analysis of Schreiner's fiction, describing how her work appropriated, parodied, feminized, and transformed traditional cultural ideas about femininity, allegory, and mythology.

Monsman, Gerald. *Olive Schreiner's Fiction: Landscape and Power*. New Brunswick, N.J.: Rutgers University Press, 1991. Examines Schreiner's art in aesthetic terms, stressing her sensitivity to nature and her philosophical ambitions. Especially useful for interpreting Waldo's aesthetic evolution and the development of Lyndall's character.

Murphy, Patricia. "Dissolving the Boundaries: Temporal Subversion in *The Story of an African Farm*." In *Time Is of the Essence: Temporality, Gender, and the New Woman*. Albany: State University of New York Press, 2001. Focuses on Schreiner's handling of time in the novel, describing how Schreiner adapted Victorian concepts about time to convey anxieties about the appearance of the "New Woman" and other gender issues.

Van Wyk Smith, Malvern, and Don MacLennan, eds. *Olive Schreiner and After: Essays on Southern African Literature in Honour of Guy Butler*. Cape Town, South Africa: D. Philip, 1983. Situates Schreiner in the tradition of white South African writing in English that she was crucial in founding.

The Story of Burnt Njal

Author: Unknown
First transcribed: Njáls Saga, thirteenth century
  (English translation, 1861)
Type of work: Historical saga
Type of plot: Adventure
Time of plot: Tenth century
Locale: Iceland

Principal characters:
NJAL, a man of law
BERGTHORA, his wife
GUNNAR, Njal's friend
HALLGERDA, Gunnar's wife
FLOSI, Njal's enemy

The Story:

Harold Grayfell rules in Norway. Hrut Heriolfsson comes out of Iceland to claim an inheritance, and he sits on the high seat of Gunnhilda, the king's mother. He is handsome and strong. He finds favor with the king as well, so that he claims his inheritance and gets a great store of rich goods while sea roving. Then he sails back to Iceland, but not before Gunnhilda puts a spell on him that he might never have pleasure living with the woman he sets his heart on.

Soon after, Hrut marries Unna, Fiddle Mord's daughter. Things do not go smoothly between Hrut and Unna, and she soon leaves him. When Mord asks at the Thing for her goods to be returned, Hrut offers to fight him instead. Mord refuses and gets great shame by his suit.

Hrut's brother Hauskuld has a fair daughter, Hallgerda, but she is hard-hearted. She marries Thorwald Oswifsson, and he is killed by Thiostolf, her foster father. Then she marries Glum, son of Olof the Hall, and he is murdered. She then sends Thiostolf to Hrut to tell of Glum's death, and Hrut strikes him dead. Fiddle Mord dies, and Unna runs through her goods. Then she asks her kinsman Gunnar Hamondsson to get back her goods from Hrut. Gunnar is the best skilled in arms of all men. His brother's name is Kolskegg.

Njal is Gunnar's friend. They swear nothing should come between them. Njal is so great a lawyer that his match is not to be found. Bergthora is his wife.

Gunnar asks Njal how to get Unna's goods, and Njal advises him to trick Hrut into summoning himself to the Thing where the suit would be tried. There Gunnar challenges Hrut to single combat, but Hauskuld makes Hrut pay the money. There is much ill feeling.

Gunnar and Kolskegg go sea roving and come back with many goods. They ride to the Thing, and there Gunnar sees Hallgerda and asks for her. Njal foretells ill from this but goes to the wedding.

At the wedding Thrain Sigfusson puts away his shrewish wife and asks for Thorgerda, Hallgerda's daughter. So there are two weddings.

Each year Gunnar and Njal have feasts for friendship's sake. Njal has it the year Bergthora insults Hallgerda and Hallgerda asks Gunnar to avenge her. Gunnar refuses and takes her home. Then Hallgerda has Bergthora's thrall killed. Gunnar pays atonement to Njal. Bergthora retaliates, and Njal pays for that death. The women urge their men on until Njal's sons are involved, but Gunnar and Njal keep their friendship.

When Otkell Skarfsson tricks Gunnar into buying a deceitful thrall, Hallgerda sends him to burn Otkell's storehouse. Gunnar offers atonement but refuses Otkell friendship. Then Otkell hurts Gunnar, and Gunnar kills Otkell. This is the beginning of Gunnar's slayings. Njal warns him not to kill more than one man in the same stock or he will invite his death.

Then Starkad, son of Bork the Waxy-toothed Blade, challenges Gunnar to a horse fight. Thorgeir Otkellsson is hurt and wants revenge against Gunnar. Starkad, his son Thorgeir, and Thorgeir Otkellsson try to ambush Gunnar, and Thorgeir

Otkellsson is killed. This is the second man slain in the same stock. Thorgeir Starkadsson swears vengeance. At the Thing the atonement is that Gunnar and Kolskegg are to go away within three years or be slain by the kinsmen of those they killed.

They make plans to go abroad, but as they ride away, Gunnar's horse throws him with his face turned toward home. When he decides not to go, Kolskegg goes alone. Gunnar is outlawed. Njal warns him that Geir the Priest is getting up a band to slay him, and Gunnar asks Njal to see after his son Hogni.

When Geir the Priest and his men come to Gunnar's house, they kill his hound Sam. Sam howls loudly before he dies, so that Gunnar is prepared. Gunnar puts up a long fight and kills two men and wounds sixteen before his enemies pull the roof off his house to get at him.

They build a cairn over Gunnar. Skarphedinn Njalsson and Hogni Gunnarsson see the cairn open, and Gunnar with a merry face sings a song before the cairn closes again. Then Skarphedinn and Hogni kill Starkad and Thorgeir Starkadsson and avenge Gunnar.

Njal's sons then go abroad, and wrongs pile up between them and Thrain Sigfusson in the Orkneys. Kari Solmundsson is with them. When they come back, Skarphedinn kills Thrain. Kettle of the Mark is Thrain's brother but Njal's son-in-law, and so Kettle and Njal make atonement. Njal takes Hauskuld Thrainsson as his foster son. Kari asks for and gets Njal's daughter Helge to wife. Then Flosi Thordsson becomes involved in the feud. He is tall and bold.

There is a change of rulers in Norway. Olaf Tryggvisson makes a change of faith and sends Thangbrand to Iceland to preach Christianity. He does that by challenging any man who speaks against the new faith. At the Thing, Thorgeir of Lightwater challenges the men for the new law, and they all make pledges. Then Njal goes to Flosi to ask his daughter Hildigunna for his foster son Hauskuld. She says she will not be wedded unless they get Hauskuld a priesthood.

Njal tries to get a priesthood for Hauskuld, but no one will sell his. At the Thing that summer, when no one can get his suit settled, Njal says it would be wiser to have a Fifth Court to take over those suits that cannot be finished in the Quarter Courts. Skapti Thorodsson then brings the Fifth Court into law. Njal begs a new priesthood for Hauskuld, and Hildigunna and Hauskuld are married.

Soon after Lyting, Thrain's sister's husband, takes offense at Hauskuld, Njal's baseborn son, and kills him. Rodny, Hauskuld's mother, places it upon Skarphedinn to avenge that death. Skarphedinn and his brothers go after Lyting and his brothers. When Njal's foster son Hauskuld makes atonement for the slaying, Aumund, Hauskuld Njalsson's base-born and blind son, comes to Lyting at the Thing and demands his share. Lyting refuses. When Aumund comes to the door, he turns short around, and his eyes are opened. Then he runs straight to Lyting and kills him with an ax. Aumund turns to go out again, and his eyes are sealed. Njal makes the atonement.

Mord Valgardsson plans to talebear before Njal's sons so that they will kill Hauskuld the Priest. A coolness springs up between Njal's sons and Hauskuld. Finally, Mord with them, Njal's sons slay Hauskuld. Njal says the next deaths will be his and those of his wife and sons.

Hauskuld's death brings his father-in-law Flosi Thordsson much grief and wrath. He gathers together a great band. Skarphedinn seeks help, and they all go to the Thing. There the atonement falls through. Flosi gathers his men for an attack with fire and sword on Njal's sons.

Njal gathers all of his sons in the house, and Flosi's band tries to master them with weapons. When the attackers wound a great many, Flosi takes fire and makes great blazes before the doors. He calls the women out, and Helgi Njalsson tries to escape with them but is killed. Bergthora stays indoors with Njal and Kari's son Thord. The three lie down on the bed with an ox hide over them. Then the fires burn hot and timbers begin to fall. Kari runs along the crossbeams and beats his way out with a burning bench. He is hidden by the smoke as he runs away. Skarphedinn tries to follow but is pinned to the wall, and Grimm falls dead in the fire. After Flosi's men are sure Skarphedinn is dead, they hear him sing a song. When men come to find them, Njal, Thord and Bergthora are not burned, but the ox hide is shriveled.

Flosi dreams that many men will die. Kari sets about getting his men together. They all go to the Thing. All who wish to avenge the burning shout their war cries. Many men are killed before an atonement is reached. Since Kari will not have that atonement cover the burning, there is another award for that. The payment covers all but Thord Karisson. Flosi and his men are to go abroad.

Thorgeir Craggeir, a kinsman, goes along with Kari. They come upon some of Flosi's men and kill them. Then Flosi makes an atonement with Thorgeir, so that Kari will be left alone. Kari says he will take it ill if Thorgeir does not make his peace. He agrees that the burning is avenged but not his son's death. Then Kari goes to the Orkneys and kills more men who set sail out of Iceland until he slays fifteen. His wife dies while he is sea roving.

Then Kari and Flosi make separate pilgrimages south for absolution. When they come home, Kari goes straight to Flosi's house. Flosi springs up and kisses Kari. Then they are fully atoned, and Flosi gives to Kari his brother's daughter Hildigunna. They live there a long time.

Critical Evaluation:

Icelanders defined sagas as the telling over and over of great ancestral feuds and battles; the sagas were often told during long winter nights. The distinction between fact and fiction was not made. Actually, the saga form had a more lofty purpose: to maintain pride in family history and to tell the stories of the ancestral heroic age and of the introduction of Christianity to Iceland. The king's sagas and the family sagas were the most popular. *The Story of Burnt Njal* (also known as *Burnt Njál*) is of the latter form. Some scholars argued up until the 1920's that the work was originally two distinct sagas, Gunnar's saga and Njal's saga. Presently it is considered to be the work of one author because of the cohesion of stylistic form and thematic structure. The saga is differentiated from the epic in that the former is prose. Otherwise there are great similarities between the Njal saga and Homer's epics. Battle scenes, festivals, and games are prevalent in both and delight the reader with their pageantry.

The Story of Burnt Njal is of the late classical period in Icelandic literary history. The romanticism and chivalry are not evident in the more skeletal earlier sagas. Njal's role of hero is that of a more ordinary man than known in the Greek epics. His initial naïveté over the deteriorating social situation and the misunderstood peace offering to Flosi conspire to cause Njal's death. He is a victim of fate and of the old code of honor, exemplified throughout the saga in his wife Bergthora. Foreshadowings in this saga are effected by employing dreams and portents, a much different literary device from the modern technique of suspense. In *The Story of Burnt Njal*, the reader is usually aware of the events to transpire. The purpose of the saga and epic forms was to retell and remind the listeners of history and myth, not, as with the moderns, to compose something completely new.

Although this Icelandic saga contains an elaborate plot and subplot structure, an abundance of characters often mentioned briefly then forgotten, and a recalling of events and names foreign and relatively unknown to modern readers, the saga provides insight into the oral tradition and the codes of a past society.

The Thing, the Icelandic assembly or parliament, was the supreme lawgiver. The Thing was established in 930 C.E. and served the Old Icelandic Commonwealth while it lasted, which was until 1262. The problem with the system and the crucial concern for the characters of the saga is that, even after being judged as correct in an audience at the Thing, those who seek justice have to carry out justice for themselves.

One of the fundamental issues relating to the execution of justice is the interplay between the heathen code of killing and revenge and the Christian idea of forgiveness. Christianity was introduced into Iceland in 1000. It is recalled in the saga by Thangbrand's journey to Iceland, which initiated that land's adoption of Christianity as the national religion. The intertwining of codes and religions again comes into play with the juxtaposition of pagan magic and Christian miracles. Ironically, often the miracles are performed not to provide healing but to carry out pagan vengeance. Kari and Flosi journey to Rome to obtain forgiveness for the bloodshed caused by their animosity, yet the reason this hostility begins involves the heathen code of honor. Thus, the saga involves not only the continuous decisions of the Thing and their often tragic aftermath but also the inception of a new religion and code of order. The narrator of this saga maintains an objective eye. Very little moralizing or psychological probing of actions is evident. The characters, six hundred in all with twenty-five main actors, are developed through their actions, a behavioristic approach, rather than by their thoughts or reflections.

The Story of Burnt Njal follows three main stories: first, the downfall of Gunnar; second, the burning of Njal and his sons; third, the exacting revenge required by Kari. The middle section, for which the saga is named, is the climax and turning point of the story. All events lead toward it, and it involves all the preceding arguments and attempted honorable reconciliations. It also reflects the breakdown of the lawmaking by the Thing into jealousy and seeming dishonor; the battle is fought essentially because of the misunderstood intentions of Njal's gift. The saga then leads away from the burning and death of Njal toward atonement at the Thing as all parties meet to arrange a settlement. Finally the saga ends on a Christian note: Forgiveness is sought from the Church, and reconciliation is effected between the enemies.

"Critical Evaluation" by Gayle Steck

Further Reading

Andersson, Theodore Murdock. "Demythologizing the Tradition: *Njáls Saga.*" In *The Growth of the Medieval Icelandic Sagas, 1180-1280.* Ithaca, N.Y.: Cornell University Press, 2006. Andersson traces the development of the Icelandic saga by examining seventeen of these works, culminating in a discussion of *The Story of Burnt Njal.* He shows how these literary works evolved from adventure tales to more abstract analyses of contemporary politics and history, and he argues that in many ways *The Story of Burnt Njal* resembles a modern novel.

Helgason, Jón Karl. *The Rewriting of "Njáls Saga": Translation, Ideology, and Icelandic Sagas.* Clevedon, England: Multilingual Matters, 1999. After providing a brief history of the saga, Helgason examines its reception in the United States, Great Britain, Denmark, Norway, and Iceland between 1861 and 1945. He describes how its various translations and revisions reflect the contemporary concerns of these countries.

Schach, Paul, trans. *The Icelandic Saga.* Lincoln: University of Nebraska Press, 1962. The chapter "Several Individual Sagas" contains a discussion of *The Story of Burnt Njal.*

Tómasson, Sverrir. "Old Icelandic Prose." In *A History of Icelandic Literature,* edited by Daisy Neijmann. Lincoln: University of Nebraska Press, in cooperation with the American-Scandinavian Foundation, 2006. *The Story of Burnt Njal* is included in this discussion of Old Icelandic prose, with information about its characters, narrative mode, structure, worldview, and the work as an example of chivalric literature.

Tucker, John. *Sagas of the Icelanders: A Book of Essays.* New York: Garland, 1989. Three different essays discuss *The Story of Burnt Njal* in detail. An excellent reference for further research.

The Story of Gösta Berling

Author: Selma Lagerlöf (1858-1940)
First published: Gösta Berlings saga, 1891 (English
 translation, 1898)
Type of work: Novel
Type of plot: Picaresque
Time of plot: Early nineteenth century
Locale: Sweden

Principal characters:
GÖSTA BERLING, a former minister
THE COUNTESS ELIZABETH, Gösta's wife
MARGARETA SAMZELIUS, the wife of a major
MARIANNE SINCLAIR, a woman in love with Gösta
CHRISTIAN BERGH, Gösta's crony

The Story:

Gösta Berling stands in the pulpit on what for him is a critical Sunday. The congregation complains of his conduct to the bishop, who thereupon comes to investigate his ministry. Gösta drinks far too much and too often. With his crony, Christian Bergh, he begins to spend more and more time in tavern taprooms, and brandy becomes a necessity for him.

That morning, he preaches his sermon as if inspired. At the end of the service, the bishop stands up and asks for complaints against the minister, but no one says a word. In his heart, Gösta feels love for his flock. As he sits up that night, thinking of the wonder that happened, Bergh comes to his window to assure him that the bishop will never trouble him again. With the intention of helping his drinking crony, Bergh drove the bishop and his attendant priests in his carriage, taking them on a wild ride, up and down hill and over plowed fields at top speed. Drawing up at their destination, he warned the bishop not to bother Gösta again. As a result, Gösta is dismissed from the church.

He becomes a beggar. In the winter he has only rags on his feet. He meets the twelve-year-old daughter of the wicked clergyman of Bro. Neglected by her father, she is hauling a heavy sled with a sack of meal for her own food. Gösta takes hold of the rope with her. When she leaves him in charge of the sled, he promptly barters both sled and meal for brandy.

Awaking from a drunken sleep, Gösta sees Margareta Samzelius, the major's wife, looking at him with compassion. Margareta, strong and rough, rules Ekeby and six estates. She was betrothed to a young man named Altringer, but her parents did not allow her to wait five years for Altringer to make his fortune, instead forcing her to marry Major Samzelius. When Altringer comes back rich and famous, Margareta becomes his mistress. At his death, he leaves his lands ostensibly to the major, but in reality to Margareta.

After great urging, Gösta becomes a pensioner, one of the group of merry wastrels who exist handsomely on Margareta's bounty. On Christmas Eve, the pensioners have a grand party, at which there is much to drink. Sintram, who is

so evil that he thinks himself the chosen of Satan, comes in dressed as the devil. He says he is going to renew his pact with Margareta. The half-drunk pensioners think uneasily of Margareta's great wealth and power. Surely something supernatural helped her. It is said that she holds her power by sacrificing the soul of one pensioner to the devil each year.

In a frightening bit of nonsense, the pensioners make a pact with the devil; no one of their number is to die that year. Once in charge of Ekeby and the six estates, the pensioners agree to conduct themselves as masters in a manner pleasing to Satan himself.

The next day, when the grouse is passed at the Christmas feast, Bergh says they are just crows, and he throws them one by one against the wall. When Margareta orders him out of the house, Bergh in revenge accuses her of being Altringer's mistress with the compliance of her husband. Margareta proudly confesses the truth of what he says. Then, to save his honor, the major disowns his wife. All the pensioners, who owe her so much, turn their faces when she asks for help. Margareta leaves her home to become a beggar.

That year, the pensioners are in charge at Ekeby. The major, indifferent to the estates, returns to his own farm. Gösta learns that Anna Stjärnhök, the rich and beautiful belle of the district, broke her engagement to a timid man named Ferdinand to become engaged to a rich old man with a bald head.

Determined to bring Anna back to Ferdinand, Gösta harries her so much at a ball that she slaps his face. That slap reveals that Anna really loves Gösta. Forgetting his duty to Ferdinand, Gösta sets out with Anna for Ekeby. On the way, however, their sleigh is followed by wolves, and they are forced to stop at Ferdinand's home for protection. Thus Gösta involuntarily brings Anna back to Ferdinand and is saved from committing a sin. Ferdinand soon dies, however, and Anna goes through a marriage ceremony with his corpse. Ever after she conceals her love for Gösta.

At a ball at Ekeby, Gösta and Marianne Sinclair take part in a tableau that presents them as lovers. Marianne, succumbing to Gösta's charm, kisses him after the tableau. Later, at the gaming table, Gösta wins all the money Marianne's father has; then, in jest, Gösta wins his consent to a betrothal with Marianne. When the father discovers that Gösta, a drunkard and an unfrocked minister, is in earnest, he is furious with his daughter.

After the ball, the pensioners find Marianne locked out by her father and half-frozen. Supposedly asleep in the guest room at Ekeby that night, the girl heard Margareta, full of wrath against her pensioners, plan a riot to drive the wastrels out. Marianne runs to a bear hunter, enlists his aid, and succeeds in breaking up the riot.

Marianne contracts smallpox on her errand, and the scars greatly mar her beauty. Not wishing Gösta to see her, she returns to her father. Gösta, thinking she jilted him and too proud to go after her, soon forgets her.

At the age of twenty, Countess Elizabeth Dohna is a carefree, sympathetic young woman married to a stupid husband. At a dance, Gösta asks her for a polka. She refuses because she heard that Gösta caused the death of Ebba, her husband's sister, who died in sorrow after hearing the story of Gösta's life. Angry at her refusal, Gösta and his friends abduct the countess and take her home. There the stupid husband sides with Gösta. The poor girl leads a miserable life. When she finally runs away to live as a peasant, the count has the marriage annulled. After she is legally a single woman again, she has a child. Not wishing to have an unnamed baby, she asks Gösta to marry her. Gösta, awed and grateful, accepts, for he loves her.

Helped by his wife, Gösta turns over a new leaf, and all the pensioners follow his lead. Ekeby rings with the smith's hammer; walls and docks are repaired. When Margareta comes back after the death of the major, she reenters Ekeby as mistress of a prosperous estate. Gösta and his wife retire to a modest cottage where Gösta earns his living as a carpenter and helps those who are in trouble; the countess serves the sick. Gösta becomes, after many years, a good man.

Critical Evaluation:

Selma Lagerlöf was born into a once prosperous Varmland family that, like most families in the district, fell on bad times. Although circumstances were straitened and the fear of poverty was a constant presence, memories of better times in the recent past were still vivid and carefully preserved as part of the family lore that Lagerlöf absorbed in anecdotes as she was growing up. In many ways, *The Story of Gösta Berling* reflects this background. The novel's characters and scenes, drawn from rural Swedish life, are reminiscent of Anton Chekhov's treatment of similar material dealing with

life in rural Russia. The loss of ancestral estates, for example, strongly affects the plot development in *The Story of Gösta Berling* as it does in Chekhov's *Vishnyovy sad* (1904; *The Cherry Orchard*, 1908) just as upper-middle-class decadence seems to direct the course of events both in Lagerlöf's novel and in Chekhov's *Tri sestry* (1901; *The Three Sisters*, 1920). Other parallels can be drawn with Lagerlöf's depiction of the deterioration of a comfortable way of life and the generous hospitality that accompanies it. So, too, does the psychology of fear—suspicion of being exploited when the security of property is lost—find Chekhovian echoes. These factors most particularly shape Lagerlöf's portrayal of the pensioners in her novel.

The Story of Gösta Berling was Lagerlöf's first and most famous novel, but it is not unique in her output, for which she won a Nobel Prize in Literature in 1909—the first woman and the first Swede to be so honored. Her later novels and tales—including *Antikrists mirakler* (1897; *The Miracles of Antichrist*, 1899), *Jerusalem I: I Dalarne* (1901; *Jerusalem*, 1915), *Jerusalem II: I det heliga landet* (1902; *The Holy City: Jerusalem II*, 1918), and *Nils Holgerssons underbara resa genom Sverige* (1906-1907; *The Wonderful Adventures of Nils*, 1907, and *The Further Adventures of Nils*, 1911) especially—also show the same concerns with the failure of the social system, the plight of the peasant, the corruption of people in positions of authority, and the eternal verities of folk wisdom. The last aspect of Lagerlöf's novels is one of her strongest and most unusual points. The folkloric qualities, expressed through supernatural elements and a great sensitivity toward nature, combine romanticism with shrewd sociopolitical insight. In *The Story of Gösta Berling* Lagerlöf's powerful imagination creates a happily reckless amalgam of unlikely, even contradictory, attitudes.

Despite apparently disparate elements in the novel, Gösta himself is the unifying force, even though in some respects he is not a credible protagonist. Lagerlöf, who seems unaware of his imperfections, observed a number of conventional taboos—mostly dealing with sex, religion, and politics—that obscured the realities of life around her and blocked her ability to deal creatively with such matters in her novels. As a result, Lagerlöf overlooked contradictions in the substantive development of her novel in pursuing situations she wanted to see occur or that she was trained, by her background, to expect. The novel must therefore be accepted on its own unconventional terms.

In Lagerlöf's time, conventional terms meant the naturalism of Émile Zola and August Strindberg. Lagerlöf chose instead to follow the timeless old truths of ancient tales and archetypal myths. Such utter indifference to contemporaneity made Lagerlöf an anomaly, but the compelling power of her art elevated her work to a level that gained her a position of respect in the literary world. Without bowing to literary fashion, she wrote a first novel that has ever since captured the attention of readers. In this work, Lagerlöf commanded a theme that is of enduring interest: Can one have fun and still be good? This question is as pertinent today as it was in the 1890's when *The Story of Gösta Berling* was first published.

Ultimately, the question confronts the sanctions of social opinion, and the definitions of "fun" and "good." To Gösta, fun is drinking and wenching. His contemporary counterpart would hardly dispute such a value system. In 1836, Nathaniel Hawthorne's "The Minister's Black Veil" exposed a previously unexplored aspect of clerical activity. Henrik Ibsen's *Brand* (1866) similarly revealed the contradictions of a clergyman caught between duty and inclination. Lagerlöf's *The Story of Gösta Berling* in 1894 came midstream in these treatments of religious crises, which continued in such later works as Sinclair Lewis's *Elmer Gantry* (1927). Lagerlöf probed this clerical dilemma, part of the larger theme of ethical responsibility, with extraordinary sensitivity and insight.

The Story of Gösta Berling is a novel that combines elements of realism to suit the fashion of the time when it was written (the characterization of Gösta is here exemplary) with elements of fantasy that suited Lagerlöf's own predilection for deferring to ancient custom and observance of traditional ways. Lagerlöf was not aware of contradictions between these two ways of viewing reality, and her novel demonstrates the level of her artistic accomplishment and of her psychological grasp of human interaction.

"Critical Evaluation" by Joanne G. Kashdan

Further Reading

Berendsohn, Walter A. *Selma Lagerlöf: Her Life and Work.* Translated by George F. Timpson. Port Washington, N.Y.: Kennikat Press, 1968. First published in German in 1927, this biography discusses the relationship between Lagerlöf's life and her books. Emphasizes her connection with Värmland, where *The Story of Gösta Berling* takes place.

Edström, Vivi. *Selma Lagerlöf.* Translated by Barbara Lide. Boston: Twayne, 1984. An accessible study by a recognized authority on Lagerlöf. Contains an overview of Lagerlöf's biography and separate chapters on her most significant works, including *The Story of Gösta Berling.* Edström discusses the form of this novel, its elements of historical reality and folklore, and its place in Swedish literary history.

Forsås-Scott, Helena. "Selma Lagerlöf." In *Swedish Women's Writing, 1850-1995.* Atlantic Highlands, N.J.: Athlone, 1997. Forsås-Scott's survey of Swedish women's writing devotes a chapter to Lagerlöf, providing feminist interpretations of *The Story of Gösta Berling* and other works.

Gustafson, Alrik. *A History of Swedish Literature.* Minneapolis, University of Minnesota Press, 1961. Places Lagerlöf's works in historical context and discusses the place of *The Story of Gösta Berling* within her own oeuvre.

_____. *Six Scandinavian Novelists.* Princeton, N.J.: Princeton University Press, 1940. A comprehensive overview of Lagerlöf's work, including a discussion of *The Story of Gösta Berling.*

Olson-Buckner, Elsa. *The Epic Tradition in Gösta Berling's Saga.* New York: Theo Gaus, 1978. In an extended analysis, Olson-Buckner points out the many points of contact between *The Story of Gösta Berling* and the conventional epic. Notes that there are structural similarities to the traditional heroic saga.

Watson, Jennifer. *Swedish Novelist Selma Lagerlöf, 1858-1940, and Germany at the Turn of the Century: O du Stern ob meinem Garten.* Lewiston, N.Y.: Edwin Mellen Press, 2004. Watson explores Lagerlöf's literary impact on German-language authors of her time, including Franz Kafka, Bertolt Brecht, Gerhardt Hauptmann, and Nelly Sachs. Includes appendix, bibliography, and index

Wivel, Henrik. *Selma Lagerlöf: Her Works of Life.* Minneapolis: Center for Nordic Studies, University of Minnesota, 1991. Contains a brief discussion of the idea of love as it is presented throughout Lagerlöf's works, including *The Story of Gösta Berling.*

Storyteller

Author: Leslie Marmon Silko (1948-   )
First published: 1981
Type of work: Short fiction and poetry

Leslie Marmon Silko's collection of short fiction and poetry, *Storyteller*, is unique in shape and composition. It literally does not fit easily on a bookshelf nor can it be easily classified, given that it consists of short fiction, poetry, Laguna Pueblo legends and myths, personal family reminiscences, and photographs. The collection comprises eight short stories by Silko; twenty-six photographs by Silko's father, Lee Marmon, and her grandfather, Henry "Grandpa Hank" Marmon; and fifty-nine lyric and narrative poems. Some of these poems are original works by Silko and others are her version of narratives concerning traditional Laguna Pueblo legend and myth. The eight short stories include Silko's first-ever published story, "The Man to Send Rain Clouds," as well as some of her most acclaimed and anthologized stories, including "Lullaby" and "Yellow Woman."

In both her literary practice and her rare interviews, Silko has emphasized that Pueblo expression is not linear but circular; she often uses the metaphor of the spiderweb to describe multiple sequences of threads, radiating from the center.

Silko begins the collection with narrative poems that relate signature events in the history of the Marmon family. The family, which operated the general merchandise store at Laguna for decades in the early twentieth century, had intermarried with Laguna Pueblo and with Latinos. A story by Aunt Susie introduces the first foray into Laguna folktale, and the mixed genres of poetry, short story, photography, and Laguna myth and legend are interweaved in the remainder of the volume, as Silko returns to recurrent themes. These themes include survival, the immanence of spirits, the importance of rain, the inevitability of periodic drought, and the compelling examples of Yellow Woman and Coyote, both as legendary figures and in their present-day personifications, in the life and culture of the Laguna Pueblos in New Mexico.

In the title short story, set in a small town in Alaska, an unnamed young Yupik woman, certainly a contemporary Yellow Woman of sorts, notices the leering looks of a Gussuck (from the term "Cossack," a word used to describe nonnative folk). She intentionally lures him across thin ice. The ice breaks, and he drowns. As the story concludes, the Yupik woman asserts to authorities that she had murdered the man, though village children who had seen the accident explain to the state trooper and the local attorney that it was indeed an accident.

"Lullaby," an oft-anthologized story, including in college readers, describes the levels of loss suffered by an elderly couple, Chato and Ayah. Most of the story describes Ayah looking for the presumably drunken Chato as a snowstorm obscures the landscape. She recalls losing their son, Jimmie, to military service. He was killed in a foreign war. She recalls losing other children in childbirth or early infancy, and recalls losing two surviving children, Danny and Ella, to U.S. Bureau of Indian Affairs officials who had tricked her into signing away her children to an American Indian boarding school. As the story concludes, the storm has passed, and the moon and stars shine down on Ayah, who is sharing her blanket with a sleeping, and perhaps dead, Chato. Ayah sings a traditional Laguna lullaby not for her lost children but for her drunken and possibly deceased husband.

Just as the traditional Yellow Woman figure returns in various iterations as a contemporary female, so, too, does the totemic Coyote figure, part of the folklore of western Indian tribes, return in the final story of this collection, this time in the guise of Sonny Boy. Sonny Boy has lost the affections of his beloved Mildred, who has married a Hopi man. In a ribald tale worthy of any Coyote myth, Sonny Boy exacts revenge on the Hopi as he presents himself as a wise man who can cure the aches and pains of Aunt Mamie—by laying hands on her and her Snow Clan kinswomen by massaging their thighs with juniper ashes. He begins with the young girls, proceeds through to the adult women, and concludes with Mrs. Sekakaku—who has refused his advances otherwise—and the afflicted Aunt Mamie. Silko intrudes into Sonny Boy's narrative consciousness at the conclusion of the story to show that he feels he has exacted his revenge on the Hopi and that his amorous proclivities are moving to a possible new chapter with the female postmaster in Laguna. Sonny Boy is clearly a Coyote at Laguna in the 1970's.

Even as the title suggests, Silko's landmark text emphasizes the importance of storytelling, the storyteller, and the listeners. The identity of the particular storyteller is not important; what is of critical importance is the story itself, the narrative and values contained therein, showing how individual stories are part of the collective stories of the people. Part of what Silko achieves in *Storyteller* is her attempt to convey a sense of the oral tradition in a piece of written literature. Silko includes many reminiscences about her Marmon forbears, supported by the twenty-six family photographs depicting a century of crossroads interactions along the ancient east-west road, later U.S. Hwy. 66, where Laguna is located. Her polyphonous voice, however, is dedicated to describing a culture and a lifestyle, not simply individuals.

The European tradition of narrative, generally linear, combines in *Storyteller* with various American Indian ritual traditions to create a multigenre text that cannot fully be described within the limits of any particular genre. Silko has been ostracized by certain groups within her tribe because she has retold sacred Laguna Pueblo stories, both in *Storyteller* and in her novel *Ceremony* (1977), which have generally not been shared with the outside world. She indeed uses such traditions to show that the Euro-Americans in her stories do not comprehend the place and purpose of the indigenous peoples of the Southwest: For example, the Roman Catholic priest in "The Man to Send Rain Clouds" never understands that the Laguna people use Catholic holy water and traditions only as an addendum to the traditional death rituals for Teofilo; and Captain Littlecock in "A Geronimo Story" vaingloriously believes that he and the Laguna Regulars, Indian scouts working for the federal troops in search of the elusive Geronimo, are forever on the verge of apprehending the legendary Jicarilla Apache, though there is no evidence in the story that the captain is capable of ever tracking him down.

Ultimately, what Silko achieves in *Storyteller* is a new approach to reading the world, a new way for the non-Laguna world to understand—through traditional myths and legends, fictional stories, photographs, and memoir—Laguna Pueblo culture and values. The inability of traditional literary criticism to classify such a text has perhaps limited the critical examination that it is due. However, its compelling message and the multiple ways the text and its principles can be accessed have kept *Storyteller* before readers, especially college students and reading groups, where the work continues to draw attention.

Richard Sax

Further Reading

Allen, Paula Gunn. *The Sacred Hoop: Recovering the Feminine in American Indian Traditions*. Rev. ed. Boston: Beacon Press, 1992. This landmark work in women's and American Indian studies includes an essay devoted to Silko's *Ceremony* rather than *Storyteller*, but this essay and others help to create a context within which *Storyteller* can be studied.

_____, ed. *Studies in American Indian Literature: Critical Essays and Course Designs*. 1983. New printing. New York: Modern Language Association of America, 1995. Collection of essays and course designs features Allen's landmark essay, "The Sacred Hoop," as well as course designs that include readings from *Storyteller*.

Arnold, Ellen L., ed. *Conversations with Leslie Marmon Silko*. Oxford: University Press of Mississippi, 2000. Sixteen interviews with the reclusive Silko showcase her creative poetics.

Barnett, Louise K., and James L. Thorson, eds. *Leslie Marmon Silko: A Collection of Critical Essays*. Albuquerque: University of New Mexico Press, 1999. This collection includes three essays devoted to interpreting *Storyteller* (by Linda Krumholz, Helen Jaskoski, and Elizabeth McHenry) as well as a bibliographical essay and other scholarly articles of interest to readers of Silko.

Fitz, Brewster E. *Silko: Writing "Storyteller" and "Medicine Woman."* Norman: University of Oklahoma Press, 2004. Fitz analyzes several of Silko's short stories, including those in *Storyteller*, focusing on the relationship between the written word and the oral storytelling tradition of Silko's family and Laguna culture.

Krupat, Arnold. "The Dialogic of Silko's *Storyteller*." In *Narrative Chance: Postmodern Discourse on Native American Indian Literature*, edited by Gerald Vizenor. Albuquerque: University of New Mexico Press, 1989. Discusses *Storyteller* from the point of view of the work of literary theorist Mikhail Bakhtin and of Native American autobiography.

Ruoff, A. LaVonne Brown. *American Indian Literatures: An Introduction, Bibliographic Review, and Selected Bibliography*. New York: Modern Language Association of America, 1990. Includes a brief but worthwhile discussion of *Storyteller*, with reference to scholarly exegesis in the "History of Written Literature" chapter.

Wiget, Andrew, ed. *Handbook of Native American Literature*. New York: Garland, 1996. Includes discussion of Silko's literary achievements, with reference to *Storyteller* in the chapter "Native American Renaissance: 1967 to Present."

The Strange Case of Dr. Jekyll and Mr. Hyde

Author: Robert Louis Stevenson (1850-1894)
First published: 1886
Type of work: Novel
Type of plot: Gothic
Time of plot: Nineteenth century
Locale: London

Principal characters:
HENRY JEKYLL, a London physician
GABRIEL JOHN UTTERSON, his counselor
RICHARD ENFIELD, Utterson's cousin
POOLE, Dr. Jekyll's manservant
HASTIE LANYON, Dr. Jekyll's close friend, a doctor

The Story:

Richard Enfield and his cousin, Gabriel John Utterson, are strolling according to their usual Sunday custom when they come upon an empty building on a familiar street. Enfield remarks that some time previously he had seen an ill-tempered man knock down and trample a small child at the doorway of the deserted building. He and other indignant bystanders had forced the stranger, who gave his name as Hyde, to pay a sum of money for the child's welfare. Enfield remembers Hyde with deep loathing.

Utterson has reasons to be interested in Hyde. He is a lawyer, and he drew up the strange will of Dr. Henry Jekyll. This will stipulates that in the event of Jekyll's death, all of his wealth will go to a man named Edward Hyde. Utterson now seeks out Hyde, the man whom Enfield had described, to discover if he is the same person who had been named heir to Jekyll's fortune.

Utterson finds Hyde, who is suspicious of Utterson's interest and shuts his door in his face. Utterson next questions Jekyll, who refuses to discuss the matter and insists that in the event of his death the will must be executed as written. Utterson fears that Hyde is an extortionist who is after Jekyll's money and will eventually murder the doctor.

About one year later, Hyde is wanted for the senseless murder of a kindly old gentleman named Sir Danvers Carew. Jekyll presents the lawyer and the police with a letter signed by Hyde, in which the murderer declares his intention of fleeing England forever. The letter ends with Hyde's apology to Jekyll for having abused his friendship.

About this time, Dr. Hastie Lanyon, who had been for years a great friend of Jekyll, becomes ill and dies. A letter addressed to Utterson is found among his papers. When Utterson opens this missive, he discovers that it contains an inner envelope that is sealed and bears the directive that it is not to be opened until after Jekyll's death. Utterson suspects that this mysterious sealed letter is also somehow connected with the evil Hyde.

One Sunday, Enfield and Utterson are again walking in the street where Enfield had seen Hyde abusing the child.

They now realize that the deserted building holds a side entrance to a laboratory that is connected to Jekyll's home. As they look up at the house, they see Jekyll sitting at a window, looking disconsolate. Then his expression seems to change, and his face takes on a grimace of horror or pain. Suddenly, he closes the window. Utterson and Enfield walk on, too overcome by what they had witnessed to be able to speak.

Not long afterward, Jekyll's manservant, Poole, contacts Utterson to speak of his concerns that, for the past week, something strange had been going on in Jekyll's laboratory. The doctor had hidden himself in his laboratory, ordering his meals to be sent in and writing curious notes demanding that Poole go to apothecaries in London in search of a mysterious drug. Poole is convinced that his master has been slain and that the murderer, not Jekyll, is hiding in the laboratory.

Utterson and Poole return to Jekyll's house and break into his laboratory with an ax. As they enter, they discover that the man in the laboratory had just killed himself by draining a vial of poison. The man is Hyde. Utterson and Poole search in vain for the doctor's body, convinced that it must be somewhere, since there is a note from Jekyll to Utterson dated this very day. In the note, Jekyll says he is planning to disappear, and he urges Utterson to read the note that Lanyon had left at the time of his death. An enclosure contains Jekyll's confession.

Utterson returns to his office to read the letters. The letter of Lanyon describes an occasion when Jekyll had sent Poole to Lanyon with a request that the doctor search for a particular drug in Jekyll's laboratory and give it to Hyde. Then, in Lanyon's presence, Hyde had taken the drug and then transformed into Jekyll. The shock of this transformation had caused Lanyon's decline in health, which led to his death.

Jekyll's own account of the horrible affair is more detailed. He had begun early in life to live a double life. Publicly, he had been genteel and circumspect; privately, however, he had practiced strange vices without restraint. Becoming obsessed with the idea that people have two personalities, he had reasoned that people are capable of having two physical beings as well. Finally, he had compounded a mixture that transformed his body into the physical representation of his evil self. He became Hyde. In this disguise he was free to haunt the lonely, narrow corners of London and to perform the darkest acts without fear of recognition.

Jekyll did everything he could to protect himself in his disguise. He cautioned his servants to let Hyde in at any hour, he took an apartment for Hyde, and he made out his will in Hyde's favor. His life proceeded safely enough until he awoke one morning in the shape of Hyde and realized that his evil self had appeared even without the drug. Frightened, he determined to cast off the persona of Hyde. He sought out better companions and tried to occupy his mind with other things. He was not strong enough, however, to continue to resist the immoral pleasures that the Hyde persona allowed him to enact. When Jekyll had finally permitted the repressed Hyde persona to emerge, Hyde was full of rage and an overpowering lust to do evil; thus, he murdered Carew.

After the murder, Jekyll had renewed his effort to abandon the nature of Hyde, but one day, walking in the park, he suddenly changed into Hyde and was forced to ask Lanyon to obtain the drug that would change him back to Jekyll. From that day on, the nature of Hyde asserted itself repeatedly. When his supply of chemicals had been exhausted and could not be replenished, Jekyll, as Hyde, shut himself up in his laboratory and experimented with one drug after another. Finally, in despair, Jekyll killed himself.

Critical Evaluation:

Robert Louis Stevenson's *The Strange Case of Dr. Jekyll and Mr. Hyde* is an important gothic-science fiction novel that follows the basic template established by Mary Wollstonecraft Shelley in *Frankenstein: Or, The Modern Prometheus* in 1818. In both novels a well-educated man conducts secret experiments that soon run out of control. The result of these experiments is the release of an uncanny double, or doppelganger, who wreaks destruction upon the immediate domestic and social circle of its creator. Both works provoke discussion about the appropriate limits of human ambition, and they question whether or not humans—as flawed individuals—should be granted unlimited scientific knowledge.

The Strange Case of Dr. Jekyll and Mr. Hyde is also linked to the gothic detective fiction form. In this mode of the detective story, multiple narrators provide competing eyewitness accounts of uncanny and disturbing events, and the rational detective figure (Mr. Utterson) must attempt to make sense of events.

The central feature of *The Strange Case of Dr. Jekyll and*

Mr. Hyde is its theme of duality. Two personalities—opposite and antagonistic—mesh within one body, and as such the novel has a rich potential for psychoanalytic criticism. In many ways, Jekyll can be seen as the superego, that portion of the human consciousness that attempts to control the physical urges of the id (here represented by Edward Hyde) and filter them through socially appropriate activities. However, when the id is repressed rather than integrated into a functioning psyche, the individual's behavior will grow increasingly erratic. It is inevitable that, in time, whatever is repressed will once again become manifest. What then occurs is what psychologists call the return of the repressed.

In Stevenson's work, Dr. Jekyll is increasingly unable to control his alter ego; his identity becomes fragmented into Jekyll and Hyde, and then the Hyde persona begins to manifest itself unexpectedly. The id, as manifested in the persona of Hyde, requires ever more extreme forms of repression (such as a complete suppression of this identity through Jekyll's refusal to take the drug that causes the transformation). The most extreme form of repression is self-annihilation, as readers see when Jekyll kills himself to repress Hyde.

A question frequently asked about the novel is the nature of what is being repressed by Jekyll. What, precisely, are the strange vices that Jekyll feels so compelled to act upon? The two most provocative answers are homosexual desire and drug abuse. Stevenson's *The Strange Case of Dr. Jekyll and Mr. Hyde* is linked to other late nineteenth century, Decadent-era works, such as Oscar Wilde's *The Picture of Dorian Gray* (1890, serial; 1891; expanded) and Bram Stoker's *Dracula* (1897). These novels explore the seamy side of London life (for example, drug use) and, in particular, explore homoerotic and homosexual themes. Jekyll, Hyde, Utterson, Enfield, Lanyon, and Sir Danvers Carew are each middle-age bachelors who, within the course of the book, never interact with women. They walk the streets of London at night and meet up with each other. They have secret lives and write secret letters with enclosed, sealed missives. From an early age, Jekyll had desires that were not socially acceptable. He was driven to create a secret identity so as to be able to act upon these irresistible urges. In the end, the cost of living a double life is too much for him, and he commits suicide.

As a novel exploring the effects of drug use, *The Strange Case of Dr. Jekyll and Mr. Hyde* reveals Jekyll's increasingly desperate need for drugs, his inability to control his body without the use of drugs, and the mood swings and physical abnormalities caused by repeated drug use, drug withdrawal, and the ever-increasing dosage needed to obtain highs.

Other critics link *The Strange Case of Dr. Jekyll and Mr. Hyde* to a particular concern of the post-Darwinian world of the late nineteenth century: the fear that British society had become too civilized, too cultured. British men, it was feared, had become effete and no longer able to lead the British Empire. This fear that British men were not "manly" enough had the potential to destabilize England's sense of leadership and cultural superiority. After all, the British defended their subjugation of other nations (particularly the "darker" peoples of Africa, India, and Asia) by insisting that the British were more highly evolved and more moral than other races and ethnicities. Hyde, who is darker, stronger, and more primitive than the effeminate Jekyll, might represent either a devolution of the human species or an interpolation of the primitive other within the confined and controlled world of British men. In either case, the logic of what is today called social Darwinism can be shown to underpin the racial and gender anxieties of *The Strange Case of Dr. Jekyll and Mr. Hyde*. Hyde is an other whose very presence threatens the safe and secure world of these men.

"Critical Evaluation" revised by Donelle Ruwe

Further Reading

Ambrosini, Richard, and Richard Dury, eds. *Robert Louis Stevenson: Writer of Boundaries*. Madison: University of Wisconsin Press, 2006. Collection of essays examining Stevenson's work. Several analyses of *The Strange Case of Dr. Jekyll and Mr. Hyde* are included in the section entitled "Evolutionary Psychology, Masculinity, and Dr. Jekyll and Mr. Hyde."

Geduld, Harry M., ed. *The Definitive "Dr. Jekyll and Mr. Hyde" Companion*. New York: Garland, 1983. An anthology offering a wide spectrum of approaches to the novel, from commentary to parodies and sequels. Appendixes list the main editions; recordings; staged, filmed, and televised versions; and published and unpublished adaptations.

Jones, William B., Jr., ed. *Robert Louis Stevenson Reconsidered: New Critical Perspectives*. Jefferson, N.C.: McFarland, 2003. Includes three essays on *The Strange Case of Dr. Jekyll and Mr. Hyde*: "'Closer than a Wife': The Strange Case of Dr. Jekyll's Significant Other" by Katherine Bailey Linehan, "The Hand of Hyde" by Richard Dury, and "Engineering Influences on Jekyll and Hyde" by Gillian Cookson.

Maixner, Paul, ed. *"The Strange Case of Dr. Jekyll and Mr. Hyde."* In *Robert Louis Stevenson: The Critical Heritage*. Boston: Routledge & Kegan Paul, 1981. This selection of opinions from Stevenson's contemporaries, while often superficial and outdated, is of historical interest. Includes Stevenson's rejoinder to his critics.

Miller, Renata Kobetts. *Recent Reinterpretations of Stevenson's "Dr. Jekyll and Mr. Hyde": Why and How This Novel Continues to Affect Us*. Lewiston, N.Y.: Edwin Mellen Press, 2005. After analyzing Stevenson's original novel, which Miller interprets as an antipatriarchal text, she provides a survey of the numerous adaptations of the work. She then focuses on two novels and a play from the late twentieth century, interviewing their authors to discuss how and why they revised Stevenson's story and why the story remains relevant.

Reid, Julia. *Robert Louis Stevenson, Science, and the Fin de Siècle*. New York: Palgrave Macmillan, 2006. Examines the influence of late-Victorian concepts of evolution on *The Strange Case of Dr. Jekyll and Mr. Hyde* and other works. Argues that an interest in primitive culture is at the heart of Stevenson's writing.

Showalter, Elaine. *Sexual Anarchy: Gender and Culture at the Fin de Siècle*. New York: Penguin, 1990. Showalter, an important feminist critic, presents a scholarly analysis that places Stevenson's novel within the context of gay culture at the end of the nineteenth century.

Stevenson, Robert Louis. *"Strange Case of Dr. Jekyll and Mr. Hyde": An Authoritative Text, Backgrounds and Contexts, Performance Adaptations, Criticism*. Edited by Katherine Linehan. New York: W. W. Norton, 2003. In addition to the text, this work contains information about the composition and production of the novel; twelve of Stevenson's letters, in which he discusses various aspects of the story; contemporary reviews and comments written after the novella was published; essays placing the work in its literary, scientific, and sociohistorical contexts; and five critical analyses.

Strange Interlude

Author: Eugene O'Neill (1888-1953)
First produced: 1928; first published, 1928
Type of work: Drama
Type of plot: Psychological realism
Time of plot: Early twentieth century
Locale: New England and New York

Principal characters:
NINA LEEDS, a neurotic woman
PROFESSOR HENRY LEEDS, her father
SAM EVANS, her husband
MRS. AMOS EVANS, his mother
GORDON EVANS, Nina's son
EDMUND DARRELL, a doctor, Nina's lover
CHARLES MARSDEN, a novelist
MADELINE ARNOLD, in love with Gordon

The Story:

Had Nina Leeds married her first love, Gordon Shaw, her whole life might be different. Gordon went off to the war in France, however, and when his plane burst into flames and crashed near Sedan, he left Nina with nothing to show for her life.

Before leaving, Gordon urged Nina to marry him, but her father objected. Now Gordon is dead, and Nina has not even the memory of one night alone with him. Instead, she has indiscriminate affairs with one soldier after another, those who like Gordon are going out to die, because she thinks she can give to others what Gordon was denied. When promiscuity fails to ease her sorrow, she returns to her father's house an embittered and lonely woman. She is particularly bitter toward her father, a professor in the university, for she suspects that her father's jealousy and irrational desire to keep her with him led to his opposing her marriage with Gordon.

Nina has an admirer in Charles Marsden, the novelist, an old friend of her father. Marsden knew Nina since she was a little girl, and he often thought of marrying her. Since, however, he is attached to his aging mother, who does not entirely approve of Nina, he never proposed. Her half-serious, half-mocking fondness for him annoys him, for it is a reminder of his own failure to accept life.

Nina has an admirer of quite a different nature in Edmund Darrell, an ambitious young physician who took an interest in Nina when she was a nurse in the hospital of which he was a staff member. Although he finds her attractive, Darrell has no intention of endangering his career by getting involved with a neurotic woman. Nevertheless, he realizes that she needs help, and he concludes that a husband and a child would be the logical solution for her difficulties. His choice is Sam Evans, scion of a well-to-do family, who is in love with Nina.

When Nina's father dies, she turns almost automatically to Marsden as a kind of surrogate. Marsden, taking his cue from Darrell, suggests Evans as a possible husband, and Nina drowsily assents. Evans marries Nina realizing that she is not in love with him, but he lives in the hope that a child will bring them closer together. About seven months after she comes to live on the Evans homestead in northern New York State, Nina finds herself pregnant, but when she confides her condition to her mother-in-law, Mrs. Evans finds it necessary to reveal what she kept hidden even from her own son: Evans's aunt, hopelessly insane, lives on the top floor of the old house, and Evans's grandmother and her father before her both died in an asylum. Overwhelmed by the situation in which she finds herself, Nina can think of no way out except to abort her child through an operation and to leave Evans. Mrs. Evans protests, pointing out that Evans needs her, that he needs the confidence a child will give him, even if this child is not his own.

While Nina ponders the situation, she encounters Darrell, just returned from Europe, and tells him about her marriage and the child. She and Darrell at last decide that it would be best for Nina to have another child, of which Darrell will be the father. Evans is delighted when he learns that his wife is to have a child. Unfortunately, Nina and Darrell are unable to proceed as rationally as they planned. Nina falls in love with Darrell, and he, despite the risk to his career, cannot tear himself away from her.

Fatherhood makes a startling change in Evans. The old look of self-conscious inferiority disappears from his face, replaced by a look of determination and confidence. Nina also changes. She becomes noticeably older, but her face wears an expression of peace and calm never seen there before. Marsden, however, changes most of all. His mother dies and he ages. His hair is almost pure white.

When Darrell returns from Europe, ostensibly because of his father's death but actually because he can no longer stay away from the woman he loves, Nina for the first time in her life feels complete, surrounded as she is by her men—her spiritual father, her husband, her lover, and her son.

The next eleven years bring yet more changes into these linked lives. Darrell and Marsden back Evans in one of his enterprises, and all become wealthy men. Darrell long ago gave up his career in medicine. Marsden, on the other hand, takes to writing genteel novels about dear old ladies and devilish bachelors, stories completely unrelated to real life.

Young Gordon Evans has no use for his real father, whom he calls Uncle Ned, and with whom he quarrels on the slightest provocation. He identifies himself completely with his mother's stories of Gordon Shaw, built up by Nina into a hero in the boy's imagination.

As time goes by, Darrell manages to break the stranglehold Nina has on his soul, devoting himself as assiduously to biology as he had formerly done to medicine. He becomes his own firm self again, impervious to all of Nina's wiles. Nina's neurotic tendencies increase, however, and she possessively opposes Gordon's marriage to Madeline, a girl of good family; she even goes so far as to consider informing Madeline of the strain of insanity in the Evans family. She grows to hate Evans and at times actively wishes for his death, a wish that is fulfilled when Evans suffers a stroke while witnessing Gordon's victory over the Navy crew.

After Evans's death, Gordon somehow cannot rid himself of the feeling that his mother never loved his father, and he remembers a time in his boyhood when he saw his Uncle Ned kiss his mother. He repressed this memory, but it reemerges one day when Gordon slaps Darrell across the face during an argument. Gordon instantly regrets his act and apologizes, and the matter ends without his realization that Evans was not his real father.

In the end, Nina is really alone. She finally gives her consent to her son's marriage to Madeline. Her own marriage to Darrell at this late date is out of the question because there are too many regretful memories between them. Nina is left alone with Marsden, who waited patiently all these years until she turns to him at last like a daughter.

Critical Evaluation:

Strange Interlude, though a very long drama, was enormously successful. The curtain went up on its nine acts at 5:30 P.M.; the evening included a supper break after the fifth act, and the final curtain did not fall until after 11 P.M. There were two touring companies and a London production for the play, which brought Eugene O'Neill his third Pulitzer Prize. In book form, the play became a best seller. Later there was a motion picture (starring Norma Shearer), and, in the middle of posthumous revival of interest in the playwright, a restaging of the play in 1963.

While its psychology came to seem somewhat dated, the play appeared fresh, experimental, and exciting in the 1920's. Its major dramatic departure, the soliloquies (in themselves scarcely new to the theater), are as long as the regular surface dialogue. The action freezes when they are delivered. The technique is a way of dramatizing the fears, drives, and obsessions below the surface of human lives that rarely see the light of day. The technique also enables O'Neill to present one of his favorite themes, that of identity conflict or division, a theme evident in many of his plays, including *The Emperor Jones* (1920), *The Hairy Ape* (1922), *All God's Chillun Got Wings* (1924), *The Great God Brown* (1926), *Days Without End* (1933), and *A Touch of the Poet* (1957). At times, as in *The Great God Brown*, O'Neill employs masks to suggest sharp conflict between our public and our private images. In *Days Without End*, he divides his hero literally in two, employing two actors to present the two sides of his hero. Sometimes, as in *Days Without End*, O'Neill seeks to heal the divisions, but elsewhere, as in *A Touch of the Poet*, he presents them as tragic facts of life.

The technique also suggests another favorite theme of O'Neill—that of the past reaching into and controlling the present. As the characters deliver their soliloquies, they seem to live not only in the moment but also in their remembered pasts. Thick heaps of time surround and control them. Past and future are always present. This theme is also present in other O'Neill plays such as *The Emperor Jones*, *Mourning Becomes Electra* (1931), and *Long Day's Journey into Night* (1956). O'Neill occasionally suggests the possibility of redemption from the past, as in *Anna Christie* (1921) and *The Fountain* (1925), but finds it increasingly difficult to do so, and his last plays are his most pessimistic.

As a character Nina Leeds suggests a figure who appears in other plays, the woman who is at once wife, mother, and lover. Nina resembles Cybele of *The Great God Brown* and Josie Hogan of *A Moon for the Misbegotten* (1947). She is the archetypal woman; she is daughter, adolescent hero worshiper, wife, mistress, and possessive mother. Each part of her being seeks expression and, frequently, gets in the way of the others, leading to much of the play's bitter torment. However, while the feminine drives are located in one person, Nina finds it necessary to satisfy these urges with different men, which leads to conflict and bitterness. Nina summarizes the conflicting drives of the play when she speaks of "God the Mother," an image of the life force, as opposed to God the Father, who is hard, arbitrary, moral.

Conflict and ambivalence appear at the very beginning of the play. Nina's hero worship is vested in the aviator Gordon Shaw who, as a youthful ideal, appropriately does not appear. He is dead when the curtain rises. As daughter, Nina lives with the genteel, withdrawn history professor Henry Leeds. Nina's father and her hero have already been in conflict, the professor in his jealousy seeing to it that Gordon goes off to war without marrying Nina. The result is that, feeling cheated and guilty, Nina retreats into nymphomania. Her father moves through a series of emotions: fear of what Nina will do, contempt for himself, resignation. A third character who appears in act 1, Charles Marsden, who suffers from a mother fixation, loathes sex but feels alternately drawn to and repelled by Nina. O'Neill early establishes him as Nina's father substitute. Thus both hero and (in the guise of Marsden) father accompany Nina through the play.

Expressing everything from hero worship to cynical depravity, Nina reacts again, exhibiting another necessary facet of a woman's being: She seeks solace in a conventional family life with yet another man, Sam Evans. Pregnant, and briefly happy in her role as would-be mother, Nina reacts against her role as wife when she discovers that she cannot have her baby. Thus it is that she calls on Edmund Darrell, who makes her happy again and supplies her with a son but discovers that his relations with Nina interfere with his career. Each of the men in the play has his own problems, urges and needs, but each is drawn into Nina's orbit as she seeks to fulfill herself.

At the end of part 1, Nina has her son, her husband, and her father-substitute, but loses her lover. Only at the beginning of part 2, and then briefly, is Nina fully in control of all her men, which gives her a momentary sense of wholeness. Quickly enough, the splintering, fragmentation, and tension resume. Ultimately, there is no escape for Nina except in the loss of her drives, yet these drives are her life. As she moves from stage to stage of her existence, nothing really changes for Nina, and nothing really changes in life—O'Neill insists—except those who play the roles. Nina finally discovers herself in her father's position, playing the possessive parent just as her father did. After Evans dies, Darrell leaves, and Gordon flies off with his fiancé, Nina returns to her father in the guise of Marsden, who can provide her with a sexless, passionless haven.

"Critical Evaluation" by Max Halperen

Further Reading

Alexander, Doris. *Eugene O'Neill's Creative Struggle: The Decisive Decade, 1924-1933*. University Park: Pennsylvania State University Press, 1992. Attempts to trace the creation of the plays to probable sources. Sees O'Neill's playwriting as an opportunity "to confront and solve" problems in his own life. Argues that *Strange Interlude* evolved from O'Neill's attempt to confront the family "lie" about his mother's drug problem and inadequacies, as well as his growing disillusionment with his second wife.

Bloom, Harold, ed. *Eugene O'Neill*. Updated ed. New York: Bloom's Literary Criticism, 2007. Includes critical essays analyzing individual plays as well as more general discussions about O'Neill's life and work.

Bogard, Travis. *Contour in Time: The Plays of Eugene O'Neill*. Rev. ed. New York: Oxford University Press, 1988. Recognizes O'Neill's plays as efforts at self-understanding. Attempts to analyze the plays in relationship to events in O'Neill's life. Excellent commentary on *Strange Interlude* and its psychological, mythical, and autobiographical elements, especially in relation to gender conflicts and attractions.

Carpenter, Frederic I. *Eugene O'Neill*. Rev. ed. Boston: Twayne, 1979. An effective, short introduction to O'Neill's life and plays, emphasizing the tragic dimension of the dramas. Sees *Strange Interlude* as a twentieth century morality play that lacks O'Neill's usual high tragic vision. Emphasizes why the play has been successful in spite of weaknesses.

Greene, James J. *Eugene O'Neill's "Strange Interlude": A Critical Commentary*. New York: Monarch Press, 1980. A brief introduction to the plot, characterization, themes, staging, strengths, and weaknesses of the play.

Manheim, Michael, ed. *The Cambridge Companion to Eugene O'Neill*. New York: Cambridge University Press, 1998. Collection of essays about O'Neill's life and works, including discussions of the theater in his time; notable stage productions of his work; his depiction of female, African, and Irish American characters; and analyses of his plays written in his early, middle, and late periods.

Sheaffer, Louis. *O'Neill: Son and Artist*. Boston: Little, Brown, 1973. Authoritative biography of O'Neill, which emphasizes the personal and autobiographical details that helped to create *Strange Interlude*. Gives special attention to the psychological and theatrical elements in this experimental drama.

Törnqvist, Egil. *Eugene O'Neill: A Playwright's Theatre*. Jefferson, N.C.: McFarland, 2004. Demonstrates how O'Neill was a controlling personality in the texts and the performances of his plays. Describes his working habits and the multiple audiences for his works. Examines the titles, settings in time and place, names and addresses, language, and allusions to other works in his dramas.

Strange Stories from a Chinese Studio

Author: Pu Songling (1640-1715)
First published: Liao-chai chih-i, 1766 (English
   translation, 1880)
Type of work: Short fiction

Despite the rationalist tradition of Confucianism, the Chinese people before the republican era were no less superstitious and credulous than were Europeans during the Middle Ages. Supernatural tales are still cultivated in Taiwan, though less extensively or seriously than they were from the mid-seventeenth to the early twentieth centuries under the Manchu Dynasty, when a great number of such collections were published and enjoyed by a wide audience. Of these collections, *Strange Stories from a Chinese Studio* is the recognized classic, superior to the rest for its style, learned allusions, wonderful mixture of humanity with the preposterous, and inventiveness. Although Pu Songling claimed in his preface that he did nothing more than copy down what he heard and edit contributions from his friends, quite a number of the stories were his creations, judging from the sophistication of sentiment and the neatness of plot. These stories, mostly supernatural in theme, rich in poetic symbolism, and deep in psychological insight, are a unique achievement in Chinese literature as studies of the feminine mind clothed in vivid imagination.

The preponderant supernatural element in these stories is far from naïve: The human nature revealed here is what is known to a wise scholar or to a passionate lover rather than to an innocent blessed with sense of wonder but little experience. Like the fairy tales of Western civilization, the stories are governed by their own logic. Supernatural intervention is common, and men associate freely with spirits. Causes are followed by effects, but not in the same manner as in the natural or everyday human world. Spirits, demons, and human beings are all under the control of the law of causation or just retribution; good deeds or evil bring forth rewards or punishments. Therefore the author believed that his stories, in spite of their weirdness, absurdity, or even, in certain cases, obscenity, had a moral purpose.

Of the 431 pieces collected here, some are short bits of curious information. The account of a chorus composed of frogs, for example, runs to no more than two lines in the original. Another account, in three lines, concerns a show with a cast of mice that perform, under masks, a puppetlike drama. Some longer ones, about a page in length, have greater human interest. In "Mr. Chu, the Considerate Husband," an old man, revived after he was thought dead, has his old spouse lie down by his side, whereupon they die together. In "The Tiger of Chao-ch'eng," a tiger, after killing a man, allows himself to be arrested, confesses his crime to the court, and agrees to serve as a son to the destitute and lonesome old mother. He constantly brings dead animals and other valuables to her door, and he sometimes comes to her house to keep her company. After her death, he is present at the funeral. When the human mourners are all frightened off, he roars terribly to give vent to his grief.

Short and comparatively artless pieces such as these can be found in other collections of a similar nature. The fame of this book rests principally on the longer tales, which the author narrates with admirable delicacy and poignancy. None is truly tragic, for one essential condition of tragedy— a belief that death is final and irrevocable—is missing here, as in many other Chinese stories. Pu Songling, apparently like his readers, did not even take death seriously; in these tales, a dead woman (most of the stories are remembered for their heroines rather than their heroes) can always in one way or another recover life or assume an animate shape. A man feels hardly any scruple about making love to a female ghost, especially when she is young and beautiful. Moreover, the ghostly heroines are often learned; their ghostly occupations are often the composition of poetry, works of great self-pity and chilliness; and they prefer a poetical, handsome young man as a lover. The poetical qualities seem to be important, too, for in one story ("The Young Gentleman Who Couldn't Spell") the ghost spurns a very good-looking young man only because he is stupid. It may be supposed that a ghost can be loved only spiritually, but in this book love means sexual love. When a man and a ghost sleep in the same bed, he may suffer from exposure to the ghostly air, but he can be cured with proper medical treatment. In one story the ghost absorbs so much vitality from her lover that she feels that life comes back to her, and she bids him reopen her grave. The coffin is decayed, but the corpse looks lifelike and feels warm. After he takes her body .home, the first words she utters after her resuscitation are: "Aren't they like a dream—these ten odd years buried there!"

A great number of stories are about spirits—the spirits of rocks, trees, flowers, frogs, snakes, fish, birds, and various mammals. The most notable is that of the fox. A fox spirit can be vicious in the popular legends, but here he, or she, is almost invariably witty, charming, highly sophisticated, and possessed of human qualities as well as of magical powers. A female fox in human shape may be only plain, as in the case of the Dowdy Fox of "The Marriage Lottery," but that is because the man she chooses is a simple peasant who, according to her, deserves neither wealth nor a beautiful mistress. In another case the fox is middle-aged and "modestly good-looking," like the celebrated Heng-niang, who lectures on the art of feminine charm and helps a disfavored wife to win back her husband's love. Most foxes, however, are young girls of unearthly beauty who have the power to cast spells but are also capable of wifely virtues and undying love. In one story, "Miss Lien-hsiang," the fox saves her human lover from the deadly influence of a female ghost. Then the rivals, both exceedingly beautiful, are reconciled, and each assumes a reincarnated form and marries the lucky man.

Indeed, few Chinese writers understood the woman's heart so fully and profoundly as did Pu Songling, who, no less than the storytellers of the Western world, was fascinated by the mystery of woman. Instead of being stiff, pale paragons of virtue or unattractive harlots, the women in this book shine with brilliance and charm. They choose their lovers freely, yet leave them when they see that they must part. Since the liberty they take is morally censurable and hardly conceivable as a theme of literature, Pu Songling solved his problem by adopting the form of the supernatural tale, thus winning praise for his fancy and style. Later readers, however, recognize the author's ghosts and his spirits of foxes or other animals as realistic portraits of the eternal woman.

There are about twenty female characters in this book who will long be remembered as among the best creations of Chinese literature. Altogether, these tales present a full gallery of portraits of women, whether human, superhuman, or subhuman; women in various moods and situations, women as lovers and wives, women with all their passion, tenderness, flirtation, perseverance, and devotion. The popularity of the tales in *Strange Stories from a Chinese Studio* has been as much the result of their strangeness as of their appeal to common humanity. The author, as a product of his age, may have intended to be simply entertaining or didactic, or both, but his genius allowed him to probe psychological depths that were often beyond the imagination of other storytellers.

Further Reading

Buber, Martin. *Chinese Tales*. Translated by Alex Page. Atlantic Highlands, N.J.: Humanities Press International, 1991. A critical introduction to translations of several of the tales provides biographical information and discusses the composition of the stories and the psychological significance of the ghosts.

Chang, Chun-shu, and Shelley Hsueh-lun Chang. *Redefining History: Ghosts, Spirits, and Human Society in P'u Sungling's World, 1640-1715*. Ann Arbor: University of Michigan Press, 1998. Examines the career, times, and ideas of Pu Songling, with special attention to historical developments in seventeenth century China. Provides an extensive analysis of *Strange Stories from a Chinese Studio*, which includes discussion of the work's structure, context within the early history of the Qing Dynasty, and its depiction of gender relations, love and passion, family and ethical values, and country life.

Ch'en, Shou-Yi. "Ch'ing Fiction." In *Chinese Literature: A Historical Introduction*. New York: Ronald Press, 1961. Describes Pu Songling's fascination with the unusual. Maintains he was a master of his craft in his command of the classical Chinese language and in the way he handled characterization and description.

Chiang, Sing-chen Lydia. *Collecting the Self: Body and Identity in Strange Tale Collections of Late Imperial China*. Boston: Brill, 2005. Analyzes the short stories of Pu Songling and other Chinese writers working in the years from 1661 through 1799. Argues that these "strange" tales, which feature ghosts, animal spirits, monsters, haunted houses, and other supernatural phenomena, reflect the era's suppressed cultural anxieties as well as their authors' ability to construct gender and identity. Two of the chapters are devoted to *Strange Stories from a Chinese Studio*.

Kow, Mei-Kao. *Ghosts and Foxes in the World of "Liaozhai zhiyi."* London: Minerva Press, 1998. Analyzes the significance of ghosts and foxes in the stories, offering Pu Songling's own explanation for their appearance. Includes discussions of ghost bureaucrats and the romantic life of ghosts.

Ma, Y. W., and J. S. M. Lau, eds. *Traditional Chinese Stories: Themes and Variations*. New York: Columbia University Press, 1978. Translations of six stories from Pu Songling's collection, along with brief critical commentary on each that places them in the context of Chinese tales about similar themes. Includes an excellent summary of the writer's literary achievement.

Plaks, Andres. "Towards a Critical Theory of Chinese Narrative." In *Chinese Narrative: Critical and Theoretical Essays*, edited by Plaks. Princeton, N.J.: Princeton University Press, 1977. Uses *Strange Studies from a Chinese Studio* as an example of a collection of tales written in elevated language that nevertheless conveys intensely personal emotions.

Zeitlin, Judith T. *Historian of the Strange: Pu Songling and* *the Chinese Classical Tale*. Stanford, Calif.: Stanford University Press, 1993. Places the writer's works in the context of Chinese narratives dealing with the fantastic and the strange. Traces the critical history of his work and provides detailed analyses of selected tales dealing with obsession, the obfuscation of boundaries between male and female, and the significance of dreams.

The Stranger

Author: Albert Camus (1913-1960)
First published: L'Étranger, 1942 (English translation, 1946)
Type of work: Novel
Type of plot: Existentialism
Time of plot: Late 1930's to early 1940's
Locale: Algeria

Principal characters:
MEURSAULT, an office worker
MARIE CARDONA, his girlfriend
RAYMOND SINTES, his friend and neighbor, a pimp
SALAMANO, another neighbor, an old man

The Story:

When Meursault is notified of his mother's death, he leaves immediately for Marengo, where she was living in the Home for Aged Persons. He is taken to the room where her coffin is placed and casually declines the doorkeeper's offer to unscrew the lid so he can look at her. Meursault spends the night there, drinking coffee, smoking, and chatting with the doorkeeper. The next day, a Friday, he attends the funeral and leaves immediately afterward to return to Algiers.

Saturday morning, Meursault goes for a swim and runs into Marie Cardona, a girl who formerly worked in his office. He invites her to a movie and later takes her to bed.

Meursault spends Sunday lounging on the balcony of his flat, smoking and watching people on the street below. The next day, returning home from work, Meursault comes upon Raymond Sintes, a young man who lives on the same floor. Raymond, who calls himself a warehouseman but is reputed to be a pimp, was just in a fight with the brother of a Moorish girl he is seeing. Believing that the girl is cheating on him, he beat her up, and her brother accosted him, seeking revenge. Raymond asks Meursault to draft a letter to entice the girl back so he can humiliate her, and Meursault agrees to help.

One afternoon, Meursault is in his room with Marie when they hear Raymond beating the girl again. A police officer is summoned. Later, Raymond asks Meursault to testify to his own knowledge that the girl was false to Raymond. Again, Meursault agrees to help, and he and Raymond go out to a café. Upon returning, they encounter another neighbor, an

old man named Salamano, whose dog ran off. Although he abused the animal mercilessly, he is weeping and fearful of what will become of him without his longtime companion.

That Sunday, Meursault and Marie accompany Raymond to the beach, where they encounter two Arabs who were following Raymond for some time. A fight breaks out, and Raymond is cut before the Arabs slip away. Later, with his wounds patched, Raymond goes walking and comes upon the Arabs again. This time, Raymond pulls a gun, but Meursault, who followed, offers to hold it to ensure a fair fight. Almost immediately, however, the Arabs vanish.

Raymond goes back to the bungalow, but Meursault—Raymond's pistol still in his pocket—stays out in the blazing afternoon sunlight and soon comes upon the Arab who stabbed Raymond. Meursault steps forward and, seeing the flash of a knife blade in a blur of light and heat, pulls the trigger. He pumps four more bullets into the Arab's inert body.

Meursault is arrested and questioned by the examining magistrate for the next eleven months, usually with a court-appointed lawyer present. The questions focus on two things: his apparent callousness at his mother's funeral and the fact that he hesitated after his first shot and then fired four more times. At one point, the magistrate displays a small silver crucifix and asks Meursault whether he believes in God. When Meursault replies matter-of-factly that he does not, the magistrate is visibly upset.

Meursault is held in prison, where he is visited by Marie,

who holds out hope for his acquittal. He soon becomes accustomed to prison life, although small privations occasionally upset him, most of all, the fact that he is not allowed to smoke. He begins to sleep sixteen to eighteen hours a day. Soon, six months pass, and he begins talking to himself without realizing it.

In June, his trial begins. One of the first witnesses called, the warden of the Home for Aged Persons in Marengo, testifies that Meursault's mother complained about her son's conduct toward her and that on the day of the funeral Meursault neither cried nor lingered by the grave. The doorkeeper is called to testify that Meursault did not want to view his mother's body. When Marie takes the stand, the prosecutor maneuvers her into admitting that her affair with Meursault began the day after his mother's funeral and that they first went to the movies to see a comedy. When Raymond attempts to exonerate his friend, he is exposed as a criminal and a pimp.

After a trial that seems almost to exclude him from its proceedings, Meursault is pronounced guilty and sentenced to death by decapitation. Meursault refuses repeatedly to see the chaplain, but one day the chaplain enters the cell without his permission and tries to talk to him about God. Meursault is patient at first, but then, becoming bored and annoyed, lashes out, cursing the chaplain and pointing out that all his supposed certainty amounts to nothing in the end. Hearing the commotion, the guards rush in to rescue the priest, leaving Meursault to drop off to sleep, exhausted.

When he awakens, he finds himself awash in a strange feeling of peace and resignation, devoid of hope and accepting of what he describes as "the benign indifference of the universe." He is content to await his execution and, in fact, hopes that it will be witnessed by a large crowd of spectators cursing him.

Critical Evaluation:

A French author born in Algeria just before the outbreak of World War I, Albert Camus considered the history of his times a history of "murder, injustice, and violence." He lost his father in the Battle of the Marne, grew up in the shadow of a world war, and participated in the next world war as a member of the French resistance movement.

Athletic and intellectually gifted, Camus played football while attending the University of Algiers, where he studied philosophy and the Greek classics, planning to become a teacher. In 1937, however, at the age of twenty-four, he was stricken with tuberculosis, which led to four years of enforced inactivity while he recuperated. During this period, he began to write and to formulate the philosophy that would underlie his novels, plays, and essays. In 1957, Camus was awarded the Nobel Prize in Literature.

As much a philosopher as a creative writer, Camus is closely associated with the atheistic branch of existentialism, a philosophy emphasizing humanity's consciousness of its mortality and its consequent need to find meaning in a universe that seems indifferent and inhospitable to such a quest. Camus believes that there is no god, hence that life has no purpose. Things—human beings, plants, animals—simply live and die as part of a natural process that has no transcendent meaning or value. Human beings are distinguished from plants and animals only by virtue of the fact that they are conscious of their own mortality. Alone among all living things, human beings know that they must die. This awareness pushes them to seek explanations, to try to find meaning in what is essentially meaningless. Camus and other thinkers describe this situation as "the absurd." Human beings—seekers of meaning in a meaningless universe—live in a condition of absurdity.

Meursault, in *The Stranger*, is not at first a seeker of meaning, nor is he particularly aware of his own mortality. He simply sleepwalks through life, as many do, ignoring the inevitability of death and the implications of mortality. Camus argues that most human beings live in this condition for as long as they can, going about their daily routines like automatons, refusing to think, seeking solace in simple physical and material pleasures. However, most are doomed to be awakened to their condition when something—the death of a loved one, perhaps, or a serious illness as in his own case—disturbs their routine.

For Meursault, the event that forces him out of his complacency is the killing of the Arab—not the murder itself, a meaningless event brought about by a natural response to the sun and danger, but its aftermath. When society condemns him, Meursault realizes that he is not being condemned for taking a human life but for refusing to accept the illusions society promotes to protect itself from having to acknowledge the absurdity of the human condition. In effect, Meursault is condemned to death for failing to weep at his mother's funeral.

After he is condemned, Meursault could fall back on the illusions proffered by society through its priests and clergymen—hucksters and shills, as Camus thought of them. To do so would have been intellectually dishonest. In fact, the novel's real turning point occurs when the priest visits Meursault in his cell. Here, for the first time, Meursault shows passion, revolting against the priest's effort to impose on him the platitudes and false certainties of religion. Meursault chooses, instead, to accept his condition; he refuses to deny the reality of his impending death. In doing so, he discovers the one tie that links him to all other beings: death. Once death, or the inevitable cessation of existence, is recognized as the single inescapable condition of existence, life, however meaningless it might ultimately be, becomes valuable. However, whatever value life has must be imposed on it; people must engage it actively. Ironically, Meursault learns this too late.

The Stranger is a deeply disturbing novel. From its famous dispassionate opening—"Mother died today. Or maybe, yesterday; I can't be sure."—to its conclusion, where Meursault expresses the hope that on the day of his execution he will be greeted by "a huge crowd of spectators," all hurling at him "howls of execration," the novel challenges assumptions about life and literature. Just when it appears that Meursault can be dismissed as a callous egoist, he reveals complexities of emotion common to all; he merely refuses to pretend to feelings he does not possess. When Meursault becomes enmeshed in the legal system, Camus shows how society is more concerned with appearances than with any meaningful concept of justice. When Meursault, instead of repenting and seeking solace in some transcendent reality, refuses to acknowledge the possibility of anything beyond the immediate facts of his situation, the heroism of his attitude is made clear.

Camus's style in this novel is disturbingly flat and objective, an anomaly for a first-person narrative. It has often been suggested that Camus was influenced by Ernest Hemingway in this respect. With this curiously flat style, Camus suggests that in an absurd universe all things have equal value. Nothing in the entire universe is intrinsically more meaningful than anything else.

Ron Carter

Further Reading

Bloom, Harold, ed. *Albert Camus's "The Stranger."* Philadelphia: Chelsea House, 2001. Collection of essays providing various interpretations of *The Stranger*, including Camus's preface to the American edition and a translation of Jean-Paul Sartre's influential explication of the novel.

Bree, Germaine, ed. *Camus: A Collection of Critical Essays.* Englewood Cliffs, N.J.: Prentice-Hall, 1962. An early collection of essays by outstanding critics.

Carroll, David. *Albert Camus, the Algerian: Colonialism, Terrorism, Justice.* New York: Columbia University Press, 2007. Analyzes Camus's novels, short stories, and political essays within the context of the author's complicated relationship with his Algerian background. Carroll concludes that Camus's work reflects his understanding of both the injustice of colonialism and the tragic nature of Algeria's struggle for independence. Includes bibliography and index.

Ellison, David R. *Understanding Albert Camus.* Columbia: University of South Carolina Press, 1990. An overview of the development of Camus's themes and writing style. Focuses on Camus as a literary man whose works embody a consistent philosophical outlook. Especially useful for first-time readers of Camus.

Hughes, Edward J., ed. *The Cambridge Companion to Camus.* Cambridge University Press, 2007. Collection of essays interpreting Camus's work, including "From *Noces* to *L'Étranger*" by Peter Dunwoodie. Other essays discuss his life and times, his formative influences, his relationship with Jean-Paul Sartre, Camus and the theater, and social justice, violence, and ethics in his work.

King, Adele, ed. *L'Étranger: Fifty Years On.* New York: St. Martin's Press, 1992. Twenty original essays by leading Camus scholars. Offers a variety of viewpoints and provides a valuable companion to a study of the novel.

Longstaffe, Moya. *The Fiction of Albert Camus: A Complex Simplicity.* New York: Peter Lang, 2007. Examines Camus's novels and short stories, discussing the coherent themes and philosophy expressed in these works. Longstaffe also describes the origins of Camus's philosophy and the narrative techniques of his fiction.

McCarthy, Patrick. *Albert Camus: "The Stranger."* 2d ed. New York: Cambridge University Press, 2004. Analyzes the strengths and weaknesses of the novel. McCarthy is especially good on the novel's political aspects and on how Camus manages to transform an unsympathetic protagonist into an Everyman.

Rhein, Phillip H. *Albert Camus.* Rev. ed. Boston: Twayne, 1989. Relates *The Stranger* to the whole of Camus's philosophy and focuses on the novel as a reflection of that philosophy. Provides an enlightening companion volume to Ellison's *Understanding Albert Camus.*

Todd, Olivier. *Albert Camus: A Life.* Translated by Benjamin Ivry. New York: Alfred A. Knopf, 1997. Using material such as unpublished letters made available after the death of Camus's widow, this detailed biography reveals much about Camus's love affairs and his many important friendships.

Stranger in a Strange Land

Author: Robert A. Heinlein (1907-1988)
First published: 1961
Type of work: Novel
Type of plot: Science fiction
Time of plot: Early twenty-first century
Locale: Bethesda, Maryland; Washington, D.C.; the
Pocono Mountains in Pennsylvania; San Francisco;
St. Petersburg, Florida

Principal characters:
VALENTINE MICHAEL "MIKE" SMITH, a human raised by
Martians
JUBAL E. HARSHAW, a lawyer who befriends Smith
ANNE,
DORCAS, and
MIRIAM, Harshaw's secretaries
LARRY, Harshaw's gardener
DUKE, Harshaw's mechanic
GILLIAN BOARDMAN, a nurse who helps Smith escape
government control
BEN CAXTON, a journalist who supports Smith's cause
JOSEPH E. DOUGLAS, secretary-general of Earth's world
government
ARCHBISHOP DIGBY, head of the Fosterite Church

The Story:

Valentine Michael Smith is conceived during a long space voyage from Earth to Mars and is born on Mars. His parents are members of the first Earth expedition to the red planet, but they are not married to each other. His mother, who is married to the expedition's medical officer, dies during childbirth, and her husband murders Michael's father with a scalpel and then kills himself soon afterward. The other members of the expedition also die shortly after landing, so Smith is raised by Martians. Culturally and psychologically, he becomes a Martian, much as the human Mowgli in Rudyard Kipling's *The Jungle Book* (1894) becomes a wolf when he is raised by wolves.

The outbreak of World War III prevents another expedition to Mars from being mounted for twenty-five years. When a second expedition does arrive on the planet, its members find Smith fully grown and bring him back to Earth. There, he presents a dilemma to the authorities: Through his human parents, he has inherited vast wealth, but, without human cultural understanding, he is not competent to control it. Further, under a legal oddity known as the Larkin Decision, Smith can be construed in terrestrial law as the owner of the entire planet Mars. To Joseph Douglas, the secretary-general of Earth's global government, the World Federation of States, Smith poses a potential threat. This potential causes Smith to be isolated—as a kind of prisoner—under various ruses. The first such ruse is medical, as Smith is kept at Bethesda Medical Center.

Ben Caxton, an investigative reporter, accuses Douglas of limiting the freedom of the man from Mars and attempts to

help Smith escape government custody. When Caxton's girlfriend, Gillian Boardman, a nurse at Bethesda, stumbles on Smith's heavily guarded hospital room, she effects the escape by disguising Smith as a nurse and taking him out of the hospital. Gillian takes Smith to Ben's apartment, but Federation authorities have already nabbed Ben, and they close in on her and Smith. Although the agents are armed, Smith easily overcomes their force with his Martian mental powers which cause his attackers simply to disappear. Frightened, Gillian flees with Smith to the Poconos retreat of Jubal Harshaw, a famed attorney, physician, and popular author with a reputation for standing up against powerful bullies if the cause appeals to him.

Intrigued by Smith, as well as by Gillian's bravery and innocence, Jubal undertakes their legal and practical defense, forcing Douglas to acknowledge Smith's legal claim to be the official representative of Mars to the Federation. It later turns out that this turn of events was planned by the Martians, who intended Smith to be their envoy to Earth. Freeing Smith from Douglas still leaves him in an ambiguous position because Smith is still a stranger to the planet of his ancestors. Harshaw sets about educating Smith—or Mike, as he has become known—on being human. Harshaw urges members of his household not to teach Mike their own cultural prejudices.

Ensconced in the bosom of Harshaw's artificial family, Mike discovers a "nest" like the ones he knew on Mars. Harshaw, whose first name means "father of many," is a father figure to the three women who act as his secretaries and housekeepers—Anne, Dorcas, and Miriam—and to the two men who keep his estate in repair, Larry and Duke. When Gillian and Mike join the household, everyone in it shares water with Mike, making them "water brothers" with the man from Mars. Mike learns about being human, while Jubal and his surrogate children learn about Mike's Martian-trained powers. He can cause things to disappear. He has complete and conscious control of his body. He can levitate, exit his body at will, and read minds.

Mike's water brothers discover the nature of these feats by learning the Martian language. They encounter a difficulty understanding the Martian verb *to grok*, which Mike uses often without translating. Its etymological meaning appears to be "to drink," but metaphorically it holds a rich variety of meaning: to understand, to contemplate, to cherish, to love, to become one with a thing or person. The metaphysical nature of Mike's teaching (although to the Martians physical and metaphysical are one) leads Mike's water brothers to view it as religion. The religious aspect of his instruction is heightened by Mike's discovery of a recently developed Earth religion, the Fosterite Church, that shares some elements of Martian beliefs. The primary shared element is the idea of "discorporation" rather than death, as the initiated choose the moment of their translation into heaven.

Mike's contact with the Fosterites proves damaging. When he meets with the head of the Fosterite Church, Archbishop Digby, Mike "grok[s] a wrongness" about the religious leader and causes him to disappear. This act, as well as the humans' inability to follow the moral codes that Mike's teaching entails, makes him a marked man and eventually the Antichrist of the Fosterites.

Mike wanders around the country with Gillian. Among other things, he works as a stage magician using his Martian powers, but fails because he lacks showmanship. In San Francisco, he has an epiphany in which he finally understands the human concepts of comedy and tragedy.

Mike starts his own religion with a temple in St. Petersburg, Florida. Either the Fosterites or a professional arsonist contracted by the Fosterites burn this temple to the ground. Finally, although Mike could escape his fate if he chose to, the Fosterites beat him to death while the police turn the other way. When Mike dies, he goes directly to Heaven, which he finds very ecumenical. Supreme Bishop Digby is already there and becomes Mike's assistant.

Critical Evaluation:

When Robert A. Heinlein completed his young adult novel *Red Planet* (1949), he felt he had enough unused background material for another book, which eventually became *Stranger in a Strange Land*. Heinlein's Mars novels, like the works of Ray Bradbury and many other science-fiction writers, followed the speculations of astronomer Percival Lowell (1855-1916), who incorrectly postulated that Mars is or was populated by an intelligent species and that canals on the planet carry scarce water from the poles to the equatorial regions. *Stranger in a Strange Land* was one of the last major science-fiction stories published before the National Aeronautics and Space Administration launched exploratory probes that invalidated Lowell's premises. Heinlein postulated Martians with mental powers so great that they previously destroyed a planet that formerly orbited the Sun between Mars and Jupiter.

In both of Heinlein's Mars novels, the sharing of water is an important bonding ritual with deep emotional significance and meaning. In *Red Planet*, Heinlein describes an instance of the water-sharing ritual among native Martians. When Jill casually gives Mike a glass of water in *Stranger in a Strange Land*, they become "water brothers" and Mike trusts her absolutely although they have just met. Jubal Harshaw's home has a swimming pool, which Mike considers the site of the ultimate religious experience. When Mike visits the Archangel Foster Tabernacle, he intentionally does not drink water.

Although Heinlein is usually associated with the political Right, he disapproved of religious fundamentalism and was deeply suspicious of organized religion in general. He was raised in Methodism, which at the time forbade playing cards, drinking alcoholic beverages, and dancing. He began to move away from this upbringing when he discovered the writings of Charles Darwin as a teenager.

The novel's title is a biblical reference from the book of Exodus, chapter 2, verse 22. The title of the first section of the novel, "His Maculate Origin," is a play on the doctrine of Immaculate Conception, which says that Mary, the mother of Jesus, was conceived without Original Sin so she could be a pure vessel for Jesus. Mike, by contrast, is conceived in an act of adultery. His name is derived from the Hebrew word *Mikael*, which means "one who is like God."

In 1940, Heinlein wrote "If This Goes On—," a cautionary tale about religious fundamentalism. His approach to criticizing religion in *Stranger in a Strange Land* and in his later book *Job: A Comedy of Justice* (1984) is satirical. This satirical element of the novel reaches its peak when Jubal, Gillian, and Mike visit the Archangel Foster Tabernacle. They enter through the Happiness Room, where they find slot machines and a bar. Then, they visit the Happy Thoughts medication chamber, where they see the preserved corpse of Foster, the religion's founder. For the service itself, they sit in a luxury box, which has adjustable seats and a waiter to provide them with refreshments. Although it is hidden from view during the service, they are told there is a giant television screen that allows the church to function as a sports bar. The service itself includes a snake dance, a sermon, door prizes, commercials, and several hymns. Heinlein considered organized religion, regardless of its factual accuracy, to be a form of entertainment. He was also impressed by the success of L. Ron Hubbard, once a science-fiction writer and Heinlein's contemporary, in founding the Church of Scientology and of Mary Baker Eddy, who founded the First Church of Christ, Scientist.

Heinlein uses place names to signify both water and Christianity. Bethesda Medical Center is a facility of the U.S. Navy, but in Heinlein's future global society the United States no longer has armed forces. The name Bethesda comes from the Bible, in which it is a pool of water in Jerusalem believed to have healing powers. San Francisco and St. Petersburg are both located on peninsulas, and both are named for Christian saints.

John R. Holmes; revised by Thomas R. Feller

Further Reading

Bloom, Harold, ed. *Science Fiction Writers of the Golden Age.* New York: Chelsea House, 1995. Provides biographical information, critical analysis, and bibliographies for Heinlein and twelve other science-fiction writers.

Franklin, H. Bruce. *Robert A. Heinlein: America as Science Fiction.* New York: Oxford University Press, 1980. This general treatment of Heinlein's fiction is more an attack on Heinlein's belief system, as well as America in general, than literary criticism. Its section on *Stranger in a Strange Land* suggests that the novel is adversely affected by a tacit Calvinism.

Heinlein, Robert A. *Grumbles from the Grave.* Edited by Virginia Heinlein. New York: Ballantine, 1990. This posthumously published selection of Heinlein's letters mentions *Stranger in a Strange Land* extensively. Chapter 14 contains letters about the novel itself, while chapter 15 features reactions to the novel.

Major, Joseph T. *Heinlein's Children: The Juveniles.* Chicago: Advent, 2006. A critical study of Heinlein's young adult fiction. The chapter on *Red Planet* points out common elements with *Stranger in a Strange Land.*

Patterson, William H., Jr., and Andrew Thornton. *The Martian Named Smith: Critical Perspectives on Robert A. Heinlein's "Stranger in a Strange Land."* Sacramento, Calif.: Nitrosyncretic Press, 2001. A detailed examination of the novel, discussing, among other topics, Heinlein and the culture of science fiction, the novel's composition and publication history, and Heinlein's use of satire, irony, and myth. Includes an appendix about the significance of names in the book.

Slusser, George Edgar. *Robert A. Heinlein: Stranger in His Own Land.* San Bernardino, Calif.: Borgo Press, 1976. Touches on all of Heinlein's fiction, and the middle third deals exclusively with *Stranger in a Strange Land.*

Stover, Leon. *Robert Heinlein.* Boston: Twayne, 1987. Critical study of Heinlein's fiction. The section on *Stranger in a Strange Land* compares it to the writing of Walt Whitman, Mark Twain, and H. L. Mencken.

Strangers and Brothers series

Author: C. P. Snow (1905-1980)
First published: 1940-1970; includes *Strangers and Brothers*, 1940 (reissued as *George Passant*, 1972); *The Light and the Dark*, 1947; *Time of Hope*, 1949; *The Masters*, 1951; *The New Men*, 1954; *Homecomings*, 1956; *The Conscience of the Rich*, 1958; *The Affair*, 1960; *Corridors of Power*, 1964; *The Sleep of Reason*, 1968; *Last Things*, 1970
Type of work: Novels
Types of plot: Bildungsroman, social realism, and political realism
Time of plot: 1914-1968
Locale: England

Principal characters:
LEWIS ELIOT, a lawyer, academic, civil servant, and writer
MARTIN ELIOT, his brother, a physicist
SHEILA KNIGHT ELIOT, his first wife
CHARLES MARCH, his rich Jewish friend, studying medicine
GEORGE PASSANT, his free-thinking mentor
ROY CALVERT, his friend, a Cambridge scholar
HERBERT GETLIFFE, a barrister
R. T. A. CRAWFORD, a scientist
DONALD HOWARD, a Cambridge fellow accused of scientific fraud
MARGARET DAVIDSON ELIOT, Eliot's second wife
ROGER QUAIFE, a conservative politician
ARNOLD SHAW, vice chancellor of a provincial university
MAURICE HOLLIS, son of Margaret Eliot by her first husband

The Stories:

Time of Hope. It is the summer of 1914, and Lewis Eliot is eight years old. Later, because of his provincial education, he comes to realize his deficiencies as a student. After falling in love with Sheila Knight, he realizes his failings as a lover. Sheila, the beautiful daughter of a self-centered clergyman and a distant mother, knows that she will never love Eliot, but his persistence leads to their marriage.

By 1933, Eliot has acquired an insightful perspective on his ambitions and his need for love. He recognizes that the legal profession does not always bring about justice and that loving someone as self-absorbed as Sheila may be rooted in some basic flaw in his own character.

Strangers and Brothers. Eliot's mentor, George Passant, a solicitor's clerk, deeply influences a circle of idealistic students. By attending Passant's group meetings and college lectures, and through his access to Passant's diary, Eliot comes to admire certain of his mentor's activities, such as helping a student retain his college scholarship. However, with time, Eliot becomes increasingly aware of Passant's limitations, such as his willingness to use his band of so-called brothers to further his own ambitions. He involves them in a scheme for deceiving investors about the circulation figures of a publication, which leads to a charge of fraud. Because Eliot is a member of the group, he gets Herbert Getliffe, a well-respected attorney, to argue the case before a jury, which returns a verdict of not guilty on all counts. Nevertheless, because of revelations about Passant's liberal

views on politics and sexual freedom, Passant loses his job at the college and his chance for advancement in a law firm.

The Conscience of the Rich. It is the 1930's, and Eliot has qualified as a barrister. In London now, he befriends Charles March, the scion of a prosperous Jewish family, who gives him the chance to see how the rich live and to speculate on their consciences. Charles's father, Leonard March, wants his son to become a lawyer, but Charles possesses a guilty conscience over his unearned wealth, and he abandons law to study to become a family physician. Eliot is more than willing to use the Marches to gain introductions to important London lawyers, hoping they will provide him with cases, through which he can build his legal reputation.

The Light and the Dark. Eliot, now a don at Cambridge, tells the tragic story of Roy Calvert, a scholar of Manicheanism whose dualistic philosophy divides the world between spirit and matter, good and evil, light and dark. His work also examines the real-world division between those persons motivated by selfishness and greed and those persons inspired by humanistic political and religious ideologies. From the outside, Calvert appears to have everything—wealth, brilliance, good looks, and scholarly success—but on the inside he is plagued by Hamlet-like depressions, which Eliot strives to mitigate, only to be rebuffed. Calvert's conflicts are brought to a head through his election as a fellow and his fascination with the dramatic successes of the Nazis. Eliot is able to dampen Calvert's attraction to Nazi power, and he experiences hope when Roy marries and the couple has a child. However, Calvert enlists in the air force, not out of patriotism but to satisfy his death wish.

The Masters. It is 1937, and there is much political maneuvering behind the election of a new master to a Cambridge college in which Eliot is a fellow. Eliot and some of his colleagues back Paul Jago, perceived as sharing their liberal humanist values, and oppose R. T. A. Crawford, a self-confident scientist who, they fear, may govern dictatorially. Intense lobbying follows, including malicious attack's on Jago's inelegant wife. It comes as a surprise when one vacillating fellow switches his vote to Crawford, who ultimately wins the mastership. On the surface, the fellows, including Jago, seem to overcome the bitter feelings engendered by the election process and agree to serve the needs of the college by cooperating with their new head.

The New Men. Martin Eliot, Lewis's brother, is a physicist who is involved in the building of the atomic bomb. Because the Germans had discovered nuclear fission, the process upon which the bomb is based, both the Americans and British feel intense urgency to create this highly destructive weapon before the Nazis. As scientists work day and night, moral concerns are pushed to the background, but they surface again as the United States develops and then uses two atomic bombs in its war against Japan. Martin soon becomes convinced that the atomic bomb is an evil weapon, but Eliot tries to dissuade his brother from going public with his antinuclear views. He succeeds in rescuing his brother's scientific career for a while, but Martin is unable to reconcile his conscience with his work, which is aimed at making Great Britain a nuclear power. Martin rejects his promising future in the atomic establishment, much to the dismay of his brother.

Homecomings. Lewis Eliot continues his search for love. His first love ends tragically, as Sheila commits suicide, and his new love for Margaret Davidson is complicated by her marriage to a good man, the pediatrician Geoffrey Hollis, and by her devotion to their son, Maurice. The progress of their affair is hindered by Margaret's moral qualms and by Eliot's involvement in government. Furthermore, they are concerned that a divorce and remarriage might damage both their reputations. Nevertheless, Eliot is determined to marry Margaret, and he is ready to adapt his conscience to the circumstances. Finally, he persuades Margaret to divorce her husband and then to marry him.

The Affair. It is the early 1950's, and Donald Howard, a young fellow, is accused of scientific fraud. Political maneuvering ensues to get the college to reverse the dismissal. Though no longer a fellow at the college, Eliot, with his legal experience, becomes convinced that an injustice has been done. At the college, academic politics mirror the Cold War politics of the outside world.

Howard is an arrogant Marxist who complicates the task of his defenders, but Eliot understands that justice should be rendered even to those who are personally and politically unappealing. Eliot is unable to achieve perfect justice for Howard, but he does prevent his dismissal. His fellowship, however, will not be renewed. This compromise proves unsatisfactory to both sides.

Corridors of Power. In 1955, Roger Quaife, a conservative politician, selects Labor Party sympathizer Eliot as an investigative associate, largely because the two share similar views on curtailing the nuclear arms race. Reaching their shared goal is compromised by Quaife's adulterous affair with the wife of a member of Parliament who opposes a nonnuclear British defense policy. Eliot understands that Quaife is a ruthless politician, willing to manipulate and discard friends and political allies to achieve power, but the ever-tolerant Eliot believes that Quaife genuinely loves his mistress and is motivated, in his public life, by a deep desire for world peace. Quaife's contradictions lead to his fall from power, and he soon marries his mistress.

The Sleep of Reason. In 1963, Eliot returns to the places of his early life. As he relives painful memories and encounters new horrors, he realizes that he must reevaluate the belief in human progress that had buttressed so much of his career. Now a full-time writer, Eliot has time to become involved in a conflict between Arnold Shaw, the vice chancellor of his old college, and certain faculty members who find Shaw authoritarian and out of touch with modern students. Through his friendships with George Passant and the Pateman family, Eliot is drawn into the lives of two students—Passant's niece, Cora Ross, and the Pateman's daughter, Katharine, who are lesbians and who are accused of the kidnapping, torture, and murder of an eight-year-old boy. Eliot agrees to serve as an adviser during the trial. The young women are convicted and sentenced to life imprisonment, forcing Eliot to understand the rationale behind the Christian doctrine of Original Sin. He also wonders whether Shaw's elitist educational program and his defense of a class society provide a way out of this moral quagmire.

Last Things. Eliot comes face-to-face with his mortality and is forced to make painful judgments about his life and character, though he continues to believe that humans create their own heavens and hells on Earth. Eliot, through his failing eyesight, cardiac problems, and a near-death experience, feels compelled to reexamine his past and renegotiate his future. He seeks the help of a priest, but he is uncomfortable discussing theological issues. He no longer sees a future for himself in government and, much to his wife's approval, he turns down a position offered to him by the Labour Party, now in power. Through discussions with family and friends, he comes to realize that he has not always been a good husband, father, colleague, or friend. His sufferings and the idea of his approaching death sometimes trouble his sleep. Still, he says that he will still have nights when he shall "go to sleep, looking forward to tomorrow."

Critical Evaluation:

Strangers and Brothers is largely the life story of Lewis Eliot, who, like C. P. Snow, was born in 1905 in a small town (the thinly disguised Leicester). In several significant ways Eliot serves as Snow's alter ego, though no strict one-to-one correspondence can be set up between the fictional and real persons. For example, Eliot had studied to become a lawyer, and Snow had studied to be a physicist. Many similarities exist as well: both were Labor Party members, had influential government positions, and were knighted. Furthermore, both managed to overcome lower middle-class family backgrounds to ascend to the heights of the British class structure.

As a sequence of novels, *Strangers and Brothers* is in the traditional of the *roman-fleuve* of such French writers as Honoré de Balzac and Marcel Proust, and of such English writers as Anthony Trollope and John Galsworthy. Snow has written that the idea for the series had a specific origin in time and place: New Year's Day, 1935, in Marseilles, France, where he envisioned a multinovel treatment of a man's life as a unified whole. At this time, he had started writing one of the novels, though he was unsure about whether it was the first of many more. He also had decided, early on, that each novel had to work on its own, apart from its place in the series. Indeed, the novels were published neither in their order of composition nor in their eventual place in Snow's overarching design. Snow himself has divided the novels into those of "direct experience," in which Eliot is the dominant character, and those of "observed experience," in which Snow tells the stories of other principal characters. *Time of Hope*, *Homecomings*, and *Last Things* are examples of direct experience, and *The Masters*, *The Affair*, and *Corridors of Power* are examples of observed experience.

Some critics have praised *Strangers and Brothers* as Snow's greatest achievement, and others have admired his unparalleled use of a first-person narrator in a panoramic novel. The American critic Alfred Kazin found the novels "remarkably intelligent." Other reviewers have noted that the quality of the novels varies considerably, from the nearly universally praised *The Masters* and the award-winning *Time of Hope* and *The New Men*, to such problematic novels as *Homecomings*, *George Passant*, and *The Sleep of Reason*, the last of which Snow admitted gave him much trouble. Three of the novels, *The Masters*, *The New Men*, and *The Affair*, have been successfully adapted for the stage, and the entire sequence, with considerable simplification of plots and numbers of characters, became an extremely successful television series in England and the United States; it then garnered more critical praise when it appeared as a DVD set.

It is understandable that, for such a massive project written over the course of thirty-five years, inconsistencies, factual errors, and other problems such as jarring differences in language crop up. Snow had attempted to remedy these problems in an omnibus edition of the series published in 1972. Nevertheless, several critics who commented on the entire cycle continued to be bothered by Snow's style of writing, which they characterized as leaden, boring, prosaic, and unemotional. Others came to Snow's defense, pointing out that his realistic presentation of facts was in keeping with such classic novelists as Trollope, whom Snow admired. Although Snow was a contemporary of such experimental stylists as Ernest Hemingway and William Faulkner, he was never attracted to modernism, theirs or that of other writers. Some have traced his direct, objective, and honest style to his background as a physicist.

Several scholars have noted that Snow is particularly successful in the novels involving subjects intimately related to his life experiences. As a trained physicist, he is believable and insightful in handling the careers and concerns of scientists. As a "poor boy" from the lower classes who made something of himself, he has an outsider's sensitivity to the weaknesses and incongruities of the hierarchical British social system. As a highly honored statesman, he has an understanding of the private and public functioning of politics. As the author of the controversial book *The Two Cultures and the Scientific Revolution* (1959), this self-described scientific humanist has been able, through his life and work, to bridge the gap between humanistic and scientific cultures. This book provoked a polemic from the literary critic F. R. Leavis, who, with a small number of like-minded scholars, were unwilling to accept Snow into the family of major novelists.

Complicating Snow's achievement has been prejudice against his liberal political views, although a growing number of critics accept his adroit management of strongly antagonistic political views in his novels. Young critics tend to think of Snow as old-fashioned, while critics from Snow's era appreciate that he had the courage and expertise to tackle subjects—such as the interactions among science, technology, and politics—that other novelists neglected. Some even predict that, as the influence of science and technology grows, the appreciation of Snow's achievement in *Strangers and Brothers* is also destined to expand and deepen.

Robert J. Paradowski

Further Reading

De la Mothe, John. *C. P. Snow and the Struggle of Modernity.* Austin: University of Texas Press, 1992. Examines Snow's exploration of the creative (and sometimes destructive) tension among science, technology, and politics.

Greacen, Robert. *The World of C. P. Snow.* New York: London House & Maxwell, 1962. This first published study of Snow argues that he was a "major talent" as a novelist. Includes a bibliography by Bernard Stone.

Heptonstall, Geoffrey. "Venturing the Real: The Significance of C. P. Snow." *Contemporary Review* 290 (Summer, 2008): 224-232. A discussion of Snow's life and work. Heptonstall describes Snow's fiction as "the territory of reason in age of excess," speaking "for decency in a culture of outrage."

Karl, Frederick R. *C. P. Snow: The Politics of Conscience.* 1963. Reprint. Carbondale: Southern Illinois University Press, 1966. Part of the Crosscurrents: Modern Critiques series, this book surveys Snow's writings up to and including *The Affair.* Helpful chronologies on the events in *Strangers and Brothers* and in Snow's life. Includes an index.

Lewis, Terrance L. *C. P. Snow's "Strangers and Brothers" as Mid-Twentieth-Century History.* New York: Peter Lang, 2009. This book, part of the American University Studies series, emphasizes the usefulness of Snow's novel sequence for an understanding of academic and political life in Britain between 1940 and 1970.

Maniyar, A. K. *The Novels of C. P. Snow.* New Delhi: Atlantic, 1991. Maniyar's analysis concentrates on one of Snow's chief themes, especially in the *Strangers and Brothers* novels: class struggle in twentieth century England. The author views Snow as a political novelist par excellence.

Shusterman, David. *C. P. Snow.* 1975. Rev. ed. New York: G. K. Hall, 1999. The author uses controversies engendered by Snow's comments in his lectures to explore similar themes in Snow's early novels and in the *Strangers and Brothers* series. Notes the interest in the series apart from their literary value. Includes notes and references, a selected bibliography, a chronology, and an index.

Thale, Jerome. *C. P. Snow.* New York: Charles Scribner's Sons, 1965. A survey of Snow's life and writings, including the first nine novels of the *Strangers and Brothers* sequence. Includes an interesting concluding chapter on Snow and his critics. Includes references and a bibliography but no index.

Strangers on a Train

Author: Patricia Highsmith (1921-1995)
First published: 1950
Type of work: Novel
Type of plot: Psychological realism
Time of plot: Late 1940's
Locale: New York City; Metcalf, Texas; Palm Beach, Florida; Connecticut; Mexico

Principal characters:
GUY HAINES, an ambitious architect
CHARLES ANTHONY BRUNO, a wealthy sociopath
ANNE FAULKNER, Haines's girlfriend and later wife
MIRIAM JOYCE HAINES, Haines's estranged wife
MRS. BRUNO, Bruno's mother
SAMUEL BRUNO, Bruno's father
ARTHUR GERARD, a private detective
OWEN MARKMAN, Miriam's lover

The Story:

Guy Haines is on his way from New York to his hometown, Metcalf, Texas, to convince his estranged wife Miriam (who is pregnant by Owen Markman) to agree to a divorce. On the train, Guy meets Charles Bruno, a flamboyant alcoholic, who, upon learning of Haines's situation, proposes to kill Miriam if Haines will kill Bruno's father in return. The crime would be perfect, Bruno insists, because no connection between the two could ever be established, and no motivation could ever be discovered. Without a motive, the police would never be able to solve either crime. Haines vacillates, but he does not agree to Bruno's plan.

In Metcalf, Haines finds Miriam more resistant to the divorce than ever. She wants to reignite their relationship and move with Haines and the unborn baby to Florida, the site of Haines's lucrative new building project. Disgusted, Haines leaves Metcalf and learns soon after that Miriam has miscarried. Later, Bruno comes to Metcalf, finds Miriam's home, follows her and two friends to the amusement park, and strangles Miriam.

Haines soon receives a note from Bruno identifying himself as the murderer. Haines does not report Bruno to the police; he waits for the police to find him. Meanwhile, Haines and Anne become engaged. Haines is unable to work, as his knowledge of Bruno's crime seems to erode his creativity. Bruno continues to call, send letters, and stalk Haines. Bruno demands that Haines complete his part of their "bargain" by killing Bruno's father. Otherwise, Bruno will speak to the authorities.

Bruno sends to Haines a deluge of maps detailing the grounds and layout of the Bruno family mansion, suggesting routes to and from the mansion, and identifying the exact spot to scale the wall surrounding it. Bruno has planned Haines's crime meticulously: He specifies the exact number of steps in the mansion, marking those that squeak and should be avoided, and he provides a poetic memory device to enable Haines to remember each detail of the plan and execute the crime without being caught. Haines delays until he wakes up early one morning to find Bruno sitting by his bed, staring at him. Haines finally agrees to kill Bruno's father, hoping to rid himself of Bruno.

On an appointed night and time, when Bruno and his mother are visiting friends in Maine, Haines, who has memorized the maps, enters the house stealthily and shoots Samuel Bruno to death. He elects not to use the large Luger weapon that Bruno has sent to him, using his own small, pearl-handled twenty-two caliber pistol instead. Haines becomes disoriented after escaping the mansion and, hearing police sirens, discovers he is lost. In a panic, Haines returns to his apartment in New York. In the weeks following the murder, Haines disposes of the gloves, overcoat, and shoes he used to commit the crime by throwing them in the garbage or off various bridges. He also disposes of the Luger.

Haines is not suspected of the murder, although Bruno sends letters to employers and friends of Haines, alleging that Haines may be more involved in the murders than was previously thought. Haines plunges into a deep depression. In June, when their new house in Connecticut is completed,

Haines and Anne get married. Haines is horrified to see Bruno at their wedding and to observe Bruno pursuing a friendship with Anne. Bruno also invites himself to their housewarming; he passes out behind a sofa and is carried to the guest room.

Haines takes a job with an architecture firm. He designs a department store, an endeavor much less prestigious than his contract in Palm Beach. He had been on the way to becoming well-known and prosperous for his impressive buildings, but his experiences have hampered his ability to work successfully.

Meanwhile, Mrs. Anthony engages private detective Arthur Gerard to search for her husband's murderer. Gerard investigates and begins to suspect that Bruno and Haines met on the train and, at that time, formulated the plan to exchange murders. After questioning everyone involved, however, Gerard ends his investigation, citing a lack of evidence to prove his theory. Exhilarated, Bruno, in Haines's absence, continues to visit Anne, who suspiciously inquires of Bruno where and when he and Haines first met. Haines, too, is relieved that Gerard is gone. Anne informs Haines that she is pregnant, and they begin to look toward the future.

Days later, Haines, Anne, Bruno, and friends are sailing, when Bruno, drunk, falls off the boat and drowns. Haines travels to Texas and talks with Owen Markman, to whom he confesses the diabolical plot hatched by Bruno and their murders of Miriam and Samuel Bruno. Haines discovers the phone has been "wired." Gerard, who has been listening in on the conversation, enters the room, and Haines surrenders to him.

Critical Evaluation:

Strangers on a Train was Patricia Highsmith's first novel and established the themes, characters, and major concerns for her twenty-two novels and eight collections of stories. Never one to cater to public taste, Highsmith was the survivor of a troubled childhood, a lesbian, and an alcoholic. She wrote out of her own early preoccupations with the idea that murderers lurk behind the masks of normalcy and routine. Making no concessions to traditional character or narrative development, Highsmith frequently concluded works with more questions than answers. As with *Strangers on a Train*, her books, written in matter-of-fact, conventional prose in an inverted crime genre, center on the interiority of her characters, and they have been more popular in Europe than in the United States. Following her death in Switzerland in 1995, however, her writings have experienced a sort of literary revival with American readers.

At age thirteen, Highsmith read *Prestupleniye i naka-*

zaniye (1866; *Crime and Punishment*, 1886), by Russian novelist Fyodor Dostoevsky (1821-1881). The novel affected her profoundly and shaped, to some degree, everything she wrote. Dostoevsky favors psychological realism and places great emphasis upon the mind and consciousness of his characters, as opposed to the natural circumstances emphasized in most realist novels. Dostoevsky stresses the duality of individuals, including contradictions and ambiguities sometimes viewed as paradoxical aspects of consciousness. The motivation behind his characters' actions are complex and uncertain. Some critics see Dostoevsky's writing and, by extension, Highsmith's as fantastic realism, in which the boundaries between external reality and internal consciousness become blurred or the two realms become interpenetrable. Other important influences on Highsmith's thought and writing include Edgar Allan Poe, whose writings ponder the relationship between realism and fantasy, and post-World War II French existentialist philosophers Jean-Paul Sartre and Albert Camus, whose works stress the absurdity of existence and the necessity, however dismal, of choice.

Highsmith distorts the traditional crime genre in *Strangers on a Train*. By telling the story from Haines's point of view, she incorporates aspects of the thriller, but those elements in her novel apply not to the crime itself or the need to see justice done, but rather to the experience of the perpetrator. In a formula that would become typical of her work, Highsmith's novel develops around the attraction-repulsion relationship of two male characters. The men, meeting accidentally, seem at first to be opposites. Haines is concerned with order, design, Plato, and traditional values. He is appalled by Bruno's bizarre offer to exchange murders. Highsmith's Bruno, perhaps by design, bears a certain resemblance to Dostoevsky's similarly stationed character in *Crime and Punishment*, who exerts strange influences over that novel's central character. Bruno assures Haines that criminal desires, including murder, are universal and appears committed to disorder and degeneracy.

Upon learning of Miriam's murder, Haines thinks of Bruno immediately and becomes overwhelmed by guilt because he did nothing to prevent it. Sleeplessness and guilt encourage Haines to consider murdering Bruno's father and leaving clues to incriminate Bruno in order to achieve a semblance of justice. When he executes the murder in his mind, Haines feels relieved. Haines, who has become contradictory, reflects Highsmith's interest in dualism, the idea that human beings are possessed of two equally inherent natures, as opposed to being essentially good and dedicated to fighting evil as an external force.

Highsmith claimed to have meditated on murder at the age of eight, and these meditations appear to have provided a basis for her later belief in and preoccupation with dualism. Consequently, her first novel is concerned with Haines's gradual realization that his plans for a life and family with Anne and his dreams of designing buildings noted for their harmony and beauty were all based upon his belief in his own goodness. As Bruno's manipulations increase, Highsmith urges readers to identify with Haines, as he begins to feel a strange attraction to Bruno, sinks into despair, and eventually accepts his own corruption. Unique among Highsmith's novels, the main character of *Strangers on a Train* is both a hero and a criminal, whereas her Tom Ripley novels focus on a main character who is more simply a criminal, albeit a charismatic one.

For all Highsmith's attention to detail in depicting the routines of everyday life, her characters behave irrationally. Although little background is provided by Highsmith for her characters, they are anchored in a realist world with homes, jobs, books, food, drinks, rituals, and events. The ordinariness of this world promotes the illusion that all is well until readers are shocked by Haines's decision not to go to the police following the murder of Miriam. Haines, who admires logic, does not turn Bruno is and can provide no good reason for not doing so. Questions inevitably arise concerning an attraction between Haines and Bruno and also concerning Bruno's apparent assumption that Haines will not report him.

Irrationality is an important force in the lives of Highsmith's characters. At one point, while committing a burglary for fun, Bruno deliberately takes things he does not want. Haines says what he intended not to say, only to discover that he has confessed to Gerard. Following his murder of Bruno's father, Haines—inexplicably to his family and friends—takes a disadvantageous job in an architecture firm in order to punish himself. Concerning these incidents and others, Highsmith merely presents the events with no explanation, insisting on portraying surface appearances that readers must interpret for themselves.

While such surface appearances tend to reinforce Highsmith's belief that anyone is capable of murder, they also belie the unseen forces at work in Haines, who no longer aims for the goals he entertained before he met Bruno. Having equated creativity with spirituality, Haines's guilt and hatred annihilate his earlier desire to create a soaring white bridge with angel wings. He grudgingly tolerates Bruno's insinuation of himself into his life, as Bruno gets to know Haines's family and friends, but he desperately attempts to erase Anne's fascination with Bruno. When Bruno drowns, however, Haines finds himself diving again and again to try to save him, as he realizes Bruno was his "brother." After Bruno dies, Haines believes he is incapable of bearing all the guilt himself, and he gives himself up.

Strangers on a Train reflects the temper of the times in which it was written, as Highsmith merges her own dark view of existence with the existential view of life that was gaining recognition in the 1940's and 1950's. Highsmith weaves the existential need for choice into her characters' absurd and irrational behaviors, juxtaposing their freedom to be individuals against the determining forces in their world. Highsmith's own voice, however bleak, represents her vision of reality within a world of literary conformity, and it should be appreciated for its authenticity.

Mary Hurd

Further Reading

Harrison, Russell. *Patricia Highsmith.* New York: Twayne, 1997. Informative discussion of Highsmith's background and all of her novels and short stories.

Highsmith, Patricia. *Plotting and Writing Suspense Fiction.* New York: St. Martin's Griffin, 2001. Not a formula book for writing suspense fiction, but a slender volume discussing how Highsmith builds suspense in her writing. Includes her own failures and also her successes as illustrations of her advice for building characters.

Lukin, Josh. "Patricia Highsmith's *Strangers on a Train* as Tragedy of Manners." *Para Doxa* 18 (2003): 157-194. Reads the novel, not as an inversion of the thriller, but as an inversion of the comedy of manners, exploring the relevance of that genre to understanding Highsmith's work.

Payne, K. "Guy and Bruno, Bruno and Guy: American Masculinity and 'Everyday' Schizophrenia in Patricia Highsmith's *Strangers on a Train.*" *The South Carolina Review* 37, no. 1 (2004): 149-156. Analyzes Highsmith's use of the homoerotic relationship between Guy and Bruno to represent the gendered fragmentation of masculine American identity. Useful for understanding the ideological implications of the author's belief in dualism.

Wilson, Andrew. *Beautiful Shadow: A Life of Patricia Highsmith.* New York: Bloomsbury, 2003. Excellently written and researched biography of Highsmith that reveals much fascinating information about a woman who preferred solitude.

The Street

Author: Ann Lane Petry (1908-1997)
First published: 1946
Type of work: Novel
Type of plot: Social realism
Time of plot: World War II
Locale: New York

Principal characters:
LUTIE JOHNSON, an ambitious black woman
BUB JOHNSON, her eight-year-old son
JIM JOHNSON, her husband
POP, her father
WILLIAM JONES, an apartment superintendent
MIN, William's live-in-companion
MRS. HEDGES, a bordello manager
BOOTS SMITH, a bandleader
JUNTO, a white power-broker

The Story:

In an attempt to provide a better life for Bub, her eight-year-old son, Lutie Johnson rents a small fifth-floor apartment in Harlem. Even as she inspects the apartment, she has misgivings, but she dismisses them, believing that this arrangement is only temporary and will allow her to advance herself and protect her son from the unseemly influences of her father's live-in companion, Min, who seems to be introducing Bub to untold vices.

Lutie's mother had died when Lutie was seven years old, leaving her to be raised by her protective and proper grandmother. Granny taught Lutie middle-class values and insisted that she marry her boyfriend straight out of high school because she was an attractive black woman whom men would see as "available."

Lutie and her husband, Jim, buy a house in Jamaica, New York, and do well until he loses his job and cannot find another. To tide them over, they become foster parents until the state removes the children. Her father, Pop, had moved in and thrown a late-night party while Jim and Lutie were away. In the aftermath of this setback, Jim becomes resentful while Lutie becomes more determined, sure that she can somehow find a way to generate income. Accordingly, she secures a job in Connecticut as a domestic. In the two years that she works for the Chandlers, she comes to believe even more strongly in the possibilities of achieving the American Dream. Jim, on the other hand, becomes demoralized and takes a lover.

Learning of Jim's infidelity, Lutie returns to New York with their son and moves in with Pop. She then finds a job at a laundry, attends night school, and ultimately secures an entry-level civil service job. While she is proud of her accomplishments, she feels that she needs a place of her own to protect her son.

Lutie rents an apartment on 116th Street, despite feeling that the superintendent, William Jones, is lusting after her as he shows her the apartment and despite feeling that Mrs. Hedges, who lives downstairs, is sizing her up and trying to figure out how to exploit her vulnerabilities. On Lutie's initial visit, she also meets Min, the seemingly spineless common-law wife of William.

Lutie soon realizes that the neighborhood (not to mention the neighbors) is not ideal, but feels it is the proper first step toward independence. Believing that, like Benjamin Franklin, she can survive on little and still advance while avoiding the pitfalls of the inner city, Lutie underestimates the power of the street, especially as it may affect Bub.

Unbeknownst to Lutie, however, William quickly befriends Bub in an attempt to get closer to Lutie. Bub welcomes the companionship and, knowing that his mother is constantly worrying about money, takes William's advice and opens a shoeshine stand, an act that angers Lutie because she fears he will set his sights too low and become a stereotypic member of the underclass.

Meanwhile, William's infatuation with Lutie spirals out of control. He not only befriends Bub and visits the apartment while Lutie is away but also resolves to kick Min out of his apartment and seduce Lutie. Min, however, recognizes his intentions and consults a root doctor, who gives her a new sense of herself and her own potential. She returns home happier than she has ever been and encouraged that she can prevent William from discarding her because of his infatuation with Lutie.

Lutie, too, receives encouragement after she visits the Junto Bar and Grill. She happens to meet Boots Smith, a local bandleader, who offers her an audition, which she eagerly accepts. After the first night, she feels as if she has secured the position of lead singer and that she will be earning enough money to move to a better neighborhood. Her dreams, however, are quickly dashed. As she returns home from the dance hall, she is confronted by William, who attempts to rape her. Mrs. Hedges rescues Lutie but then tells her that a white gentleman desires to sleep with her (an offer that offends Lutie and makes her even more eager to move). The following night, Smith explains that his boss, Junto, will not allow him to pay Lutie for her singing. She storms out of the club but does not immediately connect the comments of Mrs. Hedges and Smith. Instead, she wonders whether she is sending the wrong message.

Nevertheless, Lutie remains confident that she can advance her career and find a better home. She resolves to study for the next civil service exam and save as much money as she can. Her hunger for a better life directly affects her son. Bub, seeing the need for more income, falls victim to William, who offers him money for his participation in a mail-theft scheme that ostensibly will assist the police in catching crooks. In reality, William is merely trying to exact revenge on Lutie for spurning him sexually. He even identifies Bub to the authorities, who arrest him and take him to juvenile detention.

Lutie, desperate to help Bub, consults a lawyer who insists that she pay him two hundred dollars to ensure Bub's release. Lacking the resources, she calls Smith, who promises to help her. When she arrives at his apartment to get the money, she finds that the money comes with a price: She must sleep with Junto. Outraged, she forces Smith to make Junto leave. She then pleads again for the money, but Smith not only denies her the money unless she capitulates to Junto but also attempts to rape her. To protect herself, Lutie grabs a candlestick and vents all of her anger on his face. Realizing what she has done, she leaves the apartment and boards a train to Chicago, figuring that Bub is better off without her in his life.

Critical Evaluation:

After winning a Houghton Mifflin Literary Fellowship in 1945, Ann Lane Petry completed and published *The Street*, which quickly became a best seller—a first for a novel by an African American woman. The novel delves into the insidious affects of racism, classism, and sexism while challenging many of the stereotypical images of black women.

Although many early critics deemed *The Street* a pale imitation of Richard Wright's *Native Son* (1940), later critics analyzed how the two novels differ. They point to her incorporation of humor, popular culture, feminist issues, and gothic elements as well as many other literary conventions. They also demonstrate how her emphasis on Mrs. Hedges and Min undercuts claims that her work is a naturalist account of powerlessness.

The Street takes a hard look at the conditions that exist in urban ghettos and demonstrates how poverty, racism, and sexism come together to thwart the efforts of one black woman to preserve her dignity and protect her family. By centering the novel on a working-class woman who is attempting to attain the American Dream, Petry provides the reader with multiple insights into the obstacles that prevent black women from attaining success. Lutie fails not because she is blind to the realities around her, but because her wariness leads her to isolate herself, leaving her nowhere to turn when she faces the biggest crisis of her life. Nevertheless, Petry seems to applaud Lutie's determination and adherence to the Protestant ethic (symbolized in part by Lutie's references to Benjamin Franklin). At the same time, however, Petry's other characters suggest that perhaps Lutie might have done better had she been less intent on demonstrating that she could advance without help from others.

In this respect, it is significant that Min and Mrs. Hedges find ways to work around the system. Having no children, they have more options, but their willingness to form relationships with others seems more important to their success. Min lives with William Jones for several years until she cannot stand him any longer. With the help of Mrs. Hedges, she moves out and seems destined for a more satisfying relationship. Mrs. Hedges takes a different route after being scarred by a fire and left permanently bald. Rather than seeking a man to provide for her, she resolves to protect herself and does so by becoming Junto's business partner, identifying new ventures that will expand his empire. In the end, both Min and Mrs. Hedges seem content. Lutie, on the other hand, is left running, hoping to vanish into the anonymity of the streets of Chicago.

Petry is able to flesh out even her minor characters, marking one of the novel's many strengths. Although she employs a third-person narrator, she constantly shifts her focus, providing the reader with insights into the thoughts and lives of characters such as William, Min, Boots Smith, Mrs. Hedges, and even Bub's teacher, Miss Rinner. Despite the negative traits that Petry assigns to some of these characters, the reader gradually begins to understand both their mind-sets and their actions. This is not to say, however, that the reader must necessarily condone their behavior, but only to say that the reader comes to understand the external forces that lead them to make their choices.

Petry's use of detailed descriptions reflects not only her years as a journalist but also her appreciation for the social barriers that stymie individual ambition. From the outset, she immerses the reader into the streets of Harlem with both tactile and sensory imagery. For this reason, readers come away with a new understanding of a world that may well be foreign to them.

C. Lynn Munro

Further Reading

Bryant, Jacqueline. "Postures of Resistance in Ann Petry's *The Street*." *CLA Journal* 45, no. 4 (June, 2002): 444-459. Debunks the notion that Petry's male characters are straw men, arguing that their negative traits are part of their survival strategies.

Eby, Clare Virginia. "Beyond Protest: *The Street* as Humanitarian Narrative." *MELUS* 33, no. 1 (Spring, 2008): 33-53. Suggests the need for a broader critical perspective to appreciate the ways Petry humanizes and evokes sympathy for even her least appealing characters.

Ervin, Hazel Arnett, ed. *The Critical Response to Ann Petry*. Westport, Conn.: Praeger, 2005. Includes eight reviews of *The Street* as well as twenty-six essays, the majority of which focus on *The Street*, its array of characters, and its various thematic threads. Also includes a useful bibliography.

Holladay, Hilary. *Ann Petry*. New York: Twayne, 1996. Offers a good blend of biographical information and critical analysis, emphasizing the importance of community in Petry's work. The first three chapters and the last chapter are especially relevant.

Lubin, Alex. *Revising the Blueprint: Ann Petry and the Literary Left*. Jackson: University Press of Mississippi, 2007. The several essays in the work reevaluate Petry's writings within a leftist/Marxist framework and suggest links between Petry and the Black Arts movement of the 1960's.

Morgan, Stacy I. *Rethinking Social Realism: African American Art and Literature, 1930-1953*. Athens: University of Georgia Press, 2004. Discusses Petry in the context of black graphic artists, poets, and novelists who preserved the social realist tradition well into the 1950's.

Petry, Ann. "The Novel as Social Criticism." In *African American Literary Criticism, 1773-2000*, edited by Hazel Arnett Ervin. New York: Twayne, 1999. Discusses the labels that critics assign to various novels, noting the ways many of these labels overlap. Also dismisses the notion that the novel of social criticism is passé.

Pryse, Marjorie, and Hortense J. Spillers, eds. *Conjuring:*

Black Women, Fiction, and Literary Tradition. Bloomington: Indiana University Press, 1985. Includes essays by Bernard Bell and Marjorie Pryse that focus on Petry's juxtaposition of American myths and American realities, emphasizing her use of dramatic irony. Pryse also discusses alternative perspectives available to Lutie in *The Street.*

Shockley, Evie. "Buried Alive: Gothic Homelessness, Black Women's Sexuality, and (Living) Death in Ann Petry's *The Street.*" *African American Review* 40, no. 3 (Fall, 2006): 439-460. Explores gothic elements (including live burial, homelessness, and the living dead) to explain why Lutie's efforts to secure a stable home for herself and her son are futile.

Wesling, Meg. "The Opacity of Everyday Life: Segregation and the Iconicity of Uplift in *The Street.*" *American Literature* 78, no. 1 (March, 2006): 117-140. Argues that Petry not only transcends determinism but also critiques it just as she undercuts the viability of the American Dream for black women. Focuses on the constraints that preclude those who lack powerful friends from achieving success through individual effort.

Street Scene

Author: Elmer Rice (1892-1967)
First produced: 1929; first published, 1929
Type of work: Drama
Type of plot: Social realism
Time of plot: 1929
Locale: New York

Principal characters:
ROSE MAURRANT, a twenty-year-old woman
ANNA, her mother
FRANK, her father
SAM KAPLAN, a frustrated young intellectual
ABE, his father
SHIRLEY, his sister
HARRY EASTER, a fairly prosperous real estate agent

The Story:

It is a hot June evening in New York, and in front of an old brownstone walk-up apartment in a mean quarter of the city, residents are discussing the weather and the affairs of the day. Anna Maurrant and her lover, Sankey, a collector for the milk company, are the subjects of the gossip of a small group of residents. They are shocked at Anna's behavior—after all, she has a grown daughter. One neighbor reports that Sankey was there twice this week while Anna's husband and their daughter, Rose, were away.

The gossip ceases with the appearance of Anna and the arrival of her husband. Frank Maurrant is irritated that Rose is not yet at home and that her whereabouts are a mystery. He tells Anna that he will have to be out of town the next day; as a stagehand, he is working on a show that is opening outside New York. After the Maurrants leave, the janitor of the building quietly predicts that Frank will someday kill Sankey.

A short time later, Sam Kaplan appears. The arguments and trivial talk that pass among the occupants of the tenement bore him. A twenty-year-old college student, he is depressed over his current situation. He feels trapped by his environment, although Abe, his father, seems content with life in the tenement, reading his newspapers, criticizing the government, longing for a social revolution, and arguing politics with anyone interested. Sam will be happy to leave the tenement atmosphere at the first opportunity.

After the street clears, Rose finally arrives, escorted by Harry Easter, manager of the real estate office where she works. Easter wants to set Rose up in an apartment and take her away from her twenty-five-dollar-a-week job, but Rose refuses his offer. Easter is married, in the first place, and she is not really very fond of him. Besides, she realizes that there will be strings attached to his proposal. Easter leaves at the arrival of Frank, who lectures his daughter on her late hours. Frank, ironically enough, speaks up for family happiness, security, and proper behavior. Sam comes out and sympathizes with Rose, who knows of her mother's situation. Sam feels that neither of them belongs in this sordid atmosphere. He is even more crushed when he tries unsuccessfully to defend Rose from an amorous taxi driver who passes by; the incident adds to his bitterness, which Rose tries in vain to allay. Rose leaves Sam sitting despondently on the curb.

Bustling tenement life goes on as usual the next morning.

In the middle of the hubbub, Sam's sister Shirley warns him to spend more time on his studies and less time with Rose. Later, she asks Rose to avoid Sam. Since he is going to be a lawyer, Shirley feels he should not be distracted from his studies. Rose pleads innocence to the charge of taking Sam's mind from his work. They possibly are slightly drawn to each other, Rose does admit.

Sam's entrance leads to another conversation with Rose concerning life and death. Although Rose, unlike Sam, admits there is joy to be found in life, certainly it is not to be found in their environment. They talk of running away; it is clear that Sam is interested in Rose romantically. Rose, however, is simply interested in getting away from her surroundings.

Although Frank leaves his wife with a less-than-subtle hint that he knows what is going on in his absence, soon after his departure Anna incautiously informs Sankey that no one is at home, Rose leaving for a funeral. After a few minutes, Frank reappears, dashes inside, and kills both his wife and her lover. He emerges, torn and bloody, and escapes. Rose arrives in time to see her mother being carried through the crowd on a stretcher.

Later that afternoon, the tabloids contain full accounts of the bloody murders. Everyone in the neighborhood is talking about the killings and speculating on the whereabouts of Frank, who is still at large. Rose, returning from a grim shopping trip, declines sincere offers of help from Easter and from others. She simply does not wish to feel obligated to anyone; she and her twelve-year-old brother will soon be leaving New York. For the present, they are moving away from the tenement immediately.

An excited crowd surges down the street, heralding the appearance of two police officers and a battered Frank, who tearfully cries that he was out of his head when he committed murder. He tried to be a good father, but this is just the way things turned out. Rose and Sam eventually find themselves alone in the street. Sam, renewing his plea that he and Rose go away together, speaks of their belonging to each other. Rose, however, feels that people should never belong to anyone. If her mother had not depended on someone else for what she should have had inside her, Rose says, the tragedy might have been averted.

She tenderly explains that loving and belonging are different emotions; a person should believe in himself or herself. She tells Sam that perhaps something will work out for them when they are older and wiser. After Sam goes into the house, a sympathetic Shirley appears to say good-bye before Rose leaves for what she hopes will be a new and better life. As she leaves, a shabby-looking couple spot the vacancy notice on the building and ring for the janitor. From the wreath on the door, they decide that someone died; it is probably the reason why the apartment is being vacated.

Critical Evaluation:

Among the important American dramatists of the 1920's and early 1930's, Elmer Rice was probably second only to Eugene O'Neill in the scope of his vision and the range of his theatrical experimentation. Although he achieved some early recognition with his courtroom drama *On Trial* (1914), it was *The Adding Machine* (1923), a wildly expressionistic episodic fantasy about a harried average man, Mr. Zero, who is trapped in an eternity of meaningless, machinelike activities, which earned Rice recognition as one of the most important dramatists in the United States. Then, having written one of the best nonrealistic plays of his time, Rice realized his greatest commercial and critical success with *Street Scene*, one of the most starkly realistic plays ever put on the American stage.

In spite of their radically differing theatrical styles, *On Trial* and *Street Scene* are about the same thing: the dehumanizing effect of modern, urban, industrial society on the human spirit. In *Street Scene*, however, Rice dramatizes his thesis by showing average people in situations of painful personal suffering, instead of abstract characters in symbolic settings, which makes *Street Scene* more powerful.

Street Scene is the forerunner of the social drama of the 1930's. Before this time, what social drama the United States produced criticized only indirectly. In *Street Scene*, however, as soon as the curtain rises, before any plot is set in motion, the audience sees and feels the crowding, ugliness, noise, heat, and general agitation that constantly surrounds these urban dwellers. Such an environment is certain to bring out the worst in people; their necessary proximity guarantees conflict and violence. The situation is bad enough for the unimaginative, who are less aware of alternatives to the stifling quality of their condition, but for the more sensitive soul, who is conscious of being dehumanized, the life is doubly painful. *Street Scene* is a play about individuals who, rebelling in the most limited ways against their plight, unleash the fury that exists beneath the surface of the oppressive status quo.

The story begins with a scene of everyday life in front of the teeming tenement. This close mix of the various racial and social types quickly establishes the general atmosphere of tension, bitterness, and petty viciousness. From this agitated surface, Rice skillfully and naturally draws out one major story and a number of minor ones. The primary plot line concerns Frank Maurrant's violent attack on his wife, Anna, and her lover, Sankey. Paralleled to this is the bittersweet love affair between Frank's daughter, Rose, and Sam Kaplan, a sensitive, young Jewish neighbor. The Maurrant family story counterpoints several other action lines and character studies, such as the birth of the Buchanan baby, the eviction of the Hildebrands, Harry Easter's attempt to seduce Rose, old man Kaplan's Marxist rhetoric, and Mae Jones's open promiscuity. It is all powerfully punctuated by the constant intrusions of the neighbors who, out of boredom and petty vindictiveness, meddle whenever they can.

Although the tenement inhabitants are confined by their economic circumstances, they are even more thoroughly imprisoned by their own distorted social, racial, and religious beliefs and assumptions. All the characters retain their ethnic prejudices and cling to notions of social superiority. The worst family in the building is the most "purely American," the Joneses, with their bullying taxi-driver son, Vincent, their whorish daughter, Mae, and their most vicious of gossips, Mrs. Jones.

Frank is driven to murder his wife from a combination of half-understood frustration and residual Puritan moralism. It is clear that the Maurrants were once happy together, but time, circumstance, and Frank's distorted concept of the husband's role combine to destroy their closeness. Anna takes Sankey as a lover because she feels lost and in need of a kind word. After the killings, Frank admits that he cannot understand what it was that drove him to murder.

Rose understands and, because she does, she is the pivotal figure in the play. The romance with Sam is never really serious, because he is a bright child and she is already a mature woman. Rose alone affirms life and sees the possibility of living it meaningfully as an autonomous human being. The only answer, Rice seems to say, is to insist on one's humanity in the face of all the pressures that modern civilization can bring against it.

Further Reading

Durham, Frank. *Elmer Rice*. New York: Twayne, 1970. Discusses the long career of Elmer Rice as a microcosm of the history of dramatic writing in the United States. Centers on Rice's employment of types and techniques as an accommodation of the changing tastes and artistic demands of the theater.

Gould, Jean. "Elmer Rice." In *Modern American Playwrights*. New York: Dodd, Mead, 1966. Focuses on Rice's background in law and its incorporation in his plots. Considers his experiments with form as efforts to find a new method of dramaturgy. Asserts that both *The Adding Machine* and *Street Scene* are indictments of overmechanization.

Hogan, Robert. *The Independence of Elmer Rice*. Carbondale: Southern Illinois University Press, 1965. Laments the "unhealthy" effects of the theater as a commercial vehicle on all playwrights, especially Rice. Assesses Rice's achievements in relation to other playwrights and within the limitations of the theater itself.

Krutch, Joseph Wood. *The American Drama Since 1918*. New York: George Braziller, 1957. Classic survey of trends in American drama from 1918 to 1956. Argues that the dignifying of human beings in *Street Scene* is the antithesis of *The Adding Machine*, which posits people as ciphers victimized by the machine age.

Novick, Julius. "Elmer Rice's Multiethnic New York." In *Beyond the Golden Door: Jewish American Drama and Jewish American Experience*. New York: Palgrave Macmillan, 2008. Focuses on Rice's depiction of Jewish American characters and experiences. Discusses *Street Scene* and another of Rice's plays, *Counsellor-at-Law* (1931).

Rabkin, Gerald. "Elmer Rice and the Seriousness of Drama." In *Drama and Commitment: Politics in the American Theatre of the Thirties*. Bloomington: Indiana University Press, 1964. Evaluates *Street Scene*, *The Adding Machine*, and *The Subway* as indications of the prevailing fear that mechanistic civilization dehumanizes people. Argues that *Street Scene*, although despairing of modern life, is optimistic.

Vanden Heuvel, Michael. *Elmer Rice: A Research and Production Sourcebook*. Westport, Conn.: Greenwood Press, 1996. An overview of Rice's life and theatrical career, with plot synopses and critical commentary for *Street Scene* and his other plays. Includes a list of cast and credits for major productions.

A Streetcar Named Desire

Author: Tennessee Williams (1911-1983)
First produced: 1947; first published, 1947
Type of work: Drama
Type of plot: Tragedy
Time of plot: 1940's
Locale: New Orleans, Louisiana

Principal characters:
BLANCHE DUBOIS, a neurotic young woman in her late twenties
STELLA KOWALSKI, her younger sister
STANLEY, Stella's husband
STEVE HUBBELL,
HAROLD MITCHELL (MITCH), and
PABLO GONZALES, Stanley's poker-playing friends
EUNICE HUBBELL, Steve's wife

The Story:

Two streetcars, one named Desire, the other Cemeteries, brings Blanche DuBois on a spring afternoon to the Elysian Fields address of her sister Stella, whom she has not seen since Stella's marriage to Stanley Kowalski. Blanche, dressed in a fluttering white garden party outfit, jars with the shabbiness and menace of the neighborhood from her first appearance. The proprietress of the building admits her to the Kowalski apartment a few minutes before Stella's return. One of Blanche's weaknesses becomes immediately apparent when, after a successful search for Stanley's whiskey, she drinks a half glass of it neat.

When Stella returns, Blanche makes only a token effort to hide her dismay at her sister's new surroundings. Stella is happy with her wild man and regards Blanche's criticisms with good-humored tolerance. Blanche turns on Stella and defends herself against a fancied accusation that she allowed Belle Reve, the family mansion, to be lost. When Stanley enters some time later, he greets Blanche brusquely. When he mentions her dead husband, Blanche becomes first confused and shaken, then ill. Later, while Blanche is in the bath, Stanley and Stella are free to discuss the implications of her sudden visit. Stella asks him not to tell Blanche that she is going to have a baby. Stanley, who is suspicious over the loss of Belle Reve and imagines himself cheated of property, tears open Blanche's trunk looking for papers. Blanche enters and, using a pretext to get Stella out of the house, presents him with legal papers detailing the forfeiture of all the DuBois property. Blanche demonstrates a bewildering variety of moods in this scene, flirting with Stanley, discussing the legal transactions with calm irony, and becoming abruptly hysterical when Stanley picks up old love letters written by her dead husband. Her reaction to the news of Stella's pregnancy is reverent wonderment.

It is Stanley's poker night with three cronies, one of whom, Mitch, is a large, sentimental man who lives with his mother. Stella and Blanche enter after an evening in the French Quarter that they extend to two-thirty in the morning to keep out of the way of the poker game. They cross into the bedroom, separated only by portieres from the living room, and meet Mitch leaving the bathroom. Blanche looks after him with some interest as he returns to the game. She begins undressing in a shaft of light through the portieres that she knows will expose her to the men in the next room. She dons a robe in time for Mitch's next trip to the bathroom. Out of the game, he stops to talk to Blanche, and during their conversation she adopts an air of primness and innocence. Not wanting Mitch to see how old she really is, she asks him to cover the naked light bulb with a little Chinese lantern she bought in the French Quarter. They dance briefly to some music from the radio, but when the radio distracts the poker players, Stanley becomes violent and throws the radio out of the window, which sets off displays of temper that involve everyone in the house. Blanche and Stella flee to the upstairs apartment, leaving the men to deal with an outraged Stanley. When Stanley discovers that he is alone, he bellows up the stairway like a lost animal until Stella comes down to him.

The next morning Blanche persists in regarding as desperate a situation that Stella has long since accepted as normal. Blanche recollects an old admirer, Shep Huntleigh, who she thinks might rescue them. When Stella defends Stanley, Blanche retaliates with a long speech describing Stanley as a Stone Age man. Because the noise of his entry is covered by the sound of a train, Stanley hears the entire speech. To keep them from realizing that he overheard, he leaves and enters again. Stella runs into his arms.

Several weeks later, well into the humid Louisiana summer, Blanche is hoping for a proposal of marriage from Mitch, whom she is dating. One day, Stanley, who was been making investigations into Blanche's conduct in Laurel, Mississippi, torments Blanche with hints of what he has found out. After he leaves, a young man comes to the door to collect for the newspaper. Blanche makes tentative advances to him, and before he leaves, she kisses him very gently on the lips.

Later that evening, Blanche and Mitch return from a date. He stays on for a talk in which Blanche tells him she is hardly able to put up with Stanley's boorishness any longer. Mitch almost ends the conversation by asking Blanche how old she is. His mother wants to know. Blanche diverts his attention from her age by telling him about her husband, whom she married when they were both very young. One evening, she discovered her husband in a sexual act with an older man. Later, while they danced to the Varsouviana at a casino outside town, she confronted him with her knowledge. Rushing outside, the young man shot himself. Somehow, the mood of this speech prompts the long-awaited proposal from Mitch. Blanche is incoherent with gratitude and relief.

On Blanche's birthday, in the autumn, Stella prepares a birthday dinner, which Stanley spoils as effectively as he can. He tells Stella that Blanche was a prostitute at a disreputable hotel in Laurel, a hotel she was asked to leave, and that she lost her high school job because of an affair with a seventeen-year-old student. At first Stella refuses to believe Stanley, then she defends Blanche's behavior as a reaction to a tragic marriage. Stanley gives the same information to Mitch, who does not appear for the birthday dinner. Stanley climaxes the scene by smashing the dinner dishes on the floor and giving Blanche his birthday present, a bus ticket back to Laurel. At this point, Stella reveals that she is in labor, and Stanley takes her to the hospital.

Much later that same evening, Mitch comes to the Kowalski apartment in an ugly mood. He repeats to Blanche the lurid details of her past that he learned from Stanley. She admits them angrily and volunteers even worse episodes. In the street outside the house, an old Mexican woman sells her flowers for the dead. Even though Mitch no longer wants to marry Blanche, he begins a clumsy sexual assault on her that she repels by screaming, illogically, that the building is on fire.

With the help of Stanley's liquor, Blanche retreats into the safety of madness. By the time Stanley returns from the hospital, she is decked fantastically in scraps of old finery from her trunk. Stanley rapes her, their struggle underlined by jazz music from a neighboring bar and by a fight between a drunk and a prostitute in the street outside.

In the final scene, another poker game is in progress when Blanche is taken to an asylum. Stella cannot accept her sister's claim that Stanley raped her, for to do so would mean the end of her marriage. To persuade Blanche to leave quietly, Stella tells her that Huntleigh came for her. When Blanche sees the attendants, she is frightened at first, but then quickly responds to their kindness. Mitch rages at Stanley and has to be pulled off him by the other men. Stanley comforts Stella's weeping, and the neighborhood returns to normal, its values undisturbed.

Critical Evaluation:

Tennessee Williams was a prolific writer who published short stories, poems, essays, two novels, an autobiography, and dozens of plays. It is for his plays that he is most widely known. The most successful of these, in both commercial and critical terms, are *The Glass Menagerie* (1944), *A Streetcar Named Desire* (1947), *Cat on a Hot Tin Roof* (1955), and *The Night of the Iguana* (1961). All four received New York Drama Critics' Circle awards, and both *A Streetcar Named Desire* and *Cat on a Hot Tin Roof* won Pulitzer prizes. Although Williams received less critical acclaim in his later years, he is regarded as one of the foremost American playwrights of the twentieth century.

Williams claimed that for him writing was therapy. He was always open about his troubled family background: his father's drunken violence, the unhappy marriage of his parents, his own mental breakdown, and the insanity of his beloved sister, who as a young woman was institutionalized for the rest of her life. Williams did not hide that he was gay or that he was an abuser of alcohol and drugs. Although he denied that his writing was autobiographical, elements from his life appear frequently in his work.

In *A Streetcar Named Desire*, Williams shows the reality of people's lives, an enduring concern of his throughout his writing career. He wrote this play believing he was about to die, so he wrote about what he felt needed to be said. When it was first presented, the play was considered shocking because of its frank presentation of sexual issues.

Williams did not rely on realism alone to portray reality. In *A Streetcar Named Desire* as in other plays, he effectively uses dramatic devices to convey and enrich meanings. Most of the action of the play takes place in the Kowalskis' apartment, but there is also action in the street. This action—the Mexican woman with "flores para los muertos" and the struggle of the drunk and the prostitute—provides not only local color but also a commentary on the main action. When Blanche first arrives at the apartment, a screeching cat is heard, a minor bit of stage business that helps create a sense of Blanche's tension. The background music, too, is carefully contrived. The "Blue Piano" and the "Varsouviana" fade in and out according to what is going on in the minds of the characters, particularly Blanche. Blanche's rape is accompanied by "hot trumpet and drums."

The use of literary devices also underlines the meanings of the play. There are a number of significant names. Blanche DuBois, white woods, as Blanche herself points out "like an orchard in spring," is clearly ironic. The family plantation was Belle Reve, a "beautiful dream" now gone. The Elysian Fields address of Stella and Stanley is an ironic comment on the unheavenly reality of the place, and Blanche arrives there by means of two streetcars, Cemeteries and Desire, which foreshadow the recurring images of death and desire throughout the play.

Death and desire bring Blanche to this low point in her life. She never recovers from the devastating death of her young husband, indirectly caused by the nature of his sexual desires. The deaths of her relatives are instrumental in reducing her to poverty, as do the desires, the costly "epic fornications" of her forebears. Her own promiscuous sexual desire destroys her reputation and her professional career. The rape by Stanley, which he claims is the culmination of a perverse desire they felt for each other all along, is the act that finally pushes her into insanity.

Just as Belle Reve is a relic of the plantation system that was the cornerstone of the civilization of the Old South, so is Blanche an anachronistic leftover from that culture. She is a southern belle, born to privilege and meant to be beautiful and refined, to read poetry, to flirt, and ultimately to marry and reproduce. Blanche is born too late in the history of her family and in the history of the South to inherit this legacy: The money is gone; the values are disintegrating. She hangs on to what vestiges of gentility she can, but this serves only to alienate rather than to shield her. Tender and delicate, like the moth she resembles, Blanche is unable to survive in the harsh reality of modern society.

There is more to the character of Blanche than merely the role of pathetic victim. She, too, has been active in her destruction. As she confesses to Mitch, she was not blameless in her husband's suicide, for her cruel remark seems to have pushed him to it. "I have always depended on the kindness of strangers," she says pathetically to the doctor who leads her away, and perhaps it is a search for "kindness," some warmth of human response, that leads to her gross, self-destructive sexual promiscuity. Despite recognizing her own undeniable flaws, she makes very little attempt to disguise her contempt for those she feels are inferior to her in refinement, and she is willing to use Mitch and Stanley to provide for her. She is also cruel to Stella, the one remaining person who loves her, in criticizing Stella's husband and her way of life.

If Blanche represents defunct southern values, Stanley represents the new, urban modernity, which pays little heed to the past. If Belle Reve is not going to mean a financial in-

heritance, Stanley is no longer interested in Belle Reve. Williams's stage directions indicate that Stanley's virile, aggressive brand of masculinity is to be admired. However, Stanley, like Blanche, is an ambiguous character. His cruel intolerance of Blanche can be seen as justifiable response to her lies, hypocrisy, and mockery, but his nasty streak of violence against his wife appalls even his friends. His rape of Blanche is a horrifying and destructive act as well as a cruel betrayal of Stella. Ultimately, however, Stanley prevails. He gets rid of Blanche, who loses everything, and in the closing lines of the play, he soothes Stella's grief, and their life goes on.

"Critical Evaluation" by Susan Henthorne

Further Reading

Bauer-Briski, Senata Karolina. *The Role of Sexuality in the Major Plays of Tennessee Williams*. New York: Peter Lang, 2002. Analyzes how sexuality is a dominant element in eight plays, including *A Streetcar Named Desire*. Examines how the characters' behavior and relations with other characters are affected by their decisions to either express or repress their sexual inclinations.

Bloom, Harold, ed. *Tennessee Williams*. Updated ed. New York: Bloom's Literary Criticism, 2007. Collection of critical essays, including three focusing on *A Streetcar Named Desire*: "Desire, Death, and Laughter: Tragicomic Dramaturgy in *A Streetcar Named Desire*" by Verna Foster, "Two Transient Plays: *A Streetcar Named Desire* and *Camino Real*" by Frank Bradley, and "'Fifty Percent Illusion': The Mask of the Southern Belle in Tennessee Williams's *A Streetcar Named Desire*, *The Glass Menagerie*, and 'Portrait of a Madonna'" by George Hovis.

Falk, Signi. *Tennessee Williams*. New ed. Boston: Twayne, 1985. An introduction to both the fiction and the drama. Places Williams in the southern tradition and examines his early exploratory work; provides a good general overview with a focus on recurring character types. Includes a chronology of play productions and publications as well as a useful critical bibliography.

Hayman, Ronald. *Tennessee Williams: Everyone Else Is an Audience*. New Haven, Conn.: Yale University Press, 1993. Biographical study that examines how Williams used events from his life and characters he knew, including himself, as source material for his drama.

Londre, Felicia Hardison. "*Streetcar* Running Fifty Years." In *The Cambridge Companion to Tennessee Williams*, edited by Matthew Roudané. New York: Cambridge University Press, 1997. Comprehensive analysis of the play, explaining why it has remained popular for decades after its first performance.

Miller, Jordan Y., ed. *Twentieth Century Interpretations of "A Streetcar Named Desire."* Englewood Cliffs, N.J.: Prentice-Hall, 1971. Excellent collection of twenty essays and reviews divided into two sections that treat the play as commercial theater and as dramatic literature. Provides views from a variety of critics and includes a notebook of the director of the original production.

Paller, Michael. *Gentlemen Callers: Tennessee Williams, Homosexuality, and Mid-Twentieth-Century Broadway Drama.* New York: Palgrave Macmillan, 2005. Charts the evolution of America's acknowledgment and general acceptance of homosexuality by examining Williams's life and the plays he wrote from the 1940's through the 1970's. Describes how critics initially ignored his gay characters and how gay activists in the 1970's reviled his work.

Thompson, Judith J. *Tennessee Williams' Plays: Memory, Myth, and Symbol.* Rev. ed. New York: Peter Lang, 2002. Examines eight plays in considerable detail, including *A Streetcar Named Desire*, in terms of recurring archetypal characters and patterns of action. Interesting analysis of tragic, romantic, and comic images.

Tischler, Nancy M. *Student Companion to Tennessee Williams.* Westport, Conn.: Greenwood Press, 2000. Critical study of Williams's life, career, and work. Analyzes several plays, including *A Streetcar Named Desire*, discussing their literary styles, themes, and Williams's influences from poetry, film, religion, mythology, and personal experience.

Weales, Gerald. *American Drama Since World War II.* New York: Harcourt, Brace & World, 1962. Places Williams's work in the context of his time. Questions the world and the values that Williams depicts as those of his characters, which often represent marginalized "fugitive types."

Studs Lonigan
A Trilogy

Author: James T. Farrell (1904-1979)
First published: 1932-1935; includes *Young Lonigan: A Boyhood in Chicago Streets*, 1932; *The Young Manhood of Studs Lonigan*, 1934; *Judgment Day*, 1935
Type of work: Novel
Type of plot: Naturalism
Time of plot: June, 1916-August, 1931
Locale: Chicago

Principal characters:
STUDS LONIGAN, a street tough
PATRICK LONIGAN, his father, a contractor
MARY LONIGAN, his mother, a pious housewife
MARTIN,
FRANCES, and
LORETTA, Studs's siblings
LUCY SCANLAN, a neighborhood girl
HELEN SHIRES, a tomboy
WEARY REILLEY, the neighborhood bully
PHIL ROLFE, the husband of Frances
CATHERINE BANAHAN, Studs's fiancé
DANNY O'NEILL, a bright neighborhood youngster

The Story:

William "Studs" Lonigan, nearly fifteen years old, graduates from St. Patrick's Grammar School, "the old dump," and surreptitiously puffs a cigarette in the bathroom as he contemplates his future as son, Catholic, and American. His proud parents are satisfied with raising all of their children within the Catholic religion; they confidently count on the Church and its unquestioned authority to provide all the guidance the family needs. At a service attached to the graduation ceremony, they hear the parish priest describe very graphically the omnipresence of sin in society as well as the daily temptations of Satan's attempts to recruit adherents to unholy causes. At a party afterward, Studs and his crowd play kissing games. That night, talking over the evening's activities with his sister, Studs begins to have evil thoughts and to experience sinful feelings. He fears the imminent punishment of God; before dropping off to sleep, the youngster nervously prays and wonders about contrition.

With only the ease of summer stretching before him,

Studs aimlessly roams neighborhood streets and vaguely dreams of performing feats of heroism. He plays soccer with tomboy Helen Shires but really longs to impress Lucy Scanlan, who he hopes might witness his prowess. Studs and Helen talk about spying on a nearby "can-house," where unmentionable activities are presumed to occur. A truculent Weary Reilley joins their ball game but plays too aggressively, deliberately trying to hurt Helen, cursing at them all the while. Studs and Weary fight, and an enthusiastic crowd soon gathers to encourage the vicious battle. In standing up to the notorious Weary, the feared local bully, Studs becomes a hero and establishes his reputation as a "tough." In days following, when he walks the streets, Studs hears even the adults speaking his name; he is a celebrity. Life is promising.

Studs attracts the company of old-time street fighters and, from one of them named Old Man O'Brien, hears vigorous expressions of neighborhood prejudice, particularly that blacks and Jews are ruining the city. Studs unquestioningly accepts this view and accompanies other hoodlums on expeditions to beat and to brutalize such racial and religious interlopers. When Studs's father mildly reprimands him for staying out late, the youngster reacts with anger and ignores any attempted discipline. Studs fantasizes about a relationship with Lucy. Reflecting on the purity of Catholic girls, he spends one euphoric afternoon in Lucy's company, sitting on a tree limb while they sing and chat about the future. Studs feels that moment to be a turning point in his life. As the summer progresses, however, he often walks the streets and parks alone. Disrespectful of adult playground supervisors, Studs bullies youngsters and, after starting a fight at a baseball game, is invited by witnesses to join an older, tougher group of associates.

Studs now openly smokes and chews tobacco. He begins to drink. He stands on the street corner and joins fellow loafers in ethnic slurs, racial jokes, and sex talk that he does not quite understand. Studs regards the poolroom as home, derides school as irrelevant, and cynically wisecracks at ordinary people going about their daily business. Studs's worried father tries to instigate a man-to-man talk, but the weak attempt fails. Studs loses his virginity when he joins a "gang-shag." He feels he is a man. The ending of the summer is a violently formative experience for Studs. He dreams of some amorphous, unplanned future. He feels free but uneasy.

One year later Studs, truant and school dropout, ponders about enlisting for war service, but he and his friends are rejected. He thinks much about death even as he listens to the continued, dreary conversations of his daily associates at Charley Bathcellar's Pool Room concerning the futility of working for a living, the uselessness of education, and the joys of alcohol and sex. Angered at his son's pointless life, Patrick Lonigan puts his son to work for him as a house painter. Still, the young man's self-destructive behavior continues. Studs is a confirmed drunk, frequently having to be carried home by his friends. He is caught with the promiscuous Elizabeth Burns and horsewhipped by the girl's enraged father. As weeks and months pass, Studs's pattern for living remains unchanged. He goes from poolroom to saloon, drinks and fights, and hears and ignores sidewalk discussions of venereal disease. A frightened Studs finally examines his conscience and goes to confession after having a premonition of death. He vows to change his ways but never does; the course of his life is irretrievably set. His character hardens. Studs and his friends deliberately cripple "Jewboy" Schwartz in a game of football that ends with a riot broken up by police. He then disgraces his family with his public drunkenness on Christmas Eve, his all-night carousing precipitating an emotional family crisis on Christmas Day. Studs plunges downward.

As the months progress, the twenty-three-year-old Studs experiences a spasm of virtue. Joining the Young Men's Christian Association (YMCA), he attends respectable dances and dreams of heroic exploits. Yet, he continues to drink, fight at dances, and battle at crap games. Tenuously and unrealistically, he continues hoping for a relationship with Lucy. Studs escorts her to a dance but turns the evening into a disaster when he brutally tries to force sex on the astonished young woman. Studs moves on, righteously regarding himself as strong and denigrating as weak those who follow moral rules.

One evening in the park, Studs boxes a young opponent and is soundly beaten. The old physical Studs appears to be diminishing, but, after the bout, he and his cronies heckle social reformers and other serious political speakers at the Bug Club. Studs then gets drunk on Jamaica ginger and collapses. Not even a powerful hell-fire sermon from heated missionary Father Shannon can deflect Studs from his path. He attends a vile and decadent New Year's Eve party at which Weary is arrested for rape. The next morning, a semiconscious Studs is found lying in the gutter, his body soiled with vomit. He was robbed for eight dollars.

As time progresses, Lonigan's gang starts disappearing into death, illness, or jail. Weakened physically, Studs wonders what he might have done with his life. He becomes engaged to Catherine Banahan, a plain but stable religious young woman, and he resolves once more to change. America, however, is in the beginnings of the Great Depression, and Studs invested his meager savings in stocks that failed. His view of life now thoroughly pessimistic, Studs blames the state of things on foreigners and international bankers and feels that only a leader such as Italy's Fascist dictator Benito Mussolini can save the reeling country. Studs visits the home of his sister Frances, married to Phil Rolfe, whom Studs always regarded as unimportant. He is jealous of their apparent happiness and comfort while he, sickly and unemployed, has to walk the streets in search of a job, his father's business having gone bankrupt. Studs witnesses many scenes of the Depression: people in panic over the closing of banks, down-and-outers begging for work, and radicals talking revolution. Studs regards communists as misguided people without moral values. A disillusioned Studs fights with his upstart brother Martin, who is intent on following a street-tough path. A vanquished Studs realizes how far he has slipped, and when he presents himself as candidate for the Order of Christopher, he is maligned as "runt" and "shrimp."

During the seemingly endless days, Studs wanders the city half heartedly. When he tries to play sandlot baseball, he is physically inadequate and is ridiculed by the younger men. He escorts Catherine to the beach, to movies, and to dance marathons. After they quarrel over his selfish, thoughtless manners, however, Studs goes to a betting parlor, wins six dollars, and pays a distraught woman for sex, as she tries desperately to recoup the food money she lost. The following day Studs, mistakenly feeling he made a conquest and desiring another ego-building encounter, returns to the woman's apartment. The irate woman, shocked to see him, insults his manhood, verbally flays his character, and threatens to call the police. The disconsolate Studs makes up with Catherine and recklessly seduces her. Not long thereafter, when Catherine tells him of her probable pregnancy, Studs suggests that she have an abortion but finally acquiesces to a wedding. At the beach, however, Studs suffers a heart attack and faints in the water. His health continues to decline.

Studs interviews for several jobs; each reveals his shortcomings. He continues his careless behaviors of drinking and smoking. During one particularly chilly, rainy day, Studs sits in wet clothing through a burlesque show. He arrives home desperately ill. When his condition worsens, a terrified Catherine appeals to Mrs. Lonigan for a bedside wedding to give her unborn child a name, but Studs's mother reviles the young woman, blaming her for Studs's present deteriorated condition. Studs dies as his mother falls into hysterics and his brother and his father get drunk.

Critical Evaluation:

Studs Lonigan is a sociological case study in fiction, a stern indictment of society awash in empty cultural institutions, and a chronicle of the failed American Dream amid a fractured urban landscape. It charts, in often brutal episodes, the life and premature death of a once promising middle-class Irish Catholic American, a product of parochial education, of a devout home, and of the city streets. The action is discontinuous, with episodes sometimes moving only minutes forward but on occasion leaping ahead years. Nevertheless, the gloomy tread of inevitability stalks every page of the degenerate journey made by James T. Farrell's archetypal protagonist.

The failed authority symbols of church, home, and school dominate Studs Lonigan's landscape. Despite the principles articulated before the young man, there never evolves within him an ethical purpose or a moral center. His response to life focuses on the ephemeral fame that underscores his street identity. Studs's models become the fast-talking, luridly fascinating poolroom hacks; his poetry becomes the accessible braggadocio of the saloon. Education is for "goofs" such as Danny O'Neill, whose later commitment to radical social values testify to his humanism; civilized behavior is for the weak. Cynically, Studs concludes that everything is "crap"; a bleak nihilism comes to shroud his every attitude, even the fearful moments of halfhearted reform. His life reflects a compendium of failure. Studs's imminent death is foreshadowed by the demise of the institutions that fail to reach him and that leave a spiritual vacuum in his life, unable to deflect him from the path of self-destruction.

Indoctrinated early into the streetwise brotherhood of sadism and self-indulgence, Studs remains surrounded by an urban ambience whose very physical environment reeks of threat and violence: decrepit pool rooms, sleazy bars, greasy diners, ominous brothels, and menacing parks. The milieu about him crushes his early romantic yearnings and his potential for fulfilling heroic plans. Corrupted into an ethos of brutality and ignorance, Studs succumbs to the crude clichés of the street, and the sensual lures to his libido dominate his maturing days. In the safe haven of an escapist movie theater where he once identified with the luminous hero, Studs now sympathizes with the plight of the gangster; he feels unaccountably sad when the villain is killed. Studs, in fact, knows right from wrong; the powerful forces about him, however, easily control his will.

The theme of isolation runs through the trilogy, for "Lonewolf" Lonigan develops a psychological system for separating from his essential self and observing his own behaviors as a seemingly objective judge. He recriminates, rationalizes, and condones the behavior of Studs, a person standing against the world, superior to those people and institutions that victimized him. Studs walks alone. Even with his antisocial cronies accompanying him on immoral activities, he maintains his own counsel. Taking part in violent episodes, he remains alone in feelings of fear and guilt. Ironically, he never comes to belong anywhere, an embodiment of the alienated, the outsider. He is alone and awash in his own filth, lying in the gutter on New Year's Day, another vivid foreshadowing of decline. From page one of this trilogy, Studs's fundamental estrangement from church, family, school, and self takes its toll. He is on his inexorable journey to an early grave.

A number of urban venues aid in mirroring the deterioration and degeneration of Studs: the burlesque theater, the betting parlor, the park bench, and the dance marathon. His life filled with illusion and prejudice, Studs has no beliefs, and his solitary wanderings only serve to intensify the bigotry of his feelings. Hating himself, he nevertheless goes to the burlesque show, associating with a clientele he regards as inferior and depraved. He considers himself above the desperate patrons in the bookie-joint, for he is Studs Lonigan, brother-in-law of Phil Rolfe, one of the operators. In the park he mindlessly threatens an intelligent communist, who, Studs reasons, must oppose God and family. The dance marathon, however, epitomizes the meaningless foxtrot of death that Studs joins. Like the sick and tired dancers who barely move their feet to stay alive in the tawdry dance competition, hoping for a few dollars, Studs, too, is engaged in a marathon of sorts, his own *danse macabre*. Without reflective thought he, too, is moving his feet out of instinct; he, too, is governed by capricious laws; he, too, is without essential hope but carries vague expectations. Around and around the dancers and Studs move, surrounded by decrepitude and dissonance. To the end, Studs maintains a totally unrealistic assessment of himself, his prospects, and his talent. With his death he leaves "the old dump" of a world just as he left St. Patrick's Grammar School a decade and a half earlier.

Abe C. Ravitz

Further Reading

Beach, Joseph Warren. *American Fiction, 1920-1940*. New York: Macmillan, 1941. Farrell's fiction is examined in the context of his contemporaries. Sections dealing with themes in *Studs Lonigan* include "James T. Farrell: Tragedy of the Poolroom Loafer" and "JTF: The Plight of the Children."

Branch, Edgar M. *James T. Farrell*. New York: Twayne, 1971. A sound assessment of Farrell's achievement as well as a perceptive interpretation of his aesthetic philosophy. Two separate chapters deal with *Studs Lonigan* specifically.

_____. *Studs Lonigan's Neighborhood and the Making of James T. Farrell*. Newton, Mass.: Arts End Books, 1996. A look at the Chicago neighborhood of Farrell's youth and the inspiration for the Studs Lonigan series. Includes illustrations, maps, bibliographical references, and an index.

Fanning, Charles. "James T. Farrell and Irish-American Fiction." In *The Irish Voice in America: Two Hundred Fifty Years of Irish-American Fiction*. 2d ed. Lexington: University Press of Kentucky, 2000. Fanning, the director of Irish and Irish immigration studies at Southern Illinois University, includes a chapter on Farrell in his examination of Irish American fiction, discussing the Studs Lonigan trilogy and other works.

Farrell, Kathleen. *Literary Integrity and Political Action: The Public Argument of James T. Farrell*. Boulder, Colo.: Westview Press, 2000. Kathleen Farrell, James T. Farrell's former daughter-in-law, charts his life in the 1930's, when he, like many of his contemporaries, was involved in left-wing political causes and sought to create a socialist literature.

Frohock, William M. *The Novel of Violence in America, 1920-1950*. Dallas, Tex.: Southern Methodist University Press, 1958. In a section entitled "James T. Farrell: The Precise Content," there is an analysis of the novelist's "documentary" style of writing that is much in evidence in the trilogy.

Landers, Robert K. *An Honest Writer: The Life and Times of James T. Farrell*. San Francisco: Encounter Books, 2004. A fresh look at Farrell. This biography argues for renewed appreciation for the American naturalist, who has fallen out of popular and of critical favor.

Walcutt, Charles C. *American Literary Naturalism: A Divided Stream*. Minneapolis: University of Minnesota Press, 1956. An analytical account of naturalistic literary theory and Farrell's "aspects of telling the whole truth."

Wald, Alan M. *James T. Farrell: The Revolutionary Socialist Years*. New York: New York University Press, 1978. A thorough historical account of Farrell's intellectual roots and evolving political stance. Important for an understanding of the sociopolitical underpinnings of the trilogy.

A Study in Scarlet

Author: Sir Arthur Conan Doyle (1859-1930)
First published: 1887, serial; 1888, book
Type of work: Novel
Type of plot: Detective and mystery
Time of plot: Nineteenth century
Locale: London

Principal characters:
SHERLOCK HOLMES, the detective
DR. JOHN WATSON, his friend
JEFFERSON HOPE, an American
TOBIAS GREGSON and LESTRADE, detectives from Scotland Yard

The Story:

To many, the Afghan wars bring fame and promotion, but to John H. Watson, M.D., they bring only misfortune. He is wounded by a Jezail bullet, succumbs to enteritis during his convalescence, and after months of suffering is sent home with a pension of eleven shillings and sixpence a day. At first, Watson lives in a hotel, but his pension scarcely covers his bills. By chance, he meets an old friend, Stamford, to whom he confides his difficulties. Stamford tells him of an amateur scientist, Sherlock Holmes, who has rooms at 221B Baker Street and is looking for someone to share them. Stamford warns him that Holmes pursues unorthodox studies—one day, Stamford finds him beating a cadaver to see if bruises can be produced after death—and that he has a queer habit of making deductions from trifling details. Watson grows curious about Holmes and arranges to have Stamford introduce them. Soon after that first meeting, Watson goes to share Holmes's rooms on Baker Street.

Watson never goes out and consequently spends much time studying his new friend. He finds Holmes an amazingly contradictory man, one who knows nothing at all of literature, philosophy, or astronomy but has a profound knowledge of chemistry, anatomy, and sensational crime stories. He also plays the violin. From time to time, Holmes has visitors, but Watson never knows why they come.

One day at breakfast, Watson learns a good deal more about his friend. Holmes shows him a letter from Tobias Gregson, a Scotland Yard investigator, who asks him for help in a case of murder. A gentleman identified by his visiting cards as Enoch J. Drebber, "Cleveland, Ohio, U.S.A.," was found murdered in a deserted house in Lauriston Gardens. Holmes then explains that he is a consulting detective and that Scotland Yard asks for his help whenever an unusual case comes up that is outside police jurisdiction or too difficult.

Holmes and Watson take a cab to Lauriston Gardens to look into the affair. Holmes spends a long time outside in the road and in the yard. Watson is impatient at the delay, but Holmes examines everything carefully. Inside the house, Gregson and another detective from Scotland Yard, Le-strade, greet them and point out the body of Drebber, which is surrounded by spatters of blood. Holmes goes over the body painstakingly.

As the orderlies carry out the corpse, a woman's wedding ring falls to the floor. The Scotland Yard men are sure a woman is involved, and Lestrade is triumphant when he finds the word "Rache" printed in letters of blood on the wall. As Holmes leaves the room, he announces his findings to the detectives. The murderer is more than six feet in height and florid. He wears square-toed boots, smokes a Trichinopoly cigar, has long nails on his right hand, and drove up to the house in a four-wheeler drawn by a horse with a new shoe on his off forefoot. Further, the murder was done by poison, and "Rache" is not an abbreviation for Rachel but rather the German word meaning revenge.

Holmes read the story from the cigar ashes, the tracks, the height of the writing, and the scratches made during the writing on the wall. From the fact that the blood on the floor came from a nosebleed, for example, he deduced that the murderer has ruddy coloring. After uncovering these initial clues, however, Holmes is baffled for a time. When he advertises the wedding ring as lost, an old woman comes to claim it, who eludes him when he tries to follow her. At that point, he realizes that he is dealing with a clever opponent.

The murdered man's trail leads to his secretary, Stangerson. Gregson is sure that if he finds Stangerson, he will have the murderer. When, however, Stangerson is found dead in his hotel room, stabbed through the heart, the case begins to seem impenetrable. Gregson and Lestrade come to Holmes one night, and the three detectives and Watson go over the difficulties. Holmes is tying up a trunk preparatory to sending it away. He calls a cab to deliver it. When the bell rings, he asks the driver to come up to help with the ropes. As the man bends down, Holmes deftly slips handcuffs over his wrists. The driver is a large, vigorous man who fights as if possessed, but the four men subdue him. With a theatrical flourish, Holmes introduces him as Jefferson Hope, the murderer of Drebber and Stangerson.

Hope calms down and tells the men he has nothing to fear. He asks Watson to feel his pulse, and Watson, who immediately detects an aneurism, agrees that Hope has not long to live. Indeed, Hope never comes to trial, for he dies in less than a week, but before that he recounts his strange story.

On the great alkali plain in Utah, a man named John Ferrier and his little daughter Lucy were the only survivors of a wagon train. The two were providentially picked up by Mormons, who, under the leadership of Brigham Young, were on their way to a new settlement in the wilderness. Ferrier agreed to adopt the Mormon faith in return for being rescued, and he prospered and became a rich man; Lucy grew up to be a beautiful woman. Although he was a Mormon, Ferrier refused to take wives, and he made a vow that Lucy should never marry a Mormon. When a traveler named Jefferson Hope stopped at their house on his way to the silver mines, an attraction developed between him and Lucy. After Hope left, the Mormon elders decreed that before thirty days should elapse, Lucy must choose a husband. She was given the choice between two men, Drebber or Stangerson, who already had several wives. Ferrier sent word to Hope, who returned on the thirtieth day, and that night Hope, Ferrier, and Lucy stole out of the Mormon village and rode away toward the mountains.

Once he judged that they were far enough away, Hope left Ferrier and Lucy in camp while he went hunting. On his return, he found that Ferrier was murdered and that Lucy was gone. Hope hid near the Mormon village in the hope of rescuing Lucy, but he was thwarted by the strong, watchful Latter-day Saints. Lucy was married off to Drebber, but survived only one month. While the women watched at night over her coffin, Hope stormed in, kissed his dead love, and took the wedding ring from her finger. Then he vanished.

Shortly afterward, both Drebber and Stangerson renounced Mormonism and moved to Cleveland. They were wealthy, but they were also afraid, for they knew that Hope was pursuing them. They fled to Russia and Germany and finally ended up in London. Hope followed them from place to place. To survive in London, and in order to follow his prey conveniently, he took a job as cabdriver. When Drebber engaged him one night when he was drunk, Hope drove him to the deserted house in Lauriston Gardens. After showing Drebber the wedding ring, he took a small box from his pocket containing two pills, one harmless and one deadly. He forced Drebber to choose one and swallow it and put the other in his own mouth. Hope felt that Lucy's spirit guided the choice when Drebber died. On impulse, Hope scribbled "Rache" on the wall with the blood that gushed from his nose

in his excitement. Later, Hope found Stangerson in his hotel room and offered him the same fatal choice. Stangerson attacked him, and Hope killed him with a knife. He refused to give the name of the old woman who appeared to claim the ring. On the day he was to appear in court, Hope died from the bursting of his aneurism, but his work was done and Lucy was avenged.

Critical Evaluation:

A Study in Scarlet was Sir Arthur Conan Doyle's first full-length detective novel. His short stories had already earned him some success and recognition, but with this effort he hoped to attract the attention of critics as well as the general reading public. Doyle longed to write serious historical fiction, in which he intended to chronicle the deeds of the men and women who made England great, but he believed that he must first establish himself as a respected and popular author. *A Study in Scarlet* met with several rejections from publishers, however, before Doyle finally managed to sell it in 1886 for the modest sum of twenty-five pounds. When the book appeared the following year as part of *Beeton's Christmas Annual*, most of the London critics completely ignored it, but it soon became very popular in the United States. Encouraged by his American publisher to write another full-length Holmes adventure, Doyle revived his detective for *The Sign of Four* in 1890, which was a success on both sides of the Atlantic. The reception of this novel stimulated renewed interest in *A Study in Scarlet*, which thereupon appeared in several separate editions and assured the author's fame and the immortality of the world's first consulting detective. (*Beeton's Christmas Annual* for 1887 has become one of the rarest and most collectible works of modern fiction.)

A Study in Scarlet provides the reader with a great deal of vital information about Sherlock Holmes and Dr. John Watson, and while it lacks the polish and style of Doyle's later detective novel, *The Hound of the Baskervilles* (1901-1902), it remains one of the most popular adventures in the canon. The greatest weakness of the novel lies in Doyle's failure completely to integrate the tragic tale of Lucy Ferrier and Jefferson Hope into the narrative of the dual murder. In later stories, Doyle became a master of integrative devices, but in *A Study in Scarlet* the reader's concentration is immediately diverted by two equally fascinating tales joined together by only the flimsiest of connections.

To students of detective fiction, *A Study in Scarlet* is valuable because it presents the details of the meeting of Dr. Watson and Sherlock Holmes. In the opening pages of the novel, Doyle uses the occasion of a mutual acquaintance introducing them to each other to delineate the personalities of his two characters. Although he added a wealth of subtle details in later stories, Holmes and Watson remain fixed in readers' minds from the moment they read of the world's first consulting detective rushing up to the bemused physician with the prophetic cry "I've found it! I've found it!"

In *A Study in Scarlet*, Doyle demonstrated his ability to create a believable atmosphere through the subtle use of detail. From a careful reading of the adventures of Holmes and Watson, a serious student of Victorian culture is able to recreate the England of the last quarter of the nineteenth century. Doyle's portrait of London in all its varied aspects is particularly vivid. He did not try to create a fictional landscape or make merely random references to suggest a particular locale but incorporated his setting into each tale as an integral part of the story line—the setting itself becomes a character. Doyle is equally adept at using the events of everyday life to give his characters credibility and to create a degree of verisimilitude often missing in popular fiction. For Doyle's contemporaries, Holmes and Watson soon ceased to be the creations of a skilled novelist and became instead living human beings. Their daily routine seemed so real, their reactions to the world about them so natural, that they assumed an existence independent of their creator. In time, even Doyle became aware of this remarkable metamorphosis, though he did not always find it gratifying.

A Study in Scarlet is, above all else, an absorbing tale, particularly the portion that deals with solving the double murder. Doyle is a master of detective fiction without equal. He does not conceal information from his readers, and every clue is presented and examined in detail, yet the reader sleuth finds the solving of each crime as difficult as do the two professionals from Scotland Yard. Doyle's final solutions seem so logical and reasonable that the reader experiences the conflicting emotions of relief and frustration, while at the same time longing for one more chance to best Mr. Sherlock Holmes at his own game.

That portion of *A Study in Scarlet* that deals with the early Mormon settlement in Utah is weaker because it is based more on myth and nescience than on fact and because Doyle brings into his narrative all the popular contemporary prejudices against the Latter-day Saints. However, he accords to Jefferson Hope an honor he reserved only for those among his characters who commit crimes for noble motives: His untimely death saves Hope from an earthly tribunal.

While Holmes, Watson, Gregson, and Lestrade, who begin their long evolution here, are already rounded, full-dimensional characters, the other figures in the tale— Drebber, Stangerson, Lucy, and John Ferrier—often appear one-dimensional, familiar players in the pulp fiction of the time. Only Hope reveals greater depth of personality, but his literary life is, of course, cut short by an aortic aneurism. In his later stories, Doyle would form even his minor characters with much greater and more subtle skill, another trait that sets his work apart from traditional detective fiction.

Through his master detective, Doyle portrays the understanding of the criminal mind as a matter of scientific principles that may easily be comprehended but not easily mastered. Although Holmes is an enigmatic figure, given to unorthodox and unaccountable behavior, he is at heart a rationalist and enamored, like any enlightened nineteenth century scientist, by the idea that there is no such thing as a mystery; there are only puzzles that anyone devoted to fact can solve. Hence, his famous exclamation: "It's elementary, my dear Watson!" For Holmes, human evil and passion are not without reason and motive; they are, therefore, rational and deducible. The world is only mysterious and uncontrollable to those who will not see. Sherlock Holmes, offspring of nineteenth century enlightenment and the scientific revolution, is among the brightest—and perhaps the last—offspring of that age.

"Critical Evaluation" by Clifton W. Potter, Jr.

Further Reading

Carr, John Dickson. *The Life of Sir Arthur Conan Doyle.* New York: Harper, 1949. Considered the definitive biography of Doyle because it is based on a thorough study of Doyle's private papers by one of the masters of the mystery novel.

Doyle, Arthur Conan. *Memories and Adventures.* Boston: Little, Brown, 1924. Leaves many matters untouched and questions unanswered but provides valuable insights into the life of the author toward the end of his career.

_____. *The New Annotated Sherlock Holmes.* Vol. 3. Edited, with a foreword and notes by Leslie S. Klinger. New York: W. W. Norton, 2005-2006. Volume 3 in this three-volume set contains extensively annotated texts of *A Study in Scarlet* and three other novels, in which Klinger defines obscure terms and discusses various issues raised by each book. Additional information is provided in the appendixes that follow each novel.

Jaffe, Jacqueline A. *Arthur Conan Doyle.* Boston: Twayne, 1987. Part of Twayne's English Authors Series, this is an excellent brief introduction to Doyle's life and in particular to his works. Two chapters, "The Beginnings of a Modern Hero: Sherlock Holmes" and "The Return of Holmes," deal with Doyle's detective fiction. Includes a short but useful bibliography.

Kestner, Joseph A. *Sherlock's Men: Masculinity, Conan Doyle, and Cultural History.* Brookfield, Vt.: Ashgate, 1997. Examines aspects of masculinity in the Sherlock Holmes novels and stories. Includes an analysis of *A Study in Scarlet.*

Lycett, Andrew. *The Man Who Created Sherlock Holmes: The Life and Times of Sir Arthur Conan Doyle.* New York: Free Press, 2007. Comprehensive and detailed biography, based in part on materials in Doyle's personal archive, which were not available to researchers until 1997. Lycett describes the events of the author's life and the variety of his writings, explaining how the author who created one of the world's most rational detectives was a believer in spiritualism and the supernatural.

McLaughlin, Joseph. "Holmes and the Range: Frontiers Old and New in *A Study in Scarlet.*" *Writing the Urban Jungle: Reading Empire in London from Doyle to Eliot.* Charlottesville: University Press of Virginia, 2000. Examines how Doyle and other British writers used words and images that defined the British Empire's colonies, particularly those in Africa, to describe life in metropolitan London.

Weimer, Christopher B. "A Cervantine Reading of Conan Doyle: Interpolated Narrative in *A Study in Scarlet.*" In *Sherlock Holmes: Victorian Sleuth to Modern Hero*, edited by Charles R. Putney, Joseph A. Cutshall King, and Sally Sugarman. Lanham, Md.: Scarecrow Press, 1996. This comparison of the novel to the works of Miguel de Cervantes was one of the papers presented at a conference of the Baker Street Breakfast Club, where members offered various interpretations of the character of Sherlock Holmes.

A Study of History

Author: Arnold Toynbee (1889-1975)
First published: 1934-1961, 12 volumes
Type of work: History

Not every work that is monumental because of its size is monumental in character. Arnold Toynbee's *A Study of History*, a twelve-volume work, compels the continuing critical attention of historians, philosophers, and other students of civilizations rising and falling over time. Despite its scope, this book is not superficial; despite its author's ambition—to account for the death of civilizations—it shows no sign of a confusion between modesty and unoriginality: Considered as a theory, it is daring and illuminating.

Is the work, however, true? Most readers hesitate to enter upon a multivolume pilgrimage if the only reward is acquaintance with a scholar's laborious fancies. In the sense in which Toynbee is a philosopher of history, a philosopher of history is someone, generally a historian, who tries to make sense out of the mass of events presumed to have occurred. Proceeding from records and signs, or what are thought to be records and signs, a story of the presumed past is constructed: That is history. The story is then surveyed in an attempt to find its theme, the moral of the tale: The account of these reflections is this person's study of history.

Such a study may be true, or it may not. To be true, such a study practically requires a historian who is a genius, some-thing of a seer, and levelheaded. Such a person might discover or create an explanation of history that shows that the fortunes and accidents of history are fortunes and accidents only relative to people's ignorance. Considered in such a light, history is inevitable. Given the demands of an accurate study of history, it is more likely that, strictly speaking, a given study of history is false—that at best it approximates the truth and makes some sense to people who share something of the author's perspective. In any case, the truth of such a study is unimportant.

Not the truth of the theory, but its plausibility is what counts; not its conformity to undiscoverable facts, but its organizing power in the face of evidence. Even if a reader rejects a study of history because of its failure to make sense out of the evidence, it is still possible that the work will have had the value of showing a creative mind's response to a historical problem. That Toynbee's study has this latter value is beyond question. To some, his theory is plausible; to others, it is as clearly false; but to all, it is exciting and worthy of respect.

Toynbee's study of history led him to present and defend the thesis that "societies," not nations, are the proper concern of the historian. According to Toynbee, civilized societies—civilizations—arise in response to challenging conditions; the civilizations grow in response to further challenges; they break down, that is, cease to respond creatively, because of some idolization of the past; and finally, they disintegrate. The civilization then becomes a dominant minority, an internal proletariat (in the society, but not of it), and an external proletariat (formerly, but no longer, of the society) as a result of the failure to respond in such a way as to meet a challenge that is repeatedly presented.

The answer to the central question, Why do civilizations die? is that they die as a result of an inability to determine themselves creatively. The failure of self-determination results, if petrifaction does not set in instead, in a schism of the society that is paralleled by a schism in the soul of the member of the society.

The thesis and each point in its defense is illustrated historically in Toynbee's work. One of the values of the work comes from its ability to charm the reader into a reexamination and reappraisal of the content of history. It also introduces readers to many historical findings with which they may not have been acquainted previously.

Dispassionately considered at some distance from the wealth of historical material that gives the thesis great persuasive force, Toynbee's central claim is perhaps not as remarkable as it may seem to be while one is reading *A Study of History*. It may be that in his use of the term "civilization," Toynbee has employed a criterion by reference to which he dismisses certain societies as primitive. The analysis reveals what his use of the term "civilization" indicates: societies that grew not from favorable, but from unfavorable and challenging conditions. Similarly, it might be argued that his account of disintegration is a question-begging truism, handsomely disguised. Civilizations decline before they fall; they fall because they fall apart, and they fall apart because they can no longer hang together creatively.

The value of the study, however, is not a function of the remarkableness of the claim. Perhaps for the first time, a historian has shown civilizations, to a considerable extent, as they are: not as living organisms, not as accidents, not as the fruits of fortune—but as societies, achieving their characters as civilizations from the mode and quality of their responses to challenges, and falling apart when, either because of the absence of challenge or because of the presence of challenges too strong to be met, the society and the individuals composing it divide into irreconcilable parts. If what Toynbee presents is a truism, at least he has had the wit to see it as a truth and the historical knowledge to make it respectable. Furthermore, he has imagination and spiritual courage.

It takes spiritual courage to argue, as Toynbee does, that history is "a vision of God's creation on the move," and that the historian finds six dimensions—the three of space, then time, life, and the Spirit. He also appraises the chances that humans have in Western civilization to pursue their "true" end: glorifying God. He argues that the laws of nature do not control all of peoples' actions, but that, within limits, humans are free; perfect freedom, he adds, is to be under the law of God. Finally, he conducts a "survey of saviours" and concludes that only Jesus has made good his claim to be the son of God.

These beliefs are not unpopular; indeed, they are shared by millions. What is odd, and therefore demanding of courage, is the expression of these beliefs in a study of history, not merely as token reminders of the faith of people in Western civilization, but as necessary to both the understanding and the existence of Western civilization itself. Although it may seem strange and unhistorical to explain history by a declaration of religious faith, it is possible, even for the unbeliever, to appreciate the historical point of Toynbee's declaration of religious faith. First, as Toynbee shows, Western civilization is, for the most part, a Christian civilization. Second, if Toynbee is right in arguing that civilizations rise and grow as they make creative responses and break down and disintegrate as they fail to determine themselves, then to be born and to grow through an exercise of the proper spirit is the special business of any individual or civilization that values life and the special quality of life that creative activity provides. It is certainly excusable for a Christian scholar to make these points in Christian terms.

A particular benefit of Toynbee's spiritual approach to historical problems is his analysis of "schism in the soul" in a disintegrating society. In a growing society, people are creative or mimetic; that is, they are leaders or imitators. In a disintegrating society, however, there is an increasing tendency to substitute for creativity and mimesis, either passively or actively. For example, instead of being creative, people might be inclined either to live with abandon, to follow their impulses (the passive substitute), or to live with self-control, keeping their passions in check (the active substitute). Truancy (desertion) and martyrdom (action above and beyond the call of duty) are considered to be the passive and active substitutes, respectively, for mimesis. Toynbee also considers "the sense of drift" and the "sense of sin" as alternative substitutes for the feeling of creative advance that accompanies the growth of a civilization. His discussion of other spiritual attitudes and characteristics is intelligent and illuminating.

Toynbee refuses to be either pessimistic or optimistic

about the possibility of the survival of Western civilization. Of the twenty-eight civilizations that Toynbee finds in history, only Western civilization is not clearly disintegrating or already dead. Toynbee sees some signs of breakdown in the West, but believes they are not conclusive. He considers that the extreme destructiveness of the atomic bomb, together with the continued effort of the Christian spirit, might finally bring about a world order that will allow Western civilization to continue to grow.

Further Reading

Brewin, Christopher. "Arnold Toynbee, Chatham House, and Research in a Global Context." In *Thinkers of The Twenty Years' Crisis: Inter-War Idealism Reassessed*, edited by David Long and Peter Wilson. New York: Oxford University Press, 1995. The years between the two world wars have been called the "idealistic" phase of international-relations theory. This collection of essays examines works written during that period, including Toynbee's writings, to analyze their utopian elements and to determine if "idealistic" is an accurate description.

Herman, Arthur. "Welcoming Defeat: Arnold Toynbee." In *The Idea of Decline in Western History*. New York: Free Press, 1997. Herman, a program coordinator at the Smithsonian Institution, analyzes the writings of Toynbee and other intellectuals who have depicted the decline of Western civilization.

Mason, Henry. *Toynbee's Approach to World Politics*. New Orleans, La.: Tulane University Press, 1958. Critical analysis of Toynbee's political theories, including both positive and negative evaluations of his methodology. Surveys his study of international affairs. The appendix covers general reception and specific criticisms of *A Study of History*.

O'Hagan, Jacinta. "The Patriarchal Civilization: Arnold Toynbee's Conception of the West." In *Conceptualizing the West in International Relations: From Spengler to Said*. New York: Palgrave, 2002. Analyzes how Toynbee and thinkers such as Oswald Spengler and Edward Said have conceived of Western civilization and the role that these conceptions have played in global relations.

Perry, Marvin. *Arnold Toynbee and the Western Tradition*. New York: Peter Lang, 1996. Provides an explication of *A Study of History*, describing Toynbee's ideas about the nature, evolution, and destiny of Western civilization. Assesses Toynbee's intellectual importance, discusses his critics and admirers, and analyzes the relevance of his ideas at the end of the twentieth century.

Samuel, Maurice. *The Professor and the Fossil: Some Observations on Arnold J. Toynbee's "A Study of History."* New York: Alfred A. Knopf, 1956. Evaluates *A Study of History* and concludes that much of the work is meaningless, that many of Toynbee's historical facts are inaccurate, and that purposeful omissions create a distorted picture.

Tomlin, E. W. F., ed. Introduction to *Arnold Toynbee: A Selection from His Works*. New York: Oxford University Press, 1978. Defines and clarifies key phrases used repeatedly in *A Study of History*. Each selection includes the editor's description of the work, its background, and the major principles it contains.

The Subjection of Women

Author: John Stuart Mill (1806-1873)
First published: 1869
Type of work: Philosophy

Written in 1860-1861, *The Subjection of Women* first appeared as a pamphlet in 1869, shortly after John Stuart Mill finished a three-year term as a member of the British parliament. While a member of Parliament, Mill presented a petition for woman's suffrage (1866) and sponsored the Married Women's Property Bill (1868). After losing his seat in Parliament in the 1868 election, Mill revised his early draft of the essay and published it. Mill's primary activity in Parliament was aimed at the enfranchisement of women—their right to vote—and *The Subjection of Women* makes clear Mill's liberal feminism and his commitment to gender equality.

The Subjection of Women is divided into four chapters, each chapter presenting and supporting an aspect of Mill's argument. In chapter 1, Mill states his general aim explicitly. He challenges the common notion that women are by nature unequal to men. He explains that "the legal subordination of one sex to the other is wrong in itself, and one of the chief hindrances to human improvement," and the systematic subordination of women by men "ought to be replaced by a principle of perfect equality, admitting no power or privilege on the one side, nor disability on the other." Mill acknowledges that his views challenge accepted views and practices, but he counters by pointing out the historical foundations of subjection, that is, the conversion of "mere physical fact into a legal right." The subjection of women, then, is based on a premodern law of force, not on the modern use of reason. Since no other system has been tried, the then-present system of subjugation of the "weaker" female sex to the "stronger" male sex rests upon unproven theory, says Mill. Mill hoped to pave the way for a new system of equality, based on theory, as no practice of gender equality had as yet been allowed.

Using an analogy that angered many of his readers, Mill compares women's subordination to men to that of the slave to his master and speaks of a kind of domestic slavery to the family. Unlike the slave, however, the woman's master not only wants her labor but also her sentiments, and he conspires to bind nature and education to accomplish his desire for the loving, submissive, domestic slave over whom he, as husband, has absolute control. The relationship between men and women is merely the customary relationship, and whatever is customary appears natural. To those with power over others, their domination appears natural, perhaps even good, and appears owing to the nature of the dominated. Women's true natures cannot be verified, however, for they are repressed in some areas and unnaturally stimulated in others, according to Mill. Furthermore, women have seldom been allowed to testify to their own natures; rather, they have been described by the men who exercise power over them. Since women have never been allowed to develop naturally without the repression, stimulation, or guidance of men, a system of subordination founded on women's "natural" sensitivity and lack of more "masculine" qualities is not inherently more valid than any other system based on theory alone.

In chapter 2, Mill attacks women's status in the marriage contract, which he sees as a kind of legal bondage. All property and any income derived from marriage belonged to the husband, even if the wife had brought the property to the marriage. Additionally, only the father had legal rights over his children. A woman who left her husband could take nothing with her, not even her children. Any action she might take must have her husband's tacit approval. Indeed, Mill sees the bondage of marriage as a more profound slavery than slavery itself, not because a woman might be treated as badly as any slave—though he does not neglect the physical power the husband has over his wife and the potential for physical abuse—but because "hardly any slave . . . is a slave at all hours and all minutes." A wife and mother, on the other hand,

is available at all times to all people. No activity a wife does is considered important enough to protect her from being interrupted to meet the needs of others.

Mill argues for a marriage contract based on equality before the law and the division of powers in the home. Though in chapter 3 he makes the case for women's admission to all "functions and occupations" held by men, he does not call for a division of duties within the home. Rather, he claims that just as a man chooses a profession, a woman who marries is choosing the management of the household and the raising of the children. The latter view is seen by many feminist readers and critics as a weakness in Mill's liberal feminism, but it is not surprising that he should hold that view in the Victorian period. Mill nonetheless states that the "*power* of earning is essential to the dignity of a woman." As Mill argues for women's freedom to enter all the professions and jobs monopolized by men, he boldly attacks male self-interest, which uses women's assumed disabilities to maintain subordination in domestic life. Most men cannot tolerate the notion of living with an equal, says Mill.

One of the functions women should exercise, Mill argues, is the vote, and there is no justification for excluding women, who, as a principle of self-protection, have as much right as men to choose who is to govern them. In *The Subjection of Women* and in an earlier essay, "Enfranchisement of Women" (1851), Mill notes the new freedoms of the modern world, where birth no longer determines individual destiny. With the new freedoms of industry, of conscience, of the press, and of action and political liberty, men should not subject half of the race to restrictions that men are no longer required to tolerate. It is only women who still suffer from that "relic of an old world of thought and practice," presuppositions based on birth.

As for the mental differences said to exist between men and women, Mill attributes these to the differences in their education and circumstances, rather than to their natures. Women are trained away from, and men are trained for, certain occupations and functions. What women have done, they have proven they can do, and their capabilities for other pursuits are unknown because they are untried. Women have not been allowed entrance into most occupations; hence, there is no evidence that they cannot be as accomplished in these forbidden offices as they have been in those offices they have exercised. Mill uses royalty as an example of women's capabilities when allowed to develop. Queen Elizabeth fulfilled well the duties of the highest office in the land. Had she not inherited the throne, she would not have been permitted even the least important of political duties.

Mill attacks the traditional notion of women's nervous

susceptibility, seeing it as the overflow of unused energies and often the result of conscious or unconscious cultivation, as exemplified by the popularity and then the unpopularity of fainting spells. He counters the biological argument that because women are smaller than men and thus have smaller brains, they have inferior intellectual powers, and points out that stereotypes of women differ from one culture to another. Women are seen as voluptuous in one country, fickle in another, and cold in yet another. In regard to the lack of cultural artifacts produced by women, Mill claims that women have had insufficient time to practice those vocations that lead to such productions. Women have been trained away from what men have been trained for. Women have been trained for the social obligations of house and family and have been discouraged from creating books, art, and the like.

Mill closes chapter 3 with a strong statement: "Women cannot be expected to devote themselves to the emancipation of women, until men in considerable number are prepared to join them in the undertaking." From a practical perspective, a married woman could be legally stopped from engaging in any activity of which her husband disapproves. In chapter 4, Mill explains why an end to the subordination of women would benefit even the privileged men most likely to resist it.

Mill also posits two questions: What good would come from the proposed changes in customs and institutions? Would humanity be better off if women were free? He argues that the inequality of marriage—the only actual bondage known to law since the abolition of slavery—contradicts all the principles of the modern world. He also claims that it is damaging to boys to grow up believing that they are superior to half the human population merely because they are male, rather than through any merits of their own. If such gender preference were eliminated, children would, "for the first time in man's existence on earth, be trained in the way [they] should go," as members of a just society.

A second benefit of giving women the free use of their faculties and free choice of employment is the advantage gained by doubling the available brain trust for the advancement of humanity. By subjugating women, society is wasting half its resources. Relations between men and women would also be much improved if women were allowed to develop their faculties. Women's influence would extend beyond the boundaries of the domestic, and men and women would be better companions to one another.

The most direct benefit from an end to the subordination of women would be the "unspeakable gain in private happiness to the liberated half of the species," allowing them a life of rational freedom. Mill sees freedom as the third necessity of life, after food and clothing. Withholding from women

freedoms that are available to men is a "positive evil," says Mill, and "leaves the species less rich." Mill knows that societal change can occur after the opinions of society change. By his arguments in *The Subjection of Women* he hopes to encourage exactly that.

The Subjection of Women remains Mill's least studied work, but it has not lost its relevance with the passage of time. In his discussion of women's true nature, Mill anticipates the "nature versus nurture" debates that have continued into the twenty-first century. It is true that women in the West can vote, they can own property, and legal conditions have changed. Women have entered many of the occupations once closed to them and exercise many of the functions once the purview of men only, but Mill's goal of gender equality has yet to be completely realized. *The Subjection of Women* contains many arguments of practical use for today's feminists and other believers in individual freedom.

Linda Ledford-Miller

Further Reading

Donner, Wendy, and Richard A Fumerton. *Mill*. Malden, Mass.: Wiley-Blackwell, 2009. Part of the Blackwell Great Minds series, this biography of Mill examines his political philosophies, including his theories of gender equality and the oppression and subjugation of women.

Lonoff, Sue. "Cultivated Feminism: Mill and *The Subjection of Women*." *Philological Quarterly* 65, no. 1 (Winter, 1986): 79-102. Describes Mill as an apostle of liberal feminism rather than its prophet. A lucid examination of the rhetorical structure of his essay.

Morales, Maria H., ed. *Mill's "The Subjection of Women."* Lanham, Md.: Rowman & Littlefield, 2005. Nine essays examine the work and include discussions of Mill as a liberal and radical feminist and his ideas about marriage, marital slavery, friendship, and androgyny.

Okin, Susan Moller. *Women in Western Political Thought.* 1979. New ed. Princeton, N.J.: Princeton University Press, 1992. Examines traditional philosophical views on women expressed in Plato, Aristotle, and Jean-Jacques Rousseau. Part 4 focuses on Mill, the only one of the major liberal political philosophers to include women in the application of principles of liberalism.

Pyle, Andrew, ed. *"The Subjection of Women": Contemporary Responses to John Stuart Mill.* Bristol, England: Thoemmes Press, 1995. A collection of essays written in response to *The Subjection of Women*, including some pieces from eminent women intellectuals of the Victorian era.

Reeves, Richard. *John Stuart Mill: Victorian Firebrand.* London: Atlantic Books, 2007. An authoritative and well-received biography that recounts Mill's life, philosophy, and pursuit of truth and liberty for all.

Tulloch, Gail. *Mill and Sexual Equality.* Boulder, Colo.: Lynne Rienner, 1989. Examines *The Subjection of Women* in detail, particularly noting Mill's arguments for reconstructed marriage. Traces the development of Mill's liberal feminism and its relationship to the themes of his major works.

Suddenly Last Summer

Author: Tennessee Williams (1911-1983)
First produced: 1958; first published, 1958
Type of work: Drama
Type of plot: Psychological realism
Time of plot: 1936
Locale: New Orleans, Louisiana

Principal characters:
MRS. VIOLET VENABLE, an eccentric matriarch
DR. CUKROWICZ, a young, handsome psychiatrist
CATHARINE HOLLY, Mrs. Venable's niece
MISS FOXHILL, Mrs. Venable's secretary-companion
MRS. HOLLY, Catharine's mother
GEORGE HOLLY, Catharine's brother
SISTER FELICITY, a nun at St. Mary's Institution

The Story:

Mrs. Violet Venable summons Dr. Cukrowicz to her mansion in New Orleans's Garden District. He comes as a result of his interest in an enormous endowment from the Sebastian Venable Memorial Foundation. Mrs. Venable and Cukrowicz stroll through the exotic garden that had been the realm of Mrs. Venable's late son, Sebastian. Mrs. Venable and Cukrowicz discuss Sebastian's occupation, which she insists was Sebastian's life because "a poet's life is his work and his work is his life." She shows the doctor one of Sebastian's poems from his collection, *Poems of Summer*. She explains that her son had written only one poem a year, and it took him nine months to write a poem. The rest of the year, Mrs. Venable and Sebastian had traveled to exotic locales.

Mrs. Venable recalls one specific summer that she and Sebastian had spent in the Encantadas, where they watched sea turtle eggs hatch. As the newly hatched turtles scurried to the sea, most were devoured by birds. Cukrowicz wonders why Sebastian was fascinated by this savage display of nature. Mrs. Venable explains it was Sebastian's search for God. The doctor asks Mrs. Venable to show her a picture of Sebastian. The photographs demonstrate how Sebastian retained his youthful beauty for twenty years.

Miss Foxhill interrupts the discussion to announce the arrival of George Holly and his mother. Mrs. Venable tells Miss Foxhill to keep the Hollys upstairs. Mrs. Venable resumes her talk with the doctor, who asks her about Sebastian's personal, private life. Mrs. Venable explains that her son, while chased, had been chaste. She insists that he had been celibate. She explains that during their travels, they were always spoken of as a couple. Mrs. Venable explains that the previous summer, Sebastian had traveled with his cousin, Catharine Holly. It was during the trip to Cabeza de Lobo that Sebastian died. Catharine had a terrible reaction to his death and was institutionalized at St. Mary's. Mrs. Venable tells Cukrowicz that Catharine "babbles," vandalizing the memory of Sebastian. To stop Catharine's rantings and ravings, Mrs. Venable wants the doctor to perform a lobotomy on Catharine; insulin shock and electric shock therapies have not silenced her.

When Miss Foxhill announces that Catharine has arrived, Mrs. Venable refuses, at first, to face her. The doctor goes alone to see Catharine. He notices Catharine with Sister Felicity standing behind her. Catharine lights a cigarette. Sister Felicity insists that Catharine extinguish the cigarette, which she does in the palm of the nun's hand. Catharine recalls how Sebastian was "famished for blonds." She relates to the nun how Sebastian talked about people as if they were items on a menu. Catharine tells the nun that Sebastian lived on pills and salads.

Mrs. Holly and her son, George, greet Catharine. George reveals that Sebastian had bequeathed him and Catharine fifty thousand dollars each. Mother and son insist that Catharine never again tell the story of what happened to Sebastian in Cabeza de Lobo. Catharine insists the story is true and refuses their request.

Mrs. Venable joins the scene. Cukrowicz also arrives. Catharine knows the doctor is from Lion's View, a sanatorium where lobotomies are performed. When Mrs. Venable accuses Catharine of taking Sebastian away from her, Catharine tries to explain why she had accompanied Sebastian on his summer tour. Mrs. Venable interrupts Catharine's explanation, denying that she had suffered a stroke and insisting that Sebastian wanted Catharine to accompany him because of a scandal Catharine made over a married man at a Mardi Gras ball.

Cukrowicz asks to be left alone with Catharine. He questions her about her feelings about Sebastian. She admits that she loved her cousin, but in a "motherly way." When the doctor asks her what she wanted to save Sebastian from, she says from completing a terrible image of himself. Catharine tells the doctor the story of the scandal she caused at the Mardi Gras ball: Catharine's date was too drunk to drive her home. She went for a taxi, but a man took her by the arm and offered to drive her home. The man took her to Duelling Oaks. Catharine knew the man's intentions, but he decided against a liaison because his wife was pregnant. At home, Catharine remembered she had left Mrs. Venable's mink stole at the ballroom. She returned and then assaulted the man. Sebastian intervened and invited her to join him on his summer tour. Telling the story agitates Catharine, and Cukrowicz gives her an injection to calm her. After she is sedated, she forces a kiss on the doctor.

The entire family gathers on the terrace, and Cukrowicz coaxes an agitated Catharine to tell her story while Mrs. Venable tries to deny the truth and preserve the myth she holds of Sebastian. After Mrs. Venable promises to keep quiet, Catharine tells of an afternoon she and Sebastian spent at Cabeza de Lobo on a private beach cordoned off from a public beach by a barbed-wire fence. Catharine says she had gone for a swim in a white bathing suit that would turn transparent when wet. She soon realized she was procuring young men for Sebastian, as his mother had before her.

The following afternoons, the crowd of homeless, hungry young men at the public beach grew, waiting for Sebastian to toss them money. Sebastian grew ill at the public display and insisted that he and Catharine go north. Before they had a chance to leave, a large band of the young men formed and made loud, percussive music on crude tin instruments. The band pursued Sebastian through the streets of Cabeza de Lobo, catching him, stripping him, and cannibalizing him.

To silence Catharine, Mrs. Venable orders the doctor to take Catharine to Lion's View and "cut this hideous story from her brain." Cukrowicz suggests that the Hollys consider that Catharine's story could be true.

Critical Evaluation:

A critical and popular success, Tennessee Williams was one of the most important playwrights to emerge onto the American theatrical scene soon after World War II. Graduating from the University of Iowa in 1938, Williams earned a Rockefeller Fellowship to write *Battle of Angels* (1940). *The Glass Menagerie* (1944) won the New York Drama Critics' Circle Award for the 1945 season. He won Pulitzer Prizes for *A Streetcar Named Desire* (1947) and *Cat on a Hot Tin Roof* (1955). His plays are both regional and naturalistic with vivid, highly individual characters—debauched and debased—in drama that has an air of fantasy about it. Exotic settings and strange, often perverse personalities populate Williams's plays. Those in *Suddenly Last Summer* are excellent examples.

The play deals with homosexuality, while never using the word. Because Sebastian Venable is dead when the play begins, he is defined only by what other characters say about him. Their statements about the dead poet tend to polarize into two extremes; between these two disparate views lies the truth. It is the dead poet's homosexuality and how it affects his reputation—both when he is alive and when he is dead—that is the crux of the play. Sebastian seems both an exploitative outsider and an alienated victim.

The play weaves an interesting set of variations of the theme of exposure for gays in society. At the time the play was written, homosexuality, while no longer "the love that dare not speak its name," as English poet Lord Alfred Douglas famously called it, was not a subject openly discussed. Sebastian, both the man and poet, chose to distance himself from public recognition, in an endeavor to conceal his sexuality from society. When Cukrowicz asks to see a photograph of Sebastian, Mrs. Venable produces two of Sebastian in disguise. For twenty years, Sebastian presented a disguised face to society. This public persona is carefully guarded by Mrs. Venable, who denies the true nature of her son's sexual identity even after his death. Catharine's accusation that Mrs. Venable procured for her son during his life is counterbalanced by Mrs. Venable's actions as his self-appointed protector after his death.

Sebastian used his mother as his procurer to deny his sexuality to the society in which they lived and traveled. The summer that Sebastian chose to travel with Catharine, he broke his mother's bond. That summer Sebastian also broke the ties that bound him to tradition, youth, and the "closet": "suddenly, last summer, he wasn't young any more, and we went to Cabeza de Lobo, and he suddenly switched from the evenings to the beach." With his mother, Sebastian traveled under the cover of the night, using his mother's forceful personality to seduce men. With his cousin, Sebastian operates in the light of day, painfully aware that his youth is slipping away. He uses his cousin's youth and beauty to attract ever-more-youthful men. Soon, Sebastian no longer needs Catharine; money replaces her youth and beauty.

Sebastian's cannibalization is foreshadowed during his trip to the Encantadas. The turtles' rush to the sea to avoid the carnivorous birds overhead demonstrates the power of an untamed primal urge, not unlike the crowd's homophobic reaction in Cabeza de Lobo, an emotion that sweeps the frenzied mass into a primal act of cannibalism. Sebastian is just as powerless among the crowd as the turtles are among the carnivorous birds. In the Encantadas, playwright Williams also tries to discern the role of God in the life of a gay man. Sebastian looks for God, possibly to make some sense of a world that forced him to deny his sexual identity. He finds a savage, uncaring God. Sebastian's anger at what he finds forces him to consider his place in a society where God makes no provision for gays.

Sebastian is powerless in New Orleans society as well. As a gay man, he must suppress his sexual identity. When he finally chooses to go public, he does it outside New Orleans and becomes an object for public consumption, literally. Because he chooses to make those he desires into objects who can be bought, Sebastian becomes an exploiter in a society where he is an outsider. The young men who seek out Sebastian become representatives of their society as a whole. Their social anxiety—or homophobia—results in their consuming Sebastian in a ritual act of destroying who they adored. Sebastian then becomes the victim. He is an exploitative outsider and an alienated victim, a character Williams deftly uses to articulate the ambiguous nature of gays in society.

Thomas D. Petitjean, Jr.

Further Reading

Bauer-Briski, Senata Karolina. *The Role of Sexuality in the Major Plays of Tennessee Williams.* New York: Peter Lang, 2002. Analyzes how sexuality is a dominant element in eight Williams plays, including *Suddenly Last Summer.* Examines how the characters' behavior and relations with other characters are affected by their decisions to either express or repress their sexual inclinations.

Bruhm, Steven. "Blackmailed by Sex: Tennessee Williams and the Economics of Desire." *Modern Drama* 34, no. 4 (December, 1991): 528-537. Argues that Sebastian lives in a system of power relations he cannot control. For critics of the play, the incident in the Encantadas foreshadows Sebastian's death at Cabeza de Lobo.

Clum, John M. "The Sacrificial Stud and the Fugitive Female in *Suddenly Last Summer, Orpheus Descending,* and *Sweet Bird of Youth.*" In *The Cambridge Companion to Tennessee Williams,* edited by Matthew Roudané. New York: Cambridge University Press, 1997. Argues that these plays compose a trilogy of sorts, in which a beautiful man is a sexual martyr. Examines the dynamics and eroticism of this martyrdom and the beautiful man's relationship to a "fugitive" woman.

_____. "'Something Cloudy, Something Clear': Homophobic Discourse in Tennessee Williams." *South Atlantic Quarterly* 88, no. 1 (Winter, 1989): 161-179. Notes that *Suddenly Last Summer* weaves an interesting set of variations on the theme of exposure of the artist as gay. Sebastian's carnivorous sense of life is linked with homosexuality.

Debusscher, Gilbert. "Minting Their Separate Wills: Tennessee Williams and Hart Crane." *Modern Drama* 26, no. 4 (December, 1983): 455-476. Examines the significant literary influence of poet Hart Crane on Williams and the composition of *Suddenly Last Summer.*

Paller, Michael. *Gentlemen Callers: Tennessee Williams, Homosexuality, and Mid-Twentieth-Century Broadway Drama.* New York: Palgrave Macmillan, 2005. Charts the evolution of America's acknowledgment and general acceptance of homosexuality by examining Williams's life and his plays written between the 1940's and 1970's. Describes how critics initially ignored his gay characters and how gay activists in the 1970's reviled his work.

Spoto, Donald. *The Kindness of Strangers: The Life of Tennessee Williams.* Boston: Little, Brown, 1985. An accessible, accurate biography of Williams that discusses Williams's homosexuality and its influence on his life and works.

Thompson, Judith J. *Tennessee Williams' Plays: Memory, Myth, and Symbol.* Rev. ed. New York: Peter Lang, 2002. Traces a pattern of mythic recollection in several of Williams's plays, including *Suddenly Last Summer.*

Tischler, Nancy M. *Student Companion to Tennessee Williams.* Westport, Conn.: Greenwood Press, 2000. Critical study of Williams's life, career, and work. Analyzes several plays and discusses their literary styles, themes, and Williams's influences from poetry, film, religion, mythology, and personal experience.

Sula

Author: Toni Morrison (1931-   )
First published: 1973
Type of work: Novel
Type of plot: Psychological realism
Time of plot: 1919-1965
Locale: Medallion, Ohio

Principal characters:
SULA PEACE, the daughter of Hannah Peace
NEL WRIGHT, the daughter of Helene Wright
EVA PEACE, Sula's grandmother
HELENE WRIGHT, Nel's mother
HANNAH PEACE, the daughter of Eva Peace
SHADRACK, a World War I Veteran

The Story:

The Bottom, the black community of Medallion, Ohio, originated in the time of slavery. Through trickery, an enslaved black man had accepted a portion of higher land from his master in exchange for completing "some very difficult chores." The black man had been told by his master that the land was nearer heaven and of better quality, but it was actually less desirable and subject to erosion.

In 1919, Shadrack, an African American World War I veteran and Medallion resident, is recuperating in a military hospital; he is suffering from psychological trauma. After his discharge from the hospital, he is arrested by the police but eventually released. Following the new year in 1920, Shadrack, carrying a cowbell and a hangman's noose, walks through Medallion informing the residents that he offers them their "only chance to kill themselves." With this act, he begins National Suicide Day.

Helene Wright, another Medallion resident, was born in New Orleans to Rochelle, a "Creole whore." Helene, who was reared by her grandmother, Cecile Sabat, married Wiley Wright, the grandnephew of Cecile, and was brought north to Medallion. A civic-minded woman, Helene reared her daughter, Nel, in a protective manner. When Helene's grandmother became ill, Helene journeyed with Nel to New Orleans. They experienced segregation on their journey, and in New Orleans, Nel met her grandmother, Rochelle.

After Nel and her mother return to Medallion, Nel seems to have achieved a "new found me-ness." At this time, Nel meets Sula Peace, who loves the orderly and "oppressive neatness" of the Wright household. In contrast, Sula's home, headed by Eva Peace, is a "woolly house, where a pot of something was always cooking on the stove."

In 1921, the household of Eva Peace includes her children, Hannah and Plum, Hannah's daughter, Sula, and various "strays" such as the Deweys, three children given the same name by Eva. Eva, who had been deserted by her husband BoyBoy after five years of marriage, is rumored to have lost her leg by intentionally allowing a train to run over it so that she could collect money.

Both of Eva's children had died in tragic ways. Plum, a World War I veteran, returned in 1919 addicted to heroin. Eva sacrificed Plum by burning him to death. Hannah, a sexually liberated woman and threat to the "good" women of the town, was burned to death accidentally when she tried to light the yard on fire. Eva attempted to save her daughter, whose death was witnessed silently by Sula.

In 1922, Sula and Nel, both about twelve years of age, share a friendship that is "as intense as it was sudden." On one occasion, when they are harassed by four white boys, Sula demonstrates her resolve to fight by cutting off the tip of her own finger. Nel and Sula also share the secret of Chicken Little's accidental drowning. While playing, Sula had tossed the young boy into the river.

In 1927, Nel marries Jude Greene, a tenor in Mount Zion's Men's Quartet. Nel's marriage affects her friendship with Sula, who leaves Medallion. She returns in 1937, "accompanied by a plague of robins." While away from Medallion, Sula attends college and travels to big cities. After her return, Sula is defiant and disrespectful to Eva. Sula also contributes to the breakup of Nel's marriage by having an affair with Jude.

In 1939, Sula places Eva in Sunnydale home for the elderly. Consequently, the African American community considers Sula to be bewitched. Sula's sexual activities, her sleeping with white men and the husbands of African American women, contributes to her pariah status. At age twenty-nine, Sula meets Ajax—Albert Jacks—a man thirty-eight years of age, whose mother is a conjure woman. Sula becomes emotionally attached to Ajax through their "genuine conversations." After Ajax deserts Sula, she realizes that she had not really known him.

In 1940, Sula, who is seriously ill, is visited by Nel. They recount the past, and Nel blames Sula for having slept with

Jude. In 1941, Sula's death is "the best news folks up in the Bottom had had since the promise of work at the tunnel." The building of a home for African American elderly people is another sign of the community's revitalization. However, this hope is countered by ominous signs such as the ice storm that ruins crops, beginning a "dislocation" that Shadrack had prophesied. Shadrack and residents from Carpenter's Road march to the tunnel, where their protest ends with an accidental cave-in.

In 1965, downtown Medallion is integrated. The land in the hills, which becomes more expensive, is used for building television towers, and a golf course is even proposed. The hills are left to "the poor, the old, the stubborn—and the rich white folks."

When Nel visits Eva at the home for the elderly, Eva accuses Nel of having killed Chicken Little. Eva tells Nel that Plum, though dead, had revealed the truth about Chicken Little's drowning. Eva's revelations upsets Nel, especially when Eva says that Nel and Sula are the same, stating, "never was no difference between you."

After Nel leaves Eva, Nel begins to remember Chicken Little's death and Sula's burial. While Nel reflects, she is passed on the road by Shadrack, who is a "little shaggier, a little older" and "still energetically mad." Recollecting the past, Nel whispers to Sula as if Sula were present. Nel affirms their childhood friendship and cries "loud and long."

Critical Evaluation:

Toni Morrison is one of the most significant novelists of the postmodern period. Her novels have consistently explored the African American experience, using historical, social, and psychological themes to focus especially on the experiences of women. Morrison's first novel was *The Bluest Eye* (1970), and her 1977 novel *Song of Solomon* led to a National Book Critics' Circle Award. Her work as an editor at Random House led to the publication of *The Black Book* (1974). *Beloved* (1987) was awarded the Pulitzer Prize in fiction in 1988, and *Playing in the Dark: Whiteness and the Literary Imagination* (1992), a critical work, was a national best seller. In 1993, Morrison received the Nobel Prize in Literature.

Morrison's novels combine psychological realism, social critique, symbolism, and the mythopoetic, resulting in a style similar to Magical Realism. Although her works are not limited to social protest, Morrison is concerned with racial themes frequently encountered in African American literature. Her novels reflect the workings of communities, the dilemmas faced by these families, and the problems encountered in their relationships. She also has addressed historical issues such as nineteenth century slavery. Her fiction celebrates survival and defines black identity as multifaceted. Influenced by William Faulkner and Ralph Ellison, she uses vernacular and poetic prose to create a stylistic balance between narrative perspective and dialogue.

In *Sula*, her second novel, Morrison creates an African American community in a fictional town that, like Lorain, Ohio, the author's hometown, borders Lake Erie. Morrison's concern for history and social context are evident in *Sula*. Her critique of nineteenth century slavery is strongly implied in the ironic naming of The Bottom. By using chronological sequences, Morrison suggests how the lives of her characters relate to broader societal transitions from World War I to the desegregation and urban renewal of the 1960's. Economic disparity caused by segregation—an indirect cause of the failure of relationships—is one of the underlying central themes in the novel.

Sula, however, is not primarily concerned with the social conflict between the white and the African American communities of Medallion. The novel mostly concerns the way African American communities both include and exclude those members who have violated community mores or who have become dislocated in ways that cause them to live on the moral or social margins. The novel presents characters who each signify an adaptation to this community, a community divided by class.

Sula and Nel are reflections not only of sisterhood but also two African American families. The Wright and Peace households, one middle-class and nuclear, the other folk-centered and extended, are two reflections of the African American community. In tracing the relationship of Nel and Sula through adulthood, Morrison shows how sisterhood can be affected by the differing routes taken by African American women. Nel's pursuit of the traditional ideal—marriage and family—contrasts with the sexually liberated path chosen by Sula. Sula, although of the folk culture, eventually moves beyond that culture when she leaves Medallion.

Other characters show problematic adjustments to sociohistorical conditions and family dislocation. Shadrack represents the returning African American World War I veteran whose National Suicide Day is an ironic comment on the life chances of African Americans in 1920. Shadrack, however, becomes an accepted eccentric character who, in many respects, defines the political direction of the community in protest and collective action. Eva Peace represents the folk tradition and the continuity of African American matriarchy, which seeks to protect and maintain a family faced with the absence of the father.

One of the most important themes is African American female sexuality. Hannah and Sula are both portrayed as sexually liberated. Because of Sula's relationship with men, she is viewed as an outcast by the community. Despite her sexual freedom, she also searches for genuine love with Ajax. Also, the theme of desertion, a pattern in Morrison's fiction, is developed in *Sula*. Eva is deserted by BoyBoy, Nel by Jude, and Sula by Ajax. Though injured by desertion, Morrison's women survive and shape identities not dependent on relationships with men.

Morrison's Magical Realism is formed by a variety of elements. Natural phenomena, such as the plague of robins and the ice storm, are used as parallels to the action. She employs folkloric elements in the portrayal of Ajax's mother as a conjure woman and in the notion of Sula as bewitched. The significance of dreams, Eva's claim of having been in communication with her dead son, Plum, and Nel's attempt to communicate with Sula's spirit, are other examples of the magical dimension of the novel.

The literary style of the novel is achieved through vernacular expression and symbolism. African American vernacular gives authentic voice to Eva, Nel, and Sula. The conversation between Sula and Nel, when Nel visits Sula on her deathbed, is a reconstruction of verbal devices used by African American women. The symbolism of fire is used when Eva burns Plum and when Hannah is mysteriously destroyed by fire. Shadrack's name implies the biblical furnace and invulnerability to destruction by fire.

Sula confirmed Morrison's reputation as a gifted writer destined for both national and international acclaim. The novel remains influential because Morrison provides a spectrum of African American women and challenges romanticized portrayals of relationships. Ultimately, *Sula* does not present sisterhood as an alternative to relationships between men and women but questions that which hinders emotional bonding.

Joseph McLaren

Further Reading

Baker, Houston A. "When Lindbergh Sleeps with Bessie Smith: The Writing of Place in *Sula*." In *Toni Morrison: Critical Perspectives Past and Present*, edited by Henry Louis Gates, Jr., and K. Anthony Appiah. New York: Amistad, 1993. Addresses Morrison's naming strategies, the significance of characters, and communal place. Compares her work to that of Richard Wright, Jean Toomer, and Zora Neale Hurston.

Carby, Hazel V., ed. *Reconstructing Womanhood: The Emergence of the Afro-American Woman Novelist*. New York: Oxford University Press, 1987. Includes a thorough study of the female characters found in African American literature. Essays explore the works of African American novelists, from Harriet Jacobs, author of *Incidents in the Life of a Slave Girl* (1861), to Morrison.

Christian, Barbara. "The Contemporary Fables of Toni Morrison." In *Black Women Novelists: The Development of a Tradition, 1892-1976*. Westport, Conn.: Greenwood Press, 1980. Argues that Morrison's first two novels "chronicle the search for beauty amidst the restrictions of life, both from within and without." Maintains that the main characters search for meaning through connection with the greater world.

_____, ed. *Black Feminist Criticism: Perspectives on Black Women Writers*. 1985. New ed. New York: Teachers College Press, 1997. A compilation of criticism and commentary on the works of Morrison and other African American women writers. Includes extensive analyses of individual works as well as examinations of common traits found in the literature. Each essay contains many explanatory notes and lists of sources.

De Weever, Jacqueline. *Mythmaking and Metaphor in Black Women's Fiction*. New York: St. Martin's Press, 1992. Examines contemporary black women writers as part of the "return to myth" tradition in letters. Insists that the experience of black people in the New World cannot be told through realism or naturalism, and that Morrison uses myth to order that experience.

Ferguson, Rebecca Hope. *Rewriting Black Identities: Transition and Exchange in the Novels of Toni Morrison*. New York: Peter Lang, 2007. Examines Morrison's first eight novels, focusing on her depiction of the complex layers of African American identity. Analyzes these novels from the perspectives of feminism, poststructualism, and race-related theory. Includes a chapter on "Vision and Self in *Sula*."

Gates, Henry L., Jr., ed. *Reading Black, Reading Feminist: A Critical Anthology*. New York: Meridian/New American Library, 1990. Collection of critical essays that explore how African American women writers have affected literature. Includes contributions by Barbara Christian, Hazel V. Carby, Mae Gwendolyn Henderson. Critical analyses go far beyond the surface, examining the characters (mostly female) from Morrison's novels.

Iyasere, Solomon O., and Marla W. Iyasere, eds. *Understanding Toni Morrison's "Beloved" and "Sula."* Troy, N.Y.: Whitston, 2000. Essays include discussions of *Sula*'s "tripled plot," its woman-centered psychology, the novel as a black woman's epic, and biblical images in Morrison's novels.

Lee, Robert A. *Black Fiction: New Studies in the Afro-American Novel Since 1945*. London: Vision Press, 1980. Insightful essays explore the African American novel to identify recurring themes and techniques. Addresses *Sula* and Morrison's creation of women in this novel who do not fit common stereotypes.

Samuels, Wilfred D., and Clenora Hudson-Weems. *Toni Morrison*. Boston: Twayne, 1990. Critical study devoted to Morrison's novels up to *Beloved*. The chapter on *Sula*, "Experimental Lives: Meaning and Self in *Sula*," focuses on the outcast theme used in the portrayal of Sula and Shadrack; the development of men and women characters also is addressed.

Tally, Justine, ed. *The Cambridge Companion to Toni Morrison*. New York: Cambridge University Press, 2007. Essays examine Morrison's career. In addition to analyses of individual novels, including "*The Bluest Eye* and *Sula*: Black Female Experience from Childhood to Womanhood" by Agnes Suranyi, other essays provide more general discussions of the language and narrative technique in her novels, the critical reception of her work, and her social and literary criticism.

Summa Theologica

Author: Thomas Aquinas (1224 or 1225-1274)
First transcribed: Summa theologiae, c. 1265-1273
    (English translation, 1911-1921)
Type of work: Philosophy

This towering edifice of thought, often called simply the *Summa*, stands as a bulwark against the forces of doubt and skepticism that invaded the Western world during the late Middle Ages, toward the close of which Saint Thomas Aquinas created this great summation of philosophical and theological knowledge. In it two of the mightiest forces in the realm of human thought meet: Hellenism and Christianity. It was their first real encounter.

Simply stated, what Saint Thomas did was collect and synthesize the philosophical knowledge and thinking of previous eras and apply them to Christian theology. This was an immensely ambitious task, and the wonder is that Saint Thomas did so well with it. Though unfinished, because of the divine doctor's sudden death from illness, the *Summa* unites, or at least joins elements of thought from, the Greek, the Arabian, and the Asian traditions in a highly detailed fashion. Saint Thomas thus became a historian of philosophy; but he was a critical historian, carefully weighing and evaluating each premise and conclusion.

The largest part of this previous thought is, as might be expected, that of the Greeks. Saint Thomas is usually given the credit for having reinterpreted the philosophy of Aristotle on a Christian basis. This statement is, however, something of an oversimplification, for the reading of Aristotle and other great Greek thinkers, including Plato, was a very special one. Saint Thomas was himself a magnificent philosopher, and the *Summa* is unquestionably his book. What he did, in essence, was to organize the thought of Aristotle along Christian lines, to apply it to the problems and principles of religion. For example, some philosophers had interpreted Aristotle's *Physica* (*Physics*, 1812) as a denial of Creation; Saint Thomas saw it as merely falling short of this fundamental concept.

The *Summa* is an exceedingly long work, running into several volumes, a necessary length in order to accomplish the goal of applying Scholasticism, the prevailing philosophical influence in the thirteenth century, to religion. In doing so, Saint Thomas gave credit for ideas and lines of thought to many earlier thinkers, and he found the seeds of much thirteenth century belief in the works of previous philosophers. His work, then, is in the nature of a summary of past thinking on the highest subjects and a setting forth of the essential principles of Christian theology as he was able to formulate them from this past material and from his own conviction and thinking.

There are three main divisions of the *Summa*: the first dealing with God and the divine nature of the creation of humanity and the universe; the second, often called the Moral Philosophy of Saint Thomas, treating humanity and the goal of human life and the ways of reaching that goal; the third considering Christ and his role as Savior. Within this general framework virtually every possible subject pertaining to theology is discussed: good and evil, pleasure, knowledge, duty, property. The list is almost endless.

The method of attacking these questions is the Socratic one. A basic question is asked and the negative side of it is enforced by a fictitious opponent; then Saint Thomas undertakes to resolve the problem and explain the positive side of the contrived argument. This method, besides making for more interesting reading, tends to create an atmosphere giving fairer treatment to opposing beliefs.

The opening of the *Summa* presents a good example. In it, Saint Thomas poses the question of "Whether, Besides the Philosophical Sciences, Any Further Doctrine Is Required?" How fundamental is the divine doctor's approach can easily be seen: At the beginning of his book, he wishes first to convince the reader of the necessity for sacred doctrine. Following the question are listed two chief objections to the writing of sacred doctrine; then Saint Thomas explains the need for it and refutes each objection in turn. This tightly organized discussion is maintained throughout; in a book that is so closely reasoned it is essential.

Part of the reason for this clear organization was the fact that the *Summa* was not primarily intended for learned divines. Instead, it was written for people whom Saint Thomas called beginners, the common people in search of the truth. Also, such an intention probably had much to do with the style of the writing. Although the *Summa* is extremely long, it is praised for its economy of language, with no wasted words, no useless introduction of extraneous points of logic, and no pursuit of attenuated lines of reasoning past the point of common sense. The work is encyclopedic, not tedious.

Although much of what Saint Thomas wrote in the *Summa* has long been accepted doctrine in the Roman Catholic Church, there is for the contemporary reader considerable material that may seem remarkably up to date, for, theology aside, this book is pivotal in the history of Western philosophy. Possibly most interesting to the modern reader will be not the ethical elements, which are fairly familiar and do not seem to mark such a sharp break with earlier Greek views, but the metaphysical and epistemological aspects of the treatise. Two particularly important issues are raised by Saint Thomas in these areas, and both are in opposition to Greek thought, especially that of Plato.

The first of these concerns the very nature of reality, which is the main point of inquiry in metaphysics. While Plato saw reality as made up of essences, largely perceived as abstractions in the mind (here the "way of knowing," the central question of epistemology, enters in), Saint Thomas maintained that the basic statement was that something had being; that is, it had existence. This is the basis for an argument that has raged ever since among philosophers: Which is the supreme reality, essence or existence? Which is the more fundamental statement, what it is or that it is?

In his defense of the latter statement. Saint Thomas propounded principles that might be called Thomistic existentialism. Certainly the conflict created in the *Summa* over this question in the thirteenth century was of vital importance. Equally so was Saint Thomas's disagreement with the Platonic belief that a person is really two separate things, a soul and a body. To Saint Thomas a person was a composite, a unity composed of soul and body, both essential to one's nature.

This conflict connects with Saint Thomas's convictions about the "way of knowing" that is basic to his epistemology. Since reality is fundamentally existence rather than essence, to know this reality one must have a body—one must be able to perceive reality through the senses. Certainly Saint Thomas's statements in this area would meet with much warmer approval by most readers today than would the Greek notions concerning reality as essences, known only by abstractions in the mind. The practicality of the Thomistic viewpoint makes it appeal to scientifically minded modern thinkers.

In building this great philosophical and theological structure, Saint Thomas dealt with three of the most pressing problems in the thinking of the thirteenth century—the nature of being, of humanity, and of knowledge—and these three subjects parallel the divisions of philosophy as it is generally studied today: metaphysics, ethics, and epistemology. In approaching this skillful and subtle blending of theology and philosophy, the reader must be willing to do what nearly every philosophical writer demands: The reader must be agreeable to accepting certain general premises or principles. Without these, few philosophers can operate, and Saint Thomas is no exception. He assumes certain beliefs in his reader (the prevailing beliefs toward the close of the Middle Ages) concerning theology and religion. Granting these convictions, the reader will find in the *Summa* well-documented (quotations are frequent) and carefully reasoned statements on both sides of every issue involved in the Christian doctrine.

This work, which death ended as Saint Thomas was working on the article about the sacrament of Penance, has been widely translated into most modern languages and continues to be assiduously studied by all who wish to grasp the moment when, in the opinion of many, modern Christian theology began.

Further Reading

Bradley, Denis J. M. *Aquinas on the Twofold Human Good: Reason and Human Happiness in Aquinas's Moral Sci-*

ence. Washington, D.C.: Catholic University of America Press, 1997. Argues that Saint Thomas Aquinas was a theologian first and a philosopher second. Contends that to avoid misinterpretation, Thomas's writings should be approached from a theological, rather than a philosophical, perspective.

Chesterton, G. K. *St. Thomas Aquinas.* New York: Sheed and Ward, 1933. A superb introduction to the life and thought of Thomas, "the Angelic Doctor." Aimed at non-Christian readers, or those with little experience in theology.

D'Arcy, M. C. *St. Thomas Aquinas.* Westminster, Md.: Newman Press, 1953. Presents a good overview of Aquinas's thought on the first principle of knowledge, the nature of reality, and the existence of God. One of the most important books on Aquinas.

Davies, Brian, ed. *Aquinas's "Summa Theologiae": Critical Essays.* Lanham, Md.: Rowman & Littlefield, 2006. Collection of essays by modern scholars who interpret various aspects of *Summa Theologica,* including Thomas Aquinas's ideas about the proof of God's existence, freedom, unity of the body and soul, the nature of the intellect, and the immortality of the soul.

Gilson, Étienne. *The Christian Philosophy of St. Thomas Aquinas.* Translated by L. K. Shook. London: Victor Gollancz, 1957. Landmark study by one of the leading Thomists of the twentieth century. Presents Aquinas as a precursor to modern existentialism.

Kenny, Anthony. *Aquinas.* New York: Hill and Wang, 1980. Covers Aquinas's life in fewer than one hundred pages. Aquinas's theories are explored, including his conception of Being (which Kenny believes is hopelessly flawed) and his notion of the nature of Mind (which Kenny praises for the questions Aquinas asks). Later chapters introduce the reader to medieval categories of thought.

_____. *The Five Ways: St. Thomas Aquinas' Proofs of God's Existence.* New York: Routledge, 2003. A study of *Summa Theologica* that focuses on Thomas Aquinas's arguments for God's existence. Critically analyzes his five methods of proof, discussing what they establish and fail to establish.

Kreeft, Peter. *A Summa of the "Summa."* San Francisco: Ignatius Press, 1990. Contains essential passages from the *Summa Theologica* selected and translated by Kreeft. The extensive footnotes are lucid and generally helpful. A good starting place.

McInerny, Ralph. *Ethica Thomastica: The Moral Philosophy of Thomas Aquinas.* 1982. Rev. ed. Washington, D.C.: Catholic University of America Press, 1997. One of the finest introductions to Thomas's moral philosophy. Covers selected themes in Thomistic moral thinking, including moral goodness, judging good and evil moral actions, work of virtues, functions of conscience, and relation of ethics to religious belief.

_____. *St. Thomas Aquinas.* Boston: Twayne, 1977. An accessible study of Thomas's thought in chapters dealing with Aristotle, Boethius, whose philosophy was introduced to modern times through Thomas's writings, and Platonism. A chapter on the tasks of theology explains Thomas's distinction between believing and knowing. The book is filled with examples and includes a useful chronology of Aquinas's life plus a short, annotated bibliography.

The Sun Also Rises

Author: Ernest Hemingway (1899-1961)
First published: 1926
Type of work: Novel
Type of plot: Social realism
Time of plot: 1920's
Locale: Paris; Pamplona, Spain

Principal characters:
JAKE BARNES, an American newspaperman
LADY BRETT ASHLEY, one of the lost generation
ROBERT COHN, a young writer
MICHAEL "MIKE" CAMPBELL, Brett's fiancé
BILL GORTON, Jake's friend
PEDRO ROMERO, a Spanish bullfighter

The Story:

Jake Barnes meets Robert Cohn in Paris shortly after World War I. Somehow Jake always thinks Cohn typical of the place and the time. Cohn, the son of wealthy Jewish parents, was once the middleweight boxing champion of Prince- ton, and he never wants anyone to forget that fact. After leaving college, he married and lived unhappily with his wife until she ran off with another man. Then, he met some writers in California and decided to start a little, arty review. He also met Frances Clyne, who became his mistress. When Jake knows Cohn, he and Frances are living unhappily in Paris, where Cohn is writing his first novel. Cohn writes and boxes and plays tennis, and he is always careful not to mix his friendships. A man named Braddocks is his literary friend. Jake is his tennis friend.

Jake is an American newspaperman who fought with the Italians during the war. His own private tragedy is a war wound that emasculated him so that he can never marry Lady Brett Ashley, a young English war widow with whom he is in love. So as not to think too much about himself, Jake spends a lot of time listening to the troubles of his friends and drinking heavily. When he grows tired of Paris, he goes on fishing trips to the Basque country or to Spain for the bullfights.

One night, feeling lonely, Jake asks Georgette, a prostitute, to join him in a drink at the Café Napolitain. They dine on the Left Bank, where Jake meets a party of his friends, including Cohn and Frances. Later, Brett comes in with a group of young men. Cohn is attracted to her, and Frances is jealous. Brett refuses to dance with Cohn, however, saying that she has a date with Jake in Montmartre. Leaving a fifty-franc note with the café proprietor for Georgette, Jake leaves in a taxi with Brett for a ride to the Parc Montsouris. They talk for a time about themselves without mentioning Jake's injury, though they both think of it. At last, Brett asks Jake to drive her back to the Café Select.

The next day, Cohn corners Jake and asks him about Brett. Later, after drinking with Harvey Stone, another expatriate, on the terrace of the Café Select, Jake meets Cohn and Frances, who announces that her lover is dismissing her by sending her off to London. She abuses and taunts Cohn while he sits quietly without replying. Jake is embarrassed. The same day, he receives a telegram from his old friend Bill Gorton, announcing his arrival on the *France*. Brett goes on a trip to San Sebastian with Cohn; she thinks the excursion will be good for him.

Jake and Bill plan to go to Spain for the trout fishing and the bullfights at Pamplona. Michael Campbell, an Englishman whom Brett is to marry, also arrives in Paris. He and Brett arrange to join Jake and Bill at Pamplona. Because Cohn went to San Sebastian with Brett and because she is now staying with Mike Campbell, everyone feels that it would be awkward if Cohn accompanied Jake and Bill on their trip. Nevertheless, he decides to join them at Bayonne. The agreement is that Jake and Bill will first go trout fishing at Burguete in the mountains. Later, the whole party will meet at the Montoya Hotel in Pamplona for the fiesta.

When Jake and Bill arrive in Bayonne, they find Cohn awaiting them. Hiring a car, they drive on to Pamplona.

Montoya, the proprietor of the hotel, is an old friend of Jake because he recognizes Jake as a true aficionado of bullfights. The next morning, Bill and Jake leave by bus for Burguete, both riding atop the ancient vehicle with several bottles of wine, amid an assortment of Basque passengers. At Burguete, they enjoy good fishing in the company of an Englishman named Wilson-Harris.

Once back in Pamplona, the whole party gathers for the festival of San Fermín. The first night they go to see the bulls come in and the men let the savage animals out of the cages one at a time. Much wine makes Mike loquacious and he harps on the fact that Cohn joined the group knowing he is not wanted. At noon on Sunday, the fiesta explodes. The carnival continues for seven days. Dances, parades, religious processions, the bullfights, and much wine furnish the excitement of that hectic week. Staying at the Montoya Hotel is Pedro Romero, a bullfighter about twenty years old, who is extremely handsome. At the fights, Romero acquits himself well, and Brett falls in love with him, as she admits to Jake with embarrassment. Brett and the young man meet at the hotel, and Romero soon becomes interested in her.

Besides the bullfights, the main diversion of the group is drunken progress from one drinking spot to another. While they are in the Café Suizo, Jake tells Cohn that Brett went with the bullfighter to his room. Cohn swings at both Mike and Jake and knocks them down. After the fight, Cohn apologizes, crying all the while. He cannot understand how Brett could go off with him to San Sebastian one week and then treat him like a stranger the next time they meet. He plans to leave Pamplona the next morning.

The next morning, Jake learns that after the fight Cohn went to Romero's room and, when he found Brett and the bullfighter there together, beat Romero badly. In spite of his swollen face and battered body, Romero performs beautifully in the ring that day, dispatching a bull that had recently killed another torero. That night, after the fights, Brett leaves Pamplona with Romero. Jake gets very drunk.

As the fiesta ends, the party disperses. Bill goes back to Paris and Mike to Saint Jean de Luz. Jake is in San Sebastian when he receives a wire from Brett asking him to come to the Hotel Montana in Madrid. Taking the express, Jake meets her the next day. Brett is alone. She sent Romero away, she says, because she thinks she is not good for him. Then, without funds, she sent for Jake. She decided to go back to Mike, she tells Jake, because the Englishman is her own sort.

After dinner, Jake and Brett ride around in a taxi, seeing the sights of Madrid. This, Jake reflects wryly, is one of the few ways they can ever be alone together—in bars and cafés and taxis. Both know the ride is as purposeless as the war-wrecked world in which they live, as aimless as the drifting generation to which they belong.

Critical Evaluation:

Upon its publication in 1926, Ernest Hemingway's *The Sun Also Rises* was instantly recognized as one of the important American novels of the post-World War I period. This was in part the result of the fact that sophisticated readers identified current expatriate celebrities among the book's characters. As most of these personages faded into obscurity, however, this aspect of the novel soon lost its appeal. A more important reason for the book's success is that it perfectly captured the mood and style of the American artistic and intellectual exiles who drank, loved, and searched for meaning on the Paris Left Bank in the aftermath of that first world struggle.

The principal theme of *The Sun Also Rises* is indicated by two epigraphs. Gertrude Stein's "you are all a lost generation" encapsulates the ambiguous and pointless lives of Hemingway's exiles as they aimlessly wander about the Continent, drinking, making love, and traveling from place to place and party to party. The quote from Ecclesiastes, which gives the novel its title, implies a larger frame of reference, a sense of permanence, order, and value. If the activities of the characters seem to arise out of Stein's quotation, their search for new meanings to replace the old ones—or at least to enable them to deal with that loss—demonstrates their desire to connect with the biblical idea.

Early in the novel the hero, Jake Barnes, declines to kiss Georgette, a prostitute, on the grounds that he is "sick." "Everybody's sick. I'm sick too," she responds. This sickness motif is opposed in another early conversation Jake has, this one with Count Mippipopolous, a most vivid minor character, who tells him "that is the secret. You must get to know the values." The search for values and the willingness to pay the price, first to acquire them and then to live by them, are what separates some of Hemingway's exiles from simple, pointless hedonism. At the center of this search for values is the Hemingway hero, Jake. As in all of Hemingway's important fictions, *The Sun Also Rises* is a novel of education—of learning to live with the conditions faced.

Jake's problem is complicated by his war injury, for, having been emasculated, Jake's "affair" with Lady Brett Ashley takes on a comical aspect, as he himself freely admits. Hemingway, however, has a very serious intention. Jake's wound is a metaphor for the condition of the entire expatriate group. They have all been damaged in some fundamental way by the war—physically, morally, psychologically, or economically—and their aimless existence can be traced back to it.

The real symbolic importance of Jake's wound is that while it deprives him of the capacity to perform sexually, it does not rid him of the desire. The people in *The Sun Also Rises* fervently want meaning and fulfillment, but they lack the ability and means to find it.

The heroes in Hemingway's major works learn values in two ways: through their own actions and by contact with other characters who already know them. These exemplars understand the values either, like Count Mippipopolous, from long, hard experience or, like the bullfighter, Pedro Romero, intuitively and automatically. Those characters never articulate their values, however, they only embody them in action. Indeed, once talked about, they become, in the Hemingway lexicon, spoiled. Jake's education can be best seen in his relationship to Robert Cohn, Romero, and Brett.

Critics have speculated on why Hemingway begins the novel with a long discussion of Cohn, a relatively minor character. Clearly, Cohn embodies the old, false, romantic values that Hemingway is reacting against. While it is hard to define precisely what the important values are, it is easy to say what they are not.

In the beginning, Jake feels that Cohn is "nice and awful" but tolerates and pities him as a case of "arrested development." By the end of the book, he thoroughly hates him. Cohn's flaws include a false sense of superiority—reinforced by his pugilistic skills—and a romantic attitude toward himself and his activities that distorts his relationship with everyone around him. To reinforce this false romanticism, Cohn alters reality to suit his preconceptions. Falling in love with Brett, he refuses to see her realistically but idealizes her. When she spends a weekend with him, because she thinks it would be good for him, he treats it as a great affair and demands the rights of a serious lover, striking out at all the other men who approach her. Cohn's false perception of reality and his self-romanticization underscore his chief fault, the cardinal sin in Hemingway's view: Cohn refuses to "pay his bill."

Cohn's romantic self-image is finally destroyed by the bullfighter Romero. Affronted that Brett is taken from him, Cohn forces the young man into a prolonged fistfight. Although totally outmanned as a boxer, Romero refuses to give in to Cohn, and after absorbing considerable punishment, he rallies and humiliates his opponent by sheer will, courage, and endurance. His romantic bubble deflated, Cohn bursts into tears and fades from the novel.

It is appropriate that Cohn's false values be exposed by Romero, because his example is also central to the educations of Jake and Brett. As an instinctively great bullfighter,

Romero embodies the values in action and especially in the bullring. In a world bereft of religious certainties, Hemingway saw the bullfighter's performance as an aesthetic ceremony that substituted for obsolete religious ritual. Without transcendental meanings, human dignity must come from the manner in which individuals face their certain destiny; the bullfighter, who repeatedly does so by choice, was, for Hemingway, the supreme modern hero, providing he performed with skill, precision, style, and without falsity (that is, making it look harder or more dangerous than it really is). Shortly before the bullfight, Jake's group watches the local citizenry run with the bulls down the main street of the town. They see one man gored to death from behind. The following day, that same bull is presented to Romero, and he kills it perfectly by standing directly in front of it as he drives home his sword. This obvious symbolism states in a single image the most important of all the values, the need to confront reality directly and honestly.

It is not only Romero's example that helps to educate Jake but also Jake's involvement in the Brett-Romero affair. His role as intermediary is the result of his would-be romance with her. They are long in love and deeply frustrated by Jake's funny-sad war injury. Yet, despite the impossibility of a meaningful relationship, Jake can neither accept Brett as a friend nor cut himself off from her, although he knows that such a procedure would be the wisest course of action. She can only be a temptress to him, and she is quite accurate when she refers to herself as Circe.

The only time Jake feels whole and happy is when he and Bill Gorton take a fishing trip at Bayonne. There, in a world without women, they fish with skill and precision, drink wine (naturally chilled in the stream) instead of whiskey, relate to the hearty exuberance of the Basque peasantry, and feel serene in the rhythms of nature. Once they return to town and Jake meets Brett at San Sebastian, his serenity is destroyed.

Jake puts his group up at a hotel owned by Montoya, an old friend and the most honored bullfighting patron. Montoya is an admirer and accepts Jake as someone who truly understands and appreciates bullfighting, not only with his intellect but also with his whole being. Montoya even trusts Jake to the point of asking advice about the handling of this newest, potentially greatest young bullfighter, Romero. When Jake presents Brett to Romero, fully understanding the implications of his act, he violates Montoya's trust. Through his frustrated love for Brett, Romero is exposed to her corrupting influence. When Jake realizes his own weakness and recognizes that it cost him his aficionado status, he is left a sadder, wiser Hemingway hero.

Romero is not destroyed because Brett sends him away before she can do any damage. More than simple altruism is involved in her decision. Life with Romero holds the possibility of wholeness for her—as it holds the possibility of dissipation for him. By sending him away rather than risk damaging him, she relinquishes her last chance for health and happiness.

It is unclear whether or not Jake's insights and Brett's final moral act give meaning to the lives of these exiles. During their Bayonne fishing trip, Jake's friend Bill sings a song about "pity and irony," and that seems to be the overall tone of the book and especially of the ending: pity for the personal anguish and aimless searching of these people, but ironic detachment toward characters whose lives and situations are, at best, at least as comical as they are tragic.

"Critical Evaluation" by Keith Neilson

Further Reading

Berman, Ronald. *Fitzgerald, Hemingway, and the Twenties.* Tuscaloosa: University of Alabama Press, 2001. Berman examines the novels and short stories that Hemingway and F. Scott Fitzgerald wrote during the 1920's within the context of the decade's intellectual history, philosophy, and popular culture. Includes analysis of *The Sun Also Rises.*

Bloom, Harold, ed. *Ernest Hemingway's "The Sun Also Rises."* New York: Chelsea House, 2007. Contains a plot summary and an analysis as well as essays by Hemingway scholars who examine the characters, sexual ambiguity, and the influence of Henry James in the novel, among other topics. Also reprints the 1926 *New York Times* review of the novel.

Fantina, Richard. *Ernest Hemingway: Machismo and Masochism.* New York: Palgrave Macmillan, 2005. Focuses on Hemingway's heroes, including Jack Barnes. Fantina argues that Hemingway's male protagonists are "profoundly submissive" and display a "masochistic posture toward women."

Gandal, Keith. "*The Sun Also Rises* and 'Mobilization Wounds': Emasculation, Joke Fronts, Military School Wannabes, and Postwar Jewish Quotas." In *The Gun and the Pen: Hemingway, Fitzgerald, Faulkner, and the Fiction of Mobilization.* New York: Oxford University Press, 2008. Examines how Hemingway, William Faulkner, and F. Scott Fitzgerald, who were all deemed unsuitable for military service or command in World War I, felt emasculated by this failure and how their works of the 1920's reflect this frustration.

Hemingway Review 6, no. 1 (Fall, 1986). This special issue celebrates the sixtieth anniversary of *The Sun Also Rises*. The nine articles deal with topics as diverse as the original manuscript, Hemingway's presentation of women and war, the moral axis of the novel, and the word "sun" as title and metaphor.

Reynolds, Michael S. *"The Sun Also Rises": A Novel of the Twenties*. Boston: Twayne, 1988. An excellent overall reference accessible to the general reader. Reynolds discusses the novel's importance and critical reception and considers it from analytic, structural, historical, and thematic perspectives.

Stoneback, H. R. *Reading Hemingway's "The Sun Also Rises": Glossary and Commentary*. Kent, Ohio: Kent State University Press, 2007. A chapter-by-chapter annotation of the novel, pointing out significant details and features to enhance readers' understanding of the work.

Trogdon, Robert W., ed. *Ernest Hemingway: A Literary Reference*. New York: Carroll & Graf, 2002. A compendium of information about Hemingway, including photographs, letters, interviews, essays, speeches, book reviews, copies of some of his manuscripts-in-process, and his comments about his own work and the work of other writers.

Wagner-Martin, Linda. *Ernest Hemingway: A Literary Life*. New York: Palgrave Macmillan, 2007. Examines Hemingway's life, especially his troubled relationship with his parents. Wagner-Martin makes insightful connections among his personal life, his emotions, and his writing.

_____, ed. *Ernest Hemingway's "The Sun Also Rises": A Casebook*. New York: Oxford University Press, 2002. Contains an interview of Hemingway conducted by George Plimpton as well as essays by Hemingway scholars examining the "death of love," humor, and alcoholism in the novel, the characters of Brett Ashley and Jake Barnes, and "Hemingway, the *Corrida*, and Spain."

_____. *New Essays on "The Sun Also Rises."* New York: Cambridge University Press, 1987. Designed as a critical guide for students of American history and culture, this volume of five commissioned essays is thought-provoking yet accessible to nonspecialist readers.

The Sunken Bell

Author: Gerhart Hauptmann (1862-1946)
First produced: Die versunkene Glocke, 1896; first published, 1896 (English translation, 1898)
Type of work: Drama
Type of plot: Fantasy
Time of plot: Indeterminate
Locale: A mountain, a valley, and the paths between

Principal characters:
HEINRICH, a bell-founder
MAGDA, his wife
THEIR CHILDREN
RAUTENDELEIN, an elfin mountain sprite
OLD WITTIKIN, her grandmother, a sorceress
THE NICKELMANN, an elemental water spirit
THE VICAR,
THE SCHOOLMASTER, and
THE BARBER, representatives of the world

The Story:

In a mountain forest glade Rautendelein, a beautiful elf-child, sits singing and combing her long, golden hair while calling to a water spirit, the Nickelmann. She makes fun of the croaking froglike monster who comes out of a nearby well. Into that setting skips a faun who seems enamored of the lovely sprite and who invites her to be his love. She refuses, as if this is not her destiny. When she leaves, the wood and water sprites discuss the intrusion of man in their hallowed realms, the sprites that day forcing off the road and into a valley lake a bell meant for a mountaintop church. The bell-founder appears, quite exhausted and badly injured from his fall. He collapses before the cottage of Wittikin, a witch whom mortals in the region greatly fear. Her granddaughter, Rautendelein, strangely drawn to the thirty-year-old Heinrich, makes him a bed of straw and gives him milk to drink.

Heinrich is also drawn to this beautiful creature whose speech is song and who makes him glad to leave the mundane life below. He tried to match the musical note of her voice in his supreme creation, the bell in the lake. He calls her his sweet fantasy and the glade his real home. He begs for a dying kiss. Wittikin tells the child all mortals die while they, the mountain folk, Thor's children, must go about their immortal business.

When voices interrupt a merry troll dance, Rautendelein fears she will lose this strange man. A wood sprite answers the rescue party, which consists of a clergyman, a teacher, and a barber—envoys of the outer world of spirit, mind, and body. The Vicar, spirit-weak, cannot go on, though the Barber urges them all to leave the bewitched area and the Schoolmaster declares such an attitude mere superstition. Frightened, each addresses Wittikin, who in turn ridicules their master-worker and his trade as well as their respective callings, for she and her kind hate clanging bells and all human enterprise. The villagers carry Heinrich away as a group of elves and sprites dance furiously. Rautendelein also dances, though she tells the Nickelmann her spirit is not in it. They examine in wonder a tear from her eye, a globe of human pain. Thor flashes out and mocks her with raindrops. The Nickelmann warns her not to live with this half-man who belongs partly in their world, but she turns to the world of men.

In the meantime, the bad news reaches the bell-maker's home. Magda, Heinrich's wife, tells a neighbor what labor the task had cost her husband and then goes off to meet her husband's body, terribly disconcerted by the pallbearer appearance of the rescuers. Heinrich revives and, speaking as one already dead to his anxious wife, begs her pardon for hurts done. He renounces his great work as a misshapen thing providentially destroyed—a work for the valley rather than for the mountaintops. Saying that he now wants no part of this world of flesh, he refuses all aid and becomes unconscious. The Vicar will not seek aid from Wittikin; but Rautendelein, thought to be deaf-mute Anna from the wayside inn nearby, breathes life into the body while the villagers seek other help. Heinrich, recovering, recognizes her as nature, essential life, beauty; he will go with her onto the mountain. He declares to the returning Magda that he will live, though he is unaware of her joyful embrace.

Heinrich's presence in the mountains irritates all the supernatural folk. Taking up quarters in an abandoned glassworks, he mines ore, cuts trees, and, worst of all, makes Rautendelein his bride. The Nickelmann is jealous, though the wood sprite says she will never love a water spirit, at least not as long as Wittikin remains the bell-founder's friend. When these creatures tease Rautendelein about her earthly lover, she replies that their accursed race could by his industry and strength become renewed.

The Vicar, now dressed in mountain costume and determined on his course, interrupts this argument. He accuses the sprite of bewitching and holding Heinrich without his consent. This charge she denies. At that moment the master craftsman appears. Misled by flattery, Heinrich declares by occult signs that he is a new man, and he drinks to the Vicar's health while explaining his exuberant yet fundamental new life.

The bell-founder's vision is a chime of the finest metals that would ring by itself, through God's will and for no earthly church. The Vicar, denouncing this ecstasy, recounts Heinrich's earthly obligations to the Church and especially to his bereaved wife and children. He says it would be better if Heinrich were dead than to see him sustained by supernatural and sacrilegious beliefs. When Heinrich defends Rautendelein and his new life, the minister declares that both the people and God will crush him, that the arrow of rue will pierce though not kill him. This arrow cannot pierce him any more than his great bell could ever toll again, Heinrich declares.

Some time later Heinrich, desperately working his forge, drives his dwarf helpers to exhaustion in an attempt to create his beatific vision, to mold the ideal. As one dwarf whispers in his ear, another angrily shatters the piece on which they worked so furiously; it is imperfect. Heinrich gives them a holiday and declares all can go to the devil and he will garden, eat, drink, sleep, and die. Exhausted, he dreams that the Nickelmann ridicules his mortality, his weakness, and his uncompleted works. He thinks his old bell longs to ring out, though choked with blood and sunk so deep. He awakens in terror and calls Rautendelein for comfort; she responds by calling him her God and caressing him into illusions of immortality.

Incompleteness and imperfection goad him still, however, and he strikes out pridefully for work. He is warned not only by her but by the spirit of the wood, the faun of sensuality, and by distant voices that cry out from below. Though he thinks himself triumphant, a half remembered tolling unsettles him as the phantom forms of his two children bring him a pitcher of Magda's tears and the news that her dead hand rings the sunken bell. Heinrich renounces Rautendelein and tears himself from her.

At midnight, near the well, the weary Rautendelein meets her fate as the bride of the Nickelmann and sinks into the water. Wood and water spirits discuss the matter, and the former prophesy that a manchild will soon fill a watery cradle. Meanwhile, defiant Heinrich calls out for his loved one, ready to throw a stone at parson, barber, teacher, or sexton. Wittikin bars his way and points to a flaming, incomplete cathedral-castle. Determined to go on and yet exhausted, he drinks from the well before he attempts to reach the flaming ruins. A beloved voice sings a good-bye, although the sound is only half remembered.

Wittikin comforts Heinrich in his final minutes, tells him he was a hardy one, and grants him a boon. He drinks first a goblet of the white wine of life, which he drains to the last drop. Then he drinks a second of red, of the questing spirit. Just then Rautendelein appears, although urged back into the well by the Nickelmann. Heinrich calls for the final goblet of yellow wine, which is brought by Rautendelein. This he feels is all aspiration, sun wine poured into his veins by the evanescent one. Only in death does the master bell-founder, embraced and kissed by his great love, hear the chimes of the sun break through the night of life into the dawn of eternity.

Critical Evaluation:

This play is the most autobiographical and poetic of all the great Silesian playwright's efforts. It is about the problem of the artist against the world, the creative spirit against reality. The problem of living while maintaining standards of idealism is Gerhart Hauptmann's own very real problem, one that he did not solve. *The Sunken Bell* is a tale of two worlds that briefly overlap by virtue of a doomed love affair. The elves and elementals that populate traditional German *Märchen* (folktales) and the *Kunstmärchen* (art-folktales) of German Romanticism are very different from the gentle and benign insect-winged fairies of English art and fiction. In Teutonic mythology the world of nature-spirits was a dangerous place whose beauty and wildness were treacherous. Like the wood-sprite in the play, who lures the Vicar, the Schoolmaster, and the Barber deeper into the woods by calling for help in Heinrich's voice, the population of the other world takes a mischievous delight in confusing human beings and in leading them to destruction.

The Sunken Bell's plot is reminiscent of a famous *Kunstmärchen*, Friedrich de la Motte-Fouqué's *Undine* (1811; English translation, 1818) in which a water-sprite marries a young knight against the wishes of her own folk, who are swift to take their revenge when he proves unable to remain faithful to her. Hauptmann's play complicates this plot. Heinrich is no handsome young man free to plight his troth; he is a mature man who already has a loving wife and two children. Nor is Rautendelein's attachment to him a matter of spontaneous sympathy; she has a fervent desire to escape the claims of her own kind, embodied in the lascivious ambitions of the ugly Nickelmann. Heinrich's failure to make good his alliance with Rautendelein does not arise from lack of faith but from the fact that his ambition to make a bigger and better bell than any that has ever been made before—a bell fit for the mountaintops—destroys his mental composure.

The mountains have symbolic roles in *The Sunken Bell*. On the one hand they are wilderness regions, untamed by human culture, where the supernatural still holds sway. On the other hand, they are the heights of human aspiration and ambition. Heinrich's first bell, which falls into the lake and is lost when the wood-sprite causes the cart transporting it to lose its wheel, is a church bell. The sprites and the witch have cause to hate such bells, whose peals announce the faith that seeks to banish sprites and witches from the world.

Heinrich's conclusion—that the sunken bell is, after all, only a bell for the valleys and that a better bell might be built by one who has the means and the inspiration—is blasphemous. It is recognized as such by the angry Vicar, but it is not the Vicar's arguments that break Heinrich's resolve. Heinrich's breakdown is contrived by the jealous Nickelmann, who cunningly causes the bell to be rung underwater, so that its tolling might echo in Heinrich's overtaxed brain. Its sounding is not so much the knell of doom as the ominous clamor of his conscience, bringing forth a vision of his two children carrying a bucket of his wife's tears.

Heinrich's reasons for renouncing Rautendelein are far better than the reasons la Motte-Fouqué's knight has for renouncing Undine, and they are reasons of which a committed Christian would approve. His death might be regarded by the Vicar as the salvation of an imperiled soul, but this is not Hauptmann's opinion. There is ample evidence within *The Sunken Bell* to prove this point, but if more were needed it would only be necessary to consult Hauptmann's novel *Der Ketzer von Soana* (1918; *The Heretic of Soana*, 1923) in which a priest is converted to a doctrine of nature-worship that is pagan and poetic. Such a faith embodies everything that Rautendelein stands for.

Rautendelein's role in the play resembles the role played by hundreds of literary femmes fatales who lure good men away from the demands of duty with promises of erotic ecstasy. There is also more to her than that. Under her spell, Heinrich becomes twice the man he was before; far from abandoning himself to erotic bliss, he throws himself into his work more extravagantly than ever. She has no intention of distracting him from his labors, but instead she uses her magic to support them in every possible way, providing wealth, raw materials, and laborers. The final tragedy is as much hers as his. It is arguable that her loss is the greater, in that it will be eternal. He, after all, is always bound to die.

Hauptmann was by no means the only writer to think that humankind would lose something precious if it were to put away forever the kind of enchantments associated with folklore and to regret that the Church was committed to the annihilation of belief in sprites, fairies, and the like. Nor was he the only one to clothe such regret in the form of an adult fairy tale. What is exceptional about *The Sunken Bell* is that, through the character of Rautendelein, Hauptmann looks at the question from the side of the spirits, insisting that there is something in human beings whose absence leaves the world of spirits direly impoverished. Humans do things and make things, something that the spirits, in their immortality, often forget to do. When Heinrich finally dies, hearing the song of the sun's "bells," Rautendelein must, tragically, return to the Nickelmann. This represents, in a sense, the triumph of nonsense over sense and of idleness over accomplishment.

"Critical Evaluation" by Brian Stableford

Further Reading

Garten, Hugh F. *Gerhart Hauptmann.* New Haven, Conn.: Yale University Press, 1954. A useful general introduction to the writer and his work.

Guthke, Karl S. "The King of the Weimar Republic: Hauptmann's Role in Political Life." In *Trails in No-Man's-Land: Essays in Literary and Cultural History.* Columbia, S.C.: Camden House, 1993. Guthke views Hauptmann's literary works from the broader context of his role in German politics.

McInnes, E. O. H. "The 'Active' Hero in Gerhart Hauptmann's Dramas." In *Hauptmann: Centenary Lectures,* edited by K. G. Knight and F. Norman. London: Institute of Germanic Studies, University of London, 1964. A relevant essay in a collection that mostly deals with later works.

Maurer, Warren R. *Gerhart Hauptmann.* Boston: Twayne, 1982. A study with emphasis on Hauptmann's works. *The Sunken Bell* is discussed in chapter 6, "Folklore and Symbolism."

_____. *Understanding Gerhart Hauptmann.* Columbia: University of South Carolina Press, 1992. Excellent overview of Hauptmann's works. Chapter 4 contains a five-page discussion of *The Sunken Bell.*

Osborne, John. *Gerhart Hauptmann and the Naturalist Drama.* 2d rev. and updated ed. Amsterdam: Harwood Academic, 1998. *The Sunken Bell* is one of Hauptmann's plays included in this study of his drama; references to the play are listed in the index. Osborne's book was originally published in 1971 as *The Naturalist Drama in Germany.*

The Sunlight Dialogues

Author: John Gardner (1933-1982)
First published: 1972
Type of work: Novel
Type of plot: Psychological realism
Time of plot: Mid-1960's
Locale: Batavia, New York

Principal characters:
FRED CLUMLY, the aging chief of police of Batavia, New York
TAGGART HODGE or the SUNLIGHT MAN, a former lawyer and insane magician
WILL HODGE, SR., Taggart's older brother and an attorney in Batavia, New York
MILLIE JEWEL HODGE, Will Hodge's former wife
LUKE HODGE, Will and Millie's son
NICK SLATER, a young American Indian, companion of Taggart Hodge

The Story:

A scarfaced, bearded, and semideranged man is arrested in Batavia, New York, for writing the word "love" in the street in large white letters. Refusing to identify himself, ironically he comes to be known as the Sunlight Man, due to his cynical diatribes against, among other targets, the American legal system, Western capitalism, and the Judeo-Christian tradition. After befuddling Police Chief Clumly with his magic tricks, he easily escapes from jail, but he soon returns to free Nick Slater, a young Indian in jail for vehicular homicide. While escaping, Nick kills one of Chief Clumly's deputies. An intense, prolonged manhunt begins. Soon afterward, Nick murders Mrs. Palazzo, the landlady of Will Hodge, Sr., when she surprises Nick and the Sunlight Man, in hiding at Will's home. Nick and the Sunlight Man then flee to the farm of Luke Hodge, one of Will's sons and the Sunlight Man's nephew. While there, the Sunlight Man engages in a bizarre series of arranged meetings and "dialogues" with Chief Clumly; the Sunlight Man teases Chief Clumly with displays of magical prowess (stealing Chief Clumly's gun and mysteriously appearing and disappearing) and lecturing Chief Clumly about the disparity between human law and universal principles (the former scorned by the Sunlight Man as he alleges obedience to the latter). These secret meetings do not remain so long, and the resultant publicity subjects Chief Clumly to criticism both for meeting with the Sunlight Man and for failing to capture him. The publicity also makes Will and the other Hodge family members aware of the fact that the Sunlight Man is really Taggart, who was disbarred sixteen years earlier and who left New York after the disbarment and after having been hideously burned when his mentally ill wife set fire to their home.

The family members do not reveal the Sunlight Man's identity; they realize that Taggart returned to Batavia because his wife is now institutionalized there. The family members' conversation reveals that Taggart left years ago in order to accompany Taggart's wife as he and her brothers sought treatment for her at various mental institutions around the country; there was no alleviation of her steadily increasing illness. Two family members cannot reveal Taggart's identity because Taggart keeps Luke Hodge and Millie Hodge, Luke's mother and Will's former wife, bound and gagged at Luke's farm while Taggart constructs his magical devices and meets with, tantalizes, and lectures Chief Clumly. After several days, a neighbor, Mr. Hardesty, comes to visit, but when he recognizes Taggart as the now-notorious Sunlight Man, Nick also kills Mr. Hardesty, again without Taggart's approval—but also without his condemnation.

In the intervals between meetings with the Sunlight Man, Chief Clumly finally learns that his tormentor is Taggart Hodge. Chief Clumly traces the movements of the wife, Kathleen Paxton, from hospital to hospital, and he discovers that a man fitting the Sunlight Man's description always accompanies her. Chief Clumly then visits Kathleen, finding her virtually comatose, and at his next meeting with the Sunlight Man, Chief Clumly reveals his knowledge. He then manages to disarm Taggart, but due to Taggart's eloquent arguments and due to sympathy with the tragic circumstances which make Taggart almost insane, Chief Clumly allows Taggart to escape, despite the fact that Taggart is an accessory to several murders. Such continued failure to apprehend the Sunlight Man, despite known meetings with him, along with general neglect of his other duties in his absorption with Taggart, causes Chief Clumly to be fired by Batavia's mayor. Clumly is still convinced that Taggart deserves better than the fate the American criminal justice system would impose

on him. Taggart's philosophical arguments affect Clumly and make Clumly more humane.

Meanwhile, Taggart remembers, despite his semideranged condition, why he came back to Batavia and what he did just prior to writing "love" in the street. After his years of travel, as he attempted to help his deranged wife in defiance of her domineering and vicious father, her father found them and took Kathleen back to Batavia and had her given shock treatment. That treatment destroyed what remained of her consciousness. Taggart also remembers that he learned that Mr. Paxton had Taggart's sons killed after the fire at Taggart's home. Taggart also recalls that he strangled Kathleen's father the evening before his deranged, ironic street-writing. Aware now of his need to escape from New York before his killing of Mr. Paxton becomes known (and, in fact, Clumly already suspected), Taggart enlists Luke as a getaway driver. Luke recognizes his uncle, however, and being semisuicidal, anyway, due to the effect his parents' troubled marriage has upon him, Luke decides to drive his truck off a bridge and kill himself and Taggart, thereby preserving the Hodge family from the infamy of public awareness of Taggart's identity. A premonition causes Taggart and Nick to jump from the truck prior to the wreck, however, and they escape death. The knowledge that he indirectly caused his nephew's death deeply affects Taggart, however, and he returns to Batavia in order to surrender. Unable to resist one more trick against the police, however, Taggart steals Officer Figlow's gun and hides it in a desk drawer. Figlow finds the gun and, terrified at seeing the Sunlight Man and not realizing the Sunlight Man's peaceful intent, Figlow grabs the gun and kills Taggart. All that remains is for Clumly to deliver the speech to the Dairyman's League that he long planned; he makes the speech an eloquent, impassioned eulogy and defense of the Sunlight Man and a plea for a more concerned and enlightened American system of criminal justice.

Critical Evaluation:

Widely regarded as John Gardner's most ambitious and important novel, *The Sunlight Dialogues* operates on a very inclusive thematic level. The holistic nature of that inquiry is clarified in the prologue, in which the old, unnamed Judge, analogous to God, says, "I made that man [Chief Clumly]. I created him, you might say. I created them all." He assumes that "nothing in the world is universal any more; there is neither wisdom nor stability, and faithfulness is dead." The Judge also states his opinion that entropy (the general trend of the universe toward death and disorder) explains all those people he once knew who have since disappeared. These beliefs provide the framework for the fundamental question explored in the tragic destruction of Taggart Hodge and in the destruction indirectly wrought by him via Nick Slater. The question: In an existential universe (one lacking absolute realities or truths) in which stupidity, instability, and unfaithfulness abound, what can combat entropy? Gardner's answer is provided through the change in Chief Clumly; the change is due to his interaction with the Sunlight Man, and the change is most clearly stated in Clumly's speech to the Dairyman's League at the novel's end.

At the beginning of *The Sunlight Dialogues*, Clumly is a letter-of-the-law, inflexible automaton, "'a man of principle,' people said, which was to say as inflexible as a chunk of steel, with a heart so cold that if you touched it you'd stick as your fingers stick to iron at twenty below zero." Also, as the Sunlight Man realizes through his wife's insanity and his sons' murder, "It's sorrow that changes a man. But there was no sorrow in the life of the chief of police. That was his crime. There was only order, lifted against the world like rusty chickenwire to keep out a herd of cows." Taggart himself, in his semi-insane state after the tragedies in his family, becomes the "herd of cows," the disorder of an entropic universe, that Clumly must struggle with; the police chief immediately senses this. Clumly reports that "the old feeling came over him again, the absolute, irrational certainty that the bearded man was the sum total of all Clumly had been fighting all his life." Clumly's fight has not been highly successful, however, as crime is rampant in Batavia, and he is a virtual laughingstock on the verge of being fired. It is only when Clumly meets with and has four "dialogues" with the Sunlight Man that Clumly begins to understand the ambiguities of the diverse, disordered world that he refused previously to acknowledge (except to try to imprison as much of it as possible).

Clumly's increasing awareness, via the "dialogues," of the inadequacies of Western capitalism, the American criminal justice system, and the Judeo-Christian tradition makes him incapable of the larger injustice of arresting the Sunlight Man and costs him his job as police chief. Ironically, however, this awareness makes him a saner, wiser human being, a humanist and a moralist who finally possesses Gardner's answer to the question of how to counteract the entropic tendency of the world. After Taggart is killed by mistake, epitomizing the stupidity, instability, and unfaithfulness that characterize twentieth century existence, Clumly combats the entropy in his speech. His answer is to bemoan "the injustice of it!" (Taggart's death), to note that laws benefit "all of *us*, anyway" (his law-abiding and financially secure audience), and to warn that "the danger is, it [a society of law] can get cold. Turn ice." He further notes, "Ladies and gentlemen, we

mustn't let that happen, I feel. I feel we must all be vigilant against growing indifference to people less fortunate." The repetition of "I feel" and the emphasis upon caring about others less fortunate show that Clumly's (and Gardner's) answer to death and disorder is moral and emotional empathy, tempered by an awareness of the complexities and inherent ambiguities of modern life. This latter awareness is illustrated in Clumly's comment that "we may be wrong about the whole thing . . . the whole kaboodle. If we could look at ourselves from the eyes of history—" (Taggart has helped him to do just that). Clumly then concludes with the human empathy emphasis of the Judeo-Christian tradition, not its hierarchical law-and-order dimension, when he states that, "Blessed are the meek, by which I mean all of us, including the Sunlight Man. . . . God be kind to all Good Samaritans and also bad ones. For of such is the Kingdom of Heaven." Clumly embodies Gardner's inclusive theme, his response to an entropic universe is to look beyond laws to justice; to look beyond self-interest to concern for others; to look beyond logic to feeling; to look beyond simplistic certainty to informed relativity; and to look beyond hierarchical divisiveness to holistic acceptance. Although entropy may ultimately prevail, the importance of Gardner's *The Sunlight Dialogues* is its demonstration that the only effective response to life is, indeed, love written large in the streets of the world.

John L. Grigsby

Further Reading

Cowart, David. *Arches and Light: The Fiction of John Gardner*. Carbondale: Southern Illinois University Press, 1983. Interprets *The Sunlight Dialogues* as centered on the human struggle against universal entropy. Includes helpful genre analysis and perceptive analogizing of the work to that of Sir Thomas Malory, Dante Alighieri, and Homer.

Howell, John M. *Understanding John Gardner*. Columbia: University of South Carolina Press, 1993. Provides a thorough discussion of the history and criticism of Gardner. Chapter 3 is devoted to an analysis of *The Sunlight Dialogues*.

Morris, Gregory L. "A Babylonian in Batavia: Mesopotamian Literature and Lore in *The Sunlight Dialogues*." In *John Gardner: Critical Perspectives*, edited by Robert A. Morace and Kathryn VanSpanckeren. Carbondale: Southern Illinois University Press, 1982. A thorough explanation of the Mesopotamian history, lore, and cultural tradition underlying the four "dialogues" between the Sunlight Man and Chief Clumly; the four dialogues are the controlling structures of *The Sunlight Dialogues*.

————. *A World of Order and Light: The Fiction of John Gardner*. Athens: University of Georgia Press, 1984. Astute analysis of *The Sunlight Dialogues* as "the artistic and intellectual center" of all Gardner's fiction; Gardner explains his "governing metaphysical system" in this novel. Analyzes the complex, multilayered structure of *The Sunlight Dialogues*.

Nutter, Ronald Grant. *A Dream of Peace: Art and Death in the Fiction of John Gardner*. New York: Peter Lang, 1997. Nutter reviews Gardner's life and work, describing his thoughts on religion and peace and other aspects of his personal philosophy. He explains how Gardner was influenced by the thinking of Alfred North Whitehead and Susanne Langer.

Payne, Alison. "Clown, Monster, Magician: The Purpose of Lunacy in John Gardner's Fiction." In *Thor's Hammer: Essays on John Gardner*, edited by Jeff Henderson et al. Conway: University of Central Arkansas Press, 1985. A perceptive study of insanity in several Gardner novels. Includes detailed analysis of the symbolic divergence of the emotional idealism of the Sunlight Man and the rational practicality of Chief Clumly in *The Sunlight Dialogues*.

Silesky, Barry. *John Gardner: The Life and Death of a Literary Outlaw*. Chapel Hill, N.C.: Algonquin Books of Chapel Hill, 2004. Silesky chronicles Gardner's life and development as a writer, describing how he cultivated the image of the eccentric outsider. While the book provides some description of his major works, it focuses on the events of his life and does not provide a detailed explication of his writings.

Thornton, Susan. *On Broken Glass: Loving and Losing John Gardner*. New York: Carroll & Graf, 2000. A memoir recounting Gardner's tumultuous relationship with Thornton, whom he was set to make his third wife before he died in a motorcycle accident a few days before the planned wedding. Thornton knew Gardner during the last three years of his life, and she traces his alcoholic decline during those years.

Winther, Per. *The Art of John Gardner: Instruction and Exploration*. Albany: State University of New York Press, 1992. Discusses Gardner's literary theory and his fiction and provides insight into the philosophical bases of important characters in *The Sunlight Dialogues*. Includes a helpful discussion of Gardner's collage technique.

The Suppliants

Author: Aeschylus (525/524-456/455 B.C.E.)
First produced: Hiketides, 463 B.C.E.? (English translation, 1777)
Type of work: Drama
Type of plot: Tragedy
Time of plot: Mythical age
Locale: Argos

Principal characters:
DANAÜS, an Egyptian of Greek descent
HIS FIFTY MAIDEN DAUGHTERS
PELASGUS, the king of Argos
THE FIFTY SONS OF AEGYPTUS
BROTHER OF DANAÜS

The Story:

Danaüs and his fifty maiden daughters flee Egypt after Danaüs's brother, Aegyptus, decides that his fifty sons should take their cousins to wife. The fugitives finally reach the shores of Argos, the land of their illustrious ancestress Io, a mortal loved by Zeus. Holding olive branches wrapped in wool before an Argive altar, the maidens seek Zeus's protection of their purity. Their supplications to the father of the gods include the wish that the sons of Aegyptus might meet disaster at sea between Egypt and Argos. In fear of being forced to marry Aegyptus's sons, the maidens also invoke the wretched Procne, who was given in marriage to the perfidious Tereus and took the life of her child, Itylus, out of hatred for her husband. They repeat their supplication to Zeus to protect them from forced love, and they invoke Artemis, the goddess of chastity, to be favorable to them. They declare that they will end their lives themselves before submitting to the sons of Aegyptus. They go on to invoke not only Zeus but also Apollo, who himself was once an exile. They pray to Poseidon, god of the sea, and to Hermes, the messenger of the gods. Danaüs recalls that the gods are merciless to those who indulge in lustful pleasures.

Danaüs, observing that someone approaches, cautions his

daughters to stay near the altar and to conduct themselves with modesty. A man, followed by servants and warriors, enters the sacred area. Seeing that the maidens wear Eastern clothing and that suppliant wands were placed on the altar, he asks whence Danaüs and the young women come. Questioned in turn, he discloses that he is Pelasgus, the king of Argos. One of the maidens then tells him that they are of Argive stock, descendants of Io, the Argive woman who gave birth to a son by Zeus. Pelasgus interrupts to remark that the maidens appear to be North Africans and to resemble the Amazons rather than the Grecians.

The maiden resumes her tale, recounting that when Hera, the wife of Zeus, saw that Zeus loved the mortal Io, she transformed Io into a heifer and placed her under the guard of Argus, the many-eyed god. Hera also created a gadfly to sting Io into a miserable, wandering existence on earth. Io's wanderings took her to Memphis, Egypt, where by mystical union with Zeus—the touch of his hand—she gave birth to a son. She named him Epaphus, from the nature of his birth. Epaphus had a daughter, Libya, after whom a great stretch of North Africa was named. Libya had a son, Belus, who fathered two sons, Danaüs—the father of fifty daughters, whom the king beholds before his very eyes—and Aegyptus, the father of fifty sons.

Pelasgus, satisfied that they are of Argive stock, asks why they left Egypt. The maiden explains that they fled because they were threatened with forced marriage to their cousins; it is not so much that they hate their cousins as that they want their husbands to love them. Pelasgus, observing that in the most advantageous marriages there is no aspect of love, is not sure he can support the maidens in their cause. The maidens point to the wand-decked shrine and ask Pelasgus to heed the sign.

All the sisters plead for assistance from Pelasgus, who fears that his meddling in the affair might bring war to Argos. Apprehensive, yet anxious to help, he insists that he will have to consult his people. The suppliants answer that he is an absolute ruler and can, if he so desires, make his own decisions. They warn him to beware of the wrath of Zeus, the god who takes pity on humans in distress and is merciless with those who refuse to assist others. Still Pelasgus insists on consulting his people, for he fears to bring disaster to Argos. Even after searching deeply in his soul for an answer, he declares that the problem is one with which he alone cannot cope, that to resolve it will involve frightful sacrifices to the gods.

In despair, the maidens propose that Pelasgus use their girdles to hang them to the statues in the sacred area. Deeply disturbed, Pelasgus suggests that Danaüs gather up all of the wands and, in hopes of eliciting general Argive sympathy for the maidens, place them on altars in the city of Argos itself. Once he is assured of safe passage into the city, Danaüs accepts the suggestion and departs with the wands. When Pelasgus directs the maidens to an unhallowed area of the sacred ground, they ask how they are to be protected there from their cousins. Pelasgus, advising them to pray to the Argive gods, returns to Argos to consult with his people.

Left alone, the maidens resume their earnest prayers and invocations to Zeus. They again recall Zeus's love for their ancestress and appeal to him—who is after all responsible for their being—to save them from the lust of Aegyptus's sons.

Danaüs returns to report that to a man the Argives will defend any refugees from seizure. Pelasgus reminds the Argives that if they fail to assist and to offer sanctuary to suppliants, Zeus will send a man-eating monster to the city. The maidens sing their gratitude to the people of Argos and invoke the gods to look auspiciously upon the land.

Danaüs, standing on an elevated place in the sacred ground, sees the sons of Aegyptus approaching the shore in their ships. He calms his frightened daughters by reminding them of the Argives' promise, but when he wishes to leave them to summon help, they beg him to stay with them. He points out that it will take Aegyptus's sons some time to make proper anchorage and that there is plenty of time for him to seek aid.

After Danaüs leaves, the maidens, overcome with apprehension at the approach of their cousins, speak of the death they prefer to the enforced love that appears to be imminent. As they cry in anguish to Zeus, a messenger comes to them from the ships and, treating them with brutality, orders them to the ships. While he sneers at their frantic appeals to the Greek gods, Pelasgus comes upon the scene of violence and demands of the messenger his business. The Egyptian answers that he comes to take what belongs to him and that only force, not any fear of the Greek gods, can prevent his taking the maidens back to Egypt. Pelasgus declares that the sons of Aegyptus will have to fight to claim their captives. When the messenger asks his name, Pelasgus retorts that his name does not matter; what does matter is that the women will not be taken from Argos by force.

The messenger returns to the ships, and Pelasgus invites the maidens to take shelter with the friendly people of Argos. The maidens first seek the approval of their father, Danaüs, who advises them to treasure their chastity before their lives and gives them permission to go. Rejoicing, the daughters of Danaüs sing reverently and thankfully to Artemis, goddess of chastity. They also invoke Aphrodite, goddess of love, who they are sure will help in guiding them to marriages blessed by true love.

Critical Evaluation:

Aeschylus's *The Suppliants* brilliantly depicts strong passions and moral greatness. The play is nevertheless very difficult to interpret. For one thing, *The Suppliants* was part of a trilogy dealing with the fate of the daughters of Danaüs; the sequel plays are lost except for a few fragments. Most Greek tragedies were in the form of a trilogy, in which the related mythical stories presented in the first play were developed to a conclusion in the third. In this trilogy, the Danaids were probably central actors in all three plays. Consequently evaluation of the one surviving play is problematic. A second difficulty to interpretation is the high proportion of lyric poetry contained in the drama: nearly half of the preserved play is choral lyrics that allude to complex myths. This beautiful and allusive poetry is unusual in a drama, and yet interpretation of these mythical references is crucial to understanding the subtler themes of the work. A third challenge to appreciating *The Suppliants* is its lack of action, which is sparse even when compared with other extant Greek tragedies. As it stands, the plot seems to turn on Pelasgus's agonizing decision whether or not to protect the maidens who come to him for refuge. This focus on the king of Argos rather than on the fate of the maidens may not be what Aeschylus actually intended as the focus of the trilogy. Each of these major difficulties must be considered in evaluating Aeschylus's art in *The Suppliants*.

It is virtually certain that *The Suppliants* was the first play of a trilogy, of which *The Egyptians* and *The Danaids* were the second and third parts. Aeschylus wrote the only extant Greek trilogy, *Oresteia* (458 B.C.E.; English translation, 1777). From his practice in that work and the myth as it is known from other sources, the probable development of the Danaid trilogy can be tentatively reconstructed. It is possible that even before *The Egyptians* opens, the war between Argos and the sons of Aegyptus is over, with Pelasgus dead and Argos utterly defeated. The maidens are forced to return to Egypt, are married, and all but one murder their husbands on the wedding night. Only Hypermestra refuses out of love to kill her new husband. As in *Oresteia*, a trial probably ensued: A fragment of *The Danaids* suggests that Hypermestra is tried for disobedience in not killing her husband. However, Aphrodite intervenes and defends her by citing the invincible power of love. If this reconstruction is correct, the courageous vow of Pelasgus to protect the maidens turns out to have been futile. The resistance of the Danaids to marriage, a prominent theme in *The Suppliants*, leads to an act for which,

according to some versions of the myth, they are eternally punished in Hades by being compelled to carry water in leaky urns. The resolution in the third play may affirm the same power of matrimony and sexual union that the maidens so passionately reject in the opening play. Clearly, any first impressions of *The Suppliants* must be qualified by reference to the story as it unfolded in the complete trilogy.

In the extant play, the audience is confronted by a dense work full of allusive choral lyrics that are intended to elaborate on the plight of the Danaids. This unusual reliance on lyric once led scholars to assume that *The Suppliants* was a very early play, written perhaps as early as c. 490 B.C.E., when the dramatic possibilities of dialogue and plot were still unexplored. Subsequently, a spectacular papyrus discovery confirmed that the play was in fact first performed in the 460's, near the close of Aeschylus's career. For whatever reason, the dramatist chose to portray the situation of the Danaids, a "protagonist" in the form of fifty maidens, primarily through lyric song rather than through dramatic confrontation and dialogue. The choral songs often dwell on the story of Io, who was loved by Zeus and persecuted by Hera. Her experience of pursuit and exile is obviously a parallel to the plight of the Danaids. However, the Danaids and also the Argives and the sons of Aegyptus trace their origins back to Io. The maidens express revulsion at the idea of forced marriage to their cousins, but while their resistance to marriage may seem to suggest an assertion of women's rights, this may be an anachronistic interpretation. It is likely that Aeschylus intended the maidens to express a more common fear of the time, that of leaving childhood and accepting the role of wife and mother.

Pelasgus is undoubtedly the most interesting character in the play. He is faced with a tragic choice: either to protect the suppliants and risk war with Egypt or to return them and incur the wrath of Zeus. Some have seen his decision to champion the Danaids' cause as a mark of weakness, since it is precipitated by their threat to commit suicide on the altar of the gods. However, Aeschylus skillfully depicts a leader who is at once reluctant to endanger his people and afraid not to do what is right. Rather than himself deciding an issue with such far-reaching implications for his country, he submits his proposal to a vote of the people, who unanimously approve the plan to protect the suppliants. This detail is surely a nod to the evolution of mature Athenian democracy in the 460's, even though the action is translated to Argos in mythical times. Although their decision leads to a war that Argos loses, the Argive resolve to defend the suppliants presents a noble contrast to the use of force by the brutal Egyptians.

The Suppliants is an intense, lyrical depiction of the helpless refugees who find defenders willing to act selflessly and to take risks for what is right. A pious Greek king and his subjects take upon themselves the problems of unjustly persecuted barbarians. With its brief acknowledgment of democracy as the only proper way for a community to decide such important matters, even if the decision should have tragic consequences, the play also represents a fascinating fusion of literature and history.

"Critical Evaluation" by John M. Lawless

Further Reading

Aeschylus. *The Suppliants*. Translated by Peter Burian. Princeton, N.J.: Princeton University Press, 1991. An excellent modern translation of the play. Also provides a sound introduction to the themes and imagery of the play and includes brief notes explaining references in the translation.

Beck, Robert Holmes. *Aeschylus: Playwright Educator*. The Hague, the Netherlands: Martinus Nijhoff, 1975. Chapter 7 examines *The Suppliants* and its themes in the context of the supposed trilogy to which it belonged. Beck places particular emphasis on the moral message that the playwright may have intended with the drama.

Burian, Peter. "Pelasgus and Politics in Aeschylus' Danaid Trilogy." In *Aeschylus*, edited by Michael Lloyd. New York: Oxford University Press, 2007. Burian, who has translated *The Suppliants*, updates an article he originally published in 1974, in which he examines the character of Pelasgus and the role of the Argive political system in the tragedy.

Conacher, D. J. "*Supplices* (*The Suppliants*) and Its Trilogy." In *Aeschylus: The Earlier Plays and Related Studies*. Toronto, Ont.: University of Toronto Press, 1996. Conacher analyzes the play's themes, structure, dramatic devices, and the trilogy of which it is a part. His book also contains a more general discussion of Aeschylus's use of the chorus and imagery.

Garvie, A. F. *Aeschylus' "Supplices": Play and Trilogy*. 2d ed. Bristol, England: Bristol Phoenix, 2006. The standard work on the style, structure, and meaning of the play. Garvie tends to be cautious in his speculation about the content of the lost plays and their possible relevance for interpretation of *The Suppliants*.

Mills, Sophie. "Theseus and *The Suppliants*." In *Theseus, Tragedy, and the Athenian Empire*. New York: Oxford University Press, 1997. Mills traces the myth of Theseus, analyzing *The Suppliants* and the other dramas in which he is a character. She maintains that these plays portray Theseus as the idealized embodiment of the Athenian national character.

Spatz, Lois. *Aeschylus*. Boston: Twayne, 1982. An excellent and accessible general work on the art of Aeschylus. Chapter 4 on *The Suppliants* is especially rewarding for discussion of possible political ideas in the drama and of various themes in the choral odes.

Winnington-Ingram, R. P. *Studies in Aeschylus*. New York: Cambridge University Press, 1983. A sober and intelligent survey of Aeschylean drama that repays consultation. Chapter 4, "The Danaid Trilogy," is concerned primarily with the speculative reconstruction of the trilogy and its value for interpreting the drama. This work updates earlier work on the Danaid trilogy.

The Suppliants

Author: Euripides (c. 485-406 B.C.E.)

First produced: Hiketides, c. 423 B.C.E. (English translation, 1781)

Type of work: Drama

Type of plot: Tragedy

Time of plot: Antiquity

Locale: Eleusis, near Athens, Greece

Principal characters:
THESEUS, king of Athens
AETHRA, his mother
ADRASTUS, king of Argos
EVADNE, Capaneus's wife
IPHIS, her father
CHILDREN OF THE SLAIN CHIEFTAINS
THE GODDESS ATHENA
HERALD OF CREON
CHORUS OF ARGIVE MOTHERS

The Story:

Adrastus, the Argive king who led the disastrous war of the Seven against Thebes and alone escaped with his life, brings the mothers and the children of the slain chieftains to Athens, the most democratic and hospitable city of Greece. There they gather at the temple of Demeter at Eleusis, and when Aethra, the mother of Theseus, comes to pray, they form a ring of supplication about her, begging for help in recovering the dead bodies of their sons for burial according to the prescribed rites. The anguish of the mothers so moves Aethra that she sends at once for her own son.

The powerful young king closely cross-examines the defeated old ruler and refuses to help after discovering that Adrastus foolishly married off his daughters to quarrelsome exiles, Tydeus and Polynices, and engaged in war against Thebes despite the advice of the prophet Amphiaraus. Aethra, however, discreetly reminds her son that, although his logic is sound as far as it goes, he is nevertheless obligated by honor and the religious customs of Attica to go to the aid of all who seek proper burial and funeral rites for the dead. Theseus, recognizing the wisdom and humanity of her counsel, departs to seek a vote of the Athenian assembly on the matter.

Upon his return, Theseus announces that, with the support of the assembly, he is ready to send two messages to Creon, king of Thebes. The first is a polite request for permission to bury the dead. If this one is refused, the second is a warning that his armies are on their way. He is interrupted by the arrival of an insolent herald from Creon who demands in the name of his despot that Adrastus be driven from Athens. The herald adds that courageous wisdom calls for peace. Theseus, although detesting war, feels obligated by the ancient laws of the gods to bury the dead, by force of arms if necessary. After a heated exchange of words, the Theban herald withdraws, and Theseus prepares for battle. He rejects Adrastus's offer of aid, for he is unwilling to blend his fortunes with those of a king who brought upon himself the wrath of the gods. As Theseus marches off with his troops, the chorus chants fear of the fickleness of heaven and prays for deliverance.

Soon a messenger brings news of Theseus's victory, describing how the Athenians arrived at the Theban gates, expressed an intent to avoid war if they were permitted to bury the Argive chieftains but finally found it necessary to fight the Thebans. Theseus, refusing to enter the gates and sack the city, personally gathered together the dead bodies and washed their wounds. Adrastus, deeply moved, lamented that the Thebans did not learn the lesson of compromise from his own experience and wished that he, too, had died with his fellow warriors.

When the bodies are brought to Athens, Adrastus delivers a eulogy over each (Capaneus, Eteocles, Hippomedon, Parthenopaeus, Tydeus, and Polynices) before they are prepared for cremation on the funeral pyre. Suddenly Evadne, widow of Capaneus, appears on a rock overhanging the burning pyre, determined to be with Capaneus in death as she was in life. Her aged father, Iphis, pleads with her in vain. Dressed in festive garments, she leaps into the fire. As the children of the cremated warriors carry away the ashes in funeral urns, the grief-stricken Iphis withdraws to the dark interior of his house to die.

Marching in a funeral procession, the children (thereafter known as the Epigoni) chant an oath with the chorus to avenge their fathers. Theseus extracts from them a promise that they and all their children will always remember the kindness they received from Athens and honor the city of democracy. Before the children can carry off the ashes of their fathers, however, the goddess Athena appears in midair and calls upon Theseus not to permit the ashes to be returned to Argos. Instead, after appropriate animal sacrifices, they must be delivered to the safekeeping of the oracle at Delphi. Then, turning to the children, Athena prophesies that when they reach adulthood they will successfully sack the city of Thebes and avenge the slaughter of their fathers.

Critical Evaluation:

Euripides' *The Suppliants* explores the themes of grief, the inhumanity of war, the proper democratic model for government, justice, and civic duty. *The Suppliants* is less effective than Euripides' other antiwar play, *Trōiades* (415 B.C.E.; *The Trojan Women*, 1782) because of a weaker blend of emotional and political themes and a weaker dramatic structure. The detached episodes within the play do not allow for complex developments within the characters of Theseus and Adrastus. Moreover, Theseus's climactic victory over Creon's army occurs very early in the play. *The Suppliants* ends without a true catharsis or a denouement that is emotionally satisfying. However, the play is blessed with eloquent speeches by Theseus and by the chorus of the wives of the slain chieftains who plead for the retrieval of the bodies of the dead soldiers.

The Suppliants is more political and didactic in nature than other Greek plays dealing with themes of supplication such as Aeschylus's *Choēphoroi* (458 B.C.E.; *The Libation Bearers*, 1777), Sophocles' *Antigonē* (441 B.C.E.; *Antigone*, 1729), and Euripides' *Trojan Women*. Euripides in *The Suppliants* is motivated to show how the Athenians might avenge the loss of the Peloponnesian War against the Spartan confederacy.

The idea of supplication as practiced by the Greeks was to make humble petitions and prayers to the gods by pouring liquids, usually wine, over the graves of the dead. The chorus of Argive mothers cannot perform this sacred ritual without the corpses of their sons Amphiaraus, Capaneus, Eteocles, Hippomedon, Parthenopaeus, Tydeus, and Polynices. However, that Theseus needs to be persuaded on the grounds of justice and civic duty into helping the Argive women retrieve the bodies of the warriors does not allow for much character complexity or emotional subtlety. Aethra, Theseus's mother, at first distressed by the women's wailing and lamentation at the temple of Demeter, requests Theseus to either drive the suppliants from the land or free them from their grief by fighting Creon and stealing the bodies. "To mourn the dead/ brings honor to those who live," the women plead to Theseus. The intense mourning and funeral marching unsettle Theseus in part because the women are foreigners, not Athenians. Theseus initially resists Adrastus's request to help by pointing out that Adrastus went to Thebes to please Tydeus and Polynices—suitors of two of his daughters—while ignoring a prophecy of doom. Theseus answers that Adrastus got what he deserved when be became confused by the squabbling of Tydeus and Polynices, two young warriors hungry for power.

Only when the goddess Athena appears deus ex machina at the end is Theseus moved to act. Preservation of the laws is what holds Greece together, and the gods will be slighted if the traditional laws are not obeyed. Motivated by Athena's wishes and his own desire to win glory for Athens, Theseus finally agrees to do it. Theseus really wishes to prove that democracy (the politics of Athens) is better than oligarchy (the politics of Thebes) and to demonstrate Greek justice in action. Theseus's sense of politics and civic duty fails to match the emotional intensity of the "inhumanity of war" pleas of the Argive women, unlike Achilles' fully developed personal and political rage against Agamemnon and Hector in Homer's *Iliad* (c. 750 B.C.E.; English translation, 1611).

The appearance of Creon's herald allows Theseus to pontificate on his political motive for attacking Thebes: Citizens of Athens are free and democratic while Creon tyrannizes Thebes with his absolute rule. Theseus's speech explains that Athens is ruled by people who share equally in governmental affairs, reigning in succession without yielding power to the rich. Creon's herald counters that Thebans do not need persuasive political rhetoric to make decisions and that the poor are incapable of attending to public matters. Theseus believes that absolute monarchy is bad and that Athenian rule is the law preserving equality and freedom. While one is aware that Athenian democracy in practice excluded many people, the discussion is intriguing on theoretical grounds, even though it provides insufficient motivation to invade Thebes.

Theseus bridges the gap between politics and personality by making the abandonment of the Argive dead into a justice issue, saying that all Greeks are hurt by devaluation of the dead. Theseus is driven by his desire to obey an ancient law when earlier he wanted only to be rid of the inconvenience of wailing mothers. To honor justice, Theseus begins his war against Creon.

Similarly, Adrastus's burial catalog of the chieftains after Theseus's victory lacks emotional impact because the audience has never encountered these characters except through other plays and legends. The audience cannot empathize with the Argive women, never having known the slain warriors. Adrastus and Theseus remain undeveloped as protagonists; they do not learn from their suffering. Evadne's desires to release herself from suffering and to join her husband Capaneus on the funeral pyre are surprising only because of inadequate exposition. Again, the audience does not really know Evadne or Capaneus apart from secondhand descriptions from other characters, so Evadne's suicide produces no cathartic release or visceral identification with suffering.

That the children of the slain chieftains are commanded by Athena to grow and exact revenge against the murder of their fathers runs counter to the main purpose of the play as a statement against the cruelty of war. Thus even with Theseus's rhetorically ornamented speech about the superiority of Athenian government and justice, the goddess Athena says the sons are lion cubs and "true-born sackers of cities," disregarding Theseus's justifications for the battle. Of course, the gods always possess the power to override any mortal desire to advance justice. Blessed with Euripidean political eloquence and the passion of suffering wrought through war, *The Suppliants* is an imperfect creation but an intriguing one.

"Critical Evaluation" by Jonathan Thorndike

Further Reading

Conacher, D. J. *Euridipean Drama: Myth, Theme, and Structure*. Toronto, Ont.: University of Toronto Press, 1967. Argues against the prevailing belief that Euripides destroyed Greek drama. Maintains that, while he never accepted myth as the basis for tragedy, Euripides continually created new dramatic structures to suit new perceptions of human tragedy.

Euripides. *Suppliant Women*. With introduction, translation, and commentary by James Morwood. Oxford, England:

Aris & Phillips/Oxbow, 2007. The text of the play is presented in Greek, with the English translation on the facing pages. The introduction places the work in its historical and literary context, while the commentary clarifies allusions and references and provides other information that enhances understanding of the play.

Grube, G. M. A. "Euripides and the Gods." In *Euripides: A Collection of Critical Essays*, edited by Erich Segal. Englewood Cliffs, N.J.: Prentice-Hall, 1968. Argues that the divine framework is still an important aspect of Euripides' drama, though he used a different concept of the gods than other dramatists did.

Halleran, Michael R. *Stagecraft in Euripides*. Totowa, N.J.: Barnes & Noble, 1985. Examines specific aspects of Euripides' technique, such as stage actions, entrances, surprises, exits, and lyrics. Discusses how Euripides changed the basic structural pattern of Greek drama in many of his plays.

Harsh, Philip Whaley. *A Handbook of Classical Drama*. Stanford, Calif.: Stanford University Press, 1944. A classic survey of the range of Greek and Roman drama, arguing for the greatness of the achievement and for its influence on modern literature. Skillful thematic reading of *The Suppliants* and the Euripidean plays leading up to it.

Mendelsohn, Daniel Adam. *Gender and the City in Euripides' Political Plays*. New York: Oxford University Press, 2002. Analyzes the Athenian idea of politics and the feminine as demonstrated in *The Suppliants* and *Children of Herakles*.

Morwood, James. *The Plays of Euripides*. Bristol, England: Bristol Classical, 2002. Morwood provides a concise overview of all of Euripides' plays, devoting a separate chapter to each one. He demonstrates how Euripides was constantly reinventing himself in his work.

Zuntz, G. *The Political Plays of Euripides*. Oxford, England: Manchester University Press, 1955. Foundational study of political ideas in *The Suppliants* and other political dramas. Zuntz explains that the play greatly impressed Euripides' contemporaries and does not deserve the low status assigned to it by modern critics.

Surfacing

Author: Margaret Atwood (1939-   )
First published: 1972
Type of work: Novel
Type of plot: Psychological realism
Time of plot: 1960's
Locale: Northern wilderness of Quebec, Canada

Principal characters:
THE NARRATOR, a woman searching for her father
JOE, her lover
ANNA, the narrator's friend
DAVID, Anna's husband
PAUL, an acquaintance of the narrator

The Story:

The narrator is driving with her lover, Joe, and another couple, David and Anna, from the city where they live to a lake in the wilderness of northern Quebec. Every year as a child, the narrator and her family had returned to this lake to spend the summer on an isolated island reached only by boat. The narrator and her brother had gone to school in a different town every year because her father was a botanist who worked in several locations for industry and the government. The narrator's mother had died on the island, and her brother had fled the family.

The narrator, who had not attended her mother's funeral and is now estranged from her father, has not returned to the island for some years. A family acquaintance, Paul, who lives in the village along the lake, had contacted the narrator to say that her father, who has been living alone on the island, is missing. She does not tell her traveling companions the real purpose of the trip.

The quartet reach the village. The three friends go into a bar while the narrator talks with Paul; she learns nothing more about her father's disappearance. She buys supplies, then another villager, Evans, runs the narrator, Joe, Anna, and David in his motorboat up the lake to the island, which is two miles long. The narrator does not want to see her father, only to find out that he is all right. She claims to be estranged from her father because she had abandoned a husband and baby some years ago, for which her parents never forgave her.

When they get to the island, they find the father's boats, but no sign of him. The narrator also finds some childlike drawings and decides that her father went insane living alone. The four had planned to leave the next day, but David, the dominant member of the group, urges them to stay for a week. He enjoys this primitive life, he says, away from the city where he and Joe teach in an adult-education school. David and Anna have been married for nine years, but their relationship is filled with tension and abuse. Joe and the narrator live together, but Joe is silent, and the narrator is not sure she loves him, although Joe would like them to marry.

Soon, the narrator becomes increasingly unmoored. She feels trapped on the small island and senses her father watching her and her companions. Looking for a note or a will, she realizes the unintelligible pictures are her father's copies of rock paintings by primitive peoples who once lived on the lake, and she finds a letter from an archaeologist verifying this. She now knows that her father is sane, although she feels as if she is somehow slipping into madness herself. The four go on an overnight camping trip by canoe, so that the narrator can secretly verify the location of the pictographs. They find a dead heron, apparently killed and hung up by fishermen from the United States who fly to the lake to fish, but the narrator cannot locate the rock paintings. They return to the cabin, and the sexual tensions among the four friends increase.

The narrator goes off on her own to find a pictograph, and in diving beneath the surface of the water (the level of the lake has been raised some years ago) she sees a blurred body that reminds her both of her brother (who nearly drowned in the lake as a child) and of a baby in a bottle. The vision triggers her memory: She had not married, nor had she abandoned a husband and child; she had had an abortion during an affair with a married man, and that death has haunted her.

The pictographs, she now realizes, indicate spiritual powers the native peoples here possessed. Needing to make some kind of sacrifice to these gods for the abortion, she leaves her sweatshirt on a rock ledge. Back on the island, Paul and other men arrive by boat to say that fishermen have found her father's body; he had apparently fallen off a cliff and drowned with a heavy camera around his neck. The narrator brushes aside the information in a frantic search of the cabin for some talisman of her mother. She finds a drawing of a pregnant woman that she made as a child, which her mother had saved and which is like one of the pictographs, and feels the first beginnings of her own rebirth, her own power.

The narrator is on her final emotional descent. She makes love with Joe and feels a lost child surfacing within her; she is certain she is pregnant. She destroys the film that David and Joe had been sporadically making of this trip, a film they call Random Samples. She then hides when Evans arrives to take his friends back to the village and to their car. The three leave without her, and the narrator must break a window to get back into the cabin. She cries for the first time, burns her childhood scrapbooks and a wedding ring she wears, then smashes and slashes everything else in the cabin. She swims naked in the lake and feels clean, has a vision of her mother and then of her father, and hides when the others return to look for her. She reaches an emotional bottom when she feels she has become an animal. Joe comes back to the island and cabin once more to look for her, but he cannot find her.

Critical Evaluation:

Margaret Atwood's second published novel, *Surfacing* was immediately popular with readers, and it established the author as a major North American writer. The often-read and often-studied novel has become a touchstone for literary criticism, particularly feminist, archetypal, and psychological criticism. The novel has a number of layers: On one level it is a detective novel, on another a gothic ghost story reminiscent of both William Shakespeare's *Hamlet, Prince of Denmark* (pr. c. 1600-1601, pb. 1603) and Henry James's *The Turn of the Screw* (1898). On still another level, it is a wilderness-quest novel, and on a fourth level, it is a mythic story like that of the Greek goddess Persephone taken to live in the underworld. Through these many levels and through language—and particularly the novel's poetic use of metaphor and motif—Atwood weaves together many subtle issues and ideas.

The arc of the novel describes the narrator diving and surfacing—into herself or her psyche, into her own past, and into the Canadian wilderness. From the beginning of the story, readers sense something missing in the narrator and her friends: The narrator claims that Anna is her best friend yet has known her for only two months. David and Anna are married yet constantly try to tear each other down. The narrator lives with Joe, but she does not love him and cannot explain why they are together. It becomes clear that the novel is the narrator's spiritual quest to find her lost identity, and that her identity is tied up with her past—with her dead mother, with a father from whom she is estranged, and with her own sexual history, in particular the abortion she had some years before and has denied.

The narrator is clearly unreliable—or, better, she is like a peeling onion. She starts by saying she had been married and had abandoned her family, and that she had an abortion; she claims her brother had drowned, and then confesses that he had fled the family. As she sheds her fictions about her past she dives closer to some core self.

The novel is about the search not only for self but also for relationships; it also is about victimization in those relationships. The narrator and her brother had an antagonistic relationship growing up, their mother was never emotionally demonstrative, and their father moved the family from town to town, with no stable home except the isolated cabin on the lake. The narrator grew into adulthood filled with numbness instead of feelings and with the sense that her head had been cut off from her body—that she is two people. Friend David abuses his wife, Anna, and both men try to violate the narrator.

The novel also deals with relationships between humans and nature. David is always carping about "the Americans" destroying the wilderness, but it turns out that Canadian fishermen had killed the heron and hung it up.

On all these levels, the novel is about power—of self, relationships, and nature. The narrator needs to find the power of her own identity, and in diving into her past she finally reclaims herself. In her final descent into madness, she destroys the dominant patriarchal power structures in her life as well as her old ties to the world. The pictographs somehow give her spiritual power and help her give birth to a new self. Likewise, relationships must have a balance of power. In destroying the film in which Joe recorded one episode of David's humiliation of Anna, the narrator is trying to right that balance.

The novel ends with some resolution, but it is neither clear nor simple. In "diving" into her own past, and also into the madness she first attributed to her father, the narrator "surfaces" with a new identity; in the last chapter she seems to resolve "to refuse to be a victim." Upon seeing Joe she says that "To trust is to let go." Readers guess that she will return to civilization with Joe and begin a long healing process.

David Peck

Further Reading

Bouson, J. Brooks. *Brutal Choreographies: Oppositional Strategies and Narrative Design in the Novels of Margaret Atwood*. Amherst: University of Massachusetts Press, 1993. Bouson argues that Atwood upsets the standard ideological order by devaluing masculinity, culture, and the rational in the novel in favor of femininity, nature, and the irrational.

Howells, Carol Ann, ed. *The Cambridge Companion to Margaret Atwood*. New York: Cambridge University Press, 2006. A dozen essays on Atwood include valuable discussions of *Surfacing*. Helpful are the essays "Margaret Atwood and Environmentalism" and "Blindness and Survival in Margaret Atwood's Major Novels."

Lane, Richard J. *The Postcolonial Novel*. Malden, Mass.: Polity Press, 2006. Chapter 6, "Recording Narrative: Margaret Atwood's *Surfacing*," one of the best discussions of the novel, argues that *Surfacing* forces readers to explore "the relations between subjects and society, language and power, and the technologies of exploitation and representation."

McCombs, Judith, ed. *Critical Essays on Margaret Atwood*. Boston: G. K. Hall, 1988. Volume includes both a number of early reviews of *Surfacing* as well as several longer and later critical considerations of the novel. Especially helpful is "The Woman as Hero in Margaret Atwood's *Surfacing*."

Ozdemir, Erinc. "Power, Madness, and Gender Identity in Margaret Atwood's *Surfacing*: A Feminist Reading." *English Studies* 84 (February, 2003): 57-79. Ozdemir agrees with J. Brooks Bouson that the novel reverses traditional binary male/female oppositions but suggests that the novel also "paradoxically dramatizes a desire to destroy all dichotomies and dualistic thinking."

Rigney, Barbara Hill. *Margaret Atwood*. Totowa, N.J.: Barnes & Noble, 1987. Chapter 3, "'Border Country': *Surfacing* and *The Journals of Susanna Moodie*," examines two early Atwood novels and sees how the duality between reality and fantasy reflects political and cultural splits within Canada itself.

Stein, Karen F. *Margaret Atwood Revisited*. New York: Twayne, 1999. Volume contains a good summary of both the novel's issues and many of the best critical approaches to the work, seeing the novel as "a woman's quest" first and as "a quest for cultural identity" second.

The Surrounded

Author: D'Arcy McNickle (1904-1977)
First published: 1936
Type of work: Novel
Type of plot: Social realism
Time of plot: Early twentieth century
Locale: Flathead Indian Reservation, Montana

Principal characters:
ARCHILDE LEON, a young man of mixed race
LOUIS LEON, his brother
CATHARINE LEON, his Native American mother
MAX LEON, his Spanish father
MIKE and NARCISSE, his nephews
DAVE QUIGLEY, the sheriff

The Story:

Archilde Leon, who is making his living as a musician in Portland, returns to his family's ranch in Montana for a visit. His father, Max, lives in the big house with Archilde's sister, Agnes, and her two sons, Mike and Narcisse, while his mother, Catharine, the daughter of a Salish chief and one of the most pious women on the reservation, lives in a cabin on the property and maintains a fairly traditional Indian lifestyle. Upon his return, Archilde discovers that his brother, Louis, stole some horses and is hiding in the nearby mountains. Catharine celebrates Archilde's return by inviting several Indians, including the highly respected Modeste, an old Salish chief, over for feasting and storytelling. Max is worried about Archilde. Of all of his sons, Archilde is the one he hoped could take over the farm. Max is frustrated to discover that Archilde would rather go back to Portland and play the fiddle than stay in Montana and work the land. Max shares his concern with his confidant, the elderly priest Father Grepilloux, who offers to help Archilde with his music if he will stay and work.

To Max's surprise and delight, Archilde helps with the harvest that fall and spends time with the priests, practicing his music. These times remind Archilde of his childhood days at the Indian boarding school. He remembers one day in particular when the clouds formed a cross in the sky, and everyone knelt down before the "sign." Archilde, however, did not kneel; instead, he chose to identify with a bird he saw fly across the sky, unaware of any other "sign." During the fall harvest, Archilde's nephews, Mike and Narcisse, are rounded up and sent to the priests' school against their wishes.

Catharine decides that she wants to go deer hunting, and Archilde goes with her. While they are in the mountains, they encounter, first, Dave Quigley, the sheriff who is hunting for Louis, and then Louis himself. The three—Catharine, Archilde, and Louis—continue with their hunting until they are stopped by a game warden for hunting doe out of season.

Louis's nervous fidgeting alarms the warden, who shoots and kills Louis. When the warden gets off his horse to examine Louis's body, Catharine kills him with an ax. Archilde, stunned by these events, helps his mother bury the game warden's body and take Louis's body home, where they tell people they found him dead in the mountains.

Given the suspicious circumstances, Archilde is detained at the Government Indian Agency for some time. When he is finally released, he discovers that Max became ill at Father Grepilloux's funeral. Not long after Archilde and his father reconcile, Max dies. Archilde decides to stay on and tend his father's land, and a series of changes follows. Catharine moves back into the house, and Mike and Narcisse return from the Indian school. Mike, however, is changed; he suffers emotionally as a result of the abusive treatment he received at the school.

At the annual Fourth of July dance, Modeste arranges to have Mike assist him. Mike dances with the other Indians and seems healed by the experience. Catharine, in a meeting of tribal elders, announces that she wants to renounce her baptism. She dreamed that she died and went to the white people's heaven, where they told her to be happy, but she could not be happy because there were no Indians there; she was sent to the Indians' heaven, but the Indians would not let her enter because she was baptized. She is upset, not only by guilt at murdering the game warden but also by the loss of her son Louis, and she was been able to gain peace through confession to the priests. She asks the tribe to allow her to be whipped, according to the ancient custom, in order to pay for the wrongs she did. Archilde enjoys the afternoon Indian dancing, but in the evening he goes into town carousing with Elise, Modeste's raucous granddaughter. Eventually, the two are thrown out of the white people's dance hall.

Afraid to return to school and in an effort to keep alive what they learned at the dance, Narcisse and Mike go into the hills to live. The relationship between Archilde and Elise develops as they spend the remainder of the summer together; nonetheless, Archilde plans to leave after the fall harvest. His leaving is postponed again, however, when his mother has a stroke.

Archilde, unaware of Catharine's total return to traditional belief, sends for both a doctor and a priest. She refuses the priest and asks for Modeste instead. Before he leaves to bring Modeste, the priest informs Archilde that Catharine confessed to him the game warden's murder, and the priest prods Archilde to call in the sheriff. Archilde goes to the Indian commissioner and tells him the story, promising to return after his mother's death. As soon as Catharine dies, however, Elise, Archilde, Mike, and Narcisse disappear. Elise leads the others into the mountains, traveling a roundabout path to a place where she thinks they will be safe. One night, however, the sheriff, Dave Quigley, who was hunting them, walks into their camp. Elise very calmly offers him a cup of coffee and, going over to him, throws the hot coffee in his face and shoots him, killing him instantly. In the confusion, Mike and Narcisse escape. Elise and Archilde do not escape, however; the Indian commissioner and the tribal police officer are waiting in the bushes and step forward to arrest them.

Critical Evaluation:

D'Arcy McNickle was born on the Flathead Indian Reservation in Montana and was a member of the Confederated Salish and Kootenai tribes. As a child, he was sent to the federal Indian boarding school, where he faced punishment if he spoke an Indian language rather than English. He spent four years at the University of Montana and went on to study in Europe, both at Oxford and at the University of Grenoble. He was an anthropologist, historian, and scholar; an administrator in the Bureau of Indian Affairs, he founded the Newberry Library Center for the History of the American Indian in Chicago, which now bears his name. *The Surrounded* was his first work of fiction and is still the most readily available. It received some critical acclaim when it was first published and has become increasingly popular since it was reprinted in the 1970's.

The Surrounded has strong autobiographical overtones. The novel focuses on Archilde, through whom the readers see the identity conflicts that trouble the racially mixed hero. Archilde is caught between the white and the Indian cultures, neither of which is unambiguously good or bad, making his position even more difficult.

One of the ways that the novel emphasizes this cultural conflict is by describing many characters and events as opposing pairs. Catharine LaLoup Leon and Max Leon, for example, each present to Archilde some of the positive aspects of Indian and white culture, respectively. The Indian dancing on the Fourth of July, full of ancient meaning and beauty, is contrasted with the white people's meaningless dance in a dark, bare hall.

The novel expresses particular concern for the decline of Native American culture. McNickle describes in great detail the transformation of Mike and Narcisse as the older women prepare them for the dance, emphasizing the beauty of traditional culture. McNickle applies his expertise as an anthropologist to the detailed explanation of all the old dances, stressing each dance's particular meaning. This is contrasted with the scene at the Fourth of July dance, where white people come to laugh disrespectfully at the old men as they move slowly through the only dances that they are still allowed to do.

In addition, *The Surrounded* presents an interesting view of nature. Archilde goes into the wilderness to be alone, and nature is generally seen as an ally to the Indians, who can live in mountain caves and hunt for their food if they so choose. The scene in which Archilde sees the cloud-cross in the sky and ignores it because the bird ignores it stresses the preeminence of nature. Archilde remembers this experience and teaches this same lesson to Mike and Narcisse: If the birds are not frightened by signs and demons, they should not be either. Nature is seen as a better source of encouragement and truth than are the priests.

An interesting aspect of the novel is the presence of two especially strong female characters. Elise is reckless and determined to get what she wants. She can ride and hunt as well as any man. She takes the initiative, not only in her relationship with Archilde but also in their escape into the mountains. She, like Catharine, is not afraid to kill when Archilde is threatened. Catharine is held in high regard, not only among the Indians but also among the whites (which is one reason that Max married her in the first place). Even in her advanced age, she hunts for herself. Her death is described as a triumphant moment. She dies unafraid, surrounded by her Indian family and friends.

The plot structure of *The Surrounded* demonstrates a certain circularity and reflects the work's thematic concern for Archilde's identity. Archilde left the reservation, trying to put some distance between himself and his people. When he returns, it is only for a short and final visit. Yet, he continues to stay as he becomes increasingly entangled in events on the reservation. The apparent inaction—staying—is actually the action that helps him determine his identity as an Indian. He does not succeed in going to Portland to be a fiddler or even in running his father's farm. Archilde succeeds in finding his identity at those times when he feels most connected to his tribal heritage: at the dance and at his mother's death. His identity comes not from breaking away and succeeding in isolation but from living in his proper context, with his people and his land.

Kelly C. Walter Carney

Further Reading

Bevis, William. "Native American Novels: Homing In." In *Recovering the Word: Essays on Native American Literature*, edited by Brian Swann and Arnold Krupat. Berkeley: University of California Press, 1982. A very helpful introduction to Native American narrative structures. Discusses *The Surrounded* in the context of other Native American novels.

Cox, James H. *Muting White Noise: Native American and European American Novel Traditions*. Norman: University of Oklahoma Press, 2006. Examines novels by McNickle and other Native American writers to describe how these writers subverted and altered the traditions of the Euro-American novel and its justification of colonialism.

Kent, Alicia A. "Native Americans: Moving from Primitive to Postmodern, Mourning Dove and D'Arcy McNickle." In *African, Native, and Jewish American Literature and the Reshaping of Modernism*. New York: Palgrave Macmillan, 2007. Kent's examination of American ethnic literature during the modernist era includes this chapter focusing on works by McNickle and other Native American writers; she describes how these writers developed experimental techniques to present their own representations of American Indians.

McNickle, D'Arcy. *D'Arcy McNickle's "The Hungry Generations": The Evolution of a Novel*. Edited by Birgit Hans. Albuquerque: University of New Mexico Press, 2007. In the 1930's, McNickle wrote *The Hungry Generations*, a novel that was later revised and published as *The Surrounded*. This volume reprints both *The Hungry Generations* manuscript and *The Surrendered*, enabling readers to see the transition from manuscript to completed novel; it also features an introduction in which Hans discusses *The Hungry Generations*.

Parker, Dorothy R. *Singing an Indian Song: A Biography of D'Arcy McNickle*. Lincoln: University of Nebraska Press, 1992. A very thorough biography, including photographs as well as some literary discussion. Useful in light of the highly autobiographical nature of *The Surrounded*.

Purdy, John Lloyd. *Word Ways: The Novels of D'Arcy McNickle*. Tucson: University of Arizona Press, 1990. Takes an especially anthropological point of view and includes, in an appendix, several Salish oral stories, which are a useful supplement to *The Surrounded*.

_____, ed. *Legacy of D'Arcy McNickle: Writer, Historian, Activist*. Norman: University of Oklahoma Press, 1996. Contains eleven essays discussing the political, cultural, and literary commentary contained in three of McNickle's novels. The essays about *The Surrendered* include analyses of the elements of traditional oral narrative, the use of inherited stories, and the depiction of hunting and heroism in the novel.

Ruppert, James. *D'Arcy McNickle*. Boise, Idaho: Boise State University Press, 1962. Provides biographical information and discusses McNickle's novels as well as his ethnographic writings.

Wiget, Andrew. *Native American Literature*. Boston: Twayne, 1985. One of the most readily available general histories of Native American writing by a reputable scholar. Includes some discussion of McNickle.

Swallow Barn
Or, A Sojourn in the Old Dominion

Author: John Pendleton Kennedy (1795-1870)
First published: 1832
Type of work: Novel
Type of plot: Social realism
Time of plot: Early nineteenth century
Locale: Virginia

Principal characters:
MARK LITTLETON, the narrator
NED HAZARD, his cousin
FRANK MERIWETHER, Ned's brother-in-law
MR. ISAAC TRACY, a gentleman farmer
BEL TRACY, his daughter
HARVEY RIGGS, a Tracy kinsman

The Story:

After receiving many invitations from his cousin Ned Hazard, Mark Littleton at last feels that he can no longer put off a visit to Virginia. He leaves his mother and his sisters in New York and begins his journey south. At Swallow Barn, his cousin's home, Mark meets or renews acquaintance with a great many relatives and friends. Ned's sister married Frank Meriwether, who is now the head of the family. The estate was left to Ned. It was heavily encumbered, and Frank paid off the heaviest debts and put the plantation on a paying basis. The house is filled with Meriwether and Hazard relatives, all permanent guests. Some perform small functions as a pretense of paying their own way, but their tasks are no more than token duties kindly thought up for them so that they will feel useful.

Mark finds life in Virginia restful and pleasant, for there is an unhurried rhythm about Swallow Barn that appeals to him. The plantation is filled with slaves and freed blacks who are fiercely loyal to Frank, a good master. Indeed, everyone loves Frank for his thoughtfulness and generosity. Mark's special favorite, however, is his cousin Ned. The two young men are inseparable companions. Ned is a man of excellent spirits, always indulging in pranks and jokes. Swallow Barn will one day revert to him, but he is content to let Frank use it as his own, wanting only to have a good time without the need of responsibilities. Ned takes Mark on several excursions around the countryside and introduces him to local beauties of nature.

While Ned and Mark walk through the woods one day, they indulge in one of their favorite pastimes by singing their loudest, each trying to outdo the other. In one verse, Ned calls out the name of Bel Tracy. He is deeply chagrined when that lady, riding up unnoticed, answers him. Bel is the daughter of old Isaac Tracy, master of the neighboring estate, The Brakes. Ned's confusion at being discovered by Bel makes Mark think that his cousin feels more than friendship for her. She teases him gently about his boisterous use of her name, leaving Ned stammering in confusion. Bel is accompanied by her sister and by Harvey Riggs, a Tracy kinsman. Harvey joins in the teasing, but Mark sees at once that it is good-natured teasing and that Harvey feels great friendship for Ned.

The two parties go back to Swallow Barn, where Harvey delivers a letter from Mr. Tracy to Frank. The subject matter is of long standing, and it affords Frank some amusement. For many years, Mr. Tracy imagined himself in possession of one hundred acres of marshlands separating The Brakes from Swallow Barn. Every court in Virginia denied his claim, but the old gentleman is adamant. Frank would long

since have given him the land, for it is worthless, but he knows the old gentleman would be lost without the affair, which provides him with mental activity as he plots ways to get possession of the land. In his letter, Mr. Tracy suggests that he and Frank let their lawyers go over the matter again, the two disputants to abide by the legal decision. Frank plans to ask his lawyer to arrange matters so that Mr. Tracy will win the suit after what looks like a difficult legal maneuver.

Old Mr. Tracy is a detriment to Ned, even though Ned loves the old gentleman. He is a gentleman of the old school, dignified and sober; Ned, on the other hand, cannot repress his merry spirits. Bel, however, absorbed some of her father's dignity and is not usually very receptive to Ned's foolishness. The poor young man tries hard to change, but his disposition is almost as firm as Mr. Tracy's.

After Ned admits to Mark that he loves Bel, the two friends map out a campaign to win her heart to Ned's cause. Their plans are temporarily postponed, however, by the arrival of the lawyers who will decide the disputed land claim. The legal gentlemen afford the young men much entertainment, one being a dandy known throughout Virginia. He is pursued by two of the maiden relatives, each of whom pretends to be pursued by him. When the dandy learns of their intentions, he finishes his business and departs as quickly as possible. The settling of the suit gives everyone but old Mr. Tracy a lot of amusement. Ned is serious about the whole matter, so he loses more ground in his suit when he unwittingly makes light of the affair. It takes a great deal of clever legal terminology to fool the old man, but at last he is awarded the land and he is convinced that justice is done.

Sometimes Ned, Mark, and the others find entertainment in listening to the tales of goblins and ghosts told by old slaves on the plantation. The two families frequently give large dinner parties, when the whole community is invited to come and spend the day. Mark, thinking he will find it hard ever to return to New York and his own family, hopes to stay long enough to help Ned in his courtship of Bel. At one of the parties, Ned has a little wine and becomes more boisterous than ever, causing Bel to lose the esteem she gradually developed for him. He gains her goodwill once more by finding her pet falcon, which flew away, but later he loses her affection by engaging in a fistfight with a town bully. Harvey Riggs, joining Mark in attempts to help Ned with his suit, tells Bel that Ned fought the bully because the ruffian cast slurs on her father. Pity at last enters Bel's heart, and she treats her suitor with more favor.

Mark at last leaves Virginia and goes home to New York. Some months later, he learns that Ned was successful; Bel married him on New Year's Day. Ned writes, too, that it is as Frank feared. Old Mr. Tracy was sorry the land suit was settled and wishes to open it again. Without the pending suit, he feels like a man who lost an old and faithful friend.

Critical Evaluation:

Although John Pendleton Kennedy states definitely that *Swallow Barn* is not a novel, it is usually listed as such because of the continuous theme running through it. In reality the book is a series of sketches or dramatic episodes concerned with plantation life and manners in Virginia during the early eighteenth century; the sketches are held together by a continuity of characters and of events. *Swallow Barn*, the first work of popular fiction to be set in Virginia, was the forerunner of a large number of novels dealing with the historic background of that state.

Had Kennedy approached literature as a profession rather than as an avocation, he might have become one of America's most important nineteenth century writers; but he felt his first obligation was to his career, initially as a lawyer in Baltimore, where his second marriage allied him firmly to the business community, and, subsequently, in the face of growing political and sectional unrest, as a man of public affairs, serving terms in the Maryland House of Delegates, the U.S. House of Representatives, and as the secretary of the U.S. Navy. In between legal, business, and political commitments, he managed to write three very different novels: *Swallow Barn*; *Horse-Shoe Robinson* (1835), a historical novel about the Revolutionary War in South Carolina; and *Rob of the Bowl* (1838), a "Cavalier Romance" of Colonial Maryland. In addition, he produced numerous essays, satires, and miscellaneous writings.

For all his lightness of touch, Kennedy had very serious motives in the writing of all of his literary efforts, especially in *Swallow Barn*. Becoming progressively alarmed by the growing national tension and disunity, Kennedy hoped that this realistic, yet sympathetic portrait of southern society might foster harmony by stimulating understanding.

In its own time, *Swallow Barn* was highly praised for its realism, but Kennedy's vision of Virginia seems romanticized; indeed, the book's primary interest for a modern reader lies in the fact that it was the novel in which the myth of the old plantation South was first fictionalized. This atmosphere of serenity and pastoral elegance, described with affectionate, gentle, and humorous irony, is based on a fixed, secure society without major social or political problems. In *Swallow Barn*, the most serious issue revolves around how to give away one hundred worthless acres in a manner that will not hurt the recipient's feelings. This uncomplicated vision

of things was not, as Kennedy freely admitted, an unbiased one. The author carefully keeps the conflicts in the background—but he also makes sure they are there.

The primary conflict is the issue of slavery. The slaves at Swallow Barn and The Brakes conform to the plantation-myth stereotype; They are well-treated, contented, amusing, and affectionate. At the same time, Kennedy acknowledges the basic injustice of the system. Far from being a Southern apologist, he was a mild abolitionist, considering slavery to be both immoral and inefficient. He remained a Unionist throughout the Civil War. As a southerner living in the midst of the situation, however, he saw and felt the complexity of the issue, and probably expressed his own sentiments through Frank Meriwether, who stated that it is wrong to keep slaves, but that it would be equally wrong to "whelm them in greater evils than their present bondage." To his own personal sorrow, Kennedy lived to see the worst of his expectations realized.

Further Reading

Barnard, Philip. "Retold Legends: Washington Irving, James Kirke Paulding, and John Pendleton Kennedy." In *A Companion to American Fiction, 1780-1865*, edited by Shirley Samuels. Malden, Mass.: Blackwell, 2004. An overview of Kennedy's work, placed within the context of other American literature of the period. Includes a discussion of *Swallow Barn*.

Bohner, Charles H. "Virginia Revisited." In *John Pendleton Kennedy: Gentleman from Baltimore*. Baltimore: Johns Hopkins University Press, 1961. Discussion of Washington Irving's influence upon *Swallow Barn*'s collection of sketches, which accurately portray early nineteenth century domestic life in Virginia. The Southern plantation romance began with *Swallow Barn*, but Kennedy's partial detachment from Virginia society allowed objectivity and irony.

Hare, John L. *Will the Circle Be Unbroken? Family and Sectionalism in the Virginia Novels of Kennedy, Caruthers, and Tucker, 1830-1845*. New York: Routledge, 2002. Examines eight novels by Kennedy, William A. Caruthers, and Nathaniel Beverley Tucker, focusing on their connections to the social and political tensions of the mid-nineteenth century. Chapter 2, "Generational Progress in *Swallow Barn*," offers an analysis of this novel.

Jones, Paul Christian. "Resisting the Romance: Genre Struggle in John Pendleton Kennedy's *Swallow Barn*." In *Unwelcome Voices: Subversive Fiction in the Antebellum South*. Knoxville: University of Tennessee Press, 2005. Contradicts the stereotypical view that all antebellum southern literature is propaganda for slaveholders by focusing on Kennedy and four other writers who subverted southern tradition. Describes how *Swallow Barn* challenges romantic images of the South with its realistic depiction of the region.

Ridgely, Joseph Vincent. *John Pendleton Kennedy.* New York: Twayne, 1966. A chapter on *Swallow Barn* discusses its structure and style, including excerpts from nineteenth century reviews. Although true to Virginia life, *Swallow Barn* employs stock devices and literary sources. Kennedy's growing ambivalence toward the South precluded the possibility of a sequel.

Romine, Scott. "The Plantation Community: John Pendleton Kennedy's *Swallow Barn* and Thomas Nelson Page's *In Ole Virginia*." In *The Narrative Forms of Southern Community.* Baton Rouge: Louisiana State University Press, 1999. Demonstrates how *Swallow Barn* and several other literary works attempt to negotiate the social tensions in the antebellum south.

Tomlinson, David O. "John Pendleton Kennedy." In *Fifty Southern Writers Before 1900: A Bio-Bibliographical Sourcebook*, edited by Robert Bain and Joseph M. Flora. Westport, Conn.: Greenwood Press, 1987. Discusses Kennedy's major themes and surveys criticism of his work. Argues that Kennedy was a nationalist who feared disunion and combined his intended satire with affection for his characters and with dismay at some Virginia social customs.

The Swiss Family Robinson

Authors: Johann David Wyss (1743-1818) and Johann Rudolf Wyss (1782-1830)
First published: Der schweizerische Robinson: Oder, Der schiffbruchige schweizer-prediger und seine familie, 1812-1827 (English translation, 1814, 1818, 1820)
Type of work: Novel
Type of plot: Adventure
Time of plot: Late eighteenth century
Locale: An island near New Guinea

Principal characters:
MR. ROBINSON, a shipwrecked Swiss gentleman
MRS. ROBINSON, his wife
FRITZ,
ERNEST,
JACK, and
FRANCIS (FRANZ), their sons
EMILY MONTROSE, a shipwrecked English girl

The Story:

Of all the passengers and crew on board the ship, only the Robinson family is saved when the vessel breaks apart on a reef and the crew and other passengers jump into lifeboats without waiting for the little family to join them. As the ship tosses about, the father prays that God will spare them. There is plenty of food on board, and after they eat, the boys go to sleep, leaving the father and the mother to guard them.

In the morning their first concern is to get to the island they can see beyond the reef. With much effort, they construct a vessel out of tubs. After they fill the tubs with food and ammunition and all other articles of value they can safely carry, they row toward the island. Two dogs from the ship swim beside them, and the boys are glad they will have pets when they reach their new home.

Their first task on reaching the island is to erect a tent of sailcloth they brought from the ship. They gather moss and dry it so that they will have some protection from the ground when they sleep. They are able to find a lobster and to shoot some game, thus to add fresh food to their supplies. Since they have no utensils for eating, they use shells for spoons, all dipping out of the iron kettle that they brought from the ship. They released some geese and pigeons while they were still on the ship and brought two hens and two cocks with them. The father knows that they must prepare for a long time on the island, and his thoughts are as much on provisions for the future as for their immediate wants.

The father and Fritz, the oldest son, spend the next day exploring the island. They find gourds from which they can make dishes and spoons, and many edible fruits and roots. Coconuts, growing in abundance, provide a treat for the mother and the younger boys. Fritz captures a small monkey, which he takes back for a pet. The younger boys are enchanted with the mischievous little animal.

The Robinsons spend the next few days securing themselves against hunger and danger from wild animals. The father and Fritz make several trips to the ship in their efforts to bring ashore everything that they can possibly use. The domesticated animals on the ship are towed back to the island. There is also a great store of firearms and ammunition, hammocks for sleeping, carpenter's tools, lumber, cooking utensils, silverware, and dishes.

While the father and Fritz are salvaging these supplies, the mother and the younger boys are working on the shore, sowing seeds, examining the contents of the kegs that floated to shore, and in every way possible making the tent a more livable home. The mother and boys also explore the island to find a spot for a more permanent home. When the father and Fritz can join them, the whole family helps to construct a tree house that will give them protection from wild animals that they fear might dwell on the island.

Through the following weeks, each day brings a new adventure of some kind. There are encounters with wild birds and terrifying animals. Ernest, the second son, studied nature with great interest before their ill-fated voyage, and he identifies many of the animals and birds. They find some food that they consider luxuries—sugarcane, honey, potatoes, and spices. They fence in a secluded area for their cattle so that they might have a constant supply of milk and fresh meat. Several new dwellings are constructed to provide homes on all sides of the island. The father finds a tree that contains long threads, and after he constructs a loom, the mother is able to weave cloth for new clothing. Jack and Francis, the younger boys, contribute to the welfare of the family by helping their mother to care for the animals and thresh the grain grown from seeds brought from the ship.

Many times the family members find their labor destroyed by uncontrollable forces. Goats eat the bark off young fruit trees they planted; monkeys rob their food stores frequently; and jackals and serpents kill some of their pets. Nevertheless, they are not too discouraged, for they know that they were very fortunate to land on an island that provides food and shelter in such abundance.

About a year later they discover a cave, which becomes a home and a storage place for their supplies. The cave protects them from the rains, and their supplies are safe from intruders. They spend many enjoyable evenings reading books they salvage from the ship. The father and mother find a way to make candles from the sap of a native tree. Altogether, their lives are agreeable and happy, and each morning and evening they thank God for his goodness.

Ten years pass. The boys become young men, and Fritz often sails long distances in the canoe he constructs. One day he captures a wounded albatross and finds attached to it a note, written in English, asking someone to help an English girl who is in a cave near a volcano. The father and Fritz decide that Fritz must try to find her without telling the rest of the family of the note or the proposed search. Fritz, successful in his search, finds a girl, Emily Montrose, who was also shipwrecked as she was sailing from India to her home in England. The members of the Robinson family accept Emily as a daughter and a sister who is able to help the mother in her duties and give the boys much joy with her stories of life in India. Her own mother is dead. Emily lived in India with her father, an army officer, who sailed back to England on a different ship. She knows he is worried about her, but there is no way for her to communicate with him.

One morning, a few months later, the castaways are astonished to hear the sound of three cannon shots. Not knowing whether the sound comes from a friendly ship or from a pirate vessel, they load their small boat with firearms and sail out to investigate. There they find an English ship that was driven off course by a storm. It is impossible for this ship to take Emily back to England, but the captain promises to notify her father and to send a ship back for her. A captain, his wife, and two children, who are on board, are so enchanted with the island that they ask to be allowed to stay. It seems as if a little colony will grow there.

Six months later the ship sent by Emily's father arrives. Fritz and Francis have a great longing to see their homeland again, and since they are now mature young men, their mother and father allow them to return with Emily. Before he leaves, Fritz tells his father that he loves Emily and intends to ask her father's permission to propose marriage to her. The Robinsons, who love Emily dearly, give their blessing to their son.

The father prepares a manuscript relating their adventures and gives it to Fritz before the boy sails, in the hope that their story might be of interest to the rest of the world. The father and mother want to spend their remaining days on the island. Now that their island is known, commerce will begin and a colony could grow there. The father prays that the little colony will increase in prosperity and piety and will continue to deserve and receive the blessings of the merciful God who cared for them all so tenderly in the past.

Critical Evaluation:

Johann David Wyss's *The Swiss Family Robinson*, which was completed and edited by Wyss's son Johann Rudolf Wyss, has remained extraordinarily popular. In its various translations, editions, adaptations, and shortened versions, it has continued to delight a child audience, despite its never being highly regarded as a work of literature. This delight is carried principally by the work's adventure, beginning with the exciting shipwreck and removal to the island and continuing through the exploration of the island, the establishment of the two children-pleasing homes in a tree house and in a cave, and the battles with boa constrictors and lions, among other beasts.

The delight is perpetuated as various characters go out to explore and generally come upon some astonishing and unexpected adventure. In addition, the ingenuity of the family, both in the face of these adventures and in the desperate situation in which they find themselves, forms much of the satisfaction of the novel. Do wild animals threaten? Build a tree house. Is the vine ladder too unsteady? Build a staircase within the trunk of the hollowed tree. Is the tree house unsuitable for the rainy season? Discover a vast cave with the added bonus of an unlimited source of rock salt. The pattern of a problem followed by an ingenious solution forms much of the novel.

Something else is suggested by the many versions of *The Swiss Family Robinson*: There is a discomfort with the text. This seems to have been felt by its authors, for an early French translator was allowed to change the ending and to add some of her own episodes. Since its first publication, the story has been so augmented and altered that it is difficult to speak of a definitive text.

The problem is that much of what occurs on the island is simply ludicrous. The island seems to be blessed with animals from all over the globe, ripped out of their natural habitats and placed on the island for the benefit of the Robinson family. Tigers, found only in Asia, romp with kangaroos, found only in Australia. Elephants sport with walruses, while on the shores flamingoes trot beside penguins. Though the father claims he is no naturalist, he can identify and name the properties—as well as give the Latin name—of every plant and animal they come across, and there are plenty. On the novel's island animals have young although they seem to have no mate; dogs can change instincts in the flick of an eye, one moment tearing a monkey apart, the next allowing its young to ride its back; and albatrosses can act as carrier pigeons. These problems and the coincidence that concludes the book make the story difficult to accept.

There are other difficulties. Much of the book is heavily didactic and pious; it seems that the father cannot speak without reference to a moral aphorism. This is not so true with the boys. While it is perfectly natural for real piety to play a role

in the life of a religious family, the pious lines that flow from the father quickly become formulaic. From a literary standpoint there are more difficulties. The dialogue is stilted and unnatural, so that even an attack by a tiger is told in cold and dispassionate prose. The characters show little change or growth, despite ten years on the island. They never change in their relationships to one another, nor do the boys ever seem to mature. The narrative pace is halting and jerky; it is usually the case that no one scene or adventure develops beyond itself. One wishes for a single narrative thread, fully developed.

It may be argued, however, that the episodic nature of the book and its halting pace are intended to simulate a journal form. In fact, the father sends the manuscript back to Europe with Fritz to be published as a journal of their time on the island. The didactic and pious passages, it might be further argued, are to underscore the principal point of the book: that people are to lead industrious and productive lives, living in harmony with one another (particularly families) and with God. The Robinsons set about establishing a peaceable kingdom. In short, New Switzerland becomes a kind of Eden, where all needs are provided for, where all live in harmony, and where there is enough difficulty and danger to make life interesting. Certainly this last element dominates thematically.

A modern reader may be troubled in more ways than one by the book's manner of presenting its theme. One may ask if the island, so rich in natural resources, could be so conveniently free of a native population. A modern reader may also be put off by the slaughter of animals—a walrus (visiting, perhaps, from colder climes) is killed so that its head can adorn a canoe, and a platypus is killed because it is such an oddity. There is a strong implication that the industrious and devout family is deservedly rewarded with not only provisions but also security and harmony. This security and harmony lead the parents to decide to stay on the island for the rest of their lives. This is not to say that they despise Europe—Fritz and Franz go back to make their way, their trunks filled with pearls and spices to start them out in the world of commerce—but they certainly see the island as a kind of utopia, and they see no need to go searching for what they have already found.

Still, the story of a family struggling to survive on a deserted island continues to capture the imaginations of readers. There continues to be a place in children's literature for a story about a loving and pious family working together in harmony in order to bring about a good life for themselves.

"Critical Evaluation" by Gary D. Schmidt

Further Reading

Bashore, J. Robert. "Daniel Defoe." In *Writers for Children: Critical Studies of Major Authors Since the Seventeenth Century*, edited by Jane Bingham. New York: Charles Scribner's Sons, 1987. A comparison of *The Swiss Family Robinson* to *Robinson Crusoe* (1719), examining the enduring appeal of each to a young readership.

Fisher, Margery. *Who's Who in Children's Books*. New York: Holt, Rinehart and Winston, 1975. In a short entry, Fisher argues that rather than being simply a series of loosely connected episodes, the novel is a depiction of a natural and accustomed piety within a family context.

Glaenzer, Richard Butler. "The Swiss Family Robinson." *Bookman* 34 (1911): 139-142. Focusing on the causes for the enduring appeal of this story, Glaenzer argues that Wyss made the novel enjoyable despite a serious purpose: to instruct children. Wyss did this by emphasizing a good-natured rivalry among four young boys, thus dealing with the serious business of life in an engaging way.

Loxley, Diana. *Problematic Shores: The Literature of Islands*. London: Macmillan, 1992. A study of the nineteenth century successors to Daniel Defoe, looking at the connections between children's books and imperialism, as well as the depiction of childhood innocence by means of empty islands.

Seeyle, John. Introduction to *The Swiss Family Robinson*, by Johann David Wyss. New York: Penguin Books, 2007. Seeyle's introduction provides useful context and background for the novel, including comparisons of Wyss's book to *Robinson Crusoe* and other Robinsonades, information about Wyss's literary influences, and details about the writing and subsequent publication and translation of the work.

Sybil

Author: Benjamin Disraeli (1804-1881)
First published: 1845
Type of work: Novel
Type of plot: Political realism
Time of plot: 1837-1843
Locale: London and the north of England

Principal characters:
SYBIL GERARD, a young woman
CHARLES EGREMONT, younger brother to Lord Marney, a member of Parliament
LORD MARNEY, a wealthy landowner
LADY DELORAINE, his mother
WALTER GERARD, Sybil's father, a Chartist leader
STEPHEN MORLEY, a Chartist and an editor
BAPTIST HATTON, an antiquarian
BISHOP HATTON, his brother, a locksmith
DEVILSDUST, one of the people of Mowbray
MICK RADLEY "DANDY MICK," his friend
JOHN TROTMAN "CHAFFING JACK," an innkeeper
LORD DE MOWBRAY, supposed lord of Mowbray Castle
MR. ST. LYS, vicar of Mowbray
MR. TRAFFORD, a manufacturer, Gerard's employer
URSULA TRAFFORD, Lady Superior of Mowbray Convent, sister to Trafford and mentor to Sybil

The Story:

In the spring of 1837, the Reform Bill is in force for five years and the king, William IV, is dying. A new election is called as the youthful Queen Victoria ascends the throne. One of the new Conservative Party members of Parliament is Charles Egremont, younger brother of Lord Marney. Their mother, Lady Marney, set up her son's election and helped to defray some expenses. Egremont asks his brother to defray the rest.

While visiting the ruins of Marney Abbey, Egremont meets two unusual men, Walter Gerard and Stephen Morley, and hears Gerard's daughter, Sybil, sing. Although only brief, the meeting makes a deep impression on him. Egremont, with other family members, then goes to visit Mowbray Castle, the home of the de Mowbrays. Lord Marney wants his brother to marry Lady Joan, heir to the rich estates, thus solving Egremont's financial problems. Egremont hardly notices her.

The castle stands just outside Mowbray, a large manufacturing town in the north of England. The wretched life and amusements of the working people contrast with the high life of the castle. The only link is Mr. St. Lys, the reforming vicar of Mowbray, himself the younger son of aristocracy.

Egremont becomes interested in the political views of Gerard and Morley, who live just outside Mowbray, and he wishes to see the real living conditions of the people. Visiting Warner, an impoverished handloom weaver, with St. Lys, Egremont meets Sybil, who regularly engages in acts of charity out of Mowbray Convent.

On the Marneys' return home, the two brothers have a terrible argument about expenses and Marney's wife. Egremont walks out and, Parliament being in recess, rents a cottage near Gerard and takes on the alias of Mr. Franklin, so that he can more easily hold lengthy discussions with Gerard, Morley, and Sybil. He also visits a nearby model factory run by the Traffords who, like the Gerards, are Roman Catholics. Morley's and Gerard's views are widely different even though both are active Chartists (a working-class movement for political reform). They are both also interested in pursuing certain claims to the Mowbray estates and are seeking a Mr. Baptist Hatton, an antiquarian, whose previous research unearthed some evidence that the Gerards are the rightful owners. Morley discovers Hatton's brother in a lawless manufacturing area called Wodgate.

Egremont is then called back to London by his mother's remarriage to Lord Deloraine. Parliament sits but remains deadlocked. The Chartists march to London to present their petition to Parliament and to hold an alternative assembly. Gerard is elected a delegate with Morley and brings Sybil with him to the capital. Various chance meetings take place: Morley discovers Hatton, now grown wealthy, but who is willing to take up Gerard's claims again. Morley and Gerard call on Egremont and recognize him as Franklin. Egremont also meets Sybil on a separate encounter. The recognition of Egremont puts a distance between him and his former friends, as does his disagreement with their political views. Even so, Egremont declares his love for Sybil. She rejects him, declaring that the difference in class is unbridgeable and citing her desire to be a nun.

The Charter is finally presented to Parliament and is met with little interest or debate. Some disillusioned Chartists riot in Birmingham, and the government determines to clamp down. Egremont learns of the dangers to the Chartist leaders still left in London and warns Sybil, and she warns her father, but too late. Both are arrested. Egremont obtains her release, but her father is eventually sent to prison at York for eighteen months. Morley declares his love for Sybil. Even Hatton sees Sybil as a future wife, especially if the Gerard claims are substantiated. The vital evidence for this is locked up in Mowbray Castle, it is discovered.

An economic depression follows. Factories close or put their workers on short-time. In Lancashire there are widespread strikes. In Mowbray, two of the activists, Devilsdust and Dandy Mick, join trade unions and help plan a national strike. In nearby Wodgate, "Bishop" Hatton is converted to Chartism and immediately begins a crusade, marching on Mowbray with his workers. The Mowbray people join them, closing down the factories, including Trafford's, though only after a confrontation in which Gerard, now released from prison, acts as mediator.

Hatton and Morley are at the scene, and, through Devilsdust and Dandy Mick, direct the mob's attention to Mowbray Castle. While it is being attacked, Lord Marney's yeomanry, setting out to quell the mob, meet Gerard leading a quiet demonstration. Marney acts in a high-handed manner; Gerard is killed and, in the ensuing melee, Marney, also. Another group of yeomanry, led by Egremont, retakes Mowbray Castle, though not before the vital documents are seized. Although Morley is also killed, Mick takes the documents to the nearby convent to be given to Sybil. She, meanwhile, having previously gone to the castle, helps save its inhabitants before being trapped by the rioters. Egremont dashes in to save her.

In a final scene, Egremont, now Lord Marney, marries Sybil, whose claim to the Mowbray estates is proved. Devilsdust and Dandy Mick are set up in business and are about to prosper.

Critical Evaluation:

Sybil: Or, The Two Nations has been described as "one of few examples of the truly political novel" and is certainly one of the few novels to be written by a future British prime minister. It was written at a crucial time both for political debate over the social condition of a newly industrialized Britain and for the development of the English novel. Benjamin Disraeli believed that fiction could be used as a means of transmitting political ideas; in doing this, he extended the limits of the novel form, creating a new genre of social comment and finding new ways to document social conditions.

At the time of writing, Disraeli represented a reform element within the British Conservative Party, dubbed "young

England" (a reference perhaps to the novel's closing remark: "It is the past alone that can explain the present, and it is youth that alone can mould the remedial future"). In the novel, Disraeli depicts a Parliament marked by interparty bickering, pettiness, personal ambition, and lack of leadership. Its most serious failure is the failure to respond to Chartism, a popular movement to reform the democratic system of the country. With the accession of a young queen, Disraeli hoped that new parliamentarians would arise and put forward reforming legislation to avert the most serious consequences of a disunited country and an oppressive economic system.

Sybil: Or, The Two Nations is, in many ways, a deeply reactionary novel. It constantly returns to the Middle Ages for its social models, creating a medieval sense of race and of class (monarchy, aristocracy of various degrees, the Church, and the people). Its plea to a revitalized aristocracy to take up its leadership role reflects a doctrine of social paternalism. This doctrine is also to be found in other contemporary writers, such as Thomas Carlyle (*Chartism*, 1839) and Arthur Helps (*Claims of Labour*, 1844), and even, to an extent, in Charles Dickens. Mr. St. Lys and Mr. Trafford are clear examples of such paternalism. Egremont's political awakening stands in contrast to the political views of his brother, who represents the decayed old order. His death and the burning of Mowbray Castle symbolize the end of the old order.

Disraeli does reveal serious ambivalence. His depiction of the aristocracy, one of the best literary features of the book, and a skill derived from his earlier "silver fork" novels, suggests strongly the unreformable nature of the aristocracy, whose position rests largely, it would seem, on past social pretension, fraud, and intrigue. Baptist Hatton's efforts to restore the Gerards is seen as typically amoral. A similar ambivalence marks Disraeli's attitude to Roman Catholicism. Coming from a Jewish background, Hatton rejects Catholic claims to authority, since they fail to recognize the priority of the Old Testament in the fabric of Christianity as "fulfilled Judaism." On the other hand, his reactionary medievalism sees the medieval Catholic Church with its care for the people as ideal Christian practice, contrasted with the present Church of England, which becomes merely a part of the political system and moribund structures. Sybil's Catholicism is never criticized, though her desire to become a nun is.

The novel, dealing largely with political ideas, also depicts current events (for example, the presentation of the Charter to Parliament), and the social conditions prevalent in both town and country in the north. Degrading living and working conditions make for a degraded populace, whether such populace is controlled by capitalists (as in Mowbray) or by free association (as in Wodgate). Disraeli considers Morley's radicalism, and the trade unions, dangerous, because they rely on leadership from the people, a leadership the people are incapable of giving, and because the radicalism is secular and denies the past. In many ways, Disraeli's opinions are prophetic.

As a novelist, Disraeli makes heavy demands on his reader. Not only is his style high-flown, balanced, and antithetical, but also is his plot often melodramatic, episodic, and loose, full of subplots that go nowhere. The reader also has to support long passages of authorial comment on British history and institutions, most of which are out of reach for modern readers. Even as a historical documentary, there are gaping omissions; for example, there is no discussion on the Factory Acts or the Labor laws. The Reform Bill is treated superficially; liberal and radical views are given short shrift. Despite its shortcomings, the novel really was, in itself, a historical event, and the author's political commitment to a united society provides a dynamic that engages the reader's intellectual attention.

David Barratt

Further Reading

Braun, Thom. *Disraeli the Novelist*. Winchester, Mass.: Allen & Unwin, 1981. Concentrates on Disraeli's career as a novelist rather than as a politician. Braun seeks to reconstruct his life through his novels and to show his development as a novelist. Chapter 5 particularly relates *Sybil: Or, The Two Nations* to the political events in Disraeli's life.

Cazamian, Louis. *The Social Novel in England, 1830-1850*. Translated by Martin Fido. Boston: Routledge & Kegan Paul, 1973. Cazamian's book is the classic study of the subject. *Sybil: Or, The Two Nations* is fully treated, along with Disraeli's other two social novels. Includes bibliography and index.

Flavin, Michael. *Benjamin Disraeli: The Novel as Political Discourse*. Portland, Oreg.: Sussex Academic Press, 2005. Views Disraeli's novels as a "breeding ground" for his Conservative political ideas and activities.

Gallagher, Catherine. *The Industrial Reformation of English Fiction: Social Discourse and Narrative Form, 1832-1867*. Chicago: University of Chicago Press, 1985. Surveys the whole field of the industrial novel, with an excellent introductory discussion of "The Condition of England" question. Chapter 8 deals extensively with *Sybil: Or, The Two Nations*. Notes, bibliography, index.

Ridley, Jane. *The Young Disraeli, 1804-1846*. London: Sinclair-Stevenson, 1995. Updated biography, and one of the most objective. Draws extensively from letters and papers and demonstrates clearly that, although Egremont may represent Disraeli's political views, he does not represent Disraeli's actual life.

Schwarz, Daniel R. *Disraeli's Fiction*. New York: Barnes & Noble, 1979. Seeks to establish Disraeli's skill and importance as a novelist, describing how writing fiction actually helped form Disraeli's character.

_____. "Disraeli's Romanticism: Self-Fashioning in the Novels." In *The Self-Fashioning of Disraeli, 1818-1851*, edited by Charles Richmond and Paul Smith. New York: Cambridge University Press, 1998. Schwarz's analyses of Disraeli's novels is included in this collection of essays that examine the life and career of the young Disraeli.

Ulrich, John McAllister. "The 'Recovery' of the Past: History and (Self-) Representation in Benjamin Disraeli's *Sybil: Or, The Two Nations*." In *Signs of Their Times: History, Labor, and the Body in Cobbett, Carlyle, and Disraeli*. Athens: Ohio University Press, 2002. An examination of how Disraeli, Thomas Carlyle, and William Cobbett reacted to the economic and social crises in Victorian England by writing books in which history, labor, and the body were not signs of their times but of social stability and meaning.

T

Tala

Author: Gabriela Mistral (1889-1957)
First published: 1938
Type of work: Poetry

For fear of losing her job as a schoolteacher in provincial Chile, Lucila Godoy Alcayaga used the pseudonym Gabriela Mistral. Her writings include poetry, stories, criticism—political and literary—and numerous prose pieces, many of them political enough to have attracted unwelcome fame. Never having children of her own, she made an international reputation early in her career with elegant poems about children and motherhood. As a teacher, she devoted a significant portion of her life to young students, who included, informally, a teenager named Ricardo Reyes, who would receive, as she did, a Nobel Prize in Literature. His pen name was Pablo Neruda.

Tala was the third of four collections that Mistral published in her lifetime. *Tala* means "felling," as in the felling of trees; the title has also been translated as *Devastation*. The modest volume's proceeds went to the benefit of orphans displaced by the Spanish Civil War. This gesture was typical of Mistral, considering how strongly her poetry speaks to the nurturing of children. At the same time, her work was by turns emotional, visionary, and possessed by a sensuality that in part may account for her desire to separate her life as a poet from her life as a teacher.

By the time *Tala* was published, Mistral had seen much more of the world as a diplomat and an education consultant than she had when her first book appeared in 1922. Mistral's deep interests in children and the mystic qualities of nature remain a key element of her third collection, but the intensity of anguish that distinguished much of her previous work gives way, in *Tala*, to a more controlled sense of observation. This is not to suggest any lack of maturity in her early work, only that with *Tala*, the reader encounters an older, widely traveled poet who has come to more comfortable terms with the tragic events of life. There is an undeniable emotional drive to these poems, but the reader will find a noticeably heightened sense of the poet's journalistic eye. The collec-

tion conveys a sense of the somewhat ethereal atmosphere of life on the South American landscape. In "Riches," Mistral writes, "I have an abiding bliss/ and a lost fortune,/ one like a rose,/ the other like a thorn."

There is a touch of autobiography here, pointing to the devastating loss she suffered as a young woman in love with a man who committed suicide. Mistral's poems often deal with her grief over Romelio Ureta's death. Here, the poet's grief is merely implied, offered more as the memory of an emotion than the emotion itself. The poet has attained the necessary distance from the tragedy to apply her art to it in new ways. Earlier poems on the subject deal with recent wounds, the poet now looks at old scars. All likelihood seems to have been that Ureta and Mistral would have married and had the family the poet longed for all of her life. Mistral never did marry, creating for herself a surrogate family in every community she joined as a teacher or diplomat.

"Riches" is a brief, imagistic lyric that considers the inadvertent exchange, as it were, of the conventional family she had anticipated for the unconventional one she found. There is surely pain in this poem, but it is pain in retrospect: "I am rich with purple and with melancholy./ Oh, how beloved is the rose,/ and what a lover, the thorn!" The direct statement of her grief in Mistral's earlier work is here given over to sensory image.

"Grace" is an example of the type of work for which Mistral earned "visionary" as one of the many honorable adjectives commonly ascribed to her work. Once again, the poem's primary vehicle of expression is the image. The speaker's acute awareness of the senses seeks the reader's appeal on an affective level rather than an intellectual one. Sensory experience is made palpable; the poet shares a deceptively simple epiphany, without explanation or analysis. The reader is led to feel the poet's experience through images that appear almost surreal: "A dappled bird,/ a bird like jasper/

went rainbow/ wild/ through the carriage/ of the air./ This same early/ morning,/ the river passed by/ like a lance./ The pure and clear/ aurora remained/ dazzling/ with the wind's perfume."

The notion of grace is taken as a natural choreography, perfect and perfectly random, following the graceful, seemingly visible turns of the passing air. The wind is akin to the river, currents of natural power and beauty to which the poet is bound yet distanced from. The speaker surveys the scene in solitude, while the rest of the village sleeps. In her small revelation, the poet is similarly distant from her community. In the moment of the poem, she is part member, part outsider of both environment and society.

Mistral undertakes a surprising description of air channeled into form as wind, which then collapses back into formlessness as it reaches the open sky. The speaker "remained trembling/ on uncertain ground,/ my good news/ swept away!"

"The Air Flower" bears a very similar quality, although its discursive and confessional content is more extensive than that of "Grace." There is a dialogue between the poem's speaker and the subject of the title, in which the air flower makes a series of demands: "Climb the mountain./ I never leave the meadow./ Cut the snow white flowers,/ the tough and tender ones;/ make them mine." After her climb and search, the speaker returns with her quarry, to which the benignly imperious airflower seems to be blind. She calls for "only red flowers" next, and the speaker complies, searching through a landscape that is lush but steep, and makes for arduous searching. After the yellow flowers come the colorless, or "colored like sleep and dreams." This is the most difficult request of all. The colorless flowers cannot be found in the usual places, and the resourceful speaker must harvest them out of the air.

When this final request has been fulfilled, the poet returns with her blossoms of air and addresses the air flower figure as Queen. The Queen is now no longer bound to the meadow, moving past her servant as a sleepwalker. She subsequently follows the Queen through life, continually plucking blossoms from the air in her wake. Mistral herself characterized this poem as "my adventure with poetry." It is not surprising to find her view of her own pursuit of poetry to be an adventure in sensory experience. For Mistral, or at least for her poetry, all experience is tied to an undercurrent of natural force. "The Air Flower" raises this undercurrent to the surface, and as in "Grace," the unseen is given shape.

Consistent with Mistral's visual sense of the invisible is a strong sense of location, most often created without relying on the explicit naming of places or landmarks. Each of these poems exhibits this quality, as do "The Escape," "Confession," and "Things." "Things" considers what the poet left behind when she began her nomadic career some fourteen years before *Tala* was published. She considers "the things I never had,/ along with others/ that I no longer possess." It is difficult not to see this as a reference to the children Mistral never had, but it is just as readily possible to again feel even the most subliminal sense of the poet's distance, both emotional and geographical, from the land she loved and left behind.

Mistral's list of things includes the pastures and orchards of her childhood, "happy footsteps/ now foreign," a poem she was taught at the age of seven, and "the perfume of almond trees." She recalls an encompassing scene of early memories claiming dreams as her vehicle. Her awakening is treated as a sort of death to it all, and the poem's closure comes as something of an imagistic last will and testament, in which the poet bequeaths her past to itself.

As much as Mistral loved her homeland, and as important an element as it becomes throughout her work, *Tala* includes departure from her homeland. While she may have prized Chile especially as the cradle of her psyche and imagination, she was a committed lover and keen observer of land, sea, and nature wherever she went. "Caribbean Sea" is a deeply felt song of praise for the beauty of Puerto Rico, but before the poem's conclusion, she calls the island by the name Cordelia, after King Lear's daughter. From there, the poem becomes a longing plea to this northernmost daughter of the Caribbean to save itself: "Before my feet/ and vision fail me,/ before my skin becomes a fable,/ before my knees/ fly in the wind." The poem is footnoted with its date of composition: Philippine Independence Day.

As a resident of the United States during the Great Depression years, Mistral would have witnessed the political and economic struggles of the poor, for whom her work as a poet expresses a deep concern and sense of kinship. "Caribbean Sea" speaks directly to Puerto Rico. This rhetorical technique, called apostrophe, is a brief departure from her more common practice of describing an unnamed universal location.

It was in 1945 that the Swedish Academy awarded Mistral the Nobel Prize in Literature. She was the first South American writer to achieve this recognition. *Lagar*, the fourth and final collection of poems to appear while she was still living, would not be published for nine more years. Thus, it was on the strength of three collections and her numerous uncollected prose works that she earned this honor. The committee's citation points out the importance the slim, lyrical volume *Tala* had in affirming the value of her relatively small but eminently notable body of work.

The general consensus of critics is that Mistral was the poet of mothers and children, a poet of average people, and the first of her generation and country to speak in the idiom of those who interested her most. Many countries and many generations have had their share of poets who wrote in plain language, but precious few have done so with such remarkable craft and elegance.

Jon Lavieri

Further Reading

Agosín, Marjorie, ed. *Gabriela Mistral: The Audacious Traveler.* Athens: Ohio University Press, 2003. Collection of essays focusing on various aspects of Mistral's life and work, paying special attention to her political activism. Some of the essays discuss the death of the beloved in her poetry, the English translations of her writings, her extensive travels, and her pan-Americanism.

Bejar, Alfredo, ed. *Globe Hispanic Biographies.* Englewood Cliffs, N.J.: Globe, 1989. A collection of essay-length biographies, including one of Mistral. Not in depth, but a source for general biographical information on the poet in English, which is rare.

Fiol-Matta, Licia. *A Queer Mother for the Nation: The State and Gabriela Mistral.* Minneapolis: University of Minnesota Press, 2002. Although she never had a child, Mistral was a symbol of womanhood to many Latin Americans, who thought of her as the national schoolteacher-mother.

Fiol-Matta examines how Mistral came to occupy this position, analyzing the issues of race, gender, and sexual politics in Mistral's life, image, and poetry.

Mistral, Gabriela. *Gabriela Mistral: A Reader.* Translated by Maria Giachetti, edited by Marjorie Agosín. Fredonia, N.Y.: White Pine Press, 1993. Includes a wide selection of poems from *Tala* in English translation. Twenty-eight prose pieces provide a good view of Mistral's range.

Neruda, Pablo. *Memoirs.* Translated by Hardie St. Martin. New York: Farrar, Straus and Giroux, 1977. Chilean poet Neruda discusses his association with Mistral as his earliest mentor. Although brief, this is perhaps one of the best places to find a portrait of Mistral during the early years of her career as a teacher.

Peña, Karen. *Poetry and the Realm of the Public Intellectual: The Alternative Destinies of Gabriela Mistral, Cecília Meireles, and Rosario Castellanos.* Leeds, England: Legenda, 2007. Examines the works of three Latin American women writers, describing how they used their poetry to challenge patriarchal society by writing about gender, sexuality, and marginalized people. The chapters on Mistral also discuss her lesbian sexuality.

Rosenbaum, Sidonia Carmen. *Modern Women Poets of Spanish America.* Westport, Conn.: Greenwood Press, 1978. Offers historical perspectives and academic criticism of four poets, including Mistral. One of the more detailed examinations of Mistral among the few studies available in English.

A Tale of a Tub

Author: Jonathan Swift (1667-1745)
First published: 1704, as *A Tale of a Tub: To Which Is Added an Account of a Battle Between the Ancient and Modern Books in St. James's Library; and the Mechanical Operation of the Spirit*
Type of work: Satire and social criticism

Principal characters:
PETER, representing the pope or the Roman Catholic Church
MARTIN, representing Martin Luther, hence the Lutheran and Anglican churches
JACK, representing John Calvin, hence the Calvinist Dissenters

A Tale of a Tub has been called the greatest of English satires. The point is debatable, but the work is surely a most spirited, complex, and amusing contribution to this genre. Jonathan Swift also showed his satirical genius in *Gulliver's Travels* (1726) and in his famous essay, "A Modest Proposal" (1729), advocating the eating of infants.

Satire is written when an author wishes to attack something. Swift spent a lifetime attacking the pretensions and stupidity of the world around him. His main object in *A Tale of a Tub*, he said, was to ridicule "the numerous and gross corruptions in religion and learning." These, readers discover, include pedantic scholars, egoistic critics, fanatic literalists in religion, and clever theologians. Such people poison society with misapplication of their reasoning powers.

Swift wisely sees to it that his sense of outrage at the religious and scholarly varieties of human stupidity is complemented throughout by an elevating sense of the comic. The opening dedication to Lord Somers, for example, shows Swift in one of his contrived comic poses. In the dedication, engagingly posing as a gullible and naïve bookseller, he satirizes the excessive praise so prevalent in dedications of the time. The genius of the attempt is the fact that hyperbole itself is the method he employs.

With the second of the prefatory dedications, Swift's target becomes clearer. Addressing "His Royal Highness Prince Posterity," Swift makes a great and ironic show of ascribing great wit and literary achievement to his age. Swift has his tongue quite firmly in cheek in this passage and implies that the wise one seeks out virtue and value in all ages. Modernity alone has no just claim; what is new is not necessarily the best. Swift's position, therefore, in the "Battle of the Books" (an intellectual controversy of his time), tended to favor the ancients or the classics as opposed to the moderns.

In the subsequent preface, Swift continues with his consummate irony to excoriate the writers of his time. He explains his title. When seamen meet a whale, they throw out an empty tub to divert him lest he wreck the ship. If the ship is the ship of state and the whale represents the vast body of scurrilous and destructive writers and thinkers who "pick holes in the weak sides of religion and government," then the tale, says Swift, shall serve as a similar decoy for the wits of the day to attack.

On the surface, Swift's intention and meaning seem plain. He raises the perennial cry against two swarms of pests: the egoistic poetasters who set themselves up as wits, intellects, and critics, and the newer philosophers whose theories seem harmful to England's Christian and constitutional way of life, as in the case of Thomas Hobbes. As a conservative, a good Anglican, and a defender of the ancients, Swift was understandably angered, but latent in the argument, as is often the case with sensible Swift, is his recognition that in fact there are flaws in the existing schemes of religion and government: "a great many are hollow, and dry, and empty, and noisy, and wooden." The point here is simply that Swift's satire is distinguished not only by its sharp edge but by its double edge.

Swift proceeds through his preface by calling into play parody, well-turned phrase, artful digression, and mock diffidence—all of these in preparation for the style and the method of the treatise itself and all playing harmoniously in one of the world's great symphonies of irony. Eleven sections of the tale proper go before the conclusion. Part 1 is the introduction. With part 2, the tale officially begins, with "Once upon a time. . . ." The tale resumes in sections 4, 6, 8, and 11, with the intervening sections consisting of digressions that are called such. The tale proper contains Swift's satire on abuses in religion; the digressions satirize abuses in learning.

The introduction serves further to establish Swift's pose as a pedantic and prolific scholar. Ironically, he satirizes pedantry as he laboriously extracts allegories out of simple tales.

Swift's own tale then begins; the reader is forewarned to observe its own patterns of allegory. The characters involved are three brothers, triplets: Peter, Martin, and Jack. They represent Saint Peter (the Roman Catholic Church), Martin Luther (the Church of England, founded as a consequence of the Reformation), and John Calvin (the Dissenters). On his deathbed, their father bequeaths each a simple and durable coat to be worn carefully and never altered. The coat represents the New Testament doctrines of the early Christian Church. When the three brothers decide to become men about town, they need to remodel their coats with shoulder knots, gold lace, silver fringes, and embroidery to be in fashion. Swift focuses his satire on the sophistry and abuses of logic by which clever Peter finds in the father's will a license for these alterations.

Having thus caustically attended to Roman Catholic accretions, Swift now turns to the field of learning in his first digression. This is a biting attack on modern critics, who seek out only the worst in an author and catalog his defects. Swift ironically commends these creatures of prey, pretending to find glorious historical antecedents for their kind.

Returning now, in section 4, to the tale, Swift excoriates various institutions of the Roman Catholic Church: penance, Purgatory, private confession, holy water, papal bulls, celibacy, relics, and more. He describes each institution with great dignity and seriousness, as Swift here takes an opportunity to blend his satire on religious excesses with his satire on pedantry. Therefore, the focus of the tale is still on Peter, who styles himself Lord Peter and claims precedence over his brothers. Martin and Jack finally rebel and obtain a copy of their father's will, which made them all equal heirs. Angry Peter forces them from the house where all have been living together. Thus, the allegory recounts the Reformation.

At this high point, nothing could be more inappropriate than a digression; and so with intent the comic Swift presents a digression. With irony, he satirizes the habit of modern writers to expatiate on their own virtues and discoveries while they ridicule the ancients.

Swift records the further adventures of Martin and Jack. Martin carefully removes the fopperies from his coat and manages to get it somewhat back to its original state. Jack, however, with too great zeal, rips off the decorations with such haste that his coat is torn to rags. He envies Martin, and so these two have a disagreement. Thus is allegorized the split between Luther and the less temperate Calvinist reformers. Martin (or the established church in England) represents Swift's ideal or norm, a middle course between Peter's ingenuity and Jack's fanaticism. Swift offers another digression "in praise of digressions." The butt of the satire is the modern writer and his habit of neglecting method, style, good grammar, and originality. Instead, he compiles his mindless writings chiefly by plagiarizing and digression.

Swift returns to the tale proper and invents a fantastic sect of "Aeolists" as he continues his satire of Jack and his followers. They were wind worshipers who venerated humanity as a wind-producing machine with outlets at both ends. Swift's satire is addressed against the bombast and energy of Calvinist preachers.

Section 9 is the famous digression on madness, full of dextrous shifts in irony that have endlessly fascinated readers. Swift continues his jokes on the theme of wind by suggesting that madness occurs when malign vapors rise from the lower regions of the body to poison the brain. Both good and bad results derive from this distemper: wars, new philosophies, and all striking achievements of the human race. What happens is that one's fancy gets in control of one's reason, and imagination overwhelms common sense.

Swift, an imaginative writer, is not deriding the imagination but its misuse. Swift's argument is that when minute scholarship turns into pedantry, this is evil; but to be content with superficial knowledge is evil as well. Swift slices through the dilemma by cautioning against the most serious error, self-deception. Let one conduct one's life sensibly, understanding the full nature and implications of one's acts. Be neither superficial nor pedantic but intelligent, Swift recommends.

Section 10 blends heavy irony and lighthearted comedy as Swift attacks the hypocrisy and the self-regard of modern writers and slyly toys with the reader. With a jab at perverse scholars such as numerologists and Cabalists, he returns to his tale proper. In the tale proper, Swift lampoons fanatic, Scripture-quoting Calvinists, their doctrine of predestination, their aversion to music in churches, their insistence on simplicity, and their apparent courting of persecution. In short, Jack's increasing whims and affectations make him appear more and more like Peter, much to the dismay of both.

A rambling conclusion ends the book, after Swift successfully defends good sense in religion and in learning through the process of ridiculing aberrations. If there is a chief victim of his mockery, it is William Wotton, a scholar whose angry comments (which might have been better left unwritten) Swift gleefully adds as footnotes to subsequent editions.

Occasional use of scatology and satirical excesses flaw the work in the eyes of some critics, especially Swift's contemporaries: Swift responded in the fifth edition by making certain alterations, omitting, for example, a short synoptic piece of the tale and a digression on war, both of which followed section 9. A lengthy and angry "Apology" (or defense) also accompanied this edition. Over the years, however, critics have frequently viewed *A Tale of a Tub* as a masterpiece, a highly moral work offering an indirect recipe for the conduct of a Christian humanist.

Further Reading

Clark, John R. *Form and Frenzy in Swift's "Tale of a Tub."* Ithaca, N.Y.: Cornell University Press, 1970. Focuses on the artistry of Swift's satire, exploring *A Tale of a Tub* as "a work of mimetic art." Argues that Swift carries out his satiric intent with great originality while staying within the tradition.

Connery, Brian A., ed. *Representations of Swift.* Newark: University of Delaware Press, 2002. Collection of papers delivered at 1999 conference about Swift. Among other topics, the papers analyze *A Tale of a Tub* and discuss Swift and gender, class, and Ireland.

Fox, Christopher, ed. *The Cambridge Companion to Jonathan Swift.* New York: Cambridge University Press, 2003. Collection of essays about Swift's life and work, including discussions of Swift's religion, his language and style, his representation of women, and Swift the Irishman. "*A Tale of a Tub* and Early Prose" by Judith C. Mueller analyzes this novel.

Fox, Christopher, and Brenda Tooley, eds. *Walking Naboth's Vineyard: New Studies of Swift.* Notre Dame, Ind.: University of Notre Dame Press, 1995. The introduction discusses Swift and Irish studies, and the subsequent essays all consider aspects of Swift as an Irish writer.

Glendinning, Victoria. *Jonathan Swift: A Portrait.* New York: Henry Holt, 1998. Illuminates the life and personality of this proud and intractable man. Investigates the main events and relationships of Swift's life, providing a portrait set amid controversy and paradox.

Harth, Phillip. *Swift and Anglican Rationalism: The Religious Background of "A Tale of a Tub."* Chicago: University of Chicago Press, 1961. A learned investigation of the novel's religious background. Rejects arguments that *A Tale of a Tub* has a unity that fuses the two objects of its satire, religion and learning, in one coherent whole.

Hudson, Nicholas, and Aaron Santesso, eds. *Swift's Travels: Eighteenth-Century British Satire and Its Legacy.* New York: Cambridge University Press, 2008. Collection of essays examining the satirical style and content of Swift's work. Some of the essays discuss his work in relationship to previous satirical writing by John Dryden and others; other essays compare his work with that of Alexander Pope and assess his influence on Jane Austen, Henry Fielding, and Samuel Beckett.

Kelly, Ann Cline. *Jonathan Swift and Popular Culture: Myth, Media, and the Man.* New York: Palgrave, 2002. Chronicles the creation of Swift's literary legend in his own time and in succeeding generations. Swift realized that in "a print-contracted world, texts create authors, not the other way around," and Kelly demonstrates how the writer constructed a print persona that differed from the "real" individual.

Paulson, Ronald. *Theme and Structure in Swift's "Tale of a Tub."* New Haven, Conn.: Yale University Press, 1960. Emphasizes the moral import of *A Tale of a Tub*, stressing Swift's penetrating insight into the nature of evil. Pleads a case for Swift as an artist who gave *A Tale of a Tub* a "unified structure."

Smith, Frederik N. *Language and Reality in Swift's "A Tale of a Tub."* Columbus: Ohio State University Press, 1979. Finds in *A Tale of a Tub* two styles of language that coincide with two ways of knowing the world. Argues that Swift rejects the "intellectualized" approach in favor of the "experience-oriented."

The Tale of Genji

Author: Murasaki Shikibu (c. 978-c. 1030)
First published: Genji monogatari, c. 1004 (English translation, 1925-1933)
Type of work: Novel
Type of plot: Romance
Time of plot: Early medieval period
Locale: Japan

Principal characters:
PRINCE GENJI, the talented illegitimate son of the emperor
THE EMPEROR, Genji's father
KIRITSUBO, Genji's mother and the emperor's concubine
LADY KOKIDEN, the emperor's consort
PRINCESS AOI, Genji's first wife
UTSUSEMI and YUGAO, noblewomen in love with Genji
MURASAKI, a young girl reared by Genji

The Story:

When the emperor of Japan takes a beautiful gentlewoman of the bedchamber as his concubine, he greatly displeases his consort, the Lady Kokiden. The lot of the concubine, whose name is Kiritsubo, is not easy, despite the emperor's protection and love, for Kokiden's influence is very great. Kiritsubo therefore has little happiness in the birth of a son, although the child is beautiful and sturdy. The existence of Kiritsubo's son makes Kokiden even more antagonistic, for she fears that her own son might lose favor in the emperor's eyes and not be made heir apparent. Because of the hardships of her life among the other women of the court, Kiritsubo languishes, her health fading away until she dies.

After his mother's death, Kiritsubo's young child is placed by the emperor under the protection of the clan of Gen; the emperor also gives the child the title of Prince Genji. The boy, spirited and handsome, becomes a popular figure at the court. Even Kokiden cannot feel a great deal of ill will toward him. Genji wins a secure place for himself in the emperor's eyes, and at the age of twelve he is not only elevated to a man's estate but also given in marriage to Princess Aoi, the daughter of the minister of the left, a powerful figure at court. Genji is not impressed with his bride, nor is she entirely happy with her bridegroom, for she is four years older than he.

Genji is appointed a captain of the guard, and in this capacity he spends much of his time at the emperor's palace. Indeed, he is rarely together with his bride in their apartment in her father's home, for with his good looks, accomplishments, and position, Genji can have any woman he wants. His wife becomes very cool toward him, but Genji cares little about what Princess Aoi says or does.

One of Genji's first love affairs is with a young gentle-woman named Fujitsubo, who, like his bride, is a few years older than he. His second romantic adventure takes place at the home of a young courtier, Ki no Kami, who is honored to have Prince Genji at his home. Genji goes into the room of a pretty young matron, Utsusemi, and takes her to his own quarters. Because of Genji's rank and pleasing self, the woman does not resent this. To keep in touch with her afterward, Genji asks that her brother be appointed a member of his train, a request that is readily granted. When Utsusemi realizes that the affair cannot long continue, she breaks it off; Genji calls her his broom tree, comparing her to a Japanese shrub that at a distance promises shade but is really only a scrawny bush.

A short time later, Genji enters Utsusemi's room in an effort to try to renew his affair with her, but she is not asleep when he enters, and when she sees him she runs out of the room. Another very charming young woman is in the room, however, and she fails to awaken when Utsusemi leaves. Genji, refusing to be irritated by Utsusemi, gently wakes the other young woman, and very soon he is on the most intimate of terms with her.

One day, while visiting his foster mother, Genji makes the acquaintance of a young woman named Yugao, to whom he later makes several masked visits. She is living a rather poor existence, despite the fact that she comes from a good family. Genji becomes tired of their clandestine meetings and arranges for them to stay for a time in a deserted palace within the imperial domains. The affair ends in tragedy when, during their stay, Yugao is strangely afflicted and dies. Only with the help of his retainers and friends is Genji able to avoid a disastrous scandal.

Shortly afterward, Genji falls ill of an ague. He goes to a hermit in the mountains to seek a cure, and there he finds a beautiful little girl named Murasaki, an orphan of a good family. Seeing something of himself in little Murasaki, who is pretty and talented, Genji resolves to take her into his care. At first, Murasaki's guardians refuse to listen to Genji's plans, but he convinces them that he has only the girl's best interests at heart and will not make her a concubine at too young an age. Finally, they agree to let him shape the little girl's future, and he takes her to his own palace to live with him. Lest people misunderstand his motives, and for the sake of secrecy, Genji does not disclose to others the identity of the girl and her age, even though his various lovers and his wife become exceedingly jealous of the mysterious stranger known to dwell with Genji.

Soon after his return to the emperor's court with Murasaki, Genji is asked to dance the "Waves of the Blue Sea" at the annual festival in the emperor's court. So well does he impress the emperor with his dancing and with his poetry that he is raised to higher rank. It is clear that if the emperor only dared to do so, Genji would be named the heir apparent. Genji's star is in the ascendant, but he is very worried, for he has made Fujitsubo, the emperor's concubine, pregnant. After the baby's birth, everyone notices how much like Genji the baby looks, but to Genji's relief the likeness is credited to the fact that he and the child are both sons of the emperor. The emperor is so pleased that he makes Fujitsubo his official consort after the unexpected death of Lady Kokiden.

Genji's marriage has proceeded very badly, and he and his wife have become increasingly distanced from each other. Finally, she becomes pregnant, but her condition only seems to make her sadder. During the pregnancy, Princess Aoi's health declines, for she is consumed with hallucinations that Genji's other lovers are stealing her life from her through hatred and jealousy. As a result of her deep affliction, Princess Aoi dies in childbirth; she is much mourned by Genji, who finally has come to appreciate and love her. A year after her death, however, when Murasaki, the girl he has reared, is of suitable age to marry, Genji takes her for his wife and resolves to settle down.

Critical Evaluation:

Lady Murasaki Shikibu was the daughter of a famous provincial governor and the widow of a lieutenant in the imperial guard. As a lady-in-waiting to Empress Akiko, she was completely familiar with Nipponese court ritual and ceremony, and her knowledge of palace life is everywhere apparent in the adventures of her nobly born hero, Prince Genji.

The Tale of Genji is undoubtedly the finest example of medieval Japanese storytelling, and in it one can trace the growth of Japanese literature. In the beginning, Murasaki's romance is an adolescent affair, very much in the fairy-tale tradition of the old Japanese chronicles. As it progresses, it becomes a full-blown prose romance. It resembles the medieval prose romances of western Europe in that both genres focus on the love affairs of their heroes. *The Tale of Genji*, however, reflects the qualities of Japanese culture. Here are people whose main occupation, far removed from the arts of war and chivalry, is to live well and enjoy nature and art in all forms. In place of the idealized woman, these romances present the idealized man, in whose life women play distinctly subordinate roles.

The Tale of Genji is a long, elegant, wittily ironical court romance that is in some respects a prototype of the novel. The book is divided into parts consisting of the title section and sections titled "The Sacred Tree," "A Wreath of Cloud,"

"Blue Trousers," "The Lady of the Boat," and "The Bridge of Dreams." Although Arthur Waley's translation from the Japanese has made the work accessible to a greater audience, few Western readers generally venture beyond the first section, "The Tale of Genji," although Murasaki's style actually improves as she proceeds. The first chapter crudely imitates the manner of old court romances, but the characterizations become richer and more complex over the course of the book, and the work's overall design—depicting a moral picture of the emperor's court of Murasaki's time—becomes apparent.

The Tale of Genji presents an incomparable re-creation of life in eleventh century Japan, faithfully depicting the smallest details of the customs, ceremonies, and manners of the aristocracy. The book is also an enchanting collection of interwoven stories, some erotic and all vividly recounted. Beyond that, the work offers a psychologically honest examination of passion and pretense, and of the hearts of men and women.

The first section treats Genji, "the Shining One," as a child and young man, idealistic but often unwise as he learns the arts of courtship and love. It also introduces Murasaki (who is certainly not the author, unless by ironic contrast), first as Genji's child-concubine, then as his second wife. Her character is tentatively sketched here, though in later parts of the book she learns about the romantic and political intrigues of court life, becomes sophisticated in practicing her own wiles, and, finally (in the section titled "Blue Trousers"), dies of a lingering, wasting disease. The early section, however, treats the hero and heroine as youthful, hopeful, and inexperienced, before they fully understand how to play the cynical games of love and dissembling.

In chapter 2 of *The Tale of Genji*, the author advances the main theme of her work, the romantic education of innocent lovers. The equerry of the palace, To no Chujo, regales several noblemen, including Genji, with stories about the weakness of women. He has at last discovered that "there exists no woman of whom one can say: 'Here is perfection.'" Genji's youthful experiences tend to support this observation. Just twelve years old when he is married to the sixteen-year-old Princess Aoi, he finds more amusement in amorous adventures than in matrimonial responsibilities, and he comes to care for his wife only shortly before her untimely death. He enjoys his first dalliance with Fujitsubo (whom he later makes pregnant) and thereafter sports with the easily yielding but jealous Utsusemi; with a complaisant lady who happens, conveniently, to be sleeping in Utsusemi's bed; with Yugao; and, finally, with the child Murasaki. With the exception of Murasaki, all the women disappoint him. Murasaki, the most innocent and childlike of his lovers, is the only

one spirited, imaginative, and beautiful enough to hold his affections.

Murasaki also undergoes a romantic education. She must learn how to function in a world controlled by men without bowing too submissively to their power. When Genji brings her to the palace, he warns her, "Little girls ought to be very gentle and obedient in their ways." At this speech, the narrator wryly comments, "And thus her education was begun." Several years later, Genji takes sexual liberties with Murasaki, who is too innocent and confused either to oppose or to enjoy his attentions. Indeed, her own innocence excites his desire. As the narrator explains, "It is in general the unexplored that attracts us, and Genji tended to fall most deeply in love with those who gave him least encouragement." When Genji decides to marry the girl, she has no choice in the matter; in fact, he criticizes her lack of enthusiasm for the arrangement, since she owes so much to his friendship. Murasaki Shikibu shows how, in the closed world of the emperor's palace, where court ladies at best play submissive parts, women must develop resources of their own—both of mind and of heart—to live with dignity. By the end of *The Tale of Genji*, her heroine is already beginning to learn that lesson.

Further Reading

Bargen, Doris G. *A Woman's Weapon: Spirit Possession in "The Tale of Genji."* Honolulu: University of Hawaii Press, 1997. Provides a feminist interpretation of the "possessing spirits" in the novel, arguing that spirit possession was a female strategy to counter male empowerment and redress the imbalance of power between the sexes.

Bowring, Richard. *Murasaki Shikibu: "The Tale of Genji."* 2d ed. New York: Cambridge University Press, 2004. Provides readable information on the cultural background of the novel, including Heian politics, Murasaki's life and her fictionalization of history, and religions that influenced the novel. Discusses the work's style, language, influence, and reception.

Caddeau, Patrick W. *Appraising "Genji": Literary Criticism and Cultural Anxiety in the Age of the Last Samurai.* Albany: State University of New York Press, 2006. Assesses the novel's impact on Japanese culture through diaries, critical treatises, newspaper accounts, film adaptations, and stage productions. Focuses on a treatise by Hagiwara Hiromichi, a nineteenth century samurai whose massive study of the novel challenged traditional interpretations of the book and conventional beliefs about the nation's culture.

Field, Norma. *The Splendor of Longing in "The Tale of Genji."* 1987. Reprint. Ann Arbor: Center for Japanese Studies, University of Michigan, 2001. Focuses on many of the women characters in the novel to show how they "make" and "unmake" the hero, Genji. Includes discussions of the social, psychological, political, and aesthetic aspects of the novel.

Kamens, Edward, ed. *Approaches to Teaching Murasaki Shikibu's "The Tale of Genji."* New York: Modern Language Association of America, 1993. Following a section on materials and recommended reading, six essays suggest ways of studying *The Tale of Genji*. Problems of reading the text are discussed, and the novel is also compared with other literary works.

Keene, Donald. *Japanese Literature.* 1955. Reprint. New York: Grove Press, 1979. The definitive commentator on Japanese literature discusses the Japanese novel's indebtedness to *The Tale of Genji* and its sad obsession with mutability.

_____. *Landscapes and Portraits: Appreciations of Japanese Culture.* Palo Alto, Calif.: Kodansha International, 1971. Reprints Keene's 1967 essay "Feminine Sensibility in the Heian Era," which explores the emergence of women writers and the *kana* writing system and analyzes *The Tale of Genji* as part of this phenomenon. Includes illustrations.

Miner, Earl, ed. *Principles of Classical Japanese Literature.* Princeton, N.J.: Princeton University Press, 1985. Seven essays combine Japanese and North American viewpoints in discussing Japanese literature. Includes a discussion of whether *The Tale of Genji* is a collection rather than a single unified work and an examination of the work's structure and narrative.

Morris, Ivan. *The World of the Shining Prince: Court Life in Ancient Japan.* 1964. Reprint. New York: Kodansha International, 1994. One of the best interpretive works available on the historical and cultural milieu of *The Tale of Genji*. Chapter 9 offers an excellent biographical account of Murasaki. Includes a complete glossary listing historical figures in Murasaki's life.

Puette, William J. *"The Tale of Genji" by Murasaki Shikibu: A Reader's Guide.* 1983. Reprint. Rutland, Vt.: Charles Tuttle, 1992. Includes an informative plot summary of *The Tale of Genji*, supplemented by background chapters on topics relevant to understanding the novel. Chapter 4 provides a brief biography of Murasaki.

A Tale of Two Cities

Author: Charles Dickens (1812-1870)
First published: 1859
Type of work: Novel
Type of plot: Historical
Time of plot: French Revolution
Locale: France and England

Principal characters:
DR. MANETTE, a former prisoner in the Bastille
LUCIE MANETTE, his daughter
MR. LORRY, an agent of Tellson & Co.
CHARLES DARNAY, the Marquis St. Evrémonde
SYDNEY CARTON, a lawyer's clerk
MISS PROSS, a servant
MADAME DEFARGE, a French revolutionary
MONSIEUR DEFARGE, her husband

The Story:

The early rumblings of the French Revolution are echoing across the English Channel when, in Paris, an old man waits in an attic for his first meeting with a daughter whom he has not seen since she was a baby. With the aid of Mr. Jarvis Lorry, an agent for the Franco-British banking house of Tellson & Co., the lovely Lucie Manette is brought to Paris to be reunited with her father, who was imprisoned for eighteen years in the Bastille. Above the wineshop of Madame and Monsieur Defarge, Dr. Manette is kept secretly until his rescuers can take him safely back to England. Day after day, Madame Defarge sits outside her wineshop, knitting into a long scarf strange symbols that will later spell out a death list of hated aristocrats and enemies of the Revolution.

Five years later, Lucie sits beside her father in the courtroom of the Old Bailey, where Charles Darnay, a teacher of languages, is on trial for treasonable activities that involve his passing between France and England on secret business. A man named John Barsad brings charges against him. Lucie and her father testify that they met Darnay on the boat when they traveled from France five years earlier. The prisoner was saved when Mr. Stryver, the prisoner's counsel, pointed across the courtroom to another man, Sydney Carton, who so resembled the prisoner that legal identification of Darnay was shaken and Mr. Stryver was able to secure an acquittal for the prisoner. Carton's relationship to Stryver is that of the jackal to the lion; the alcoholic, aimless Carton writes the cases that Stryver pleads in court.

Lucie and her father live in a small tenement under the care of their maid, Miss Pross, and their kindly friend, Mr. Lorry. Jerry Cruncher, the porter at Tellson & Co. and a secret resurrectionist, is often helpful. Darnay and Carton become frequent callers in the Manette household, after the trial that brought them together.

In France, the fury of the people grows. Monseigneur the Marquis St. Evrémonde is driving in his carriage through the countryside when he carelessly kills a child of a peasant named Gaspard. The nobleman returns to his castle to meet his nephew, Charles Darnay, who is visiting from England. Darnay's views differ from those of his uncle. Darnay knows that his family committed grave injustices, and he begs his uncle to make amends. Monseigneur the Marquis haughtily refuses. That night, the marquis is murdered in his bed.

Darnay returns to England to seek Dr. Manette's permission to court Lucie. In order to construct a bond of complete honesty, Darnay attempts to tell the doctor his true French name, but Manette fearfully asks him to wait until the morning of his marriage before revealing it. Carton also approaches Lucie with a proposal of marriage. When Lucie refuses, Carton asks her always to remember that there is a man who will give his own life to keep a life she loves beside her.

In France, Madame Defarge knits the story of the hated St. Evrémondes into her scarf. Gaspard was hanged for the assassination of the marquis; Monseigneur's house must be destroyed. Barsad, the spy, brings news that Lucie will marry Darnay, the nephew of the marquis. This news disturbs Defarge, for Dr. Manette, a former prisoner of the Bastille, holds a special honor in the eyes of the revolutionists.

Lucie and Darnay are married. Carton becomes a loyal friend of the family. Time passes, and tiny Lucie arrives. When the child is six years old, in the year 1789, the French people storm the Bastille. At the Bastille, Defarge goes to the cell where Dr. Manette was a prisoner and extracts some papers hidden behind a stone in the wall.

One day, while Darnay is talking to Mr. Lorry at Tellson & Co., a letter addressed to the Marquis St. Evrémonde is placed on Mr. Lorry's desk. Darnay offers to deliver it to the proper person. When he is alone, he reads the letter. It is from an old family servant who is imprisoned by the revolutionists. He begs the Marquis St. Evrémonde to save his life. Darnay realizes that he must go to Paris. Only Dr. Manette knows of Darnay's family name, and the doctor is sworn to secrecy.

Darnay and Mr. Lorry go to Paris, the latter to look after the French branch of Tellson & Co. Shortly after his arrival, Darnay is seized as an undesirable immigrant after Defarge orders his arrest. Mr. Lorry is considerably upset when Lucie and Dr. Manette suddenly arrive in Paris. Some of the doctor's friends inform him of Darnay's arrest. The old man feels that his own imprisonment in the Bastille will win the sympathy of the revolutionists and enable him to save his son-in-law.

After fifteen months of waiting, Darnay is brought to trial. Because he is able to prove himself innocent of harming the French people, he is freed but forbidden to leave France. A short time later, he is again arrested, denounced by Defarge and one other person whose name the officer refuses to disclose.

While shopping one day in the Paris market, Miss Pross and Jerry Cruncher, who are in Paris with Lucie and Mr. Lorry, meet a man who causes Miss Pross to scream in amazement and Jerry to stare in silent astonishment. The man is Solomon, Miss Pross's lost brother. Jerry remembers him as Barsad, the man who was a spy-witness at the Old Bailey. Carton arrives on the scene at that moment, and he is able to force Barsad to come with him to the office of Tellson & Co. for a private conference. Barsad fears detection of his duplicity, for he is now an employee of the Republican French Government. Carton and Jerry threaten to expose him as a former spy for the English government, the enemy of France. Carton makes a deal with Barsad.

When Darnay is once more brought before the tribunal, Defarge testifies against him and names Dr. Manette as the other accuser. Defarge produces the papers that he found in Dr. Manette's cell in the Bastille. Therein the doctor wrote the story of his arrest and imprisonment because he learned of a secret crime committed by a St. Evrémonde against a woman of humble birth and her young brother. His account is enough to convict Darnay. Sentenced for the crimes of his ancestors, Darnay, the young St. Evrémonde, is condemned by the tribunal to the guillotine.

Carton now begins to visit the Defarge wineshop, where he learns that Madame Defarge is the sister of the woman ruined by St. Evrémonde years before. With the help of the false Barsad, he gains admittance to the prison where Darnay was taken. There he drugs the prisoner and, still aided by the cowed Barsad, has him carried from the cell, himself remaining behind. The resemblance between the two will allow him to pass as Darnay and prevent discovery of the aristocrat's escape.

Madame Defarge goes to the lodgings of Lucie and Dr. Manette to denounce them. Only Miss Pross is there; the others, including Darnay, are already on their way to safety. To keep Madame Defarge from learning of their escape, Miss Pross struggles with the furious woman when she demands admittance to Lucie's apartment. Madame Defarge is killed when her pistol goes off. Miss Pross is deaf for the rest of her life. Lucie and Darnay return safely to England. Carton dies at the guillotine, giving his own life for the happiness of those he loved.

Critical Evaluation:

The central paradox of *A Tale of Two Cities* is that its action involves one of the most important political events of modern European history—and perhaps of its entire history—the French Revolution, while the values of the novel are ultimately antipolitical. Politics and history, neither of which Charles Dickens renders with great faithfulness, loom as a necessity from which his characters must flee to save their souls. Throughout the novel, Dickens reminds his readers that all acts, whether magnanimous or petty, shrink to nothing when viewed in a cosmic context. Indeed, for him, the goal of politics—the finding of a just community—is an absurd one in this world. To paraphrase Sydney Carton's famous last speech: It is a far better thing to die and join such a community in heaven—the existence of which Dickens cannot with certainty assert—than to engage with society. *A Tale of Two Cities* demonstrates that Dickens's political will, wan in his previous novels, is finally exhausted.

In this regard and in one of the first substantial essays dealing with Dickens's art and thought, published a year before *A Tale of Two Cities* was completed, Walter Bagehot said,

Mr. Dickens has not infrequently spoken, and what is worse, he has taught a great number of parrot-like imitators to speak, in what really is, if they knew it, a tone of objection to the necessary constitution of human society.

Dickens's strength, Bagehot agreed, appears in the quality of his moral cry, his protest against the injustices of society; yet, as he said, the novelist never indicates how these inequalities might be removed.

By the time of *A Tale of Two Cities*, distinguished by its outrage against the tyranny of both the governors and the governed, Dickens clearly indicates that society cannot be made to progress or even be substantially ameliorated. For him, the great grasp for freedom by the French people, for example, goes finally unsung, drowned out by the terrible cacophony of the guillotine. To Dickens's unwillingness to accept the "necessary constitution of human society," then, must be added his refusal to understand and accept the necessarily slow and painful processes of history.

In his early comic and satiric novels, such as *Pickwick Papers* (1836-1837), *Nicholas Nickleby* (1838-1839), and *Oliver Twist* (1837-1839), Dickens's simple stance of protest carried with it a zestful anger that was both invigorating and liberating; but as he grew more serious in his artistic intent, beginning with *Dombey and Son*, completed in 1848, and continuing through *David Copperfield* (1849-1850), *Bleak House* (1852-1853), *Hard Times* (1854), and *Little Dorrit* (1855-1857), for many readers his masterpiece, he lost his sense of the efficacy of the human will to deal with the complexities of a modern, industrial society. His gradual loss of faith was accompanied by a diminishing moral energy; his imagination seemed unable to create viable and pertinent responses to a civilization increasingly encroaching on individual freedom. Particularly in *Little Dorrit*, the novel published immediately before *A Tale of Two Cities*, readers are stunned as well as enervated by the hopelessness of the conclusion.

There is a significant scene in *A Tale of Two Cities* that appears at the conclusion of book 1 and is relevant to Dickens's social despair. After Dr. Manette has been saved from the Bastille and is on the way from Paris to London, his rescuer, Mr. Jarvis Lorry, asks him, "I hope you care to be recalled to life?" Dr. Manette answers, "I can't say." In some ways, the question is never answered by the doctor, for at the novel's conclusion his mind clouds permanently from the effects of his sufferings. If to be "recalled to life" means to be called back into civilization and history, then the novel implies that the doctor's answer is "No." The quality of life in society is actually no better, Dickens seems to claim, than perpetual imprisonment in the Bastille, and humans are caught up in an undertow of events that leaves them helpless; their imagination, intelligence, and will are useless when pitted against politics.

Indeed, the novelist goes further than this in his view of the ineptitude of human beings. If they consent to join in the machinations of society, Dickens asserts, they must inevitably expect to be corrupted. It is a tragic view, unrelieved by a belief in human dignity, or in the human ability to attain nobility through exertion of will. The readers of *A Tale of Two Cities*, left with Dickens's vision of unmitigated tragedy, remain unconsoled in their own existence, which is inextricably bound up with the demands of history and politics.

The consolation that Dickens does offer takes the form of a vague promise of supernatural communion and a picture of human fellowship and love. The fellowship, composed of Dr. and Lucie Manette, Charles Darnay and Sydney Carton, and the minor characters of Mr. Lorry, Miss Pross, and Jerry Cruncher, provides a sanctuary within the confines of history. There affection, trust, and sacrifice stand opposed to the hate, treachery, and tyranny of the world.

"Critical Evaluation" by David L. Kubal

Further Reading

Beckwith, Charles E., ed. *Twentieth Century Interpretations of "A Tale of Two Cities."* Englewood Cliffs, N.J.: Prentice-Hall, 1972. A collection of scholarly critical essays followed by commentaries on the novel by such literary figures as George Bernard Shaw and George Orwell.

Bloom, Harold, ed. *Charles Dickens's "A Tale of Two Cities."* New York: Chelsea House, 2007. Collection of essays providing scholarly analyses of the novel.

Cotsell, Michael A., ed. *Critical Essays on Charles Dickens's "A Tale of Two Cities."* New York: G. K. Hall, 1998. The essays were written in the nineteenth and twentieth centuries and include excerpts from books about the French Revolution; character analyses; and discussions of the representation of women, alternatives to "bourgeois individualism," and the "purity of violence" in the novel.

Glancy, Ruth. *"A Tale of Two Cities": Dickens's Revolutionary Novel.* Boston: Twayne, 1991. A detailed study that places the novel in its historical and literary context and provides a careful analysis of the plot.

_____, ed. *Charles Dickens's "A Tale of Two Cities": A Sourcebook.* New York: Routledge, 2006. A collection that enhances understanding of the novel. Offers a contextual overview, contemporary documents about the French Revolution, nineteenth century reviews of the book, twentieth century interpretations, and analyses of key passages.

Hardy, Barbara. *Dickens and Creativity.* London: Continuum, 2008. Focuses on the workings of Dickens's creativity and imagination, which Hardy argues is at the heart of his self-awareness, subject matter, and narrative. *A Tale of Two Cities* is discussed in chapter 11, "Assertions of Style: Rhythm and Repetition in *A Tale of Two Cities* and *Our Mutual Friend.*"

Jordan, John O., ed. *The Cambridge Companion to Charles Dickens.* New York: Cambridge University Press, 2001. Essays examine Dickens's life and times, analyze his novels, and discuss Dickens in relation to language, gender, family, domestic ideology, the form of the novel, illustration, theater, and film.

Kaplan, Fred. *Dickens: A Biography.* New York: William Morrow, 1988. Scholarly and well-written. It is particularly valuable in addressing Dickens's personal identification with the characters of Sydney Carton and Charles Darnay.

Nelson, Harland S. *Charles Dickens.* Boston: Twayne, 1981. An excellent introduction to Dickens's life and works.

Paroissien, David, ed. *A Companion to Charles Dickens.* Malden, Mass.: Blackwell, 2008. Collection of essays discussing Dickens as a reformer, Christian, and journalist. Also examines Dickens and the topics of gender, technology, and the United States. Includes the essay *"A Tale of Two Cities"* by Paul Davis.

The Talented Mr. Ripley

Author: Patricia Highsmith (1921-1995)
First published: 1955
Type of work: Novel
Type of plot: Psychological thriller
Time of plot: Early 1950's
Locale: New York City, Italy, France, Monte Carlo, and Greece

Principal characters:
TOM RIPLEY, an ambitious but poverty-stricken young man
DICKIE GREENLEAF, a man of Tom's age, the scion of a wealthy shipbuilder, and a would-be painter
MARGE SHERWOOD, Dickie's American companion and hopeful girfriend, an aspiring writer
FREDDIE MILES, a jet-set friend of Dickie, son of a hotel-chain owner
HERBERT GREENLEAF, Dickie's father
EMILY GREENLEAF, Dickie's mother
CLEO DOBELLE, Tom's New York friend and confidant
ALVIN MCCARRON, an American private detective hired by Herbert Greenleaf
AUNT DOTTIE, Tom's aunt, who raised him after his parents died

The Story:

Tom Ripley is trying to survive in New York City. He has to rely on his wits while living off menial work. Between jobs, he engages in illegal scams and lives among shady people. One day, wealthy Herbert Greenleaf approaches Tom—who casually knows his son Dickie—to persuade him to travel to Italy and convince his wastrel son to return home. Tom eagerly accepts Mr. Greenleaf's offer of a round-trip ticket and six hundred dollars in spending money. Arriving in Mongibello, Tom runs into Dickie and Marge on the beach; the couple seems indifferent to him until Tom tells them the truth about why he is there and keeps them entertained. Dickie invites Tom to share his luxurious house. Tom accepts, to the chagrin of Marge, who lives separately and sees Tom as an impediment to her romance with Dickie.

Tom and Dickie, who resemble one another, become fast friends and travel widely together, usually without Marge. They run into Freddie Miles, a wealthy acquaintance of Dickie who reminds his chum about a scheduled winter skiing party in Cortina. Tom, thrilled to be living a leisurely life he could only dream about before, covets Dickie's fine clothes, expensive possessions, and a monthly allowance of five hundred dollars.

The friendship between the two men becomes strained after Tom is discovered wearing Dickie's best clothes, admiring himself in a mirror. Dickie cruelly repeats Marge's suggestion that Tom might be homosexual; Tom hotly denies it. The friendship crumbles further after Tom attempts to involve Dickie in a drug-smuggling scheme. Dickie begins to spend more time with Marge and shuns Tom; Tom daydreams about eliminating Dickie. Because Marge is busy

working on a book, Dickie consents to accompany Tom to San Remo. There, they rent a small motorboat and head into the Ligurian Sea. While they undress to swim, Tom beats Dickie to death with an oar, sinks his body with the anchor, and scuttles the boat near shore.

Tom returns to Mongibello. He tells Marge that Dickie has moved to Rome and is gathering his belongings. Tom reinforces his story by forging letters from Dickie to Marge and the Greenleafs, writing on Dickie's distinctive typewriter and in Dickie's style. In Rome, Tom forges Dickie's signature to collect his monthly allowance. He wears Dickie's clothes as he travels to France on Dickie's passport. Back in Rome, as Dickie, he rents a plush apartment, knowing that wealthy Americans are exempt from reporting changes of address, and lives in quiet comfort, traveling whenever and wherever he pleases.

Freddie Miles, however, tracks down the apartment Tom has rented and shows up unannounced. He sees Tom, dressed in Dickie's clothes and wearing Dickie's jewelry, and grows suspicious. Before Freddie can do anything, however, Tom bludgeons him to death with a heavy ashtray. That night, Tom half-walks, half-carries the corpse downstairs and stuffs it into Freddie's sports car. Tom leaves the body at a cemetery, where it is discovered the following morning.

For days afterward, Tom plays a dangerous game with the police—who are investigating not only the murder of Freddie but also the disappearance of Tom Ripley—with Marge, and with other acquaintances. He continues to impersonate Dickie, and, before disposing of Dickie's typewriter, he composes a will. In it, Dickie leaves everything he owns to

Tom. When Marge shows up at the apartment, Tom plays himself, the concerned friend. Tom claims to be living with Dickie and pretends to be bewildered by events. As soon as Marge leaves, Tom flees town, moving to Venice. Finally, it becomes too risky to continue playing Dickie, so he reverts to Tom Ripley and reports to the Venice police. Since Tom has reappeared, the police develop a new theory: Dickie killed Freddie, is in hiding, and may have committed suicide. Marge comes to Venice, and Tom generously lets her stay in his apartment.

Mr. Greenleaf shows up in Italy with a private investigator named McCarron and wants to see Tom. Back at Tom's apartment, Marge finds Dickie's jewelry and questions Tom about it. Clutching a shoe he intends to use to kill her if she does not believe him, Tom insists Dickie gave him the jewelry. Luckily, Marge believes him and becomes convinced that Dickie could have committed suicide. McCarron questions Tom and seems satisfied with his answers. Mr. Greenleaf leaves for Rome to continue the search for Dickie. Several months later, Tom, now visiting Greece, receives a letter from Mr. Greenleaf: He is convinced his son is either dead from his own hand or in hiding, and he will honor his son's request that Tom inherit everything.

Critical Evaluation:

The Talented Mr. Ripley introduced perhaps the most charming and complex sociopathic serial killer literature has ever known. If nothing else, Tom Ripley is one of few characters of his ilk worthy of having a suspenseful, blackly humorous series devoted to his devious and sometimes violent exploits. In *Ripley Under Ground* (1970), *Ripley's Game* (1974), *The Boy Who Followed Ripley* (1980), and *Ripley Under Water* (1991), Patricia Highsmith periodically revisited her creation, developing and exploring the limits of his amorality. Despite his dark side, Tom has many admirable qualities and talents. He is good with numbers. He can imitate other people and drop chameleon-like into any role. He is an excellent forger. He has a good sense of humor. He is clever, resourceful, an eager learner, and adaptable. Tom has his flaws, too: the remnants of a conscience, a fear of water, ambivalence about his sexuality, and total ruthlessness. Like his creator, Tom Ripley has expatriate tendencies, preferring the genteel, slower-paced ambiance of Europe to the bustle of America.

In the first Ripley novel, Highsmith established what proved to be ground rules for the other volumes that followed. The dispassionate third-person narrative provides readers enough distance to avoid identifying too completely with the antiheroic protagonist, yet it is close enough to maintain sympathy toward him. Tom's progression from minor crook to murderer has a certain twisted logic. It is understandable that he, orphaned as an infant and raised by an insensitive, cruel aunt, would long for more than he has at the beginning of the story. It is unsurprising that a young man such as Tom might turn to petty crime in desperation, and that he would fear exposure and incarceration. It is not farfetched that he who has had nothing all his life might go to extraordinary lengths to acquire the trappings of the good life and do whatever was necessary to hold on to them. Tom may resort to murder, but it is a protective measure, not a compulsion.

Highsmith's simple, straightforward prose, with few stylistic embellishments—characteristic of an unsophisticated young man willing to take extreme risks to achieve his desires—propels the story forward, adding believability by its plainness. Descriptions of seascapes or restaurant scenes or brutal murders are treated with equally unemotional, matter-of-fact declarative sentences, and, because readers cannot anticipate the transition from harmless to harmful, the sense of menace is ratcheted up from passage to passage.

In tracking the nefarious adventures of Tom Ripley in his quest to transform himself from an unimportant nobody into a person of means—a gentleman—the author explores several interrelated themes. Highsmith pays homage to Henry James's *The Ambassadors* (1903), the story of a man who, like Ripley, is sent to Europe to fetch a wayward son. Highsmith has Tom Ripley ask for the James book several times during the novel, to remind readers where the idea for the story originally came from, and she uses it to draw contrasts between the lifestyles of the rich and poor.

Another theme from literary tradition is the doppelganger, or double. Throughout *The Talented Mr. Ripley*, Tom mirrors his perfect model, Dickie Greenleaf. They are already the same age, nearly identical in height and weight, and have similar hair color and features. Tom studies Dickie while he is alive, copying his mannerisms, his walk, the intonation of his voice, and his signature. After Dickie's death, Tom—a pragmatist who knows that two objects cannot occupy the same space at the same time—poses as his late friend, travels under Dickie's passport, styles his lightened hair to match Dickie's, dresses in Dickie's clothes, and wears his rings. Dickie's interrupted life in essence continues, only in Tom's body.

Questions of sexuality abound in the novel, perhaps reflecting the tumultuous nature of the bisexual Highsmith's personal life. It is suggested that Tom's attraction to Dickie or other handsome men goes beyond mere admiration. When the subject comes up between them, Tom and Dickie vehemently deny they are "queer." By his thoughts and deeds, Tom seems almost asexual: Though he appreciates her attractive features and figure, he expresses contempt for Marge, treats her cruelly, and considers killing her, and he murders Dickie. Though he may form a long-lasting relationship (as he does in later books), it is evident that the only person he truly loves is himself.

The novel weaves together several threads: the slippery nature of identity, alienation from society, and dependence upon self. Identity, as Tom aptly demonstrates, is simply a matter of perspective: If one believes one is who one claims to be, one can convince others to believe it, too. Deception is a matter, not of putting on a disguise, but of adopting an attitude. Ultimately, people such as Tom, with much to answer for, succumb to paranoia and withdraw from the mainstream, unable to fully trust anyone else, deaf to all but the voices that echo in their own heads.

Jack Ewing

Further Reading

Harrison, Russell. *Patricia Highsmith*. New York: Twayne, 1997. An entry in the United States Authors series, which is aimed at advanced high school students and up, this critical interpretation and discussion of the author's work includes a brief biography, a time line of events, an index, and a bibliography.

Highsmith, Patricia. *Plotting and Writing Suspense Fiction*. Reprint. New York: St. Martin's Griffin, 2001. A manual of tips, techniques, and advice for would-be suspense writers, based on Highsmith's experience in plotting and story development, spiced with incidents from her own life and the author's pungent philosophy.

Mawer, Noel. *Critical Study of the Fiction of Patricia Highsmith: From the Psychological to the Political*. Studies in American Literature 65. Lewiston, N.Y.: Edwin Mellen Press, 2004. This analysis of the author's work employs both cultural and personal analyses to examine psychological themes found in Highsmith's short and long fiction.

Meaker, Marijane. *Highsmith: A Romance of the Fifties*. San Francisco: Cleis Press, 2003. An intimate and not particularly flattering portrait of the author by one of Highsmith's former lovers; told against the backdrop of the lesbian culture of the 1950's.

Schenkar, Joan. *The Talented Miss Highsmith: The Secret Life and Serious Art of Patricia Highsmith*. New York: St. Martin's Press, 2009. This biography gives a full portrait of the writer, with contributions from her work, her private papers, and her friends.

Smith, Andrew. *Beautiful Shadow: A Life of Patricia Highsmith*. New York: Penguin Bloomsbury, 2004. A biography based on Highsmith's diaries, notebooks, and letters that illuminates the author's life in relation to her work, and vice versa.

Tuss, Alex. "Masculine Identity and Success: A Critical Analysis of Patricia Highsmith's *The Talented Mr. Ripley* and Chuck Palahniuk's *Fight Club*." *Journal of Men's Studies* 12, no. 2 (January 1, 2004): 93-103. Compares Highsmith's novel to Palahniuk's, examining each author's representation of the relationship between masculinity and material success.

Tales of Ise

Author: Unknown
First published: Ise monogatari, tenth century (English translation, 1968)
Type of work: Short fiction
Type of plot: Love
Time of plot: Ninth century
Locale: Japan

Principal characters:
THE NARRATOR, a man who loves love
HIS WIFE, the daughter of Aritsune
VARIOUS WOMEN

The Story:

Not too many years after the capital is moved from Nara to Kyoto, in 794, there lives a man who loves love. Shortly after his maturity rite (which at that time was usually at the age of eleven) and when the boy grows four and a half feet tall, the youth goes falcon hunting at Kasuga in the former capital. There he happens to see two beautiful sisters and sends them a poem. The poem begins the description of the love life of this man. Later, he meets and begins to visit a performer in the imperial court. When their love affair is exposed, the woman is made unavailable by the simple expediency of placing her in service at court where, in 866, she becomes the consort of the Emperor Seiwa.

Tiring of life in the capital, the man goes on a trip to eastern Japan, but he goes no farther than the border of Ise and Owari Provinces when he becomes homesick and composes poems to express his nostalgia. He meets an itinerant priest, sees Mount Fuji for the first time, and composes a poem. Entering the province of Musashi, at the Sumida River that runs through present-day Tokyo, he composes a celebrated poem of nostalgia concerning the oystercatcher birds. In Musashi he also meets and is attracted to various women. Later he wanders through the region to the northeast, where he makes love to the local country women.

Friends since early childhood, the man and the daughter of Aritsune eventually marry, but Narihira does not long remain faithful to her. Scattered through the episodes, however, are hints that cause the reader to believe that she manages to draw him back to her after each infidelity.

In another story, there is the eternal triangle involving two men and one woman, with the usual tragic results. The woman in this case waits three years for the return of a man who leaves to make his fortune in the capital. Meanwhile, she is courted by a second man, who finally wins her promise of marriage. The first man, returning on the wedding night, learns what happened during his absence and leaves the woman with his blessing. Following him, she loses her life.

There is, in another story, a weakling son of good family and a household maid. In another, a young woman is in love but too shy to make her feelings known. She dies with her love unrequited as a result. Two faithless people have an affair, each sends the other poems charging the other with faithlessness. A beloved wife has a husband who is so busy with his duties at court that she feels neglected and goes with another man to the country. Eventually the husband is appointed an imperial emissary to an important shrine and there meets the woman, who is by then the wife of a country official. She realizes her mistake and becomes a nun. There is the story of an elderly woman, the mother of three sons, who is amorously starved but too diffident to say so openly, so she tells her sons of her craving as something she dreamed. The third son alone is sympathetic to his mother's plight, and he arranges for her to meet the handsome narrator.

From the earliest times it was the custom for the emperor to appoint through divination an unmarried imperial princess to serve as the head priest at important shrines. In the narrator's time the head priest of the great shrine of Ise is Princess Yasuko, second daughter of Emperor Montoku. Her appointment, made in 859, lasts until 876. Sometime after her appointment, there appears in Ise a handsome inspector in the guise of a falcon hunter. The priest, having received word of his arrival on official matters, greets him with special kindness; the meeting leads to their falling in love with each other. For the sake of discretion she waits until nighttime before paying him a visit, and she leaves long before dawn. That same morning a messenger arrives from her with a poem, the gist of which is "Did you come to see me last night, or was it I who went to see you? I do not remember. Nor do I know whether it was all a dream, or was real."

The narrator replies with another poem setting a tryst for that evening, but the governor of the province gives an all-night banquet; thus the narrator's plans are thwarted. On the following day it is necessary for him to continue his tour of inspection. The lovers part, promising each other in poems to meet again, somewhere, sometime.

So the stories of love go, ending with the poem that might be roughly translated "Long have I known/ That this last journey must be made,/ But little did I know/ That it might be so soon."

Critical Evaluation:

The *Tales of Ise* belongs to a Heian period (794-1186) genre that is referred to in Japanese as *uta monogatari* (poem tales). Most of the Japanese poetry of this period was short, usually only five lines adding up to a total of approximately thirty-one syllables. These were often occasional poems for which a headnote might clarify the subject or detail the circumstances of composition. In the poem tale, such as the *Tales of Ise*, the compiler or compilers created prose settings for the poems or for groups of poems. In some cases these settings were completely unrelated to the actual circumstances of the poems' composition. Sometimes groups of episodes might be centered on the same character or similar situations, but there was no overall unity to the narrative. Thus *Tales of Ise* is within its genre in having no narrative that may be summarized with much coherence. The narrator's presence in much of the book is the source of what unity it possesses.

The poem tale has some similarities to another genre of the period, the imperial anthology of poetry. These were anthologies commissioned by emperors and edited by the leading poets of the day. The longest section of an imperial anthology was the five books devoted to love poetry. This section describes a typical love affair from the first meeting to the inevitably unhappy ending. Thus the editor of the anthology used the selected poetry to craft a portrait of an aesthetic ideal in the courtly life of the Heian period. The *Tales of Ise* has no such organizing principle. The only link between many of the episodes is the unidentified hero, a "certain person," the "man of old," who is gallant, elegant, charming, and above all witty. The *Tales of Ise* does go much further than the anthology in anchoring its portraits of love in a realistic world populated by realistic people. In this sense the poem tale can be seen as bridging the gap between poetry and the great flourishing of the novel that would soon take place in Japan. This flowering culminated in the greatest achievement of classical Japanese literature, Lady Murasaki Shikibu's *Genji monogatari* (c. 1004; *The Tale of Genji*, 1925-1933).

The exact origin or authorship of the *Tales of Ise* is unknown. Considering the lack of organizing principle, it seems likely that the *Tales of Ise* is the product of several authors over some period of time. Certain groups of episodes form short biographical sketches focusing on events in the life of Ariwara no Narihira (825-880), however, so there is speculation that these episodes may have been the original core of the work.

The fragmentary structure of the poem tale makes it nearly impossible to pinpoint any single theme in this work. However, a careful reading of the *Tales of Ise* can provide one of the clearest statements of the ideal of courtly elegance that was so important to Heian culture. For this reason this collection of subtle little vignettes was one of the most influential works in traditional Japanese literature. In spite of the lack of a theme, there is an unmistakable tone to the work.

The work shows a great sensitivity to beauty, a sensitivity that is tinged with grief over beauty's passing and the passing of time. This tone is an essential part of the aesthetics of Japanese literature in the Heian period. A good example of this sensitivity can be found in a famous episode from the *Tales of Ise* in which a young man, presumably Narihira, has been visiting a certain woman who was in service to the Empress. Suddenly the lady has been moved away. Although he knows where she is, he cannot visit her. In the early spring of the next year, when the plum trees are in bloom, the young man visits the place where he originally met the young lady. Unable to recapture the past, he is overcome with grief and composes this poem: "Is this not the moon?/ This spring, is it not the/ spring of old?/ Myself alone, only I/ am the same as before." The poem suggests metaphysical interpretation in a way that is unusual for Japanese poetry of this period. The nuances are difficult to capture in translation, but the poem first asks the rhetorical question: Are not the moon and the spring different this year? They are not, but since they appear so different, perhaps it is the author who has changed. The overall impressions from the poem are of time passing, uncertainty, and subjectivity. From the context, the subject is grief over the end of a brief but intense love affair. Perhaps more than any other single poem in the work, this poem forms the clearest statement of what might be called a theme in the *Tales of Ise*.

Love is the thread that unites most of the episodes in the *Tales of Ise*, but often it is the art of poetry that forms the real subject matter. Later generations looked on the *Tales of Ise* almost as a poetic guide, a "how to" manual for the elegant courtier and his lady, each pursuing their numerous affairs. Of course, since Japanese poetry is such a highly conventional verse form, often poems were only slight variations on common themes or images. In later times borrowing became formalized as poets would take two or three lines from a well-known poem and give them a new twist by adding several lines of new composition. Eventually much of the sentiment that is expressed in the poetry of the *Tales of Ise* would become nothing more than trite convention. In the *Tales of Ise*, however, there is still a sense of freshness that provides much of the charm for this pivotal work in traditional Japanese literature.

"Critical Evaluation" by Jon W. La Cure

Further Reading

Carter, Steven. D. "Claiming the Past for the Present: Ichijo-Kaneyoshi and *Tales of Ise*." In *Rhetoric and the Discourses of Power in Court Culture: China, Europe, and Japan*, edited by David R. Knechtges and Eugene Vance. Seattle: University of Washington Press, 2005. Carter describes how Ichijo-Kaneyoshi, a fifteenth century Japanese court regent and patron of the arts, influenced the reception of the work.

Harris, H. Jay, trans. Introduction to *The Tales of Ise*. Rutland, Vt.: Charles E. Tuttle, 1972. This translation also has a running commentary on each episode. The introduction gives background information and summarizes the speculations about the origins and authorship of the text.

Keene, Donald. *Seeds in the Heart: Japanese Literature from Earliest Times to the Late Sixteenth Century*. New York: Henry Holt, 1993. Gives a picture of the probable circumstance of the composition of the *Tales of Ise*, the text as it is now, and other poem tales of the period.

McCullough, Helen Craig. *Tales of Ise: Lyrical Episodes*

from Tenth-Century Japan. Stanford, Calif.: Stanford University Press, 1968. This complete translation of the work is scholarly and readable. There is a lengthy introduction to the *Tales of Ise* and to the poetry and poets of the early Heian period.

Mostow, Joshua S. "Modern Constructions of *Tales of Ise*: Gender and Courtliness." In *Inventing the Classics: Modernity, National Identity, and Japanese Literature*, edited by Haruo Shirane and Tomi Suzuki. Stanford, Calif.: Stanford University Press, 2000. Mostow examines how interpretations of *Tales of Ise* have responded to Japan's changing fortunes since the nineteenth century, demonstrating that gender played a central role in the poem's reception.

Okada, H. Richard. *Figures of Resistance: Language, Poetry, and Narrating in "The Tale of Genji" and Other Mid-Heian Texts*. Durham, N.C.: Duke University Press, 1991. Has a chapter devoted to the *Tales of Ise* that deals with the political and social background of the work.

Tahara, Mildred M., trans. Introduction to *Tales of Yamato: A Tenth Century Poem-Tale*. Honolulu: University Press of Hawaii, 1980. This translation of another major tenth century poem tale has a short introduction and a succinct history of Japanese literature in an appendix.

Tales of Odessa

Author: Isaac Babel (1894-1940)
First published: Odesskie rasskazy, 1931 (English translation, 1955)
Type of work: Short fiction
Type of plot: Comic realism
Time of plot: Early twentieth century
Locale: Moldavanka district, Odessa, Russia

Principal characters:
BENYA KRIK, a criminal boss
DVOIRA, his sister
ZILYA EICHBAUM, his first wife
SENDER EICHBAUM, a rich Jewish merchant, Zilya's father
RUBIN OSIPOVICH TARTAKOVSKY, a rich Jewish merchant
JOSEPH MUGINSTEIN, his clerk
FROIM GRACH, a criminal boss
BASYA GRACH, his daughter, and Benya's second wife
LYUBKA SCHNEIWEISS, an innkeeper

The Story:

Benya Krik is the boss of the Jewish criminals in Moldavanka, a district in Odessa, Russia. One day, he writes to Sender Eichbaum, a rich Jewish merchant in town, demanding twenty thousand rubles. After Eichbaum ignores the attempt at extortion, Krik and his accomplices raid Eichbaum's property and begin killing his cows. Eichbaum rushes outside to try to stop the killing, and so does his daughter Zilya, wearing only a low-cut blouse. Eichbaum pays Krik to go away, but two days later the gangster returns, returns the money, and asks to marry Zilya. After some persuasion, Eichbaum consents.

A new police chief has resolved to raid Krik's house on the day the gangster's forty-year-old sister, Dvoira, plans to marry. A groom had to be bought with the money Krik extorted from Eichbaum because Dvoira is forty years old and has a goiter. On the day of the wedding, a messenger brings Krik the news of the impending raid. Krik and a few friends leave the wedding for half an hour and then return. The lavish wedding feast is soon interrupted by smoke from the burning police station.

A local rabbi explains how Krik was named king of the Moldavanka gangsters. As a young man, Krik asked to join the gang of Froim Grach, then the leader of Odessa's Jewish underworld. As a test, Grach had told him to rob the rich merchant Rubin Osipovich Tartakovsky, who was so powerful that he had been nicknamed Jew-and-a-half. The story continues: Krik first writes a threatening letter demanding money. Tartakovsky's humorous reply goes astray. Angered by a lack of response, Krik robs Tartakovsky's factory, in the course of which one of the thieves, Savka Butris, kills clerk Joseph Muginstein.

Although Muginstein's death is ultimately Krik's fault, Tartakovsky is made to pay Muginstein's mother five thousand rubles as compensation; Krik also grants her a pension for life. He also arranges an extravagant funeral for both Muginstein and Butris, who is killed either by Krik or by a member of his gang. At the funeral, Krik delivers a brief and somewhat incoherent eulogy, then drives off in his red car. Someone watching the proceedings pronounces Krik the king for his bravado and grand gestures, and the title stuck.

Grach's daughter Basya returns to her father after spending her first twenty years with her grandmother. She wants to marry Solomonchik Kaplun, the son of a grocer, but Solomonchik's parents insist that he marry a grocer's daughter. Grach asks Lyubka Schneiweiss, the innkeeper, her advice about whom his daughter should marry. She recommends that Basya marry the already-married Krik. When Krik at last emerges, the two men arrange the wedding, which includes making the Kapluns pay two thousand rubles toward Basya's dowry.

Critical Evaluation:

The four stories of *Tales of Odessa* first appeared in various journals between 1921 and 1924. Isaac Babel continued to write other pieces using the same characters and settings; the last of these works was not published until 1964. These tales recount adventures among the Jewish underworld of the Moldavanka district of the port city of Odessa in the period just before the 1917 Russian Revolution.

In "Odessa" (1916), Babel contrasts the gloom of St. Petersburg's authors with the sunlight of Nikolai Gogol's Ukrainian stories. In the collection *Tales of Odessa*, Babel, emulating Gogol, presents a world filled with color that reflects the vividness of the city and its inhabitants. Human sweat is the color of blood. Basya wears an orange dress; Benya Krik goes courting in an orange suit. The sun is pink or purple, and the sky turns as red as a red-letter day. Froim Grach has red hair, and Krik drives a red car. Lyubka's son has legs the color of raspberries. The gangsters look like hummingbirds in their suits. Even the dead Muginstein turns green as grass.

Babel's Odessa resembles the land of Cockaigne, an imaginary place of luxury. At Dvoira's wedding, the guests enjoy turkeys, chicken, geese, fish, fish soup, rum, cigars, and oranges. The guests reciprocate by throwing money, rings, and necklaces onto golden trays waiting to receive their tributes. Dvoira sits on a mountain of pillows. Sixty chanters sing at Joseph Muginstein's funeral, which is attended by hundreds, perhaps thousands, of mourners. Everything and everyone is larger than life. Rubin Osipovich Tartakovsky is taller than the biggest police officer and fatter than the heaviest Jewish woman. Basya herself weighs more than 180 pounds.

Drawing on both Gogol and traditional Jewish humor,

Babel writes about the underdog, the schlemiel. Whereas Sholem Aleichem and other Jewish writers of the period show the misfortunes that beset such a character, Babel's underdogs triumph. For example, when Tartakovsky is pursued during a pogrom, a group of Jews going to a funeral take a machine gun from a coffin and disperse the anti-Semites. When police threaten to arrest Krik, he and his gang burn down the police station. In these comic tales, Jewish defeat invariably turns to victory. In a world of pogroms and anti-Semites, Babel creates a topsy-turvy world in which a Jew is king.

Babel's Jews are not rabbis, scholars, or martyrs, and they are not poor tradesmen like Aleichem's Tevya the milkman. Rather, Babel's Jews emerge as crafty and powerful figures who act as a law unto themselves. Because the rich, proud Kapluns insult Basya Grach, they must contribute two thousand rubles to her dowry. Without recourse to the legal system, Krik makes amends for Savka Butris's killing of Muginstein. Most of the luxuries at Dvoira's wedding feast are contraband, as are the provisions at Lyubka's inn.

Heightening the humor of the characters and their adventures is Babel's style. Names can be funny: Lyubka's last name, Schneiweiss, means "snow white," a multilevel irony given her behavior and underworld associates. *Krik* means "yell." Babel's metaphors, too, are comic, as when he likens the newly married Dvoira and her groom to a cat and mouse.

Even the manner in which the stories are told enhances the comedy. Though only one story, "How Things Were Done in Odessa," contains an internal narrator, all rely on devices of orality, such as digression, repetition, and interpolated tales. Babel introduces typical Yiddish phrases and jokes, as when Krik tells Grach to stop wasting time smearing kasha (groats) on the table, a metaphor for pointless arguing. In that same story, Krik apologizes to Muginstein's mother by noting that even God makes mistakes. It would have been better for God to have put the Jews in Switzerland rather than in Russia, where they are persecuted. Meticulously crafted, the stories that make up *Tales of Odessa* are masterpieces of the short-story genre.

Joseph Rosenblum

Further Reading

Bloom, Harold, ed. *Isaac Babel*. Philadelphia: Chelsea House, 2004. A collection of essays that examines Babel's work. Includes a biographical introduction by Bloom and discussion of Babel's melding of art and reality in his writings. Part of Bloom's Major Short Story Writers series.

Carden, Patricia. *The Art of Isaac Babel*. Ithaca, N.Y.: Cornell University Press, 1972. Offers close readings of the stories. Less biographically oriented than James E. Fallen's 1974 study, *Isaac Babel*.

Ehre, Milton. *Isaac Babel*. Boston: Twayne, 1986. Surveys Babel's life and literary output. Includes an annotated bibliography of criticism.

Fallen, James E. *Isaac Babel: Russian Master of the Short Story*. Knoxville: University of Tennessee Press, 1974. Linking Babel's writings and life, Fallen places the stories within the context of Jewish and modernist literature.

Freidin, Gregory, ed. *The Enigma of Isaac Babel: Biography,*

History, Context. Stanford, Calif.: Stanford University Press, 2009. This collection of scholarly essays examines Babel's life and art, the first work to do so "since the fall of communism and the opening of Soviet archives." Includes a preface, notes, and an index.

Hallett, Richard. *Isaac Babel*. New York: Frederick Ungar, 1973. A critical biography tracing Babel's development as a writer.

Mendelsohn, Danuta. *Metaphor in Babel's Short Stories*. Ann Arbor, Mich.: Ardis, 1982. A study of Babel's use of language.

Tales of Soldiers and Civilians

Author: Ambrose Bierce (1842-1914?)
First published: 1891
Type of work: Short fiction

Ambrose Bierce wrote volumes of acid, satirical prose in his long career as a journalist and even managed to get a somewhat pretentious twelve-volume edition of his collected works published. Most of it, because of its time-bound nature, was doomed to oblivion by the time the edition appeared. One of his works that continues to survive is the collection of short stories titled *Tales of Soldiers and Civilians*. Bierce's literary reputation rests largely on this book.

The bland title of the collection stands in ironic contrast to the vision of life that informs the stories themselves. Indeed, Bierce seems to have attached bland, noncommittal titles to most of his stories intentionally. Titles such as "Chickamauga," "An Occurrence at Owl Creek Bridge," and "The Mocking-Bird" tell little of the macabre nature of these tales. Bierce seems to have chosen his mild titles with deliberate irony. When this volume was reprinted in 1898, it was given a more meaningful title, *In the Midst of Life*. The irony is clearer and more indicative of the true content of the book: In the midst of life is death.

Death is the sole absolute of this book, the common denominator of each story, and the final proposition in a logic of ruthless necessity. Each protagonist is part of a greater logic; each is subordinate to the plot, and each is cursed. Death is separated from life, is raised up as a separate principle antagonistic to life, and becomes an entity in its own right. Death is seen as a hostile specter rather than as a normal part of life. As such, death seeks to conquer life rather than to aid it. Death then becomes an inevitable victor that "has all seasons for his own," as Bierce was fond of remarking.

Against such a powerful antagonist, the heroes become victims in a web of cruel necessity, shadow figures drawn into the Valley of the Shadow; as such, they are depicted with sharp, relentless strokes. Bierce's heroes are essentially lonely men who derive their reality from the fear they experience. These men are cursed and driven by the logic of their curses. Their strongest motivation is fear, an all-pervasive anxiety that frequently annihilates them. The success of each story depends on its ability to arouse this same fear in the reader.

In consequence, Bierce places a great value on courage in the face of death. He is acute enough, however, to see that courage is not so much fearlessness as it is a greater fear overcoming a lesser fear, in most cases a fear of dishonor overcoming a fear of death. Courage, then, is the faith that one's honor is more important than one's life. Frequently the heroes Bierce admires court death with an awesome recklessness. His heroes are inevitably damned. There is no escape, no transcendence, and no salvation from the macabre situations into which they are drawn. Their dooms are inescapable facts, and the measure of their manhood is expressed in how they meet death.

Bierce's vision of life is fatalistic, but there is more to it than that. Avenging Furies hover about his stories, but they are not the same Furies that haunted Orestes. Bierce is nihilistic, but inevitably there is a macabre humor in his nihilism. The acid, satirical touch that colors the rest of Bierce's work is present here as well. Bierce's Furies are diabolical jesters who love irony more than they love the wretched human spirit. His Furies are divine practical jokers who drum "Dixie" and "John Brown's Body" on the human skull for laughs. One can scarcely tell whether the shriek one senses in Bierce's prose is that of humor or that of horror.

Bierce's grotesque wit serves as a relief from the horror of his situations. A related technique that serves the same purpose is his ironic stance, one that removes him from the petty human scene and separates him from the terror of his heroes. Bierce assumes a godlike attitude that determines the objective nature of his prose. He uses a naturalistic style that is precise in diction, spare in depiction, and ironic in narration.

In effect, Bierce takes on the cruel role of the Furies in narrating his stories, and the tone of his prose is frigid, caustic, and inhuman. It is precisely this emotional sterility, this godlike irony, that makes his stories so powerfully chilling. If, for example, Bierce were to sympathize with his heroes, the reader would have pathos rather than terror. The very lack of an appropriate emotional response in the narration stimulates to an excessive degree the proper emotional response in the reader. The fact that Bierce himself was caustic, cruel, and sharp, demanding perfection of his fellow human beings, admirably served his limited artistic abilities and enabled him to focus his talent on evoking both terror and humor.

Tales of Soldiers and Civilians is, as the title suggests, divided into two parts: war stories and mystery stories. The two types of stories develop Bierce's vision of life in different literary directions. The war tales anticipate the work of Ernest Hemingway, while the civilian stories anticipate more modern horror-tale writers such as H. P. Lovecraft. Beyond a doubt, Bierce reached his artistic peak in the soldier tales. War stories provided the perfect medium for someone of his character and experience. First of all, Bierce had served in the U.S. Civil War, and undoubtedly his stories draw much of their vigor from his firsthand experience. His depictions of various battles and their effects have an unmistakable aura of reality. His description of war is hauntingly vivid and stands in marked contrast to the maudlin accounts found in the vast bulk of Civil War writings.

Second, war tales provided an acceptable outlet for Bierce's obsessions with fear, courage, and death. These leitmotifs could be presented naturally in tales of soldiers. Since war abounds in abnormal situations, Bierce could write naturally about a man killing his twin brother, about a son killing his father, and about an artilleryman killing his wife. In the context of their stories, these plots become necessary accidents, part of some divine causality. Third, Bierce's naturalistic style is admirably suited to describing the limited vision of the soldier in war, a vision that is not permitted the luxury of feeling pity and that must avoid all contemplation. It is a vision, moreover, that must concentrate on immediate objectives and on carrying out specific orders. Finally, the army subjugates individuals to the mass. Deeds of fear and courage are the only acts by which a soldier is individualized and judged. Bierce's characters draw their reality from the ways they face death. Each hero undergoes an ordeal, which means death either for him or for someone close to him, and that test determines his character. Apart from that ordeal, Bierce's characters are lifeless puppets dancing to meretricious plots.

Bierce's war stories are his best. Nowhere else did he achieve such a perfect fusion of form and content, except perhaps in his aphorisms. In quality, the tales are superior to nearly all of the other short fiction that was being written during the nineteenth century in the United States. In many instances, they anticipate or rival Hemingway's stories. Actually, many points of comparison can be drawn between Bierce and Hemingway: Both show obsession with fear, courage, and death; both use a crisp, ironic prose to communicate their vision; both find expression in stories of war; both present character tested through some ordeal; and both possess a cruel and evocative power—a power that at times gives their fiction a haunting quality as vivid as a nightmare. Bierce's war tales, particularly "Chickamauga," "An Occurrence at Owl Creek Bridge," "One Kind of Officer," and "Killed at Resaca," are first-rate for what they attempt to do.

His civilian stories, however, fall somewhat short of the high standards he achieves in his war tales. The reason for this diminished quality is that Bierce attempts to impose on his stories of civilians the same vision of life that pervades his soldier tales, and the grafting is not always successful. Pictures of war provide the perfect literary vehicle for his outlook, because war abounds in pathological situations. When he tries to impose this vision on civilian reality, however, the imperfections of plot, the implausibilities, and the grotesqueness show up much more glaringly. The trick endings do not come off nearly as successfully. The characters and plots never match those of the war stories. To inject a pathological fear into stories about civilians requires great skill. What Bierce did succeed in doing with the civilian stories was to extend the then relatively new prose genre of the short mystery tale. In this lesser genre, Bierce comes off rather well when compared with later writers working in this vein, and his stories continue to hold their own in the anthologies. Where Bierce is successful in turning his neuroses into fine artistic stories, he has few equals in suspense, evocative power, clarity, and irony.

Further Reading

Blume, Donald T. *Ambrose Bierce's Civilians and Soldiers in Context: A Critical Study*. Kent, Ohio: Kent State University Press, 2004. Presents analysis of each of the nineteen stories in the collection and points out the interrelated meanings and themes in the tales.

Davidson, Cathy N., ed. *Critical Essays on Ambrose Bierce*. Boston: G. K. Hall, 1982. Collection of essays on Bierce's work includes early criticism written by H. L. Mencken and Van Wyck Brooks.

Knight, Melinda. "Cultural Radicalism in the American Fin de Siècle: Cynicism, Decadence, and Dissent." *Connecticut Review* 14 (Spring, 1992): 65-75. Shows how Bierce and several other marginalized "aesthetes and decadents" repudiated values held by cultural and business leaders in the 1890's. Notes how Bierce attacked democracy, genteel realism, prudery, and would-be reformers.

Morris, Roy, Jr. *Ambrose Bierce: Alone in Bad Company*. New York: Crown, 1995. Objective biography interweaves Bierce's writings with an account of his life, pointing out the parallels between the unhappiness of that life and Bierce's dark literary vision.

Owens, David M. *The Devil's Topographer: Ambrose Bierce and the American War Story*. Knoxville: University of Tennessee Press, 2006. Examines Bierce's twenty-two war stories, demonstrating how they reflect his participation in the Civil War and his development as a soldier rather than as a writer. Also assesses Bierce's contributions to American short fiction.

Woodruff, Stuart C. *The Short Stories of Ambrose Bierce: A Study in Polarity*. Pittsburgh, Pa.: University of Pittsburgh Press, 1964. Presents an informative introductory survey of Bierce's tales.

Tales of the South Pacific

Author: James A. Michener (1907?-1997)
First published: 1947
Type of work: Novel
Type of plot: Historical realism
Time of plot: 1942-1943
Locale: South Pacific islands

Principal characters:
THE COMMANDER, a U.S. Navy first lieutenant
TONY FRY, a first lieutenant (junior grade)
EMILE DE BECQUE, a French planter
LATOUCHE BARZAN, the Frenchman's daughter
BUS ADAMS, a Navy pilot
NELLIE FORBUSH, a Navy nurse
LUTHER BILLIS, a Navy construction battalion officer
JOE CABLE, a U.S. Marine lieutenant
BLOODY MARY, a Tonkinese entrepreneur
LIAT, her daughter

The Story:

American, British, and Australian naval and marine forces face life and death in the South Pacific during World War II. An American naval lieutenant, the Commander, observes and relates the stories of the Tonkinese, the officers, the nurses, and the enlisted men he encounters. Navy lieutenant Tony Fry involves himself in everything from dealing with the survivors of the *Bounty* crew, to providing whiskey to the troops, to cohabiting with the Tonkinese and eventually marrying one of them. His death on the beach at Kuralei is particularly hard for the Commander, who admires Tony and even envies him.

In "The Milk Run," Lieutenant Bus Adams, a daredevil pilot, describes spending seven hours on the water after being shot down during a cleanup mission. His rear gunner is killed, and he is under heavy bombardment from the Japanese. Upon hearing of Adams's plight, an admiral orders his immediate rescue regardless of the cost. The rescue, involving New Zealand and American pilots, bombers, fighters, and PT boats, eventually costs $600,000. Adams admits it is a lot of money but is truly grateful he is the beneficiary.

In "Those Who Fraternize," Adams is having a love affair with Latouche Barzan, one of four beautiful part-Javanese sisters and the daughter of a French plantation owner. Renowned for her lavish dinners and for entertaining the officers, she also is independent and freethinking. When Tony Fry arrives at the plantation, Latouche falls in love with him. Bus is heartbroken but accepts the inevitable and also accepts her gift of another French woman. He then attends the wedding of Tony and Latouche.

"Our Heroine" concerns twenty-two-year-old Navy nurse Nellie Forbush from Little Rock, Arkansas. She earlier has deftly dealt with a married lothario intent on seducing her. In the New Hebrides, she and the other nurses are pursued by the officers and lusted after by the enlisted men. Numerous instances of rape and near rape are reported, as well as tales of heroes who defend the women.

Life changes for Nellie when she meets Emile De Becque, a French plantation owner. In spite of a twenty-year age difference, they are immediately attracted, and Emile decides she has been worth the wait. He proposes and she accepts. Then, she hears Bus Adams's story of "The Frenchman's Daughter." Emile has four grown daughters by Javanese, Polynesian, and Tonkinese mothers whom he never married. Shocked but not deterred, Nellie agrees to go with Emile to his plantation. There, she is introduced to four more daughters, ages seven to eleven, whose mothers were Tonkinese and Polynesian and whom Emile had not married.

Nellie is dumbstruck. Her southern heritage has taught her that, since these children are not white, they are taboo. She tells herself that she cannot marry a man who has slept with women of color and has children of color. Her heart is broken, and she asks Emile to drive her home, but she is finally convinced to stay for dinner, where she is enchanted by the girls' chatting and their manners. As she and Emile drive to her quarters, they are attacked by four would-be rapists. Emile overpowers them and gets Nellie home safely. Regretfully, she tells him that they can never marry.

Later that evening, Nellie confesses her doubts to another nurse, contemplates accepting a proposal from a boy back home, and finally reminds herself that she enlisted to learn to live with other people and see the world. She realizes how preposterous her prejudices have been and rushes to the plantation, Emile, and his daughters.

"Fo' Dolla'" recounts the relationship between Marine lieutenant Joe Cable, the Tonkinese beauty Liat whom he loves, and her enterprising mother Bloody Mary. Mary, whose nickname derives from the bloody-looking betal juice that has permanently stained her mouth, runs a kiosk at which she sells grass skirts, toy canoes, seashells, shrunken heads, and anything else she can convince the men to buy. Lieutenant Cable is ordered to shut down Mary's kiosk. Even

so, Mary is highly impressed with Joe, who is tall, lean, blond, attractive, and educated. He in turn finds her amusing and enterprising. Through Mary, Joe discovers the island of Bali-ha'i, where he meets Liat. With the assistance of Seabee (construction battalion) officer Luther Billis—an ubiquitous presence throughout the tales—Joe takes every opportunity to be with Liat on the island.

Mary implores Joe to marry her daughter, but, torn between his passion and the cultural mores engrained in him, he finally realizes he cannot overcome his prejudices. He volunteers for a duty that will take him into combat and away from the woman he loves but cannot marry. As a final token, Joe gives Liat a man's watch and convinces her to make love one last time. When he leaves, Mary hurls the watch to the ground, curses the lieutenant, and makes an obscene gesture. Liat is left to her fate as the wife of a short, fat, pompous, French plantation owner.

In "A Cemetery at Hoga Point," the Commander visits a plateau overlooking the sea where 281 fighting men are buried. Two black men serve as caretakers, and the Commander questions one of them about his position and the graveyard's occupants. In one of the graves lies Lieutenant Joe Cable. The caretaker provides details of Joe's turmoil after he left Liat and his death on a beachhead. Meanwhile, the war goes on.

Critical Evaluation:

James A. Michener, one of the United States' most prolific writers, began his career with the publication of <i>Tales of the South Pacific</i> in 1947. Although raised as a Quaker, he had a strong love of his country and joined the U.S. Navy in 1942. He was stationed in the South Pacific from 1944 to 1945. There, he observed and wrote about the natives, the islands, the fighting men, the romances, the prejudices, the battles, and the intrigues he witnessed.

While the book consists of nineteen short stories, the author deemed it a novel because of its continuity of characters, setting, and themes, particularly its focus on the ravages of prejudice. The Pulitzer Prize committee sidestepped the question and awarded Michener the five-hundred-dollar Pulitzer Prize in fiction in 1947.

Michener, an orphan, was taken in at about age three by Mabel Michener and raised with as many as eight other orphans. At one point, Michener lived in a poorhouse, and at fourteen he began hitchhiking across the United States, meeting people of all backgrounds. He never learned who his parents were, but he was accepted as a Michener and used that name and a false birth certificate to enlist in the Navy. After graduating from Swarthmore College and doing graduate research at numerous universities, Michener taught in Pennsylvania and Colorado. He then became an associate editor for the Macmillan Company.

It was World War II that changed Michener's life. Having been assigned to the Solomon Islands as a Navy lieutenant, he determined to bring his observations of courage, humor, and tragedy to the reading public. After *Tales of the South Pacific* was published to favorable—albeit few—reviews, composer Richard Rogers, lyricist Oscar Hammerstein II, director Josh Logan, and producer Leland Hayward offered the author five hundred dollars for the rights to produce a musical based on two of the tales. Michener refused the initial offer but settled, prophetically, for royalties from the play. *South Pacific* (pr., pb. 1949) was a smash hit and also won a Pulitzer Prize.

The two stories chosen for the musical were "Fo' Dolla'" and "Our Heroine," both of which center around ingrained racial prejudice. It was suggested by some viewers of the play that the antiracist song "You've Got to Be Carefully Taught" was not what audiences expected in a musical and should be cut. Hammerstein refused, and Michener thanked him for doing so.

As an avowed liberal, Michener abhorred prejudice, whether racial or sexual. He focused in his tales not only on the doubts of Nellie Forbush and Joe Cable but also on the situations faced by the women, both South Pacific islanders and American nurses, who are in danger of rape and other abuses. The indigenous peoples also are shown as being treated with contempt by the French plantation owners and some of the military personnel. In *Tales of the South Pacific*, this prejudice is countered by Nellie's decision to marry Emile, by Tony's marriage to the biracial Latouche, and by the characterization of Bloody Mary—one of the most memorable and likable of Michener's characters.

The Commander narrates thirteen of the nineteen tales in the novel. Realizing the Commander's limited access to all the stories he wished to tell, however, Michener changed point of view for the other six stories. Two of these are narrated by pilot Bus Adams and four are narrated in the third person. One of the third-person tales, "Our Heroine," is the story of Nellie and Emile. By switching point of view for this tale, Michener allows readers to witness the turmoil and anguish Nellie experiences as she faces her conflicting feelings for Emile and his biracial children.

Michener was an avid reader and admired Ernest Hemingway for his terse style and especially for his use of familiar rather than obscure words. Certainly, *Tales of the South Pacific* is written in a straightforward, readable style. Contrary to many later war novels, there is little cursing. In fact,

once the manuscript was submitted and accepted for publication, Michener was told by his English editor that "G.I. talk" was unacceptable. Therefore, substitutions for the offending words were found.

Although in his autobiography Michener decries the use of dialect in his novels, he does employ the rhetorical device in *Tales of the South Pacific*. For example, the final tale, "A Cemetery at Hoga Point," consists of a conversation between the Commander and a black grave keeper who speaks in heavy African American dialect. Bloody Mary and other natives also speak in dialect.

This debut novel is not replete with the lengthy details of history, flora, fauna, and other background features for which Michener later became renowned. It does, however, vividly portray what he witnessed in the South Pacific and provides readers with memorable characters and adventures. Michener did not begin his writing career until he was about forty, and he died in 1997. In the fifty or so years during which he was active, he published more than thirty novels, numerous nonfiction works, art critiques, and an extensive autobiography.

Josephine M. Lee

Further Reading

Day, A. Grove. *James Michener.* New York: Twayne, 1964. Reflections on Michener by his friend and the coauthor of *Rascals in Paradise* (1957). Contains a helpful chronology along with notes and references.

Hayes, John P. *James A. Michener: A Biography.* Indianapolis, Ind.: Bobbs-Merrill, 1984. Contains some interesting anecdotes about Michener's two years in the South Pacific, reaction to *Tales of the South Pacific*, and staging of the musical *South Pacific*.

May, Stephen J. *Michener: A Writer's Journey.* Norman: University of Oklahoma Press, 2005. Chapters 5-7, covering 1940-1949, center on the writing and staging of *Tales of the South Pacific*. The foreword is written by Ernest Hemingway's daughter-in-law and gives some insight into the relationship between the two authors.

Michener, James A. *James A. Michener's Writers' Handbook: Explorations in Writing and Publishing.* New York: Random House, 1992. Contains Michener's own extensive notes and guidelines on writing a novel and his autobiography. Also has a section of "Questions Most Frequently Asked by Would-Be Writers."

_____. *Literary Reflections.* Austin, Tex.: State House Press, 1993. A collection of previously written essays and two poems. Michener describes some of the people responsible for his love of literature and art. Four essays are devoted to famous writers, including Ernest Hemingway, Margaret Mitchell, Marcus Goodrich, and Truman Capote.

_____. *The World Is My Home: A Memoir.* New York: Random House, 1992. Michener's autobiography, published five years before his death. The first seven chapters cover his personal life and the second seven discuss his career. Provides interesting insights into his upbringing, his politics, and his writing style.

The Talisman

Author: Sir Walter Scott (1771-1832)
First published: 1825
Type of work: Novel
Type of plot: Historical
Time of plot: Twelfth century
Locale: The Holy Land

Principal characters:
KING RICHARD THE LION-HEARTED, the ruler of England
SIR KENNETH, the Knight of the Couchant Leopard
EL HAKIM SALARIN, a Muslim physician
THEODORICK OF ENGADDI, a hermit
QUEEN BERENGARIA, Richard's wife
LADY EDITH PLANTAGENET, Richard's kinswoman
CONRADE, the marquis of Montserrat
THE GRAND MASTER OF THE KNIGHTS TEMPLARS

The Story:

Sir Kenneth, the Knight of the Couchant Leopard, is one of the knights who follows King Richard the Lion-Hearted to the Holy Land during the Third Crusade. At the time, Richard is ill with a fever, and the Council of Kings and Princes has sent Kenneth on a mission to Theodorick of Engaddi, a religious hermit who acts as a go-between for both Christians and Muslims. Richard is not aware of the mission, for the other leaders in the Crusade are jealous of him and his power, and they resent his high-handed methods and his conceit. In the desert, Kenneth meets and fights with a Saracen, an infidel who does not know at first that Kenneth carries a pass from Saladin, the leader of the Muslims. Neither warrior is injured in the fight, and since at the time there is a truce between the Christians and the Muslims, they continue their journey together. The Saracen promises to conduct Kenneth to Theodorick's convent retreat.

Theodorick shows Kenneth a crypt containing a piece of the cross of Christ. As the knight kneels before the holy relic, a group of nuns, novices, and others living at the convent come into the holy place singing and strewing flowers. One of the robed ladies, King Richard's kinswoman Lady Edith Plantagenet, several times passes by him at his devotions, each time dropping a single rose at his side. Although she and Kenneth have never spoken, they love each other. Marriage is impossible for them, however, because Lady Edith is related to the English king and Kenneth is only a poor Scottish knight. Both his low birth and his nationality form a barrier between them, for England and Scotland are constantly at war. Edith is at the convent because she is one of the ladies attending Richard's wife, Queen Berengaria, who is on a pilgrimage to pray for the king's recovery.

Forcing himself to put Lady Edith out of his mind, Kenneth delivers his message to Theodorick, who promises to carry it to Saladin. When Kenneth returns to Richard's camp, he brings with him El Hakim, a Muslim physician. Saladin has sent this learned man to cure Richard's fever, for although the two rulers are enemies, they respect each other's valor and honor. El Hakim uses a talisman to make a potion that brings down the king's fever. Still weak but restored to health, Richard is grateful to Kenneth for bringing the physician but furious with him for acting as a messenger for the Council of Kings and Princes without his knowledge. Richard feels certain that the other leaders will soon withdraw from the Crusade, for the Christians are greatly outnumbered by the infidels. It will be impossible for Richard to continue the war with his small band of followers.

The other leaders are growing increasingly restless and dissatisfied. Two of them in particular wish to see Richard disgraced: Conrade, the marquis of Montserrat, wants to gain a principality in Palestine for himself, and the Grand Master of the Knights Templars wants Richard killed and out of the way. The other leaders merely want to give up the Crusade and return to their homes. Conrade's sly hints and slurs against Richard move the archduke of Austria to place his flag next to Richard's standard on the highest elevation in the camp. Learning of this act, Richard rises from his bed and, though still weak, tears down the archduke's flag and stamps on it. Then he orders Kenneth to guard the English flag and see to it that no other flag is placed near it.

Queen Berengaria has grown bored with life in the camp. She sends Kenneth a false message saying that Edith wants him to come to her tent. He is bewildered by the message and torn between his love for Edith and his duty to King Richard. At last, overwhelmed by love, he leaves his trusted dog on guard and walks to Edith's tent. There he overhears the plotters giggling over their joke. When Edith learns of the trick, she disclaims any part in it and sends Kenneth at once back to his post. There he finds the royal standard of England gone and his dog apparently on the verge of death.

El Hakim appears suddenly and says that he can cure the animal with his talisman. He also offers to take Kenneth to the Muslim camp to escape the king's wrath, but Kenneth refuses to run away. Instead, he confesses his desertion to Richard and is instantly condemned to death. Everyone tries to save him: The queen even confesses to the trick she played on him, but Richard will not be moved. Kenneth refuses to plead his own cause; he believes that he deserves to die for deserting his post. In preparation for his execution, he asks for a priest and makes his confession. Then El Hakim asks the king for a boon in return for saving the royal life with his talisman. He is granted the favor he requests: the privilege of taking Kenneth with him when he leaves Richard's camp. Kenneth is thus saved from death and becomes an outcast from the Christian camp.

The other leaders of the Crusade continue their scheming to rob Richard of his power. At last, the Grand Master persuades Conrade to join him in a plot to kill the king. They capture a dervish—a member of a wild tribe of desert nomads who are rabidly devout Muslims—disguise him, and send him, pretending to be drunk, to Richard's tent. The king's guards are lax, but one of the gifts that Saladin has sent the king, a mute Nubian slave, is extremely loyal to him. As the assassin raises his poniard to strike the king, the slave dashes him to the ground. In the scuffle, the Nubian receives an arm wound from the dagger. Richard knows that the knife's blade has probably been poisoned, and he sucks the slave's wound to save him from the poison's effects.

The grateful slave writes a note promising that if Richard will have all the leaders pass in review, he, the slave, can identify the one who stole the royal flag. The slave is, in reality, Kenneth in disguise. After curing Kenneth's dog, El Hakim had told the knight that the animal undoubtedly could identify his assailant. Richard agrees to the plan for seeking out the culprit, and as the suspected plotters pass by in review, the dog attacks Conrade of Montserrat. Conrade denies his guilt, but Richard declares that his innocence can be decided only by trial of arms. The king asks Saladin to choose a neutral ground for the match and courteously invites Saladin to be present at the combat to test Conrade's innocence or guilt.

At the place of combat, where Richard and Saladin meet for the first time without their battle armor, Saladin is revealed to be El Hakim. Richard confesses that he had known the slave to be Kenneth, whom he also names as the king's champion. In the fight, Conrade is seriously wounded and is hastily carried away by the Grand Master of the Knights Templars, who fears that Conrade will reveal the whole plot against the king. Richard then reveals to the queen and Lady Edith that Kenneth is really David, the earl of Huntingdon and prince royal of Scotland. The king has learned his true identity from one of Kenneth's retainers. The noble knight, having vowed not to reveal himself until the Crusaders have taken the Holy City, has refused to break his oath even to save his life.

The king promises to give Kenneth Edith's hand in marriage, although their betrothal belies Theodorick's earlier prophecy that Edith would marry Saladin. Abashed, the old hermit confesses that he interpreted the signs incorrectly. His vision had been that a kinswoman of the king would marry Richard's enemy in a Christian marriage. Theodorick had thought his vision meant that Saladin would be converted and marry Edith. The true prophecy was that the king's kinswoman would marry Kenneth, a Scot and thus an enemy of the English king; being Christians, they would have a Christian wedding.

At a noontime repast provided by Saladin in honor of his friends, Saladin kills the Grand Master of the Knights Templars because he has learned that the Grand Master, while bending over Conrade to hear his confession, stabbed Conrade with a dagger so that he could not confess the plot against Richard. Richard and Saladin both realize that the Crusade has failed and that the Christian forces can never hope to overcome the Saracens. The two men part as friends, each honoring the other's skill and valor. A short time later, Edith and Kenneth are married, and Kenneth receives the lucky talisman as a wedding gift from Saladin. Although the magic token later effects some cures in Europe, it never again has the power it had in the hands of the famous infidel.

Critical Evaluation:

The Talisman contains all the ingredients of a romantic adventure: faraway lands, love, mystery, chivalric courage, and daring. Sir Walter Scott weaves these ingredients together with his usual skill and brings the various subplots together in the final scenes. As is his custom, he makes history serve his own purposes by inventing characters and situations and blending them with real people and historical events. The result is a masterful combination of fact and fiction that makes it possible for readers to ignore any discrepancies and simply enjoy the well-told tale.

The Talisman functions very effectively as entertainment, but it also operates on a more important level of expression. Throughout his life, Scott was committed to moral truth; he chose the historical novel as the medium for his artistic expression because the genre encompasses the facts of time as well as the truths of morality that endure the tests of time. Furthermore, he was a thoroughly eighteenth century man, concerned with the triumph of reason over passion and with proper conduct in an orderly society. These are the elements that inform *The Talisman*.

Using a particular historical period as the framework for each of his novels, Scott seeks to reveal an era or a way of life representative of that particular period and to demonstrate the relationship between past and present, thereby pointing out attitudes, conflicts, and behavior common to all human beings at all stages of history. To create the historical setting, Scott introduces a character who embodies the period or manner of life with which the novel is concerned, thus avoiding unnecessary detail. In *The Talisman*, King Richard represents the chivalric code and way of life as it was known in England during the Middle Ages. Richard also represents the excess pride and imprudence that can infect anyone, which shows that certain attitudes, weaknesses, and behavior patterns are universal to humankind. Similarly, Sir Kenneth represents the seeker of order and honor through proper conduct. Saladin, although a pagan, symbolizes the object of Sir Kenneth's quest. Clearly, Scott's approach to history relies less on facts than on general historical context. He realized that a reader required more than fact and that reality must be altered and improved to correspond with the desire for unexpected developments. Scott did not abuse history, as he has sometimes been accused of doing, but he made use of it as narrative fiction demanded.

Scott's dual purpose in *The Talisman* is at once to reveal the decadence of the chivalric code and to determine if there is intrinsic value in it. To this end, King Richard the Lion-Hearted symbolizes chivalry, its ceremony, and its power over individuals. This power has become tainted, however, as

evidenced by Richard's impetuosity and prideful acts; he represents the fanaticism that blocks clear, rational thought. Honor, as represented in Richard, has become an empty ritual, arising from rashness rather than judicious thought and conduct. Moreover, the presence of such evil forces as the Grand Master and the marquis of Montserrat further demonstrates the degenerate state of the chivalric order.

To illustrate this deterioration most clearly, an antithetical figure, Saladin, is presented as a basis for comparison. He represents the rationality, fidelity, and compassion that are missing in the Crusaders' camp. Saladin does not symbolize a code, but rather the honor that evolves from the organic growth of right conduct nourished by the use of reason and common sense. The character who experiences the influences of both forces and must choose between them is Sir Kenneth, who occupies the middle ground. From the beginning, he is susceptible to the positive influence of Saladin, as is required for the young knight's structural role. Already schooled in the chivalric code and displaying the narrow vision that brings with it, Kenneth meets Saladin, disguised as Sheerkohf, in a duel and emerges victorious in might but not in honor. Afterward, Kenneth doubts the Saracen's sincerity in offering peace between them. When Saladin convinces him of the earnestness of his pledge, the "confidence of the Muslim" makes Kenneth "ashamed of his own doubts." Thereafter, Saladin's wisdom, rationality, and sense of honor affect Kenneth's development.

Saladin's impact on Sir Kenneth succeeds largely through the Saracen's many disguises. Just as King Richard's irrational interpretation of the chivalric code holds sway over the young knight principally for reasons of rank, so too Saladin's influence is an artificial imposition because of his sovereignty. It is Scott's purpose to show that reason, prudence, and moral conduct must grow organically from within the individual rather than be imposed by external forces or rituals. Scott illustrates this truth in disguising Saladin as El Hakim, the wise Muslim healer. In this role, Saladin appears as a more common individual, like Kenneth, and one who has objectively witnessed the course of events leading to the young knight's conviction and impending execution. The Saracen tries to reason with Kenneth, pointing out that it is foolish to die for a crime of which he is not entirely guilty. In any case, the knight's guilt is to some extent the result of Richard's pride, which has created the precariousness of the situation in the first place. Kenneth ignores the Saracen's advice, and it is his irrational adherence to the code of honor based on ritual, not careful thought and action, that induces El Hakim to bargain with Richard and his rash pride for the young knight's life. The Saracen's wise and compassionate intervention enables him to convince Kenneth later that it is more practical to stay alive and redeem himself and his reputation by revealing the real culprit to King Richard and to the entire camp.

Shortly thereafter, when El Hakim spurs Kenneth and himself away from the attacking band of Templars in the desert, the Saracen demonstrates to Sir Kenneth that more good can be gained in living and accomplishing their positive goals than in dying foolishly at the hands of the traitorous Templars. When El Hakim becomes identified with Sheerkohf, a character with whom Kenneth can relate more closely because of their previous relationship, Kenneth begins to recognize the value of Saladin's code of honor, based more positively on reason, common sense, and prudent action. Sheerkohf convinces Kenneth that he is free to choose whatever path he wishes to follow, either to wander off aimlessly or to move forward in seeking his redemption. As Sheerkohf unfolds his plan to disguise Sir Kenneth as a mute Ethiopian slave and thus secretly to infiltrate the Crusaders' camp and reveal the real thief of England's banner, the young knight this time chooses to follow the Saracen's advice. He is beginning to absorb the value derived from reason and prudence and to appreciate the efficacy of judicious thought and self-restrained action. From this point on, the positive resolution of the conflict is inevitable.

Richard seems to learn the lessons of prudence and self-restraint, and the victorious Sir Kenneth enjoys his rewards: the announcement of his real identity and sovereignty and the hand of Lady Edith Plantagenet in marriage. The positive influence of Saladin's character becomes clear as he is identified by all concerned with his various disguises and his valuable deeds; his impact is apparent also in Kenneth's potential as a great leader, for the young knight has matured largely because of Saladin's influence. As a final act in the story, the talisman—essentially the symbol of reason, order, and correct conduct—is transferred from East to West, from pagan to Christian, to carry on the magical curative work that it had already begun. This somewhat ironic turn reaffirms Scott's belief that human beings, regardless of origin, share a common nature throughout history and that reason and order in society, by exposing the imprudence of outdated codes such as chivalry, transcend the boundaries of race, creed, nationality, and time.

"Critical Evaluation" by Larry K. Bright

Further Reading

D'Arcy, Julian Meldon. *Subversive Scott: The Waverley Novels and Scottish Nationalism.* Reykjavík, Iceland: Vigdís Finnbogadóttir Institute of Foreign Languages, University of Iceland, 2005. Demonstrates how Scott's novels contain dissonant elements, undetected manifestations of Scottish nationalism, and criticism of the United Kingdom and its imperial policy.

Hayden, John O., ed. *Walter Scott: The Critical Heritage.* New York: Barnes & Noble, 1970. Collection of essays includes information on the initial critical reception of *The Talisman.* Provides reviews dating from 1805 to an 1883 article on Scott written by Mark Twain.

Irvine, Robert P. "The State, the Domestic, and National Culture in the Waverley Novels." In *Enlightenment and Romance: Gender and Agency in Smollett and Scott.* New York: Peter Lang, 2000. Analyzes the fiction of Scott and Tobias Smollett within the context of the emergence of the social sciences and the dominance of novels written by female authors in the eighteenth century. Describes how Smollett and Scott adapted the feminine romance and the domestic novel to assert control over the narrative structure of their novels.

Johnson, Edgar. *Sir Walter Scott: The Great Unknown.* 2 vols. New York: Macmillan, 1970. Extensively researched biography explores Scott both as a man and as a writer. Provides a reading of *The Talisman* that focuses on Scott's misrepresentation of history and historical figures. An excellent introductory source.

Lincoln, Andrew. *Walter Scott and Modernity.* Edinburgh: Edinburgh University Press, 2007. Examines Scott's novels and poems, arguing that these were not works of nostalgia; instead, Scott used the past as a means of exploring modernist moral, political, and social issues. Includes discussion of *The Talisman.*

Shaw, Harry E., ed. *Critical Essays on Sir Walter Scott: The Waverley Novels.* New York: G. K. Hall, 1996. Collection of essays published between 1858 and 1996 discusses the series of novels that includes *The Talisman.* Walter Bagehot's 1858 article addresses Scott's rationalism, his subversion of the literary form in his fiction, and what his work meant to Victorian readers. Caroline McCracken-Flesher's essay "Recuperation of Cannon Fodder: Walter Scott's *The Talisman*" examines this novel.

Talley Family Saga

Author: Lanford Wilson (1937-   )
First produced: 1978-1981; includes *Fifth of July*, 1978; *Talley's Folly*, 1979; *Talley and Son*, 1981 (as *A Tale Told*); first published, *Fifth of July*, 1978 (revised, 1982); *Talley's Folly*, 1979; *Talley and Son*, 1986
Type of work: Drama
Type of plot: Psychological realism
Time of plot: July 4, 1944, *Talley's Folly* and *Talley and Son*; July 4/5, 1977, *Fifth of July*
Locale: Lebanon, Missouri

Principal characters:
CALVIN STUART TALLEY, the family patriarch
CHARLOTTE "LOTTIE" TALLEY, his daughter
ELDON TALLEY, son of Calvin Talley
NETTA TALLEY, wife of Eldon Talley
KENNETH "BUDDY" TALLEY, SR., and TIMMY TALLEY, sons of Eldon and Netta
OLIVE TALLEY, wife of Buddy
SALLY TALLEY FRIEDMAN, daughter of Eldon and Netta
MATT FRIEDMAN, husband of Sally Talley
KENNETH TALLEY, JR., son of Buddy and Olive
JUNE TALLEY, daughter of Buddy and Olive
JED JENKINS, lover of Kenneth Talley, Jr.
JOHN and GWEN LANDIS, friends of Kenneth, Jr., and June
SHIRLEY TALLEY, daughter of June Talley and John Landis

The Story:

Talley and Son. It is sunset, July 4, 1944. The Talley family learns from a telegram delivered by Harley Campbell that Eldon Talley's youngest child, Timmy, was killed in the Pacific in World War II. Family members argue with one another over the family fortune, the importance of war heroes, the decision whether to sell the clothing factory to the out-of-state Delaware Industries, and the difficulty of grief. The eldest Talley, Calvin, is senile, so his son, Eldon, assumes power of attorney for the family businesses, the local bank, and the factory, which he co-owns with Harley.

After Avalaine Platt, the illegitimate daughter of the family's laundry woman, accuses Eldon of being her father, Calvin tricks the unsuccessful handyman Emmet Young into marrying Avalaine; he will work as head cutter at the clothing factory. When Eldon and Harley object, Calvin says that he will not allow Young to work for him; instead, if Harley consents, the family will sell the factory to Delaware Industries and thus rid the Talley family of possible scandal. The factory will then move to Louisiana.

Although Eldon disagrees with his father and threatens to use his power to prevent losing the factory, he convinces Harley to sell him all the Campbell shares from the local bank. This enables the Talley family to control the bank. Before this point, Eldon hoped Timmy would return to work in the factory. Calvin and his daughter, Lottie, remind him that neither Timmy nor his brother, Buddy, were ever truly interested in the clothing industry. Timmy's interest in the family business was a way to obtain the love and approval of his father.

Eldon's daughter, Sally, appears. Aunt Lottie, who encouraged Matt Friedman to take Sally away from the Talley clan, convinces her to elope with him without telling anyone. Lottie does not inform Sally of Timmy's death until after the marriage. As the agreement between Harley and Eldon concerning the bank is finalized, Sally packs. Sally exits, but not before Eldon sees her. Ironically, although everyone in the family, except for Aunt Lottie, is anti-Semitic, Eldon allows her to leave, telling her he hopes she is not making a mistake. The play ends with Lottie and Timmy (in his role as narrator) reflecting on the deterioration of the house—and, by implication, of the family.

Talley's Folly. At the Talley family boathouse, Matt Friedman and Sally Talley discuss their relationship, World War II, the Talley family, and each other's dreams and aspirations. Although Sally protests that she does not love Matt, it is clear that she does. Sally recognizes that she is the family misfit. She works as a nurse in an army hospital, is outspoken like her Aunt Lottie, and is fired from teaching Sunday school. She also defends Matt against the family's anti-Semitic prejudice. Her father, Eldon, and her brother, Buddy, are most suspicious of Matt's socialistic ideas, which come into direct conflict with the money-making, capitalistic patriarchs. In the past Sally was expected to wed Harley, son of the equally powerful Campbell, until she learns she is barren and thus is neither a financial nor a social asset. Matt, a bachelor in his forties, loves Sally, who is twelve years younger, and fights for her. Sally is reluctant to marry Matt because she cannot have his children; ironically, Matt does not want any children since he thinks the world is much too horrible. Despite Matt and Sally's obvious differences and disagreements, the two agree to marry.

Fifth of July. In 1977, Kenneth Jr., his sister, June, his lover, Jed Jenkins, his niece, Shirley, and his Aunt Sally reunite with June and Ken's friends, Gwen and John Landis. The Landises, Ken, and June all attended Berkeley during the turbulent 1960's and were actively involved in antiwar protests. Hoping for a better United States, they realized the impossibility of achieving a utopian democratic society that valued the individual human being. Ken served in Vietnam for a cause in which he did not believe—and lost both his legs.

Ken, without the consent of his family or the devoted Jed, decides to sell the family home to John, a horrible capitalist. John and Gwen plan to make the house a recording studio. A singer and a drug addict, Gwen hopes to continue her rise to the top. Ken recently fell down in front of a classroom of high school students and thus loses all confidence in himself. He does not want to take a position teaching English at the local high school and live on the Talley farm. Aunt Sally, whose husband, Matt, died recently, wishes to scatter his ashes into the lake. Jed, who loves and cultivates the land, scatters the ashes in his rose garden on the Talley property. Ken's decision to sell the family estate is much more difficult than expected. Ken learns that his best friends (including his former lover, John) ran away to Europe without him rather than wait until he could accompany them. He regains his self-confidence and appreciation of family ties when he learns of John's betrayal and when John accidentally knocks him down. Ken cannot sell the land to one for whom honor, family, and love of nature mean nothing. Sally will live at the house with the gay couple. Ken changes his mind; he will not sell.

Ken's refusal to sell the Talley home to an outsider and Shirley's dreams for the future demonstrate that there is still hope for the Talley family. He will return to teaching—his lifelong ambition—and Shirley, by rejecting her ill-bred and corrupt father to remain with the Talley clan, might become the most famous person in Missouri history.

Critical Evaluation:

Lanford Wilson's trilogy about the Talley family traces their spiritual decline in the 1940's to their renewed hope and optimism in the late 1970's. *Talley's Folly* and *Talley and Son* take place on July 4, 1944, when the family learns that Eldon's youngest child, Timmy, has been killed. In addition, family outcast Sally agrees on that day to marry Matt Friedman, a man of Russian-Jewish descent. *Fifth of July* may be viewed as the completion of the saga.

Of the three Talley plays, *Fifth of July* and *Talley's Folly* have received the most critical attention, with *Talley's Folly* winning the Pulitzer Prize in drama in 1980. *Fifth of July*, which was first performed Off-Broadway by the Circle Repertory Company in April, 1978, and ran for 168 performances, was revised, with significant changes, and reopened on Broadway in November, 1980, for a longer run.

The plots of *Talley and Son* and *Talley's Folly* overlap, but *Talley's Folly* is far less plot-driven. Set at the family boathouse, *Talley's Folly* is a romantic comedy in which only two characters, Matt and Sally, discuss their relationship, World War II, the Talley family, and each other's dreams and aspirations.

The events of *Talley and Son* and *Talley's Folly* stress two complementary conflicts. Each is concerned with family—most particularly the role a family plays in contributing to and inhibiting the growth of individual members. *Talley and Son* demonstrates the importance of the father-son relationship, and *Talley's Folly* emphasizes the effects of family estrangement on the individual. Timmy, the narrator of the former play, represents the failure of the Talley patriarchs, Eldon and Calvin Stuart Talley, to consider family bonds as more important than money and power. The elder Talley is portrayed as a powerful and corrupt figure in the history of Lebanon; he does whatever he can to protect the family name and to maintain control. Eldon has inherited many of his traits. For example, he has fathered a child out of wedlock but is unwilling to take responsibility. None of the sons is able to relate well to his father or to become the son for which his father wished.

Sally's conflict in *Talley's Folly* concerns whether she should rebel against her patriarchal family and marry an outsider. Thus, while the title *Talley and Son* emphasizes the importance of familial male bonding, both plays stress the failure of mothers and fathers to teach their children humane values. The mother figures—Olive, Buddy's wife, Aunt Lottie, and Netta, Eldon's wife—have, like their husbands, contributed to the family's decline through their own spiritual weakness. Lottie is, however, the strongest rebel; she recognizes the flaws of her father and her brother—and the inherent problems in the capitalistic American dream—but is physically and emotionally incapable of caring for herself. Her inner strength is clear, nevertheless, when she tells Sally she will rebel vicariously through her niece's marriage. Lottie serves as a mother figure to Sally, hoping she will reject their family's corrupt values. Sally's own mother, Netta, is too neurotic to take care of herself or her family effectively, though her outbursts at Eldon show that she could, were she to allow herself, stand up against him for his extramarital affairs.

In *Fifth of July*, family plays a significant role as well, although the play advocates a broader definition of family. Aunt Sally influences and cares for Shirley, June's daughter. She becomes the clan's matriarch since Olive and Buddy moved to California, forsaking home and the past. The ideal gay relationship between Ken and Jed may perhaps be the first in an American drama glorifying the values of family and tradition. On the one hand, *Fifth of July* critiques the American dream of capitalism, showing the flaws of the capitalists John and Gwen Landis in, for example, the harshness and vulgarity of their language and in their immoral betrayal of Ken during the Vietnam War. On the other hand, the American dream of individualism, of land, of family, and of home triumph in the historically latest Talley play.

All three plays criticize American concepts of masculinity, male-female relationships, and heroism, but *Fifth of July* most fully explores the effects of war. Although the other two Talley plays touch on antiwar sentiment (particularly evident in the cruelty and violence of Timmy's death), *Fifth of July* directly confronts the Vietnam War, the concept of American heroism, and the idealism of those who protested the Vietnam conflict. Vietnam symbolizes for Wilson the failure of American men and women to acknowledge fundamental problems within the American psyche. As Ken and John try to convince Wes, John and Gwen's sidekick, that by definition "Heroic actions must have saving results," Wilson ironically emphasizes that for Vietnam there was no such effect—that for Ken, like so many others who fought for the United States, his sacrifice was futile. Although World War II had positive results, Vietnam failed miserably—as did the antiwar and related Civil Rights movements—in achieving the American Dream. The personal sacrifices of Timmy and his nephew, Ken, Jr., are underappreciated when the wars are over.

Each of the Talley plays affirms idealism while warning Americans against the effects of materialism, capitalism, and war on the American psyche. All the play's conflicts emerge from a lack of humane concern for family and for those outside the family. Like many American dramatists, Wilson fears that money and materialism lead to objectification of the human being and to denial of the most basic of American values, the worth of the individual.

D. Dean Shackelford

Further Reading

Adler, Thomas P. "The Artist in the Garden: Theatre, Space, and Place in Lanford Wilson." In *Modern Dramatists: A Casebook of Major British, Irish, and American Playwrights*, edited by Kimball King. New York: Routledge, 2001. Demonstrates how in Wilson's plays, the most important places are not visually depicted but are absent from the stage.

Barnett, Gene A. *Lanford Wilson*. Boston: Twayne, 1987. Provides useful interpretations of individual characters, the major themes, and other elements of the Talley plays. Includes bibliography.

Bigsby, Christopher. "Lanford Wilson." In *Contemporary American Playwrights*. New York: Cambridge University Press, 1999. An overview of Wilson's life and work, providing biographical details, discussion of his literary influences, and analyses of individual plays, including those in the Talley trilogy. Describes how Wilson's plays are characterized by a "bruised lyricism, a poetry generated out of inarticulation of prosaic lives."

Cooperman, Robert. "The Talley Plays and the Evolution of the American Family." In *Lanford Wilson: A Casebook*, edited by Jackson R. Bryer. New York: Garland, 1994. Excellent study of the Talley plays, emphasizing the changing social mores affecting the family. Describes Wilson's trilogy as a history of the American family. Asserts that *Fifth of July* represents the integration of traditional and modern families and thus offers hope.

Herman, William. "Down and Out in Lebanon and New York: Lanford Wilson." In *Understanding Contemporary American Drama*. Columbia: University of South Carolina Press, 1987. Offers an interpretive and biographical introduction to Wilson. Emphasizes the connections between the plays, which show Wilson's American optimism. Includes bibliography.

Jacobi, Martin J. "The Comic Vision of Lanford Wilson." *Studies in the Literary Imagination* 21, no. 2 (Fall, 1988): 119-134. A useful analysis of the comedy in several Wilson plays, including *Fifth of July* and *Talley's Folly*. Focuses primarily on how to classify the plays based on their endings.

Martine, James J. "Charlotte's Daughters: Changing Gender Roles and Family Structures in Lanford Wilson." In *Lanford Wilson: A Casebook*, edited by Jackson R. Bryer. New York: Garland, 1994. Analyzes the intersection of changing family and gender roles in the Talley plays. Sees Sally as the central figure of the Talley plays, tracing the evolution of the Talley women from Aunt Lottie to Shirley.

Monroe, R. E. "The Outsider in Lanford Wilson's Rural Plays." *Journal of American and Comparative Cultures* 25, nos. ½ (Spring, 2002): 166-171. Focuses on three rural plays, including *Talley & Son*. Describes how these plays depict individual and community character and feature outsiders who are truth-tellers.

Radavich, David. "Rabe, Mamet, Shepard, and Wilson: Mid-American Male Dramatists in the 1970's and '80's." *Midwest Quarterly* 48, no. 3 (Spring, 2007): 342-358. Examines the work of Wilson and three other playwrights from the Midwest, focusing on their depiction of men's relations with each other and with women. Analyzes the Talley plays, maintaining that, unlike the characters in the other playwrights' work, Wilson's male characters "seem comfortable" in their masculinity.

Williams, Philip Middleton. *A Comfortable House: Lanford Wilson, Marshall W. Mason, and the Circle Repertory Theatre.* Jefferson, N.C.: McFarland, 1993. Focuses on the Talley plays, emphasizing the collaboration between Wilson and Mason.

Tamar

Author: Robinson Jeffers (1887-1962)
First published: 1924
Type of work: Poetry
Type of plot: Psychological
Time of plot: World War I
Locale: Near Carmel, California

Principal characters:
TAMAR CAULDWELL, a young woman
LEE CAULDWELL, her brother
DAVID CAULDWELL, her father
JINNY CAULDWELL, David's sister
STELLA MORELAND, the sister of David's dead wife
WILL ANDREWS, Tamar's suitor

The Poem:

Injured when his horse stumbles and falls over a sea cliff, young Lee Cauldwell is nursed back to health by his sister, Tamar. Lee, who has lived a wild and dissolute life, vows to give up his drinking and debauchery. He and Tamar become devoted to each other during his convalescence, so much so that Lee jealously warns a former suitor of his sister to stay away from her. Old David Cauldwell, Lee and Tamar's father, fears what might result from the isolation of his family. His fears are confirmed when the brother and sister, after swimming in the river, are drawn to each other.

The Cauldwell family members are a peculiar group. In addition to David and his two children, the family includes two old women: Jinny Cauldwell and Stella Moreland. Aunt Jinny, the mentally disabled sister of David, is cared for by Aunt Stella, the sister of David's dead wife. Through the confused mumblings of Jinny, Tamar realizes that an incestuous relationship occurred years before between David and his sister Helen.

A short time later, Tamar discovers that she is pregnant. Rather than admit that Lee is the father of her child, she deliberately seeks out and seduces her former suitor, Will Andrews. Disgust and revulsion grow in her until she hates her two lovers and, most of all, herself. She feels that she will lose her mind if she does not talk to someone.

Aunt Stella is a medium through whom the voices of the dead sometimes speak. In desperation, Tamar appeals to Stella to let her speak to Helen. That evening she and Stella, with Jinny between them, steal down to the seashore so that they will not be discovered by the men. Stella gradually falls into a trance, and through her lips Tamar hears the voice of a man who tells her that the coastline country was once the land of the Indians, where their gods used to come to them. He orders Tamar to strip and dance so that the gods will come again. Against her will, Tamar dances to strange guttural chants from the lips of the entranced woman. After a while the chanting ceases, and Tamar returns slowly to her senses. Then through the lips of Stella she hears the voice of Helen taunting her for the shameful display. The voice, after warning Tamar that she will lose her child, tells her that a fire Tamar set earlier in the family's cabin will be quenched before it fulfills its purpose of destroying the corruption of the Cauldwell family. Then, in a mournful voice, Helen tells Tamar of the horror of death, of her longing for life, and of her need to haunt Tamar as long as she lives, because Tamar possesses life. On the shore, unassisted by anyone and in great pain, Tamar suffers a miscarriage.

Back in the cabin once more, Tamar can scarcely restrain the hatred she feels for her family. All pity has left her, and all love. In order to revenge herself on Helen, she tempts her old father with her beauty. Through the medium of Stella, Helen curses Tamar and pleads with her not to commit that ultimate folly.

Lee, who has returned to his drinking, enlists in the army, but Tamar is determined not to let him go. She tells him that the child she had carried was not his; rather, the father was Will Andrews, who had visited her late at night after she set a lighted lamp in her window as a signal. Tamar taunts Lee until he lashes her with a whip.

When Will Andrews comes to the cabin that night, Tamar tells him that Lee is to leave the following day for the army and would like to say good-bye to him. The meeting between the two men is cool but amiable. While Lee is out of the room, Tamar shows Will her lash wounds and tells him that she has lost his child through the outrages that both her father and Lee have perpetrated upon her. When Lee returns with his father, Will accuses him of those atrocities. In turn, Lee accuses Will of having attempted to set fire to their home. Tamar, who herself is responsible, says nothing but goads the men on to fight with her smiles and wordless encouragement to Will. As they struggle, Lee stabs Will with a knife.

Helen, through the person of Stella, tries to save old David Cauldwell from the destroying forces of hate and evil, but he refuses to heed her warnings. Downstairs, the simpleminded Jinny, alone and disturbed, is attracted by the light of a candle. She carries it to the window, where the flame sets fire to the blowing curtains. Her dying shrieks attract the attention of those upstairs. Lee tries to run to her, but Tamar clings to him and will not let him go. Will, dying, drags himself as far as the window. Stella rushes out into the flaming hall and perishes. The old man prays brokenly, groveling on the floor. Lee makes one last effort to escape, but Tamar, glorying in the destruction of her three lovers, embraces him until the flames consume them all.

Critical Evaluation:

Robinson Jeffers was the son of an Old Testament theologian who gave him a classical education in Europe and in the United States. After beginning graduate studies first in medicine and then in forestry, Jeffers concluded that he wanted to become a poet, but he did not find his own voice in verse until he and his wife settled in the small town of Carmel, California, at the northern end of the spectacular sweep of coast known as Big Sur, with its towering highlands, wild rivers and creeks, abundant wildlife, and crashing surf. He built a stone dwelling, Tor House, and next to it Hawk Tower, made of boulders from the shore below the house. Jeffers built the tower to please his wife, Una, who admired the towers of Ireland; he named it for his favorite animal, whose intense awareness and frightening ferocity seemed to Jeffers emblematic of life at its most intense.

Jeffers had found not only a home but also a locale for his poems. The dramatic landscape, with its tall mountains falling abruptly into the immense, boiling ocean, an arena for the struggle of animal and marine life, seemed to cry out for tragedy like all beautiful places, to paraphrase another poem by Jeffers. Directly across the mouth of the Carmel River from Tor House lies Point Lobos, its wild beauty now preserved as a state park. Here Jeffers places *Tamar*, the story of the Cauldwell family; the poem is the first of many long narrative poems through which he presents his poetic themes and develops his philosophical viewpoint.

The themes of Jeffers's long poems involve the fatal effects of human passion, which is always egocentric and, therefore, self-destructive, not only for the people who indulge that passion but also for those around them—usually a family. This passion is acted upon in a natural setting of beauty and power, a reminder that people are part of nature and thus are driven by impulses and instincts beyond their control or understanding. They are also subject to forces outside themselves—forces that eventually defeat and destroy them. This assessment of the human condition is bleak, but the philosophical viewpoint that Jeffers adopts goes beyond that bleak position. Passion, violence, sin, and death are not just elements in people's lives; they are also elements that enable the universe to live, grow, die, and combine again to be reborn. As humans, as part of nature, people cannot escape this fate. Furthermore—and here Jeffers differs from many Romantic poets—there is no point in people complaining about these elements or trying futilely to change them. People might as well "be angry at the sun for setting/ If these things anger you" (*Be Angry at the Sun*, 1941). Jeffers's position is similar to that of classical Stoicism. He feels that if people abandon the human perspective and think cosmically, which Jeffers calls "inhumanism," they may be at peace because they can then see the entire cycle of life as something transcendent and magnificent, fraught though it may be with violence and flux.

The Bible and the Greek tragedy are the models for Jeffers's narrative poems. Tamar Cauldwell has the same name as two Tamars in the Old Testament; one was raped by her brother (Samuel 13), and the other deceived her father-in-law into fathering her child (Genesis 38). Jeffers's character has qualities of both these literary forebears, although she has not been raped by her brother; instead, she has willingly entered into a sexual relationship with him, and she has seduced her father and a third lover, the last in order to cover up the cause of her pregnancy.

Tamar Cauldwell's sin is worse than those of the biblical Tamars; she chooses to be incestuous and takes not one but two other lovers. Jeffers uses human sexuality, and particularly incest, as a symbol of people's fatal self-involvement. Tamar is the first of a series of Jeffers's characters who recognize that sin and pain are not, as Fyodor Dostoevski or Friedrich Nietzsche might say, a necessity; instead, Jeffers's characters recognize that sin and pain are inevitable.

Tamar embraces, even revels in, her own excesses, but she also knows that acknowledging her guilt does not free her from the consequences of sin; she dies along with the others when the purifying fire, which wipes out the old to make way for the new, envelops the house. The fire is accidentally set by Jinny, who thinks of a candle as a beautiful plaything; this incident emphasizes the role of chance and accident in the life of the world and the creatures in it.

Jeffers was familiar with the work of classical scholars such as Francis Macdonald Cornford and Jane Ellen Harrison, who theorized that the Greek tragedy and the myths that it dramatized grew out of fertility rituals. Jeffers was also familiar with the comparative mythological work of Sir James George Frazer, whose speculations in *The Golden Bough* (1890) about the interrelatedness of world religions and myths also informed T. S. Eliot's *The Waste Land* (1922). The difference between Eliot and Jeffers is that Eliot imposed a mythic structure on an urban, modern landscape, whereas Jeffers saw the mythic patterns growing up out of the land and the sea before him. For Jeffers, the California coast was a great stage on which the drama of existence was played out daily. *Tamar* is the most powerful work in a series of works in which he investigates the implications of this cosmic process.

"Critical Evaluation" by Jim Baird

Further Reading

Brophy, Robert J. *Robinson Jeffers: Myth, Ritual, and Symbol in His Narrative Poems*. Cleveland, Ohio: Case Western Reserve University Press, 1973. Shows Jeffers's use of Greek myth and world mythology to establish his view of humankind as fated to endure pain and suffering. Includes a chapter devoted to discussion of *Tamar*.

_____. "*Tamar, The Cenci*, and Incest." *American Literature* 42, no. 2 (May, 1970): 241-244. Investigates the connections between Jeffers and the Romantics through the incest theme as it appears in both *Tamar* and Percy Bysshe Shelley's drama *The Cenci*.

_____, ed. *Robinson Jeffers: Dimensions of a Poet*. New York: Fordham University Press, 1995. Collection of essays offers various interpretations of Jeffers's poems, including *Tamar*. Topics addressed include Jeffers's uses of history, the female archetype in his work, and his relationship to Carmel and Big Sur, California.

Carpenter, Frederic I. "The Poetry of Myth: The Long Poems." In *Robinson Jeffers*. New York: Grosset & Dunlap, 1962. Analyzes all Jeffers's long narratives, with particular focus on *Tamar*. Offers an excellent short introduction to Jeffers's work.

Hunt, Tim. "The Problematic Nature of *Tamar, and Other Poems*." In *Centennial Essays for Robinson Jeffers*, edited by Robert Zaller. Newark: University of Delaware Press, 1991. Shows how Jeffers's poetic concerns are reflected in his revision of *Tamar* and the other poems in the volume in which it was first collected.

McClintock, Scott. "The Poetics of Fission in Robinson Jeffers." *CLIO: A Journal of Literature, History, and the Philosophy of History* 37, no. 2 (Spring, 2008): 171-191. Analyzes the transformation of Jeffers's poetics from a metaphysical philosophy of inhumanism to his use of more violent imagery influenced by the development of nuclear weapons during the Cold War.

Zaller, Robert. "The Birth of the Hero." In *The Cliffs of Solitude*. New York: Cambridge University Press, 1983. Presents a psychological reading of the character of Tamar as well as discussion of Jeffers's other major protagonists.

Tamburlaine the Great

Author: Christopher Marlowe (1564-1593)
First produced: Part 1, c. 1587; part 2, 1587; first published, 1590
Type of work: Drama
Type of plot: Tragedy
Time of plot: Fourteenth century
Locale: Asia

Principal characters:
TAMBURLAINE, the Scythian conqueror
ZENOCRATE, his wife
BAJAZETH, the emperor of the Turks
CALLAPINE, his son
MYCETES, the king of Persia
COSROE, his brother
THERIDAMAS,
TECHELLES, and
USUMCASANE, followers of Tamburlaine
ORCANES, the king of Natolia

The Story:

When Mycetes becomes king of Persia, his brother, Cosroe, tells him openly that he is not fit for the office. Among Mycetes' greatest concerns are the raids of Tamburlaine, the Scythian shepherd who became a bandit. Because it is rumored that this robber chief aspires to rule the East, Mycetes sends Theridamas with a thousand troops to capture Tamburlaine, and he orders another lord named Menaphon to follow Theridamas. Cosroe sarcastically points out to the king that Menaphon is needed in Babylon, where the province is about to revolt against a sovereign as inferior as Mycetes. At this insult, Mycetes threatens he will be revenged against his brother.

Menaphon asks Cosroe if he is afraid of the king's threat, but Cosroe assures the Persian lord that there is a plot afoot to make Cosroe himself emperor of Asia. He claims that it hurts him to witness the scorn now heaped on Persia, which formerly awed the entire world. Soon afterward, the revolt Cosroe predicts takes place. The rebellious lords offer Cosroe the crown, and he sets out to annex the thousand troops of Theridamas and conquer his brother Mycetes.

On a Scythian hill, Tamburlaine is holding Zenocrate, the daughter of the sultan of Egypt. He speaks grandly of kingdoms he will conquer, and Techelles and Usumcasane echo his boasts, vowing to follow Tamburlaine to the death. The ambitious leader is in love with Zenocrate, and he promises her all the wealth and power in his kingdom. Suddenly, Mycetes' thousand horse troops attack Tamburlaine's five hundred foot soldiers. When Theridamas accosts the Scythian, he is so impressed with his appearance and with Tamburlaine's visions of mighty kingdoms and power that the outlaw is able to persuade Theridamas to become an ally.

Cosroe prepares to send troops to join Tamburlaine and Theridamas by the river Araris and there to engage the forces of Mycetes, who is fuming with rage at the revolt. Meander, a follower of Mycetes, conceives the proposal that he who conquers Tamburlaine will be offered the province of Albania, and he who takes Theridamas can have Media. Mycetes stipulates, however, that Cosroe be captured alive. Mycetes is convinced that the followers of the bandit Tamburlaine can be bribed to desert their leader, since he purchased their loyalty by bribes in the first place.

When Cosroe meets Tamburlaine, the Scythian boasts of his great future; Theridamas indicates to Cosroe that he believes in Tamburlaine's ability. Certain of victory, Cosroe promises Techelles and Usumcasane rewards for their deeds, and, indeed, Mycetes is defeated. After the victory, Tamburlaine then bribes Theridamas, Techelles, and Usumcasane with a promise of kingdoms of their own if they will attack Cosroe. Marveling at Tamburlaine's arrogance and daring, Cosroe prepares for battle. Cosroe is wounded in battle, and Tamburlaine, gloating over his easy conquest, proclaims himself king of Persia.

At the court in Algiers, the kings of Fez, Morocco, and Algiers fume at the thought that a bandit took Persia and is now forcing them to raise their siege of Greek Constantinople. Bajazeth, king of the Turks, dispatches a message to Tamburlaine, threatening him if he dares set foot in Africa. Meanwhile the kings plan to take Greece by siege.

Zenocrate slowly grows to admire Tamburlaine, who is now plotting the conquest of the Turkish kings. Zabina, wife of Bajazeth, sneers at Zenocrate and calls her a concubine. After subduing Bajazeth, Tamburlaine makes Zabina Zenocrate's attendant slave. To show his might, Tamburlaine puts Bajazeth in a cage and uses it as a footstool. Bajazeth and Zabina continue, however, to hurl disdainful remarks and threats at him.

The next victim of the Scythian's lust for power is the sultan of Egypt, Zenocrate's father. As Tamburlaine's armies prepare to take Damascus, Zenocrate gently asks her lover to deal kindly with the city of her father, but he refuses. Zenocrate grieves until Tamburlaine promises not to harm her father when Damascus falls. By now the Scythian conqueror loves Zenocrate dearly. While ordering three emissaries from Damascus to be killed, he thinks of his beloved's beauty and tenderness. Zenocrate herself is torn between her conscience, which revolts against her lord's cruelty, and her love for him.

When Tamburlaine brings the sultan to Zenocrate alive, the conqueror promises to give the sultan's kingdom back to him if Zenocrate will accept the title of queen of Egypt. She readily accepts this condition and Tamburlaine begins planning the wedding.

By this time, Bajazeth and Zabina killed themselves by dashing their heads against the bars of the cage in which Tamburlaine imprisoned the Turkish monarch. Orcanes, the king of Natolia, preparing for a battle with Sigismund, the king of Hungary, learns that Tamburlaine is mustering an attack. He sends for all the Christian rulers of Europe to form an alliance against an invasion by the Scythian. The former enemies Sigismund and Orcanes the Mohammedan enter into a pact of friendship with the rulers of Buda and Bohemia.

Callapine, son of Bajazeth and a prisoner of Tamburlaine, is guarded by Almeda, whom the young prince bribes with offers of wealth and power if he will help him escape. Tamburlaine and Zenocrate by now have three sons, Calyphas, Amyras, and Celebinus. Calyphas expresses a desire to lead a peaceful life with his mother.

The treaty of the monarchs against Tamburlaine does not hold. When Orcanes withdraws his troops from his campaign against the Christians, Sigismund is urged by his allies to attack Orcanes. Orcanes is trapped, for he is at the same time preparing to attack Tamburlaine. The betrayed monarch, crying for his enemies' Christ to help him defeat the traitors, prepares to defend himself. In the battle, Sigismund is killed and Orcanes emerges the victor.

Zenocrate becomes ill. When she dies, Tamburlaine is overcome with such grief that he will not have her buried until after his own death. Escaping with the aid of Almeda, Callapine returns to his father's kingdom and marshals the allies to defeat Tamburlaine and avenge Bajazeth's death. Inconsolable in his grief for Zenocrate, Tamburlaine prepares to fight the forces of Callapine. The Scythian's sons, Amyras and Celebinus, are eager for battle, but Calyphas, who dislikes bloodshed, refuses to join the fighting.

After he vanquishes his Turkish enemies, Tamburlaine returns to his camp and wrathfully stabs Calyphas, who remained in his tent all the while. The Turkish monarchs are bridled like horses and, under Tamburlaine's whip, forced to pull his carriage. The conqueror then takes Babylon, which leads to terrible plunder, rape, and murder. Tamburlaine is now mad with lust and power. Only Callapine is still able to oppose him.

Finally, Tamburlaine falls ill with a mysterious malady, and his physician declares that he is dying. After crowning his son Amyras monarch of his empires, the dying conqueror sends for Zenocrate's hearse. Bidding his son to reign with power, Tamburlaine, the scourge of God, leans over his beloved Zenocrate's coffin and dies.

Critical Evaluation:

A study of driving ambition, *Tamburlaine the Great* is also notable for the dignity and beauty of Christopher Marlowe's lines. The poetry of the play is all the more remarkable for being among the first written in English blank verse. Marlowe wrote with so much original invention, that for a time many scholars believed him the author of some plays now attributed to William Shakespeare. It is safe to say that Marlowe is the best of the pre-Shakespearean playwrights.

Marlowe's turbulent life ended tragically, and perhaps characteristically, in a barroom brawl with a man named Ingram Frizer. Even though he was only twenty-nine when he died, Marlowe managed to set a precedent for the development of English drama by leaving behind a model of Senecan dramatic form. His first production, *Tamburlaine the Great*, more a dramatic masque than a play, was a milestone of early Elizabethan drama. Certainly Shakespeare must have been influenced, especially in *Julius Caesar* (pr. c. 1599-1600, pb. 1623), by the conjunction of "Nature," "Fortune," and "stars" in the construction of Tamburlaine's character. Above all, Marlowe made blank verse the accepted mode of Elizabethan theatrical expression, both to reflect delicate grace and to pronounce such mighty lines as, "Even as when windy exhalations/ Fighting for passage, tilt within the earth." The character Tamburlaine is shown capable of a certain tenderness because of Marlowe's poetic versatility. As the hero says to Zenocrate, "With milk-white harts upon an ivory sled/ Thou shalt be drawn amidst the frozen pools,/ And scale the icy mountains' lofty tops,/ Which with thy beauty will be soon resolv'd."

Basing his drama on the history of Timur the Lane (1336-1406), a Mongol conqueror and descendant of Genghis Khan, Marlowe constructed his first Herculean hero as a bloodthirsty personification of the Renaissance spirit of boldness, defiance, and determination who tests the limitations of human ability. Invulnerable to all attacks but that of death, Tamburlaine moves toward his goals undaunted by considerations of destiny or accidental circumstances. He is the master of his own destiny simply because he decides to be and finds no one strong enough to deny him his ambitions. He says to Theridamas, "Forsake thy king, and do but join with me/ And we will triumph over all the world:/ I hold the Fates bound fast in iron chains,/ And with my hand turn Fortune's wheel about." Here is the hubris of classical Athenian tragedy, but with a difference: Tamburlaine is not struck down because of it; instead, he succeeds in everything he has time to undertake. One of the most effective moments of part 2, which is overall less compelling than part 1, is the passage in act 5 when Tamburlaine says, "Give me a map; then let me see how much/ Is left for me to conquer all the world." Only physical inevitabilities bring Marlowe's hero low, although it is clear that he becomes somewhat vulnerable once he gains love and possessions and sons.

He succeeds in attaining his goals because he regards the world and every thing and every person in it as an object. It is not surprising that his mighty, rhetorical speeches are filled with references to crimson robes, meteors, jewels, vermilion tents, and gold crowns. There is, in fact, a close connection between Tamburlaine's rhetoric and his achievements. He is godlike in the sense that what he says he does; his words become deeds. It is not surprising that he regards even Zenocrate's dead body as an object "Embalm'd with cassia, ambergris, and myrrh/ Not lapp'd in lead, but in a sheet of gold." It is but another splendid, colorful object under his control to preserve or to destroy. In the same vein, he uses his victims as horses to pull his chariots. Tamburlaine is the egotistic dream of the Renaissance epitomized: "Of stature tall, and straightly fashioned/ Like his desire, lift upwards and divine." In the correspondence between his appearance and his character there is a prediction of William Shakespeare's *Hamlet*, but the difference between the two heroes—Tamburlaine does not falter in his purpose for a moment—is much more striking than any similarities.

From the very beginning, after Tamburlaine steps into the power vacuum created by Mycetes' insufficiency (which is described as the inability to use "great and thundering speech"), the play is a series of episodic atrocities, connected only by the unswerving ambition of the hero. The action of the play has as such little to recommend it by way of originality or structural genius. The hero is both the center and the continuity of the work. Cosroe calls him the model of humanity, as Shakespeare was to call his Hamlet and his Brutus. One of Tamburlaine's most sympathetic characteristics is his never waning enthusiasm—the *sprezzatura* of the Italian Renaissance:

> TAMB.: What say my other friends? Will you be kings?
> TECH.: Ay, if I could, with all my heart, my lord.
> TAMB.: Why, that's well said, Techelles, so would I.

Combined with this essential enthusiasm is Tamburlaine's expression of a typically Renaissance longing for the infinite of something, whether it be the infinite knowledge sought by Faustus, the infinite riches desired by the Jew of Malta, or Tamburlaine's insatiable thirst for power. Marlowe's prologue promises that the hero will be seen "threatening the world with high astounding terms," and all three last words have thematic significance. Tamburlaine's description of himself as "the chiefest lamp of all the earth" is the most explicit indication that he desires to join the company of the stars, that is, to escape from earth and wander among realms unknown to ordinary humans. The root of the word "astounding" is related to the intensely rhetorical nature of Tamburlaine's every speech. Indeed, his approach to stellar glory is primarily through the flamboyant energy of his language—Marlowe's "mighty line." It is no coincidence that Tamburlaine is rarely seen in action but usually in speech.

Finally, the word "terms" draws the thematic structure together and indicates the boundaries and limitations of human experience and behavior that Tamburlaine means to break through and cast aside with his speech. This explains why his victims are always so startled. He has no respect for ordinary conventions and not only does the most outlandish things to kings and generals but also slays them. However, it is just as important to note that Tamburlaine has no divine aspirations. What he seeks to accomplish remains human: "A god is not so glorious as a king:/ I think the pleasures they enjoy in heaven/ Cannot compare with kingly joys in earth." It is for his successful extension of human terms that Tamburlaine becomes a seminal character in the development of English Renaissance drama.

"Critical Evaluation" by Kenneth John Atchity

Further Reading

Battenhouse, Roy W. *Marlowe's Tamburlaine: A Study in Renaissance Moral Philosophy*. 1941. Reprint. Nashville, Tenn.: Vanderbilt University Press, 1964. Battenhouse contends that the play upholds traditional morality and the Christian worldview.

Cheney, Patrick, ed. *The Cambridge Companion to Christopher Marlowe*. New York: Cambridge University Press,

2004. Collection of essays, including discussions of Marlowe's life, his place in the twenty-first century, his literary style, gender and sexuality in his work, and his reception and influence. Mark Thornton Burnett provides an analysis of *Tamburlaine the Great*.

Deats, Sara Munson, and Robert A. Logan, eds. *Placing the Plays of Christopher Marlowe: Fresh Cultural Contexts*. Burlington, Vt.: Ashgate, 2008. Collection of critical essays analyzing Marlowe's plays. The numerous references to *Tamburlaine the Great* are listed in the index.

Hopkins, Lisa. *Christopher Marlowe, Renaissance Dramatist*. Edinburgh: Edinburgh University Press, 2008. An introduction to Marlowe's plays, discussing their themes, theatrical contexts, and performance histories from 1587 through 2007; Marlowe's relationship to William Shakespeare; and Marlowe's theatrical achievements. The references to *Tamburlaine the Great* are listed in the index.

Knoll, Robert E. "Caesarism." In *Christopher Marlowe*. New York: Twayne, 1969. A good starting place for the general reader. Knoll considers the hero appealing in his diabolic aspirations.

Levin, Harry. "The Progress of Pomp." In *The Overreacher: A Study of Christopher Marlowe*. Cambridge, Mass.: Harvard University Press, 1952. One of the most influential books on Marlowe. Presents the Marlovian hero as a rebel and explores the use of language and irony in *Tamburlaine the Great*.

Oz, Avraham, ed. *Marlowe*. New York: Palgrave Macmillan, 2003. Collection of essays about Marlowe's plays, including "Faces of Nation and Barbarism: Prophetic Mimicry and the Politics of *Tamburlaine the Great*" by Avraham Oz.

Ribner, Irving, ed. *Christopher Marlowe's Tamburlaine Part One and Part Two: Text and Major Criticism*. New York: Odyssey Press, 1974. A comprehensive book on the plays. Features an authoritative text edited and glossed by Ribner. Reprints eleven influential essays, including one from Ellis-Fermor's milestone 1927 book on Marlowe, and concludes with a useful bibliography. The final essay by Kenneth Friedenreich surveys the critical history of the plays.

The Taming of the Shrew

Author: William Shakespeare (1564-1616)
First produced: c. 1593-1594; first published, 1623
Type of work: Drama
Type of plot: Comedy
Time of plot: Sixteenth century
Locale: Padua, Italy

Principal characters:
BAPTISTA, a rich gentleman of Padua
KATHARINA, his shrewish daughter
BIANCA, another daughter
PETRUCHIO, Katharina's suitor
LUCENTIO, a student in love with Bianca
TRANIO, his servant
VINCENTIO, Lucentio's father
GREMIO and HORTENSIO, Lucentio's rivals
A PEDANT

The Story:

As a joke, a beggar is carried, while asleep, to the house of a noble lord and there dressed in fine clothes and waited on by many servants. The beggar is told that he is a rich man who, in a demented state, has imagined himself to be a beggar, but who is now restored to his senses. The lord and his court have great sport with the poor fellow, to the extent of dressing a page to pose as the beggar's rich and beautiful wife and presenting the supposed woman to him as his dutiful and obedient spouse. The beggar, in his stupidity, assumes his new role as though it were his own, and he and his lady settle down to watch a play prepared for their enjoyment.

Lucentio, a young man, and Tranio, his servant, have journeyed to Padua so that Lucentio can study in that ancient city. Tranio persuades his master that life is not all study and work and that he should find pleasures also in his new residence. On their arrival in the city, Lucentio and Tranio encounter Baptista and his daughters, Katharina and Bianca. These three are accompanied by Gremio and Hortensio, young gentlemen both in love with gentle Bianca. Baptista, however, will not permit his younger daughter to marry until someone takes Katharina off his hands. Although Katharina is wealthy and beautiful, she is such a shrew that no suitor will have her. Baptista, not knowing how to control his sharp-tongued daughter, announces that Gremio or Hortensio must find a husband for Katharina before either can woo Bianca. He charges them also to find tutors for the two girls, that they might be skilled in music and poetry.

Unobserved, Lucentio and Tranio witness this scene. At first sight, Lucentio also falls in love with Bianca, and he determines to have her for himself. His first act is to exchange clothes with Tranio, so that the servant appears to be the master. Lucentio then disguises himself as a tutor in order to woo Bianca without her father's knowledge.

About the same time, Petruchio arrives in Padua. He is a rich and noble man of Verona, come to Padua to visit his friend Hortensio and to find for himself a rich wife. Hortensio tells Petruchio of his love for Bianca and of her father's decree that she cannot marry until a husband is found for Katharina. Petruchio declares that the stories told about spirited Katharina are to his liking, particularly the account of her great wealth, and he expresses a desire to meet her. Hortensio proposes that Petruchio seek Katharina's father and present his family's name and history. Hortensio, meanwhile, plans to disguise himself as a tutor and thus plead his own cause with Bianca.

The situation grows confused. Lucentio is disguised as a tutor, and his servant, Tranio, is dressed as Lucentio. Hortensio is also disguised as a tutor. Petruchio is to ask for Katharina's hand. Also, unknown to anyone but Katharina and Bianca, Bianca loves neither Gremio nor Hortensio and swears that she will never marry rather than accept one or the other as her husband.

Petruchio easily secures Baptista's permission to marry his daughter Katharina, for the poor man is only too glad to have his older daughter finally wed. The courtship of Petruchio and Katharina is a strange one indeed, a battle of wits, words, and wills. Petruchio is determined to bend Katharina to his will, but Katharina scorns and berates him with a vicious tongue. Nevertheless, she has to obey her father's wish and marry Petruchio, and the nuptial day is set. Then Gremio and Tranio, the latter still believed to be Lucentio, vie with each other for Baptista's permission to marry Bianca. Tranio wins because he claims more gold and vaster lands than Gremio can declare. In the meantime, Hortensio and Lucentio, both disguised as tutors, woo Bianca.

As part of the process by which he seeks to tame Katharina, Petruchio arrives late for his wedding, and when he does appear he wears old and tattered clothes. Even during the wedding ceremony Petruchio acts like a madman, stamping, swearing, and cuffing the priest. Immediately afterward he drags Katharina away from the wedding feast and takes her to his country home, there to continue his scheme to bend her to his will. He gives her no food and no time for sleep, all the while pretending that nothing he has is good enough for her. In fact, he all but kills her with kindness. Before he is through, Katharina agrees that the moon is the sun and that an old man is a woman.

Bianca falls in love with Lucentio, whom she thinks to be her tutor. In chagrin, Hortensio throws off his disguise, and he and Gremio forswear their love for any woman so fickle. Tranio, still hoping to win Bianca for himself, finds an old pedant to act the part of Vincentio, Lucentio's father. The false father argues his son's cause with Baptista until that lover of gold promises his daughter's hand to Lucentio, as he thinks, but in reality to Tranio. When Lucentio's true father appears on the scene, he is considered an impostor and is almost put in jail for his deceit. The real Lucentio and Bianca, meanwhile, have been married secretly. Returning from the church with his bride, Lucentio reveals the whole plot to Baptista and the others. At first Baptista is angry about the way in which he has been duped, but Vincentio speaks soothingly to him and soon cools his rage.

Hortensio, in the meantime, has married a rich widow. To celebrate these weddings, Lucentio gives a feast for all the couples and the fathers. Following the feast, after the ladies have retired, the three newly married men enter into a bet: Each wagers one hundred pounds that, of the three new wives, his own wife will most quickly obey his commands. Lucentio sends first for Bianca, but she sends word that she will not come. Then Hortensio sends for his wife, but she too refuses to obey his summons. Petruchio then orders Katharina to appear, and she comes instantly to do his bidding. At his request, she also forces Bianca and Hortensio's wife to go to their husbands. Baptista is so delighted with his older daughter's meekness and willing submission that he adds another twenty thousand crowns to her dowry. Katharina tells them all that a wife should live only to serve her husband and that a woman's heart and tongue ought to be as soft as her body. Petruchio has tamed the shrew forever.

Critical Evaluation:

Although it is not possible to determine the dates of composition of William Shakespeare's plays with absolute certainty, it is generally agreed that the early comedy *The*

Taming of the Shrew was probably written after *The Two Gentlemen of Verona* (pr. c. 1594-1595) and before *A Midsummer Night's Dream* (pr. c. 1595-1596, pb. 1600). Even at this early date, Shakespeare shows himself to be a master of plot construction. Disregarding the classical unity of action, which forbade subplots, for a more enlightened concept of unity, Shakespeare creates two distinct lines of action, each derived from a different source, and integrates them into a unified dramatic whole. A single source for the main plot of Petruchio's taming of Katharina has not been found.

Misogynistic stories abounded in Shakespeare's time, stories of men exercising their "rightful" dominance over women. One in particular, a ballad titled *A Merry Jest of a Shrewd and Curst Wife, Lapped in Morel's Skin* (printed c. 1550), tells the story of a shrewish wife who is beaten bloody by her husband and then wrapped in the salted skin of a plow horse named Morel. Like Kate, this wife has a younger sister who is the favorite of their father. If Shakespeare used this ballad as a source for the main plot of this play, it is obvious that he toned it down greatly, substituting psychological tactics for physical brutality. Nevertheless, some stage versions of *The Taming of the Shrew* have emphasized Petruchio's physical mistreatment of Katharina. The eighteenth century English actor David Garrick as Petruchio threatened Katharina with a whip. Some critics even today see in this play an unacceptable male chauvinism. One must remember that Shakespeare lived and wrote in a patriarchal world in which the father ruled the family and the husband ruled the wife. Much in this play reflects the patriarchal nature of Elizabethan society, but Katharina's strength of character may mitigate charges of male chauvinism against Shakespeare.

The source for the underplot, the wooing of Bianca by various suitors, is George Gascoigne's *Supposes* (pr. 1566). The heroine in Gascoigne's play is made pregnant by her lover, but she remains completely chaste in *The Taming of the Shrew*. Shakespeare also dispenses with the source's character of the bawdy nurse and modifies the harsh satire that Gascoigne directs at Dr. Cleander, the pantaloon, who represents the degeneracy of "respectable" society. For this character Shakespeare substitutes Gremio, a wealthy old citizen of Padua who would marry Bianca but is thwarted by the young Lucentio. These changes are typical of Shakespeare, in whose plays sexual relationships are virtually always sanctified by marriage and in whose comedies satire is usually genial or at least counterbalanced by good humor.

The Taming of the Shrew is the only play by Shakespeare that has an "induction," or anterior section, that introduces the main action. In the induction, which is set in Shakespeare's native Warwickshire, an unconscious drunken tinker named Sly is taken to the house of a lord, dressed in fine clothes, and made to think he is a lord who has been comatose for fifteen years. Convinced he is indeed a lord, Sly begins to speak in blank verse and agrees to watch a play performed by traveling players, namely, *The Taming of the Shrew*. At the end of the first scene, Sly is already bored with the play and exclaims, "Would 'twere done!" He is never heard from again.

This induction, which at first sight appears irrelevant, dramatizes a recurring theme in all of Shakespeare's comedies and the central theme of this play: the deceptiveness of appearances. Sly mistakes the opulence of his surroundings for his true reality and thinks he is a lord rather than a poor tinker of Burton-heath. In the play proper, many of the characters pose as people other than themselves and are responded to in guises not of their true nature. In the subplot, Lucentio, in order to woo Bianca, trades places with his servant Tranio and further takes on the role of Cambio, a schoolmaster hired by Gremio, to woo Bianca for himself. Hortensio, another suitor to Bianca, assumes the role of Litio, a music teacher, to gain access to her. Late in the action, a pedant is coerced to play the role of Vincentio, the father of Lucentio. When the true Vincentio appears on the scene, the disguises of the subplot are finally revealed.

In the major plot the theme of illusion is not as literal, but it is no less important. Katharina, the shrew, has played her part for so long that everyone believes she is an irritable and hateful woman. Conversely, Bianca, her sister, is universally regarded as sweet and of a mild disposition. Neither image is totally true. Bianca has to be told twice by her father to enter the house in the first scene, indicating that she is not as tractable as she is thought to be. Katharina, in her first meeting with Petruchio, does not protest when he tells her father that they will be married on Sunday. She remains silent, indicating that she has tacitly accepted him. In the final scene, the true natures of Katharina and Bianca come out for everyone to see. It is Bianca who is the disobedient wife, and it is Katharina who gives a disquisition on the perfect Elizabethan wife. Whether her speech is to be taken at face value or as a statement of irony is debatable.

Petruchio has come "to wive it wealthily in Padua." He is a rip-roaring fortune hunter who will wed any woman who is rich enough, "Be she as foul as was Florentius's love/ As old as Sibyl, and as curst and shrewd/ As Socrates' Xanthippe." He is overwhelming in speech and manner and completely unintimidated by Katharina's reputation as a shrew. He annihilates her resistance with his outlandish actions. At his country house outside Padua, he mistreats his servants unconscionably, demonstrating to Katharina the kind of behavior that she has displayed. He then deprives her of sleep, food, and drink, as one would tame a falcon. Finally, he deprives her of fine clothing. By his example, she is led to see her own unreasonable behavior. She at last decides to submit to her husband's demands rather than persist in her perverse behavior. *The Taming of the Shrew* is a perennially popular stage production that can be performed and interpreted in various ways, depending on the inclinations of the directors.

"Critical Evaluation" by Robert G. Blake

Further Reading

Aspinall, Dana E., ed. *"The Taming of the Shrew": Critical Essays.* New York: Routledge, 2002. Compilation presents critical essays on the play as well as reviews of stage, screen, and television adaptations. Topics addressed include metamorphoses, marriage and genre, and power in the play.

Bloom, Harold, ed. *William Shakespeare's "The Taming of the Shrew."* New York: Chelsea House, 1988. Collection of essays provides discussion of the play based in various modern critical approaches, including feminism and deconstruction.

Davies, Stevie. *William Shakespeare: "The Taming of the Shrew."* New York: Penguin Books, 1995. Critical analysis of the play reassesses its language and the text of the folio. Places the play's depiction of radical feminism within the context of a sixteenth century war between the sexes that reached its climax in the 1590's, when feminists and antifeminists engaged in a major "pamphlet war."

Hamilton, Sharon. "Plighted Cunning, Playing the Good Girl Role: *The Taming of the Shrew* and *King Lear.*" In *Shakespeare's Daughters.* Jefferson, N.C.: McFarland, 2003. Discusses how Bianca deceives her father by pretending to be a dutiful daughter.

Holderness, Graham. *Shakespeare in Performance: "The Taming of the Shrew."* New York: Manchester University Press, 1989. Examines four different productions of the play, including the 1967 film directed by Franco Zeffirelli and starring Elizabeth Taylor and Richard Burton and a British 1980 television adaptation starring John Cleese. Focuses on the importance of the performance of Shakespeare's works.

Kidnie, Margaret Jane. *"The Taming of the Shrew": A Guide to the Text and Its Theatrical Life.* New York: Palgrave Macmillan, 2006. Handbook provides an overview of the play and discusses its text, sources, early performances, cultural context, and key productions and performances on stage and in film.

Wells, Stanley, ed. *The Cambridge Companion to Shakespeare Studies.* New York: Cambridge University Press, 1986. Excellent resource for any student of Shakespeare's work. Includes biographical information on the playwright and covers such topics as the conventions and beliefs of Elizabethan England.

Wynne-Davies, Marion, ed. *"Much Ado About Nothing" and "The Taming of the Shrew."* New York: Palgrave, 2001. Includes five essays about *The Taming of the Shrew*, including "The Turn of the Shrew" by Joel Fineman, "Renaissance Family Politics and Shakespeare's *The Taming of the Shrew*" by Karen Newman, and "A Shrew for the Times" by Diana E. Henderson.

Tarr

Author: Wyndham Lewis (1882-1957)
First published: 1918; revised, 1928
Type of work: Novel
Type of plot: Psychological realism
Time of plot: About 1910
Locale: Paris

Principal characters:
FREDERICK TARR, an English artist
BERTHA LUNKEN, Tarr's fiancé and a German art student
OTTO KREISLER, a German artist
ANASTASYA VASEK, a Russian
LOUIS SOLTYK, a Pole

The Story:

Frederick Tarr, an English artist living in Paris, is engaged to a young German woman, Bertha Lunken, a student in the Parisian art schools. Tarr dislikes Germans, although he knows a great many of them in Paris. It is his theory that either one has to be very intimate with them or one has to learn how to put up with them when one is not intimate. Not wishing to have it known that he is engaged to Bertha, he is on the point of breaking with her, for he considers her a dolt. He justifies his strange attitude on the grounds that all of his finer feelings go into his art, which leaves nothing over for sex. He admits that his taste in women is deplorable.

After a conversation with a friend during which he explains his theory, Tarr goes to his fiancé's apartment. He feels some remorse for his treatment of Bertha, but he was attracted by her bourgeois-bohemian absurdities and her Germanic floridity and unwittingly became too involved. Now, he feels, a break has to be made. He, however, underestimates the intensity of feeling that Bertha developed for him. The scene in the apartment, carefully decorated with sham art that Tarr loathes, is comic yet tragic. Tarr cannot help feeling that he is treating Bertha shabbily, yet he is passionately convinced that marriage is not for him. Nor did he expect such floods of tears; but somehow the break is accomplished, and Tarr departs with the promise to see Bertha again after a few days.

Otto Kreisler, an impecunious German artist, lives on a small allowance grudgingly doled out by his father. He just returned from a trip to Italy and is more than usually hard up. Four years before, Otto made the mistake of marrying off an old sweetheart to his father. Since he refuses his father's urgings that he give up art, return to Germany, and settle down into business, the monthly check, in revenge, is sent at irregular intervals. At this point, he is concerned with pawning his portmanteau as the result of failure to borrow money from an affluent compatriot, Ernst Volker. On his return from Italy, Kreisler discovers, to his horror, that his position as the recipient of Volker's bounty is taken by a Pole, Louis Soltyk, and that no more money can be expected. He already owes Volker fifteen hundred marks. It is the psychological effect of lack of money that, by indirect means, propels Kreisler toward his final tragedy.

In a mood of discouragement—the check from home is late again—he goes to the Café Vallet for lunch. By chance, he finds himself at the same small table with an extraordinarily beautiful young woman who, after some preliminary conversation, explains that she is Anastasya Vasek and that she escaped to Paris from her parents' bourgeois home. Kreisler is strongly attracted to her, because to him women are a kind of emotional pawnshop where he can dump his sorrows. With German sentimentality, he thinks of love as sorrowful. Determined to follow up that chance meeting, and despite the fact that his evening clothes are in pawn, he accepts an invitation from a member of the German colony, Fraulein Lipmann, to join her group at a dance at a club in the neighborhood. On the afternoon before the dance, he finds Anastasya sitting with Soltyk in a cafe. Again, he decides, the Pole is interfering in his affairs.

Driven by a kind of persecution mania, Kreisler deliberately makes a fiasco of the evening. On the way to the dance, he finds himself walking with Bertha and somewhat behind the other members of the party. Again, their peculiar German psychologies interact; he wishes to avenge himself through her on the more affluent guests; she feels that he is suffering and that she should make a sacrifice to console him. So Kreisler kisses her roughly, and she permits the kiss. They are seen by the other Germans, who are walking ahead. Kreisler arrives at the dance, dressed in rumpled morning clothes and still under the spell of his mania; he behaves abominably, insults nearly every woman present, and is almost thrown out. Worse, Anastasya laughs at him, turning his admiration to hate. The next morning, when the long-awaited allowance arrives accompanied by a command to return to Germany, Kreisler replies to his father that he will kill himself in exactly one month.

Shortly afterward, Bertha receives a letter from Tarr, informing her that he heard of the episode with Kreisler and that he is leaving for London. Furthermore, the "Kreisler affair" embroiled Bertha with her German friends. In a dreary mood, she goes out to buy lunch and meet Kreisler; after some conversation, she accepts his invitation to visit a café the following evening. This curious act is a defense against her friends; it is part of her theory that he is in distress, and it will contradict the story, now current, that his outrageous behavior was the result of Anastasya's snub. Furthermore, her meeting with Kreisler will be a kind of revenge on Tarr. She succeeds in convincing herself that she is being driven into this strange friendship. Eight days later, in Kreisler's studio, he possesses her by force, and the situation that she created becomes suddenly tragic. Kreisler comes to her apartment, offers to shoot himself, and finally departs after swearing to be her eternal servant. With her usual sentimentality, Bertha feels uplifted, as if together they did something noble.

Meanwhile, Tarr merely moves to the Montmartre district, where he feels that he can work in peace. He continues to frequent his old section with its German colony so that he can keep an eye on Bertha. Inevitably, he meets Anastasya, and just as inevitably, he encounters Bertha and Kreisler together. He cannot resist joining this pair; their "Germanness" gives him an ironic pleasure. Kreisler is baffled by the Englishman's sudden friendship that leads Tarr to join him at a café evening after evening, and he finds his Teutonic solemnity not equal to the situation. Fearful of being driven mad, he threatens the Englishman with a whip, when Tarr goes to his room, and then pushes him out the door.

Tarr and Anastasya become attracted to each other. During this time, they have long conversations about life and art. A storm, however, is gathering. One evening Tarr, who joins Kreisler and a Russian at a café, sees the German jump from his seat, rush across the room to a group of Russians and Poles, and slap Soltyk's face. That afternoon, Kreisler meets Anastasya and Soltyk; in a cold fury, he strikes Soltyk. Then he challenges the Pole to a duel. After much excited conversation, the challenge is accepted.

The duel next morning is another mixture of comedy and tragedy. The seconds are trying to effect an honorable compromise when Kreisler's mood suddenly changes: He offers to forgive Soltyk if the latter will kiss him. As he leans forward, the enraged Pole leaps upon him; they fall to the ground, and the seconds begin fighting among themselves. When the dust settles, Soltyk's friends try to lead him away, but they are stopped by Kreisler, who still holds his pistol. A Pole strikes at him; Kreisler fires and kills Soltyk. Kreisler flees. Five days later, penniless and hungry, he reaches a village near the border and is put in jail. In a last display of his disordered temperament, he hangs himself in his cell. His father pays the exact sum demanded by the town for the burial.

Meanwhile in Paris, Tarr and Anastasya rapidly become involved in an affair, and Tarr continues to see Bertha in decreasing "doses" as though he is taking medicine. As he is about to give her up, she tells him that she is pregnant and that the child is Kreisler's. Out of pity, Tarr marries her, but he lives with Anastasya. Two years later, Bertha divorces him to marry an eye doctor. Tarr never marries Anastasya. He has three children by another woman.

Critical Evaluation:

Wyndham Lewis is probably the least known of the great modernist authors and artists. A sometime colleague of Ezra Pound; an acquaintance of T. S. Eliot, James Joyce, and Gertrude Stein; and a campaigner for innovation in the arts of painting and literature, Lewis lost fame by turning on these and other allies, who, understandably, became less than enthusiastic about promoting his reputation. His feud with the literary Sitwell family, for example, whose portraits he painted, undoubtedly lost him many commissions. His output as painter, novelist, poet, philosopher, and controversial pamphleteer was prodigious. His father was American, and his mother English; Lewis was born on a yacht moored in Canadian waters. He thus was a citizen of three countries. After his parents separated when he was an infant, Lewis was raised in England by his English mother. He was educated at Rugby, a famous public school, and at London's Slade School of Art. *Tarr* is his first novel.

Lewis has been called the foremost English prose stylist of his century. In *Tarr*, his skill and his rigorous aesthetic are well in evidence. His painting, of the Futuristic stamp, but which Lewis, more to name his own movement than to create a necessary distinction, termed vorticist, is hard-edged and done with dizzying perspective. One finds a similar technique in *Tarr*. Eliot remarked that Lewis's novel was a war of points-of-view, not only in its content but also in its form. The style of the writing alters according to which of the major characters predominates in any given chapter.

It needs to be remarked here that there are a number of texts of this novel. In 1918 alone, three different versions were published: a serialized one, an American edition, and the English edition. In 1928, Lewis issued a revision of the American version. The reprint novel that is most widely available is based on the 1918 American text and provides an exhaustive variant table. Lewis uses various devices as "distancers," so that readers are frequently reminded by these unfamiliar signs that they are reading a text, not being hypnotized into ignoring one. To the same end, Lewis loads his prose with startling words and phrases, that insist on their status as artifice. The distinction between nature and art forms the subject of several exchanges in the novel. Furthermore, Kreisler and Bertha have too much nature in them, whereas Anastasya, like Tarr, is able to separate herself.

The writing is not replete with sensuous detail. Frederick Tarr is ascetic rather than sensuous in his aesthetics, as was Lewis. Tarr, being self-invented, evinces another article of Lewis's Futurist faith, that one needs to rid oneself of the past and begin anew, to be unnatural, unorganic, to break the inertia of the species. Personality, Lewis argues, is developed to overcome that which is imposed by birth and environment. It is noteworthy that the tragic events in the novel are brought about by the persistence of traditions that have outlived their time—dueling, the notion that a woman is a man's possession. These events arise from the conflict of the present with the past. Lewis needs to make this historical break evident, and *Tarr* embodies this need. The reader is kept aware at all times that the novel is art. The discomfort the text can cause is a deliberate calculation on its author's part. People must wake up, the aesthetic argument underlying *Tarr* implies, and cease to function as automata of nature. To be truly human is to invent oneself, to be efficient, a modern, a machine. Kreisler, a Romantic, has much that is old-fashioned, mechanical, and inefficient in his behavior. His suicide, ironically, moves like clockwork. Old-fashioned, too, is Kreisler's vision of himself as a pawn of fate. He is the villain of the story, because he is an embodiment of much that his creator found reprehensible.

In art, however, evil is often more engaging than good, and the sections with Kreisler in them are far and away the most readable portions. This may well be part of Lewis's calculation also: The hypnotized individual is presented in hypnotic prose. There is more of Kreisler than Tarr in the book, and Lewis himself was later to remark that he should have named the book after the German.

To one way of reading, the book is an allegory. Kreisler, in his envy of the civilized, in his passionate blindness, in his march toward death and destruction, represents the Germany of 1914. Kreisler is resentful of the Frenchified culture of the Poles, fearful of the power of Russia, baffled by the detachment of the English. All these elements—the Polish, the Russian, and the English, as well as the German—formed the tragic forces of World War I. Allegorical reading alone will not neatly contain the many meanings of this difficult, stimulating, and idiosyncratic novel, which, like a mobile, can turn a different aspect toward readers each time they open the book.

"Critical Evaluation" by David Bromige

Further Reading

Chapman, Robert. *Wyndham Lewis: Fictions and Satires.* New York: Barnes & Noble, 1973. Contains an excellent analysis of *Tarr*, particularly regarding the relations among the principal characters. Disagrees with those critics who have said that to reject the ideas of Frederick Tarr is to reject the novel.

Gąsiorek, Andrzej. *Wyndham Lewis and Modernism.* Tavistock, England: Northcote House/British Council, 2004. Introduction to Lewis's life and work as both a writer and a painter, including his participation in the vorticist movement, his commitment to early avant-gardism, and his eventual movement away from modernism and toward a theory of satire. Examines his opinions on gender, sexuality, politics, society, and the commodification of culture and aesthetics.

Jameson, Fredric. *Fables of Aggression: Wyndham Lewis, the Modernist as Fascist.* Rev. ed. Brooklyn, N.Y.: Verso Books, 2008. Jameson maintains that Lewis differs from other modernist writers because he was a political novelist. He provides a framework with which to examine these political novels, focusing on Lewis's use of language as both a symbolic and a political act.

Materer, Timothy. *Wyndham Lewis, the Novelist.* Detroit, Mich.: Wayne State University Press, 1976. Discusses the role of humor, the genesis of Frederick Tarr, and the dynamics between Tarr the "satiric commentator" and Kreisler the "tragic protagonist."

Peppis, Paul. *Literature, Politics, and the English Avant-Garde: Nation and Empire, 1901-1918.* New York: Cambridge University Press, 2000. Lewis figures prominently in Peppis's discussion of avant-garde literature in early twentieth century England. Peppis describes the impact of nationalism and imperialism on vorticism, and in a separate chapter he analyzes "anti-individualism and fictions of national character" in *Tarr*.

Pritchard, William H. *Wyndham Lewis.* New York: Twayne, 1968. Finds that the interest in *Tarr* lies less in the plot than in the restlessness and self-involvement of the characters, and the stylistic differences they engender.

Wragg, David A. *Wyndham Lewis and the Philosophy of Art in Early Modernist Britain: Creating a Political Aesthetic.* Lewiston, N.Y.: Edwin Mellen Press, 2005. A reevaluation of Lewis's works up to the 1930's, analyzing the philosophical and art historical aspects of his writings and how these elements contribute to readers' understanding of his political ideas. Useful for advanced students and readers with prior knowledge of literary history and critical theory.

Tartuffe

Author: Molière (1622-1673)
First produced: Tartuffe: Ou, L'Imposteur, 1664; first published, 1669 (English translation, 1732)
Type of work: Drama
Type of plot: Comedy
Time of plot: Seventeenth century
Locale: Paris

Principal characters:
ORGON, a wealthy former officer of the King's Guard
MADAME PERNELLE, his mother
ELMIRE, his wife
DAMIS, his son
MARIANE, his daughter
VALÈRE, Mariane's lover
DORINE, Mariane's maid
CLÉANTE, Orgon's brother-in-law
TARTUFFE, a hypocrite

The Story:

Orgon's home is a happy one. Orgon is married to Elmire, a woman much younger than he, who adores him. His two children by a former marriage are fond of their stepmother, and she of them. Mariane, the daughter, is engaged to be married to Valère, a very eligible young man, and Damis, the son, is in love with Valère's sister.

Then Tartuffe comes to live in the household. Tartuffe is a penniless scoundrel whom the trusting Orgon found praying in church. Taken in by his words and his pretended religious fervor, Orgon has invited the hypocrite into his home. As a consequence, the family is soon thrown into chaos. Once established, Tartuffe proceeds to change their normal, happy mode of life to a very strict one. He sets up a rigid Puritan regimen for the family and persuades Orgon to force his daughter to break her engagement to Valère in order to marry Tartuffe. He says that she needs a pious man to lead her in a righteous life.

Valère is determined that Mariane will marry no one but himself, but unfortunately Mariane is too spineless to resist Tartuffe and her father. Confronted by her father's orders, she remains silent or remonstrates only weakly. As a result, Tartuffe is cordially hated by almost every member of the family, including Dorine, the saucy, outspoken servant, who does everything in her power to break the hold the hypocrite has secured over her master. Dorine hates not only Tartuffe but also his valet, Laurent, for the servant imitates the master in everything. In fact, the only person other than Orgon who likes and approves of Tartuffe is Orgon's mother, Madame Pernelle, who is the type of Puritan who wishes to withhold from others pleasures in which she herself would not indulge.

Madame Pernelle highly disapproves of Elmire, maintaining that in her love for clothes and amusements Orgon's wife is setting her family a bad example that Tartuffe is trying to correct. Actually, Elmire is merely full of the joy of living, a fact that her mother-in-law is unable to perceive. Orgon

himself is little better. When he is informed that Elmire has fallen ill, his sole concern is for the health of Tartuffe. Tartuffe, however, is in fine health, stout and ruddy-cheeked. For his evening meal, he consumes two partridges, half a leg of mutton, and four flasks of wine. He then retires to his warm and comfortable bed and sleeps soundly until morning.

Tartuffe's romantic designs are not really on the daughter, Mariane, but on Elmire herself. One day, after Orgon's wife has recovered from her illness, Tartuffe appears before her. He compliments Elmire on her beauty and even goes so far as to lay his hand on her knee. Damis, Orgon's son, observes all that goes on between them from the cabinet where he is hidden. Furious, he reveals to his father what he has seen, but Orgon refuses to believe him. The wily Tartuffe has so completely captivated Orgon that Orgon orders his son to apologize to Tartuffe. When Damis refuses, Orgon, violently angry, drives the young man from the house and disowns him. To show his confidence in Tartuffe's honesty and piety, Orgon signs a deed of trust turning his estate over to Tartuffe's management and announces his daughter's betrothal to Tartuffe.

Elmire, embittered by the behavior of this impostor in her house, resolves to unmask him. She persuades Orgon to hide under a cloth-covered table to see and hear for himself the real Tartuffe. Then she entices Tartuffe, disarming him with the assurance that her foolish husband will suspect nothing. Emboldened, Tartuffe pours out his heart to her, leaving no doubt as to his intention of making her his mistress. Disillusioned and outraged when Tartuffe asserts that Orgon is a complete dupe, the husband emerges from his hiding place, denounces the hypocrite, and orders him from the house. Tartuffe defies him, reminding Orgon that according to the deed of trust, the house now belongs to Tartuffe.

Another matter makes Orgon even more uneasy than the possible loss of his property. He had been in possession of a box that was given to him by a friend, Argas, a political criminal now in exile. It contains important state secrets, the revelation of which would mean a charge of treason against Orgon and certain death for his friend. Orgon has foolishly entrusted the box to Tartuffe, and he fears the use the villain might make of its contents. Orgon informs his brother-in-law, Cléante, that he will have nothing further to do with pious men and that, in the future, he will shun them like the plague. Cléante, however, points out that such an extreme reaction is the sign of an unbalanced mind. He says that it is not fair to cast aspersions on religion itself simply because a treacherous vagabond is masquerading as a religious man.

The next day, Tartuffe follows through on his threat, using his legal right to Orgon's property to force Orgon and his family from their house. Madame Pernelle cannot believe Tartuffe guilty of such villainy, and she reminds her son that, in this world, virtue is often misjudged and persecuted. When the sheriff's officer arrives with the notice of eviction, however, even she finally believes that Tartuffe is a villain.

The crowning indignity comes when Tartuffe takes to the king the box containing the state secrets and orders are issued for Orgon's immediate arrest. Fortunately, before the king has a chance to examine the contents of the box, he recognizes Tartuffe as an impostor who has committed crimes in another city. Therefore, because of Orgon's loyal service in the army, the king annuls the deed that Orgon made turning his property over to Tartuffe and returns the box to Orgon unopened.

Critical Evaluation:

Molière wrote *Tartuffe* not to condemn organized religion or religious people but rather to condemn hypocrisy and to instruct audiences, through the use of humor, on the importance of moderation, common sense, and clear thinking in all areas of life. Although the play was originally condemned as an outright attack on religion and devout people, a proper reading suggests just the opposite. Religion is not the problem; rather, the misuse of religion for personal gain at the expense of innocent, unsuspecting people is Molière's concern. Works such as *Tartuffe* in fact help to protect and promote religion by exposing impostors for who they really are and demonstrating the real danger they pose to society when they go unchallenged.

The play's major emphasis is on the silly yet serious results of failing to act with common sense. The reactions of the various characters of the play to the hypocrite, Tartuffe, serve to remind the audience of the importance of clear thinking in a world where some people will take advantage of simple thinking and blind trust. The play reinforces the golden virtue of "moderation in all things." Excess, even in

service of the most sacred faith, leads to ridiculous conclusions and potentially catastrophic actions.

The comic way in which the story unfolds, from seemingly harmless simple belief about religious doctrine to eventual trust in the absurd notion that Tartuffe should be in control of the family's finances and estate, is a warning to all people to avoid letting others take advantage of them through their own lack of careful observation and scrutiny of human behavior. Orgon is unable to see the absurdity of the restrictions that Tartuffe places on his family. Ordinarily a reasonable and capable man, Orgon becomes so enamored of Tartuffe's manner and so dazzled by his rhetoric that he jeopardizes family, wealth, societal position, and eventually his own faith in the value of religion for the sake of appeasing the manipulative hypocrite. Molière clearly understood the dangers of false piety.

The play sets forth the theme of the importance of a well-ordered soul living in a well-ordered society under the virtue of reason. The comical yet serious unraveling of Orgon's professional and personal life at the hands of Tartuffe is the vehicle for the author's implicit appeal for reason and order in personal interactions and societal institutions. As Molière shows, when individuals such as Orgon ignore common sense and become infatuated with charismatic figures, the results can be tragic. Orgon's relationship with Tartuffe leads directly to the breakdown of his relationship with his son, the growth of mistrust between Orgon and his wife, personal embarrassment, and financial problems. These troubles have adverse effects on everyone in Orgon's life and, by extension, on society as a whole. The dishonest intentions of one man wreak havoc on many lives. Through the comic manner in which he tells the story, the playwright reinforces the idea that Orgon's difficulties could have been avoided. Tartuffe and his kind have power only when ordinary citizens willfully give up their ability to think for themselves.

In the end, the audience sees Orgon as remorseful for foolishly placing his trust in Tartuffe; he is also angry. In his anger, he inappropriately asserts that religion has been the cause of all the calamity that he and his family have undergone. Cléante, however, reminds Orgon that the real problem is not religion but the misuse of religion by impostors. Through Cléante's final speech, Molière reinforces the validity of appropriate religious expression by the truly devout.

"Critical Evaluation" by Kenneth E. Hada

Further Reading

Bermel, Albert. *Molière's Theatrical Bounty: A New View of the Plays*. Carbondale: Southern Illinois University Press,

1990. Provides original interpretations of the plays, partly designed to help actors think about the characters' motivations. Discusses the possibility of a sexual relationship between Tartuffe and Orgon; explains why Dorine can speak so freely to her master.

Hall, H. Gaston. *Comedy in Context: Essays on Molière*. Jackson: University Press of Mississippi, 1984. Analyzes Molière's work thematically. Especially informative on the historical background of the religious issues raised by *Tartuffe* as well as on the social customs of the time in which the play was first produced.

Hawcroft, Michael. *Molière: Reasoning with Fools*. New York: Oxford University Press, 2007. Examines the characters in Molière's plays whom Hawcroft calls *raisonneurs*—the thoughtful, witty, and resourceful friends of the foolish protagonists. Analyzes the *raisonneur*'s role as brother-in-law and polemicist in *Tartuffe*.

Koppisch, Michael S. *Rivalry and the Disruption of Order in Molière's Theater*. Madison, N.J.: Fairleigh Dickinson University Press, 2004. Argues that Molière's plays involve rivalries that eventually collapse the characters' differences. Chapter 3 examines the interdependence of Tartuffe and Orgon.

McCarthy, Gerry. *The Theatres of Molière*. New York: Routledge, 2002. Places Molière's life and work within the context of the French theater of his time. Discusses the productions of some of his plays, including the actors, scenery, and costumes.

Mander, Gertrud. *Molière*. Translated by Diana Stone Peters. New York: Frederick Ungar, 1973. Includes descriptions and analyses of fourteen plays and an informative detailed chronology of the playwright's life. Examines why Molière's contemporaries found *Tartuffe* so threatening and disturbing.

Polsky, Zachary. *The Comic Machine, the Narrative Machine, and the Political Machine in the Works of Molière*. Lewiston, N.Y.: Edwin Mellen Press, 2003. Examines the nature of seventeenth century French comedy by analyzing the works of Molière. Discusses the moralism and political context of Molière's plays and describes the use of speech, voice, and body in their performance. Includes a detailed analysis of *Tartuffe*.

Racevskis, Roland. *Time and Ways of Knowing Under Louis XIV: Molière, Sévigné, Lafayette*. Lewisburg, Pa.: Bucknell University Press, 2003. Examines the new technology of time measurement in seventeenth century France and its impact on French society and writers. Analyzes the depiction of time in *Tartuffe*.

Scott, Virginia. *Molière: A Theatrical Life*. New York: Cambridge University Press, 2000. Chronicles Molière's life and provides an overview of his plays, placing them within the context of seventeenth century French theater.

Walker, Hallam. *Molière*. Updated ed. Boston: Twayne, 1990. Examines *Tartuffe* within the context of religious controversies of the period as well as in terms of its artistic antecedents. Argues that Molière achieved new psychological realism and artistic complexity with this play. Discusses as a central theme of the play Orgon's willingness to punish himself and his family, which Tartuffe exploits but does not create.

The Task

Author: William Cowper (1731-1800)
First published: 1785
Type of work: Poetry

The first popular poetic success of William Cowper was *The Task*, which was also his first major venture in blank verse. For the fifty-four-year-old recluse, the reception of his poem must have had a salutary effect, for he went on to become, according to his greatest champion, Robert Southey, "The most popular poet of his generation."

Cowper's place in literary history is often in dispute. He was born exactly one hundred years after John Dryden and completed his best work in the year of Samuel Johnson's death. He neither aspired to become poet laureate nor wished to be the critical arbiter of his day. In many ways, however, he was the successor of both Dryden and Johnson. Cowper's blank verse is perhaps the best between that of seventeenth century poet John Milton and William Wordsworth's work in the early nineteenth century; his criticism expresses dissatisfaction with the extreme formalism of his age and anticipates, in some measure, the nineteenth century revolt against neoclassicism. He is usually said to be a writer of this transition toward Romanticism and realism.

His first work of any magnitude, *Olney Hymns* (1779), he undertook with his evangelical friend, the Reverend John Newton, while living at Olney with the Unwin family. "Oh! for a closer walk with God" is the most beautiful of his hymns.

Although Cowper's writing of the then-fashionable couplet was not successful, his early verse was at least simple. He objected strenuously to Alexander Pope's influence, which resulted in the highly ornamented versification of that age. Several long poems in this genre, published in 1782, serve as a kind of prelude to *The Task*. "Table Talk," written in rather abstract couplets, is a dialogue concerning the political, social, moral, and literary topics of the day. Here Cowper's dislike for the artifice of the eighteenth century is quite clear, and he damns most of the literary cults with faint praise, at the same time urging a return to God and nature for inspiration. "The Progress of Error" outlines the follies of high life and living as these affect the social structure: In this work he suggests a return to Christianity for the solutions to vexing problems. "Truth" extends Cowper's religious beliefs almost as if his distant relation, the cleric John Donne, were making himself felt. Cowper's thesis in the poem is that pride is truth's greatest foe, while humility will uplift humankind. In "Expostulation," he particularly decries anti-Semitism and urges England to remove this mote from the public eye. "Hope" and "Charity" celebrate God's nature (not the human nature of the Age of Reason) as the proper study, or at least reflection, of humanity. Satirically, he contrasts humanity's ways with God's. Another poem of this early group is "Retirement," an apology for his life as a recluse, his justification for giving up a life of action for the contemplative life of the poet.

In 1783, one of Cowper's intimate friends, Lady Austen, urged him to abandon the restrictive couplet form for blank verse. Cowper tells of this happening in the "Advertisement" of *The Task*:

> A lady, fond of blank verse, demanded a poem of that kind from the author, and gave him the SOFA for a subject. He obeyed; and, having much leisure, connected another subject with it; and, pursuing the train of thought to which his situation and turn of mind led him, brought forth at length, instead of the trifle heat first intended, a serious affair—a Volume!

This volume of five thousand lines is divided into six parts: "The Sofa," "The Time-Piece," "The Garden," "The Winter Evening," "The Winter Morning Walk," and "The Winter Walk at Noon." The poem's success was immediate, launching for the middle-aged poet a career and a reputation.

The sofa that Cowper describes in the opening lines is the effete summation of humanity's efforts to indulge in comforts, a human failing the poet presents with good humor. He leaves the sofa, as he says, "for I have lov'd the rural walk" with a good companion at his side. It is immediately apparent that the poet's work is to justify humanity's ways to God: "The task of new discov'ries falls on me," he suggests as he goes abroad. The next lines indicate that he will not countenance romantic illusions of the peasant's hard life or such poetic effusion of his age that tend to overlook the sordid, the cruel, or the ungodly. In comparing country and town, he sets up a dichotomy that persists throughout the poem: God creates and people destroy.

In "The Time-Piece," about expediency, Cowper takes a long look at institutions, especially political. After a close examination of events now forgotten, he remarks in a memorable line, "England, with all thy faults, I love thee still." The England he loves is the nation of an earlier, more virtuous, simpler time. He examines public figures, especially ministers, and finds them wanting. He suggests that God must be in every heart, Christ in every act. The river Ouse he describes as a symbol of immortality and ease.

"The Garden" brings the poet to the eternal verities of nature and causes him to celebrate family life and domestic happiness. Within this poem is the parable of Cowper ("I was a stricken deer, that left the herd") who, wounded by society, retired to a life of religious contemplation. From this vantage point, he asks people to be humane and Christian, to eschew wars, to learn wisdom. "Who loves a garden loves a greenhouse too," is his plea to humanity to cultivate simple pleasures in a rural setting: "Health, leisure, means t' improve it, friendship, peace" are what he thinks worthwhile. He concludes with a harsh renunciation of the city.

Continuing his statement of conflicting interests, in "The Winter Evening," Cowper compares the tragic news of the world with the simple man who delivers the post, unmoved. So should one live, the poet says, interested and sympathetic but apart; nothing is pleasanter than a winter night spent with good friends in good talk and before a good fire. Again, the town appears as the corrupter, its poison filtering down in the form of fashions spoiling the simple folk and altering the landscape. Although there are consolations in poetry, especially Milton's, rural life brings more compensations and inspiration.

"The Winter Morning Walk," a bracing though aesthetic experience, restores the poet's good humor as he observes beasts and people under winter's thrall. Cowper sees in winter a hope for immortality, for as the seeds and hibernating creatures wait out the ice, so humanity is bound in history. He next shames the greats of history as tyrants of oppression and great countries as slaveholders:

> Tis liberty alone that gives the flow'r
> Of fleeting life its lustre and perfume
> He is a freeman whom the truth makes free,
>   and all are slaves besides.

This is the substance of his argument. He concludes with an apostrophe to godly graces and offers thanks to God.

Finally, in "The Winter Walk at Noon," the poet uses sonorous polysyllables to celebrate village bells as symbols of harmonious living—and offers also a backward glance at his own life. He describes the winter landscape in an ode to the cold, crisp season. In memorable passages, he anticipates the spring. Finally, he justifies the life of the rambler, the contemplative life of the poet who sounds the note of God's truth, whether of castigation or exaltation.

Further Reading

Brunström, Conrad. *William Cowper: Religion, Satire, Society.* Lewisburg, Pa.: Bucknell University Press, 2004. Reconsiders Cowper's work within the context of eighteenth century political and religious culture. Brunström views Cowper not as a "pre-Romantic," or an old-fashioned Calvinist living in a more secular age, but as a writer who understood the increasingly emotional quality of the era's religious discourse and expressed that emotion in his work.

Feingold, Richard. *Nature and Society: Later Eighteenth-Century Uses of the Pastoral and Georgic.* New Brunswick, N.J.: Rutgers University Press, 1978. Studies *The Task* in relation to Cowper's views on society. By analyzing the poem from both pastoral and georgic perspectives, Feingold establishes that Cowper's primary concerns are issues and conditions of contemporary life.

Free, William N. *William Cowper.* New York: Twayne, 1970. This comprehensive study of Cowper devotes one chapter to *The Task.* Biographical sources are cited to illustrate how Cowper's personal experiences influenced the theme, structure, tone, and metaphors of his poem. Includes chronology and selected bibliography.

King, James. *William Cowper: A Biography.* Durham, N.C.: Duke University Press, 1986. Cowper's poetic ambitions and literary career are the focus of this study. Good starting point for critical analysis of Cowper's poetry.

Newey, Vincent. *Cowper's Poetry: A Critical Study and Reassessment.* New York: Barnes & Noble, 1982. Exhaustive treatment of many of Cowper's poems, including *The Task.* Meticulous examination of Cowper's diction, tone, and syntax yields excellent interpretations of Cowper's most popular, as well as his less celebrated, poetry.

_____. "Cowper's Prospects: Self, Nature, Society." In *Romanticism and Religion from William Cowper to Wallace Stevens*, edited by Gavin Hopps and Jane Stabler. Burlington, Vt.: Ashgate, 2006. Focuses on Cowper as an early Romantic writer. Includes analysis of *The Task.*

Priestman, Martin. *Cowper's "Task": Structure and Influence.* New York: Cambridge University Press, 1983. Compares Cowper and other eighteenth century poets, illuminating the differences and similarities between Cowper and his contemporaries.

Terry, Richard. "Mock-Heroic and Grace: The Case of Cowper." In *Mock-Heroic from Butler to Cowper: An English Genre and Discourse.* Burlington, Vt.: Ashgate, 2005. Terry traces the development of the mock-heroic genre of English literature in the seventeenth and eighteenth centuries. In addition to his chapter on Cowper, he discusses the mock-heroic qualities in *The Task* on pages 27-29.

A Taste of Honey

Author: Shelagh Delaney (1939-   )
First produced: 1958; first published, 1959
Type of work: Drama
Type of plot: Psychological realism
Time of plot: 1950's
Locale: Salford, Lancashire, England

Principal characters:
HELEN, a "semi-whore"
JOSEPHINE (JO), her teenage daughter
PETER, Helen's boyfriend
THE BOY (JIMMIE), Jo's black boyfriend
GEOFFREY (GEOFF), a gay art student

The Story:

Helen and her daughter Jo are moving into a comfortless apartment in a Salford slum. Jo complains about the place, but Helen says they can afford nothing better. They bicker constantly about everything from Helen's drinking and many boyfriends to the cold, their frequent moves, and Jo's determination to quit school after Christmas. Helen complains about feeling sick. In unpacking, Helen finds some drawings Jo has done and thinks them quite good, but Jo resents even her mother's praise.

Peter, a brash car salesman, arrives in search of Helen, who has been avoiding him. Peter had not known before that Helen has a teenage daughter (and is thus older than he thought) but he nevertheless asks Helen to marry him. Helen seems tempted to say yes. Jo brings them coffee and continues to make sarcastic comments. While Peter tells dirty jokes, Jo tries to discourage him from marrying Helen; he leaves without having received an answer. While the two women prepare for bed, Helen asks Jo what she thinks about her marrying Peter. Jo tells her mother that she considers it ridiculous.

Shortly before Christmas, Jo's boyfriend, a black sailor, walks her home from school. When he tries to kiss her, she says no, though she enjoys his kisses. He proposes marriage, and she agrees. He gives her a cheap ring and asks what her mother will think, especially about his race. Jo says that she does not care how her mother might react. Nevertheless, she decides to wear the ring on a ribbon around her neck, under her clothes. Jo tells him that after she leaves school she will go to work in a bar and move out of her mother's home as soon as possible. They arrange to meet later.

When Jo returns home, Helen guesses that she has been seeing a boyfriend. Jo asks to be told her real birth date, who her natural father was, and when Helen's husband had thrown Helen and Jo out. Helen avoids answering and abruptly announces that she is going to marry again. When Peter arrives, Jo sarcastically calls him "Daddy" and says that his marrying Helen is crazy. While Helen is getting ready, Jo attacks Peter. She looks at the photographs in his

wallet, including some of other women, and derides Peter and Helen for wanting to marry. Jo is convinced that Helen and Peter will be away for several days, during which Jo, not for the first time, will be left alone. She complains about her mother's neglect, and Helen criticizes her for her jealousy. Peter and Helen leave, and Jo falls onto the bed, crying.

Jo's boyfriend enters the apartment and, thinking Jo might be ill, fixes her some medicine. Jo tells him that Helen and Peter are getting married and asks him to stay with her over Christmas. They begin kissing as the lights fade.

After a time, Helen returns, carrying boxes of wedding finery. Because Jo is in pajamas, Helen notices Jo's ring and berates her for spending time with her boyfriend in the apartment. While arranging for her own wedding, she begs Jo not to ruin her life by getting married. Jo again asks about her father. Helen reveals that he was sweet but mentally retarded; they had made love only once. Helen tells Jo that they will see each other after her honeymoon, and Jo wishes Helen good luck.

In early summer, a noticeably pregnant Jo and Geoff, an art student, return to her apartment from a fair. Geoff has been evicted from his apartment (perhaps for being gay), so Jo has invited him to stay with her. He, too, notices her drawings. They discuss Jo's pregnancy, her decision against abortion, her finances, and whether she should tell her mother about the baby, especially since Helen presumably now has money. Jo absolutely refuses to let Helen know. Geoff sings nursery rhymes and asks about the baby's father; Jo claims he is an African prince. As she is falling asleep, Jo tells Geoff that he is like a big sister to her.

A month or two later, Geoff is still living with Jo, helping to prepare for the baby. He seems far more nurturing than Jo, who says she hates babies. Geoff says that he stays because someone has to care for Jo. He asks her to marry him, regardless of any physical relationship, but Jo refuses. She suggests that he leave and then reconsiders. Helen arrives, and Geoff asks her not to reveal to Jo that he contacted her. Helen and Jo immediately begin bickering. When Jo implies that her morals are no worse than Helen's, Helen tries to hit Jo, who flees from her. Geoff tries to intervene, but Helen chases him out. Then, somewhat calmer, she tells Jo that she has brought money to help out with the baby. Jo resentfully tells Helen that the "mother-love act" is too late. Peter arrives, drunk. He insults everyone in turn, including Helen for being old and for giving Jo "his" money. When Helen invites Jo to stay with them, Peter rejects the idea and they begin to quarrel. Helen eventually leaves with Peter, who takes back the money Helen had given Jo.

In September, Geoff is giving the apartment a thorough cleaning in preparation for the baby, which is nearly due. Jo suddenly feels frightened. When Geoff comforts her, she compares him favorably with her mother; he replies that, in some ways, Jo is just like Helen. He gives Jo a doll to practice her mothering skills, but she says the doll is the wrong color and throws it down. Then she tells the truth about her baby's father, Jimmie. Geoff again proposes marriage; again she puts him off. Helen arrives, evidently ready to move back in with Jo. She criticizes all of Geoff's efforts, insults him, and sends him away. Alone with Jo, she reveals that Peter has discarded her for a younger woman. When Geoff returns, Helen all but throws him out, so he leaves again, apparently for good.

Jo awakes from a nap and calls out for Geoff. She tells Helen that her baby will be black. Helen is appalled and walks out. Singing one of Geoff's nursery rhymes, Jo watches her go.

Critical Evaluation:

Shelagh Delaney, who wrote *A Taste of Honey* at the age of eighteen, clearly drew on aspects of her own experience to create the world of the play. Like Jo, she grew up in a gritty Lancashire town and left school at sixteen to work at various menial jobs. By identifying closely with her character Jo, Delaney was able to present an adolescent's perspective with uncanny accuracy. The incessant conflicts with her mother—with their fluid mixture of sarcasm, sensitivity, neediness, sullen rebelliousness, and longing for affection—are especially believable. In the dialogue between Helen and Jo, Delaney reflects tensions common to most mother-daughter relationships, regardless of geography or class. The play also evokes the perpetual "now" of adolescence and the sense of drifting in the present and of being neither child nor adult. As Jo puts it, "I really am [contemporary], aren't I? I really do live at the same time as myself, don't I?" Significantly, Jo speaks of herself in question form, which accurately mirrors her uncertainty about who she is and what she wants from life.

The play's focus on life from Jo's perspective comes at a price, however, and the scenes with Helen can give the audience an uneasy sense that the author is settling old scores. Helen always appears unsympathetic, with Jo her victim. Their dialogue sounds so real that it might have been quoted verbatim from actual quarrels between Delaney and her mother, unmodified by artistic insight. The male characters fare even worse than Helen. They float, shadowlike, at the periphery of Jo's small world, fulfilling functions in the plot but having no real lives of their own. The audience does not even learn the name of Jo's boyfriend until the second act, after he is long gone. Peter stands in for all the men who have cheated Jo of her mother's affection over the years, while Geoff sets a standard of good mothering that Helen (or almost any real human being) could never actually achieve. The play shows all the characters as Jo sees them, almost exclusively in terms of their relationship to her. While this self-centered worldview has resonance for the adolescent in everyone, it could be said to lack the complex insights of a more mature artist.

A Taste of Honey nevertheless represents a remarkable achievement for a young woman writing her first play in the mid-1950's, a time when "angry young men" were dominating the English theater. Following John Osborne's *Look Back in Anger* (pr. 1956), plays about working-class life became enormously popular, but hardly any were given a female perspective. In these "kitchen-sink" dramas, women were usually nurturing mother surrogates, objects of frustrated male rage, or (quite often) both. How to be a real man in the postwar, welfare-state world remained the central question for an entire generation of new playwrights. Delaney had the originality to examine the same social milieu while focusing on working-class women.

Although *A Taste of Honey* won prizes, became a hit onstage and in film, and continues to be performed, Delaney's contribution has been largely overlooked or marginalized. In the context of "angry" theater, her interest in women and mothering has been treated as less relevant than issues of masculine violence. Feminist theater criticism has considered Delaney a foremother who prefigured important themes but never achieved her full promise. Some, holding Delaney's youth and inexperience against her, regard the play as a fluke and attribute its success mostly to director Joan Littlewood's modifications and insights. The failure of Delaney's subsequent play, *The Lion in Love* (pr. 1960), and her later abandonment of the stage have confirmed these opinions. She continued to write, however, primarily for television and film, a choice that seems reasonable given the way her work uses music and "cinematic" emotional close-ups.

The high quality of her screenplay for the film *Dance with a Stranger* (1985) should refute charges that her early success was an accident. In her later works, Delaney retained her bitter humor, her insight into characters, especially women, and her impressive gift for pungent dialogue.

A Taste of Honey remains relevant for the way in which it focuses on women's emotional struggles with motherhood and their sexuality. The similarities of Helen's and Jo's experiences (working in bars, pregnancy and single motherhood at an early age, desertion or rejection by men, bare economic subsistence) compellingly convey the tragic cycle of poverty, child neglect, and hopeless alienation from mainstream society, problems that certainly continued after the 1950's. The play also marks one of the earliest positive stage portrayals of a gay male character; neither a joke nor a stereotype, Geoff retains his human dignity and freely nurtures those who need him. In addressing these issues, Delaney blazed a trail for other playwrights, both male and female.

Susan Wladaver-Morgan

Further Reading

De Jongh, Nicholas. "Out of Bondage Towards Being." In *Not in Front of the Audience: Homosexuality on Stage.* New York: Routledge, 1992. Examines *A Taste of Honey* in the light of gay and lesbian studies and finds in Geoff a recognition of the full humanity of the gay character unusual for its time. Notes that, however tentatively, the play marks the beginnings of a revolt against conventional relationships and for personal liberation.

Dyer, Rachel. "'We're Coming Home': Accent(uat)ing Nostalgia in Kathleen Jamie's *Autonomous Region* and Shelagh Delaney's *A Taste of Honey*." In *Devolving Identities: Feminist Readings in Home and Belonging*, edited by Lynne Pearce. Burlington, Vt.: Ashgate, 2000. Presents a feminist analysis of the play, focusing on its representations of gender and regional identity.

Esche, Edward J. "Shelagh Delaney's *A Taste of Honey* as Serious Text." In *The Death of the Playwright? Modern British Drama and Literary Theory*, edited by Adrian Page. New York: St. Martin's Press, 1992. Discusses the play as modern tragedy, not as an uplifting piece for high school students. Esche relies on a particular stage production for some of his interpretation.

Jellicoe, Ann. "Motherhood and Masculinity." In *Look Back in Gender: Sexuality and the Family in Post-War British Drama*, edited by Michelene Wandor. London: Methuen, 1987. Examines *A Taste of Honey* from a feminist perspective that would not have been available to Delaney in 1958 and observes that while the play violates a number of taboos, the old values still rule. Discusses how the play, especially in its treatment of relationships between women, marks a significant departure from the established conventions of the British theater as it existed at the time.

Komporaly, Jozefina. *Staging Motherhood: British Women Playwrights, 1956 to the Present*. New York: Palgrave Macmillan, 2006. *A Taste of Honey* is one of the plays analyzed in this examination of the depiction of motherhood in the plays of British women playwrights.

Taylor, John Russell. *The Angry Theatre: New British Drama*. New York: Hill & Wang, 1962. Places Delaney's work in the context of the theatrical revolution following John Osborne's *Look Back in Anger*. Offers an especially interesting comparison of Delaney's original script with the workshop version produced by Joan Littlewood that formed the basis of the printed text.

Wellwarth, George E. "The Drama of Alienated Youth: Shelagh Delaney." In *The Theater of Protest and Paradox: Developments in the Avant-Garde Drama*. Rev. ed. New York: New York University Press, 1971. Discusses how, like many of the important plays of its period, *A Taste of Honey* presents loneliness as the human condition. Praises Delaney's dialogue but finds her plotting weak.

Tell Me a Riddle

Author: Tillie Olsen (1912-2007)
First published: 1961
Type of work: Short fiction

The Stories:

"I Stand Here Ironing": A woman is ironing her laundry, but the real action occurs in her mind, in which she is speaking about a phone call from her daughter Emily's school. Mother recalls Emily's infancy, when she was abandoned by her father during the Great Depression, and her own regret that she has to leave the child with a neighbor while she works. Even after she finds a night job so that she can be with Emily during the day, she soon has to leave the child with her husband's relatives to work full-time.

At the age of two, Emily returns to her mother, only to be placed in a day nursery until social workers can send her to an institution, where she grows even more isolated and uncertain. Home again, she remains quiet and distant. Mother feels terrible guilt for these events beyond her control and their effect on her daughter.

Emily, now a teenager, has developed a surprising gift for acting, and audiences love her. Still, mother worries that nothing can come of it because of her difficult early years. Mother hopes that the school official will understand and help her daughter learn "that she is more than this dress on the ironing board, helpless before the iron."

"Hey Sailor, What Ship?": Whitey, a sailor ashore in San Francisco, visits his good friends Lennie and Helen, the only family he has had since he saved Lennie's life during the bitter longshoremen's strike of 1934. In an alcoholic daze, Whitey is taken home by Lennie and put to bed on the couch. Helen and their younger daughters are fond of Whitey, but Jeannie, the eldest, is ashamed of him.

Whitey awakes to tremors and food and a note left by Helen. The note says that the children will be home soon after school to stay with him, but he flees in confusion. Five days later, he returns with gifts and food. All quickly realize that he is more than drunk—he is very ill—and call a doctor friend to examine him.

Little Allie loves Whitey, proudly showing him his photograph as a handsome young man. For her, he recites a patriotic Filipino poem, "El Ultimo Adiós" ("the last farewell"). His body is failing, he is dying, but he cannot stay—the urge to drink is too powerful.

"O Yes": In the troubled 1950's, at the beginning of the Civil Rights movement, Helen and her middle daughter,

Carol, who are white, are invited to the Baptist church of Carol's African American friend, Parialee (Parry) Phillips, who is to be baptized. The two mothers are friends, and their daughters have been close throughout childhood, but now they have entered middle school and Carol is embarrassed, fearing that a black classmate in the choir might report her presence at the church to friends at school. As the congregation works itself into ecstasy with the preacher, Carol is startled by a woman's scream.

Almost fainting, Carol cannot handle the intense emotions of the parishioners. Parry's mother patiently tries to explain their customary worship to the tearful girl, but at home, her older sister, Jeannie, is skeptical, hardened at age seventeen. Actually, Carol and Parry are separating. Parry is learning "jivetalk" and growing away from Carol (and Carol from Parry). Painfully aware of racism, both girls feel awkward, but in a sense Carol is the one being baptized. The two mothers regret that their adolescent daughters cannot yet move beyond that separation, as they themselves had done.

"Tell Me a Riddle": An elderly Russian-immigrant couple, David and Eva, have been married forty-seven years and have seven children. Now, David wants to sell the house and move into The Haven, a cooperative for the elderly, where he will be free of responsibilities. Eva, although wanting to be free of responsibilities, too, refuses to leave her home, saying that she wants to stay "because eighteen hours a day I ran. And you never scraped a carrot or knew a dish towel sops." He switches on the television to drown out her voice; she turns off her hearing aid. They argue bitterly over the potential sale of the house, although at night, in their sleep, they still cuddle next to each other.

Eva's occasional fatigue increases; she often stays in bed. Eventually they discover that she requires gallbladder surgery, which reveals a greater problem: cancer. Although David says he cannot face her illness, he does, concealing his grief from Eva. As she recuperates, he decides to take her for a final visit to her children and grandchildren. They fly to Ohio, to their daughter Vivi.

Grandmother Eva cannot hold Vivi's newborn—she sweats, stiff and awkward, resisting the emotional surge of responsibility for a tiny life: "Never again to be forced to move to the rhythms of others." David loves the baby, happily singing to the child. As Eva becomes stronger, she is able to tidy up, trying to help her exhausted daughter, but she will not feed or care for the children. She begs to go home. Instead, David takes her to Los Angeles, to a seaside apartment that Lennie had arranged for them. Their granddaughter, Jeannie, commutes from her job as a visiting nurse. The city's pollution sickens Eva, but she loves the beach until she tells a long-ago friend that she is dying.

Jeannie brings Eva a child-shaped cookie, a *pan de muerto* lovingly made by the mother of a dead three-year-old child. Jeannie resigns her job to stay with her weakened grandmother, who can no longer travel. Lennie and Helen arrive as Eva's fever returns. Too ill to move to a hospital, she remains in the apartment, often with delirious, fragmented memories of her girlhood in Russia. As Eva suffers, she recalls songs of the revolution, singing snatches of the old socialist hymn "These Things Shall Be." David abandons his concerns about money; for his wife's sake, not his, he hopes for her quick death. In Eva's final agony, Jeannie consoles her grandparents.

Critical Evaluation:

Written in the 1950's, before the full flowering of the women's movement, the four loosely related stories of Tillie Olsen's *Tell Me a Riddle* have become American classics. "Tell Me a Riddle," the collection's title story, received an O. Henry Award for best American short story in 1961.

Olsen, the daughter of immigrants who had fled czarist Russia after the revolution of 1905, offers an intimate glimpse into the lives of the working-class poor from the 1930's through the 1950's. Plot is of little relevance here; character predominates, and Olsen makes frequent use of stream of consciousness as she follows their unspoken, sometimes incoherent thoughts.

Several critics believe that Olsen's best work is that which is closest to autobiography. In the 1930's, as a member of the Young Communist League, she had been arrested for organizing packinghouse workers and spent a month in jail. In *Tell Me a Riddle*, the book by which she will be best remembered, many of the characters and events parallel those in her own life: involvement with the labor movements of the 1930's; combining motherhood with jobs in factories and slaughterhouses; an infant daughter, like Emily, taken from her after the father deserted them; unmoored, lonely alcoholics like Whitey; and the hard death of her mother from cancer. Although Olsen's writing was influenced by her beliefs, her politics evolved from socialism to something closer to

humanism, and she did not proselytize. She had choses to illustrate the problems through literature.

In addition to being a proletarian writer of the working poor who had been effectively silenced by her culture, Olsen was a feminist. In the 1950's, when her youngest child began school and she could write full-time, popular American culture emphasized the nuclear family and strict gender roles. Irving Howe, an early critic reviewing *Tell Me a Riddle* in 1961, stereotyped Olsen as a woman who relied on her "narrow" experiences as a housewife and mother. However, in *Tell Me a Riddle*, she speaks for many who have been neither seen clearly nor taken seriously, who have been silenced because of their gender or their working-class status, or because of the menial work they do; and even though American culture has gradually changed, her work remains relevant, speaking with clarity, sincerity, and passion.

Joanne McCarthy

Further Reading

Cardoni, Agnes Toloczko. *Women's Ethical Coming-of-Age: Adolescent Female Characters in the Prose Fiction of Tillie Olsen*. Lanham, Md.: University Press of America, 1998. A survey of Olsen's adolescent female characters, comparing and contrasting their milieux. Includes a bibliography and an index.

Frye, Joanne S. *Tillie Olsen: A Study of the Short Fiction*. New York: Twayne, 1995. Frye's thoughtful examination of the stories in *Tell Me a Riddle*, especially "Hey Sailor, What Ship?" Includes an extended conversation with Olsen, focusing specifically on these stories.

Nelson, Kay Hoyle, and Nancy Huse, eds. *The Critical Response to Tillie Olsen*. Westport, Conn.: Greenwood Press, 1994. A collection of the most important articles, reviews, and parts of books about Olsen, arranged in chronological order. Includes essays from a variety of approaches on the stories "I Stand Here Ironing," "Tell Me a Riddle," and "O Yes."

Pearlman, Mickey, and Abby H. P. Werlock. *Tillie Olsen*. Boston: Twayne, 1991. The first book-length interpretation of Olsen's work offers a 1987 interview with Olsen, a chronology, and a chapter-long analysis of each story and the nonfiction *Silences* (1978). Chapter 2 contains a well-researched biographical sketch. The authors also challenge errors made by various critics.

Reid, Panthea. *Tillie Olsen: One Woman, Many Riddles*. New Brunswick, N.J.: Rutgers University Press, 2010. A comprehensive biographical account of Olsen's life and work based on diaries, letters, manuscripts, private documents, resurrected public records, and interviews. Also corrects fabrications and myths about Olsen.

Rosenfelt, Deborah Silverton, ed. *Tell Me a Riddle/Tillie Olsen.* New Brunswick, N.J.: Rutgers University Press, 1995. Consists of the footnoted title story, two essays by Olsen, and seven critical essays on her life, political activism, and writing. Confirms that the conditions that historically discouraged women from writing are similar to those facing Eva in "Tell Me a Riddle."

Schultz, Lydia A. "Flowing Against the Traditional Stream: Consciousness in Tillie Olsen's 'Tell Me a Riddle.'"

MELUS 22, no. 3 (Fall, 1997): 113-131. A detailed investigation of the stream-of-consciousness technique as it is used in this story. The developing "stream" the reader follows is that of the marriage between Eva and David, through which Olsen reveals David's emerging empathy for his wife.

Trensky, Anne. "The Unnatural Silences of Tillie Olsen." *Studies in Short Fiction* 27 (Fall, 1990): 509-516. A thematic analysis of "Tell Me a Riddle" that explores Olsen's concern with the cultural silences that have stifled so many women.

The Tell-Tale Heart

Author: Edgar Allan Poe (1809-1849)
First published: 1843
Type of work: Short fiction
Type of plot: Horror
Time of plot: 1840's
Locale: An American village

Principal characters:
THE NARRATOR, a man whose madness drives him to murder
THE OLD MAN, in the care of the narrator, and his victim

The Story:

A man insists that he is not mad. In spite of being dreadfully nervous, he also insists that his senses, especially his hearing, have been heightened rather than destroyed. He claims that the calm and healthy way he will tell the following story is evidence of his sanity.

He admits that he cannot say when the idea to kill the old man had come into his mind. He says he had no reason, nor passion, for killing him; the old man had never harmed or insulted him. He did not want his money. He says he loved the old man. He thinks he killed him because of the old man's eye, like the eye of a vulture, a pale blue eye that made the old man's blood run cold.

The narrator says that he had never been kinder to the old man than he had been during the week before he killed him. He tells the following story: Before the murder, every night at midnight, he makes a small opening in the old man's chamber door and puts a small closed lantern inside. Taking an hour to slowly place his head in the opening so he can see the old man, he opens the lantern, allowing the light to shine on the vulture eye. He does this for seven nights, but because the eye is always closed, he does not become enraged by it. In great detail, he praises himself for his cunning, asks his listener if a mad person could have been so clever as he, and even tells the listener that he or she would have laughed if they had seen how methodically he had opened the door and placed the lantern inside the old man's chamber.

On the eighth night, he tells the listener, he once again puts the lantern inside the chamber, but this time his finger slips, making a noise that wakens the old man, who then cries out. For an hour, the narrator waits; then he hears a groan and recognizes it as the groan of mortal terror, a sound he, too, has made in the night. He slowly opens the crevice in the lantern until the light falls on the open vulture eye. Still he waits, knowing the old man's terror must be extreme. He hears a sound like that of a watch inside cotton and thinks it is the beating of the old man's terrified heart. Imagining that the sound is so loud it could be heard by a neighbor, he bursts inside the chamber, pulls the old man to the floor, and suffocates him with the bedding. He then cuts up the corpse and puts the body parts under the floor, replacing the boards so cleverly so that no one could ever see anything wrong.

Proud that a tub had caught all of the old man's blood, he then cleans up the crime scene and prepares to go to bed when he hears a knock at the door. Three men who identify themselves as police tell him that neighbors had reported hearing a shriek in the night. He smiles and says it was his own shriek in a dream. He tells the officers that the old man is out, visiting in the country, then takes them through the house, leading them to the old man's bedchamber. He brings in chairs for them to sit on, placing his own chair right over the spot where the corpse is hidden beneath the floorboards.

He answers the officers' questions, cheerily, but then thinks he hears a ringing in his ears, which gets louder and more distinct. Finally, he thinks that the noise is not from within his ears but from beneath the flooring. He becomes more and more agitated, pacing, swearing, and grating his chair upon the floor over the body. He thinks the police can hear the sound also, and that they are pretending they do not, making a mockery of his own horror. Finally, he feels he must scream or die. He shrieks loudly, admitting the murder and insisting the officers pull up the planks to reveal the beating of the old man's "hideous heart."

Critical Evaluation:

There are two physical settings in Edgar Allan Poe's "The Tell-Tale Heart": the house the narrator shares with the old man where the murder takes place and the location from which the narrator tells his story, presumably a prison or an asylum for the criminally insane. However, the most important setting for the story is within the obsessed mind of the narrator. The old man is hardly more than the evil eye that so infuriates the narrator, the source of his mysterious obsession.

The central question on which the story depends is, why does the narrator kill the old man? He says he has no personal animosity toward him, that he does not want his money, that the old man has not injured him in any way. In fact, he says he loves the old man. The only reason he can give is the evilness of the old man's eye. Although some critics have suggested that the eye is the "evil eye" of superstition, which the narrator feels threatens him, there is no way to understand his motivation except to say the narrator must be mad. Still, the reader feels compelled to try to understand the method and meaning of the madness. For Poe, there is no meaningless madness in a short story.

The key to understanding the mysterious motivation in the story is Poe's concept of a central idea or effect around which everything else coheres, like an obsession that can be identified on the principle of repetition. Thus, if the reader is alert to repetitions in the story, these repeated themes become the clues to the mystery. Determining motifs foregrounded by repetition helps the reader distinguish between details that

are relevant to the central theme and those that merely provide an illusion of reality. Poe, the creator of the detective story, was well aware of the importance of discovering all those details that matter in a case and then constructing a theory based on their relationship to each other

To understand what the eye means in the story, the reader must take Poe's advice in his essays and reviews on short fiction and determine how all the various details in the story seem bound together to create one unified theme and effect. In addition to the details about the eye, there are two other sets of details repeated throughout the story: the narrator's identification with the old man and the idea of time. When the narrator sticks his head in the old man's chamber at night and hears him groan, he says he knows what he is feeling, for he himself has felt the same terror many times himself. At the moment the narrator kills the old man, as well as the moment when he confesses the crime, he thinks he hears the beating of the old man's heart; however, of course, what he hears is the beating of his own heart. When the police question him about the old man's scream in the night, he says it was his own in a bad dream.

The narrator makes several references to time. The beating of the old man's heart sounds like the ticking of a watch wrapped in cotton; the old man is said to listen to death watches (a kind of beetle that makes a ticking sound) in the wall; time seems to slow down and almost stop when he sticks his head in the old man's chamber. To understand this obsession with time and its association with the beating of a heart, the reader must relate it to the title and ask, what tale does a heart tell? The answer is that the tale every heart tells is that of time—time inevitably passing, every beat of one's heart bringing one closer to death. As in many other Poe stories, "The Tell-Tale Heart" suggests that when one becomes aware of the ultimate destiny of all living things—that humans are born only to die—time becomes the enemy that must be defeated at all costs.

By connecting the repeated theme of the narrator's identification with the old man to the obsession with the eye, the reader can conclude that what the narrator wishes to destroy is not the eye but that which sounds like "eye" (after all, he says that his sense of sound especially has been heightened). That is, the word "eye" sounds like the word "I," the self. This connection relates in turn to the theme of time. The only way one can escape the inevitability of time is to destroy that which time would destroy—the self. However, to save the self from time by destroying the self is a paradox that the narrator can only deal with by displacing his need to destroy himself (the I) to a need to destroy the eye of the old man. By destroying the old man's eye, the narrator indirectly does succeed in destroying himself—ultimately by exposing himself as a murderer. Of course, one could say, this is madness; indeed it is. However, it is madness and motivation with meaning, a meaning that Poe wishes us to discover by careful reading of the story.

One of Poe's major contributions to the development of the short story was his conception of plot not merely as a series of events, one thing after another, but as the calculated organization of all those details in the story that relate to and revolve around a central theme. It is no wonder that his own obsession with this aesthetic principle would lead him to create that great "reader" of hidden plot or pattern, Auguste Dupin, who would later become the model for Sir Arthur Conan Doyle's great detective Sherlock Holmes. "The Tell-Tale Heart" is indeed a murder mystery in which the narrator concocts a plot to kill the old man. However, the real plot of the story is Poe's elaborate pattern of psychological obsession and displacement, as one man tries to accomplish what all human beings wish to do—defeat the ticking of the clock that marks one's inevitable movement toward death.

Charles E. May

Further Reading

Ackroyd, Peter. *Poe: A Life Cut Short*. London: Chatto & Windus, 2008. Ackroyd, a novelist, provides a concise chronicle of Poe's brief, unhappy life.

Fisher, Benjamin F. *The Cambridge Introduction to Edgar Allan Poe*. New York: Cambridge University Press, 2008. An introductory overview of Poe's literary career and writings. Describes how Poe's fiction advanced from gothic fantasy to more sophisticated explorations of human psychology.

Gargano, James W. "The Theme of Time in 'The Tell-Tale Heart.'" *Studies in Short Fiction* 5 (1968): 378-382. Gargano argues that the story is a ruse perpetuated by the protagonist against himself and claims the real villain in the story is time.

Kennedy, J. Gerald. *A Historical Guide to Edgar Allan Poe*. New York: Oxford University Press, 2001. Considers the tensions between Poe's otherworldly settings and his representations of violence, delivers a capsule biography situating Poe in his historical context, and addresses topics such as Poe's sensationalism and his relationships to gender constructions. Includes a bibliographical essay, a chronology of Poe's life, a bibliography, illustrations, and an index.

May, Charles E. *Edgar Allan Poe: A Study of the Short Fiction*. Boston: Twayne, 1991. An introduction to Poe's short stories that attempts to place them with the nineteenth century short narrative tradition and within the context of Poe's aesthetic theory. Suggests Poe's contributions to the short story in terms of his development of detective fiction, fantasy, satire, and self-reflexivity.

Pritchard, Hollie. "Poe's 'The Tell-Tale Heart.'" *Explicator* 61, no. 2 (Spring, 2003). Argues that the narrator's madness in "The Tell-Tale Heart" is sadomasochism, that he gets pleasure from killing the old man. Noting that egocentrism is at the heart of sadomasochism, Pritchard suggests that the final pleasure the narrator receives is the prideful telling of his crime.

Robinson, E. Arthur. "Poe's 'The Tell-Tale Heart.'" *Nineteenth-Century Fiction* 19 (1965): 369-388. Discusses the narrator's psychological identification with the old man and the motif of the extensions of subjective time, both of which are linked in the story. Argues that the theme of the story is self-destruction through subjectivity.

Shen, Dan. "Edgar Allan Poe's Aesthetic Theory, the Insanity Debate, and the Ethically Oriented Dynamics of 'The Tell-Tale Heart.'" *Nineteenth-Century Fiction* 63, no. 3 (December, 2008): 321-345. Claims that "The Tell-Tale Heart" reflects an interaction, characteristic of Poe's stories, between structurally unified dramatic irony and the historical "insanity defense" controversy.

Wing-chi Ki, Magdalen. "Ego Evil and 'The Tell-Tale Heart.'" *Renascence* 61, no. 1 (Fall, 2008): 25-38. Discusses the relationship between ego and the eye in the story. Claims that the story foregrounds different stages of "ego-evil," as the narrator defines himself through the narcissistic eye and the enigmatic gaze of the other.

The Tempest

Author: William Shakespeare (1564-1616)
First produced: 1611; first published, 1623
Type of work: Drama
Type of plot: Fantasy
Time of plot: Fifteenth century
Locale: An island in the sea

Principal characters:
PROSPERO, the rightful duke of Milan
MIRANDA, his daughter
FERDINAND, son of the king of Naples
ARIEL, a spirit, Prospero's servant
CALIBAN, Prospero's slave
ALONSO, the king of Naples
SEBASTIAN, Alonso's brother
ANTONIO, the duke of Milan, Prospero's brother
GONZALO, a philosopher, who saves the lives of Prospero
and Miranda

The Story:

Alonso, the king of Naples, is returning from the wedding of his daughter to a foreign prince when his ship is overtaken by a terrible storm. In his company are Duke Antonio of Milan and other gentlemen of the court. As the gale rises in fury and it seems certain the vessel will split and sink, the noble travelers are forced to abandon ship and trust to fortune in the open sea.

The tempest is no chance disturbance of wind and wave. It was raised by a wise magician, Prospero, when the ship sails close to an enchanted island on which he and his lovely daughter, Miranda, are the only human inhabitants. Theirs is a sad and curious history. Prospero is the rightful duke of Milan, but being devoted more to the study of philosophy and magic than to affairs of state, he gave much power to his ambitious brother, Antonio, who twelve years earlier seized the dukedom with the aid of the crafty Neapolitan king. Prospero and his small daughter were set adrift in a boat by the conspirators, and they would have perished miserably had not Gonzalo, an honest counselor, secretly stocked the frail craft with food, clothing, and some of the books Prospero valued most.

The exiles drift at last to an island that is the refuge of Sycorax, an evil sorceress. There Prospero found Caliban, her son, a strange, misshapen creature of brute intelligence, able only to hew wood and draw water. In addition, there were many good spirits of air and water who became obedient to Prospero's will when he freed them from torments to which the sorceress Sycorax had condemned them. Chief among these is Ariel, a lively sprite.

Prospero, using his magic arts to draw the ship bearing King Alonso and Duke Antonio close to his enchanted island, orders Ariel to bring the whole party safely ashore, singly or in scattered groups. Ferdinand, King Alonso's son, is moved by Ariel's singing to follow the sprite to Prospero's rocky cell. Miranda, who does not remember ever seeing a human face other than her father's bearded one, at first sight falls deeply in love with the handsome young prince, and he with her. Prospero is pleased to see the young people so attracted to each other, but he conceals his pleasure, speaks harshly to them, and, to test Ferdinand's mettle, commands him to perform menial tasks.

Meanwhile Alonso, Sebastian, Antonio, and Gonzalo wander sadly along the beach, the king in despair because he believes his son drowned. Ariel, invisible in the air, plays solemn music, lulling to sleep all except Sebastian and Antonio. Drawing apart, they plan to kill the king and his counselor and make Sebastian tyrant of Naples. Watchful Ariel awakens the sleepers before the plotters can act.

On another part of the island, Caliban, carrying a load of wood, meets Trinculo, the king's jester, and Stephano, the royal butler, both drunk. In rude sport they offer a drink to Caliban. Tipsy, the loutish monster declares he will be their slave forever.

Like master, like servant. Just as Sebastian and Antonio plot to murder Alonso, so Caliban, Trinculo, and Stephano scheme to kill Prospero and become rulers of the island. Stephano is to be king, Miranda his consort, and Trinculo and Caliban will be viceroys. Unseen, Ariel listens to their evil designs and reports the plan to Prospero.

Miranda disobeys her father's injunction on interrupting Ferdinand in his task of rolling logs and the two exchange lovers' vows, which are overheard by the magician. Satisfied with the prince's declarations of devotion and constancy, Prospero leaves them to their happy company. He and Ariel go to mock Alonso and his followers by showing them a banquet that vanishes before the hungry castaways can taste the rich dishes. Then Ariel, disguised as a harpy, reproaches them for their conspiracy against Prospero. Convinced that Ferdinand's death is punishment for his own crime, Alonso is moved to repentance for his cruel deed.

Returning to his cave, Prospero releases Ferdinand from his task. While spirits dressed as Ceres, Iris, Juno, nymphs, and reapers entertain Miranda and the prince with a pastoral masque, Prospero suddenly remembers the schemes being entertained by Caliban and the drunken servants. Told to punish the plotters, after tempting them with a display of kingly garments, Ariel and his fellow spirits, now in the shapes of fierce hunting dogs, drive the plotters howling with pain and rage through bogs and briar patches.

Convinced that the king of Naples and his false brother Antonio repented the evil deed they did him years before, Prospero commands Ariel to bring them into the enchanted circle before the magician's cell. With strange, beautiful music, Ariel lures the king, Antonio, Sebastian, and Gonzalo to the cell, where they are astonished to see Prospero in the appearance and dress of the wronged duke of Milan. Prospero confirms his identity, orders Antonio to restore his dukedom, and severely warns Sebastian not to plot further against the king. Finally, he takes the repentant Alonso into the cave, where he sees Ferdinand and Miranda playing chess. A joyful reunion follows between father and son, and the king is completely captivated by the beauty and grace of Miranda. During this scene of reconciliation and rejoicing, Ariel appears with the master and boatswain of the wrecked ship, who report the vessel safe and ready to continue the voyage. Ariel drives the three grotesque conspirators into the cell, where Prospero releases them from their spell. Caliban is ordered to prepare food and set it before the guests, and Prospero invites his brother and the king of Naples and his entourage to spend the night in his cave.

Before he leaves the island, Prospero dismisses Ariel from his service, leaving that sprite free to wander as he wishes. Ariel promises calm seas and auspicious winds for the voyage back to Naples and Milan, from where Prospero will journey to take possession of his lost dukedom and to witness the marriage of his daughter and Prince Ferdinand.

Critical Evaluation:

The Tempest, written toward the close of William Shakespeare's career, is a work of fantasy and courtly romance, the story of a wise old magician, his beautiful, unworldly daughter, a gallant young prince, and a cruel, scheming brother. It contains all the elements of a fairy tale in which ancient wrongs are righted and true lovers live happily ever after. The play is also one of poetic atmosphere and allegory. Beginning with a storm and peril at sea, it ends on a note of serenity

and joy. None of Shakespeare's other dramas holds so much of the author's mature reflection on life itself.

Early critics of *The Tempest*, concerned with meaning, attempted to establish symbolic correlations between the characters Prospero, Ariel, Caliban, and Miranda and such qualities as imagination, fancy, brutality, and innocence. Others considered the play in terms of its spectacle and music, comparing it to the masque or commedia dell'arte. Most critics read into Prospero's control and direction of all the characters—which climaxes with the famous speech in which he gives up his magic wand—Shakespeare's own dramatic progress and final farewell to the stage.

In the mid-twentieth century, criticism began to explore different levels of action and meaning, focusing on such themes as illusion versus reality, freedom versus slavery, revenge versus forgiveness, time, and self-knowledge. Some suggested that the enchanted island where the shipwreck occurs is a symbol of life itself: an enclosed arena wherein are enacted a range of human passions, dreams, conflicts, and self-discoveries. Such a wide-angled perspective satisfies both the casual reader wishing to be entertained and the serious scholar examining different aspects of Shakespeare's art and philosophy.

This latter view is consonant with one of Shakespeare's principal techniques, which he employs in all of his work: the analogy between microcosm and macrocosm. This Elizabethan way of looking at things simply meant that the human world mirrored the universe. In the major tragedies, this correspondence is shown in the pattern between order and disorder, usually with violent acts (the murder of Caesar, the usurpation of the throne by Richard III, Claudius's murder of Hamlet's father, Macbeth's killing of Duncan) correlated with a sympathetic disruption of order in the world of nature. Attendant upon such human events therefore are such natural phenomena as earthquakes, strange beasts, unaccountable storms, voices from the sky, and witches. The idea that the world is but an extension of the mind, and that the cosmic order in turn is reflected in human beings, gives validity to diverse interpretations of *The Tempest* and, as a matter of fact, encompasses many of them.

The initial storm or "tempest" invoked by Prospero, which wrecks the ship, finds analogy in Antonio's long-past usurpation of Prospero's dukedom and his setting Prospero and Miranda adrift at sea in a storm in the hope they will perish. When, years later, the court party—Alonso, Sebastian, Antonio, and Ferdinand, along with the drunken Stephano and Trinculo—is cast upon the island, its "meanderings," pitfalls, and enchantments make it a place where everyone will go through a learning process and most come to greater self-knowledge.

Illusions on this island, which include Ariel's disguises, the disappearing banquet, and the line of glittering costumes that delude Stephano, Trinculo, and Caliban, find counterparts in the characters' illusions about themselves. Antonio comes to believe he is the rightful duke; Sebastian and Antonio, deluded by ambition, plan to kill Alonso and Gonzalo and make Sebastian tyrant of Naples. The drunken trio of court jester, butler, and Caliban falsely see themselves as future conquerors and rulers of the island. Ferdinand is tricked into believing that his father drowned and that Miranda is a goddess. Miranda, in turn, nurtured upon illusions by her father, knows little of human beings and their evil. Even Prospero must come to see he is not master of the universe and that revenge is not the answer after all. He must move to a higher reality, in which justice and mercy have greater power.

It has been noted that the island holds different meanings for different characters. Here again is an illustration of the analogy between microcosm and macrocosm. The characters with integrity see it as a beautiful place; honest Gonzalo, for example, thinks it might be a utopia. Sebastian and Antonio, however, whose outlook is soured by their villainy, characterize the island's air as perfumed by a rotten swamp. Whether a character feels a sense of freedom or of slavery is conditioned not just by Prospero's magic but by the individual's view of the island and his or her own makeup. The loveliest descriptions of the island's beauty and enchantment come from Caliban, the half-human, who knew its offerings far better than anyone else before his enslavement by Prospero.

Perhaps in few of his other plays did Shakespeare create a closer relationship between the human and the natural universes. In *The Tempest*, beauty and ugliness, good and evil, and cruelty and gentleness are matched with the external environment, and everything works toward a positive reconciliation of the best in both humans and nature. This harmony is expressed by the delightful pastoral masque Prospero stages for the young lovers, in which reapers and nymphs join in dancing, indicating the union of the natural with the supernatural. The coming marriage of Ferdinand and Miranda also foreshadows such harmony, as do the repentance and forgiveness demonstrated by the major characters.

It may be true, as Prospero states in act 5, that upon the island "no man was his own," but he also confirms that understanding comes like a "swelling tide," and he promises calm seas for the homeward journey, after which all will presumably take up the tasks and the responsibilities of their respective station with improved perspective. As Prospero renounces his magic, Ariel is freed to return to the elements, and Caliban, true child of nature, is left to regain harmony with his world. Perhaps the satisfaction experienced by

Shakespeare's audiences results from the harmony between humans and nature that illuminates the close of the play.

"Critical Evaluation" by Muriel B. Ingham

Further Reading

Cobb, Christopher J. "Unceasing Transformation: Further Tests of Romance in *The Tempest, Henry VIII*, and *The Two Noble Kinsmen*." In *The Staging of Romance in Late Shakespeare: Text and Theatrical Technique*. Newark: University of Delaware Press, 2007. Describes Shakespeare's late plays, including *The Tempest*, as part of the tradition of staged romance in the English Renaissance theater. Argues that Shakespeare's late plays were theatrical experiments in which he extended and reformed this tradition.

French, Marilyn. *Shakespeare's Division of Experience*. New York: Summit Books, 1981. French sees the play as Shakespeare's attempt to synthesize themes from his earlier works and finally propound a theory of justice that satisfies the hierarchical imperatives he previously set out. An examination of gender roles plays a significant part in her attempts to explicate Shakespeare's universe. Caliban is presented as representative of colonized peoples.

Griffiths, Trevor R. *"The Tempest."* New York: Palgrave Macmillan, 2007. Handbook providing an overview of the play. Discusses its text, sources, early performances, cultural context, key productions and performances on stage and on film, and critical assessments. Examines how other writers and political thinkers have adapted *The Tempest* to develop their own ideas.

Kermode, Frank. *William Shakespeare: The Final Plays*. London: Longmans, Green, 1963. Kermode sees this play as the most classically unified of Shakespeare's late works; he finds a repetition of earlier themes, including "guilt and repentance, the finding of the lost, forgiveness, the renewal of the world, [and] the benevolence of unseen powers."

Lindley, David. "Music, Masque and Meaning in *The Tempest*." In *The Court Masque*. New York: Manchester University Press, 1984. Examines the masque as a unique Renaissance art form and uncovers the role music plays in *The Tempest* to assert and deny power.

Lyne, Raphael. *Shakespeare's Late Work*. New York: Oxford University Press, 2007. Provides a detailed reading of *The Tempest* and other plays written at the end of Shakespeare's career, placing them within the context of his oeuvre. Argues that the late works have a distinct identity, defined as an ironic combination of belief and skepticism regarding faith in God, love of family, reverence for monarchs, and the theatrical depiction of truth.

Murphy, Patrick M., ed. *"The Tempest": Critical Essays.* New York: Routledge, 2001. Chronicles the critical history of the play from the seventeenth to the late twentieth centuries. Includes eight original essays approaching the play from a variety of modern critical perspectives, including feminism, deconstruction, performance theory, cultural materialism, and postcolonialism.

Peterson, Douglas L. *Time, Tide, and Tempest: A Study of Shakespeare's Romances.* San Marino, Calif.: Huntington Library, 1973. Places *The Tempest* in the context of Shakespeare's romance plays. Explores the themes and motifs of redemption and natural order, which elaborated on Shakespeare's earlier vision.

Smith, Hallett Darius, ed. *Twentieth Century Interpretations of "The Tempest": A Collection of Critical Essays.* Englewood Cliffs, N.J.: Prentice-Hall, 1969. Provides viewpoints and interpretations of *The Tempest* by sixteen critics, including A. C. Bradley and Northrup Frye. Includes a chronology of important dates and a bibliography.

The Temple

Author: George Herbert (1593-1633)
First published: 1633
Type of work: Poetry

Sir Richard Herbert, an aristocrat of Norman descent, died when his son George was three years old. His ten children were reared by their mother, who is known to have been a wise, witty, generous, and religious woman. John Donne said, "Her house was a court in the conversation of the best." Too frail for the family profession of soldiering, George Herbert was early guided toward the priesthood by his mother. He was not ordained until 1630, but Magdalen Herbert seems to have influenced the course of his life as much as Donne influenced his poetry. The first sonnets he wrote were addressed to her, and in them he vowed to devote himself to religious poetry.

The Latin verses that Herbert wrote at Cambridge are full of classical allusion. In *The Temple*, the main body of his English verse, he eschewed all archaic references and poetic rhetoric as studiously as Donne did himself. From Donne he also learned to transmute thought into feeling so that the intellectual concept becomes the emotional experience of the poem. Like Donne's, his rhythms are colloquial; his imagery, although not often as dramatic as that of Donne, is similarly practical, concrete, and arresting.

Herbert's range was narrower than Donne's, for he wrote only religious poetry and none that was tortuous or complicated. Though Herbert can be said to have a moral simplicity, however, his work is anything but simple. Within his one central preoccupation, his thought is varied. In his last letter to Nicholas Ferrar, to whom he sent the manuscript of *The Temple*, he described his poems as "a picture of the many spiritual conflicts that have passed betwixt God and my soul, before I could subject mine to the will of Jesus my master, in whose service I have now found perfect freedom." His anguish was not caused by the possibility that he had lost his faith or was threatened with damnation but by the idea that he should prove not to be a good and worthy servant to God. Herbert's greatest temptation was worldly ambition.

At Cambridge, Herbert's relaxation was music; he played the lute and wrote accompaniments to his Latin poems. This interest is evident in the vocabulary and also in the rhythm of many of his poems. Some, like his version of the Twenty-third Psalm, were written to be sung. In "Easter," the lute is an image for the body of Christ on the cross:

> The cross taught all wood to resound his name,
> Who bore the same.
> His stretched sinews taught all strings, what key
> Is best to celebrate this most high day.

The equation in the second stanza of the Crucifixion and the lute communicates the glory and pathos of Easter. The eager invocations to the poet's own heart and lute in the first stanza are found also in the third, which carries the full implications of the previous image and reinforces it:

> Consort both heart and lute, and twist a song
> Pleasant and long:
> Or since all musick is but three parts vied,

And multiplied;
O let thy blessed Spirit bear a part,
And make up our defects with his sweet art.

Ambition for worldly acclaim is as recurrent in Herbert's poetry as is music. In *The Temple* he often analyzes the delights of success, and the rejection of these delights is as meaningful poetically as it was in his life. In "The Pearl," Herbert speaks of his knowledge of learning, honor, and pleasure, and he concludes each stanza with the refrain "Yet I love thee." In the last stanza, the value of such knowledge is justified and explained: It renders his love of God significant and reasoned. "Therefore not sealed but with open eyes/ I flie to thee." This quality of quietness, certitude, and moral simplicity at the end of many of Herbert's poems gives them peculiar power. A controlled and intense late poem of rebellion contemplated, "The Collar" reflects at its close Herbert's complete humility and devotion in spite of all ambition and restlessness. The poem describes all that was lost:

> Sure there was wine,
> Before my sighs did drie it: there was corn,
> Before my tears did drown it.
> Is the yeare onely lost to me?
> Have I no bayes to crown it?
> No flowers, no garlands gay? all blasted?
> All wasted?
> Not so, my heart: but there is fruit,
> And thou hast hands.
> Recover all thy sight-bloom age
> On double pleasures: leave thy cold dispute
> Of what is fit, and not forsake thy cage. . . .

The poem is forceful, quick, and argumentative, and at the height of its fierceness the poet interrupts himself: "Methought I heard one calling, *Childe:*/ And I reply'd, *My Lord.*"

Herbert's devotion to God is usually expressed with this humility and with a sensitive awareness of personal unworthiness. The ability to love is itself a gift of God. The search for a way of service is complemented by Herbert's intense consciousness of the sacrificial nature of Christ's life. In the sonnet "Redemption," the poet records a search for Christ first in heaven, then in earth's palaces, cities, and courts, and finally finds him in a rabble of thieves and murderers: "there I him espied,/ Who straight, *Your suit is granted*, said, and died."

The common meeting grounds between people and their mundane activities and possessions are a great source of imagery to Herbert. His lyrics are probably his greatest poetry,

and their structure, imagery, vocabulary, and rhythm all encompass one dominant idea, which, after the thought that inspired the lyric has been thoroughly explored, is finally, exactly, and directly communicated. Herbert's poems have total unity, and the impression of ease—in craftsmanship, not of feeling—is obtained by the logical and perceptive argument. Technically, this effect is most often achieved in the development of the images. In "Vertue," the clear and sensuous expression of the death of the day and a rose and of the spring that is composed of days and roses, "A box where sweets compacted lie," leads to an image of natural strength where the virtuous soul "Like season'd timber; never gives." The penultimate line, following logically from the timber image, uses a most commonplace object, coal, as a continuation of it, and reverberates with the conviction of the immortality of the soul: "But though the whole world turn to coal,/ Then chiefly lives."

In "Affliction (I)," Herbert's feeling of unworthiness is clearly related to his ill health. There is a carefully balanced argument: At first, loving God was a joyous experience, and Herbert uses the metaphor of a furnished house to express his contentment: "Thy glorious household stuff did me entwine." After the first rapture, in which there was no room for fear, sorrow and sickness overcame him. This situation was partly improved when he turned from "the way that takes the town" and won "Academic praise." Then, lest he should "too happie be" in his unhappiness, God sent him further sickness. "Thus does thy power cross-bias me." A note of rebellion sounds at the seemingly contradictory demands of God, but the poem concludes: "Ah my deare God! though I am clean forgot,/ Let me not love me, if I love thee not."

Herbert's poetry is a constant communing with God, and it presents a great variety of moods. The firm tone of "Affliction (I)" can be contrasted with the delicacy and gentleness of "Love (III)," in which the alternating long and short lines illustrate the hesitancy of a soul yearning for God's love and yet not able to grasp it because of its own inadequacies. The tenderness of love is implicit in the words "welcome," "sweetly," "smiling," and "quick-eyed love." Flat monosyllables convey the soul's guilt in "sinne," "slacke," "marr'd," and "shame." Yet love made the eyes that call themselves unworthy, and love bore the blame for the sin; love encourages the soul until it can accept these things and the gift of love itself: "You must sit down, sayes Love, and taste my meat:/ So I did sit and eat."

Another poem in which the length of line echoes the feeling is "Easter Wings." The affected device of writing a poem in the shape of "wings"—and it was in the early editions printed vertically on the page—is in this instance effective.

The first and last lines of both verses are long, and each verse has middle lines of only two words each. This arrangement conveys in reading the rise and fall of the lark's song, which is the image for the Fall of Man and his resurrection in Christ. "Easter Wings" is the best of the poems in which Herbert uses some trick to illustrate his meaning. Other examples are "The Altar" and "Paradise."

Donne's influence on Herbert's poetry can thus also be seen in the variety of his lyrical forms, the directness of his language, and his less learned but equally arresting imagery. In contrast to Donne's poetry, Herbert's is essentially peaceful. His poems never end on a note of desperation. His way of thinking and his sensibility, by which he perceives the nuances in an idea and the connections between varied images and then fuses these to communicate feeling, is essentially metaphysical. The quiet tone of Herbert's poetry, with its power of persuasion by gentle argument, is entirely original and something for which, as the "Jordan" poem tell us, he consciously strove and beautifully achieved:

> As flames do work and winde, when they ascend;
> So did I weave myself into the sense.
> But while I bustled, I might hear a friend
> Whisper, *How wide is all this long pretence!*
> There is in love a sweetness readie penn'd:
> Copie out only that, and save expense.

Herbert had great influence on other seventeenth century poets: Henry Vaughan borrowed from him extensively, and Richard Crashaw called his own first volume *The Steps to the Temple*. Herbert was, together with the other metaphysical poets, criticized in the eighteenth century, yet Alexander Pope, although disliking his poetic method, in his *Essay on Man* (1733-1734) appears to have been influenced by Herbert's philosophy. Samuel Coleridge restored critical favor to Herbert and consequently profoundly influenced Gerard Manley Hopkins, and the twentieth century responded with delight to all the metaphysical poets.

Further Reading

Bloch, Chana. *Spelling the Word: George Herbert and the Bible*. Berkeley: University of California Press, 1985. Provides a thoroughly documented and accessible examination of Herbert's allusions, echoes, and borrowings from the Bible and of his creative transformations of biblical texts.

Fish, Stanley E. "Letting Go: The Dialectic of Self in Herbert's Poetry." In *Self-Consuming Artifacts: The Experience of Seventeenth Century Literature*. 1972. Reprint. Pittsburgh, Pa.: Duquesne University Press, 1998. Discusses Herbert's lyrics from the perspective of a reader's response, emphasizing their dramatic qualities and inconclusiveness. Remains one of the most controversial and provocative studies of Herbert.

Judge, Jeannie Sargent. *Two Natures Met: George Herbert and the Incarnation*. New York: Peter Lang, 2004. Examines how the spiritual conflict described in *The Temple* reflects Herbert's belief in the incarnation of Jesus Christ as his confidant, primary audience, and divine lord.

McKenzie, Tim. *Vocation in the Poetry of the Priest-Poets George Herbert, Gerard Manley Hopkins, and R. S. Thomas*. Lewiston, N.Y.: Edwin Mellen Press, 2003. Examines the vocational conflicts of the three poet-priests and how these conflicts are reflected in their work. Concludes that Herbert, Hopkins, and Thomas were "holy fools" who communicated to others the nature of God.

Roberts, John R., ed. *Essential Articles for the Study of George Herbert's Poetry*. Hamden, Conn.: Archon Books, 1979. Collection of thirty-four essays represents some of the most influential critical and scholarly approaches to Herbert. Contains many revealing and influential discussions of such topics as Herbert's style, the structure of *The Temple*, and relevant intellectual and theological contexts for the work.

Summers, Joseph H. *George Herbert: His Religion and Art*. 1954. Reprint. Cambridge, Mass.: Harvard University Press, 1968. Excellent study of Herbert's poetry relates it to his life, times, and religion. Provides a fine introduction to Herbert's complex form, his search for the proper language of devotion, and his broad Anglican theology.

Vendler, Helen. *The Poetry of George Herbert*. Cambridge, Mass.: Harvard University Press, 1975. Presents close readings, some detailed, of nearly all of Herbert's lyrics. Emphasizes Herbert's formal skill, which is often manifested in the poems in "reinventions," subtle and dramatic shifts in tone and theme.

Young, R. V. *Doctrine and Devotion in Seventeenth-Century Poetry: Studies in Donne, Herbert, Crashaw, and Vaughan*. Rochester, N.Y.: D. S. Brewer, 2000. Argues against other critics' approach to seventeenth century devotional poetry from the perspective of Protestant theology and postmodern theory. Examines the work of Herbert and the other poets from the perspective of Continental Catholic devotional literature and theology, demonstrating how the ideas and poetic devices in the English poets' works are also evident in the Catholic poetry of France and Spain and the theology of Saint Augustine and Thomas Aquinas.

The Temple of the Golden Pavilion

Author: Yukio Mishima (1925-1970)
First published: Kinkakuji, 1956 (English translation, 1959)
Type of work: Novel
Type of plot: Psychological realism
Time of plot: Mid-twentieth century
Locale: Kyoto, Japan

Principal characters:
MIZOGUCHI, a Zen Buddhist acolyte and student at the Golden Temple
TSURUKAWA, his friend and fellow student
KASHIWAGI, another friend and fellow student
FATHER DOSEN, the superior at the temple

The Story:

The son of a Zen Buddhist monk, Mizoguchi is haunted by his father's admiration of the beautiful Temple of the Golden Pavilion. Mizoguchi himself is not beautiful. He is a stutterer and describes himself as ugly, but he considers himself a great artist. When a naval cadet visits Mizoguchi's middle school, the boy scratches the fine scabbard of the cadet's sword for no particular reason other than envy.

When Mizoguchi tries to confront Uiko, an attractive young woman who lives nearby, she teases him about his stuttering, and he curses her. A few months later she hides in a temple with her lover, a deserter from the navy, and when the military police find them, the lover shoots her and then kills himself. Mizoguchi, however, is not especially disturbed by the tragedy.

When his father takes him to visit the Golden Temple, Mizoguchi is disappointed; he finds that he actually prefers a model of the temple to the real thing. His ailing father's main intent, however, is to introduce his son to the temple's superior, Father Dosen, who will become Mizoguchi's teacher. Shortly afterward, his father dies, and Mizoguchi feels no particular grief, nor does he feel sorry for his mother, who, he knows, had once been unfaithful to his father. This event, which he witnessed as a boy, caused him to despise both parents and is likely the origin of his own self-loathing.

As an acolyte or student of Zen during the last year of World War II, Mizoguchi forms a friendship with an outgoing, likable student named Tsurukawa, but he continues to feel alienated by the beauty of the temple and drawn to a life of evil. One evening, Mizoguchi sees a tea ceremony in which a beautiful woman uses milk from her breast for a young army officer's cup, and he is struck by the mystery of the event.

During the American military occupation of Japan following the war, a drunken U.S. soldier insists that Mizoguchi step on the stomach of a prostitute outside the temple. Mizoguchi finds a strange pleasure in doing so, and he maliciously passes on to Father Dosen the carton of cigarettes that the soldier gives him. After the prostitute has a miscarriage, she extorts money from the superior, and later she commits suicide. Mizoguchi feels no guilt over what has happened; in fact, he takes a certain evil pleasure in it.

Although Father Dosen knows what happened, he sends Mizoguchi to attend Otani University, where the young man meets the cynical, clubfooted Kashiwagi, an intellectual who detects immediately that Mizoguchi is a virgin and afraid of women. When Mizoguchi tries to have sex with a woman Kashiwagi provides for him, the image of the Golden Temple intervenes and leaves him impotent. Upon returning from that outing, Mizoguchi learns that Tsurukawa has been killed in an accident (later revealed to be a suicide).

Kashiwagi enjoys flower arranging and playing the flute, and he despises literature and architecture because they represent lasting and immutable forms of beauty. In fact, Kashiwagi prefers art forms noted for their "uselessness." One afternoon, the beautiful woman whom Mizoguchi had long ago seen offering her breast milk to a soldier (who was later killed in the war) turns up at Kashiwagi's apartment, and he treats her brutally. Mizoguchi follows her to her home and tells her about seeing her years before, but when she offers him her breast, he sees it transformed into the Golden Temple and is again struck impotent. The eternal beauty of the temple stands between him and mortal beauty, but it also stands as a challenge to him, and after this Mizoguchi resolves to "rule" over the temple.

Increasingly, Mizoguchi feels no kinship with anyone or anything but the temple, which becomes his focus in life. When he discovers Father Dosen with a geisha, he tries to blackmail the superior, but to no avail, and he begins to do poorly in his studies. He takes delight in not being understood, and in the fall of 1948 he runs off. As he faces the wildness of the Sea of Japan, he realizes his mission in life is to burn down the Golden Temple.

At age twenty-one, in the spring of 1950, Mizoguchi has a run-in with Kashiwagi when he presses Father Dosen on one of Mizoguchi's IOUs, but the superior pays it. The superior's threat to expel Mizoguchi frees him to pursue his scheme, and Kashiwagi's malicious revelation that Tsurukawa's death was a suicide prompted by an unhappy love provides an additional incentive. Subsequently, Mizoguchi takes the superior's money and pays for a prostitute with it instead of paying off Kashiwagi. He is able to consummate the sexual act, but it offers him no satisfaction, as he can see the beauty of the day changing before his eyes and realizes that everything, including the woman, is destined to die.

Shortly after the outbreak of the Korean War, Mizoguchi buys arsenic and a knife, intending to set fire to the temple and then commit suicide. Just before he lights the fire, Mizoguchi contemplates the beauty of the temple one last time and recognizes that it is a dream of perfection that can never be completed; it will always pursue the next unknown beauty. Paradoxically, then, nothingness is "the very structure of this beauty." The beauty of the Golden Temple never ceases, and it is unsurpassed. Mizoguchi also recalls a Buddhist proverb: When you meet the Buddha, kill the Buddha. He sees that he must burn the temple "precisely because it [is] so futile" to do so. Sitting on a hill overlooking the burning temple, Mizoguchi discards the knife and arsenic, lights a cigarette, and tells himself he wants to live.

Critical Evaluation:

Yukio Mishima based *The Temple of the Golden Pavilion* on an actual event, the destruction of the famous temple (completed in about 1398), a Japanese national treasure, by a disturbed monk in 1950. The temple was quickly rebuilt, and awareness of that fact, at least among Japanese readers, could have a significant impact on how one interprets the novel. That is, one could argue that Mizoguchi fails in the end to destroy beauty and that in fact the temple is simply transformed. In the first three years after the novel appeared, it sold some 300,000 copies in Japan and was adapted into a successful play as well.

If it were not for the fact that it is narrated in the first person by the main character, who revels in his psychopathology, the novel might qualify as symbolic allegory. The temple is apparently a symbol of eternal and changeless beauty in an unstable and ugly world. Mizoguchi himself is the embodiment of the ugliness of the world. The constant threat of death and destruction is pervasive in the novel, which begins in the middle of World War II and ends at the start of the Korean War.

Every beautiful person or thing in the novel appears vulnerable. Every beauty is on the verge of transformation into ugliness or death or annihilation. Mizoguchi's mother seems an ugly peasant to him, and his father seems to be wasting away before he dies of a hemorrhage. The beautiful Uiko is killed by her desperate lover; the handsome and upbeat Tsurukawa, whom Mizoguchi believes to be a positive image of his own dark self, commits suicide; any beautiful act (flower arranging or playing the flute) associated with Kashiwagi is compromised by the character's cruelty. Father Dosen's involvement with geisha girls demonstrates, as Mizoguchi sees it, the failure of religion or philosophy to deal effectively with the devastating impact of change and obliteration. When he destroys the temple, Mizoguchi performs an act of destruction that has an element of evil as an alternative to the artistic or godlike act of creation. Ironically, then, his burning of the temple can be seen as a great act of personal, individual heroism and self-expression. Mizoguchi has rid himself of his obsession and regained the desire to live.

Those familiar with Mishima's biography will detect parallels between him and his nihilistic protagonist. Although he was able to avoid military service during World War II, Mishima later created a paramilitary organization. A brilliant student, he was physically weak as a young man, but he later took up bodybuilding and became a successful actor. He was fascinated with swordplay (kendo) and the samurai code of Bushido, which emphasizes loyalty and acts of courage. Apparently gay, he nevertheless married and fathered two children. His ambivalent sexuality appears in many characters, but especially in Mizoguchi. Mishima ended his life dramatically when his paramilitary Tatenokai (shield society) occupied the offices of a general of the Japanese Defense Force. At the end of this demonstration he committed suicide and had himself beheaded by one of his comrades. Although suicide figures only tangentially in this novel, it could be argued that Mizoguchi's final act is self-destructive, and it certainly reflects Mishima's interest in acts of violence.

The Temple of the Golden Pavilion may also be read as a philosophical novel concerned with the nature of art, and perhaps especially with its limitations. Drawn between the life of the artist and that of the soldier, to use the terms broadly, Mishima became increasingly frustrated with the limitations of the former and infatuated with the active life represented by the latter. Mizoguchi also finds himself unable to yield to art, unable to accept the flaws in the work that every artist must endure, presumably because the evidence of experience is too much for him. This novel attains the stature of tragedy, then, because like many great tragic heroes, Mizoguchi can find no resolution to the dilemma of life except destruction. Arguably, Mishima's death as a man of action, as a soldier who was also an artist haunted by beauty, was similarly tragic. Readers must decide for themselves whether Mizoguchi is worthy of their sympathies, whether he is comparable, for example, to such tragic heroes as Hamlet, Othello, and Faust, or whether his disillusioned nihilism makes him an unsympathetic antihero.

Ron McFarland

Further Reading

Keene, Donald. *Five Modern Japanese Novelists*. New York: Columbia University Press, 2003. Examination of the lives and works of five Japanese novelists presents Keene's personal recollections of the writers as well as literary and cultural analyses of their works. Devotes a chapter to Mishima.

Nathan, John. *Mishima: A Biography*. 1974. Reprint. Cambridge, Mass.: Da Capo Press, 2000. Reprint of a classic biography includes a new preface. Nathan knew Mishima personally and professionally, and he provides a detailed and balanced portrait of the writer.

Piven, Jerry S. *The Madness and Perversion of Yukio Mishima*. Westport, Conn.: Praeger, 2004. Psychological study of Mishima traces the events of his life—most notably his early childhood, spent largely in his grandmother's sickroom—to provide a better understanding of the author and his works. Chapter 6 is devoted to a discussion of *The Temple of the Golden Pavilion*.

Scott-Stokes, Henry. *The Life and Death of Yukio Mishima*. New York: Farrar, Straus and Giroux, 1974. Biography

provides ample material for readers interested in exploring the parallels between Mishima and Mizoguchi.

Starrs, Roy. *Deadly Dialectics: Sex, Violence, and Nihilism in the World of Yukio Mishima*. Folkestone, England: Japan Library, 1994. Discusses Mizoguchi as "rising heroically from passive to active nihilism" and argues that there is "relief and catharsis" in the ending of *The Temple of the Golden Pavilion*.

Ueda, Makoto. *Modern Japanese Writers and the Nature of Literature*. Stanford, Calif.: Stanford University Press, 1976. Includes discussion of *The Temple of the Golden Pavilion* that focuses on the work as a philosophical novel and on the role of the novelist as psychiatrist. Provides information on many details of Mishima's life.

Wolfe, Peter. *Yukio Mishima*. New York: Frederick Ungar, 1989. Includes commentary on *The Temple of the Golden Pavilion* that discusses Mizoguchi's act as one of self-betrayal.

Yamanouchi, Hisaaki. *The Search for Authenticity in Modern Japanese Literature*. New York: Cambridge University Press, 1978. Argues for the separation of Mishima from his protagonist in *The Temple of the Golden Pavilion*, even though Mishima himself was nihilistic and often felt estranged from life.

Yourcenar, Marguerite. *Mishima: A Vision of the Void*. 1986. Reprint. Chicago: University of Chicago Press, 2001. Yourcenar, herself a novelist, analyzes Mishima's works and argues that the author's life was "an exhausting climb" toward what he perceived as its proper end. Includes discussion of *The Temple of the Golden Pavilion*.

The Temptation of Saint Anthony

Author: Gustave Flaubert (1821-1880)
First published: La Tentation de Saint Antoine, 1874 (English translation, 1895)
Type of work: Novel
Type of plot: Historical
Time of plot: Fourth century
Locale: Egypt

Principal characters:
SAINT ANTHONY
HILARION, his disciple
THE DEVIL
THE QUEEN OF SHEBA
TERTULLIAN
MONTANUS
APOLLONIUS

The Story:

Anthony has lived the life of a hermit for more than thirty years and now has come almost to the point of despair. He is extremely weary of life and of the world as he sees it from the limited point of view of his cell high in the mountains. At one time people had made pilgrimages to see him and be advised by him; these same people had furnished him with whatever money and clothing he needed. Everyone stopped coming years ago, however, and Anthony has begun to fear that his life is worthless. He then begins to long for the money, women, and goods of this world through which he might regain some sort of recognition and pleasure.

One night Anthony's solitude becomes too much. He remembers his early life as a monk, with its adventures and successes, and he thinks of the things he might have done if he had not become a hermit. At last he decides that it is merely his own stubbornness that keeps him alone in the mountains. Rather than allow himself to be guilty of such a sin, he prepares to depart, but he gets no farther than the cleared area in front of his cell. Realizing that he has almost yielded to temptation, he throws himself onto the ground. Then, in order to regain his strength and courage, he reads from the Acts of the Apostles and tries to think. His mind, however, keeps coming back to worldly matters that still tempt him.

Anthony then begins to review in his mind the things that are a credit to him in this world, the good works of his life. He praises himself for hardships he has suffered and for the things he has denied himself. Again, he begins to feel sorry for himself; the desire for the money, goods, and women he was earlier denied becomes unbearable. He falls into a trance, and while he lies on the ground the Devil appears, his wings spread like those of a giant bat to reveal beneath them the seven deadly sins. Anthony awakes hungry and thirsty. Taking up a scrap of bread, which is all that he can find to eat in his cell, he throws it on the ground in anger. Then there appears before him a table laden with all manner of meat and fruit from which he might satisfy himself. As he watches, the table grows, and delicacies he has never seen before appear on it. Anthony almost indulges himself, but he realizes in time that this also is the work of the Devil. When he kicks the table, it disappears.

Soon afterward Anthony finds on the ground a silver cup that has a gold coin at the bottom of it. When he picks up the coin, another coin appears, and then another, until the cup fills and begins to overflow. As Anthony watches, he begins to dream of the power that could be his because of so much wealth. He soon sees himself as second in power only to the emperor, and he begins to think of the revenge he could take on all his enemies. He even imagines himself as the emperor, taking precedence in Church affairs over the fathers of the Council of Nicaea. During this time, however, his bodily form has become more and more degraded, until at last he sees himself as a beast. At this point, he awakes.

Anthony flogs himself furiously for indulging in such sinful dreams, but as he is doing so he becomes aware of the arrival of a caravan. Soon the Queen of Sheba presents herself before him with many promises of love and luxury, the only condition being that Anthony must give up his solitary life and live with her. Although she uses all of her feminine charms to lure him away, Anthony firmly resists the temptation she offers.

After she has disappeared, Anthony notices that a child, whom he supposed has been left behind by the caravan, is standing in the doorway of his cell. The child is Hilarion, a former disciple. As Anthony watches, the child grows to the height of a man and begins accusing the saint of leading a sinful life. He charges that Anthony's abnegation is merely a subtle form of corruption, that his solitude simply frees him from the outbreak of his lusts, and that he only thinks he holds all the wisdom of the world because he is too lazy to learn anything new. When Anthony defends himself by saying that the Scriptures hold all the wisdom necessary for anyone, Hilarion points out various contradictions in the New Testament. He then tempts Anthony by offering to lead him to a knowledge of the Unknown, the sources and secrets of life. At this point Anthony falls into another trance.

When he again becomes aware of his surroundings, he finds himself in a large congregation that includes all the great heretics of history, each propounding his own theories of God and the universe. Some suggest that God is feminine. Others are devoutly following one aspect of Christianity, such as drinking the blood of Christ, while completely ignoring all other aspects. Some are warming their naked bodies by an open fire in order to show the purity of Adam in paradise. Soon a man dressed as a Carthaginian monk leaps into the middle of the crowd, names them all for the impostors they are, and drives them away. Anthony recognizes the monk as Tertullian and rushes forward to meet him, but he finds, instead, a woman seated alone on a bench.

The woman begins to talk about Montanus, whom she believes to be the incarnation of the Holy Ghost. When Anthony suggests that Montanus is dead, Montanus appears before them in the form of a black man. Then follows another succession of people, each propounding a different heresy, until a woman called Marcellina suggests that she can cause Christ himself to appear if she invokes him with the aid of a silver image. When she is put to the test, however, only a python appears. It quickly wraps itself around Anthony, and the people begin to proclaim him the Christ. Anthony swoons in horror.

When he awakes again, he finds himself in prison with the early Christians who were thrown to the lions, and he finds himself wishing that he too could give his life to God in such a way. Then Simon appears before him with a woman; Simon claims that she is the embodiment of all the infamous women of history and that she has now been cleansed through him. He offers Anthony the secret of his magic but disappears at the mention of holy water. Apollonius and his disciple then appear before Anthony and offer to describe the long road to salvation and immortality. Anthony is about to yield to their eloquence, but he draws back in horror when Apollonius begins to describe his visions and his power of curing the sick and predicting the future. These prove the hardest to resist of the temptations offered thus far; it is not until Anthony clings to the Cross and prays that Apollonius and his disciple disappear.

Nevertheless, Apollonius's taunts that Anthony's fear of the gods keeps him from knowing them awakens in him a desire to see them. Hilarion then causes to appear before him the gods of all ages. When Anthony laughs at them, Hilarion points out that there is an element of truth in each one, a fact that causes Anthony to grieve that these false religions can so easily lead one astray. He himself almost succumbs to the beauty of Olympus and the Greek gods, but he is able to repel their images by repeating the Apostles' Creed. Although Anthony has seen and learned enough of the false gods, the vision continues until he confesses to a desire to see the Devil. He hopes that his horror of Satan will rid him forever, once there is a confrontation, of such an evil. When the Devil appears, Anthony is immediately filled with regret, but it is too late to recall his wish.

The Devil carries Anthony into space in order to show him that humankind and the world are not the center of the universe, that there are no limits to space and no purpose in its being. While the two engage in a discussion on the nature of God, the Devil attempts to dispel all of Anthony's beliefs in divine goodness, love, and infinite power. He tries to show that before they can understand a God that has no limitations whatsoever, people must first understand the infinite. Spreading his wings to cover all space, the Devil shows himself to be infinite and calls upon Anthony to believe in him and curse God. Only by raising his eyes in a last desperate movement of hope is the saint able to rid himself of this evil.

When Anthony next awakes, the figures of Death and Lust confront him, each begging him to come and escape the ugliness of this world. Refusing to yield, Anthony is no longer disturbed by what had seemed the disparateness of all things. As dawn begins to break, he no longer feels afraid; he enjoys life once more. When the clouds roll back and he sees the face of Jesus Christ in the middle of the sun, he makes the sign of the Cross and resumes his prayers.

Critical Evaluation:

Gustave Flaubert began writing the first version of *The Temptation of Saint Anthony* on May 24, 1848, nine days after a communist uprising in Paris had briefly overturned the French government. He completed it on September 12, 1849, nine weeks after the French had restored Pius IX to the papal throne in spite of all Giuseppe Garibaldi had done to prevent it. Flaubert was, however, persuaded by his friends that the work was something unsuitable for public consumption, and he put it away. He turned his attention to a much more prosaic tale of temptation, *Madame Bovary* (1857; English translation, 1886), before returning to *The Temptation of Saint Anthony* in 1856. The resulting second draft was also shelved. The version that he published in 1874 was very different, being rather more compact and much more distanced as well as having a markedly different ending.

Critics who hail Flaubert as the parent of French naturalism and *Madame Bovary* as a masterpiece of realism tend to dismiss *The Temptation of Saint Anthony* as a kind of aberration, but the posthumous publication of Flaubert's earlier writings has revealed that it was a natural culmination of that work. In "Rêve d'enfer" (a dream of hell), written in 1837, for example, an alchemist encounters Satan, who also appears briefly in the rhapsodic "La danse des morts" (the dance of death, 1838) before giving a very elaborate account of himself in the phantasmagoric drama "Smarh" (wr. 1839), which almost qualifies as a preliminary sketch for *The Temptation of Saint Anthony*. The subject matter of *The Temptation of Saint Anthony* was decided when Flaubert saw Pieter Brueghel's painting on the theme in 1845. The novel is the last and best of a series, then, in which the character and power of the Devil are minutely examined. The Devil is the central character of the story; Saint Anthony is merely a convenient lens through which the Devil's works can be viewed.

Flaubert was wont to reply, when asked whether he had a model in mind for Emma Bovary, that she was himself. What he presumably meant by that was that his own imagination had been excited by romantic notions of much the same kind as those that lead her astray. As she does, he became desperate for a means of escaping from the appalling dullness of provincial life. He found his escape not so much in the various expeditions to the East that took him away from his mother's house as in the work of literary composition in which he immersed himself profoundly—perhaps more profoundly than any other writer. When he prepared the 1874 version of *The Temptation of Saint Anthony* for publication he was in his fifties and his triumph over temptation was secure enough so that the Devil had become a figure of abstract interest whose devices he could describe and analyze in a relatively clinical fashion. In the 1874 version the Devil is not personally present in the final section, the last illusions that he sends are chimerical, and the final ecstatic revelation climaxes with a tranquil vision of Jesus. In the earlier versions, by contrast, the Devil remains present in person after waving aside his last illusions (science and the seven deadly sins), and his laughter continues to mock Anthony's desperate prayer to the end. The final version has Anthony proclaiming, "O bliss! bliss!" The earlier ones have him wailing, "Pity! Pity!" Such is the distance a man may travel between youth and maturity.

In all its versions, *The Temptation of Saint Anthony* is an allegory of self-discovery in which religious faith is a sturdy but not invulnerable construction battered by all the doubts that intellect and imagination can raise. Flaubert differs sharply from other writers of Faustian fantasies in taking it for granted that the temptations of wealth and sex—the former represented by the cup and the coins and the latter by the Queen of Sheba and Ennoïa (the companion of Simon Magus)—are by no means the most powerful levers that can be applied against virtue. When other writers add further lures to these two old favorites (and very few have seen the need), they tend to do so in terms of some search for more extreme sensations. Flaubert, however, is much more interested in the intellectual temptations of paganism and heresy. The bribery implicit in Simon's magic is easy enough to resist, but the mockery of Apollonius of Tyana is not, and the grandiose vision of the scientific cosmos displayed by the Devil is harder still to resist. This astonishing intellectual reach—reflected in the imaginative ambition of the melodrama—makes the work a masterpiece.

In the 1874 text, the wonders of nature, which provide the final challenge to Anthony's piety, are quickly redrawn into the perverted image of the Chimera and the Sphinx. Anthony's rejection of his tempters is represented as a victory, in stark contrast to the 1848-1849 text and the 1856 text, which rule any such victory impossible. In the earlier versions the Devil wins, not by carrying Anthony off to hell in the vulgar manner of some Gothic shocker but by granting him the intellectual legacy of his discoveries and condemning him to live with the sound of diabolical laughter forever resounding in his ears.

It is understandable that a novel first composed during Europe's year of revolutions should have a much sharper awareness of the vulnerability of religious and political faiths than one prepared for publication in a relatively peaceful year, when stability seemed to have been restored after the horrors of the Paris Commune of 1871. The real change was, however, in the author's own attitude. He had found his own particular domestic stability and intellectual security. Whether he had achieved this state by compromise or capitulation, and whether it was a triumph or a defeat, must remain a matter of opinion. The decision as to which of the various versions of *The Temptation of Saint Anthony* to rank most highly will follow in train. Critics who prefer the sobriety of middle age to the recklessness of youth, and the safety of careful conservatism to the hazards of radicalism, inevitably agree with Flaubert's friends that the first version should have been hidden from public view, and perhaps that it should have remained hidden forever; others are free to have different opinions.

"Critical Evaluation" by Brian Stableford

Further Reading

Brombert, Victor. *The Novels of Flaubert: A Study of Themes and Techniques.* Princeton, N.J.: Princeton University Press, 1966. Thorough examination of Flaubert's works includes a chapter devoted to *The Temptation of Saint Anthony.*

Donato, Eugenio. *The Script of Decadence: Essays on the Fictions of Flaubert and the Poetics of Romanticism.* New York: Oxford University Press, 1993. Chapter 4, "Gnostic Fictions," includes an elaborate discussion of the temptations offered by the heretics in *The Temptation of Saint Anthony.*

Ginsburg, Michal Peled. *Flaubert Writing.* Stanford, Calif.: Stanford University Press, 1986. Chapter 2 includes a detailed critique of *The Temptation of Saint Anthony.*

Porter, Laurence M., ed. *A Gustave Flaubert Encyclopedia.* Westport, Conn.: Greenwood Press, 2001. Alphabetically arranged collection of articles focuses on Flaubert's literary works and their sources. Provides information about the places and characters in his fiction, nineteenth century history, and the writers who influenced and were influenced by Flaubert.

Troyat, Henri. *Flaubert.* Translated by Joan Pinkham. New York: Viking Press, 1992. Thorough, engrossing biography reconstructs Flaubert's life based on the novelist's prodigious correspondence with his family and friends.

Unwin, Timothy, ed. *The Cambridge Companion to Flaubert.* New York: Cambridge University Press, 2004. Collection of essays offers analyses of all of Flaubert's works as well as discussions of his life, his place in literary history, his writing process, and other aspects of his fiction. In the final essay, "Flaubert, Our Contemporary," noted novelist Mario Vargas Llosa assesses Flaubert's continued relevance.

Wall, Geoffrey. *Flaubert: A Life*. New York: Farrar, Straus, and Giroux, 2002. Critically acclaimed, highly readable narrative biography offers many previously unpublished details about Flaubert's life and works.

Williams, Tony, and Mary Orr, eds. *New Approaches in Flaubert Studies*. Lewiston, N.Y.: Edwin Mellen Press, 1999. Contributors to this collection of essays provide fresh interpretations of Flaubert's works. Mary Neiland's essay "*La Tentation de saint Antoine* and the Works of Flaubert" examines *The Temptation of Saint Anthony*. Other topics addressed in the volume include Flaubert's depictions of gender roles, his use of flower figures and other imagery, and his classical influences.

The Tenant of Wildfell Hall

Author: Anne Brontë (1820-1849)
First published: 1848
Type of work: Novel
Type of plot: Social realism
Time of plot: Early nineteenth century
Locale: England

Principal characters:
HELEN GRAHAM, in reality Helen Huntingdon, the tenant
FREDERICK LAWRENCE, her landlord
ARTHUR HUNTINGDON, her first husband
GILBERT MARKHAM, her second husband

The Story:

Gilbert Markham, a young gentleman farmer, is immediately interested when a strange tenant comes to Wildfell Hall. Mrs. Graham, as her neighbors know her, is young and beautiful, and her demand for seclusion arouses great curiosity among the local gentry. She is particularly criticized for the way in which she cares for her small son, Arthur, whom she will not allow out of her sight. Gilbert's mother declares the child will become the worst of milksops.

On his first visit to Wildfell Hall, Gilbert learns that Mrs. Graham is a landscape painter of considerable ability and that she is concealing her whereabouts from her former friends. Her air of secrecy arouses both his curiosity and sympathy. Avoiding the attentions of Eliza Millward, the vicar's daughter, for whom he until then showed a preference, Gilbert spends much of his time in the company of the young widow. He accompanies her and young Arthur on long walks to find scenes for Mrs. Graham to paint. His friends attempt to discourage his attentions to the tenant of Wildfell Hall. There is a rumor that she is having an affair with Frederick Lawrence, her landlord, and Lawrence himself assures Gilbert that he will fail in his attentions to Mrs. Graham. When he tries to tell her of his growing affection, Mrs. Graham insists that Gilbert regard her simply as a friend.

After the vicar, Mr. Millward, accuses the widow of improper conduct, Gilbert visits her, declares his love, and wins from her a promise that she will reveal her secret to him. Later that night, however, he overhears Mrs. Graham in a mysterious discussion with her landlord that leads him to suspect that the rumors about them are true. Gilbert thereupon resolved to have no more to do with her. On his next encounter with Lawrence, Gilbert strikes his rival and wounds him severely.

When Gilbert meets Mrs. Graham a short time later, she gives him a copy of her journal to read. The journal, beginning in 1821, tells the story of Helen Graham's life for the past six years. It opens with an account of her meeting with Arthur Huntingdon, whom she loved despite her aunt's claim that the young man was wild and wayward. Her aunt, with whom she made her home, took her away so that she could see no more of the objectionable Huntingdon, but by a miscalculation, the unwelcome suitor was invited to their summer home for partridge hunting. Helen married Huntingdon that autumn, only to find, shortly afterward, that her husband's true character was exactly as her aunt described. He was a drunkard, a man incapable of high principle or moral responsibility. She began to be contemptuous of him, and he responded with growing indifference toward her. Every year, Huntingdon spent several months in London, always returning weakened by dissipation. At home he held long hunting parties for his dissolute companions. Despite Helen's hopes, the birth of their son did nothing to change his way of life.

When Helen's father died, she was greatly disturbed by her husband's callous attitude toward her grief. The scenes of drunken debauchery continued in her home, and one day she discovered her husband making love to Lady Lowborough, a visitor in their house. When she demanded a separation for herself and her child, Huntingdon refused. To keep the affair from becoming known to others, Helen at last decided to stay with her husband.

Fearing that Huntingdon was corrupting their son and alienating his affections from her, Helen finally began to make her plans to escape. During that time she had to fight off a would-be lover of her own, Mr. Hargrave, who was determined to win her. She hoped to find refuge in a place where her husband could not find her and legally take her child from her. Her pride kept her from appealing to her brother or to her uncle and aunt. After Huntingdon learned of her plan from reading her journal, he had her watched constantly, and he refused to let her have any money in her possession.

Her position became unendurable, however, when Huntingdon brought his mistress into the house on the pretext of providing a governess for young Arthur. Helen determined to ask her brother to let her occupy rooms in the old and now unused family home. She made her escape without money or resources, taking only her son with her.

The journal ends with Helen's arrival at Wildfell Hall. Reading this account, Gilbert realizes that Frederick is the brother mentioned several times in the diary. He at once seeks out Helen to renew his suit; despite his entreaties, however, she insists that they should not see each other again. Gilbert goes to see her brother, whom he treated so harshly at their last meeting. The reconciliation between the two men is prompt and sincere.

A short time later, the whole community learns the secret of the tenant of Wildfell Hall. Huntingdon falls from his horse, and his wife, learning of his serious condition, goes to his house at Grassdale to look after him. Frederick tells Gilbert that Huntingdon received her ungraciously but that she is determined to stay with him out of a sense of duty.

Despite her care, however, Huntingdon secures a bottle of wine and drinks it in defiance of his doctor's orders. His indiscretion brings on a relapse that ends in his death.

Several months later, Gilbert hears that Helen's uncle died and that she went to live with her aunt at Staningley. More than a year passes before he dares to go to her. He finds her at Staningley, and the welcome of young Arthur is as joyous as Helen's is warm and gracious. She and Gilbert are married a short time later.

Critical Evaluation:

Begun in autumn 1846, shortly after the completion of *Agnes Grey* (1847), Anne Brontë's *The Tenant of Wildfell Hall* retains the social realism of the earlier work but adds a new complication of plot and a heightened sense of the dramatic. The chronological narrative, concentration on a single character, and subdued tone of the first novel here give way to a sophisticated structure that reveals increased complexity in themes, narrative techniques, and style.

The principal arguments in the preface to the second edition indicate the novel's two principal themes. Brontë expresses her desire "to tell the truth, for truth always conveys its own moral," and she pleads for the equality of male and female authors. Her comments correspond to her novel's themes of moral behavior and sexual equality.

The novel is closer to the Enlightenment than to Romanticism in its insistence on reason and moderation and in its depiction of the evil consequences of excess. The latter is shown in the degradation of Arthur Huntingdon, who appears first as a rakish but amusing and sophisticated man of the world but rapidly sinks to debauched reveler, brutal husband, and, finally, to the desperate alcoholic whose ravings indicate fear of a God in whom he does not believe but whom he cannot dismiss. Brontë, drawing on the observation of her brother, Branwell Brontë, shows clearly that Huntingdon's collapse results from an addiction. Huntingdon's addiction, however, is exacerbated by a failure of reason. Devoid of intellectual interests, Huntingdon is characterized by a fundamental unseriousness, and the lightheartedness that initially makes him a witty entertainer eventually leads to a callous indifference to others and a readiness to turn any situation, however serious, into a jest.

Huntingdon is not the only character who acts without reason and self-control. His dissolute friends share his proclivities, the only exception being the despondent Lowborough, who finally overcomes the addictions of gambling, alcohol, and laudanum. Helen herself, ignoring all warnings and drawn by a physical attraction that she does not fully recognize but that Brontë presents unmistakably, marries impetuously, believing that she can reform Huntingdon. The young Gilbert Markham harbors irrational suspicions, which lead him to a rejection of Helen and to violence against Lawrence.

Feminist issues form the second major theme. Brontë makes a forceful case for the independence and the equality of women in showing that while Huntingdon declines into fatuous alcoholism, Helen matures into a reasoning, self-disciplined individual who is determined to maintain some control. When she locks her bedroom door against Huntingdon the night of their first quarrel, this anticipates her later rejection of all sexual relations with him. When she finally leaves the abusive marriage, she defies the Victorian social code that required a wife to remain with her husband whatever his behavior. In subsequently demanding a written contract awarding her custody of her son, Helen affirms the rights of mothers, which were not legally recognized until the passage of the Infants' Custody Bill in 1839.

After the separation, Helen achieves both financial and intellectual independence. Huntingdon controls her property, but she manages to support herself by her painting. Again she defies convention since, although the Victorians regarded painting as a suitable drawing-room accomplishment for ladies, they reserved for men the serious pursuit of art as a profession. Helen's trials also bring her intellectual independence. Naturally spirited, she learns how to assert herself. Her quiet demeanor does not prevent her from challenging received opinions, most notably in her discussion with Mrs. Markham on the need to bring up boys and girls in the same way. In her marriage to Gilbert, the reader must suppose that Helen will not relinquish her hard-won independence but rather that theirs is an equal union. Earlier, Gilbert tells his mother that he will not expect his future wife to subordinate herself to his wishes and his comforts.

Divided into three sections, the novel presents two narrative voices. The first section is told by Gilbert, now middle-aged, recounting events of his youth in letters to his friend Halford. Entering imaginatively into the mind of her male persona, Brontë shows how Gilbert develops from naïve egotism to a maturity marked by sensitivity and patience. This initial point of view introduces Helen as the impressive, mysterious stranger who arouses suspense at the same time that it establishes the character of the mature heroine.

The second section is the diary Helen gives to Gilbert, which provides an intimate depiction of her first marriage, shows her moral growth, and becomes a means of instruction for Gilbert. Thus enabled to understand Helen's real self, Gilbert learns about the possible pitfalls of marriage and so is better prepared for a different kind of union himself.

The third section reverts to Gilbert's narrative, supplemented by letters from Helen to her brother. The perspective alternates between Helen and Gilbert until the final scene, which brings the lovers together in the plot as the two voices blend in an open and harmonious dialogue.

In keeping with the novel's realistic mode and personal viewpoint, Brontë's style is plain and straightforward but enhanced by descriptions, irony, and symbols. The descriptions are imaginative and keenly observed and range from the gloom of the crumbling old hall to the delights of a spring morning. Occasional ironic humor sharpens the social satire, as in Gilbert's portrait of the Reverend Millward or Helen's account of her youthful conversations with her aunt. Symbols are used dramatically to reinforce character and theme.

In Hargrave's chess game with Helen, both players recognize that his real object is her seduction: The scene suggests that Hargrave sees his relationship with her as both a contest that he is determined to win and a game in which he is not required to act responsibly. The winter rose that Helen offers to Gilbert, recalling the earlier rose she picked for him, is in fact a proposal and an emblem of her heart, which, like the rose, survived storms and hardships.

The Tenant of Wildfell Hall is remarkable for its outspokenness in developing its themes and treating its subject. Brontë's unflinching honesty in portraying and deromanticizing the darker side of human nature, her serious moral sense, and her confident feminism make this a remarkable mid-Victorian novel.

"Critical Evaluation" by Muriel Mellown

Further Reading

Frawley, Maria H. "The Female Saviour in *The Tenant of Wildfell Hall*." *Brontë Society Transactions* 20, part 3 (1991): 133-143. Examines the novel in light of the Victorian ideology of woman as savior or angel in the house and shows that Helen both submits to and struggles against this conventional role.

Ingham, Patricia. *The Brontës*. London: Longman, 2003. This collection of essays that examine the Brontë sisters' work from the perspective of feminism, Marxism, and postcolonialism includes two pieces about *The Tenant of Wildfell Hall*: "Gender and Layered Narrative in *Wuthering Heights* and *The Tenant of Wildfell Hall*" by N. M. Jacobs and "Siblings and Suitors in the Narrative Architecture of *The Tenant of Wildfell Hall*" by Tess O'Tolle.

Jay, Betty. *Anne Brontë*. Tavistock, England: Northcote House/British Council, 2000. Reevaluates Brontë's novels and poetry from the perspective of feminism and other twentieth century critical theories.

Langland, Elizabeth. "The Voicing of Feminine Desire in Anne Brontë's *The Tenant of Wildfell Hall*." In *Gender and Discourse in Victorian Literature and Art*, edited by Antony Harrison and Beverly Taylor. DeKalb: Northern Illinois University Press, 1992. Analyzes the use of two narrators and shows how Gilbert finally adopts Helen's perspective. The narrative techniques are a means of refuting the idea of woman's redemptive spirituality and of providing a way for a woman to voice her desire.

Matus, Jill. "'Strong Family Likeness': *Jane Eyre* and *The Tenant of Wildfell Hall*." In *The Cambridge Companion to the Brontës*, edited by Heather Glen. New York: Cambridge University Press, 2002. This comparison of novels by Anne and her sister Charlotte is included in this collection of essays about the Brontë sisters.

Nash, Julie, and Barbara A. Suess, eds. *New Approaches to the Literary Art of Anne Brontë.* Burlington, Vt.: Ashgate, 2001. Collection of essays, the majority of which offer various interpretations of *The Tenant of Wildfell Hall* and *Agnes Grey.*

Thormahlen, Marianne. "The Villain of Wildfell Hall: Aspects and Prospects of Arthur Huntingdon." *Modern Lan-*

guage Review 88, part 4 (October, 1993): 831-841. Places the work in its historical context and analyzes Huntingdon's character in the light of contemporary theology, social developments, and science.

Torgerson, Beth E. *Reading the Brontë Body: Disease, Desire, and the Constraints of Culture.* New York: Palgrave Macmillan, 2005. Examines how the Brontë sisters' literary depictions of illness and disease reflect Victorian attitudes and their personal experiences. Includes analyses of *The Tenant of Wildfell Hall* and *Agnes Grey.*

Tender Is the Night

Author: F. Scott Fitzgerald (1896-1940)
First published: 1934
Type of work: Novel
Type of plot: Social realism
Time of plot: 1920's
Locale: Europe

Principal characters:
DICK DIVER, a psychiatrist
NICOLE, his wife
ROSEMARY HOYT, an actor
TOMMY BARBAN, a professional soldier

The Story:

Rosemary Hoyt is just eighteen years old, dewy fresh and full of the promise of beautiful maturity. In spite of her youth, she is already a famous actor, and her film *Daddy's Girl* is all the rage. She has traveled to the south of France with her mother for a rest after having become very ill as a result of her diving repeatedly into a Venice canal during the shooting of the motion picture.

At the beach, Rosemary meets Dick Diver and suddenly realizes that she is in love. After she becomes well acquainted with the Divers, she also comes to like Diver's wife, Nicole, a strikingly beautiful woman, and Dick and Nicole's two children. Rosemary's mother approves of Dick. At one of the Divers's famous parties, Rosemary tells Dick outright that she loves him, but he makes light of her declaration.

During the party another guest, Mrs. McKisco, sees Nicole behaving hysterically in the bathroom, and on the way home she tries to talk about it with her husband and Tommy Barban, a war hero. Tommy makes her keep silent. Resenting Tommy's interference, Mr. McKisco provokes a quarrel with him that ends in a duel in which several shots are exchanged but no one is hurt. Rosemary is greatly moved by the incident.

Rosemary travels to Paris with the Divers, where they all attend a round of parties and tours. She makes frequent ad-

vances to Dick, but he puts her off, apathetically, until one day a young college man tells of an escapade in which Rosemary was involved. Then Dick begins to desire the young woman. Although their brief love affair is confined to furtive kisses in hallways, Nicole becomes suspicious.

An acquaintance of Dick, Abe North, a brawling composer, offends two black men and involves a third in the dispute. While Dick is in Rosemary's hotel room, Abe brings one of the black men to the room to ask Dick's help in resolving the mess. Dick goes with Abe to his own room, leaving the black man in the corridor. The two other black men then kill the waiting man and lay his bleeding body on the bed in Rosemary's room. When the body is found, Dick carries it into the hall and then takes Rosemary's bedspread to his bathtub to wash it out. Seeing the bloody bedspread, Nicole becomes hysterical and accuses Dick of many infidelities. Her breakdown is like the one Mrs. McKisco had earlier witnessed.

Some years before, Dick had been doing research in advanced psychology in a clinic in Zurich. There he one day met a pathetic but beautiful patient, young Nicole Warren. At first merely attracted to her professionally, Dick later learned the cause of her long residence in the clinic. Nicole came from a wealthy Chicago family. When she was eleven, her mother died, and after that her father initiated an incestuous relationship with her, which led to Nicole's breakdown. Her father, too cowardly to kill himself as he had planned, had placed her in the Zurich clinic. For many reasons, Dick became Nicole's tower of strength; with him she was almost normal. Finally, motivated by pity and love, Dick married her. For a time, he had been able to maintain her in a healthy equilibrium, and the marriage seemed to be a success. This was aided by the fact that Nicole's family was rich—in fact, Nicole's older sister was able to buy Dick a partnership in the clinic where he first met Nicole.

For some time after the episode involving Rosemary, Nicole is quite calm but too withdrawn. Then she receives a letter, written by a neurotic woman, accusing Dick of misdeeds with his female patients. The accusations are baseless, but Nicole believes them and has another relapse. She leaves her family at a country fair and becomes hysterical while riding on the Ferris wheel.

At one time, Dick had shown great promise as a writer and as a psychiatrist. His books had become standard reference sources, and many of his colleagues considered him a genius. After Nicole's hysterical fit on the Ferris wheel, however, he no longer seems able to do real work. One reason for this is Nicole's increasing wealth, which means that Dick does not have to work. At the age of thirty-eight, still a handsome and engaging man, he begins to drink heavily.

On several occasions, Nicole is embarrassed by her husband's drunken behavior. She does her best to prevent his drinking and, in so doing, begins to gain strength of her own. For the first time since her long stay at the clinic, she comes to have an independent life, a life apart from Dick's influence.

Dissatisfied with the life he is leading, Dick decides to go away by himself for a while. He runs into Tommy Barban, still a reckless, strong, professional soldier, who has just had a romantic escape from Russia. While still separated from his wife, Dick receives word that his father has died. He goes back to the United States for the funeral, and the visit is a nostalgic experience. His father had been a gentle clergyman, living a narrow life; in contrast to Dick, he had roots, and he was buried among his ancestors. Dick thinks about how he has lived a rootless, unfettered life for so many years, and he almost determines to remain in the United States.

On the way back to meet his family, Dick stops in Naples. At his hotel, he meets Rosemary again. She is busy making another motion picture, but she manages to find time to see him. No longer as innocent as she once was, she proves an easy sexual conquest. Dick also meets Nicole's older sister in Naples.

One night, Dick drinks far too much and becomes embroiled in a dispute with a chiseling taxi driver. When he refuses to pay an exorbitant fare, a fight breaks out, and Dick is arrested. The police captain unfairly takes the side of the taxi driver, and, blind with rage, Dick strikes a police officer. In return, he is severely beaten by the Fascist carabinieri. Thinking that his eye has been gouged out, Dick gets word to Nicole's sister, who brings all her influence to bear on the consul to have her brother-in-law released from police custody.

Back in Zurich, Dick is busy for a time working at the clinic. On a professional visit to Lausanne, he learns to his surprise that Nicole's father is there, very near death. When the dying man expresses a wish to see his daughter again, Dick sends for Nicole. Strangely enough, the weakened father still cannot face his daughter. In a despairing frenzy, the old man escapes from the hospital and disappears.

Dick continues to go downhill. He consistently drinks too much, and at one point one of his patients, objecting to the smell of liquor on his breath, creates a scene. Finally, Dick is forced to surrender his partnership in the clinic. With no job, he wanders restlessly. He and his wife, he realizes, have less and less in common. At last, after Dick has disgraced his family many times with his drunken scenes, Nicole begins to welcome the attentions of Tommy Barban. She no longer needs Dick, and she looks forward confidently to an independent life with Tommy. After he and Nicole are divorced, Dick moves to the United States. Nicole hears word of him occasionally. He becomes an unsuccessful general practitioner, moving from one small town to another.

Critical Evaluation:

In his literary work, F. Scott Fitzgerald is a retrospective oracle. He describes an age of individuals who came on the scene and burned themselves out even before they were able to conceptualize themselves. His first published novel, *This Side of Paradise* (1920), is autobiographical and describes the early Jazz Age, with its vague values of money, beauty, and a distorted sense of social propriety. His masterpiece, *The Great Gatsby*, came in 1925, and *Tender Is the Night* fictionalizes the personal and social disintegration that followed the success that *The Great Gatsby* had brought Fitzgerald.

In addition to describing the glamour, excitement, and frenetic pursuit of the good life between the two world wars, *Tender Is the Night* contains a masterful attempt at thematic telescoping. Beyond his potential as a fictional character, Dick Diver serves a double function in the novel: He is, on the largest scale, a mid-twentieth century American equivalent of the tragic hero, and he also represents the complex disintegration of the American individual during a precarious point in history.

In many ways, Diver's fall follows Aristotle's formula for classical tragedy: He is an isolated hero upon whom an entire community of individuals depends to give necessary form to their lives, yet he has a tragic flaw, a lack of perspective and introspection. (He is once told by a classmate, "That's going to be your trouble—judgment about yourself.") He represents the individual in his role as a psychiatrist, a person who is expected to understand human motivation. Ever since the precipitating element, Nicole's case, "drifted into his hands," he has been at the mercy of fate, and his fall is monumental, from an elevated position in life into failure and anonymity. Most significant, Diver has a perception of his own tragic importance. He realizes that he is losing his grip on situations, and even though he recognizes some of the possible consequences of his actions, he is not equipped psychologically to combat them.

Dick Diver, however, is not a strictly tragic figure; at most, he is the sort of tragic hero that America would allow in the 1920's, but it is in this capacity that Diver serves to describe the disintegration of the American character. Dick is not simply symbolic of an American; his character is individualized to represent what an American with his exemplary vulnerabilities could become in certain circumstances. Diver and his companions create their own mystique to avoid the realities of a world thrown into, and extracting itself from, war. Their frenetic rites and the aura in which the compatriots hide ultimately form the confusion that grows larger than Diver, unleashing itself and swallowing him.

Diver and the American character at this time are incomplete; each is detrimentally eclectic and depends for support on props such as music, money, and material possessions. Incompleteness nourishes Diver's paternalistic assimilation of portions of the personalities that surround him and depend on him. His need to be needed, however, causes him to assimilate more weaknesses than strengths, and the organic process is abortive. The American character is presented as being a limited, possessive one. There is a sense of something existing beyond Diver's intellectual and emotional reach that could have proved to be his salvation. Fitzgerald emphasizes the eclectic and incomplete nature of the American during this era by interweaving elements of the romantic, the realistic, and the didactic when describing the actions and motivations of his characters. The result presents a severely realistic emotional conflict that sporadically explodes several characters, including Diver, into psychological chaos.

Diver also functions as the pivotal character of the plot itself. Fitzgerald relays Diver's decline quite convincingly and succeeds in providing the reader subliminally with the correct formula for observing Diver's actions and their consequences. In the first three chapters of the novel, the reader is taught, through Nicole's exemplary case, to appreciate the importance of psychological analysis, to isolate the "precipitating factor" in a character's development, and then to consider that factor's influence on subsequent actions. The reader thus becomes equipped to transfer these premises to observations of Diver. Throughout the duration of the novel, Diver is driven by a need to be needed, which leads him increasingly into circumstances that involve him directly and cause him almost voluntarily to allow his energy to be sapped.

Tender Is the Night is a psychological novel that is more successful than most novels of its type, partly because of Fitzgerald's handling of time. Time serves horizontal, linear, and vertical purposes in the novel. In linear time, the reader has an advantage that Diver does not have. (This was not so in earlier drafts of the novel.) The reader knows that Diver grows older, that Rosemary matures and finds other interests, and that Nicole eventually recovers from her illness, but these are circumstances of which Diver is ignorant. Time also functions vertically, making the notion of thematic telescoping possible. Diver is not cognizant of the passing of time until his plunge is in its advanced stages. As Diver gradually acknowledges time and the vast gap between his "heroic period" and his encroaching anonymity, his thematic function passes from that of the purely tragic figure to that of the national character and, finally, to that of the flawed individual Dick Diver, who learns to accept his situation.

"Critical Evaluation" by Bonnie Fraser

Further Reading

Blazek, William, and Laura Rattray, eds. *Twenty-first Century Readings of "Tender Is the Night."* Liverpool, England: Liverpool University Press, 2007. Collection of essays addresses topics such as the novel's narrative vision, Fitzgerald's style, the life of the American expatriate, and some short precursors to *Tender Is the Night.*

Bloom, Harold, ed. *F. Scott Fitzgerald.* Updated ed. New York: Chelsea House, 2006. Essay collection examines Fitzgerald's fiction, including *Tender Is the Night.*

Bruccoli, Matthew J. *The Composition of "Tender Is the Night": A Study of the Manuscripts.* Pittsburgh, Pa.: University of Pittsburgh Press, 1963. Definitive study of the text of the novel provides a comprehensive analysis of the seventeen drafts that Fitzgerald produced. Notes significant changes between versions and thus offers valuable evidence of the forces that influenced Fitzgerald's creative process.

Bruccoli, Matthew J., with Judith S. Baughman. *Reader's Companion to F. Scott Fitzgerald's "Tender Is the Night."* Columbia: University of South Carolina Press, 1996. Discusses the genesis, creation, publication, and critical reception of *Tender Is the Night.* Includes a lengthy section of notes explaining the many references in the novel.

Curnutt, Kirk. *The Cambridge Introduction to F. Scott Fitzgerald.* New York: Cambridge University Press, 2007. Provides a concise overview of Fitzgerald's life and work and offers discussions of his composition process; the major themes, characters, plots, and motifs in his fiction; the critical reception of the works; and modern Fitzgerald studies.

Gale, Robert L. *An F. Scott Fitzgerald Encyclopedia.* Westport, Conn.: Greenwood Press, 1998. Presents a wealth of information, including brief biographies of all of Fitzgerald's significant family members, friends, and acquaintances; plot summaries of all of his fictional works; and brief descriptions of every named person in his works.

LaHood, Marvin J., ed. *"Tender Is the Night": Essays in Criticism.* Bloomington: Indiana University Press, 1969. Offers a wide variety of criticism, ranging from discussions of theme, symbolism, and dialogue to psychological topics. Two of the essays discuss connections between Fitzgerald and John Keats.

Metzger, Charles R. *F. Scott Fitzgerald's Psychiatric Novel: Nicole's Case, Dick's Case.* New York: Peter Lang, 1989. Intriguing psychoanalytic study of the novel examines Nicole and Dick's mental symptoms, discusses the effectiveness of their treatments, and debates whether they recovered from their psychological problems.

Prigozy, Ruth, ed. *The Cambridge Companion to F. Scott Fitzgerald.* New York: Cambridge University Press, 2002. Collection of essays examines various aspects of Fitzgerald's life and work. Topics addressed include his critical reputation, the portrayal of women in his fiction, and his work in Hollywood. Milton R. Stern's *"Tender Is the Night* and American History" focuses on this novel.

Stern, Milton R. *Critical Essays on F. Scott Fitzgerald's "Tender Is the Night."* Boston: G. K. Hall, 1986. Provides two discussions of Fitzgerald's text as well as critical responses to the novel in chronological order, beginning with contemporary reviews from the 1930's. Includes valuable essays by Matthew J. Bruccoli, Malcolm Cowley, and Arthur Mizener, among others.

_____. *"Tender Is the Night": The Broken Universe.* New York: Twayne, 1994. Provides literary and historical context for the novel as well as a reading of various types of identities in the novel. Includes an informative chronology of the events of Fitzgerald's life.

Tess of the D'Urbervilles
A Pure Woman Faithfully Presented

Author: Thomas Hardy (1840-1928)
First published: 1891
Type of work: Novel
Type of plot: Philosophical realism
Time of plot: Late nineteenth century
Locale: England

Principal characters:
JACK DURBEYFIELD, a poor worker
TESS, his daughter
ALEC D'URBERVILLE, her betrayer
ANGEL CLARE, her husband

The Story:

It is a proud day when Jack Durbeyfield learns that he is descended from the famous D'Urberville family. Durbeyfield never does more work than necessary to keep his family supplied with meager food and himself with beer, but from that day on, he ceases doing even that small amount of work. His wife joins him in thinking that such a high family should live better with less effort, and she persuades their oldest daughter, Tess, to visit the Stoke-D'Urbervilles, a wealthy family who assumed the D'Urberville name because no one else claimed it. It is her mother's hope that Tess would make a good impression on the rich D'Urbervilles and perhaps a good marriage with one of the sons.

When Tess meets her supposed relatives, however, she finds only a blind mother and a dapper son who makes Tess uncomfortable by his improper remarks to her. The son, Alec, tricks the innocent young Tess into working as a poultry maid; he does not let her know that his mother is unaware of Tess's identity. After a short time, Tess decides to avoid Alec and look for work elsewhere to support her parents and her brothers and sisters. Alec, however, manages at last to get her alone and then rapes her.

When Tess returns to her home and tells her mother of her terrible experience, her mother's only worry is that Alec is not going to marry Tess. She works in the fields, facing the slander of her associates bravely. Her trouble is made worse by the fact that Alec follows her from place to place. By traveling to different farms during the harvest season, Tess manages to elude Alec long enough to give birth to her baby without his knowledge. The baby does not live long, however, and a few months after its death, Tess goes to a dairy farm far to the south to be a dairymaid.

At the dairy farm, Tess is liked and well treated. Angel Clare, a pastor's son who rejected the ministry to study farming, is also at the farm. It is his wish to own a farm someday, and he is working on different kinds of farms so that he can learn something of the many kinds of work required of a general farmer. Although all the dairymaids are attracted to Angel, Tess interests him the most. He thinks her a beautiful and innocent young maiden. Tess feels that she is wicked, however, and rejects the attentions Angel pays to her. She urges him to turn to one of the other girls for companionship. It is unthinkable that the son of a minister would marry a dairymaid, but Angel does not care much about family tradition. Despite her pleas, he continues to pay court to Tess. At last, against the wishes of his parents, Angel asks Tess to be his wife. He loves her, and he realizes that a farm girl will be a help to him on his own land. Although Tess is in love with Angel by this time, the memory of her night with Alec causes her to refuse Angel again and again. At last, his insistence, coupled with the written pleas of her parents to marry someone who can help the family financially, wins her over, and she agrees to marry him.

On the night before the wedding, which Tess postpones many times because she feels unworthy, she writes Angel a letter, revealing everything about herself and Alec. She slips the letter under his door; she is sure that when he reads it, he will renounce her forever. In the morning, however, Angel acts as tenderly as before, and Tess loves him more than ever for his forgiving nature. When she realizes that Angel did not find the letter, she attempts to tell him about her past. Angel only teases her about wanting to confess, thinking that such a pure girl could have no black sins in her history. They are married without Angel learning about Alec and her dead baby.

On their wedding night, Angel tells Tess about an evening of debauchery in his own past. Tess forgives him and then tells about her affair with Alec, thinking that he will forgive her as she did him; but such is not the case. Angel is at first stunned and then so hurt that he cannot even speak to Tess. Finally, he tells her that she is not the woman he loves, the one he married, but a stranger with whom he cannot live, at least for the present. He takes her to her home and leaves her there. Then he goes to his own home and on to Brazil, where he plans to buy a farm. At first, neither Tess nor Angel tells their parents the reason for their separation. When Tess finally tells her mother, the ignorant woman blames Tess for losing her husband by confessing something he need never to know.

Angel leaves Tess some money and some jewels that were given to him by his godmother. Tess puts the jewels in a bank; she spends the money on her parents. When it is gone, her family goes hungry once more, for her father still thinks himself too highborn to work for a living. Again, Tess goes from farm to farm, performing hard labor in the fields to get enough food to keep herself and her family alive.

While she is working in the fields, she meets Alec again. He met Angel's minister father and, repenting his evil ways, became an itinerant preacher. The sight of Tess, for whom he always lusted, causes a lapse in his new religious fervor, and he begins to pursue her once again. Frightened, Tess writes to Angel, sending the letter to his parents to forward to him. She tells Angel that she loves him and needs him and that an enemy is pursuing her. She begs him to forgive her and to return to her.

The letter takes several months to reach Angel. Meanwhile, Alec is so kind to Tess and so generous to her family that she begins to relent in her feelings toward him. At last, when she does not receive an answer from Angel, she writes him a note saying that he is cruel not to forgive her and that now she will not forgive his treatment of her. Then she goes to Alec again and lives with him as his wife.

It is thus that Angel finds her. He comes to tell her that he forgives her and that he still loves her. When he finds her with Alec, however, he turns away, more hurt than before.

Tess, too, is bitterly unhappy. She now hates Alec because once again he is the cause of her husband's repudiation of her. Feeling that she could find happiness only if Alec is dead, she stabs him as he sleeps. Then she runs out of the house and follows Angel, who is aimlessly walking down a road leading out of the town. When they meet and Tess tells him what she did, Angel forgives her everything, even the murder of Alec, and they go on together. They are happy with each other for a few days, although Angel knows that the authorities will soon find Tess.

When the officers finally find them, Tess is asleep. Angel asks the officers to wait until she awakens. As soon as she opens her eyes, Tess sees the strangers and knows that they came for her and that she will be hanged, but she is not unhappy. She had a few days with the husband she truly loves, and now she is ready for her punishment. She stands up bravely and faces her captors. She is not afraid.

Critical Evaluation:

Best remembered as the chronicler of the fictional Wessex, England, Thomas Hardy is considered one of the greatest novelists of the late nineteenth century. Born and raised in a small hamlet in Dorset, Hardy moved to London as a young man and spent most of the rest of his life as an urban professional. He remained part enthralled and part troubled about his native Wessex, however, and wrote with passion about industrialization, the movement of labor to the cities (or the exile of rural people in search of a living), the destruction of agricultural economies (and the ways of life dependent on them), and social dislocation. Almost all of Hardy's best-known novels contrast the social conditions of urban and rural people. While his novels are complex and often deeply tragic, his poems often are eulogies to the rural landscapes he loved.

Tess of the D'Urbervilles was inspired by Hardy's concerns over the fragility of the English rural worker's livelihood. The novel was also shockingly honest for its day in its presentation of women's sexuality and power. Tess's unrelenting victimization, often considered the novel's most serious flaw, is, in part, Hardy's indictment of Victorian values, which put the blame of economic deprivation on the poor, and the blame for sexual exploitation on the exploited (women). The theme of sexual exploitation is closely interwoven with the story of Wessex's decline.

Tess's troubles begin with her parents' economic condition; they are representatives of the disaffected and drunken villagers whose houses will soon fall to larger farms mass-producing crops for mass consumption. The novel is strewn with images of the Wessex countryside being gobbled up by machinery (the harvesting machine, for example, that is symbolically referred to as the "grim reaper"), rail tracks, and new farm enclosures. The uncertainty of Tess's parents' fate contributes to their irresponsibility. Since they are drunk at Rolliver's Inn, Tess embarks on a journey with the beehives to the market; this is the journey on which she falls asleep and accidentally kills the family's horse in a collision.

The loss of the horse, in turn, prompts Tess to work for her family's upkeep. The events that follow, culminating in her psychological disintegration and final criminal act, are rooted in a cause that is not Tess's fault—her parents' drunken irresponsibility—and perhaps not even her parents' fault; rather, the tragic plot is set in motion by an economic set of circumstances. These economic conditions have social and psychological effects. Hardy's frankness regarding money was also denounced in his day. Tess, abandoned by her husband, returns to Alec only when she is at a loss to care for her mother and younger siblings.

This is not to say that all the mistakes and wrongs perpetrated in the novel have an economic basis. The rural-urban dislocations generated by England's economic circumstances play a large part in Tess's life. Alec D'Urberville is the city-bred, cultured, streetwise man who takes advantage of Tess. Her rape and later seduction can be read as a metaphor for the city's ruthless exploitation of the country. Angel Clare is educated in the city, and he develops fine sensibilities that unrealistically construct Tess into an ethereal and pure being (he likens her to Demeter). The unrealistic nature of Angel's expectations makes him unable to forgive her for not being a virgin. Alec and Angel both manipulate Tess: the former through sexual and economic exploitation, and the latter through myths and idealistic moral constructs. Hardy continually draws readers' attention to, and calls on readers' compassion for, his female protagonist. The men who exploit her—representative of the deeds and words, respectively, that oppress women—are brought under the readers' critical gaze. In a broad sense, the female is associated with the rural. For example, in one of the first scenes traveling students, of whom Angel is one, survey and "penetrate" the countryside in which Tess dances with the village maidens. Hardy's imagery evokes conceptions of power in the act of the urban gaze focusing on the rural, doubling as Angel's gaze on Tess.

The novel ends a tragedy. Unlike the protagonists of classic tragedies, the protagonist in this tragedy bears very little of the blame for her fate. Her mistakes are at best innocence, helplessness, and an overdeveloped sense of responsibility toward her loved ones. For many critics, such helplessness makes Tess a flawed, almost unrealistic, character. In any case, her fate must be read as a symbolic representation of the social power dynamics that Hardy criticizes. The novel is more than a simple realistic account of a fallen milkmaid.

Hardy is considered to be a realistic, naturalistic writer. His style has been described as cinematic, painterly, and pictorial because of its elaborate and meticulous renditions of landscape and architecture. Some of the ways in which readers make meaning of his narratives—for example, Tess as a symbol—do not fall into the realistic tradition, however, and Hardy's best novels may be read on many levels in addition to those of realistic or naturalistic fiction. *Tess of the D'Urbervilles* may also be read for its historical, moral, satirical, and aesthetic concerns.

"Critical Evaluation" by Bishnupriya Ghosh

Further Reading

Casagrande, Peter J. *Tess of the D'Urbervilles: Unorthodox Beauty.* New York: Twayne, 1992. Focuses on Hardy's intertwining of beauty and ugliness, of moral and aesthetic issues. Examines Victorian attitudes toward women, Tess's "terrible beauty," and parallels between her suffering and the horse's death. Analyzes Angel as a mix of convention and newness.

Kramer, Dale, ed. *The Cambridge Companion to Thomas Hardy.* New York: Cambridge University Press, 1999. An introduction and general overview of all Hardy's work and specific demonstrations of Hardy's ideas and literary skills. Individual essays explore Hardy's biography, aesthetics, and the impact on his work of developments in science, religion, and philosophy in the late nineteenth century. The volume also contains a detailed chronology of Hardy's life and Linda M. Shire's essay "The Radical Aesthetic of *Tess of the D'Urbervilles*."

Kramer, Dale, and Nancy Marck, eds. *Critical Essays on Thomas Hardy: The Novels.* Boston: G. K. Hall, 1990. Discusses Hardy's plots and rhetoric, with focus on individual novels. Good essay on Hardy's understanding of Tess as a woman, examining Victorian debates and postromantic ideas. Treats awareness of language as a shaping force.

McEathron, Scott, ed. *Thomas Hardy's "Tess of the d'Urbervilles": A Sourcebook.* New York: Routledge, 2005. Contains essays and poems by Hardy, some contemporary reviews of the novel, and modern critical essays, including examinations of the postmodern characteristics and color and movement in the novel and an analysis of Tess's rape. Explicates key passages from the novel.

Millgate, Michael. *Thomas Hardy: A Biography Revisited.* New York: Oxford University Press, 2004. This biography enhances and replaces Millgate's 1982 biography, considered to be one of the best and most scholarly Hardy biographies available. Includes bibliography and index.

Moore, Kevin Z. *The Descent of the Imagination: Postromantic Culture in the Later Novels of Thomas Hardy.* New York: New York University Press, 1990. Uses language and cultural dominance issues to discuss Tess's quest for beauty and freedom.

Page, Norman, ed. *Oxford Reader's Companion to Hardy.* New York: Oxford University Press, 2000. An encyclopedia containing three hundred alphabetically arranged entries examining Hardy's work and discussing his family and friends, important places in his life and work, his influences, critical approaches to his writings, and a history of his works' publication. Also includes a chronology of his life, lists of places and characters in his fiction, a glossary, and a bibliography.

Tomalin, Claire. *Thomas Hardy.* New York: Penguin, 2007. This thorough and finely written biography by a respected Hardy scholar illuminates the novelist's efforts to indict the malice, neglect, and ignorance of his fellow human beings. Tomalin also discusses aspects of his life that are apparent in his literary works.

Vigar, Penelope. *The Novels of Thomas Hardy: Illusion and Reality.* London: Athlone Press, 1974. Analyzes Hardy's techniques and style. Examines *Tess of the D'Urbervilles* in terms of Hardy's notion of imaginative flights that emerge from visual effects. Examines the novel's structure in terms of its contrasts—Tess's purity and guilt, reality and perceptions.

Wright, Terence. *Tess of the D'Urbervilles.* Atlantic Highlands, N.J.: Humanities Press, 1987. Summarizes critical approaches to *Tess of the D'Urbervilles*, providing an overview of criticism of the novel. Synthesizes some of the best criticism, emphasizing importance of place, ambiguity of causes, human insignificance, and the inevitability of human tragedy, with Tess representing individual and larger tragedy.

Tevye the Dairyman
Or, The Two Nations

Author: Sholom Aleichem (Sholom Naumovich
   Rabinowitz, 1859-1916)
First published: Tevye der Milkhiger, 1894-1914
   (English translation, 1949, 1987)
Type of work: Short fiction

Tevye the Dairyman is a collection of eight stories published by the Yiddish writer Sholom Aleichem between 1894 and 1914. The first Tevye story appeared in the Warsaw yearbook *Der Hoyzfraynt*. A fragment titled "Vekhalaklakoys," written in 1914 and published shortly before the author's death in 1916, deals with Tevye but is generally not included in the list of the Tevye stories. The collection *Tevye's Daughters* was published in 1949; it contains the eight Tevye stories. *Tevye the Dairyman and Railroad Stories* was published in 1987. *Tevye the Dairyman* is considered by some to be a loose, episodic novel about the changes that were overwhelming Eastern European Jewish life at the beginning of the twentieth century. Tevye recounts his gradual loss of control over his family, his continued questioning of God's motives, and the appropriation of his community and livelihood by forces beyond his control. The stories are the basis for the popular stage musical *Fiddler on the Roof* (1964; the title comes not from Sholom Aleichem but from a Marc Chagall painting). While many are familiar with Tevye through the theatrical version, *Tevye the Dairyman* is of greater depth.

The stories are purportedly verbatim reportage of personal anecdotes and reflections that Tevye shares with the author in occasional meetings through the years. The tone is conversational and familiar, and Tevye often refers to the place, time, and circumstances of meeting. In an ironic twist, Tevye often pleads with Sholom Aleichem that the intimate details of his life not be published to the world.

The first story, "Tevye Strikes It Rich," is a genial tale in which a good deed reaps the humble dairyman wealth beyond imagination. Returning to his village of Kasrilevke from a round of deliveries to Boiberik, where the rich Jews from Yehupetz summer in their dachas, Tevye meets two wealthy Jewish women who engage him to drive them home. Once arrived, the women and their families thank Tevye with a generous tip and a cartload of food. He rushes home to his wife Golde and they ponder how to enjoy their newfound riches.

The story introduces many of the elements that mark the entire collection. Tevye's mode of expression is painstakingly circuitous; he constantly digresses to philosophize or to quote, and in many cases misquote, Jewish scripture and wisdom. He is a master of oxymoron and paradox, as when he says, "He's only human too, don't you think, or why else would God have made him a horse?" He is also adept at hyperbole, as in "The shadows of the trees were as long as the exile of the Jews." Tevye is defined by his spiraling thought process and wry speech.

At each turn, whether dealing with the women or his horse or his wife, Tevye is endearingly skeptical and ornery. His contempt for the upper classes is evident, yet he fawns when there is money to be made; his is an odd mix of acceptance and opportunism. His thoughts never stray long from metaphysics, for Tevye is a traditional Jew, constantly searching for God's wisdom in the slightest twist of fortune. He is often more apt to curse than to thank his creator, but Tevye's faith is firm. He knows that there is divine wisdom he cannot understand, and that the best he can do with his miserable lot is to accept it with a modicum of good cheer.

In the second story, "The Bubble Bursts," Tevye loses the small fortune he gained by foolishly trusting it to the speculating care of his cousin Menachem Mendl. Menachem takes a hundred rubles, promising to turn it into thousands, and then disappears. After being admonished by his wife, "Tevye . . . don't just stand there doing nothing. Think!" Tevye sets off to Yehupetz in search of Menachem. When Tevye finally finds him, after some small adventures, he learns that his cousin lost all the money. In the end, Tevye interprets his bad luck as a confirmation from God of his place in the great scheme of things.

The first two stories trace equal motions, one forward and one backward. In the next stories, the emotional heart of *Tevye the Dairyman* comes into focus. Tevye has seven daughters. (In some of the stories, the number is unclear. Scholars speculate that Sholom Aleichem originally intended a story about each daughter, but ultimately wrote about only five.) As a poor father of daughters, a primary concern is how

Tevye will marry them into happiness and reasonable prosperity. In his culture, matches are made by matchmakers and negotiated by fathers. Tevye comes to learn that such traditions are precarious at best.

In "Modern Children," the third story, Tevye arranges a lucrative match for his oldest daughter Tsaytl with the wealthy widower butcher Layzer Wolf. Tsaytl, however, is heartbroken at the prospect, and Tevye relents, and later invents a prophetic nightmare to sway his wife Golde away from the match. Then Motl the poor tailor informs Tevye that he and Tsaytl are in love and plan to marry. While Tevye cannot conceive of a young couple making such a decision on their own, without deferring to matchmakers or parents, he ultimately gives his blessing.

This story begins the account of the unraveling of tradition and of paternalism. Tevye cannot stand firm against his daughters' tears. As he is buffeted with the persistence and emotions of those around him, he debates in his mind the wisdom of the old ways and the brazenness of the new. In his humorously doubtful and self-effacing way, he searches for God's will in each moment. Tevye sees the story end well, with Tsaytl married happily to a good, although not wealthy, man.

Hodl is Tevye's second daughter, and she lends her name to the fourth story, in which the stakes are raised. Not only does Hodl choose her mate, a visiting student named Pertchik, but also she goes off with him to Siberia, where he is exiled for his revolutionary activities.

For the first time in *Tevye the Dairyman*, the tone in "Hodl" becomes pained. Tevye always protected his wife and daughters from unpleasant truths; now, as Hodl leaves, she has secrets, confidential information, that she cannot share with him. At the train station, Tevye bids Hodl farewell and she acknowledges that they may never meet again. Having maintained a stoic front, Tevye cannot endure the heartbreak any longer.

That did it! I couldn't keep it in a second longer. You see, just then I thought of my Hodl when I held her as a baby in my arms . . . she was just a tiny thing then . . . and I held her in these arms . . . please forgive me . . . if . . . if I . . . just like a woman . . . but I want you to know what a Hodl I have! You should see the letters that she writes me . . . she's God's own Hodl, Hodl is . . . and she's with me right here all the time . . . deep, deep down . . . there's just no way to put it into words. . . .

You know what, Pani Sholom Aleichem? Let's talk about something more cheerful. Have you heard any news of the cholera in Odessa?

From this point on, humor and pain go hand in hand. Sholom Aleichem's humor is a way of understanding the developing crisis of Eastern European Jewry. He neither belabors nor belittles that crisis; rather, he attempts to convey faithfully both the farce and the tragedy that he witnesses.

In the fifth and sixth stories, "Chava" and "Shprintze," Tevye loses his next two daughters in even more devastating ways. When Chava chooses to marry a non-Jew, Tevye comes up against a wall that he cannot surmount. He declares her dead to him and refuses any further contact. He even flees in panic when he comes upon her alone in the forest. This time, when he beseeches Sholom Aleichem, "you're not to breathe a word about this, or put any of it in your books!" Tevye is articulating the unspoken fears of a threatened people.

Then Tevye's fourth daughter, Shprintze, falls in love with the son of a rich Jewish widow. At last, Tevye believes, one of his daughters is making a brilliant match, but soon Tevye is accused of scheming to entrap the young man. The wedding is canceled, Shprintze is heartbroken, and one day Tevye arrives home to find her drowned in the river. Here, the prose becomes taut and subtle; much of the pain of Shprintze's suicide is conveyed indirectly.

In the last two stories, the unraveling of Tevye's world is complete. In "Tevye Leaves for the Land of Israel," his wife Golde has died, and his fifth daughter Beilke marries a wealthy Jew named Podhotzur. Tevye finally has a well-married daughter, but she abandons him, supporting her husband's desire to exile the aging dairyman to Israel. Beilke will not question her husband's lust for reputation, a reputation that has no room for impoverished in-laws. Always looking at the bright side, Tevye accepts his exile and is eager to return to the ancestral homeland in Palestine.

He never goes, however, because Motl the tailor dies and Tevye must look after his eldest daughter Tsaytl, and her children. In "Get Thee Out," Tevye likens himself to Abraham in the Bible, being ordered by God to leave his home. Podhotzur loses his fortune, and he and Beilke leave for America, and now Tevye, Tsaytl, and her children are being driven from Kasrilevke. As they prepare to leave, Tsaytl reminds Tevye of the child that he so long ago banished, and he turns around to face his third daughter, Chava, whom he pronounced dead for marrying a non-Jew. He admits, "you know as well as I do that no matter what a child may have done, when it stands there looking right through you and says 'Papa'. . . ." Tevye ultimately leaves it to Sholom Aleichem and to the reader to intuit whether he embraces her in his arms or issues the biblical order "lekh-lekho," or "get thee out."

The reunion is the emotional conclusion of the collection, a catharsis amid social dissolution. The irony continues: Local Russians, under pressure to conduct a pogrom on their Jewish population, give their well-loved Tevye the option of breaking his own windows. The humor is fitting for a man ennobled by his humility and firm in the conviction that all the blessings and ills that visit him are the expression of God's wisdom and will.

Barry Mann

Further Reading

Frieden, Ken. "Tevye the Dairyman and His Daughters' Rebellion." In *Classic Yiddish Fiction: Abramovitsh, Sholem Aleichem, and Peretz.* Albany: State University of New York Press, 1995. Frieden, a professor of Judaic studies at the State University of New York, examines the Tevye stories and other works by Sholom Aleichem.

Gittleman, Sol. *From Shtetl to Suburbia: The Family in Jewish Literary Imagination.* Boston: Beacon Press, 1978. Discusses Aleichem and others as pioneers of the tradition. The extended chapter on Aleichem examines the crisis of contemporary family life as conveyed through the Tevye stories.

Liptzin, Solomon. *The Flowering of Yiddish Literature.* New York: T. Yoseloff, 1963. Offers an exhaustive historical narrative of Yiddish literature from the 1860's to World War I. The chapter on Aleichem examines the historical, literary, and social values of his work.

Miron, Dan. *The Image of the Shtetl, and Other Studies of Modern Jewish Literary Imagination.* Syracuse, N.Y.: Syracuse University Press, 2000. Miron's study of the representation of the Jewish world focuses heavily on the major works of Sholom Aleichem, including the Tevye stories.

Samuel, Maurice. *The World of Sholom Aleichem.* New York: Alfred A. Knopf, 1943. Samuel re-creates Sholom Aleichem's milieu, with explorations of Tevye's personality, landscape, philosophy, and family life. A very anecdotal volume that includes warm retellings of the Tevye stories.

Waife-Goldberg, Marie. *My Father, Sholom Aleichem.* New York: Simon & Schuster, 1968. An interesting and revealing memoir by Sholom Aleichem's daughter, full of anecdotes about Sholom Aleichem and examining the parallels between him and his fictional persona, Tevye.

Wisse, Ruth R. *The Schlemiel as Modern Hero.* Chicago: University of Chicago Press, 1971. This slim book includes a chapter on Sholom Aleichem entitled "Ironic Balance for Psychic Survival," in which Wisse discusses the uses of irony and satire and the polarization of faith and fact as reflected in Tevye's philosophical dialogues.

Tex

Author: S. E. Hinton (1948-　　)
First published: 1979
Type of work: Novel
Type of plot: Social realism
Time of plot: 1970's
Locale: Tulsa, Oklahoma

Principal characters:
TEX MCCORMICK, a fourteen-year-old boy
MASON, his brother
POP, their father
JOHNNY COLLINS, Tex's best friend
JAMIE, Johnny's younger sister
BOB, Johnny's older brother
COLE, Johnny's father
LEM PETERS, a friend of the McCormick boys
MISS CARLSON, Tex's teacher
NEGRITO, Tex's horse

The Story:

Tex McCormick loves his horse, Negrito. He returns home from school and is surprised that his older brother Mason is also home. Mason is a senior, the star of the basketball team, and is hoping to get into a good college, possibly with a basketball scholarship. Tex knows that, if Mason skipped practice, either he is sick or something is wrong. When Tex confronts him, Mason admits to selling Negrito and his own horse, Red. Their father, Pop, is out on the rodeo circuit and has not written or sent money home in four months. Mason had no other choice. They needed money to pay their bills.

Tex is outraged when Mason breaks the news. The brothers argue, and the fight turns physical. Mason is angry that their financial situation has gotten this bad, and he takes his anger out on Tex. When the fists stop flying, Mason tries to apologize. Tex insists that he is going to get the horses back, that their father never would have allowed this to happen. Mason is amazed that Tex does not see that he was forced to take drastic measures precisely because Pop is not home.

Tex vows to find the horses and get them back. He leaves the house to search for them. He meets up with his best friend, Johnny Collins, and Johnny's younger sister, Jamie. He tells them what Mason did. They try to talk him out of looking for the horses, but Tex will not listen. Mason comes looking for Tex and drags him back home.

That weekend, the fair begins. Bob, Johnny's older brother, drives Tex and Johnny to the city and drops them off at the fair. The boys meet Jamie and her friend. The girls talk the boys into having their fortunes told. The fortuneteller reads Tex's palm, telling him that he will be one of the "people who stay" and that he will not get Negrito back. Tex is not sure what she means by "people who stay."

Tex and Johnny continue to get into trouble, both in and out of school. Cole Collins, Johnny's father, deems Tex to be a bad influence. Mason takes offense at Cole's judgment because Johnny is just as much of a troublemaker as Tex is. One of Mason's old friends, Lem Peters, stops by to announce the birth of his son. Lem wants to share his good news with the Collins kids, so Tex sneaks him into the Collins house. The boys are happy to hear Lem's news. Jamie is the realist of the group and doubts raising a baby will be easy. When she makes a wisecrack about Lem's parenting skills, it does not go over well. Tex comes to her defense. Tex struggles to understand why he has begun to look at Jamie differently. He is starting to notice girls, and Jamie is becoming more than his best friend's sister.

Tex and Mason take a trip into the city. Mason has to go to the doctor for some tests. Mason learns that he has an ulcer, likely caused by the recent financial stress. The brothers visit Lem while they are in town and find out that he has been dealing drugs in order to support his family. On the way home, Mason lets Tex drive the truck. Tex stops to pick up a hitchhiker, unaware that the man is wanted by the police.

The hitchhiker pulls a gun on Mason and tells the brothers that he has shot someone to finally settle an old score. Tex notices that they are being followed by the police and drives the truck into a ditch. The hitchhiker is shot and killed by the police. The boys' adventure with the hitchhiker makes the eve-

ning news. Pop sees the story on television in Dallas; he calls the boys and tells them he is coming home. Tex is thrilled, while Mason is angry.

Pop returns and gets into an argument with Mason almost immediately. Pop starts making promises, including promising Tex that he will get Negrito back. Pop comes through with the money eventually, but when Tex and Mason try to buy Negrito back his new owners refuse to sell. Tex is angry with Mason all over again. Tex says some hurtful things to Mason and realizes for the first time that hurting someone can feel good.

Tex gets into more trouble at school. Pop shows up late for a meeting with the principal and another argument with Mason ensues. This time, Mason airs some dirty laundry, proclaiming that Pop is not Tex's biological father. Pop does not deny the accusation. Tex is shocked by the revelation and leaves school.

Tex runs into Lem. Lem asks him to tag along while he clears up a misunderstanding with one of his customers. Tex agrees to go along because he does not want to go home. They arrive at an apartment. Lem tries to smooth things over, but it is not going well. When Tex tries to leave, one of the men shoots him. Tex grabs the gun and prepares to shoot back, but he cannot go through with it. The two escape, and Tex tells Lem that he was shot. Lem panics. If he takes Tex to the hospital, the police might find out about the drugs. Tex calls the Collins house for help. Lem calls his wife and tells her to get rid of their drugs. Tex loses consciousness as Lem pleads for him to hang on. While Tex is in the hospital, Pop tells him about his biological father. Tex also learns that Cole called the ambulance and saved Tex's life.

In the spring, Mason decides not to go to college, but Tex tells Mason that he has to go. Tex does not want Mason to resent him for the rest of his life. He believes he can take care of himself now, and he already has a summer job lined up. Tex accepts the fortuneteller's prediction: Mason will go because he needs to, but Tex will stay.

Critical Evaluation:

S. E. Hinton's first three novels generated mixed reviews of her skill as a writer. While the critics could not deny that her stories were commercial successes, some of them felt that her characters and plot lines were not always believable. With the writing of *Tex*, Hinton challenged herself to prove the naysayers wrong. This time, Hinton's goal was to write a book in which the plot events did not overshadow her hero's journey. She sought to portray the maturation and growth of Tex McCormick over the story's time line.

It took Hinton nearly three and a half years to write *Tex*.

She was not suffering from writers' block as she had after *The Outsiders* (1967) was published. Instead, Hinton took her time constructing the novel, taking great care to ensure that the flow of events and the characters' interactions would be smooth and not forced. Hinton's efforts paid off with the creation of Tex McCormick. Of all her characters, Tex comes closest to resembling a living, breathing human being.

In *Tex*, Hinton reexamines themes covered in her previous novels. The fortuneteller's prediction about "people who go and people who stay" is another way of framing Hinton's recurring theme of the loss of innocence. When Tex and Mason discuss going to the fair, Tex is surprised that Mason does not want to go. Mason has outgrown the fair. "I'll think the Fair is fun no matter how old I get," Tex responds. It is Tex's way of retaining his innocence. The "people who go" are the ones who have grown up or are not content with life as it is. They need to move on.

In each of Hinton's novels, many of the characters are figured as orphans. Some, like the Curtis brothers in *The Outsiders*, are literally orphans. Others have parents who are absent due to illness or an addiction such as alcoholism. This absence leaves them feeling empty and searching for a place where they belong. Some find solace in friendships. Some, such as Rusty James in *Rumble Fish* (1975), are incapable of finding a place where they fit in. Tex thinks he belongs because he has Mason and Pop. When he finds out that Pop is not his biological father, he becomes orphaned for a time. Tex's reaction to the news is measured, almost purposeful. Later, when Pop tells Tex about his mother's infidelity, Tex asks if this is the reason why Pop always paid more attention to Mason. Tex hopes that Pop's answer will be "no." He still wants to belong to Pop. When Pop answers, "I reckon," Tex has to face the fact the he may never have belonged in the first place. This story line relates to another of Hinton's recurring themes, questioning the role fate plays in life.

Hinton returns to fate and destiny as the guiding forces in Tex's life. However, unlike Rusty James, Tex has not resigned himself to the notion that he is doomed from the start. Instead, Tex figures out how to use fate to his advantage. When he realizes that he is one who will "stay," he does not believe that is necessarily a bad thing. Tex is where he wants to be and finds freedom in embracing his destiny. Tex beats fate at its own game by refusing to be victimized by it.

In *That Was Then, This Is Now* (1971), Hinton brought back a few of her characters from *The Outsiders* in cameo appearances. This led some reviewers to believe the second novel was a sequel, despite the fact that, other than the cameos, the two stories were unrelated. The cameos were used to illustrate Bryon's growth over the course of the novel. Hinton uses this device again in *Tex*, though she is not as direct about identifying the cameo characters by name. A careful reader may notice that the hitchhiker Tex picks up is actually Mark Jennings from *That Was Then, This Is Now*. The hitchhiker speaks of breaking out of prison in order to settle an old score, and he shoots a man (presumably Bryon, also from the previous novel) to exact his revenge. However, after spending so many years hating Bryon and planning for that moment, when it finally comes, he cannot finish the job.

After the hitchhiker is killed and Tex returns to school, he learns that his teacher, Miss Carlson, went to the hitchhiker's funeral. When he asks her how she knew him, Miss Carlson identifies the hitchhiker as Mark, a person she used to know. Tex apologizes to her for what happened. When she tells him that she is "sad, but not surprised," Hinton shows readers how Mark's attitude led to his demise and how Miss Carlson did not let the past define her. She chose to move on with her life and did not become a victim of fate.

Reviewers were full of praise for Tex, acknowledging Hinton's maturing style and dedication to her craft. Any doubts about Hinton's skill as a novelist were finally dispelled. Tex went on to win many awards, including an American Library Association Best Books for Young Adults citation in 1979, a New York Public Library Books for the Teen-Age citation in 1980, and an American Book Award nomination in 1981. In 1982, Tex also received a Sue Hefly Award from the Louisiana Association of School Libraries and a nomination for the California Reading Association's Young Reader Medal.

Martel Sardina

Further Reading

Daly, Jay. *Presenting S. E. Hinton*. Boston: Twayne, 1989. A comprehensive analysis of Hinton's works. Contains an author biography, individual chapters focused on each of her young adult novels, literary criticism, and supplemental information about the film adaptations of her books.

Hinton, S. E. *Some of Tim's Stories*. New York: Speak/Penguin Group USA, 2007. Contains interviews with Hinton discussing her young adult novels, their film adaptations, and her most recent works.

Howard, Todd. *Understanding "The Outsiders."* San Diego, Calif.: Lucent Books, 2001. A comprehensive look at the novel, including literary criticism.

Wilson, Antoine. *The Library of Author Biographies: S. E. Hinton*. New York: Rosen, 2003. Provides an overview of Hinton's works. Contains an author interview, selected book reviews, and a list of awards each book received.

Thanatopsis

Author: William Cullen Bryant (1794-1878)
First published: 1817; enlarged, 1821
Type of work: Poetry

William Cullen Bryant's poem "Thanatopsis" is considered to be the best of a number of poems he wrote on the subject of death. More noteworthy, however, is the fact that this poem established Bryant's reputation as a poet. That is not to say, however, that the poet was an overnight success. The *North American Review*, the periodical in which the poem first appeared, had a small circulation. Furthermore, according to one of Bryant's biographers, "Thanatopsis" was actually submitted to the publisher by the poet's father, and, since it was printed anonymously, one editor thought that the poem had been written by Bryant's father, Dr. Peter Bryant. Also, in the early nineteenth century, American readers were just beginning to develop an appreciation of the kind of Romanticism that the poem exhibits.

After his reputation was established, however, Bryant was sometimes called the "American Wordsworth" because, like the British Romantic poet William Wordsworth, he excelled in creating effective descriptions of nature. It is interesting to note that Bryant was acknowledged as the foremost poet in the United States even before his poems had been collected into a single volume; they had been published only singly in magazines and newspapers over a period of some fifteen years. One writer commented that Bryant had "been placed by common consent at the head of the list of American poets."

Like many of his contemporaries, Bryant did not earn a living exclusively from writing poetry. Influential in civic and political affairs, he was a lawyer and, for more than fifty years, editor of the *New York Evening Post*. That such a busy man could produce a poem judged to be of such high quality was in itself an outstanding achievement.

"Thanatopsis" filled one of the needs of Bryant's generation very well. Written during the early days of American nationhood, when there was not yet any real sense of a national past, the very size of the young country contributing to a sense of isolation, this poem provided reflections on topics that had real relevance to the citizenry: human mortality, the perception of death as separation, and the transience of life. "Thanatopsis" was thus sensitive to and in tune with the feelings of the times.

The poem is divided into three main sections. It has been noted that, whether Bryant was consciously aware of doing so or not, he structured the poem in the traditional rhetorical form of the "plain style" sermon that had been brought by settlers to New England during colonial days. This style provided for a three-part division, the parts dealing, in turn, with doctrine, reasons, and uses. The first section (lines 1-30) provides the philosophical background, or "doctrine," of the poem. Nature personified—that is, given human qualities, such as the ability to speak a language—is established as an authority to speak to humanity through its "still voice": "To him who in the love of nature holds/ Communion with her visible forms, she speaks/ A various language." The major problem to be resolved is that of coming to terms with the fact that everyone must eventually die. To relieve the fear that often accompanies thoughts of death, Nature can speak with a "various language." These variations include a "voice of gladness," a "smile and eloquence of beauty," and a "gentle sympathy" that is soothing and healing, offering consolation that "steals away" the fear. The "voice" in the poem then submits that when thoughts of death and burial become overwhelming, one should "go forth, under the open sky" and listen to what Nature has to say.

The "doctrine" that the poem teaches is that death means a total loss of human evidence: "Surrendering up Thine individual being, shalt thou go/ To mix forever with the elements." Some critics have criticized this passage as indicating that Bryant was not writing a Christian poem in which a faith in immortality and a hope of being eternally with God in heaven provides consolation. Actually, some people wrote letters of gratitude to Bryant for the consolation that the poem had given them; these people interpreted the poem as being a religious one.

The middle, or "reason," section of the poem (lines 31-72) becomes something of a debate, providing justification for the reason people should not view death as an isolation that forever separates. It argues against the reasons humanity would give for not wanting to face death. The dead are not alone; rather, they may actually be in more distinguished company than they have been accustomed to in life:

> Thou shalt lie down
> With patriarchs of the infant world—with kings,
> The powerful of the earth—the wise, the good,
> Fair forms, and hoary seers of ages past,
> All in one mighty sepulchre.

Furthermore, a return to Nature (that is, burial in the earth) means that all of the beauties of nature—the hills and vales, the "venerable woods" and "meadows green," the majestic rivers, the "complaining brooks," and even the "old ocean" itself—provide "solemn decorations" on "the great tomb of man" over which the sun never ceases to shine.

Another argument against the grave as consigning one to eternal isolation is that all the people living on the earth at a given time are but a "handful" compared to the number of the "slumbering" dead who are literally spread throughout the earth. It is just a matter of time until all will share the experience of death. Death should thus be thought of as something of a joyful reunion with those who have gone before.

To counter the possibility that an individual may die with no one taking note of the departure, with life going on gaily as if that person had never lived, Nature would say not to worry, for all of those still living on earth will one day come to the same end: "Yet all these shall leave/ Their mirth and their employments, and shall come/ And make their bed with thee." No one is exempt: Young and old alike "shall one by one be gathered" to join those who have departed earlier.

Like the Puritan sermon, the final section of the poem (lines 73-81) is analogous to the "uses" or application of the truths of the earlier sections. It "teaches" that if one is to face death without fear, one must, in life, prepare to be able to look on death at least with equanimity if not with enthusiasm. That preparation consists of taking seriously the admonition to live in such a way that, when death comes, one does not experience it as a prisoner taken in the night to some "dungeon" or "narrow house"—a coffin—and lowered into a grave, with no hope of escape. Rather, with an "unfaltering trust," one may compare going to the grave with preparing to lie down peacefully for a nap with the full expectation of having pleasant dreams.

In addition to using the Puritan sermon form innovatively, the poem reveals the use of a pattern of contrast, contradiction, and paradox in its development. For example, the intellectual and the emotional are juxtaposed to good effect. Impersonal references to details that suggest grief and loss are plentiful: "thoughts of the last bitter hour," "sad images of the stern agony, and shroud, and pall." However, there are unmistakably emotional undertones to these references.

Another example of this pattern in the poem is seen in the way the eternal, or permanent, aspect of nature is contrasted with the transient, or short-lived. The sun, the hills, the rivers, the forests, the ocean—elements that are perceived as timeless—are juxtaposed with references to the impermanence of humanity: "Earth, that nourished three, shall claim/ Thy growth, to be resolv'd to earth again." Also seen in this pas-

sage is the paradox that, even as Nature consoles with her "voice of gladness" and comes to humanity "with a mild and healing sympathy," it is "Earth, that nourished thee," who comes to "claim thy growth." The same Nature that is a consoler is thus also seen as Nature the enemy, who claims the lives of human beings. The graves of the dead, which become "one mighty sepulchre" and "the great tomb of man" that is decorated by all of the splendid beauty of nature, are also the "sad abodes of death" where "the oak shall send his roots abroad, and pierce thy mould."

Yet another paradox is that the poem is simultaneously a lesson on dying and a lesson on living. In order to learn the lesson of dying well, it is necessary to learn how to live well, and in "Thanatopsis" this involves living with such a perspective that death is seen as a natural, not a fearful, conclusion to life.

By 1825, Bryant had formulated his theory about poetry, which he shared in his "Lectures on Poetry" produced in 1825 and 1826. He believed that the "great spring of poetry" is emotion and that the source of poetic inspiration is nature. To his credit, the connections that Bryant made between "things of the moral and of the natural worlds," later known as the doctrine of analogies or correspondences, were made more than ten years before the theory would become a central tenet of American literary criticism.

It is important to realize that, in its day, both "Thanatopsis" and its writer played a central role in the formation of the character of a national literature. American politician and writer Richard Henry Dana, Jr., has been credited with commenting that "no one on this side of the Atlantic is capable of writing such verses," referring to Bryant and "Thanatopsis." At that time, it was assumed that American poetry had not yet matured sufficiently to produce a poem that could so favorably be compared to the poems of well-established British poets such as Wordsworth. Another critic of Bryant's era detected in "Thanatopsis" "the literature of the new nation, as distinct from colonial literature." To the large extent that this appraisal was accurate, the poem has carved for itself a permanent place in American literary history.

Victoria Price

Further Reading

Brodwin, Stanley, and Michael D'Innocenzo. *William Cullen Bryant and His America: Centennial Conference Proceedings, 1878-1978.* New York: AMS Press, 1983. Provides a broad background against which to study "Thanatopsis." One chapter focuses on the role that Bryant and this poem played in the development of American literature.

Brown, Charles Henry. *William Cullen Bryant*. New York: Charles Scribner's Sons, 1971. Addresses early influences on Bryant and his concept of death. Discusses the confusion over the authorship of "Thanatopsis" and traces the evolution of the poem to its final form. Illustrations include an autographed manuscript of "Thanatopsis."

Godwin, Parke. *A Biography of William Cullen Bryant*. 2 vols. 1883. Reprint. New York: Russell & Russell, 1967. Bryant's son-in-law discusses the events that led to the publication of "Thanatopsis," placing the writing of this and Bryant's other poetry within the context of the events of the poet's life.

Harrington, Joseph. "Re-birthing 'America': Philip Freneau, William Cullen Bryant, and the Invention of Modern Poetics." In *Making America, Making American Literature: Franklin to Cooper*, edited by A. Robert Lee and W. M. Verhoeven. New York: Rodopi, 1996. Discussion of Bryant's poetry is part of a collection of essays examining the development of American literature from the 1770's through the 1820's.

McLean, Albert F., Jr. *William Cullen Bryant*. Updated ed. New York: Twayne, 1989. Chapter 3, "The Poem of Death," is devoted to "Thanatopsis." The structure, tone, intent, and uses of language in the poem are discussed thoroughly. Includes a chronology of Bryant's life.

Muller, Gilbert H. *William Cullen Bryant: Author of America*. Albany: State University of New York Press, 2008. Biography discusses Bryant as a "first-rate poet" who helped define the idea of American democratic culture. Includes discussion of "Thanatopsis."

Peckham, H. H. *Gotham Yankee: A Biography of William Cullen Bryant*. New York: Russell & Russell, 1971. Addresses Bryant's attitudes toward life and death in order to place "Thanatopsis" in context. Compares this poem with other poems about death, especially Robert Blair's "The Grave."

That Evening Sun

Author: William Faulkner (1897-1962)
First published: 1931, as "That Evening Sun Go Down"
Type of work: Short fiction
Type of plot: Social realism
Time of plot: Late nineteenth and early twentieth centuries
Locale: Jefferson, Yoknapatawpha County, Mississippi

Principal characters:
NANCY, the Compson's laundress
JESUS, Nancy's husband
DILSEY, the Compson's servant
MR. COMPSON
MRS. COMPSON
CADDY, their daughter
JASON, their youngest son
QUENTIN, their oldest son and the story's narrator

The Story:

The twenty-four-year-old Quentin Compson recalls changes that have taken place in the town of Jefferson, Mississippi, over the last fifteen years. He thinks of the African American laundresses, or washerwomen, who used to wash white families' laundry fifteen years ago, in 1899. They would pick up bundles of clothing from families such as the Compsons and carry the bundles on their heads to and from their cabins. More recently, the process has come to involve transporting laundry by automobile, though the work is still done by African American women. Quentin recalls a series of events that occurred in 1899.

As a nine-year-old and the eldest of the three Compson children, Quentin observes his family's interactions with Nancy, a washerwoman who lives in a cabin on the other side of the ditch in "Negro Hollow." Nancy washes for the Compsons and cooks for them when Dilsey, their regular servant, is ill. Her estranged husband Jesus lives on the margins of both the African American and the white communities. He bears a permanent scar across his face, the result of a razor cut from a fight, presumably one of many fights in which he has participated.

Nancy has a confrontation with a white man named Mr. Stovall. On Main Street in the middle of the day in front of several townspeople, she accosts the bank clerk and church deacon for not paying her money she is owed for sexual favors. Stovall knocks Nancy to the ground and kicks her in the face, knocking out several of her teeth, before she is taken to jail for an undisclosed reason. While in Jefferson's jail, Nancy sings about her troubles and tries to hang herself. The jailer accuses her of using cocaine, sees that she is pregnant, and proceeds to beat her for her behavior anyway.

After she is released, Nancy is visited by Jesus in the Compsons' kitchen. Speaking in sexual innuendos, their discussion focuses on her pregnancy and the father's identity. Nancy makes it clear that Jesus is not the father, and he threatens to kill whoever is. Knowing that Jesus would not confront Stovall because of the consequences (he likely would be lynched), Nancy grows increasingly afraid of her husband, whom she believes actually wants to kill her out of jealousy. Jesus then disappears, apparently heading to Memphis to see another woman.

The Compsons arrange a pallet in their kitchen for Nancy, who refuses to return to her cabin since she believes Jesus is lying in wait for her in the ditch. She even sleeps one night in the children's room. When Dilsey returns to work, Mrs. Compson refuses to allow Nancy to remain any longer. Bemoaning her plight, she expresses herself in a way Quentin describes as "a sound that was not singing and not unsinging." Terrified to go home alone, Nancy convinces the children to come to her cabin with her. She tells them a story that mirrors her own situation, desperately trying to entertain them to keep them by her.

Five-year-old Jason becomes upset and wants to return home, as Quentin and seven-year-old Caddy grow increasingly uneasy. Eventually, Mr. Compson arrives. He is sympathetic to Nancy's fears but does not believe she is in imminent danger. He takes his children home, leaving Nancy alone. She is so convinced that Jesus will return no matter what she does that she leaves the door to her cabin open, seemingly resigned to her fate, but she keeps the light burning, because she does not want to be killed in the dark.

Critical Evaluation:

During a career as a writer spanning five decades, 1949 Nobel laureate William Faulkner wrote nineteen novels and more than seventy short stories. As one of his most anthologized stories, "That Evening Sun" demonstrates the best elements of Faulkner's fictional technique and augments his achievements as a modern American writer. The original manuscript was titled "Never Done No Weeping When You Wanted to Laugh" and told from Nancy's point of view.

The story was reworked to be told from a child's perspective and retitled "That Evening Sun Go Down" for its initial 1931 publication in H. L. Mencken's *American Mercury* magazine. The story again was retitled with the omission of

the last two words and was revised and reprinted in subsequent collections of the author's short stories, including *These Thirteen* (1931)*, Collected Stories* (1950), and *Selected Short Stories* (1962).

Nancy's story is filtered through the perceptions of children. The young Compsons observe the story's events as they unfold, but they understand very little of what is happening to Nancy or its significance. Nevertheless, in the process of recreating conversations between his parents and Nancy, Nancy and Jesus, Nancy and Dilsey, and Nancy and the children, Quentin captures his family's ineffectual attempts to calm and protect her. Lacking closure and resolution, Nancy's fate is not disclosed at the story's end, but there are signs, including a bloody hog bone left by Jesus on the kitchen table, that she will be killed.

The story's title is a phrase taken from "St. Louis Blues," a popular blues song written in 1914 by composer, singer, and bandleader W. C. Handy, with whom Faulkner would have been familiar. "That Evening Sun" is one of four stories written by Faulkner in which he incorporates elements from blues music into his fiction for literary purposes. The other three are two novels, *Soldier's Pay* (1926) and *Sartoris* (1929), and "Pantaloon in Black," part of the short story sequence *Go Down, Moses* (1942).

Set in Mississippi's northern hill country in Faulkner's imagined Yoknapatawpha County, "That Evening Sun" vividly depicts social relations in the Jim Crow South. The story's narrator, the twenty-four-year-old Quentin Compson, has grown up as a member of a privileged white family; he has been directly exposed to and absorbed a way of life that assumes people of color will fulfill subservient roles without protest. The experiences recounted in this story also relate to what Quentin's experiences as a main character in the novel *The Sound and the Fury* (1929), written before "That Evening Sun," when Quentin is a student at Harvard University. The outcome of Nancy's plight anticipates Quentin's suicide in the novel (a suicide that inexplicably takes place five years before Quentin turns twenty-four). Common to both the story and the novel as well are the characters Caddy and Nancy. Each is the victim of sexist behavior. What happens to Nancy in the story and Caddy in the novel shows how gender issues parallel those of race and class.

"That Evening Sun" is primarily Nancy's story, but it is a story readers enter and understand only indirectly because Nancy does not tell her story in her own words. Instead, by having Quentin tell her story, Faulkner keeps his readers distanced from the world Nancy inhabits. By not giving her voice directly, Faulkner has Quentin objectify her situation. This strategy also parallels his strategy in *The Sound and the*

Fury, in which Faulkner tells Caddy's story through her three brothers and an omniscient narrator, rather than giving her a voice of her own.

Quentin's narration is as an observer more than as a participant, showing how the two halves of this Jim Crow milieu intersect and are inextricably interwoven yet remain separate, distinct, and forever unequal. The literal divide in the story is symbolized by the ditch that separates Nancy's cabin from the Compsons' house. Nancy must continue to cross this ditch, not only for her livelihood but also for her survival.

Since she is unable to convince other characters that her fears are justified, Nancy's situation becomes a dilemma she can neither avoid nor evade. Marginalized by everyone around her, Nancy becomes self-destructive. Being referred to in racist epithets and even calling herself these words, she becomes the victim and the scapegoat of a system of oppression that is self-perpetuating. Unlike the female singer in Handy's song who will find a way to overcome her lover's transgressions and win him back, Nancy's blues, a "singing" and a "not singing," are never fully articulated, so no one, not even a more mature Quentin looking back in time, understands her predicament.

Living on the margins of society, Nancy never is protected by the law, and Jesus remains an outlaw. Inevitably, the jealousy they show toward each other leads to retribution and violence. Literally and figuratively, the hog bone placed by Jesus on the kitchen table is a sign that he will return to take her life. In the context of African American folklore manifested as hoodoo, Jesus has conjured Nancy, but only she knows it.

Similar to the way Faulkner recreates the Compson family in *The Sound and the Fury*, he resurrects Nancy as Nancy Mannigoe in *Requiem for a Nun* (1951). Ironically, Nancy sacrifices her own life in this story so that her white employer, Temple Drake, can search for a degree of forgiveness for her own actions.

Published at the beginning of his most prolific decade as a writer, "That Evening Sun" remains one of Faulkner's best short stories. His use of an adolescent narrator to portray Nancy's haunting, tragic life and its consequences anticipates equally engaging narrative strategies and moving subject matter in such novels as *Light in August* (1932) and *Absalom, Absalom!* (1936)—the latter of which also features Quentin Compson as a narrator.

Kevin Eyster

Further Reading

Blotner, Joseph H. *Faulkner: A Biography.* Rev. ed. New York: Vintage, 1991. Originally published in 1974 in two volumes, Blotner's meticulous study of Faulkner's life and writing is the most thoroughly written biography of the author. This volume updates the original publication, adding new material.

Brown, May Cameron. "Voice in 'That Evening Sun': A Study of Quentin Compson." In *Critical Essays on William Faulkner: The Compson Family*, edited by Arthur F. Kinney. Boston: G. K. Hall, 1982. Emphasizes Quentin's role in the story and how his recalling of events recreates the voices of those involved. Also makes connections to Quentin's character in *The Sound and the Fury*.

Ferguson, James. *Faulkner's Short Fiction*. Knoxville: University of Tennessee Press, 1991. Discusses Faulkner's accomplishments as a short-story writer in relation to his success as a novelist. Analyzes the stories individually, while considering them in the order in which they were written and revised, published and republished.

Gartner, Carol B. "Faulkner in Context: Seeing 'That Evening Sun' Through the Blues." *Southern Quarterly* 34, no. 2 (Winter, 1996): 50-58. Explores the story in the context of blues music, making a case for Faulkner's exposure to and understanding of this musical genre. Argues that the story is more Nancy's than Quentin's.

Hamblin, Robert W. "Before the Fall: The Theme of Innocence in Faulkner's 'That Evening Sun.'" *Notes on Mississippi Writers* 11 (1979): 86-94. Offers an allegorical reading of the story, explaining how its representation of innocence can be read on different levels.

Kuyk, Dirk, Jr., Betty M. Kuyk, and James A. Miller. "Black Culture in William Faulkner's 'That Evening Sun.'" *Journal of American Studies* 20 (1986): 33-50. Foregrounds Nancy and Jesus's relationship in the context of African and African American cosmologies. Shows how the Compsons are incapable of understanding these worldviews.

Matthews, John T. "Faulkner's Narrative Frames." In *Faulkner and the Craft of Fiction*, edited by Doreen Fowler and Ann J. Abadie. Jackson: University Press of Mississippi, 1989. Considers the story in the light of Faulkner's experimentation with point of view and narrative technique throughout his literary canon, specifically his ability to create stories within stories.

Skei, Hans H. *Reading Faulkner's Best Short Fiction*. Columbia: University of South Carolina Press, 1999. An analysis of twelve stories, including their publication history, by one of the premier scholars of Faulkner's short stories. Each chapter shows how the stories can be read closely through the lens of reader-response criticism. A helpful introduction for readers coming to the stories for the first time.

Towner, Theresa M. *The Cambridge Introduction to William Faulkner.* New York: Cambridge University Press, 2008. One of the best introductions available to Faulkner's fiction, analyzing his novels and stories, including "That Evening Sun," and their critical background.

Zender, Karl F. "'That Evening Sun': Marginality and Sight." In *William Faulkner's Short Fiction: An International Symposium*, edited by Hans H. Skei. Oslo, Norway: Solum Forlag, 1997. A close reading of the story showing how the theme of perception and metaphors of sight and seeing and their lack contribute to cultural misunderstandings and fatal consequences.

That Was Then, This Is Now

Author: S. E. Hinton (1948-   )
First published: 1971
Type of work: Novel
Type of plot: Social realism
Time of plot: Late 1960's
Locale: Tulsa, Oklahoma

Principal characters:
BRYON DOUGLAS, a sixteen-year-old boy
MRS. DOUGLAS, his mother
MARK JENNINGS, his best friend
CHARLIE, owner of Charlie's Bar
M&M CARLSON, a thirteen-year-old boy
CATHY, his older sister, who becomes Bryon's girlfriend
ANGELA SHEPARD, Bryon's former girlfriend
TIM and CURLY, Angela's older brothers
MIKE CHAMBERS, a teenager Mrs. Douglas befriends
    during one of her hospital stays
PONYBOY CURTIS, the object of Angela's affections

The Story:

Bryon and Mark are best friends. They have lived together with Bryon's mother ever since Mark's parents shot each other in a drunken brawl. The boys hang out at Charlie's Bar and earn money by hustling pool. Charlie tells the pair that M&M, a younger Hippie boy, is looking for them. Bryon and Mark find M&M in time to stop Curly Shepard and his Greaser gang from beating M&M up. The "Hippies" are a new group and the lines between the two former groups, the "Greasers" and "Socs," are becoming blurred.

The following day, Bryon and Mark visit Bryon's mother in the hospital. While there, Bryon meets Cathy Carlson, M&M's older sister, who works in the snack bar. Bryon is taken with Cathy and hopes to see her again. Bryon and Mark also visit Mike Chambers, a boy Bryon's mother befriends. Mike is recovering from a beating after being falsely accused of harming a young African American girl. Mike tells Bryon and Mark what happened, how he actually saved the girl from being harassed by a group of whites. Mike drove the girl home and his car was surrounded by a group of African American kids. They pulled him from the car and nearly beat him to death when the girl lied, claiming Mike hurt her. De-

spite the beating, Mike does not hate African Americans. When he thinks about it from the girl's viewpoint, he can almost understand why she lied. After the visit ends, Bryon and Mark discuss Mike's misfortune. Mark does not share Mike's understanding of the factors that caused the girl to lie. Mark states that if anyone ever hurt him like that, he would hate them forever.

Mrs. Douglas's hospital stay causes financial stress. The boys are forced to look for jobs, but they do not have much luck. Bryon asks Charlie for a job. Charlie refuses because Bryon is underage. Charlie also doubts Bryon's honesty in certain areas, though he does trust Bryon enough to loan him his car so Bryon can take Cathy to a school dance.

At the dance, Bryon's former girlfriend, Angela Shepard, starts a fight intending to punish Ponyboy Curtis for failing to respond to her advances. Unfortunately, Mark is the unintended recipient of a bottle to the head. Bryon leaves Cathy at the dance and goes with Mark to the hospital. Mark gets stitched up. Ponyboy hotwires Charlie's car and brings Cathy to the hospital. Bryon takes over driving duty, dropping off Ponyboy and Cathy and finally taking Mark home. The boys stay up talking. Mark tells Bryon that even though they are not blood relations, he feels like they are "real" brothers.

After Mark recovers, the boys go to Charlie's Bar to make some money hustling pool. Bryon manages to hustle a couple of Texans, who are not happy to lose their money. The Texans wait for the boys outside, intent on teaching them a lesson. Charlie realizes the boys are in trouble and attempts to save them. The boys witness Charlie's death when the Texans shoot him.

In the weeks that follow, the boys struggle to make sense of Charlie's death. Meanwhile, the financial strife at home grows worse. Mrs. Douglas is hospitalized again. Mark gives Mrs. Douglas money but will not reveal where it is coming from. Mark grows distant. Bryon finds himself frequently turning to Cathy for support instead.

M&M disappears. Bryon and Cathy search but do not find him. Bryon and Mark get Angela drunk and cut her hair as payback for Mark's injury in the earlier fight. Mark is jealous of Cathy, and the distance between the boys grows. Bryon questions whether he knows who Mark really is. The Shepard brothers beat Bryon up for cutting Angela's hair, but, instead of retaliating, Bryon chooses to deal with them by not hating them, a lesson learned from Mike's experience with the African Americans who beat him.

Mark lets it slip that he might know where M&M is. By the time M&M is found, he is on a bad acid trip. He is hallucinating and scared. Bryon and Cathy take him to the hospital. The doctors try to treat him, but there is no guarantee that he will make a full recovery. Later that night, Bryon discovers a container of pills in Mark's room. He realizes that Mark has been making money selling drugs and may even be the one responsible for M&M's condition. Bryon calls the police and turns Mark in.

Mark is sentenced to five years in the state reformatory. Bryon distances himself from everyone, including Cathy. Later, Bryon visits Mark in prison. Mark tells Bryon that he hates him. Bryon tries to apologize but Mark will not listen. Bryon pleads for forgiveness, reminding Mark of their friendship and brotherly bond. Mark turns Bryon's words against him when he says, "Like a friend once told me, 'That was then, and this is now.'" Bryon leaves, numb and worn out, wishing to be a kid again, at an age when he seemed to have all the answers.

Critical Evaluation:

Critics praised S. E. Hinton's sophomore effort. *That Was Then, This Is Now* was voted one of the Best Books for Young Adults by the American Library Association in 1971. Some incorrectly called the book a sequel to *The Outsiders* (1967),

possibly due to cameo appearances by characters from the earlier novel, such as Ponyboy Curtis, Tim Shepard, and Curly Shepard. The central story of Mark and Bryon's friendship has no relation to the events portrayed in *The Outsiders*. The appearance of the established characters is used to illustrate that times have changed, a literal interpretation of the title.

That Was Then, This Is Now is a more controlled novel than its predecessor, perhaps as a result of Hinton's process in writing it. After the success of *The Outsiders*, Hinton struggled with writer's block for nearly three years. When she was writing for fun, it was easy, but when writing became Hinton's "real" job, she was overwhelmed with the prospect of writing something as good as *The Outsiders*. Hinton was able to beat the block when her future husband, David Inhofe, demanded that she start writing again and set a quota of two pages per day.

Hinton claims that she writes stories based on characters rather than problems because over time problems will change while characters endure. However, *That Was Then, This Is Now* incorporates many "problems" into its plot. Hinton tackles race relations, drug abuse, and teenage violence. Instead of preaching concrete solutions to readers, Hinton lets her characters muddle through these tough issues and allows her readers to draw their own conclusions about how to best solve these problems. Perhaps this is the reason that Hinton's works resonate so well with the young adult audience. Teenagers do not want adults telling them what to do in real life. It would be presumptuous for an author to subject readers to that kind of treatment in fiction.

Hinton's decision to incorporate cameo appearances by characters from *The Outsiders* is a curious one. Tim and Curly Shepard are minor characters in *The Outsiders*. They are mentioned early on in the book as rivals who are looking for Dally to settle a score. When push comes to shove and the rumble between the Greasers and Socs occurs, the Shepards fight side by side with Ponyboy and company. They join forces to defeat the Socs, their common enemy.

In *That Was Then, This Is Now*, the Shepards beat Bryon in retaliation for cutting Angela's hair. They act as readers would expect them to act given their history. Readers do not learn anything new about the Shepards as a result of this interaction. However, their appearance is necessary to illustrate how Bryon has grown over the course of the story. Mark wants revenge, but Bryon does not. Bryon does not hate them for beating him up; instead, he realizes that he probably deserved the beating and that future attacks would not solve anything. It is time to move on.

Ponyboy's appearance is interesting, because readers get

to see him from a different point of view than that of the earlier novel. Bryon dislikes Ponyboy, perhaps out of jealousy over his breakup with Angela. Readers may find it hard to dislike Ponyboy if they have already encountered him as a hero in *The Outsiders*. As Ponyboy continues to demonstrate heroic qualities through his actions, such as bringing Cathy to the hospital after Mark is injured, even Bryon finds it hard not to like him. At the end of the novel when Bryon learns that Ponyboy and Cathy are now a couple, he cannot help but hope that the pair will be happy together.

Some of the themes Hinton explored in *The Outsiders* are reexamined from an alternate point of view in *That Was Then, This Is Now*. In *The Outsiders*, Hinton conveyed the importance of retaining innocence and not becoming jaded by the world. In *That Was Then, This Is Now*, she turns the world upside down by proclaiming times are changing: Her characters must grow with them or be left behind. Gone are the days of the idealistic dreamers who watched sunsets. Growing up means having to make tough decisions. The story of how Mark and Bryon's friendship changes over time proves that, despite one's hopes, retaining childhood innocence is impossible. The events that unfold represent Hinton's attempt to illustrate why this is the case.

Hinton's theme of honor among the lawless takes a different turn when Bryon ultimately betrays Mark by turning him in for dealing drugs. Bryon has to stand up for what he personally believes is right, even though that means betraying his best friend. This theme also exists in other crime stories, in which many criminals themselves revile some crimes, particularly crimes against children. It is interesting to note which crimes are deemed acceptable and which ones are deemed to be wrong.

Hinton's theme of bridging the gap between rich and poor also takes a different turn with the introduction of the Hippies in *That Was Then, This Is Now*. There are still Greasers and Socs (poor kids and rich kids), but neither group quite knows what to make of the Hippies. Hippies wear their hair long, like Greasers, but they will not fight back when jumped.

Mark and Bryon decide that they are better off just leaving them alone. The days of the rumbles are ending and somehow they are managing to peacefully coexist, though that coexistence may be only temporary.

Hinton also touches on the price of loyalty. Mark stays loyal to Bryon throughout the book, despite Bryon's relationship with Cathy. Bryon's betrayal blindsides Mark. He is unable to understand how his best friend and surrogate brother could justify such an action.

Hinton uses animal imagery throughout the course of the novel, continually giving Mark the characteristics of a lion. Early references describe Mark as a "friendly lion," or an "innocent lion." Over the course of the story, the descriptions change to "dangerous lion," or "jungle animal." The change in descriptions mirrors the emotional closeness or distance between Mark and Bryon. By the end of the novel, Hinton's comparison to a "dangerously caged lion" captures Mark's hatred and rage over being sent to prison. Hinton delves deeper into the price of loyalty and the use of animal imagery becomes even more prominent in *Rumble Fish* (1975), her third novel.

Martel Sardina

Further Reading

Daly, Jay. *Presenting S. E. Hinton*. Boston: Twayne, 1989. A comprehensive analysis of Hinton's works. Contains an author biography, individual chapters focused on each of her young adult novels, literary criticism, and supplemental information about the film adaptations of her books.

Hinton, S. E. *Some of Tim's Stories*. New York: Speak/Penguin Group USA, 2007. Contains interviews with Hinton discussing her young adult novels, their film adaptations, and her most recent works.

Wilson, Antoine. *The Library of Author Biographies: S. E. Hinton*. New York: Rosen, 2003. Provides an overview of Hinton's works. Contains an author interview, selected book reviews, and a list of awards each book received.